PROFESSIONAL
COOKING

Photography *by*

J. GERARD SMITH

Illustrations *by*

STEVE JENKINS

THIRD EDITION

PROFESSIONAL COOKING

WAYNE GISSLEN

JOHN WILEY & SONS, INC.

NEW YORK   CHICHESTER   BRISBANE   TORONTO   SINGAPORE

Publisher: Margaret K. Burns
Senior Editor: Claire Thompson
Editorial Production: Micheline Frederick, Frank Grazioli, Jacqueline A. Martin.
Production Assistant: Liane Carita
Text Design: Karin Gerdes Kincheloe
Text Illustrations: Steve Jenkins
Black and White and Color Photography: J. Gerard Smith
Illustration Manager: Dean Gonzalez
Manufacturing Manager: Jane Bennett
Text Composition: Publication Services
Color Separations: Professional Litho
Printed and bound by Von Hoffman Press, Inc.

Library of Congress Cataloging-in-Publication Data

Gisslen, Wayne, 1946–
    Professional cooking / Wayne Gisslen. — 3rd ed.
      p.   cm.
    Includes bibliographical references and index.
    ISBN 0-471-59300-1 (Trade). — ISBN 0-471-59301-X (College)
    1. Quantity cookery.   2. Food services   I. Title
TX820.G54 1995
641.5´7—dc20   94-21756
                                                       CIP

Printed in the United States of America
10 9 8 7 6 5 4 3 2

To **MARY ELLEN**

PREFACE

*T*he third edition of *Professional Cooking* represents a further refinement of the popular text that, in its first two editions, has helped to train more than 200,000 cooks and chefs. The incorporated revisions will help make the text even more useful in preparing students for work in modern kitchens.

Users of earlier editions of *Professional Cooking* will recognize at once that the most prominent change in the third edition is the use of hundreds of new color photographs, replacing most of the black-and-white photos of previous editions. With the use of color, the concise, step-by-step illustrations of manual techniques have been made even clearer. As before, the techniques are shown from the point of view of the person performing them, making it easier for the student to comprehend them at a glance.

These photographs support and reinforce the systematic presentation of cooking theory and techniques, which remain the heart of the book.

ABOUT THIS BOOK

The book has a dual goal: *understanding*—that is, an understanding of cooking theory, of how to cook—and *performing*—that is, the mastery of a set of manual skills and the ability to apply them to a wide range of cooking styles and products.

The current revision retains the second edition's basic structure and organization, which created the flexibility that has made *Professional Cooking* adaptable to nearly any course of study. The basic cooking methods (dry-heat methods, moist-heat methods, and so on) are introduced early on. Then, within each of the main cooking chapters, the material is arranged by cooking method.

Thus, for those curricula that are organized by cooking method, it is a simple matter to select the appropriate sections—for example, moist-heat methods—from the meat, poultry, fish, and vegetable chapters. At the same time, the arrangement of the chapters by product type enables the instructor to emphasize how the basic cooking methods differ as they are applied to different products.

The new *Professional Cooking* focuses, as did the earlier editions, on the development of flexible skills, which are essential for success in a cooking career. Modern food service is evolving rapidly, and there is a tremendous variety of establishments on the scene today, from the executive dining room to the school cafeteria, from the simplest short-order coffee shop to the most exclusive restaurant or club, from kitchens that make extensive use of convenience foods to those that use only fresh produce. The graduate who understands the workings of foods and the interplay among ingredients, cooking methods, cost factors, and other elements can function successfully in any type of food service operation.

The Role of the Chef–Instructor

No textbook, of course, can serve as a substitute for practical kitchen experience. Furthermore, a book cannot replace an experienced chef-instructor, who can give practical demonstrations, supervise students' work, answer questions, and give advice and assistance as the need arises. Every instructor has had unique experience and has developed special techniques and procedures. Many chefs, in fact, disagree with one another on a number of points. Although this book presents methods and recipes that are widely used and accepted, many instructors will prefer procedures that differ from some of those explained in this text, and they may wish to supplement the recipes in this book with some of their own. Throughout the book, the instructor's input is encouraged. Exposure to a variety of recipes and techniques can only enrich the students' education and enhance the depth of their experience.

The Recipes

The recipes in this book are planned and organized to reinforce the basic skills that the student is learning. In each case, specific recipes follow a discussion of theories, guidelines, and general procedures applicable to a defined category of foods and/or cooking methods. Students are encouraged, by means of recipe variations, to see how they can apply these procedures to other ingredients, and to see the similarities and differences among various preparations.

In the preparation of this new edition, each of the more than 900 recipes (including approximately 400 main recipes and over 500 variations) was carefully evaluated with respect to its fit in the total picture. Because the purpose of the text is to teach fundamental cooking techniques, it is important to illustrate these techniques—and to allow the student to experience them—with fundamental, straight-forward recipes that reveal the connection between general theory and specific application in the most direct way. Retaining most of the recipes of earlier editions serves this purpose better than replacing them with recipes that may seem at first glance to be more stylish or *au courant,* or introducing many recipes with complexities that obscure the basic principles being taught.

What makes a dish feel modern is as much a matter of presentation as it is of ingredients or recipe instructions. How an item, along with its garnish and sauce, is plated can make it look rustic or elegant, simple or elaborate, traditional or modern. For this revision, the discussion of food presentation in Chapter 22 has been enhanced to include information on modern plating styles. As the examples illustrated by the accompanying photographs show, as simple an item as a sautéed chicken breast can be as stylish as a complicated dish requiring exotic or expensive ingredients.

Readers are urged to study Chapter 5, "The Recipe: Its Structure and Its Use," before actually proceeding with any of the recipes, so that they will not only know how to use the recipes in this book but will also understand the structure and limitations of the many kinds of recipes they will be using in their careers.

While every culinary program has different requirements, the recipes in this book should be adaptable to any purpose. Most major recipes are written for 24 or 25 portions, a quantity that can be converted easily to higher or lower yields if necessary. Those recipes requiring more costly ingredients, those that are generally made to order, or those that are more complex are written for smaller yields, such as 10 or 12 portions. In addition, variations often indicate ingredient substitutions, so that the recipes will fit different budgetary requirements and different local or regional tastes.

The metric quantities in the recipes have been reworked to correspond more closely to practices in Canada. In some cases, this has meant slight changes in ingredient proportions. Testing has shown, however, that the resulting changes in the finished products are very small or negligible, generally no greater than the changes caused by the normal fluctuations of ingredient quality or by the use of pots of different sizes.

Sanitation and Safety

Another important addition to the text is an introduction to the Hazard Analysis Critical Control Point (HACCP) system. This approach to food sanitation and safety is becoming widely adopted throughout the food service industry, so it is important that students become familiar with it.

Features

Pronunciation Guides and Glossary

Much kitchen terminology is taken from French. Phonetic guides are included for difficult words, giving the approximate pronunciation using English sounds. (Exact rendering is impossible in many cases, because French has a number of sounds that don't exist in English.) Because food workers must be able to communicate with each other, definitions of terms introduced in the text are summarized in a glossary at the end of the book.

Format

This book is designed to be readable and useful. The format emphasizes and highlights key points in bold type, italics, and numbered sequences, so that basic information can be located and reviewed at a glance.

Realistic Procedures

Although supported by discussions of cooking theory, procedures given here are based on actual practices in the industry. Attention is given not just to quantity production but also to the special problems of cooking to order. Presentation and service of the finished product are considered in detail as is pre-preparation or *mise en place,* so essential to the organization of a working restaurant. At the same time, the major emphasis is on quality, too often neglected in the quest for convenience.

Even a book as large as this one cannot possibly contain all a cook needs to know. Other information is included if it has a direct bearing on kitchen and bakeshop work. More specialized information, such as stewarding and managerial skills, has to be omitted. Also, more advanced techniques, particularly those belonging to *garde manger,* are beyond the scope of this book. Finally, although much of what we talk about is strongly influenced by the cooking of other nations, especially France, the practices discussed are those of American food service.

Wayne Gisslen

ACKNOWLEDGMENTS

*T*he preparation of the third edition was made possible by the collaboration of many individuals to whom I owe a debt of gratitude. Foremost among these is Jim Smith, whose photography is the principle feature of this revision. Without his skills and his patience, this project would not have been possible. Thanks, also, to Anne Smith for her invaluable assistance and for the warm hospitality during the many weeks I spent in the Smiths' home and studio.

I am grateful, too, for special assistance provided by Chef Daniel Smith and by Margaret Smith, owners of the Thymes restaurant, Kingston, New York, for helping us obtain essential ingredients and equipment and for providing wise counsel; by Chef-Instructor Larry De Vries, Crocus Plains Regional Secondary School, Brandon, Manitoba, for his helpful information about Canadian culinary and educational practices; by Joan Garvin and Sam Kadko, for suggesting many ideas I was able to use to improve this book; and by J. A. Henckels Zwillingswerk, for providing knives and other equipment used in photography.

Thanks to Lou Haverilla, Assistant Vice President–Customer Education at IBP, Inc. and to Tonya Parravano and the National Live Stock and Meat Board for providing photographs for Chapter 10.

Most of all, I am grateful to my wife, Mary Ellen Griffin, for innumerable ideas, suggestions, and critical appraisals, not to mention the motivation and moral support that enabled me to complete this project.

In acknowledging the assistance of those who supported this latest revision, I must not neglect to express once more my gratitude to those fine professionals who were instrumental in helping me to develop *Professional Cooking* from concept to finished book and who generously offered their advice, criticisms, and suggestions for improvement: Philip Panzarino, New York City Technical College, Brooklyn, New York; Mike Jung, Hennepin Technical Center—North Campus, Brooklyn Park, Minnesota; and William Petsch, Pinellas Vocational Technical Institute, Clearwater, Florida. I also thank Eberhart Werthman and Gary Lensing, St. Paul Technical Vocational Institute, and Jeff Larson and Jim Curtis, White Bear Lake (916) Vo-Tech, who shared their ideas and educational philosophies, and Anne Bailey and Samantha Durell, who assisted me in testing recipes.

Finally, I wish to say thank you to Robert Pirtle and Judith Joseph, my first editors, who first made *Professional Cooking* possible; to the staff at John Wiley & Sons, Micheline Frederick, Frank Grazioli, Jacqueline Martin, and Karin Kincheloe, who have put so much talent and effort into this book; and especially to my editor, Claire Thompson, whose unstinting support, assistance, and encouragement I value highly.

Reviewers

I would like to acknowledge the following instructors who have contributed to this book over three editions by suggesting revisions and additions.

George Akau
Clark College
Vancouver, WA

Angela M. Anderson
Miami Dade Community College
Miami, FL

Robert Anderson
Des Moines Area Community College
Ankeny, IA

Alan Argulski
Genesee Community College
Batavia, NY

Moses Ball
Atlantic Vocational-Technical Center
Coconut Creek, FL

Joseph L. Belvedere Jr.
Paul Smith's College
Paul Smiths, NY

George J. Bissonette
Pikes Peak Community College
Colorado Springs, CO

Pete Bordi
Penn State University
University Park, PA

Harsha Chacko
University of New Orleans
New Orleans, LA

Daniel Charna
Ashland College
Ashland, OH

Jesse Clemons
State Technical Institute at Memphis
Memphis, TN

Alec O. Cline
American Culinary Federation, Inc.
Redwood City, CA

Michael M. Collins
San Jacinto College
Pasadena, TX

Randall Colman
Sullivan County Community College
Loch Sheldrake, NY

Mike Costello
St. Cloud Area Vocational-Technical Institute
St. Cloud, MN

William J. Daly
State University of New York at Cobleskill
Cobleskill, NY

Juanita M. Decker
Waukesha County Technical Institute
Pewaukee, WI

Marian Dobbins
Tucson, AZ

Dale Dunham
Oklahoma State University
Okmulgee, OK

Evan Enowitz
Grossmont College
El Cajon, CA

Fred T. Faria
Johnson & Wales University
Providence, RI

Robyn L. Flipse
Brookdale Community College
Lincroft, NJ

Sandra Flowerday
Educational Consultant
Charlotte, MI

Sandra Foley
Gogebic Community College
Ironwood, MI

Willard L. Geach
Long Beach City College
Long Beach, CA

Joan W. Geerken
State University of New York at Cobleskill
Cobleskill, NY

James Goering
El Centro College
Dallas, TX

Jeff Graves
Purdue University
West Lafayette, IN

Juliet Groux
West Liberty State College
West Liberty, WV

John D. Hedley
Los Angeles Trade-Technical College
Los Angeles, CA

Rosemary L. Hedlund
Des Moines Area Community College
Ankeny, IA

Iris Helveston
State of Florida
Department of Education
Tampa, FL

Maynard G. Hemmah
Moorhead Area Vocational-Technical Institute
Moorhead, MN

Margaret A. Howard
Sheridan Vocational-Technical Center
Hollywood, FL

Lynn Huffman
Texas Tech University
Lubbock, TX

Daniel K. Jeatran
Milwaukee Area Technical College
Milwaukee, WI

Frank F. Johnson, Jr.
University of South Florida
Tampa, FL

Roosevelt Johnson
Sidney North Colver Vocational-Technical
  Institute
New Orleans, LA

Todd Jones
Mattatuck Community College
Waterbury, CT

Mike Jung
Hennepin Technical Center
Brooklyn Park, MN

Tom King
Cabrillo College
Aptos, CA

Suzanne Little, M. S., R. D.
San Jacinto College
Pasadena, TX

Shirley Lotze
Western Wisconsin Technical Institute
LaCrosse, WI

Robert M. Lyna
Southern Maine Vocational-Technical Institute
South Portland, ME

Sylvia Marple
University of New Hampshire
Durham, NH

Valeria S. Mason
State Department of Education
Gainesville, FL

John McDonald
St. Augustine Technical Center
St. Augustine, FL

Terence F. McDonough
Erie Community College
Buffalo, NY

Marcia W. McDowell
Monroe Community College
Rochester, NY

Linda McDuffie
North Seattle Community College
Seattle, WA

Robert McLean
The Fay School
Southboro, MA

Ann Miglio
Williamsport Area Community College
Williamsport, PA

Harold O. Mishoe
Southern Maine Vocational-Technical
   Institute
South Portland, ME

Ken W. Myers
University of Minnesota-Crookston
Crookston, MN

Kathy Niemann
Portland State University
Portland, OR

William T. Norvell
William Rainey Harper College
Palatine, IL

Gary Page
Grand Valley State College
Allendale, MI

Philip Panzarino
New York City Technical College
Brooklyn, NY

Richard Petrello
Withlacoochee Vocational-Technical Center
Inverness, FL

William F. Petsch
Pinellas Vocational Technical Institute
Clearwater, FL

Michael Piccinino
Shasta College
Redding, CA

Larry Richardson
Hinds Junior College–Jackson Branch
Jackson, MI

Neil Rittenaur
North Dakota State College of Science
Wahpeton, ND

Hubert E. Robert
Holyoke Community College
Holyoke, MA

Ricardo G. Saenz
Renton Vocational-Technical Institute
Renton, WA

Robert R. Santos
Maui Community College
Kahului, HI

Frank Schellings
Diablo Valley College
Pleasant Hill, CA

David Schneider
Macomb Community College
Mt. Clemens, MI

Charlotte Schwyn
Delta College
Stockton, CA

Roy John Sharp
Portland Community College
Portland, OR

William Sprowl
Mt. San Jacinto College
San Jacinto, CA

Nancy S. Steryous
St. Petersburg Vocational-Technical Institute
St. Petersburg, FL

Siegfried Stober
Joliet Junior College
Joliet, IL

Peter Sugameli
Wayne Community College
Detroit, MI

Julia Sullivan
Copiah-Lincoln Jr. College
Wesson, MI

William Thornton
St. Phillips College
San Antonio, TX

Robin W. Turner
State University of New York at Delhi
Delhi, NY

Jerry L. Vincent
Johnson County Community College
Overland Park, KS

Barbara Vredeveld
Iowa Western Community College
Council Bluffs, IA

R. G. Werth
Asheville-Buncombe Technical College
Asheville, NC

J. William White
Pinellas County School System
St. Petersburg, FL

Doris Wilkes
Florida Hospitality Education Program
The Florida State University
Tallahassee, FL

Ronald Zabkiewicz
South Technical Education Center
Boynton Beach, FL

Roland Zwerger
Elgin Community College
Elgin, IL

CONTENTS

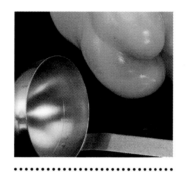

PART TWO
STOCKS, SAUCES, AND SOUPS
119

PART THREE

MEAT, POULTRY, AND FISH

193

PART FOUR
VEGETABLES AND GRAINS
379

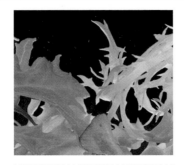

PART FIVE
THE PANTRY AND OTHER SPECIAL SUBJECTS
473

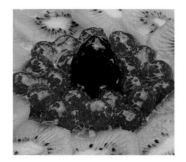

PART SIX
THE BAKESHOP
653

RECIPE TABLE OF CONTENTS

PROFESSIONAL
COOKING

PART ONE

INTRODUCTION TO PROFESSIONAL COOKING

A student of the culinary arts masters a great deal of knowledge in addition to cooking theory and techniques. An understanding of the subjects in this part is important to an accomplished cook.

The Food Service Industry

Sanitation and Safety

Tools and Equipment

Basic Cooking Principles

The Recipe: Its Structure and Its Use

The Menu

Pre-preparation

CHAPTER 1

THE FOOD SERVICE INDUSTRY

This is an exciting time to be starting a career in food service. It is a time when interest in dining and curiosity about new foods are increasing rapidly. There are more new restaurants every year. Many restaurants are busy every night, and restaurant chains number among the nation's largest corporations. The chef, once considered a domestic servant, has become respected as an artist and skilled craftsperson.

The growth of the food service industry creates a demand for thousands of skilled people every year. But it is not simply the opportunity of finding a job that attracts so many people. A food service career is challenging and exciting, and, above all, provides the chance to find real satisfaction in doing a job well.

Unfortunately, many people see only the glamorous side of food service and fail to understand that this is a tiny part of the picture. The public does not often see the years of training, the long hours, and the tremendous pressures that lie behind every success.

This chapter gives you a brief overview of modern food service, including how it got to where it is today and where it is headed. The main purpose of this book is to teach basic cooking techniques. But before you start your practical studies, it is good to know a little about the profession you are entering.

After reading this chapter, you should be able to

1. Discuss the development of modern food service, including the effects of recent food and equipment technology.

2. Identify the major stations in a classical kitchen.

3. Discuss the factors that influence the organization of modern kitchens.

4. Work in a professional manner.

A SHORT HISTORY OF MODERN FOOD SERVICE

The value of history is that it helps us understand the present and the future. In food service, a knowledge of our professional heritage helps us to see why we do things as we do, how our cooking techniques have been developed and refined, and how we can continue to develop and innovate in the years ahead.

The Origins of Classical and Modern Cuisine

Quantity cookery has existed for thousands of years, as long as there have been large groups of people to feed, such as armies. But modern food service began at the time of the French Revolution in 1793. Before this time, the great chefs were employed in the houses of the French nobility. With the revolution and the end of the monarchy, many chefs, suddenly out of work, opened restaurants in and around Paris to support themselves.

The great chef of this time was *Marie-Antoine Carême* (1784–1833), whose career spanned the first 30 years of the nineteenth century. Carême is credited as the founder of classical cuisine. As a young man, he learned all the branches of cooking, and he dedicated his career to refining and organizing culinary techniques. His many books contain the first really systematic account of cooking principles, recipes, and menu making.

As a chef to kings, heads of state, and wealthy patrons, Carême became famous as the creator of elaborate, elegant display pieces, the ancestors of our modern wedding cakes, sugar sculptures, and ice and tallow carvings. But it was Carême's practical and theoretical work as an author and chef that was responsible, to a large extent, for bringing cooking out of the middle ages and into the modern period.

Escoffier

Georges Auguste Escoffier (1847–1935) was the great chef of this century and is revered by chefs and gourmets as the father of twentieth-century cookery. His two main contributions were the simplification of classical cuisine and the classical menu and the reorganization of the kitchen.

It is hard to believe that Escoffier's elaborate multicourse banquets are a simplification of anything. But in the typical banquet menu of the eighteenth century, each course consisted of as many as 20 separate dishes—or more!—mostly a variety of meats and poultry, all placed on the table at once. Guests helped themselves to the few dishes they could reach. Carême began the reform, but Escoffier brought the menu into the twentieth century.

Escoffier rejected what he called the "general confusion" of the old menus in which sheer quantity seemed to be the most important factor. Instead, he called for order and diversity and emphasized the careful selection of one or two dishes per course, dishes that would follow one another harmoniously and that would delight the taste with their delicacy and simplicity.

Escoffier's books and recipes are still important reference works for professional chefs. The basic cooking methods and preparations we study today are based on Escoffier's work.

Escoffier's second major achievement, the reorganization of the kitchen, resulted in a streamlined workplace that was better suited for turning out the simplified dishes and menus that he instituted. The system he established is still in use today, especially in large hotels and full-service restaurants, as we will discuss later in this chapter.

Modern Developments

Today's kitchens look much different from those of Escoffier's day, even though our basic cooking principles are the same. Also, the dishes we eat have gradually changed, due to the innovations and creativity of modern chefs. The process of simplification and refinement, to which Carême and Escoffier made monumental contributions, is still going on, adapting classical cooking to modern conditions and tastes.

Many developments in the twentieth century have made changes in the food service industry.

Development of New Equipment

We take for granted such basic equipment as gas and electric ranges and ovens and electric refrigerators. But even these essential tools did not exist until fairly recently. The easily controlled heat of modern cooking equipment, as well as motorized food cutters, mixers, and other processing equipment, have greatly simplified food production.

Research and technology continue to produce sophisticated tools for the kitchen. Some of these products, such as tilting skillets and steam-jacketed kettles, can do many jobs and are popular in many kitchens. Others can do specialized tasks rapidly and efficiently, but their usefulness depends on volume, because they are designed to do only a few jobs.

Modern equipment has enabled many food service operations to change their production methods. With sophisticated cooling, freezing, and heating equipment, it is possible to do some preparation farther in advance and in larger quantities. Some large multiunit operations prepare food for all their units in one large central commissary. The food is prepared in quantity, packaged, chilled or frozen, and then heated or cooked to order in the individual units.

Development and Availability of New Food Products

Modern refrigeration and rapid transportation caused revolutionary changes in eating habits. For the first time, fresh foods of all kinds—meats, fish, vegetables, and fruits—became available all year. Exotic delicacies can now be shipped from anywhere in the world and arrive fresh and in peak condition.

The development of preservation techniques, not just refrigeration but also freezing, canning, freeze drying, vacuum packing, and irradiation, increased the availability of most foods and has also made affordable some foods that were once rare and expensive.

Techniques of food preservation also have had another effect. It has now become possible to do some or most of the preparation and processing of foods before shipping rather than in the food service operation itself. Thus, convenience foods have come into being. Recently, convenience foods have accounted for an increasing share of the total food market.

Some professional cooks think of new convenience food products and new equipment as a threat to their own positions. They fear that these products will eliminate the need for skilled chefs, because everything will be prepared or will be done by machine. However, it still requires skill and knowledge to handle convenience products properly. The quality of the product as served depends on how well the cook handles it. Furthermore, many new food products and new types of equipment are intended to do work that takes little or no skill, such as peeling potatoes or puréeing vegetables. Convenience foods and advanced equipment free cooks from some of the drudgery so that they have more time to spend on those jobs that require skill and experience.

Sanitary and Nutritional Awareness

The development of the sciences of microbiology and nutrition had a great impact on food service. One hundred years ago there was little understanding of the causes of food poisoning and food spoilage. Food handling practices have come a long way since Escoffier's day.

There was also little knowledge of nutritional principles in the last century. Today, nutrition is an important part of a cook's training. Customers are also more knowledgeable, and the demand for healthful, well-balanced menus is growing.

Modern Cooking Styles

All these developments have helped change cooking styles, menus, and eating habits. The evolution of cuisine that has been going on for hundreds of years still continues. Changes occur not only because of technological developments, such as the ones just described, but also because of our reactions to culinary traditions.

Two opposing forces can be seen at work throughout the history of cooking. One is the urge to simplify, to eliminate complexity and ornamentation, and instead to emphasize the plain, natural tastes of basic, fresh ingredients. The other is the urge to invent, to highlight the creativity of the chef, with an accent on fancier, more complicated presentations and procedures. Both these forces are valid and healthy; they continually refresh and renew the art of cooking.

Recent history provides an example of these trends. Reacting to what they saw as a heavy, stodgy, overly complicated classical cuisine, a number of French chefs in the late 1960s and early 1970s became famous for a style called *nouvelle cuisine* ("new cooking"). They rejected many traditional principles, such as a dependence on flour to thicken sauces, and instead urged simpler, more natural flavors and preparations, with lighter sauces and seasonings and shorter cooking times. Very quickly, however, this new, "simpler" style became extravagant and complicated, famous for strange combinations of foods and fussy, ornate arrangements and designs. By the 1980s, many people were already saying that nouvelle cuisine was dead.

It isn't dead, of course, any more than the cuisine of Escoffier is dead. The best achievements of nouvelle cuisine have taken a permanent place in the classical tradition. Meanwhile, many of the excesses have already been forgotten. It is probably fair to say that most of the best new ideas and the lasting accomplishments have been those of classically trained chefs with a solid grounding in the basics.

In America, our traditional dishes and regional specialties are the product of cooking traditions brought over by immigrant settlers, combined with the indigenous ingredients of a bountiful land. For many years, critics often argued that most American menus offered the same monotonous, mediocre food. Recently, by contrast, American cooking has become fashionable, and almost any local specialty is declared "classic." The fact is, however, that in any country one finds both good and bad food. It takes a skilled cook with a knowledge of the basics to prepare exceptional food, whether it is American, classical French, or any other.

The growth of American food service holds great promise for new cooks and chefs. Technology will continue to make rapid changes in our industry, and men and women are needed who can adapt to these changes and respond to new challenges. Although automation and convenience foods will no doubt grow in importance, there will always be a need for imaginative chefs who can create new dishes and develop new techniques and styles and for skilled cooks who can apply both old and new techniques to produce high-quality foods in all kinds of facilities, from restaurants and hotels to schools and hospitals.

THE ORGANIZATION OF MODERN KITCHENS

The Basis of Kitchen Organization

The purpose of kitchen organization is to assign or allocate tasks so that they will be done efficiently and properly and so that all workers will know what their responsibilities are.

The way a kitchen is organized depends on several factors.

1. *The menu.*

    The kinds of dishes to be produced obviously determine the jobs that need to be done. The menu is, in fact, the basis for the entire operation. Because of its importance, we devote a whole chapter to a study of the menu (Chapter 6).

2. *The type of establishment.*

    The major types of food service establishments are listed as follows:

    Hotels
    Institutional kitchens
      Schools
      Hospitals
      Employee lunchrooms
      Military feeding
      Correctional institutions
    Catering and banquet services

Fast-food restaurants
Full-service restaurants

3. *The size of the operation (the number of customers and the volume of food served).*

4. *The physical facilities, including the equipment in use.*

The Classical Brigade

As you learned earlier in this chapter, one of Escoffier's important achievements was the reorganization of the kitchen. He divided the kitchen into departments or stations, based on the kinds of foods they produced. A station chef was placed in charge of each department. In a small operation, the station chef may be the only worker in the department. But in a large kitchen, each station chef might have several assistants.

This system, with many variations, is still used today, especially in large hotels with traditional kinds of food service. The major positions are as follows:

1. The *chef* is the person in charge of the kitchen. In large establishments this person has the title of *executive chef.* The executive chef is a manager who is responsible for all aspects of food production, including menu planning, purchasing, costing, and planning work schedules.

2. The *sous chef* (**soo** shef) is directly in charge of production. Because the executive chef's responsibilities require spending a great deal of time in the office, the sous chef takes command of the actual production and the minute-by-minute supervision of the staff.

    Both the sous chef and executive chef have had many years of experience in all stations of the kitchen.

3. The *station chefs* or *chefs de partie* are in charge of particular areas of production. The following are the most important station chefs:

    a. The *sauce chef* or *saucier* (so-see-**ay**) prepares sauces, stews, and hot hors d'oeuvres, and sautés foods to order. This is usually the highest position of all the stations.

    b. The *fish cook* or *poissonier* (pwah-so-**nyay**) prepares fish dishes. (This station may be handled by the saucier in some kitchens.)

    c. The *vegetable cook* or *entremetier* (awn-truh-met-**yay**) prepares vegetables, soups, starches, and eggs. Large kitchens may divide these duties among the *vegetable cook,* the *fry cook,* and the *soup cook.*

d. The *roast cook* or *rotisseur* (ro-tee-**sur**) prepares roasted and braised meats and their gravies and broils meats and other items to order. A large kitchen may have a separate *broiler cook* or *grillardin* (gree-ar-**dan**) to handle the broiled items. The broiler cook may also prepare deep-fried meats and fish.

e. The *pantry chef* or *garde manger* (gard-mawn-**zhay**) is responsible for cold foods, including salads and dressings, pâtés, cold hors d'oeuvres, and buffet items.

f. The *pastry chef* or *patissier* (pa-tees-**syay**) prepares pastries and desserts.

g. The *relief cook, swing cook,* or *tournant* (toor-**nawn**) replaces other station heads.

4. *Cooks and assistants* in each station or department help with the particular duties that are assigned to them. For example, the assistant vegetable cook may wash, peel, and trim vegetables. With experience, assistants may be promoted to station cooks and then to station chefs.

Modern Kitchen Organizations

As you can see, only a large establishment needs a staff like the classical brigade just described. (In fact, some large hotels have even larger staffs, with other positions such as separate day and night sous chefs, assistant chef, banquet chef, butcher, baker, and so on.)

Most modern operations, on the other hand, are smaller than this. The size of the classical brigade may be reduced simply by combining two or more positions where the work load allows it. For example, the *second cook* may combine the duties of the sauce cook, fish cook, soup cook, and vegetable cook.

A typical medium-size operation may employ a chef, a second cook, a broiler cook, a pantry cook, and a few cooks' helpers.

A *working chef* is in charge of such operations not large enough to have an executive chef. In addition to being in charge of the kitchen, the working chef also handles one of the production stations. For example, he or she may handle the sauté station, plate foods during service, and help out on other stations when needed.

Small kitchens may have only a chef, one or two cooks, and perhaps one or two assistants who handle simpler jobs such as washing and peeling vegetables.

In many small operations, the *short-order cook* is the backbone of the kitchen during service time. This cook may handle the broiler, deep fryer, griddle, sandwich production, and even some sautéed items. In other words, the short-order cook's responsibility is preparation of foods that can be quickly prepared to order.

By contrast, establishments such as school cafeterias may do no cooking to order at all. Stations and assignments are based on the requirements of quantity preparation rather than cooking to order.

Skill Levels

The preceding discussion is necessarily very general, because there are so many different kinds of kitchen organizations. Titles vary also. The responsibilities of the worker called the second cook, for example, are not necessarily the same in every establishment. Escoffier's standardized system has evolved in many different directions.

One title that is often misunderstood and much abused is that of *chef.* The general public tends to refer to anyone with a white hat as a chef, and people who like to cook for guests in their homes refer to themselves as amateur chefs.

Strictly speaking, the name *chef* should be reserved for one who is *in charge of a kitchen* or a part of a kitchen. The word *chef* is French for chief or head. Studying this book will not make you a chef. That is a title that must be earned by experience not only in preparing food but also in managing a staff and in planning production. Use the word *chef* with respect, because when you become a chef, you will want the same respect.

Skills required of food production personnel vary not only with the job level but also with the establishment and the kind of food prepared. The director of a hospital kitchen and the head chef in a French restaurant need different skills. The skills needed by a short-order cook in a coffee shop are not exactly the same as those needed by a production worker in a school cafeteria. Nevertheless, we can group skill levels into three general categories.

1. Supervisory. The head of a food service kitchen, whether called executive chef, head chef, working chef, or kitchen director, must have management and supervisory skills as well as a thorough knowledge of food production. A leadership position requires an individual who understands organizing and motivating people, planning menus and production procedures, controlling costs and managing budgets, and purchasing food supplies and equipment. Even if they do no cooking at all, people in these positions should be experienced cooks, so that they can schedule production, instruct workers, and control quality. Above all, the chef must be able to work well with people, even under extreme pressure.

2. Skilled and technical. While the chef is the head of an establishment, the cooks are the backbone. These workers carry out the actual food production. Thus, they must have knowledge of and experience in cooking techniques, at least for all the dishes made in their own department. In addition, they must be able to work well with their fellow workers and to coordinate with other departments. Food production is a team activity.

3. Entry level. Entry-level jobs in food service usually require no particular skills or experience. Workers in these jobs are assigned such work as washing vegetables and preparing salad greens. As their knowledge and experience increase, they may be given more complex tasks and eventually become skilled cooks. Many executive chefs began their careers as pot washers who got a chance to peel potatoes when the pot sink was empty.

Beginning at entry-level positions and working one's way up with experience has been the traditional method of advancing in a food service career. Today, however, many cooks are graduates of 1- or 2-year cooking schools. But even with such an education, many new graduates begin at entry-level positions. This is as it should be and certainly should not be seen as a discouragement. Schools teach general cooking knowledge, while every food service establishment requires specific skills, according to its own menu and its own procedures. Experience as well as theoretical knowledge are needed to be able to adapt to "real life" working situations. But students who have studied and learned well should be able to work their way up much more rapidly than the beginners with no knowledge at all.

STANDARDS OF PROFESSIONALISM

What does it take to be a good food service worker?

The emphasis of a food service education is on learning a set of skills. But in many ways, *attitudes* are more important than skills, because a good attitude will help you not only to learn skills but also to persevere and to overcome the many difficulties you will face in your career.

The successful food service worker follows an unwritten code of behavior and set of attitudes we call *professionalism.* Let's look at some of the qualities that a professional must have.

Positive Attitude toward the Job

In order to be a good professional cook, you have to like it and want to do it well. Being serious about your work doesn't mean you can't enjoy it. But the enjoyment comes from the satisfaction of doing your job well and making everything run smoothly.

Any experienced chef knows the stimulation of the rush: when it's the busiest time of the evening, the orders are coming in so fast you can hardly keep track of them, and every split second counts—then, when everyone digs in and works together and everything "clicks," there's real excitement in the air. But this excitement comes only when you work for it.

A cook with a positive attitude works quickly, efficiently, neatly, and safely. Professionals have pride in their work and want to make sure that the work is something to be proud of.

Staying Power

Food service requires physical and mental stamina, good health, and a willingness to work hard. It is hard work. The pressures can be intense and the hours long and grueling. You may be working evenings and weekends when everyone else is playing. And the work can be monotonous. You might think it's real drudgery when you have to hand shape two or three dozen dinner rolls for your baking class, but wait until you get that great job in the big hotel and are told to make 3,000 canapés for a party.

Ability to Work with People

Few of you will work in an establishment so small that you are the only person on the staff. Food service work is teamwork, and it's essential to be able to work well on a team and to cooperate with your fellow workers. You can't afford to let ego problems, petty jealousy, departmental rivalries, or personal feelings about other people get in the way of doing the job well. In the old days, many chefs were famous for their temper tantrums. Fortunately, self-control is more valued today.

Eagerness to Learn

There is more to learn about cooking than you will learn in a lifetime. But isn't it great to try? The greatest chefs in the world are the first to admit that they have more to learn, and they keep working, experimenting, and studying.

The food service industry is changing so rapidly that it is vital to be open to new ideas. No matter how good your techniques are, you might learn an even better way.

Experience

One of America's most respected chefs has said, "You don't really know how to cook a dish until you have done it a thousand times."

There is no substitute for years of experience. Studying cooking principles in books and in schools can get your career off to a running start. You may learn more about basic cooking theories from your chef instructors than you could in several years of working your way up from washing vegetables. But if you want to become an accomplished cook, you need practice, practice, and more practice. A diploma will not make you a chef.

Dedication to Quality

These days there seems to be something around called "gourmet" food. It's hard to say exactly what that is. Apparently, the only thing so-called "gourmet" foods have in common is high price.

The only distinction it makes sense to make is between well-prepared food and poorly prepared food. There is good roast duckling à l'orange and there is bad roast duckling à l'orange. There are good hamburgers and french fries, and there are bad hamburgers and french fries.

Whether you work in a fancy French restaurant, a fast-food restaurant, a college cafeteria, or a catering house, you can do your job well or you can do it not so well. The choice is yours.

High quality doesn't necessarily mean high price. It costs no more to cook green beans properly than to overcook them. But in order to produce quality food, you must *want* to. It is not enough to know how to.

Good Understanding of the Basics

Experimentation and innovation in cooking are the order of the day. Brilliant chefs are breaking old boundaries, inventing dishes that would have been unheard of years ago. There seems to be no limit to what can be tried.

However, the very chefs who seem to be most revolutionary are the first to insist on the importance of solid grounding in basic techniques and in the classic methods practiced since Escoffier's day. In order to innovate, you have to know where you are starting from.

For the beginner, knowing the basics will help you take better advantage of your experience. When you watch a practiced cook at work, you will understand better what you are seeing and will know what questions to ask.

In order to play great music on the piano, you first have to learn to play scales and exercises.

That's what this book is about. It's not a course in French cooking or American cooking or gourmet cooking or coffee shop cooking. It's a course in the basics. When you finish the book, you will not know everything. But you should be ready to take good advantage of the many rewarding years of food service experience ahead of you.

TERMS FOR REVIEW

Carême	sous chef	rotisseur	tournant
Escoffier	station chef	grillardin	working chef
nouvelle cuisine	saucier	garde manger	short-order cook
chef	poissonier	patissier	professionalism
executive chef	entremetier		

QUESTIONS FOR DISCUSSION

1. Escoffier is sometimes called the father of modern food service. What were his most important accomplishments?

2. Discuss several ways in which modern technology has changed the food service industry.

3. What is the purpose of kitchen organization? Is the classical system of organization developed by Escoffier the best one for all types of kitchens: Why or why not?

4. True or false: A cook in charge of the sauce and sauté station in a large hotel needs to have supervisory skills as well as cooking skills. Explain your answer.

5. True or false: If a culinary arts student in a professional school studies hard, works diligently, gets top grades, and shows real dedication, he or she will be qualified to be a chef upon graduation. Explain your answer.

SANITATION
AND SAFETY

In the last chapter, we talked
about professionalism in food service. Professionalism is an attitude
that reflects pride in the quality of your work. One of the most important ways of
demonstrating professional pride is in the area of sanitation and safety. Pride in quality
is reflected in your appearance and work habits. Poor hygiene, poor grooming
and personal care, and sloppy work habits are nothing to be proud of.

Even more important, poor sanitation and safety can
cost a lot of money. Poor food handling procedures and unclean kitchens
cause illness, unhappy customers, and even fines, summonses, and lawsuits. Increased
food spoilage raises food costs. Poor kitchen safety results in injuries,
medical bills, and work days lost.

Finally, poor sanitation and safety habits show lack of respect
for your customers, for your fellow workers, and for yourself.

In this chapter you will study the causes of food-borne
diseases and kitchen injuries, and you will learn ways of preventing
them. Prevention, of course, is the most important part. It is not as important to
be able to recite the names of disease-causing bacteria as it is to
be able to prevent their growth in food.

After reading this chapter, you should be able to

1. Prevent food poisoning and food-borne diseases by exercising proper hygiene, food handling and storage techniques, cleaning and sanitizing procedures, and pest control.

2. Develop safe work habits to prevent injuries and avoid common hazards in the kitchen.

SANITATION

Rules of personal hygiene and sanitary food handling are not just rules invented to make your life difficult. There are good reasons for all of them. Instead of starting this chapter with lists of rules, we will first talk about the causes of food-borne diseases. Then, when we get to the rules, you will know why they are important. This will make them easier to remember and to practice.

The rules that are presented in this chapter are only basic guidelines. Local health departments will have more detailed regulations. *All food service operators are responsible for knowing the health department regulations in their own cities and states.*

The information presented in this chapter is practical, not merely theoretical. It should not merely be learned but put to use systematically. One effective system that food service establishments can use to ensure food safety is called the Hazard Analysis Critical Control Point (HACCP) system. It is a practical program that identifies possible danger points and sets up procedures for corrective action. HACCP is introduced later in this chapter.

. . . .

INTRODUCTION TO MICROBIOLOGY

Most food-borne diseases are caused by *bacteria,* tiny one-celled plants so small that they can be seen only under a microscope.

Microbiology is the study of microscopic forms of life, including bacteria. Studying this chapter will not make you a microbiologist. In fact, some of the information in the next several pages you may forget very quickly—names like *Clostridium perfringens,* for instance. The importance of these first sections is not simply to exercise your memory for difficult facts, *it is to help you understand how and why disease-causing bacteria grow and spread, so that you are better able to prevent food-borne disease.*

Kinds of Bacteria

Bacteria are everywhere, in the air, in the water, in the ground, on our food, on our skin, inside our bodies. Scientists have various ways of classifying and describing these bacteria. As food workers, we are interested in a way of classifying them that may be less scientific but is more practical to our work.

1. *Harmless bacteria.* Most bacteria fall into this category. They are neither helpful nor harmful to us. We are not concerned with them in food sanitation.

2. *Beneficial bacteria.* These bacteria are helpful to us. For example, many live in the intestinal tract, where they fight harmful bacteria, aid the digestion of food, and produce certain nutrients. In food production, bacteria make possible the manufacture of many foods including cheese, yogurt, and sauerkraut.

3. *Undesirable bacteria.* These are the bacteria that are responsible for food spoilage. They cause souring, putrefying, and decomposition. These bacteria may or may not cause disease, but they have a built-in safety factor: they announce their presence by means of sour odors, sticky or slimy surfaces, and discoloration. As long as we use common sense and follow the rule "when in doubt, throw it out," we are relatively safe from these bacteria.

   We are concerned with these bacteria for two reasons:

   a. Food spoilage costs money.
   b. Food spoilage is a sign of improper food handling and storage. This means that the next kind of bacteria is probably present.

4. *Disease-causing bacteria, or pathogens.* These are the bacteria that cause most food-borne illness, the bacteria that we are most concerned with.

   Pathogens do not necessarily leave detectable odors or tastes in food. In other words, you can't tell if food is contaminated by smelling, tasting, or looking at it. The only way to protect food against pathogenic bacteria is by proper hygiene and sanitary food handling and storage techniques.

Bacteria Growth

Bacteria multiply by splitting in half. Under ideal conditions for growth, they can double in number every 15 to 30 minutes. This means that one single bacterium could multiply to a million in less than 6 hours!

Conditions for Growth

1. *Food.* Bacteria require some kind of food in order to grow. They like many of the foods we do.

2. *Moisture.* Bacteria require water in order to absorb food. Dry foods will not support bacterial growth. Foods with a very high salt or sugar con-

tent are also relatively safe, because these ingredients make the bacteria unable to use the moisture present.

3. **Temperature.** Bacteria grow best at warm temperatures. *Temperatures between 45°F and 140°F (7°C and 60°C) will promote the growth of disease-causing bacteria.* This temperature range is called the *Food Danger Zone.*

    Note: Some health departments advocate 40°F (4°C) as the lower limit of the Food Danger Zone. Check with your local authorities.

4. **Acidity or alkalinity.** In general, disease-producing bacteria like a neutral environment, neither too acid nor too alkaline.

5. **Air.** Most bacteria require oxygen to grow. These are called *aerobic.* Some bacteria are *anaerobic,* which means they can grow only if there is no air present, such as in metal cans. Botulism, one of the most dangerous forms of food poisoning, is caused by anaerobic bacteria.

6. **Time.** When bacteria are introduced to a new environment, they need time to adjust to their surroundings before they start growing. This time is called the *lag phase.* If other conditions are good, the lag phase may last about 1 hour or somewhat longer.

    If it weren't for the lag phase, there would be much more food-borne disease than there is. This time delay makes it possible to have foods at room temperature *for very short periods* in order to work on them.

Think of most of the foods sitting around a kitchen: a bowl of chicken salad sitting on the counter, waiting for lunch service; a sheet pan full of fresh chickens that a prep cook was working on before she got interrupted by the chef, who needed something else done; a coconut cream pie set on the dessert cart to tempt customers. All the conditions are perfect. Any self-respecting germ would love to move in and start raising a family.

Locomotion

Bacteria do not have feet. They can move from place to place in only one way: they must be carried.

Foods can become contaminated by any of the following means:

Hands

Coughs and sneezes

Other foods

Equipment and utensils

Air

Water

Insects

Rats and mice

Protection against Bacteria

Because we know how and why bacteria grow, we should now be able to keep them from growing. Because we know how bacteria get from place to place, we should now know how to keep them from getting into our food.

There are three basic principles of food protection against bacteria. These principles are the reasons behind nearly all the sanitation techniques that we discuss in the rest of this chapter.

1. **Keep bacteria from spreading.**
    Don't let food touch anything that may contain disease-producing bacteria, and protect food from bacteria in the air.

2. **Stop bacteria from growing.**
    Take away the conditions that encourage bacteria to grow. In the kitchen, our best weapon is temperature. *The most effective way to prevent bacterial growth is to keep foods below 45°F (7°C) or above 140°F (60°C).* These temperatures won't necessarily kill bacteria; they'll just slow down their growth greatly.

3. **Kill bacteria.**
    Most disease-causing bacteria are killed if they are subjected to a temperature of 170°F (77°C) for 30 seconds or higher temperatures for shorter times. This fact enables us to make food safe by cooking and to sanitize dishes and equipment with heat. The term *sanitize* means to kill disease-causing bacteria.

    Certain chemicals also kill bacteria. These may be used for sanitizing equipment.

FOOD-BORNE DISEASES

As you know, most food-borne illnesses are caused by bacteria. But there are other causes, too. This section summarizes the main food-borne diseases in the United States. For each disease, pay particular attention to the way it is spread, the foods involved, and the means of prevention.

Bacterial Diseases

There are two kinds of diseases caused by bacteria: intoxications and infections.

Intoxications are caused by poisons (toxins) that the bacteria produce while they are growing in the food. It is these poisons, not the bacteria themselves, that cause the diseases.

Infections are caused by bacteria (or other organisms) that get into the intestinal system and attack the body.

The first two diseases we discuss, botulism and staphylococcus food poisoning, are intoxications. The third, *Escherichia coli*, can be either an intoxication or an infection. The rest are infections.

Botulism

Caused by toxins produced by the bacteria *Clostridium botulinum*, botulism attacks the nervous system and is usually *fatal*, even if only a small amount of poisoned food is eaten. The bacteria are anaerobic (do not grow in air) and do not grow in high-acid foods. Most outbreaks are caused by improper canning techniques. The toxin (although not the bacteria) is destroyed by boiling (212°F/100°C) for 20 minutes.

Source of bacteria: soil on vegetables and other foods.

Foods usually involved: home-canned, low-acid vegetables (very rarely in commercially canned foods).

Prevention: use only commercially canned foods. Discard *without tasting* any bulged or damaged cans or foods with off odors.

Staphylococcus Food Poisoning (Staph)

Caused by toxins produced in foods by the bacterium *Staphylococcus aureus*, staph is probably the most common food poisoning, characterized by nausea, vomiting, stomach cramps, diarrhea, and prostration.

Source of bacteria: usually food workers.

Foods usually involved: custards and desserts made with dairy products, potato salad, protein salads, ham, hollandaise sauce, many other high-protein foods.

Prevention: good hygiene and work habits. Do not handle foods if you have an illness or infection. Clean and sanitize all equipment. Keep foods below 45°F or above 140°F.

Escherichia coli

This bacterium causes severe illness, either as an intoxication or an infection. Severe abdominal pain, nausea, vomiting, diarrhea, and other symptoms result from *E. coli* intoxication. As an infection, *E. coli* causes intestinal inflammation and bloody diarrhea. While the illness normally lasts from one to three days, it can lead to long-term illness in some cases.

Source of bacteria: intestinal tracts of humans and some animals, especially cattle; contaminated water.

Foods usually involved: raw or undercooked red meats; unpasteurized dairy products; sometimes fish from contaminated water, prepared foods such as mashed potatoes and cream pies.

Prevention: cook foods, including red meats, thoroughly; avoid cross-contamination. Practice good hygiene.

Salmonella

The food infection caused by salmonella bacteria exhibits symptoms that are similar to those of staph poisoning, though the disease may last longer. Most poultry carry this bacteria.

Source of bacteria: contaminated meats and poultry; fecal contamination by food workers.

Foods usually involved: poultry, meats, eggs, poultry stuffings, gravies, raw foods, shellfish from polluted waters.

Prevention: good personal hygiene. Proper food storage and handling. Insect and rodent control. Wash hands and sanitize all equipment and cutting surfaces after handling raw poultry. Use certified shellfish.

Clostridium Perfringens

This is another infection characterized by nausea, cramps, stomach pain, and diarrhea. The bacteria are hard to destroy because they are not always killed by cooking temperatures.

Source of bacteria: soil, fresh meats, human carriers.

Foods usually involved: meats and poultry, reheated or unrefrigerated gravies and sauces.

Prevention: keep foods hot (above 140°F) or cold (below 45°F).

Streptococcal (Strep) Infections

The symptoms of this disease are fever and sore throat.

Sources of bacteria: coughs, sneezes, infected food workers.

Foods usually involved: any food contaminated by coughs, sneezes, or infected food workers and then served without further cooking.

Prevention: do not handle food if you are infected. Protect displayed food (salad bars, pastry carts, etc.) from customers' sneezes and coughs.

Other Food Infections

Infectious Hepatitis

This is a severe disease that can last for many months. It is caused by a virus.

Source of contamination: shellfish from polluted waters, infected food workers.

Foods usually involved: shellfish eaten raw, any food contaminated by an infected person.

Prevention: good health and hygiene. Use only certified shellfish from safe waters.

Trichinosis

This disease is often mistaken for the flu at first, but it can last for a year or more. It is caused by a tiny worm that becomes imbedded in the muscles.

Source of contamination: infected pork from hogs that ate unprocessed garbage.

Foods usually involved: pork products.

Prevention: cook all pork products to an internal temperature of at least 150°F (65°C). To be on the safe side, many authorities recommend 165°F (74°C).

Chemical Poisoning

Except for lead poisoning, the following diseases show their symptoms very quickly, usually within less than 30 minutes of eating the poisoned food. To prevent these diseases, do not use the materials that cause them.

1. **Antimony.**   Caused by storing or cooking acid foods in chipped grey enamelware.

2. **Cadmium.**   Caused by cadmium-plated ice cube trays or containers.

3. **Cyanide.**   Caused by silver polish containing cyanide.

4. **Lead.**   Caused by lead water pipes, solder containing lead, or utensils containing lead.

5. **Copper.**   Caused by unclean or corroded copper utensils, acid foods cooked in unlined copper utensils, or carbonated beverages in contact with copper tubing.

6. **Zinc.**   Caused by foods cooked in zinc-plated (galvanized) utensils.

PERSONAL HYGIENE

Earlier in this chapter we said that most food-borne disease is caused by bacteria. Now we change that statement slightly to say that *most food-borne disease is caused by bacteria spread by food workers.*

The first step in preventing food-borne disease is good personal hygiene. Even when we are healthy we have bacteria all over our skin and in our nose and mouth. Some of these bacteria, if given the chance to grow in food, will make people ill.

1. Do not work with food if you have any communicable disease or infection.

2. Bathe or shower daily.

3. Wear clean uniforms and aprons.

4. Keep hair neat and clean. Always wear a hat or hairnet.

5. Keep mustaches and beards trimmed and clean. Better yet, be clean shaven.

6. Wash hands and exposed parts of arms before work and as often as necessary during work, including:

    a. After eating, drinking, or smoking.
    b. After using the toilet.
    c. After touching or handling anything that may be contaminated with bacteria.

7. Cover coughs and sneezes, and then wash hands.

8. Keep your hands away from your face, eyes, hair, and arms.

9. Keep fingernails clean and short. Do not wear nail polish.

10. Do not smoke or chew gum while on duty.

11. Cover cuts or sores with clean bandages.

12. Do not sit on worktables.

FOOD STORAGE

The following rules of safe food storage have two purposes:

To prevent contamination of foods.

To prevent growth of bacteria that may already be in foods.

Temperature control is an important part of food storage. Perishable foods must be kept out of the *Food Danger Zone*—45°F to 140°F (7°C to 60°C)—as much as possible, because these temperatures support bacterial growth. See Figure 2.1 for a chart of important temperatures.

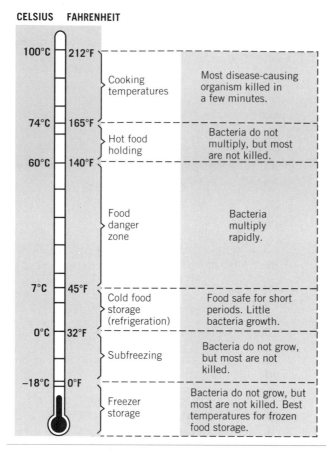

CELSIUS   FAHRENHEIT

100°C	212°F	Cooking temperatures — Most disease-causing organism killed in a few minutes.
74°C	165°F	Hot food holding — Bacteria do not multiply, but most are not killed.
60°C	140°F	
		Food danger zone — Bacteria multiply rapidly.
7°C	45°F	Cold food storage (refrigeration) — Food safe for short periods. Little bacteria growth.
0°C	32°F	
		Subfreezing — Bacteria do not grow, but most are not killed.
−18°C	0°F	
		Freezer storage — Bacteria do not grow, but most are not killed. Best temperatures for frozen food storage.

FIGURE 2.1   **Important temperatures in sanitation and food protection.**

Dry Food Storage

Dry food storage pertains to those foods not likely to support bacterial growth in their normal state. These foods include

> Flour
>
> Sugar and salt
>
> Cereals, rice, and other grains
>
> Dried beans and peas
>
> Ready-prepared cereals
>
> Breads and crackers
>
> Oils and shortenings
>
> Canned and bottled foods (unopened)

1. Store dry foods in a cool, dry place, off the floor, away from the wall, and not under a sewer line.

2. Keep all containers tightly closed to protect from insects, rodents, and dust. Dry foods can be contaminated, even if they don't need refrigeration.

Freezer Storage

1. Keep frozen foods at 0°F (−18°C) or lower.

2. Keep all frozen foods tightly wrapped or packaged to prevent freezer burn.

3. Label and date all items.

4. Thaw frozen foods properly. These methods may be used:

   a. In refrigerator.
   b. Under cold running water.
   c. In a microwave oven, if the item is to be cooked or served immediately.

   Do not thaw at room temperature, because the surface temperature will go above 45°F (7°C) before the inside is thawed, resulting in bacterial growth.

Refrigerator Storage

1. Keep all perishable foods below 45°F (7°C).

2. Do not overcrowd refrigerators. Leave space between items so that cold air can circulate.

3. Keep refrigerator doors shut except when removing or putting in foods.

4. Keep shelves and interiors of refrigerators clean.

5. Store raw and cooked items separately if possible.

6. If raw and cooked foods must be kept in the same refrigerator, keep cooked foods *above* raw foods. If cooked foods are kept below raw foods, they can become contaminated by drips and spills. Then, if they are not to be cooked again before serving, they may be hazardous.

7. Keep refrigerated foods wrapped or covered and in sanitary containers.

8. Do not let any unsanitary surface, such as the bottoms of other containers, touch any food.

9. Chill foods as quickly as possible over ice or in a cold water bath before placing in refrigerator. A gallon of stock placed in a refrigerator hot off the stove may take 10 hours to go below 45°F, giving bacteria plenty of time to grow.

10. When holding foods such as protein salads in a cold bain marie or refrigerated table for service, do not heap the food above the level of the container. The food above this level will not stay cold enough.

Hot Food Holding

1. To keep foods hot for service, use steam tables or other equipment that will keep all parts of all foods *above 140°F (60°C)* at all times.

2. Keep foods covered.

3. Bring foods to holding temperature as quickly as possible by using ovens, steamers, range-top pots and pans, or other cooking equipment. Do not warm up cold foods by placing them directly in the steam table. They will take too long to heat and bacteria will have time to grow.

4. Do not let ready-to-eat foods come in contact with any contaminated surface.

FOOD HANDLING AND PREPARATION

We face two major sanitation problems when handling and preparing food. The first is *cross-contamination,* which is the transfer of bacteria to food from another food or from equipment or work surfaces.

The second problem is that, while we are working on it, food is usually at a temperature between 45°F and 140°F, or the Food Danger Zone. The lag phase of bacteria growth (p. 15) helps us a little, but to be safe we must keep foods out of the danger zone whenever possible.

1. Start with clean, wholesome foods from reputable purveyors. Whenever applicable, buy government-inspected meats, poultry, fish, dairy, and egg products.

2. Handle foods as little as possible. Use tongs, spatulas, or other utensils instead of hands when practicable.

3. Use clean, sanitized equipment and worktables.

4. Clean and sanitize cutting surfaces and equipment after handling raw poultry, meat, fish, or eggs and before working on another food.

5. Clean as you go. Don't wait until the end of the workday.

6. Wash raw fruits and vegetables thoroughly.

7. When bringing foods out of refrigeration, do not bring out more than you can process in an hour.

8. Keep foods covered whenever possible unless in immediate use.

9. Do not let any perishable foods remain in the temperature danger zone for more than 1 hour.

10. Boil leftover gravies, sauces, soups, and vegetables before serving.

11. Don't mix leftovers with freshly prepared foods.

12. Chill all ingredients for protein salads and potato salads *before* combining.

13. Chill custards, cream fillings, and other hazardous foods as quickly as possible by pouring them into shallow, sanitized pans, covering them, and refrigerating. Do not stack the pans.

14. Cook all pork products to an internal temperature of at least 150°F (65°C).

CLEANING AND SANITIZING EQUIPMENT

Cleaning means removing visible soil. *Sanitizing* means killing disease-causing bacteria. Two ways of killing bacteria are by *heat* and by *chemicals.*

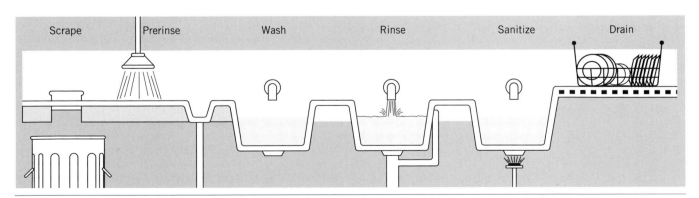

FIGURE 2.2   **Setup of three-compartment sink for manual dishwashing.**

Manual Dishwashing

Figure 2.2 shows the setup of a three-compartment sink for washing dishes, glassware, and eating utensils by hand.

Procedure

1. ***Scrape and prerinse.***

    The purpose of this step is to keep the wash water cleaner longer.

2. ***Wash.***

    Use warm water at 110°F to 120°F (43°C to 49°C) and a good detergent. Scrub well with a brush to remove all traces of soil and grease.

3. ***Rinse.***

    Use clean, warm water to rinse off detergent. Change the water frequently, or use running water with an overflow, as in Figure 2.2.

4. ***Sanitize.***

    Place utensils in a rack and immerse in hot water at *170°F (77°C) for 30 seconds.* (A gas or electric heating element is needed to hold water at this temperature.)

5. ***Drain and air dry.***

    Do not towel dry. This may recontaminate utensils. Do not touch food contact surfaces of sanitized dishes, glasses, and silverware.

Mechanical Dishwashing

The steps in washing dishes by machine are the same as in the hand method, except that the machine does the washing, rinsing, and sanitizing.

Procedure

1. Scrape and prerinse.

2. Rack dishes so that dishwasher spray will strike all surfaces.

3. Run machine for a full cycle.

4. Sanitizing temperatures:
    180°F (82°C) for machines that sanitize by heat.
    140°F (60°C) for machines that sanitize by chemical disinfectant.

5. Air dry and inspect dishes. Do not touch food contact surfaces.

Washing Kitchen Utensils and Equipment

1. Use the same three-compartment sink setup and procedure as for manual dishwashing.

2. Do not use scouring powder or steel wool. These may make scratches where bacteria can hide. Also, pieces of steel wool break off and can remain in the pan and thus get into food.

3. Utensils with baked-on foods should be scraped and prerinsed, soaked in the first compartment to loosen the baked-on food, then scraped and prerinsed again.

4. Sanitizing of kitchen equipment may be done with *chemical disinfectants* instead of heat. Use an approved disinfectant, and follow the instructions on the label.

Cleaning and Sanitizing Stationary Equipment and Work Surfaces

1. Unplug electric equipment before cleaning. You could seriously injure yourself if you accidentally hit the power switch while you are cleaning a piece of equipment.

2. Disassemble equipment when possible. (This obviously doesn't apply to such equipment as worktables.) All immersible parts should be cleaned and sanitized like kitchen utensils.

3. Wash all food contact surfaces, using a detergent solution and *clean* cloths.

4. Sanitize all surfaces with a double-strength sanitizing solution and with clean cloths used only for this purpose.

5. Allow to air dry.

6. Reassemble equipment.

RODENT AND INSECT CONTROL

Rats, mice, flies, and cockroaches can spread disease by contaminating food and food contact surfaces. Any sign of rodent or insect infestation is usually considered a serious violation of health codes.

There are four basic methods of pest control. We start with the most important and most effective.

Build Them Out

1. Block all possible rodent entrances, including structural defects in the building.

2. Put screens on all windows and doors.

3. Make sure all doors are self-closing, or install fly fans or air curtains.

4. Inspect incoming supplies for signs of insect infestation.

Eliminate Harborage and Breeding Places

1. Repair holes in walls or floors, or any other structural defects.

2. Eliminate narrow spaces between and behind equipment, counters, or other fixtures, and hollow spaces made by false bottoms in counters, cabinets, etc.

3. Store food and supplies off the floor.

4. Seal all cracks and crevices. Repair loose tiles, wall coverings, and so on.

5. Remove all fly breeding places inside and out: garbage, manure, general filth.

Eliminate Food Supplies

1. Keep all foods tightly covered or wrapped.

2. Keep garbage containers tightly covered, and use metal (ratproof) garbage cans.

3. Clean up all spilled food.

4. General sanitation: keep floors, walls, and equipment clean.

Exterminate

Hire a qualified, licensed exterminator, who knows how to use poisons, insecticides, and traps. Most poisons should not be used in a food production operation, so it's better not to do the job yourself.

Extermination is only a temporary solution. For permanent freedom from rodents and insects, you must rely on the other methods of control.

SETTING UP A SYSTEM FOR FOOD SAFETY

Once you have learned the information in the first part of this chapter, you must apply it in the kitchen.

Many food service operations have designed food safety systems that enable food workers to keep a close check on food items whenever there is a risk of contamination or of the growth of pathogens. In the most effective systems, nothing is left to chance. At each stage of food production and storage, workers refer to written guidelines that explain what standards to look for and what action to take if the foods don't meet those standards. Having a written set of guidelines helps everyone avoid costly mistakes.

The HACCP System

One effective food safety system is called the *Hazard Analysis Critical Control Point* system, or HACCP. Versions of this system are being widely adopted throughout the food service industry.

The following discussion is a brief introduction to some of the basic concepts of HACCP. For a detailed explanation, you may refer to published materials such as *Applied Foodservice Sanitation*, fourth edition, a project of the Educational Foundation of the National Restaurant Association (see Bibliography, p. 801). The discussion below is based on information presented in that book.

The Flow of Food

HACCP begins with a concept called the *flow of food*. This term refers to the movement of food through a food service operation, from receiving through various stages of storage, preparation, and service, until it gets to the final consumer.

The flow of food is different for each item being prepared. Some menu items involve many steps. For example, a luncheon dish of creamed chicken and vegetables over rice might have the following steps:

> Receiving raw ingredients (chicken, vegetables, cream, rice, etc.)
>
> Storing raw ingredients
>
> Preparing ingredients (washing, cutting, trimming, etc.)
>
> Cooking
>
> Holding and serving
>
> Cooling and storing leftovers
>
> Reheating, holding, and storing leftovers

Even the simplest items undergo several steps. For example, a cake that is bought already prepared from a commercial baker and served as dessert will go through at least the following steps on its way to the customer:

> Receiving
>
> Storing
>
> Serving

Hazards and Critical Control Points

At each of these steps, as foods flow through the operation, there are risks that can lead to dangerous conditions, which are called *hazards*. These hazards can be divided into three categories:

- *Contamination,* such as cross-contamination from a soiled cutting surface; torn packaging that permits insect infestation; working on food without washing hands; spilling cleaning chemicals on food.

- *Growth of bacteria and other pathogens* due to such conditions as inadequate refrigeration or storage, and holding hot foods below 140°F (60°C).

- *Survival of pathogens or the continued presence of toxins,* usually because of inadequate cooking or heating or inadequate sanitizing of equipment and surfaces.

Note that these hazards correspond to the sanitation techniques discussed on page 15 (keep bacteria from spreading, stop bacteria from growing, kill bacteria). The important difference is that the hazards addressed by HACCP include chemical and other hazards in addition to disease-causing organisms.

At each step where there is a risk of one of these hazards, it is possible to take some action that will eliminate the hazard or reduce it to a minimum. Such actions are called *critical control points.* In simple language, setting up an HACCP system starts with reviewing the flow of food to figure out where something might go wrong and then deciding what can be done about it. In the language of HACCP, these steps are called "assessing the hazards" and "identifying critical control points."

Setting Standards and Following Procedures

The next step in designing an HACCP food safety system is setting up procedures for critical control points. At each critical control point, food workers need to know what standards have to be met, what procedures to follow to meet the standards, and what to do if they aren't met. To reduce the chances for making mistakes, these standards and procedures are written out. Whenever possible, they should be included in the operation's recipes.

Some procedures are general ones and include the sanitation rules discussed earlier in this chapter. For example: wash hands before handling food and after handling raw foods; hold foods above 140°F (60°C) or below 45°F (7°C). Others apply to specific items. For example: roast a particular meat to an internal temperature of at least 165°F (74°C).

Careful observation is needed to know when standards are met. This often involves *measuring.* The only way to know, for example, that a roast has reached the required internal temperature is to measure it, using a clean, sanitized thermometer.

Managers must ensure that all employees are trained to follow procedures and have the equipment to do the job.

Once these procedures are developed, additional steps in setting up an HACCP system are important to ensure that the system is effective: monitoring critical control points, taking corrective action if procedures are not followed, keeping records of all aspects of the system, and verifying that the system is working.

As this brief introduction to HACCP implies, establishing such a system to control all aspects of food production requires more information than this chapter has space for. Refer to the book mentioned at the beginning of this section for a comprehensive discussion.

SAFETY

Kitchen work is usually considered a relatively safe occupation, at least in comparison with many industrial jobs. Nevertheless, the kitchen has many hazards. Minor injuries from cuts and burns are very common, and more serious injuries are all too possible. The quantity of very hot equipment and of powerful machinery, combined with the busy, sometimes frantic pace, makes it important for everyone to work carefully and with constant attention to rules of safety.

THE SAFE WORKPLACE

Most of this section is concerned with ways that workers can prevent certain kinds of accidents, such as cuts, burns, and falls. However, it is much easier to develop and practice habits that prevent accidents if safety is built into the workplace.

Building Safety into the Kitchen

The management of a food service operation must see to it that the structure and equipment have necessary safety features.

1. Structure, equipment, and electric wiring in good repair.

2. Adequate lighting on work surfaces and in corridors.

3. Nonslip floors.

4. Clearly marked exits.

5. Equipment supplied with necessary safety devices.

6.   Heat-activated fire extinguishers over cooking equipment, especially deep fryers.

7.   Conveniently located emergency equipment, such as fire extinguishers, fire blanket, and first aid kit.

8.   Clearly posted emergency telephone numbers.

9.   Smooth traffic patterns to avoid collisions between workers.

Building Safety into the Worker

Safety is more than just memorizing all the rules in this chapter. Safety is an attitude, a matter of professionalism. True professionals work safely because it's part of their attitude toward their craft. They are proud of their work and want to do it as well as possible. Many accidents are caused by carelessness, by lack of attention, and by clowning around in the kitchen.

PREVENTING CUTS

1.   Keep knives sharp. A sharp knife is safer than a dull one, because it requires less pressure and is less likely to slip.

2.   Use a cutting board. Do not cut against a metal surface. Place a damp towel under the board to keep it from slipping.

3.   Pay attention to your work when using a knife or cutting equipment.

4.   Cut away from yourself and other workers.

5.   Use knives only for cutting, not for such jobs as opening bottles.

6.   Don't try to catch a falling knife. Step back and let it fall.

7.   Don't put knives in a sink, under water, or any place where they can't be seen.

8.   Clean knives carefully, with the sharp edge away from you.

9.   Store knives in a safe place, such as in a rack, when not in use.

10.   Carry a knife properly. Hold it beside you, point down, with the sharp edge back and away from you. Don't swing your arm. Whenever possible, carry knives in a sheath. Warn people when you are walking past them with a knife in hand.

11.   Keep breakable items, such as dishes and glassware, out of the food production area.

12.   Don't put breakable items in the pot sink.

13.   Sweep up, don't pick up, broken glass.

14.   Discard chipped or cracked dishes and glasses.

15.   Use special containers for broken dishes and glasses. Don't throw them in with other garbage.

16.   If there is broken glass in the sink, drain it before trying to take out the glass.

17.   Remove all nails and staples when opening crates and cartons, and dispose of them.

PREVENTING BURNS

1.   Always assume a pot handle is hot. Don't just grab it with your bare hand.

2.   Use dry pads or towels to handle hot pans. Wet ones will create steam, which can burn you.

3.   Keep pan handles out of the aisle, so people won't bump into them. Also, keep handles away from open flames of gas burners.

4.   Don't fill pans so full that they are likely to spill hot foods.

5.   Get help when moving heavy containers of hot food.

6.   Open lids away from you to let steam escape safely.

7.   Use care when opening compartment steamers.

8.   Make sure gas is well vented before trying to light ovens or pilot lights. Strike matches *before* turning on the gas. Also, strike matches away from yourself.

9.   Wear long sleeves and double-breasted jackets to protect yourself from spilled or spattered hot foods or fat. Also, wear sturdy leather shoes with closed toes.

10.   Dry foods before putting them in frying fat, or hot fat may splatter on you.

11.   When placing foods in hot fat, let them fall away from you, so that fat will not splash on you.

12.   Keep liquids away from the deep fryer. If a liquid were spilled into the fryer, the suddenly created steam could spray hot fat on anyone nearby.

13.   Always warn people when you are walking behind them with hot pans or when you are walking behind someone who is working with hot items.

14.   Warn service people about hot plates.

PREVENTING FIRES

1. Know where fire extinguishers are located and how to use them.

2. Use the right kind of fire extinguisher. There are three classes of fires, and fire extinguishers should be labeled according to the kind of fire for which they can be used.

    a. Class A fires: wood, paper, cloth, ordinary combustibles.
    b. Class B fires: burning liquids, such as grease, oil, gasoline, solvents.
    c. Class C fires: switches, motors, electrical equipment, and so forth.

    Never use water or a Class A fire extinguisher on a grease fire or electrical fire. You will only spread the fire.

3. Keep a supply of salt or baking soda handy to put out fires on range tops.

4. Keep hoods and other equipment free from grease buildup.

5. Don't leave hot fat unattended on the range.

6. Smoke only in designated areas. Do not leave burning cigarettes unattended.

7. If a fire alarm sounds and if you have time, turn off all gas and electric appliances before leaving the building.

8. Keep fire doors closed.

9. Keep exits free from obstacles.

PREVENTING INJURIES FROM MACHINES AND EQUIPMENT

1. Do not use any equipment unless you understand its operation.

2. Use all guards and safety devices on equipment. Keep slicing machine set at zero (blade closed) when not in use.

3. Don't touch or remove food from any kind of equipment while it is running, not even with a spoon or spatula.

4. Unplug electric equipment before disassembling or cleaning.

5. Make sure the switch is off before plugging in equipment.

6. Do not touch or handle electric equipment, including switches, if your hands are wet or if you are standing in water.

7. Wear properly fitting clothing and tuck in apron strings to avoid getting them caught in machinery.

8. Use equipment only for the purpose intended.

9. Stack pots and other equipment properly on pot racks, so that they are stable and not likely to fall.

PREVENTING FALLS

1. Clean up spills immediately.

2. Throw salt on a slippery spot to make it less slippery, while a mop is being fetched.

3. Keep aisles and stairs clear and unobstructed.

4. Don't carry objects too big to see over.

5. Walk, don't run.

6. Use a safe ladder, not chairs or piles of boxes, to reach high shelves or to clean high equipment.

PREVENTING STRAINS AND INJURIES FROM LIFTING

1. Lift with the leg muscles, not the back. Figure 2.3 shows proper lifting techniques.

2. Don't turn or twist the back while lifting, and make sure your footing is secure.

3. Use a cart to move heavy objects long distances, or get help.

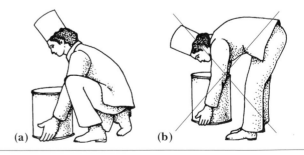

FIGURE 2.3 **Proper lifting technique. (a) Squat on one knee, then lift with the leg muscles. (b) Do not bend over and lift with the back.**

TERMS FOR REVIEW

bacteria	sanitation	salmonella	HACCP
pathogen	intoxication	trichinosis	flow of food
aerobic	infection	Food Danger Zone	hazard
anaerobic	botulism	cross-contamination	critical control point
lag phase	staph	sanitize	Class A, B, and C fires

QUESTIONS FOR DISCUSSION

1. True or false: holding food in a steam table above 140°F (65°C) kills disease-causing bacteria and eliminates the problem of food poisoning. Explain your answer.

2. True or false: canning foods eliminates air so disease-causing bacteria can't grow. Explain your answer.

3. Which of the following foods can become contaminated by disease-causing organisms?

Chocolate eclairs	Dinner rolls
Potato salad	Shrimp cocktail
Roast beef	After-dinner mints
Lettuce	Saltine crackers
Turkey sandwich	Rice pudding

4. How often should you wash your hands when working on food?

5. Why is temperature control one of the most effective weapons against bacterial growth? What are some important temperatures to remember?

6 What is the importance of cleaning and sanitizing equipment and cutting boards immediately after working on raw poultry?

7. You are making egg salad, and you have just cooked the eggs. What is your next step *before* chopping the eggs and mixing them with the other ingredients? Why?

8. Is it possible for a dish to be clean but not sanitized? Sanitized but not clean?

9. Explain the concepts of *hazards* and *critical control points*. Give at least three examples of each.

CHAPTER 3

TOOLS AND EQUIPMENT

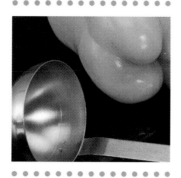

Thorough knowledge
of equipment is essential for success in the kitchen. Few food service
operations depend on nothing more than a range and oven, an assortment of pots
and pans, and knives and other hand tools. Modern technology continues
to develop more and more specialized and technically advanced
tools to reduce kitchen labor.

Much of this equipment is so complex
or so sophisticated that only first-hand instruction and practice
will teach you how to operate it effectively and safely. Other items, especially
hand tools, are simple and need no explanation but require much
practice to develop good manual skills.

There is a vast array of specialized equipment that
is available for today's kitchens. It would take a large book, not just a
short chapter, to explain all of the many items you will come in contact with in
your career—items such as pasta machines, crêpe machines, burger formers, breading
machines, cookie droppers, beverage machines, Greek gyro broilers, doughnut
glazers, conveyor fryers, and so on. In this technological age, nearly every
year brings new types of tools to simplify various tasks.

This chapter introduces you to the most commonly used
equipment in food service kitchens. It cannot, in this short space, serve as an
operating manual for every model of every machine you will use. It cannot take the
place of demonstration by your instructor and of actual experience.

*After studying this chapter, you should be able to understand the safe
and efficient use of standard kitchen equipment.*

INTRODUCTION TO QUANTITY FOOD EQUIPMENT

Before we look at specific items, we must first consider some points relating to the use of equipment in general.

Food Equipment Can Be Dangerous

Modern cooking and food processing equipment has an extraordinary capacity to burn, cut, smash, mangle, and amputate various parts of the tender human body. If this sounds like a harsh way to begin a chapter, it is not meant to intimidate you or scare you but to inspire a healthy respect for the importance of proper safety and operating procedures.

Never use a piece of equipment until you are thoroughly familiar with its operation and all its features. You must also learn how to know when a machine is not operating correctly. When this happens, shut it down immediately and report the malfunction to a supervisor.

Not All Models Are Alike

Each manufacturer introduces slight variations on the basic equipment. While all convection ovens operate on the same basic principles, each model is slightly different, if only in the location of the switches. It is important to study the operating manual supplied with each item or to be "broken in" by someone who already knows that item well and has operated it.

Cleaning Is Part of the Operating Procedure

Thorough, regular cleaning of all equipment is essential. Most large equipment can be partially disassembled for cleaning. Again, every model is slightly different. Operating manuals should give these procedures in detail. If a manual is not available, you must get the information from someone who knows the equipment.

Conserve Energy

At one time it was standard procedure for the chef to turn on the ovens and ranges first thing in the day and keep them on all day. Today high energy costs have made such practices very expensive. For-tunately, modern equipment has shorter preheating times.

Know the preheating time for all your cooking equipment, so you don't need to turn it on before it's necessary. Plan production so that high energy-using equipment is not on for long periods when not in use.

Your Hands Are Your Best Tools

Machines are intended to be labor-saving devices. However, the usefulness of specialized processing equipment often depends on the volume of food it handles. It takes less time for a cook to slice a few pounds of onions by hand than to set up a slicing attachment, pass the onions through it, and then break down and clean the equipment. This is why it is so important to develop good manual skills.

COOKING EQUIPMENT

Range Tops

The range is still the most important piece of cooking equipment in the kitchen, even though many of its functions have been taken over by other tools, such as steamers, steam kettles, tilting skillets, and ovens.

Types of Cook Tops (Figures 3.1, 3.2)

1. *Open elements* (burners), either electric coils or gas flames. Advantages: fastest to heat and can be turned off after short use. Disadvantage: cook-top space is limited to one pot per burner.

FIGURE 3.1 **Open burner gas range with griddle.**

FIGURE 3.2   **Flat-top range (at right).**

2. *Flat top or hot top* (light weight). Burners covered with steel plate. More cook space is available. Top will support moderately heavy weights.

3. *Heavy-duty flat top.* Burners covered with heavy cast steel. The top will support many heavy pots. A thick top requires longer preheating. Set burners for different levels, and adjust cooking heat by moving pots to different spots on the top.

Do's and Don'ts

1. Make sure gas pilots are lit before turning on burners. If burners do not light, turn off gas and allow the gas to ventilate before trying again to light pilots or burners.

2. Adjust air intake so that gas flames are blue with a white tip, for maximum heat.

3. Do not keep flat-top ranges on high heat unless items are being cooked over them. Damage to tops could result.

Ovens

The oven and the range top are the two workhorses of the traditional kitchen, which is why the two are so often found in the same units (Figures 3.1, 3.2). Ovens are enclosed spaces in which food is heated usually by hot air or, in some newer kinds of ovens, by microwaves or infrared radiation.

In addition to roasting and baking, ovens can do many of the jobs normally done on the range top. Many foods can be simmered, stewed, braised, or poached in the oven, freeing the range top and the chef's attention for other tasks.

There are many other kinds of ovens beyond those discussed here, but many of them are for specialty or high-volume uses. These include *conveyor* *ovens,* which carry foods through the oven on a steel conveyor belt; *holding ovens* or warmers, which are designed to hold many types of foods at serving temperatures for extended periods without drying out or overcooking (this category includes ovens that also cook the food, then automatically switch to holding temperature); and high-volume *roll-in ovens,* with large doors into which one can roll carts loaded with trays of food.

Conventional Ovens

These ovens operate simply by heating air in an enclosed space. The most common ovens are part of the range unit, although separate oven units or ovens as part of a broiler unit are also available. *Stack ovens* (Figure 3.3) are units that consist of individual shelves arranged one above the other. Pans are placed directly on the oven deck rather than on wire shelves. Temperatures are adjustable for each separate unit.

Do's and Don'ts

Many of these points apply to other types of ovens as well.

1. Preheat ovens thoroughly, but no longer than necessary, to avoid excess energy use.

2. To avoid high energy loss and interruption of cooking, do not open the door any more than necessary.

FIGURE 3.3   **Stack or deck ovens.**

3. Space items well to allow for heat circulation.

4. Be sure the pilot light is on before turning on gas ovens.

Convection Ovens (Figure 3.4)

These ovens contain fans that circulate the air and distribute the heat rapidly throughout the interior. Because of the forced air, foods cook more quickly at lower temperatures. Also, shelves can be placed closer together than in conventional ovens, without blocking the heat flow.

Do's and Don't's

1. For most products, set the temperature 25°F to 50°F (15°C to 30°C) lower than for conventional ovens. Check manufacturer's recommendations.

2. Watch cooking times closely. The forced heat cooks more quickly and tends to dry out some foods excessively if they are overcooked. Shrinkage of roasts is greater than in a conventional oven.

3. Many models of convection ovens should not be operated with the blower switch off or the motor may burn out.

4. The forced air of a convection oven may deform some soft items. Cake batters, for example, develop ripples. Check manufacturer's recommendations.

Revolving Ovens

These large ovens, also called *reel ovens*, are large chambers containing many shelves or trays on a

FIGURE 3.4   **Convection oven.**

ferris-wheel type attachment. This oven eliminates the problem of hot spots or uneven baking, because the mechanism rotates the foods throughout the oven.

Revolving ovens are used in bakeshops and in high-volume operations.

Slow-Cook-and-Hold Ovens

While the traditional oven is nothing more than a heated box equipped with a thermostat, some modern ovens have more sophisticated features, such as computerized, electronic controls and special probes that sense when a roast is done and tell the oven to switch from cooking temperature to holding temperature.

Many of these ovens are designed to be especially useful for low-temperature roasting (see p. 220). The sensitive controls make it possible to cook at steady, reliable temperatures of 200°F (95°C) or lower and to hold foods at 140°F (60°C) for long periods. Large cuts of meat take many hours to roast at a low temperature like 200°F (95°C). By setting the controls in advance, the operator can even let meats roast overnight, unattended.

These ovens are available as convection ovens and as regular, stationary-air ovens.

Combination Steamer Ovens

A relatively new kind of oven is one that can be operated in three different modes: as a convection oven, as a convection steamer (see p. 34), and, with both functions on at once, as a high-humidity oven. Injecting moisture into an oven while roasting meats can help to reduce shrinkage and drying.

Barbecue Ovens or Smoke Ovens

Barbecue ovens are like conventional ovens, but with one important difference: they are able to produce wood smoke, which surrounds the food and flavors it while it bakes or roasts. Special woods, such as hickory, mesquite, or various fruit woods such as apple or cherry, must be added to the smoke-producing part of the oven, according to the manufacturer's instructions. This device is usually nothing more complicated than an electric heating element that heats small blocks or chips of the wood so that they are hot enough to smoke but not hot enough to burst into flame.

Depending on the model, various cooking features are available. Thus, ovens may have smokeless roast/bake cycles, cold-smoke cycles (with the smoke element on but the oven off), holding cycles, and broiling capabilities.

Infrared or Reconstituting Ovens

These units contain quartz tubes or quartz plates that generate intense infrared heat. Infrared ovens are used primarily for reconstituting frozen foods. They bring large quantities of foods to serving temperature in a short time. The heat is even and controllable.

Microwave Ovens (Figure 3.5)

In these ovens, special tubes generate microwave radiation, which creates heat inside the food. Microwave cooking is discussed in detail in Chapter 4.

Broilers and Salamanders

Broilers are sometimes called overhead broilers to avoid confusing them with grills. Overhead broilers generate heat from above; food items are placed on a grate beneath the heat source. Broiling is a favorite way of preparing steaks, chops, chicken, and many other items.

Heavy-duty broilers (Figure 3.6) produce very high heat and consume vast quantities of energy. Some broilers are said to go as high as 2000°F (1100°C) at the burner.

Foods must be watched closely to avoid burning. Cooking temperature is adjusted by raising or lowering the grate that holds the food.

Salamanders (Figure 3.7) are small broilers used primarily for browning or glazing the tops of some items. They may also be used for broiling small quantities during off-peak hours. Salamanders are usually mounted above the range.

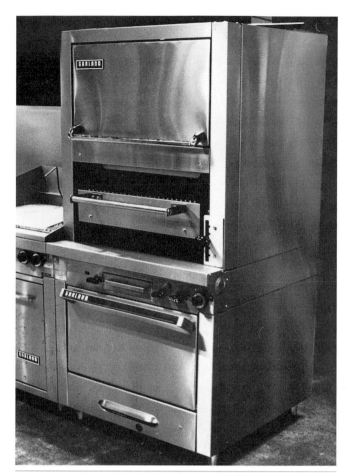

FIGURE 3.6   **Heavy-duty broiler.**

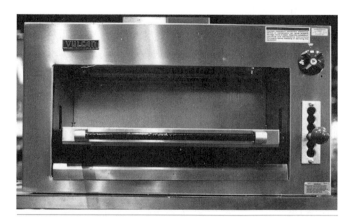

FIGURE 3.7   **Salamander.**

FIGURE 3.5   **Microwave oven.**

Grills

Grills are used for the same cooking operations as broilers, except the heat source is below the grid that holds the food rather than above it (Figure 3.8). Many people favor the taste of grilled foods, because of the "charcoal" taste that is actually created by smoke from meat fats that drip into the heat source.

FIGURE 3.8 **Gas grill.**

Although smoke from meat fats creates the taste that people associate with grilled foods, actual wood smoke flavors, such as hickory or mesquite smoke flavor, can be added to foods if those woods are burned in the grill under the food. In order to do this, you must use a grill designed to burn such fuels.

Types

There are many different models of grills in use. The major differences in operation are due to the difference in heat source—gas, electricity, or charcoal.

To operate, set different areas for different temperatures, and place foods in appropriate areas for cooking temperatures desired. Keep grills clean, since the high temperatures can easily start grease fires.

Griddles

Griddles are flat, smooth, heated surfaces on which food is cooked directly. Pancakes, French toast, hamburgers and other meats, eggs, and many potato items are the foods most frequently cooked on a griddle. Griddles are available as separate units or as part of a range top (Figure 3.1).

Clean griddle surfaces after every use, so that they will cook at peak efficiency. Polish with a griddle stone or griddle cloth until the surface shines. Follow the grain of the metal to avoid scratching.

Condition griddles after each cleaning or before each use, to create a no-stick surface and to prevent rusting. Procedure: spread a thin film of oil over the surface and heat to 400°F (200°C). Wipe clean and repeat until griddle has a smooth, no-stick finish.

Rotisseries

Rotisserie broilers cook meats and other foods by turning them slowly in front of electric or gas-powered heating elements. Even though classical cooking theory categorizes spit-cooking as roasting, these cookers are more closely related to broilers, because the foods are cooked by the infrared heat of the elements.

Although they are especially suitable for chicken and other poultry, rotisseries can be used to cook any meats that can be fastened to a spit.

Both enclosed (ovenlike) rotisseries and open or unclosed units are available. Small units hold about 8 chickens, and sizes range all the way to very large models that can hold as many as 70 chickens.

Because the heating elements are on the side (or sometimes above), the fats and juices don't drip into the flames as they do with grills. Drip pans catch juices, which can be used for basting or gravy making.

Deep Fryers

A deep fryer has only one use—to cook foods in hot fat. Yet because of the popularity of fried foods, this function is an important one.

Standard deep fryers (Figure 3.9) are powered by either gas or electricity and have thermostatic controls that maintain fat at preset temperatures.

Automatic fryers remove food from the fat automatically after a preset time.

Pressure fryers are covered fry kettles that fry foods under pressure. Foods cook faster, even at a lower fat temperature.

Do's and Don'ts

Frying procedures and care of frying fat are discussed in detail in Chapter 4. The following points relate to the operation of the equipment.

1. When filling kettles with solid fats, set thermostat at 250°F (120°C) until the fat has melted enough to cover the heating elements.

2. Keep kettles filled to the fill line.

3. Make sure drain valve is shut before adding fat to the empty kettle.

FIGURE 3.9   **Deep fryers.**

4. Check accuracy of the thermostat regularly by reading the fat temperature with a thermometer.

Cleaning

Cleaning procedures differ greatly, depending on the model. Here is a general procedure.

1. Shut off power.

2. Drain fat through a filter into a dry container (unless you are discarding it). Be sure the container is large enough to hold all the fat before you start.

3. Flush food particles from sides and bottom of kettle with some of the hot fat.

4. Wash kettle with a mild detergent solution. If kettles are not removable, turn on fryer and bring detergent solution almost to a boil (beware of foaming over). Scrub with a stiff brush.

5. Drain and rinse thoroughly with clean water.

6. Dry kettle, heating elements, and baskets thoroughly.

7. Refill with strained or fresh fat.

Tilting Skillet

The tilting skillet, also known as the *tilting brazier* and *tilting fry pan,* is a versatile and efficient piece of equip-ment. It can be used as a griddle, fry pan, brazier, stew pot, stock pot, steamer, and bain marie or steam table.

The tilting skillet is a large, shallow, flat-bottomed pot. Or, to look at it another way, it is a griddle with 6-inch-high sides and a cover. This skillet also has a tilting mechanism that enables liquids to be poured out of it. Power may be gas or electric.

Clean the skillet immediately after each use, before food has time to dry on. Add water, turn on the skillet to heat it, and scrub thoroughly.

Steam-Jacketed Kettles

Steam-jacketed kettles, or steam kettles, are sometimes thought of as stock pots that are heated not just on the bottom but on the sides as well. This comparison is only partly accurate, because steam kettles heat much more quickly and have more uniform and controllable heat than pots on the range.

Types

Steam kettles range in capacity from 2 gallons to over 100 gallons. Some large institutional kettles are 4,000 gallons. *Tilt* or *trunnion kettles* (Figure 3.10) can be

FIGURE 3.10   **Small tilt (trunnion) kettle.**

tilted for emptying, either by turning a wheel or pulling a lever. *Nontilt* kettles are emptied by a spigot and drain on the bottom. Heat is controlled by regulating the steam flow or by adjusting the thermostat. Steam may be from an outside source or self-generated.

Exercise caution when operating all steam equipment. Steam can cause serious burns.

Clean immediately after use to avoid drying on food, as for tilting skillets. Disassemble spigot and drain, and clean with a bottle brush.

Steam Cookers

Steam cookers are ideal for cooking vegetables and many other foods rapidly and with minimum loss of nutrients and flavor. For this reason, they are becoming more common in both large and small kitchens.

Types

Pressure steamers (Figure 3.11) cook foods under a pressure of 15 pounds per square inch (high-pressure steamers), or 4 to 6 pounds per square inch (low-pressure steamers). They are operated by a timer, which shuts the equipment off after a preset time. The door cannot be opened until the pressure returns to zero.

Pressureless or *convection steamers* (Figure 3.12) do not operate under pressure. Jets of steam are directed at the food to speed the heat transfer, just as the fan in a convection oven speeds cooking. The door can be opened any time during cooking.

FIGURE 3.12 **Convection steamer.**

All steamers hold standard-size counter pans (12 × 20 inches) or fractions thereof. Capacity of steamers varies from one to many pans.

Operation of steamers varies greatly, depending on the model. Check operating manuals, and be sure you understand a particular model well before attempting to operate it.

Caution is important with all steam equipment, because of the danger of severe burns.

PROCESSING EQUIPMENT

Mixers

Vertical mixers (Figure 3.13) are important and versatile tools for many kinds of food mixing and processing jobs, both in the bakeshop and in the kitchen.

Types

Bench-model mixers range from 5- to 20-quart capacity. Floor models are available as large as 140 quarts. Adaptor rings enable several sizes of bowls to be used on one machine. Most mixers have three operating speeds.

FIGURE 3.11 **Pressure steamer.**

FIGURE 3.13   **Mixer.**

Agitator Attachments (Figure 3.14)

There are three main mixing attachments, plus some specialized ones. The *paddle* is a flat blade used for general mixing. The *wire whip* is used for such tasks as beating cream and eggs and making mayonnaise. The *dough arm* is used for mixing and kneading yeast doughs.

Do's and Don't's

1. Make sure bowl and mixing attachment are firmly in place before turning on machine.

2. Make sure you are using the right size attachment for the bowl. Using a 40-quart paddle with a 30-quart bowl could cause serious damage. Sizes in quarts are marked on the sides of large bowls and on the tops of attachments.

3. Turn off machine before scraping down the bowl or inserting a spoon, scraper, or hand into the bowl. Mixer motors are powerful and can cause serious injury.

4. Turn off machine before changing speeds.

Food Cutter

The food cutter or food chopper, familiarly known as the "buffalo chopper," is a common piece of equipment used for general chopping of foods. A variety of attachments (described in the next section) make it a versatile tool.

FIGURE 3.14   **Mixer attachments: (a) whip, (b) paddle, (c) dough arm.**

General Operation

Food is placed in a rotating bowl, which carries the food to a pair of knives that are spinning rapidly under a cover. The fineness of the cut depends on how long the food is left in the machine.

Do's and Don't's

1. Always make sure the machine is completely assembled before use.

2. Cover lock knob must be closed before machine can be turned on.

3. Never try to reach under the bowl cover while the machine is running.

4. For uniform chopping, place food in bowl all at one time.

5. Keep knives sharp. Dull knives will bruise food rather than cut it cleanly.

Attachments for Mixers and Food Chopper

The following are the most common of the many attachments designed to fit both the food chopper and the vertical mixer.

1. The *food grinder* (Figure 3.15) is used mostly for grinding meats, although other moist foods may be ground also. Food is forced through a feed tube into a screw, which pushes the food through holes in a plate, where it is cut by a rotating blade. The size of the holes regulates the fineness of the grind.

Make sure the rotating blade is attached properly, cutting edge out, when assembling the grinder.

2. The *slicer/shredder* (Figure 3.16) consists of a hopper and lever that feeds the food into a rotating disk or plate. The plate cuts or shreds the food and drops it into a receiving container. The slicing plate may be adjusted to cut various thicknesses.

3. The *dicer* attachment forces foods through a grid-type blade that cuts them into perfect dice. Different size blades may be used.

Slicer

The slicer is a valuable machine because it slices foods more evenly and uniformly than can be done by hand. Thus it is valuable for portion control and for reducing cutting loss.

Types

Most modern slicers have blades set at an angle (Figure 3.17). Slices fall away from these blades with less breaking and folding than from vertical blades.

With manual machines, the operator must move the carriage back and forth to slice the food. Automatic machines move the carriage with an electric motor.

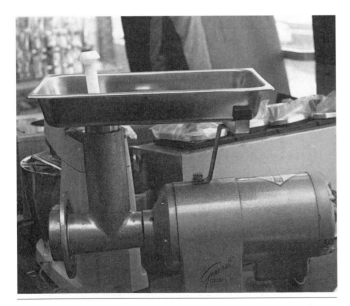

FIGURE 3.15 Grinder attachment (on separate motor).

FIGURE 3.16 Slicer/shredder attachment.

FIGURE 3.17   **Slicer.**

Do's and Don't's

1. Be sure the machine is properly assembled before using.

2. Always use the end weight to press the food against the blade. This protects the hand from serious cuts and also provides a more even pressure on the food, for more uniform slices.

3. Set the thickness control knob at zero when the machine is not in use or is being cleaned.

4. Always unplug the machine before dismantling and cleaning.

5. Keep the blade sharp with the sharpening stones provided with the slicer.

Vertical Cutter/Mixer and Food Processor

The vertical cutter/mixer (VCM) is like a large, powerful, high-speed blender. It is used to chop and mix large quantities of foods very rapidly. It can also be used for puréeing (soups, for example) and for mixing liquids.

Types

VCMs range in size from 15 to 80 quarts. The small models have a hand-operated mixing baffle, which moves the foods into the blades. Larger machines have automatic baffles.

Food processors, like the ones popular today in home kitchens, actually were used in commercial kitchens, especially in Europe, years before the home

models were introduced. The professional models (Figure 3.18) are from two to four times larger than the home models. Since they are much smaller than VCMs, they are not well suited to high-volume work. Instead, they are mostly used for specialized tasks, such as puréeing raw meats and fish for delicate pâtés and mousses.

Do's and Don't's

1. Watch processing times closely. Chopping times are very short, so an extra second can make cabbage soup out of cole slaw.

2. Make sure the machine is properly assembled before use.

3. After turning machine off, allow the blades to come to a full stop before opening the cover.

4. Keep the blades sharp. Dull blades bruise food.

HOLDING AND STORAGE EQUIPMENT

Hot Food Holding Equipment

Several types of equipment are used to keep food hot for service. This equipment is designed to hold foods above 140°F (60°C) in order to prevent the growth of

FIGURE 3.18   **Food processor.**

bacteria that can cause disease. Because food continues to cook at these temperatures, it should be held for as short a time as possible.

1. *Steam tables* (Figure 3.19) are standard holding equipment for serving lines. Standard-size counter pans or hotel pans are used as inserts to hold the foods. Flat or domed covers may be used to cover the foods.

    Check water levels in steam tables periodically, to make sure they don't go dry. (Electrically heated counters that operate dry—without steam—are also available.)

2. A *bain marie* is a hot water bath. Containers of foods are set on a rack in a shallow container of water, which is heated by electricity, gas, or steam. The bain marie is used more in the production area, while the steam table is used in the service area.

3. *Overhead infrared lamps* are used in service areas to keep plated food warm before it is picked up by the service staff. They are also used for keeping large roasts warm.

    Foods dry out quickly under holding lamps. This is a disadvantage for almost all foods except for french fries and other deep-fried foods, which lose their crispness if they are kept moist.

Cold Food Storage Equipment

The quality of the food you serve depends to a great degree on refrigeration equipment. By keeping foods cold, usually below 40°F (5°C), the refrigerator

(known in the trade as the "cooler" or the "box") guards against spoilage and bacterial growth.

Freezers are used to hold foods for longer times, or to store foods purchased in frozen form.

There are so many sizes, models, and designs of refrigeration equipment that it would be futile to try to describe them all here.

To enable refrigerators and freezers to work at top efficiency, observe the following rules:

1. Place items far enough apart and away from inside walls of refrigerator so that cold air can circulate. Freezers, on the other hand, work most efficiently when they are full.

2. Keep the door closed as much as possible. When storing or removing an item, do it quickly and shut the door.

3. Keep stored foods well wrapped or covered, to prevent drying and transfer of odors. (Meats are an exception to this rule; see p. 217.)

4. Keep refrigerators spotlessly clean.

POTS, PANS, AND CONTAINERS

Metals and Conductivity

A good cooking utensil should distribute heat evenly and uniformly. If it does not, it will develop hot spots that are likely to burn or scorch the food being cooked. Two factors affect a pan's ability to cook evenly:

Thickness of the metal. A heavy-gauge pot cooks more evenly than one made of thin metal. Thickness is most important on the bottom.

FIGURE 3.19 **Steam table.**

Kind of metals. Different metals have different conductivity, which means the speed at which they transfer heat. The following materials are used for cooking equipment:

1. *Aluminum* is used for most cooking utensils in food service kitchens. It is a very good conductor, and its light weight makes pots and pans easy to handle. Because it is a relatively soft metal, it should not be banged around or abused.

   Do not use aluminum for storage or for long cooking of strong acids, because it reacts chemically with many foods. Also, it tends to discolor light-colored foods such as sauces, especially if they are stirred or beaten with a metal spoon or whip.

   Pans made of *anodized aluminum,* sold under such brand names as Calphalon, have surfaces that are harder and more corrosion-resistant than regular aluminum pans do. Although this is not, strictly speaking, a no-stick finish, it is less porous than untreated aluminum, so foods are less likely to stick. Also, it is more resistant to acids than regular aluminum, and it will not discolor light-colored foods. Its disadvantages are that it is more expensive and not quite as durable as standard aluminum.

2. *Copper* is the best heat conductor of all and was once widely used for cooking utensils. However, it is extremely expensive and requires a great deal of care. Also it is very heavy. Today it is used mostly for show.

   Copper reacts chemically with many foods to create poisonous compounds, so copper pans must be lined with another metal, such as tin or stainless steel.

3. *Stainless steel* is a poor heat conductor. Cooking pots and pans made of it tend to scorch foods easily. Stainless steel is ideal for storage containers, because it will not react with foods as aluminum does. It is also used for low-temperature cooking or holding equipment, such as steamer pans and counter pans, where scorching or hot spots are not a problem.

   Stainless steel pots and pans are also available with a heavy layer of copper or aluminum bonded to the bottom. This feature gives you the advantages of stainless steel (its hardness, durability, and the fact that it does not react with acid foods or discolor light sauces) with the heat-conducting qualities of copper or aluminum. These pans are usually expensive.

4. *Cast iron* is a favorite material with many chefs, because of its ability to distribute heat evenly and to maintain high temperatures for long periods. It is used in griddles and heavy skillets. Cast iron cracks easily if dropped. It rusts very quickly unless kept properly conditioned and dry (see p. 559 for conditioning pans).

5. *Porcelain enamel-lined pans* should not be used. In fact, they are forbidden by some health departments. They scratch and chip easily, providing good hiding places for bacteria. Also, certain kinds of grey enamel can cause food poisoning if chipped.

6. *No-stick plastic-type coatings,* known by various brand names such as Teflon and Silverstone, provide a very slippery finish, but one that requires a lot of care because it is easily scratched. Do not use metal spoons or spatulas with this equipment. Many chefs keep a set of no-stick egg pans and use them for no other purpose.

   Because more customers are requesting low-fat foods, no-stick coatings are increasing in popularity. They enable cooks to sauté foods with little or no fat.

7. *Glass* and *earthenware* have limited use in commercial kitchens, because they are very breakable. They are very poor conductors of heat but are resistant to corrosion and food acids.

Pots and Pans and Their Uses

1. **Stock pot.** A large, deep, straight-sided pot for preparing stocks and simmering large quantities of liquids (Figure 3.20). Stock pots with spigots

FIGURE 3.20 **Stock pot.**

(Figure 3.21) allow liquid to be drained off without disturbing the solid contents or lifting the pot. Sizes: 8 to 200 quarts (or liters).

2. **Sauce pot.** Round pot of medium depth (Figure 3.22). Similar to stock pots, but shallower, making stirring or mixing easier. Used for soups, sauces, and other liquids. Sizes: 6 to 60 quarts (or liters).

3. **Brazier.** Round, broad, shallow, heavy-duty pot with straight sides (Figure 3.23). Used for browning, braising, and stewing meats. Sizes: 11 to 30 quarts (or liters).

4. **Saucepan.** Similar to a small, shallow, light sauce pot, but with one long handle instead

of two loop handles (Figure 3.24). May have straight or slant sides. Used for general range-top cooking. Sizes: 1½ to 15 quarts (or liters).

5. **Sauté pan, straight sided.** Similar to a shallow, straight-sided saucepan, but heavier (Figure 3.25). Used for browning, sautéing, and frying. Also used for cooking sauces and other liquids when rapid reduction is required, because of broad surface area. Sizes: 2½ to 5 inches (65–130 mm) deep; 6 to 16 inches (160–400 mm) in diameter.

6. **Sauté pan, slope sided.** Also called fry pan (Figure 3.26). Used for general sautéing and frying of meats, fish, vegetables, and eggs. Sloping sides allow the cook to flip and toss items without using a spatula, and they make it easier to

FIGURE 3.21 **Stock pot with spigot.**

FIGURE 3.22 **Sauce pot.**

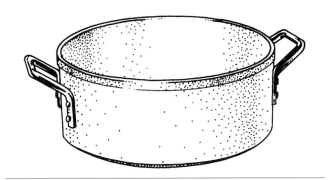

FIGURE 3.23 **Brazier.**

FIGURE 3.24 **Saucepan.**

FIGURE 3.25 **Straight-sided sauté pan.**

get at the food when a spatula is used. Sizes: 6 to 14 inches (160–360 mm) top diameter.

7. **Cast iron skillet.** Very heavy, thick-bottomed fry pan (Figure 3.27). Used for pan frying when very steady, even heat is desired.

8. **Double boiler.** Lower section, similar to a stock pot, holds boiling water. Upper section holds

FIGURE 3.26 **Slope-sided sauté pan.**

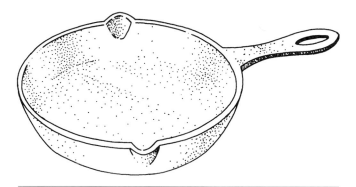

FIGURE 3.27 **Cast iron skillet.**

FIGURE 3.28 **Double boiler.**

foods that must be cooked at low temperatures and cannot be cooked over direct heat (Figure 3.28). Size of top section: 4 to 36 quarts (or liters).

9. **Sheet pan** or **bun pan.** Shallow (1 inch or 25 mm deep) rectangular pan (Figure 3.29) for baking cakes, rolls, and cookies, and for baking or broiling certain meats and fish. Sizes: 18 × 26 inches (full pan); 18 × 13 inches (half pan) (46 × 66 cm and 46 × 33 cm, respectively).

10. **Bake pan.** Rectangular pan about 2 inches deep (Figure 3.30). Used for general baking. Comes in a variety of sizes.

11. **Roasting pan.** Large rectangular pan, deeper and heavier than bake pan (Figure 3.31). Used for roasting meats and poultry.

12. **Hotel pan,** also called **counter pan, steam table pan,** or **service pan.** Rectangular pans usually

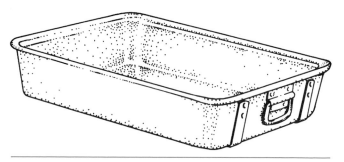

FIGURE 3.29 **Sheet pan.**

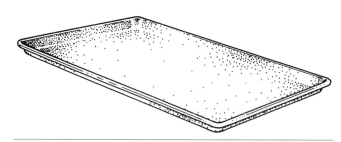

FIGURE 3.30 **Bake pan.**

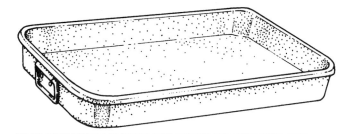

FIGURE 3.31 **Roasting pan.**

made of stainless steel (Figure 3.32). Designed to hold foods in service counters. Also used for baking and steaming, and foods can then be served from same pan. Also used for storage. Standard size: 12 × 20 inches. Fractions of this size (½, ⅓, etc.) are also available. Standard depth: 2½ inches (65 mm). Deeper sizes are also available. (Standard metric pan is 325 × 530 mm.)

13. **Bain marie insert,** usually called simply *bain marie.* Tall, cylindrical stainless steel containers (Figure 3.33). Used for storage and for holding foods in bain marie (water bath). Sizes: 1 to 36 quarts (or liters).

14. **Stainless steel bowl.** Round bottom bowl. Used for mixing and whipping, for production of hollandaise, mayonnaise, whipped cream, egg white foams. Round construction enables whip to reach all areas. Comes in many sizes.

MEASURING DEVICES

The following equipment is discussed in terms of U.S. measurements. Comparable items in metric units are also available.

1. *Scales.* Most recipe ingredients are measured by weight, so accurate scales are very important. *Portion scales* (Figure 3.34) are used for measur-

ing ingredients as well as for portioning products for service. The baker's *balance scale* is discussed in Chapter 24.

2. *Volume measures* used for liquids have lips for easy pouring (Figure 3.35). Sizes are pints, quarts, half gallons, and gallons. Each size is marked off into fourths by ridges on the sides.

3. *Measuring cups* are available in 1-, ½-, ⅓-, and ¼-cup sizes. They can be used for both liquid and dry measures.

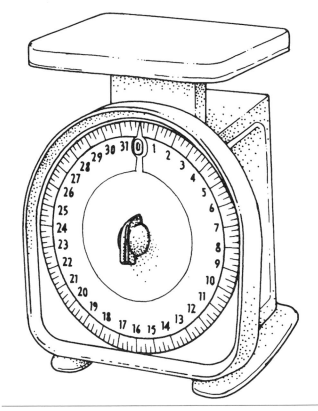

FIGURE 3.34 **Portion scale.**

FIGURE 3.32 **Hotel pan.**

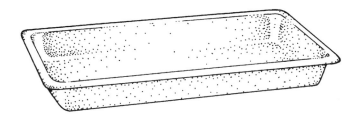

FIGURE 3.33 **Bain marie inserts.**

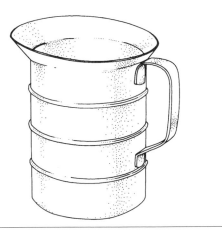

FIGURE 3.35 **Liquid volume measure.**

TABLE 3.1   **Scoop Sizes**

Scoop Number	U.S. Measure		Metric Measure	
	Volume	Approximate Weight	Volume	Approximate Weight
6	⅔ cup	5 oz	160 mL	140 g
8	½ cup	4 oz	120 mL	110 g
10	3 fl. oz	3–3½ oz	90 mL	85–100 g
12	⅓ cup	2½–3 oz	80 mL	70–85 g
16	¼ cup	2–2½ oz	60 mL	60–70 g
20	1½ fl. oz	1¾ oz	45 mL	50 g
24	1⅓ fl. oz	1⅓ oz	40 mL	40 g
30	1 fl. oz	1 oz	30 mL	30 g
40	0.8 fl. oz	0.8 oz	24 mL	23 g
60	½ fl. oz	½ oz	15 mL	15 g

Note: Weights vary greatly with different foods, depending on how compact they are. Best practice is to weigh a spoonful of an item before proceeding with portioning.

4. *Measuring spoons* are used for measuring very small volumes: 1 tablespoon, 1 teaspoon, ½ teaspoon, and ¼ teaspoon. They are used most often for spices and seasonings.

5. *Ladles* are used for measuring and portioning liquids (Figure 3.36). The size, in ounces, is stamped on the handle.

6. *Scoops* come in standard sizes and have a lever for mechanical release (Figure 3.37). They are used for portioning soft solid foods. Scoop sizes are listed in Table 3.1. The number of the scoop indicates the number of level scoopfuls per quart (or liter). In actual use a rounded scoopful is often more practical, so exact weights will vary.

7. *Thermometers* measure temperatures. There are many kinds for many purposes.

   a. A *meat thermometer* (Figure 3.38) indicates internal temperature of meats. It is inserted before cooking and left in the product during cooking.

   b. An *instant-read thermometer* (Figure 3.39) will give readings within a few seconds of being inserted in a food product. It reads from 0°F to 220°F. Many chefs carry these in their

FIGURE 3.36   **Ladles.**

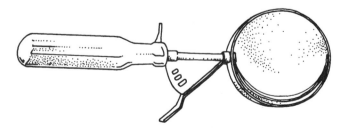

FIGURE 3.37   **Scoop.**

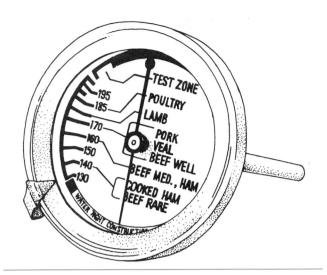

FIGURE 3.38   **Meat thermometer.**

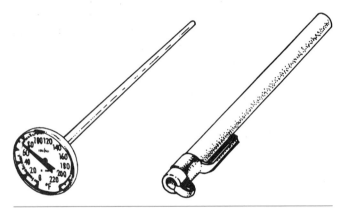

FIGURE 3.39   **Instant-read thermometer.**

jacket pockets like a pen, ready whenever needed. Instant-read thermometers must not be left in meats during roasting, or they will be damaged.

   c. *Fat thermometers* and *candy thermometers* test temperatures of frying fats and sugar syrups. They read up to 400°F.

   d. Special thermometers are used to test the accuracy of oven, refrigerator, and freezer thermostats.

KNIVES, HAND TOOLS, AND SMALL EQUIPMENT

Knife Materials

The metal that a knife blade is made of is an important consideration, since the metal must be able to take and hold a very fine edge.

1. *Carbon steel* is the traditional favorite, because it can be honed to an extremely sharp edge. Its disadvantages are that it corrodes and discolors easily, especially when used with acid foods and onions. Also, it discolors some foods (such as hard-cooked eggs) and may leave a metallic taste.

2. *Stainless steel* will not rust or corrode, but it is much harder to sharpen.

3. *High-carbon stainless steel* is a relatively new alloy that combines the best aspects of carbon steel and stainless steel. It takes an edge almost as well as carbon steel, and it will not rust, corrode, or discolor. Knives made of this material are highly prized and are relatively expensive.

Knife Handles

The *tang* is the portion of the metal blade that is inside the handle. The best-quality, most durable knives have a *full tang*, which means that the tang runs the *full length* of the handle.

Knives and Their Uses

1. *French knife* or *chef's knife* (Figure 3.40).   Most frequently used knife in the kitchen, for general purpose chopping, slicing, dicing, and so on. Blade is wide at the heel and tapers to a point. Blade length of 10 inches (260 mm) is most popular for general work. Larger knives are for heavy cutting and chopping. Smaller blades are for more delicate work.

   This is your most important tool, so you must learn to handle it and care for it well. Chapter 7 explains its use in detail.

2. *Utility* or *salad knife* (Figure 3.41).   Narrow, pointed knife 6 to 8 inches (160–200 mm) long. Used mostly for pantry work, cutting and preparing lettuce, fruits, and so on. Also useful for carving roast chicken and duck.

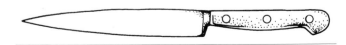

FIGURE 3.40   **French knife or chef's knife.**

FIGURE 3.41   **Utility knife.**

3. ***Paring knife*** (Figure 3.42).   Small pointed blade 2 to 4 inches (50–100 mm) long. Used for trimming and paring vegetables and fruits.

4. ***Boning knife*** (Figure 3.43).   Thin, pointed blade about 6 inches (160 mm) long. Used for boning raw meats and poultry. Stiff blades are used for heavier work. Flexible blades are used for lighter work and for filleting fish.

5. ***Slicer*** (Figure 3.44).   Long, slender, flexible blade up to 14 inches (360 mm) long. Used for carving and slicing cooked meats.

6. ***Serrated slicer*** (Figure 3.45).   Like a slicer, but with serrated edge. Used for cutting breads, cakes, and similar items.

7. ***Butcher knife*** (Figure 3.46).   Heavy, broad, slightly curved blade. Used for cutting, sectioning, and trimming raw meats in the butcher shop.

8. ***Scimitar*** or ***steak knife*** (Figure 3.47).   Curved, pointed blade. Used for accurate cutting of steaks.

9. ***Cleaver*** (Figure 3.48).   Very heavy, broad blade. Used for cutting through bones.

10. ***Oyster knife*** (Figure 3.49).   Short, rigid, blunt knife with dull edge. Used for opening oysters.

11. ***Clam knife*** (Figure 3.50)   Short, rigid, broad-bladed knife with a slight edge. Used for opening clams.

12. ***Vegetable peeler*** (Figure 3.51).   Short tool with a slotted, swiveling blade. Used for peeling vegetables and fruits.

13. ***Steel*** (Figure 3.52).   Not a knife, but an essential part of the knife kit. Used for truing and maintaining knife edges. (See Chapter 7 for use of the steel.)

14. ***Cutting board.***   This is an important partner to the knife. Hard wood boards are favored by many chefs. Hard rubber or plastic boards are thought to be more sanitary, but there is some evidence that bacteria survive longer on plastic

FIGURE 3.42   **Paring knife.**

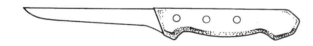

FIGURE 3.43   **Boning knife.**

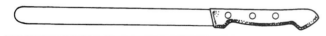

FIGURE 3.44   **Slicer.**

FIGURE 3.45   **Serrated slicer.**

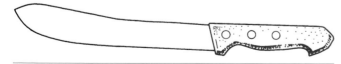

FIGURE 3.46   **Butcher knife.**

FIGURE 3.47   **Scimitar.**

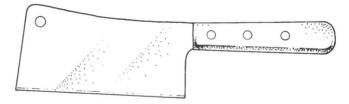

FIGURE 3.48   **Cleaver.**

FIGURE 3.49   **Oyster knife.**

FIGURE 3.50   **Clam knife.**

FIGURE 3.51   **Vegetable peeler.**

FIGURE 3.52   **Steel.**

and rubber than on wood. Cutting boards must be kept very clean.

Note: In some communities, wooden boards are prohibited by health regulations.

Hand Tools and Small Equipment

1. *Ball cutter, melon ball scoop,* or *parisienne knife* (Figure 3.53).   Blade is a small, cup-shaped, half sphere. Used for cutting fruits and vegetables into small balls.

2. *Cook's fork* (Figure 3.54).   Heavy, two-pronged fork with a long handle. Used for lifting and turning meats and other items. Must be strong enough to hold heavy loads.

3. *Straight spatula* or *palette knife* (Figure 3.55). A long flexible blade with a rounded end. Used mostly for spreading icing on cakes and for mixing and bowl scraping.

4. *Sandwich spreader* (Figure 3.56).   A short, stubby spatula. Used for spreading fillings and spreads on sandwiches.

5. *Offset spatula* (Figure 3.57).   Broad blade, bent to keep hand off hot surfaces. Used for turning and lifting eggs, pancakes, and meats on griddles, grills, sheet pans, and so on. Also used as a scraper to clean bench or griddle.

6. *Rubber spatula* or *scraper* (Figure 3.58).   Broad, flexible rubber or plastic tip on long handle. Used to scrape bowls and pans. Also used for folding in egg foams or whipped cream.

7. *Pie server* (Figure 3.59).   A wedge-shaped offset spatula. Used for lifting pie wedges from pan.

8. *Bench scraper* or *dough knife* (Figure 3.60).   A broad, stiff piece of metal with a wooden handle

FIGURE 3.58   **Rubber spatula.**

FIGURE 3.53   **Ball cutter.**

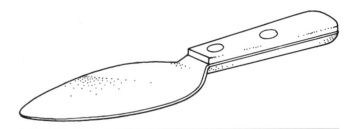

FIGURE 3.59   **Pie server.**

FIGURE 3.54   **Cook's fork.**

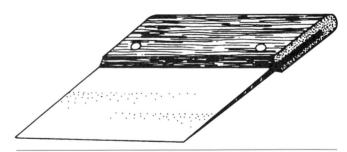

FIGURE 3.60   **Bench scraper.**

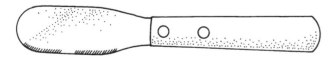

FIGURE 3.55   **Straight spatula.**

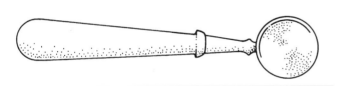

FIGURE 3.56   **Sandwich spreader.**

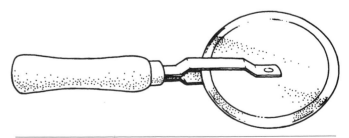

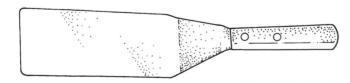

FIGURE 3.57   **Offset spatula.**

FIGURE 3.61   **Pastry wheel.**

on one edge. Used to cut pieces of dough and to scrape workbenches.

9. *Pastry wheel* or *wheel knife* (Figure 3.61). A round, rotating blade on a handle. Used for cutting rolled-out doughs and pastry and baked pizza.

10. *Spoons: solid, slotted,* and *perforated* (Figure 3.62). Large stainless steel spoons, holding about 3 ounces. Used for stirring, mixing, and serving. Slotted and perforated spoons are used when liquid must be drained from solids.

11. *Skimmer* (Figure 3.63). Perforated disc, slightly cupped, on a long handle. Used for skimming froth from liquids and for removing solid pieces from soups, stocks, and other liquids.

12. *Tongs* (Figure 3.64). Spring-type or scissor-type tools used to pick up and handle foods.

13. *Wire whip* (Figure 3.65). Loops of stainless steel wire fastened to a handle. There are two kinds of whips:

   a. Heavy whips are straight, stiff, and have relatively few wires. Used for general mixing, stirring, and beating, especially heavy liquids.
   b. Balloon whips or piano wire whips have many flexible wires. Used for whipping eggs, cream, and hollandaise, and for mixing thinner liquids.

14. *China cap* (Figure 3.66). Cone-shaped strainer. Used for straining stocks, soups, sauces, and other liquids. Pointed shape allows the cook to drain liquids through a relatively small opening.

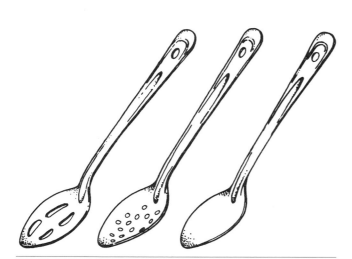

FIGURE 3.62   **Spoons: slotted, perforated, solid.**

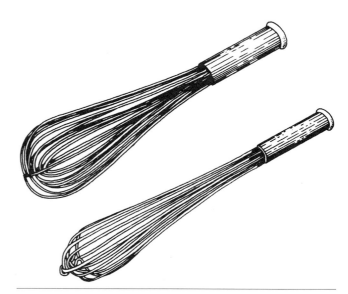

FIGURE 3.65   **Wire whips.**

FIGURE 3.63   **Skimmer.**

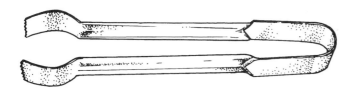

FIGURE 3.64   **Tongs.**

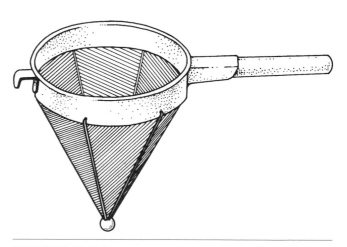

FIGURE 3.66   **China cap.**

15. ***Fine china cap*** or ***chinois (shee-nwah)*** (Figure 3.67). China cap with very fine mesh. Used when great clarity or smoothness is required in a liquid.

16. ***Strainer*** (Figure 3.68). Round-bottomed, cup-shaped strainer made of screen-type mesh or of perforated metal. Used for straining pasta, vegetables, and so on.

17. ***Sieve*** (Figure 3.69). Screen-type mesh supported in a round metal frame. Used for sifting flour and other dry ingredients.

18. ***Colander*** (Figure 3.70). Large perforated bowl made of stainless steel or aluminum. Used to drain washed or cooked vegetables, salad greens, pasta, and other foods.

19. ***Food mill*** (Figure 3.71). A tool with a hand-turned blade that forces foods through a perforated disk. Interchangeable disks have different coarseness or fineness. Used for puréeing foods.

20. ***Grater*** (Figure 3.72). A four-sided metal box with different sized grids. Used for shredding and grating vegetables, cheese, citrus rinds, and other foods.

21. ***Zester*** (Figure 3.73). Small hand tool used for removing the colored part of citrus peels in thin strips.

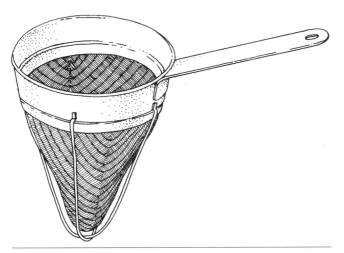

FIGURE 3.67 **Chinois.**

FIGURE 3.68 **Strainer.**

FIGURE 3.70 **Colander.**

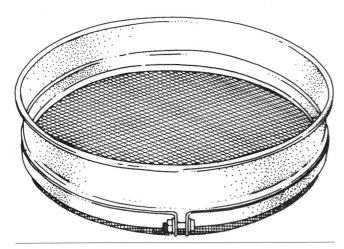

FIGURE 3.69 **Sieve.**

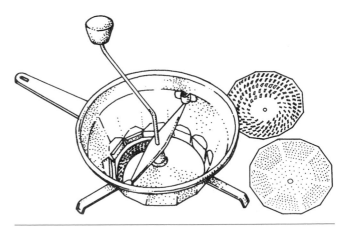

FIGURE 3.71 **Food mill.**

22. **Channel knife.** Small hand tool used mostly in decorative work. See Figure 22.2 to see how it is used.

23. **Pastry bag** and **tubes** (Figure 3.74). Cone-shaped cloth or plastic bag with open end that can be fitted with metal tubes or tips of various shapes and sizes. Used for shaping and decorating with items such as cake icing, whipped cream, duchesse potatoes, and soft dough.

24. **Pastry brush** (Figure 3.75). Used to brush items with egg wash, glaze, etc.

25. **Can opener** (Figure 3.76). Heavy-duty food service type can openers are mounted on the edge of the workbench. They must be carefully cleaned and sanitized every day to prevent contamination of foods. Replace worn blades, which can leave metal shavings in the food.

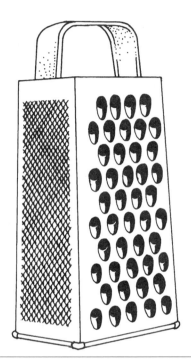

FIGURE 3.72   **Box grater.**

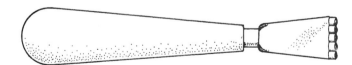

FIGURE 3.73   **Zester.**

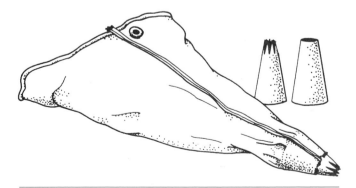

FIGURE 3.74   **Pastry bag and tubes.**

FIGURE 3.75   **Pastry brush.**

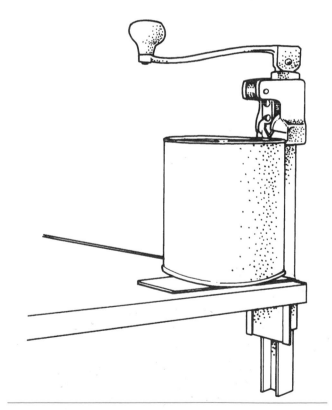

FIGURE 3.76   **Can opener.**

BASIC COOKING PRINCIPLES

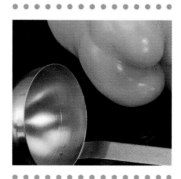

No written recipe can be 100 percent accurate. No matter how carefully a recipe is written, the judgment of the cook is still the most important factor in making a preparation turn out well. A cook's judgment is based on experience, on an understanding of the raw materials available, and on knowledge of basic cooking principles.

This chapter deals with basic principles. You will learn about what happens to food when it is heated, about how food is cooked by different cooking methods, and about rules of seasoning and flavoring. It is important to understand the theories so that you can then put them into practice successfully in the kitchen.

After reading this chapter, you should be able to

1. Name the most important components of foods and describe what happens to them when they are cooked.

2. Describe the ways in which heat is transferred to food in order to cook it.

3. List the factors that affect cooking times.

4. Explain the differences between moist-heat cooking methods, dry-heat cooking methods, and dry-heat methods using fat.

5. Describe each basic cooking method used in the commercial kitchen.

6. List the rules for achieving good quality in deep-fried foods.

7. Understand the basic principles for using seasonings and flavorings to create good-tasting foods.

HEAT AND FOOD

To cook food means to heat it in order to make certain changes in it. Skillful cooks know exactly what changes they want to make and what they have to do to get them right. To learn these cooking skills, it is important for you to know why foods behave as they do when heated. For this you have to study a little theory to support your practice in the kitchen.

Perhaps not all the parts in this section will make sense to you at first. But they should become clearer to you after you have thought about them in relation to specific techniques, as demonstrated by your instructor. Later in your studies, when you are learning about cooking meats, fish, vegetables, and other foods, review this section from time to time. Not only will you understand it better, but it should help you make more sense out of the procedures you are learning and practicing.

. . . .

EFFECTS OF HEAT ON FOODS

Foods are composed of proteins, fats, carbohydrates, and water, plus small amounts of other compounds such as minerals (including salt), vitamins, pigments (coloring agents), and flavor elements. It is important to understand how these components react when heated or mixed with other foods. You will then be better equipped to correct cooking faults when they occur and to anticipate the effects of changing cooking methods, cooking temperatures, or ingredient proportions.

In other words, when you know *why* foods behave as they do, you can then understand *how* to get them to behave as you want them to.

Proteins

1. Protein is a major component of meats, poultry, fish, eggs, milk, and milk products. It is present in smaller amounts in nuts, beans, and grains.

2. *Coagulation.* As proteins are heated, they become firm, or *coagulate*. As the temperature increases, they shrink, become firmer, and lose more moisture. Exposure of proteins to excessive heat toughens them and makes them dry.

Most proteins complete coagulation or are "cooked" at 160°F to 185°F (71°C to 85°C).

3. *Connective tissues* are special proteins that are present in meats. Meats with a great deal of connective tissue are tough, but some connective tissues are dissolved when cooked slowly with moisture. By cooking tough meats properly, therefore, they can be made more tender. These techniques are explained in Chapter 10.

4. *Acids,* such as lemon juice, vinegar, and tomato products, do two things to proteins:

   a. They speed coagulation.
   b. They help dissolve some connective tissues.

Carbohydrates

1. Starches and sugars are both carbohydrates. Both compounds are present in foods in many different forms. They are found in fruits, vegetables, grains, beans, and nuts. Meats and fish also contain a very small amount of carbohydrate.

2. For the cook, the two most important changes in carbohydrates caused by heat are caramelization and gelatinization.

   a. *Caramelization* is the browning of sugars. The browning of sautéed vegetables and the golden color of bread crust are forms of caramelization.
   b. *Gelatinization* occurs when starches absorb water and swell. This is a major principle in the thickening of sauces and in the production of breads and pastries.

   Acids inhibit gelatinization. A sauce thickened with flour or starch will be thinner if it contains acid.

Fruit and Vegetable Fiber

1. *Fiber* is the name for a group of complex substances that give structure and firmness to plants. This fiber cannot be digested.

2. The softening of fruits and vegetables in cooking is in part the breaking down of fiber.

3. Sugar makes fiber more firm. Fruit cooked with sugar keeps its shape better than fruit cooked without sugar.

4. Baking soda (and other alkalis) make fiber softer. Vegetables should not be cooked with

baking soda because they become mushy and lose vitamins.

Fats

1. Fats are present in meats, poultry, fish, eggs, milk products, nuts and whole grains, and, to a lesser extent, in vegetables and fruits. Fats are also important as cooking mediums, as for frying.

2. Fats can be either solid or liquid at room temperature. Liquid fats are called oils. Melting points of solid fats vary.

3. When fats are heated, they begin to break down. When hot enough, they deteriorate rapidly and begin to smoke. The temperature at which this happens is called the *smoke point,* and it varies for different fats. A stable fat—one with a high smoke point—is an important consideration in deep-fat frying.

Minerals, Vitamins, Pigments, and Flavor Components

1. Minerals and vitamins are important to the nutritional quality of the food. Pigments and flavor components are important to a food's appearance and taste and may determine whether the food is appetizing enough to eat. So it is important to preserve all these elements.

2. All of these components may be leached out, or dissolved away, from foods during cooking.

3. Vitamins and pigments may also be destroyed by heat, by long cooking, and by other elements present during cooking.

4. It is important, then, to select cooking methods that preserve, as much as possible, a food's nutrients and appearance. This will always be a consideration when cooking techniques are explained in the remainder of this book.

HEAT TRANSFER

In order for food to be cooked, heat must be transferred from the heat source (such as a gas flame or an electric element) to and through the food. Understanding the ways in which heat is transferred and the speed at which it is transferred helps the cook control the cooking process.

Heat is transferred in three ways: conduction, convection, and radiation.

Conduction

Conduction occurs in two ways:

1. When heat moves directly from one item to something touching it. For example: from the top of the range to a soup pot placed on it, from the pot to the broth inside, and from the broth to the solid food items in it.

2. When heat moves from one part of something to an adjacent part of the same item. For example: from the exterior of a roast to the interior, or from a sauté pan to its handle.

Different materials conduct heat at different speeds. Heat moves rapidly through copper and aluminum, more slowly in stainless steel, slower yet in glass and porcelain. Air is a very poor conductor of heat.

Convection

Convection occurs when heat is spread by the movement of air, steam, or liquid (including hot fat). There are two kinds of convection:

1. **Natural.** Hot liquids and gases rise, while cooler ones sink. Thus, in any oven, kettle of liquid, or deep-fat fryer there is a constant, natural circulation that distributes heat.

2. **Mechanical.** In convection ovens and convection steamers, fans speed the circulation of heat. Thus, heat is transferred more quickly to the food, and the food cooks faster.

Stirring is a form of mechanical convection. Thick liquids cannot circulate as quickly as thin ones, so the rate of natural convection is slower. This explains in part why it is so easy to scorch thick soups and sauces. The heat is not carried away from the bottom of the pan quickly enough, so it stays concentrated on the bottom and scorches the food. Stirring redistributes the heat and helps prevent this. (Using heavy pots made of a material that conducts heat well also helps prevent scorching, because the pot conducts the heat more quickly and evenly all across the bottom and up the sides.)

Radiation

Radiation occurs when energy is transferred by waves from the source to the food.

The waves themselves are not actually heat energy, but are changed into heat energy when they strike the food being cooked. (Light waves, radio waves, and X rays are examples of radiation not used for cooking.)

Two kinds of radiation are used in the kitchen:

1. *Infrared.* Broiling is the most familiar example of infrared cooking. In a broiler, an electric element or a ceramic element heated by a gas flame becomes so hot that it gives off infrared radiation, which cooks the food. There are also high-intensity infrared ovens designed to heat food rapidly.

2. *Microwave.* In microwave cooking, the radiation generated by the oven penetrates part way into the food, where it agitates the molecules of water. The friction caused by this agitation creates heat, which cooks the food.

   a. Because microwave radiation affects only water molecules, a completely waterless material will not heat up in a microwave oven. Plates become hot only when heat is *conducted* to them by hot foods.

   b. Because most microwaves penetrate no more than about 2 inches into foods, heat is transferred to the center of large pieces of food by *conduction,* just as in roasting.

Cooking with microwaves is discussed in more detail later in this chapter.

COOKING TIMES

It takes time to heat a food to a desired temperature, the temperature at which a food is "done" (meaning that the desired changes have taken place). This time is affected by three factors:

1. *Cooking temperature.*

   This means the temperature of the air in the oven, the fat in the fryer, the surface of a griddle, or the liquid in which a food is cooking.

2. *The speed of heat transfer.*

   Different cooking methods transfer heat at different rates, as shown by these examples:

   Air is a poor conductor of heat, while steam is much more efficient. A jet of steam (212°F/

100°C) will easily burn your hand, but you can safely reach into an oven at 500°F (260°C). This is why it takes longer to bake potatoes than to steam them.

A convection oven cooks faster than a conventional oven, even if both are set at the same temperature. The forced air movement transfers heat more rapidly.

3. *Size, temperature, and individual characteristics of the food.*

   For example:

   A small beef roast cooks faster than a large one.

   A chilled steak takes longer to broil than one at room temperature.

   Fish items generally cook more quickly than meats.

Because there are so many variables, it is very difficult or even impossible to determine exact cooking times in most recipes. Different ovens, fryers, and steamers, for example, may transfer heat more or less efficiently or have different recovery times. Roasting charts that give cooking times for various cuts of meat can be used only as guidelines, and the cook must use his or her judgment to make the final determination of doneness. This matter of cooking times will be discussed again in the next chapter.

COOKING METHODS

Cooking methods are classified as "moist heat" and "dry heat."

Moist-heat methods are those in which the heat is conducted to the food product by water (including stock, sauces, etc.) or by steam.

Dry-heat methods are those in which the heat is conducted without moisture, that is, by hot air, hot metal, radiation, or hot fat. We usually divide dry-heat methods into two categories: without fat and with fat.

Different cooking methods are suited to different kinds of foods. For example, some meats are high in connective tissue and will be tough unless this tissue is broken down slowly by moist heat. Other meats are low in connective tissue and are naturally tender. They are at their best and juiciest when cooked with dry heat to a rare or medium-done stage.

There are many other factors to consider when choosing cooking methods for meats, fish, and vegetables, such as the flavor and appearance imparted by browning, the flavor imparted by fats, and the firmness or delicacy of the product. These factors will be taken up as individual foods are discussed in later chapters.

The basic cooking methods are summarized here. Practical application to different foods will be discussed in detail in the remainder of the book and reinforced by your instructors' demonstrations and your own experience and practice.

. . . .

MOIST-HEAT METHODS

Poach, Simmer, and Boil

To poach, simmer, and boil all mean to cook a food in water or a seasoned and flavored liquid. The temperature of the liquid determines the method.

1. To *boil* means to cook in a liquid that is bubbling rapidly and is greatly agitated. Water boils at 212°F (100°C) at sea level. No matter how high the burner is turned, the temperature of the liquid will go no higher.

    Boiling is generally reserved for certain vegetables and starches. The high temperature would toughen the proteins of meats, fish, and eggs, and the rapid bubbling breaks up delicate foods.

2. To *simmer* means to cook in a liquid that is bubbling very gently. Temperature is about 185°F to 205°F (85°C to 96°C).

    Most foods cooked in a liquid are simmered. The higher temperatures and intense agitation of boiling are detrimental to most foods. The word "boiled" is sometimes used as a menu term, as when simmered fresh beef is called "boiled beef."

3. To *poach* means to cook in a liquid, usually a small amount, that is hot but not actually bubbling. Temperature is about 160°F to 180°F (71°C to 82°C).

    Poaching is used to cook delicate foods such as fish and eggs out of the shell. It is also used to partially cook foods such as variety meats, in order to eliminate undesirable flavors and to firm up the product before final cooking.

4. A rule of thumb: whether a food is to be simmered or boiled, the liquid is often brought to a full boil at first. This compensates for the lowering of the temperature when the food items are added. The heat is then adjusted to maintain a steady temperature.

5. To *blanch* means to cook an item partially and very briefly, usually in water, but sometimes by other methods (as when french fries are blanched in deep fat).

    There are two ways of blanching in water:

    a. Place the item in cold water, bring to a boil, simmer briefly. Cool the item by plunging it into cold water.

    Purpose: to dissolve out blood, salt, or impurities from certain meats and bones.

    b. Place the item in rapidly boiling water and return the water to the boil. Remove the item and cool in cold water.

    Purpose: to set the color and destroy harmful enzymes in vegetables, or to loosen the skins of tomatoes, peaches, and similar items for easier peeling.

6. Altitude note: The boiling point of water decreases as altitude above sea level is increased. At 5,000 feet (1,500 meters) above sea level, water boils at about 203°F (95°C). Thus, it takes longer to boil foods at high altitudes, because the temperature is lower.

Steam

To *steam* means to cook foods by exposing them directly to steam.

1. In quantity cooking, this is usually done in special steam cookers, which are designed to accept standard-size pans. Steaming can also be done on a rack above boiling water. This method is more cumbersome, however, and is only occasionally used in food service. Cooking in a steam-jacketed kettle is not steaming, because the steam does not actually touch the food.

2. Steaming also refers to cooking an item tightly wrapped or in a covered pan, so that it cooks in the steam formed by its own moisture. This method is used in cooking items *en papillote,* wrapped in parchment paper (or foil). "Baked" potatoes wrapped in foil are actually steamed.

3. Steam at normal pressure is 212°F (100°C), the same as boiling water. However, it carries much more heat than boiling water and cooks very

rapidly. Cooking times must be carefully controlled to avoid overcooking.

4. A *pressure steamer* is a steam cooker that holds in steam under pressure. The temperature of the steam then goes higher than 212°F (100°C), as the following chart shows:

Pressure	Steam Temperature
5 psi (pounds per square inch)	227°F (106°C)
10 psi	240°F (116°C)
15 psi	250°F (121°C)

Because of these temperatures, pressure steaming is an extremely rapid method of cooking and must be very carefully controlled and timed.

5. Steaming is widely used for vegetables. It cooks them rapidly, without agitation, and minimizes the dissolving away of nutrients that occurs when vegetables are boiled.

Braise

To *braise* means to cook covered in a small amount of liquid, usually after preliminary browning. In almost all cases, the liquid is served with the product as a sauce.

1. Braised meats are usually browned first using a dry-heat method such as pan-frying. This gives a desirable appearance and flavor to the product and to the sauce.

2. Braising also refers to cooking some vegetables, such as lettuce or cabbage, at low temperature in a small amount of liquid, without first browning in fat, or with only a light preliminary sautéing.

3. Foods being braised are usually not completely covered by the cooking liquid. The top of the product is actually cooked by the steam held in the covered pot. Pot roasts, for example, are cooked in liquid that covers the item by one-third to two-thirds. The exact amount depends on how much sauce is needed for service. This method yields a flavorful, concentrated sauce.

4. In some preparations, especially of poultry and fish, no liquid is added. This is still considered braising, since steam is trapped by the cover and the item cooks in its own moisture and in the moisture of other ingredients such as vegetables.

5. Braising may be done on the range or in the oven. Oven-braising has three major advantages:

   a. Uniform cooking. The heat strikes the braising pot on all sides, not just the bottom.
   b. Less attention required. Foods braise at a low, steady temperature, without having to be checked constantly.
   c. Range space is free for other purposes.

DRY-HEAT METHODS

Roast and Bake

To *roast* and to *bake* means to cook foods by surrounding them with hot, dry air, usually in an oven. Cooking on a spit in front of an open fire may also be considered roasting.

Roasting usually applies primarily to meats and poultry.

Baking applies to breads, pastries, vegetables, and fish. It is a more general term than roasting.

1. Cooking *uncovered* is essential to roasting. Covering holds in steam, changing the process from dry-heat to moist-heat cooking, such as braising or steaming.

2. Meat is usually roasted on a rack (or, if it is a rib roast, on its own natural rack of bones). The rack prevents the meat from simmering in its own juices and fat. It also allows hot air to circulate all around the product.

3. When roasting in a conventional oven, the cook should allow for uneven temperatures by occasionally changing the position of the product. The back of the oven is often hotter because heat is lost at the door.

4. To *barbecue* means to cook with dry heat created by the burning of hardwood or by the hot coals of this wood. In other words, barbecuing is a roasting or grilling technique requiring a wood fire.

   Authentic, traditional American barbecue is done in wood-burning ovens or pits, but these are not really practical for the average restaurant that wants to add some barbecued items to the menu. So today, most barbecuing is done in specially designed smoke ovens or cookers. In principle, these units work like regular ovens, except that they also have devices that heat small pieces of hardwood to produce smoke. Foods should be suspended in the ovens or placed on racks so that the smoke can contact all surfaces.

Technically, the foods cooked in these units cannot be said to be barbecued, since the heat is created by electric or gas burners. But because of the wood smoke, the results can be nearly identical.

Broil

To *broil* means to cook with radiant heat from above.

Note: The terms broiling, grilling, and griddling are sometimes confused. Grilling (see next) is often called broiling, and griddling is called grilling. This book uses the terms that refer to the equipment used. Thus, broiling is done in a broiler, grilling on a grill, and griddling on a griddle.

1. Broiling is a rapid, high-heat cooking method that is usually used only for tender meats, poultry, and fish and for a few vegetable items.

2. Note the following rules of broiling:

    a. Turn heat on full. Cooking temperature is regulated by moving the rack nearer to or farther from the heat source.

    b. Use lower heat for larger, thicker items, and for items to be cooked well done. Use higher heat for thinner pieces and for items to be cooked rare. This is done so that the inside and outside are done to the desired degree at the same time. It takes practice and experience to cook foods of different thickness to the right degree of doneness inside with the desired amount of surface browning.

    c. Preheat the broiler. This helps to sear the product quickly, and the hot broiler will make the desired grill marks on the food.

    d. Foods may be dipped in oil to prevent sticking and to minimize drying. (This may not be necessary if the food is high in fat.) Care should be taken, as too much oil on a hot broiler grate may cause a fire.

    e. Turn foods over only once, to cook from both sides but to avoid unnecessary handling.

3. A low-intensity broiler called a *salamander* is used for browning or melting the top of some items before service.

Grill, Griddle, and Pan-broil

Grilling, griddling, and pan-broiling are all dry-heat cooking methods that use heat from below.

1. *Grilling* is done on an open grid over a heat source, which may be charcoal, an electric element, or a gas-heated element. Cooking temperature is regulated by moving the items to hotter or cooler places on the grill. Grilled meats should be turned to achieve desired grill markings, just as in broiling.

2. *Griddling* is done on a solid cooking surface called a griddle, with or without small amounts of fat to prevent sticking. The temperature is adjustable and is much lower (around 350°F/177°C) than on a grill. In addition to meats, items such as eggs and pancakes are cooked on a griddle.

    Grooved griddles have a solid top with raised ridges. They are designed to cook like grills, but to create less smoke. Meats cooked on a grooved griddle do not have the "charcoal-grilled" flavor imparted by smoke from burning fats.

3. *Pan-broiling* is like griddling, except it is done in a sauté pan or skillet instead of on a griddle surface. Fat must be poured off as it accumulates, or the process would become pan-frying. No liquid is added, and the pan is not covered, or else the item would steam.

DRY-HEAT METHODS USING FAT

Sauté

To *sauté* means to cook quickly in a small amount of fat.

1. The French word *sauter* means "to jump," referring to the action of tossing small pieces of food in a sauté pan (see Figure 17.1). However, larger foods, such as slices of meat and pieces of chicken, are sautéed without actually being tossed in the pan.

2. Note these two important principles:

    a. Preheat the pan before adding the food to be sautéed. The food must start cooking at high heat, or it will begin to simmer in its own juices.

b. Do not overcrowd the pan. Doing so lowers the temperature too much, and again the food begins to simmer in its own juices.

3. Meats to be sautéed are often dusted with flour to prevent sticking and to help achieve uniform browning.

4. After a food is sautéed, a liquid such as wine or stock is often swirled in the pan to dissolve browned bits of food sticking to the bottom. This is called *deglazing*. This liquid becomes part of a sauce served with the sautéed items.

Pan-fry

To *pan-fry* means to cook in a moderate amount of fat in a pan over moderate heat.

1. Pan-frying is similar to sautéing, except that more fat is generally used and the cooking time is longer. The method is used for larger pieces of food, such as chops and chicken pieces, and the items are not tossed by flipping the pan as they often are in sautéing.

2. Pan-frying is usually done over lower heat than sautéing, because of the larger pieces being cooked.

3. The amount of fat depends on the food being cooked. Only a small amount is used for eggs, for example, while as much as an inch (2.5 cm) or more may be used for pan-fried chicken.

4. Most foods must be turned at least once for even cooking. Some larger foods may be removed from the pan and finished in the oven, to prevent excessive surface browning. This method of finishing in the oven is also used to simplify production when large quantities of foods must be pan-fried.

Deep-fry

To *deep-fry* means to cook a food submerged in hot fat. Quality in a deep-fried product is characterized by the following properties:

Minimum fat absorption

Minimum moisture loss (that is, not overcooked)

Attractive golden color

Crisp surface or coating

No off flavors imparted by the frying fat

Many foods are dipped in a breading or batter before frying. This forms a protective coating between food and fat and helps give the product crispness, color, and flavor. Obviously, the quality of the breading or batter affects the quality of the finished product (see Chapter 7, pp. 114–115).

Guidelines for Deep-frying

1. ***Fry at proper temperatures.*** Most foods are fried at 350°F to 375°F (175°C to 190°C). Excessive greasiness in fried foods is usually caused by frying at too low a temperature.

2. ***Don't overload the baskets.*** Doing so greatly lowers the fat temperature.

3. ***Use good quality fat.*** The best fat for frying has a *high smoke point* (the temperature at which the fat begins to smoke and to break down rapidly).

4. ***Replace about 15 to 20 percent of the fat with fresh after each daily use.*** This extends frying life.

5. ***Discard spent fat.*** Old fat loses frying ability, browns excessively, and imparts off flavors.

6. ***Avoid frying strong and mild-flavored foods in the same fat, if possible.*** French fries should not taste like fried fish.

7. ***Fry as close to service as possible.*** Do not leave foods in the basket above the fry kettle, and do not hold under heat lamps for more than a few minutes. The foods' moisture quickly makes the breading or coating soggy.

8. ***Protect fat from its enemies:***
   Heat. Turn fryer off or to a lower holding temperature (200°F to 250°F/95°C to 120°C) when not in use.

   Oxygen. Keep fat covered between services, and try to aerate the fat as little as possible when filtering.

   Water. Remove excess moisture from foods before frying. Dry baskets and kettle thoroughly after cleaning. Keep liquids away from the fryer to prevent accidental spills.

   Salt. Never salt foods over the fat.

   Food particles. Shake loose crumbs off breaded items before placing over fat. Skim and strain fat frequently.

   Detergent. Rinse baskets and kettle well after cleaning.

Pressure Frying

Pressure frying means deep-frying in a special covered fryer that traps steam given off by the foods being cooked and increases the pressure inside the kettle.

In a standard fryer, even though the fat may be at 350°F (175°C), the temperature inside the food will not rise above 212°F (100°C), the boiling point of water. Just as in a pressure steamer, a pressure fryer raises this temperature and cooks the food more quickly, without excessive surface browning. At the same time, the fat temperature can be lower, 325°F (165°C) or less.

Pressure frying requires accurate timing, because the product cannot be seen while it is cooking.

MICROWAVE COOKING

Microwave cooking refers to the use of a specific tool rather than to a basic dry-heat or moist-heat cooking method. This equipment is used mostly for heating prepared foods and for thawing either raw or cooked items. However, it can be used for primary cooking as well.

Different models of microwave ovens range in power from about 500 watts up to about 2,000 watts. The higher the wattage, the more intense the energy it puts out and the faster it will heat foods. Most models have switches that allow you to cook at different power levels.

One of the most important advantages of the microwave oven in à la carte cooking is that it enables you to heat individual portions of many foods to order quickly and evenly. Instead of keeping such foods as stews hot in the steam table, where they gradually become overcooked, you can keep them refrigerated (either in bulk or in individual portions) and reheat each order as needed. This is perhaps the main reason why most restaurants have one or more microwave ovens, even though they may not use them for primary cooking.

Because the microwave oven is a unique tool in food service, the cook should observe the following special points regarding its use:

1. Small items will not brown in a standard microwave. Large roasts may brown somewhat from the heat generated in the item itself. Some models of microwave ovens have added browning elements that use conventional heat.

2. Watch timing carefully. Overcooking is the most common error in microwave use. High energy levels cook small items very rapidly.

3. Large items should be turned once or twice for even cooking.

4. An on–off cycle is often used for large items to allow time for heat to be conducted to the interior.

5. If your equipment has a defrost cycle (which switches the oven to lower power), use this cycle rather than full power to thaw frozen foods. Lower power enables the item to thaw more evenly, with less danger of partially cooking it. If your oven does not have this feature, use an on–off cycle.

6. Sliced, cooked meats and other items that are likely to dry out in the microwave should be protected either by wrapping them loosely in plastic or wax paper or by covering them with a sauce or gravy.

7. Because microwaves act only on water molecules, foods with a high water content, such as vegetables, heat faster than denser, drier foods, such as cooked meats.

8. Foods at the edge of a dish or plate heat faster than foods in the center. This is because they are hit by rays bouncing off the walls of the oven as well as by rays directly from the energy source. Therefore

   a. Depress the center of casseroles so that the food is not as thick there as at the edges. This will help it heat more evenly.
   b. When you are heating several foods at once on a plate, put the moist, quick-heating items like vegetables in the center and the denser, slower-heating items at the edges.

9. Because microwaves do not penetrate metal, aluminum foil and other metals shield foods from the radiant energy. For example, a potato wrapped in foil will not cook in a microwave oven.

With older machines, it was a general rule not to put any metal in the oven, since the radiation could bounce off the metal and damage the magnetron (the oven's generator). With newer machines, it is possible to heat foods in foil pans and to shield certain parts of the food by covering them with pieces of foil, so that they do not overheat. Follow the procedures recommended by the manufacturer.

Because microwaves cook so rapidly, they will not break down the connective tissues of less tender meats. Slow, moist cooking is necessary for dissolving these connective tissues.

The more food that is placed in a microwave at once, the longer the cooking time. Thus, the primary advantage of microwave cooking—speed—is lost with large roasts and other large quantities.

SUMMARY OF COOKING TERMS

The following is an alphabetical list of terms that describe ways of applying heat to foods. Basic cooking methods described earlier are included, as well as more specific applications of these basic methods.

BAKE. To cook foods by surrounding them with hot, dry air. Similar to ROAST, but the term *baking* usually applies to breads, pastries, vegetables, and fish.

BARBECUE. (1) To cook with dry heat created by the burning of hardwood or by the hot coals of this wood. (2) Loosely, to cook over hot coals, such as on a grill or spit, often with a seasoned marinade or basting sauce.

BLANCH. To cook an item partially and very briefly in boiling water or in hot fat. Usually a pre-preparation technique, as to loosen peels of vegetables, fruits, and nuts, to partially cook french fries or other foods before service, to prepare for freezing, or to remove undesirable flavors.

BOIL. To cook in water or other liquid that is bubbling rapidly, about 212°F (100°C) at sea level and at normal pressure.

BRAISE. (1) To cook covered in a small amount of liquid, usually after preliminary browning. (2) To cook (certain vegetables) slowly in a small amount of liquid without preliminary browning.

BROIL. To cook with radiant heat from above.

DEEP-FRY. To cook submerged in hot fat.

DEGLAZE. To swirl a liquid in a sauté pan, roast pan, or other pan to dissolve cooked particles of food remaining on the bottom.

DRY-HEAT COOKING METHODS. Methods in which heat is conducted to foods without the use of moisture.

FRY. To cook in hot fat.

GLAZE. To give shine to the surface of a food, by applying a sauce, aspic, sugar, or icing, and/or by browning or melting under a broiler or salamander or in an oven.

GRIDDLE. To cook on a flat, solid cooking surface called a griddle.

GRILL. To cook on an open grid over a heat source.

MOIST-HEAT COOKING METHODS. Methods in which heat is conducted to foods by water or other liquid (except fat) or by steam.

PAN-BROIL. To cook uncovered in a skillet or sauté pan without fat.

PAN-FRY. To cook in a moderate amount of fat in an uncovered pan.

(EN) PAPILLOTE. Wrapped in paper (or sometimes foil) for cooking, so that the food is steamed in its own moisture.

PARBOIL. To cook partially in a boiling or simmering liquid.

PARCOOK. To cook partially by any method.

POACH. To cook very gently in water or other liquid that is hot but not actually bubbling, about 160°F to 180°F (71°C to 82°C).

REDUCE. To cook by simmering or boiling until the quantity of liquid is decreased, often done to concentrate flavors.

ROAST. To cook foods by surrounding them with hot, dry air, in an oven or on a spit in front of an open fire.

SAUTÉ. To cook quickly in a small amount of fat.

SEAR. To brown the surface of a food quickly at a high temperature.

SIMMER. To cook in water or other liquid that is bubbling gently, about 185°F to 205°F (85°C to 96°C).

STEAM. To cook by direct contact with steam.

STEW. To simmer a food or foods in a small amount of liquid, which is usually served with the food as a sauce.

SWEAT. To cook slowly in fat without browning, sometimes under a cover.

THE ART OF SEASONING AND FLAVORING

*P*eople eat because they enjoy the flavors of good food, not just because they must fill their stomachs to stay alive. Appearance, texture, and nutrition are important, too, but good taste is the first mark of good cooking.

Enhancement and adjustment of flavors is one of a cook's most critical tasks, a task requiring experience and judgment. Unfortunately, the fine art of seasoning and flavoring is too often one of the most abused.

The most important flavors of a particular preparation are the flavors of its main ingredients. Roast beef should taste like roast beef, green beans like green beans, sole stuffed with crabmeat like sole and crabmeat. It's a fact of life, however, that plain foods generally are a little bland to most palates, so the cook's job is to perk up the taste buds with a few added ingredients, so that the beef tastes more like beef, the green beans more like green beans.

. . . .

SEASONING AND FLAVORING DEFINED

Strictly speaking, there is a difference between seasoning and flavoring.

Seasoning means enhancing the natural flavor of the food, without significantly changing its flavor. Salt is the most important seasoning ingredient.

Flavoring means adding a new flavor to a food, changing or modifying the original flavor.

The difference between seasoning and flavoring is often one of degree. For example, salt is usually used only to season, not to flavor. But in the case of potato chips or pretzels the salt is so predominant that it can be considered an added flavoring. On the other hand, nutmeg is normally used for its distinctive flavor, but just a dash can perk up the flavor of a cream sauce without actually being detectable to most people.

Basic Rule of Seasoning and Flavoring

Your main ingredients are your main sources of flavor. Use good-quality main ingredients, handle all foods with care, and employ correct cooking procedures.

Badly prepared foods cannot be rescued by a last-minute addition of spices. The function of spices, herbs, and seasonings is to heighten and to give extra interest to the natural flavors of foods, not to serve as main ingredients or to cover up natural flavors.

WHEN TO SEASON AND FLAVOR

Seasoning

1. The most important time for seasoning liquid foods is at the end of the cooking process.

    The last step in most recipes, whether written or not, is "adjust the seasoning." This means that you have to first taste and evaluate the product. Then you must decide what should be done, if anything, to improve the taste. Often a little salt in a stew or a dash of fresh lemon juice in a sauce is enough.

    The ability to evaluate and correct flavors takes experience, and it is one of the most important skills a cook can develop.

2. Salt and other seasonings are also added at the beginning of cooking, particularly for larger pieces of food, when seasonings added at the end would not be absorbed or blended in, but would just sit on the surface.

3. Adding some of the seasoning during the cooking process also aids in evaluating the flavor at any step along the way.

4. Do not add very much seasoning if it will be concentrated during cooking, as when a liquid is reduced.

Flavoring

Flavoring ingredients can be added at the beginning, middle, or end, depending on the cooking time, the cooking process, and the flavoring ingredient.

1. Only a few flavorings can be added successfully at the end of cooking. Fresh (not dried) herbs, sherry or flamed brandy, and condiments like prepared mustard and Worcestershire sauce can be.

2. Most flavorings need heat to release their flavors and time for the flavors to blend.

    a. Whole spices take longest.
    b. Ground spices release flavors more quickly and thus don't require as long a cooking time.

3. Too much cooking results in loss of flavor. Most flavors, whether in spices or in main ingredients, are *volatile*, which means they evaporate when heated. That is why you can smell food cooking.

We can conclude that herbs and spices should cook with the foods long enough to release their flavors but not so long that their flavors are lost. If cooking times are short, you can generally add spices and herbs at the beginning or middle of cooking time. On the other hand, if cooking times are long, it is usually better to add them in the middle or toward the end of cooking time.

Note: Food safety experts recommend adding spices and herbs at least 30 minutes before the end of cooking, so that any microorganisms they might carry will be destroyed.

COMMON SEASONING AND FLAVORING INGREDIENTS

Any food product can be used as a flavoring ingredient, even meat (as when crumbled bacon is added to sautéed potatoes, or diced ham is included in a mirepoix). Sauces, which are compound preparations containing many flavoring ingredients, are themselves used as flavorings for meat, fish, vegetables, and desserts.

We obviously cannot treat all possible flavoring ingredients here, but we discuss some of the most important ones as follows. A survey of herbs and spices is provided in Table 4.1. Ingredients used primarily in the bakeshop are discussed in Chapter 24.

1. *Salt* is the most important seasoning ingredient. Don't use too much. You can always add more, but you can't take it out.

2. *Pepper* comes in three forms: white, black, and green. They are actually the same berry but processed differently. (Black pepper is picked unripe; white is ripened and the hull is removed; green peppercorns are picked unripe and are preserved before their color darkens.)

   a. Whole and crushed *black pepper* is used primarily in seasoning and flavoring stocks and sauces, and sometimes red meats. Ground black pepper is used in the dining room by the customer.

   b. Ground *white pepper* is more important as a seasoning in the food service kitchen. Its flavor is slightly different from that of black pepper, and it blends well (in small quantities) with many foods. Its white color makes it undetectable in light-colored foods.

   c. *Green peppercorns* are fairly expensive and are used in special recipes, primarily in luxury restaurants. The types packed in water, brine, or vinegar (those in water and in brine have better flavor) are soft. Wet-pack peppercorns are perishable; water-packed peppercorns will keep only a few days in the refrigerator after they are opened, while the others will keep longer. Green peppercorns are also available freeze-dried.

3. *Red pepper* or *cayenne* is completely unrelated to black and white pepper. It belongs to the same family as paprika and fresh sweet bell peppers. Used in tiny amounts, it gives a spicy hotness to sauces and soups, without actually altering the flavor. In larger amounts, it gives both heat and flavor to many spicy foods, such as those of Mexico and India.

4. *Lemon juice* is an important seasoning, particularly for enlivening the flavor of sauces and soups.

5. *Parsley*, *chives*, and sometimes *mint* and *dill* are the only *fresh herbs* used in most food service operations. The fresh products should be used instead of the dried whenever possible. Their flavor is greatly superior. Parsley, both whole leaf and chopped, is also important as a garnish.

6. *Onion*, *garlic*, *shallots*, and other members of the onion family, as well as *carrots* and *celery*, are used as flavorings in virtually all stations of the kitchen except the bakeshop. Try to avoid the use of dried onion and garlic products. They have less flavor and the fresh product is always available.

7. *Wine*, *brandy*, and other alcoholic beverages are used to flavor sauces, soups, and many entrées. Brandy should be boiled or flamed to eliminate the high percentage of alcohol, which would be unpleasant in the finished dish. Table wines usually need some cooking or reduction (either separately or with other ingredients) to produce the desired flavors. Fortified wines like sherry and madeira, on the other hand, may be added as flavorings at the end of cooking.

8. *Prepared mustard* is a blend of ground mustard seed, vinegar, and other spices. It is used to flavor meats, sauces, and salad dressings and as a table condiment. For most cooking purposes, European styles such as Dijon (French) or Dusseldorf (German) work best, while the bright-yellow American ballpark style is more appropriate as a table condiment than as a cooking ingredient. There is also a coarse, grainy style that is sometimes called for in specialty recipes.

9. Grated *lemon and orange rind* are used in sauces, meats, and poultry (as in duckling a l'orange), as well as in the bakeshop. Only the colored outer portion, called the *zest*, which contains the flavorful oils, is used. The white pith is bitter.

10. *MSG*, or *monosodium glutamate*, is a flavor enhancer widely used in oriental cooking. MSG doesn't actually change the flavor of foods but acts on the taste buds. It has a bad reputation for causing chest pains and headaches in some individuals.

USING HERBS AND SPICES

Definitions

Herbs are the leaves of certain plants that usually grow in temperate climates.

Spices are the buds, fruits, flowers, bark, seeds, and roots of plants and trees, many of which grow in tropical climates.

The distinction is often confusing, but it is not as important to know which flavorings are spices and which are herbs as it is to use them skillfully.

Guidelines for Using Herbs and Spices

1. Be familiar with each spice's aroma, flavor, and effect on food. Looking at a spice chart, including the one in this book, is no substitute for familiarity with the actual product.

2. Store spices in a cool place, tightly covered in opaque containers. Heat, light, and moisture deteriorate herbs and spices rapidly.

3. Don't use stale spices and herbs, and don't buy more than you can use in about 6 months. Whole spices keep longer than ground, but both lose much flavor after 6 months.

4. Be cautious after you have replaced old spices. The fresher products are more potent, so the amount you used before might now be too much.

5. Use good-quality spices and herbs. It doesn't pay to economize here. The difference in cost is only a fraction of a cent per portion.

6. Whole spices take longer to release flavors than ground spices, so allow for adequate cooking time.

7. Whole herbs and spices for flavoring a liquid are tied loosely in a piece of cheesecloth (called a *sachet*) for easy removal.

8. When in doubt, add less than you think you need. You can always add more, but it's hard to remove what you've already added.

9. Except in dishes like curry or chili, the spices should not dominate. Often they should not even be evident. If you can taste the nutmeg in the creamed spinach, there's probably too much nutmeg.

10. Herbs and spices added to uncooked foods such as salads and dressings need several hours for flavors to be released and blended.

11. Taste foods before serving, whenever possible. How else can you "adjust the seasoning"?

Table 4.1 is not a substitute for familiarity with the actual products. Eventually you should be able to identify by aroma, taste, and appearance any spice on your shelf without looking at the label.

TABLE 4.1   **Herbs and Spices**

Product	*Market Forms*	*Description*	*Examples of Use*
Allspice	Whole, ground	Small brown berry; flavor resembles blend of cinnamon, cloves, and nutmeg	Sausages and braised meats, poached fish, stewed fruits, pies, puddings
Anise seed	Whole, ground	Small seed; licorice flavor	Cookies, pastries, breads
Basil	Crushed leaves	Aromatic leaf; member of mint family	Tomatoes and tomato dishes, pesto (Italian basil sauce), egg dishes, lamb chops, eggplant, peas, squash

(Continues)

TABLE 4.1   **Herbs and Spices** *(Continued)*

Product	Market Forms	Description	Examples of Use
Bay leaves	Whole	Stiff, dark green, oblong leaves; pungent aroma	One of the most important herbs; used in stocks, sauces, stews, braised meats
Caraway seed	Whole	Dark brown, curved seeds; familiar rye bread seasoning	Rye bread, cabbage, sauerkraut, pork, cheese spreads, eastern European dishes
Cardamom	Whole pod, ground seed	Tiny brown seeds inside white or green pod; sweet and aromatic; expensive	Pickling, Danish pastries, curries
Cayenne (red pepper)	Ground	Ground form of hot red pepper; looks like paprika, but is extremely hot	In small amounts in many sauces, soups, meat, fish, egg, and cheese dishes (see p. 62)
Celery seed	Whole, ground, ground mixed with salt (celery salt)	Tiny brown seeds with strong celery flavor	Salads, cole slaw, salad dressings, tomato products
Chervil	Crushed leaves	Herb with mild flavor of parsley and tarragon	Soups, salads, sauces, egg and cheese dishes
Chili powder	Ground blend	Blend of spices including cumin, chili peppers, oregano, garlic	Chili and Mexican dishes, egg dishes, appetizers, ground meat
Chives	Fresh, dried, frozen	Grasslike herb with onion flavor	Salads, egg and cheese dishes, fish, soups
Cinnamon	Sticks, ground	Aromatic bark of cinnamon or cassia trees	Pastries, breads, desserts, cooked fruits, ham, sweet potatoes, hot beverages
Cloves	Whole, ground	Dried flower buds of a tropical tree; pungent, sweet flavor	Whole: marinades, stocks, sauces, braised meats, ham, pickling; ground: cakes, pastries, fruits
Coriander	Whole, ground	Round, light brown, hollow seed, slightly sweet, musty flavor	Pickling, sausage, pork, curried dishes, gingerbread
Cumin seed	Whole, ground	Small seed resembling caraway, but lighter in color	Ingredient of curry and chili powders; sausages and meats; egg and cheese dishes
Curry powder	Ground blend	A mixture of 16 to 20 spices, including red pepper, turmeric, cumin, coriander, ginger, cloves, cinnamon, black pepper; different brands vary greatly in flavor and hotness	Curried dishes, eggs, vegetables, fish, soups, rice
Dill	Crushed leaves (called "dill weed"), whole seed	Herb and seed with familiar "dill pickle" flavor; seed is more pungent than the herb	Seed: pickling, sauerkraut, soups; herb: salads, cheese dishes, fish and shellfish, some vegetables
Fennel	Whole seed	Greenish-brown seeds similiar in flavor to anise, but larger size	Italian sausage, tomato sauce, fish
Garlic	Fresh: whole bulbs; dried: granulated, powder, and mixed with salt	Strong, aromatic member of onion family; fresh bulbs composed of many small cloves	Wide variety of foods

TABLE 4.1 *(Continued)*

Product	Market Forms	Description	Examples of Use
Ginger	Whole, ground (also fresh and candied or crystallized)	Light brown, knobby root of ginger plant	Baked goods and desserts, fruits, curried dishes, braised meats; fresh: in Chinese and other oriental dishes
Juniper berries	Whole	Slightly soft, purple berries with "piney" flavor; principal flavoring of gin	Marinades, game dishes, sauerkraut
Mace	Whole ("blade"), ground	Orange outer covering of nutmeg; similiar flavor, but milder	Baked goods, desserts, fruits, sausages, pork, fish, spinach, squash, other vegetables
Marjoram	Crushed leaves	Grey-green herb with pleasant aroma and slightly minty flavor, similar to oregano but much milder	Pâtés and ground meats, braised meats, sauces, roast lamb, poultry and poultry stuffings
Mint	Leaves	Aromatic herb with familiar cool flavor; two varieties: spearmint and peppermint	Lamb, fruits, tea and fruit beverages, peas, carrots, potatoes
Mustard seed	Whole, ground (also prepared mustard; see p. 62)	Very pungent seed in two varieties: white or yellow, and brown. Brown is stronger.	Cheese and egg dishes, pickling, meats, sauces and gravies
Nutmeg	Whole, ground	Sweet, aromatic kernel of nutmeg fruit	Soups, cream sauces, chicken, veal, many vegetables (spinach, mushrooms, squash, potatoes), desserts, custards, breads, pastries
Oregano	Leaves, ground	Pungent herb, known as the "pizza herb"	Italian and Mexican dishes, tomato products
Paprika	Ground	Ground form of a dried, sweet red pepper. Spanish variety is brighter in color, mild in flavor; Hungarian is darker and more pungent.	Spanish: used (or overused) primarily as garnish on light-colored foods; Hungarian: goulash, braised meats and poultry, sauces
Parsley	Fresh: whole sprigs, in bunches; dried: in flakes	Most widely used herb. Dark green curly or flat leaves with delicate, sweet flavor	Almost all foods (see p. 62)
Pepper, black and white	Whole (peppercorns); ground fine, medium, or coarse	Small black or creamy white, hard berry. Pungent flavor and aroma	Most widely used spice (see p. 62)
Pepper, red	(see cayenne)		
Poppy seed	Whole	Tiny blue-black seeds with faint but distinctive flavor	Garnish for breads and rolls, buttered noodles; ground: in pastry fillings
Rosemary	Whole	Light green leaves resembling pine needles	Lamb, braised meats and poultry, soups, tomato and meat sauces
Saffron	Whole (threads)	Red stigma of saffron crocus. Gives bright yellow color to foods. Mild distinctive flavor. Very expensive.	Should be steeped in hot liquid before use. Rice dishes, poultry and seafoods, bouillabaisse, baked goods

(Continues)

TABLE 4.1 **Herbs and Spices** *(Continued)*

Product	Market Forms	Description	Examples of Use
Sage	Whole, rubbed (finer consistency than whole leaves), ground	Pungent grey-green herb with fuzzy leaves	Pork, poultry, stuffings, sausage, beans, tomatoes
Savory	Crushed leaves	Fragrant herb of mint family; summer savory is preferred to winter	Many meat, poultry, fish, egg, and vegetable dishes
Sesame seeds	Whole (hulled or unhulled)	Small yellowish seed with nutlike taste. Familiar hamburger bun garnish. High oil content.	Bread and roll garnish
Tarragon	Crushed leaves	Delicate green herb with flavor that is both minty and licorice-like	Béarnaise sauce, tarragon vinegar, chicken, fish, salads and dressings, eggs
Thyme	Crushed leaves, ground	Tiny brownish-green leaves; very aromatic	One of the most important and versatile of herbs; stocks, soups, sauces, meats, poultry, tomatoes
Turmeric	Ground	Intense yellow root of ginger family; mild but distinctive peppery flavor	A basic ingredient of curry powder; pickles, relishes, salads, eggs, rice

TERMS FOR REVIEW

coagulation	infrared	braise	sauté
connective tissues	microwave	roast	pan-fry
caramelization	poach	bake	deep-fry
gelatinization	simmer	barbecue	seasoning
fiber	boil	broil	flavoring
smoke point	blanch	grill	volatile
conduction	steam	griddle	herb
convection	en papillote	pan-broil	spice
radiation			

QUESTIONS FOR DISCUSSION

1. Your broiler cook has just broiled a codfish fillet that turned out dry, rubbery, and shrunken. Explain what happened to it.

2. Why might adding some tomato product to a beef stew help make the meat more tender?

3. You are roasting a large quantity of ducklings and must use both your conventional ovens and your convection oven. You set all the ovens at the same temperature, but find the ducklings in the convection oven are done first. Why?

4. Arrange the following cooking methods into three groups, depending on whether they are moist-heat methods, dry-heat methods without fat, and dry-heat methods with fat: braising, roasting, deep-frying, sautéing, poaching, steaming, broiling, pressure frying, grilling, simmering.

5. What are some advantages of braising a pan of Swiss steaks in the oven instead of on the range?

6. A cook in your restaurant is roasting several pans of chickens. He thinks they are browning too fast and he covers the pans with foil to keep the chickens from browning too much more. What is wrong with this?

7. You are sautéing some beef tenderloin tips for stroganoff, and you suddenly find that the meat is simmering in liquid rather than sautéing. What did you do wrong?

8. Your customers complain that your french fries are too greasy and soggy. How can you correct the problem?

9. What is meant by the phrase "adjust the seasoning"?

10. What is wrong with adding whole caraway seed to a portion of goulash just before serving?

THE RECIPE: ITS STRUCTURE AND ITS USE

Recipes are important tools for the cook because they are a means of recording and passing along essential information. Learning to cook without being able to consult recipes would be like learning to play the piano without written music.

In spite of their importance, written recipes have many limitations, as we will discuss in this chapter. No matter how detailed a recipe may be, it assumes that you already have certain knowledge—that you understand the terminology it uses, for example, and that you know how to measure ingredients.

In this chapter, we discuss various kinds of recipes and their structure, and we learn how recipes are used in a commercial kitchen. In particular, we examine techniques for measuring ingredients and portions, for converting recipes, and for calculating food cost with the aid of written recipes.

After reading this chapter, you should be able to

1. Understand the problems and limitations of written recipes and the importance of using judgment when you cook.

2. Discuss the structure and functions of standardized recipes.

3. Use and understand the recipes in this book to practice basic cooking techniques.

4. Measure ingredients and portions.

5. Use metric measurements.

6. Convert recipes to higher or lower yields.

7. Perform yield cost analyses.

8. Calculate raw food costs.

THE WRITTEN RECIPE

The Uses and Limitations of Recipes

A *recipe* is a set of instructions for producing a certain dish. In order to duplicate a desired preparation, it is necessary to have a precise record of the ingredients, their amounts, and the way in which they are combined and cooked. This is the purpose of a recipe.

Many people believe that learning to cook means simply learning recipes. Knowledgeable cooks, on the other hand, are able to prepare food without written recipes, if they have to, because they have a good understanding of basic principles and techniques. A recipe is a way of applying basic techniques to specific ingredients.

If you have read the preceding chapter, or have even casually leafed through this book, you know that it is not just a book of recipes. Although there are hundreds of recipes in this book, they take up a relatively small part of it. Your main concern will be learning techniques and procedures that you will be able to apply to any recipe.

The main purpose of learning basic cooking principles is not to be able to cook without recipes, however, but to understand the recipes you use. As we said in the beginning of this chapter, every recipe assumes that you have certain knowledge, so that you can understand the instructions and follow them correctly.

Some recipes supply very little information and some supply a great deal. But no matter how detailed it is, a written recipe can't tell you everything, and some judgment by the cook is always required. There are several reasons for this:

1. *Food products are not uniform.*

   Food ingredients are natural products, so they are not uniform like machine bolts, ball-point pens, or typing paper. One tomato may be riper than another, one carrot tenderer or sweeter than another, one oyster saltier than another. Such variations may affect how the ingredients are handled, how long they are cooked, what proportions are needed, and how much seasoning is required.

2. *Kitchens do not have the same equipment.*

   Different pans distribute heat at different rates. Different broilers heat to different temperatures. Liquid evaporates from wide pots faster than from tall, narrow ones, and so on.

3. *It is impossible to give exact instructions for many processes.*

   How do you set the burner if the instructions say "Cook over medium heat"? How thick is a "thick" sauce? How long do you broil a rare steak?

The difference between an experienced cook and a beginning cook is the ability to make judgments about these variables.

Standardized Recipes

1. *Definition.*

   A *standardized recipe* is a set of instructions describing the way a particular establishment prepares a particular dish. In other words, it is a customized recipe developed by an operation for the use of its own cooks, using its own equipment, to be served to its own patrons.

2. *The structure of a standardized recipe.*

   Recipe formats differ from operation to operation, but nearly all of them try to include as much precise information as possible. The following details are usually listed:

   a. Name of the recipe.
   b. Yield, including total yield, number of portions, and exact portion size.
   c. Ingredients and exact amounts, listed in order of use.
   d. Equipment needed, including measuring equipment, pan sizes, portioning equipment, and so on.
   e. Directions for preparing the dish. Directions are kept as simple as possible.
   f. Preparation and cooking times.
   g. Directions for portioning, plating, and garnishing.
   h. Directions for breaking down the station, cleaning up, and storing leftovers.

3. *The function of standardized recipes.*

   An operation's own recipes are used to control production. They do this in two ways:

   a. *They control quality.* Standardized recipes are very detailed and specific. The reason for this is to ensure that the product is the same every time it is made and served, no matter who cooks it.
   b. *They control quantity.* First, they indicate precise quantities for every ingredient and

how they are to be measured. Second, they indicate exact yields and portion sizes, and how the portions are to be measured and served.

4. ***The limitations of standardized recipes.***

Standardized recipes have the same problems as any recipes—the problems that we discussed earlier regarding variations in foods, equipment, and vagueness of instructions. These problems can be reduced by writing the recipe carefully, but they cannot be eliminated. Even if an operation uses very good standardized recipes, a new employee making a dish for the first time will usually require some supervision, to make sure he or she interprets the instructions the same way as the rest of the staff. These limitations don't invalidate standardized recipes. If anything, they make exact directions even more important. But they do mean that experience and knowledge are still very important.

Instructional Recipes

The recipes in this book are *not* standardized recipes. Remember that a standardized recipe is a recipe that is custom made for a particular operation. The recipes in this book are obviously not.

The purpose of a standardized recipe is to direct and control the production of a particular food item. Directions must be as complete and exact as possible.

The purpose of the instructional recipes in this book is to teach basic cooking techniques. They provide an opportunity for you to practice, with specific ingredients, the general procedures you have learned.

If you glance at any of the recipes in this book, you will see that they do not contain all the features of a standardized recipe, as described in the previous section. In particular, you will see the following differences:

1. ***Instructions for preparation.***

In most cases, recipes in this book follow a discussion of a basic procedure. The recipes are examples of the general procedure, and they give you experience in applying what you have learned. The information you are given in the recipe instructions is intended primarily to encourage you to think and to learn a technique, not just to turn out a product. You should consult your instructor when you have a question about a procedure.

2. ***Variations and optional ingredients.***

Many recipes are followed by variations. These are actually whole recipes, given in very abbreviated terms. It would be possible to write them out as separate, full-length recipes. (You are encouraged to do this before preparing a variation, as a learning experience.)

Giving them as variations rather than as separate recipes encourages you to see the patterns behind the recipes. Again, you are learning techniques, not just recipes. You develop a lot more understanding of what you are doing if you see Spanish rice and Turkish pilaf, for example, or coconut cream pie and chocolate pudding as variations of the same basic techniques rather than as separate, unrelated recipes.

Your instructors may have their own variations, or they may wish to make changes in the basic recipes, in order to teach you certain points. Unlike standardized recipes, instructional recipes are not engraved in stone.

Cooking with Judgment

When you make a recipe for the first time, you should be applying your knowledge and thinking about the recipe in relation to the skills you have. In particular, you should determine the following points:

1. ***What are the basic cooking methods?***

When you read the recipe for sauerbraten (see p. 262), you will quickly figure out that the cooking method used is braising (even if the word "braise" is never used in the recipe). Then you should review in your mind everything you know about basic braising procedures.

2. ***What are the characteristics of the ingredients?***

If the sauerbraten recipe calls for bottom round of beef, for example, you should ask yourself, "What do I know about bottom round? Is it lean or fatty? Tough or tender? How do these traits affect cooking?"

3. ***What are the functions of the ingredients?***

What does the vinegar do in the sauerbraten recipe? What about the vegetables? The gingersnaps?

When you have gained more experience, you will be able to easily answer these questions. You will know what ingredients contribute to flavor, to texture, or to body and how they do it.

4. What are the cooking times?

Most of the recipes in this book do not give cooking times, except as general guidelines to help you plan production. This is because cooking times are too variable to be stated exactly.

Instead, you will learn how to test for doneness by observing changes in the product. You must be able to judge when a product has reached the right temperature, the proper texture or consistency, or the desired taste.

When you learn to cook with judgment, you will be able to cook with most recipes, even poorly written ones. You will be able to see what might be wrong with a new recipe before you try it and will be able to make adjustments in it. You will know how to substitute ingredients or use different equipment. You will even be able to create new recipes.

Remember we said that some recipes supply very little information and depend largely on the cook's knowledge. With enough experience, you will even be able to cook from recipes like the following, a complete recipe for Fillets of Sole Bercy, quoted in its entirety from *Le Repertoire de la Cuisine*, a favorite book used by chefs in classical French cooking: "Poached with shallots and chopped parsley, white wine and fish stock. Reduce the stock, add butter, and coat the fish, glaze."

MEASUREMENT

Many restaurants budget a profit of 10 percent or less. This means that a sandwich selling for $3.00 makes a profit of only 30 cents. If the cook happens to put a half ounce too much meat in the sandwich, the operation is probably losing money on it. No wonder so many restaurants go out of business.

Careful measurement is one of the most important parts of food production. It is important for consistent quality each time a recipe is prepared and served. And it is important for cost controls.

There are two important kinds of measurement in the kitchen:

Ingredient measurement

Portion measurement, or portion control

Ingredient Measurement

Weight

Weighing is the most accurate method of measuring ingredients. It is the method used for most solid ingredients.

Accurate scales are necessary for weighing. Small portion scales are often used in the kitchen because of their convenience. Balance scales are used in the bakeshop (see pp. 656–657 for procedure).

Procedure for Weighing Ingredients on a Portion Scale

1. Place receiving container, if any, on the scale.

2. Set the scale so that it reads *zero*.

3. Add the item being weighed to the container (or place on scale, if no container is used) until the scale reads desired weight.

To be able to weigh ingredients, you must observe the difference between AP (as purchased) weight and EP (edible portion) weight.

AP weight is the weight of the item as purchased, before any trimming is done.

EP weight is the weight after all nonedible or nonservable parts have been trimmed off.

Recipes sometimes specify which weight they are referring to. When they don't, you must judge from the instructions.

1. If a recipe calls for "2 lb potatoes" and the first instruction is "scrub, peel, and eye the potatoes," then you know that AP weight is called for.

2. If the recipe calls for "2 lb peeled, diced potatoes," then you know that the EP weight is called for. You will need more than 2 lb AP.

Volume

Volume measures are used for liquids. Measuring a liquid by volume is usually faster than weighing it, and accuracy is good.

Solid ingredients are usually not measured by volume since they cannot usually be measured accurately by this method. One pint of chopped onions will vary considerably in weight, depending on how large or small they are cut and whether the volume measure is filled loosely or packed.

Dry ingredients such as flour or sugar are usually weighed in the bakeshop. However, they are sometimes measured by volume in the kitchen, when speed is more important than accuracy. To measure dry ingredients by volume, fill a dry-volume measure until the ingredient is mounded over the top. Then level it off with a spatula or other straight edge.

Very small quantities, such as ¼ teaspoon salt, are measured by volume when the amount is too small to weigh.

Count

Measuring ingredients by count is done in these circumstances:

1. When units are in fairly standard sizes. Examples: 6 large eggs for a pancake batter; 8 parsley stems for a stock.

2. When serving portions are determined by numbers of units. Examples: 1 baked apple per portion; 6 fried shrimp per portion.

Portion Control

Portion control is the measurement of portions to ensure that the correct amount of an item is served. In order for portion control to be carried out, cooks and service personnel must be aware of proper portion sizes. These facts are usually indicated on the house recipes and on the working menu used in the kitchen and service area.

Portion Control in Preparation

Portion control actually begins with the measuring of ingredients. If this is not done correctly, then the yield of the recipe will be thrown off.

When portions are determined by count—1 hamburger patty, 2 tomato slices, 1 wedge of pie—then the units must be measured or cut according to instructions: 4 ounces of meat per patty; ¼ inch slices of "5 × 6" tomatoes; 8 equal wedges per pie.

Portion Control in Plating and Service

Portioning for service may be done by the cook, as in a short-order restaurant, or by the service personnel, as in a cafeteria. The following tools and techniques are used.

1. *Count.*

    Examples: 1 slice of ham per order; 5 shrimp per order. This is very accurate if cutting and other prep work have been done correctly.

2. *Weight.*

    Example: 4 ounces of sliced ham per order. A portion scale must be at the serving station for this method of portion control.

3. *Volume.*

    Ladles, scoops, and kitchen spoons come in standard sizes and are used for portioning. The exact size of the ladle or scoop must be determined in advance and indicated on service instructions.

    Kitchen spoons, either solid or perforated, are not as accurate for portioning but are often used for convenience and speed. You must be able to judge by eye how full to fill the spoon (rounded, heaped, etc.). Check a spoonful on a portion scale from time to time to make sure you are being consistent.

4. *Even division.*

    Example: cutting a pie into 8 equal wedges; cutting a pan of lasagne 4 by 6 to make 24 equal portions.

5. *Standard fill.*

    Standard-size dishes, cups, or glasses are filled to a given level, as judged by eye. Example: a glass of orange juice. This is actually a form of volume measure.

Units of Measure

The system of measurement used in the United States is very complicated. Even though we have used the system all our lives, we still sometimes have trouble remembering things like how many fluid ounces in a quart or how many feet in a mile.

Table 5.1 lists abbreviations used in this book. Table 5.2 lists equivalents among the units of measure used in the kitchen. You should memorize these very thoroughly, so you don't have to lose time making simple calculations.

TABLE 5.1   **Abbreviations of U.S. Units in This Book**

Pound	lb
Ounce	oz
Gallon	gal
Quart	qt
Pint	pt
Cup	cup (abbreviation not used)
Fluid ounce	fl. oz or oz
Tablespoon	tbsp
Teaspoon	tsp
Inch	in.

TABLE 5.2 Units of Measure—U.S. System

Weight
1 pound	= 16 ounces

Volume
1 gallon	= 4 quarts
1 quart	= 2 pints
	or
	4 cups
	or
	32 (fluid) ounces
1 pint	= 2 cups
	or
	16 (fluid) ounces
1 cup	= 8 (fluid) ounces
1 (fluid) ounce	= 2 tablespoons
1 tablespoon	= 3 teaspoons

Length
1 foot	= 12 inches

Note: One fluid ounce (usually called, simply, "ounce") of water weighs one ounce. One pint of water weighs one pound.

The Metric System

The United States is the only major country that uses the complex system of measurement we have just described. Other countries use a much simpler system called the metric system. Some day we will probably be using the metric system in our kitchens, so it is a good idea to become familiar with it.

Basic Units

In the metric system, there is one basic unit for each type of measurement:

The *gram* is the basic unit of weight.

The *liter* is the basic unit of volume.

The *meter* is the basic unit of length.

The *degree Celsius* is the basic unit of temperature.

Larger or smaller units are made very simply by multiplying or dividing by 10, 100, 1000, and so on. These divisions are expressed by *prefixes*. The ones you will need to know are

kilo- (kill-o) = 1000

deci- (dess-i) = 1/10

centi- (sent-i) = 1/100

milli- (mill-i) = 1/1000

Once you know these basic units, there is no longer any need for complicated tables like Table 5.2. Table 5.3 summarizes the metric units you will need to know in the kitchen.

Converting to Metric

Most people think that the metric system is much harder to learn than it really is. This is because they think about metric units in terms of U.S. units. They read that there are 28.35 grams in an ounce, and they are immediately convinced that they will never be able to learn metrics.

Do not worry about being able to convert between U.S. and metric units. This is a very important point to remember, especially if you think that the metric system might be hard to learn.

The reason for this is very simple. You will usually be working in either one system or the other. You will rarely, if ever, have to convert from one to the other. (An exception might be if you have equipment based on one system, and you want to use a recipe written in the other.) When American kitchens change to the metric system, you will use scales that measure in grams and kilograms, volume measures that measure in liters and deciliters, and thermometers that indicate degrees Celsius. And you will use recipes that indicate these units. You will not have to worry about how many grams in an ounce. All

TABLE 5.3 Metric Units

Basic Units

Quantity	Unit	Abbreviation
Weight	gram	g
Volume	liter	L
Length	meter	m
Temperature	degree Celsius	°C

Divisions and Multiples

Prefix/Example	Meaning	Abbreviation
kilo-	1000	k
kilogram	1000 grams	kg
deci-	1/10	d
deciliter	0.1 liter	dL
centi-	1/100	c
centimeter	0.01 meter	cm
milli-	1/1000	m
millimeter	0.001 meter	mm

you will have to remember is the information in Table 5.3.

To become accustomed to working in metric units, it is helpful to have a feel for how large the units are. The following equivalents may be used to help you visualize metric units. They are not exact conversion factors. (When you need exact conversion factors, see Appendix 1.)

A *kilogram* is slightly more than 2 pounds.

A *gram* is about 1/30 ounce. (A half teaspoon of flour weighs a little less than a gram.)

A *liter* is slightly more than a quart.

A *deciliter* (100 milliliters) is slightly less than a half cup.

A *centiliter* (10 milliliters) is about 2 teaspoons.

A *meter* is slightly more than 3 feet.

A *centimeter* is about 3/8 inch.

0°C is the freezing point of water (32°F).

100°C is the boiling point of water (212°F).

An increase or decrease of *1 degree Celsius* is equivalent to about 2 degrees Fahrenheit.

Metric Recipes

American industry will no doubt completely adopt the metric system some day. Many recipe writers are already eager to get a head start and are printing metric equivalents. As a result, you will see recipes calling for 454 grams of potatoes, 28.35 grams of butter, or a baking temperature of 191°C. No wonder people are afraid of the metric system!

Kitchens in metric countries do not work with such impractical numbers, any more than we normally use figures like 1 lb 1¼ oz potatoes, 2.19 oz butter, or a baking temperature of 348°F. That would defeat the whole purpose of the metric system, which is simplicity and practicality. If you have a chance to look at a French cookbook, you will see nice, even numbers like 1 kg, 200 g, and 4 dL.

The metric equivalents in the recipes in this book are rounded off. What's more, they are not always rounded off in the same way. In some places you may see 1 pound rounded off to 500 grams, in other places to 450 grams. The object is to keep the proportions and the total yield as close as possible, while arriving at practical measurements. Unfortunately, it is not always possible to keep the proportions exactly the same, because the U.S. is not a decimal-based system like the metric system. In some cases, the metric quantities may produce slightly different results due to these varying proportions, but

these differences are small. If you have U.S. equipment, you will use the U.S. units, and if you have metric equipment, you will use the metric units. You should rarely have to worry about converting between the two.

CONVERTING RECIPES

Unless you are working in an operation that uses only its own standardized recipes, you will very frequently be required to convert recipes to different amounts. For example, you may have a recipe for 50 portions of Swiss steak, but you need only 25 portions.

Converting recipes is a very important technique. It is a skill you will probably need to use many times in this book. There is no "best" yield to write recipes for, since every operation, every school, and every individual has different needs.

Nearly everyone instinctively can double a recipe or cut it in half. It seems more complicated, though, to change a recipe from 10 to 18 portions, say, or from 50 to 35. Actually, the principle is exactly the same: you multiply each ingredient by a number called a conversion factor, as follows:

Procedure for Converting Total Yield

1. Divide the desired yield by the recipe yield:

$$\frac{\text{new yield}}{\text{old yield}} = \text{conversion factor}$$

2. Multiply each ingredient quantity by the conversion factor:

$$\text{conversion factor} \times \text{old quantity} = \text{new quantity}$$

In order to do this in the U.S. system, you will usually have to convert all weights to ounces and all volumes to fluid ounces. (This is not necessary in the metric system.)

Example 1: You have a recipe for 10 portions of Broccoli Mornay, requiring 3 lb AP broccoli and 2½ cups Mornay sauce. Convert to 15 portions.

$$\frac{\text{new yield}}{\text{old yield}} = \frac{15}{10} = 1.5$$

Broccoli: 3 lb = 48 oz
48 oz × 1.5 = 72 oz = 4 lb 8 oz
Sauce: 2½ cups = 20 oz
20 oz × 1.5 = 30 oz = 3¾ cups

Problems in Converting Recipes

For the most part, these conversion procedures work very well. But when you make some very large conversions—from 10 to 400 portions, for example, or from 500 to 6—you may encounter some problems.

For example, you may have to make major equipment changes, like from a 2-quart sauce pot to a large steam kettle. Consequently, you have to adjust your techniques and sometimes even ingredients. Evaporation rates may be different, thickening agents may need increasing or decreasing, seasonings and spices may have to be cut back. Or sometimes quantities may be too large or too small to mix properly.

This is one more example of the importance of cooking with judgment. Experienced chefs develop a feel for these problems over the years. When you make such adjustments on converted recipes, be sure to make a note of them for future reference.

Although there are no fixed rules you can learn for these adjustments, it is possible to list the most common types of problems encountered, so that you can be on the alert for them when making recipe conversions. In general, most of the pitfalls fall into one of the following categories:

Measuring

This is most often a problem when you are expanding small recipes, such as when you want to take a consumer recipe for four portions and adapt it to a high-volume operation such as a large cafeteria. Many such recipes use volume measures for both solids and liquids. As we explained earlier, volume measurement of solids is very inaccurate. Of course, small inaccuracies can become large ones when a recipe is multiplied. Therefore, it is important to be cautious and to test it carefully when you are converting a recipe that uses volume measures for solid ingredients.

This problem is largely avoided when all solids are measured by weight. But such items as spices and seasonings may be too small to be measured accurately by weight. For this reason, it is usually a good idea to cut back on spices and salt in a converted recipe. You can always add more later if you taste the product and decide it needs more seasoning.

Surface and Volume

If you have studied geometry, you may remember that a cube with a volume of 1 cubic foot has a top surface area of 1 square foot. But if you double the volume of the cube, the top surface area is not doubled but is in fact only about one and a half times as large.

What in the world, you ask, does this have to do with cooking? Consider the following example.

Suppose you have a good recipe for a half gallon of cream soup, which you normally make in a small soup pot. You want to make 16 gallons of the soup, so you multiply all ingredients by a conversion factor of 32 and make the soup in a steam kettle. To your surprise, not only do you end up with more soup than you expected, but it turns out rather thin and watery. What happened?

Your converted recipe has 32 times as much volume to start, but the amount of surface area has not increased nearly as much. Since the ratio of surface area to volume is less, there is less evaporation. This means that there is less reduction and less thickening, and the flavors are not as concentrated. To correct this problem, you would have to use less stock, preferably one that is also more concentrated.

Suppose instead that you made the expanded recipe in a tilting skillet. In this case, there is so much surface area that the liquid would evaporate very quickly, resulting in an overly thickened and overly seasoned soup.

Differences in surface area and volume can cause other problems as well. Food service operations have to be more careful than home cooks do about food spoilage and the Food Danger Zone (Chapter 2), because large volumes of food cool down and heat up much more slowly than small volumes do.

For the same reason, a home baker worries about keeping a bread dough warm so that it will ferment, but a commercial baker worries about keeping a dough cool enough so that it doesn't ferment too fast. This is because a large batch of dough has so much volume in comparison with its surface area that it tends to retain heat rather than cool down quickly to room temperature.

Equipment

When you change the size of a recipe, you must often change the equipment, too. This change often means that the recipe does not work in the same way. Cooks must be able to use their judgment to anticipate these problems and to modify their procedures to avoid them. The example just given, of cooking a large batch of soup in a steam kettle or in a tilting skillet, is one example of the kinds of problems that can arise when you change cooking utensils.

Other problems can arise because of mixers or other processing equipment. For example, if you break down a salad dressing recipe to make only a small quantity, you might find that there is so little liquid in the mixing machine that the beaters don't blend the ingredients properly.

Or you might have a recipe for a muffin batter that you usually make in small quantities and mix the batter by hand. When you increase the recipe greatly, you find you have too much to do by hand. Therefore, you use a mixer but keep the mixing time the same. Because the mixer does the job so efficiently, you overmix the batter and end up with poor-quality muffins.

Many mixing and stirring jobs can be done only by hand. This is easy with small quantities but very difficult with large batches. The result is often an inferior product. On the other hand, some handmade products are better if they are done in large batches. It is hard, for example, to make a very small batch of puff pastry, because the dough cannot be rolled and folded properly.

Time

Some people make the mistake of thinking that if you double a recipe, you must also double the cooking time. That this is an error can be shown by a simple example. Assume that it takes 15 minutes to cook a steak in a broiler. If you put two steaks in the broiler, it still takes 15 minutes to cook them, not 30 minutes.

If all other things are equal, cooking times stay the same when a recipe is converted. Problems arise, however, because all other things are not always equal. For example, a large pot of liquid takes longer to bring to a boil than a small pot. Therefore, the total cooking time is longer.

On the other hand, a big kettle of vegetable soup that you are making ahead for tomorrow's lunch takes longer to cool down than a small pot. Meanwhile, the vegetables continue to cook in the retained heat during the cooling. In order to avoid overcooking, you may need to undercook the large batch slightly.

In cases where the cooking time must be increased, you sometimes might find that you have to increase the amount of herbs and spices. This is because the flavors are volatile (see p. 62), and more flavor is lost because of the increased cooking time. (Another answer to this problem is to add the spices later.)

Changing recipe sizes can affect not only cooking times but also mixing times. The best way to avoid this problem is to rely not on printed cooking and mixing times but on your own judgment and skills to tell you when a product is properly cooked or properly blended.

Recipe Problems

Many recipes have flaws, either in the quantities or types of ingredients or in the cooking procedures. When the item is made in small quantities, these flaws may not be noticeable, or the cook may almost unconsciously or automatically make adjustments during production. When the recipe is multiplied, however, the flaws may suddenly become apparent and the product quality is lower. The only solution here is to carefully test recipes and to have a good understanding of basic cooking principles.

FOOD COST

Food service operations are businesses. This means that someone in the operation has to worry about budgets, cost accounting, bills, and profits. Usually this is the job of the manager, while the cook takes care of food production.

The cooks have a great deal of responsibility for food cost controls, however. They must always be conscious of accurate measurement, portion control, and careful processing, cooking, and handling of foods to avoid excess trimming loss, shrinkage, and waste.

The manager, on the other hand, is concerned with determining budgets, calculating profits and expenses, and so on. We cannot deal with these subjects here, since this is a book about food preparation. But you may encounter them later in your studies or in your career.

Every cook should understand three areas of cost accounting, however—doing yield analyses, calculating raw food cost or portion cost, and using food cost percentages.

Food Cost Percentages

An individual operation's food cost percentage is usually determined by the budget. The chef is interested in this figure, because it tells him or her whether the menu prices and the costs for each item are in line.

The food cost percentage of a menu item equals the raw food cost or portion cost divided by the menu price:

$$\text{percentage} = \frac{\text{food cost}}{\text{menu price}}$$

You can use this figure in two ways:

1. If you know the menu price and want to see what your food cost should be in order to be within the budget, multiply the menu price by the percentage:

food cost = menu price × percentage

Example: Menu price is $6.75 and food cost percentage is 35%.

35% = 0.35

6.75 × 0.35 = $2.36

2. If you know the food cost and want to determine what the menu price should be at a particular percentage, divide the cost by the percentage:

$$\text{menu price} = \frac{\text{food cost}}{\text{percentage}}$$

Example: Food cost is $1.60 and food cost percentage is 40%.

$$\frac{\$1.60}{40\%} = \frac{\$1.60}{0.40} = \$4.00$$

Yield Cost Analysis

In order to calculate portion costs of recipes, you must first determine the costs of your ingredients. For many ingredients, this is relatively easy. You just look at your invoices or at price lists from your purveyors.

Many recipes, however, specify trimmed weight rather than the weight you actually pay for. For example, a stew might call for 2 pounds of sliced onions. Let's say that you pay 24 cents a pound for onions, and to get 2 pounds of sliced onions, you need 2¼ pounds of untrimmed onions. In order to calculate the cost of the recipe correctly, you have to figure out what you actually paid for the onions. In this case, the true cost is 54 cents (2¼ lb times $.24 per lb), not 48 cents (2 lb times $.24 per lb).

The following are two frequently used abbreviations that you must understand:

- AP stands for *as purchased*. This means the untrimmed quantity, in the same form in which it is purchased. This is the amount that you pay for.

- EP stands for *edible portion*. This means the raw, uncooked quantity after all trimming is done. This is the quantity that you actually cook.

In the case of fruits and vegetables, the best way to determine AP quantities for use in costing recipes is to make a note of them when you are preparing the item. Tables of vegetable and fruit trimming yields in Chapters 16 and 19 will also help you. (Chapter 16 explains how to use these figures.)

In the case of ingredients such as meats and fish, figuring the cost can be a little more complicated. If you buy precut, portion control steaks of fish fillets and use them just as you receive them, your AP and EP costs are the same. But if you buy whole loins of beef or whole fish and cut them yourself, you have to do a yield cost analysis in order to determine your actual costs.

The examples discussed in the remainder of this chapter use U.S. measures. For metric examples, see Appendix 4, page 797.

Raw Yield Test

Suppose you work in a restaurant that serves veal scaloppine. The restaurant buys whole legs of veal. It is your job to bone out the veal, trim off all fat and connective tissue, separate the muscles at the seams, and cut the large pieces into scaloppine.

A typical whole leg of veal might weigh 30 lb, at a price of $5.00 a pound, for a total cost of $150.00. After finishing your trimming and cutting, you find you have 18 lb of veal scaloppine. How do you figure the cost per pound of this meat?

The simplest example would be if you threw away all the trimmings, bones, and scrap meat. Then you would know that your 18 lb of veal cost you $150.00. Dividing $150 by 18 lb gives you a cost per pound of $8.33.

But in your restaurant, you don't throw away the trimmings. You make stock with the bones, grind up the small trimmings for meatballs, use the larger trimmings for veal stew, and sell the fat to the fat collector who picks up all your waste fat once a week. Now you must do a yield test to figure your costs.

Table 5.4 shows a typical form that you might use for a yield test. For simplification, the blanks in the form are of two types. The dotted lines are to be filled in by reading your invoices and by taking the weights from your actual yield test. The solid lines are to be filled in by doing calculations.

Note that in Table 5.5 the form has been filled in with the results of a yield test on a leg of veal. We will go through the form step by step.

The executive chef in this restaurant fills out the first two lines, based on the invoice, gives you the form, and requests you to do the test. You fill out the rest of the form, beginning with blank 1 on the third line. You proceed as follows:

1. Weigh the whole leg of veal and enter the weight in blank 1. Copy the price per pound and total cost from line 2 to blanks 2 and 3.

   Note that blank 3 can also be arrived at by multiplying the weight by the price per pound. However, suppose the veal were left in the cooler for several more days and dried out a bit. The weight then might be 29½ pounds. By multiplying 29.5 by $5.00, you would get a total cost of $147.50. But since the price you paid was actually $150, it is important to use that figure and not fill in the blank by multiplying.

2. Break down the veal into all its component parts and record the weights of the trim and waste

TABLE 5.4   **Raw Yield Test Form**

Item . . . .   Test number . . . .   Date . . . .

Purveyor . . . .   Price per pound . . . .   Total cost . . . .

AP weight (1) . . . .   Lb price (2) . . . .   Total cost (3) . . . .

Trim, salvage, and waste:

Item	Weight	Value/lb	Total Value (lb × value)
(4)	. . . .	. . . .	_____
(5)	. . . .	. . . .	_____
(6)	. . . .	. . . .	_____
(7)	. . . .	. . . .	_____
(8)	. . . .	. . . .	_____
(9)	. . . .	. . . .	_____
(10)	. . . .	. . . .	_____

Total Weight
(4 thru 10)   (11) _____

Total Value
(4 thru 10)   (12) _____

Total yield of item   (13) . . . .

Net cost (3 minus 12)   (14) _____

Cost per lb (14 divided by 13)   (15) _____

Percentage of increase (15 divided by 2)   (16) _____

---

starting in blank 4. In this case, there are only six items: fat, bones, small meat scraps for grinding, meat for stew, unusable waste, and cutting loss.

Record the weight of the finished scaloppine in blank 13.

(What is *cutting loss?* This is not something you can actually weigh. However, there is always some loss of weight due to particles of meat and fat sticking to the cutting board, to drying, and to other factors. So when you add up all your weights, you find that they total less than 30 lb. To determine cutting loss, add up blanks 4 through 8 and blank 13. Subtract this total from line 1.)

3. Enter the values per pound of the trim, salvage, and waste on lines 4 through 10. In this case, these numbers are given to you by the executive chef from the invoices:

The fat collector pays 12 cents a pound for waste fat.

When you have to buy extra bones for your stock pot, you have to pay 38 cents a pound for them, so this is their value to you. This is also the figure you will use when you cost out your stock recipe. If you didn't make stock and threw out the bones, you'd enter zero in this blank.

Similarly, the values entered for ground veal and stew meat are the prices you'd have to pay if you bought them.

TABLE 5.5 **Completed Raw Yield Test Form**

Item .... veal leg to scalop .... Test number .... 3 .... Date .... 3/16/94 ....

Purveyor .... ABC Meats .... Price per pound ...... $5.00 ...... Total cost ...... $150 ......

AP weight (1) .... 30 lb .... Lb price (2) ...... $5.00 ...... Total cost (3) .... $150 ....

Trim, salvage, and waste:

	Item	Weight	Value/lb	Total Value (lb × value)
(4)	fat	2½ lb	$ .12	$ .30
(5)	bone	3 lb 5 oz	$ .38	$1.26
(6)	ground veal	2 lb 2 oz	$4.89	$10.39
(7)	stew meat	3 lb	$5.29	$15.87
(8)	unusable trim	14 oz	0	0
(9)	cutting loss	3 oz	0	0
(10)				

Total Weight (4 thru 10) (11) ___ 12 lb ___   Total Value (4 thru 10) (12) ___ $27.82 ___

Total yield of item (13) .... 18 lb ....

Net cost (3 minus 12) (14) _____ $122.18 _____

Cost per lb (14 divided by 13) (15) _____ $6.79 _____

Percentage of increase (15 divided by 2) (16) _____ 1.36 (136%) _____

Unusable trim and cutting loss have no value, so you enter zero.

4. Calculate the total values of each item on lines 4 through 10 by multiplying the weight by the value per pound. Note that this particular form tells you how to do all the calculations.

5. Add the weights in lines 4 through 10 and enter the total in blank 11. Add the total values in lines 4 through 10 and enter this figure in blank number 12.

6. Subtract the total value of all the trim (blank 12) from the price you paid for the veal (blank 3). This gives you the net cost of your 18 pounds of scaloppine.

7. To find the cost per pound of the scaloppine, divide the net cost (blank 14) by the weight (blank 13). This is the figure you will use in costing recipes for veal scaloppine.

8. The percentage of increase in the last line is determined by dividing the net cost per pound (blank 15) by the price per pound of the whole leg (blank 2). This figure can be used as follows:

Suppose next week you buy another leg of veal from the same purveyor, but the price has gone up to $5.29. Instead of doing another yield test, you can simply multiply this new price by the percentage of increase ($5.29 times 1.36), to get a new cost per pound of $7.19.

Cooked Yield Test

Earlier we introduced two important abbreviations, AP (as purchased) and EP (edible portion). A third expression sometimes used is AS, meaning *as served*. When foods such as fruits are served raw, AS may be the same as EP. But if the food is cooked, these weights are different.

In the case of the veal scaloppine, your recipe portions, and therefore your portion costs, are based on raw weight. For example, your scaloppine recipe might call for 5½ ounces of raw meat per portion.

In some cases, on the other hand, your portions may be based on cooked weight. This is most often true of roasts. For example, let's say you buy whole fresh hams, bone and trim them, and serve them as roasts, allowing 6 ounces of sliced, cooked meat per portion. To arrive at your cost, you will have to do a cooked yield test, as illustrated by Tables 5.6 and 5.7. (This form may be printed on the same sheet of

---

TABLE 5.6   Cooked Yield Test Form

Item .... Test number .... Date ....

AP price per lb ....

Cooking temperature ....

Net raw weight   (1) .... Net cost per lb   (2) ....

Total net cost   (3) ....

Weight as served   (4) ....

Cooked cost per lb (3 divided by 4)   (5) _____

Shrinkage (1 minus 4)   (6) _____

Percentage of shrinkage (6 divided by 1)   (7) _____

Total percentage of cost increase   (5 divided by AP price per lb)   (8) _____

TABLE 5.7   Completed Cooked Yield Test Form

Item .... roast fresh ham .... Test number .... 2 ...... Date .... 9/4/94 ...

AP price per lb .... $3.49 ....

Cooking temperature .... 325 ....

Net raw weight   (1) .... 12 lb ..... Net cost per lb   (2) .... $3.93 ....

Total net cost   (3) .... $47.16 ....

Weight as served   (4) .... 8 lb 4 oz ....

Cooked cost per lb (3 divided by 4)   (5) _____ $5.72 _____

Shrinkage (1 minus 4)   (6) _____ 3¾ lb _____

Percentage of shrinkage (6 divided by 1)   (7) _____ 31% _____

Total percentage of cost increase   (5 divided by AP price per lb)   (8) _____ 164% _____

paper as the raw yield test form, so that an operation can have a complete cost analysis on one form.)

This form has been filled in with the results of a cooked yield test done on a roast, boneless fresh ham. Let's assume that this same ham has already had a raw yield test done on it.

The first half of the form, through blank 3, is filled in before the test starts. The numbers for blanks 1, 2, and 3 are taken from the raw yield test form, but you should double-check the net raw weight by weighing the item again before roasting.

Enter the total weight of cooked ham served in blank 4. You arrive at this figure by recording the total number of portions served and multiplying this number by the portion size. Let's say that 22 portions are served at 6 ounces each. This gives us a total of 132 ounces (22 times 6), or 8¼ pounds.

You might be tempted to simply weigh the whole roast after cooking and trimming. Remember, though, that there will be some waste—crumbs on the slicer or cutting board, spillage of juices, and so on. It is more accurate to record the weight that you actually sell.

If this had been a bone-in roast, you would have another reason to carve the meat before weighing, because you could not include the weight of the bone in your as-served figure.

The remaining blanks on the form are determined by doing the calculations, just as you would do the calculations for the raw yield test.

Portion Costs

Portion cost or *raw food cost* is the total cost of all the ingredients in a recipe, divided by the number of portions served:

$$\text{portion cost} = \frac{\text{cost of ingredients}}{\text{number of portions}}$$

We will cost out a sample recipe to show you how the procedure works. First, note the following points and keep them in mind when you are calculating portion costs. Many errors in costing are caused by forgetting one of these points.

1. Costs must be based on AP (as purchased) amounts, even though recipes often give EP (edible portion) quantities. These terms are explained in the preceding section.

2. Include *everything*. That means the lemon wedge and parsley garnish for the fish fillet, the cream and sugar that go with the coffee, and the oil that was used for pan-frying the eggplant. These are sometimes called *hidden costs*.

   Seasonings and spices are a typical example of hidden costs that are difficult to calculate. Some operations add up the cost of all seasonings used in a year and divide that by the total food cost to get a percentage. This percentage is added to each item. For example, if the cost of an item is $2.00 and the seasoning cost percentage is 5%, the total cost is $2.00 plus 5% of $2.00, or $2.10.

   Other hidden costs can be calculated in the same way. For example, you could figure out your cost percentage for frying fat and add the percentage to all deep-fried foods.

   Some restaurants take an arbitrary figure for all hidden costs, usually from 8 to 12 percent, and add this to all menu items.

3. Record the number of portions *actually served*, not just the number the recipe is intended to serve. If the roast shrank more than you expected during cooking, or if you dropped a piece of cake on the floor, those costs still have to be covered.

Example: Costing a Recipe
Item: Baked Rice

Ingredient Amount	Recipe Quantity	AP Quantity	Price	Total
Rice, long grain	4 lb	4 lb	$0.62/lb	$2.48
Butter	12 oz	0.75 lb	1.97/lb	1.48
Onions	1 lb	1.2 lb	0.36/lb	0.43
Chicken stock	4 qt	4 qt	0.25/qt	1.00
Salt	1 oz	¹⁄₁₆ lb	0.15/lb	0.01
		Total cost		$5.40
		Number of portions		50
		Cost per portion		$0.11

Note: Cost of chicken stock is determined by costing out the operation's recipe for chicken stock.

Procedure for Calculating Portion Cost

1. List ingredients and quantities of recipe as prepared.

2. Convert the recipe quantities to AP (as purchased) quantities.

3. Determine the price of each ingredient (from invoices, price lists, etc.). The units in this step and in step 2 must be the same in order for you to do the calculation.

4. Calculate the total cost of each ingredient by multiplying the price per unit by the number of units needed.

5. Add up the ingredient costs to get the total recipe cost.

6. Divide the total cost by the number of portions served to get the cost per portion.

TERMS FOR REVIEW

recipe	meter	milli-	EP weight
standardized recipe	degree Celsius	raw food cost	AS weight
portion control	kilo-	portion cost	yield test
gram	deci-	food cost percentage	hidden cost
liter	centi-	AP weight	

QUESTIONS FOR DISCUSSION

1. What are some reasons why written recipes can't be 100 percent exact and must depend on the cook's judgment? Select two or three recipes (from this book or any other) and try to determine where they depend on the cook's judgment.

2. What is the purpose of a standardized recipe?

3. What are the three basic ways of measuring ingredients? Which method is used for most solid ingredients, and why?

4. What is the first step in portion control? List four other techniques in portion control.

5. Make the following conversions in the U.S. system of measurement:

   3½ pounds = _____ ounces

   6 cups = _____ pints

   8½ quarts = _____ fluid ounces

   ¾ cup = _____ tablespoons

   46 ounces = _____ pounds

   2½ gallons = _____ fluid ounces

   5 pounds 5 ounces divided by 2 = _____

   10 teaspoons = _____ fluid ounces

6. Make the following conversions in the metric system:

   1.4 kilograms = _____ grams

   53 deciliters = _____ liters

   15 centimeters = _____ millimeters

   2590 grams = _____ kilograms

   4.6 liters = _____ deciliters

   220 centiliters = _____ deciliters

7. Turn to the recipe for Swedish Meatballs on page 265. Convert it to yield 35 portions.

8. Discuss the main types of problems you may face when converting recipe yields.

9. What is the difference between AP weight and EP weight? Explain how these terms are related to calculating costs per portion of menu items.

10. The following problems are calculations with food cost percentages, portion cost, and menu price. For each problem, two of these figures are given. Find the third.

	Food cost percentage	Portion cost	Menu price
a.	____	$1.24	$4.95
b.	40%	____	$2.50
c.	30%	$2.85	____

CHAPTER 6

THE MENU

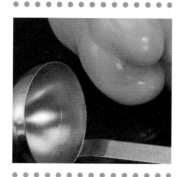

A menu is a list of dishes
served or available to be served at a meal. To the customer in a restaurant,
it is a list of dishes from which to make selections for a meal. To the cook it is a list of
dishes to be prepared. But our familiarity with the menu simply as a list of foods
tends to hide its importance as a management tool.

Nearly every aspect of the operation of a food
service business depends on the menu. In fact, it is fair to say that it is the
single most important document in the business. Purchasing, production, sales, cost
accounting, labor management, even the kitchen layout and equipment
selection of a new facility, all are based on the menu.

You can see why it is essential to pay careful attention to
the writing of the menu and why so many factors are considered. In this chapter
we discuss these factors from the point of view of kitchen production. How does one
construct a menu that builds sales by offering the best choices to the customer
and that also promotes efficiency and productivity?

After reading this chapter, you should be able to

1. Explain how the makeup of a menu depends on the type of meal and on the institution using it.

2. Describe the differences between static and cycle menus, and between à la carte and table d'hôte menus.

3. List the various courses that may appear in modern menus.

4. Devise balanced menus that contain an adequate variety of foods and that can be efficiently and economically prepared.

5. Bring an awareness of basic nutritional principles to the construction of menus.

MENU FORMS AND FUNCTIONS

Menus must be planned for the people eating the food. This sounds like a simple rule, but it is frequently forgotten. You must never forget that the customer is the main reason for being in business.

This rule means that, in most operations, the taste and preferences of the cooks or chefs are of little importance when planning the menu. True, there are some restaurants that exist primarily as showcases for the chef's own artistry, but they are rare. Instead, the tastes and preferences of the clientele must be given top priority if the business is to succeed. The kind of clientele the business serves will influence the form the menu takes.

The Clientele

Type of Institution

Each kind of operation has a different menu, because each serves the needs of different clientele:

Hotels must provide a variety of service for their guests, from budget-minded tourists to business people on expense accounts, from quick breakfast and sandwich counters to elegant dining rooms and banquet halls.

Hospitals must satisfy the dietary needs of the patients.

Schools must consider the ages of the students and their tastes and nutritional needs.

In-plant food services need menus that offer substantial but quickly served food for working customers.

Catering and banquet operations depend on menus that are easily prepared for large numbers but that are lavish enough for parties and special occasions.

Fast food and take-out operations require limited menus featuring inexpensive, easily prepared, easily served foods for people in a hurry.

Full-service restaurants range from simple neighborhood diners to expensive, elegant French restaurants. Menus, of course, must be planned according to the customers' needs. Trying to institute a menu of high-priced, luxurious French foods in a café situated in a working-class neighborhood will probably not succeed.

Customer Preferences

Even facilities with captive audiences, such as school cafeterias and hospital kitchens, must produce food that is appealing to their customers and in sufficient variety to keep them from getting bored with the same old things. Grumbling about the food is a favorite sport among students, but at least it can be kept to a minimum.

Restaurants have an even harder job, because their customers don't just grumble if they don't like the selections. They don't come back. Americans are becoming more and more interested in trying unfamiliar foods, especially ethnic foods. Nevertheless, tastes vary in different regions of the country, in different neighborhoods, in different age groups, and in different social and ethnic backgrounds. Foods that are enjoyed by some people are completely rejected by others.

Prices must be kept in line with the customers' ability and willingness to pay. Prices will, of course, place limits on what foods can be offered.

Kind of Meal

Menus will vary not only for different kinds of operations but for different meals as well.

Breakfast

Breakfast menus are fairly standard across the country. A restaurant has to offer the usual selection of fruits, juices, eggs, cereals, pancakes, waffles, breakfast meats, plus regional specialties like Southern grits, because this is what customers want and expect. In addition, featuring one or two unusual items on the menu—such as an English muffin topped with creamed crabmeat and a poached egg, a special kind of country ham, or an assortment of freshly made fruit sauces or syrups for the pancakes and waffles—often attracts additional customers. Breakfast menus must feature foods that can be prepared quickly and eaten in a hurry.

Lunch

The following factors are important to consider when planning lunch menus.

1. *Speed.* Like breakfast customers, luncheon diners are usually in a hurry. They are generally working people who have a limited time to eat. Foods must be prepared quickly and be easy to serve and eat. Sandwiches, soups, and salads are important items on many lunch menus.

2. *Simplicity.* Menu selections are fewer, and fewer courses are served. In many cases customers select only one course. Luncheon specials—combinations of two or three items, such as soup and a sandwich or omelet and salad, offered at a single price—satisfy the need for simplicity and speed.

3. Variety. In spite of the shortness of the menu and the simplicity of the selections, luncheon menus must have variety. This is because many customers eat at the same restaurant several times a week, or even every day. In order to keep the menu short, many operations offer several different luncheon specials every day, so there is always something new on the menu.

Dinner

Dinner is usually the main meal and is eaten in a more leisurely fashion than either breakfast or lunch. Of course, some people are in a hurry in the evening, too, but in general people come to a restaurant to relax over a substantial meal. Dinner menus offer more selections and more courses. Not surprisingly, prices and check averages are also higher than at lunch.

Types of Menus

Static and Cycle Menus

A *static menu* is one that offers the same dishes every day. These menus are used in restaurants and other establishments where the clientele changes daily or where there are enough items listed on the menu to offer sufficient variety.

A *cycle menu* is one that changes every day for a certain period; after this period the daily menus repeat in the same order. For example, a 7-day cycle menu will have a different menu every day for a week and will repeat each week. This kind of menu is used in such operations as schools and hospitals, where the number of choices must be kept small. The cycle menu is a way of offering variety.

Some restaurants use a menu that is part cycle and part static. This means that they have a basic menu of foods prepared every day, plus a repeating series of daily specials to offer more variety without putting too much strain on the kitchen.

À la Carte and Table d'Hôte

An *à la carte* menu is one in which each individual item is listed separately, with its own price. The customer makes selections from the various courses and side dishes to make up a meal. (Note: The term *à la carte* is also used to refer to cooking to order, as opposed to cooking ahead in large batches.)

Table d'hôte (pronounced tobble dote) originally meant a fixed menu with no choices—like a meal you would be served if you were invited to someone's home for dinner (the term *table d'hôte* means "the host's table"). Banquet menus are familiar examples of this kind of menu.

Table d'hôte has also come to refer to a menu that offers a selection of complete meals at given prices. In other words, a customer may choose from among several selections, each of which includes an entrée and side dishes plus other courses, such as appetizer, salad, and dessert. There is a single "package price" for each full meal selection.

Many restaurants use a combination of à la carte and table d'hôte selections. For example, a steak house may include salad, potato, vegetable, and beverage with the entrée choice, while additional dishes like appetizers and desserts may be offered at extra cost.

Closely related to the table d'hôte menu is the *prix fixe* (pree fix), meaning "fixed price," menu. On a pure prix fixe menu, there is only one price given. Each guest may choose one selection from each course offered, and the total meal will cost the single price indicated. Often on such menus there are a few items, featuring costly ingredients, that carry an extra charge, called a *supplement*. The supplement is usually indicated in parentheses after the listing. It is best to limit the number of supplements as much as possible. Too many extra charges on a prix fixe menu can leave customers frustrated and angry.

BUILDING THE MENU

A *course* is a food or group of foods served at one time or intended to be eaten at the same time. In a restaurant the courses are normally served in sequence, allowing enough time for a course to be eaten before the next is served. In a cafeteria, the customers may select all their courses at once—appetizer, salad, main dish and vegetables, and dessert, for example—but will eat them in a particular order.

In the following pages we discuss the various principles that apply to planning the courses that make up a menu. The main purpose of these principles is to lend variety and interest to a meal. They are not merely arbitrary rules that you must follow for no reason.

The Classical Menu

Today's menus are descendants of elaborate banquet menus served in the nineteenth and early twentieth centuries. These menus had 12 or more courses, and the various sequences of the courses were well established by tradition.

The following sequence of courses is typical of one that may have been served at a great banquet early in this century.

1. Cold hors d'oeuvre   small, savory appetizers

2. Soup   clear soup, thick soup, or broth

3. Hot hors d'oeuvre   small, hot appetizers

4. Fish   any seafood item

5. Main course or   a large cut of roasted or braised meat,
    pièce de resistance   usually beef, lamb, or venison, with
                            elaborate vegetable garnishes

6. Hot entrée   individual portions of meat or poultry,
                            which have been broiled, braised,
                            pan-fried, etc.

7. Cold entrée   cold meats, poultry, fish, pâté,
                            and so on

8. Sorbet   a light ice or sherbet, sometimes
                            made of wine, to refresh the appetite
                            before the next course

9. Roast   usually roasted poultry, accompanied
                            by or followed by a salad

10. Vegetable   usually a special vegetable preparation,
                            such as artichokes or asparagus, or a
                            more unusual vegetable such as
                            cardoons

11. Sweet   what we call "dessert": cakes and tarts,
                            pudding, soufflés, etc.

12. Dessert   fruit and cheese and sometimes small
                            cookies or petits fours

Modern Menus: Courses and Arrangement

Such extensive classical menus are rarely served today. Even grand, elegant banquets comprising many courses are usually shorter than the menu we just described. However, if you study that menu, you will be able to see the basic pattern of modern menus hiding amidst all those courses.

The main dish is the centerpiece of the modern meal. If the meal consists of only one dish, it is considered the main course, even if it is a salad or a bowl of soup. There is usually only one main course, although large banquets may still have more than one, such as a poultry dish followed by a meat dish.

One or more dishes may be served before the main dish. These are usually light in character, so that the customer is not satiated before the main course.

Study the following diagram of the modern menu and compare it to the classical menu. The notes that follow the diagram explain several aspects that may be puzzling. Then, in the next sections we discuss how to select specific dishes for each course to arrive at a balanced menu.

The Modern Menu

First courses	Appetizer
	Soup
	(Fish)
	Salad
Main dish	Meat, poultry, or fish
	Vegetable accompaniment
Dessert dishes	Salad
	Fruits and cheeses
	Sweets

Notes

- Appetizer, soup, and salad are the three courses usually served before the main course. One, two, or all three of them may be served, and they are usually served in this order. Thus, meals may have the following courses:

Appetizer	Soup	Salad
Main dish	Main dish	Main dish
Appetizer	Soup	Appetizer
Soup	Salad	Salad
Main dish	Main dish	Main dish

Appetizer
Soup
Salad
Main dish

- A fish course is sometimes included in more formal dinners, after appetizer and soup courses. It should be a relatively small portion, and the main dish should not also be fish.

- Salads may be served either before or after the main course (but not both). In more traditional meals, they are served after the main course to refresh the appetite before the cheese and sweet courses. Serving the salad before the main course is a comparatively recent invention.

- Sometimes one or more of the first courses is served at the same time as the main dish, possibly on the same plate. This is especially popular on luncheon menus, where quick service is desired. Thus, you will find soup and sandwich combinations, salad and omelet combinations, and so on.

- If both cheese and sweets are served for dessert, they may come in either order. English menus have cheese after the sweets, while French menus generally place the sweets last.

Variety and Balance

Balancing a menu means providing enough variety and contrast so that the meal holds interest from the first course to the last. To balance a menu, you must develop a feeling for which foods complement each other or provide pleasing contrasts. And you must avoid repeating flavors and textures as much as possible.

These principles apply whether you are planning a banquet menu, where the diners have no choices; a school cafeteria menu, where there are only a few choices; or a large à la carte menu, where there are many choices.

Of course, with an à la carte menu, the customers' own choices determine how balanced their own meals are. There's nothing wrong with listing a creamed dish among the appetizers and another creamed dish among the main dishes. But you should offer enough choices so that the customers can easily select balanced meals if they desire. In other words, if half the appetizers and half the entrée selections are served in a cream sauce, you're not offering enough variety.

The following factors must be considered in balancing a menu.

1. **Flavors.**

Don't repeat foods with the same or similar tastes. This applies to any predominant flavors, whether of the main ingredient, of the spices, of the sauce, and so on. For example,

   a. Don't serve broiled tomato halves with the main dish if the appetizer has a tomato sauce.
   b. Don't serve both a spicy, garlicky appetizer and a spicy, garlicky main dish. On the other hand, don't make everything too bland.
   c. Unless you operate a specialty restaurant like a steak house or a seafood restaurant, balance the menu among meats (beef, pork, lamb, veal), poultry, and fish.
   d. Acid or tart foods are often served as accompaniments to fatty foods, because they help cut the fatty taste. This is why applesauce and pork, mint sauce and lamb, or orange sauce and duckling are such classic combinations.

2. **Textures.**

Texture applies to the softness or firmness of foods, their feel in the mouth, whether or not they are served with sauces, and so on. Don't repeat foods with the same or similar texture. For example,

   a. Serve a clear soup instead of a thick soup if the main course is served with a cream sauce. On the other hand, a cream soup goes well before a simple sautéed or broiled item.
   b. Don't serve too many mashed or puréed foods, unless you are running a baby-food restaurant.
   c. Don't serve too many heavy, starchy items.

3. **Appearance.**

Serve foods with a variety of colors and shapes. Colorful vegetables are especially valuable for livening up the appearance of meats, poultry, fish, and starches, which tend to be mostly white or brown. (Creating attractive food is discussed in Chapter 22.)

There are so many possible combinations of foods that it is impossible to give rules that will cover all of them. Besides, creative chefs are continually experimenting with new combinations, breaking old rules, and coming up with exciting menus. Years of experience, however, are required to develop this kind of creativity and a feel for what makes certain combinations work. In the meantime, pay close attention to the principles discussed.

Kitchen Capabilities and Availability of Foods

Physical conditions place limitations on your menu. Depending on your equipment, on your labor force, and on the foods available to you, certain items will be inconvenient, difficult, or even impossible to serve.

Equipment Limitations

Know the capacities of your equipment and plan menus accordingly. If your broiler capacity is 200 steaks an hour, and you plan a banquet menu for 400 people, with broiled shrimp as an appetizer and broiled steaks as a main course, you're in big trouble.

Spread the work load evenly among your equipment. If you have ovens, a broiler, and a fryer, balance the roasted and braised items, the broiled items, and the fried items. Don't let the broiler stand idle while orders are backed up at the deep fryer. Also, using a variety of cooking methods adds variety of taste and texture to the menu.

Personnel Limitations

Spread the work load evenly among the workers. As with equipment, you don't want the fry cook to have more than he or she can handle, while the broiler cook has little to do.

Spread the work load throughout the day. Balance the cooked-to-order items against the cooked-ahead items, so that you don't have to do everything at the last minute.

Offer items that the cooks are able to prepare. Don't put items on the menu that are above the skill level of the staff.

Availability of Foods

Use foods in season. Foods out of season are more expensive, often lower in quality, and their supply is undependable. Don't put asparagus on the menu if you can't get good asparagus.

Use foods locally available. Fresh seafood is the most obvious example of a food that is hard to get in some parts of the country, unless you—and your customers—are willing to pay premium prices.

Complete Utilization of Foods

You can't afford to throw food away, any more than you can afford to throw money away. Total utilization of foods must be planned into menus. Whether or not this is done can make or break a food service operation.

1. *Use all edible trim.*

   Unless you use only portion control meats, poultry, and fish and only frozen and canned vegetables, you will have edible trim. You can either throw it away and call it a loss, or you can use it and make money on it.

   Plan recipes that utilize these trimmings and put them on the menu. For example:

   a. Use small meat scraps for soups, chopped meat, pâtés, creamed dishes, croquettes.
   b. Use larger meat trimmings for soups, stews, braised items.
   c. Use bones for stocks and soups.
   d. Use vegetable trimmings for purées, soups, stews, stocks, fillings for omelets and crêpes.
   e. Use day-old breads for stuffings, breading, French toast, croutons, meat extender.

2. *Don't add an item to the menu unless you can use the trimmings.*

   This is really the same as number 1, looking from the opposite angle. In other words, don't put rissolé potatoes on your menu unless you also plan to serve an item that uses the trimmings, such as whipped potatoes or croquettes.

3. *Plan production to avoid leftovers.*

   The best way to use up leftovers is not to create them in the first place. Handling food twice—once as a fresh item and once as a leftover—is more expensive and time consuming than handling it once, and it almost always results in loss of quality. Limited menus—that is, with fewer selections—decrease the likelihood of leftovers.

4. *Plan ahead for use of leftovers.*

   Careful planning of production can keep leftovers to a minimum. But some leftovers are almost inevitable, and it's better for your costs to use them than to throw them out.

   Whenever you put an item on the menu that could become a leftover, you should have a recipe ready that will use the leftovers. This is better than being surprised with leftovers that you don't know what to do with.

   For example, if you served roast chicken for dinner one day, you might plan on chicken à la king or chicken salad for a luncheon special the next day.

   Remember to handle all leftovers according to proper sanitary procedures.

5. *Eliminate "minimum-use" perishable ingredients.*

"Minimum-use" ingredients are those that are used in one or two items on your menu. For example, an operation might serve chicken breast topped with sautéed mushrooms but not use mushrooms in any other item. When the ingredient is perishable, the result is a high percentage of spoilage or waste.

This situation can be remedied in any of three ways.

a. Change the recipe to eliminate the minimum-use ingredient.
b. Eliminate the item from the menu.
c. Add other items to the menu using the ingredient.

Be careful not to unbalance the menu, however, by using an ingredient in too many dishes. Try to avoid both extremes.

Menu Accuracy

When you have selected the items you want to include on your menu, be sure to label them accurately. Giving misleading names to menu items is not only dishonest and unfair to the customer, it is actually illegal in some localities that have adopted "Truth in Menu" laws, and you can be prosecuted for fraud. Furthermore, customers who feel confused or cheated may not come back.

Calling something chicken salad if it is made with turkey, veal cutlet if it is made with pork, or whipped cream if it is actually artificial whipped topping is such obvious mislabeling that it can hardly be accidental. However, some kinds of menu inaccuracies result not from intentional deception but from simple misunderstanding. In particular, look out for these types of labeling problems:

1. *Point of origin.*

If your menu lists "Maine lobsters," they must be from Maine. Roquefort dressing must be made with Roquefort cheese from Roquefort, France. Idaho potatoes must be from Idaho. On the other hand, generally accepted names or names that indicate type rather than origin can be used. For example: Swiss cheese, French bread, Swedish meatballs.

2. *Grade or quality.*

U.S. Choice and U.S. Fancy are names of grades, and you'd better be using those grades if you say

you are. Incidentally, the word prime in "Prime Rib" indicates a cut, not a grade. But if you say "U.S. Prime Rib," you are now talking about a grade.

3. *"Fresh."*

If you call something fresh, it must be fresh, not frozen, canned, or dried. There is no such thing as "fresh frozen."

4. *"Imported."*

An item labeled "imported" must come from outside the country.

5. *"Homemade."*

The word *homemade* means that the item was made on the premises. Adding a few fresh carrots to canned vegetable soup does not make it homemade.

6. *Size or portion.*

If you indicate a portion size on the menu, be sure you serve that size (within allowable tolerances). A "10-ounce steak" must weigh at least 10 ounces before cooking (9½ ounces would be within allowable tolerance). "Jumbo shrimp" are not just big shrimp. They are a specific size.

Some other common violations are the following:

Listing "maple syrup" and serving maple-flavored syrup.

Listing "Coke" (a brand name) and serving another brand of cola.

Listing "butter" and serving margarine.

Listing coffee or breakfast cereal "with cream" and serving milk.

Listing "ground round" and serving other ground beef.

NUTRITIONAL CONSIDERATIONS

Menu planners must have a basic understanding of nutrition, because the human body requires a variety of foods in order to function and to be healthy.

The food service worker's responsibility to provide nutritious food and well-balanced menus depends in part on the operation. School and hospital food services must, of course, plan menus carefully to meet basic nutritional needs. A qualified dietitian is usually required in such establishments.

The obligations of restaurateurs are more subtle. Because they are in business to sell food, they must offer foods that will attract customers. Those who plan menus are as concerned with presenting attractive, flavorful foods as they are with serving nutritious foods. Also, if the menu is à la carte, there is no way to ensure that a customer will order items that will make up a nutritionally balanced meal.

But restaurateurs do have an obligation to offer a choice. That is, menus should be planned so that customers can order well-balanced meals if they desire. People are becoming more concerned with fitness and health, so a nutritiously balanced menu may even help attract customers.

Nutrients

1. Nutrients are certain chemical compounds that are present in foods and that fulfill one or more of the following functions:

   a. Supply energy for body functions.
   b. Build and replace cells that make up body tissues.
   c. Regulate body processes.

2. There are six categories of nutrients:

   a. Carbohydrate
   b. Fats
   c. Proteins
   d. Vitamins
   e. Minerals
   f. Water

In addition, there is a substance in foods that is not, strictly speaking, a nutrient, but that is necessary for healthful body functioning:

   g. Fiber

Calories

The *calorie* is a unit of measurement used to measure energy. It is defined as the amount of heat needed to raise the temperature of 1 kilogram of water by 1°C.

Remember that one of the functions of nutrients is to supply energy to the body. The calorie is used to measure how much energy certain foods will supply for these functions. In our overfed society, calories have come to be viewed as something to be avoided. Nevertheless, without sufficient food energy we could not live.

Carbohydrates, proteins, and fats can be used by the body to supply energy:

   1 gram of carbohydrate supplies 4 calories
   1 gram of protein supplies 4 calories
   1 gram of fat supplies 9 calories

Kinds of Nutrients and Their Importance

Each of the nutrients that we listed earlier has certain characteristics and functions in the body. These are discussed below in general terms. For a summary of individual nutrients and the foods in which they are found, see Table 6.1.

Carbohydrates

Carbohydrates are the most important source of food energy. *Starches* are complex carbohydrates. They are found in such foods as grains, bread, peas and beans, and many vegetables and fruits. *Sugars* are simple carbohydrates. They are found in sweets, and, to a lesser extent, in fruits and vegetables.

Most authorities believe that complex carbohydrates are better for you than simple carbohydrates.

TABLE 6.1 **Major Nutrients**

Nutrient	Major Dietary Sources	Functions in the Body
Carbohydrates	Grains (including breads and pasta) Dried beans Potatoes Corn Sugar	Major source of energy (calories) for all body functions. Necessary for proper utilization of fats. Unrefined carbohydrates supply fiber, important for proper waste elimination.
Fats	Meats, poultry, and fish Dairy products Eggs Cooking fats and shortening Salad dressings	Supplies food energy (calories). Supplies essential fatty acids. Carries fat-soluble vitamins.

(Continues)

TABLE 6.1   **Major Nutrients** *(Continued)*

Nutrient	Major Dietary Sources	Functions in the Body
Proteins	Meats, poultry, and fish Milk and cheese Eggs Dried beans and peas Nuts	Major building material of all body tissues. Supplies energy (calories). Helps make up enzymes and hormones, which regulate body functions.
Vitamin A	Liver Butter and cream Green and yellow vegetables and fruits Egg yolks	Helps skin and mucous membranes resist infection. Promotes healthy eyes and makes night vision possible.
Thiamin (Vitamin B_1)	Pork Whole grains and fortified grains Nuts Legumes Green vegetables	Needed for utilization of carbohydrates for energy. Promotes normal appetite and healthy nervous system. Prevents beriberi.
Riboflavin (Vitamin B_2)	Organ meats Milk products Whole grains and fortified grains	Needed for utilization of carbohydrates and other nutrients. Promotes healthy skin and eyes.
Niacin (a B vitamin)	Liver Meat, poultry, and fish Legumes	Needed for utilization of energy foods. Promotes healthy nervous system, skin, digestion. Prevents pellagra.
Vitamin B_{12}	Most animal and dairy products	Promotes healthy blood and nervous system.
Vitamin C (ascorbic acid)	Citrus fruits Tomatoes Potatoes Dark green, leafy vegetables Peppers, cabbage, and broccoli Cantaloupe Berries	Strengthens body tissues. Promotes healing and resistance to infection. Prevents scurvy.
Vitamin D	Fortified milk products Formed in skin when exposed to sunlight	Necessary for utilization of calcium and phosphorus to promote healthy bones, teeth, and muscle tissue
Vitamin E	Unsaturated fats (vegetable oils, nuts, whole grains, etc.)	Protects other nutrients.
Calcium	Milk products Leafy vegetables Canned fish with bones	Forms bones and teeth. Necessary for healthy muscles and nerves.
Iron	Liver and red meat Raisins and prunes Egg yolks Leafy vegetables Dried beans Whole grains	Needed for formation of red blood cells.

This is partly because starchy foods also have many other nutrients, while sweets have few other nutrients. Also, there is some evidence that a lot of sugar in the diet may contribute to heart and circulatory diseases.

The term *fiber* refers to a group of carbohydrates that cannot be used by the body. Therefore, fiber supplies no food energy. However, it is important for the proper functioning of the intestinal tract and the elimination of body waste. In addition, there is evidence that sufficient dietary fiber helps prevent some kinds of cancers. Fruits and vegetables, especially if raw, and whole grains supply dietary fiber.

Fats

Fats supply energy to the body in highly concentrated form. Also, some fatty acids are necessary for regulating certain body functions. Third, fats act as carriers of fat-soluble vitamins (vitamins A, D, E, and K).

Fats may be classified as saturated and unsaturated. *Saturated fats* are solid at room temperature. *Unsaturated fats,* also known as oils, are liquid at room temperature. Health experts believe that unsaturated fats are more healthful and that saturated fats may contribute to heart disease.

Animal products—meats, poultry, fish, eggs, dairy products—and solid shortenings are the major sources of saturated fats. Unsaturated fats are found mostly in vegetable products—nuts, whole grains, salad and cooking oils, and some fruits and vegetables.

Cholesterol is a fatty substance that has been closely linked with heart disease, because it collects on the walls of arteries and blocks the flow of blood to the heart and other vital organs. It is found only in animal products and is especially high in egg yolks, butter fat, and organ meats such as liver and brains. In addition, the human body can manufacture its own cholesterol, so not all the cholesterol in the blood is necessarily from foods. Nevertheless, experts generally agree that it is best to keep the cholesterol in the diet as low as possible.

Protein

Proteins are known as the building blocks of the body. They are essential for growth, for building body tissues, and for basic body functions. They can also be used for energy if the diet does not contain enough carbohydrates and fats.

Proteins consist of substances called *amino acids.* The body is able to manufacture many of them, but there are eight amino acids that it cannot manufacture and must get from foods. A food protein that contains all eight essential amino acids is called a *com-plete protein.* Meats, poultry, fish, eggs, and dairy products contain complete proteins.

Proteins that lack one or more of these essential amino acids are called *incomplete proteins.* Foods high in incomplete proteins include nuts, grains, and dried beans and other legumes. Foods that, *if eaten together,* supply all the amino acids are called *complementary proteins.* For example, cornmeal tortillas topped with chili beans supply complete protein, because the corn supplies the amino acids lacking in the beans. Beans and rice are another example of complementary proteins.

Vitamins

Vitamins are present in foods in extremely small quantities, but they are essential for regulating body functions. Unlike proteins, fats, and carbohydrates, they supply no energy, but some of them must be present in order for energy to be utilized in the body. Also, lack of certain vitamins causes diseases called *deficiency diseases.*

Vitamins are classified as *water soluble* and *fat soluble.* The water-soluble vitamins (the B vitamins and vitamin C) are not stored in the body and must be eaten every day. Foods containing these vitamins should be handled so that vitamins are not dissolved into the cooking water and lost (as discussed in Chapter 16).

Fat-soluble vitamins (A, D, E, and K) can be stored in the body, so they do not need to be eaten every day, as long as the total amount eaten over a period of time is sufficient.

Minerals

Minerals, like vitamins, are also consumed in very small quantities and are essential for regulating certain body processes. The most important minerals in the diet are calcium, phosphorus, iron, copper, iodine, sodium, and potassium.

Sodium, a component of table salt, is somewhat of a health problem, not because we don't get enough of it, but because many people get too much. Too much sodium is thought to contribute to high blood pressure. Health authorities are trying to convince people to reduce the sodium in their diets, primarily by salting foods less.

The Balanced Diet

In order to stay healthy, we must consume a varied diet that contains all the essential nutrients. In addition, we must limit our intake of foods that can be harmful in large quantities. Although researchers still have much to learn about nutrition and our knowledge is constantly changing, there is some strong evidence about what good eating patterns are. According to federal health agencies, the following guidelines are suggested for maintaining a healthful diet. It should be noted that these are only general recommendations for people who are already healthy and want to stay that way. They are not necessarily for those who need special diets because of disease or other abnormal conditions.

1. **Eat a variety of foods.**

   The greater variety of foods we eat, the more likely we are to get all the nutrients we require. A diet that includes daily selections from each of the following food groups helps to ensure a balanced diet. These food groups form what is known as the food pyramid. The number of daily servings of each group is indicated.

   Milk, yogurt, and cheese (2–3 servings)

   Meat, poultry, fish, dried beans, eggs, and nuts (2–3 servings)

   Vegetables (3–5 servings)

   Fruits (2–4 servings)

   Bread, cereals, rice, and pasta (6–11 servings)

2. **Maintain healthy weight.**

   People who are greatly overweight are more likely to develop certain chronic diseases, such as high blood pressure, heart disease, and strokes. Anyone who consumes more calories than he or she burns off will gain weight. The only way to lose weight is to take in fewer calories than you burn.

   Rather than depending on crash diets, it is usually better to lose weight slowly and gradually, to develop better habits of eating, and to increase your physical activity. To get all the nutrients you need while cutting down on calories, cut down on foods that are high in calories but low in nutrients, especially fat and fatty foods, sugar and sweets, and alcohol.

3. **Choose a diet that is low in fat, saturated fat, and cholesterol.**

   As mentioned above, high fat intake, especially of saturated fats and cholesterol, is associated with such conditions as heart disease and high blood pressure. Although there are other factors contributing to these diseases, such as heredity and smoking, following this recommendation should increase the chances of staying healthy.

   In a recommended diet, no more than about 30 percent of the calories would be in the form of fat. In the average American diet, about 40 percent of the calories are from fat.

4. **Choose a diet with plenty of vegetables, fruits, and grain products.**

   If you decrease your fat intake as recommended in point 3, you will need a larger proportion of carbohydrates in your diet to supply energy. The nutritional advantages of complex carbohydrates over refined ones and of fiber in the diet are discussed in the preceding section on nutrients. Vegetables, fruits, and grains are dietary sources of starch and fiber, as well as of vitamins and minerals.

5. **Use sugars only in moderation.**

   On average, each American consumes well over 100 pounds of sweeteners a year, not only as table sugar but also in candies, sweets, jams, jellies, soft drinks, ice cream, breakfast cereals, flavored milks, catsup, and so on. Too much sugar contributes to tooth decay and provides "empty calories," adding to overweight and obesity problems without supplying significant amounts of important nutrients.

6. **Use salt and sodium only in moderation.**

   Sodium, as noted earlier, appears to contribute to high blood pressure. For people who already have high blood pressure, it is especially important to cut down on sodium in the diet. The best ways to do this are to decrease the use of salt in the kitchen and at the table and to limit the intake of prepared foods that are high in salt, such as potato chips, salted nuts, pretzels, pickled foods, cured meats, and salty condiments like soy sauce.

7. **If you drink alcoholic beverages, do so in moderation.**

   Alcoholic beverages are high in calories while providing few other nutrients. Heavy drinking may cause a variety of serious diseases. Moderate drinking—one or two drinks a day—appears to do little harm and may in fact be of some benefit.

Cooking Healthful Meals

Restaurateurs and chefs are becoming more and more attentive to people's health and diet concerns. Many of them are reexamining their menus, modifying some of their cooking practices, and adding new, healthful items to their menus. Some have developed new menus that are specially planned to follow as closely as possible the seven recommendations listed previously.

An increased health consciousness has affected the way we think about food and the way we cook. Professional cooks are making their foods more healthful in several ways:

1. *Using less fat in cooking.*

    Cooking methods that require no added fat, such as simmering, poaching, baking, steaming, and grilling, can be considered the most healthful.

    For sautéing, no-stick pans are becoming more widely used, because little or no fat is needed. With regular pans, one can be careful to use as little fat as possible.

    Grilling is popular because it can be done without first coating the food with fat. If this is done, however, one must be very careful not to let the food dry out.

2. *Using the freshest, highest-quality foods possible.*

    In order to prepare delicious foods with little or no added salt and with less reliance on high-fat, high-sodium sauces and condiments, it is important to use high-quality natural ingredients at their peak of flavor. Healthful cooking means letting the true flavors of foods dominate.

    To enhance natural flavors without added salt, cooks are using more fresh herbs, hot seasonings such as chilies, ginger, and pepper, and flavorful ingredients like garlic, browned onions, and flavored vinegars.

3. *Modifying portion sizes.*

    It is not necessary to feature huge slabs of meat to serve satisfying meals. Smaller portions of well-trimmed meat, poultry, or fish, nicely balanced on the plate with an assortment of attractive, fresh vegetables and complex carbohydrates are likely to be more healthful.

    Sauces often get the blame for adding calories to a meal, but if a sauce is flavorful, you don't need much. Make a better sauce and serve less of it. Also, if a sauce isn't too thick, it won't cling as heavily to the food, and a little will go a longer way.

4. *Using nutritional information.*

    Studying the nutritional content of foods aids in planning healthful menus. There are many publications available that list nutritional contents of most common food items. Some restaurants have even hired the part-time services of registered dietitians to analyze their menus and give advice on how to make their food more healthful.

    Hiring a dietitian is of course not practical for every operation. On the other hand, a basic awareness of nutrition will help every professional minimize the fat, cholesterol, and sodium and maximize the nutritional content and balance in the foods they serve.

TERMS FOR REVIEW

static menu	course	calorie	cholesterol
cycle menu	minimum-use ingredient	carbohydrate	complete protein
à la carte	fresh	fiber	complementary protein
table d'hôte	imported	saturated fat	vitamin
prix fixe	homemade	unsaturated fat	

QUESTIONS FOR DISCUSSION

1. What role is played by the chef's favorite dishes when a menu is written?

2. What are the main differences between breakfast, lunch, and dinner menus?

3. Which of the following are most likely to have static menus?

Fast-food restaurant
High school cafeteria
Employee lunchroom
Army mess
French restaurant

4. The following menus are made up of dishes prepared from recipes in this book. Evaluate each one for variety and balance.

   Clear vegetable soup
   Green salad with French dressing
   Chicken fricassée
       Cauliflower au gratin

   Scotch broth
   Cucumber and tomato salad
   Roast rack of lamb with spring vegetables

   Oysters casino
   Vichyssoise
   Broiled steak
       Baked potato
       Buttered green beans

   Cream of mushroom soup
   Macaroni and ham salad
   Veal scaloppine à la creme
       Broccoli mornay
       Rice pilaf

   Oxtail soup
   Coleslaw
   Beef pot roast
       Braised green cabbage
       Bouillon potatoes

   Gazpacho
   Tomato and avocado salad
   Chicken croquettes, Suprême sauce
       Baked acorn squash
       Duchesse potatoes

5. What is the best solution to the problem of using up leftovers? What is the next best solution?

6. What are the U.S. government's seven dietary guidelines for Americans? Discuss.

7. As a cook, what are some ways that you can reduce the fat and sodium content of your menu offerings?

8. How can you ensure a nutritionally balanced menu without actually calculating the nutrient content of every item?

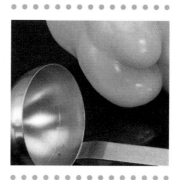

CHAPTER 7

PRE-PREPARATION

To be successful in the food service industry, cooks need more than the ability to prepare delicious, attractive, and nutritious foods. They must have a talent for organization and efficiency. In any kitchen there are a great many tasks to be completed over a given time and by a limited number of workers. No matter when these tasks are done, they all must come together at one crucial point: service time. Only if pre-preparation has been done thoroughly and systematically will service go smoothly.

Good chefs take pride in the thoroughness and quality of their pre-preparation, or mise en place (pronounced meez-on-plahss). This French term, meaning "everything put in place," has become almost a professional password in American kitchens, because food service professionals understand its importance to the success of the establishment.

This chapter deals with the basic concepts of pre-preparation, as well as a number of specific operations that are normally part of the mise en place.

After reading this chapter, you should be able to

1. Explain the importance of carefully planned pre-preparation.

2. Describe the steps in planning for pre-preparation.

3. Explain the difference in preparation requirements for set meal service and extended meal service.

4. Keep sharp edges on your knives.

5. Use a chef's knife to perform basic cutting techniques.

6. Understand basic precooking and marinating procedures.

7. Set up and use a standard breading station.

8. Handle convenience foods in pre-preparation operations.

MISE EN PLACE: "EVERYTHING READY"

*E*ven on the simplest level, pre-preparation is necessary. If you prepare only one short recipe, you must first

- Assemble your tools.
- Assemble your ingredients.
- Wash, trim, cut, prepare, and measure your raw materials.
- Prepare your equipment (preheat oven, line baking sheets, etc.).

Only then can you begin the actual preparation.

When many items are to be prepared in a commercial kitchen, the situation is much more complex. Dealing with this complexity is the basis of kitchen organization.

. . . .

PLANNING AND ORGANIZING FOR PRE-PREPARATION

The Problem

Every food service operation faces a basic conflict between two unavoidable facts:

1. There is far too much work to do in a kitchen to leave until the last minute, so some work must be done ahead.

2. Most foods are at their best quality immediately after preparation, and they deteriorate as they are held.

The Solution

To solve this problem, the chef must plan the pre-preparation carefully. Planning generally follows these steps:

1. **Break each menu item down into its stages of production.**

Turn to any recipe in this book. Note that the procedures are divided into a sequence of steps, which must be done in a certain order to make a finished product.

2. **Determine which stages may be done in advance.**

a. The first step of any recipe, whether written or not, is always part of advance preparation: *assembling and preparing the ingredients.* This includes cleaning and cutting produce, cutting and trimming meats, and preparing breadings and batters for frying.

b. Succeeding steps of a recipe may be done in advance *if they can then be held without loss of quality.*

c. Final cooking should be done as close as possible to service, for maximum freshness.

Frequently separate parts of a recipe, such as a sauce or a stuffing, are prepared in advance, and the dish is assembled at the last minute.

In general, items cooked by dry-heat methods, such as broiled steaks, sautéed fish, and french-fried potatoes, do not hold well. Large roasts are an important exception to this rule. Items cooked by moist heat, such as braised beef, soups, and stews, are usually better suited to reheating or holding in a steam table. Very delicate items should always be freshly cooked.

3. **Determine the best way to hold the item at its final stage of pre-preparation.**

a. Sauces and soups are frequently kept hot, above 140°F (60°C), for service in steam tables or other holding equipment. Many foods such as vegetables, however, should be kept hot for only short periods, because they quickly become overcooked.

b. Refrigerator temperatures, below 40°F (4°C), are best for preserving the quality of most foods, especially perishable meats, fish, and vegetables, before final cooking or reheating.

4. **Determine how long it takes to prepare each stage of each recipe. Plan a production schedule beginning with the preparations that take the longest.**

Many operations can be carried on at once, because they don't all require your complete attention the full time. It may take 6 to 8 hours to make a stock, but you don't have to stand and watch it all that time.

5. **Examine recipes to see if they might be revised for better efficiency and quality as served.**

For example,

a. Instead of preparing a full batch of green peas and holding for service in the steam table, you might blanch and chill them and then heat portions to order in a sauté pan, steamer, or microwave oven.

b. Instead of holding a large batch of veal scaloppine in mushroom sauce in the steam table, you might prepare and hold the sauce, sauté the veal to order, combine with a portion of the sauce, and serve fresh from the pan.

Caution: Unless you are in charge of the kitchen, do not change a recipe without authorization from your supervisor.

The Goal

The goal of pre-preparation is to do as much work in advance as possible *without loss of quality.*

At service time, all energy can then be used for finishing each item immediately before serving, with the utmost attention to quality and freshness.

Many preparation techniques in common use are designed for the convenience of the cooks at the expense of quality. Remember, quality should always take highest priority.

PREPARATION FOR SET MEAL SERVICE AND EXTENDED MEAL SERVICE

Set Meal Service

*   All customers eat at one time.
*   Often called "quantity cooking" because large batches are prepared in advance.
*   Examples: school cafeterias, banquets, employee dining rooms.

The traditional method of set meal preparation, still widely used, has been to prepare the entire quantity of each item in a single large batch and to keep it hot for the duration of the meal service. This method has two major disadvantages:

*   Deterioration of quality due to long holding.
*   Large quantities of leftovers.

Modern high-speed equipment, such as pressure steamers, convection ovens, infrared ovens, and microwave ovens, make possible a system called *small-batch cooking.* Quantities needed are divided in smaller batches, placed in pans ready for final cooking or heating, and then cooked only as needed. Its advantages are as follows:

*   Fresher food, because it is not held so long.
*   Fewer leftovers, because pans not needed are not cooked.

Small-batch cooking also accommodates items prepared in advance and frozen or chilled for storage.

Extended Meal Service

*   Customers eat at different times.
*   Often called "à la carte cooking" because customers usually select items from a written menu ("carte" in French).
*   Examples: restaurants, short-order counters.

Individual items are cooked "to order" rather than cooked ahead, but pre-preparation is extensive, down to the final cooking stage.

The short-order cook, for example, must have everything ready to go: cold meats, tomatoes and other sandwich ingredients sliced and arranged, spreads prepared and ready, hamburger patties shaped, garnishes prepared, and so on. If the cook has to stop during service to do any of these things, orders will back up and service will get behind.

A steak that takes 10 minutes to broil may be cut and trimmed in advance, but broiling should be started 10 minutes before it is to be served.

Obviously, if the last step in a recipe is to braise the item for 1½ hours, one cannot wait until an order comes in before beginning to braise. An experienced cook will estimate very closely how many orders will be needed during the meal period and prepare a batch that, ideally, will be finished just when service begins.

Preparation Techniques Are Adapted to Style of Service

Note the differences in these two methods for Chicken Chasseur. In both cases, the final product is chicken in a brown sauce with mushrooms, shallots, white wine, and tomatoes.

1. *Quantity method—Chicken Chasseur:*
    Brown chicken in fat; remove.
    Sauté shallots and mushrooms in same fat.
    Add flour to make a roux.
    Add white wine, tomatoes, brown stock, seasonings; simmer until thickened.
    Add chicken; braise until done.

2. *À la carte method—Chicken Chasseur:*

Prepare Sauce Chasseur in advance; hold in bain marie.

For each order:

Brown chicken in sauté pan; finish cooking in oven.

Deglaze pan with white wine; reduce.

Add one portion of sauce; add chicken and simmer briefly; serve.

CLEANING AND CUTTING THE RAW MATERIALS

ROUGH PREP

Rough prep means the preliminary processing of ingredients to the point at which they can be used in cooking.

Rough prep usually applies to fresh vegetables and fruits, as they usually require much washing and trimming. Meats and other ingredients also may require cutting and trimming. (Some operations do much of their own meat cutting; others buy ready-cut portion control meats.) Vegetable, meat, poultry, and seafood chapters contain detailed information on preliminary preparation of specific items.

USING THE KNIFE

There are many kinds of labor-saving equipment for cutting, chopping, and slicing fresh foods. Chapter 3 lists the basic kinds.

The chef's knife or French knife, however, is still the cook's most important and versatile cutting tool. The knife is more precise than a machine. Unless you are cutting a large quantity, the knife can even be faster. Cleaning a large machine takes time.

To get the best use out of your knife, *you must learn to keep it sharp and to handle it properly.*

Keeping a Sharp Edge

The Sharpening Stone

A stone is the best tool for sharpening a chef's knife. Electric sharpeners wear away too much of your expensive knife, and they do not make as good an edge.

Follow these guidelines:

1. Hold the blade at a constant 20° angle to the stone, as shown in Figure 7.1.

2. Make light, even strokes, the same number on both sides of the blade.

3. Sharpen in one direction only, to get a regular, uniform edge.

4. Do not oversharpen.

5. Finish with a few strokes on the steel (see next section), then wipe the blade clean.

Figure 7.2 illustrates one of several sharpening methods. There are other good ones, too, and your instructor may prefer a method not illustrated here.

The Steel

This tool is used not to sharpen the edge but to *true the edge* (to perfect it, or to smooth out irregularities) and to *maintain the edge* (to keep it sharp as it is used).

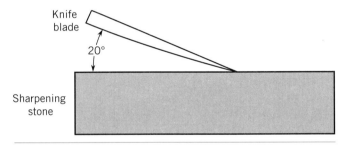

FIGURE 7.1 **When sharpening a knife, hold the blade at a 20° angle to the stone.**

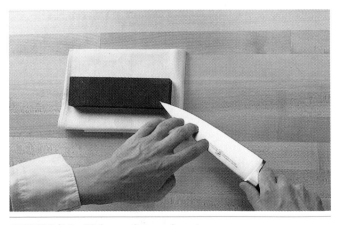

FIGURE 7.2 **Using a sharpening stone.**
(a) Hold the knife firmly. Start with the tip of the knife against the stone as shown, and hold the edge against the stone at a 20° angle. Use the guiding hand to keep an even pressure on the blade.

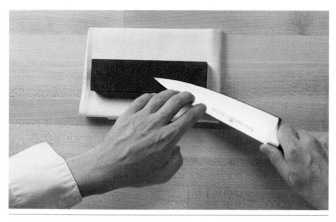

(b) Start to draw the knife over the stone. Press very gently on the blade.

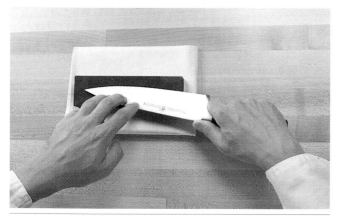

(c) Keep the motion smooth, using even, light pressure.

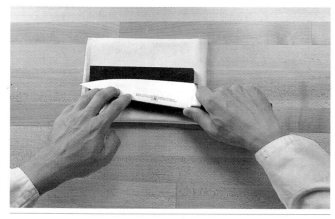

(d) Draw the knife across the stone all the way to the heel of the blade.

Observe these guidelines for using the steel:

1. Hold the blade at a constant 20° angle to the steel, just as when using the stone (Figure 7.1). A smaller angle will be ineffective. A larger one will dull the edge.

2. Make light strokes. Do not grind the knife against the steel.

3. Make even, regular strokes. Alternate each stroke first on one side of the blade, then on the other.

4. Use no more than five or six strokes on each side of the blade. Too much steeling can actually dull the blade.

5. Use the steel often. Then you will rarely have to sharpen the knife on the stone.

Figure 7.3 illustrates one of several steeling methods. This one is popular, but several others are equally correct. Carefully observe your instructors' demonstrations of their preferred methods.

FIGURE 7.3 **Using a steel.**
(a) Hold the steel and knife away from your body. With the knife in a vertical position, and, at a 20° angle to the steel, touch the steel with the heel of the blade.

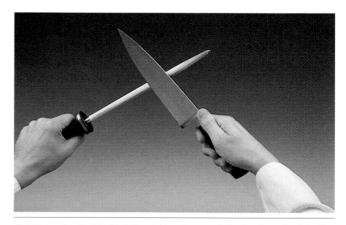

(b) Pass the knife lightly along the steel, bringing the blade down in a smooth arc. *(Continues)*

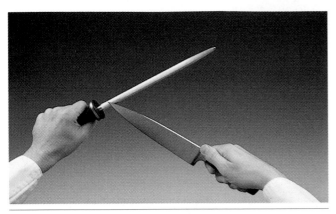

(c) Complete the movement. Do not strike the guard of the steel with the tip of the blade.

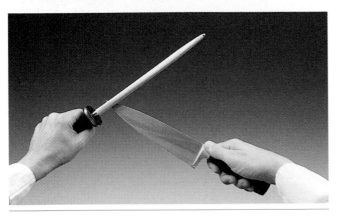

(d, e, f) Repeat the motion on the other side of the steel.

Handling the Knife

The Grip

A proper grip gives you maximum control over the knife. The proper grip increases your cutting accuracy and speed, it prevents slipping, and it lessens the chance of an accident. The type of grip you use depends in part on the job you are doing and the size of the knife.

The grip illustrated in Figure 7.4 is one of the most frequently used for general cutting and slicing. Many chefs feel that actually grasping the blade with the thumb and forefinger in this manner gives them greatest control.

Holding the knife may feel awkward at first, but practice will make it seem natural. Watch your instructors demonstrate the grips they use, then practice under their supervision.

The Guiding Hand

While one hand controls the knife, the other hand controls the product being cut. Proper positioning of the hand will do three things:

1. **Hold the item being cut.**

   In Figure 7.5, the item is held firmly so that it will not slip.

2. **Guide the knife.**

   Note that the knife blade slides against the fingers. The position of the hand controls the cut.

3. **Protect the hand from cuts.**

   Fingertips are curled under, out of the way of the blade.

FIGURE 7.4   **Grasping the blade of the knife between the thumb and forefinger gives the worker good control over the blade.**

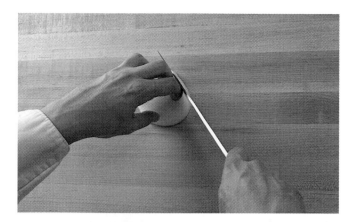

FIGURE 7.5   The position of the guiding hand, which holds the item being cut or sliced and also guides the blade, from two points of view.

Cutting Techniques

Different parts of the blade are appropriate for different purposes, as shown in Figure 7.6. (Note: Prying off bottle caps is not a function of any part of the knife.)

1. *Slicing.*

   Two basic slicing techniques are illustrated in Figures 7.7 and 7.8.

2. *Dicing.*

   Figure 7.9 shows the steps in dicing a product, here using a potato as an illustration.

3. *Dicing an onion.*

   Dicing an onion presents a special problem for cutting because it is in layers, not a solid piece. This technique is illustrated in Figure 7.10.

4. *Peeling grapefruit.*

   This technique, as shown in Figure 7.11, can also be used for peeling yellow turnips or other round vegetables and fruits with heavy peels.

5. *Chopping.*

   This chopping technique is used to cut up a product when no specific shape is needed. Figure 7.12 illustrates chopping parsley.

FIGURE 7.6   **Using different parts of the knife blade.** **(a) The tip of the knife, where the blade is thinnest and narrowest, is used for delicate work and small items.**

(b) The center of the blade is used for most general work.

(c) The heel of the knife is used for heavy or coarse work, especially when greater force is required.

FIGURE 7.7 Slicing technique 1.
(a) The knife starts at a sharp angle, with the tip of the knife on the cutting board.

FIGURE 7.8 Slicing technique 2.
(a) The blade starts at a 45° angle, with the tip on the cucumber, against the fingers of the guiding hand.

(b) The knife moves forward and down to slice through the carrot.

(c) The knife finishes the cut against the board. For the second slice, the heel of the knife is raised and pulled backward, but the tip always stays on the board.

(b, c) Slice downward and forward through the item.

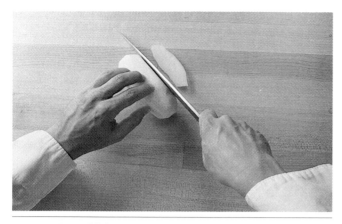

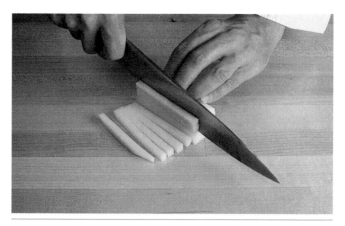

(d) Looking from this angle shows how the slices have been stacked up.

FIGURE 7.9   **Dicing a potato.**
(a) Square off the peeled, eyed potato by cutting a slice from all sides. Use the trimmings for mashed potatoes or soup.

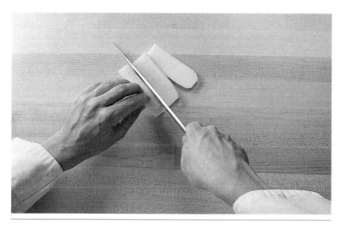

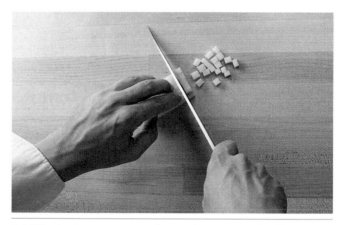

(e) Pile the batonnets together and cut across in slices ¼ inch apart. You now have perfect ¼-inch dice.

(b) Cut the potato into even slices of the desired thickness. Here we are making a ¼-inch dice, so the slices are ¼ inch thick.

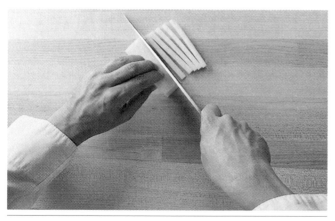

(c) Stack the slices and again slice across the stack in even ¼-inch slices. You now have batonnet potatoes, slightly smaller than regular french fries. Slices ⅛ inch thick would have given you allumette potatoes.

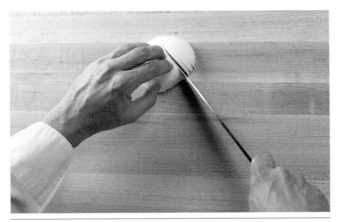

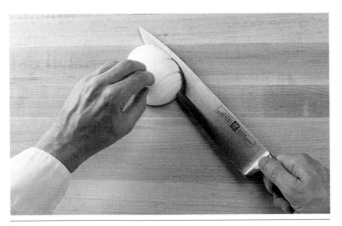

FIGURE 7.10 **Dicing an onion.**
(a) Cut the peeled onion in half lengthwise, through the root end. Place one-half on the cutting board, cut side down.

(b) With the root end away from you, make a series of vertical lengthwise cuts. Do not cut through the root end. The closer together you make the cuts, the smaller the dice will be.

(c) Holding the onion carefully at the top, make a few horizontal cuts toward but not through the root end, which is holding the onion together.

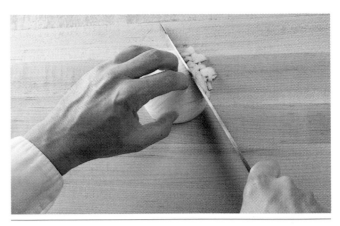

(d) Finally, slice across the onion to separate it into dice. Again, the closer together the cuts, the smaller the dice.

(e) Continue making slices almost to the root end. The root end may be rough cut for mirepoix to be used for stocks, sauces, and roasts.

FIGURE 7.11   **Peeling a grapefruit.**
(a) Cut off the ends of the grapefruit and turn it on a flat end so that it will be stable. Slice off a section of the peel, following the contour of the grapefruit.

(b) Make sure the cut is the proper depth to remove the peel but not to waste the product.

(c) Continue making slices around the grapefruit until all the peel is removed.

(d) The fruit can then be sliced or sectioned. (The remaining pulp is squeezed for juice.)

FIGURE 7.12   **Chopping with a French knife.**
Holding the tip of the knife against the cutting board, rock the knife rapidly up and down. At the same time, gradually move the knife sideways across the product on the board, so that the cuts pass through all parts of the pile of food. After several cuts, redistribute the pile and begin again. Continue until the product is chopped as fine as you want.

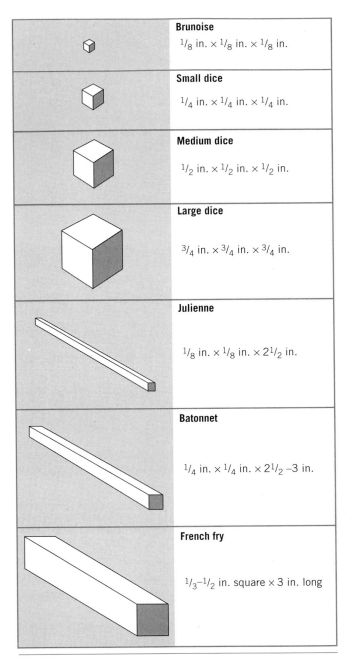

Brunoise		$\frac{1}{8}$ in. × $\frac{1}{8}$ in. × $\frac{1}{8}$ in.
Small dice		$\frac{1}{4}$ in. × $\frac{1}{4}$ in. × $\frac{1}{4}$ in.
Medium dice		$\frac{1}{2}$ in. × $\frac{1}{2}$ in. × $\frac{1}{2}$ in.
Large dice		$\frac{3}{4}$ in. × $\frac{3}{4}$ in. × $\frac{3}{4}$ in.
Julienne		$\frac{1}{8}$ in. × $\frac{1}{8}$ in. × $2\frac{1}{2}$ in.
Batonnet		$\frac{1}{4}$ in. × $\frac{1}{4}$ in. × $2\frac{1}{2}$ –3 in.
French fry		$\frac{1}{3}$–$\frac{1}{2}$ in. square × 3 in. long

FIGURE 7.13 **Basic cuts and shapes.**
(a) **Brunoise (broon-wahz):** ⅛ in. × ⅛ in. × ⅛ in. **(3 mm × 3 mm × 3 mm).**
(b) **Small dice:** ¼ in. × ¼ in. × ¼ in. **(6 mm × 6 mm × 6 mm).**
(c) **Medium dice:** ½ in. × ½ in. × ½ in. **(12 mm × 12 mm × 12 mm).**
(d) **Large dice:** ¾ in. × ¾ in. × ¾ in. **(2 cm × 2 cm × 2 cm).**
(e) **Julienne (or allumette potatoes):** ⅛ in. × ⅛ in. × 2½ in. **(3 mm × 3 mm × 6 cm).**
(f) **Batonnet:** ¼ in. × ¼ in. × 2½–3 in. **(6 mm × 6 mm × 6–7.5 cm).**
(g) **French fry or pomme frite:** ⅓–½ in. square × 3 in. long **(8–12 mm square × 7.5 cm long).**

BASIC CUTS AND SHAPES

Cutting food products into uniform shapes and sizes is important for two reasons:

1. It ensures even cooking.

2. It enhances the appearance of the product.

Figure 7.13 shows some common shapes, with their names and dimensions.

The following terms describe other cutting techniques:

Chop: to cut into irregularly shaped pieces.

Concasser (con-cass-say): to chop coarsely.

Mince: to chop into very fine pieces.

Emincer (em-man-say): to cut into very thin slices (does not mean "to mince").

Shred: to cut into thin strips, either with the coarse blade of a grater (manual or power) or with a chef's knife.

PRELIMINARY COOKING AND FLAVORING

*A*dvance preparation often requires certain precooking and flavoring of ingredients to make them ready for use in the finished recipe.

On the most obvious level, if a recipe for chicken salad calls for cooked, diced chicken, you must first cook the chicken before you can proceed with the recipe. A complete cooking procedure, in such a case, is part of the mise en place or pre-preparation.

·············

BLANCHING AND PARCOOKING

Partial cooking is a significant part of advance preparation. It requires a degree of culinary skill and judgment to determine when and how much cooking is necessary or desirable.

Partial cooking may be done by any moist-heat or dry-heat methods. Commonly used are simmering or boiling (parboiling), steaming, and deep-frying (especially for potatoes). The term *blanching* may mean any of these methods, but it usually implies *very brief* cooking.

There are four main reasons for blanching or parcooking:

1. ***To increase holding qualities.***

    Heating helps preserve foods by

    a. Destroying bacteria that cause spoilage.
    b. Destroying enzymes that discolor foods (as when potatoes turn brown) and help them deteriorate.

2. ***To save time.***

    It takes less time to finish parboiled vegetables for service than it does raw vegetables. Large batches of foods may be blanched and chilled, and individual portions then finished to order.

    Items such as roast duck, which would take too long to cook completely to order, are often roasted half to three-fourths done, then finished as the orders are received.

3. ***To remove undesirable flavors.***

    Some variety meats and certain strong-flavored vegetables such as rutabaga are sometimes blanched to make them milder and more acceptable to the customer.

4. ***To enable the product to be processed further.***

    For example: vegetables and fruits such as tomatoes and peaches, as well as some nuts, are blanched to loosen the skins for peeling.

    Sweetbreads are blanched so that they will be firm enough for slicing and breading or other kinds of handling.

MARINATING

To marinate means to soak a food product in a seasoned liquid in order to

1. Flavor the product.

2. Tenderize the product.

Note: The tenderizing effect of the acids in the marinade is relatively small. It is still essential to match the proper cut of meat with the proper cooking techniques for greatest tenderness.

The marinade can also serve as the cooking medium and become part of the sauce. Vegetable marinades, called vinaigrettes, are served cold with the vegetables as salads or hors d'oeuvres, without further cooking or processing.

Marinades have three categories of ingredients.

1. ***Oil.***

    Oil helps preserve the meat's moisture. Sometimes it is omitted, especially for long marinations, when the oil would only float on top, out of contact with the product being marinated.

    Tasteless vegetable oils are used when a neutral flavor is required. Specialty oils, such as olive oil, are used to add flavor to the item being marinated.

2. ***Acid***—from vinegar, lemon juice, wine.

    Acid helps tenderize protein foods.

    It carries flavors (its own and dissolved flavors from spices and herbs).

3. ***Flavorings***—spices, herbs, vegetables.

    A wide choice is available, depending on the purpose.

    Whole spices release flavors more slowly, so they are more suitable for long marinations.

Kinds of Marinades

1. ***Cooked.*** Used when long keeping quality is important. Modern refrigeration has made cooked marinades less widely used. An advantage of cooked marinades is that spices release more flavor into the marinade when it is cooked.

2. ***Raw.*** Most widely used for long marination under refrigeration. For example, see the recipe for Sauerbraten, page 262.

3. ***Instant.*** There is a wide variety of flavors and purposes. Used for marinating a few minutes up to several hours or overnight. For example, see the recipe for London Broil, page 241.

Guidelines for Marinating

1. Marinate under refrigeration (unless product is to be cooked in only a few minutes).

2. The thicker the product, the longer it takes for the marinade to penetrate. Some foods are marinated a week or longer.

3. Use an acid-resistant container, such as stainless steel, glass, crockery, or some plastics.

4. Tie spices in a cheesecloth bag (sachet) if easy removal is important.

5. Cover product completely with marinade. When marinating small items a short time, you may use less liquid, but you must then turn the product frequently for even penetration.

PREPARATION FOR FRYING

Most foods to be deep-fried, with the major exception of potatoes, are first given a protective coating of breading or batter. This coating serves four purposes:

1. It helps retain moisture and flavor in the product.

2. It protects the fat against the moisture and salt in the food, which speed deterioration of frying fat.

3. It protects the food from absorbing too much fat.

4. It gives crispness, flavor, and good appearance to the product.

....

BREADING

Breading means coating a product with bread crumbs or other crumbs or meal before deep-frying, pan-frying, or sautéing. The most widely used method for applying these coatings is called the *Standard Breading Procedure.*

The Three Stages of the Standard Breading Procedure

1. *Flour.* Helps the breading stick to the product.

2. *Egg wash.* A mixture of eggs and liquid, usually milk or water. More eggs give greater binding power, but increase the cost. A small quantity of oil is occasionally added to the egg wash.

3. *Crumbs.* Combine with the egg wash to create a crisp, golden coating when fried. Fine, dry bread crumbs are most often used and give good results. Other products used are fresh bread crumbs, crushed corn flakes or other cereal, cracker meal, and cornmeal.

Procedure for Proper Breading

Figure 7.14 illustrates a station setup for the Standard Breading Procedure.

1. Dry the product to get a thin, even coating of flour.

2. Season the product . . . or season the flour (step 3) for greater efficiency. Do not season the crumbs. The presence of salt in contact with the frying fat helps break down the fat and shorten its life.

3. Dip the product in flour to coat evenly. Shake off excess.

4. Dip in egg wash to coat completely. Remove. Let excess drain off, so that crumb coating will be even.

5. Dip in bread crumbs. Cover with crumbs and press gently on product. Make sure it is coated completely. Remove. Carefully shake off excess.

6. Fry immediately, or hold for service.

7. To hold for later service, place in a single layer on a pan or rack and refrigerate. Do not hold very moist items, such as raw clams or oysters. The breading will quickly become soggy.

8. Strain egg wash and sift flour and crumbs as often as necessary to remove lumps.

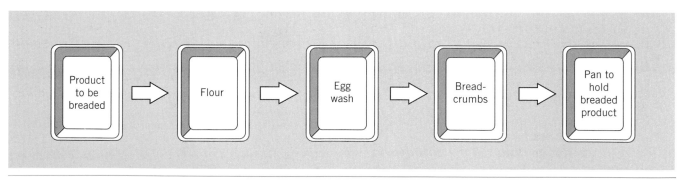

FIGURE 7.14 Setup of station for standard breading procedures.
Right-handed cooks work from left to right.
Left-handed cooks work from right to left.

For small items like scallops and oysters, breading may be done with the aid of a series of wire baskets placed in the flour, wash, and crumbs, instead of by hand. The procedure is the same, except that the baskets are used to lift and shake small quantities of the product and to transfer them to the next basket.

To keep one hand dry during breading, use your right hand (if you are right handed; left-handed persons reverse the procedure) only for handling the flour and crumbs. Use your other hand for handling the product when it is wet.

DREDGING WITH FLOUR

Purpose

The purpose of dredging is to give a thin, even coating of flour to a product.

Meats to be sautéed or pan-fried are often dredged with flour to give them an even, brown color and to prevent sticking.

Vegetables such as sticks of zucchini are sometimes coated only in flour before deep-frying, to give them a light golden color and very thin coating.

Procedure

Follow steps 1 to 3 of Standard Breading Procedure, above.

BATTERS

Batters are semiliquid mixtures containing flour or other starch. They are used in deep-frying to give a crisp, flavorful coating. There are many different formulas and variations for batters.

1. Many different liquids are used, including milk, water, or beer.

2. Eggs may or may not be used.

3. Thicker batters make thicker coatings. Too thick a batter will make a heavy, unpalatable coating.

4. Leavenings are frequently used to give a lighter product. These may be:

   a. Baking powder.
   b. Beaten egg whites.
   c. Carbonation from the beer or seltzer used in the batter.

Three recipes for basic, typical batters are given in the recipe for Deep-Fried Onion Rings, page 425. These batters may be used on a wide variety of products.

HANDLING CONVENIENCE FOODS

Convenience foods are playing an increasingly prominent role in the food service industry. Their use has become so important that no student of professional cooking can afford to be without knowledge of them.

A convenience food may be defined as *any product that has been partially or completely prepared or processed by the manufacturer.* In other words, when you buy a convenience product, you are having the manufacturer do some or all of your pre-preparation for you.

Of course, you must pay for this service, as reflected in the price of the product. Although buying the convenience product will likely cost you more than buying the raw materials, you save in increased kitchen efficiency. As you will remember from Chapter 5, labor costs as well as food costs must be figured into your menu prices.

Processed foods for restaurants and institutions range from partially prepared items that can be used as components in your recipes, such as frozen fish fillets, peeled potatoes, concentrated stock bases, and frozen puff pastry dough, to fully prepared items that need only be reconstituted or served as is, such as frozen prepared entrées and frozen pies and pastries. Some items, like frozen french fries, have wide acceptance, while other more fully prepared foods continue to be resisted by both customer and operator.

In general, the more completely a product has been prepared by the manufacturer, the less it will reflect the individuality of the food service operator—the less opportunity the cooks have to give it their own character and quality.

Is a stock made from "scratch" better than a product made from a convenience base? Most quality-conscious chefs would probably answer Yes! But the correct answer is, "Not if the homemade stock is poorly made." No matter what products you use, there is no substitute for quality and care. The fresh product is potentially the best, but not if it is badly stored or handled. Convenience foods also need proper handling to maintain their quality.

Considering convenience foods as normal products with part of the preprep completed, rather than as totally different kinds of products unlike your normal raw materials, is the key to understanding and handling them properly. *Convenience products are not a substitute for culinary knowledge and skill.* They should be a tool for the good cook rather than a crutch for

Clear vegetable soup with cranberry beans (page 166).

PART TWO

STOCKS, SAUCES, AND SOUPS

* * *

*S*tocks are the foundation of cooking, and they are essential to most sauces and soups. The preparations introduced in these chapters are among the most basic of the chef's art.

Stocks and Sauces

Soups

CHAPTER 8

STOCKS AND SAUCES

The importance of stocks in the
kitchen is indicated by the French word for stock: *fond*, meaning foundation or
base. In classical cuisine, the ability to prepare good stocks is the most basic of all skills,
because so much of the work of the entire kitchen depends on them. A good stock
is the foundation of soups, sauces, and most braised foods and stews.

In the modern American kitchen, stocks have lost much of the
importance they once had. In the first place, increased reliance on portion control
meats has made bones for stock a rarity in most establishments. Second, making stocks requires
extra labor, which most restaurants today aren't able to provide. Finally, more food
today is served without sauces, so stocks aren't seen to be quite as necessary.

Nevertheless, the finest cuisine still depends on soups and sauces
based on high-quality stocks. So stock making remains an essential skill that you
should learn early in your training. Stocks and sauces are almost never served by
themselves but are components of many other preparations. You will need to
refer to this chapter in connection with many other subjects.

After reading this chapter, you should be able to

1. Prepare basic mirepoix.
2. Use a sachet or spice bag for flavoring liquids.
3. Prepare white veal or beef stock, chicken stock, fish stock, and brown stock.
4. Cool and store stocks correctly.
5. Prepare meat, chicken, and fish glazes.
6. Evaluate and use convenience bases.
7. Explain the functions of sauces.
8. Prepare white, blond, and brown roux and use them to thicken liquids.
9. Prepare and use beurre manié.
10. Thicken liquids with cornstarch and other starches.
11. Prepare and use egg yolk and cream liaison.
12. Finish a sauce with raw butter (monter au beurre).
13. Prepare the five leading sauces: Béchamel, Velouté, Brown Sauce or Espagnole, Tomato, and Hollandaise.
14. Prepare small sauces from leading sauces.
15. Prepare simple and compound butters.
16. Prepare miscellaneous hot and cold sauces and pan gravies.

121

STOCKS

*T*he preparation of stocks has been simplified in many ways since the days of Escoffier, although this does not mean that it demands less care or skill. Few chefs today bother to tie vegetables for a stock into a bundle, for example. They're going to be strained out anyway. The number and variety of ingredients is usually not as great as it once was. Nor is it common to cook stocks for as many hours as were once thought necessary. All these details will be taken up one by one in this section.

A stock may be defined as a clear, thin (that is, unthickened) liquid flavored by soluble substances extracted from meat, poultry, and fish, and their bones, and from vegetables and seasonings. Our objective in preparing stocks is to select the proper ingredients and then to extract the flavors we want. In other words, combine the correct ingredients with the correct procedure.

....

INGREDIENTS

Bones

Bones are the major ingredient of stocks (except water, of course). Most of the flavor and body of stocks is derived from the bones of beef, veal, chicken, fish, and occasionally lamb, pork, ham, and game. (Vegetable stocks, an exception, draw their flavor entirely from vegetables; see p. 124.)

The kinds of bones used determine the kind of stock.

Chicken stock, of course, is made from chicken bones.

White stock is made from beef or veal bones or a combination of the two. Chicken bones or even pork bones are sometimes added in small quantity.

Brown stock is made from beef or veal bones that have been browned in an oven.

Fish stock is made from fish bones and trimmings left over after filleting. Bones from lean white fish give the best stock. Fat fish are not normally used. The term *fumet* is often used for a flavorful fish stock.

Lamb, game, turkey, and other stocks have specialized uses.

In Chapter 4, we discussed a group of proteins called connective tissue. Remember that some of these proteins are dissolved when cooked with slow, moist heat. In Chapter 10, "Understanding Meats," there is more information about these substances. There are two basic facts that you should learn and understand:

1. When certain connective tissues (called collagen) break down, they form *gelatin*. This gives body to a stock, an important feature of its quality. A well-made stock will thicken or even solidify when chilled.

2. *Cartilage* is the best source of gelatin in bones. Younger animals have more cartilage in their skeletons. As they become older, this hardens into solid bone, which is harder to dissolve into stocks. *Knuckle bones*, on the joints of major bones, have a lot of cartilage and are valued in stock making. Neck bones and shank bones are also used a great deal.

Cut large bones into pieces about 3 inches (8 centimeters) long. This exposes more surface area and aids extraction. Also, the bones are easier to handle.

Meat

Because of its cost, meat is rarely used in stock making any more. (Exception: chicken hearts and gizzards are often used in chicken stock.)

Occasionally a broth is produced as a result of simmering meat or poultry, as when fowl is cooked for dishes like creamed chicken. This broth can then be used like a stock. However, the chicken is considered the object of the game in this case. The broth is just a by-product.

In this book we use the word *broth* to mean a flavorful liquid obtained from the simmering of meats and/or vegetables.

Mirepoix

Aromatic vegetables are the second most important contributors of flavor to stocks. (In the case of vegetable stocks, they are the most important.)

Mirepoix (pronounced meer-pwah) is a combination of onions, carrots, and celery. It is a basic flavoring preparation that is used in all areas of cooking, not only for flavoring stocks, but also for sauces, soups, meats, poultry, fish, and vegetables. (The classical mirepoix of decades ago contained a wider variety of ingredients, sometimes including ham or bacon, leeks and other vegetables, and one or more fresh herbs. The modern version is considerably simplified.)

Learn the following proportions well. Mirepoix is a basic preparation that you will need throughout your career.

Mirepoix

To Make:	1 Pound	400 Grams
Onions	8 oz	200 g
Celery	4 oz	100 g
Carrots	4 oz	100 g

A *white mirepoix,* made without carrots, is used when it is necessary to keep the stock as colorless as possible. Mushroom trimmings may be added to white mirepoix. When cost permits, it is a good idea to include some leeks in the mirepoix, in place of part of the onions. They give an excellent flavor.

In vegetable stocks, a variety of other vegetables is used in addition to or in place of the traditional mirepoix; see page 124 for a brief discussion.

Cutting Mirepoix

Chop the vegetables coarsely into relatively uniform-sized pieces. Since mirepoix is rarely served, it is not usually necessary to cut it neatly.

The size depends on how long it will cook. If the mirepoix will cook a long time, as for beef stock, cut into large pieces (1 to 2 inches). Cutting into small pieces is necessary for releasing flavors in a short time, as when used for fish stock.

Acid Products

Acids, as noted in Chapter 4 (p. 52), help dissolve connective tissues. Thus, they are sometimes used in stock making to extract flavor and body from bones.

Tomato products contribute flavor and some acid to brown stocks. They are not used for white stocks, because they would give an undesirable color. Also, when making brown stocks, be careful not to add too much tomato, because this may make the stock cloudy.

Wine is occasionally used, especially for fish stocks. Its flavor contribution is probably more important than its acidity.

Scraps and Leftovers

In some kitchens a stock pot is kept going all day, and various scraps are constantly being thrown in. This may or may not be a good idea.

Scraps may be used in stocks if they are *clean, wholesome, and appropriate to the stock being made.* If done correctly, stock making is a good way of utilizing trimmings that would otherwise be thrown out. It is better to save trimmings and use them in a planned way rather than to throw them into the stock randomly.

A stock pot is not a garbage disposal, and the final product is only as good as the ingredients and the care that go into it.

Seasonings and Spices

1.   *Salt* is usually not added when making stocks. Stocks are never used as is, but are reduced, concentrated, and combined with other ingredients. If salt had been added, it might become too concentrated. Some chefs salt stocks *very lightly,* because they feel it aids in extracting flavor.

2.   *Herbs and spices* should be used only lightly. They should never dominate a stock or have a pronounced flavor.

Herbs and spices are usually tied in a cheesecloth bag called a *sachet* (pronounced sa-shay; French for "bag"). The sachet is tied by a string to the handle of the stock pot so it can be removed easily at any time.

Bouquet garni is another important term, generally used for a sachet that contains no spices, but only herbs, such as parsley, thyme, bay leaf, and celery leaves. The word "bouquet" derives from the practice of tying fresh herbs in a bundle with string rather than in cheesecloth. Obviously, this cannot be done with dried herbs.

The following seasonings, in varying quantities, are commonly used for stocks:

Thyme

Bay leaves

Peppercorns

Parsley stems

Cloves, whole

Garlic (optional)

Ingredient Proportions

The following proportions are basic, effective, and widely used, but they are not an iron-clad rule. Nearly every chef will have some variations.

White Stock (Including Chicken Stock)

To Make:	1 Gallon	4 Liters
Bones	5–6 lb	2½–3 kg
Mirepoix	1 lb	500 g
Water	5–6 qt	5–6 L
Sachet	1	1

Brown Stock

To Make:	1 Gallon	4 Liters
Bones	5–6 lb	2½–3 kg
Mirepoix	1 lb	500 g
Tomato product	8 oz	250 g
Water	5–6 qt	5–6 L
Sachet	1	1

Fish Stock

To Make:	1 Gallon	4 Liters
Bones	4–6 lb	2–3 kg
Mirepoix	8 oz	250 g
Water	1 gal	4 L
White wine	8 oz	250 mL
Sachet	1	1

Many cooks use ratios to help them remember the basic proportions, as follows:

Bones	50%
Mirepoix	10%
Water	100%

Ingredients for Vegetable Stocks

Vegetable stocks, made without any animal products, play an important role in vegetarian cooking and are also used in more traditional kitchens, in response to customers' requests for light, healthful dishes. The basic ingredients for vegetable stocks are vegetables, herbs and spices, water, and sometimes wine.

Ingredients and proportions can vary greatly. For example, if you want a particular flavor to predominate, use a larger quantity of that vegetable. For example, if you want a broth tasting primarily of asparagus, use a large quantity of asparagus to make it, with smaller quantities of more neutral vegetables (like onion and celery) to round out the flavor. For a more neutral, all-purpose vegetable stock, avoid strong-flavored vegetables and use more balanced proportions of the various ingredients.

A few additional guidelines for making vegetable stocks or broths:

1. Starchy vegetables such as potatoes, sweet potatoes, and winter squash make a stock cloudy. Use them only if clarity is not important.

2. Some vegetables, especially strong-flavored ones, are best avoided. Brussels sprouts, cauliflower, and artichokes can overwhelm a stock with a strong flavor or odor. Dark green, leafy vegetables, especially spinach, develop an unpleasant flavor when cooked for a long time. Beets turn a stock red.

3. Cook long enough to extract flavors, but not so long that flavors are lost. Best cooking times are 30 to 45 minutes.

4. Sweating the vegetables in a small amount of oil before adding water gives them a mellower flavor, but this step can be omitted. Butter can be used if it is not necessary to avoid all animal products.

PROCEDURES

Making stock may seem at first glance to be a simple procedure. However, there are many steps involved and a rather complicated set of reasons for each. If you are to be successful at making consistently good stocks, you must understand not only what to do, but why you are doing it.

The following outlines give procedures for making basic stocks as well as the reasons for every step. After learning these procedures, and checking with your instructors for any modifications or variations they may have, you will then be able to turn to the individual recipes, where the steps are given again, but without explanations.

Blanching Bones

In Chapter 4, we discussed proteins coagulating when heated. Many proteins dissolve in cold water but solidify into small particles or into froth or scum when heated. It is these particles that make a stock cloudy. Much of the technique of stock making involves avoiding cloudiness to produce a clear stock.

The purpose of blanching bones is to rid them of some of the impurities that cause cloudiness. The bones of *young animals*, especially veal and chicken, are highest in blood and other impurities that cloud and discolor stocks.

Chefs disagree on the importance of blanching. Many feel that it is needed to produce clear white stocks. Others feel that blanching causes valuable flavors to be lost. Fish bones, at any rate, are not blanched because of their very short cooking time.

Procedure for Blanching Bones

1. **Rinse bones in cold water.**

   This washes off blood and other impurities from the surface. It is especially important if the bones are not strictly fresh.

2. **Place bones in stock pot or steam-jacketed kettle and cover with cold water.**

   Impurities dissolve more readily in cold water. Adding hot water would retard extraction.

3. **Bring the water to a boil.**

   As the water heats, impurities solidify (coagulate) and rise to the surface as scum.

4. **Drain the bones and rinse them well.**

   The bones are now ready for the stock pot.

Preparing White Stocks

A good white stock has rich, full flavor, good body, clarity, and little or no color. Chicken stocks may have a light yellow color.

Procedure for Preparing White Stocks

1. **Cut the bones into 3- to 4-inch (8–10 cm) pieces.**

   This exposes more surface area and helps extraction. A meat saw is used to cut heavy veal and beef bones. Fish and chicken bones don't need to be cut, but whole carcasses should be chopped up for more convenient handling.

2. **Rinse the bones in cold water. (If desired, chicken, veal, or beef bones may be blanched.)**

   This removes some impurities that cloud the stock or, if the bones are old, give an off taste.

3. **Place bones in stock pot or steam-jacketed kettle and add cold water to cover.**

   Starting in cold water speeds extraction. Starting in hot water delays it, because many proteins are soluble in cold water but not in hot.

4. **Bring water to a boil, then reduce to a simmer. Skim the scum that comes to the surface.**

   Skimming is very important for a clear stock because the scum (which is fat and coagulated protein) will cloud the stock if it is broken up and mixed back into the liquid.

5. **Add the chopped mirepoix and the herbs and spices.**

   Remember, the size you cut mirepoix depends on how long it is to be cooked.

6. **Do not let the stock boil. Keep it at a low simmer.**

   Boiling makes the stock cloudy, because it breaks up solids into tiny particles that get mixed into the stock.

7. **Skim the surface as often as necessary during cooking.**

8. **Keep the water level above the bones. Add more water if the stock reduces below this level.**

   Cooking bones exposed to air will turn dark and thus darken or discolor the stock. Also, they do not release flavor into the water if the water doesn't touch them.

9. **Simmer for recommended length of time:**

Beef and veal bones	6 to 8 hours
Chicken bones	3 to 4 hours
Fish bones	30 to 45 minutes

   Most modern chefs do not simmer stocks as long as earlier generations of chefs did. It is true that longer cooking will extract more gelatin, but gelatin isn't the only factor in a good stock. Flavors begin to break down or degenerate after a period of time. The above times are felt to be the best for full flavor, while still getting a good portion of gelatin into the stock as well.

10. **Skim the surface and strain off the stock through a china cap lined with several layers of cheesecloth.**

    Adding a little cold water to the stock before skimming stops the cooking and brings more fat and impurities to the surface.

11. **Cool the stock as quickly as possible, as follows:**

    a. Set the pot in a sink with blocks or some other object under it. This is called *venting*. It allows cold water to flow under the pot as well as around it.

    b. Run cold water into the sink, but not higher than the level of the stock or the pot will become unsteady. An overflow pipe keeps the water level right and allows for constant circulation of cold water (see Figure 8.1).

    c. Stir the pot occasionally so that all the stock cools evenly. Hang a ladle in the pot so that you can give it a quick stir whenever you pass the sink, without actually taking extra time to do it.

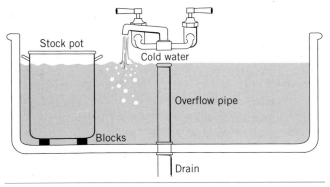

FIGURE 8.1 **Setup for cooling stocks in a cold-water bath.**

Cooling stock quickly and properly is very important. Improperly cooled stock can spoil in 6 to 8 hours, because it is a good breeding ground for bacteria.

Do not set the hot stock in the walk-in or, worse yet, the reach-in. All that heat and steam will overload the refrigerator and may damage other perishables as well as the equipment.

12. When cool, refrigerate the stock in covered containers. Stock will keep 2 to 3 days if properly refrigerated.

RECIPE 1 Basic White Stock

Yield: 2 gal (8 L)

U.S.	Metric	Ingredients	Procedure
10–12 lb	5–6 kg	Bones: chicken, veal, or beef	1. Review instructions for stock preparation (pp. 125–126).
10–12 qt	10–12 L	Cold water Mirepoix:	2. If beef or veal bones are whole, cut them into 3–4 in. (8–10 cm) pieces with a meat saw. Rinse the bones in cold water.
1 lb	500 g	Onion, chopped	
8 oz	250 g	Carrot, chopped (optional)	3. Blanch the bones: place them in a stock pot, cover with cold water, and bring to a boil. Drain and rinse.
8 oz	250 g	Celery, chopped Sachet:	
1	1	Bay leaf	4. Place the bones in the stock pot and cover with cold water. Bring to a boil, reduce heat to simmer, and skim the scum carefully.
¼ tsp	1 mL	Thyme	
¼ tsp	1 mL	Peppercorns	5. Add the mirepoix and sachet ingredients (tied in cheesecloth).
6–8	6–8	Parsley stems	
2	2	Whole cloves	6. Simmer for required length of time, skimming the surface as often as necessary. Beef and veal: 6–8 hours Chicken: 3–4 hours Add water if necessary to keep bones covered.
			7. Strain through a china cap lined with several layers of cheesecloth.
			8. Cool the stock, vented, in a water bath and refrigerate.

Variations

1A. Prepare **White Lamb Stock, Turkey Stock,** and **Ham Stock** according to the basic procedure, substituting the appropriate bones.

1B. *Vegetable Stock:* Omit the bones. Reduce the water to 9 qt (9 L). Use half the quantity of onions and celery in the basic recipe. Add the following ingredients: ½ oz (15 g) garlic, chopped; 4 oz (125 g) leeks; 8 oz (250 g) mushrooms, sliced; 2 oz (60 g) fennel, sliced. Sweat the onion, garlic, and leek in ½ oz (15 mL) olive oil before adding the remaining ingredients. Cook the stock 30–45 minutes.

Preparing Brown Stocks

The difference between brown stocks and white stocks is that the bones and mirepoix are browned for the brown stock. This causes a few complications, as you will see. But except for these differences, the procedure is essentially the same.

Two methods for browning are given below.

Procedure for Preparing Brown Stocks

1. Cut the bones in 3- to 4-inch pieces, as for white stock. Veal and/or beef bones are used for brown stock.

2. Do not wash or blanch the bones. The moisture would hinder browning.

3. Place the bones in a roasting pan in one layer and brown in a hot oven 375°F (190°C) or higher. The bones must be well browned to color the stock sufficiently. This takes over an hour. Some chefs prefer to oil the bones lightly before browning.

4. When the bones are well browned, remove them from the pan and place in stock pot. Cover with cold water and bring to a simmer.

5. Drain and reserve the fat from the roasting pan. Deglaze the pan by adding water and stirring

---

RECIPE 2   Basic Brown Stock

Yield: 2 gal (8 L)

U.S.	Metric	Ingredients	Procedure
10–12 lb	5–6 kg	Bones: veal or beef	1. Review instructions for stock preparation (pp. 127–128).
10–12 qt	10–12 L	Cold water	
			2. If bones are whole, cut into 3- to 4-inch (8–10 cm) pieces with a meat saw.
			3. Place the bones in a roasting pan in a hot oven (400°F/200°C) and brown them well.
			4. Remove bones from pan and place in a stock pot. Cover with water and bring to a simmer. Skim and let stock continue to simmer.
			5. Drain and reserve the fat in the roasting pan. Deglaze the pan with water and add to stock pot.
		Mirepoix:	6. Toss the mirepoix with some of the reserved fat and brown well in the oven.
1 lb	500 g	Onion, chopped	
8 oz	250 g	Carrot, chopped	7. Add the browned mirepoix, the tomato product, and the sachet to the stock pot.
8 oz	250 g	Celery, chopped	
1 lb	500 g	Tomatoes or tomato purée	8. Continue to simmer for a total cooking time of 6 to 8 hours, skimming the surface as necessary. Add water as needed to keep bones covered.
		Sachet:	
1	1	Bay leaf	
¼ tsp	1 mL	Thyme	
¼ tsp	1 mL	Peppercorns	9. Strain through a china cap lined with several layers of cheesecloth.
6–8	6–8	Parsley stems	
2	2	Whole cloves	10. Cool the stock, vented, in a cold-water bath and refrigerate.

Variations

2A. Prepare **Brown Lamb Stock** and **Game Stock** according to the basic procedure, substituting the appropriate bones.

RECIPE 3   Fish Stock or Fumet

Fish stock may be made according to the same recipe as for white stock. The following method yields a slightly more flavorful stock, due to the preliminary sweating of mirepoix and bones in the butter and to the addition of wine.

Yield: 1 gal (4 L)

U.S.	Metric	Ingredients	Procedure
1 oz	30 g	Butter	1. Butter the bottom of a heavy stock pot or sauce pot. Place the mirepoix in the bottom of the pot and the bones over the top of it. Cover the bones loosely with a round of brown paper or parchment.
		Mirepoix:	
4 oz	125 g	Onion, chopped fine	
2 oz	60 g	Celery, chopped fine	
2 oz	60 g	Carrot, chopped fine (optional)	2. Set the pot over low heat and cook slowly for about 5 minutes, until the bones are opaque and begin to exude some juices.
2 oz	60 g	Mushroom trimmings (optional)	
4–6 lb	2–3 kg	Bones from lean fish	3. Add the wine, bring to a simmer, then add water to cover, and the sachet.
8 oz	250 mL	White wine (dry)	
1 gal	4 L	Cold water	4. Bring to a simmer again, skim, and let simmer for 30 to 45 minutes.
		Sachet:	
½	½	Bay leaf	
¼ tsp	1 mL	Peppercorns	5. Strain through a china cap lined with several layers of cheesecloth.
6–8	6–8	Parsley stems	
1	1	Whole clove	6. Cool, vented, in a cold-water bath and refrigerate.

over heat until all the brown drippings are dissolved or loosened. Add to stock pot.

6. While the stock is getting started, place the mirepoix in the roasting pan with some of the reserved fat and brown the vegetables well in the oven. (See alternative procedure below.)

7. When the water in the stock pot comes to a simmer, skim and continue as for white stock.

8. Add the browned vegetables and the tomato product to the stock pot. If desired, they may be held out until 3 to 4 hours before the end of the cooking time.

9. Continue as for white stock.

Alternative Procedure

The mirepoix may be browned with the bones. When the bones are half browned, add the mirepoix to the pan and continue roasting until bones and vegetables are browned. Tomato may be added toward the end of browning time, but exercise caution—tomato purée burns easily.

Some chefs use this method because it eliminates some steps. Others prefer to brown the mirepoix separately so that it can be added to the stock later in the cooking time.

REDUCTIONS AND GLAZES

Stocks are concentrated by boiling or simmering them to evaporate part of the water. This is called *reduction* or reducing.

Reduction is an important technique in sauce making and in many other areas of cooking, because it produces a more flavorful product by concentrating it. A reduced stock also has more body, because the gelatin is concentrated.

What Are Glazes?

• A *glaze* or *glace* (French word pronounced glahss) is a stock that is reduced until it coats the back of a spoon. It is so concentrated—reduced by three-fourths or more—that it is solid and rubbery when refrigerated.

Glazes are used as flavorings in sauce making and in some meat, poultry, fish, and vegetable preparations. Only small amounts are needed because they are so concentrated.

Kinds of Glazes

1. Meat glaze or *glace de viande* (glahss duh vee awnd)—made from brown stock.

2. Chicken glaze or *glace de volaille* (voh lye)—made from chicken stock.

3. Fish glaze or *glace de poisson* (pwah sohn)—made from fish stock.

Procedure for Preparing Glazes

1. Reduce the stock over moderate heat.

2. Skim the surface frequently.

3. When reduced by half to two-thirds, strain into a smaller, heavy saucepan and continue to reduce over lower heat until it is syrupy and coats a spoon.

4. Pour into containers, cool, cover, and refrigerate.

5. Glazes will keep for several weeks or longer if properly stored. They may also be frozen.

   Glazes diluted to original strength do not taste like the stocks they were made from. The long cooking changes the flavors somewhat.

CONVENIENCE BASES

The cost, both in time and materials, of making stocks in modern kitchens has lead to the widespread use of concentrated convenience products known as bases. These are diluted with water to make flavored liquids similar to stocks.

Glazes can be considered to be bases, and in fact they are the original bases, used long before today's manufacturers started producing convenience products.

Judging Quality

Bases vary greatly in quality. The best ones are composed mainly of meat extracts. These are perishable products and need to be refrigerated.

Many bases are made primarily from salt, however—an expensive way to buy salt, we might add.

Read the list of ingredients. Avoid products that list salt first. The best way to judge the quality of a base is to dilute it and compare its flavor to a well-made stock.

Using Bases

Bases can be improved with little labor by simmering the diluted or made-up product for a short time with some mirepoix, a sachet, and a few bones or meat trimmings if possible. This helps to give a fresher, more natural taste to a highly processed product.

Bases are also added to stocks to supplement them when there is only a small quantity of stock on hand.

In addition, bases are sometimes added to weak stocks to give them more flavor, but this is not as good a practice as making the stock properly in the first place.

Using bases requires taste and judgment, just as in other areas of cookery. If used without care and restraint, they can detract from the quality of your cooking. But, used carefully, bases can be a valuable tool in some situations. Always taste and evaluate as you cook.

There is no substitute for a well-made stock. But it is also true that a good base may be better than a poorly made stock. It all depends on the skills you are learning now.

SAUCES

Like stocks, sauces have lost some of the importance they once had in commercial kitchens, except, of course, in the best restaurants serving what may be considered luxury cuisine. Some of this decline is due to changes in eating habits and to increased labor costs.

However, much of this change is due to misunderstanding. How many times have you heard someone say, "I don't go for all those sauces all over everything; I like good simple food." No doubt this person puts catsup—a sweetened tomato sauce—on hamburgers, gravy on mashed potatoes, and tartar sauce on fried fish.

The misunderstandings arise from poorly made sauces. No one likes thick, pasty cream sauces on vegetables or oversalted but otherwise flavorless brown sauces gumming up their meat. But just because some cooks made bad sauces is no reason to reject all sauce cookery.

In fact, many chefs feel that good sauces are the pinnacle of all cooking, both in the skill they require and in the interest and excitement they can give to food. Very often, the most memorable part of a really fine meal is the sauce that enhances the meat or fish.

A sauce works like a seasoning. It enhances and accents the flavor of the food; it should not dominate or hide the food.

A good cook knows that sauces are as valuable as salt and pepper. Even a simple grilled steak is made even better when it has an added touch, something as simple as a slice of seasoned butter melting on it, or as refined as a spoonful of Béarnaise sauce.

No matter where you work, sauce making techniques are basic skills you will need in all your cooking. Croquettes, soufflés, and mousses have sauces as their base, nearly all braised foods are served with sauces made of their cooking liquids, and basic pan gravies, certainly favorites everywhere, are made with the same techniques as the classic sauces.

. . . .

UNDERSTANDING SAUCES

The Functions of Sauces

A sauce may be defined as a flavorful liquid, usually thickened, which is used to season, flavor, and enhance other foods.

A sauce adds the following qualities to foods:

1. Moistness

2. Flavor

3. Richness

4. Appearance (color and shine)

5. Interest and appetite appeal

The Structure of Sauces

The major sauces we consider here are made of three kinds of ingredients.

A liquid, the body of the sauce

A thickening agent

Additional seasoning and flavoring ingredients

To understand sauce making, you must learn first how to prepare these components and then how to combine them into finished sauces.

Liquid

A liquid ingredient provides the body or base of most sauces. There are five liquids or bases on which most sauces are built, and the resulting sauces are called Leading Sauces or Mother Sauces.

White stock (chicken, veal, or fish)—for Velouté Sauces

Brown stock—for Brown Sauce or Espagnole (ess pahn yohl)

Milk—for Béchamel

Tomato plus stock—for Tomato Sauce

Clarified butter—for Hollandaise

The most frequently used sauces are based on stock. The quality of these sauces depends on the stock-making skills you learned in the previous section.

Thickening Agents

A sauce must be thick enough to cling lightly to the food. Otherwise it will just run off and lie in a puddle in the plate. This doesn't mean that it has to be heavy and pasty.

Starches are the most common thickening agents, but there are others as well. We will discuss each of these in detail.

Other Flavoring Ingredients

Although the liquid that makes up the bulk of the sauce provides the basic flavor, other ingredients are added to make variations on the basic themes and to give a finished character to the sauces.

Adding specified flavoring ingredients to basic sauces is the key to the whole catalog of classic sauces. Most of the hundreds of sauces listed in the standard repertoires are made by adding one or more flavoring ingredients to one of the five basic sauces or leading sauces.

As in all of cooking, sauce making is largely a matter of learning a few building blocks and then building with them.

ROUX

Starches as Thickeners

1. Starches are the most common and most useful thickeners used in sauce making. Flour is the principal starch used in sauce making. Other starches available to the chef include cornstarch, arrowroot, waxy maize, instant or pregelatinized starch, bread crumbs, and other vegetable and grain products like potato starch and rice flour. These will be discussed later.

2. Starches thicken by *gelatinization,* which, as was discussed in Chapter 4, is the process by which starch granules absorb water and swell to many times their original size.

Another important point made in Chapter 4 is that acids inhibit gelatinization. Whenever possible, do not add acid ingredients to sauces until the starch has fully gelatinized.

3. Starch granules must be separated before heating in liquid, to avoid lumping. If granules are not separated, lumping occurs because the starch on the outside of the lump quickly gelatinizes into a coating that prevents the liquid from reaching the starch inside.

Starch granules are separated in two ways:

a. Mixing the starch with fat.

This is the principle of the *roux,* which we discuss now, and of *beurre manié,* which we will see in the next section.

b. Mixing the starch with a cold liquid.

This is the principle used for other starches, such as cornstarch. It can also be used with flour, but as we will learn later, it makes an inferior sauce. A mixture of raw starch and cold liquid is called a *slurry.*

Roux Ingredients

Roux (pronounced roo) is a *cooked* mixture of *equal parts by weight* of fat and flour.

Fat

The cooking fats employed for making roux are as follows:

Clarified butter is preferred for the finest sauces because of its flavor. The butter is clarified (p. 147) because the moisture content of whole butter tends to gelatinize some of the starch and make the roux hard to work.

Margarine is widely used in place of butter because of its lower cost. However, its flavor is inferior to butter and does not make as fine a sauce. The quality of margarine varies from brand to brand.

Animal fats, such as chicken fat, beef drippings, and lard, are used when their flavor is appropriate to the sauce. Thus, chicken fat can be used for chicken velouté, and beef drippings can be used for beef gravy. When properly used, animal fats can enhance the flavor of a sauce.

Vegetable oil and *shortening* can be used for roux but since they add no flavor, they are not preferred. Solid shortening also has the disadvantage of having a high melting point, which gives it an unpleasant "fuzzy" feeling in the mouth. It is best reserved for the bakeshop and the fry kettle.

Today roux-thickened sauces are often condemned for health reasons because of the fat content of the roux. It should be remembered, however, that when a roux-bound velouté or brown sauce is properly made, most of the fat is released and skimmed off before the sauce is served.

Flour

The thickening power of flour depends in part on its starch content. Bread flour has less starch and more protein than cake flour. Eight ounces of cake flour have the same thickening power as 10 ounces of bread flour.

Bread flour frequently is used for general cooking purposes in commercial kitchens, and most sauce recipes in this book, as well as in other books, are based on bread flour or on all-purpose flour, which has similar thickening power. Proportions of roux to liquid must be adjusted if another flour is used.

Flour is sometimes browned dry in the oven for use in brown roux. A heavily browned flour has only one-third the thickening power of unbrowned flour.

In addition to starch, wheat flour also contains proteins and other components. As a roux-thickened sauce is simmered, these components rise to the surface as scum. They can then be skimmed off. Sauces are generally simmered for a time even after the starch is completely gelatinized, so that these "impurities" can be cooked off. This improves the texture, gloss, and clarity of a sauce.

Ingredient Proportions

Correct amounts of fat and flour—*equal parts by weight*—are important to a good roux. There must be enough fat to coat all the starch granules, but not too much. In fact, Escoffier called for even less fat than our standard proportions (8 oz fat to 9 oz flour).

A good roux should be stiff, not runny or pourable. A roux with too much fat is called a slack roux. Using excess fat not only increases the cost of the roux unnecessarily, but the excess fat rises to the top of the sauce, where it either is skimmed off or makes the sauce look "greasy."

Preparing Roux

A roux must be cooked so that the finished sauce does not have the raw, starchy taste of the flour. There are three kinds of roux, depending on how much they are cooked.

White roux is cooked for just a few minutes, just enough to cook out the raw taste. Cooking is stopped as soon as the roux has a frothy, chalky, slightly gritty appearance, before it has begun to color. White roux is used for Béchamel and other white sauces based on milk.

Blond roux, or pale roux, is cooked a little longer, just until the roux begins to change to a slightly darker color. Cooking must then be stopped. Blond roux is used for veloutés, sauces based on white stocks. The sauces have a pale ivory color.

Brown roux is cooked until it takes on a light brown color and a nutty aroma. Cooking must take place over low heat so that the roux browns evenly without scorching. For a deeper brown roux, the flour may be browned in an oven before adding to the fat. A heavily browned roux has only about one-third the thickening power of white roux, but contributes flavor and color to brown sauces.

Basic Procedure for Making All Roux

1. Melt fat.

2. Add correct amount of flour and stir until fat and flour are thoroughly mixed.

3. Cook to required degree for white, blond, or brown roux.

    Cooking is done in a saucepan on top of the stove, and the roux is stirred for even cooking. Use low heat for brown roux, moderate heat for white or blond roux. Large quantities may be baked in an oven. Some restaurants make up batches large enough to last for several days or a week.

Incorporating the Roux

Combining the roux and liquid to obtain a smooth, lump-free sauce is a skill that takes practice to master. It's a good idea to practice the various techniques with water, under the guidance of your instructor, so that you have a good idea of what you are doing before you start working with valuable stocks.

General Principles

Liquid may be added to roux, or roux may be added to liquid.

The liquid may be hot or cooled, but not ice cold. A very cold liquid will solidify the fat in the roux.

The roux may be warm or cold, but not sizzling hot. Adding a hot liquid to a very hot roux causes spattering and possibly lumps.

Within these general guidelines, there is room for a number of variations. Two of them are described here. Since successful use of roux is largely a matter of experience, you are advised to profit from your instructors' experience when they demonstrate these techniques or whichever methods they prefer.

Equipment note: Stainless steel pans are best for white sauces. Whipping in an aluminum pan makes the sauce grey.

Procedures

Method 1:   Adding Liquid to Roux

This method is used when a roux is made up specifically for the one sauce, gravy, or soup being prepared.

1. Use a heavy sauce pot to prevent scorching either the roux or the sauce.

2. When the roux is made, remove the pan from the fire for a few minutes to cool slightly.

3. Slowly pour in the liquid, all the while beating vigorously with a wire whip to prevent lumps from forming.

    If the liquid is hot (such as simmering milk for Béchamel sauce), you will have to beat especially well, because the starch will gelatinize quickly.

    If the liquid is cool, you can add a quantity of it, beat to dissolve the roux, then add the remainder of the liquid, hot or cool.

4. Bring the liquid to a boil, continuing to beat well. The roux does not reach its full thickening power until near the boiling point.

5. Simmer the sauce, stirring from time to time, until all the starchy taste of the flour has been cooked out.

    This will take at least 10 minutes, but the flavor and consistency of the sauce will improve if it is cooked longer. Many chefs feel that 20 minutes of simmering is a bare minimum. Others cook some sauces for an hour or longer.

6. When the sauce is finished, it may be kept hot in a bain marie or cooled for later use. Either way, it should be covered or should have a thin film of butter melted onto the top to prevent a skin from forming.

Roux Proportions in Sauces

Sauce	Butter	Flour	Roux	Liquid
Thin or light	6 oz/190 g	6 oz/190 g	12 oz/375 g	1 gal/4 L
Medium	8 oz/250 g	8 oz/250 g	1 lb/500 g	1 gal/4 L
Thick or heavy	12 oz/375 g	12 oz/375 g	1½ lb/750 g	1 gal/4 L

Method 2:   Adding the Roux to the Liquid

Many restaurants make up large batches of roux to last all day or even all week. This method may be used in these situations.

1.   Bring the liquid to a simmer in a heavy pot.

2.   Add a small quantity of roux and beat vigorously with a whip to break up all lumps.

3.   Continue to beat small quantities into the simmering liquid until the desired consistency is reached. Remember that roux must simmer for a time to thicken completely, so do not add roux too quickly or you will risk overthickening the sauce.

4.   Continue to simmer until the roux is cooked out and no starchy taste remains.

5.   If the sauce is to simmer a long time, underthicken it, because it will thicken as it reduces.

Proportions of Roux to Liquid

The table above indicates the quantities of roux needed to thicken 1 gallon or 4 liters of liquid to thin, medium, and thick consistencies.

How thick is a thick sauce? Obviously, these are not precise, scientific terms that can be defined easily. Experience can be the only teacher in this case. This is another good reason to practice with roux and water, so that you can, with experience, produce the exact consistency you want.

You also have available the techniques of dilution and reduction to adjust the consistency of a sauce (see p. 134), and you will learn how to use *beurre manié* and other thickening agents.

OTHER THICKENING AGENTS

Starches

1.   *Beurre manié* (pronounced burr mahnyay) is a mixture of equal parts soft, raw butter and flour worked together to form a smooth paste. It is used for quick thickening at the end of cooking, to finish a sauce. The raw butter adds flavor and gives a sheen to the sauce when it melts.

To use, drop very small pieces into a simmering sauce and stir with a whip until smooth. Repeat until desired consistency is reached. Simmer just a few minutes more to cook the flour and remove from the fire.

2.   *Whitewash* is a thin mixture of flour and cold water. Sauces made with whitewash have neither as good a flavor nor as fine a texture as those made with roux. *Whitewash is not recommended for use.*

3.   *Cornstarch* produces a sauce that is almost clear, with a glossy texture.

To use, mix with cold water or other cold liquid until smooth. Stir into the hot liquid. Bring to a boil and simmer until the liquid turns clear and there is no starchy taste. Do not boil for a long period or the starch may break down and the liquid will thin out. Sauces thickened with cornstarch may thin out if held on the steam table for long periods. Cornstarch is used extensively in sweet sauces to accompany certain meats, as well as in desserts and dessert sauces. It has roughly twice the thickening power of flour.

4.   *Arrowroot* is used like cornstarch, but it gives an even clearer sauce. Its use is limited by its high cost.

5.   *Waxy maize* is used for sauces that are to be frozen. Flour and other starches break down and lose their thickening power when frozen. Waxy maize does not. It is handled like cornstarch.

6.   *Pregelatinized or instant starches* have been cooked, or gelatinized, then redried. Thus, they will thicken a cold liquid without heating. These starches are rarely used in sauce making but frequently used in the bakeshop.

7.   *Bread crumbs* and other crumbs will thicken a liquid very quickly because they have already been

cooked, like instant starches. Bread crumbs may be used when smoothness of texture is not desired. A common example is the use of gingersnap crumbs to thicken sauerbraten gravy.

Egg Yolk and Cream Liaison

Egg yolks have the power to thicken a sauce slightly due to coagulation of egg proteins when heated.

Caution must be used when thickening with egg yolks because of the danger of curdling. This happens when the proteins coagulate too much and separate from the liquid.

Pure egg yolks coagulate at about 140°F to 158°F (60°C to 70°C). For this reason, they are beaten with heavy cream before use. This raises their curdling temperature to 180°F to 185°F (82°C to 85°C). (Note that this is still well below the boiling point.) The heavy cream also adds thickness and flavor to the sauce.

Egg yolks have only a slight thickening power. The liaison is used primarily to give richness of flavor and smoothness of texture to a sauce and only secondarily to give a slight thickening. Also, because of the instability of the egg yolks, it is used only as a finishing technique.

Procedure for Using a Liaison

1. Beat together the egg yolks and cream in a stainless steel bowl. Normal proportions are 2 to 3 parts cream to 1 part egg yolks.

2. Very slowly add a little of the hot liquid to the liaison, beating constantly. This is known as *tempering.*

3. Off the heat, add the warmed, diluted liaison to the rest of the sauce, stirring well as you pour it in.

4. Return the sauce to low heat to warm it gently, but do not heat it higher than 180°F (82°C) or it will curdle. In no circumstances should it boil.

5. Hold for service above 140°F (69°C) for sanitation reasons, but lower than 180°F (82°C).

Egg Yolk Emulsification

Egg yolks are also used as the thickening agent for Hollandaise and related sauces, but in this case the principle is entirely different. The entire procedure will be discussed in detail when we get to the Hollandaise family of sauces, page 149.

FINISHING TECHNIQUES

Remember that the three basic elements of a finished sauce are a liquid, a thickening agent, and additional seasoning and flavoring ingredients. We have discussed in detail how liquids are combined with thickening agents to make the basic sauces. In the next part we will look at the way families of sauces are built upon these bases by the addition of flavoring ingredients.

There are a great many ways of modifying or adding to a sauce. Among these methods are a number of basic techniques that are used over and over again for making sauces. Before we study the structure of the sauce families, it will be helpful to look at these basic finishing techniques.

Reduction

1. *Using reduction to concentrate basic flavors.*

   If we simmer a sauce for a long time, some of the water is evaporated. The sauce becomes more concentrated, and the resulting product is more flavorful. This is the same technique used when making glazes from stocks. Some reduction takes place in nearly all sauces, depending on how long they are simmered.

2. *Using reduction to adjust textures.*

   Concentrating a sauce by reduction also thickens it, because only the water evaporates, not the roux or other solids. A skilled sauce chef uses both reduction and dilution to give a sauce the precise texture being sought. If a sauce is too thin, it may be simmered until it reaches desired thickness. Or the chef may add a large quantity of stock or other liquid to a thickened sauce to thin it out greatly, and then simmer it again until it is reduced to just the right consistency. By doing this, the chef has also given more flavor to the sauce.

3. *Using reduction to add new flavors.*

   If we can add a liquid to a sauce and then reduce it to concentrate it, why can't we reduce a liquid first and then add it to a sauce?

   In fact, this is one of the most important techniques in sauce making. We have already mentioned that glazes—reduced stocks—are used to flavor sauces. Reductions of other liquids, especially red and white wines, are used a great deal in this way.

   Skip ahead to the recipe for Bordelaise Sauce, page 144. Note how the red wine is cooked down with shallots, pepper, and herbs to one-fourth its original volume. Not only is the flavor of the wine concentrated, but it also extracts flavor from the other spices. This reduction is a very powerful flavoring agent that gives Bordelaise Sauce its distinctive taste. Reduction allows you to add a great deal of flavor to a sauce without adding much liquid.

Terminology

To reduce by one-half means to cook away one-half of the volume, so that half is left.

To reduce by three-fourths means to cook away three-fourths of the volume, so that only one-fourth is left.

To reduce au sec (pronounced oh seck) means to reduce until dry or nearly dry.

Straining

If you have learned how to use a roux properly, you should be able to make a smooth, lump-free sauce. However, to bring a sauce's texture to perfection, to create the velvety smoothness that is important to a good sauce, straining is necessary. Even a slight graininess that you can't see, you can still feel on your tongue.

Straining through a china cap lined with several layers of cheesecloth is effective. Very fine sieves are also available for straining sauces. Straining is usually done before final seasoning.

Deglazing

To *deglaze* means to swirl a liquid in a sauté pan or other pan to dissolve cooked particles of food remaining on the bottom.

This term was discussed in relation to the basic technique of sautéeing in Chapter 4, and again in connection with the production of brown stock. It is also an important technique for finishing sauces that accompany sautéed items.

A liquid such as wine or stock is used to deglaze a sauté pan and then reduced by one-half or three-fourths. This reduction, with the added flavor of the pan drippings, is then added to the sauce that is served with the item.

Enriching with Butter and Cream

1. *Liaison.*

   In addition to being a thickening agent, the liaison of egg yolks and cream is used to finish a sauce by giving it extra richness and smoothness.

2. *Heavy cream.*

   Heavy cream has long been used to give flavor and richness to sauces. The most obvious example is adding cream to basic Béchamel Sauce to make Cream Sauce.

3. *Butter.*

   A useful enriching technique, both in classical and in modern cooking, is called finishing with butter, or *monter au beurre* (pronounced mohn tay oh burr).

   To finish a sauce with butter, simply add a few pieces of softened butter to the hot sauce and swirl it in until it melts. The sauce should then be served immediately; if it is allowed to stand, the butter may separate out.

   Finishing a sauce with butter gives it a little extra shine and smoothness, as well as adding to it the rich, fresh taste of raw butter.

Seasoning

Whether or not a sauce is to be given a final enrichment of liaison, cream, or butter, it must be checked carefully for seasonings before serving. Remember that the last step in any recipe, whether written or not, is "adjust the seasonings."

1. *Salt* is the most important seasoning for sauces. *Lemon juice* is also very important. These two seasonings emphasize the flavors that are already there by stimulating the taste buds. *Cayenne* and *white pepper* are perhaps third and fourth in importance.

2. *Sherry* and *Madeira* are frequently used as final flavorings. These wines are added at the end of cooking (unlike red and white table wines, which must be cooked in a sauce) because their flavors are easily evaporated by heat.

SAUCE FAMILIES

Leading Sauces

One more time, let's look at the three basic building blocks of sauce cookery, this time from a slightly different angle.

Liquid + thickening agent = Leading Sauce

Leading Sauce + additional flavorings = Small Sauce

We have talked about five basic liquids for sauces: milk, white stock, brown stock, tomato purée (plus stock), and clarified butter. From these we get our

CHART 8.1 **The Leading Sauces**

Liquid	Thickening Agent	Leading Sauce
Milk	+ White roux	= Béchamel Sauce
White stock (veal, chicken, fish)	+ White or blond roux	= Velouté (veal velouté, chicken velouté, fish velouté)
Brown stock	+ Brown roux	= Brown Sauce or Espagnole
Tomato plus stock	+ (Optional roux)	= Tomato Sauce
Butter	+ Egg yolks	= Hollandaise

Note: Roux is not used in all tomato sauces, since tomato purée is naturally thick.

five Leading Sauces, also known as Mother Sauces, as shown in Chart 8.1.

To these five sauces, we add one more: *Fond Lié* (pronounced fone lee ay), meaning "thickened stock." It is sometimes used in place of Espagnole.

Brown stock + cornstarch = Fond Lié

You should understand that these charts are a bit oversimplified. Most of these sauces have a few other ingredients for flavoring. Yet knowing this basic structure is the key to making sauces.

Small Sauces

The major Leading Sauces—Béchamel; Veal, Chicken, and Fish Veloutés; and Espagnole—are rarely used by themselves as sauces. They are more important as the bases for other sauces, called Small Sauces. Tomato Sauce and Hollandaise are used as they are, but they, too, are important as bases for Small Sauces.

Let's expand our sauce family chart one more generation to include some examples of the Small Sauces, to show the relationships (see Chart 8.2).

Chart 8.2 is probably a little more complicated than you had expected, because of the extra arrows and the extra category of Secondary Leading Sauces. These are relatively easy to explain.

1. *Secondary Leading White Sauces.*

   These three sauces—Allemande, Suprême, and White Wine—are really finished sauces, like other Small Sauces. But they are used so often to build other Small Sauces that they rate a special category.

   For example, to make Suprême Sauce, you add cream to Chicken Velouté.

   To make Albufera Sauce, you can add meat glaze (glace de viande) to your Suprême Sauce.

Or, if you don't have Suprême Sauce, you can make it by adding both cream and meat glaze to Chicken Velouté. This is why there are two sets of arrows in the chart.

Allemande, Suprême, and White Wine sauces are also known as the *Main Small Sauces*. If the concept of Secondary Leading White Sauces seems too confusing at first, you may simply think of them as small sauces. The important thing is to understand how the sauces are derived.

2. *Demiglaze.*

   a. Demiglaze is defined as half brown sauce plus half brown stock, reduced by half. (In French it is know as *demi-glace*, pronounced dem me glahss.) Most chefs prefer Demiglaze to Espagnole as a base for Small Sauces because of its more concentrated, more fully developed flavor.

      It is possible to make Small Sauces directly from Espagnole, but they will not be as fine.

   b. Some modern chefs feel that Espagnole is too heavy for modern tastes and that lighter sauces are required. These chefs prepare Demiglaze from Fond Lié, by reducing it with mirepoix, white wine, and seasonings, or by simply reducing by half a very flavorful brown stock.

      In other words, Demiglaze may be considered to be a well-flavored brown stock, reduced by half ("demi" means "half"), thickened with roux or cornstarch or left unthickened (except by natural gelatin).

3. *Small Sauces listed twice.*

   Notice, for example, that Mushroom Sauce is listed under both Chicken Velouté and Fish

CHART 8.2   **The Small Sauces**

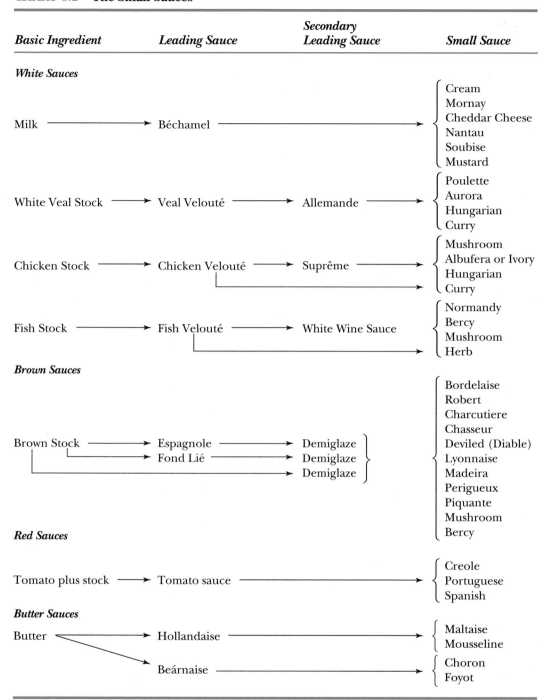

Basic Ingredient	Leading Sauce	Secondary Leading Sauce	Small Sauce
White Sauces			
Milk	Béchamel		Cream Mornay Cheddar Cheese Nantau Soubise Mustard
White Veal Stock	Veal Velouté	Allemande	Poulette Aurora Hungarian Curry
Chicken Stock	Chicken Velouté	Suprême	Mushroom Albufera or Ivory Hungarian Curry
Fish Stock	Fish Velouté	White Wine Sauce	Normandy Bercy Mushroom Herb
Brown Sauces			
Brown Stock	Espagnole Fond Lié	Demiglaze Demiglaze Demiglaze	Bordelaise Robert Charcutiere Chasseur Deviled (Diable) Lyonnaise Madeira Perigueux Piquante Mushroom Bercy
Red Sauces			
Tomato plus stock	Tomato sauce		Creole Portuguese Spanish
Butter Sauces			
Butter	Hollandaise		Maltaise Mousseline
	Beárnaise		Choron Foyot

Velouté. This means that you should use the stock of the product you are serving with the sauce. Mushroom Sauce for chicken should be made out of Chicken Velouté, for fish, out of Fish Velouté. To be even more confusing, there is a Mushroom Sauce made with Brown Sauce. There are also both a white and a brown Bercy

sauce. These are considered unrelated sauces that happen to have the same name.

4. ***Hollandaise and Béarnaise.***

These are essentially two variations of the same kind of sauce, with different flavorings. Each has its own small family of Small Sauces.

Standards of Quality for Sauces

1. **Consistency and body.**

   Smooth, with no lumps.

   Not too thick or pasty, but thick enough to coat the food lightly.

2. **Flavor.**

   Distinctive but well-balanced flavor.

   Proper degree of seasoning.

   No starchy taste.

   The flavor should be selected to enhance or complement the food (such as Suprême Sauce with chicken or White Wine Sauce with fish) or to provide a pleasing contrast (such as a Béarnaise Sauce with grilled beef or Raisin Sauce with ham).

3. **Appearance.**

   Smooth, with a good shine.

   Good color for its type (rich, deep brown for brown sauce, pale ivory for velouté, white—not grey—for cream sauce).

Other Sauces

As usual, not everything fits into one package. In addition to the five major sauce families, there are a number of other preparations that don't follow these basic patterns. We will encounter these later in the chapter.

These other preparations include these groups:

1. *Simple and compound butters,* including simple browned butter as well as butter combined with different flavorings.

2. *Pan gravies,* or sauces made with the pan drippings of the meat or poultry they are served with.

3. *Miscellaneous hot sauces,* which are not made like any of the five basic sauces. These include such things as Raisin Sauce (for ham) and Sour Cream Sauce.

4. *Miscellaneous cold sauces* include not only sauces for meats, like Cumberland Sauce and Horseradish Sauce, but also Vinaigrettes, Mayonnaise, and their variations, covered in Chapter 19.

PRODUCTION

Béchamel

The classic version of the standard white sauce, Béchamel, was made with lean veal and herbs and spices simmered with the sauce for an hour or with white veal stock added to the sauce and then reduced. This is rarely done today.

Nevertheless, the plain Béchamel used today—simply milk and roux—can be improved by simmering the sauce with onion and spices. These may be omitted, of course, but the sauce will have less flavor.

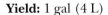

RECIPE 4 **Béchamel Sauce**

Yield: 1 gal (4 L)

U.S.	Metric	Ingredients	Procedure
		Roux:	1. Review instructions for making and incorporating roux (pp. 132–133).
8 oz	250 g	Clarified butter	
8 oz	250 g	Bread flour	2. Heat the butter in a heavy sauce pot over low heat. Add the flour and make a white roux. Cool the roux slightly.
1 gal	4 L	Milk	
1	1	Small whole onion, peeled	
1	1	Whole clove	3. In another saucepan, scald the milk. Gradually add it to the roux, beating constantly.
1	1	Bay leaf, small	
		Salt	4. Bring the sauce to a boil, stirring constantly. Reduce heat to a simmer.
		Nutmeg	
		White pepper	

RECIPE 4   **Béchamel Sauce** *(Continued)*

U.S.	Metric	Ingredients	Procedure
			5. Stick the bay leaf to the onion with the clove and add to the sauce. Simmer at least 15 minutes, or if possible, for 30 minutes or more. Stir occasionally while cooking.
			6. Adjust the consistency with more hot milk, if necessary.
			7. Season *very lightly* with salt, nutmeg, and white pepper. Spice flavors should not dominate.
			8. Strain the sauce through a china cap lined with cheesecloth. Cover or spread melted butter on surface to prevent skin formation. Keep hot in a bain marie, or cool in cold-water bath for later use.

Variations

Light Béchamel: Use 12 oz (375 g) roux.

Heavy Béchamel: Use 1½ lb (750 g) roux.

Small Sauces

For each of the following sauces, add the ingredients indicated to *1 qt (1 L) Béchamel Sauce.* Season to taste.

4A. Cream Sauce: 4 to 8 oz (125 to 250 mL) heavy cream, heated or tempered.

4B. Mornay Sauce: 4 oz (125 g) grated Gruyère cheese and 2 oz (60 g) Parmesan, stirred in until just melted. Finish, off heat, with 2 oz (60 g) raw butter. Thin out with a little hot milk, if necessary, or use a stock or broth appropriate for the dish being prepared.

   Mornay Sauce for Glazing or Gratinéeing: Finish Mornay Sauce with liaison of 2 egg yolks and 2 oz (60 mL) heavy cream.

4C. Cheddar Cheese Sauce: 8 oz (250 g) cheddar cheese, ½ tsp (2 mL) dry mustard, 2 tsp (10 mL) Worcestershire Sauce.

4D. Mustard Sauce: 4 oz (125 g) prepared mustard.

4E. Soubise Sauce: 1 lb (500 g) onions, finely diced, cooked slowly in 2 oz (60 g) butter without browning. Simmer with sauce 15 minutes, and force through a fine sieve.

4F. Tomatoed Soubise Sauce: Add 1 pt (500 mL) thick tomato purée to 1 qt (1 L) Soubise Sauce.

4G. Nantua Sauce: 6 oz (175 g) shrimp butter (p. 148), 4 oz (125 mL) heavy cream.

(**Note:** Classic Nantua Sauce is made with crayfish, not readily available in all parts of the United States.)

Velouté

The three velouté sauces are the bases of many variations. Instructions for the Small Sauces indicate which of the three to use. If more than one are given, the choice depends on what you are serving it with.

Note: In the United States, Chicken Velouté is used much more often than Veal Velouté. Many of the sauces at one time made with veal stock are now made with chicken stock.

RECIPE 5   Velouté Sauce (Veal, Chicken, or Fish)

Yield: 1 gal (4 L)

U.S.	Metric	Ingredients	Procedure
		Roux:	1. Review instructions for making and incorporating roux (pp. 132–133).
8 oz	250 g	Clarified butter	
8 oz	250 g	Bread flour	2. Heat the butter in a heavy sauce pot over low heat. Add the flour and make a blond roux. Cool the roux slightly.
5 qt	5 L	White stock, hot (veal, chicken, or fish)	
			3. Gradually add the hot stock to the roux, beating constantly. Bring to a boil, stirring constantly. Reduce heat to a simmer.
			4. Simmer the sauce very slowly for an hour. Stir occasionally, and skim the surface when necessary. Add more stock if needed to adjust consistency.
			5. Do not season velouté, since it is not used as is but as an ingredient in other preparations.
			6. Strain through a china cap lined with cheesecloth. Cover or spread melted butter on surface to prevent skin formation. Keep hot in a bain marie, or cool in a cold-water bath for later use.

RECIPE 6   White Wine Sauce

Yield: 1 gal (4 L)

U.S.	Metric	Ingredients	Procedure
1 pt	500 mL	White wine (dry)	1. Reduce the wine by half in a saucepan.
1 gal	4 L	Fish Velouté	2. Add the velouté and simmer until reduced to desired consistency.
1 pt	500 mL	Heavy cream, hot	
4 oz	125 g	Butter	3. Slowly stir in the hot (or tempered) cream.
		Salt	
		White pepper	4. Remove from heat and swirl in the raw butter, cut into pieces.
		Lemon juice	
			5. Season to taste with salt, white pepper, and a few drops of lemon juice.
			6. Strain through cheesecloth.

RECIPE 7   **Suprême Sauce**

Yield: 1 gal (4 L)

U.S.	Metric	Ingredients	Procedure
1 gal	4 L	Chicken Velouté	1. Place the velouté in a saucepan and simmer over moderate heat until reduced by about one-fourth. Stir occasionally.
1 qt	1 L	Heavy cream	
4 oz	125 g	Butter	
		Salt	2. Pour the cream into a stainless steel bowl and temper it by slowly stirring in a little of the hot sauce. Stir this mixture slowly back into the sauce in the pan and return the sauce just to a simmer.
		White pepper	
		Lemon juice	
			3. Swirl in the raw butter, cut into pieces. Season to taste with salt, white pepper, and a few drops of lemon juice.
			4. Strain through cheesecloth.

RECIPE 8   **Allemande Sauce**

Yield: 1 gal (4 L)

U.S.	Metric	Ingredients	Procedure
1 gal	4 L	Veal Velouté (see note)	1. Review instructions for incorporating liaison (p. 134).
		Liaison:	
8	8	Egg yolks	2. Place the velouté in a saucepan and simmer a few minutes over moderate heat until slightly reduced.
1 pt	500 mL	Heavy cream	
1 oz	30 mL	Lemon juice	3. Beat the egg yolks and cream together in a stainless steel bowl.
		Salt	
		White pepper	4. Temper the liaison by *slowly* beating in about one-third of the hot sauce. Then slowly stir this mixture back into the sauce in the pan.
			5. Reheat to just below simmering. Do not boil.
			6. Add lemon juice, salt, and white pepper to taste and strain through cheesecloth.

Note: Allemande Sauce, strictly speaking, should be made with Veal Velouté. However, since Chicken Velouté is much more common in the United States, Allemande Sauce and the small sauces derived from it are often made with Chicken Velouté.

Small Sauces

For each of the following sauces, add the listed ingredients to 1 qt (1 L) *Veal, Chicken,* or *Fish Velouté, Suprême Sauce, Allemande Sauce,* or *White Wine Sauce* as indicated. Season the sauce to taste.

9A. *Poulette:* Simmer 8 oz (250 g) *white* mushrooms or mushroom trimmings with velouté when making *Allemande.* Make Allemande, strain. Finish with 2 tbsp (30 mL) chopped parsley and lemon juice to taste.

9B. *Aurora:* Add 6 oz (175 g) tomato purée to 1 qt (1 L) *Veal* or *Chicken Velouté, Suprême Sauce,* or *Allemande Sauce.*

9C. *Hungarian:* Sweat 2 oz (60 g) minced onion and 1 tbsp (15 mL) paprika in 1 oz (25 g) butter until soft. Add ½ cup (100 mL) white wine and reduce by half. Add 1 qt (1 L) *Veal* or *Chicken Velouté,* simmer 10 minutes, and strain.

9D. *Ivory or Albufera:* Add 2 oz (60 g) meat glaze (glace de viande) to 1 qt (1 L) *Suprême Sauce.*

9E. *Curry:* Cook 4 oz (125 g) mirepoix, cut brunoise, in 1 oz (25 g) butter until tender but not brown. Add 1 tbsp (15 mL) curry powder, 1 crushed garlic clove, pinch of thyme, ½ bay leaf, 2 to 4 parsley stems and cook another minute. Add 1 qt (1 L) *Veal, Chicken,* or *Fish Velouté.* Simmer 20 minutes, add ½ cup (125 mL) cream, strain, and season with salt and lemon juice.

9F. *Mushroom:* Sauté 4 oz (125 g) sliced mushrooms in 1 oz (25 g) butter, adding 1 tbsp (15 mL) lemon juice to keep them white. Add to *Suprême, Allemande,* or *White Wine Sauce* or to appropriate velouté.

9G. *Bercy:* Reduce by two-thirds: 2 oz (60 g) chopped shallots and ½ cup (125 mL) white wine. Add 1 qt (1 L) *Fish Velouté,* reduce slightly, and finish with 2 oz (60 g) raw butter, 2 tbsp (30 mL) chopped parsley, and lemon juice to taste.

9H. *Herb:* To *White Wine Sauce* add chopped parsley, chives, and tarragon to taste.

9I. *Normandy:* To 1 qt (1 L) *Fish Velouté,* add 4 oz (125 mL) mushroom cooking liquid (or 4 oz/125 g mushroom trimmings) and 4 oz (125 mL) oyster liquid or fish fumet. Reduce by one-third. Finish with a liaison of 4 egg yolks and 1 cup (250 mL) cream. Strain and swirl in 3 oz (75 g) raw butter.

9J. *Anchovy:* Follow the instructions for Normandy Sauce, but in place of the raw butter used to finish the sauce, substitute 6 oz (175 g) Anchovy Butter.

9K. *Shrimp:* To 1 qt (1 L) *White Wine Sauce,* add 4 oz (125 g) shrimp butter and a dash of cayenne. If desired, garnish with 4 oz (125 g) diced, cooked shrimp.

9L. *Venetian:* Combine ½ cup (125 mL) each of white wine and tarragon vinegar, ½ oz (15 g) chopped shallots, and 2 tsp (10 mL) chervil. Reduce by two-thirds. Add 1 qt (1 L) *White Wine Sauce* and simmer 2–3 minutes. Strain. Add tarragon to taste.

9M. *Horseradish:* Add 2 oz (60 g) drained horseradish, ½ cup (125 mL) heavy cream and 2 tsp (10 mL) dry mustard dissolved in 1 oz (30 mL) vinegar to 1 qt (1 L) *Velouté* made with beef or veal stock or broth from Boiled Beef (p. 254).

Espagnole or Brown Sauce

As one glance at the procedure for making Espagnole will tell you, this sauce is more complicated than Béchamel or Velouté. Because it is the starting point for the hearty, flavorful sauces that accompany red meats, it is necessary to give it extra flavor and richness with mirepoix. Some chefs even add more browned bones and cook the sauce as long as a stock.

Note how the roux is made in the following recipe. Though there is mirepoix cooking in the fat, the basic principle is the same as when you make a simple roux in a separate pot.

RECIPE 10 **Brown Sauce or Espagnole**

Yield: 1 gal (4 L)

U.S.	Metric	Ingredients	Procedure
		Mirepoix:	1. Sauté the mirepoix in the butter until well browned.
1 lb	500 g	Onions, medium dice	
8 oz	250 g	Carrots, medium dice	2. Add the flour and stir to make the roux. Continue to cook until the roux is browned.
8 oz	250 g	Celery, medium dice	
8 oz	250 g	Butter	
8 oz	250 g	Bread flour	3. Gradually stir in the brown stock and tomato purée, stirring constantly until the mixture comes to a boil.
6 qt	6 L	Brown stock	
8 oz	250 g	Tomato purée	
		Sachet:	4. Reduce heat to simmer and skim the surface. Add the sachet and let simmer for about 2 hours, until the sauce is reduced to 1 gal (4 L). Skim as often as necessary.
½	½	Bay leaf	
¼ tsp	1 mL	Thyme	
6–8	6–8	Parsley stems	
			5. Strain through a china cap lined with several layers of cheesecloth. Press on the mirepoix gently to extract their juices.
			6. Cover or spread melted butter on surface to prevent skin formation. Keep hot in a bain marie, or cool in a cold-water bath for later use.

RECIPE 11 **Fond Lié or Jus Lié**

Yield: 1 qt (1 L)

U.S.	Metric	Ingredients	Procedure
1 qt	1 L	Brown stock	1. Bring the stock to a boil in a saucepan. Reduce heat to a simmer.
1 oz	30 g	Cornstarch or arrowroot	
			2. Dissolve the starch in a small amount of cold stock or water. Stir it into the simmering stock.
			3. Simmer until thickened and clear.

Variation

For added flavor, the stock sometimes is reduced with browned mirepoix and tomato (as for Espagnole) before being thickened. Browned bones may also be added.

RECIPE 12 **Demiglaze**

Yield: 1 gal (4 L)

U.S.	Metric	Ingredients	Procedure
1 gal	4 L	Brown Sauce	1. Combine the sauce and stock in a saucepan and simmer until reduced by half.
1 gal	4 L	Brown stock	
			2. Strain through a chinois (fine china cap) or a regular china cap lined with cheesecloth. Cover to prevent a skin from forming. Keep hot in a bain marie, or cool in a cold-water bath for later use.

Small Sauces

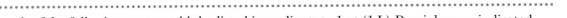

For each of the following sauces, add the listed ingredients to 1 qt (1 L) Demiglaze, as indicated.

12A. **Bordelaise:** Reduce by three-fourths: 1 cup (250 mL) dry red wine, 2 oz (60 g) chopped shallots, ¼ tsp (1 mL) crushed peppercorns, a pinch of thyme, and ½ bay leaf. Add 1 qt (1 L) Demiglaze, simmer 15 to 20 minutes, and strain. Swirl in 2 oz (60 g) raw butter, cut in pieces. Garnish with diced or sliced beef marrow, poached in salted water.

12B. **Marchand de Vin** (Wine Merchant)**:** Reduce 6 oz (200 mL) red wine and 2 oz (60 g) chopped shallots by three-fourths. Add 1 qt (1 L) Demiglaze, simmer, and strain.

12C. **Robert:** Cook 4 oz (125 g) chopped onion in butter without browning. Add 1 cup (250 mL) white wine and reduce by two-thirds. Add 1 qt (1 L) Demiglaze and simmer 10 minutes. Strain and add 2 tsp (10 mL) dry mustard and a pinch of sugar dissolved in a little lemon juice.

12D. **Charcutière:** Garnish Robert Sauce with sour pickles, cut julienne.

12E. **Chasseur:** Sauté 6 oz (175 g) sliced mushrooms and 2 oz (60 g) minced shallots in 2 oz (60 g) butter. Add 1 cup (250 mL) white wine and reduce by three-fourths. Add 1 qt (1 L) Demiglaze and 8 oz (250 g) diced tomato. Simmer 5 minutes and add 2 tsp (10 mL) chopped parsley.

12F. **Diable (Deviled):** Reduce by two-thirds: 8 oz (250 mL) white wine, 4 oz (125 g) chopped shallots, ½ tsp (2 mL) crushed peppercorns. Add 1 qt (1 L) Demiglaze and simmer 20 minutes. Season with cayenne to taste and strain.

12G. **Madeira:** Reduce 1 qt (1 L) Demiglaze by about ½ cup (100 mL). Add 3 to 4 oz (100 mL) Madeira wine.

12H. **Perigueux:** Garnish Madeira Sauce with finely diced truffle.

12I. **Port Wine:** Follow instructions for Madeira Sauce, but use port wine instead of Madeira.

12J. **Italian Sauce:** Sauté 1 lb (500 g) finely chopped mushrooms and ½ oz (15 g) minced shallots in 2 oz (60 g) butter until all moisture is evaporated. Add 1 cup (250 mL) white wine and reduce by half. Add 1 oz (30 g) tomato paste and 1 qt (1 L) Demiglaze and simmer 10 minutes. Add 2 tbsp (30 mL) chopped parsley.

12K. **Mushroom:** Sauté 8 oz (250 g) sliced mushrooms and 1 oz (30 g) minced shallots in 2 oz (60 g) butter until browned. Add 1 qt (1 L) Demiglaze and simmer about 10 minutes. Add 2 oz (60 mL) sherry and a few drops of lemon juice.

12L. **Bercy:** Reduce by three-fourths: 1 cup (250 mL) dry white wine and 4 oz (125 g) chopped shallots. Add 1 qt (1 L) Demiglaze and simmer 10 minutes.

Small Sauces *(Continued)*

12M. Piquante: Reduce by two-thirds: 4 oz (125 g) minced shallots, 4 oz (125 mL) wine vinegar, and 4 oz (125 mL) white wine. Add 1 qt (1 L) Demiglaze and simmer until slightly reduced. Add 2 oz (60 g) capers, 2 oz (60 g) sour pickles cut brunoise, 1 tbsp (15 mL) chopped parsley, and ½ tsp (2 mL) tarragon.

12N. Lyonnaise: Sauté 4 oz (125 g) onions in 2 oz (60 g) butter until slightly browned. Add ½ cup (125 mL) white wine vinegar and reduce by half. Add 1 qt (1 L) Demiglaze and simmer 10 minutes.

Tomato Sauce

Two basic tomato sauces are given, one made with roux and one without roux. In addition, a third tomato sauce, much simpler to prepare, is included with the pasta recipes in Chapter 18.

RECIPE 13   **Tomato Sauce I (with Roux)**

Yield: about 1 gal (4 L)

U.S.	Metric	Ingredients	Procedure
4 oz	125 g	Salt pork, diced	1. In a heavy saucepan over medium heat, sauté the salt pork in butter until partially rendered.
2 oz	60 g	Butter	
4 oz	125 g	Onion, med. dice	
2 oz	60 g	Carrots, med. dice	2. Add the onion, carrot, and celery and sauté until they are slightly softened.
2 oz	60 g	Celery, med. dice	
4 oz	125 g	Bread flour	3. Add the flour, stir to make a roux, and cook until the roux is just lightly browned.
1½ qt	1½ L	White stock	
2 qt	2 L	Tomatoes, canned	
2 qt	2 L	Tomato purée, canned	4. Slowly add the stock, while stirring, and bring to a boil. Add the tomatoes and tomato purée and again bring to a boil. Reduce heat to a simmer.
		Sachet:	
1	1	Bay leaf	
2	2	Garlic cloves, crushed	
¼ tsp	1 mL	Thyme	
1	1	Clove	5. Add the sachet. Simmer over very low heat for 1 to 1½ hours, until sauce is reduced to desired consistency.
½ tsp	2 mL	Peppercorns, crushed	
		Salt	
1 tbsp	30 mL	Sugar	6. Remove sachet and strain sauce or pass through a food mill. Season to taste with salt and sugar.

Note: Tomato Sauce scorches easily, so heat must be very low. The sauce may be cooked in a slow oven (300°F/150°C) loosely covered to reduce the danger of scorching.

Variation

13A. Seasoned Tomato Purée: Prepare as in basic recipe, but omit flour, use only 1½ pt (750 mL) stock, and reduce to desired thickness.

RECIPE 14   Tomato Sauce II (without Roux)

Yield: 1 gal (4 L)

U.S.	Metric	Ingredients	Procedure
4 oz	125 g	Bacon	1. Render the bacon in a heavy sauce pot, but do not brown it.
8 oz	250 g	Onion, med. dice	
8 oz	250 g	Carrots, med. dice	2. Add the onion and carrot and sauté until slightly softened, but do not brown.
4 qt	4 L	Tomatoes, canned or fresh, coarsely chopped	
2 qt	2 L	Tomato purée, canned	3. Add the tomatoes and their juice, the tomato purée, bones, and sachet. Bring to a boil, reduce heat, and simmer over very low heat (see note to Tomato Sauce I) for 1½ to 2 hours, until reduced to desired consistency.
1 lb	500 g	Ham bones or browned pork bones	
		Sachet:	
2	2	Garlic cloves, crushed	
1	1	Bay leaf	4. Remove sachet and bones. Strain sauce or pass it through a food mill.
¼ tsp	1 mL	Thyme	
¼ tsp	1 mL	Rosemary	
¼ tsp	1 mL	Peppercorns, crushed	5. Adjust the seasoning with salt and a little sugar.
		Salt	
		Sugar	

Tomato Sauce III

See Tomato Sauce for Pasta, page 461.

Small Sauces

For each of the following sauces, add the listed ingredients to 1 qt (1 L) Tomato Sauce, as indicated.

14A. Portugaise (Portuguese): Sauté 4 oz (125 g) onions, cut brunoise, in 1 oz (30 mL) oil. Add 1 lb (500 g) tomato concassé (see p. 396) and 1 tsp (5 mL) crushed garlic. Simmer until reduced by about one-third. Add 1 qt (1 L) Tomato Sauce I or II, adjust seasonings, and add 2 to 4 tbsp (30 to 60 mL) chopped parsley.

14B. Spanish: Lightly sauté in oil without browning: 6 oz (175 g) onion, small dice; 4 oz (125 g) green pepper, small dice; and 1 clove garlic, chopped fine. Add 4 oz (125 g) sliced mushrooms and sauté. Add 1 qt (1 L) Tomato Sauce II and season to taste with salt, pepper, and hot red pepper sauce.

14C. Creole: Sauté in oil: 4 oz (125 g) onion, small dice; 4 oz (125 g) celery, sliced; 2 oz (60 g) green pepper, small dice; 1 tsp (5 mL) chopped garlic. Add 1 qt (1 L) Tomato Sauce II, 1 bay leaf, pinch of thyme, ½ tsp (2 mL) grated lemon rind. Simmer 15 minutes. Remove bay leaf and season to taste with salt, pepper, and cayenne.

Butter Sauces

The fifth Leading Sauce is Hollandaise. Hollandaise and its cousin Béarnaise are unlike the sauces we have been studying, because their major ingredient is not stock or milk, but butter.

Before tackling the complexities of Hollandaise, we will first look at simpler butter preparations used as sauces.

1. *Melted butter.*

   This is the simplest butter preparation of all, and one of the most widely used, especially as a dressing for vegetables.

   Unsalted or sweet butter has the freshest taste and is ideal for all sauce making.

2. *Clarified butter.*

   Butter consists of butterfat, water, and milk solids. *Clarified butter* is purified butterfat, with water and milk solids removed. It is necessary for many cooking operations. Clarified butter is used in sautéing, because the milk solids of unclarified butter would burn at such high temperatures. It is used in making Hollandaise, because the water of unclarified butter would change the consistency of the sauce.

Procedure for Clarifying Butter

Method 1

1. Melt the butter in a heavy saucepan over moderate heat.

2. Skim the froth from the surface.

3. Carefully pour off the clear melted butter into another container, leaving the milky liquid at the bottom of the saucepan.

Method 2

1. Melt the butter in a heavy saucepan over moderate heat.

2. Skim the froth from the surface.

3. Leave the pan on the heat and continue to skim the froth from the surface at intervals. The water in the bottom will boil and gradually evaporate.

4. When the butter looks clear and no longer forms a scum on top, strain off the butter through a cheesecloth into another container.

   You will need 1¼ lb of raw butter to make 1 lb clarified butter; 1 lb raw butter yields 12 to 13 oz clarified butter.

3. *Brown Butter.*

   Known as Beurre Noisette (nwah zett) in French, this is whole melted butter that has been heated until it turns light brown and gives off a nutty aroma. It is usually prepared at the last minute and served over fish, white meats, eggs, and vegetables.

   Care must be taken not to burn the butter, since the heat of the pan will continue to brown it even after it is removed from the fire.

4. *Black Butter.*

   Black Butter, or Beurre Noir (nwahr), is made like Brown Butter but heated until it is a little darker, and flavored with a few drops of vinegar. Capers, chopped parsley, or both are sometimes added.

   To avoid dangerous spattering of the vinegar in the hot butter, many chefs pour the butter over the food item, then deglaze the pan with the vinegar and pour that over the item.

5. *Meunière Butter.*

   This is served with fish cooked à la Meunière (see p. 359). Brown Butter is seasoned with lemon juice and poured over the fish, which has been sprinkled with chopped parsley.

   As in the case of Black Butter, dangerous spattering can result when moisture is added to hot butter. To avoid this, cooks often sprinkle the lemon juice directly on the fish before pouring on the Brown Butter.

6. *Compound butters.*

   Compound butters are made by softening raw butter and mixing it with various flavoring ingredients. The moisture is then rolled into a cylinder in waxed paper.

   Compound butters have two main uses:

   a. Slices of the firm butter are placed on hot grilled items at service time. The butter melts over the item and sauces it.
   b. Small portions are swirled into sauces to finish them and give them a desired flavor.

   Easy as they are to make, compound butters can transform a plain broiled steak into a truly special dish.

   The favorite compound butter for steaks is Maitre d'Hotel Butter (may truh doh tel). Other variations are given after the recipe.

7. *Beurre Blanc.*

   Beurre Blanc is a sauce made by whipping a large quantity of raw butter into a small quantity of a flavorful reduction of white wine and

RECIPE 15 Maitre d'Hotel Butter

Yield: about 1 lb (500 g)

U.S.	Metric	Ingredients	Procedure
1 lb	500 g	Butter	1. Using a mixer with the paddle attachment, beat the butter at low speed until it is smooth and creamy.
¼ cup	60 mL	Chopped parsley	
1½ oz	50 mL	Lemon juice	
pinch	pinch	White pepper	2. Add the remaining ingredients and beat slowly until completely mixed.
			3. Roll the butter into a cylinder about 1 inch (2½ cm) thick in a sheet of parchment or waxed paper. Chill until firm.
			4. To serve, cut slices ¼ inch (½ cm) thick and place on broiled or grilled items just before service.

Variations

For each kind of seasoned butter, add to 1 lb (500 g) butter the listed ingredients *instead of* the parsley, lemon juice, and pepper.

15A. Anchovy Butter: 2 oz (60 g) anchovy fillets, mashed to a paste.

15B. Garlic Butter: 1 oz (30 g) garlic, mashed to a paste (see p. 393).

15C. Escargot (Snail) Butter: Garlic Butter plus ½ cup (125 mL) chopped parsley, salt, white pepper.

15D. Shrimp Butter: ½ lb (250 g) cooked shrimp and shells, ground very fine. Force shrimp butter through a fine sieve to remove pieces of shell.

15E. Mustard Butter: 3–4 oz (100 g) Dijon-style mustard.

15F. Herb Butter: Chopped fresh herbs to taste.

15G. Scallion or Shallot Butter: 2 oz (60 g) minced scallions or shallots.

15H. Curry Butter: 4–6 tsp (20–30 mL) curry powder heated gently with 1 oz (30 g) butter and then cooled.

RECIPE 16 Beurre Blanc

Yield: 1 qt (1 L)

U.S.	Metric	Ingredients	Procedure
1 pt	500 mL	Dry white wine	1. Combine the wine, vinegar, and shallots in a saucepan. Reduce until there is about 2 oz (60 mL) liquid remaining.
3 oz	100 mL	White wine vinegar	
2 oz	60 g	Shallots, chopped	
2 lb	1 kg	Cold butter	2. Cut the butter into small pieces.
		Salt	3. Add the butter to the hot reduction. Set the pan over moderately high heat and whip vigorously. When the butter is nearly all melted and incorporated, remove from the heat and continue to whip until smooth.
			4. Season to taste. The shallots may be left in the sauce or strained out.
			5. Hold the sauce in a warm, not hot, place until served. Stir or whip it from time to time.

vinegar, so that the butter melts and forms an emulsion with the reduction. The technique is basically the same as *monter au beurre* (p. 135) except that the proportion of butter to liquid is much greater.

Beurre Blanc should be held at a warm, not a hot, temperature and stirred or whipped from time to time so that the fat and water do not separate. For more stable mixtures of fat and water—called emulsions—see the discussion of Hollandaise, below.

Hollandaise and Béarnaise

Hollandaise is considered an egg-thickened sauce, but the egg doesn't thicken by coagulation as it does in a liaison or in a custard sauce. Instead, it works by emulsification.

An *emulsion* is a uniform mixture of two unmixable liquids. In the case of Hollandaise, the two liquids are melted butter and water (including the water in the lemon juice or the vinegar reduction). The two stay mixed and thick because the butter is beaten into tiny droplets and the egg yolks hold the droplets apart. You will encounter emulsion again when you prepare mayonnaise and other salad dressings in Chapter 14.

Two recipes for Hollandaise are given. The first is the classic version, flavored with lemon and with a reduction of vinegar, shallots, and pepper. The second, flavored with just lemon juice, is used more often today because it is quicker and easier.

Guidelines for Preparing Hollandaise and Béarnaise

Students tend to be afraid of Hollandaise because it has a reputation for being difficult to make. True, some precautions are necessary to avoid overcooking the eggs and for getting the right consistency. But if you follow the instructions in the recipe carefully and keep in mind these guidelines, you should have no trouble.

Many of these rules have one object in common: Don't overcook the egg yolks, or they will lose their ability to emulsify.

1. *Cool the reduction before adding the yolks, or they will overcook.*

2. *Use the freshest eggs possible for the best emulsification.*

3. *Beat the yolks over hot water.*

   An experienced cook is able to beat them over direct heat, if care is taken, without making scrambled eggs. Until you have gained some confidence, it is safer to use a hot water bain marie, even though it is slower.

4. *Use a round-bottomed stainless steel bowl.*

   The whip must be able to reach all the eggs to beat them evenly. Also, stainless steel will not discolor the sauce or give it a metallic flavor.

5. *Have the butter warm but not hot, or it may overcook the eggs. If it is too cool, it might solidify.*

6. *Add the butter slowly at first.*

   The yolks can only absorb a little at a time. Add a few drops at first and beat in thoroughly before adding more. If you add butter faster than it can be absorbed, the emulsion may break.

7. *Don't add more butter than the egg yolks can hold.*

   Remember this standard proportion:

   6 egg yolks per pound (450 g) of clarified butter

8. *Broken or curdled Hollandaise can be rescued.*

   First try adding a teaspoon of cold water and beating vigorously. If this doesn't work, start over with a couple of egg yolks and repeat the procedure from step 6 in the recipe, adding the broken sauce as you would the butter.

Holding Hollandaise Sauce

Hollandaise Sauce, as well as other sauces in this family, poses a special safety problem. It must be kept warm for service, but it needs to be held below 140°F (60°C) so that the eggs don't curdle. Unfortunately, bacteria grow quickly in this temperature range. Therefore, extra care must be taken to avoid foodborne diseases.

The following sanitation procedures must be observed to avoid the danger of food poisoning:

1. Make sure all equipment is perfectly clean.

2. Hold sauce no longer than 1½ hours. Make only enough to serve in this time, and discard any that is left over.

3. Never mix an old batch of sauce with a new batch.

4. Never hold Hollandaise or Béarnaise—or any other acid product—in aluminum. Use stainless steel containers.

Recipes for Hollandaise and Béarnaise sauces begin on page 151.

Pan Gravies

Pan gravy is a sauce made with juices or drippings of the meat or poultry with which it is being served. Standard pan gravies are similar to brown sauces. Instead of being made with Espagnole or Demiglaze as a base, however, they are made from pan drippings plus roux plus stock or water and sometimes milk or cream.

Jus (pronounced zhoo) refers to unthickened juices from a roast. When the roast is served with these clear, natural juices, it is said to be served *au jus* (oh zhoo), meaning "with juice." Stock is usually added to the pan juices so that there is enough quantity to serve.

The preparation of both gravy and jus are properly part of meat cookery, and recipes and detailed procedures are included in the meat and poultry chapters.

Now that you have studied sauce making in detail, however, it will be helpful to give a general procedure for making pan gravies, so that you can see how similar it is to making brown sauce and how the same techniques you have just learned are applied to a different product.

Basic Procedure for Making Pan Gravy

Method 2 has fewer steps, but Method 1 is actually quicker for large quantities and gives greater control over final consistency.

Method 1

1. ***Remove the roast from the roasting pan.***

   If you have not added mirepoix to the pan during roasting, you can do so now.

2. ***Clarify the fat.***

   Set the roasting pan over high heat and cook until all the moisture has evaporated, leaving only the fat, mirepoix, and the brown (caramelized) drippings. Pour off and save the fat.

3. ***Deglaze the pan.***

   Pour stock or other liquid into the roasting pan. Stir over heat until caramelized drippings are dissolved.

4. ***Combine with stock and simmer.***

   Pour the deglazing liquid, plus mirepoix, into a large pot with desired amount of stock. Simmer until mirepoix is well cooked. Skim the surface well to re move fat and scum.

5. ***Make a roux or, alternatively, a slurry of arrowroot or cornstarch and water.***

   For roux, measure enough of the fat from step 2 to make the correct amount of roux for the volume of gravy. Make a blond or brown roux, as desired. For starch slurry, see page 131.

6. ***Thicken the gravy with the roux or starch slurry.***

7. ***Strain.***

8. ***Adjust seasonings.***

Method 2

1. Remove roast from roasting pan.

2. Clarify the fat.

3. Add flour to roasting pan and make a roux.

4. Add stock. Stir until thickened and pan is deglazed.

5. Strain, and skim excess fat.

6. Adjust consistency, if necessary, with more stock or more roux.

7. Season.

RECIPE 17   **Hollandaise Sauce I**

Yield: 1 qt (1 L)

U.S.	Metric	Ingredients	Procedure
2½ lb	1125 g	Butter	1. Review the guidelines for preparing Hollandaise and Béarnaise.
			2. Clarify the butter (see p. 147). You should have about *2 lb (900 g) clarified butter*. Keep the butter warm but not hot.
¼ tsp	1 mL	Peppercorns, crushed	3. Combine the peppercorns, salt, and vinegar in a saucepan and reduce until nearly dry (*au sec*). Remove from heat and add the cold water.
¼ tsp	1 mL	Salt	
3 oz	100 mL	White vinegar or wine vinegar	
2 oz	60 mL	Cold water	4. To make it easier to beat with a wire whip, it is best now to transfer this diluted, cooled reduction to a stainless steel bowl. Use a clean rubber spatula to make sure you transfer all the flavoring material to the bowl.
12	12	Egg yolks	
2–4 tbsp	30–60 mL	Lemon juice	
		Salt	
		Cayenne	5. Add the egg yolks to the bowl and beat well.
			6. Hold the bowl over a hot-water bath and continue to beat the yolks until they are thickened and creamy.
			7. Remove the bowl from the heat. Using a ladle, slowly and gradually beat in the warm, clarified butter. Add the butter drop by drop at first. If the sauce becomes too thick to beat before all the butter is added, beat in a little of the lemon juice.
			8. When all the butter has been added, beat in lemon juice to taste and adjust seasoning with salt and cayenne. If necessary, thin the sauce with a few drops of warm water.
			9. Strain through cheesecloth and keep warm (not hot) for service. Hold no longer than 1½ hours (see p. 149).

RECIPE 18 Hollandaise Sauce II

Yield: 1 qt (1 L)

U.S.	Metric	Ingredients	Procedure
2½ lb	1125 g	Butter	1. Review the guidelines for preparing Hollandaise and Béarnaise. 2. Clarify the butter (see p. 147). You should have about *2 lb (900 g) clarified butter.* Keep the butter warm but not hot.
12 2 oz 3 oz	12 60 mL 100 mL	Egg yolks Cold water Lemon juice Salt Cayenne	3. Place the egg yolks and cold water in a stainless steel bowl and beat well. Beat in a few drops of lemon juice. 4. Hold the bowl over a hot-water bath and continue to beat until they are thickened and creamy. 5. Remove the bowl from the heat. Using a ladle, slowly and gradually beat in the warm butter. Add the butter drop by drop at first. If the sauce becomes too thick to beat before all the butter is added, beat in a little of the lemon juice. 6. When all the butter has been added, beat in lemon juice to taste and adjust seasoning with salt and cayenne. If necessary, thin the sauce with a few drops of warm water. 7. Keep warm (not hot) for service. Hold no longer than 1½ hours (see p. 149).

Small Sauces

18A. *Maltaise:* To 1 qt (1 L) Hollandaise, add 2 to 4 oz (60 to 125 mL) orange juice (from blood oranges if possible) and 2 tsp (10 mL) grated orange rind. Serve with asparagus.

18B. *Mousseline:* Whip 1 cup (250 mL) heavy cream until stiff and fold into 1 qt (1 L) Hollandaise.

RECIPE 19   **Béarnaise Sauce**

Yield: 1 qt (1 L)

U.S.	Metric	Ingredients	Procedure
2½ lb	1125 kg	Butter	1. Review the guidelines for preparing Hollandaise and Béarnaise.
			2. Clarify the butter (see p. 147). You should have about *2 lb (900 g) clarified butter.* Keep the butter warm but not hot.
2 oz	60 g	Shallots, chopped	3. Combine the shallots, vinegar, tarragon, and peppercorns in a saucepan and reduce by three-fourths. Remove from the heat and cool slightly.
1 cup	250 mL	White wine vinegar	
2 tsp	10 mL	Tarragon	
1 tsp	5 mL	Peppercorns, crushed	
12	12	Egg yolks	4. To make it easier to beat with a wire whip, it is best now to transfer this reduction to a stainless steel bowl. Use a clean rubber spatula to make sure you get it all. Let the reduction cool a little.
			5. Add the egg yolks to the bowl and beat well.
			6. Hold the bowl over a hot-water bath and continue to beat the yolks until they are thickened and creamy.
			7. Remove the bowl from the heat. Using a ladle, slowly and gradually beat in the warm, clarified butter. Add the butter drop by drop at first. If the sauce becomes too thick to beat before all the butter is added, beat in a little lemon juice or warm water.
			8. Strain the sauce through cheesecloth.
		Salt	9. Season to taste with salt, cayenne, and a few drops of lemon juice. Mix in the parsley and tarragon.
		Cayenne	
		Lemon juice	
2 tbsp	30 mL	Chopped parsley	10. Keep warm (not hot) for service. Hold no longer than 1½ hours (see p. 149).
1 tsp	5 mL	Tarragon	

Small Sauces

19A. Foyot: Add 2 oz (60 g) melted meat glaze (glace de viande) to 1 qt (1 L) Béarnaise.

19B. Choron: Add 2 oz (60 g) tomato paste to 1 qt (1 L) Béarnaise.

Miscellaneous Hot Sauces

RECIPE 20 **Sour Cream Sauce**

Yield: 1 qt (1 L)

U.S.	Metric	Ingredients	Procedure
8 oz	250 g	Onions, cut brunoise	1. Sauté the onion in butter until light brown.
2 oz	60 g	Butter	
2 oz	60 mL	White wine (dry)	2. Add the wine and reduce by three-fourths.
2½ pt	1.2 L	Sour cream	
		Lemon juice	3. Stir in the sour cream and simmer until reduced to desired consistency, about 5 minutes.
		Cayenne	
		Salt	
		White pepper	4. Season to taste with a few drops of lemon juice and a little cayenne, salt, and pepper.

RECIPE 21 **Applesauce**

Yield: about 1 qt (1 L)

U.S.	Metric	Ingredients	Procedure
4 lb	2 kg	Apples (see note)	1. Cut the apples into quarters and remove the cores. Skins may be left on, because they will be strained out later. (Red peels will color the sauce pink.) Dice the apples coarsely.
		Sugar (see step 4)	
		Lemon juice	2. Place the apples in a heavy saucepan with about 2 oz (60 mL) of water. Cover.
			3. Set the pan over low heat and cook the apples slowly until very soft. Stir occasionally.
			4. Add sugar to taste. The amount needed depends on the sweetness of the apples, but the sauce should be tart, not too sweet.
			5. Add a little lemon juice to taste.
			6. Pass the sauce through a food mill.
			7. If the sauce is too thin or watery, let simmer uncovered until thickened.
			8. Serve warm or cold with roast pork or duck.

Note: Use tart cooking apples such as Romes. Do not use Red Delicious.

RECIPE 22   **Barbecue Sauce**

Yield: ½ gal (2 L)

U.S.	Metric	Ingredients	Procedure
1 qt	1 L	Tomato purée	1. Place all ingredients in a heavy saucepan and bring to a boil. Reduce heat and simmer about 20 minutes, until slightly reduced and flavors are well blended. Stir occasionally during cooking so the sauce does not scorch on the bottom.
1 pt	500 mL	Water	
⅔ cup	150 mL	Worcestershire sauce	
½ cup	125 mL	Cider vinegar	
½ cup	125 mL	Vegetable oil	
8 oz	250 g	Onion, chopped fine	
4 tsp	20 mL	Garlic, chopped fine	2. Adjust seasoning.
2 oz	60 g	Sugar	
1 tbsp	15 mL	Dry mustard	
2 tsp	10 mL	Chili powder	
1 tsp	5 mL	Black pepper	
		Salt	

Note: This sauce is not intended to be eaten "as is," but to be cooked with other foods. See recipe for Barbecued Spareribs (p. 232) and Barbecued Pork Sandwich (p. 535).

RECIPE 23   **Sweet and Sour Sauce**

Yield: 1 qt (1 L)

U.S.	Metric	Ingredients	Procedure
1 qt	1 L	Chicken stock, cold	1. Place ½ cup of the stock in a bowl and mix with the cornstarch to make a paste.
¼ cup	60 mL	Cornstarch	
8 oz	250 g	Sugar	2. Place the remaining stock or water in a saucepan and add the sugar and soy sauce. Bring to a boil, stirring to dissolve the sugar.
2 oz	60 mL	Soy sauce	
4 oz	125 g	Green or red pepper, small dice	
4 oz	125 g	Onion, small dice	3. Stir in the cornstarch mixture and simmer until thickened and clear.
½ cup	125 mL	Red wine vinegar	
½ tsp	2 mL	Ginger	4. Add the vegetables and ginger and simmer until the vegetables are tender.
		Salt	
		White pepper	5. Add the vinegar. Simmer another minute.
			6. Season to taste with salt and white pepper.

Miscellaneous Cold Sauces

RECIPE 24 Cumberland Sauce

Yield: 1 qt (1 L)

U.S.	Metric	Ingredients	Procedure
3	3	Oranges	1. Carefully cut the zest (colored peel) from the oranges and lemons. Remove only the colored part, not the white part underneath, which is bitter. Juice the oranges and lemons for step 3.
3	3	Lemons	
			2. Cut the peels into julienne. Blanch them in simmering water for 10 minutes and drain.
1½ lb	800 g	Red currant jelly	3. Melt the jelly in a saucepan and stir in the wine.
6 oz	200 mL	Port wine	
6 oz	200 mL	Orange juice (from step 1)	4. Mix the mustard and ginger with a little of the orange juice to make a paste. Add the spices and the rest of the juices to the pan. Bring to boil.
3 oz	100 mL	Lemon juice (from step 1)	
1½ tsp	7 mL	Dry mustard	5. Remove from the heat and add salt and cayenne to taste.
¼ tsp	1 mL	Ginger	
		Salt	6. Add the blanched peels and cool the sauce.
		Cayenne	

RECIPE 25 Tartar Sauce

Yield: about 1 qt (1 L)

U.S.	Metric	Ingredients	Procedure
4 oz	125 g	Dill pickles or sour gherkins	1. Chop the pickles and onions very fine. Chop the capers if they are large, or leave whole if small.
2 oz	60 g	Onions	
2 oz	60 g	Capers	2. Press the pickles and capers in a fine sieve or squeeze out in a piece of cheese-cloth so that they don't make the sauce too liquid.
1 qt	1 L	Mayonnaise	
2 tbsp	30 mL	Chopped parsley	
			3. Combine all ingredients in a stainless steel bowl and mix well.

Variation

25A. *Rémoulade Sauce:* Add 1 tbsp (15 mL) anchovy paste or mashed anchovies to Tartar Sauce.

RECIPE 26 **Horseradish Sauce (Sauce Raifort)**

Yield: about 1 qt (1 L)

U.S.	Metric	Ingredients	Procedure
2 cups	500 mL	Heavy cream	1. Whip the cream until stiff, but do not overwhip.
½ cup	125 mL	Prepared horseradish, drained	2. Mix the horseradish with a little of the whipped cream, then fold into the rest of the cream.
		Salt	3. Season to taste with salt.

Note: This sauce should be made just before service.

RECIPE 27 **Cocktail Sauce**

Yield: 2 qt (2 L)

U.S.	Metric	Ingredients	Procedure
1 qt	1 L	Catsup	1. Combine all ingredients and mix.
2½ cups	600 mL	Chili sauce	2. Chill.
1 cup	250 mL	Prepared horseradish	3. Serve as a dip with shrimp, crab, lobster, raw clams, or raw oysters.
4 oz	125 mL	Lemon juice	
2 tbsp	30 mL	Worcestershire sauce	
dash	dash	Hot red pepper sauce	

RECIPE 28 **Mignonette Sauce**

Yield: 1 qt (1 L)

U.S.	Metric	Ingredients	Procedure
1 qt	1 L	Wine vinegar	1. Combine all ingredients.
8 oz	250 g	Shallots, brunoise	2. Chill.
1 tsp	5 mL	Salt	3. Serve 1 oz (30 mL) per portion as a cocktail sauce for oysters or clams on the half shell.
1 tsp	5 mL	White pepper	
2 tsp	5 mL	Tarragon	

TERMS FOR REVIEW

stock	sauce	au sec	Fond Lié
broth	slurry	deglaze	clarified butter
mirepoix	roux	monter au beurre	Brown Butter
sachet	white roux	Leading Sauce	compound butter
bouquet garni	beurre manié	Small Sauce	emulsion
venting	whitewash	Béchamel	pan gravy
reduction	demiglaze	Velouté	jus
glaze	liaison	Espagnole	au jus
glace de viande			

QUESTIONS FOR DISCUSSION

1. Which bones make a more gelatinous stock, beef or veal?

2. The stock pot is often considered to be a good way to use trimmings from meats and vegetables. Do you agree? Explain.

3. How should vegetables for mirepoix be cut?

4. Explain the importance of blanching bones before making stocks.

5. Why should stock not be boiled? What about covering the stock pot?

6. Explain the procedure for cooling stock. Why is it important?

7. Why is an understanding of stocks important even if you work in an establishment that uses only bases?

8. You have just prepared a Suprême Sauce, but your supervisor says it's too thin. It must be served in 5 minutes. What can you do to correct it?

9. What are the two methods for preparing starches so that they can be incorporated into hot liquids? Why are they necessary, and how do they work?

10. Why is it necessary to be able to thicken a sauce with a roux without making lumps, if the sauce is going to be strained anyway?

11. You are preparing a gravy for a batch of swiss steaks that are to be frozen for later use. What thickening agent will you use?

12. Name the five Leading Sauces and their major ingredients. List at least two Small Sauces made from each.

13. What precautions must be taken when finishing and holding Allemande Sauce?

14. What are the similarities between Espagnole and pan gravy? Differences?

15. What precautions are necessary when making Hollandaise to avoid overcooking the eggs or curdling the sauce?

CHAPTER 9

SOUPS

The popularity of soups today may
be due to increased nutrition consciousness, to a desire for simpler or lighter meals,
or to an increased appreciation of how appetizing and satisfying soups can be. Whatever
the reasons, they emphasize the importance of soup-making skills.

If you have already studied the preparation of stocks and sauces in Chapter 8,
you now have at your disposal the major techniques for the preparation of soups: you know
how to make stocks and how to use thickening agents such as roux and liaison.

In addition, a few other techniques are necessary for you to master
before you are able to prepare all the different types of soups that are popular in
the United States today. As in sauce making, a few basic techniques are the building
blocks that you can use to create a wide variety of appetizing soups.

After reading this chapter, you should be able to

1. Describe the major categories of soups.

2. Serve soups properly.

3. Prepare clarified consommé.

4. Prepare vegetable soups and other clear soups.

5. Prepare cream soups.

6. Prepare purée soups.

7. Prepare bisques, chowders, specialty soups, and national soups.

UNDERSTANDING SOUPS

Soup, according to the dictionary, is a liquid food derived from meat, poultry, fish, and vegetables. This definition is all right as far as it goes, but there's a lot it doesn't tell us. Is a stock, straight from the stock pot, a soup? Is beef stew liquid enough to be called soup?

We're interested more in production techniques than in definitions. However, a few more definitions will be necessary before we can go into the kitchen, so that we can talk to each other in the same language. Definitions aren't rules, so don't be alarmed if you hear other books or chefs use these terms differently. What matters is that you learn the techniques and are able to adapt them to many uses.

. . . .

CLASSIFICATIONS OF SOUPS

Soups can be divided into three basic categories: clear or unthickened soups, thick soups, and special soups that don't fit the first two categories.

Most of these soups, no matter what their final ingredients may be, are based on stock. Thus, the quality of the soup depends on the stock-making skills discussed in Chapter 8. *Chicken stock* is the most frequently used soup stock in this country.

Clear Soups

These soups are all based on a clear, unthickened broth or stock. They may be served plain or garnished with a variety of vegetables and meats.

1. *Broth* and *bouillon* are two terms used in many different ways, but in general they both refer to simple, clear soups without solid ingredients. We have already defined *broth* (Chapter 8) as a flavorful liquid obtained from the simmering of meats and/or vegetables.

2. *Vegetable soup* is a clear, seasoned stock or broth with the addition of one or more vegetables and sometimes meat or poultry products and starches.

3. *Consommé* is a rich, flavorful stock or broth that has been clarified to make it perfectly clear and transparent. The process of clarification is a technique that we will study in detail.

Far from being just a plain old cup of broth, a well-made consommé is considered one of the greatest of all soups. Its sparkling clarity is a delight to the eye, and its rich, full flavor, strength, and body make it a perfect starter for an elegant dinner.

Thick Soups

Unlike clear soups, thick soups are opaque rather than transparent. They are thickened either by adding a thickening agent such as a roux, or by puréeing one or more of their ingredients to provide a heavier consistency.

1. *Cream soups* are soups that are thickened with roux, beurre manié, liaison, or other added thickening agents and have the addition of milk and/or cream. They are similar to Velouté and Béchamel sauces—in fact, they may be made by diluting and flavoring either of these two leading sauces.

   Cream soups are usually named after their major ingredient, such as Cream of Chicken or Cream of Asparagus.

2. *Purées* are soups that are naturally thickened by puréeing one or more of their ingredients. They are not as smooth and creamy as cream soups.

   Purées are normally based on starchy ingredients. They may be made from dried legumes (such as Split Pea Soup) or from fresh vegetables with a starchy ingredient such as potatoes or rice added. Purées may or may not contain milk or cream.

3. *Bisques* are thickened soups made from shellfish. They are usually prepared like cream soups and are almost always finished with cream.

4. *Chowders* are hearty American soups made from fish, shellfish, and/or vegetables. Although they are made in many different ways, they usually contain milk and potatoes.

5. *Potage* is a term sometimes associated with certain thick, hearty soups, but it is actually a general term for soup. A clear soup is called a *potage clair* in French.

Specialty and National Soups

This is a catch-all category that includes soups that don't fit well into the main categories and soups that are native to particular countries or regions.

1. Specialty soups are distinguished by unusual ingredients or methods, such as Turtle Soup, Gumbo, Peanut Soup, and Cold Fruit Soup.

2. Cold soups are sometimes considered specialty soups, and in fact some of them are. But many other popular cold soups, such as jellied consommé, cold cream of cucumber soup, and Vichyssoise (vee shee swahz) are simply cold versions of basic clear and thick soups.

SERVICE OF SOUPS

Standard Portion Sizes

Appetizer portion: 6 to 8 oz (200 to 250 mL).

Main course portion: 10 to 12 oz (300 to 350 mL).

Temperature

Serve hot soups hot, in hot cups or bowls.

Serve cold soups cold, in chilled bowls, or even nested in a larger bowl of crushed ice.

Holding for Service

Strangely enough, some chefs who take the greatest care not to overcook meats or vegetables will nevertheless keep a large kettle of soup on the steam table all day. You can imagine what a vegetable soup is like after 4 or 5 hours at these temperatures.

1. Small-batch cooking applies to soups as well as to other foods. Heat small batches frequently to replenish the steam table with fresh soup.

2. Consommés and some other clear soups can be kept hot for longer periods if the vegetable garnish is heated separately and added at service time.

Garnish

Soup garnishes may be divided into three groups.

1. *Garnishes in the soup.*

   Major ingredients, such as the vegetables in clear vegetable soup, are often considered as garnishes.

Consommés are generally named after their garnish, such as Consommé Brunoise, containing vegetables cut into brunoise shape (⅛-inch dice).

Vegetable cream soups are usually garnished with carefully cut pieces of the vegetable from which they are made.

This group of garnishes includes meats, poultry, seafood, pasta products, and grains such as barley or rice.

These garnishes are treated as part of the preparation or recipe itself, not as something added on.

2. *Toppings.*

   Clear soups are generally served without toppings, to let the attractiveness of the clear broths and the carefully cut vegetables speak for themselves. Occasional exceptions are toppings of chopped parsley or chives.

   Thick soups, especially those that are all one color, are often decorated with a topping. Toppings should be placed on just before service, so that they won't sink or lose their fresh appearance. Their flavors must be appropriate to the soup.

   Do not overdo soup toppings. The food should be attractive in itself.

   Topping suggestions for thick soups:

   Fresh herbs (parsley, chives), chopped

   Sliced almonds, toasted

   Grated cheese

   Sieved egg yolks

   Chopped or riced egg whites

   Croutons

   Grated parmesan cheese

   Crumbled bacon

   Paprika

   Sour cream or whipped cream

3. *Accompaniments.*

   American soups are traditionally served with crackers. In addition to the usual saltines, some other suggestions for crisp accompaniments are

Melba toast	Profiteroles (tiny
Corn chips	unsweetened
Breadsticks	cream puff shells)
Cheese straws	Whole-grain wafers

CLEAR SOUPS

CONSOMMÉ

When we define consommé as a clarified stock or broth, we are forgetting the most important part of the definition. The name consommé means, literally, "completed" or "concentrated." In other words, a consommé is a strong, concentrated stock or broth. In classical cuisine, this was all that was necessary for a stock to be called a consommé. In fact, two kinds were recognized: ordinary (or unclarified) consommé and clarified consommé.

Rule number one for preparing consommé is that the stock or broth must be strong, rich, and full flavored. Clarification is second in importance to strength. A good consommé, with a mellow but full aroma and plenty of body (from the natural gelatin) that you can feel in your mouth, is one of the great pleasures of fine cuisine. But clarification is an expensive and time-consuming procedure, and, quite frankly, it's not worth the trouble if the soup is thin and watery.

How Clarification Works

Coagulation of proteins was an important subject in our discussion of stock making, because one of our major concerns was how to keep coagulated proteins from making the stock cloudy. Strangely enough, it is this same process of coagulation that enables us to clarify stocks to perfect transparency.

Remember that some proteins, especially those called albumins, will dissolve in cold water. When the water is heated, they gradually solidify or coagulate and rise to the surface. If we control this process very carefully, these proteins will collect all the tiny particles that cloud a stock and will carry them to the surface. The stock is then left perfectly clear.

If, on the other hand, we are not careful, these proteins will break up as they coagulate and will cloud the liquid even more, just as they can do when we make stock.

Basic Ingredients

The mixture of ingredients we use to clarify a stock is called the *clearmeat* or the *clarification*.

1. *Lean ground meat* is one of the major sources of protein that enables the clearmeat to do its job. It also contributes flavor to the consommé.

It must be lean, because fat is undesirable in a consommé. Beef shank, also called shin beef, is the most desirable meat because it is high in albumin proteins as well as in flavor and in gelatin, and it is very lean.

Beef and/or chicken meat are used to clarify chicken consommé. Meat is *not* used, obviously, to make fish consommé. Ground lean fish may be used, but it is normal to omit flesh altogether and use only egg whites.

2. *Egg whites* are included in the clearmeat because, being mostly albumin, they greatly strengthen its clarifying power.

3. *Mirepoix* and other seasoning and flavoring ingredients are usually included because they add flavor to the finished consommé. They do not actually help in the clarification, except possibly to give solidity to the raft. The *raft* is the coagulated clearmeat, floating in a solid mass on top of the consommé.

The mirepoix must be cut into fine pieces so that it will float with the raft.

A large amount of a particular vegetable may be added if a special flavor is desired, as in, for example, Essence of Celery Consommé.

4. *Acid ingredients*—tomato products for beef or chicken consommé, lemon juice or white wine for fish consommé—are often added, because the acidity helps coagulate the protein. They are not absolutely necessary—the heat will coagulate the protein anyway—but many chefs like to use them.

Procedure for Preparing Consommé

1. Start with a well-flavored, cold, strong stock or broth.

If your stock is weak, reduce it until it is concentrated enough, then cool it before proceeding, or plan on simmering the consommé longer to reduce while clarifying.

2. Select a heavy stock pot or soup pot, preferably one with a spigot at the bottom. The spigot enables you to drain off the finished consommé without disturbing the raft.

3. Combine the clearmeat ingredients in the soup pot and mix them vigorously.

4. Optional step: mix in a small amount of cold water or stock—about 4 to 8 oz per pound (250

to 500 mL per kg) of meat—and let stand 30 to 60 minutes. This allows more opportunity for the proteins that do the clarifying to dissolve out of the meat.

Note: Chefs disagree on the importance of this step. Some let the mixture stand overnight in the refrigerator. Others skip this step altogether. Check with your instructor.

5. Gradually add the cold, degreased stock and mix well with the clearmeat.

    The stock must be cold so that it doesn't cook the proteins on contact.

    Mixing distributes the dissolved proteins throughout the stock, so that they can collect all the impurities more easily.

6. Set the pot over a moderately low fire and let it come to a simmer very slowly.

7. Stir the contents occasionally so that the clearmeat circulates throughout the stock and doesn't burn to the bottom.

8. When the simmering point is approaching, stop stirring. The clearmeat will rise to the surface and form a raft.

9. Move to lower heat so that the liquid maintains a slow simmer. Do not cover.

    Boiling would break up the raft and cloud the consommé. The same principle operates in stock making.

10. Let simmer 1½ hours, without disturbing the raft.

11. Strain the consommé through a china cap lined with several layers of cheesecloth.

    If you are not using a stock pot with a spigot, ladle the consommé out carefully, without breaking up the raft.

    Let the liquid drain through the cheesecloth by gravity. Do not force it, or fine particles will pass through and cloud the consommé.

12. Degrease.

    Remove all traces of fat from the surface. Strips of clean brown paper passed across the surface are effective in absorbing every last speck of fat, without absorbing much consommé.

13. Adjust the seasonings.

    Kosher salt is preferred to regular table salt because it has no impurities or additives that could cloud the stock.

Emergency Procedures

1. **Clarifying hot stock.**

    If you do not have time to cool the stock properly before clarifying, at least cool it as much as you can. Even 10 minutes in a cold-water bath will help. Then, mix ice cubes or crushed ice with the clearmeat. This will help keep it from coagulating when the hot stock hits it. Proceed as in the basic method.

    Finally, review your production planning so that you can avoid this emergency in the future.

2. **Clarifying without meat.**

    In a pinch, you can clarify a stock with egg whites alone. Use at least three or four egg whites per gallon (4 liters) of stock, plus some mirepoix if possible. Great care is necessary, because the raft will be very fragile and easily broken up.

    Egg whites and mirepoix alone are often used for clarifying fish stocks.

3. **Failed clarification.**

    If the clarification fails because you let it boil, or for some other reason, it can still be rescued, even if there is no time for another complete clarification.

    Strain the consommé, cool it as much as you can, then slowly add it to a mixture of ice cubes and egg whites. Carefully return to a simmer as in the basic method, and proceed with the clarification.

    This should be done in emergencies only. The ice cubes dilute the consommé, and the egg white clarification is risky.

4. **Poor color.**

    Beef or veal consommé, made from brown stock, should have an amber color. It is not dark brown like canned consommé. Chicken consommé is a very pale amber.

    It is possible to correct a pale consommé by adding a few drops of caramel color to the finished soup. But for best results, check the color of the stock before clarification. If it is too pale, cut an onion in half and place it cut side down on a flat-top range until it is black, or char it under a broiler. Add this to the clearmeat. The caramelized sugar of the onion will color the stock.

RECIPE 29 **Consommé**

....

Yield: 1 gal (4 L)   **Portions**: 16   **Portion size**: 8 oz (250 mL)
                                                              20   6 oz (200 mL)

U.S.	Metric	Ingredients	Procedure
1 lb	500 g	Lean beef, preferably shin, ground	1. Review the information on preparing consommé, pages 162–163.
		Mirepoix, chopped into small pieces:	2. Combine the beef, mirepoix, egg whites, tomatoes, herbs, and spices in a tall, heavy stock pot. Mix the ingredients vigorously with a wooden paddle or a heavy whip.
8 oz	250 g	Onion	
4 oz	125 g	Celery	
4 oz	125 g	Carrot	
8 oz	250 g	Egg whites	
8 oz	250 g	Canned tomatoes, crushed	
6–8	6–8	Parsley stems, chopped	
pinch	pinch	Thyme	
1	1	Bay leaf	
2	2	Whole cloves	
½ tsb	2 mL	Peppercorns, crushed	
5 qt	5 L	Cold beef or veal stock (brown or white)	3. Add about a pint of cold stock and stir well. Let stand about 30 minutes. (Optional step: see pp. 162–163 for explanation.)
			4. Gradually stir in the remaining stock. Be sure the stock is well mixed with the other ingredients.
			5. Set the pot on moderately low heat and let it come to a simmer very slowly. Stir occasionally.
			6. When the simmering point is approaching, stop stirring.
			7. Move the pot to lower heat and simmer very slowly for about 1½ hours. Do not stir or disturb the raft that forms on top.
			8. Very carefully strain the consommé through a china cap lined with several layers of cheesecloth.
			9. Degrease thoroughly.
			10. Season to taste.

Variations

29A. Double Consommé: Use twice the quantity of beef in the basic recipe. Add 8 oz (250 g) leeks to the mirepoix.

29B. Chicken Consommé: Use chicken stock instead of beef or veal stock. Add to the clearmeat 8 oz (250 g) chicken trimmings (such as wing tips and necks) which have been chopped and browned in a hot oven. Omit tomato and add 1 oz (30 mL) lemon juice.

RECIPE 29   Consommé *(Continued)*

29C. Cold Jellied Consommé: Unflavored gelatin must often be added to consommé to make jellied consommé. The amount needed depends on the strength of the stock and on the amount of jelling desired. Classically, a chilled consommé is only half jelled, more like a thick syrup. Some people, however, prefer a gelatin content high enough to solidify the consommé. In the following guidelines, use the lower quantity of gelatin for a semi-jelled soup, the higher quantity for a fully jelled soup. Also, for tomatoed consommé (Madrilène), increase the gelatin slightly, because the acidity of the tomatoes weakens the gelatin.

1. If the stock is thin when cold, add 1–2 oz (30–60 g) gelatin per gallon (4 L).
2. If the stock is slightly jelled and syrupy when cold, add ½–1 oz (15–30 g) gelatin per gallon (4 L).
3. If the stock is jelled when cold, no gelatin is needed. Or add up to ½ oz (15 g) per gallon (4 L) if a firmer texture is desired.

Gelatin may be added to the clearmeat (in step 2 of the recipe). This is the best method, because there is no danger of clouding the consommé. It may also be added to the finished consommé after softening it in cold water. See page 512 for instructions on the use of gelatin.

29D. Consommé Madrilène: Increase the tomatoes in the basic recipe to 24 oz (750 g). Use beef, veal, or chicken stock. Serve hot or jellied.

29E. Essence of Celery Consommé: Increase the celery in the basic recipe to 1 lb (500 g).

29F. Consommé au Porto: Flavor the finished consommé with 6–8 oz (200–250 mL) port wine per gallon (4 L).

29G. Consommé au Sherry: Flavor the finished consommé with 6–8 oz (200–250 mL) sherry wine per gallon (4 L).

RECIPE 30   Garnished Consommés

For the following consommés, prepare and cook the garnish separately. At service time, add one or two tablespoons of the garnish to each portion. See page 112 for description of cuts.

30A. Consommé Brunoise: Onion or leek, carrot, celery, and turnip (optional), cut brunoise. Sweat lightly in butter and simmer in a little consommé until tender.

30B. Consommé Julienne: Onion or leek, carrot, and celery, cut julienne. Prepare like Brunoise garnish.

30C. Consommé Printaniere: Small dice of spring vegetables: carrot, turnip, celery, green beans. Prepare like Brunoise garnish.

30D. Consommé Paysanne: Thin slices of leeks, carrots, celery, turnip, and cabbage. Prepare like Brunoise garnish.

30E. Consommé with Pearl Tapioca: Cooked pearl tapioca.

30F. Consommé Vermicelli: Cooked broken vermicelli (very thin spaghetti).

VEGETABLE SOUPS

Clear vegetable soups are made from a clear stock or broth, not necessarily clarified, with the addition of one or more vegetables and sometimes meat or poultry and/or pasta or grains. Most vegetable soups are made from meat or poultry stock or broth. Meatless or vegetarian soups are made from vegetable broth or water.

Guidelines for Preparing Vegetable Soups

Procedures for making these soups are not complicated. Most of them are made simply by simmering vegetables in stock until done. But care and attention to details are still necessary for producing a quality soup.

1. *Start with a clear, flavorful stock.*

   This is one reason it's important to be able to make stocks that are clear, not cloudy.

2. *Select vegetables and other ingredients whose flavors go well together.*

   Don't just throw in everything you've got. Judgment, combined with experience, must be used to create a pleasing combination. Five or six vegetables are usually enough. More than that just make a jumble.

3. *Cut vegetables uniformly.*

   Neat, careful cutting means uniform cooking and attractive appearance. Sizes of cuts are important, too. Pieces should be large enough to be identifiable, but small enough to eat conveniently with a spoon.

4. *Cooking vegetables slowly in a little butter before combining with liquid improves their flavor and gives the soup a mellower, richer taste.*

5. *Cook starches such as grains and pasta separately and add to the soup later.*

   Cooking them in the soup makes it cloudy. Potatoes are sometimes cooked directly in the soup, but they should be rinsed of excess starch after cutting, if you want to keep the soup as clear as possible.

6. *Observe differences in cooking times.*

   Add long-cooking vegetables first, short-cooking vegetables near the end. Some vegetables, like tomatoes, need only be added to the hot soup after it is removed from the fire.

7. *Don't overcook.*

   Some cooks feel that soups must be simmered a long time to extract flavors into the liquid. But you should already have done this when you made the stock! Vegetables in soup should be no more overcooked than vegetable side dishes, especially since the soup will probably spend a longer time in the steam table.

RECIPE 31 Clear Vegetable Soup

Yield: 6 qt (6 L)   **Portions:** 24   **Portion size:** 8 oz (250 mL)

U.S.	Metric	Ingredients	Procedure
6 oz	175 g	Butter or chicken fat	1. Heat the butter in a heavy sauce pot over medium low heat.
1½ lb	750 g	Onions, small dice	
1 lb	500 g	Carrots, small dice	2. Add the onions, carrots, celery, and turnip. Sweat the vegetables in the butter over low heat until they are about half cooked. Do not let them brown.
1 lb	500 g	Celery, small dice	
12 oz	375 g	Turnip, small dice	
6 qt	6 L	Chicken stock	3. Add the stock. Bring to a boil and skim carefully. Simmer until vegetables are just barely tender.
1 lb	500 g	Drained canned tomatoes, coarsely chopped	
		Salt	4. Add the tomatoes and simmer another 5 minutes.
		White pepper	5. Degrease the soup and season with salt and white pepper.
12 oz	375 g	Frozen peas, thawed	6. Just before serving, add the peas.

RECIPE 31   **Clear Vegetable Soup** *(Continued)*

● ●

Variations

31A. Other vegetables may be used in addition to or in place of one or more of the vegetables in the basic recipe.

Add with the vegetables sweated in butter:

Leeks	Green cabbage
Rutabagas	Parsnips

Add to the simmering soup, timing the addition so that all the vegetables are done at the same time:

Potatoes	Lima beans
Green beans	Corn

31B. Other cuts may be used for the vegetables instead of small dice, such as batonnet, julienne, or paysanne (see p. 112).

31C. Vegetable Rice Soup: Add 1½ to 2 cups (350 to 500 mL) cooked rice to the finished soup.

31D. Chicken Vegetable Rice Soup: Add 12 oz (375 g) cooked, diced chicken to Vegetable Rice Soup.

31E. Vegetable Beef Soup: Use beef stock instead of chicken stock. Add 12 oz (375 g) cooked diced beef when the tomatoes are added. Also, add the juice from the tomatoes.

31F. Vegetable Beef Barley Soup: Add 1½ to 2 cups (350 to 500 mL) cooked barley to Vegetable Beef Soup.

● ●

RECIPE 32   **Cabbage Soup**

● ●

Yield: 6 qt (6 L)   **Portions:** 24   **Portion size:** 8 oz (250 mL)

U.S.	Metric	Ingredients	Procedure
1¼ lb	625 g	Onion, sliced thin	1. In a heavy stock pot or sauce pot, sweat the onions in the butter until they begin to soften.
4 oz	125 g	Butter	
2½ lb	1250 g	Cabbage, shredded (see p. 392 for technique)	2. Add the cabbage and stir to coat it with fat. Continue to sweat the vegetables until the cabbage is about half cooked.
6 qt	6 L	Brown stock	
		Salt	3. Add the brown stock and bring to a boil. Reduce heat to a simmer.
		Pepper	4. Simmer about 20 minutes, until the cabbage is tender.
			5. Season to taste with salt and pepper.
6 tbsp	100 mL	Chopped parsley	6. At service time, stir in the chopped parsley.
1 qt	1 L	Sour cream	7. Top each portion with a spoonful of sour cream. (Do not add sour cream until immediately before the soup is served.)

● ●

RECIPE 33   **Mushroom Barley Soup**

Yield: 6 qt (6 L)   **Portions:** 24   **Portion size:** 8 oz (250 mL)

U.S.	Metric	Ingredients	Procedure
8 oz	250 g	Barley	1. Cook the barley in boiling water until tender. Drain.
10 oz	300 g	Onion, brunoise	2. In a heavy sauce pot or stock pot, sweat the vegetables in the fat until they are about half cooked. Do not let them brown.
5 oz	150 g	Carrot, brunoise	
5 oz	150 g	White turnip, brunoise	
2 oz	60 g	Butter or chicken fat	3. Add the chicken stock. Bring to a boil. Reduce heat and simmer until the vegetables are just tender.
5 qt	5 L	Chicken stock	
2 lb	1 kg	Mushrooms, diced	4. While the soup is simmering, sauté the mushrooms briefly in fat without letting them brown.
4 oz	125 g	Butter or chicken fat	
		Salt	5. Add the mushrooms and the drained, cooked barley to the soup. Simmer another 5 minutes.
		White pepper	
			6. Degrease the soup. Season to taste with salt and pepper.

OTHER CLEAR SOUPS

In addition to vegetable soups, there are many other clear or unthickened soups known to various cuisines. They range from simple broths to elaborate concoctions of meats, vegetables, starches, and other ingredients. Although many of them contain vegetables, we don't classify them as vegetable soups because other ingredients are generally more prominent.

RECIPE 34   **Chicken Noodle Soup**

Yield: 6 qt (6 L)   **Portions:** 24   **Portion size:** 8 oz (250 mL)

U.S.	Metric	Ingredients	Procedure
10 oz	300 g	Egg noodles	1. Cook the noodles in boiling, salted water. (See procedure for cooking pasta, p. 460.) Drain and rinse in cold water.
10 oz	300 g	Cooked chicken meat	
6 qt	6 L	Chicken stock	2. Cut the chicken into small dice.
		Salt	3. Bring the stock to a simmer. Season to taste with salt and white pepper. If stock doesn't have enough flavor, add more stock and reduce to concentrate the flavor.
		White pepper	
			4. Just before service, add the chicken and noodles to the stock. Let them heat through before serving.
		Chopped parsley	5. Garnish each portion with a little chopped parsley.

RECIPE 34   **Chicken Noodle Soup** *(Continued)*

Note: See poultry chapter (p. 303) for preparing "boiled" chicken and broth for use in soups. Other leftover cooked chicken may also be used.

Variations

34A. Beef Noodle Soup: Prepare as in basic recipe, using beef and beef stock.

34B. Chicken or Beef Noodle Soup with Vegetables: Before adding the chicken and noodles, simmer 10 oz (300 g) diced carrots and 5 oz (150 g) diced celery in the stock until tender.

RECIPE 35   **Brunswick Soup**

Yield: 6 qt (6 L)   **Portions:** 24   **Portion size:** 8 oz (250 mL)

U.S.	Metric	Ingredients	Procedure
10 oz	300 g	Onions, small dice	1. In a heavy pot, sweat the onions in the butter until about half cooked. Do not brown.
1 oz	30 g	Butter or oil	
5 qt	5 L	Chicken stock	
1¼ lb	600 g	Tomato concassé	2. Add the chicken stock and bring to a boil. Simmer about 10 minutes.
1¼ lb	600 g	Lima beans, frozen	
1¼ lb	600 g	Okra, fresh or frozen, cut in ¼-in. (½ cm) pieces	3. Add the remaining vegetables and the chicken. Simmer until the vegetables are tender, about 10–15 minutes.
1 lb	475 g	Corn, frozen	
1¼ lb	600 g	Cooked chicken meat and giblets, small dice	4. Season to taste with salt and white pepper.

RECIPE 36   **Chicken Tomato Bouillon**

Yield: 6 qt (6 L)   **Portions:** 24   **Portion size:** 8 oz (250 mL)

U.S.	Metric	Ingredients	Procedure
6 qt	6 L	Chicken stock	1. Place the stock, juice, celery, onion, basil, and thyme in a sauce pot. Bring to a boil.
2 qt	2 L	Tomato juice	
8 oz	250 g	Celery, chopped	
8 oz	250 g	Onion, chopped	
1½ tsp	7 mL	Basil	2. Simmer about 45 minutes, until vegetables are soft and flavors are well blended.
½ tsp	2 mL	Thyme	
		Salt	
		Pepper	3. Strain and season with salt, pepper, and a pinch of sugar.
		Sugar	
		Chopped parsley or chives	4. Garnish each portion with a light sprinkling of parsley or chives.

Variations

36A. Chicken Tomato Bouillon with Rice: Add 2 cups (500 mL) cooked rice at service time.

36B. Cold Chicken Tomato Bouillon: Chill the soup and add a few drops of lemon juice to taste. Serve each portion with a spoonful of sour cream.

RECIPE 37 Oxtail Soup

Yield: 6 qt (6 L)   **Portions:** 24   **Portion size:** 8 oz (250 mL)

U.S.	Metric	Ingredients	Procedure
6 lb	2.7 kg	Oxtails	1. Using a heavy chef's knife, cut the oxtails into sections at the joints.
		Mirepoix:	
10 oz	300 g	Onion, medium dice	2. Place the oxtails in a bake pan and brown in a 450°F (230°C) oven. When they are partially browned, add the mirepoix to the pan and brown it along with the oxtails.
5 oz	150 g	Carrot, medium dice	
5 oz	150 g	Celery, medium dice	
6 qt	6 L	Brown stock (see note)	3. Place the oxtails and mirepoix in a stock pot with the stock.
		Sachet:	
1	1	Bay leaf	
pinch	pinch	Thyme	4. Pour off the fat from the pan in which the meat was browned. Deglaze the pan with a little of the stock and add this to the stock pot.
6	6	Peppercorns	
2	2	Whole cloves	
1	1	Garlic clove	5. Bring to a boil. Reduce heat to a simmer and skim well. Add the sachet.
			6. Simmer until the meat is tender, about 3 hours. Add a little water if necessary during cooking to keep the meat completely covered.
			7. Remove the pieces of oxtail from the broth. Trim the meat off the bones and dice it. Place it in a small pan with a little of the broth. Keep warm if the soup is to be finished immediately, or chill for later use.
1¼ lb	600 g	Carrots, small dice	8. Strain the broth. Degrease carefully.
1¼ lb	600 g	White turnip, small dice	9. Sweat the carrots, turnips, and leeks in the butter until about half cooked.
10 oz	300 g	Leeks, white part only, cut julienne	
4 oz	125 g	Butter	10. Add the broth. Simmer until vegetables are tender.
10 oz	300 g	Tomatoes (canned), drained, coarsely chopped	11. Add the tomatoes and the reserved oxtail meat. Simmer another minute.
2 oz	60 mL	Sherry (optional)	12. Add the sherry, if desired. Season to taste with salt and pepper.
		Salt	
		Pepper	

Note: Water is sometimes used instead of stock. If this is done, brown 4–5 lb (about 2 kg) of beef or veal bones with the oxtails and simmer in the soup with them. Double the quantity of mirepoix.

Variation

Oxtail soup is often clarified. Chill the broth after step 7 and clarify like consommé. See pages 162–163 for procedure.

THICK SOUPS

CREAM SOUPS

Learning to cook professionally, as you have already heard, is not learning recipes but learning basic techniques that you can apply to specific needs.

The basic techniques of sauce making were discussed in Chapter 8. If we tell you that cream soups are simply diluted Velouté or Béchamel sauces, flavored with the ingredient for which they are named, you should almost be able to make a cream of celery soup without any further instructions.

It's not quite that simple. There are some complications, but they are mostly a matter of detail. You already know the basic techniques.

The Classic Cream Soups

In the great kitchens of several decades ago, cream soups were exactly as we have just described: diluted, flavored sauces. In fact, what we now call cream soups were divided into two groups, veloutés and creams.

1. Velouté soups consisted of

    Velouté Sauce
    Puréed flavoring ingredient
    White stock, to dilute
    Liaison, to finish

2. Cream soups consisted of

    Béchamel Sauce
    Puréed flavoring ingredient
    Milk (or white stock), to dilute
    Cream, to finish

These methods were natural to large kitchens that always had quantities of Velouté and Béchamel sauces on hand. Making a soup was simply a matter of finishing off a sauce.

Modern cooks view these methods as being complicated, and have devised other methods that seem simpler. But most of the sauce steps are involved—you still have to thicken a liquid with roux (or other starch), cook and purée the ingredients, and add the milk or cream.

The classical method is still important to learn. It will give you more versatility, it makes an excellent soup, and besides, it really isn't any harder or longer, in the final analysis. In addition, you will learn two other methods much in use today.

But first, we will consider a frequently encountered problem with cream soups.

Curdling

Because cream soups contain milk or cream or both, curdling is a common problem. The heat of cooking and the acidity of many of the other soup ingredients are the causes of this curdling.

Fortunately, there is one fact we can use to avoid curdling: *roux and other starch thickeners stabilize milk and cream.* Caution is still necessary, because soups are relatively thin and do not contain enough starch to be completely curdle proof.

Observe the following guidelines to help prevent curdling:

1. Do not combine milk and simmering soup stock without the presence of roux or other starch. Do one of the following:

    a. Thicken the stock before adding milk.
    b. Thicken the milk before adding it to the soup.

2. Do not add cold milk or cream to simmering soup. Do one of the following:

    a. Heat the milk in a separate saucepan.
    b. Temper the milk by gradually adding some of the hot soup to it. Then add it to the rest of the soup.

3. Do not boil soups after milk or cream has been added.

Standards of Quality for Cream Soups

1. *Thickness.* About the consistency of heavy cream. Not too thick.

2. *Texture.* Smooth; no graininess or lumps (except garnish, of course).

3. *Taste.* Distinct flavor of the main ingredient (asparagus in Cream of Asparagus, etc.). No starchy taste from uncooked roux.

Basic Procedures for Making Cream Soups

The following methods apply to most cream soups. Individual ingredients may require some variations.

Method 1

1. Prepare Velouté Sauce or Béchamel Sauce (pp. 138–141), using roux.

2. Prepare main flavoring ingredients. Cut vegetables into thin slices. Sweat them in butter about 5 minutes to develop flavor. *Do not brown.* Green leafy vegetables must be blanched before stew-

ing in butter. Cut poultry and seafood into small pieces for simmering.

3. Add flavoring ingredients from step 2 to Velouté or Béchamel and simmer until tender. Exception: finished tomato purée is added for cream of tomato; further cooking is not necessary.

4. Skim any fat or scum carefully from the surface of the soup.

5. Purée the soup. Pass it through a food mill and strain in a fine china cap, or just strain in a fine china cap, pressing down hard on the solid ingredients to force out liquid and some of the pulp. Soup should be very smooth.

   Poultry and seafood ingredients may be puréed or reserved for garnish.

6. Add hot white stock or milk to thin the soup to proper consistency.

7. Adjust seasonings.

8. At service time, finish with liaison (p. 134) or heavy cream.

Method 2

1. Sweat vegetable ingredients (except tomatoes) in butter; do not let them color.

2. Add flour. Stir well to make a roux. Cook the roux for a few minutes, but do not let it start to brown.

3. Add white stock, beating with a whip as you slowly pour it in.

4. Add any vegetables, other solid ingredients, or flavorings that were not sautéed in step 1.

5. Simmer until all ingredients are tender.

6. Skim any fat that has risen to the surface.

7. Purée and/or strain (as in Method 1).

8. Add hot white stock or milk to thin soup to proper consistency.

9. Adjust seasonings.

10. At service time, finish with heavy cream or liaison.

Method 3

1. Bring white stock to a boil.

2. Add vegetables and other flavoring ingredients. If desired, some or all of the vegetables may first be cooked slowly in butter for a few minutes to develop flavors.

3. Simmer until all ingredients are tender.

4. Thicken with roux, beurre manié, or other starch.

5. Simmer until no starch taste remains.

6. Skim fat from surface.

7. Purée and/or strain (as in Method 1).

8. Add hot or tempered milk and/or cream. A light cream sauce may be used, if desired, to avoid thinning the soup or curdling the milk.

9. Adjust seasonings.

RECIPE 38   Cream of Mushroom Soup (Cream Soup Method 2)

Yield: 6 qt (6 L)   **Portions:** 24   **Portion size:** 8 oz (250 mL)

U.S.	Metric	Ingredients	Procedure
12 oz	375 g	Butter	1. Review cream soup guidelines and Method 2.
12 oz	375 g	Onion, chopped fine	
1½ lb	750 g	Mushrooms, chopped	2. Heat the butter in a heavy sauce pot over moderate heat.
9 oz	275 g	Flour	
			3. Add the onions and mushrooms. Sweat the vegetables without letting them brown.
			4. Add the flour and stir to make a roux. Cook the roux for a few minutes, but do not let it start to brown.

RECIPE 38 **Cream of Mushroom Soup (Cream Soup Method 2)** *(Continued)*

U.S.	Metric	Ingredients	Procedure
4½ qt	4½ L	White stock, chicken or veal, hot	5. Gradually beat in the stock. Bring to a boil, stirring with a whip as it thickens. 6. Simmer until vegetables are very tender. 7. Skim the soup carefully. 8. Pass the soup through a food mill to purée it. 9. Pass the puréed soup through a fine china cap or through cheesecloth.
3 pt approximately	1½ L	Hot milk Salt White pepper	10. Add enough hot milk to the soup to bring it to the proper consistency. 11. Heat the soup again, but do not let it boil. 12. Season to taste.
3 cups 6 oz	750 mL 175 g	Heavy cream, hot Optional garnish: Mushrooms, brunoise, sautéed in butter	13. At service time, add the cream. Add the garnish, if desired.

Variations, Method 2

For each variation, replace the mushrooms with the vegetable and quantity indicated. See the note to the variations for Cream of Celery Soup, page 174.

38A. Cream of Asparagus: 3 lb (1.5 kg) asparagus.

38B. Cream of Broccoli: 3 lb (1.5 kg) broccoli.

38C. Cream of Carrot: 3 lb (1.5 kg) carrots.

38D. Cream of Cauliflower: 3 lb (1.5 kg) cauliflower.

38E. Cream of Celery: 3 lb (1.4 kg) celery.

38F. Cream of Corn: 3 lb (1.4 kg) whole kernel corn.

38G. Cream of Cucumber: 3 lb (1.5 kg) peeled, seeded cucumber.

38H. Cream of Green Pea: 3 lb (1.5 kg) frozen peas. Add after step 5.

38I. Cream of Spinach: 3 lb (1.5 kg) fresh or 2 lb (900 g) frozen spinach. Blanch, drain, and add after step 5.

38J. Cream of Watercress: 1½ lb (750 g) watercress.

38K. Cream of Chicken: 6 oz (175 g) celery and 6 oz (175 g) carrot. Use strong chicken stock. Add 6 oz (175 g) cooked chicken meat, cut into julienne or fine dice, to the finished soup after straining.

RECIPE 39 **Cream of Celery Soup (Cream Soup Method 1)**

| **Yield:** 6 qt (6 L) | | **Portions:** 24 | | **Portion size:** 8 oz (250 mL) |

U.S.	Metric	Ingredients	Procedure
3 lb	1.5 kg	Celery, small dice	1. Review cream soup guidelines and Method 1.
12 oz	375 g	Onion, small dice	
3 oz	90 g	Butter	2. Sweat the celery and onions in the butter in a heavy sauce pot until they are almost tender. Do not let them brown.
4½ qt	4½ L	Velouté Sauce, made with chicken or veal stock (see note)	3. Add the velouté to the pot. Simmer until the vegetables are very tender.
			4. Skim any fat or scum from the soup.
			5. Pass the soup through a food mill to purée it.
			6. Pass the purée soup through a fine china cap or through cheesecloth.
3 pt approximately	1½ L	Hot milk *or* white stock	7. Add enough hot milk or stock to bring the soup to the proper consistency.
		Salt	8. Heat the soup again, but do not let it boil.
		White pepper	
			9. Season to taste.
3 cups	750 mL	Heavy cream, hot	10. At service time, add the cream. Add the garnish if desired.
		Optional garnish:	
6 oz	175 g	Celery, julienne, cooked	

Note: Béchamel may be used in place of Velouté if desired. This is often done for vegetarian menus.

Variations, Method 1

For the following cream soups, make the substitutions in the basic recipe as indicated. Frozen and canned vegetables may be used where appropriate, in place of fresh. Also, trimmings may be used if they are clean and of good quality, such as the bottom ends of asparagus or broccoli stalks.

39A. Cream of Asparagus: Use 3 lb (1.5 kg) asparagus stalks in place of celery. Optional garnish: cooked asparagus tips.

39B. Cream of Broccoli: Use 3 lb (1.5 kg) broccoli in place of celery. Optional garnish: small cooked broccoli florets.

39C. Cream of Carrot: Use 3 lb (1.5 kg) carrots in place of celery. Garnish: chopped parsley.

39D. Cream of Cauliflower: Use 3 lb (1.5 kg) cauliflower in place of celery. Optional garnish: tiny, cooked cauliflower florets.

RECIPE 39 **Cream of Celery Soup (Cream Soup Method 1)** *(Continued)*

39E. *Cream of Corn:* Use 3 lb (1.5 kg) whole kernel corn (fresh, frozen, or canned) in place of the celery. Do not sweat the corn with the onions. Instead, sweat the onions alone, add the velouté, then add the corn. Garnish: corn kernels.

39F. *Cream of Cucumber:* Use 3 lb (1.5 kg) peeled, seeded cucumber in place of celery. Optional garnish: small, diced, cooked cucumber.

39G. *Cream of Mushroom:* Use 1½ lb (750 g) mushrooms in place of celery. Optional garnish: julienne, brunoise, or sliced cooked mushrooms.

39H. *Cream of Pea:* Use 3 lb (1.5 kg) frozen green peas in place of celery. Do not sweat the peas with the onions, but add them after the velouté has been added.

39I. *Cream of Spinach:* Use 3 lb (1.5 kg) fresh spinach or 2 lb (900 g) frozen spinach in place of celery. Do not sweat the spinach with the onion. Blanch it, drain it well, and add it to the velouté in step 3.

39J. *Cream of Watercress:* Use 1½ lb (750 g) watercress in place of celery.

39K. *Cream of Chicken:* Reduce celery to 6 oz (175 g) and add 6 oz (175 g) carrot (note that, together with the onion, this makes 1½ lb (750 g) mirepoix). Use a Velouté Sauce made with a strong, flavorful chicken stock. After the soup is strained, add 6 oz (175 g) cooked chicken meat, cut into julienne or fine dice.

Cold Cream Soups

Most cream soups are delicious cold as well as hot. For example, Cold Cream of Cucumber Soup is a special favorite in summer. Procedure:

1. Chill soup after step 9 in recipe.
2. Add cold cream after soup is well chilled.
3. Dilute with extra milk, cream, or stock if soup becomes too thick.
4. Season carefully. Cold foods require more seasonings.

RECIPE 40 **Cream of Broccoli Soup (Cream Soup Method 3)**

Yield: 6 qt (6 L)		**Portions:** 24	**Portion size:** 8 oz (250 mL)

U.S.	Metric	Ingredients	Procedure
4½ qt	4½ L	White stock, chicken or veal	1. Bring the stock to a boil in a heavy sauce pot.
3 lb	1.5 kg	Broccoli (fresh or frozen), chopped	2. Add the broccoli and onion. (Optional: Vegetables may be sweated in butter first, to develop flavors.)
12 oz	375 g	Onion, chopped fine	
			3. Simmer until the vegetables are tender. *Do not overcook* or the broccoli will lose its fresh, green color.
9 oz	275 g	Butter, clarified	4. Combine the butter and flour in a saucepan to make a roux. Cook the roux a few minutes, but do not let it color. Cool the roux slightly. (Note: Beurre manié may be used instead of roux.)
9 oz	275 g	Flour	
			5. Beat the roux into the soup. Simmer until no starch taste remains.
			6. Pass the soup through a food mill and then through a fine china cap or cheesecloth.
3 pt approximately	1½ L	Hot milk	7. Add enough hot milk to bring the soup to proper consistency.
		Salt	8. Heat the soup again, but do not let it boil.
		White pepper	9. Season to taste.
3 cups	750 mL	Heavy cream, hot	10. At service time, add the heavy cream. If desired, add the garnish.
6 oz	175 g	Optional garnish: Small broccoli florets, cooked	

Variations, Method 3

For other cream soups, replace the broccoli with 3 lb (1.4 kg) of any of the following:

Asparagus
Carrots
Cauliflower
Celery
Corn
Green peas
Spinach

RECIPE 41 **Cream of Tomato Soup**

Yield: 6 qt (6 L)   **Portions:** 24   **Portion size:** 8 oz (250 mL)

U.S.	Metric	Ingredients	Procedure
4 oz	125 g	Salt pork, diced	1. In a heavy sauce pot, cook the salt pork over medium heat to render the fat.
4 oz	125 g	Onion, medium dice	
2 oz	60 g	Carrots, medium dice	2. Add the onion, carrot, and celery. Sweat until they are slightly softened.
2 oz	60 g	Celery, medium dice	
2 oz	60 g	Flour	3. Add the flour and stir to make a roux. Cook the roux a few minutes.
3 qt	3 L	White stock	
2 lb	1 kg	Canned tomatoes	4. Slowly beat in the stock. Bring to a boil, stirring while the liquid thickens slightly.
2 lb	1 kg	Tomato purée	
		Sachet:	
1	1	Bay leaf	5. Add the tomatoes, tomato purée, and sachet. Simmer about 1 hour.
pinch	pinch	Thyme	
1	1	Whole clove	6. Strain through a china cap. Press down on the solids with a ladle to force out all the juices and some of the pulp. (Alternative method: pass through a food mill, then strain.)
2	2	Peppercorns, crushed	
			7. If the soup is being made ahead, chill the tomato base and proceed to the next step just before service.
2 qt	2 L	Cream Sauce, hot	8. Return the tomato base to the sauce pot and bring back to a simmer.
		Salt	
		White pepper	9. Stir in the hot cream sauce.
			10. If the soup is too thick, thin out with a little stock.
			11. Season to taste with salt and pepper.

Variations

If you study this recipe, you will see that the first part (through step 6) is basically the same as Tomato Sauce I (p. 145) but with more mirepoix. It also contains much more stock, which makes it thinner than a sauce.

The recipe can be broken down as follows:

    1 part   Tomato sauce
    1 part   Stock
    1 part   Cream Sauce

Using this formula, you can also make Cream of Tomato Soup from Tomato Sauce II, from Seasoned Tomato Purée (variation following Tomato Sauce I), or from canned tomato sauce. You can also make it from canned tomato purée, if you simmer it with extra herbs, seasonings, and mirepoix. Check all seasonings and flavors carefully when using canned, prepared products.

PURÉE SOUPS

Techniques

Purée soups are made by simmering dried or fresh vegetables, especially high-starch vegetables, in stock or water, then puréeing the soup. Thus, they are relatively easy to prepare. Puréed soups are not as smooth and refined as cream soups but are heartier and coarser in texture and character.

Techniques vary greatly, depending on the ingredients and the desired result.

Basic Procedure for Making Purée Soups

1. Sweat mirepoix or other fresh vegetables in fat.

2. Add liquid.

3. Add dried or starchy vegetables.

4. Simmer until vegetables are tender. Fresh vegetables should be completely cooked but not overcooked or falling apart.

5. Purée soup in a food mill.

   Variation: Some soups made from dried legumes, such as bean soup, are not puréed but are served as is or slightly mashed up.

6. Purée soups are generally not bound with an added starch but rely on the starches present in the vegetables. Some fresh vegetable purées, however, settle out. These may be thickened with a little starch if desired.

7. Add cream if required.

8. Adjust seasonings.

RECIPE 42 **Purée of Carrot Soup (Potage Crecy)**

Yield: 6 qt (6 L) **Portions:** 24 **Portion size:** 8 oz (250 mL)

U.S.	Metric	Ingredients	Procedure
4 oz	125 g	Butter	1. Heat the butter in a heavy sauce pot over moderately low heat.
4 lb	2 kg	Carrots, small dice	
1 lb	500 g	Onions, small dice	2. Add the carrots and onions. Sweat the vegetables until they are about half cooked. Do not let them brown.
5 qt	5 L	Chicken stock or white veal stock	
1 lb	500 g	Potatoes, small dice	3. Add the stock and potatoes. Bring to a boil.
		Salt	
		White pepper	4. Simmer until the vegetables are tender.
			5. Purée the soup by passing it through a food mill.
			6. Bring the soup back to a simmer. If necessary, add more stock to thin out the soup to the proper consistency.
			7. Season to taste.
		Optional:	8. If desired, finish soup with hot cream at service time.
1½–2 cups	350–500 mL	Cream, hot	

Variations

42A. Rice may be used in place of potatoes as the binding agent in the above recipe or in any of the variations below *except* Purée of Potato, Purée of Potato and Leek, and Purée of Watercress. Use 8 oz (250 g) raw rice in place of 1 lb (500 g) potatoes. The soup must be simmered until the rice is very soft.

42B. Purée of Cauliflower Soup (Purée Dubarry): Use 4 lb (2 kg) cauliflower in place of carrots.

***RECIPE 42* Purée of Carrot Soup (Potage Crecy)** *(Continued)*

42C. *Purée of Celery or Celery Root Soup:* Use 4 lb (2 kg) celery or celery root in place of carrots.

42D. *Purée of Jerusalem Artichoke Soup:* Use 4 lb (2 kg) Jerusalem artichokes in place of carrots.

42E. *Purée of Potato Soup (Potage Parmentier):* Omit carrots from basic recipe, add 10 oz (300 g) leeks to the onion, and increase the potatoes to 5 lb (2.5 kg).

42F. *Purée of Potato and Leek Soup:* Use 2 lb (1 kg) leeks in place of the carrots. Increase the potatoes to 2½ lb (1.25 kg).

42G. *Purée of Turnip Soup:* Use 4 lb (2 kg) white turnips in place of carrots.

42H. *Purée of Watercress Soup:* Prepare like Purée of Potato Soup, but add 5 bunches watercress, chopped, when the potatoes are almost tender.

42I. *Purée of Mixed Vegetable Soup:* Decrease carrots to 1¼ lb (600 g). Add 10 oz (300 g) each of celery, turnips, leeks, and cabbage.

42J. *Potage Solferino:* Combine equal parts Purée of Potato and Leek Soup, and Cream of Tomato Soup.

***RECIPE 43* Purée of Green Pea Soup**

Yield: 6 qt (6 L) **Portions:** 24 **Portion size:** 8 oz (250 mL)

U.S.	Metric	Ingredients	Procedure
4 oz	125 g	Butter	1. Heat the butter in a heavy sauce pot over moderately low heat.
10 oz	300 g	Onions, fine dice	
4 qt	4 L	Chicken stock	2. Add the onions and sweat them without letting them brown.
6 lb	3 kg	Frozen peas	
pinch	pinch	Sugar	3. Add the stock and bring to a boil.
		Salt	4. Add the peas and sugar. Simmer until the peas are soft, about 5 minutes.
		White pepper	
2½ cups	600 mL	Heavy cream, optional	5. Pass the soup through a food mill.
			6. Return the soup to a simmer. Add additional stock if necessary, to bring to proper consistency.
			7. Adjust seasoning.
			8. At service time, heat the heavy cream and stir into the soup.

RECIPE 44 **Purée of Split Pea Soup**

Yield: 6 qt (6 L)   **Portions:** 24   **Portion Size:** 8 oz (250 mL)

U.S.	Metric	Ingredients	Procedure
6 oz	175 g	Salt pork	1. Cut the salt pork into fine dice or pass through a grinder.
		Mirepoix:	
10 oz	300 g	Onion, small dice	2. Cook the salt pork slowly in a heavy sauce pot to render the fat. Do not brown the pork.
5 oz	150 g	Celery, small dice	
5 oz	150 g	Carrot, small dice	
			3. Add the mirepoix and sweat in the fat until the vegetables are slightly softened.
6 qt	6 L	Ham stock (see note)	4. Add the ham stock and ham bone. Bring to a boil.
1	1	Ham bone or ham hock (optional)	
3 lb	1.5 kg	Green split peas	5. Rinse the split peas under cold water. Drain in a strainer and add to the stock. Also add the sachet.
		Sachet:	
1	1	Bay leaf	
2	2	Whole cloves	6. Cover and simmer until the peas are tender, about 1 hour.
6	6	Peppercorns	
		Salt	7. Remove the ham bone and sachet.
		Pepper	8. Pass the soup through a food mill.
			9. Bring the soup back to a simmer. If it is too thick, bring it to proper consistency with a little stock or water.
			10. Season to taste.
			11. If a ham hock was used, trim off the meat. Dice it and add it to the soup.

Note: Water may be used if ham stock is not available. In this case, the optional ham bone or ham hock should be used to provide flavor. Simmer the water and bone together for an hour or more before making the soup, to extract more flavor.

Variations

Other dried vegetables are made into soups using the same procedure. Most dried beans should be soaked in cold water overnight to reduce cooking time. (Split peas may be soaked, but they cook quickly enough without soaking.)

44A. Purée of White Bean Soup: Use 3 lb (1.5 kg) navy beans. Soak the beans overnight. Use chicken or veal stock in place of ham stock.

44B. Purée of Yellow Split Pea Soup: Use yellow split peas instead of green.

44C. Purée of Lentil Soup: Use 3 lb (1.5 kg) lentils. Soak overnight. Use either ham stock or white stock. Garnish with diced cooked bacon or ham or sliced frankfurters.

44D. Purée of Kidney Bean Soup: Use 3 lb (1.5 kg) red kidney beans. Soak them overnight. Use white stock, and add 2½ cups (600 mL) red wine to the soup when the beans are almost tender. Garnish with croutons sautéed in butter.

44E. Purée of Black Bean Soup: Use 3 lb (1.5 kg) black turtle beans. Soak them overnight. Use white stock and use the optional ham bone. Add 8 oz (250 mL) Madeira or sherry to the finished soup. Garnish with lemon slices and chopped hard-cooked egg.

RECIPE 44 **Purée of Split Pea Soup** *(Continued)*

....

44F. *Purée Mongole:* Combine 3 qt (3 L) Purée of Green Split Pea Soup and 2 qt (2 L) tomato purée, preferably Seasoned Tomato Purée, page 146 (canned tomato purée is also acceptable). Dilute to proper consistency with about 1–2 qt (1–2 L) white stock. Garnish with cooked peas and with cooked julienne of carrots and leeks.

44G. *Nonpuréed Bean Soups:* Prepare any of the above soups as directed, but purée only about one-fourth of the beans. Add this purée to the soup as a thickening agent.

....

RECIPE 45 **Navy Bean Soup**

....

Yield: 6 qt (6 L)		**Portions:** 24		**Portion size:** 8 oz (250 mL)

U.S.	*Metric*	*Ingredients*		*Procedure*
2 lb	1 kg	Dried navy beans		1. Soak the beans overnight in cold water.
4 oz	125 g	Bacon, diced		2. Place the bacon in a heavy sauce pot over medium heat. Render the fat from the bacon, but do not cook until crisp.
4 oz	125 g	Onions, small dice		
8 oz	250 g	Carrots, small dice		
8 oz	250 g	Celery, small dice		3. Add the vegetables and cook over low heat until almost tender.
4 oz	125 g	Leeks, sliced		
3	3	Garlic cloves, chopped		
5 qt	5 L	Stock or water		4. Add the stock or water and the ham hock. Bring to a boil.
1	1	Ham hock		
1	1	Bay leaf		5. Drain the beans and add them to the liquid. Also add the bay leaf, thyme, and pepper.
½ tsp	2 mL	Thyme		
½ tsp	2 mL	Pepper		
				6. Cover and simmer until the beans are tender.
1 qt	1 L	Canned tomatoes, with juice, crushed		7. Add the tomatoes to the soup and simmer another 15 minutes. Remove the bay leaf.
				8. Remove the ham hock from the soup. Cut off and dice the meat and add it to the soup. Discard the bones.
				9. Mash the beans lightly with a paddle or pass about one-fourth of the beans through a food mill. Add this purée back to the soup to thicken it.
				10. If the soup is too thick, thin it out with a little stock.
				11. Adjust the seasoning.

....

RECIPE 46 **Vichyssoise (Cold Leek and Potato Soup)**

....

Yield: 6 qt (6 L)   **Portions:** 24   **Portion size:** 8 oz (250 mL)

U.S.	Metric	Ingredients	Procedure
3 lb	1.5 kg	Leeks, white part only	1. Cut the leeks and potatoes into thin slices.
3 lb	1.5 kg	Potatoes, peeled	
6 oz	175 g	Butter	2. Sweat the leeks in butter without letting them brown.
4½ qt	4½ L	Chicken stock	
		Salt	3. Add the stock and potatoes and bring to a boil. Simmer until vegetables are tender.
		White pepper	
			4. Pass the soup through a food mill and then through a fine china cap or cheesecloth. Vichyssoise should be very smooth.
			5. If soup is too thick, add a little stock to bring to proper consistency.
			6. Chill the soup thoroughly.
			7. Adjust the seasonings.
4–5 cups	1–1¼ L	Heavy cream	8. At service time, stir in the heavy cream.
		Garnish; chopped chives	9. Garnish each portion with chopped chives.

Variation

Water is sometimes used instead of stock. Leeks are flavorful enough to make a delicious soup even without stock.

....

BISQUES

A bisque is a cream soup made with shellfish. At one time bisques were thickened with rice, but today they are more frequently thickened with roux. Bisques are made basically like other cream soups, but they seem more complex because of the handling of the shell-fish and the variety of flavoring ingredients often used. Expensive to prepare and rich in taste, they are considered luxury soups.

The term bisque has come to be used for a great variety of other soups, primarily because the word sounds nice. In this book we reserve the term for shellfish cream soups.

RECIPE 47 **Shrimp Bisque**

Yield: 2 qt (2 L)   **Portions:** 10   **Portion size:** 6 oz (200 mL)

U.S.	Metric	Ingredients	Procedure
1 oz	30 g	Butter	1. Heat the butter in a saucepan over medium heat.
2 oz	60 g	Onions, brunoise	
2 oz	60 g	Carrots, brunoise	2. Add the onions and carrots. Sauté until they are lightly browned.
1 lb	500 g	Small shrimp, shells on	
small piece	small piece	Bay leaf	3. Add the shrimp, bay leaf, thyme, and parsley stems. Sauté until the shrimp turn red.
pinch	pinch	Thyme	
4	4	Parsley stems	
1 oz	30 g	Tomato paste	4. Add the tomato paste and stir well.
2 oz	60 mL	Burnt brandy (see note)	5. Add the brandy and wine. Simmer until reduced by half.
6 oz	200 mL	White wine	
			6. Remove the shrimp. Peel and devein them. Return the shells to the saucepan.
			7. Cut the shrimp into small dice and reserve for garnish.
1 qt	1 L	Fish Velouté	8. Add the Fish Velouté and stock to the saucepan. Simmer 10 to 15 minutes.
1 pt	500 mL	Fish stock	
1 cup	250 mL	Heavy cream, hot	9. Strain. Return the soup to the saucepan and bring back to a simmer.
		Salt	
		White pepper	10. At service time add the hot cream and the diced shrimp. Season to taste.

Note: Burnt brandy is brandy that has been heated in a saucepan and flamed (carefully) to burn off the alcohol.

Variations

This recipe is based on Method 1 for making cream soups (pp. 171–172), because it uses velouté as a base. You can also use fish stock instead of velouté and thicken the soup in other ways:
1. Beat in a beurre manié (p. 133), a little at a time, after step 8, until properly thickened.
2. Stir in a cornstarch slurry (cornstarch in cold water), a little at a time.
3. Simmer 2 oz (60 g) rice in 1 pt (500 mL) of the stock, until the rice is completely cooked. Liquidize in a blender or force through a fine sieve to purée the rice, and add to the soup. (This is the classical method.)

To reduce food cost, you may reduce the quantity of shrimp and add extra shrimp shells for flavor. *Or,* instead of using all the cooked shrimp for garnish, save most of them for another use.

Paprika is often used instead of tomato paste to color and flavor bisques. Substitute 1 tbsp (15 mL) of Spanish paprika for the 1 oz (30 g) of tomato paste.

47A. Lobster Bisque: In place of shrimp, use live lobster, cut up as shown in Figure 14.9. (Or to reduce food costs, use crushed lobster shells or rock lobster tails.)

CHOWDERS

Chowders are chunky, hearty soups that are so full of good things that they sometimes are more like stews than soups. Many chowders are simply cream soups or purée soups that are not puréed but left chunky. Like other specialty regional soups, chowders resist being categorized. However, most of them are based on fish or shellfish or vegetables, and most contain potatoes and milk or cream.

RECIPE 48   **Potato Chowder**

Yield: 6 qt (6 L)   **Portions:** 24   **Portion size:** 8 oz (250 mL)

U.S.	Metric	Ingredients	Procedure
8 oz	250 g	Salt pork	1. Grind the salt pork or cut into very fine dice.
12 oz	375 g	Onions, medium dice	
3 oz	90 g	Celery, medium dice	2. Render the pork fat in a heavy sauce pot.
4 oz	125 g	Flour	
			3. Add the onions and celery. Cook in the fat over moderate heat until nearly tender. Do not brown.
			4. Add the flour. Stir into the fat to make a roux. Cook the roux slowly for 4–5 minutes, but do not let it brown.
3½ qt	3½ L	Chicken stock	5. Using a wire whip, slowly stir in the stock. Bring to a boil, stirring to make sure the liquid is smooth.
3 lb	1.5 kg	Potatoes, medium dice	
			6. Add the potatoes. Simmer until all the vegetables are tender.
3 pt	1½ L	Milk, hot	7. Stir in the hot milk and cream.
1 cup	250 mL	Heavy cream, hot	8. Season to taste with salt and white pepper.
		Salt	
		White pepper	
		Chopped parsley	9. Sprinkle each portion with a little chopped parsley for garnish.

Variations

48A.   *Corn Chowder:* Version 1. Prepare as in basic recipe, but reduce potatoes to 2¼ lb (1.1 kg). When vegetables are tender, add 3 lb (1.5 kg) frozen or drained canned whole kernel corn. (If using canned corn, replace part of the chicken stock with the corn liquid.)

Version 2. Prepare as in basic recipe, but reduce potatoes to 1½ lb (750 g). Add 3 lb (1.5 kg) canned cream-style corn when vegetables are tender.

RECIPE 49 New England Clam Chowder

Yield: 6 qt (6 L)   **Portions:** 24   **Portion size:** 8 oz (250 mL)

U.S.	Metric	Ingredients	Procedure
2 qt	2 L	Canned, minced clams, with their juice or fresh shucked clams, with their juice (see note)	1. Drain the clams. If you are using fresh clams, chop them, being sure to save all the juice.
1½ qt	1½ L	Water	2. Combine the juice and water in a saucepan. Bring to a boil. 3. Remove from the heat and keep the liquid hot for step 7.
10 oz	300 g	Salt pork, ground or cut into fine dice	4. In a heavy sauce pot or stock pot, render the salt pork over medium heat.
1 lb	500 g	Onions, small dice	5. Add the onions and cook slowly until they are soft, but do not brown.
4 oz	125 g	Flour	6. Add the flour and stir to make a roux. Cook the roux slowly for 3–4 minutes, but do not let it brown.
2 lb	1 kg	Potatoes, small dice	7. Using a wire whip, slowly stir the clam liquid and water into the roux. Bring to a boil, stirring constantly to make sure the liquid is smooth. 8. Add the potatoes. Simmer until tender. (If you are using large, tough "chowder" clams, pass them once through a grinder and add them with the potatoes.)
2½ qt	2½ L	Milk, hot	9. Stir in the clams and the hot milk and cream. Heat gently but do not boil.
1 cup	250 mL	Heavy cream, hot Salt White pepper	10. Season to taste with salt and white pepper.

***Note*:** If whole clams in the shell are used, you will need about 8–10 qt (8–10 L). Scrub them well. Combine with the 1½ qt (1½ L) water in a stock pot and simmer until the shells are open. Remove the clams from the shells and chop. Strain the liquid.

Variations

49A. *Manhattan Clam Chowder:* Substitute 4 oz (125 mL) oil or 4 oz (125 g) butter for the salt pork. Add 10 oz (300 g) celery, small dice; 10 oz (300 g) carrots, small dice; and 1 tsp (5 mL) chopped garlic to the onions in step 5. Omit flour. Instead of milk, use 2½ qt (2½ L) chopped canned tomatoes and their juices. Omit cream.

49B. *New England Fish Chowder:* Follow the procedure for New England Clam Chowder, but omit clams and water. Use 3 qt (3 L) fish stock instead of the clam juice and water mixture in step 7. Remove all skin and bones from 1¼ lb (625 g) haddock fillets. Cut into ¾ inch (2 cm) chunks. Add to the finished soup and *keep hot* (do not boil) until the fish is cooked, about 5 minutes.

SPECIALTY SOUPS AND NATIONAL SOUPS

RECIPE 50 **French Onion Soup Gratinée**

Yield: 7½ qt (7½ L) **Portions:** 24 **Portion size:** 10 oz (300 mL)

U.S.	Metric	Ingredients	Procedure
4 oz 5 lb	125 g 2.5 kg	Butter Onions, sliced thin	1. Heat the butter in a stock pot over moderate heat. Add the onions and cook until they are golden. Stir occasionally. Note: The onions must cook slowly and become evenly browned. This is a slow process and will take about 30 minutes. Do not brown too fast or use high heat.
6½ qt 4–6 oz	6½ L 125–175 mL	Beef stock, or half beef and half chicken stock Salt Pepper Sherry (optional)	2. Add the stock and bring to a boil. Simmer until the onions are very tender and the flavors are well blended, about 20 minutes. 3. Season to taste with salt and pepper. Add the sherry, if desired. 4. Keep the soup hot for service.
 1½ lb	 750 g	French bread (see procedure) Gruyère or Swiss cheese, or a mixture, coarsely grated	5. Cut the bread into slices about ⅜ inch (1 cm) thick. You will need 1 or 2 slices per portion, or just enough to cover the top of the soup in its serving crock. 6. Toast the slices in the oven or under the broiler. 7. For each portion, fill an individual service soup crock with hot soup. Place one or two slices of the toast on top, and cover with cheese. Pass under the broiler until the cheese is bubbling and lightly browned. Serve immediately.

Variation

Onion soup may be served without gratinéeing, and with cheese croutons prepared separately. Toast the bread as in basic recipe. Place on a sheet pan. Brush lightly with butter and sprinkle each piece with grated cheese. (Parmesan may be mixed with the other cheese.) Brown under the broiler. Garnish each portion with one cheese crouton. (This method is less expensive because it uses much less cheese.)

RECIPE 51   **Borscht**

Yield: 6 qt (6 L)   **Portions:** 24   **Portion size:** 8 oz (250 mL)

U.S.	Metric	Ingredients	Procedure
2 lb	1 kg	Beef brisket or shank (see note)	1. Simmer the beef in the water or stock until tender.
3½ qt	3½ L	Water or beef stock	2. Remove the cooked beef from the broth and cut it into small dice.
			3. Measure the broth and, if necessary, add water to bring it back up to 3 qt (3 L).
			4. Return the meat to the broth.
4 oz	125 g	Butter	5. Heat the butter in a heavy pot. Add the onion, leeks, and the cabbage. Cook slowly in the butter for about 5 minutes.
8 oz	250 g	Onion, sliced thin	
8 oz	250 g	Leeks, white part and about ½ inch (1 cm) of green, cut julienne	
8 oz	250 g	Cabbage, shredded	
2 No. 2½ cans		Beets (about 60 oz/ 1.7 kg) (see note)	6. Drain the beets and save the juice. Grate the beets on a coarse grater, or chop them fine.
4 oz	125 g	Tomato purée	7. Add the mixture of onions, leeks, and cabbage, the beets, beet juice, tomato purée, vinegar, and sugar to the meat and broth.
4 oz	125 mL	Vinegar	
2 tbsp	30 g	Sugar	
		Salt	
		White pepper	8. Bring to a boil and simmer until the vegetables are tender.
			9. Season to taste with salt, white pepper, and more vinegar if desired.
		Sour cream	10. Serve each portion topped with a spoonful of sour cream.

Note: Leftover cooked beef may be used. In this case, use 16 to 20 oz (500 to 625 g) cooked beef and use stock, not water.

   If fresh raw beets are used, shred or grate them and sweat them with the onions.

Variations

51A. Cold Borscht: Omit beef. Strain soup through a china cap, pressing down on the vegetables to force out all juices. Chill the soup and add lemon juice to taste. Serve with sour cream.

RECIPE 52 **Minestrone**

Yield: 6 qt (6 L) **Portions:** 24 **Portion size:** 8 oz (250 mL)

U.S.	Metric	Ingredients	Procedure
4 oz	125 mL	Olive oil	1. Heat the oil in a heavy pot over medium heat.
1 lb	500 g	Onions, sliced thin	
8 oz	250 g	Celery, small dice	2. Add the onions, celery, carrots, and garlic. Sweat them in the oil until they are almost tender. Do not brown.
8 oz	250 g	Carrots, small dice	
2 tsp	10 mL	Garlic, chopped	
8 oz	250 g	Green cabbage, shredded (see p. 392 for technique)	3. Add the cabbage and zucchini. Stir to mix the vegetables. Continue to sweat them for another 5 minutes.
8 oz	230 g	Zucchini, medium dice	
1 lb	500 g	Canned tomatoes, crushed	4. Add the tomatoes, stock, and basil. Bring to a boil, reduce heat, and simmer until the vegetables are almost cooked. (Do not overcook. The soup will continue to cook when the pasta is added.)
5 qt	5 L	White stock	
1 tsp	5 mL	Basil	
6 oz	175 g	Small macaroni, such as ditalini	5. Add the pasta and continue to simmer the soup until the pasta is cooked.
1½ lb	750 g	Drained, canned cannellini or other white beans (two No. 2 cans)	6. Add the beans and bring the soup back to a boil.
			7. Add the parsley. Season to taste with salt and pepper.
¼ cup	60 mL	Chopped parsley	
		Salt	
		Pepper	
		Parmesan cheese, grated	8. Just before service, stir in the Parmesan cheese, *or* serve the cheese separately.

RECIPE 53 **Avgolemono**

Yield: 6 qt (6 L) **Portions:** 24 **Portion size:** 8 oz (250 mL)

U.S.	Metric	Ingredients	Procedure
6 qt	6 L	Chicken stock	1. Bring the stock to a boil in a large sauce pot or in a stock pot.
8 oz	250 g	Rice, raw	2. Place the rice in a strainer and rinse under cold water. Add to the stock. Simmer until the rice is cooked.
			3. Remove from heat.

RECIPE 53 **Avgolemono** (*Continued*)

U.S.	Metric	Ingredients	Procedure
8	8	Liaison: Eggs, beaten Lemon juice Salt White pepper Chopped parsley	4. Just before serving, beat the eggs with the lemon juice in a stainless steel bowl. 5. Gradually beat in about 1 pt (500 mL) of the hot soup to temper the liaison. Stir the mixture back into the soup. 6. Return the soup to the heat and warm it up to below the simmering point. *Do not boil,* or the soup will curdle. 7. Season to taste with salt and pepper. 8. At service time, top each portion with a little chopped parsley.
6 oz	200 mL		

RECIPE 54 **Scotch Broth**

Yield: 6 qt (6 L)   **Portions:** 24   **Portion size:** 8 oz (250 mL)

U.S.	Metric	Ingredients	Procedure
6 qt	6 L	White lamb stock	1. Bring 1 qt (1 L) of the stock to a boil in a saucepan.
4 oz	125 g	Barley	2. Add the barley and cover the pan. Simmer until tender.
1½ lb	750 g	Lean, boneless lamb shoulder or shank, cut in small dice	3. Bring the remaining 5 qt (5 L) of stock to a boil in another pot. 4. Add the lamb and cover the pot. Simmer until the meat is almost tender.
4 oz	125 g	Butter	5. Heat the butter in a heavy pot over medium heat. Add the vegetables and sweat them in the butter until nearly tender. 6. Add the lamb and stock from step 4. Simmer until the meat and vegetables are tender. 7. Add the cooked barley and stock from step 2. Simmer about 5 minutes, until the flavors are well blended. 8. Season to taste with salt and pepper.
12 oz	375 g	Onions, brunoise	
8 oz	250 g	Carrots, brunoise	
8 oz	250 g	Celery, brunoise	
4 oz	125 g	Leeks, brunoise	
4 oz	125 g	Turnips, brunoise Salt White pepper	
		Chopped parsley	9. At serving time, sprinkle each portion with a little chopped parsley.

RECIPE 55 Gazpacho

Yield: 2½ qt (2½ L) **Portions:** 12 **Portion size:** 6 oz (200 mL)

U.S.	Metric	Ingredients	Procedure
2½ lb	1.2 kg	Tomatoes, peeled and chopped fine	1. If a blender is available, combine all ingredients in the blender and process until liquified.
1 lb	500 g	Cucumbers, peeled and chopped fine	
8 oz	250 g	Onions, peeled and chopped fine	2. If a blender is not available, combine all ingredients except the olive oil. Pass through a food mill. If a smoother soup is desired, then pass through a fine sieve. Rub the solids through the sieve to purée them. Place the mixture in a stainless steel bowl. Using the wire whip, slowly beat in the olive oil.
4 oz	125 g	Green peppers, seeded and chopped fine	
½ tsp	2 mL	Crushed garlic	
2 oz	60 g	Fresh white breadcrumbs	
1 pt	500 mL	Cold water or tomato juice	
3 oz	90 mL	Red wine vinegar	
4 oz	125 mL	Olive oil	
		Salt	3. Add salt, pepper, and cayenne or pepper sauce to taste.
		Pepper	
		Cayenne or hot red pepper sauce	4. If necessary, adjust the tartness by adding a little lemon juice or vinegar.
		Lemon juice or vinegar	5. Chill the soup thoroughly.
		Garnish:	6. Combine garnish ingredients in a small bowl or bain marie.
2 oz	60 g	Onion, small dice	
2 oz	60 g	Cucumber, small dice	7. At service time, ladle 6 oz (200 mL) gazpacho into chilled soup cups. Top with 1–2 tbsp (15–30 g) diced vegetable garnish. If desired, gazpacho may be served with ice cubes.
2 oz	60 g	Green pepper, small dice	

TERMS FOR REVIEW

clear soup	purée soup	potage	clearmeat
vegetable soup	bisque	national soup	coagulation
consommé	chowder	clarification	raft
cream soup			

QUESTIONS FOR DISCUSSION

1. You have 3 gallons (12 liters) of vegetable soup in the walk-in, prepared by a cook on the morning shift. You are going to serve the soup this evening, and your dinner service lasts from 6 until 10 P.M. How should you prepare the soup for service?

2. What are the most important characteristics of a good consommé?

3. Why is it important not to boil consommé during clarification?

4. What is the function of egg whites in clearmeat? Mirepoix? Tomato product?

5. In what order would you add the following items to a vegetable soup during cooking?

Carrots	Shredded cabbage
Barley	Diced cooked beef
Tomatoes	

6. Using Method 1 or 2, describe how you would prepare Cream of Watercress Soup.

A trio of broiled dishes: deviled chicken (page 296), lobster (page 356), and London broil (page 241) with broiled tomato (page 423).

PART THREE

MEAT, POULTRY, AND FISH

. . . .

. . . . *On* most dinner plates, the most important element
is a serving of one of the foods considered in these chapters. They require
most of a cook's time and supply most of a meal's satisfaction.

Understanding Meats

Cooking Meats

Understanding Poultry

Cooking Poultry

Understanding Fish and Shellfish

Cooking Fish and Shellfish

CHAPTER 10

UNDERSTANDING MEATS

Meat is muscle
tissue. It is the flesh of domestic animals (cattle, hogs, and lambs) and of
wild game animals (such as venison).

Meat is the mainstay of the American diet. As a cook, chef,
or food service operator, you will be spending more of your time and money on
meats than on any other food.

It is important, then, to understand meats thoroughly in order
to cook them well and profitably. Why are some meats tender and some tough?
How can you tell one cut from another when there are so many? How do
you determine the best way to cook each cut?

In order to answer questions like these, it is helpful to start at
the most basic level of composition and structure. We will then proceed to
discuss grading and inspection, basic cuts, and appropriate cooking and storage
methods. Only then will we be able to best approach the individual cooking
methods and recipes presented in the following chapters.

After reading this chapter, you should be able to

1. Describe the composition and structure of meat and tell how it relates to meat selection and cooking methods.

2. Use the federal meat inspection and grading system to help you select and purchase meats.

3. Explain the significance of aging meats.

4. Identify the primal cuts of beef, lamb, veal, and pork, and list the major fabricated cuts obtained from each of them.

5. Select appropriate cooking methods for the most important meat cuts, based on the meat's tenderness and other characteristics.

6. Determine doneness in cooked meat.

7. Store meats for maximum shelf life.

COMPOSITION, STRUCTURE, AND BASIC QUALITY FACTORS

COMPOSITION

Muscle tissue consists of three major components: water, protein, and fat.

Water

Water is about 75 percent of muscle tissue. With such a high percentage of water in meat, you can see why *shrinkage* can be a big problem in cooking meat. Too much moisture loss means dry meat, loss of weight, and loss of profit.

Protein

Protein is an important nutrient and the most abundant solid material in meat. About 20 percent of muscle tissue is protein.

As we learned in Chapter 4, protein *coagulates* when it is heated. This means it becomes firmer and loses moisture. Coagulation is related to doneness: when protein has coagulated to the desired degree, the meat is said to be "done." Doneness will be discussed later in this chapter.

Too high heat *toughens* protein.

Fat

Fat accounts for up to 5 percent of muscle tissue.

Of course, there can be more fat surrounding the muscles. A beef carcass can be as much as 30 percent fat.

Because of health and dietary concerns, many meat animals are being bred and raised with a lower fat content than in past years. Nevertheless, a certain amount of fat is desirable for three reasons:

1. *Juiciness.*

   Marbling is fat that is deposited within the muscle tissue. The juiciness we enjoy in well-marbled beef is due more to fat than to moisture.

   Surface fat protects the meat—especially roasts—from drying out during cooking as well as in storage. Adding surface fats where they are lacking is called *barding*.

2. *Tenderness.*

   Marbling separates muscle fibers, making them easier to chew.

3. *Flavor.*

   Fat is perhaps the main source of flavor in meat. A well-marbled Prime (top grade) steak tastes "beefier" than the same cut of a lower grade.

Carbohydrate

Meat contains a very small amount of carbohydrate. From the standpoint of nutrition, its quantity is so small that it is insignificant. It is important, however, because it plays a necessary part in the complex reactions that take place when meats are browned by roasting, broiling, or sautéing. Without this carbohydrate, the desirable flavor and appearance of browned meats would not be achieved.

STRUCTURE

Muscle Fibers

Lean meat is composed of long, thin muscle fibers bound together in bundles. These determine the *texture* or *grain* of a piece of meat. Fine-grained meat is composed of small fibers bound in small bundles. Coarse-textured meat has large fibers.

Feel the cut surface of a tenderloin steak, and compare its smooth texture to the rough cut surface of brisket or bottom round.

Connective Tissue

Muscle fibers are bound together in a network of proteins called *connective tissues*. Also, each muscle fiber is covered in a sheath of connective tissue.

It is very important for the cook to understand connective tissue for one basic reason: *connective tissue is tough.* To cook meats successfully, you should know

- Which meats are high in connective tissue and which are low.

- What are the best ways to make tough meats tender.

1. *Meats are highest in connective tissue if*

   a. They come from muscles that are more exercised. Muscles in the legs, for example, have more connective tissue than muscles in the back.

   b. They come from older animals. Veal is tenderer than meat from a young steer, which in turn is tenderer than meat from an old bull or cow. (Young animals have connective tissue, too, but it becomes harder to break down as the animal ages.)

2. Meats high in connective tissue can be made more tender by using proper cooking techniques.

    There are two kinds of connective tissue: *collagen,* which is white in color, and *elastin,* which is yellow.

    a. *Collagen.*

    Long, slow cooking in the presence of moisture breaks down or dissolves collagen by turning it into gelatin and water. Of course, muscle tissue is about 75 percent water, so moisture is always present when meats are cooked. Except for very large roasts, however, long cooking by a dry-heat method has the danger of evaporating too much moisture and drying out the meat. Therefore, *moist-heat cooking methods at low temperatures are most effective for turning a meat high in connective tissue into a tender, juicy finished product.*

    Other factors also help tenderize collagen:

    Acid helps dissolve collagen. Marinating meat in an acid mixture, or adding an acid such as tomato or wine to the cooking liquid, helps tenderize.

    Enzymes are naturally present in meats. They break down some connective tissue and other proteins as meat ages (see *aging,* p. 198). These enzymes are inactive at freezing temperatures, slow acting under refrigeration, active at room temperature, and destroyed by heat above 140°F (60°C).

    Tenderizers are enzymes such as papain (extracted from papaya), which are added to meats by the cook or injected into the animal before slaughter. Exercise care when using enzyme tenderizers. Too long an exposure at room temperature can make the meat undesirably mushy.

    b. *Elastin.*

    Older animals have a higher proportion of elastin than younger animals.

    Elastin is not broken down in cooking. Tenderizing can be accomplished only by *removing the elastin* (cutting away any tendons) and by mechanically *breaking up the fibers,* as in

    Pounding and cubing (cubed steaks).

    Grinding (hamburger).

    Slicing the cooked meat very thin against the grain (as in London broil).

INSPECTION AND GRADING

Cooks and food service operators are assisted in their evaluation of meats by a federal inspection and grading system.

Inspection

1. Inspection is a *guarantee of wholesomeness,* not of quality or tenderness. It means that the animal was not diseased and the meat is clean and fit for human consumption.

2. It is indicated by a round stamp (Figure 10.1).

3. It is required by federal law—all meat must be inspected.

Quality Grading

1. Grading is a *quality* designation.

2. It is indicated by a shield stamp (Figure 10.2).

3. It is *not required by law.* (Some packers use a *private grading system* and give different brand names to different grades. Reliability of private grades depends on the reputation of the packer.)

Quality grading is based on the texture, firmness, and color of the lean meat, the age or maturity of the animal, and the marbling (the fat within the lean).

FIGURE 10.1   **USDA inspection stamp for meat.**

FIGURE 10.2   **USDA grade stamp for meat.**

All these factors must be considered together. For example, old, tough meat can still have marbling, but it would rate a low grade because of the other factors. Table 10.1 summarizes USDA meat grades.

Yield Grading

In addition to quality grading, beef and lamb are graded according to how much usable meat in proportion to fat they have. The meatiest grade is Yield Grade 1. Poorest yield (much exterior fat) is Yield Grade 5.

Pork is yield graded from 1 to 4, but most pork is sold already cut and trimmed.

Veal, which has little fat, is not yield graded.

AGING

"Green" Meat

Soon after slaughter, an animal's muscles stiffen, due to chemical changes in the flesh. This stiffness, called *rigor mortis,* gradually disappears. Softening takes 3 to 4 days for beef, less time for smaller carcasses like veal, lamb, and pork. This softening is caused by *enzymes* in the flesh.

Green meat is meat that has not had enough time to soften. It is tough and relatively flavorless. Because it takes several days for meats to reach the kitchen from the slaughterhouse, green meat is seldom a problem, except when meat is frozen while still green.

Aged Meat

Enzyme action continues in muscle tissue even after meat is no longer green. This tenderizes the flesh even more and develops more flavor. Holding meats in coolers under controlled conditions to provide time for this natural tenderizing is called *aging.*

Beef and lamb can be aged, because high-quality carcasses have enough fat cover to protect them from bacteria and from drying. Veal has no fat cover, so it is not aged. Pork does not require aging.

The three major types of aging are described as follows:

1. **Dry aging.** Aging does not mean just storing meat in your refrigerator. *There is a difference*

TABLE 10.1 **USDA Meat Grades**

Characteristics	Beef	Veal	Lamb	Pork
Highest quality, highest price, limited supply.	Prime	Prime	Prime	Pork used in food service is very consistent in quality and is not quality graded. It is inspected for wholesomeness and graded for yield.
High in quality, generally tender and juicy. Abundant supply. Widely used in food service as well as in retail.	Choice	Choice	Choice	
Lean meat, not as fine or tender. Economical. Can be tender and flavorful if cooked carefully. Used in many institutional food service operations.	Select	Good	Good	
Least frequently used in food service. Highest of these grades are sometimes used in institutional food service. Lowest of these grades are used by canners and processors.	Standard Commercial Utility Cutter Canner	Standard Utility Cull	Utility Cull	

Note: Quality varies within grades. For example, the best Choice beef is close to Prime, while the lowest Choice beef is close to Select.

between aged meat and old meat. Temperature must be carefully monitored. Air flow and humidity must be controlled, because bacteria will grow on cut surfaces if there is too much moisture. Ultraviolet lights are sometimes used in aging coolers to kill bacteria and mold.

2. *Fast aging.*   To speed aging, meat can be held at a higher temperature and humidity for a shorter time. Ultraviolet lights to control bacteria are especially important in fast aging. Most fast-aged meat is sold on the retail market rather than to food service establishments.

3. *Vacuum-pack aging.*   The modern trend is to break down carcasses into smaller cuts and wrap them in air- and moisture-proof plastic bags. This is called *Cryovac aging.* The wrapping protects meats from bacteria and mold and prevents weight loss due to drying. (However, Cryovac-aged meats often lose more weight in cooking than do dry-aged meats.) Of course, meats in Cryovac must be refrigerated.

Aging increases tenderness and flavor. An off taste is not characteristic of aged meat. *If a meat smells or tastes spoiled, it probably is.* Sometimes meats in Cryovac have a musty aroma when first opened, but this disappears quickly.

Aging costs money. Storage costs, weight losses due to drying, heavier trimming due to dried and discolored surfaces, all add to the price of aged meat (although Cryovac aging costs less than dry aging). As a meat purchaser, you will have to decide how much quality is worth how much cost for your particular establishment.

UNDERSTANDING THE BASIC CUTS

Meat cuts are based on two factors:

1. The muscle and bone structure of the meat.

2. Uses and appropriate cooking methods of various parts of the animal.

Food service suppliers may follow a set of specifications called Institution Meat Purchase Specifications (IMPS). (IMPS, including numbers and names of cuts, are the same as the National Association of Meat Purveyors Specifications, or NAMPS.) All cuts

are described in detail and listed by number. This simplifies purchasing, since you can order by number for exactly the cut you want.

AVAILABLE FORMS: CARCASSES, PARTIAL CARCASSES, PRIMALS, AND FABRICATED CUTS

Beef, lamb, veal, and pork may be purchased in some or all of these forms.

Carcasses

The carcass is the whole animal, minus entrails, head, feet, and hide (except pork, which has only the entrails and head removed). Whole carcasses are rarely purchased by food service operators, because of the skill and labor required in cutting and because of the problem of total utilization.

Sides, Quarters, Foresaddles, Hindsaddles

These represent the first step in breaking down a carcass.

Again, these larger cuts are no longer frequently used in food service. Fewer establishments are cutting their own meats.

1. Beef is split first through the backbone into sides. Sides are divided between the 12th and 13th ribs into forequarter and hindquarter.

2. Veal and lamb are not split into sides but are divided between ribs 12 and 13 into foresaddle and hindsaddle.

   Note: A new cutting style has been developed for lamb. In this method, the foresaddle and hindsaddle are divided after the 13th rib. For more information, see the chart of lamb cuts on page 210. The new style cuts and the traditional style are available, according to the customers' needs.

3. Pork carcasses are not divided in this way. They are cut directly into primal cuts (below).

Primal or Wholesale Cuts

These are the primary divisions of quarters, foresaddles, hindsaddles, and carcasses. These cuts are still used to some extent in food service, because they

1. Are small enough to be manageable in many food service kitchens.

2. Are still large enough to allow a variety of different cuts for different uses or needs.

3. Are easier to utilize completely than quarters or halves.

Each primal may be *fabricated,* or cut up and trimmed, in several different ways. They are always the starting point for smaller cuts. For this reason it will benefit you to be able to identify each one. Study the charts and photos in Figures 10.3 through 10.6. (Please note that the lamb chart in Figure 10.5 shows the traditional cuts, not the new cuts mentioned previously.) Learn the names of the primals, their location on the carcass, and the most important cuts that

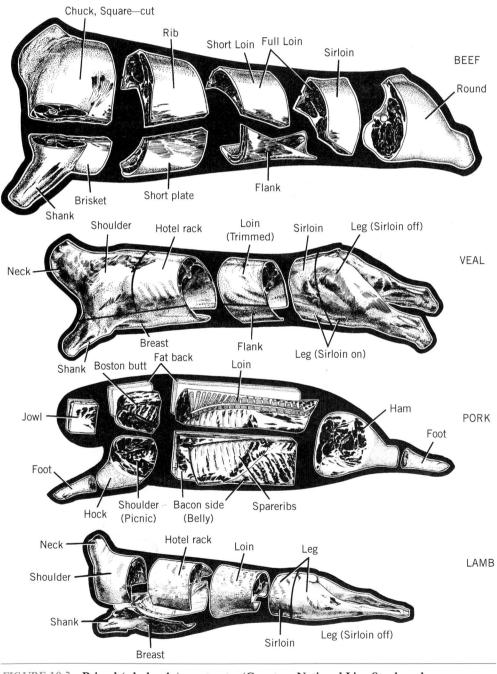

FIGURE 10.3 **Primal (wholesale) meat cuts. (Courtesy National Live Stock and Meat Board.)**

come from each. Then, whenever you work with a piece of meat, try to identify it exactly and match it with its primal cut.

Fabricated Cuts

Primal cuts are fabricated into smaller cuts for roasts, steaks, chops, cutlets, stewing meat, ground meat, and so forth, according to individual customer requirements and, if applicable, IMPS/NAMPS specifications.

The amount of trim and exact specifications can have many variations. For example, a beef primal rib is trimmed and prepared for roasting at least nine different ways.

Portion control cuts are ready-to-cook meats, cut according to customer's specifications. Steaks and chops are ordered either by weight per steak

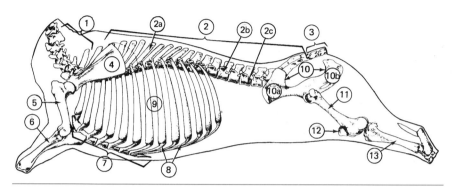

FIGURE 10.4   Beef bone structure. (Courtesy National Live Stock and Meat Board.)

1. **Neck bone**	4. **Blade bone**	10. **Pelvis**
2. **Backbone**	5. **Arm bone**	10a. **Hip bone**
2a. **Feather bone**	6. **Fore shank bone**	10b. **Rump or aitch bone**
2b. **Finger bone**	7. **Breast bone**	11. **Leg or round bone**
2c. **Chine bone**	8. **Rib cartilage**	12. **Knee cap**
3. **Tail bone**	9. **Ribs**	13. **Hind shank bone**

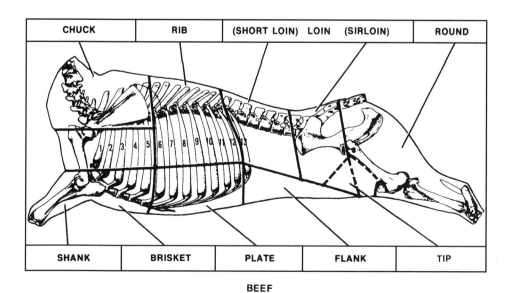

FIGURE 10.5   Primal (wholesale) cuts and their bone structure. (Courtesy National Live Stock and Meat Board.) *(Continues)*

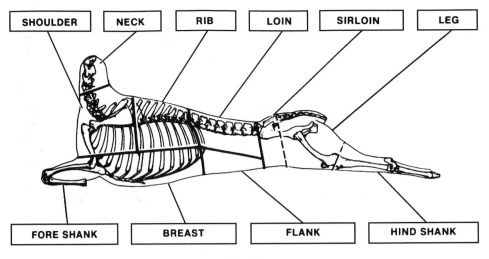

| SHOULDER | NECK | RIB | LOIN | SIRLOIN | LEG |

| FORE SHANK | BREAST | FLANK | HIND SHANK |

LAMB

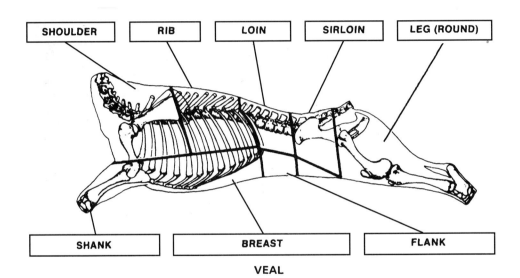

| SHOULDER | RIB | LOIN | SIRLOIN | LEG (ROUND) |

| SHANK | BREAST | FLANK |

VEAL

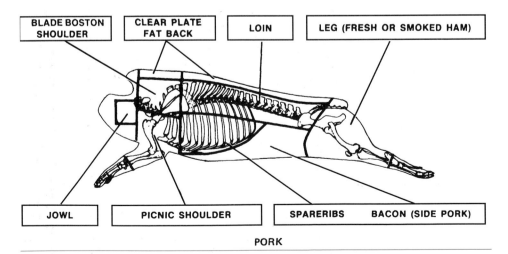

| BLADE BOSTON SHOULDER | CLEAR PLATE FAT BACK | LOIN | LEG (FRESH OR SMOKED HAM) |

| JOWL | PICNIC SHOULDER | SPARERIBS | BACON (SIDE PORK) |

PORK

FIGURE 10.5 **(Continued)**

or by thickness. Portion control cuts require the least work for the cook of all meat cuts. They are also the most expensive per pound of all categories of cuts.

BONE STRUCTURE

Knowing the bone structure of meat animals is essential for:

1. **Identification of meat cuts.**

   The distinctive shapes of the bones are often the best clue to the identification of a cut. Note how the shapes of the bones in Figure 10.6 help your recognition.

2. **Boning and cutting meats.**

   Bones are often surrounded by flesh. You will need to know where they are even if you can't see them.

3. **Carving cooked meats.**

   Same reason as for number 2.

Study the chart of the beef skeleton in Figure 10.4 and learn the names of the major bones. Then compare the charts in Figure 10.5. You will see that the bone structures for all the animals are identical (except for pork, which has more than 13 ribs). Even the names are the same.

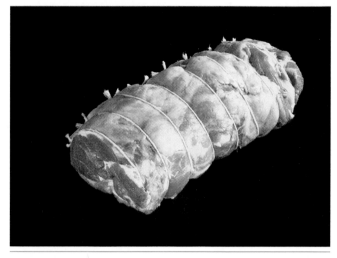

(b) Lamb boneless shoulder, rolled and tied.

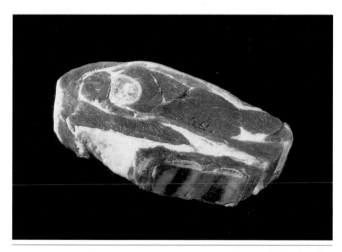

(c) Lamb arm chop.

FIGURE 10.6 **Typical primal and fabricated cuts of beef, lamb, veal, and pork. (Courtesy IBP, Inc., Dakota City, Nebraska, and the National Live Stock and Meat Board)**

(a) Lamb square-cut shoulder, whole.

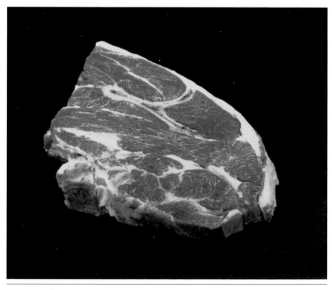

(d) Lamb blade chop. *(Continues)*

(e) Beef chuck, boneless, separated into blade, clod, and arm.

(f) Pork butt.

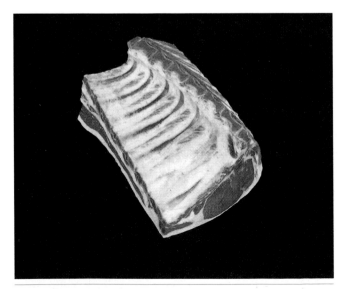

(g) Beef rib, roast ready.

(h) Beef rib steak.

(i) Veal rib roast.

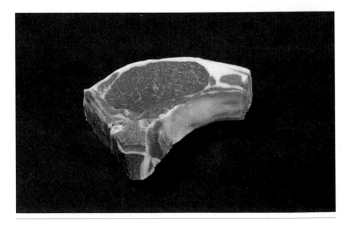

(j) Lamb rib chop.

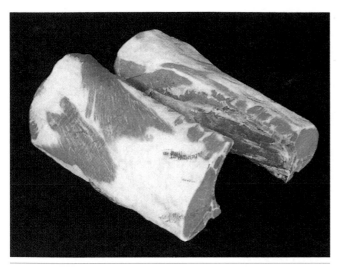

(k) Pork rib half and loin half roasts.

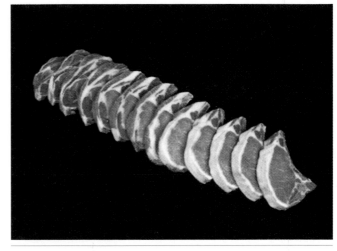

(n) Pork rib chops.

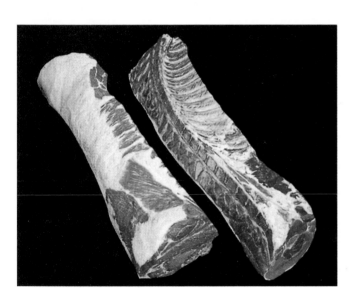

(l) Full pork loin (includes rib).

(o) Beef loin.

(m) Pork tenderloin.

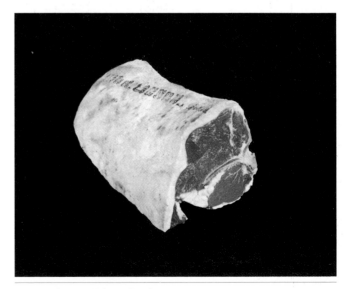

(p) Beef short loin. *(Continues)*

(q) Beef T-bone steak.

(t) Beef boneless strip loin.

(r) Beef porterhouse steak.

(u) Lamb loin roast.

(s) Beef tenderloin, trimmed.

(v) Lamb loin chop.

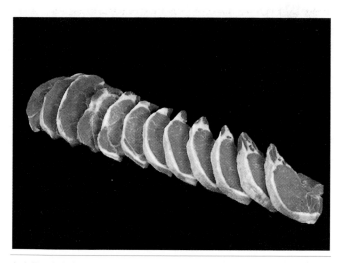

(w) Pork loin chops.

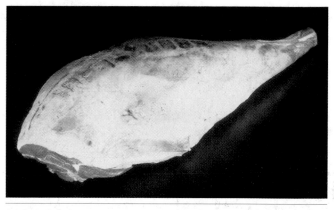

(z) Lamb, whole leg.

(x) Beef outside (bottom) round.

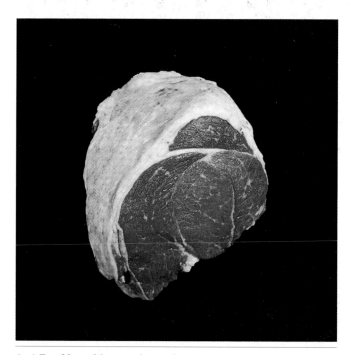

(aa) Beef knuckle, untrimmed.

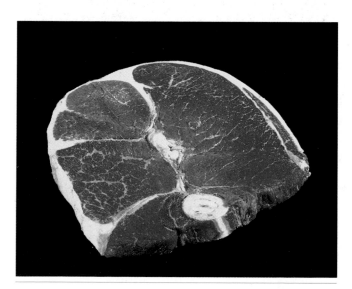

(y) Beef round steak.

(bb) Beef inside (top) round. *(Continues)*

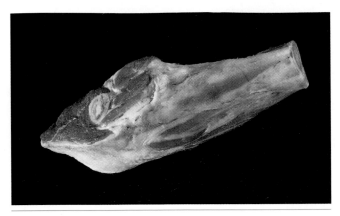

(cc) Lamb foreshank.

(ee) Beef flank steak.

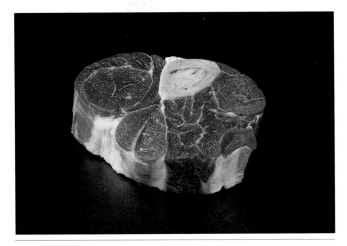

(dd) Beef shank cross cuts.

(ff) Veal breast.

BEEF, LAMB, VEAL, AND PORK CUTS

Beef Primal Cuts and Fabricated Cuts

Primal	Major Bones	Common Fabricated Cuts	Primary Cooking Methods
Forequarter			
Chuck (square cut)	Ribs 1–5	Shoulder clod	Moist heat
	Blade bone	Triangle	
	Backbone (including chine and feather bones)	Boneless inside chuck	
		Chuck tender	
		Chuck short ribs	
	Neck bones	Cubed steaks	
	Arm bone	Stew meat	
		Ground chuck	
Brisket	Rib bones	Boneless brisket and corned beef brisket	Moist heat
	Rib cartilage		
	Breast bone	Ground beef	
Shank	Shank bone	Stew meat	Moist heat
		Ground beef	

Note: Square-cut chuck, brisket, and shank, in one piece, are called *cross-cut chuck.*

Primal	Major Bones	Common Fabricated Cuts	Primary Cooking Methods
Rib	Ribs 6–12	Rib roasts ("prime rib")	Dry heat
	Backbone (chine and feather bones)	Rib steaks	
		Short ribs	Moist heat
Short plate	Rib bones	Short ribs	Moist heat
	Tip of breast bone	Stew meat	
	Rib cartilage	Ground beef	
Hindquarter			
(Full loin)		Full tenderloin (to have tenderloin in one piece, it must be stripped out of loin before loin is split into short loin and sirloin)	Dry heat
Short loin	Rib 13	Club steaks	Dry heat
	Backbone [chine, feather bones, finger bones (see note 1)]	T-bone steaks	
		Porterhouse steaks	
		Strip loin	
		Strip loin steaks	
		Short tenderloin	
Sirloin	Backbone	Top sirloin butt	Dry heat
	Hip bone (part of pelvis)	Bottom sirloin butt	
		Butt tenderloin	
Flank	Tip of rib 13	Flank steak	Moist heat (exception: flank steak cooked as London broil)
		Ground beef	
Round	Round (leg) bone	Knuckle (sirloin tip)	Moist heat and dry heat
	Aitch bone (part of pelvis)	Inside (top) round	
		Outside (bottom) round	
	Shank bone	Eye of round (part of outside round)	
	Tail bone	Rump	
		Hind shank	

Note 1: Finger bones are the short horizontal bones attached to those chine bones that have no ribs attached. They are the stems of the T's in T-bones.

Lamb Primal Cuts and Fabricated Cuts

Primal	Major Bones	Common Fabricated Cuts	Primary Cooking Methods
Foresaddle			
Shoulder	Ribs 1–4 or 1–5 (see note 2) Arm Blade Backbone (chine and feather bones) Neck bones	Shoulder roasts Shoulder chops Stew meat Ground lamb	Moist heat and dry heat
Breast and shank	Rib bones Breast bone Shank bone	Riblets Breast Stew meat Ground lamb	Moist heat
Hotel rack	Ribs 5–12 or 6–13 (see note 2) Backbone	Rib roast (rack) Crown roast Rib chops	Dry heat
Hindsaddle			
Loin (with or without flank)	Rib 13 (optional; see note 2) Backbone (chine, feather bones, finger bones)	Loin roast Loin chops	Dry heat
Leg	Backbone Tail bone Pelvis (hip bone, aitch bone) Round bone Hind shank	Leg roast Leg chops Sirloin chops Shank	Dry heat Moist heat

Note: Hotel rack and loin attached are called *lamb back;* used mostly for chops.

Note 2: Lamb foresaddles are divided between ribs 4 and 5, unlike beef and veal, which are divided between ribs 5 and 6. Thus, the rack or rib section of lamb has 8 ribs; beef and veal, 7 ribs. In the new, optional style of cutting, the carcass is divided into foresaddle and hindsaddle after the 13th rib, and the foresaddle is divided between ribs 5 and 6. The rack thus contains ribs 6–13.

Veal Primal Cuts and Fabricated Cuts

Primal	Major Bones	Common Fabricated Cuts	Primary Cooking Methods
Foresaddle			
Shoulder (square cut)	Ribs 1–5 Blade bone Backbone (chine and feather bones) Neck bones Arm bone	Shoulder roasts Shoulder chops Shoulder clod steaks Cubed steaks Stew meat Ground veal	Moist heat and dry heat
Breast	Rib bones Rib cartilage Breast bone	Boneless breast Cubed steaks Ground veal	Moist heat
Shank	Shank bone	Shank cross cuts (osso buco)	Moist heat
Hotel rack	Ribs 6–12 Backbone (chine and feather bones)	Rib roast (rack) Rib chops	Dry heat and moist heat

Note: Hotel rack plus connecting portions of breast is called a *bracelet.*

Veal Primal Cuts and Fabricated Cuts *(Continued)*

Primal	Major Bones	Common Fabricated Cuts	Primary Cooking Methods
Hindsaddle			
Loin (with or without flank)	Rib 13 Backbone (chine, feather bones, finger bones)	Saddle (loin roast) Loin chops	Dry heat and moist heat
Leg	Backbone Tail bone Pelvis (hip bone, aitch bone) Round bone Hind shank	Leg roasts Scaloppine or cutlets Shank cross cuts (osso buco)	Dry heat Moist heat

Note: Hotel rack and loin attached are called *veal back*; used mostly for chops.

Pork Primal Cuts and Fabricated Cuts

Primal	Major Bones	Common Fabricated Cuts	Primary Cooking Methods
Shoulder picnic	Shoulder (arm) bone Shank bone	Fresh and smoked picnic Hocks Ground pork Sausage meat	Moist heat
Boston butt	Blade bone (rib bones, back and neck bones are removed)	Butt steaks Shoulder roasts Daisy (smoked) Ground pork Sausage meat	Dry heat and moist heat
Loin	Rib bones (see note 3) Backbone (chine, feather bones, finger bones) Hip bone	Loin roast Loin and rib chops Boneless loin Country-style ribs Canadian-style bacon (smoked)	Dry heat and moist heat
Ham	Aitch bone Leg bone Hind shank bone	Fresh ham Smoked ham Ham steaks	Dry heat and moist heat
Belly	None	Bacon	Dry heat and moist heat
Spareribs	Rib bones Breast bone	Spareribs	Moist heat
Fatback and clear plate	None	Fresh and salt fatback Salt pork Lard	(Used as cooking fats)
Jowl	None	Jowl bacon	Moist and dry heat
Feet	Foot bones		Moist heat

Note 3: Pork has more than 13 ribs (unlike beef, lamb, and veal) due to special breeding to develop long loins.

SELECTING MEATS FOR YOUR OPERATION

Deciding Which Forms to Purchase

Whether you buy whole carcasses, fabricated cuts, or anything in between, depends on four factors:

1. How much meat-cutting skill do you or your staff have?

2. How much work and storage space do you have?

3. Can you use all cuts and lean trim on your menu?

4. Which form gives you the best *cost per portion,* after figuring in labor costs?

Meat purveyors can usually cut meat more economically than food service operators, because they deal in large volume. Carcasses or primal cuts cost less per pound than fabricated cuts, but they have more waste (fat and bone) and they require more labor (which costs money). However, some operators still do some of their own cutting, depending on how they can answer the four questions above. They feel that cutting their own meat gives them greater control over quality.

Some compromises are available. If you want the quality of freshly cut steaks, for example, you might buy boneless strip loins and cut your own steaks to order. You need not buy primal loins.

Specifications

When buying meat, you will need to indicate the following specifications:

1. *Item name.*

Include IMPS/NAMPS number if applicable.
Example: 173 Beef Short Loin, Regular

2. *Grade.*

Example: U.S. Choice
(You may also want to specify division of grade, such as the upper half or lower half of U.S. Choice.)

3. *Weight range:* for roasts and large cuts.

Portion weight or thickness (not both): for steaks and chops.

4. *State of refrigeration: chilled or frozen.*

5. *Fat limitations: average thickness of surface fat.*

Example: ¾ inch average, 1 inch maximum. (Does not apply to veal.)

COOKING AND HANDLING MEATS

TENDERNESS AND APPROPRIATE COOKING METHODS

The heat of cooking affects tenderness in two ways:

1. It tenderizes connective tissue, if moisture is present and cooking is slow.

2. It toughens protein. Even meats low in connective tissue can be tough and dry if cooked at excessively high heats for too long.

The Principle of Low-Heat Cooking

1. High heat toughens and shrinks protein and results in excessive moisture loss. Therefore, low-heat cooking should be the general practice for most meat cooking methods.

2. Broiling seems to be a contradiction to this rule. The reason that carefully broiled meat stays tender is that it is done quickly. It takes time for the heat to be conducted to the interior of the meat, so the inside never gets very hot. Meat broiled well done, however, is likely to be dry.

3. Roasts cooked at low temperatures have better yields than those roasted at high heat. That is, they shrink less and lose less moisture.

4. Because liquid or steam is a better conductor of heat than air, moist heat penetrates meat quickly. Therefore, to avoid overcooking, meat should be simmered, never boiled.

Breaking Down Connective Tissue

Remember that connective tissue is highest in muscles that are more frequently exercised and in more mature animals.

Look again at the principal cooking methods (column 4) in the table of meat cuts (p. 209). You should detect a pattern of tender cuts, cooked primarily by dry heat; slightly less tender cuts, cooked sometimes by dry and sometimes by moist heat; and least tender cuts, cooked almost always by moist heat.

1. *Rib and loin cuts.*

Always the tenderest cuts, used mostly for roasts, steaks, and chops.

Beef and lamb. Because these meats are often eaten rare or medium done, the rib and loin are used almost exclusively for roasting, broiling, and grilling.

Veal and pork.   Pork is generally eaten well done, and veal is most often eaten well done, although many people prefer it slightly pink in the center. Therefore, these meats are occasionally braised, not to develop tenderness but to help preserve juices. Veal chops, which are very low in fat, may be broiled if great care is taken not to overcook them and dry them out. A safer approach is to use a method with fat, such as sautéing or pan-frying, or to use moist heat.

2. ***Leg or round.***

Beef.   The cuts of the round are less tender and are used mostly for braising.

High-grade Prime or Choice rounds can also be roasted. The roasts are so large that, roasted at low temperatures for a long time, the beef's own moisture helps dissolve collagen. Inside round (top round) is favored for roasts because of its size and relative tenderness.

Beef round is very lean. It is best roasted rare. Lack of fat makes well-done round taste dry.

Veal, lamb, and pork.   These meats are from young animals and therefore are tender enough to roast.

Legs make excellent roasts, since large muscles with few seams and uniform grain allow easy slicing and attractive portions.

Figure 10.7 shows the muscle structure of the round seen in cross section. A center-cut steak from a whole round of beef, lamb, veal, or pork has this same basic structure.

3. ***Chuck or shoulder.***

Beef.   Beef chuck is a tougher cut that is usually braised.

Veal, lamb, and pork.   These are most often braised but are young enough to be roasted or cut into chops for broiling. Shoulder roasts are not the most desirable because they consist of many small muscles running in different directions. Therefore, they do not produce attractive, solid slices.

4. ***Shanks, breast, brisket, and flank.***

These are the least tender cuts, even on young animals, and are almost always cooked by moist heat.

Shanks are very desirable for braising and simmering, since their high collagen content is converted into much gelatin that gives body to braising liquids and good eating quality to the meat.

Beef flank steaks can be broiled (as London broil) if they are cooked rare and cut across the grain into thin slices. This cuts the connective tissue into chewable pieces (see mechanical tenderization, p. 197).

5. ***Ground meat, cubed steaks, and stew meat.***

These can come from any primal cut. They are usually made from trimmings, although whole chucks are sometimes ground into chopped meat. Ground meat and cubed steaks can be cooked by dry or moist heat, since they have been mechanically tenderized. Stew meat is, of course, cooked by moist heat.

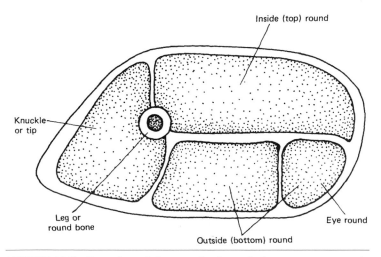

FIGURE 10.7   **Location of the muscles in a whole center-cut round steak of beef, veal, lamb, or pork.**

Other Factors Influencing Choice of Cooking Methods

1. **Fat content.**

Meats high in fat, such as Prime beef or lamb, are generally cooked without added fat, such as by roasting or broiling.

Meats low in fat, such as veal, are often cooked with added fat to prevent dryness. Sautéing, pan-frying, or braising are generally preferable to broiling for veal chops that are cooked well done.

Fat can be added to lean meats in two ways:

a. *Barding.*   Tying slices of fat, such as pork fatback, over meats with no natural fat cover, to protect them while roasting.

b. *Larding.*   Inserting strips of fat with a larding needle into meats low in marbling.

These two techniques were developed in Europe when meats were much leaner and not as tender. They are not often used with today's tender, grain-fed meats. These techniques are useful, however, when cooking lean game such as venison.

2. **Developing tenderness is not the only goal of cooking.**

Other goals are

a. Developing flavor.

b. Preventing excessive shrinkage and nutrient loss.

c. Developing appearance.

You will often have to compromise to get a balanced result. For example, preliminary browning of a roast at high heat increases shrinkage but may be desirable for some roasts to develop flavor and appearance.

Searing and "Sealing"

Searing

The purpose of searing meats at high heat is to create desirable flavor and color by browning the meats' surfaces. It was long believed that searing the surface of meat "seals the pores," keeping in juices.

This does not actually happen. Meat does not have pores but is an open network of fibers. Think of the surface of a steak as resembling the cut end of a thick rope. There are no pores to seal. It is true that heavy browning creates a kind of crust on the surface of the meat, but this crust is no more waterproof than an unbrowned surface.

Roasts cooked from the start at a low temperature retain more juices than roasts that are seared at high heat first.

Steaks, chops, and cutlets cooked very quickly at high heat retain more moisture at first because the intense heat instantly evaporates the juices from the surface of the meat and forces internal juices further into the meat. This permits browning, because moisture would create steam and inhibit browning. However, overcooked steaks will be dry whether or not the steak was seared.

Blanching and "Sealing"

Dropping meat into boiling water doesn't "seal the pores" either. What actually happens is this: Many proteins dissolve in cold water. When heated, these proteins coagulate and become froth or scum on the surface of the water. When meat is placed into boiling water, some of the protein coagulates inside that meat and not as much is carried out of the meat with the lost moisture. Prolonged cooking will shrink meat as much if started in boiling water as if started in cold water.

Cooking Frozen Meats

Some sources recommend cooking some meats from the frozen state, without thawing, in order to eliminate drip loss that occurs during defrosting.

However, it is usually better to thaw before cooking, because of the following reasons:

1. Frozen meats lose no moisture from defrosting but lose more during cooking. The total loss is about the same as for thawed meats. Besides, the perception of juiciness depends as much or more on fat content than on moisture content.

2. Cooking frozen meats complicates the cooking process and requires adjustments in procedure. It is possible for roasts to be cooked on the outside but still be frozen in the center. Frozen steaks, too, are more difficult to cook evenly than thawed steaks. Thawed meats, on the other hand, are handled like fresh meats.

3. Cooking frozen meats requires extra energy, and energy is expensive. A hard-frozen roast may take three times as long to cook as a thawed roast.

DONENESS

Definitions

The meaning of the term "doneness" depends on whether the cooking method uses dry heat or moist heat.

Fresh Meats

1. Check in purchases on arrival to ensure that purchased meat is of good quality.

2. Do not wrap tightly. Bacteria and mold thrive in moist, stagnant places. Air circulation inhibits their growth. Store loosely, but cover cut surfaces to prevent excessive drying.

3. Do not open Cryovac-wrapped meats until ready to use.

4. Store at 32°F to 36°F (0°C to 2°C). Meat does not freeze until about 28°F (–2°C).

5. Keep meats separated in cooler (and on worktable) to avoid cross-contamination.

6. Use as soon as possible. Fresh meats keep well for only 2 to 4 days. Ground meats keep even less well, because so much surface area is exposed to bacteria. Cured and smoked products may keep up to a week.

    Frequent deliveries are better than long storage.

7. Do not try to rescue meats that are going bad by freezing them. Freezing will not improve the quality of spoiling meat.

8. Keep coolers clean.

Frozen Meats

1. Wrap frozen meats well to prevent freezer burn.

2. Store at 0°F (–18°C) or colder.

3. Rotate stock—first in, first out. Frozen meats do not keep indefinitely. Recommended shelf life, at 0°F (–18°C), for beef, veal, and lamb: 6 months; for pork: 4 months (pork fat turns rancid easily in the freezer).

4. Defrost carefully. Tempering in the refrigerator is best. Defrosting at room temperature encourages bacterial growth.

5. Do not refreeze thawed meats. Refreezing increases loss of quality.

6. Keep freezers clean.

TERMS FOR REVIEW

coagulation	inspection	Cryovac	portion control cuts
marbling	grading	Institution Meat Purchase	barding
connective tissue	yield grade	Specifications	larding
collagen	green meat	primal cuts	doneness
elastin	aging	fabricated cuts	carry-over cooking

QUESTIONS FOR DISCUSSION

1. Many people assume that the leaner a meat is, the better it is. Do you agree? Explain.

2. What is connective tissue? Why is it important for the cook to understand connective tissue?

3. Flank steak (beef) is very high in connective tissue, yet it is often broiled and served in thin slices as London broil. How is this possible?

4. You are in charge of a large hospital food service. Why might you choose USDA Select grade beef for making pot roast and stew?

5. Why are portion control meats so widely used in food service, even though their per-pound cost is higher?

6. Can you explain why veal loin, a tender cut, is sometimes braised, while veal shoulder, a less tender cut, is sometimes roasted?

7. Which of the following cuts would you be more likely to braise? Which might you roast? Beef chuck, lamb shanks, veal rib, beef rib, pork shoulder, corned beef brisket, ground pork, beef strip loin, lamb leg.

8. Table 10.2 indicates the internal temperature of rare roast beef as 130°F (54°C). Why, then, would you remove a roast rib from the oven when the temperature on the meat thermometer reads 115°F (46°C)?

9. Why are weight/time roasting charts inadequate for determining the doneness of roast meats?

CHAPTER 11

COOKING MEATS

This chapter presents basic cooking methods as they apply to beef, lamb, veal, and pork. It is important that you have read and understood the basic material in Chapter 10, especially the sections on matching particular cuts to appropriate cooking methods, and on testing for doneness. If necessary, please review those sections, as well as the discussion of basic cooking methods in Chapter 4.

The procedures given here are general ones. Be aware that these procedures may be modified slightly in specific recipes. Nevertheless, the basic principles still hold. In addition, your instructors may wish to show you variations or methods that differ from those presented here.

The recipes that follow each of the procedures for roasting, sautéing, braising, and so on are intended to illustrate the basic techniques. Each time you prepare one of these recipes, you should be thinking not just about that one product but about the techniques you are using, and how they can be applied to other products. It is helpful to compare the recipes in each section, to see how they are alike and how they are different. This way you will be learning to cook, not just to follow recipes.

After reading this chapter, you should be able to

1. Cook meats by roasting and baking.
2. Cook meats by broiling, grilling, and pan-broiling.
3. Cook meats by sautéing, pan-frying, and griddling.

4. Cook meats by simmering.
5. Cook meats by braising.
6. Cook variety meats.

ROASTING AND BAKING

Remember the definitions of *roast* and *bake* (Chapter 4): to cook foods by surrounding them with hot, dry air, usually in an oven. Roasting is a dry-heat method. No water is used, and the meat is not covered so that steam can escape.

In principle, roasting meats is a simple procedure. The prepared cut of meat is placed in an oven at a selected temperature, and it is removed when done. What could be easier?

However, there are many variables, and chefs often disagree about proper roasting procedures, especially when it comes to the fine points. In this section you will learn a roasting procedure that you can apply to most meats. But first we will discuss in more detail several of the points of disagreement and some of the variations that are possible.

Seasoning

Salt added to the surface of meat just before roasting will penetrate the meat only a fraction of an inch during cooking. The same is true of the flavors of herbs and spices. In the case of a beef rib roast, where most of the surface is either fat or bone, there will be no penetration at all. You will have salty fat, salty bones, and salty pan drippings, but the meat will be unseasoned. Also, salt added just before roasting retards browning, because the salt draws moisture to the surface.

There are several alternatives to seasoning just before cooking:

1. Season several hours or a day in advance to give the seasonings time to penetrate.

2. Season the roast after cooking.

3. Don't season at all, but carefully season the gravy or juices (jus) that are served with the meat.

With smaller cuts of meat, such as beef tenderloin or rack of lamb, the chef may season just before roasting, because the meat is not as thick and each customer receives a larger share of seasoned, browned surface.

Temperature

Low-Temperature Roasting

As we discussed on page 214, it was once thought that starting the roast at a high temperature "seals the pores" by searing the surface, thus keeping in more juices.

We now know that this is not the case. Repeated tests have shown that *continuous roasting at a low temperature* gives a superior product with

1. Less shrinkage.

2. More flavor, juiciness, and tenderness.

3. More even doneness from outside to inside.

4. Greater ease in carving.

Low-roasting temperatures generally range from 200°F to 325°F (95°C to 160°C), depending on

1. The size of the cut. The larger the cut, the lower the temperature. This ensures that the outer portion is not overcooked before the inside is done.

2. The operation's production schedule. Lower temperatures require longer roasting times, which may or may not be convenient for a particular operation.

Searing

If a well-browned, crusted surface is desired for appearance, such as when the roast is to be carved in the dining room, a roast may be started at high temperature (400°F to 450°F/200°C to 230°C) until it is browned. The temperature should then be lowered to the desired roasting temperature and the meat roasted until done, as for low-temperature roasting.

High-Temperature Roasting

Very small pieces of meat that are to be roasted rare may be cooked at a high temperature. The effect is similar to broiling: a well-browned, crusted exterior and a rare interior. The meat is in the oven for so short a time that there is little shrinkage. Examples of cuts that may be roasted at a high temperature are rack of lamb and small sections of beef tenderloin.

Convection Ovens

If a convection oven is used for roasting, the temperature should be reduced about 50°F (25°C). Many chefs prefer not to use convection ovens for large roasts, because the drying effect of the forced air seems to cause greater shrinkage. On the other hand, convection ovens are very effective in browning and are good for high-temperature roasting.

Fat Side Up or Fat Side Down

Roasting meats fat side up provides continuous basting as the fat melts and runs down the sides. This method is preferred by perhaps the majority of chefs, although there is not complete agreement.

In this book we use the fat-side-up method. In the classroom, you should be guided by the advice of your instructor.

Basting

Basting is unnecessary if the meat has a natural fat covering and is roasted fat side up. For lean meats, *barding* will have the same effect. This means covering the surface of the meat with a thin layer of fat, such as sliced pork fatback or bacon.

If a roast is basted by spooning pan drippings over it, use only the fat. Fat protects the roast from drying, while moisture washes away protective fat and allows drying.

Use of Mirepoix

Mirepoix is often added during the last part of the roasting time to flavor the roast and to add extra flavor to the pan juices.

Many chefs feel, however, that the mirepoix adds little if any flavor to the roast and is actually harmful because the moisture of the vegetables creates steam around the roast. Mirepoix can be more easily added when the gravy is being made. And if no gravy or juice is to be served there may be no need for mirepoix at all.

The use of mirepoix is more important for white meats—veal and pork—because, being usually cooked well done, they lose more juices and need a good gravy or jus to give them moistness and flavor.

Gravy and Jus

The general procedures for making pan gravy are given in Chapter 8 (p. 150). Read or review this section if necessary. The procedure for making jus, given here in the recipe for roast prime ribs of beef au jus, is the same except that no roux or other thickening agents are used. In other words, use the methods for making pan gravy (p. 150) but eliminate steps 5 and 6 from Method 1, and step 3 from Method 2.

Basic Procedure for Roasting Meats

1. Collect all equipment and food supplies.

   Select roasting pans that have low sides (so moisture vapor does not collect around the roast) and that are just large enough to hold the roast. If pans are too large, drippings will spread out too thin and burn.

2. Prepare or trim meat for roasting. Heavy fat coverings should be trimmed to about ½ inch (1 cm) thick.

3. If desired, season meat several hours ahead or the day before.

4. Place meat fat side up on a rack in the roasting pan. The rack holds the roast out of the drippings. Bones may be used if no rack is available. Bone-in rib roasts need no rack, because the bones act as a natural rack.

5. Insert a meat thermometer (clean and sanitary) so that the bulb is in the center of the meat, not touching bone or fat. (Omit this step if you are using an instant-read thermometer.)

6. Do not cover or add water to the pan. Roasting is a dry-heat cooking method.

7. Place meat in oven, which has been preheated to desired temperature.

8. Roast to desired doneness, allowing for carry-over cooking.

9. If desired, add mirepoix to the pan during the last half of the cooking period.

10. Remove roast from oven and let stand in a warm place 15 to 30 minutes. This allows the juices to be reabsorbed through the meat so that less juice is lost when the meat is sliced. Also, resting the meat makes slicing easier.

11. If the meat must be held, place in an oven or warmer set no higher than the desired internal temperature of the roast.

12. While the roast is resting, prepare jus or pan gravy from the drippings. Mirepoix may be added to the drippings now if it was not added in step 8.

13. Slice the roast as close as possible to serving time. In almost all cases, slice the meat against the grain, for tenderness.

RECIPE 56   Roast Rib of Beef au Jus

Yield: 10 lb (4½ kg) boneless,   **Portions:** 25   **Portion size:** 6½ oz (175 g)
    trimmed meat   20   8 oz (225 g)
                                                                                       1½ oz (50 mL) jus

U.S.	Metric	Ingredients	Procedure
20 lb	9 kg	Beef rib, roast ready, bone in (one average size rib roast)	1. Place the meat fat side up in a roasting pan. 2. Insert a meat thermometer so that the bulb is in the center of the meat, not touching bone or fat. 3. Place in a preheated 300°F (150°C) oven. Roast until rare or medium done, as desired, *allowing for carry-over cooking.* Thermometer readings: Rare: 120°F (49°C) Medium: 130°F (54°C) (Outer slices will be more done than center.) Roasting time will be at least 3–4 hours. 4. Remove the meat from the pan and let stand in a warm place 30 minutes before carving.
		Mirepoix:	5. Drain off all but about 3–4 oz (100 g) of the fat from the roasting pan. Be careful to retain any juices in the pan. Add the mirepoix to the pan.
8 oz	250 g	Onions	
4 oz	125 g	Carrots	6. Set the pan over high heat and cook until mirepoix is brown and moisture has evaporated, leaving only fat, mirepoix, and browned drippings.
4 oz	125 g	Celery	
			7. Pour off any excess fat.
2 qt	2 L	Brown stock Salt Pepper	8. Pour about a pint of stock into the roasting pan to deglaze it. Stir over heat until brown drippings are dissolved. 9. Pour the deglazing liquid and mirepoix into a sauce pot with remaining stock. Simmer until mirepoix is soft and liquid is reduced by about one-third. 10. Strain through a china cap lined with cheesecloth into a bain marie. Skim fat carefully. Season to taste with salt and pepper. 11. For service, stand the roast on its widest end. Cut down beside the bones to free the meat, and slice the meat across the grain. 12. Serve each portion with 1½ oz (50 mL) jus.

RECIPE 56   **Roast Rib of Beef au Jus** *(Continued)*

Variations

56A. Rib-eye roll, top round, sirloin, or **strip loin** may be roasted by the same procedure. Roast these cuts on a rack.

56B. Roast Beef with Gravy: Roast desired cut of beef according to the basic recipe. Prepare gravy according to the following recipe.

RECIPE 57   **Roast Beef Gravy**

Yield: approx. 1½ qt (1.5 L)   **Portions:** 25   **Portion size:** 2 oz (60 mL)

U.S.	Metric	Ingredients	Procedure
		Pan drippings from roast beef (previous recipe)	1. After removing the roast, add the mirepoix to the drippings in the roasting pan.
		Mirepoix:	2. Set the pan over high heat and cook until mirepoix is brown and moisture has evaporated, leaving only fat, mirepoix, and browned drippings.
8 oz	250 g	Onions	
4 oz	125 g	Carrots	
4 oz	125 g	Celery	
			3. Pour off and save the fat.
2 qt	2 L	Brown stock	4. Deglaze the pan with some of the stock. Pour the deglazing liquid and mirepoix into a sauce pot with remaining stock. Add the tomato purée. Bring to a boil and reduce heat to a simmer.
4 oz	125 g	Tomato purée	
4 oz	125 g	Flour	5. Make a brown roux with the flour and 4 oz (125 g) of the reserved fat. Cool the roux slightly and beat it into the simmering stock to thicken it.
		Salt	
		Pepper	6. Simmer 15 to 20 minutes, until all raw flour taste is cooked out and liquid is reduced slightly.
		Worcestershire sauce	
			7. Strain through a china cap into a bain marie.
			8. Season to taste with salt, pepper, and Worcestershire sauce.

Variation

57A. Jus Lié: Omit tomato paste and roux. Thicken liquid with 1½ oz (50 g) cornstarch or arrowroot blended with ½ cup (100 mL) cold water or stock.

RECIPE 58 **Roast Stuffed Shoulder of Lamb**

Portions: 10   **Portion size:** 5 oz (150 g) meat
                                                and stuffing
                                            2 oz (60 mL) gravy

U.S.	Metric	Ingredients	Procedure
		Stuffing:	1. Sauté the onion and garlic in oil until soft. Remove from heat and cool.
4 oz	125 g	Onion, fine dice	
1 tsp	5 mL	Garlic, chopped fine	
2 oz	60 g	Olive oil, veg. oil, *or* butter	2. Combine onion and garlic with remaining stuffing ingredients and mix lightly.
3 oz (about 2 cups)	100 g	Soft, fresh bread crumbs	
⅓ cup	80 mL	Chopped parsley	
½ tsp	2 mL	Rosemary	
¼ tsp	1 mL	Black pepper	
½ tsp	2 mL	Salt	
1	1	Egg, beaten	
1	1	Boneless lamb shoulder, about 4 lb (1.8 kg)	3. Lay the lamb shoulder out flat, fat side down.
		Oil	4. Spread the lamb with the stuffing and roll it up. Tie the roll tightly.
		Salt	
		Pepper	5. Rub the meat with oil, salt, pepper, and rosemary.
		Rosemary	
			6. Place the meat on a rack in a roasting pan. Insert a meat thermometer into the thickest part of the meat (not into the stuffing).
			7. Place in a 325°F (165°C) oven. Roast the meat about 1½ hours.
		Mirepoix:	8. Place the mirepoix in the bottom of the roasting pan. Baste the meat with fat and continue to roast until the thermometer reads 160°F (71°C). Total cooking time is about 2½ hours.
4 oz	125 g	Onions, chopped	
2 oz	60 g	Carrots, chopped	
2 oz	60 g	Celery, chopped	
			9. Remove the roast from the pan and let stand in a warm place.
2 oz	60 g	Flour	10. Set the roasting pan over high heat to clarify the fat and finish browning the mirepoix. Drain off about three-fourths of the fat.
1 qt	1 L	Brown beef stock or lamb stock	
4 oz	125 g	Tomatoes, canned	
		Salt	11. Add the flour to the pan to make a roux, cooking it until it is brown.
		Pepper	

RECIPE 58   **Roast Stuffed Shoulder of Lamb** *(Continued)*

U.S.	Metric	Ingredients	Procedure
			12. Stir in the stock and tomatoes and bring to a boil. Simmer, while stirring, until the gravy is thickened and reduced to about 1½ pints (750 mL).
			13. Strain and skim excess fat.
			14. Season to taste with salt and pepper.
			15. Slice the roast crosswise, so that each slice contains stuffing in the center. When slicing, be careful to keep the slices from falling apart. Serve each portion with 2 oz (60 mL) gravy.

Variations

58A. Roast Boneless Shoulder of Lamb: Roast tied, boneless lamb shoulder as in basic recipe, without stuffing.

58B. Roast Leg of Lamb: Prepare leg of lamb for roasting as shown in Figure 11.1. Rub with oil, salt, pepper, rosemary, and garlic. Roast as in basic recipe (without stuffing) to rare, medium, or well-done stage. Leg of lamb may be served with natural juices (au jus) instead of thickened gravy, if desired. Approximate yield: 8 lb (3.6 kg) AP leg of lamb yields about 3½ lb (1.6 kg) cooked meat. Yield is less if cooked well done. See Figure 11.2 for carving technique.

58C. Roast Leg of Lamb Boulangère: 1½ hours before lamb is done, transfer the meat to a rack over a pan of Boulangère Potatoes (p. 441) and finish cooking.

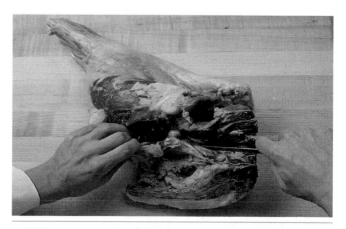

FIGURE 11.1   **Preparing leg of lamb for roasting. Fresh hams may be prepared using the same basic technique. (a) Begin by removing the hip and tail bones.**

(b) With a sharp-pointed boning knife, cut along the hip bone to separate bone from meat. Always cut against the bone. *(Continues)*

(c) Continue until the hip and tail bones are completely removed. Note the round ball joint at the end of the leg bone in the center of the meat.

(f) Full leg of lamb, ready for roasting. The end of the shank bone and part of the shank meat have been removed.

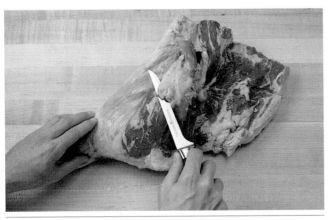

(d) Trim off excess external fat, leaving a thin covering.

(g) The leg may be tied into a more compact shape.

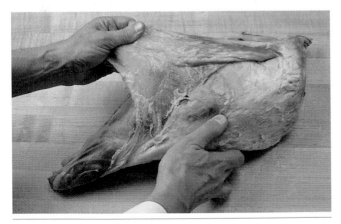

(e) Pull off the skin or "fell" on the outside of the leg.

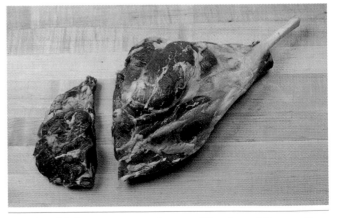

(h) The sirloin portion may be cut off and used for another purpose, such as shish kebabs.

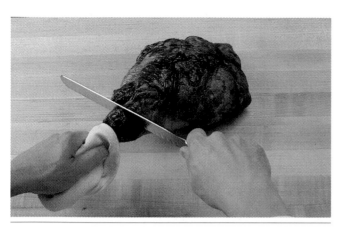

FIGURE 11.2 **Carving a leg of lamb. Hams and other leg roasts may be carved using the same basic technique shown here.**

(a) Place the roast on a clean, sanitary cutting board. Begin by making a vertical cut through to the bone about 1 inch from the end of the shank meat. The small collar of shank meat forms a guard to protect the hand in case the knife slips.

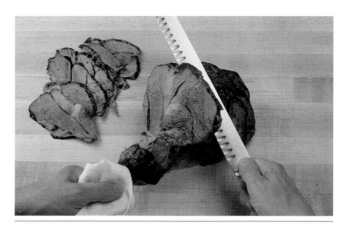

(c) When slices become too large, angle the knife.

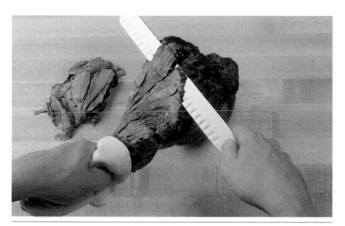

(b) Using long, smooth strokes, cut thin slices on a slight bias as shown.

(d) Then take alternating slices from different sides of the roast as shown. When the top of the roast has been completely sliced, turn over and repeat the procedure on the bottom of the roast.

RECIPE 59 **Roast Rack of Lamb**

| | | **Portions:** 8 | **Portion size:** 2 chops |
| | | | 1 oz (30 mL) jus |

U.S.	Metric	Ingredients	Procedure
2	2	Racks of lamb, 8 ribs each Salt Pepper Thyme	1. Prepare lamb for roasting as shown in Figure 11.3. 2. Place any trimmed-off bones in the bottom of a roasting pan. Place the meat fat side up on top of the bones. Season with salt, pepper, and thyme. 3. Place in hot oven (450°F/230°C) and roast to desired doneness. Rack of lamb is usually roasted rare or medium. Test doneness with a meat thermometer or by the touch method as for steaks. Total time will be about 30 minutes. 4. Remove the lamb from the roasting pan and hold in a warm place. Leave bones in pan. 5. Set the roasting pan over moderate heat to caramelize the juices and clarify the fat. Pour off the fat.
2 cloves 1 pt	2 cloves 500 mL	Garlic, chopped White or brown veal stock	6. Add the garlic to the pan and cook 1 minute. 7. Deglaze the pan with the stock and reduce by half. Strain, degrease, and season to taste. 8. Cut the meat between the ribs into chops. Serve 2 chops per portion with 1 oz (30 mL) jus.

Variations

59A. *Rack of Lamb aux Primeurs* (with spring vegetables): Place the two racks on one or two heated serving platters. Garnish the platters with an assortment of spring vegetables, cooked separately: tournéed carrots, tournéed turnips, buttered peas, green beans, rissolé potatoes. Pour the jus into a warm gooseneck or sauceboat. Carve and serve the meat, vegetables, and jus in the dining room.

59B. *Rack of Lamb Persillé:* Prepare as in basic recipe. Combine the ingredients for Persillade (pear-see-yahd), listed below. Before carving and serving, spread the top (fat side) of each rack with 1 tbsp (15 g) soft butter. Pack the persillade onto the top of the racks and brown under the salamander.

Persillade:

   4 cloves garlic, minced
   2 oz (60 g) fresh bread crumbs (about 1 cup)
   ⅓ cup (80 mL) chopped parsley

FIGURE 11.3 **Preparing rack of lamb for roasting.**
(a) Begin by cutting down on both sides of the featherbones all the way to the chine bone.

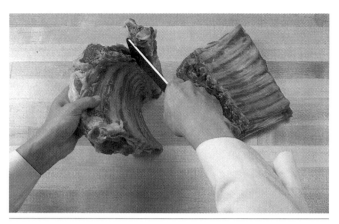

(d) Repeat the procedure on the other side of the chine.

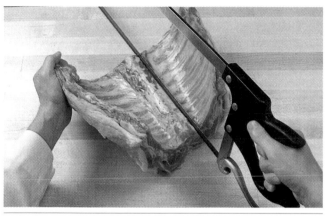

(b) If a meat saw is available, turn the rack over and cut through the rib bones at the points where they attach to the chine bone.

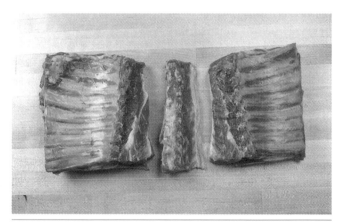

(e) The two halves are separated from the chine.

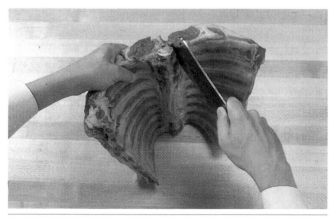

(c) If a meat saw is not available, a cleaver can be used. Stand the roast up on end and, with a cleaver, cut through the rib bones at the point where they join the chine bone. This will separate one rack.

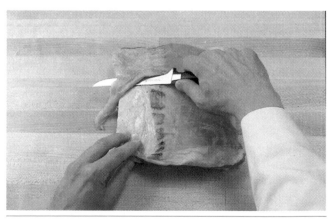

(f) Trim excess fat from the top of the meat, leaving a thin protective covering. During this step you should also remove the shoulder blade cartilage, which is embedded in the layers of fat. *(Continues)*

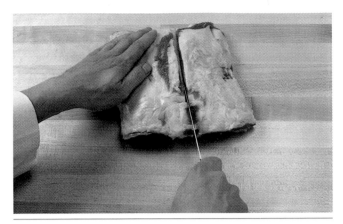

(g) To trim the fat and meat from the ends of the bones (called "frenching" the bones), first cut through the fat in a straight line down to the bone, keeping the cut about an inch (2.5 cm) from the tip of the eye muscle.

(i) The roast is trimmed and ready to cook.

(h) Score the membrane covering the rib bones. Pull and cut the layer of fat from the bones.

RECIPE 60   **Roast Loin of Pork**

		Portions: 25	**Portion size:** 1 chop, about 7 oz (200 g) with bone 2 oz (60 mL) gravy

U.S.	Metric	Ingredients	Procedure
17 lb	7.7 kg	Pork loins, center cut, bone in Salt Pepper	1. With a meat saw, cut off the chine bones so that the loins can be carved into chops after roasting.
1 tsp	5 mL	Sage Mirepoix:	2. Rub the pork with salt, pepper, and sage.
8 oz	250 g	Onion	3. Place the cutoff chine bones in a roasting pan. Place the pork loins fat side up on top of the bones. Insert a meat thermometer into the thickest part of the muscle.
4 oz	125 g	Carrot	
4 oz	125 g	Celery	
			4. Place in oven at 325°F (165°C) and roast 1 hour.
			5. Place mirepoix in bottom of pan and continue to roast until the thermometer reads 160°F (71°C). Total cooking time is about 2 to 2½ hours.
			6. Remove roast from pan and hold in a warm place.
2½ qt	2.5 L	Chicken stock, veal stock, or pork stock	7. Set the roasting pan over moderate heat and cook until moisture has evaporated and mirepoix is well browned. Drain off and reserve fat.
5 oz	150 g	Flour Salt Pepper	8. Deglaze the pan with the stock and pour the contents into a sauce pot. Skim well.
			9. Make a brown roux with the flour and 5 oz (150 g) of the pork fat. Thicken the gravy with the roux and simmer 15 minutes, until thickened and slightly reduced.
			10. Strain the gravy and adjust the seasonings.
			11. Cut the roast into chops between the rib bones. Serve each portion with 2 oz (60 mL) gravy.

Variations

Other pork cuts may be roasted as in basic recipe: full loin, loin ends, boneless loin, fresh ham, shoulder.

60A. Roast Pork with Cream Gravy: Prepare as in basic recipe, but use 1½ qt (1.5 L) stock to deglaze pan, and add 1 qt (1 L) milk. Finish gravy with 1 cup (250 mL) hot heavy cream.

RECIPE 61 **Barbecued Spareribs**

U.S.	Metric	Ingredients	Procedure
			Portions: 24 **Portion size:** 10 oz (300 g) (cooked weight)
18 lb	8.5 kg	Fresh pork spareribs	1. Weigh the spareribs and cut them into 12-oz (350-g) portions.
2½ qt	2.5 L	Barbecue Sauce (p. 155)	2. Place the ribs in roasting pans with the inside of the ribs down.
			3. Place the ribs in a slow oven (300°F/ 150°C). Bake for 1 hour (see note).
			4. Drain fat from pans. Spoon about a cup of the sauce over the ribs to coat them with a thin layer. Turn them over and coat with more sauce.
			5. Bake 45 minutes. Turn and coat the ribs with the remaining sauce. Bake until tender, about 30 to 60 minutes more.
			6. Serve the portions whole or cut into 1- or 2-rib pieces for easier eating.

Note: Spareribs are often covered with boiling water and simmered for 30 minutes before baking. This is not necessary to cook the ribs and may result in the loss of some flavor and nutrients, but it does speed the cooking time. If ribs are simmered, omit the preliminary baking (step 3). Ribs may also be finished on a grill or under a broiler.

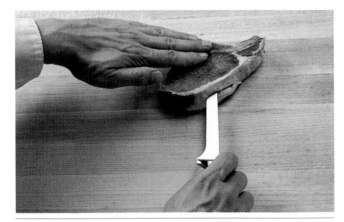

FIGURE 11.4 **For stuffed pork chops, cut a pocket in the chops as shown.**

RECIPE 62   **Baked Stuffed Pork Chops**

··

Portions: 25   **Portion size:** 1 chop
2 oz (60 mL) gravy

U.S.	Metric	Ingredients	Procedure
25 1½ lb	25 750 g	Prunes, pitted Basic Bread Stuffing (p. 318)	1. Soak the prunes in hot water 15 minutes. Drain and cool. 2. Prepare the stuffing and add the prunes. Keep refrigerated until ready to use.
25	25	Pork chops, cut thick (at least ¾ inch, 2 cm) Oil Salt Pepper	3. Cut a pocket in the pork chops as shown in Figure 11.4. 4. Stuff the pockets with the prune stuffing, using 1 prune per chop. Fasten the openings with picks or skewers. 5. Oil a bake pan and place the chops in it. Brush them with oil and season with salt and pepper. 6. Place the chops under the broiler just until lightly browned. 7. Transfer the pan to an oven at 350°F (175°C) and bake for about ½ hour, until chops are cooked through. 8. Remove the chops from the pan and place in a hotel pan for holding. *Remove picks.*
8 oz 3½ pt 2 oz	250 mL 1.75 L 60 mL	Water or white wine Brown sauce or Demiglaze Sherry (optional)	9. Deglaze the bake pan with the water or wine, degrease, and strain it into the hot brown sauce. 10. Bring to a boil and reduce the sauce slightly to bring to the proper consistency. 11. Add the sherry (if used) and adjust seasoning. 12. Serve 1 chop per portion, with 2 oz (60 mL) gravy.

··

RECIPE 63 Baked Ham with Raisin Cider Sauce

Portions: 25 **Portion size:** 5 oz (150 g) ham
2 oz (60 mL) sauce

U.S.	Metric	Ingredients	Procedure
15 lb	7 kg	Smoked ham	1. Place the ham(s) in a stock pot with enough water to cover. Bring to a boil and reduce heat to a simmer. Simmer for 1 hour. Drain.
			2. Cut off skin and excess fat. Leave fat covering about ½ inch (1 cm) thick. Score the fat with a knife.
3–4 tbsp	45–60 mL	Prepared mustard	3. Place the ham fat side up in a roast or bake pan. Spread with a thin layer of prepared mustard. Mix the sugar and cloves and sprinkle over the ham.
6 oz	175 g	Brown sugar	
¼ tsp	1 mL	Ground cloves	
			4. Bake at 350°F (175°C) about 1 hour. (*Caution:* Sugar burns easily, so check ham after 30 or 45 minutes.)
1½ qt	1.5 L	Apple cider	5. Place cider, raisins, sugar, nutmeg, and lemon rind in a saucepan and simmer 5 minutes.
8 oz	250 g	Raisins, seedless	
3 oz	100 g	Brown sugar	
½ tsp	2 mL	Nutmeg	6. Mix cornstarch with a little cold water or cold cider and stir into the sauce. Simmer until thickened.
1 tsp	5 mL	Grated lemon rind	
6 tbsp	50 g	Cornstarch	
		Salt	7. Add salt to taste.
			8. Slice ham (as for leg of lamb, Figure 11.2). Serve 5-oz (150-g) portion with 2 oz (60 mL) sauce on the side.

Note: Amount of cooking required depends on type of ham. *Aged country hams* must be soaked 24 hours in cold water, scrubbed, and simmered about 20 minutes per pound (500 g). Hams labeled "tenderized" or "ready to cook" may be baked without simmering (starting with step 2) or may be just blanched before baking (place in cold water, bring to a boil, and drain).

Variations

63A. Ham with Brown Cider Sauce: When ham is baked, drain fat from pan and deglaze with 1½ pt (750 mL) cider. Add 1½ qt (1.5 L) Demiglaze or Espagnole and simmer until reduced and thickened. Flavor to taste with mustard and a little sugar.

63B. Fruit-glazed Ham: Omit mustard-sugar glaze. During last half of baking, spoon fruit preserves (apricot, pineapple, or peach) over ham to glaze.

RECIPE 64   **Baked Meat Loaf**

Portions: 25   **Portion size:** 4 oz (125 g)

U.S.	Metric	Ingredients	Procedure
1 lb	500 g	Onions, fine dice	1. Sauté the onions and celery in oil until tender. Remove from pan and cool thoroughly.
8 oz	250 g	Celery, fine dice	
2 oz	60 mL	Oil	
12 oz	375 g	Soft bread crumbs	2. In a large bowl, soak the bread crumbs in the liquid.
12 oz	375 mL	Tomato juice *or* stock *or* milk	
7½ lb	3.75 kg	Ground beef	3. Add the sautéed vegetables, the meat, eggs, salt, and pepper. Mix *gently* until evenly combined. Do not overmix.
5	5	Eggs, beaten slightly	
1 tbsp	15 mL	Salt	
½ tsp	2 mL	Black pepper	4. Form the mixture into 2 or 3 loaves in a bake pan, or fill loaf pans with the mixture.
			5. Bake at 350°F (175°C) about 1 to 1½ hours, until done. Test with a meat thermometer for internal temperature of 165°F (74°C).
3 pt	1.5 L	Tomato Sauce *or* Spanish Sauce *or* Creole Sauce *or* Sour Cream Sauce	6. For service, cut the loaves into 4-oz (125-g) slices. Serve with 2 oz (60 mL) sauce per portion.

Variations

Use 5 lb (2.5 kg) ground beef and 2½ lb (1.25 kg) ground pork instead of all beef. Be sure to cook until well done.

64A. Italian-Style Meat Loaf: Add the following ingredients to the basic mix:
   4 tsp (20 mL) chopped garlic, sautéed with the onion
   1 oz (30 g) parmesan cheese
   ⅔ cup (150 mL) chopped parsley
   1½ tsp (7 mL) basil
   1 tsp (5 mL) oregano

64B. Salisbury Steak: Divide basic meat mixture into 6-oz (175-g) portions. Form into thick, oval patties and place on sheet pan. Bake at 350°F (175°C) for about 30 minutes.

64C. Baked Meatballs: Divide basic meat mixture or Italian-Style Meat Loaf mixture into 2½-oz (75-g) portions using a No. 16 scoop. Form into balls and place on sheet pans. Bake at 350°F (175°C). May be served with tomato sauce over pasta.

BROILING, GRILLING, AND PAN-BROILING

Broiling and grilling are dry-heat cooking methods, which use very high heat to cook meat quickly. Properly broiled meats have a well-browned, flavorful crust on the outside, and the inside is cooked to the desired doneness and still juicy.

It may be helpful to think of broiling and grilling as browning techniques rather than cooking techniques. This is because the best, juiciest broiled meats are those cooked to the rare or medium-done stage. Because of the intense heat, it is difficult to broil meats to the well-done stage and still keep them juicy. Pork and veal, which are usually eaten well done, are generally better griddled, sautéed, or braised than broiled or grilled. (Veal can be broiled successfully if the customer prefers it still a little pink inside.)

For best results, only high-quality, tender cuts with a good fat content should be broiled.

Temperature Control

The object of broiling is not just to cook the meat to the desired doneness but also to form a brown, flavorful, crusty surface.

The goal of the broiler cook is to create the right amount of browning—not too much or too little—by the time the inside is cooked to the desired doneness. To do this, you must broil the item at the right temperature.

In general, *the shorter the cooking time, the higher the temperature,* or else the meat won't have time to brown. The longer the cooking time, the lower the temperature, or the meat will brown too much before the inside is done.

Cooking time depends on two factors:

1. The desired doneness.
2. The thickness of the cut.

In other words, a well-done steak should be cooked at a lower heat than a rare one. A thin steak cooked rare must be broiled at a higher temperature than a thick one cooked rare.

To control the cooking temperature of a broiler, raise or lower the rack. On a grill, set different areas for different temperatures and grill meats in the appropriate area.

Seasoning

As for roasting, chefs disagree on when to season. Some feel that meats should not be seasoned before broiling. This is because salt draws moisture to the surface and retards browning. Others feel that seasoning before broiling improves the taste of the meat, because the seasonings become part of the brown crust rather than something sprinkled on afterward.

Until you have gained some experience as a broiler cook, it may be safest not to season before broiling. But you should be aware that it is done.

One way around this problem is to serve the meat with a *seasoned butter* (p. 148). Another option is to marinate the meat in seasoned oil 30 minutes before broiling.

Procedure for Broiling or Grilling Meats

In a broiler, the heat source is above the food. In a grill, the heat is below the food. Except for this difference, the basic procedure is the same for both.

Make sure you understand how to test broiled meats for doneness (p. 216) before starting.

1. Collect and prepare all equipment and food supplies. If necessary, score the fatty edges of meats to prevent curling.

2. Preheat the broiler or grill.

3. Dip the meat in oil, let excess drip off, and place the item on the broiler or grill. The oil helps prevent sticking and keeps the product moist. It may be unnecessary for meats high in fat. Using too much oil can cause grease fires.

4. When one side is brown and the meat is cooked halfway, turn it over with a fork (piercing only the fat, *never the meat,* or juices will be lost) or with tongs. Figure 11.5 illustrates the technique for grill-marking steaks and other meats.

5. Cook the second side until the meat is cooked to the desired doneness.

6. Remove from broiler or grill and serve immediately.

Pan-broiling

Broiling very thin steaks (minute steaks) to the rare stage is difficult because the heat is not high enough to form a good brown crust without overcooking the inside.

Pan-broiling in a heavy iron skillet is an answer to this problem:

Procedure

---

1.   Preheat an iron skillet over a high flame until it is very hot. Do not add fat. (The pan should, of course, be well seasoned.)

2.   Proceed as for grilling. Pour off any fat that accumulates during cooking, if necessary.

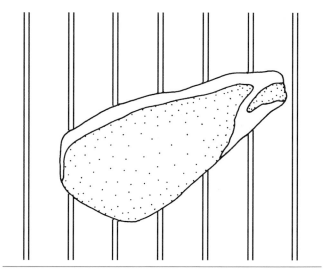

(b) When the meat is about one-fourth done, turn the meat about 60° to the angle shown. Do not turn it over.

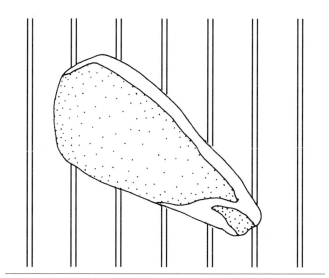

FIGURE 11.5 **Grill-marking steaks.**
(a) Place the meat on a preheated grill at an angle as shown.

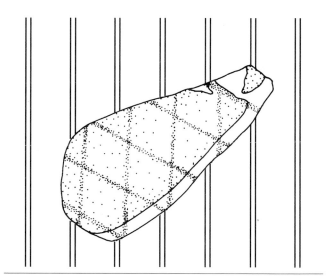

(c) When the steak is about half done, turn it over. The grill marks will appear as shown.

RECIPE 65 **Broiled Steak Variations**

Yield: as required

U.S.	Metric	Ingredients	Procedure
		Beef steaks, such as	1. Review guidelines and procedures for broiling meats.
		Rib	
		Rib eye	2. Cut, trim, and prepare steaks as necessary. Ready-to-cook, portion-control steaks usually need no prep.
		Strip loin	
		Tenderloin	
		Club	3. Place oil in a small hotel pan. Dip steaks in oil and let excess drip off.
		Porterhouse	
		T-bone	4. Place steaks on preheated grill or broiler.
		Sirloin	
		Chopped beef patties	5. When steak is about one-fourth done, turn it about 60 degrees to grill mark it (see Figure 11.5).
		Salad oil	
			6. When steak is half done, turn over and complete the cooking to desired doneness. If turning with a fork, pierce the fat, not the meat, or juices will be lost.
		Suggested sauces:	7. Remove steak from broiler and serve immediately on a hot plate. Serve with appropriate sauce or garnish. Serve the sauce on the side or in a sauceboat (except for seasoned butters). Do not cover steak completely with sauce.
		Maitre d'Hotel Butter	
		Garlic Butter	
		Anchovy Butter	
		Bordelaise Sauce	
		Chasseur Sauce	
		Madeira Sauce	
		Perigueux Sauce	
		Mushroom Sauce (brown)	
		Bercy Sauce (brown)	
		Lyonnaise Sauce	
		Béarnaise Sauce	
		Foyot Sauce	
		Choron Sauce	

RECIPE 66   **Broiled Lamb Chops**

Prepare as for broiled steaks, using rib, loin, or shoulder chops.

RECIPE 67   **Broiled Lamb Patties**

| **Portions:** 25 | | **Portion size:** 5 oz (150 g) | |

U.S.	Metric	Ingredients	Procedure
6 oz	175 g	Onions, chopped fine	1. Sauté the onion in oil until tender. Do not brown. Cool thoroughly.
2 oz	60 g	Salad oil	
6½ lb	3.25 kg	Ground lamb	2. Combine all ingredients except bacon in a bowl. Mix gently until evenly combined. Do not overmix.
8 oz	250 g	Soft, fresh bread crumbs	
10 oz	300 mL	Milk	3. Scale the meat into 5-oz (150-g) portions. Form the portions into thick patties (about ¾ inch (2 cm) thick).
½ cup	30 g	Chopped parsley	
1½ tsp	7 mL	Basil	
2½ tsp	12 mL	Salt	4. Wrap a strip of bacon around each pattie and fasten with picks.
1 tsp	5 mL	White pepper	
25 strips	25 strips	Bacon	5. Broil the patties under moderate heat until done, turning once (see note).
			6. Remove picks before serving.

Note: Patties may be browned under the broiler, arranged on a sheet pan, and finished in the oven at 375°F (190°C).

Variations

Ground ***Beef*** or ***Veal*** may be used instead of lamb.

RECIPE 68 **Shish Kebab**

Portions: 25			**Portion size:** 6 oz (175 g)

U.S.	Metric	Ingredients	Procedure
10 lb	4.5 kg	Lamb leg, boneless, trimmed	1. A day before cooking, trim any remaining fat and connective tissue from the lamb. Cut into 1-inch (2½-cm) cubes. Keep all the cubes the same size for even cooking.
		Marinade:	
1 qt	1 L	Olive oil, or part olive and part vegetable oil	2. Combine the marinade ingredients and pour over the lamb in a hotel pan. Mix well. Refrigerate overnight.
½ cup	125 mL	Lemon juice	3. Drain the meat and weigh out 6-oz (175-g) portions. Thread each portion onto a skewer.
5	5	Garlic cloves, crushed	
4 tsp	20 mL	Salt	
1½ tsp	7 mL	Pepper	4. Place skewers on a grill or broiler rack and broil at moderate heat until medium done, turning over once when they are half cooked.
1 tsp	5 mL	Oregano	
			5. To serve, place each portion on a bed of Rice Pilaf (p. 456). The skewers should be removed by the waiter in the dining room or by the cook in the kitchen.

Note: Shish kebabs are sometimes made with vegetables (onions, green peppers, cherry tomatoes, mushrooms) on the same skewer with the meat. However, it is easier to control cooking times if vegetables are broiled on separate skewers. Also, the meat is less likely to steam in the moisture from the vegetables.

FIGURE 11.6 **Slicing London Broil flank steak.**
(a) Holding the knife at a sharp angle, slice the meat in very thin slices across the grain. Use a table fork or kitchen fork to hold the meat steady. Some chefs slice the meat toward the fork.

(b) Others prefer to slice away from the fork. The final result is the same.

RECIPE 69   London Broil

| | **Portions:** 24 | | **Portion size:** 5 oz (150 g) |

U.S.	Metric	Ingredients	Procedure
10 lb	4.75 kg	Flank steak (5 steaks) Marinade:	1. Trim all fat and connective tissue from beef.
1 pt	500 mL	Vegetable oil	2. Combine the marinade ingredients in a hotel pan. Place steaks in the pan and turn them so they are coated with oil. Cover and refrigerate for at least 2 hours.
2 oz	60 mL	Lemon juice	
2 tsp	10 mL	Salt	
2 tsp	10 mL	Black pepper	
1 tsp	5 mL	Thyme	
			3. Remove the meat from the marinade and place in a preheated broiler or grill. Broil at high heat about 3 to 5 minutes on each side, until well browned outside but rare inside (see note).
			4. Remove from broiler and let rest 2 minutes before slicing.
			5. Slice the meat very thin on a sharp angle across the grain (see Figure 11.6).
1½ qt	1.5 L	Mushroom Sauce (brown) (p. 144).	6. Weigh 5-oz (150-g) portions. Serve each portion with 2 oz (60 mL) sauce.

Note: Flank steak should be broiled rare. If cooked well done it will be tough and dry.

Variations

Thick-cut steaks from the round or chuck are sometimes used for London Broil.

69A. *Teriyaki-Style London Broil:* Marinate the steaks in a mixture of the following ingredients: 2½ cups (600 mL) Japanese soy sauce, 6 oz (200 mL) vegetable oil, 4 oz (125 mL) sherry, 6 oz (175 g) chopped onion, 2 tbsp (30 g) sugar, 2 tsp (10 mL) ginger, 1 crushed clove garlic. Marinate at least 4 hours or, preferably, overnight. Broil as in basic recipe.

RECIPE 70 **Glazed Ham Steak with Fruit**

		Portions: 25	**Portion size:** 1 steak, 5 oz (150 g)

U.S.	Metric	Ingredients	Procedure
5 oz	150 g	Brown sugar	1. Combine the sugar, mustard, water, lemon juice, and butter in a small saucepan and heat just until the sugar is dissolved. Remove from heat and set aside.
2½ tsp	12 mL	Dry mustard	
2 oz	60 mL	Water	
3 oz	90 mL	Lemon juice	
1 oz	30 g	Butter	
25	25	Ham steaks or slices, 5 oz (150 g) each	2. Dip ham steaks in oil, if desired, and let excess oil drip off. Place steaks on broiler rack and broil on each side just until lightly browned. Precooked ham needs only to be heated through. Do not overcook.
		Salad oil (optional)	
50	50	Apricot halves	
		or	
25	25	Pineapple slices	3. Top each ham steak with one, two, or three pieces of fruit (depending on size) and brush the ham and fruit with the sugar mixture. (This should be done without removing the steaks from the broiler grid. Just pull the grid out while you are working on the steaks.)
		or	
75	75	Peach slices	
			4. Return the steaks to the broiler just long enough to glaze the surface and heat the fruit.

Variation

To prepare ham steaks in the oven, arrange the steaks on an oiled sheet pan, top with fruit, brush with glaze, and bake until hot and lightly browned.

SAUTÉING, PAN-FRYING, AND GRIDDLING

If you review the general definitions of sautéing, pan-frying, and griddling in Chapter 4, you will see that the differences among these methods are largely a matter of degree. Sautéing uses high heat and a small amount of fat and is usually used for small pieces of food. Pan-frying uses moderate heat, a moderate amount of fat, and is usually employed with larger items, such as chops. But at what point does moderate heat become high heat, and a small amount of fat become a moderate amount of fat? It is impossible to draw an exact dividing line between sautéing and pan-frying.

Each time you cook a piece of meat, you must judge how much heat and how much fat to use to do the job best. This depends on the kind of food and the size of the pieces. Following are some guidelines to help you make the right judgments.

Guidelines for Sautéing, Pan-frying, and Griddling

1. Use only tender cuts for sautéing.

2. Smaller or thinner pieces of meat require higher heat. The object is to brown or sear the meat in the time it takes to cook it to the desired doneness. Very small or thin pieces cook in just a few moments.

3. If large or thick items are browned over high heat, it may be necessary to finish them at lower heat to avoid burning them.

4. The amount of fat needed is the amount required to conduct the heat to all surfaces so that the item cooks evenly. Flat items need much less fat than irregularly shaped items like chicken pieces.

   Sautéing small pieces of meat requires little fat because the items are tossed or flipped so that all sides come in contact with the hot pan.

5. When sautéing small pieces of food, do not overload the pan, and do not flip or toss the food more than necessary. This will cause the temperature to drop too much and the meat will simmer in its own juices instead of sauté.

6. Use clarified butter or oil or a mixture for sautéing. Whole butter burns easily.

7. Dredging meats in flour promotes even browning and helps prevent sticking. Flour meats immediately before cooking, not in advance, or the flour will get pasty. Also, shake off excess flour before adding meat to the pan.

8. When pan-frying several batches, strain or skim the fat between batches. Otherwise, burned food particles from previous batches may mar the appearance of the meat.

9. Griddling and pan-frying are preferable to broiling and grilling for cooking pork and veal chops, because the lower temperatures keep these meats moister when cooked well done. Hamburgers cooked well done are also moister if cooked on a griddle.

General Procedures for Sautéing and Pan-frying Meats

The following procedures are presented side by side, so that you can compare them. Keep in mind that these are the two extremes and that many recipes require a procedure that falls somewhere between the two.

The procedure for pan-frying applies to *griddling* as well, although only a small amount of fat can be used on a griddle.

Sautéing

1. Collect all equipment and food supplies.
2. Prepare meats as required. This may include dredging with flour.
3. Heat a small amount of fat in a sauté pan until very hot.
4. Add the meat to the pan. Do not overcrowd the pan.
5. Brown the meat on all sides, flipping or tossing it in the pan as necessary, so that it cooks evenly.
6. Remove meat from pan and drain excess fat, if any. Deglaze the pan with stock, wine, or other liquid to dissolve the browned bits of food sticking to the bottom. Finish the sauce according to the recipe.
7. Serve the meat with the sauce, or return the meat to the sauce to reheat *briefly* and coat it with the sauce. Do not let it cook in the sauce. Serve.

Pan-frying

1. Collect all equipment and food supplies.
2. Prepare meats as required. This may include breading or dredging with flour.
3. Heat a moderate amount of fat in a sauté pan or skillet until hot.
4. Add the meat to the pan.
5. Brown the meat on one side. Turn it with a spatula and brown the other side. Larger pieces may need to be finished at reduced heat after browning. Or, if required, they may finish cooking, uncovered, in the oven.
6. Serve immediately.

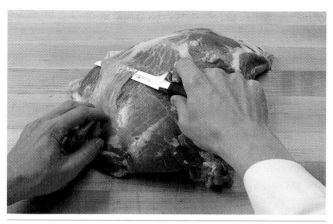

FIGURE 11.7 **Trimming and cutting veal for scaloppine. (a) Remove all tendons and connective tissue (silverskin) from the veal. Slip the point of a thin boning knife under the skin. Angle the edge of the blade upward against the skin and cut it away carefully, without cutting through the meat.**

(d) . . . leave it attached.

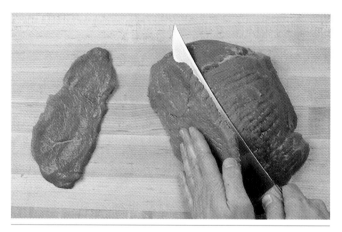

(b) Holding the blade of the knife at an angle if necessary to get a broader slice, cut *across the grain* of the meat as shown to make thin slices.

(e) Then cut a second slice the same way, but cut all the way through.

(c) Broader slices can be cut from narrower pieces of meat by butterflying. Cut the slice almost through the meat but . . .

(f) A butterflied scaloppine is twice as large as a single slice. Unfortunately, it has a seam in the center that often detracts from the appearance of the finished dish, unless the veal is breaded or covered with a topping.

RECIPE 73 **Pork Chops Charcutière**

| | **Portions:** 24 | | **Portion size:** 6 oz (175 g) chop |
| | | | 2 oz (60 mL) sauce |

U.S.	Metric	Ingredients	Procedure
24	24	Pork chops, 6 oz (175 g) each Oil	1. Trim excess fat from chops if necessary. 2. Add enough oil to a skillet or sauté pan or to a griddle to make a thin film. Heat over moderate heat. 3. Place the chops in the hot pan or on griddle and cook until browned and about half done. Turn over and cook until well done and browned on the second side.
1½ qt	1.5 L	Charcutière Sauce (p. 144)	4. Place the chops on hot dinner plates for service (or place them in a hotel pan if they must be held). 5. Spoon a ribbon of sauce (2 oz/60 mL) around each plated chop, and serve.

Variations

73A. Pork Chops Robert: Use Robert Sauce instead of Charcutiére Sauce.

73B. Pork Chops Piquante: Use Piquante Sauce.

73C. Veal Chops may be cooked by the same basic procedure and served with an appropriate sauce, such as a well-seasoned Demiglaze or a mixture of Demiglaze and cream. Other suggestions: Ivory Sauce, Hungarian Sauce, Mushroom Sauce (white), Aurora Sauce.

(g) If desired, pound the cutlet to an even thickness with a cutlet mallet. This helps to disguise the seam in a butterflied cutlet.

RECIPE 74 **Tournedos Vert-pré**

Portions: 1			**Portion size:** 5–6 oz (150–175 g)

U.S.	Metric	Ingredients	Procedure
1 oz 2	30 g 2	Clarified butter Tournedos (see note) 2½–3 oz (75–90 g) each	1. Heat the butter in a small sauté pan over moderately high heat.
2 slices	2 slices	Maitre d'Hotel Butter (p. 148) Watercress Allumette Potatoes (p. 449)	2. Place the tournedos in the pan and cook until well browned on the bottom and about half cooked.
			3. Turn the meat over and continue to cook until rare or medium done, according to customer's request.
			4. Place the tournedos on a hot dinner plate and top each with a slice of Maitre d'Hotel Butter. Garnish the plate with a portion of Allumette Potatoes and a generous bunch of watercress. Serve immediately, while the butter is still melting.

Note: Tournedos (singular form: one tournedos, pronounced TOOR-nuh-doe) are small tenderloin steaks cut about 1½ inches (4 cm) thick. The same recipe may be used for fillet steaks, which are larger but thinner cuts from the tenderloin.

Variations

74A. *Tournedos Béarnaise:* Pan-fry tournedos as in basic recipe, and serve with Béarnaise Sauce.

74B. *Tournedos Bordelaise:* Pan-fry as in basic recipe. Top each steak with a slice of poached beef marrow, and coat lightly with Bordelaise Sauce.

74C. *Tournedos Chasseur:* Pan-fry as in basic recipe. Plate the steaks and deglaze the sauté pan (drained of cooking fat) with ½ oz (15 mL) white wine. Add 2 oz (60 mL) Chasseur Sauce, bring to a simmer, and pour around the tournedos.

74D. *Tournedos Rossini:* Pan-fry as in basic recipe. Set the tournedos on croutons (rounds of bread cut the same size as the steaks and fried in butter till golden). Top each steak with a slice of pâté de foie gras (goose liver pâté) and a slice of truffle (if available). Coat lightly with Madeira Sauce.

RECIPE 75   Sautéed Tenderloin Tips with Mushrooms in Red Wine Sauce

Portions: 10   **Portion size:** 7 oz (200 g)

U.S.	Metric	Ingredients	Procedure
2½ lb	1.2 kg	Beef tenderloin tips, trimmed of all fat	1. Cut the beef into thin slices, cutting across the grain on the bias.
2 oz	60 mL	Oil	2. Heat the oil in a sauté pan over high heat until almost to the smoke point. Sauté the beef quickly, until well browned but not overcooked. It should be still pink inside. If necessary, sauté in several batches or in more than one pan, to avoid overcrowding the pan.
			3. Remove the meat from the pan and discard excess fat.
2 oz	60 g	Clarified butter	4. Heat the clarified butter in the sauté pan and sauté the mushrooms until lightly browned. Remove from pan.
1 lb	500 g	Mushrooms, sliced thick	
4 oz	125 mL	Red wine, dry	5. Deglaze the pan with the red wine and reduce by about half.
1½ pt	750 mL	Demiglaze or Brown Sauce, hot	6. Add the Demiglaze or Brown Sauce. Also, add any juices that have collected under the meat and the mushrooms.
		Salt	
		Pepper	7. Bring the sauce to a boil and cook briefly until reduced to desired consistency. Season.
			8. Add the beef and mushrooms to the sauce and bring just to a simmer. Remove from heat and serve immediately in casserole dishes. Garnish with toast points (p. 599).

Note: Less tender cuts of beef may be used if the meat is simmered in the sauce until tender. The item will then be braised rather than sautéed.

Variations

75A. *À la Carte Service:* Preprep: Sauté mushrooms and add to Demiglaze. Deglaze mushroom pan with wine and add to sauce. For each order: Sauté 4 oz (125 g) beef and combine with 3 oz (100 mL) sauce.

75B. *Beef Tenderloin Tips Chasseur:* Prepare as in basic recipe, except omit mushrooms; use white wine instead of red; and use Chasseur Sauce instead of Demiglaze.

75C. *Beef Sauté à la Deutsch:* Prepare as in basic recipe, except during preprep sauté the following in butter and add to the Demiglaze: 12 oz (375 g) onions cut julienne, 6 oz (175 g) green peppers cut julienne, and ½ tsp (2 mL) chopped garlic. (For à la carte service, the mushrooms may also be added at this point, although they will be a little fresher if cooked at the last minute.)

RECIPE 76 **Beef Stroganoff**

Portions: 10		**Portion size:** 6 oz (175 g)	

U.S.	Metric	Ingredients	Procedure
2 oz	60 g	Clarified butter	1. Heat the butter in the sauté pan and sauté the onion and mushrooms briefly without letting them get brown.
4 oz	125 g	Onions, brunoise	
8 oz	250 g	Mushrooms, sliced	
2 oz	60 mL	White wine (see note)	2. Add the white wine and reduce by half over high heat.
1 oz	30 g	Tomato paste	
2 tsp	10 mL	Prepared mustard	3. Stir in the mustard and tomato paste. Then add the Demiglaze. Reduce over high heat until thickened.
1½ pt	750 mL	Demiglaze or Brown Sauce	
1¼ cups	300 mL	Sour cream	4. Stir in the sour cream and season to taste. Keep the sauce hot in a bain marie.
		Salt	
		Pepper	
2½ lb	1.25 kg	Beef tenderloin tips, trimmed of all fat, cut into thin strips, about 1½ by ½ inch (3 by 1 cm)	5. Heat the oil in a sauté pan over high heat until almost to the smoke point. Sauté the beef quickly, until well browned but not overcooked. It should still be pink inside. If necessary, sauté in several batches or in more than one pan, to avoid overcrowding the pan.
2 oz	60 mL	Oil	6. Remove the meat from the pan and discard excess fat.
			7. Add the sour cream sauce to the pan and bring to a simmer. Stir in the meat and adjust the seasoning.
			8. Serve immediately with noodles or spaetzle (p. 470).

Note: Wine may be omitted if necessary. Deglaze pan with a mixture of equal parts water and vinegar (white or wine vinegar). Check seasoning of finished dish very carefully; season with a little lemon juice if desired.

Less tender cuts of meat may be used in this preparation if the meat is simmered in the sauce until tender. The item will then be braised rather than sautéed.

SIMMERING

Simmering is not a frequently used cooking method for meats. Part of the reason that simmered meats are not as popular may be that they lack the kind of flavor caused by browning with dry heat.

However, simmering is used effectively for certain less tender cuts for which browning is either not desired or not appropriate. Popular examples of simmered meats are cured products such as ham and corned beef, fresh or cured tongue, fresh beef brisket, and white stews such as veal blanquette.

The term *stewing* is used to mean cooking small pieces of meat either by simmering or by braising (a composite method that includes both browning and simmering). Stews cooked by braising are covered in the next section.

One difference between stews and many other simmered meats is that stews are served in a sauce or gravy made of the cooking liquid.

Basic Procedure for Simmering Meats

1. Collect all equipment and food supplies.

2. Prepare meat for cooking. This may include cutting, trimming, or tying.

3. Prepare the cooking liquid:

    a. For fresh meats, start with boiling liquid.
    b. For cured and smoked meats, start with cold liquid to help draw out some of the salt from the meats.
    c. For both kinds of meats, there must be enough liquid to cover the meat completely.

4. Place the meat in the cooking liquid and return (or bring) to a boil.

5. Reduce heat to a simmer and skim the surface. Meat must never boil for any length of time. Simmering results in a tenderer, juicier product.

6. Simmer until the meat is tender, skimming as necessary. Mirepoix or other flavorings may be added during cooking, if required.

7. If the meat is to be served cold, cool it in its cooking liquid to retain moistness. Cool rapidly in a cold-water bath, as for stocks.

RECIPE 77   **Simmered Corned Beef**

		Portions: 15	**Portion size:** 3 oz (90 g)

U.S.	Metric	Ingredients	Procedure
5 lb	2.5 kg	Corned beef brisket	1. Trim excess fat from corned beef if necessary.
			2. Place the beef in a stock pot or steam kettle. Cover with cold water.
			3. Bring to a boil and reduce heat to a simmer. Simmer until the meat feels tender when pierced with a fork. Cooking time will be about 2 to 3 hours.
			4. To hold and serve hot, place the cooked meat in a steam table pan and add some of the cooking liquid to keep it moist. To serve, cut the meat across the grain into thin slices, holding the knife at an angle to get broader slices. Serve with Horseradish Sauce or prepared horseradish.
			5. To serve cold, cool the beef, with some of its cooking liquid to keep it moist, in a cold-water bath. When cool, remove from the liquid and refrigerate, covered. Slice and serve on sandwiches or with potato salad and pickles. Cold corned beef may be reheated in its cooking liquid.

Variations

77A. *New England Boiled Dinner:* Serve hot corned beef with cabbage wedges, potatoes, turnips, carrots, and small white onions, cooked separately in some of the beef cooking broth, and with fresh or canned whole red beets, cooked or heated separately.

77B. *Glazed Corned Beef:* When corned beef is tender, drain and place in a bake pan. Spread the top with 1 oz (30 g) prepared mustard and sprinkle with 3 oz (90 g) brown sugar. Bake at 350°F (175°C) until glazed, about 20 minutes.

RECIPE 78 **Blanquette of Veal**

		Portions: 25	**Portion size:** 5 oz (150 g)

U.S.	Metric	Ingredients	Procedure
10 lb	5 kg	Boneless, trimmed veal breast, shoulder, or shank	1. Cut the veal into 1-inch (2½-cm) dice. 2. Blanch the meat: Place in a sauce pot and cover with cold water. Bring to a boil, drain, and rinse the meat under cold water (see note).
1	1	Medium onion, stuck with 2 cloves	3. Return the meat to the pot and add the onion, bouquet garni, and salt.
		Bouquet garni:	4. Add enough stock to just cover the meat.
1 rib	1 rib	Celery	5. Bring to a boil, skim, cover, and lower heat to a slow simmer.
1	1	Carrot, small	
1	1	Leek, small (optional)	6. Simmer until meat is tender, about 1½ hours. Skim when necessary.
5–6	5–6	Parsley stems	
1	1	Bay leaf	7. Strain off the stock into another pan. Reserve the meat and discard the onion and bouquet garni.
pinch	pinch	Thyme	
4 tsp	20 mL	Salt	
2½ qt (approximately)	2.5 L	White veal stock	
		Roux:	8. Reduce the stock to about 2½ pt (1.25 L).
4 oz	125 g	Butter, clarified	
4 oz	125 g	Flour	9. Meanwhile, prepare a white roux with the butter and flour. Beat into the stock to make a velouté sauce, and simmer until thickened and no raw flour taste remains.
		Liaison:	
5	5	Egg yolks	
1 pt	500 mL	Heavy cream	10. Remove the sauce from the heat. Beat the egg yolks and cream together, temper with a little of the hot sauce, and stir into the sauce.
		Lemon juice	
		Nutmeg	
		White pepper	11. Combine the sauce and meat and heat gently but do not boil.
			12. Season to taste with a few drops of lemon juice, a pinch of nutmeg and white pepper, and more salt if needed.

Note: Blanching eliminates impurities that discolor the sauce. This step can be omitted, but the product will have a less attractive appearance.

Variations

*78A. **Blanquette of Lamb:*** Prepare as in basic recipe, using lamb shoulder or shank.

*78B. **Blanquette of Pork:*** Prepare as in basic recipe, using pork shoulder or butt.

RECIPE 79   **Irish Lamb Stew**

Portions: 16   **Portion size:** 8 oz (250 g) meat, vegetables, and broth

U.S.	Metric	Ingredients	Procedure
3½ lb	1.75 kg	Lean, boneless lamb shoulder or shanks	1. Cut meat into 1-inch (2½-cm) cubes.
3 pt (approximately)	1.5 L	Water or white lamb stock	2. Bring the water to a boil in a large, heavy sauce pot. Add the lamb. There should be just enough liquid to cover the meat; add more liquid if necessary.
1	1	Small onion stuck with 2 cloves	
		Sachet:	3. Return to a boil, reduce heat to a simmer, and skim the scum carefully.
1	1	Bay leaf	
1 clove	1 clove	Garlic	4. Add the onion stuck with cloves, the sachet ingredients tied in a piece of cheesecloth, and salt to taste. Simmer 1 hour.
4	4	Whole peppercorns	
6	6	Parsley stems	
¼ tsp	1 mL	Thyme	
		Salt	
1 lb	500 g	Onions, sliced thin	5. Add the onion, leek, and potatoes. Continue to simmer until the meat is tender and the vegetables are cooked. The potatoes should break down somewhat and thicken the stew.
8 oz	250 g	Leeks (white part) sliced	
2 lb	1 kg	Potatoes, peeled and sliced thin	
		Chopped parsley	6. Remove and discard the sachet and the onion stuck with cloves. Correct the seasoning.
			7. Garnish each portion with chopped parsley.

Variation

Carrots and white turnips may be cooked with the stew or cooked separately and added as a garnish.

RECIPE 80 **Simmered Fresh Beef Brisket ("Boiled Beef")**

Portions: 25			**Portion size:** 4 oz (125 g)

U.S.	Metric	Ingredients	Procedure
10 lb	5 kg	Fresh beef brisket, well trimmed	1. Place beef in a stock pot with enough boiling water to cover. Return the water to a boil, reduce heat to a simmer, and skim the scum carefully.
		Mirepoix:	
8 oz	250 g	Onion, coarsely chopped	2. Add the mirepoix and seasonings.
4 oz	125 g	Carrot, coarsely chopped	3. Simmer until the meat is tender when tested with a fork.
4 oz	125 g	Celery, coarsely chopped	4. Transfer the meat to a steam table pan and add enough of the broth to barely cover, to keep the meat moist, or cool the meat with some of the broth in a cold-water bath and refrigerate.
2 cloves	2 cloves	Garlic	
1	1	Bay leaf	
½ tsp	2 mL	Peppercorns	
2	2	Whole cloves	
6	6	Parsley stems	5. To serve, cut the meat into thin slices across the grain. Slice at an angle to make the slices broader. Serve each portion with Horseradish Sauce (p. 142), prepared horseradish, or mustard and with boiled vegetables, such as carrots, potatoes, or turnips.
		Salt	
			6. Strain the broth and save for soups or sauces. If desired, use some of the broth to make Horseradish Sauce to accompany the meat.

Variations

80A. ***Beef tongue*** (fresh, cured, or smoked), ***beef shank,*** various cuts of ***beef chuck, beef short ribs, fresh or smoked ham, pork shoulder,*** or ***lamb shoulder and leg*** may be cooked using the same method.

80B. ***Simmered Pork Shoulder with Cabbage:*** Cook *fresh* or *smoked* pork shoulder or pork butt as in basic recipe. Cut 5 lb (2.3 kg) cabbage (for 25 portions) into wedges and simmer in some of the pork broth. Serve each portion of meat with a cabbage wedge. For 25 4-oz (125-g) portions, use about 15 lb (7.5 kg) bone-in, skin-on shoulder.

BRAISING

Braising is a combination of dry-heat and moist-heat cooking methods. Meats are first browned or seared in fat or in a hot oven, then simmered in a flavorful liquid until tender.

The popularity of properly braised items is due to the flavor imparted by the browning and by the sauce made from the braising liquid. Clearly, the quality of a braised meat depends greatly on the quality of the stock the meat is cooked in. Other liquids used in braising include wine, marinades, tomato product, and occasionally water.

Popular Types of Braised Meat Dishes

1. ***Large cuts.***

   Large cuts of meat braised whole, sliced, and served with a sauce or gravy are sometimes called *pot roasts.*

2. ***Individual portion cuts.***

   Meats may be cut into portion sizes before braising instead of afterward. When portion cuts of beef round are braised in a brown sauce, the process is sometimes called *swissing,* and the product is called Swiss steak.

   Other braised portion cut meats include short ribs, lamb shanks, and pork chops.

3. ***Stews.***

   Stews are made of meats cut into small pieces or cubes. Most stews are made by braising, but some are cooked by simmering only, without first browning or searing the meat.

   Stews are usually made with enough liquid or gravy to cover the meat completely while cooking. However, there are also "dry" stews, which are braised in their own juices or in a very little added liquid.

   Brown stews are made by browning the meat thoroughly before simmering. *Fricassées* are white stews made by cooking white meat in fat over low heat, without letting it brown, and then adding liquid. Compare this to a *blanquette,* which is a white stew made by simmering the meat in stock without first cooking it in fat. The cooking method for blanquettes, therefore, is simmering rather than braising.

   Many other dishes can be classified as braised stews, even if we don't normally think of them that way. Chili, for example, is a braised dish made of finely cut or ground beef or pork. Even meat sauce for spaghetti (p. 461) is actually a braised meat or a stew.

Many chefs prefer to use the term "braising" only for large cuts of meat. However, the basic cooking method—using first dry heat, then moist heat—is the same for small cuts as well.

Guidelines for Braising Meats

The basic principle of braising, then, is a combination of searing or browning and then simmering. This process accomplishes two things: it cooks the meat, and it produces a sauce. (You will use some of your saucemaking techniques when you braise meats.)

Before giving basic procedures that apply to most popular braised meats, first we will discuss a number of factors that affect the quality of the finished product.

1. ***Seasoning.***

   The meat may be seasoned before browning or it may receive its seasonings from the cooking liquid while braising. But remember that salt on the surface of meat retards browning. Also, herbs may burn in the high heat necessary for browning.

   Marinating the meat for several hours or even several days before browning is an effective way to season, because the seasonings have time to penetrate.

2. ***Browning.***

   Dry the meat thoroughly before browning. Small pieces for stew may be dredged in flour for better browning. In general, red meats are well browned; white meats are browned less heavily, usually until they are golden.

3. ***Amount of braising liquid.***

   The amount of liquid to be added depends on the type of preparation and on the amount of sauce required for serving. Do not use more liquid than necessary, or the flavors will be less rich and less concentrated.

   Pot roasts usually require about 2 oz (60 mL) sauce per portion, and this determines the amount of liquid needed. The size of the braising pot used should allow the liquid to cover the meat by one-third to two-thirds.

   Stews usually require enough liquid to cover the meat.

   Some items are braised with no added liquid. They are browned and then covered, and the item cooks in its own moisture, which is trapped in by the pan lid. Pork chops are frequently cooked in this way. If roasted, sautéed or pan-fried items are covered during cooking, they become, in effect, braised items.

4. *Vegetable garnish.*

Vegetables to be served with the meat may be cooked along with the meat or cooked separately and added before service.

If the first method is used, the vegetables should be added just long enough before the end of cooking for them to be cooked through but not overcooked.

5. *Adjusting the sauce.*

Braising liquids may be thickened by a roux either before cooking (Method 2) or after cooking (Method 1). In some preparations the liquid is left unthickened or is naturally thick, such as tomato sauce.

In any case, the sauce may require further adjustment of its consistency by

a. Reducing.
b. Thickening with roux or beurre manié or other thickening agent.
c. Addition of a prepared sauce, such as demiglaze or velouté.

Basic Procedures for Braising Meats

Method 1

1. Collect all equipment and food supplies.

2. Cut or trim meat as required. Dry it thoroughly. For stews, the meat may be dredged with flour.

3. Brown the meat thoroughly on all sides in a heavy pan with a small amount of fat, or in an oven.

4. Remove meat from pan and brown mirepoix in the fat left in the pan.

5. Return the meat to the pan and add required amount of liquid.

6. Add sachet or other seasonings and flavorings.

7. Bring liquid to a simmer, cover the pot tightly, and simmer in the oven or on top of the range until the meat is tender.

Oven braising provides more uniform heat. Temperatures of 250°F to 300°F (120°C to 150°C) are sufficient to maintain a simmer. Do not let boil.

8. Remove meat from the pan and keep it warm.

9. Prepare a sauce or gravy from the braising liquid. This usually includes the following:

a. Skim fat.
b. Prepare a brown roux with this fat or with another fat if desired.
c. Thicken the braising liquid with the roux. Simmer until the roux is cooked thoroughly.
d. Strain and adjust seasonings.

10. Combine the meat (sliced or whole) with the sauce.

Method 2

1. Collect all equipment and food supplies.

2. Prepare meat for cooking, as required.

3. Brown meat thoroughly in a heavy pan with fat or in a hot oven.

4. Remove meat from pan (if required) and brown mirepoix in remaining fat.

5. Add flour to make a roux. Brown the roux.

6. Add stock to make a thickened sauce. Add seasonings and flavorings.

7. Return meat to pan. Cover and simmer in oven or on range until meat is tender.

8. Adjust sauce as necessary (strain, season, reduce, dilute, etc.).

Method 3: Fricassées

1. Follow Method 2, EXCEPT:

a. Do not brown the meat. Cook it gently in the fat without browning.
b. Add flour to the meat in the pan and make a blond roux.

2. Finish the sauce with a liaison of egg yolks and cream.

RECIPE 81 **Swiss Steak**

			Portions: 25		Portion size: 5 oz (150 g) meat

Portion size: 5 oz (150 g) meat
2 oz (60 mL) sauce

U.S.	Metric	Ingredients	Procedure
25	25	Beef round steaks, 5 oz (150 g) each	1. Dry the meat so it will brown more easily.
8 oz	250 mL	Oil	2. Heat the oil in a heavy skillet until very hot. Brown the steaks well on both sides. Transfer the browned steaks to a braising pan or bake pan.
10 oz	300 g	Onion, brunoise	3. Add the onion to the fat in the skillet and sauté until lightly browned.
5 oz	150 g	Bread flour	4. Stir in the bread flour to make a roux. Cook until the roux is browned.
2½ qt	2.5 L	Brown stock	5. Stir in the stock and tomato purée and simmer until the sauce thickens. Add the bay leaves and season to taste with salt and pepper.
5 oz	150 mL	Tomato purée	
2	2	Bay leaves	
		Salt	6. Pour the sauce over the steaks. Cover and braise in the oven at 300°F (150°C) until tender, about 2 hours.
		Pepper	
			7. Transfer the steaks to a hotel pan for service.
			8. Strain the sauce (optional). Degrease. Adjust the seasoning and consistency and pour over the steaks.

Variations

Steaks and other variations may be braised in a prepreared Brown Sauce or Espagnole, instead of a specially made sauce. Omit steps 3, 4, and 5.

81A. Swiss Steaks in Tomato Sauce: Reduce flour to 2½ oz (75 g). For braising liquid, use 2½ pt (1.25 L) brown stock, 2½ lb (1.25 kg) chopped canned tomatoes with their juice, and 1¼ lb (625 g) tomato purée. Season with bay leaf, oregano, and basil. After removing cooked steaks, reduce sauce to desired consistency. Do not strain. Garnish each portion with chopped parsley.

81B. Swiss Steaks with Sour Cream: Prepare as in basic recipe. When steaks are cooked, finish the sauce with 1 pt (500 mL) sour cream, 2½ oz (75 mL) Worcestershire sauce, and 2 tbsp (30 g) prepared mustard.

81C. Swiss Steaks in Red Wine Sauce: Prepare as in basic recipe, but add 1 pt (500 mL) dry red wine to the braising liquid.

81D. Braised Short Ribs: Allow one 10-oz (300-g) piece per portion. Tie (see Figure 11.8). Braise as in basic recipe, but add 5 oz (150 g) each celery and carrot to the onion to make 1¼ lb (600 g) mirepoix. If desired, replace the tomato purée with 1 lb (500 g) chopped canned tomatoes.

81E. Braised Oxtails: Allow 1 lb (500 g) oxtails per portion. Cut into sections at joints. Prepare like Braised Short Ribs.

81F. Braised Lamb Shanks: Allow 1 lamb shank per portion. Prepare like Braised Short Ribs. Add chopped garlic to mirepoix if desired.

FIGURE 11.8 **Tie short ribs as shown, so that the meat will stay on the bone during cooking.**

RECIPE 82 Beef Pot Roast

Portions: 25   **Portion size:** 4 oz (125 g) meat
                                                        2 oz (60 mL) sauce

U.S.	Metric	Ingredients	Procedure
10 lb	5 kg	Beef bottom round, well trimmed (see note)	1. Dry the meat so that it will brown more easily. Heat the oil in a brazier over high heat and brown the meat well on all sides. Remove from pan. (Alternative method: brown meat in a very hot oven.)
4 oz	125 mL	Oil	
		Mirepoix:	2. Add the mirepoix to the brazier and brown it.
8 oz	250 g	Onions, med. dice	
4 oz	125 g	Celery, med. dice	3. Add the tomato product, the stock, and the sachet ingredients tied in cheesecloth. Bring to a boil, cover, and place in a preheated oven set at 300°F (150°C), or just hot enough to maintain a simmer.
4 oz	125 g	Carrots, med. dice	
6 oz	175 g	Tomato purée	
		or	
12 oz	375 g	Tomatoes, canned	
2½ qt	2.5 L	Brown stock	4. Braise the meat until tender, about 2–3 hours.
		Sachet:	
1	1	Bay leaf	5. Remove meat from pan and keep warm for service in a covered pan. Discard sachet. (See alternate method of service, next page.)
pinch	pinch	Thyme	
6	6	Peppercorns	
1 clove	1 clove	Garlic	
4 oz	125 g	Bread flour	6. Skim the fat from the braising liquid and reserve 4 oz (125 g) of it.
			7. Make a brown roux with the flour and the reserved fat. Cool the roux slightly.
			8. Bring the braising liquid to a simmer and beat in the roux. Simmer the sauce at least 15 to 20 minutes, until thickened and reduced slightly.
			9. Strain the sauce and adjust the seasonings.
			10. Slice the meat across the grain. The slices should not be too thick. Serve each 4-oz (125-g) portion with 2 oz (60 mL) sauce.

RECIPE 82   **Beef Pot Roast** *(Continued)*

Note: Other cuts of beef from the round, or from the chuck or brisket may be used instead of bottom round. Braised round makes the best slices, but it tends to be dry. Chuck and brisket are moister when braised, because they have a higher fat content.

For quicker, more uniform cooking and easier handling, cut meats for braising into 5–7 lb (2–3 kg) pieces.

Variations

Alternative method of service: Cool beef as soon as cooked. For service, slice cold meat on electric slicer and arrange in hotel pans. Add sauce, cover pans, and reheat in oven or steamer. Individual portions may also be reheated to order in the sauce.

82A. ***Braised Beef Jardinière:*** Garnish the finished product with 1 lb (500 g) each carrots, celery, and turnips, all cut batonnet and boiled separately, and 1 lb (500 g) pearl onions, boiled and sautéed until brown.

82B. ***Bouef à la Mode:*** Replace the oil (for browning the beef) with diced bacon. Add 1 pt (500 mL) red wine to braising liquid. (Classical boeuf à la mode is cooked with a calf's foot to provide gelatin, and the sauce is not thickened.)

82C. ***Braised Lamb Shoulder:*** Prepare boned, rolled shoulder of lamb according to the basic recipe. Use either regular brown stock or brown lamb stock.

RECIPE 83   **Pork Chops Creole**

	Portions: 25		**Portion size:** 1 chop, 6 oz (175 g)
			3 oz (100 mL) sauce

U.S.	Metric	Ingredients	Procedure
25	25	Pork chops, 6 oz (175 g) each	1. Brown the pork chops on both sides in a small amount of oil over high heat.
		Oil	2. Arrange the chops in a bake pan.
2½ qt	2.5 L	Creole Sauce (p. 146)	3. Bring the sauce to a boil and pour over the chops.
			4. Cover the pan loosely and place in oven at 325°F (165°C). Cook until the chops are tender, about 1 hour.
			5. Adjust seasoning. Serve 1 chop with 3 oz (100 mL) sauce.

Note: Rice is the ideal accompaniment to this dish.

Variations

83A. Pork chops may be braised in other sauces, such as Robert, Chasseur, Piquante (add capers, pickles, and herbs *after* cooking the pork), Tomato, or Barbecue.

RECIPE 84   Beef Stew

Portions: 25			**Portion size:** 8 oz (250 g)

U.S.	Metric	Ingredients	Procedure
6 lb	3 kg	Beef chuck, boneless and well trimmed of fat	1. Cut the meat into 1-inch (2½-cm) cubes.
4 oz	125 mL	Oil	2. Heat the oil in a brazier until very hot. Add the meat and brown well, stirring occasionally to brown all sides. If necessary, brown the meat in several small batches to avoid overcrowding the pan.
1 lb	500 g	Onion, fine dice	
2 tsp	10 mL	Garlic, chopped	
4 oz	125 g	Flour	
8 oz	250 g	Tomato purée	3. Add the onion and garlic to the pan and continue to cook until onion is lightly browned.
2 qt	2 L	Brown stock	
		Sachet:	
1	1	Bay leaf	4. Add the flour to the meat and stir to make a roux. Continue to cook over high heat until the roux is slightly browned.
pinch	pinch	Thyme	
small sprig	small sprig	Celery leaves	
			5. Stir in the tomato purée and stock and bring to a boil. Stir with a kitchen spoon as the sauce thickens.
			6. Add the sachet. Cover the pot and place in an oven at 325°F (165°C). Braise until the meat is tender, about 1½–2 hours.
1 lb	500 g	Celery, EP	7. Cut the celery and carrots into large dice.
1½ lb	750 g	Carrots, EP	8. Cook the celery, carrots, and onions separately in boiling salted water until just tender.
1 lb	500 g	Small pearl onions, EP	
8 oz	250 g	Tomatoes, canned, drained and coarsely chopped	9. When meat is tender, remove the sachet and adjust seasoning. Degrease the sauce.
8 oz	250 g	Peas, frozen, thawed	10. Add celery, carrots, onions, and tomatoes to the stew.
		Salt	
		Pepper	11. Immediately before service, add the peas. Or garnish the top of each portion with peas.

Note: For more elegant service, remove the cooked meat from sauce before adding the vegetables. Strain the sauce, and pour it back over the meat.

Variations

Vegetables for garniture may be varied, as desired.

84A. Beef Stew with Red Wine: Prepare as in basic recipe, but use 2½ pt (1.25 L) dry red wine and 1½ pt (750 mL) brown stock instead of 2 qt (2 L) brown stock.

84B. Boeuf Bourguignon: Prepare Beef Stew in red wine, using rendered salt pork or bacon fat instead of oil. (Cut the pork into batonnet shapes, sauté until crisp, and save the cooked pork for garnish.) Increase garlic to 2 tbsp (30 mL).

Garnish: Omit vegetable garnish (celery, carrots, pearl onions, tomatoes, and peas) indicated in basic recipe, and substitute lardons (cooked salt pork or bacon pieces), small mushroom caps browned in butter, and boiled pearl onions browned in butter. Serve with egg noodles.

RECIPE 84   **Beef Stew** (*Continued*)

84C. *Brown Lamb Stew* or *Navarin of Lamb*: Prepare as in basic recipe, using lamb shoulder instead of beef chuck. Increase garlic to 2 tbsp (30 mL).

84D. *Brown Veal Stew*: Prepare as in basic recipe, using veal shoulder or shank.

84E. *Brown Veal with White Wine*: Prepare Brown Veal Stew, replacing 1 pt (500 mL) of the stock with white wine.

84F. *Beef Pot Pie*: Fill individual casserole dishes with stew and vegetable garnish. Top with pie pastry (p. 745). Bake in hot oven (400–450°F/200–225°C) until crust is brown.

Veal Fricassée
Pork Fricassée

See Chicken Fricassée variations, page 311.

RECIPE 85   **Chile Con Carne**

	Portions: 24			**Portion size:** 8 oz (250 g)

U.S.	*Metric*	*Ingredients*	*Procedure*
2½ lb	1.25 kg	Onion, small dice	1. Sauté the onion, pepper, and garlic in oil in a heavy sauce pot until tender but not browned. Remove from the pot.
1¼ lb	625 g	Green pepper, small dice	
1 oz	30 g	Garlic, chopped	2. Add the meat to the pot and brown over high heat, breaking the meat up with a spoon as it browns. Drain off the fat.
4 oz	125 g	Oil	
5 lb	2.5 kg	Ground beef	
	1 No. 10 can	Tomatoes	3. Return the vegetables to the pot and add the remaining ingredients.
10 oz	300 g	Tomato paste	
2½ pt	1.25 L	Brown stock	
3 oz	90 g	Chili powder	4. Simmer uncovered until the chili has reduced to desired thickness, about 45 to 60 minutes. Stir occasionally during cooking period.
		Salt	
		Pepper	

Variation

85A. *Chili with Beans*: Add 4 lb (2 kg) (drained weight) cooked or canned, drained kidney beans or pinto beans about 15 minutes before end of cooking.

RECIPE 86 **Sauerbraten**
....

Portions: 25   **Portion size:** 4 oz (125 g)

2 oz (60 mL) sauce

U.S.	Metric	Ingredients	Procedure
10 lb	5 kg	Beef bottom round, trimmed (see note) Marinade:	1. Place the trimmed beef in a nonmetallic crock or barrel.
1 qt	1 L	Red wine vinegar	2. Add all the marinade ingredients to the crock. If the meat is not completely covered by the liquid, add equal parts vinegar and water until it is. Cover.
1 qt	1 L	Water	
1 lb	500 g	Onion, sliced	
8 oz	250 g	Carrots, sliced	3. Refrigerate for 3 to 4 days. Turn the meat in the marinade every day.
2 cloves	2 cloves	Garlic, chopped	
2 oz	60 g	Brown sugar	
2	2	Bay leaves	
3	3	Whole cloves	
1 tsp	5 mL	Peppercorns, crushed	
2 tsp	10 mL	Salt	
		Vegetable oil, if needed for browning meat	4. Remove the meat from the marinade. Dry the meat thoroughly with towels.
			5. Brown the meat on all sides. This may be done on the range in an iron skillet, on a very hot griddle, under the broiler, or in a brazier in a hot oven.
			6. Place the meat in a braising pan. Strain the marinade. Add the vegetables to the meat and enough of the liquid to cover the meat by half. Cover and braise in a 300°F (150°C) oven until the meat is tender, about 2 to 3 hours.
			7. Remove the meat from the braising liquid and transfer to a hotel pan. Set aside.
8 oz	250 mL	Red wine	8. Strain 2 qt (2 L) of the braising liquid into a saucepan and skim off fat. Bring to a boil. Reduce to about 1½ qt (1.5 L).
4 oz	125 g	Gingersnap crumbs	
			9. Add wine and boil another 2–3 minutes.
			10. Reduce heat to a simmer and stir in the gingersnap crumbs. Simmer another 3–4 minutes. Remove from heat and let stand 5 minutes to allow the crumbs to be completely absorbed.
			11. Slice the meat across the grain. Serve 4 oz (125 g) meat per portion, overlapping the slices on the plate. Ladle 2 oz (60 mL) sauce over meat.

RECIPE 86   **Sauerbraten** *(Continued)*

Note: If you are preparing this item in large quantities and are using whole bottom round (called gooseneck), separate the eye of round from the bottom round, and cut the bottom round in half lengthwise, so that the two pieces are about the size of the eye of round.

Brisket or chuck may also be used for sauerbraten. They will not make as attractive slices, but the eating quality will be very good.

Variation

86A. Sauerbraten with Sour Cream Gravy: Marinate and braise meat as in basic recipe. Prepare gravy through step 8. Thicken the sauce with a roux made of 4 oz (125 g) butter or beef fat, 4 oz (125 g) flour, and 2 oz (60 g) sugar. Cook the roux until well browned and thicken the sauce. Omit wine and add 8 oz (250 mL) sour cream.

RECIPE 87   Hungarian Goulash (Veal, Beef, or Pork)

Portions: 25		**Portion size:** 8 oz (250 g)	

U.S.	Metric	Ingredients	Procedure
7½ lb	3.75 kg	Boneless, lean meat: Veal (shoulder, shank, or breast), *or* beef (chuck), *or* pork (shoulder or butt)	1. Cut the meat into 1-inch (2½-cm) cubes. 2. Heat the fat in a brazier and sauté the meat until lightly seared on all sides. 3. Add the onions and cook over moderate heat to sweat the onions. Continue to cook until most of the liquid that forms is reduced.
5 oz	150 mL	Oil, lard, or rendered beef suet	4. Add the paprika, garlic, and caraway seeds and stir.
2½ lb	1.25 kg	Onions, fine dice	
5 tbsp	75 mL	Hungarian paprika	
2 tsp	10 mL	Garlic, crushed	
½ tsp	2 mL	Caraway seeds	
10 oz	300 g	Chopped, drained canned tomato or tomato purée	5. Add the tomato and stock, cover, and simmer until the meat is almost tender, about 1 hour in the oven (325°F/165°C) or on the range.
2½ qt	2.5 L	White stock	
2½ lb EP	1.25 kg EP	Potatoes, medium dice Salt	6. Add the potatoes and continue to cook until the meat and potatoes are tender. 7. The potatoes will thicken the sauce slightly, but if necessary, reduce the sauce slightly. Degrease and season to taste. 8. Serve with spaetzle or noodles.

RECIPE 88 **Meat Curry**

....

		Portions: 25		**Portion size:** 8 oz (250 g)

U.S.	Metric	Ingredients	Procedure
9 lb	4.5 kg	Boneless, lean meat: lamb (shoulder, breast, or leg), *or* beef (chuck), *or* veal (shoulder, shank, or breast)	1. Cut the meat into 1-inch (2½-cm) cubes. 2. Heat the oil in a brazier over medium heat and add the meat. Cook the meat in the fat, stirring occasionally, until seared on all sides, but only lightly browned.
8 oz	250 mL	Oil	
2½ lb	1.25 kg	Onions, medium dice	3. Add the onions and garlic to the pan. Sauté until softened, but do not brown.
2 tbsp	30 mL	Garlic, chopped	
5 tbsp	75 mL	Curry powder (see note)	4. Add the spices and salt and stir. Cook 1 minute.
1 tbsp	15 mL	Coriander, ground	
2½ tsp	12 mL	Paprika	
1 tsp	5 mL	Cumin, ground	
1 tsp	5 mL	Pepper	
½ tsp	2 mL	Cinnamon	
2	2	Bay leaves	
2 tsp	10 mL	Salt	
4 oz	125 g	Flour	5. Stir in the flour to make a roux and cook another 2 minutes.
2 qt	2 L	White stock	6. Add the stock and tomatoes. Bring to a boil while stirring.
10 oz	300 g	Tomato concassé	7. Cover and simmer slowly in the oven (300°F/150°C) or on top of the range until the meat is tender (1 to 1½ hours).
8 oz	250 mL	Heavy cream, hot	8. Degrease, discard the bay leaf, and add the cream. Adjust the seasonings.
		Boiled or steamed rice Condiments (suggested): Raisins Chutney Peanuts or cashews Chopped scallions or onions Diced pineapple Diced banana Diced apple Shredded coconut Poppadums	9. Serve with rice and with an assortment of 4 or more condiments in small bowls.

Note: If desired, increase curry powder to taste and omit other spices (except bay leaf).

....

RECIPE 89 Swedish Meatballs

Portions: 25		**Portion size:** 3 meatballs, 5 oz (150 g) cooked weight 2 oz sauce (60 mL)	

U.S.	Metric	Ingredients	Procedure
10 oz 2 oz	300 g 60 mL	Onion, chopped fine Oil	1. Sauté the onions in oil until tender, but not brown. Cool thoroughly.
10 oz 2½ cups 10	300 g 625 mL 10	Dry bread crumbs Milk Eggs, beaten	2. Combine the bread crumbs with the milk and egg and let soak for 15 minutes.
5 lb 1¼ lb 2½ tsp ½ tsp ½ tsp 2 tbsp	2.5 kg 625 g 12 mL 2 mL 2 mL 30 g	Ground beef Ground pork Dillweed Nutmeg Allspice Salt	3. Add the cooked onion and the crumb mixture to the meat in a mixing bowl. Add the spices and salt and mix gently until well combined. 4. Portion the meat with a No. 20 scoop into 2-oz (60-g) portions. Roll into balls and place on a sheet pan. 5. Brown in a 400°F (200°C) oven.
2 qt 2½ cups 1 tsp	2 L 625 mL 5 mL	Brown Sauce, hot Light cream, hot Dillweed	6. Remove meatballs from sheet pan and place in bake pans in a single layer. 7. Add the hot cream and dill to the hot Brown Sauce and pour over the meatballs. 8. Cover the pans and bake at 325°F (165°C) for 30 minutes, until the meatballs are cooked. 9. Skim fat from sauce. 10. Serve 3 meatballs and 2 oz (60 mL) sauce per portion.

COOKING VARIETY MEATS

Variety meats, also known as *offal,* include various organs, glands, and other meats that don't form a part of the dressed carcass of the animal.

For cooking purposes, we can divide the most popular variety meats into two groups:

Glandular meats	Muscle meats
Liver	Heart
Kidneys	Tongue
Sweetbreads	Tripe
Brains	Oxtails

Liver

Calf's liver is the most prized, because it is tender and delicate in flavor. It is easily recognized by its pale,

pinkish color. Most calf's liver is served pan-fried, sautéed, or broiled.

Beef liver is darker, stronger in flavor, and tougher. It is also pan-fried or broiled, and it is frequently braised.

Pork liver is also available, but it is used mostly in pâtés and sausages.

1. *Preparation.*

Remove outer skin.

Slice on the bias about ¼ inch (½ cm) thick. Slicing is easier if liver is partially frozen. Remove tough membranes.

2. *Cooking.*

Cook to order. Do not cook ahead.

To broil: Brush with (or dip in) oil or melted butter. Broil according to basic procedure for meats.

To pan-fry, griddle, or sauté: Dredge in seasoned flour. Cook in desired fat over moderately high heat.

Do not overcook, unless customer requests well done. To be moist, liver must be slightly pink inside. Liver cooked well done is very dry.

Serve with bacon, french fried or smothered onions, or seasoned butter.

Kidneys

Veal and lamb kidneys are the most popular, especially in more elegant restaurants. They are usually prepared by sautéing and broiling.

Beef kidneys are stronger in flavor and less tender. They are often cooked by braising and served in specialty items like steak and kidney pie.

Before cooking, split kidneys in half lengthwise and remove the white fatty tissue and veins in the center.

Sweetbreads

Sweetbreads are the thymus glands of calves and young beef animals. (The gland gradually disappears as the animal matures.) They are considered a delicacy and are often expensive. Sweetbreads are very mild in flavor and delicate in texture. They are usually braised or breaded and sautéed in butter.

Before cooking, sweetbreads should be prepared according to the following procedure:

1. Soak in several changes of cold water for several hours or overnight. This removes blood, which would darken the meat when cooked.

2. Blanch in simmering salted water for 10 minutes. Some chefs like to add a little lemon juice or vinegar to the water to preserve whiteness and make the meat firmer.

3. Refresh under cold water and peel off membranes and connective tissue.

4. Press between two trays, with a light weight on top, and refrigerate for several hours.

5. Prepare for cooking:
   a. For braising, leave whole or cut into large dice.
   b. For breading and sautéing, split in half horizontally. Pass through Standard Breading Procedure.

Brains

Brains are not a popular item but are delicate in both flavor and texture. Calf's brains are the most frequently used.

Brains are very perishable and should be cooked as soon as possible. They are also very fragile and must be handled carefully.

Brains must be preprepared according to the following procedure. They may then be served hot with Black Butter (p. 147) or cooled and then dipped in batter, deep-fried, and served with tomato sauce.

1. Soak in fresh water, as for sweetbreads.

2. Peel off outer membrane (this may be done before or after poaching).

3. Poach 20 minutes in court bouillon made of 1 oz (25 mL) lemon juice or vinegar per pint (500 mL) salted water, plus a bouquet garni.

4. Drain and serve immediately, or cool in fresh, cold water.

Muscular Variety Meats

Heart, tongue, oxtails, and tripe are made of muscle tissue, just like other meats from the carcass. They are all tough, however, and must be cooked for a long time by simmering or braising in order to be made tender.

1. *Heart,* usually from veal or beef, is very tough and lean. It can be braised or simmered, or it may be ground and added to chopped meat for casserole dishes and meat loaves.

   Before cooking, trim coarse fibers and veins inside and at top.

2. Cooked beef *tongue* is popular as a cold, sliced meat for sandwiches. It may be fresh, cured, or smoked. Veal and lamb tongues are also available.

   After simmering, remove skin and trim gristle at base of tongue before slicing.

3. *Oxtails* contain flavorful meat and a rich gelatin content, making them highly desirable for soups and stews.

   To disjoint oxtails, cut into sections at the joints with a French knife or butcher knife. Do not use a cleaver, or you may splinter the bones.

4. *Tripe* is the muscular stomach lining of the beef animal (although lamb and pork tripe are sometimes available in ethnic markets). Honeycomb tripe is the most popular.

   Most tripe that comes from the market has been partially cooked, but it still requires several hours of simmering to be made tender.

RECIPE 90 **Sautéed Sweetbreads**
....

	Portions: 10		**Portion size:** 4 oz (125 g)

U.S.	Metric	Ingredients	Procedure
2½ lb	1.25 kg	Sweetbreads, blanched, trimmed, and pressed according to the procedure on page 266. Standard Breading Procedure: Flour Egg wash Bread crumbs Clarified butter Butter, raw	1. Slice the sweetbreads in half horizontally. 2. Season the sweetbreads and pass through Standard Breading Procedure. 3. Heat the butter in a skillet and sauté the sweetbreads over medium heat until browned on both sides. Place on dinner plates. 4. Heat the raw butter in sauté pan until lightly browned (beurre noisette). Pour a little of the browned butter over each portion. Serve immediately.

Variation

Omit breading. Simply dredge the sweetbreads in flour before sautéing.

....

RECIPE 91 **Braised Sweetbreads**
....

	Portions: 10		**Portion size:** 3½ oz (100 g) sweetbreads (cooked weight) 2 oz (60 mL) sauce

U.S.	Metric	Ingredients	Procedure
3 lb	1.5 kg	Sweetbreads	1. Prepare (blanch and trim) sweetbreads according to the procedure on page 266. Leave them whole or cut into uniform serving pieces.
2 oz	60 g	Butter	
		Mirepoix:	2. Heat the butter in a large sauté pan (straight sided). Add the mirepoix and cook over medium heat until lightly browned.
6 oz	175 g	Onion, medium dice	
3 oz	90 g	Carrot, medium dice	3. Place the sweetbreads on top of the mirepoix and pour in the Demiglaze.
3 oz	90 g	Celery, medium dice	4. Cover tightly and place in oven at 325°F (165°C) until the sweetbreads are very tender and well flavored with the sauce, about 45–60 minutes.
3½ pt	750 mL	Demiglaze, hot	
			5. Remove the sweetbreads from the sauce and place in a hotel pan.
			6. Bring the sauce to a rapid boil and reduce slightly. Strain and adjust seasoning. Pour over sweetbreads.

....

RECIPE 92 **Broiled Lamb Kidneys with Bacon**

....

| | | | **Portions:** 10 | **Portion size:** 2 kidneys |
| | | | | 2 strips bacon |

U.S.	Metric	Ingredients	Procedure
20	20	Bacon strips	1. Cook the bacon on a griddle or in the oven on a sheet pan until crisp. Drain fat and keep bacon warm.
20	20	Lamb kidneys	
		Melted butter or oil	2. Split the kidneys in half lengthwise and cut out white fat and gristle in center.
		Salt	
		Pepper	3. Arrange the kidneys on skewers, 4 half kidneys per skewer.
			4. Brush the kidneys well with melted butter or oil and season with salt and pepper.
			5. Broil the kidneys under high heat, turning once, until browned on the outside but still slightly rare. (Test by pressing with finger, as for testing steaks.)
			6. Serve immediately with 2 slices of bacon per portion. Mustard is often served with kidneys.

....

RECIPE 93 **Calf's Liver Lyonnaise**

....

			Portions: 10	**Portion size:** 1 slice liver
				1½ oz (50 g)
				onion garnish

U.S.	Metric	Ingredients	Procedure
2 lb	1 kg	Onions	1. Peel and slice the onions.
3 oz	90 g	Butter	2. Heat the butter in a sauté pan and add the onions. Sauté them over medium heat until tender and golden brown.
1 cup	250 mL	Demiglaze or strong brown stock	
		Salt	3. Add the Demiglaze or stock and cook a few minutes, until the onions are nicely glazed. Season to taste.
		Pepper	
			4. Place in a bain marie and keep warm for service.
10 slices	10 slices	Calf's liver, ¼ inch (6 mm) thick (about 4 oz/125 g each)	5. Season the liver and dredge in flour. Shake off excess flour.
		Salt	6. Pan-fry the liver in butter or oil over moderate heat until browned on both sides and slightly firm to the touch. Do not overcook or use high heat.
		Pepper	
		Flour	7. Serve each portion with 1½ oz (50 g) of the onion mixture.
		Clarified butter or oil	

....

RECIPES USING COOKED MEATS

In addition to the following recipes, see also:

Ham Croquettes, page 321

Ham and Cheese Croquettes, page 321

Scalloped Potatoes with Ham, page 440

Chef's Salad, page 508

Ham Salad and variations, page 502

Beef Salad, page 502

Corned Beef Salad, page 502

Barbecued Pork or Beef Sandwiches, page 535

Numerous soup recipes, Chapter 9

RECIPE 94   **Stuffed Peppers**

			Portions: 24	**Portion size:** ½ pepper
				4 oz (125 g) filling
				2 oz (60 mL) sauce

U.S.	Metric	Ingredients	Procedure
12	12	Green peppers, large	1. Cut the peppers in half lengthwise. Remove seeds and core.
			2. Blanch the peppers in boiling salted water or in a steamer for 4 to 5 minutes. (Peppers must be only partially cooked and still crisp and firm.) Cool quickly in cold water.
12 oz	375 g	Rice	3. Cook the rice by boiling, steaming, or baking (see p. 454). Cool.
12 oz	375 g	Onion, fine dice	4. Sauté the onions and garlic in oil until lightly browned. Cool.
1½ tsp	7 mL	Chopped garlic	
3 oz	90 mL	Oil	5. Combine the rice, onions, meat, and Tomato Sauce. Season to taste.
2¼ lb	1 kg	Ground cooked meat (beef, veal, pork, or lamb)	
			6. Fill each pepper half with 4 oz (125 g) meat mixture.
1 pt	500 mL	Tomato Sauce	
		Salt	
		Pepper	
		Stock or water	7. Arrange peppers in bake pans and add about ¼ inch (½ cm) stock or water to the bottom of the pan (do not pour it on the peppers).
3 pt	1.5 L	Tomato Sauce	
			8. Bake at 350°F (175°C) for 30–45 minutes, until hot and the tops are browned.
			9. Serve 1 pepper half per portion, with 2 oz sauce.

RECIPE 95   Sweet and Sour Pork

	Portions: 25		**Portion size:** 6 oz (175 g)
U.S.	*Metric*	*Ingredients*	*Procedure*
5 lb	2.3 kg	Cooked pork	1. Cut the pork into ½-inch (1-cm) dice.
10 oz	300 mL	Soy sauce	2. Mix the pork with the soy sauce so that it is all coated. Marinate (in refrigerator) for an hour.
4 oz	125 mL	Oil	
2½ qt	2.5 L	Sweet and Sour Sauce	
1 lb	450 g	Pineapple chunks	3. Drain the pork and sauté in oil over high heat until browned. Drain all fat from pan.
			4. Add Sweet and Sour Sauce and simmer 15 minutes. Add pineapple and heat through. Serve with boiled rice.

RECIPE 96   Beef Hash

	Portions: 25		**Portion size:** 8 oz (250 g)
U.S.	*Metric*	*Ingredients*	*Procedure*
1½ lb	750 g	Onions, fine dice	1. Sauté onions in oil in a sauté pan until tender.
4 oz	125 mL	Oil	
6 lb	3 kg	Cooked beef	2. Cut beef and potatoes into very small dice. Add onions and mix.
6 lb	3 kg	Cold, peeled boiled potatoes	
1–2 cups	250–500 mL	Beef stock	3. Add just enough stock to moisten the hash lightly. Amount needed depends on moistness of the beef.
		Salt	
		Pepper	4. Season to taste with salt and pepper.
			5. Place mixture in a lightly oiled bake pan. Bake in a 350°F (175°C) oven until heated through, about 30 minutes. Hold for service in the steam table.

Note: Proportions of beef and potatoes may be varied, depending on food cost requirements.

Variations

96A. Pan-fried Hash: Prepare hash through step 4. Pan-fry individual portions to order on a griddle or in a small sauté pan.

96B. Corned Beef Hash: Prepare as in basic recipe, using cooked corned beef.

96C. Ham Hash: Prepare as in basic recipe, using cooked smoked ham.

Any of the following ingredients may be added to the basic recipe:

1. 10 oz (300 g) diced green pepper, sautéed with the onion.
2. 10 oz (300 g) diced celery, sautéed with the onion.
3. Tomato purée, tomato sauce, or catsup in place of the stock.

RECIPE 97   Macaroni, Ham, and Cheese Casserole

· ·

Portions: 25   **Portion size:** 6 oz (175 g)

U.S.	Metric	Ingredients	Procedure
2 lb	900 g	Elbow macaroni	1. Cook macaroni in boiling salted water until tender (see p. 460 for method). Drain and rinse in cold water.
2 lb	900 g	Cooked ham	
3 qt	3 L	Cheddar Cheese Sauce	2. Cut ham into small dice.
		Paprika	3. Mix ham and macaroni until evenly combined. Add the Cheese Sauce and mix.
			4. Pour mixture into a buttered hotel pan or bake pan. Cover the pan with foil. Bake at 350°F (175°C) about 20 minutes, until hot.
			5. Uncover and sprinkle with paprika. Bake another 10 minutes uncovered.

TERMS FOR REVIEW

persillade	stew	fricassée	goulash
London broil	New England boiled dinner	blanquette	variety meats
shish kebab	pot roast	navarin	sweetbreads
tournedos	Swiss steak	sauerbraten	tripe
stroganoff			

QUESTIONS FOR DISCUSSION

1. List four advantages of roasting at a low temperature.

2. When might you use high temperatures for roasting?

3. What is the purpose of basting?

4. In the recipe for Baked Meat Loaf (p. 235), why are the sautéed vegetables cooled after cooking in step 1?

5. Which steaks require the highest broiler heat, thick ones or thin ones? Steaks to be cooked rare or steaks to be cooked well done?

6. Why is it important not to overload the pan when sautéing meats?

7. Why is the menu term "boiled beef" inaccurate?

CHAPTER 12

UNDERSTANDING POULTRY

The versatility, the popularity,
and the relatively low cost of poultry items make them ideal for all kinds
of food service operations, from elegant white-tablecloth restaurants to cafeterias and
fast-food restaurants. Also, chicken and turkey are becoming very popular
among diet-conscious people, because chicken and turkey are lower
in fat and cholesterol than other meats.

Learning about poultry is, in some ways, easier than
learning about meats like beef and lamb. Because chickens, turkeys, and other
poultry are much smaller, they are not cut up in such detail.

However, poultry has its own unique cooking
problems, so it is important that the student observe both the similarities and
the differences between meat and poultry.

After reading this chapter, you should be able to

1. Explain the differences between "light meat" and "dark meat," and describe how these differences affect cooking.

2. Use four techniques that help keep chicken or turkey breast moist while roasting.

3. Identify any domestic poultry item with reference to its kind, class, and style.

4. Store poultry items properly.

5. Determine doneness in cooked poultry.

6. Truss poultry for cooking.

7. Cut up chicken into parts.

COMPOSITION AND STRUCTURE

The flesh of poultry is muscle tissue, as is the flesh of beef, lamb, veal, and pork. Its composition and structure are essentially the same as those of meat.

Review the section on meat composition and structure (Chapter 10, pp. 196–197). Remember that muscle tissue is composed of

Water (about 75%)

Protein (about 20%)

Fat (up to 5%)

Other elements, including carbohydrate, in small quantities

Remember that muscles consist of *muscle fibers,* held together in bundles by *connective tissue.*

Maturity and Tenderness

We learned in Chapter 10 that the tenderness of a piece of meat—or poultry—is related to *connective tissue* and that connective tissue increases with

- Use or exercise of the muscle.
- Maturity or age of the animal or bird.

1. Use or exercise is of less concern in poultry. Most poultry is so young that it is relatively tender throughout. However, there are some differences, discussed in the next section, "'light meat' and 'dark meat.'"

2. *Maturity* is a major consideration when selecting poultry. Young, tender birds are cooked by dry-heat methods, such as broiling, frying, and roasting, as well as by moist-heat methods. Older, tougher birds need slow, moist heat to be made palatable.

Maturity is the major factor in categorizing each kind of poultry (see p. 276).

"Light Meat" and "Dark Meat"

Poultry is not divided up into many small cuts as are meats. Chicken and turkey, however, are usually thought of as consisting of two kinds of parts, depending on the color of the meat. These color differences reflect other differences:

"Light meat"—breast and wings

Less fat

Less connective tissue

Cooks faster

"Dark meat"—legs (drumsticks and thighs)

More fat

More connective tissue

Takes longer to cook

Duck and goose have all dark meat, but the same differences in connective tissue hold true.

The cook must observe these differences when preparing poultry.

1. *Cooking whole birds.*

Everyone has tasted chicken or turkey breast so dry it was difficult to swallow. In fact, light meat is overcooked more often than not, because it cooks faster than the legs and is done first. In addition, the breast has less fat than the legs, so it tastes much drier when cooked (or overcooked).

A major problem in roasting poultry is cooking the legs to doneness without overcooking the breast. Chefs have devised many techniques to help solve this problem. Here are some of them.

a. Roasting breast down for part of the roasting period. Gravity draws moisture and fat to the breast rather than away from it.

b. Basting with fat only, not with water or stock. Fat protects from drying, but moisture washes away protective fat.

c. Barding, or covering the breast with a thin layer of pork fat. Usually done with lean game birds.

d. Separating breast from leg sections and roasting each for a different time. Often done with large turkeys.

2. *Cooking poultry parts.*

Many recipes have been devised especially for certain poultry parts, such as wings, drumsticks, and boneless chicken breast. These recipes take into account the different cooking characteristics of each part. For example, flattened boneless chicken breasts can be quickly sautéed and remain juicy and tender. Or turkey wings, when braised, release enough gelatin to help make a rich sauce.

Many of these items have especially high customer appeal, especially boneless chicken breast, and are served in the most elegant restaurants.

Several of the chicken and turkey recipes in Chapter 13 are for specific parts. Those that use cut-up whole chickens can easily be adapted for specific parts. For example, you may want to buy whole chickens, braise the leg sections, and reserve the breasts for other preparations.

INSPECTION AND GRADING

Like meat, poultry is subject to federal inspection and grading. (Note: Unlike for meats, poultry inspection and grading stamps are not stamped on the birds but are printed on tags and packing cases.)

Inspection

1. A guarantee of wholesomeness (fit for human consumption).
2. Indicated by a round stamp (Figure 12.1).
3. Required by law.

Grading

1. Based on quality.
2. Indicated by a shield stamp and letter grade (Figure 12.2).
3. Not required by law.

U.S. grades are A, B, and C (A being the best). They are based on

Shape of carcass (lack of defects).

Amount of flesh.

Amount of fat.

FIGURE 12.1   USDA inspection stamp for poultry.

FIGURE 12.2   USDA grade stamp for poultry.

Pinfeathers (present or absent).

Skin tears, cuts, broken bones.

Blemishes and bruises.

Most poultry used in food service is Grade A. Lower grades are used by canners and processors.

CLASSIFICATION AND MARKET FORMS

The following terms are used to classify poultry:

Kind—the species, such as chicken, turkey, or duck.

Class—the subdivision of kind, depending on age and sex. Table 12.1 describes kinds and classes of domestic poultry.

Style—the amount of cleaning and processing.
   Live: almost never purchased in food service.
   Dressed: killed, bled, and plucked. Also rarely seen in food service.
   Ready to cook: dressed and eviscerated, with head and feet removed.

   a. Whole.
   b. Cut up, or parts.

State of refrigeration—chilled or frozen.

HANDLING AND STORAGE

Fresh Poultry

1. Fresh poultry is extremely perishable. It should arrive packed in ice and be kept in ice until used.
2. Ideally, use it within 24 hours of receiving, never more than 4 days.
3. Poultry often carries salmonella bacteria. Wash all equipment and cutting surfaces after handling poultry to avoid contamination of other foods.

Frozen Poultry

1. Store frozen poultry at 0°F (−18°C) or lower until ready to thaw.
2. Thaw in original wrapper in refrigerator, allowing 1 to 2 days for chickens, 2 to 4 days for larger birds. If pressed for time, thaw in cold, running water in original wrapper.
3. Do not refreeze thawed poultry.

TABLE 12.1 **Domestic Poultry Classes and Characteristics**

Kind/Class	Description	Age	Weight Range
Chicken			
Rock Cornish game hen	Special breed of young chicken, very tender and delicate.	5–6 weeks	¾–2 lb (0.34–0.9 kg)
Broiler or fryer	Young chicken of either sex. Tender flesh and flexible cartilage. Smooth skin.	9–12 weeks	Broiler: 1½–2½ lb (0.7–1.1 kg) Fryer: 2½–3½ lb (1.1–1.6 kg)
Roaster	Young chicken of either sex. Tender flesh and smooth skin, but less flexible cartilage.	3–5 months	3½–5 lb (1.6–2.3 kg)
Capon	Castrated male chicken. Flesh very tender and well flavored. Large breast. Expensive.	Under 8 months	5–8 lb (2.3–3.6 kg)
Hen or fowl	Mature female. Tough flesh and coarse skin. Hardened breastbone cartilage.	Over 10 months	3½–6 lb (1.6–2.7 kg)
Cock or rooster	Mature male. Coarse skin. Tough, dark meat.	Over 10 months	4–6 lb (1.8–2.7 kg)
Turkey			
Fryer-roaster	Young bird of either sex. Tender flesh, smooth skin, and flexible cartilage.	Under 16 weeks	4–9 lb (1.8–4 kg)
Young turkey (hen or tom)	Young turkeys with tender flesh but firmer cartilage.	5–7 months	8–22 lb (3.6–10 kg)
Yearling turkey	Fully matured turkey that is still reasonably tender.	Under 15 months	10–30 lb (4.5–14 kg)
Mature turkey or old turkey (hen or tom)	Old turkey with tough flesh and coarse skin.	Over 15 months	10–30 lb (4.5–14 kg)
Duck			
Broiler or fryer duckling	Young tender duck with soft bill and windpipe.	Under 8 weeks	2–4 lb (0.9–1.8 kg)
Roaster duckling	Young tender duck with bill and windpipe that are just starting to harden.	Under 16 weeks	4–6 lb (1.8–2.7 kg)
Mature duck	Old duck with tough flesh and hard bill and windpipe.	Over 6 months	4–10 lb (1.8–4.5 kg)
Goose			
Young goose	Young bird with tender flesh.	Under 6 months	6–10 lb (2.7–4.5 kg)
Mature goose	Tough old bird.	Over 6 months	10–16 lb (4.5–7.3 kg)
Guineas			
Young guinea	Domestic relatives of the pheasant. Young birds are tender, old ones are tough.	About 6 months	¾–1½ lb (0.34–0.7 kg)
Mature guinea		Up to 12 months	1–2 lb (0.45–0.9 kg)
Pigeons			
Squab	Very young pigeons with light, tender meat.	3–4 weeks	Under 1 lb (0.45 kg)
Pigeon	Older pigeons with tough, dark meat.	Over 4 weeks	1–2 lb (0.45–0.9 kg)

DONENESS

Poultry is almost always cooked well done. Many cooks, however, cannot tell the difference between well done and overcooked. Chicken and turkey are low in fat, so they quickly become dry and unpalatable when overcooked. Even duck and goose, which are very fatty, taste dry and stringy if cooked too long.

Many skilled chefs with years of experience can often tell the doneness of a roast chicken or turkey just by looking at it. Until you have gained that much experience, you should rely on other methods.

For Large Roasted Birds

Internal temperature of 180°F (82°C), tested with a thermometer, is the most accurate guide. The thermometer should be inserted into the thickest muscle of the inner part of the thigh, away from the bone.

The thigh is tested rather than the breast, because the thigh is the last part of the bird to become fully cooked.

For Smaller Birds, Cooked by Any Method

Doneness of smaller birds is determined in the following ways.

1. Looseness of joints. The leg will move freely in its socket.

2. Clear juices. Juices inside the cavity of a roasted bird will be clear yellow rather than cloudy and red or pink.

3. Flesh separating from bone. Muscles will *begin* to pull away from bones, especially breast bone and leg bones. Excessively shrunken flesh means it's overcooked and dry.

4. Firmness to touch. Test with finger pressure as you would a steak (see p. 216). Especially useful method for sautéed boneless chicken breasts.

Not recommended: Do not test by piercing deeply with a fork and twisting the flesh. Too many valuable juices will be lost.

TRUSSING METHODS

Trussing means tying the legs and wings against the body to make a compact, solid unit. It has two main purposes:

1. Even cooking. Extended legs and wings cook too quickly.

2. More attractive appearance, especially when presented or served whole or carved in the dining room.

One of many trussing methods is illustrated in Figure 12.3. Your instructor may wish to show you other methods.

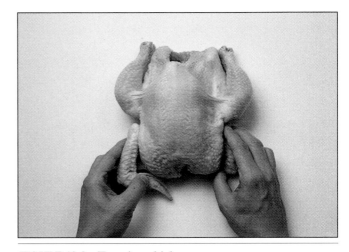

FIGURE 12.3 **Trussing chicken.**
(a) Place the chicken breast up with the neck end toward you. Tuck the first joint of the wings behind the back.

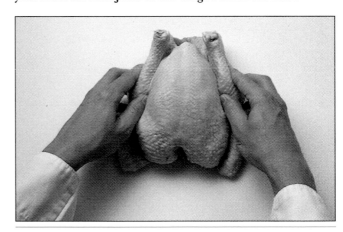

(b) Press the legs forward and down against the body.

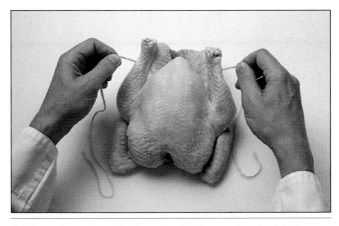

(c) Pass the center of a length of twine under the hip bone just ahead of the tail. *(Continues)*

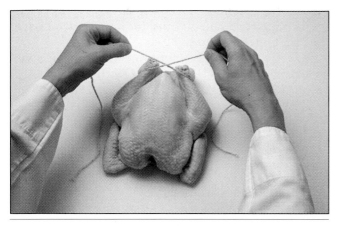

(d) Bring the twine up and across the ends of the legs.

(g) Tie the twine tightly.

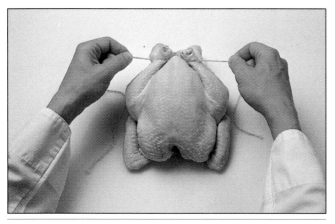

(e) Pass the twine under the ends of the legs as shown and pull tight.

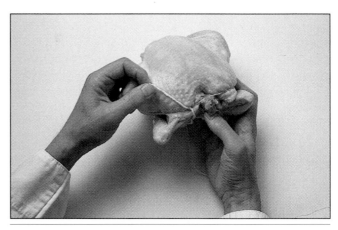

(h) The stub of the neck holds the twine in place, preventing it from slipping behind the back.

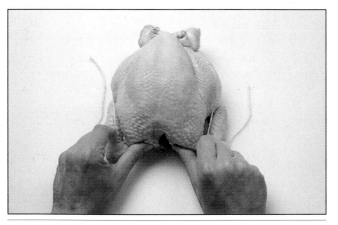

(f) Bring the ends of the twine toward the neck end of the bird. Pull firmly on the twine while pressing on the breast portion with the thumbs as shown.

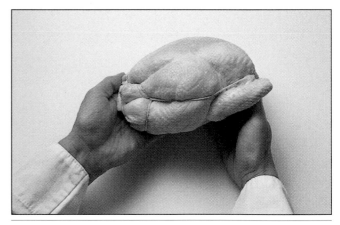

(i) The trussed chicken.

CUTTING UP CHICKEN

There are many different ways of cutting up chickens. Every chef has his or her own preferred methods. Some of these methods are illustrated, step by step, in Figures 12.4, 12.5, and 12.6. They show how to split a chicken for broiling and how to cut up whole chickens into quarters and eighths, for both bone-in parts and semiboneless pieces.

As for meats, it is important to know the bone structure of chicken in order to cut it up. The best way to learn this is to practice cutting chickens.

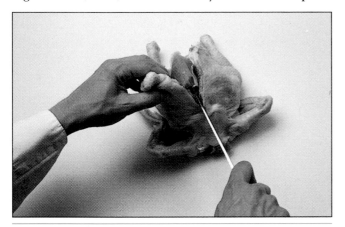

FIGURE 12.4   **Splitting chicken for broiling.**
(a) Hold the chicken up by the tail. Cut through the bones to one side of the backbone, all the way to the neck.

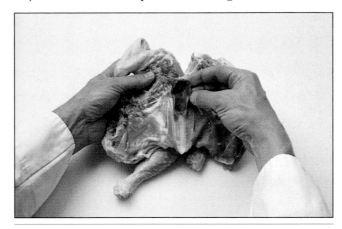

(d) Pull out the breast bone or keel bone. This helps the chicken lie flat and cook evenly.

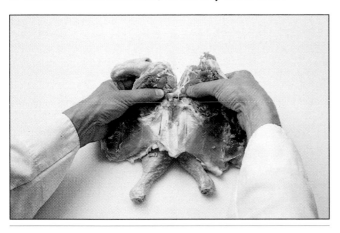

(b) Split the chicken open.

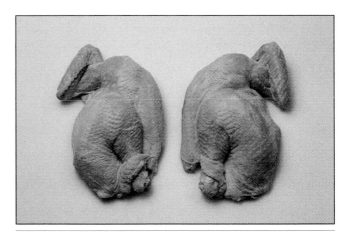

(e) For a portion size of one-half chicken, cut the chicken in half down the center of the breast. Make a split in the skin below the leg and slip the end of the leg through it as shown, to hold the chicken in shape.

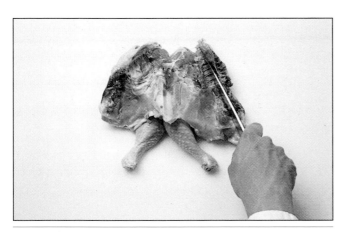

(c) Cut off the backbone as shown.

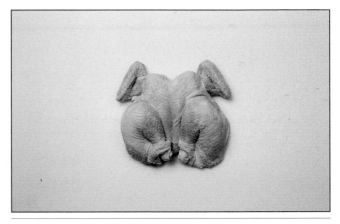

(f) Portion-size cornish game hens are left whole.

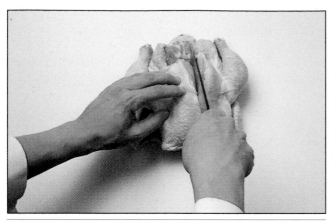

FIGURE 12.5 **Cutting chicken into quarters and eighths, bone in.**
(a) Place the chicken on the cutting board breast up. Split the chicken down the center of the breast with a heavy knife, as shown.

(d) Cut through the skin between the leg and the breast.

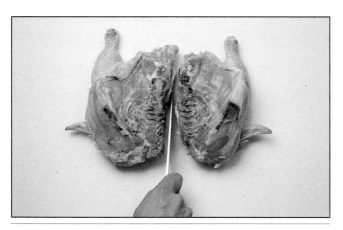

(b) Spread the chicken open and cut through the bones on one side of the backbone.

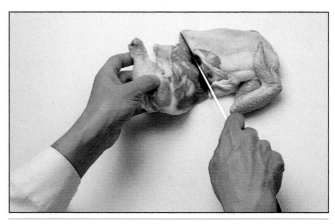

(e) Pull the leg back and cut off the entire leg section. Repeat with the other half. The chicken is now in quarters.

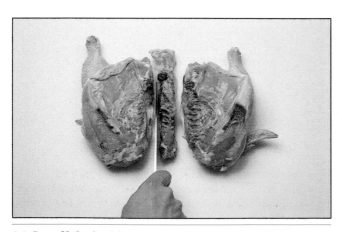

(c) Cut off the backbone completely. Save for stocks.

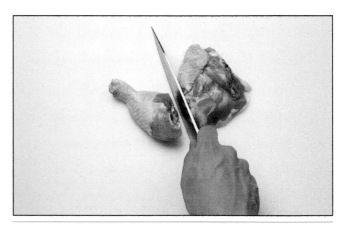

(f) To cut into eighths, cut the drumstick and thigh apart at the joint.

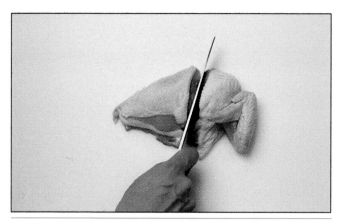

(g) Cut the breast and wing quarter into two equal pieces. (Another method is to simply cut off the wing.)

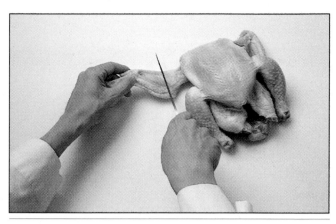

FIGURE 12.6   **Cutting up chickens, semiboneless. (a) Cut off the wings at the second joint. Save for stocks.**

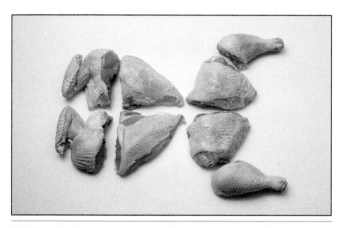

(h) The chicken cut into eighths. Note that the first joint of each wing has been cut off.

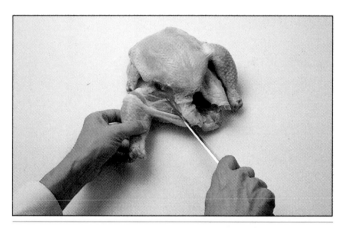

(b) Cut through skin between the leg and body.

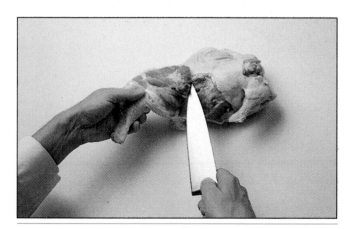

(c) Turn the chicken on its side and pull the leg back. Carefully start to cut the flesh from the bone, being sure to get the "oyster," the little nugget of tender meat in the hollow of the hip bone. Cut through the ligaments at the hip joint. *(Continues)*

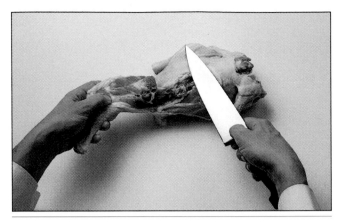

(d) Holding the chicken steady with the knife, pull off the leg. Repeat with the other leg.

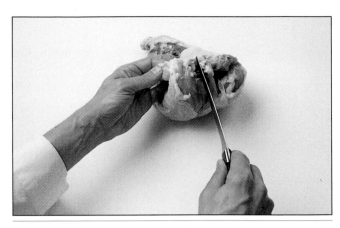

(g) Holding the chicken by the wing, cut through the wing joint.

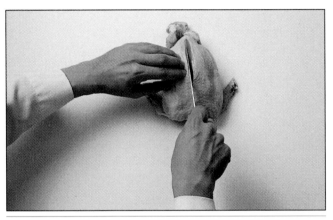

(e) Turn the breast portion upright. Cut down along one side of the ridge of the breast bone to separate the breast meat from the bone.

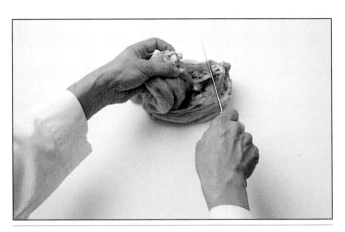

(h) Holding the carcass steady with the knife, pull back on the wing and breast meat.

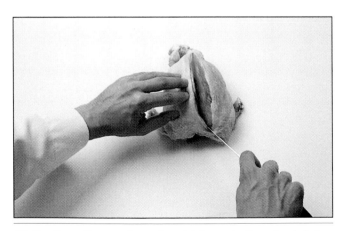

(f) Continue the cut along the wish bone to the wing joint.

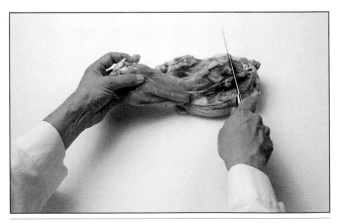

(i) Pull the breast meat completely off the bone. Be sure to hold on to the small "tenderloin" muscle inside the breast so that it doesn't separate from the rest of the meat. Repeat with the other side.

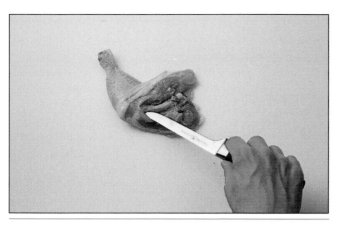

(j) If desired, remove the thigh bone. Cut down along both sides of the bone to separate it from the meat.

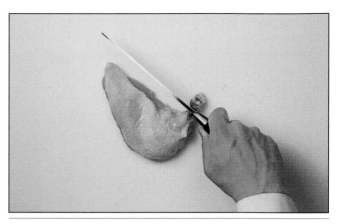

(l) For a neater appearance, chop off the end of the wing bone with the heel of the knife.

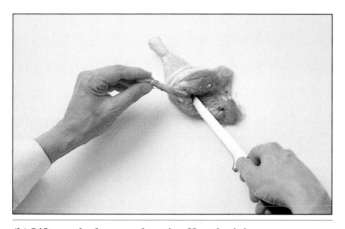

(k) Lift out the bone and cut it off at the joint.

(m) The cut-up chicken. From left: breast portions without and with wing bone; leg portions without and with thigh bone; wing sections and carcass for stock pot. The drumstick and thigh (bone-in) may be cut apart at the joint, as in Figure 12.5.

TERMS FOR REVIEW

maturity	kind	broiler/fryer	hen
light and dark meat	class	roaster	fowl
inspection	style	capon	trussing
grading			

QUESTIONS FOR DISCUSSION

1. Why are hens or fowl not roasted in commercial kitchens?

2. Why is the breast section so often dry when whole chickens and turkeys are roasted? Can you suggest some ways to remedy this problem?

3. Give a brief description of each of the following classes of poultry. Be sure to mention relative tenderness and approximate size.

Capon	Young tom turkey
Roaster duckling	Rock Cornish game hen
Broiler/fryer	Yearling turkey
Roaster	Hen or fowl

4. How should fresh and frozen poultry be stored?

5. Describe five methods for determining doneness in poultry items.

6. What is the purpose of trussing poultry?

CHAPTER 13

COOKING POULTRY

The muscle tissue of poultry,
as we have said, has basically the same structure as the muscle tissue
of meat animals. In particular, the breast meat of chicken and turkey is so
similar to veal that they are interchangeable in many recipes.

Imaginative cooks realize that even when two meats are quite
different—chicken and beef, for example—interesting new dishes can
be made by making substitutions that might seem unusual. For example, it is possible
to make a delicious chili from chicken or turkey meat, a preparation that has
the added advantage of having a lower food cost than beef chili.

Because the basic cooking methods for poultry are the same
as for meat, they are not repeated here. But you may want to review them
before proceeding with any of the recipes in this chapter. Also, please review
the discussion of light and dark meat (p. 274) in the previous chapter,
as well as the methods for testing doneness (p. 277).

After reading this chapter, you should be able to

1. Cook poultry by roasting and baking.

2. Cook poultry by broiling and grilling.

3. Cook poultry by sautéing, pan-frying, and deep-frying.

4. Cook poultry by simmering and poaching.

5. Cook poultry by braising.

6. Prepare dressings and stuffings.

ROASTING AND BAKING

The general procedures for roasting and baking meats also apply to poultry, as illustrated by the following recipes. However, there are some differences in the ways poultry items are handled. The guidelines below should be observed.

Remember that poultry items are almost always cooked well done (except for certain game birds).

Seasoning and Basting

1. Seasonings and, if desired, a little mirepoix or a bouquet garni should be placed inside the cavity. You need to season the skin only if the skin is to be served and eaten, since the seasonings will not penetrate the skin.

2. Oil the skin before roasting to help in browning and to protect against drying. The skin may be basted with *fat only* during roasting, but this is unnecessary if the bird is roasted breast down (and turned breast up just to brown, at the end of the roasting period).

   Basting is beneficial for large turkeys, which must be subjected to dry heat for several hours. If you baste large poultry during roasting, do it every 20 to 30 minutes. More frequent basting results in the loss of a great deal of heat from the oven, because the door is opened so frequently.

3. Basting is unnecessary for duck and goose, which have a great deal of fat under the skin. These birds are usually roasted breast up for that reason.

Temperature

Selection of roasting temperature depends on the product being roasted.

1. *Low-temperature roasting* is used for large items such as turkeys and capons. It results in a tender, juicy product.

   Large turkeys are best roasted at 250°F (120°C). However, since cooking times may be too long for some operations, it is sometimes necessary to roast at 300°F to 325°F (150°C to 160°C) to fit the production schedule. Or, if overnight roasting is practical, another possibility is to roast 20- to 30-lb birds at 200°F to 225°F (95°C to 105°C).

   Smaller items such as roasting chickens are usually roasted at 300°F to 350°F (150°C to 175°C). Sometimes small items roasted at a low temperature do not brown well by the time they are done. In such cases, the heat can be turned up for a few minutes when they are almost done, in order to brown them.

2. The *searing* method may be used for chickens under 4 to 5 pounds (2 kg) and for baked chicken parts. That is, start at 450°F (230°C) for 15 minutes, then reduce to 250°F to 325°F (120°C to 160°C). These small items cook so quickly that continuous roasting at a low temperature would produce very little browning.

   Ducks and geese also may be started at a high temperature in order to melt off some of the heavy fat layer under the skin and to make the skin brown and crisp.

3. *High-temperature roasting* is used for small items such as squab and game birds, which are often served rare. Cornish hens may also be "flash roasted." The cooking time for small items is so short that they do not dry out, unless overcooked.

   Ducks may also be roasted at a continuously high temperature (400°F to 425°F/200°C to 220°C), because their fat content protects them from drying. Great care should be used to prevent overcooking, however, because this can happen very quickly at these temperatures.

Baked Poultry

Roasting and baking are the same process. Cutting up the chicken doesn't change the cooking method. Baked chicken or turkey parts are treated like roasted poultry.

Chicken parts are sometimes coated with seasoned crumbs or flour and rolled in fat before baking. Such products are sometimes misleadingly called "oven fried," because of their resemblance to breaded fried chicken.

RECIPE 98   **Roast Chicken with Natural Gravy**

| | **Portions:** 24 | **Portion size:** ¼ chicken |
| | | 2 oz (60 mL) jus |

U.S.	Metric	Ingredients	Procedure
6	6	Chickens, 3–3½ lb (1.4–1.6 kg) each Salt Pepper Oil or butter Mirepoix:	1. Remove giblets from chickens. Check inside cavities to make sure they have been well cleaned. Reserve giblets for other use.
6 oz	175 g	Onion, medium dice	2. Season the insides of the chickens with salt and pepper.
3 oz	90 g	Carrots, medium dice	3. Truss the chickens (see Figure 12.3).
3 oz	90 g	Celery, medium dice	4. Rub the outside of the chickens with oil or butter (butter promotes faster browning). Season the skin with salt and pepper, since it will be served with the meat.
			5. Place the mirepoix in a roasting pan. Place a rack over the mirepoix, and place the chickens breast down on the rack.
			6. Place the chickens in an oven preheated to 450°F (230°C). After 15 minutes (not longer) turn the heat down to 325°F (165°C).
			7. When the chickens have been in the oven for 45–60 minutes, turn them breast side up. Baste with the fat in the roasting pan and finish roasting. Total cooking time is about 1½ hours.
			8. Remove the chickens from the roasting pan and hold them in a warm place for service.
3 qt	3 L	Strong chicken stock	9. Set the roasting pan on the range over high heat and brown the mirepoix well, but do not let it burn. Pour off the fat.
2 oz	60 g	Cornstarch	
2 oz	60 mL	Cold water or stock Salt Pepper	10. Add the stock to deglaze the pan. Boil until the gravy is reduced by about one-third. Degrease carefully.
			11. Stir the cornstarch with the cold water or stock. Stir it into the gravy. Bring to a boil and simmer until thickened.
			12. Strain into a bain marie, using a china cap lined with cheesecloth. Season carefully with salt and pepper.
			13. Quarter the chickens, or carve them as shown in Figure 13.1. Serve a quarter chicken with 2 oz (60 mL) gravy.

(Continues)

RECIPE 98 **Roast Chicken with Natural Gravy** *(Continued)*

Variations

98A. Roast Herbed Chicken: Place 3–4 parsley stems and a pinch each of tarragon and marjoram in the cavity of each bird. After turning the chicken breast up in the roasting pan, rub the skin with chopped parsley, tarragon, and marjoram.

98B. Roast Chicken with Gravy: Save 4 oz (125 g) of the fat skimmed from the juices and make a blond roux with the fat and 4 oz (125 g) bread flour. Beat the roux into the juices and simmer until thickened.

98C. Roast Chicken with Cream Gravy: Prepare as in basic recipe, but use only 1½ qt (1.5 L) chicken stock. Boil until reduced to 1 qt (1 L) and strain (step 9). Add 1 qt (1 L) hot milk and thicken with 8 oz (250 g) blond roux. Finish with 4 oz (125 mL) heavy cream.

RECIPE 99 **Baked Chicken**

		Portions: 24	**Portion size:** ¼ chicken

U.S.	Metric	Ingredients	Procedure
8 oz	250 g	Flour	1. Combine the flour and seasonings in a pan.
5 tsp	25 mL	Salt	2. Dry the chicken pieces with paper towels if they are wet. Dredge in the seasoned flour.
½ tsp	2 mL	White pepper	
2 tsp	10 mL	Paprika	3. Dip the chicken in the fat, so that all sides are coated. Let excess drip off.
½ tsp	2 mL	Thyme	
15 lb	7 kg	Fryer chicken parts or quarters (see note)	4. Arrange the chicken pieces on a sheet pan or in bake pans, skin side up. If using both dark and light meat parts, place them on separate pans.
1 lb	500 g	Melted butter, oil, or a mixture of butter and oil	5. Bake the chicken at 350°F (175°C) until done, about 1 hour.

Note: If you are starting with whole chickens, cut them into quarters or eighths as shown in Figure 12.5. Any chicken parts may be used for this recipe. For example, you might bake just the legs and use the breasts and wings for other preparations.

Variations

99A. Baked Herbed Chicken: Add 1 tbsp (15 mL) tarragon, 1 tsp (5 mL) marjoram, 2 tbsp (30 mL) chives, and 2 tbsp (30 mL) dry parsley to the flour mixture. Omit paprika.

99B. Baked Rosemary Chicken: Prepare as in basic recipe. After placing chicken parts in bake pans, sprinkle with rosemary, about 4 tsp (20 mL) for 25 portions. Fifteen minutes before chicken is done, sprinkle with 3–4 oz (90–125 mL) lemon juice.

99C. Baked Chicken Parmesan: Instead of flour for dredging, use 1 cup (100 g) parmesan cheese mixed with 1½ cups (150 g) fine dry bread crumbs. Season as in basic recipe.

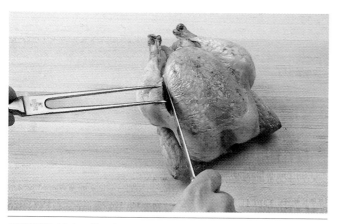

FIGURE 13.1   Carving roast chicken.
(a) Place the chicken on a clean, sanitary cutting board. Cut through the skin between the leg and the breast sections.

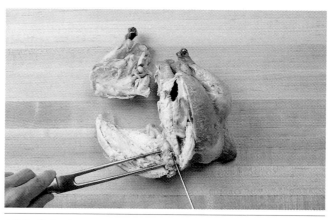

(d) Pull the breast section away from the bone. With the knife, cut through the joint where the wing bone is attached to the body. Separate the breast and wing section completely from the carcass. Repeat steps *a* through *d* on the other side of the chicken.

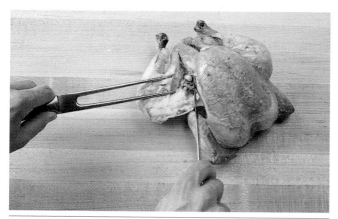

(b) Pull the leg away from the body of the chicken with the fork. Using the knife, cut between the thigh bone and the hip to separate the leg completely.

(e) Cut the wings from the breast portions, and cut the drumsticks apart from the thighs.

(c) Hold the chicken steady by bracing the backbone with the fork. Cut through the breast between the two halves, just to one side of the keel bone.

RECIPE 100 **Roast Turkey with Giblet Gravy**

Yield: about 7 lb (3.5 kg) sliceable meat

	Portions:	Portion size:
	22	5 oz (150 g)
	28	4 oz (125 g)
	36	3 oz (100 g)

U.S.	Metric	Ingredients	Procedure
1	1	Turkey, dressed, 20 lb (10 kg) Salt Pepper Oil	1. Remove giblets from cavity of turkey. Check inside of turkey to make sure it has been well cleaned. Lock the wings in place by twisting the wing tips behind the back of the turkey. 2. Season the inside of the turkey with salt and pepper. Rub the skin thoroughly with oil. 3. Place the turkey on one side in a roasting pan, on a rack if possible (see note). 4. Place in an oven preheated to 325°F (165°C). (Lower temperatures are preferable if production schedule permits. See p. 286 for explanation.) 5. Roast for 1½ hours. Turn the turkey on the other side. Roast another 1½ hours. Baste turkey with drippings (fat only) every 30 minutes.
			6. While turkey is roasting, place turkey heart, gizzard, and neck in a saucepan. (Reserve the liver for another use, or add to bread dressing.) Cover the giblets with water and simmer until very tender, about 2–3 hours. Reserve the broth and the giblets for gravy.
		Mirepoix:	7. Turn the turkey breast up. Place the mirepoix in the pan.
8 oz	250 g	Onions, chopped medium	8. Return the turkey to the oven and continue to roast. Baste occasionally by spooning the fat in the pan over the turkey.
4 oz	125 g	Carrots, chopped medium	
4 oz	125 g	Celery, chopped medium	9. Turkey is done when a thermometer inserted into the thickest part of the inside of the thigh reads 180°F (82°C). Total roasting time is about 5 hours. (See Chapter 12 for discussion of how to determine doneness.) 10. Remove the turkey from roasting pan and let stand in a warm place at least 15 minutes before carving.

RECIPE 100 **Roast Turkey with Giblet Gravy** *(Continued)*

U.S.	Metric	Ingredients	Procedure
3 qt 6 oz	3 L 175 g	Chicken stock, hot Bread flour Salt Pepper	11. Drain off and save the fat from the roasting pan. 12. Set the roasting pan with the mirepoix and drippings on the range to reduce the moisture and brown the mirepoix. Brown lightly if a light gravy is desired. Brown heavily if a dark gravy is desired. 13. Deglaze the pan with about a quart of the chicken stock. Pour into a saucepan with the rest of the stock and the giblet broth (from step 5). Bring to a simmer. Degrease well. 14. Make a blond roux with the flour and 6 oz (175 g) of the fat from the roasting pan. Beat the roux into the gravy to thicken it. 15. Simmer at least 15 minutes, until the gravy is smooth and no raw flour taste remains. Strain and season. 16. Chop or dice the giblets very fine and add to the gravy. 17. Slice the turkey and serve desired portion with 2 oz (60 mL) gravy. See Figure 13.2 for slicing techniques. For quantity service, see procedures demonstrated in Figure 13.3.

Note: Because of the difficulty of handling large turkeys, many chefs do not use a rack. Also, large turkeys are easier to turn if they are placed first on one side, then on the other, rather than breast down.

For more even cooking, separate leg and thigh sections from breast section. Roast dark and light meat on separate pans, if many turkeys are being prepared. Remove each part from oven when done.

Variations

100A. ***Roast Capons and Large Chickens:*** Prepare like roast turkey. Reduce roasting time, depending on size of bird. A 6-lb (2.7-kg) bird will require about 3 hours at 325°F (65°C).

100B. ***Roast Turkey, Chicken, or Capon with Cream Gravy:*** Prepare as in basic recipe, but use half stock and half milk for the gravy, instead of all stock. When gravy is finished, add 8 oz (250 mL) heavy cream.

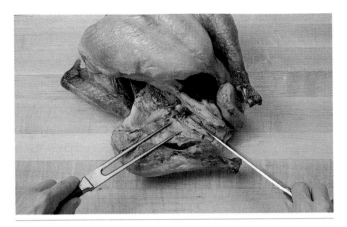

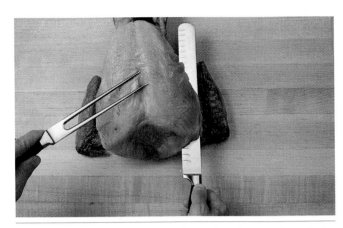

FIGURE 13.2 **Carving roast turkey.**

(a) **Place the turkey on a clean, sanitary cutting board. Cut through the skin between the leg and body. Pull the leg outward with a fork. The leg should pull off easily, but use the knife as necessary to separate the thigh from the hip.**

(d) **Make a horizontal cut just above the wing, cutting all the way through to the bones of the body cavity. This cut helps the breast slices separate evenly.**

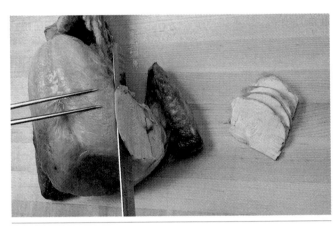

(b) **Cut the drumstick and thigh apart at the joint. Repeat with other leg.**

(e) **With long, smooth strokes, cut the breast into thin slices.**

(c) **Cut the meat from the drumstick and thigh in thin slices.**

(f) When the slices become too large, change the angle of the knife slightly as shown. Continue until both sides of the breast are completely sliced.

FIGURE 13.3 **Quantity service of roast turkey and dressing.**
(a) Using a scoop, place measured portions of baked dressing in hotel pans as shown or on sheet pans.

(g) An alternative method is to cut off an entire half breast in one piece. This piece can then be sliced as shown. Cut across the grain, holding the knife at an angle to get broader slices.

(b) Place measured portions of dark meat slices on top of the mounds of dressing.

(c) Place light meat slices on last, using the best-looking slices for the tops. Cover the pans. Refrigerate if they are to be held for later service. To serve, ladle a small amount of stock over the portions to keep them moist, and reheat, covered, in a moderate oven. Ladle 2 oz (60 mL) gravy over the portions when served.

RECIPE 101 **Roast Duckling à l'Orange**

Portions: 8   **Portion size:** ¼ duckling

U.S.	Metric	Ingredients	Procedure
2	2	Ducks, about 5 lb (2.3 kg) each Salt Pepper	1. Make sure the ducklings are well cleaned. Use the neck, gizzard, and heart in preparing the sauce (step 5); save the liver for another use. 2. Season the cavities with salt and pepper. 3. Place the ducks breast up on a rack in a roasting pan. (Caution: Do not use baking sheets or shallow pans. The pans must be deep enough to hold the large quantity of fat from the ducks.) 4. Place the pan in an oven heated to 450°F (230°C). After 15 minutes, turn the heat down to 375°F (190°C) and continue roasting until the ducks are done, about 1½ hours in all (see note).
1½ pt 3 1½ oz 3 oz ¼ cup	750 mL 3 50 mL 90 g 60 mL	Brown Sauce or Fond Lié Oranges Lemon juice Sugar Wine vinegar or white vinegar	5. While the duck is roasting, prepare the sauce. Add the duck neck and giblets (except liver) to the Brown Sauce and simmer about an hour, until reduced to 1 pt (500 mL). Strain and keep the sauce hot. 6. Peel the zest (colored part of the peel) from the oranges in long strips. Cut them into julienne. Blanch the zests in boiling water for 5 minutes. Drain and cool in cold water. Drain again and reserve the zest. 7. Squeeze enough juice from the oranges to measure 4 oz (125 mL). Add to the lemon juice and set aside. 8. Heat the sugar in a small saucepan over low heat, until the sugar melts. As soon as it starts to turn a golden caramel color, add the vinegar (keep your face turned away!) and the fruit juices. Simmer until the caramel is dissolved and the liquid is reduced by about half. 9. Add the Brown Sauce and bring to a simmer. 10. If the sauce is too thin, adjust consistency by adding a little additional Brown Sauce and reducing. Sauce should be just thick enough to coat lightly. It should not be heavy or pasty.
2 oz	60 mL	Optional: Orange liqueur, such as Curaçao	11. If desired, add the liqueur and simmer a few minutes.

RECIPE 101   **Roast Duckling à l'Orange** *(Continued)*

U.S.	Metric	Ingredients	Procedure
½ cup	125 mL	Chicken stock or white wine	12. When the ducks are done, remove them from the pan. (Check to be sure they are done by pouring out the juices in the cavity into a pan. There should be no trace of pink in the juices.)
			13. Drain off all the fat from the roasting pan.
			14. Deglaze the pan with the stock or wine, stirring to dissolve all the brown drippings.
			15. Reduce the liquid by half. Degrease and strain into the sauce. Adjust the seasonings of the sauce.
			16. Cut the ducks into 8 pieces each.
		Optional garnish: Peeled orange sections	17. To serve, place one breast piece and one leg piece on each plate, garnish the top with some of the blanched orange peels, and ladle on 2 oz (60 mL) sauce. Garnish the plate with orange sections, if desired.

Note: Duck may be roasted at a continuous temperature (from 325°F to 400°F/160°C to 200°C). If the skin is not brown and crisp enough by the time the duck is almost done, the oven may be turned to high (450°F/230°C) for a few minutes.

Variations

Duck may be roasted according to the basic recipe (steps 1–4) and served without a sauce, or simply with applesauce (p. 154). Special seasonings create different products, such as the following recipe:

101A. Roast Duckling, Bohemian Style: Season the cavity of each duck with salt, pepper, and about ½ tsp (2 mL) caraway seeds. Place on rack in roasting pan and season the breast with salt, pepper, and another ½ tsp (2 mL) caraway. Roast as in basic recipe. Serve without sauce, but with Sauerkraut (p. 417) or Braised Red Cabbage (p. 416) and Potato Dumplings (p. 469).

BROILING AND GRILLING

Tender, young poultry items may be cooked on the grill or broiler using the same procedure as for steaks and chops.

Use lower temperatures than for meats. The outside can be burned very easily before the inside is cooked through. For quantity production, broiled chicken is sometimes finished in the oven on sheet pans, preferably on racks.

Start poultry pieces skin side down. This helps to keep flavorful juices from dripping out. Brush generously with melted butter or other fat before and during broiling.

Since the skin of broiled chicken is often eaten, it may be seasoned before cooking.

RECIPE 102 Broiled Chicken

			Portions: 10		Portion size: ½ chicken

U.S.	Metric	Ingredients	Procedure
5	5	Chickens—broilers, about 2 lb (900 g) each	1. Split the chickens in half and prepare for broiling as shown in Figure 12.4.
4 oz	125 mL	Melted butter (or oil) Salt Pepper	2. Brush the chickens on both sides with melted butter. Season with salt and pepper.
			3. Place the chickens skin side down on broiler rack (or on grill). Broil at moderately low heat until the chicken is half cooked and well browned on one side.
			4. Turn the chickens over. (Use tongs or fork, but do not pierce the flesh with the fork.) Continue to broil until the chicken is done (no pink near thigh bone) and well browned on second side. (See first variation below for oven method.)
			5. Remove from broiler. To serve, place half a chicken on dinner plate, skin side up.

Variations

102A. Broiled Chicken, Quantity Method: For large quantities, or for bigger chickens (quartered instead of halved), use slightly higher heat (set the broiler rack higher), and broil until browned on both sides, as in basic recipe. Remove from broiler and place in bake pans or on sheet pans. Finish cooking in the oven at 325–350°F (165–175°C).

102B. Broiled Rock Cornish Game Hen: Remove backbones from hens and prepare for broiling (see Figure 12.4*f*). Broil as in the basic recipe for any of the variations. Serve one hen per portion.

102C. Broiled Tarragon Chicken: Before brushing with melted butter, rub each chicken half with ¼ tsp (1 mL) tarragon and 1–2 tsp (5–10 mL) chopped fresh parsley. Broil as in basic recipe.

102D. Broiled Deviled Chicken (Poulet à la Diable): When chicken is almost completely cooked, brush tops (skin side) of chicken lightly with prepared mustard and sprinkle with fresh bread crumbs (about 1 tbsp (15 mL) mustard and 1 oz (30 g) bread crumbs per portion). Return to broiler to brown crumbs. Serve with 2 oz (60 mL) Deviled Sauce (p. 144) per portion.

SAUTÉING, PAN-FRYING, AND DEEP-FRYING

Because chicken and turkey are lean, tender meats, cooking in fat is an appropriate and a popular way to prepare them. The procedures for sautéing and pan-frying meats apply to chicken as well. Also please note the following guidelines that apply particularly to poultry items.

Sautéing

1. Boneless chicken breasts, thin slices of turkey breast, and other quick-cooking items are ideal for sautéing.

2. Larger items, such as bone-in chicken cut into eighths, are harder to cook to doneness by sautéing, because they need longer cooking times. Such items are often browned by sautéing, then finished by another method, such as baking or braising.

3. In classical cuisine, there are preparations for chicken called *sautés,* many of which are actually made by braising. The basic procedure for sautéing meats is used, except that the chicken is only partially cooked by sautéing. It is then finished by simmering briefly in the sauce made by deglazing the pan. Recipes for this kind of preparation are included under "Braising."

Pan-frying

1. Pan-fried chicken is usually breaded or floured before cooking, for even browning and crispness.

2. About ¼ inch (½ cm) or more of fat in the pan is needed to pan-fry chicken.

3. The side that is to be face up on the plate should be browned first, for best appearance. This is called the *presentation side*. For chicken pieces, this is usually the skin side.

4. After browning on all sides over moderately high heat, lower the heat so that the chicken will cook to doneness without overbrowning. Pan-fried chicken takes about 30 to 45 minutes to cook.

Deep-frying

1. The procedure for deep-frying is like that for pan-frying, except that the item doesn't have to be turned, because it is submerged in the hot fat. Review page 58 for deep-frying instructions.

2. Pieces from small chickens (under 2½ lb/1 kg) are best for deep-frying. Larger pieces require such a long cooking time that the surface may brown too much.

   If necessary, fried items may be finished in the oven.

3. Fry chicken at 325°F to 350°F (160–175°C) for even cooking.

RECIPE 103   **Pan-fried Chicken**

| | | | Portions: 24 | Portion size: ½ chicken |
| | | | 48 | ¼ chicken |

U.S.	Metric	Ingredients	Procedure
12	12	Chickens, 2½ lb (1.1 kg) each	1. Cut chickens into 8 pieces as shown in Figure 12.5.
1 lb	450 g	Flour	2. Place the flour in a small hotel pan and season with salt and pepper.
5 tsp	25 mL	Salt	
1 tsp	5 mL	White pepper	3. Pour about ¼ inch (½ cm) of oil into enough heavy iron skillets to hold all the chicken in a single layer. Heat over moderately high heat.
			4. Dredge the chicken pieces in the seasoned flour and shake off excess.
			5. Place the pieces, skin side down, in the hot oil. Let the pieces fall away from you to avoid splashing hot oil on yourself.
			6. Fry the chicken until golden brown on the bottom. Turn the pieces with tongs and brown the other side.
			7. Lower the heat slightly to avoid overbrowning. Continue to cook the chickens, turning once or twice more, until cooked through. Breast meat cooks faster than leg meat—remove it when it is done. Total cooking time will be from 20 to 40 minutes, depending on size of chickens and temperature of fat.
			8. Remove chicken from pan and drain well. Place on hot dinner plates, or hold for service in counter pans. Do not cover pans or hold too long, or chicken will lose its crispness.

(Continues)

RECIPE 103 **Pan-fried Chicken** *(Continued)*

Variations

For slightly crustier, browner chicken, dip in milk before dredging in flour.

103A. Alternative Method, Quantity Service: Brown chickens in hot oil as in basic recipe. Place on sheet pans or in bake pans, skin side up, and finish cooking in a 350°F (175°C) oven.

103B. Country-style Fried Chicken: Fry chickens as in basic recipe. For 24 portions: pour all but 4 oz (125 g) fat from the pans. Add 4 oz (125 g) flour and make a blond roux. Stir in 2½ qt (2.5 L) milk and bring to a boil. Stir constantly as the gravy thickens. Simmer a few minutes to eliminate all raw starch taste, and season with salt and white pepper. Adjust the consistency with stock, water, or additional milk, if necessary. Strain. Serve the chicken with gravy and mashed potatoes.

RECIPE 104 **Breaded Chicken Cutlets**

Follow the recipe for Breaded Veal Cutlets, page 244, using boneless chicken breasts, lightly flattened with a meat mallet, in place of veal. Use slightly lower heat to avoid overbrowning—chicken breasts are thicker and take longer to cook than veal cutlets.

If desired, leave wing bone in. Chop off the end of the bone with the heel of a heavy chef's knife.

RECIPE 105 **Breaded Turkey Cutlets**

Follow the recipe for Breaded Veal Cutlets, page 244, using sliced boneless turkey breast. To prepare the turkey, bone and skin fresh turkey breast. Slice the cutlets the same way you would cut veal, as shown in Figure 11.7. Turkey is increasingly popular for use in many meat recipes, because of its lower cost as compared to the high cost of veal and other meats.

RECIPE 106 **Turkey Scaloppine**

Follow the recipes for Veal Marsala, page 245, or any of the variations. Cut the turkey as for Turkey Cutlets (Recipe 105).

RECIPE 107   **Sautéed Boneless Breast of Chicken with Mushroom Sauce**

Portions: 10   **Portion size:** 1 chicken breast,
                                                 about 4 oz (125 g)
                                                 2 oz (60 mL) sauce

U.S.	Metric	Ingredients	Procedure
10	10	Boneless chicken breasts, from five 3½ lb (1.6 kg) chickens	1. If you are starting with whole chickens, first cut off the wings and use for another purpose. Remove the breasts as shown in Figure 12.6. Remove the skin from the breasts.
2 oz	60 g	Clarified butter Salt White pepper	2. Add enough clarified butter to a sauté pan to just cover the bottom with a thin film. Place on the range over moderate heat.
2 oz	60 g	Flour for dredging	3. While the pan is heating, season the chicken breasts and dredge in flour. Shake off excess flour.
			4. Place the breasts in the hot pan, presentation side (that is, the side that had the skin on) down.
			5. Sauté over moderate heat until lightly browned and about half cooked. (The heat must be regulated so that the chicken doesn't brown too fast.)
			6. Turn the chicken over and complete the cooking.
			7. Remove the chicken from the pan and place on hot dinner plates for service. Keep warm.
10 oz	300 g	Mushrooms (white), sliced	8. Add the mushrooms to the pan and sauté briefly. After a few seconds, before the mushrooms start to darken, add the lemon juice. Toss the mushrooms in the pan as they sauté.
1 oz	30 mL	Lemon juice	
2½ cups	600 mL	Suprême Sauce, hot	9. Add the Suprême Sauce to the pan and simmer for a few minutes, until reduced to the proper consistency. (The juices from the mushrooms will dilute the sauce.)
			10. Ladle 2 oz (60 mL) sauce over each portion and serve immediately.

Variations

107A. Alternative (Quick) Method: Sauté the chicken as in basic recipe. Plate and ladle 2 oz (60 mL) prepared Mushroom Sauce (p. 142, made with Suprême Sauce as a base) over each portion.

107B. Other Sauces based on chicken stock may be used in place of Mushroom Sauce to serve with sautéed chicken breasts, including Suprême, Aurora, Hungarian, or Ivory.

RECIPE 108 **Deep-fried Chicken**

Portions: 24   **Portion size:** ½ chicken

U.S.	Metric	Ingredients	Procedure
12	12	Chickens about 2 lb (900 g) each	1. Cut chickens into 8 pieces as shown in Figure 12.5.
		Standard Breading Procedure (see note):	2. Set up breading station: seasoned flour, egg wash, and crumbs (see p. 114).
8 oz	250 g	Flour	3. Pass the chicken through the Standard Breading Procedure.
2 tsp	10 mL	Salt	
1 tsp	5 mL	White pepper	4. Heat the fat in a deep-fryer to 325–350°F (165–175°C).
2	2	Eggs	
2½ cups	600 mL	Milk	5. Fry the chicken until golden brown and cooked through. Fry light meat and dark meat pieces in separate baskets, since the light meat cooks faster.
1½ lb	750 g	Dry bread crumbs	
			6. Remove from the fat, drain well, and serve immediately.

Note: Quantities given for breading materials are only guidelines. You may need more or less, depending on the shapes of the chicken pieces, the care used in breading, and other factors. In any case, you will need enough so that even the last piece to be breaded can be coated easily and completely.

Variations

108A. Alternative Method: For larger chickens or for quantity service, brown the chicken in the deep-fryer. Drain, place on sheet pans, and finish in the oven at 350°F (175°C).

108B. Fried Chicken Maryland: Fry the chicken as in basic recipe. Serve each portion with the following sauce and garnish:

 2 oz (60 mL) Cream Sauce, Suprême Sauce, or Horseradish Sauce made with Béchamel, placed on the plate *under* the chicken.

 2 strips crisp bacon (p. 567), placed in a cross on top of the chicken.

 2 corn fritters (p. 426).

 2 banana quarters, breaded and fried.

RECIPE 109   **Chinese Style Chicken with Peppers and Nuts**

Portions: 12   **Portion size:** 6 oz (175 g)

U.S.	Metric	Ingredients	Procedure
2½ lb	1.2 kg	Boneless, skinless chicken meat, raw	1. Remove all fat from the chicken. Cut into ½-inch (1-cm) dice.
1 lb	450 g	Green or red peppers	2. Cut the peppers in half and remove the core and seeds. Cut into strips ¼ inch (½ cm) wide.
1 lb	450 g	Scallions	
3 tbsp	45 mL	Cornstarch	
4 oz	125 mL	Soy sauce	3. Cut off the roots and withered parts of the green tops of the scallions. Split the scallions in half lengthwise and cut into 1-inch (2½-cm) pieces. Combine with the green peppers.
4 oz	125 g	Walnut pieces or unsalted peanuts	
¼ tsp	1 mL	Ground ginger	
⅛ tsp	0.5 mL	Cayenne	4. Stir the cornstarch with the soy sauce until smooth.
1½ cups	350 mL	Chicken broth or water	
			5. Have the remaining ingredients ready in separate containers. Everything must be ready before starting to cook, because cooking takes only a few minutes.
2 oz	60 mL	Oil	6. Heat half the oil in a large sauté pan or skillet until very hot, almost smoking.
			7. Add the peppers and scallions and sauté rapidly for about 2 minutes, until the vegetables are only slightly cooked. Remove from pan.
			8. Add the remaining oil to the pan and again get it very hot.
			9. Add the chicken and sauté rapidly until no longer pink. If the chicken sticks to the pan, use a spatula to stir.
			10. Add the nuts, ginger, and cayenne and sauté another minute.
			11. Quickly stir the cornstarch mixture (the starch settles out) and add it and the stock or water to the pan. Stir to deglaze the pan and bring to a simmer.
			12. Add the sautéed vegetables and simmer just until heated through. Correct the seasonings.
			13. Serve immediately with boiled or steamed rice.

RECIPE 110   **Chicken Breasts Parmesan**

Portions: 10		**Portion size:** 1 chicken breast about 4 oz (125 g)	

U.S.	Metric	Ingredients	Procedure
3 oz	90 g	Flour	1. Place the flour in a small counter pan and season with salt and white pepper.
1 tsp	5 mL	Salt	
½ tsp	2 mL	White pepper	2. Beat the eggs in a bowl and mix in the parmesan cheese and milk. Place the bowl next to the seasoned flour when ready for service.
4	4	Eggs	
3 oz	90 g	Parmesan cheese	
1 oz	30 mL	Milk	
10	10	Boneless, skinless chicken breasts, from five 3½ lb (1.6 kg) chickens	3. Flatten the chicken breasts lightly with a meat mallet.
			4. If cooking to order, select a sauté pan just large enough to hold the number of portions being cooked in a single layer. If cooking all the chicken breasts at once, use a very large skillet or enough sauté pans to hold all the breasts in a single layer.
4 oz	125 mL	Clarified butter	
			5. Place the pan (or pans) over moderate heat and add enough clarified butter to just cover the bottom.
			6. Dip the chicken breasts in the flour and shake off excess. Dip in the cheese batter, turning the pieces to coat both sides.
			7. Cook over moderate heat until the bottom is golden. Turn the pieces over. Reduce the heat to low and continue to cook until the chicken is cooked through. It should feel somewhat firm when done.
20	20	Lemon slices	8. Place each portion on a hot plate and top with two lemon slices. Serve immediately.

Variation

110A. Alternative Method: As soon as the first side is browned, turn the pieces over, cover the pans, and place in an oven at 350°F (175°C) for 8–10 minutes. This procedure requires less attention from the cook, an advantage in a busy kitchen.

RECIPE 111   **Sautéed Chicken Livers with Bacon and Onions**

		Portions: 10	**Portion size:** 4 oz (125 g) livers, plus garnish

U.S.	Metric	Ingredients	Procedure
10 strips	10 strips	Bacon	1. Cut the bacon strips in half. Place them in a sauté pan and fry over low heat until crisp.
1¼ lb	625 g	Onions, sliced	
2½ lb	1.25 kg	Chicken livers, cleaned and cut in half	2. Remove the bacon from the pan and drain. Pour off and save the bacon fat, leaving about 1 oz (30 g) in the pan for the next step.
½ tsp	2 mL	Rosemary	3. Place the pan over high heat and add the onions. Sauté until browned. Remove the onions from the pan.
		Salt	
		Pepper	4. Add another ounce of bacon fat to the pan and place over high heat.
			5. Quickly dry the chicken livers with paper toweling and place in the hot pan. Sauté until browned on all sides.
			6. Add the rosemary and continue to sauté until the livers are cooked through but still pink inside.
			7. Add the onions back to the pan and toss with the livers until blended together and hot. Season to taste with salt and pepper. (Caution: The bacon fat will be salty.)
			8. Plate and garnish each portion with two half strips of bacon.

SIMMERING AND POACHING

Simmering and poaching are both methods of cooking in a liquid. The major difference is the temperature. In simmering, the liquid is a little below the boiling point and bubbling very gently. In poaching, the temperature is even lower, and the liquid is not really bubbling. Also, less liquid is usually used for poaching.

Simmering

1. The simmering method is used to cook fowl and other tough items, which require long cooking in moist heat to be made tender. Cooking time is about 2½ hours.

2. The cooking liquid is usually water, seasoned with salt and most often with mirepoix and herbs.

3. Simmered fowl yields a rich, flavorful broth. The meat can be used for soups, creamed dishes, casseroles, salads, and similar preparations.

4. Start the fowl in *cold water* if a flavorful soup is your main objective. Start with *hot water* to retain more flavor in the meat.

Poaching

1. The poaching method is used to gently cook tender poultry in order to retain moisture and to develop a light, subtle flavor. Cooking time is usually very short, because the product is naturally tender.

2. The cooking liquid is usually stock, sometimes with the addition of wine and other flavorings and seasonings. Cold liquid is added to the poultry product in the pan to cover part way, and the pan must be covered to retain steam. Covering also helps to prevent drying and discoloration.

3. After cooking, the liquid may be used to make a sauce, such as Suprême Sauce, to serve with the cooked product.

4. It is important to drain the poultry well after cooking, or any remaining liquid may spoil the appearance of the sauce on the plate.

5. Poaching may be done on the range top or in the oven. Oven poaching provides more even heat.

RECIPE 112   "Boiled" Fowl

This preparation and the variation that follows are usually not served as is. Instead, they are the basis for several of the other recipes in this section that call for simmered or cooked chicken or turkey and for chicken or turkey stock or velouté. The cooked meat can also be used for chicken or turkey salads.

Yield: about 4½–5 lb (2–2.3 kg) cooked meat

U.S.	Metric	Ingredients	Procedure
3	3	Fowls, about 5 lb (2.3 kg) each	1. Truss the fowls. This step is optional but recommended because it keeps the chicken from falling apart, especially if you are cooking more than one in the pot.
		Mirepoix:	
8 oz	250 g	Onion, coarsely chopped	2. Place the fowl in a stock pot.
4 oz	125 g	Celery, coarsely chopped	3. Add boiling water to cover and return to a boil. Skim the scum carefully.
4 oz	125 g	Carrots, coarsely chopped	4. Add the mirepoix and sachet.
		Sachet:	5. Simmer until the fowl feels tender when pressed on the thigh, about 2½ hours.
1	1	Bay leaf	6. If the chicken and broth are to be used immediately for another preparation, remove the fowl from the liquid. Place in another pan and keep covered until needed. Strain the broth.
6	6	Parsley stems	
¼ tsp	1 mL	Peppercorns	
2	2	Whole cloves	
1 tsp	5 mL	Salt	
			7. If the chicken and broth are not needed right away, leave the chicken in the broth and cool quickly in a cold-water bath, as for cooling stocks (p. 125). When completely cool, remove the fowl and refrigerate, covered. Strain the broth and refrigerate.
			8. To use, disjoint the fowl, remove all bones and skin, and dice or cut as required.

Variation

112A. Simmered Chicken or Turkey: Simmer young chickens or turkey as in basic recipe. They may be whole or disjointed. A 3-lb (1.4-kg) chicken will take about 45–60 minutes. Turkey will take about 1½–3 hours, depending on size. Do not overcook young poultry, and do not let the liquid boil.

RECIPE 113   **Chicken or Turkey Pot Pie**

Portions: 25   **Portion size:** 3 oz (90 g) meat
2 oz (60 g) vegetables
4 oz (125 mL) sauce

U.S.	Metric	Ingredients	Procedure
5 lb	2.3 kg	Cooked chicken or turkey meat (light and dark meat)	1. Cut the chicken or turkey into ¾-inch (1-cm) dice.
12 oz	350 g	Potatoes, medium dice	2. Cook the vegetables separately in boiling salted water. Drain and cool.
12 oz	350 g	Carrots, medium dice	
12 oz	350 g	Tiny white onions, peeled	3. Season the velouté to taste with salt and pepper.
12 oz	350 g	Peas	4. Prepare the pastry and cut out circles to cover the tops of casserole serving dishes. (You will need about 2 oz (60 g) pastry per portion.)
3 qt	3 L	Chicken Velouté	
		Salt	
		Pepper	
25	25	Flaky pie pastry covers (p. 745)	5. Divide the light and dark meat evenly among individual serving casseroles (3 oz/90 g per portion).
			6. Divide the vegetables evenly among the casseroles (about ½ oz/15 g per portion of each vegetable).
			7. Ladle about 4 oz (125 mL) velouté into each casserole.
			8. Top the dishes with the pastry. Cut holes in the centers to allow steam to escape.
			9. Place the dishes on a sheet pan. Bake at 400°F (200°C) until the crust is well browned.

Variations

Vegetable ingredients may be varied as desired. Other vegetables that may be used include celery, mushroom caps, and lima beans.

113A. ***Chicken or Turkey Stew:*** Prepare the meat, vegetables, and velouté as in basic recipe. Omit pastry. Combine the ingredients in a sauce pot and bring to a simmer. Hold for service.

RECIPE 114   **Chicken or Turkey à la King**

Portions: 25   **Portion size:** 8 oz (250 g)

U.S.	Metric	Ingredients	Procedure
10 oz	300 g	Butter, clarified	1. Heat the butter in a sauce pot over medium heat. Add the onions and green pepper and sauté just until the vegetables start to become tender. Do not let them brown.
3 oz	90 g	Onion, brunoise	
10 oz	300 g	Green pepper, small dice	
8 oz	250 g	Flour	2. Add the flour and stir to make a roux. Cook the roux gently for a few minutes, but do not let it brown.
2½ qt	2.5 L	Chicken or turkey stock	
2½ cups	625 mL	Milk, hot	3. With a whip, stir in the chicken stock. Bring to a boil, stirring constantly as the sauce thickens.
			4. Stir in the hot milk. Simmer for 15 to 20 minutes to cook out the starch taste and to reduce the liquid slightly.
1 lb	500 g	Mushrooms, sliced	5. Sauté the mushrooms in butter very quickly, without letting them brown. Add them to the sauce.
4 oz	125 g	Butter, clarified	
2½ cups	625 mL	Light cream, hot	
4 oz	125 g	Drained canned pimientos, small dice	6. Stir in the hot cream. Also add the pimiento and the chicken. Stir in gently to avoid breaking up the meat.
5 lb	2.3 kg	Cooked chicken or turkey meat, ½-inch (1-cm) dice	7. Bring just to a simmer. Add sherry, salt, and pepper to taste.
4 oz	125 mL	Sherry wine	8. Serve in patty shells (p. 761) or with rice.
		Salt	
		Pepper	

Variations

Chicken à la King may be made with preprepared velouté sauce. Add chicken meat, sautéed or blanched vegetables, light cream, and seasonings to velouté and bring to a simmer.

*114A. **Creamed Chicken or Turkey with Mushrooms:*** Omit peppers, pimientos, and sherry from basic recipe. Season *lightly* with nutmeg. Optional: Substitute milk for the chicken stock.

*114B. **Chicken or Turkey Shortcake:*** Prepare Creamed Chicken or Turkey with Mushrooms. Add 10 oz (300 g) cooked diced carrots and 10 oz (300 g) cooked peas. Serve over biscuits (p. 700).

RECIPE 115   **Chicken or Turkey Tetrazzini**

Portions: 25   **Portion size:** 7 oz (200 g)
                                      chicken and sauce
                                      4 oz (125 g)
                                      spaghetti

U.S.	Metric	Ingredients	Procedure
5 lb	2.3 kg	Cooked chicken or turkey meat	1. Cut the chicken or turkey into strips about 2 × ¼ × ¼ inches (5 × ½ × ½ cm).
2 qt	2 L	Chicken Velouté	2. Bring the velouté to a simmer in a saucepan.
2 lb	900 g	Mushrooms, sliced	
6 oz	175 g	Butter	3. Sauté the mushrooms quickly in butter, but do not brown them. Add them to the sauce.
3	3	Egg yolks, beaten	
2½ cups	600 mL	Cream	4. Combine the egg yolk with the cream to make a liaison. Temper with a little of the hot sauce, then stir into the remaining sauce in the pan.
2–3 oz	60–90 mL	Sherry	
		Salt	5. Add the chicken or turkey meat. Bring the mixture to just below the simmering point. Do not boil.
		White pepper	
			6. Add the sherry and season to taste with salt and pepper. Keep the sauce hot in a bain marie. Do not let it boil.
2½ lb	1.25 kg	Spaghetti, spaghettini, or vermicelli	7. Cook the spaghetti in 1 gal (4 L) of boiling salted water until al dente. Drain in a colander and rinse under cold water. (See p. 460 for pasta cooking methods.)
as needed		Butter	8. Lightly butter the insides of individual service casseroles.
8 oz	250 g	Parmesan cheese, grated	9. Place a portion (4 oz/125 g) of spaghetti in each dish. Top with a 7-oz (200-g) portion of chicken and sauce.
			10. Sprinkle the tops with parmesan cheese. Run under the broiler until browned. Serve immediately.

RECIPE 116 **Poached Chicken Breast Princesse**

Portions: 24				**Portion size:** ½ chicken breast 2 oz (60 mL) sauce plus garnish	

U.S.	Metric	Ingredients		Procedure	
24	24	Boneless, skinless half chicken breasts, from twelve 3-lb (1.2-kg) chickens	1.	Select a baking pan just large enough to hold the chicken breasts in a single layer. Butter the inside of the pan.	
as needed		Butter Salt White pepper	2.	Season the chicken breasts with salt and pepper. Place them in the pan, presentation side (that is, the side that had the skin on) up.	
¼ cup	60 mL	Lemon juice	3.	Sprinkle with the lemon juice and add enough chicken stock to barely cover the chicken.	
1½ qt approximately	1.5 L	Chicken stock, cold			
			4.	Cover the chicken with a buttered piece of parchment or waxed paper.	
			5.	Bring to a simmer on top of the stove. Finish poaching in a 325°F (165°C) oven or over low heat on the stove. Cooking time will be 5–10 minutes.	
			6.	Remove the chicken breasts from the liquid. Place them in a hotel pan, cover, and keep them warm.	
		Beurre manié:	7.	Reduce the poaching liquid over high heat to about 2½ pt (1.1 L).	
3 oz	90 g	Butter, softened			
3 oz	90 g	Flour	8.	Knead the butter and flour together to make a beurre manié (p. 133).	
2½ cups	600 mL	Heavy cream, hot Salt	9.	With a wire whip, beat the beurre manié into the simmering stock to thicken it. Simmer a minute to cook out any starchy taste.	
			10.	Add the hot cream to the sauce. Season to taste.	
72	72	Asparagus tips, cooked, hot	11.	Place each chicken breast, well drained, on a plate and coat with 2 oz (60 mL) sauce. Garnish with 3 asparagus tips. Serve immediately.	

RECIPE 116   **Poached Chicken Breast Princesse** *(Continued)*

Variations

116A. ***Alternative Method:*** Poach the chicken as in basic recipe. Plate immediately and coat with preprepared Suprême Sauce. Save poaching liquid for next day's sauce.

116B. ***Poached Chicken Breast Florentine:*** Poach the chicken as in basic recipe. Place each portion on a bed of buttered spinach (well drained). Coat with Mornay Sauce. Optional: Sprinkle with parmesan cheese and brown under the broiler.

116C. ***Other sauces*** may be used to coat poached chicken breasts, including

Allemande
Aurora
Hungarian
Ivory
Mushroom

RECIPE 117   **Chicken Blanquette I**

			Portions: 25	**Portion size:** 5 oz (150 g)

U.S.	Metric	Ingredients	Procedure
5 lb	2.5 kg	Cooked chicken meat, 1-inch (2½-cm) dice	1. Combine the chicken with the sauce and bring to a simmer.
2½ pt	1.1 L	Chicken Velouté Liaison:	2. Remove from the heat. Beat the egg yolks and cream together. Temper with a little of the hot sauce, and stir into the sauce.
5	5	Egg yolks	
1 pt	500 mL	Heavy cream	3. Return the pot to the heat and bring to just below the simmer. Do not boil.
		Lemon juice	
		Nutmeg	4. Season to taste with a few drops of lemon juice, a pinch each of nutmeg and white pepper, and salt.
		White pepper	
		Salt	

Variations

117A. ***Chicken Blanquette II:*** Follow the recipe for Veal Blanquette, page 252. Use 12 lb (6 kg) disjointed chicken (raw) in place of the 10 lb veal. Use chicken stock instead of veal stock.

117B. ***Chicken Blanquette à l'Ancienne (Ancient Style):*** Garnish each portion with two cooked pearl onions and one cooked mushroom cap, fluted if possible (see p. 596).

117C. ***Chicken Blanquette Brunoise:*** Add to the sauce: 4 oz (125 g) each of carrot, celery, and leeks or onions, all cut brunoise and sautéed lightly in butter.

117D. ***Chicken Blanquette Argenteuil:*** Garnish each portion with 3 cooked asparagus tips.

BRAISING

A moist-heat cooking method, braising may be used to tenderize tough poultry products. Also, as for veal and pork, it can be used to provide moistness and flavor to tender poultry items. Coq au vin, the well-known braised chicken in red wine, was originally made with tough old rooster (coq), but today the same recipe is applied to tender young chicken.

Poultry products are braised using the same procedures as for meats, except that mirepoix is frequently omitted. Other flavoring ingredients may be used instead, depending on the recipe. Methods 1 and 2 (p. 256) are used when the chicken is to be browned. Method 3 (p. 256) is used for fricassées, white stews in which the chicken is sautéed without browning.

If you review the procedure for sautéing meats (p. 243), you will see that if the product is not completely cooked when browned in step 5, then finished cooking by simmering it in the sauce in step 7, the result is a braised item. This procedure may be used for classical "sautés," actually braised items. (An alternative method is to finish cooking the chicken or meat in a covered pan in the oven while you are making the sauce. This is also braising, because the cover holds in moisture.)

RECIPE 118   Chicken Fricassée

| | **Portions:** 24 | | **Portion size:** ¼ chicken |
| | | | 3 oz (90 mL) sauce |

U.S.	Metric	Ingredients	Procedure
6	6	Chickens, 2½–3 lb (1.1–1.4 kg) each	1. Cut the chicken into 8 pieces each. Season with salt and white pepper.
		Salt	
		White pepper	2. Melt the butter in a brazier over moderate heat.
6 oz	175 g	Butter	
12 oz	350 g	Onion, cut brunoise	3. Add chicken and onion. Sauté very lightly so that the chicken is seared on all sides, but *do not brown.*
6 oz	175 g	Flour	4. Add the flour and stir so that it combines with the fat to make a roux. Cook another 2 minutes, without browning.
3 qt approximately	3 L	Chicken stock	
		Bouquet garni:	5. Gradually stir in enough stock to cover the chicken. Bring to a simmer, while stirring, until the sauce thickens.
1	1	Bay leaf	
1	1	Small piece of celery	
4	4	Parsley stems	6. Add the herbs, tied in cheesecloth (bouquet garni).
¼ tsp	1 mL	Thyme	
			7. Cover and place in a slow oven (300°F/150°C) or over very low heat on the range. Cook until tender, about 30–45 minutes.

RECIPE 118   **Chicken Fricassée** *(Continued)*

U.S.	Metric	Ingredients	Procedure
5	5	Liaison: Egg yolks, beaten	8. Remove the chicken from the sauce and keep it warm in a covered pan.
1 pt	500 mL	Heavy cream	9. Degrease the sauce. Reduce it over high heat to proper thickness. You should have about 2 qt (2 L) sauce. Strain through cheesecloth.
2 tbsp	30 mL	Lemon juice Salt White pepper Nutmeg	10. Combine the egg yolks and cream. Temper with a little hot sauce, and add the liaison to the sauce. Bring to just below the simmer. Do not boil.
			11. Season to taste with lemon juice, salt, white pepper, and nutmeg. Pour the sauce over the chicken.

Variations

118A. Chicken Fricassée with Tarragon: Add 1 tbsp (15 mL) tarragon to the Bouquet Garni.

118B. Chicken Fricassée à l'Indienne: Add 4 tbsp (60 mL) curry powder when making the roux.

118C. Fricassée of Turkey Wings: Prepare as in basic recipe, using one or two turkey wings per portion, depending on size. Cut large turkey wings into two pieces.

118D. Veal Fricassée: Prepare as in basic recipe, using 10 lb (4.5 kg) boneless veal shoulder, cut into large dice. Use white veal stock.

118E. Pork Fricassée: Use 10 lb (4.5 kg) boneless, diced pork and pork, veal, or chicken stock.

118F. Fricassée à l'Ancienne:
118G. Fricassée Brunoise: } Use same garnishes as Chicken Blanquette variations (p. 309).
118H. Fricassée Argenteuil:

RECIPE 119   Chicken Chasseur

Portions: 10   **Portion size:** ½ chicken
3 oz (90 mL) sauce

U.S.	Metric	Ingredients	Procedure
5	5	Chicken, 2–2¼ lb (0.9–1 kg) each (see note)	1. Cut the chickens into 8 pieces. Season the chicken with salt and pepper.
		Salt	2. Heat the oil in a brazier or large sauté pan. Brown the chicken well on all sides.
		Pepper	
2 oz	60 mL	Oil	3. Remove the chickens from the pan. Cover and keep them hot.
2 oz	60 g	Shallots or onions, cut brunoise	4. Add the shallots and mushrooms to the pan and sauté lightly without browning.
8 oz	250 g	Mushrooms, sliced	5. Add the white wine and reduce by three-fourths over high heat.
8 oz	250 mL	White wine	
1½ pints	750 mL	Demiglaze	6. Add the Demiglaze and tomatoes and bring to a boil. Reduce slightly. Season with salt and pepper.
8 oz	250 g	Tomato concassée, fresh *or*	
4 oz	125 g	Drained, chopped canned tomatoes	7. Place the chickens in the sauce. Cover and simmer slowly on the stove or in the oven at 325°F (165°C), about 20 to 30 minutes, until done.
		Salt	
		Pepper	
2 tbsp	30 mL	Chopped parsley	8. When the chicken is done, remove it from the pan and reduce the sauce slightly over high heat. Add the chopped parsley and check the seasonings.
			9. Serve ½ chicken (2 pieces dark meat and 2 pieces light meat) per portion. Cover with 3 oz (90 mL) sauce.

Note: Large chickens may be used, if desired. For 3½-lb (1.6-kg) chickens, use ¼ chicken per portion (1 piece dark meat and 1 piece light meat).

Variations

119A. Alternative Method: Brown chickens as in basic recipe. Drain excess fat. Add 1 qt (1 L) preprepared Chasseur Sauce and finish cooking the chickens as in basic method.

119B. Chicken Bercy: Method 1: Prepare as in basic recipe, but omit the mushrooms and tomato. Method 2: Brown chickens as in basic recipe. Add 1 qt (1 L) preprepared Bercy Sauce and simmer the chickens until done.

119C. Chicken Portugaise: Method 1: Prepare as in basic recipe, but omit the mushrooms and wine. Use 4 oz (125 g) onions (brunoise) and add 1 tsp (5 mL) chopped garlic. Substitute Tomato Sauce for the Demiglaze. Method 2: Brown chicken as in basic recipe. Add 1 qt (1 L) Portugaise Sauce and simmer the chicken until done.

119D. Chicken Hongroise: Prepare as in basic recipe, but sauté chicken only lightly. Do not brown. Omit mushrooms and wine. Use Hungarian (Hongroise) Sauce instead of Demiglaze. When the chicken is cooked, add 4–6 oz (125–175 mL) heavy cream (tempered or heated) to the sauce. Omit parsley garnish. Serve with rice pilaf.

RECIPE 120 Chicken Cacciatora

| | | Portions: 25 | | Portion size: 8–10 oz (250–300 g) chicken |
| | | | | 3 oz (90 mL) sauce |

U.S.	Metric	Ingredients		Procedure
15–17 lb	7.5–8 kg	Broiler-fryers, disjointed	1.	If starting with whole chickens, cut into eighths as shown in Figure 12.5.
1 lb	500 g	Flour	2.	Place the flour in a pan and season with salt and pepper.
2 tbsp	30 mL	Salt		
1½ tsp	7 mL	Pepper	3.	Dredge the chicken in the flour. Shake off excess.
8 oz	250 mL	Oil		
			4.	Heat the oil in a large sauté pan or skillet. Add the chicken pieces and brown well on all sides over high heat.
			5.	Remove the chicken from the pan and place in a brazier.
1¼ lb	600 g	Onion, sliced thin	6.	Pour about 5 oz (150 mL) of the oil used to brown the chickens into a sauce pot. (Discard the rest of the oil, but keep the sauté pan handy.)
1 lb	500 g	Green pepper, cut into thin strips (batonnet)		
5 oz	150 g	Celery, thin strips (batonnet)	7.	Add the onion, green pepper, celery, carrot, and garlic. Sweat until nearly tender.
5 oz	150 g	Carrot, cut brunoise		
2 tbsp	30 mL	Garlic, chopped fine	8.	Add the wine, tomatoes, tomato paste, and herbs. Bring to a boil.
1 cup	250 mL	White wine or Marsala		
2½ qt	2.5 L	Tomatoes (canned), crushed, with their juice	9.	Add a ladleful of the sauce to the pan in which the chickens were browned. Deglaze the pan and pour the liquid back into the sauce. Simmer about 5 minutes.
8 oz	250 g	Tomato paste		
2	2	Bay leaves	10.	Pour the sauce over the chickens. Bring to a boil. Cover the pan and finish cooking in a 300°F (150°C) oven or over low heat on the stove. Cooking will take 30–45 minutes.
½ tsp	2 mL	Basil		
			11.	When the chicken is tender, remove it from the sauce and place in a hotel pan.
			12.	Degrease the sauce. Reduce the sauce over high heat until thickened to desired consistency. Adjust seasoning. Pour over the chicken.

Variation

Sauté 1½ lb (700 g) mushrooms with the onions and peppers. Omit carrots and celery.

RECIPE 121 **Braised Duckling with Sauerkraut**

Portions: 12   **Portion size:** ¼ duckling
                                     4 oz (125 g) kraut

U.S.	Metric	Ingredients	Procedure
3	3	Ducklings, 5 lb (2.2 kg) each	1. Cut the ducklings into 8 pieces, the same way you would disjoint a chicken. (See Figure 12.5.) Trim off all excess fat.
2 oz	60 mL	Oil	
			2. Heat the oil in a sauté pan or brazier. Place the duck pieces in the pan skin side down, and cook over moderately high heat until the skin is well browned. A great deal of fat will render out.
			3. Turn the pieces over and continue to brown on all sides.
			4. Drain off all the fat from the pan. Turn all the duck pieces skin side up.
		Bouquet garni:	5. Tie the herbs in a cheesecloth bag and place in the pan with the duck.
1	1	Bay leaf	
½ tsp	2 mL	Thyme	6. Cover the pan and place in a 325°F (165°C) oven for about 30 minutes. Do not add any liquid. The duck will cook in its own juices.
6–8	6–8	Parsley stems	
½ recipe (about 3 lb/1.5 kg)		Braised Sauerkraut (p. 417)	7. While the duck is cooking, prepare the sauerkraut, but cook it only 30 minutes.
			8. Remove the duck from its pan and bury it in the partially cooked kraut. Carefully degrease the duck pan without losing any of the juices. Pour the juices over the duck and kraut.
			9. Cover and continue braising the duck and kraut for another hour.
			10. When done, remove the duck and place in a hotel pan or on a serving platter. Remove the kraut with a slotted spoon and place in another hotel pan, or around the duck on the platter.
			11. Degrease the juices. Pour some of the juices over the duck and some over the sauerkraut.

Variation

121A. Braised Duckling with Cabbage: Prepare as in basic recipe, but substitute ½ recipe Braised White or Green Cabbage (p. 416) for the ½ recipe Sauerkraut.

RECIPE 122   **Paprika Chicken**

Portions: 24   **Portion size:** ¼ chicken
3 oz (90 mL) sauce

U.S.	Metric	Ingredients	Procedure
4 oz	125 mL	Oil	1. Heat the oil in a skillet and brown the chicken *lightly* on all sides.
6	6	Chickens, disjointed, 3–3½ lb (1.4–1.6 kg) each	
			2. Remove the chicken from the pan and place in a brazier.
1½ lb	700 g	Onions, chopped fine	3. Add the onion and green pepper to the fat in the pan. Sauté until soft but not browned.
1 lb	450 g	Green pepper, small dice	
2 oz	60 g	Flour	4. Add the flour and stir to make a roux. Cook the flour slowly for a few minutes.
6 tbsp	90 mL	Hungarian paprika	
1 pt	500 mL	Chicken stock	5. Add the paprika and stir to blend in.
1 lb	450 g	Canned tomatoes, crushed	6. Stir in the chicken stock, tomatoes, and salt. Bring to a boil. Sauce will be very thick at this point.
2 tsp	10 mL	Salt	
			7. Pour the sauce over the chicken. Cover and simmer over very low heat or in a 325°F (165°C) oven until the chicken is tender, about 30–40 minutes.
1 pt	500 mL	Sour cream	8. When the chicken is tender, remove it from the sauce and place in a hotel pan.
			9. Degrease the sauce. Stir in the sour cream. Simmer a minute, but do not boil. Adjust the seasonings.
			10. Pour the sauce over the chicken in the hotel pan.
			11. Serve with egg noodles, spaetzle (p. 470), or rice.

RECIPE 123   Coq au Vin

Portions: 12   **Portion size:** ¼ chicken
                                                        2½ oz (75 mL) sauce

U.S.	Metric	Ingredients		Procedure
12 oz	350 g	Salt pork or slab bacon	1.	Cut the salt pork or bacon into batonnet shapes, 1 × ¼ × ¼ inch (2 × ½ × ½ cm).
1 oz	30 mL	Oil	2.	Place the bacon pieces in a saucepan. Cover with cold water. Bring to a boil and drain.
			3.	Add the oil to a large sauté pan and place over moderate heat. When hot, add the blanched bacon. Sauté until lightly browned. Remove with a slotted spoon and set aside.
3	3	Chickens, 3½ lb (1.6 kg) each, cut into 8 pieces	4.	Increase the heat to high. Add the chickens to the fat remaining in the pan and brown well on all sides. Remove the chicken from the pan.
24	24	Tiny white onions, peeled and parboiled	5.	Add the onions and mushrooms to the pan and sauté until browned. Remove with a slotted spoon and set aside with the bacon pieces. Pour off the fat from the pan.
1½ lb	700 g	Small mushroom caps		
1 qt	1 L	Red wine (dry)	6.	Add the wine and stock to the pan and bring to a boil.
1 pt	500 mL	Chicken stock		
		Bouquet garni:	7.	Add the thyme, bay leaf, and garlic, tied in a piece of cheesecloth.
½ tsp	2 mL	Thyme		
1	1	Bay leaf	8.	Return the chicken to the pan. Bring the liquid back to a boil. Cover and cook in a 300°F (150°C) oven or over very low heat on top of the stove until chicken is done, about 30–40 minutes.
4	4	Large garlic cloves, crushed		
		Beurre manié:	9.	Remove the chicken from the cooking liquid and place in a heated pan or on a serving platter. Garnish with the mushrooms, onions, and bacon pieces.
2 oz	60 g	Butter, softened		
2 oz	60 g	Flour	10.	Degrease the cooking liquid carefully.
		Chopped parsley	11.	Place over high heat and boil until the liquid is reduced to about 1 qt (1 L).
			12.	Mix the butter and flour to make beurre manié. Beat in the beurre manié a little at a time, just enough to thicken the sauce lightly. Strain the sauce over the chicken and garnish.
			13.	At service time, sprinkle each portion with a little chopped parsley.

RECIPE 124   Arroz con Pollo (Spanish Rice with Chicken)

| | | Portions: 24 | Portion size: ¼ chicken |
| | | | 5 oz (150 g) rice |

U.S.	Metric	Ingredients	Procedure
6	6	Chickens, 3 lb (1.4 kg) each	1. Cut the chickens into 8 pieces each.
3 oz	90 mL	Olive oil	2. Heat the olive oil in a large sauté pan. Brown the chickens on all sides. Transfer the pieces to a brazier as they are browned. Drain off and discard about one-third of the fat in the pan.
1 lb	500 g	Onion, small dice	3. Place the onion, green pepper, and garlic in the sauté pan in which the chicken was browned. Sauté over medium heat until the vegetables are almost tender.
1 lb	500 g	Green peppers, medium dice	
4 tsp	20 mL	Garlic, chopped fine	
2 tsp	10 mL	Paprika	
1 qt	1 L	Long-grain rice, raw	4. Add the paprika and rice and stir until the grains are coated with fat.
3 pt	1.5 L	Chicken stock	
2 lb	900 g	Fresh tomatoes, 1-inch (2½-cm) dice *or*	5. Add the stock and tomatoes. Bring to a boil. Season the liquid to taste with salt and pepper.
1½ lb	700 g	Canned tomatoes, diced	
		Salt	6. Pour the contents of the pan over the chicken in the brazier. Cover and place in a 325°F (165°C) oven until the rice and chicken are cooked, about 20–30 minutes.
		Pepper	
1¼ lb	600 g	Frozen peas, thawed	7. At service time, stir in the peas and garnish the top with pimiento strips.
4 oz	125 g	Pimientos, cut into thin strips	

DRESSINGS AND STUFFINGS

Stuffing chickens and turkeys is usually not practical in production kitchens. Baking the "stuffing" separately gives better results, for these reasons:

1. **Safety.**   Stuffing inside a bird is an ideal breeding ground for bacteria that cause food poisoning.

2. **Quality.**   Additional roasting time is needed to heat the stuffing through. The result is often overcooked poultry.

3. **Practicality.**   Filling poultry with stuffing and then removing it after roasting is impractical, time-consuming, and messy.

Stuffing that is baked separately is usually called "dressing."

Is poultry ever stuffed? Yes. Small birds served whole as one or two portions can be stuffed and often are. Stuffed Cornish hens or small game birds such as quail are popular items.

Basic Ingredients of Dressings

1. Starch base, such as bread or rice.

2. Aromatic vegetables, generally onions and celery.

3. Fat, such as butter or chicken fat, for sautéing the vegetables and for providing richness.

Dressings for chicken and turkey, which are lean, may require more fat than dressings for duck and goose, which are fatty.

4. Liquid, usually stock, to provide moisture.

5. Seasonings, herbs, and spices.

6. Eggs, sometimes added as a binder, but not always necessary.

7. Other ingredients for flavor, character, and bulk, such as:

Sausage	Chestnuts
Oysters	Fruits
Giblets	Nuts

Guidelines for Making Dressings

1. All ingredients that require cooking must be completely cooked before combining with other dressing ingredients. They will cook very little more during baking or roasting.

2. Cool all ingredients before combining, to avoid growth of dangerous bacteria.

3. Never let baked or unbaked dressing stay in the Food Danger Zone (45°F to 140°F/7°C to 60°C) longer than an hour.

   a. Refrigerate unbaked dressing if not to be baked immediately.

RECIPE 125 **Basic Bread Dressing**

Yield: about 4 lb (2 kg)

U.S.	Metric	Ingredients	Procedure
1 lb	500 g	Onion, small dice	1. Sauté the onion and celery lightly in the fat until tender but not browned. Cool thoroughly.
½ lb	250 g	Celery, small dice	
½ lb	250 g	Fat such as butter, chicken fat, or bacon fat	2. Cut the bread into small cubes. (If desired, crusts may be trimmed first.)
2 lb	1 kg	White bread, 2 days old	3. Combine the bread and cooked vegetables in a large stainless steel bowl. Add the herbs and seasonings and toss gently until all ingredients are well mixed.
1 oz	30 g	Chopped parsley	
1 tsp	5 mL	Sage	
½ tsp	2 mL	Thyme	
½ tsp	2 mL	Marjoram	4. Add the stock a little at a time, and mix the dressing lightly after each addition. Add just enough to make the dressing slightly moist, neither dry nor soggy. Adjust the seasonings.
½ tsp	2 mL	White pepper	
2 tsp	10 mL	Salt	
1–2 pt	0.5–1 L	Chicken stock, cold	5. Place in a greased bake pan and bake at 375°F (190°C) until hot at the center, about 1 hour.

Variations

*125A. **Sausage Dressing:*** Cook 1 lb (500 g) crumbled pork sausage meat, drain, and cool. Use some of the drained fat to cook the vegetables for the dressing. Add the cooked sausage to the dressing before adding the stock.

*125B. **Chestnut Dressing:*** Reduce the bread to 1½ lb (750 g). Add 1 lb (500 g) cooked, coarsely chopped chestnuts to the dressing before adding the stock.

*125C. **Mushroom Dressing:*** Cook 2 lb (1 kg) sliced mushrooms with the onion and celery, and proceed as in basic recipe.

*125D. **Giblet Dressing:*** Add ½ lb (250 g) cooked, chopped chicken or turkey gizzards and hearts to the dressing before adding the stock.

*125E. **Cornbread Dressing:*** Substitute cornbread for all or part of the white bread in Basic Bread Dressing or Sausage Dressing.

b. Hold baked dressing above 140°F (60°C) for service, or chill as rapidly as possible.

c. Reheat baked dressing rapidly in oven or steamer to an internal temperature of 180°F (82°C).

4. Bake dressings in shallow pans (2 inches/5 cm deep) for rapid cooking, to get it above the Danger Zone quickly.

5. Do not overmix bread dressings, or they will become pasty. Toss ingredients together lightly.

6. For light texture, do not pack dressings into baking pans. Spoon it loosely.

7. If you stuff poultry instead of baking the dressing separately, fill the birds loosely. Do not pack. Stuffings expand during cooking.

RECIPES USING COOKED POULTRY

In addition to the following recipes, see also

Chicken or Turkey Salad, page 500.

Chef's Salad, page 508.

Recipes for poultry cooked by simmering, in this chapter.

RECIPE 126 **Chicken or Turkey Curry**

Portions: 25			**Portion size:** 6 oz (175 g)

U.S.	Metric	Ingredients	Procedure
6 lb	2.7 kg	Cooked chicken or turkey meat	1. Cut the chicken into ½-inch (1-cm) dice.
2 qt	2 L	Curry Sauce (p. 142)	2. Combine the meat and sauce in a saucepan. Bring to a simmer. Simmer slowly for about 10 minutes, so that the chicken can absorb some of the flavor of the sauce.
			3. Serve a 6-oz (175-mL) ladle of curry per portion, over boiled or steamed rice. (See p. 264 for condiments to be served with curry.)

Variations

Other cooked or leftover meats and fish may be used in place of chicken, such as lamb, veal, shrimp, or a firm flaked fish such as cod.

RECIPE 127 **Chicken or Turkey Croquettes**

Portions: 24

Portion size: 2 croquettes,
2 oz (60 g) each
2 oz (60 mL) sauce

U.S.	Metric	Ingredients	Procedure
8 oz	250 g	Clarified butter or chicken fat	1. Heat the fat in a heavy sauce pot. Add the onion and celery and sauté over medium heat until tender.
8 oz	250 g	Onion, chopped fine	
4 oz	125 g	Celery, chopped fine	2. Stir in the flour to make a roux. Cook the roux slowly a few minutes without browning. Remove from heat and let cool slightly.
8 oz	250 g	Flour	
1 qt	1 L	Chicken stock or milk, hot	
3 lb	1.4 kg	Cooked chicken or turkey meat, chopped very fine or passed through a grinder	3. Beat in the hot stock or milk. Bring the mixture to a boil, stirring constantly. The mixture will become very thick. Simmer 5 minutes, while stirring, to cook the flour completely.
		Salt	
		White pepper	4. Add the chicken or turkey and blend in thoroughly. Heat the mixture to a simmer, stirring constantly. It should be very thick. If not, cook a few minutes, while stirring, to dry it out.
		Nutmeg	
2	2	Eggs, beaten	
¼ cup	60 mL	Chopped parsley	
			5. Season to taste with salt, white pepper, and just a trace of nutmeg.
			6. Remove from the heat and quickly stir in the beaten egg and parsley.
			7. Spread the mixture into a shallow pan. Cover with a piece of oiled parchment or waxed paper and chill the mixture thoroughly.
		Standard Breading Procedure: Flour Egg wash Bread crumbs Oil for deep frying	8. Using a No. 20 scoop, divide the mixture into 2-oz (60-g) portions. Shape into cone shapes. (Note: Cone-shaped scoops are available that do this all in one step.)
			9. Pass the croquettes through the Standard Breading Procedure (see p. 114).
			10. Deep-fry at 350°F (175°C) until golden brown.
1½ qt	1.5 L	Suprême Sauce *or* Poulette Sauce *or* Mushroom Sauce (white)	11. Serve 2 croquettes per portion, with 2 oz (60 mL) sauce. Ladle a thin band across the croquettes and pour the rest of the sauce around them. Do not cover completely with the sauce.

RECIPE 127   **Chicken or Turkey Croquettes** *(Continued)*

Variations

127A.   **Chicken and Rice Croquettes:**   Use 2 lb (900 g) chicken meat and 1 lb (500 g) cooked rice.

127B.   **Ham Croquettes:**   Use ham instead of chicken or turkey. Add 2 tbsp (30 mL) prepared mustard to the mixture, and double the amount of parsley. Serve with Mustard Sauce or Cheddar Cheese Sauce.

127C.   **Ham and Cheese Croquettes:**   Add 12 oz (350 g) grated cheddar cheese to Ham Croquette mixture.

127D.   **Salmon or Tuna Croquettes:**   Use well-drained canned salmon or tuna instead of chicken or turkey. Use milk, not stock. Season the mixture to taste with dill weed. Serve with Herb Sauce, Creole Sauce, or Mushroom Sauce (made with Fish Velouté).

QUESTIONS FOR DISCUSSION

1. Describe the three roasting methods discussed in this chapter: low-temperature roasting, searing, and high-temperature roasting. When are they used?

2. True or false: Chicken should be broiled at a lower temperature than steaks. Explain your answer.

3. What is meant by the term "presentation side"?

4. Why is it difficult to cook large chicken pieces by deep-frying? How can this problem be solved?

5. What are the differences between simmering and poaching, as applied to poultry?

6. Give three reasons for baking dressing in a separate pan rather than stuffing it into roast poultry.

CHAPTER 14

UNDERSTANDING FISH AND SHELLFISH

At one time, fresh fish was
enjoyed only in limited areas—along the sea coast and, to a lesser extent,
around lakes and rivers. Today, thanks to modern refrigeration and freezing
technology, fish products are enjoyed across the country all year.

For the cook, the difficulties of understanding fish
and shellfish are in some ways the reverse of those for meat. With meat,
we are presented with only a few animals, but a bewildering array of cuts from
each. With fish, there are only a few "cuts," but hundreds of species,
each with its own characteristics and cooking requirements.

For this reason, it is especially important that students
learn the basic principles of structure, handling, and cooking, so that they
can utilize the many varieties of seafood in a systematic way.

Fish products are divided into two categories: fin fish,
or fish with fins and internal skeletons, and shellfish, or fish with external shells
but no internal bone structure. Since they have many differences, it is
helpful to look at them separately, as we do in this chapter.

After reading this chapter, you should be able to

1. Explain how the cooking qualities of fish are affected by its lack of connective tissue.
2. Determine doneness in cooked fish.
3. Select appropriate cooking methods for fat and lean fish.
4. Recognize the basic market forms of fish.
5. Dress and fillet round fish and flatfish.
6. Recognize common varieties of fin fish in American food service.
7. Check fish for freshness.
8. Store fish and fish products properly.
9. Understand the popular varieties of shellfish, including their characteristics, handling, and special cooking procedures.
10. Open oysters and clams, split lobster, and peel and devein shrimp.

FIN FISH

COMPOSITION AND STRUCTURE

The edible flesh of fish, like that of meat and poultry, consists of water, proteins, fats, and small amounts of minerals, vitamins, and other substances. The differences, however, are perhaps more important than the similarities.

Fish has very little connective tissue. This is one of the most important differences between fish and meat. It means that

1. *Fish cooks very quickly*, even at low heat (just enough heat to coagulate the proteins).

2. *Fish is naturally tender.* Toughness is the result not of connective tissue but of the toughening of the protein by high heat.

3. *Moist-heat cooking methods* are used not to create tenderness but *to preserve moistness* and provide variety.

4. *Cooked fish must be handled very carefully* or it will fall apart.

SPECIAL PROBLEMS IN COOKING FISH

Doneness and "Flaking"

When fish is cooked, the flesh breaks apart into its natural separations. This is called "flaking." Most books, somewhat misleadingly, say that fish is done when it flakes *easily.* Unfortunately, some cooks interpret this as meaning "nearly falling apart." Because fish continues to cook in its retained heat even when removed from the fire, it is often dreadfully overcooked by the time it reaches the customer. *Fish is very delicate and is easily over-cooked.*

Observe these tests for doneness:

1. The fish *just separates* into flakes; that is, it is beginning to flake but does not yet fall apart easily.

2. If bone is present, the flesh separates from the bone, and the bone is no longer pink.

3. The flesh has turned from translucent to opaque (usually white, depending on the kind of fish).

Remember, the major flaw in fish preparation is *overcooking.*

Cooking Fat Fish and Lean Fish

The fat content of fish ranges from 0.5 percent to 20 percent.

Lean fish are those that are low in fat. Examples: Flounder, sole, cod, red snapper, bass, perch, halibut, pike.

Fat fish are those that are high in fat. Examples: Salmon, tuna, trout, butterfish, mackerel.

Cooking Lean Fish

Since lean fish has almost no fat, it can easily become very dry, especially if overcooked. It is often served with sauces to enhance the moistness and give richness.

Moist-heat methods. Lean fish is especially well suited to poaching. This method preserves moistness.

Dry-heat methods. Lean fish, if it is broiled or baked, should be basted with butter or oil. Take special care not to overcook, or the fish will be dry.

Dry-heat methods with fat. Lean fish may be fried or sautéed. The fish gains palatability from the added fat.

Cooking Fat Fish

The fat in these fish enables them to tolerate more heat without becoming dry.

Moist-heat methods. Fat fish, like lean fish, can be cooked by moist heat. Poached salmon and trout are very popular.

Dry-heat methods. Fat fish are well suited to broiling and baking. The dry heat helps eliminate some excessive oiliness.

Dry-heat methods with fat. Large fat fish, like salmon, or stronger-flavored fish, like bluefish or mackerel, are rarely cooked in fat. Smaller ones, like trout, are often pan-fried. Take care to avoid excessive greasiness. Drain the fish well before serving.

CUTTING FISH

Market Forms

Fish are available in several forms, as illustrated in Figure 14.1. Or they may be cut by the cook into these forms, depending on how they are to be cooked.

Buying Processed Fish versus Cutting Them Yourself

Most food service establishments purchase fish in the forms in which they intend to cook them. They find it less expensive to pay the purveyor to do the cutting than to hire and train the personnel and to allocate the storage and work space to do it in-house.

Some restaurants still buy whole fish. Here are a few reasons why they do:

1. Their clientele demands it. Some high-priced luxury restaurants stake their reputations on using only the freshest, most unprocessed ingredients. They are able to charge enough to cover their high labor costs.

2. They are in the heart of a fresh fish market, where fresh whole fish, delivered daily, are economical. They can best take advantage of seasonal bargains.

3. They are high-volume specialty restaurants and find it more economical to clean the fish themselves and watch the market for the best prices every day.

4. They make fish stocks and use the bones.

5. They serve the whole fish. Examples: Sautéed or poached trout presented whole; whole cold poached fish as a buffet display.

Your purchasing decisions will depend on what you plan to do with the fish and what forms are most economical for those purposes.

(d) Steaks: cross-section slices, each containing a section of backbone.

FIGURE 14.1 **Market forms of fish.**
(a) Whole or round: completely intact, as caught.

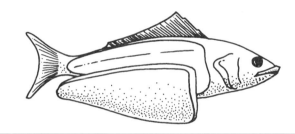

(e) Fillets: boneless sides of fish, with skin on or off.

(b) Drawn: viscera removed.

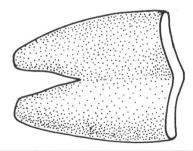

(f) Butterflied fillets: both sides of a fish still joined, but with bones removed.

(c) Dressed: viscera, scales, head, tail, and fins removed.

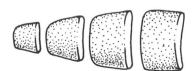

(g) Sticks: cross-section slices of fillets.

Dressing and Filleting

Although most of you will work with ready-to-cook fish products, you should know how to clean and fillet whole fish.

1. ***Dressing.***   Figure 14.2 illustrates how to dress a whole fish.

2. ***Filleting.***   There are two basic shapes of fish: flatfish (like flounder and sole) and round fish (like cod and trout). They are filleted differently: flatfish have four fillets, round fish have two. Figures 14.3 and 14.4 show the two different methods for filleting these fish.

FIGURE 14.2   **Dressing a fish.**
(a) Scale the fish. Lay the fish flat on work surface. Rub a scaling tool or the back of a knife against the scales, from tail to head. Repeat until all scales are removed. Rinse. (Exceptions: Trout, with very tiny scales, and scaleless fish, like catfish, are not scaled.)

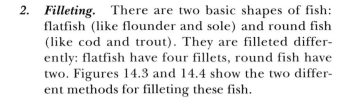

(c) Cut off tail and fins. Scissors are easiest to use.

(b) Eviscerate. Slit the belly and pull out viscera. Rinse cavity.

(d) Remove head. Cut through flesh just behind gills. Cut or break backbone at the cut and pull off head.

(e) The fish is dressed.

FIGURE 14.3   Filleting flatfish.
(a) Use a thin-bladed, flexible knife. Cut off the head, just behind the gills. (This step is optional.)

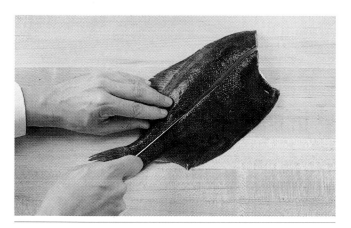

(b) Make a cut from head to tail just to one side of the center line, down to the backbone.

(c) Turn the knife so that it is almost parallel to the table. Making long, smooth cuts, cut horizontally against the backbone toward the outer edge of the fish. Gently separate the fillet from the bone.

(d) Remove the fillet completely. Repeat to remove the three remaining fillets.

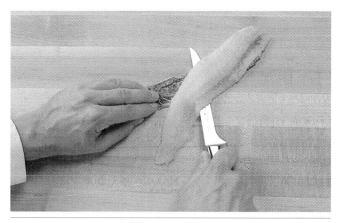

(e) To skin, place fillet skin side down on the work surface, with the tail pointing toward you. Holding the skin at the tail end, slide the knife between the skin and flesh, scraping against the skin to avoid cutting into the fillet. Note: Dover or English sole is skinned before filleting: cut through the skin at the tail. Holding the tail with one hand, peel off the skin toward the head. Caution: Do not do this with flounder. You will tear the flesh.

FIGURE 14.4   **Filleting round fish.**
(a) Cut into the top of the fish along one side of the backbone, from head to tail. Cut against the bone with smooth strokes of the knife to separate the flesh from the bone.

(b) Cut under the flesh toward the tail; detach it.

(c) Cut along the curved rib bones and finish detaching the fillet at the head end. Turn the fish over and repeat to remove the second fillet. Lightly run your finger along the flesh side of the fillets to see if any bones remain in them. Pull out any you find. Skin the fillets as for flatfish.

VARIETIES AND CHARACTERISTICS

There are hundreds of varieties of fish eaten around the world. However, relatively few species account for the majority of the fish used in American food service. Following are some of the most common varieties that are used fresh. Some of these are illustrated in Figure 14.5.

Saltwater Fish—Flatfish

These are all very popular in commercial kitchens. Flatfish have lean, white flesh and a mild, delicate flavor. They are all very flat, oval in shape, with both eyes on one side of the head.

Flounder

> Type: Lean.
>
> Varieties: Winter flounder, lemon sole, grey sole, sand dab.
>
> Characteristics: White flesh; fine flakes; mild, sweet flavor.
>
> Weight: ½ to 5 lb (0.2 to 2.3 kg).

Sole (Dover sole or English sole)

> Type: Lean.
>
> Characteristics: Narrower, more elongated than flounder. Flesh similar to flounder, but firmer in texture. One of the most prized of all fish. Expensive.
>
> Weight: 1 to 2 lb (0.5 to 1 kg).

Halibut

> Type: Lean.
>
> Characteristics: Looks like a giant flounder, with thicker flesh, delicate flavor. Cut into steaks and fillets.
>
> Weight: 4 to 100 lb and up (2 to 45 kg).

Turbot

> Type: Lean.
>
> Characteristics: Large, broad flatfish. White, firm, delicate flesh.
>
> Weight: 1 to 25 lb (0.5 to 11 kg).

Saltwater Fish—Round Fish

Black Sea Bass

> Type: Lean.
>
> Characteristics: Small, black-skinned fish with firm, delicate, sweet white flesh.
>
> Weight: Up to 3 lb (1.5 kg).

FIGURE 14.5 **Popular fish varieties.**
(a) Flounder.

(b) Dover sole.

(c) Black sea bass.

Bluefish

Type: Fat.

Characteristics: Flavorful, oily flesh that is bluish when raw, greyish when cooked. Abundant and inexpensive.

Weight: 1 to 10 lb (0.5 to 4.5 kg).

Cod

Type: Lean.

Varieties: Small, young cod is called *scrod.*

Characteristics: Lean, white, delicately flavored flesh with large flakes. Most important food fish in the United States. Most fish sticks and similar items are made from cod.

Weights: Scrod: 1 to 2½ lb (0.5 to 1 kg). Cod: 2½ to 25 lb and up (1 to 11 kg).

Grouper

Type: Lean.

Characteristics: Firm white fish similar in texture and flavor to large red snapper.

Weight: Up to 700 lb (300 kg), but most groupers on the market weigh 5 to 15 lb (2.3 to 7 kg).

(d) Bluefish.

(e) Cod. *(Continues)*

Haddock

Type: Lean.

Varieties: Finnan haddie is smoked haddock, not a separate kind of fish.

Characteristics: Similar to cod, but generally smaller.

Weight: 1 to 5 lb (0.5 to 2.3 kg).

Mackerel

Type: Fat.

Varieties: Spanish and Boston mackerel are the most common small varieties. King mackerel or king fish is larger, usually cut into steaks.

Characteristics: Fat, firm flesh with rich flavor and slightly dark color.

Weight: ½ to 5 lb (0.2 to 2.3 kg).

Monkfish

Also known as lotte, anglerfish, bellyfish.

Type: Lean.

Characteristics: Large, ugly fish, but only tail is used. White, very firm flesh with fine texture, somewhat like lobster. Rich flavor. Holds up well in soups and stews, but dries out easily if cooked dry without fat.

Weight: 5 to 50 lb (2.3 to 23 kg).

Ocean Perch

Type: Lean.

Varieties: Many. Red-skinned varieties (redfish) are especially popular and more expensive.

Characteristics: Mild, somewhat bony.

Weight: Depends on variety, but typically about 1 lb (0.5 kg).

(f) Grouper.

(h) Spanish mackerel.

(g) Boston mackerel.

(i) Monkfish.

Pompano

Type: Fat.

Characteristics: Small fish with rich, sweet-flavored flesh. Expensive.

Weight: ¾ to 2 lb (0.3 to 1 kg).

Porgy

Type: Lean.

Characteristics: Small, oval fish. Sweet and mild, but quite bony.

Weight: Up to 2 lb (1 kg).

Red Snapper

Type: Lean.

Characteristics: Firm, delicate, sweet white flesh with large flakes. Large coarse bones. Skin is red. Highly prized, and popular in restaurants.

Weight: 1 to 15 lb (0.5 to 7 kg).

Salmon

Type: Fat.

Varieties: Atlantic, chinook, sockeye, coho, chum, humpback.

Characteristics: Rich, pink-to-red flesh with somewhat "meaty" texture and flavor. One of the most prized of all fish. Much is canned or smoked.

Weight: 4 to 25 lb (2 to 11 kg).

Note: Salmon may also be classed as a fresh-water fish, because it swims up rivers to spawn.

Shad

Type: Fat.

Characteristics: Oily, rich flavor and very many bones in several rows in each fillet. Its roe (egg sacs) are especially prized. Fresh shad is highly seasonal (February to June).

Weight: 1½ to 5 lb (0.7 to 2.3 kg).

(j) Pompano.

(l) Red snapper.

(k) Porgy.

(m) Salmon. *(Continues)*

Shark

Type: Fat.

Varieties: Mako shark is the variety usually used.

Characteristics: Firm texture, similar to swordfish, but softer and a little moister and with finer grain; less expensive. Has cartilage skeleton, no bones. Usually cut into steaks.

Weight: 25 to 40 lb (11 to 18 kg).

Striped Bass

Type: Lean.

Characteristics: Firm, white, delicately flavored fish with large flakes.

Weight: 1 to 10 lb (0.5 to 4.5 kg).

Swordfish

Type: Fat.

Characteristics: Very large, fat fish with dense "meaty," not flaky, texture. High yield. Sold mostly as steaks. Expensive.

Weight: Up to 1000 lb (450 kg).

Tilefish

Type: Lean.

Characteristics: Firm, sweet, mild white flesh, pinkish when raw. Used mostly for steaks, but smaller ones can be filleted or poached whole.

Weight: 4 to 8 lb (1.8 to 3.6 kg).

Tuna

Type: Fat.

Varieties: Yellowfin and bluefin have red flesh, grey when cooked. Albacore has pink flesh, off-white when cooked. Some other varieties also available.

Characteristics: Meaty texture and appearance. Belly cuts much fattier than back ("loin"). Red-fleshed varieties often served raw as sashimi or sushi. When cooked, usually cut into steaks and grilled. Should not be cooked well done or will be very dry.

Weight: Depends on variety. May be several hundred pounds.

Weakfish

Also called sea trout.

Type: Lean.

Characteristics: Mild, light grey flesh with soft texture.

Weight: Up to 10 lb (4.5 kg).

(n) Striped bass.

(o) Tilefish.

(p) Weakfish.

Whiting

Type: Lean.

Characteristics: Fragile, white flesh with mild flavor. Fillets must be handled carefully or they will break up.

Weight: ¼ to 3 lb (0.1 to 1.4 kg).

(q) Whiting.

Freshwater Fish

Catfish

Type: Lean to fat.

Varieties: Bullhead is similar but is not the same species.

Characteristics: Firm flesh with abundant flavor. Layer of fat directly under skin. Catfish has no scales and is usually skinned before frying or pan-frying. Farmed catfish is milder and usually leaner than wild catfish.

Weight: 1 to 8 lb (0.5 to 3.6 kg).

Perch

Type: Lean.

Varieties: Yellow perch is the most common. Walleyed pike is actually a perch, not a pike.

Characteristics: Mild-flavored, flaky, white flesh with firm texture and fine grain.

Weight: ½ to 5 lb (0.2 to 2.3 kg).

Pike

Type: Lean.

Varieties: Northern pike is most common in the United States. Walleyed pike is not a pike but a perch.

Characteristics: Firm white flesh similar to perch, but not as thick, and with many small bones.

Weight: 2 to 12 lb (1 to 5.4 kg).

Trout

Type: Fat.

Varieties: Lake trout, river trout, brook trout, rainbow trout, many local varieties.

Characteristics: Soft, fine-textured flesh with rich, delicate flavor. Color of flesh may be white, pink, or reddish.

Weight: Lake trout: 4 to 10 lb (2 to 4.5 kg). Others: ½ to 3 lb (0.2 to 1.4 kg).

Whitefish

Type: Fat.

Characteristics: Flaky, white flesh with somewhat sweet flavor.

Weight: 1½ to 6 lb (0.7 to 2.7 kg).

(r) Catfish.

(s) Trout.

(t) Whitefish.

HANDLING AND STORAGE

Fish and shellfish are some of the most perishable foods you will handle. It is especially important to store them carefully and use them quickly. The "fishy" taste that turns many people away from fish is actually a sign of decomposition. Fresh fish should taste and smell sweet and fresh.

Because fresh fish is not federally inspected (unlike meats and poultry), it is up to you to check for quality. Guidelines for checking fish quality are summarized in Table 14.1.

Storing Fresh Fish

Objectives

1. To maintain temperature of 30°F to 34°F (–1°C to +1°C).

2. To keep the fish moist.

3. To prevent fish odors and flavors from being transferred to other foods.

4. To protect the delicate flesh from being bruised or crushed.

Methods

1. On crushed ice—the preferred method. Use drip pans to allow for drainage of melted ice. Change ice daily. Cover container or store in separate box away from other foods.

   Whole fish should be drawn as soon as possible, because the entrails deteriorate quickly. Whole or drawn fish are not wrapped. Cut fish (fillets, steaks, portions) should be wrapped or left in original moistureproof wrap.

2. In refrigerated box at 30°F to 34°F (–1°C to +1°C)—if crushed ice storage is not available or practical. Wrap all fish or leave in original moistureproof wrap.

Storage Time

Fresh fish may be stored for 1 or 2 days. If it must be kept longer, you may (1) wrap and freeze it immediately or (2) cook and then refrigerate it for later use in recipes calling for cooked fish.

Check stored fish for freshness just before you use it. Even if it was fresh when received, it may not be fresh after a few days in storage.

Frozen, Canned, and Other Processed Fish

Federal Inspection

Some of the processed fish products are inspected and graded by the U.S. Department of Commerce. This service is voluntary, although new regulations for inspection of fresh and processed seafood are under consideration at the time this is being written. *Inspection* assures cleanliness, wholesomeness, safety, and accuracy of labeling. *Grading* indicates that the product meets quality standards for appearance, flavor, and uniformity.

Frozen Fish

Frozen seafood products account for more of the fish served today than does fresh. If it were not for the wide availability of these frozen seafood products, commercial kitchens would serve much less fish than they do.

Checking Quality

1. Frozen products should be frozen when received, not thawed.

2. Look for fresh, sweet odor or none at all. Strong, "fishy" odor means poor handling.

3. Items should be well wrapped, with no freezer burn.

4. Some frozen fish is *glazed* with a thin layer of ice to prevent drying. Check for shiny surface to

---

TABLE 14.1   **Checklist for Fish Freshness**

Characteristics	Fresh Fish	Not-so-Fresh Fish
Odor	Fresh and mild, no off odors	Strong "fishy" odor
Eyes	Clear, shiny, bulging	Cloudy, sunken
Gills	Red or pink	Grey or brown
Texture of flesh	Firm, elastic	Soft, dents easily
Scales	Shiny, tight on skin	Loose, not shiny

Note: Because most fish is not purchased whole or dressed but as fillets, steaks, or other portions, odor must be your primary check for freshness.

make sure glaze has not melted off or evaporated.

Storage

1. Store at 0°F (–18°C) or colder.

2. Keep well wrapped to prevent freezer burn.

3. Maximum storage time:

   Fat fish: 2 months.

   Lean fish: 6 months.

4. Rotate stock—first in, first out.

Thawing and Handling

1. *Frozen raw fish.*

   a. Thaw in refrigerator, never at room temperature. Allow 18 to 36 hours, depending on size. Alternative method, if pressed for time: Keep in original moistureproof wrapper and thaw under cold running water.

   b. Small pieces (fillets, steaks, portions) up to 8 oz (250 g) can be cooked from frozen state to make handling easier and to prevent excessive drip loss. Large fish should be thawed for more even cooking from surface to interior.

   c. Fillets or other portions that are to be breaded or prepared in some other way before cooking may be partially thawed (for example, for a few seconds in a microwave), then prepped and cooked. They will handle more easily than if fully thawed.

   d. Handle thawed fish as you would fresh fish.

   e. Do not refreeze.

2. *Breaded and battered fish, fully prepared entrées, and other frozen, prepared fish items.*

   a. Read and follow package directions.

   b. Most of these items are cooked from the frozen state, usually in the deep-fryer, oven, microwave, or steamer.

Canned Fish

1. Check cans for signs of damage. Discard swollen cans (or return to the supplier).

2. Store like other canned goods, in a cool, dry place.

3. Opened canned fish should be placed in covered containers, labeled with the contents and date, and refrigerated. It will keep for 2 or 3 days.

SHELLFISH

*S*hellfish are distinguished from fin fish by their hard outer shells and their lack of backbones or internal skeletons.

There are two classifications of shellfish:

Mollusks are soft sea animals that live inside a pair of hard, hinged shells. (There are other kinds of mollusks with no shell, such as squid and octopus, and with one shell, such as snails and abalone; but they are of less importance in food service.)

Crustaceans are animals with segmented shells and jointed legs.

. . . .

MOLLUSKS

The most important mollusks in commercial kitchens are oysters, clams, mussels, and scallops.

Oysters

Characteristics

1. Oysters have rough, irregular shells. The bottom shell is slightly bowl shaped. The top shell is flat.

2. The flesh of the oyster is extremely soft and delicate and contains a high percentage of water.

3. Oysters are available all year, even in months without an "R" in their names, but they are at their best in the fall, winter, and spring.

4. There are four main varieties in the United States:

   Eastern: Known by many local names, depending on their origin.

   Olympia: Very small, from the Pacific coast.

   Belon: European oyster now grown in North America.

   Japanese: Very large, from Pacific coast.

Market Forms

1. Live, in the shell.

2. Shucked—fresh or frozen. Shucked oysters are graded by size as follows.

Grade	*Number per Gallon* (3.8 liters)
Extra Large or Counts	160 or fewer
Large or Extra Selects	161 to 210
Medium or Selects	211 to 300
Small or Standards	301 to 500
Very Small	Over 500

3.   Canned—rarely used in food service.

Checking Freshness

1.   Oysters in the shell must be alive to be good to eat. Tightly closed shells, or shells that close when jostled, indicate live oysters. Discard dead ones.

2.   Live or shucked oysters should have a very mild, sweet smell. Strong odors indicate spoilage.

Opening Oysters

1.   Scrub shells thoroughly before opening.

2.   Oysters to be served raw must be opened in a way that leaves the bottom shell intact and the tender oyster undamaged. The technique illustrated in Figure 14.6 is one common way of opening oysters. Your instructor may wish to show you another method.

3.   Oysters to be cooked may be opened by spreading them on a sheet pan and placing them in a hot oven *just* until the shells open. Remove from shells and cook immediately. Discard any that do not open.

Storage

1.   Keep live oysters in a cold, wet place, in the cartons or sacks in which they arrived. They should keep at least 1 week.

2.   Store fresh shucked oysters in the original container in refrigerator at 30°F to 34°F (−1°C to 1°C). They will keep up to a week.

3.   Keep frozen oysters in freezer, at 0°F (−18°C) or colder, until ready for use. Thaw in refrigerator for 24 hours or more, depending on size of container.

Cooking Oysters

1.   Cook just enough to heat through to keep oysters juicy and plump. Overcooking makes them shrunken and dry.

2.   Cooking methods: Poaching, deep-frying, baking on the half shell with toppings, in soups and stews.

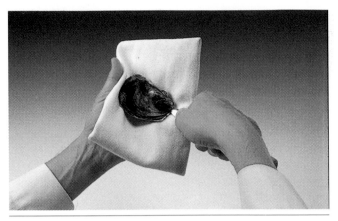

FIGURE 14.6   **Opening oyster.**

(a) Examine the shell to see that it is tightly closed, indicating a live oyster. Rinse shell under cold, running water. Hold oyster in left hand, as shown. (Left handers will hold oyster in right hand.) You may hold the oyster with a towel to protect your hand. Hold oyster knife near the tip as shown. Insert knife between the shells near the hinge.

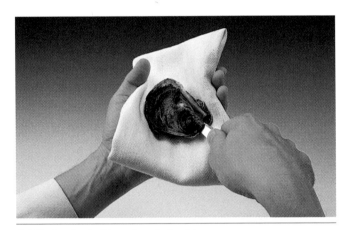

(b) Twist the knife to break the hinge.

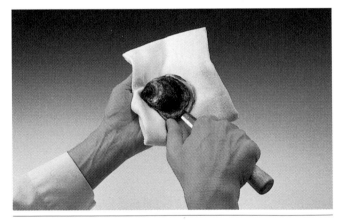

(c) Slide the knife under the top shell and cut through the *adductor* muscle (which closes the shells) near the top shell. Try not to cut the flesh of the oyster or it will lose plumpness. Remove the top shell.

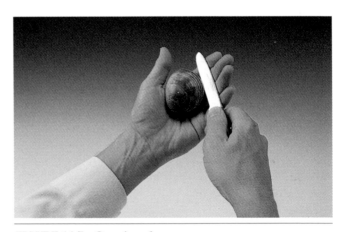

(d) Carefully cut the lower end of the muscle from the bottom shell to loosen oyster. Remove any particles of shell from the oyster before serving.

Clams

Characteristics

There are two major kinds of clams from the East coast: *hard shell* and *soft shell*. The West coast also has some local varieties.

1. Hard-shell clams or quahogs. These go by different names, depending on size.

   Littlenecks are the smallest. They are tenderest for eating raw or for steaming.

   Cherrystones are medium sized, and perhaps the most common. They can be eaten raw and are good for steaming, though tougher than littlenecks.

   Chowders, the largest, are also called quahogs in the Northeast. Rather tough, they are chopped for cooking in chowders or cut into strips for frying.

2. Soft-shell clams. These are sometimes called longnecks, because of the long tube that protrudes from between the shells. They have very thin shells that do not close completely.

   They are also called *steamers*, because the usual way to serve them is to steam them and serve them with their own broth and with melted butter for dipping.

Market Forms (Hard-Shell Clams)

1. Live, in the shell.
2. Shucked, fresh or frozen.
3. Canned, whole or chopped.

Checking Freshness

Same as for oysters. Clams in the shell must be alive. Live and shucked clams should smell fresh.

Opening Clams

1. Scrub shells thoroughly before opening.

2. Hard-shell clams are sometimes sandy inside, and soft-shell clams nearly always are. They can be "flushed" as follows:

   a. Make a salt brine, using ⅓ cup salt per gallon of water.
   b. Soak the clams in the brine for 20 minutes.
   c. Drain and repeat until the clams are sand free.
   d. Some chefs put cornmeal in the water and refrigerate the clams in it for a day. The clams eat the cornmeal and expel the sand.
   e. Rinse in fresh water before using.

3. Opening hard-shell clams is different from opening oysters. This technique is illustrated in Figure 14.7.

4. Like oysters, clams to be cooked may be opened by spreading on sheet pans and placing in a hot oven *just* until the shells open. Discard any that do not open.

Storage

Same as for oysters.

FIGURE 14.7 **Opening clams.**
(a) Examine the shell to see that it is tightly closed, indicating a live clam. Rinse shell under cold, running water. Avoid jostling the clam too much, or it will "clam up" tighter. Hold clam in left hand as shown (or in right hand if you are left handed). Place the sharp edge of the clam knife against the crack between the shells. *(Continues)*

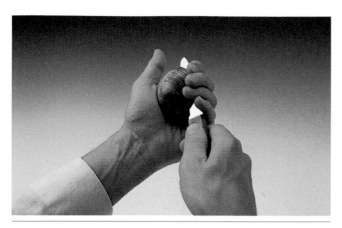

(b) Squeeze with the fingers of the left hand, forcing the knife between the shells.

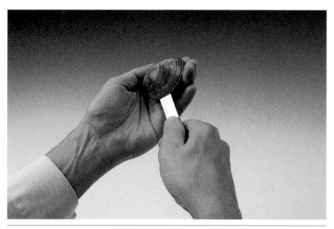

(c) Change the angle of the blade as shown in the illustration and slide the knife against the top shell to cut the adductor muscles (clams have 2, oysters have only 1). Be careful not to cut or pierce the soft clam.

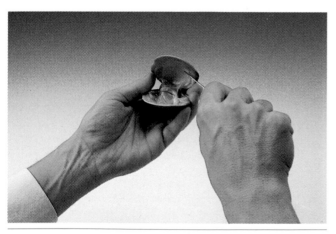

(d) Open the clam and finish detaching the meat from the upper shell.

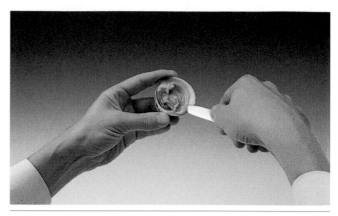

(e) Cut the muscles against the lower shell to loosen the clam completely. Discard top shell. Remove any particles of shell from the clam before serving.

Cooking Clams

1. Clams become very tough and rubbery if over-cooked. Cook just enough to heat through.

2. When steaming clams in the shell, steam just until shells open.

3. Cooking methods: Steaming, poaching, deep-frying, baking on the half shell with toppings, simmering in soups and chowders.

Mussels

Characteristics

1. Mussels resemble small, black or dark blue clams. Their shells are not as heavy as clam shells.

2. The flesh of the mussel is very soft and is yellowish or yellow-orange in color.

3. Mussels are most widely available in coastal areas where they are harvested. They are most plentiful from October to April.

Market Forms

Most mussels are sold live, in the shell. Many are also sold shucked and packed in brine.

Checking Freshness

1. Like oysters and clams, mussels must be alive to be good to eat. Check for tightly closed shells, or shells that just close when jostled.

2. Discard any mussels that are very light in weight or seem to be hollow. Also, discard any that are much too heavy—they are probably full of sand.

Cleaning

1. Clean shells thoroughly:

   Scrub well under cold, running water.

   Scrape off barnacles, if any, with a clam knife.

   Remove the "beard," a fibrous appendage protruding from between the shells.

2. Mussels are usually sandy inside. They should be soaked in brine and flour or cornmeal like clams (see previous section) to rid them of sand.

Storage

Keep refrigerated (32°F to 35°F/0°C to 2°C) and protect from light. Store in original sack and keep sack damp.

Cooking

Unlike oysters and clams, mussels are almost never served raw. They are usually steamed and served in their cooking broth, in soups, or chilled and served with mayonnaise-type sauces. Cook only until shells open and mussels are heated through. Do not overcook. Discard any that are not open after cooking.

Scallops

Characteristics

1. Scallops are almost always sold shucked. The only part we usually eat is the adductor muscle, which closes the shell. If live scallops in the shell are available, leave the orange, crescent-shaped coral attached to the adductor muscle when shucking.

2. There are two main kinds of scallops:

   Bay scallops: small, with delicate flavor and texture; expensive; 32 to 40 per pound (70 to 88 per kilogram) on the average.

   Sea scallops: larger, not as delicate as bay scallops, but still tender unless overcooked; 10 to 15 per pound (22 to 33 per kilogram) on the average.

3. Scallops are creamy white in color and have a sweet flavor.

4. They are available all year.

Market Forms

1. Fresh, shucked. Sold by the gallon or pound.

2. Frozen.

   a. IQF (individually quick frozen).
   b. In 5-lb (2.3-kg) blocks.

Checking Freshness

A sweet, clean smell is a sign of freshness. Strong "fishy" odor or a brownish color is a sign of age or spoilage.

Handling

1. Shucked scallops can be cooked without any further preparation. They are improved, however, if you pull off the small, tough tendon or sinew on the side of each scallop.

2. Large sea scallops are sometimes cut into smaller pieces before cooking.

Storage

Keep scallops covered and refrigerated (30°F to 34°F/–1°C to +1°C). Do not let them rest directly on ice, or they will lose flavor and become watery.

Cooking Scallops

Scallops are cooked in almost every way that fish are cooked. The most popular methods are sautéing, deep-frying, broiling, and poaching.

CRUSTACEANS

The most important crustaceans in commercial kitchens are lobsters, rock lobsters or langoustes, shrimp, and crabs.

Lobsters

Characteristics

1. The northern lobster is perhaps the most prized shellfish in this country. It has a large, flexible tail, four pairs of legs, and two large claws. Its shell is dark green or bluish green but turns red when cooked.

2. Meat from the tail, claws, and legs is eaten. It is white and sweet, with a distinctive taste. Claw meat is considered especially good. The coral (roe or eggs), which is dark green when raw and red when cooked, and the green tomalley (liver) in the thorax or body portion are also eaten.

3. Lobsters are classified by weight.

Chicken	1 lb (450 g)
Quarters	1¼ lb (575 g)
Selects	1½ to 2¼ lb (675 to 1025 g)
Jumbos	over 2½ lb (1130 g)

(b) Cut off the legs and claws.

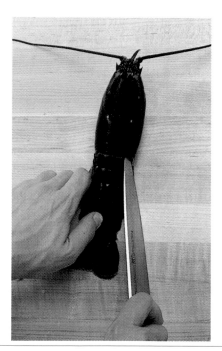

(c) Remove the tail section from the thorax, either by breaking it off or by inserting the knife behind the thorax as shown and cutting through the flesh.

(d) Cut the thorax in half lengthwise.

(e) Remove and discard the stomach, a sac just behind the eyes.

(f) Remove the tomalley and coral for use in the sauce to accompany the lobster.

(g) Cut the tail into pieces where the segments join. This is a small lobster. Large tails should be cut into more pieces (at least 4 or 5), so that each piece is not too large.

(h) The cut-up lobster, ready to cook.

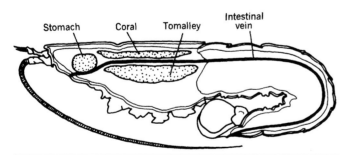

FIGURE 14.10   **Cross-section of a female lobster, showing the location of the stomach, tomalley, coral, and vein.**

Storage

1. Live lobsters can be kept in two ways:

   a. Packed in moist seaweed or in moist, heavy paper, kept in a cool place.
   b. In salt water. Special lobster tanks are used in restaurants for display and for allowing

customers to select their own lobster. Air must be bubbled through the water to keep the lobsters alive.

2. Cooked lobster meat must be covered and refrigerated at 30°F to 34°F (–1°C to 1°C). It is very perishable and should be used in 1 or 2 days.

Cooking Lobsters

1. Lobster meat becomes tough if cooked at too high a temperature or for too long. Boiling too long will also make the meat dry. Whole lobster is usually cooked by dropping into boiling water and then simmering for 5 to 6 minutes per pound (500 g). For jumbo lobsters, reduce the cooking time slightly.

2. Whole or cut-up lobster can be cooked by simmering in water or court bouillon, simmering in sauce or soup, sautéing, baking, or broiling.

Rock Lobsters

Characteristics

1. Rock lobsters are also known as spiny lobsters or langoustes. They are warm-water relatives of northern lobsters but have no claws. Only the tails are marketed, sold as *lobster tails*.

2. The flesh of the rock lobster tail is similar to that of the northern or Maine lobster, but it is drier and coarser, with less flavor.

3. Rock lobster tails weigh from 2 to 12 oz (60 to 340 g).

4. *Langoustines* or langostinos are smaller relatives of the rock lobster. These small shellfish are often marketed as *rock shrimp*. When out of the shell, they look like shrimp, but their flavor is milder and sweeter than that of shrimp. The term "scampi" (plural form of "scampo") refers not to shrimp but to a variety of langoustine from Italian waters. The name scampi is often used, incorrectly, for large shrimp broiled with butter and garlic.

Market Forms

Nearly all rock lobster tails are sold IQF (individually quick frozen).

Handling and Cooking

1. Rock lobsters are handled and cooked much like northern lobsters. Most common cooking methods are steaming, simmering, and broiling.

2. Tails to be broiled will be moister if poached for 5 minutes before splitting and broiling.

3. Tails steamed or simmered whole should have the shells split before serving as a convenience to the customer.

Shrimp

Characteristics

1. Shrimp are small crustaceans that look somewhat like tiny, clawless lobsters. Only the tail is marketed and eaten, as a rule.

2. There are many varieties, depending on where caught, but the particular variety is usually of little importance to the cook.

3. Shrimp are classified by count per pound; the higher the count, the smaller the shrimp. (For example, "16/20" means 16 to 20 per pound.) Classification systems are different for different markets.

4. Large shrimp are more expensive per pound, but they require less work to peel and devein.

5. Yield: 1 lb of raw shrimp (tails) in the shell yield about ½ lb peeled, cooked shrimp.

6. The term "prawn" is sometimes used for large shrimp, sometimes for langoustines (see p. 343). Use of the term varies from region to region.

Market Forms

1. "Green shrimp" are raw shrimp in the shell.

    a. Fresh: Not widely available, except near source of supply.
    b. Frozen: In 5-lb (2.3-kg) blocks.

2. P/D (peeled, deveined): Usually IQF (individually quick frozen).

3. PDC (peeled, deveined, and cooked): Usually IQF.

    Note: IQF shrimp are usually *glazed* (see p. 334).

Checking Freshness

1. Frozen shrimp should be solidly frozen when received.

2. Glazed shrimp should be shiny, with no freezer burn.

3. All shrimp should smell fresh and sweet. A strong "fishy" or iodine smell indicates age or spoilage.

Storing

1. Like other frozen fish, shrimp should be kept frozen at 0°F (−18°C) or lower until ready for use.

2. Thaw in refrigerator, allowing sufficient slack time.

3. Fresh or thawed shrimp in the shell are stored on crushed ice, like whole fish.

4. Peeled shrimp lose soluble nutrients and flavor when stored unwrapped on ice. They should be wrapped before placing on ice or covered and simply refrigerated.

Handling

1. Shrimp served hot must normally be peeled and deveined before cooking. Figure 14.11 shows how.

2. Shrimp to be served cold may be peeled after cooking to preserve flavor.

3. Large shrimp are sometimes butterflied, as shown in Figure 14.11*f*. This is done for appearance (makes shrimp seem larger, with more surface area for breading) and to speed cooking by reducing thickness.

Cooking Shrimp

Like most shellfish, shrimp become tough and rubbery when cooked at too high a heat. Shrimp can be cooked by simmering, deep-frying, sautéing, broiling, and baking.

Crabs

Six kinds of crabs are important in commercial kitchens.

1. *Alaskan king crab.* Largest of the crabs, weighing from 6 to 20 lb (2.7 to 9 kg). The meat can be removed in large chunks, making it especially attractive to serve in restaurants. It is expensive.

2. *Alaskan snow crab.* Smaller than the king crab. Often used as a less expensive substitute.

3. *Dungeness crab.* Another West coast crab, weighing 1½ to 4 lb (0.7 to 1.8 kg). The meat is very sweet.

4. *Blue crab.* Small crab from the East coast, weighing about 5 oz. Most frozen crabmeat is from blue crabs.

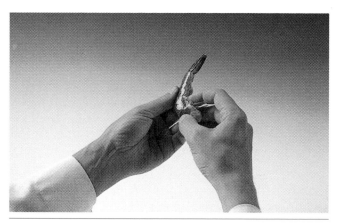

FIGURE 14.11 Peeling and deveining shrimp.
(a) Pull off the "legs" with forefinger.

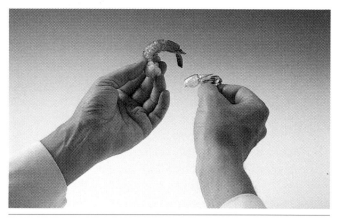

(d) For most other preparations, the tail section of the shell is removed.

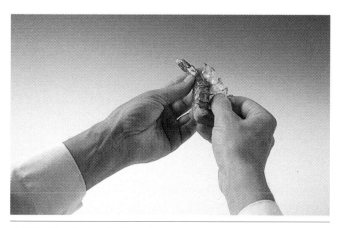

(b) Peel back the shell as shown and remove.

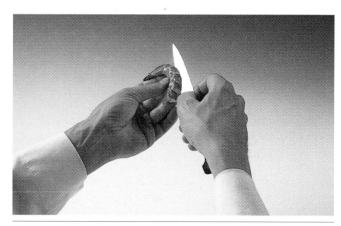

(e) With a paring knife, make a shallow cut down the back of the shrimp and pull out the intestinal vein, which is just below the surface.

(c) For deep-fried and broiled shrimp, the tail section of the shell is left on for appearance. It also gives the cook something to hold when dipping the shrimp in batter.

(f) To butterfly shrimp, make the cut in step (e) deeper, so that the shrimp can be spread open as shown.

5. **Soft-shell crab.**   Actually a molting blue crab, harvested before the new shell has hardened. It is sautéed or fried and eaten shell and all; only the gills and head are removed.

6. **Stone crabs.**   Popular in the Southeast. Only the claws are eaten.

Market Forms

1. Live. Crabs taste best when fresh, but very few (except soft-shell crabs) are purchased live, because of the labor required to pick the meat. An average blue crab yields less than an ounce of meat.

2. Cooked, frozen, in the shell.
   King crab legs, whole and split.
   Snow and stone crab claws.
   Soft-shell crabs, whole.

3. Cooked, frozen meat. All varieties.

Freshness and Storage

1. Live crabs should be kept alive until cooked. They are packed in damp seaweed and kept cool.

2. Frozen crabmeat should be treated like any other frozen fish. It is very perishable when thawed.

Handling and Cooking

1. Hard-shell crabs are picked of their meat after cooking.
   a. Simmer 10 to 15 minutes in salted water (½ cup salt per gallon). Cool rapidly in ice water.
   b. Break off the pointed shell on the underside (called the apron) and remove the top shell.
   c. Remove and discard the spongy gills and the stomach, which is just behind the eyes.
   d. Pick out the body meat.
   e. Crack the legs and claws with a mallet or the back of a heavy knife and pick out the meat.

2. Soft-shell crabs.
   a. With a knife or shears, cut off the head section, just behind the eyes.
   b. Lift the pointed, outside corners of the top shell and pull out the spongy gills.
   c. Cut off the apron, the small flap on the underside.
   d. The crab may then be dredged in flour for sautéing or breaded or battered for deep-frying.

3. Frozen crabmeat.
   a. Crabmeat is usually very watery. You may need to squeeze out excess moisture before cooking. Whenever possible, save the liquid for use in sauces and soups.
   b. Frozen crabmeat is already cooked. It needs only to be heated through to be prepared for serving.

Crayfish

Crayfish or *crawfish* (the preferred term in the southern U.S.) are freshwater relatives of the lobster. Not long ago they were used almost exclusively in southern regional cuisine and in elegant French restaurants. With the spreading popularity of southern cuisines, including Creole and Cajun, they have become more widely available.

Crayfish are marketed live and frozen (peeled tail meat or whole).

MISCELLANEOUS SEAFOOD

Several other seafood items play a role in food service kitchens. They are classified with fish, even though some of them spend part or all of their lives on land, like frogs and snails.

1. *Squid* are classified as mollusks, even though they have no shell. They must be skinned and eviscerated, and the head and beak are discarded. The hollow body and the tentacles are eaten. Somewhat chewy, squid are cut up and either fried quickly or simmered for about 45 minutes in a seasoned liquid or sauce.

2. *Snails or escargots* are popular hors d'oeuvres when baked in their shells with a highly seasoned butter. Fresh snails require long, slow cooking before being baked with escargot butter, but canned snails are fully cooked and ready to prepare. Canned snails can be improved, however, by first simmering them in white wine and seasonings.

3. *Frogs' legs* are often compared to chicken in taste and texture (but then, so are a lot of things). Only the hind legs are used, and they are sold in pairs. They may be sautéed, deep-fried, or poached and served with a sauce.

TERMS FOR REVIEW

fin fish	dressed	adductor muscle	rock shrimp
shellfish	fillet	coral	scampi
flaking	flatfish and round fish	tomalley	prawn
lean and fat fish	mollusks	langoustine	crayfish
drawn	crustaceans		

QUESTIONS FOR DISCUSSION

1. Fish has very little connective tissue. How does this affect the ways in which you handle it and cook it?

2. Based on what you learned about fat and lean fish and about individual species of fish, can you suggest at least one cooking method for each of the following?

Mackerel	Salmon
Cod	Perch
Flounder	Swordfish
Trout	Whitefish
Red snapper	Halibut

3. List and describe the major market forms of fresh fish.

4. What are the differences between filleting flatfish and round fish? Describe or demonstrate.

5. You have just received delivery of fresh whole red snapper and fresh cod fillets. What should you check before accepting the shipment? After accepting them, what do you do with them?

6. You are making a casserole of shrimp with a prepared Newburg sauce and frozen, glazed cooked shrimp. When you add the frozen shrimp to the sauce, it thins out so much it is no longer usable. Why did this happen, and how could you have prevented it?

7. What is the most important indication of freshness in fresh oysters, clams, lobsters, and crabs? Describe how you would preserve this freshness.

8. How does opening oysters differ from opening clams, and how is it similar?

9. What happens to most kinds of shellfish when they are overcooked?

BAKING

Whole fish and fish portions may be cooked by baking in an oven. Although large whole fish may be baked, this is usually not practical in volume food service. The method is more often used with steaks and fillets and with small fish. It is also a popular method for preparing shellfish such as stuffed clams or oysters.

Baking is often combined with other cooking methods. For example, partially broiled fish can be finished by baking. Baked fish casseroles are usually made with cooked fish. These recipes are included at the end of the chapter.

Guidelines for Baking Fish

1. Fat fish are best for baking, because they are less likely to dry out.

2. Lean fish may be baked successfully if great care is taken not to overcook them. Basting with butter or oil helps prevent drying.

3. In most cases, baking temperatures are from 350°F to 400°F (175°C to 200°C). Large fish are best baked at the lower end of this range, so that they will bake more evenly.

    It is also possible to bake thin fillets or slices of fillets (cut like scaloppine) at very high temperatures. Great care must be used in this case, because the fish may cook in a minute or less, and a few seconds too long might ruin the fish. The effect of the high heat is almost like broiling, and the normal guidelines for broiling thin fish fillets should be followed, as explained in the next section.

4. It is not possible to give specific baking times, because fish vary so much in shape and composition. Different ingredients and types of baking pans will also affect the baking time. The following guideline is helpful, however: Measure the thickness of the fish at the thickest point. At 400°F (200°C), baking time will be about 10 minutes per inch (2.5 cm) of thickness.

5. Serving baked fish with a sauce or seasoned butter enhances its moistness and improves palatability. Serving with lemon also enhances the fish.

6. If fish is baked with a moist topping or sauce, strictly speaking it is no longer a dry-heat method. However, because the basic procedure is the same, it is treated like baking fish dry.

Procedure for Baking Fish

1. Collect all equipment and food supplies.

2. Prepare and season fish (whole, steaks, fillets) as directed in recipe.

3. Place fish on oiled or buttered baking sheets. Brush tops with oil or butter.

    Alternative method: Dip fish in oil or melted butter to coat both sides. Place on baking sheets.

4. Apply toppings, if desired. Examples: seasoned bread crumbs, lemon slices, mushrooms or other vegetable garnish, and sauces.

5. Bake at 350°F to 400°F (175°C to 200°C) until done. If the fish is lean and doesn't have a moist topping, baste with oil or butter during baking.

Moist Baking or Braising

As we noted above, if fish is baked with moist ingredients or with liquids, strictly speaking it is not a dry-heat method, although such preparations are included in this section. In French cooking, baking fish—usually whole fish or large pieces—with vegetables and liquid is called braising. To avoid confusion with the braising method as applied to meats, however, we will avoid that term and refer to such dishes as baked.

This procedure is the same as the basic procedure for baking fish as described above, with the following special features:

1. The baking pan should be just large enough to hold the fish, so that you will not need too much liquid.

2. The bottom of the pan is buttered or oiled and then covered with a layer of sliced or chopped vegetables, such as carrots, onions, shallots, and mushrooms. The vegetables may be raw or first sautéed gently in butter or oil. The fish is then placed on top of the vegetables.

3. A small amount of liquid is frequently added, such as equal parts wine and fish stock. Just enough liquid is used to cover the fish about halfway or less. During baking, the fish is basted with this liquid.

4. The fish may be baked uncovered or covered only lightly. It should not be covered tightly,

however, because the liquid must be able to reduce somewhat, so that it will become more concentrated and more flavorful. Remember also that more liquid will be released from the fish, diluting the cooking liquid.

5. For service, the fish is removed from the dish. The liquid is strained, degreased, reduced, and

finished in various ways, such as by adding butter, cream, or velouté sauce.

You can see that this is a sort of combination technique. Because it often uses wine and other liquids, the method is in some ways similar to poaching in wine, as explained on page 366.

RECIPE 128   Baked Cod Fillets Portugaise

| | | | Portions: 24 | Portion size: 5 oz (150 g) fish |
| | | | | 2 oz (60 mL) sauce |

U.S.	Metric	Ingredients	Procedure
24	24	Cod fillets, 5-oz (150-g) portions	1. Place cod fillets on a well-oiled baking sheet or bake pan, flesh side up (that is, skin side down).
⅓ cup	75 mL	Lemon juice	
8 oz	250 mL	Melted butter or oil	2. Brush the fish lightly with lemon juice. Then brush generously with the butter or oil and season lightly with salt and pepper.
		Salt	
		White pepper	
			3. Place the pan in a preheated 350°F (175°C) oven until done, about 10 to 15 minutes.
			4. Halfway through the cooking time, check the fish and, if the tops appear to be drying out, brush with more butter or oil.
1½ qt	1.5 L	Portuguese Sauce (p. 146)	5. Serve each portion with 2 oz (60 mL) sauce. Nap the sauce across the center of the portion. Do not cover the entire fillet.

Variations

Many other fish may be baked according to the basic recipe, such as

Haddock (fillets or steaks)   Halibut (steaks or fillets)
Snapper (fillets)   Bluefish (fillets)
Bass (fillets)   Mackerel (fillets)
Pike (fillets)   Salmon (fillets or steaks)
Perch (fillets)   Swordfish (steaks)
Flounder (fillets)   Whitefish (fillets)

Other appropriate sauces may be used, such as
Melted Butter
Beurre Noisette
Maitre d'Hotel Butter
Tomato and tomato-based sauces such as Creole (not for salmon or for very delicate fish like flounder)
Mustard (for strong flavored fish only, such as mackerel or bluefish)
Curry (not for salmon or other fat fish)

RECIPE 129 **Baked Fish with Tomatoes and Mushrooms**

		Portions: 10	**Portion size:** 1 fish

U.S.	Metric	Ingredients	Procedure
10	10	Small whole fish, about 12 oz (375 g) each (see note) Salt Pepper Thyme	1. Scale and clean the fish but leave the heads on. Season the fish inside and out with salt and pepper, and put a small pinch of thyme and a sprig of parsley in the cavity of each.
10	10	Parsley sprigs	
		Olive oil	2. Select as many baking pans as necessary to just hold the fish in a single layer. Oil the pans with a little olive oil.
8 oz	250 g	Onion, small dice	
1 oz	30 g	Shallots, minced	3. Sauté the onions and shallots in a little olive oil for about a minute. Add the mushrooms and sauté lightly.
8 oz	250 g	Mushrooms, chopped	
1 lb	500 g	Tomato concassée	4. Put the sautéed vegetables and the tomatoes in the bottoms of the baking pans.
8 oz	250 mL	Dry white wine	
			5. Put the fish in the pans. Oil the tops lightly. Pour in the wine.
			6. Bake at 400°F (200°C) until the fish is done. The time will vary but will average around 15 to 20 minutes. Baste often with the liquid in the pan.
			7. Remove the fish and keep them warm until they are to be plated.
			8. Remove the vegetables from the pans with a slotted spoon and check for seasonings. Serve a spoonful of the vegetables with the fish, placing it under or alongside each fish.
			9. Strain, degrease, and reduce the cooking liquid slightly. Just before serving, moisten each portion with a tablespoon or two of the liquid.

Note: Many types of fish can be used, including sea bass, red snapper, porgy, perch, and trout. As an alternative, use thick steaks or thick pieces of fillet from larger fish such as cod or tilefish.

Variation

*129A. **Baked Fish à la Menagère:*** Use butter instead of olive oil. Substitute sliced leeks for part or all of the onion. Omit the tomatoes. Add 4 oz (125 g) sliced carrot and cook it with the leek. Slice the mushrooms instead of chopping them, and add them to the pan raw. Add 1 cup (250 mL) fish stock along with the wine. After straining and reducing the cooking liquid in step 9, thicken it very lightly with a little beurre manié. Enrich the sauce with a little raw butter or cream.

RECIPE 130   **Baked Stuffed Mackerel**

		Portions: 10		**Portion size:** 1 fish, with stuffing
U.S.	Metric	Ingredients		Procedure
10	10	Mackerel, about 8–12 oz (250–375 g) each *or* other small fish	1.	Fillet the fish (see p. 328, Figure 14.4), but leave the skin on.
8 oz	250 g	Bread crumbs, fresh	2.	Combine the crumbs, butter, and herbs in a bowl. Toss lightly until mixed.
3 oz	90 mL	Melted butter		
1 tbsp	15 mL	Chopped parsley	3.	Mix the beaten egg, lemon zest, and lemon juice. Add to the crumbs and mix gently. Season to taste.
½ tsp	2 mL	Thyme		
1	1	Egg, beaten		
¼ tsp	1 mL	Grated lemon zest		
2 oz	60 mL	Lemon juice		
		Salt		
		Oil or melted butter	4.	Place 10 fillets (that is, half of each fish) on a well-oiled baking sheet, skin side down.
			5.	Top each fillet with 1½ oz (50 g) of the stuffing. (Portion with a No. 24 scoop.) Shape the stuffing to fit the length of the fish.
			6.	Place the second fillet on top and press down lightly.
			7.	Brush fish with oil or melted butter.
			8.	Bake at 350°F (175°C) until done, about 15–20 minutes.

RECIPE 131   **Baked Pike Fillets English Style**

		Portions: 25		**Portion size:** 1 fillet, 5–6 oz (150–175 g)
U.S.	Metric	Ingredients		Procedure
25	25	Pike fillets, 5–6 oz (150–175 g)	1.	Brush the fillets lightly with the lemon juice and season with salt and pepper.
2½ oz	75 mL	Lemon juice	2.	Dip both sides of each fillet in the butter and then in the bread crumbs. Press the crumbs on lightly so they adhere.
		Salt		
		White pepper		
10 oz	300 mL	Melted butter	3.	Place the fillets on a baking sheet, flesh side up (skin side down).
1½ lb or as needed	700 g	Bread crumbs, dry		
			4.	Place pan in oven at 400°F (200°C) and bake until fish is done and crumbs are lightly browned.
25	25	Lemon wedges	5.	Serve immediately, with lemon wedges.

Variation

131A. Herbed Baked Fish: Combine 6 tbsp (90 mL) chopped parsley and 1½ tsp (7 mL) marjoram with the bread crumbs.

RECIPE 132 Baked Clams Oreganata

Portions: 10

Portion size: 3 clams
(appetizer portion)

U.S.	Metric	Ingredients	Procedure
30	30	Cherrystone clams	1. Open the clams (see Figure 14.7 for technique). Catch the juice in a bowl.
			2. Remove the clams from the shell. Place them in a strainer over the bowl of juice. Let them drain 15 minutes in the refrigerator. Save the 30 best half shells.
			3. Chop the clams into small pieces.
2 oz	60 mL	Olive oil	4. Heat the oil in a sauté pan. Add the onion and garlic. Sauté about 1 minute but do not brown.
1 oz	30 g	Onions, shallots, or scallions, chopped fine	
1 tsp	5 mL	Garlic, chopped fine	5. Add *half* the clam juice and reduce by three-fourths over high heat.
1 oz	30 mL	Lemon juice	6. Remove from the heat and add the lemon juice, crumbs, parsley, oregano, and white pepper. Mix gently, to avoid making the crumbs pasty.
10 oz	300 g	Bread crumbs, fresh	
1 tbsp	15 mL	Chopped parsley	
¾ tsp	3 mL	Oregano	
⅛ tsp	0.5 mL	White pepper	7. Taste and adjust seasonings if necessary. (Clams are usually very salty.)
⅓ cup	25 g	Parmesan cheese	8. Cool the mixture. Mix in the chopped clams.
		Paprika	9. Fill the 30 clam shells with the mixture. Sprinkle with parmesan cheese and (very lightly!) with paprika.
			10. Place on a sheet pan and refrigerate until needed.
10	10	Lemon wedges	11. For each order, bake 3 clams in a hot oven (450°F/230°C) until they are hot and the top is brown.
			12. Garnish with lemon wedge.

Note: Clams and oysters are often baked on a bed of rock salt to hold them steady. The rock salt also holds heat well.

BROILING

Like baking, broiling is a dry-heat method. Therefore, many of the same precautions are necessary, as the following guidelines indicate.

Guidelines for Broiling Fish

1. Because of the intense heat of the broiler, great care is needed to avoid overcooking the fish.

2. Use small slices or fillets for broiling.

3. Fat fish is best for broiling, since it doesn't get as dry as lean fish. However, all fish (fat or lean) should be coated with a fat before broiling to reduce drying.

4. Lean fish may be dredged in flour before dipping in melted butter or oil. The flour forms a crust, which helps retain moisture.

5. Instead of dredging with flour, fish may be coated with fat and then with bread crumbs or cornmeal. This also forms a flavorful crust.

6. Broil fish to order and serve immediately.

7. Broiled fish may be garnished *lightly* with paprika if more color is desired. But don't overdo it. One of the most common faults in broiling or baking fish is coating them with a heavy layer of paprika, which ruins the delicate flavor of the fish.

8. Thick cuts should be turned once during broiling in order to cook evenly. Thin pieces may be arranged on an oiled pan and broiled on one side only. Lobster is also broiled without turning.

9. Serve broiled fish with lemon and/or with a seasoned butter. Tartar Sauce is also appropriate.

Procedure for Broiling Fish

1. Collect all equipment and food supplies.

2. Prepare the fish as required: season and coat with oil or butter, with flour and then fat, or with fat and then bread crumbs.

3. Preheat broiler.

4. Broil thick cuts on both sides, turning once. Broil thin pieces on one side only.

5. Serve immediately, with appropriate sauce and garnish.

RECIPE 133   Broiled Fish Steaks Maitre d'Hotel

....

Portions: as needed   **Portion size:** 5–6 oz (150–175 g)

U.S.	Metric	Ingredients	Procedure
as needed		Fish steaks, 5–6 oz (150–175 g) each (see note) Salt White pepper Oil or melted butter	1. Season the steaks with salt and pepper. 2. Place the oil or melted butter in a small pan. Dip both sides of the steaks in it to coat completely. 3. Place on the rack of a preheated broiler. Broil under medium heat until half cooked. Turn over with a spatula. At this point it may be necessary to brush the tops of the steaks with more oil or butter if they are becoming dry. 4. Complete the cooking on the second side.
as needed		Maitre d'Hotel Butter Lemon wedges	5. Plate up the fish. Place a slice of seasoned butter on top of each steak. Garnish the plate with a lemon wedge. Serve immediately.

Note: Salmon, tuna, and swordfish steaks are ideal for broiling, but they are also expensive. Some other fish steaks that may be broiled include cod, haddock, halibut, king mackerel, and large bluefish.

Fillets may also be broiled using this recipe if they are thick or firm enough to avoid breaking up on the grill.

Variations

For lean white fish (halibut, cod, etc.), dredge in flour and shake off excess before dipping in the melted butter or oil. Broil as in basic recipe.

Other compound butters may be used in place of Maitre d'Hotel Butter.

For fat fish, omit the butter and serve the fish with a small quantity of flavorful vinaigrette.

....

RECIPE 134 Broiled Lobster

....

	Portions: 1			Portion size: 1 lobster

U.S.	Metric	Ingredients		Procedure
1	1	Live lobster, 1–1½ lb (450–700 g)	1.	Split the lobster as shown in Figure 14.8. Remove and discard the stomach (just behind the eyes) and the vein that runs through the tail. The liver and coral may be left in or removed and added to the stuffing (step 3), as desired.
1 tsp	5 mL	Shallot, chopped fine	2.	Sauté the onion in the butter just until it starts to become tender.
1 tbsp	15 g	Butter		
1 oz	30 g	Bread crumbs, dry	3.	Optional step: Chop the lobster coral and liver (tomalley) and add to the pan. Sauté just until it becomes firm, about 10–20 seconds.
3 tbsp	45 mL	Chopped parsley		
		Salt	4.	Add the bread crumbs and brown them lightly in the butter. Remove from the heat.
		Pepper		
			5.	Add the parsley. Season the crumbs with salt and pepper.
		Melted butter	6.	Place the lobster shell side down on a small sheet pan or in a shallow bake pan. Fill the body cavity with the crumb mixture. Do not put the crumbs over the tail meat.
			7.	Brush the tail well with melted butter.
			8.	Place a few of the legs on top of the stuffing. If the lobster was split by the first method shown in Figure 14.8g, weight the end of the tail down to keep it from curling.
			9.	Place the lobster under the broiler at least 6 inches (15 cm) from the heat. Broil until the crumbs are well browned.
			10.	At this point the lobster will probably not be completely cooked, unless it is very small and the broiler heat very low. Place the pan with the lobster in a hot oven to finish cooking.
2 oz	60 mL	Melted butter	11.	Remove the lobster from the heat and serve immediately with a small cup of melted butter and with lemon garnish.
		Lemon wedges		

Variation

134A. Broiled Rock Lobster Tail: Rock lobster is usually very dry if broiled like lobster. A better method is to poach it in salted water (see pp. 363–364) until just cooked. Then split the tails, brush with butter, and run under the broiler for 1–2 minutes.

....

RECIPE 135 **Oysters Casino**

		Portions: 12	**Portion size:** 3 oysters
			(appetizer portion)

U.S.	Metric	Ingredients	Procedure
36	36	Oysters	1. Open oysters as shown in Figure 14.6. Discard top shell.
			2. Place oysters on a sheet pan or in a shallow bake pan (see note).
½ lb	225 g	Butter	3. Place the butter in the bowl of a mixer and beat with the paddle attachment until soft and smooth.
2 oz	60 g	Green pepper, chopped fine	
1 oz	30 g	Pimiento, chopped fine	4. Add the green pepper, shallots, parsley, and lemon juice. Mix until evenly combined. Season to taste with salt and pepper. (Casino butter can be rolled in parchment, refrigerated or frozen, and sliced to order.)
1 oz	30 g	Shallots, chopped fine	
¼ cup	60 mL	Chopped parsley	
1 oz	30 mL	Lemon juice	
		Salt	
		White pepper	
9 strips	9 strips	Bacon	5. Cook the bacon in the oven or on the griddle until about half cooked. Drain.
			6. Cut each strip into 4 pieces.
			7. Place about 2 tsp (10 mL) of the butter mixture on top of each oyster.
			8. Top each oyster with a piece of bacon.
			9. Run the oysters under the broiler until the bacon is brown and the oysters are hot. Do not overcook.

Note: Broiled or baked oysters and clams are often placed on beds of rock salt to hold them steady.

Variation

135A. ***Clams Casino:*** Prepare as in basic recipe, using cherrystone or littleneck clams.

RECIPE 136   Broiled Shrimp, Scampi Style

| | | **Portions:** 10 | **Portion size:** 4½ oz (125 g) |

U.S.	Metric	Ingredients	Procedure
50	50	Shrimp, size 16–20 per pound	1. Peel, devein, and butterfly the shrimp as shown in Figure 14.11. Leave tails on.
			2. Place shrimp in individual service casserole dishes or in a shallow bake pan, tails up and cut side down. (Shrimp will curl more when cooked, so tails will stand up as shrimp are broiled.)
			3. Keep refrigerated until needed.
6 oz	175 g	Butter	4. Heat butter and oil in a saucepan until the butter is melted.
½ cup	125 mL	Oil, preferably olive oil (see note)	
1 tbsp	15 mL	Garlic, chopped very fine	5. Add the garlic, lemon juice, parsley, salt, and pepper.
1 oz	30 mL	Lemon juice	6. Pour the butter sauce over the shrimp.
2 tbsp	30 mL	Chopped parsley	7. Place under the broiler at medium heat. Broil until the tops are lightly browned. (Don't worry if the tips of the tails burn a little; this is normal.)
		Salt	
		Pepper	
			8. Transfer the shrimp to the oven above the broiler for a few minutes to finish cooking.

Note: All butter may be used, instead of a mixture of butter and oil. Or, if you are using a good quality olive oil, use more oil and less butter or all olive oil.

Serve this dish with rice or with plenty of bread to soak up the flavorful butter.

Variations

The shrimp can be marinated for an hour or two in the oil, chopped garlic, lemon juice, and seasonings. Add the butter at cooking time. Or omit the butter when cooking, and serve small cups of garlic butter on the side.

136A. Shrimp Brochettes: Marinate the shrimp as indicated above. Put the shrimp on skewers and broil, basting several times with the marinade and melted butter.

136B. Broiled Scallops: Place the scallops in individual service casseroles (5–6 oz/150–175 g per portion). Top each portion with 1 tbsp (15 mL) dry bread crumbs. Pour the butter sauce over the scallops and broil as in basic recipe.

136C. Broiled Fish Fillets or Steaks with Garlic Butter: Use fillets or steaks of any lean, white fish. Place fish on sheet pans and prepare according to procedure for Broiled Scallops, using the bread crumbs.

SAUTÉING AND PAN-FRYING

As in meat cookery, the exact distinction between sautéing and pan-frying fish is impossible to draw. For many purposes the two terms are used interchangeably.

A classic method for sautéing fish is called *à la meunière* (mun yair). In this preparation, the product is dredged in flour and sautéed in clarified butter or oil. It is then plated and sprinkled with lemon juice and chopped parsley, and freshly prepared, hot brown butter (beurre noisette) is poured over it. When the hot butter hits the lemon juice, it creates a froth. The fish should then be served at once.

Other sautéed fish preparations call for standard breading procedure or for dredging the fish with a product other than flour, such as cornmeal. Also, a variety of garnishes may be used.

The procedures and variations just described apply to most popular sautéed and pan-fried fish recipes. In general, because most types of fin fish are so delicate, especially if filleted, they do not lend themselves to a great many sautéing variations. On the other hand, firm shellfish like shrimp and scallops are easier to sauté, and there is a greater variety of recipes for them.

Guidelines for Sautéing and Pan-frying Fish and Shellfish

1. Lean fish are especially well suited to sautéing, because the cooking method supplies fat that the fish lack.

   Fat fish may also be sautéed, as long as you take care not to get the fish too greasy.

2. Sautéed fish is usually given a coating of flour, breading, or other starchy product before sautéing. This forms a crust that browns attractively, enhances the flavor, and helps hold the fish together and prevent sticking.

3. Fish may be soaked in milk briefly before dredging in flour. This helps the flour form a better crust.

4. Clarified butter or oil are the preferred fats for sautéing and pan-frying. Whole butter is likely to burn, unless the fish items are very small.

5. Use a minimum of fat. About ⅛ inch (3 mm), or enough to cover the bottom of the pan, is enough.

6. Small items, such as shrimp or scallops, are sautéed over high heat. Larger items, such as whole fish, require lower heat to cook evenly.

7. Very large fish may be browned in fat, then finished in the oven, uncovered.

8. Brown the most attractive side—the presentation side—first. For fillets, this is usually the flesh side or the side against the bone, not the skin side.

9. Handle fish carefully during and after cooking to avoid breaking the fish or the crisp crust.

10. Sauté or fry to order and serve immediately.

Procedure for Cooking Fish à la Meunière

1. Collect all equipment and food supplies.

2. Heat a small amount of clarified butter in a sauté pan.

3. Season the fish and dredge in flour. Shake off excess.

4. Place fish in pan, presentation side down.

5. Sauté the fish, turning once with a spatula, until both sides are brown and the fish is just cooked through.

6. Remove the fish from the pan with a spatula and place on serving plate, presentation side up.

7. Sprinkle fish with lemon juice and chopped parsley.

8. Heat some raw butter in the sauté pan until it turns light brown. Pour it over the fish immediately.

9. Serve at once.

RECIPE 137   **Fillets of Sole Meunière**

| | | | **Portions:** 10 | **Portion size:** 4 oz (125 g) |

U.S.	Metric	Ingredients	Procedure
20	20	Sole fillets, 2 oz (60 g) each Salt White pepper	1. Have all ingredients ready, but do not season and flour the fish until immediately before cooking.
3 oz 6 oz	90 g 175 g	Flour Clarified butter or oil, or a mixture of butter and oil	2. Unless you are cooking to order, use as many sauté pans as necessary to hold all the fillets, or cook them in several batches. Place the sauté pans over medium heat, so that they will be ready as soon as the fish is floured.
			3. Season the fillets with salt and pepper. Place the clarified butter in the hot pans to heat. Dredge the fish in flour and shake off excess. Place the fish in the pans flesh side (presentation side) down.
			4. Sauté until lightly browned. Turn over with a spatula and brown the other side. Be careful not to break the fillets when turning.
			5. Remove the fillets from the pan with a spatula, being careful not to break them. Plate up the fish on hot dinner plates.
1 oz	30 mL	Lemon juice	6. Sprinkle the fish with lemon juice and chopped parsley.
¼ cup	60 mL	Chopped parsley	
5 oz	150 g	Butter	7. Heat the butter in a small saucepan or sauté pan until it turns light brown (beurre noisette).
20	20	Slices of peeled lemon	
			8. Pour the hot butter over the fish.
			9. Quickly place a lemon slice on top of each fillet and serve immediately.

Variations

Other white fish fillets may be cooked by the same procedure.

Placing fish in milk before dredging in flour helps form an attractive, well-browned crust. However, the fish must be drained well before flouring, or the flour coating may be heavy and pasty.

137A.   *Fillets of Fish Doré:* Sauté the fish as in the basic recipe, but serve without the lemon juice, chopped parsley, and beurre noisette. Garnish the plate with lemon and parsley sprig. ("Doré" means "golden.")

137B.   *Trout Meunière:* Prepare whole, drawn trout as in basic recipe. Dip fish in milk before dredging in flour to form a better crust.

137C.   *Fish Sauté Amandine:* Prepare as in basic recipe. Brown sliced almonds in the butter used for garnishing. Omit garnish of lemon slices, and garnish plate with lemon wedges.

RECIPE 137   **Fillets of Sole Meunière** *(Continued)*

··

Variations

137D. Fish Sauté Grenobloise: Prepare as in basic recipe. Garnish the fish with capers and diced, peeled lemon sections, in addition to the chopped parsley, before pouring on the brown butter.

137E. Sautéed Soft Shell Crabs: Prepare as in basic recipe. Serve 2 per portion. Chopped parsley and lemon slices may be omitted.

··

RECIPE 138   **Sautéed Scallops with Tomato, Garlic, and Parsley**

··

			Portions: 10	Portion size: 4 oz (125 g)

U.S.	Metric	Ingredients	Procedure	
2½ lb	1.25 kg	Bay or sea scallops	1.	If you are using sea scallops and they are very large, cut them in halves or quarters. Dry the scallops with paper towels.
2 oz	60 mL	Olive oil		
2 oz	60 mL	Clarified butter	2.	Heat the oil and butter in a large sauté pan until it is very hot.
2 tsp	10 mL	Garlic, chopped fine		
4 oz	125 g	Drained, chopped canned or fresh tomato	3.	Place the scallops in the sauté pan and sauté quickly. Shake the pan often to keep the scallops from sticking.
¼ cup	60 mL	Chopped parsley Salt	4.	When the scallops are about half cooked, add the garlic. Continue to sauté until the scallops are lightly browned.
			5.	Add the tomato and parsley and sauté a few seconds, just enough to heat the tomato.
			6.	Add salt to taste and serve immediately.

Variations

Omitting the tomato makes a slightly different but equally good dish.

138A. Sautéed Shrimp: Use peeled, deveined shrimp. Sauté as in basic recipe.

··

RECIPE 139   **Spicy Shrimp or Scallop Sauté**

Portions: 10			**Portion size:** 4 oz (125 g)

U.S.	Metric	Ingredients	Procedure
1 tsp	5 mL	Paprika	1. Mix together all the spices, herbs, and salt.
¼ tsp	1 mL	Cayenne	
¼ tsp	1 mL	Black pepper	2. If the shrimp or scallops are wet, dry them with paper towels. If you are using sea scallops and they are large, cut them into halves or quarters.
½ tsp	2 mL	White pepper	
¼ tsp	1 mL	Thyme	
¼ tsp	1 mL	Basil	
¼ tsp	1 mL	Oregano	3. Toss the shrimp or scallops with the dry seasonings.
½ tsp	2 mL	Salt	
2½ lb	1.25 kg	Peeled, deveined shrimp, or scallops	4. Sauté the onion and garlic in a little clarified butter until they are tender and only lightly browned. Remove them from the pan and set them aside.
6 oz	175 g	Onion, sliced	
1 clove	1 clove	Garlic, chopped	
		Clarified butter	5. Add a little more butter to the pan and sauté the seafood just until it is cooked.
			6. Return the onion and garlic to the pan and toss to combine. Serve immediately, accompanied by white rice.

Variation

For spicy fish fillets, season them well with the dry seasoning mix in the basic recipe. Then dredge them in flour and sauté as for meunière.

DEEP-FRYING

Deep-frying is perhaps the most popular method of preparing fish in this country. While fried fish may not be the most subtle or refined preparation, it can be of very high quality if the fish is fresh and not overcooked, the frying fat is of good quality, and the item is served without delay after cooking.

Lean fish—either small whole fish or small portions such as fillets or sticks—and shellfish such as shrimp, clams, oysters, and scallops are best for deep-frying.

Fish to be fried is breaded or battered to protect the fish from the frying fat and to protect the frying fat from the fish. Also the breading or batter provides a crisp, flavorful, and attractive coating.

Frozen breaded fish portions are widely used. They should be fried without thawing.

Fried fish is usually served with lemon and/or a cold sauce such as tartar, remoulade, or cocktail sauce on the side.

Frying and breading procedures have been discussed in detail in Chapter 7. There is no need to repeat them here, but you should review those sections if necessary. Also, the batter recipes on page 425 are suitable for fish as well as for vegetables.

RECIPE 140 Fried Breaded Fish Fillets

Portions: 25 **Portion size:** 4 oz (125 g)

U.S.	Metric	Ingredients	Procedure
		Standard Breading Procedure (see note):	1. Set up breading station (see p. 114): Place the flour in one pan, the eggs beaten with milk in a shallow bowl, and the bread crumbs in another pan.
4 oz	125 g	Flour	
4	4	Whole eggs, beaten	
1 cup	250 mL	Milk	
1¼ lb	625 g	Bread crumbs, dry	
25	25	4-oz (125-g) fillets of lean, white fish, such as Haddock Perch Pike Bass Sole Flounder Salt White pepper	2. Season the fish lightly with salt and white pepper. 3. Bread the fish fillets by passing them through the flour, egg wash, and crumbs. Press the crumbs on firmly. (See p. 114 for detailed breading instructions.) 4. Fry the fillets in deep fat heated to 350°F (175°C) until golden brown.
25	25	Parsley sprigs	5. Drain and serve immediately. Garnish each portion with a parsley sprig and a lemon wedge. Serve with 1 oz (25 mL) Tartar Sauce.
25	25	Lemon wedges	
25 oz	750 mL	Tartar Sauce	

Note: Quantities given for breading materials are only guidelines. You may need more or less, depending on the shapes of the fish pieces, the care used in breading, and other factors. In any case, you will need enough so that even the last piece to be breaded can be coated easily and completely.

Variations

Breaded fish fillets may also be pan-fried in butter or oil (see previous section).

140A. ***Fried Breaded Scallops:*** Prepare as in basic recipe. Use wire baskets in the breading station to simplify the procedure, as explained on page 115.

140B. ***Fried Breaded Shrimp:*** Peel, devein, and butterfly shrimp as shown in Figure 14.11*f.* Leave tails on. Bread and fry as in basic recipe.

140C. ***Fried Oysters or Clams:*** Prepare like scallops.

POACHING AND SIMMERING IN COURT BOUILLON

Poaching is cooking in a liquid at very low heat. Fillets and other small portions are sometimes cooked in a small amount of fish fumet and/or wine and served with a sauce made of the poaching liquid. Whole fish and thick steaks may be cooked in a seasoned liquid called a court bouillon. The liquid is not used to make a sauce, and the fish may be served hot or cold. Because these are two distinct procedures, we discuss them separately.

Court bouillon may be defined as water containing seasonings, herbs, and usually an acid, used for cooking fish. The name means "short broth" in French, so called because it is made quickly, unlike stocks.

In quantity food service, this method is perhaps used most often for cooking large whole fish that are to be decorated and served cold on a buffet. Slightly higher, simmering temperatures are used for cooking crustaceans, such as lobster, crab, and shrimp.

The famous preparation called *truit au bleu* (blue trout) is made by poaching trout that are alive up until cooking time. The fish must be alive and must not be washed in order for the fish to turn blue. Live fish have a protective slippery coating on the skin, and the blue color results from the vinegar in the court bouillon reacting with this coating.

Guidelines for Poaching Fish in Court Bouillon

1. Both fat and lean fish may be cooked by this method.

2. Seasoned liquid for cooking fish may be as simple as salted water. More often, however, it contains flavoring ingredients such as spices, herbs, and mirepoix, and acid ingredients such as lemon juice, vinegar, and white wine.

3. Cook flavoring ingredients in court bouillon to extract flavors before cooking fish.

4. Cooking temperature is 160°F to 180°F (70°C to 80°C), well below boiling. A temperature of 160°F is sufficient to cook fish, and it reduces the likelihood of overcooking. Higher temperatures are harmful to the delicate texture and flavor of fish.

    Lobsters, crabs, and shrimp may be cooked at a *simmer*, because their textures are not so fragile. The terms "boiled lobster" and "boiled fish" are often used but inaccurate. They should never be boiled.

5. Start shellfish, small fish, and portion cuts in hot liquid to preserve flavors. Start large fish in cold liquid to cook more evenly and to avoid

sudden contractions that would split the skin and spoil the appearance.

6. Special fish poachers with racks are best for poaching. They allow the fish to be removed from the liquid without damage. If these utensils are not available, wrap fish in cheesecloth so it can be lifted out easily, or tie the fish loosely to a board.

7. Serve poached fish with an appropriate sauce, such as Hollandaise for hot fish and a mayonnaise-base sauce for cold fish. Mild vinaigrettes go well with both hot and cold poached fish.

Procedure for Poaching Fish in Court Bouillon

1. Collect all equipment and food supplies.

2. Prepare court bouillon.

3. Place the fish in a suitable pan with liquid to cover.
    Start small fish and portions in simmering liquid.
    Start shellfish in boiling liquid.
    Start large fish in cold liquid.

4. Cook fish at below the simmer, 160°F to 180°F (70°C to 80°C). Lobsters, crabs, and shrimp may be cooked at a gentle simmer.

5. If fish is to be served hot, remove from liquid and serve immediately.

6. If fish is to be served cold, stop the cooking by adding ice to the liquid, and cool the fish in the court bouillon to retain moisture.

RECIPE 141   **Court Bouillon for Fish**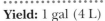

Yield: 1 gal (4 L)

U.S.	Metric	Ingredients	Procedure
1 gal	4 L	Water	1. Combine all ingredients in a stock pot or sauce pot and bring to a boil.
8 oz	250 mL	White vinegar, wine vinegar, *or* lemon juice	
8 oz	250 g	Onions, sliced	2. Reduce heat and simmer 30 minutes.
4 oz	125 g	Celery, sliced	3. Strain and cool.
4 oz	125 g	Carrots, sliced	
2 oz	60 g	Salt	
½ tsp	2 mL	Peppercorns, crushed	
1	1	Bay leaf	
¼ tsp	1 mL	Thyme	
10–12	10–12	Parsley stems	

RECIPE 142   **Poached Whole Fish**

....

			Portions: 10		**Portion size:** 4 oz (125 g)

U.S.	Metric	Ingredients	Procedure
5 lb	2.5 kg	Drawn fish *or*	1. Place the clean dressed or drawn fish on the lightly oiled rack of a fish poacher. Or, if a rack is unavailable, wrap the fish in cheesecloth or tie it loosely on a board so that it can be lifted out when cooked.
4 lb	2 kg	Dressed fish (1 large or 2 or more smaller fish. See note.)	
3 qt or as needed	3 L	Court Bouillon, cold	2. Place the fish in the poaching pan and pour in enough cold court bouillon to cover the fish completely.
			3. Set the pan over moderately low heat and slowly bring barely to a simmer.
			4. Reduce heat to very low and cook the fish at below the simmering point until done. The fish will feel firm, not mushy, at its thickest part, and the backbone, as seen inside the cavity, will no longer be pink. Total cooking time will vary from 5 to 20 minutes, depending on the size of the fish and exact cooking temperature. In general, plan on about 8–10 minutes for every inch of thickness at the thickest point.
		Suggested sauces: Hollandaise Mousseline Beurre noisette Herb vinaigrette	5. For serving hot: Remove fish from liquid, drain well, and serve immediately with choice of sauce. For serving cold: Add ice to the court bouillon to stop the cooking. Cool the fish rapidly in the liquid and refrigerate. Drain when chilled.

Note: For attractive presentations, such as for buffet work, fish is often poached with the head on. Suggested fish for poaching whole:

Haddock	Red snapper	Striped bass
Cod	Salmon	Trout

Variations

*142A. **Poached Fish Steaks:*** Prepare as in basic recipe, except start with boiling court bouillon. Drain the cooked fish, remove skin and center bone, and serve immediately, with selected sauce. Suggested fish steaks: cod, haddock, halibut, turbot, salmon.

*142B. **"Boiled" Shellfish*** (lobster, crab, shrimp): Prepare as for fish steaks, using *salted water, court bouillon,* or *acidulated water* (4 oz lemon juice and ½ oz salt per quart of water, or 125 mL lemon juice and 15 g salt per liter). Water may simmer when cooking shellfish.

....

POACHING IN FUMET AND WINE

Fish poached in white wine is rightly considered one of the stars of classical cuisine. If well prepared, it can be one of the most exquisite dishes on the menu.

This method of preparation is best for lean, delicate white fish, such as sole, halibut, turbot, haddock, cod, pike, and perch. It is also used for salmon and trout. The fish is always served with a sauce made from the poaching liquid.

The procedure and recipe given here are for fillets of sole au vin blanc (in white wine). This is the basic preparation, and most other poached fish recipes are variations on it. Many of the variations involve only different garnishes.

Because of the delicacy of flavors, this preparation requires good quality fish and well made stock, and the wine should have a good flavor. A very cheap, bad tasting wine will spoil the dish.

Procedure for Poaching Fish in Fumet and Wine

1. Collect all equipment and food supplies. Select a pan just large enough to hold the fish portions in a single layer. This will enable you to use a minimum amount of poaching liquid. Also, use a pan with low, sloping sides. This makes it easier to remove the fragile cooked fish from the pan.

2. Butter the bottom of the pan and sprinkle with chopped shallots.

3. Arrange the fish portions in the pan in a single layer. Season them lightly.

4. Add enough fish fumet and white wine to almost cover the fish. Use as little liquid as necessary, so the flavor will be more concentrated and less reduction will be required later.

5. Cover the fish with a piece of buttered parchment or other paper and cover the pan with a lid. The paper holds in the steam to cook the top of the fish. It is sometimes omitted if the pan has a tight lid, but it does help to cook more evenly.

6. Bring the liquid just to a simmer and finish poaching in the oven at moderate heat. Thin fillets will cook in just a few minutes. Fish may be poached on top of the range, but the oven provides more even, gentle heat from both top and bottom.

7. Drain the liquid into a wide pan and keep the fish warm. After a few minutes of standing, more liquid will drain from the fish. Add this to the rest.

8. Reduce the poaching liquid over high heat to about one-fourth its volume.

9. Add fish velouté and heavy cream and bring to a boil. Adjust seasoning with salt, white pepper, and lemon juice.

10. Strain the sauce.

11. Arrange the fish on plates for service, coat with the sauce, and serve immediately.

Variations in Sauce Production

Using a preprepared velouté, as in the standard method just given, makes the sauce production very quick, and the procedure can easily be used for cooking to order.

An alternative method may be used if no velouté is available or if a large quantity of fish is being poached for banquet service:

1. Use a larger quantity of fumet and wine for cooking the fish, and reduce it only by about half, depending on the amount of sauce needed.

2. Thicken the liquid with roux or beurre manié and simmer until no raw starch taste remains.

3. Finish the preparation as in the basic method.

Another method, which has recently become popular, uses no starch thickener. Instead, the reduced poaching liquid is lightly bound with heavy cream or raw butter:

- To bind the sauce with cream, add about 2 oz (60 mL) or more heavy cream per portion to the reduced cooking liquid and continue to reduce until the sauce is lightly thickened.

- To bind with butter, whip raw butter into the reduced cooking liquid as for *monter au beurre* (p. 135). Use about ½ oz (15 g) butter or more per portion.

A further variation is known as *à la nage*, which means "swimming." To serve poached seafood à la nage, reduce the cooking liquid only slightly; season and strain it carefully. If desired, enrich the liquid with a very small quantity of butter or leave it unenriched. Serve the seafood with the liquid in a soup plate or other plate deep enough to hold the juices.

Glazing

Poached fish is sometimes glazed before serving. This is done as follows:

1. According to the particular recipe, combine the finished sauce with egg yolk, Hollandaise Sauce, and/or lightly whipped cream. Or combine the reduction of the cooking liquid with Mornay Sauce instead of Fish Velouté.

2. Coat the fish with the sauce and run the plate or platter under the salamander or broiler for a few seconds, until golden brown.

Note: It's a good idea to test a little of the sauce under the salamander before coating the fish, to make sure it will brown.

RECIPE 143   **Sole Vin Blanc (Poached Fillets of Sole in White Wine Sauce)**

Portions: 25		**Portion size:** 4 oz (125 g) fish	
		2 oz (60 mL) sauce	

U.S.	Metric	Ingredients	Procedure
6¼ lb	3 kg	Sole fillets: 50 fillets, 2 oz (60 g) each	1. Fold the fillets in half or roll them up, starting with the large end (see Figure 15.1). Be sure that the skin side of the fillet is on the inside of the fold or the roll (called *paupiette*).
3 oz	90 g	Butter	
3 oz	90 g	Shallots, fine dice	
10 oz	300 mL	White wine	2. Butter the inside of shallow hotel pans or bake pans. Sprinkle with the shallots. Lay the fillets on top of the shallots in a single layer.
2½ cups or as needed	600 mL	Fish stock	
			3. Pour the wine into the pan and add enough stock to almost cover the fish.
			4. Butter a piece of parchment or waxed paper cut the same size as the pan. Cover the fish closely with it, buttered side down. Cover the pan.
			5. Set the pan on the range and bring just barely to a simmer. DO NOT BOIL.
			6. Place the pan in a hot oven (400°F/ 200°C) and cook the fish until it is just barely done, about 5 minutes.
			7. Drain the poaching liquid into a broad sauté pan. Keep the fish covered in a warm, not hot, place. If more liquid collects under the fish as it stands, add this to the rest.
3½ pt	1.75 L	Fish Velouté	8. Reduce the poaching liquid over high heat to about one-fourth its volume.
12 oz	375 mL	Heavy cream	
		Lemon juice	9. Add the velouté and heavy cream. Bring to a boil. Reduce to about 2½ pt (1.25 L).
		Salt	
		White pepper	10. Season the sauce to taste with salt, white pepper, and a few drops of lemon juice. Strain.
			11. To serve, place 2 fillets on a dinner plate and coat with 2 oz (60 mL) sauce.

(Continues)

RECIPE 143 **Sole Vin Blanc** *(Continued)*

Variations

Any lean white fish may be poached using this recipe or any of the variations below, including:

Halibut	Cod	Perch
Turbot	Pike	Scallops
Haddock		

143A. ***À la Carte Service, Fast Method:*** Poach fish as in basic recipe. Plate the fish as soon as it is cooked. Coat it with a *preprepared White Wine Sauce.* The poaching liquid may be reused throughout the service period, then used to make velouté for the next day's sauce. Other sauces based on Fish Velouté or Béchamel may be used instead of White Wine Sauce:

Bercy	Normandy	Nantua
Herb	Mushroom	Mornay

143B. ***Glazed Poached Fish:*** Prepare as in basic recipe. Immediately before serving, fold 1 pt (500 mL) Hollandaise and 8 oz (250 mL) heavy cream, whipped, into the sauce. Coat the fish and brown it quickly under the salamander.

143C. ***Poached Fish Bonne Femme:*** Add 1½ lb (700 g) sliced mushrooms to the shallots in the poaching pan. Poach as in basic recipe. Do not strain the sauce.

143D. ***Poached Fish Duglére:*** Add 1½ lb (700 g) tomato concassée (pp. 396–397) and 4 tbsp (60 mL) chopped parsley to the pan when poaching the fish. Poach as in basic recipe. Omit heavy cream, but stir 5 oz (150 g) raw butter into the sauce before serving. Do not strain.

143E. ***Poached Fish Mornay:*** Strain the reduced poaching liquid (after step 8) and add a little of it to a thick Mornay Sauce for glazing (p. 139), just enough to thin it to the desired consistency. Coat the fish with the sauce and brown under the salamander or broiler.

Note: Scallops are often prepared à la Mornay and served in scallop shells with a Duchesse Potato border. The dish is called *Coquille St. Jacques Mornay. (St. Jacques* is the French term for scallop, and *coquille* means "shell.")

143F. ***Poached Fish Florentine:*** Prepare like Poached Fish Mornay, but place the cooked fish on beds of cooked, buttered spinach before coating with sauce.

143G. ***Seafood à la Nage:*** Double the quantity of fish stock. Omit the velouté and heavy cream. After poaching, reduce the cooking liquid only slightly. Season carefully and strain. Serve the seafood with the broth.

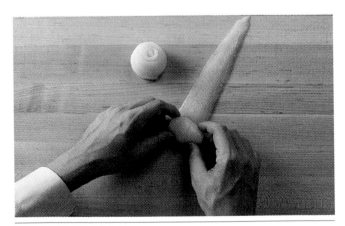

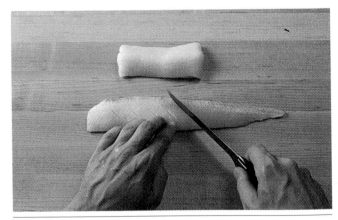

FIGURE 15.1 **Rolling and folding sole fillets.**
(a) To make "paupiettes" or rolled fillets of sole, lay fillets on work surface with white, flesh side down (skin side up). Starting at the large end, roll up tightly. As the fish cooks, the connective tissues on the skin side shrink and keep the roll tight. If you roll the fillet skin side out, it unrolls as it cooks.

(b) If the fillets are to be poached flat or folded, first make a series of very shallow cuts in the skin side as shown. This helps keep the tissues from shrinking and deforming the fillet. Fold so that flesh side is out (skin side on the inside).

MIXED COOKING TECHNIQUES

The Basic Technique

The recipes included in this section are so varied that it would be confusing to give a procedure that would cover all of them. They are all grouped together here because they have two basic things in common:

1. The item cooks in its own juices and, usually, a small amount of added liquid.

2. The item is served with its flavorful cooking liquid.

In some cases, enough liquid is added to barely cover, and the item simmers. In other cases, little liquid is added and the item cooks in the steam trapped by the pot lid.

The French term *étuver* (ay too vay) is used for this kind of procedure. The word is usually translated as "stew," but this may be misleading. More precisely, it means "to cook or steam in its own juices" or "to sweat."

Variations

Note the following three variations that are represented by the recipes in this section.

1. The product is cooked for a few minutes in fat over low heat, along with mirepoix or onion, to begin extracting juices. A little liquid is then added, the pot is covered, and the item is cooked. Example: Fisherman's Stew.

2. The product is sautéed over high heat. Then other ingredients and liquids are added and the item is cooked, covered, over low heat. Example: Lobster Americaine.

3. The product is simply placed in a pot with liquids and flavoring ingredients. The pot is covered, and the item is steamed or simmered. Example: Mussels Marinière.

Cooking en Papillote

An unusual version of variation 3 just cited is called *cooking en papillote* (on poppy-yote), or in paper. The fish item, plus flavoring ingredients and sauce, is tightly enclosed in a piece of parchment so that steam cannot escape. When it is heated, the item steams in its own moisture. All the juices, flavors, and aromas are held inside the paper, which is not opened until it is placed before the customer.

Sometimes a starch-thickened sauce is used in cooking fish en papillote. In this case the fish is usually precooked (poached) so that it will not exude juices that will dilute and spoil the sauce. The problem with this method is that the fish is often overcooked by the time it reaches the customer.

Compartment Steaming

Several precautions should be observed if you cook fish and shellfish in a compartment steamer.

1. Watch the cooking time very carefully. Fish cooks quickly, especially in the high heat of a steamer, and is easily overcooked.

2. Avoid pressure steaming of fish and shellfish, if possible. The high temperatures toughen fish protein very quickly. Such items as lobster tails can become very rubbery.

3. Use solid pans to retain juices, and use the juices for sauces and soups.

RECIPE 144   Lobster à l'Americaine

··

Portions: 2   **Portion size:** ½ lobster

U.S.	Metric	Ingredients	Procedure
1	1	Live lobster, about 1½ lb (700 g)	1. Cut up the lobster as shown in Figure 14.9.
1 oz	30 g	Butter, softened	2. Remove the tomalley (liver) and coral (if any). Mash them in a small bowl with the soft butter.
2 oz	60 mL	Oil	3. Heat the oil in a sauté pan and add the lobster pieces. Sauté over high heat until the shells turn red.
1 tbsp	15 mL	Shallot, chopped fine	
½ tsp	2 mL	Garlic, chopped fine	
2 oz	60 mL	Brandy	4. Drain off the oil by tilting the pan and holding the lobster in with the pan lid.
6 oz	200 mL	White wine	
4 oz	125 mL	Fish stock	5. Add the shallot and garlic to the pan. Sauté for a few seconds.
4 oz	125 g	Tomato concassée *or*	
2 oz	60 g	Tomato purée	6. Remove from the heat (to avoid burning yourself if the brandy flares up) and add the brandy. Return to the heat and add the wine, fish stock, tomato, chopped parsley, tarragon, and cayenne.
1 tbsp	15 mL	Chopped parsley	
¼ tsp	1 mL	Tarragon	
pinch	pinch	Cayenne	

7. Cover the pan and simmer until the lobster is cooked, about 10–15 minutes.

8. Remove the lobster from the cooking liquid and place it on a serving platter or in broad soup plates for service. The meat may be left in the shell or removed from the shell, as desired.

9. Reduce the cooking liquid over high heat to about 6 oz (175 mL).

10. Remove from the heat and stir in the mixture of butter, tomalley, and coral from step 2. Heat the sauce gently for a minute, but do not boil or it will curdle. Adjust the seasoning.

11. Strain the sauce and pour it over the lobster. Serve immediately.

Variations

144A. Lobster Newburg: (Note: See p. 376 for Seafood Newburg using cooked shellfish.) Prepare through step 4. Omit remaining ingredients. Instead, add 1 tbsp (15 mL) brandy, 3 tbsp (45 mL) sherry or Marsala or Madeira wine, and 3 oz (100 mL) fish stock. Cover and simmer as in basic recipe. Remove lobster meat from shells and discard shells. Reduce cooking liquid by half and add 1 cup (250 mL) heavy cream *or* light Cream Sauce. Reduce the sauce slightly and finish by adding the mixture of butter, tomalley, and coral (step 10 of basic recipe). If desired, flavor with more sherry. Pour sauce over the lobster meat.

144B. Shrimp: May be cooked using the main recipe or the variation. They should be shelled before combining with the finished sauce.

··

RECIPE 145   **Moules Mariniére (Steamed Mussels)**

....

Portions: 10

U.S.	Metric	Ingredients	Procedure
7 lb	3.2 kg	Mussels, in shells	1. Scrub the mussels well with a stiff brush and remove the beards. Clean them well by soaking them according to the procedure given in Chapter 14.
3 oz	90 g	Shallots or onions, chopped fine	
6	6	Parsley stems	
¼ tsp	1 mL	Pepper	2. Place the mussels in a stock pot or large sauce pot. Add the onions or shallots, parsley stems, pepper, and wine.
1 cup	250 mL	White wine	
			3. Cover the pot and set it over moderately high heat. Cook until the mussels open, about 5 minutes.
¼ cup	60 mL	Chopped parsley	4. Drain the mussels and strain the liquid through cheesecloth into a broad saucepan. Bring to a boil.
3 oz	90 g	Butter	
		Salt	
		Lemon juice	5. Add the parsley and butter. Swirl the liquid in the pan until the butter is melted. Season to taste with salt and a few drops of lemon juice.
			6. For service, remove the top shells of the mussels (or leave them on, if desired). Place the mussels in broad soup plates and pour the sauce over them.

Variations

145A. Steamed Mussels (without wine): Substitute water for the wine and add 2 oz (60 mL) lemon juice. Increase the onion or shallot to 6 oz (175 g) and add 3 oz (90 g) sliced celery.

145B. Mussels in Cream: Prepare the basic recipe. Reduce the cooking liquid by half and add 1 cup (250 mL) heavy cream *or* a liaison of 2 egg yolks and 1 cup (250 mL) heavy cream.

....

RECIPE 146 **Mackerel en Papillote**

....

		Portions: 1	**Portion size:** 4 oz (125 g)

U.S.	Metric	Ingredients	Procedure
1	1	Mackerel fillet, 4 oz (125 g) (see note)	1. Cut out a piece of parchment in a heart shape, as shown in Figure 15.2. (Foil may be used instead of parchment.) The piece must be big enough to hold the fish and still have room for crimping the edges. Oil the parchment and place on the work bench oiled side down. (If using foil, place it oiled side up.)
2 tsp	10 mL	Melted butter	
		Salt	
		White pepper	
2 tsp	10 mL	Chopped parsley	2. Place the fillet on one side of the heart. Brush with melted butter and sprinkle with salt, pepper, parsley, marjoram, and chopped shallot. Lay the lemon slices on top.
pinch	pinch	Marjoram	
1 tsp	5 mL	Shallots, chopped very fine	
2	2	Thin lemon slices	
			3. Fold and crimp the parchment as shown in the illustration, to enclose the fish tightly.
			4. Place the folded package in a sauté pan or, if several orders are being done at once, on a sheet pan. Set on the range to start the cooking.
			5. As soon as the paper begins to puff, place the pan in a hot oven (450°F/ 230°C). Bake until the parchment is puffed and browned, about 5–8 minutes. (If the paper doesn't brown, you may run it under the broiler for a second.)
			6. Serve immediately. The parchment should be cut open in front of the customer.

Note: Pompano or bluefish may be used.

Variation

Instead of the parsley, shallots, and lemon slices, top fillets with a thin layer of duxelles (p. 415).

....

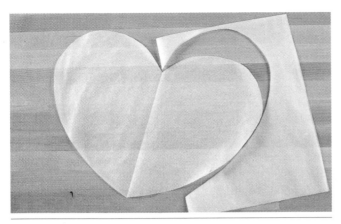

FIGURE 15.2 **Preparing foods en papillote.**
(a) **Cut out a heart-shaped piece of parchment. This is done by folding a sheet of parchment in half and cutting half a heart from the folded side. Oil or butter the parchment and place on the work surface oiled side down.**

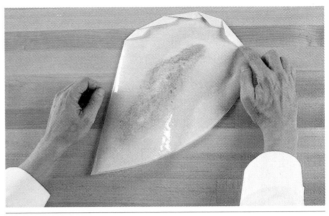

(d) **Continue crimping around the edge. Each crimp holds the previous one in place.**

(b) **Place the fish fillet or other item plus any sauce, topping, or seasoning, on one side of the heart.**

(e) **When you reach the bottom of the heart, fold the point under to hold it in place. The papillote is now ready for cooking.**

(c) **Fold over the other half of the heart. Starting at the top of the fold, make a small crimp in the edges as shown.**

RECIPE 147 **Fisherman's Stew**

Portions: 10   **Portion size:** (see step 9)

U.S.	Metric	Ingredients	Procedure
2 lb	900 g	Fish steaks or fillets (see note for suggested fish)	1. Cut the fish into 3-oz (90-g) serving pieces.
10	10	Clams, in shell	2. Scrub the clams and mussels well.
20	20	Mussels, in shell (or 10 more clams)	3. Cut the lobster tails in half lengthwise with a heavy chef's knife. Remove the intestinal vein.
5	5	Lobster tails, small (or use 10 large shrimp)	
4 oz	125 mL	Olive oil	4. Heat the oil in a heavy sauce pot or large straight-sided sauté pan.
8 oz	250 g	Onions, sliced	
8 oz	250 g	Leeks, julienne	5. Add the onions, leeks, garlic, and fennel. Sweat them in the oil for a few minutes.
2 tsp	10 mL	Garlic, chopped	
¼ tsp	1 mL	Fennel seed	
12 oz	350 g	Tomato concassée *or* drained, chopped canned tomato	6. Add the pieces of fish and the lobster tails (or shrimp). Cover and cook over low heat for a few minutes to begin extracting juices from the fish.
2 qt	2 L	Fish stock	7. Remove the cover and add the clams and mussels.
4 oz	100 mL	White wine (optional but recommended)	
2	2	Bay leaves	8. Add the tomato, fish stock, wine, bay leaves, parsley, thyme, salt, and pepper. Cover and bring to a boil. Reduce heat, and simmer about 15 minutes, until the clams and mussels are open.
2 tbsp	30 mL	Chopped parsley	
¼ tsp	1 mL	Thyme	
2 tsp	10 mL	Salt	
¼ tsp	1 mL	Pepper	
		French bread slices, dry or toasted	9. To serve, place 2 or 3 thin slices of French bread in the bottoms of soup plates. For each portion, place a piece of fish, 1 clam, 2 mussels, and half of 1 lobster tail in each plate. Ladle 8 oz (250 mL) broth over the fish.

Note: Any firm fish may be used, such as halibut, cod, haddock, sea bass or striped bass, red snapper, or mackerel. Avoid delicate fish like flounder or sole, which break up easily during cooking.

If desired, reduce or eliminate shellfish from the recipe and increase the quantity of fish.

RECIPES USING COOKED FISH

In addition to the following recipes, see also

Salmon or Tuna Croquettes, page 321.

Dilled Shrimp Salad and variations, page 503.

Shrimp or Crab in Avocado, page 509.

RECIPE 148 Seafood Casserole au Gratin

		Portions: 25	Portion size: 6 oz (175 g)
U.S.	*Metric*	*Ingredients*	*Procedure*
3¾ lb	1.7 kg	Cooked, flaked cod or other firm, white fish	1. Pick over the fish and shellfish to make sure it contains no bones or pieces of shell.
2½ lb	1.1 kg	Cooked crabmeat, shrimp, scallops, or lobster meat, or a mixture of any of these	2. Heat the butter in a wide saucepan or straight-sided sauté pan. Add the fish and shellfish. Sauté lightly over moderate heat until the fish is heated through and coated with butter.
4 oz	125 g	Butter	3. Add the Mornay Sauce and bring just to a simmer. Taste and adjust seasonings.
2 qt	2 L	Mornay Sauce, hot	
4 oz	125 g	Parmesan cheese	4. Ladle 6-oz (175-g) portions into individual service casseroles. Sprinkle with parmesan cheese.
			5. Heat under the broiler at low heat until the tops are lightly browned.

Variations

Other combinations of seafood may be used. If desired, use all fish or all shellfish.

Other sauces may be used instead of Mornay, including

Cream Sauce
Cheddar Cheese Sauce
Nantua Sauce
White Wine Sauce
Mushroom Sauce (made from Fish Velouté)

148A. *Salmon or Tuna Casserole:* Use drained, canned salmon or tuna, and use Cream Sauce, Cheddar Cheese Sauce, or Mushroom Sauce (made with Fish Velouté) instead of Mornay Sauce. Combine the parmesan cheese with an equal quantity of buttered bread crumbs before topping. If desired, prepare in a bake pan instead of individual casseroles.

RECIPE 149 Seafood Newburg

Portions: 25			**Portion size:** 7 oz (200 g)	

U.S.	Metric	Ingredients	Procedure	
2½ lb	1.2 kg	Cooked sea scallops	1.	If the sea scallops are large, cut them in half or quarters.
2½ lb	1.2 kg	Cooked crabmeat	2.	Pick over the crabmeat to make sure there are no pieces of shell. If there are large pieces of meat, cut them into ½-in. (1-cm) dice.
1¼ lb	600 g	Cooked, peeled shrimp		
4 oz	125 g	Butter		
2½ tsp	12 mL	Paprika		
8 oz	250 mL	Sherry	3.	Cut the shrimp in half lengthwise.
2½ qt	2.5 L	Cream Sauce, hot	4.	Heat the butter in a large saucepan or sauté pan. Add the paprika and the seafood. Sauté over moderate heat until heated through and coated lightly with butter.
		Salt		
		White pepper		
			5.	Add sherry and simmer for a minute.
			6.	Add the Cream Sauce and bring to a simmer. Season to taste with salt and white pepper.
			7.	Serve with rice or in patty shells.

Variations

Different proportions of seafood may be used. Lobster meat may also be included.

149A. Seafood Curry: Omit paprika and sherry. Substitute Curry Sauce (made with Fish Velouté) for the Cream Sauce. Garnish with toasted, sliced almonds, if desired.

RECIPE 150 **Cod Cakes**

			Portions: 25	**Portion size:** 2 cakes, 2½ oz (75 g) each

U.S.	Metric	Ingredients	Procedure
4 lb	1.8 kg	Cooked cod	1. Flake the fish until it is well shredded.
4 lb	1.8 kg	Potato purée (p. 434)	2. Combine with the potato, egg, and egg yolk. Mix well.
3	3	Whole eggs	
2	2	Egg yolks	3. Season to taste with salt, pepper, and a little ground ginger.
		Salt	
		White pepper	
pinch	pinch	Ginger	4. Scale the mixture into 2½-oz (75-g) portions. Shape into round, slightly flattened cakes.
		Standard Breading Procedure:	
		Flour	5. Pass the cakes through Standard Breading Procedure.
		Egg wash	
		Bread crumbs	6. Deep-fry at 350°F (175°C) until golden brown.
		Tomato Sauce *or* Tartar Sauce	7. Serve 2 cakes per portion. Accompany with Tomato Sauce or Tartar Sauce.

Variations

150A. *Salmon or Tuna Cakes:* Prepare as in basic recipe, using well-drained canned salmon or tuna.

If you have Duchesse Potato mixture on hand, simply combine equal parts fish and duchesse mixture. No additional eggs are needed, since the potatoes already contain eggs.

TERMS FOR REVIEW

meunière	au bleu	étuver
court bouillon	à la nage	en papillote

QUESTIONS FOR DISCUSSION

1. What major precaution must be taken when baking or broiling lean fish?

2. Describe the procedure for cooking fish à la meunière.

3. Which side of a fish fillet is the "presentation side"?

4. What techniques can you use for lifting whole poached fish out of court bouillon without breaking it or damaging its appearance?

5. What temperatures are best for poaching fish?

6. What is one advantage of using the oven to poach fish fillets?

7. Describe two methods for making a finished sauce out of the cooking liquid (fumet and wine) used for poaching fish fillets.

Fettuccine with vegetables, page 463

PART FOUR

VEGETABLES AND GRAINS

Vegetables, potatoes, pastas, and grains add more than nutritional value to meals. Properly and imaginatively prepared, they contribute flavor, texture, and eye appeal. The foods in this part are assuming ever greater prominence on modern menus.

Understanding Vegetables

Cooking Vegetables

Potatoes and Other Starches

CHAPTER 16

UNDERSTANDING VEGETABLES

Vegetables have long been
abused and neglected, relegated to the minor roles of unimportant side dishes,
to be taken or left, or not even noticed on the table.

Today, however, the lowly vegetables are beginning to
be appreciated, not only for their nutritional importance, but for the variety,
flavor, eye appeal, and even elegance and sophistication that they bring to the menu.
Modern cooks owe it to themselves and their customers to treat vegetables
with understanding, respect, and imagination.

Because they are so perishable, vegetables require extra care
from receiving to service. *Freshness* is their most appealing and attractive quality, and
one must be especially careful to preserve it. The goals of proper vegetable cookery
are to preserve and enhance their fresh flavor, texture, and color, to prepare
and serve vegetables that are not just accepted but sought after.

After reading this chapter, you should be able to

1. Control texture, flavor, color, and nutritional changes when cooking vegetables.
2. Prepare and serve vegetables cooked to their proper doneness.
3. Judge quality in cooked vegetables, based on color, appearance, texture, flavor, seasonings, and appropriateness of combination with sauces or other vegetables.
4. Perform pre-preparation for fresh vegetables.
5. Calculate yields based on trimming losses.
6. Check quality of frozen, canned, and dried vegetables.
7. Prepare vegetables for service by the batch cooking method and the blanch and chill method.
8. Store fresh and processed vegetables correctly.

CONTROLLING QUALITY CHANGES DURING COOKING

As a cook, you have a choice of many different kinds of vegetables and many different cooking methods. Not surprisingly then, you are also faced with the necessity of learning many different rules for cooking vegetables.

Many guides to vegetable cookery simply present you with a long list of rules to memorize. You should be able to understand the principles more easily, however, if you first learn how vegetables change as they are cooked and how to control those changes. In other words, we suggest that you not just memorize what to do, but understand why you do it.

Cooking affects vegetables in four ways. It changes the following:

1. Texture.
2. Flavor.
3. Color.
4. Nutrients.

How much these four characteristics change determines if your final product is attractive and delicious to the customer or if it will end up in the garbage. You can control these changes if you understand how they happen.

Unfortunately, there is still some legitimate controversy among chefs about proper vegetable cooking techniques. Modern technology has not yet solved all the problems that experienced chefs tackle successfully every day in the kitchen.

················

CONTROLLING TEXTURE CHANGES

Changing the texture is one of the main purposes of cooking vegetables.

Fiber

The fiber structure of vegetables (including cellulose and pectins) gives them shape and firmness. Cooking softens some of these components.

The *amount of fiber* varies

1. In different vegetables. Spinach and tomatoes have less than carrots and turnips, for example.

2. In different examples of the same vegetables. Old, tough carrots have more fiber than young, fresh carrots.

3. In the same vegetable. The tender tips of asparagus and broccoli have less fiber than their tougher stalks.

Fiber is made *firmer* by

1. *Acids.* Lemon juice, vinegar, and tomato products, when added to cooking vegetables, extend the cooking time.

2. *Sugars.* Sugar strengthens cell structure. You will use this principle primarily in fruit cookery. For firm poached apples or pears, for example, cook in a heavy syrup. For applesauce, cook apples until soft before sweetening.

Fiber is *softened* by

1. *Heat.* In general, longer cooking means softer vegetables.

2. *Alkalis.* *Do not add baking soda* to green vegetables. Not only does it destroy vitamins, but it makes the vegetables unpleasantly mushy.

Starch

Starch is another vegetable component that affects texture.

1. *Dry starchy foods* like dried legumes (beans, peas, lentils), rice, and macaroni products must be cooked in sufficient water so that the starch granules can absorb moisture and soften. Dried beans are usually soaked before cooking to replace lost moisture.

2. *Moist starchy vegetables* like potatoes and sweet potatoes have enough moisture of their own, but they must still be cooked until the starch granules soften.

Doneness

A vegetable is said to be done when it has reached the desired degree of tenderness. This stage varies from vegetable to vegetable. Some, such as winter squash, eggplant, and braised celery, are considered properly cooked when they are quite soft.

Most vegetables, however, are best cooked very briefly, until they are crisp-tender or *al dente* (firm to the bite). At this stage of tenderness they not only have the most pleasing texture, but they retain maximum flavor, color, and nutrients.

Guidelines for Achieving Proper Doneness in Vegetables

1. Don't overcook.

2. Cook as close to service as possible. Holding vegetables in a steam table continues to cook them.

3. If vegetables must be cooked in advance, slightly undercook them, cool rapidly in cold water, drain, and refrigerate, then reheat to order.

4. For uniform doneness, cut into uniform sizes before cooking.

5. Vegetables with both tough and tender parts need special treatment, so that the tender parts are not overcooked by the time the tougher parts are done.

   For example,

   Peel the woody stalks of asparagus.

   Peel or split broccoli stalks.

   Pierce the base of brussels sprouts with a sharp knife.

   Remove heavy center stalks of lettuce leaves before braising.

6. Don't mix batches of cooked vegetables. They are likely to be cooked to slightly different doneness.

CONTROLLING FLAVOR CHANGES

Cooking Produces Flavor Loss

Many flavors are lost during cooking, by dissolving into the cooking liquid and by evaporation. The longer a vegetable is cooked, the more flavor it loses.

Flavor loss can be controlled in several ways:

1. Cook for as short a time as possible.

2. Use boiling salted water. Starting vegetables in boiling water shortens cooking time. The addition of salt helps reduce flavor loss.

3. Use only enough water to cover to minimize leaching. Note that this rule contradicts rule 1, because adding vegetables to a small quantity of

water lowers the temperature more, so cooking time is extended. Save your questions on this until you have finished the sections on color and nutritional changes.

4. Steam vegetables whenever appropriate. Steam cooking reduces leaching out of flavor and shortens cooking time.

Strong-flavored Vegetables

With certain strong-flavored vegetables, it is desirable to lose some of their flavors to make them more appealing to the taste. These include the onion family (onions, garlic, leeks, shallots), the cabbage family (cabbage, brussels sprouts, cauliflower, broccoli), and some root vegetables (turnips, rutabagas).

When cooking strong-flavored vegetables, leave uncovered to allow these flavors to escape, and use larger amounts of water.

Cooking Produces Flavor Change

Cooked vegetables do not taste like raw vegetables, because cooking produces certain chemical changes. As long as the vegetables are not overcooked, this change is desirable. It produces the flavors one looks for in vegetable dishes.

Overcooking produces undesirable changes in members of the cabbage family. They develop a strong, unpleasant flavor. Cabbage and its relatives should be cooked quickly, uncovered.

Cooking and Sweetness

Young, freshly harvested vegetables have a relatively high sugar content that makes them taste sweet. As they mature, or as they sit in storage, the sugar gradually changes to starch. This is especially noticeable in corn, peas, carrots, turnips, and beets.

To serve sweet-tasting vegetables:

1. Try to serve young, fresh vegetables that have been stored for as short a time as possible.

2. For older vegetables, especially those just listed, add a small amount of sugar to the cooking water to replace lost sweetness.

CONTROLLING COLOR CHANGES

It is important to preserve as much natural color as possible when cooking vegetables. Because customers may reject or accept a vegetable only on the basis of its appearance, it can be said that its visual quality is as important as its flavor or nutritional value.

Pigments are compounds that give vegetables their color. Different pigments react in different ways to heat and to acids and other elements that may be present during cooking, so it is necessary to discuss them one at a time. Table 16.1 summarizes this information.

White Vegetables

White pigments, called *flavones*, are the primary coloring compounds in potatoes, onions, cauliflower, and white cabbage, and the white parts of such vegetables as celery, cucumbers, and zucchini.

White pigments stay white in acid and turn yellow in alkaline water. To keep vegetables such as cauliflower white, add a little lemon juice or cream of tartar to the cooking water. (Don't add too much, though, as this may toughen the vegetable.) Covering the pot also helps keep acids in.

Cooking for a short time, especially in a steamer, helps maintain color (and flavor and nutrients as well). Overcooking or holding too long in a steam table turns white vegetables dull yellow or gray.

Red Vegetables

Red pigments, called *anthocyanins*, are found in only a few vegetables, mainly red cabbage and beets. Blueberries also are colored by these red pigments. (The red color of tomatoes and red peppers is due to the same pigments that color carrots yellow or orange.)

Red pigments react very strongly to acids and alkalis.

> *Acids* turn them a brighter red.
>
> *Alkalis* turn them blue or blue-green (not a very appetizing color for red cabbage).

Red beets and red cabbage, therefore, have their best color when cooked with a small amount of acid. Red cabbage is often cooked with tart apples for this reason.

When a strongly acid vegetable is desired, such as Harvard Beets or Braised Red Cabbage, add just a small amount of acid at first. Acids toughen vegetables and prolong cooking time. Add the rest when the vegetables are tender.

Red pigments dissolve easily in water. This means

TABLE 16.1 **Vegetable Color Changes During Cooking**

Color	Examples of Vegetables	Cooked with Acid	Cooked with Alkali	Overcooked
White	Potatoes, turnips, cauliflower, onions, white cabbage	White	Yellow	Yellowish, gray
Red	Beets, red cabbage (not tomatoes, whose pigment is like that in yellow vegetables)	Red	Blue or blue-green	Greenish blue, faded
Green	Asparagus, green beans, lima beans, broccoli, brussels sprouts, peas, spinach, green peppers, artichokes, okra	Olive green	Bright green	Olive green
Yellow (and orange)	Carrots, tomatoes, rutabagas, sweet potatoes, squash, corn	Little change	Little change	Slightly faded

- Use a short cooking time. Overcooked red vegetables lose a lot of color.

- Use only as much water as is necessary.

- Cook beets whole and unpeeled, with root and an inch of stem attached, to protect color. Skins easily slip off cooked beets.

- When steaming, use solid pans instead of perforated pans to retain the red juices.

- Whenever possible, serve the cooking liquid as a sauce with the vegetable.

Green Vegetables

Green coloring, or *chlorophyll*, is present in all green plants. Green vegetables are very common in the kitchen, so it is important to understand the special handling required by this pigment.

Acids are enemies of green vegetables. Both *acid* and *long cooking* turn green vegetables to a drab olive-green.

Protect the color of green vegetables by

- Cooking uncovered to allow plant acids to escape.

- Cooking for the shortest possible time. Properly cooked green vegetables are tender-crisp, not mushy.

- Cooking in small batches rather than holding for long periods in a steam table.

Steaming is rapidly becoming the preferred method for cooking green vegetables. Steam cooks food rapidly, lessens the dissolving out of nutrients and flavor, and does not break up delicate vegetables. Overcooking, however, can occur very rapidly in steamers.

DO NOT use baking soda to maintain green color. Soda destroys vitamins and makes texture unpleasantly mushy and slippery.

How much water to use when boiling? A large quantity of water helps dissolve plant acids, helps preserve colors, and speeds cooking. But some cooks feel that an excessive amount of nutrients are lost. See the next section for further discussion.

Yellow and Orange Vegetables

Yellow and *orange* pigments, called *carotenoids*, are found in carrots, corn, winter squash, rutabaga, sweet potatoes, tomatoes, and red peppers. These pigments are very stable. They are little affected by acids or

alkalis. Long cooking can dull the color, however. Short cooking not only prevents dulling of the color, but preserves vitamins and flavors.

CONTROLLING NUTRIENT LOSSES

Vegetables are an important part of our diets because they supply a wide variety of essential nutrients. They are our major sources of vitamins A and C and are rich in many other vitamins and minerals. Unfortunately, many of these nutrients are easily lost.

Six factors are responsible for most nutrient loss:

1. High temperature.

2. Long cooking.

3. Leaching (dissolving out).

4. Alkalis (baking soda, hard water).

5. Plant enzymes (which are active at warm temperatures but are destroyed by high heat).

6. Oxygen.

Some nutrient loss is inevitable, because it is rarely possible to avoid all of these conditions at the same time. For example,

- Pressure steaming shortens cooking time but the high temperature destroys some vitamins.

- Braising uses low heat but the cooking time is longer.

- Baking eliminates leaching out of vitamins and minerals, but the long cooking and high temperature cause nutrient loss.

- Boiling is faster than simmering, but the higher temperature can be harmful, and the rapid activity can break up delicate vegetables and increase loss through leaching.

- Cutting vegetables into small pieces decreases cooking time but increases leaching by creating more exposed surfaces.

- Even steaming allows some leaching out of nutrients into the moisture that condenses onto the vegetables and then drips off.

Cooking in a Little Liquid versus a Lot of Liquid

This is an area of controversy with good arguments on both sides.

1. Using a lot of liquid increases vitamin loss by leaching. One should use just enough liquid to cover, and the cooking liquid should then be saved for reheating the vegetables or for stocks or soups.

2. Using a little liquid increases cooking time. When the vegetables are combined with the small quantity of boiling water, the temperature is lowered greatly and the vegetables must sit in warm water while it again heats up. Also, plant enzymes may destroy some vitamins before the water again becomes hot enough to destroy them.

Tests have shown that, for these reasons, no more nutrients are lost when vegetables are cooked in a lot of water than when vegetables are cooked in just enough water to cover.

When cooking green vegetables, there is an added advantage to using a lot of water. Plant acids are more quickly diluted and driven off, better preserving the color.

The best cooking methods, nutritionally, are usually those that produce the most attractive, flavorful products.

- They are more likely to be eaten. Discarded vegetables benefit no one, no matter how nutritious they are.

- Factors that destroy nutrients are often those that also destroy color, flavor, and texture.

GENERAL RULES OF VEGETABLE COOKERY

Now that you understand *how* vegetables change as they cook, let's summarize that information in some general rules. You should now be able to explain the reasons for each of these rules.

- Don't overcook.

- Cook as close to service time as possible and in small quantities. Avoid holding for long periods on a steam table.

- If the vegetable must be cooked ahead, undercook slightly and chill rapidly. Reheat at service time.

- Never use baking soda with green vegetables.

- Cut vegetables uniformly for even cooking.

- Start with boiling, salted water when boiling vegetables.

- Cook green vegetables and strong-flavored vegetables uncovered.

- To preserve color, cook red and white vegetables in a slightly acid (not strongly acid) liquid. Cook green vegetables in a neutral liquid.

- Do not mix batches of cooked vegetables.

STANDARDS OF QUALITY IN COOKED VEGETABLES

1. *Color.*

   Bright, natural colors.

   Green vegetables, in particular, should be a fresh, bright green, not olive green.

2. *Appearance on plate.*

   Cut neatly and uniformly. Not broken up.

   Attractively arranged or mounded on plate or dish.

   Not swimming in its cooking water.

   Imaginative and appropriate combinations and garnishes are always well received.

3. *Texture.*

   Cooked to the right degree of doneness.

   Most vegetables should be crisp-tender, not overcooked and mushy, but not tough or woody either.

   Vegetables intended to be soft (potatoes, squash, sweet potatoes, tomatoes, vegetable purées) should be cooked through, with a pleasant, smooth texture.

4. *Flavor.*

   Full, natural flavor and sweetness, sometimes called "garden-fresh" flavor. Strong-flavored vegetables should be pleasantly mild, with no off-flavors or bitterness.

5. *Seasonings.*

   Lightly and appropriately seasoned. Seasonings should not be too strong and not mask the natural "garden" flavors.

6. *Sauces.*

   Butter and seasoned butters should be fresh and not used heavily; vegetables should not be greasy.

   Cream sauces and other sauces should not be too thick or too heavily seasoned. As with seasonings, sauces should enhance, not cover up.

7. *Vegetable combinations.*

   Interesting combinations attract customers.

Flavors, colors, and shapes should be pleasing in combination.

Vegetables should be cooked separately and then combined, to allow for different cooking times.

Acid vegetables (like tomatoes) added to green vegetables will discolor them. Combine just before service.

HANDLING FRESH, FROZEN, CANNED, AND DRIED VEGETABLES

FRESH VEGETABLE PRE-PREPARATION

Washing

1. Wash all vegetables thoroughly.

2. Root vegetables that are not peeled, such as potatoes for baking, should be scrubbed very well with a stiff vegetable brush.

3. Wash green, leafy vegetables in several changes of cold water. Lift the greens from the water, so that the sand can sink to the bottom. Pouring off into a colander dumps the sand back onto the leaves.

4. After washing, drain well and refrigerate lightly covered. The purpose of covering is to prevent drying, but covering too tightly cuts off air circulation. This can be a problem if the product is stored more than a day, because mold is more likely to grow in a damp, closed space. Use a drain insert in the storage container to allow drainage.

Soaking

1. With a few exceptions, do not soak vegetables for long periods. Flavor and nutrients leach out.

2. Cabbage, broccoli, brussels sprouts, and cauliflower may be soaked for 30 minutes in cold, salted water to eliminate insects, if necessary.

3. Limp vegetables can be soaked briefly in cold water to restore crispness.

4. Dried legumes are soaked for several hours before cooking to replace moisture lost in drying. Dried beans will absorb their weight in water.

Peeling and Cutting

1. Peel most vegetables as thinly as possible. There are many nutrients just under the skins.

2. Cut into uniform pieces for even cooking.

3. Peel and cut as close to cooking time as possible to prevent drying and loss of vitamins through oxidation.

4. For machine paring, sort vegetables for evenness of size to minimize waste.

5. Treat vegetables that brown easily (potatoes, eggplant, artichokes, sweet potatoes) with an acid, such as lemon juice, or with an antioxidant solution, or hold under water until ready to use (some vitamins and minerals will be lost).

6. Save edible trim for soups, stocks, and vegetable purées.

Trimming Loss: Calculating Yields and Amounts Needed

Table 16.2 lists, in the last column, the percentage yield for each vegetable. This figure indicates, on the average, how much of the AP (as purchased) weight is left after pre-prep to produce the ready-to-cook item, or EP (edible portion) weight. You can use this figure to do two basic calculations.

1. *Calculating yield.*

    Example. You have 10 lb AP brussels sprouts. Percentage yield after trimming is 80%. What will your EP weight be?

    First, change the percentage to a decimal number by moving the decimal point two places to the left.

    $$80\% = 0.80$$

    Multiply the decimal by your AP weight to get EP yield.

    $$10 \text{ lb} \times 0.80 = 8 \text{ lb}$$

2. *Calculating amount needed.*

    Example. You need 10 lb EP brussels sprouts. How much untrimmed vegetables do you need?

    Change the percentage to a decimal number.

    $$80\% = 0.80$$

    Divide the EP weight needed by this number to get the AP weight.

    $$\frac{10 \text{ lb}}{0.80} = 12.5 \text{ lb}$$

TABLE 16.2 **Fresh Vegetable Pre-preparation**
(*Note:* Since fruits are handled in the pantry more than in the vegetable kitchen, the table of fruit pre-preparation is included in Chapter 19.)

Product	Quality Indicators and Pre-preparation	Percentage Yield
Artichokes, globe	Quality Indicators (Q.I.): Compact, tight leaves; heavy for size; few or no brown blemishes.	80% (whole, trimmed)
	Prep.: Wash. Cut 1 inch off tops. Cut off stem and lower leaves. Scrape out choke (fuzzy center) with melon ball cutter. (Removal of choke can be done before or after cooking.) Dip in lemon juice immediately. To trim bottoms, see Figure 16.1.	30% (bottoms only)
Artichokes, Jerusalem	Wash and peel off brown skin.	80%
Asparagus	Q.I.: Tightly closed tips; firm, not withered, stalks.	55%
	Prep.: Break off woody lower ends. Remove lower scales, which may harbor sand, or peel lower part of stalk. Figure 16.2 shows an alternative method. Tips may be cut to uniform lengths and/or tied in bundles for cooking.	
Beans, dried	Prep.: Pick over to remove bad beans and foreign particles. Soak overnight in three times their volume of cold water.	
Beans, green or wax	Q.I.: Firm and straight, with few shriveled ends; even color, without blemishes. Should be tender and crisp enough to break when bent to 45° angle. Enclosed seeds should be small, not large and bulging.	88%
	Prep.: Wash. Cut or snap off ends. Remove any spots. Leave whole or cut into desired lengths.	

(Continues)

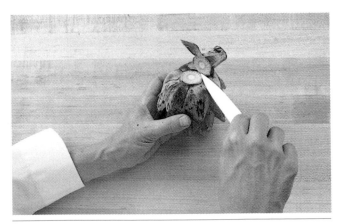

FIGURE 16.1 **Trimming artichoke bottoms.**
(a) Cut or break off the stem flush with the bottom of the artichoke, as shown.

(b) Break off the outer leaves.

(c) Or you may trim the outer leaves off with a knife as shown, being careful not to cut into the base of the artichoke.

(f) With a ball cutter or tablespoon, scrape out the fuzzy choke.

(d) Cut off the remaining leaves above the base.

(g) A trimmed artichoke bottom on the left; a trimmed whole artichoke on the right. Note that the points of the leaves have been cut off and center choke removed.

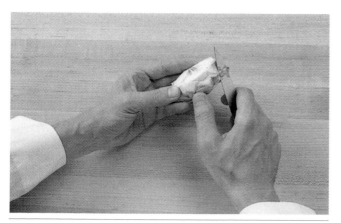

(e) With a paring knife, trim off the green outer peel to give the base a smooth, neat appearance.

FIGURE 16.2   Trimming asparagus.
(a) With a vegetable peeler, pare the stalk from about 2 inches (5 cm) below the tip down to the base.

(c) Another method used by many chefs is to break off the stems first . . .

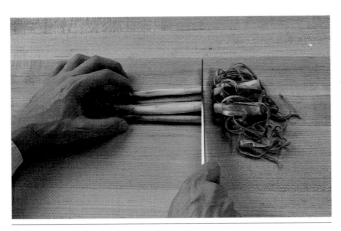

(b) Then cut or break off the hard, woody bottoms of the stems.

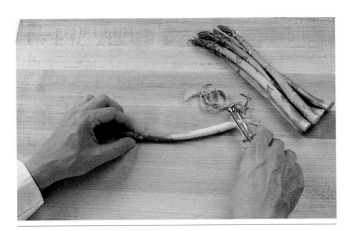

(d) . . . and then peel the stem.

TABLE 16.2   Fresh Vegetable Pre-preparation *(Continued)*

Product	Quality Indicators and Pre-preparation	Percentage Yield
Beans, lima	Q.I.: Shelled beans should be plump, with tender skins.	40%
	Prep.: Shell, wash, and drain.	
Beets	Q.I.: Firm, round, uniform size; smooth skin. Tops, if any, should be fresh or just wilted, but not yellow or deteriorated. Large, rough beets are often woody.	40–45% (75% if purchased without tops)
	Prep.: Cut off tops, leaving 1 inch of stem attached to beets. Leave roots on. Scrub well. Steam or boil before peeling.	

*TABLE 16.2   **Fresh Vegetable Pre-preparation (Continued)***

Product	Quality Indicators and Pre-preparation	Percentage Yield
Broccoli	Q.I.: Dark green, tightly closed buds. Prep.: Wash well. Soak in salted water 30 minutes if necessary to remove insects. Split large stalks into smaller sizes for portioning. Split thick stalks part way for faster cooking, or cut tops from stalks. Tougher stalks may be peeled (Figure 16.3).	65–75%
Brussels sprouts	Q.I.: Bright green; tight heads; uniform size. Prep.: Trim bottom ends and remove yellowed outer leaves (but don't cut off too much of the bottom or you will lose too many leaves). For more even cooking, pierce base with sharp knife point. Rinse well. Soak in cold salted water 30 minutes if necessary to remove insects.	80%
Cabbage, white, green, or red	Q.I.: Firm head, heavy for size. Good color. Crisp leaves. Leaves finely ribbed. Prep.: Remove coarse or discolored outer leaves. Remove core and rinse whole, or cut into quarters and then remove core. For wedges, core is left in, but with bottom trimmed, to hold sections together. (See Figure 16.4.)	80%
Carrots	Q.I.: Bright orange color; crisp, straight, and well shaped; smooth surface. Large carrots are sometimes woody. Prep.: Trim top and bottom ends. Pare with hand peeler or in machine.	75–80% *(Continues)*

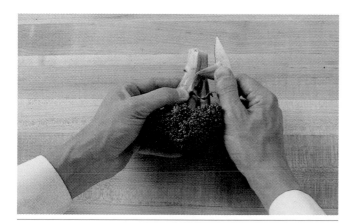

FIGURE 16.3   **Prepare tough bottoms of broccoli stalks by pulling off the fibrous peel as shown.**

TABLE 16.2 **Fresh Vegetable Pre-preparation** *(Continued)*

Product	Quality Indicators and Pre-preparation	Percentage Yield
Cauliflower	Q.I.: White color, not yellow or brownish; fine grained, tightly closed buds; fresh green, well-trimmed leaves. Prep.: Remove leaves and trim tough part of stalk. Cut away discolored parts. Wash. Soak in salted water 30 minutes if necessary to remove insects. Separate into florets, leaving portion of center stalk attached to each one, to minimize trim loss. If cooking whole, cut out center of stalk for more even cooking.	55%
Celery	Q.I.: Straight, compact, well trimmed; fresh green color. Prep.: Cut off root end. Separate stems and scrub well. Reserve leaves and tough outer stems for stocks, soups, mirepoix. Ribbed outer side of stems may be peeled to remove strings.	75%
Celery root (knob celery or celeriac)	Q.I.: Firm and heavy. Large ones are often soft and spongy in center. Prep.: Wash well, peel, and cut as desired.	75%
Corn (on cob)	Q.I.: Fresh, moist husks, not dry; no worm damage; kernels well filled, tender, and milky when punctured. Prep.: Strip off husks, remove silk, and cut off bottom stump. Cut into 2 or 3 sections as desired. Keep refrigerated and use as soon as possible.	28% (after husking and cutting from cob)
Cucumbers (slicing type)	Q.I.: Firm, crisp, dark green, well shaped. Yellow color means overmature. Prep.: Wash. Trim ends. Peel if skin is tough or has been waxed.	75–95% depending on peeling

FIGURE 16.4 **Cutting and shredding cabbage.**
(a) Cut the cabbage head into quarters. Then cut out the core as shown.

(b) With a French knife, cut into thin shreds.

TABLE 16.2   **Fresh Vegetable Pre-preparation (Continued)**

Product	Quality Indicators and Pre-preparation	Percentage Yield
Eggplant	Q.I.: Shiny, dark purple color; heavy and plump; without blemishes or soft spots.	90% (75% if peeled)
	Prep.: Wash. Trim off stem end. Peel if skin is tough. Cut just before use. Dip in lemon juice (or antioxidant solution) to prevent discoloration.	
Garlic	Q.I.: Skin may be white or pink. No brown spots, soft spots, or spoilage; dry skin; no green shoots.	88%
	Prep.: Separate cloves one by one as needed, or strike whole bulb with heel of hand to separate. To peel cloves, crush slightly with side of heavy knife. Peel and trim root end. (See Figure 16.5.)	

(Continues)

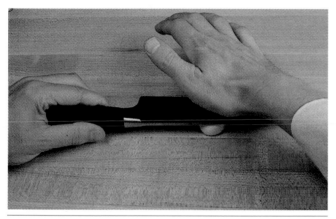

FIGURE 16.5   **Peeling and crushing garlic.**
(a) Place the garlic on the worktable. Hold a broad knife blade over it as shown and strike it firmly with the palm of the hand.

(c) Chop or mince the garlic.

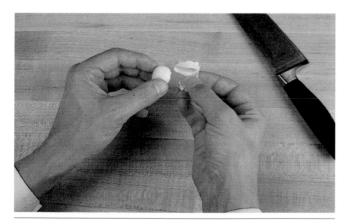

(b) The garlic can now be peeled easily.

(d) To make a paste of the garlic, sprinkle it with salt and mash it firmly with the *back* of the knife blade.

TABLE 16.2   **Fresh Vegetable Pre-preparation** *(Continued)*

Product	Quality Indicators and Pre-preparation	Percentage Yield
Kohlrabi	Q.I.: Uniform light green color; 2–3 inches in diameter. Crisp and firm. No woodiness. Prep.: Peel like turnips, being sure to remove full thickness of skin.	55%
Leeks	Q.I.: Fresh green leaves; 2–3 inches of white. White part should be crisp and tender, not fibrous. Prep.: Cut off roots and green tops. Cut deeply through white part, separate the layers slightly, and wash very carefully to remove all embedded soil. (See Figure 16.6.)	50%
Lettuce	See Chapter 19 for full description of salad greens.	75%

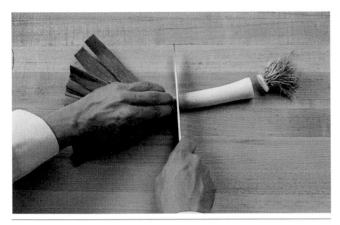

FIGURE 16.6   **Cleaning leeks.**
(a) Trim off the root end and as much of the green as desired.

(c) Spread apart the layers as shown. Carefully wash out all embedded dirt under running water.

(b) Make one or two deep cuts to within an inch (2½ cm) of the root end.

TABLE 16.2   *Fresh Vegetable Pre-preparation (Continued)*

Product	Quality Indicators and Pre-preparation	Percentage Yield
Mushrooms	Q.I.: Firm, white caps, closed at the stem. Stems should be relatively short. No dark spots, bruises, or mold. Prep.: Trim bottoms of stems. Just before cooking, wash quickly in cold water; drain well. If you desire to keep the mushrooms white, add a small amount of acid (lemon juice, vinegar, ascorbic acid) to the rinse water.	90%
Okra	Q.I.: Tender, full pods, not dry or shriveled. Ridges should be soft. Seeds should be soft and white. Uniform green color. Prep.: Wash. Trim ends. Slice or leave whole.	82%
Onions, dry	Q.I.: Clean, hard, well shaped; no mold or black fungus; no green shoots. Skins should be very dry. Prep.: Cut off root and stem ends. Peel. Wash. Cut or slice as needed. (See Figure 7.10.)	90%
Onions, green (scallions)	Q.I.: Fresh, crisp green tops; little or no bulb formation at white part. Prep.: Cut off roots and wilted ends of green tops. Amount of green left on varies with different recipes or uses.	60–70%
Parsley	Q.I.: Bright green, unwilted leaves with no rot. Prep.: Wash well and drain. Remove yellow leaves and large stems (save stems for stocks). Separate into sprigs for garnish, or chop leaves.	85%
Parsnips	Q.I.: Firm, smooth, well shaped, with light, uniform color. Large ones are often woody. Prep.: Refrigerating for 2 weeks develops sweetness. Trim ends and peel. Rinse.	70–75%
Peas (green and black-eyed)	Q.I.: Firm, fresh, moderately filled-out pods. Prep.: Shell and rinse. (Peas are not often purchased in the pod by food service operations, because of the labor required for shelling.)	40%
Peas, edible pod	Q.I.: Fresh green color, crisp pods, no blemishes. Prep.: Remove stem end. Pull off strings at side veins. (Both the flat, Chinese snow peas and full-pod variety called sugar snap peas are available. Expensive.)	90%
Peppers, sweet (green or red)	Q.I.: Shiny green or red color; well shaped; no soft spots or shriveling. Prep.: Wash. Cut in half lengthwise and remove core, seeds, and white membranes. Or leave whole (as for stuffed peppers) and cut out core from the end.	82%

(Continues)

TABLE 16.2 **Fresh Vegetable Pre-preparation** *(Continued)*

Product	Quality Indicators and Pre-preparation	Percentage Yield
Potatoes, white	See Chapter 18.	80%
Potatoes, sweet (including "yams")	Q.I.: Clean, dry surface. Firm, not shriveled or blemished. Fat, regular shapes are preferable because of less waste in trimming and portioning.	80%
	Prep.: Scrub, boil or steam, and then peel. May be peeled before cooking, but must be dipped in antioxidant to prevent discoloring. Machine paring is wasteful with irregular shapes.	
	Note: There are two basic varieties of sweet potatoes. The variety that has a moister, deeper orange flesh is sometimes referred to, inaccurately, as "yam." The two varieties are interchangeable for most purposes. True yams are an entirely different vegetable, with starchy, white flesh. They are not often seen in this country, except in Hispanic and some other ethnic markets.	
Radishes	Q.I.: Firm, tender, and crisp, with good shape and color.	90%
	Prep.: Cut off root and stem ends. Wash.	
Rutabagas	See turnips.	
Spinach and other greens	Q.I.: Fresh, crisp, dark green leaves. No rot or slime or badly bruised leaves. Short stems.	50–70%
	Prep.: Remove stems and damaged leaves (Figure 16.7). Wash in several changes of water. Use large quantity of water and lift spinach up and down to float off sand and dirt. Lift from water and drain well.	

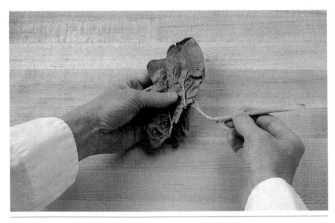

FIGURE 16.7 **When trimming spinach leaves, remove the heavy center rib along with the stem.**

FIGURE 16.8 **Preparing tomato concassée.**
(a) Blanch and peel the tomato and cut it in half crosswise. Gently squeeze out the seeds as shown. *(Continues)*

TABLE 16.2   **Fresh Vegetable Pre-preparation** *(Continued)*

Product	Quality Indicators and Pre-preparation	Percentage Yield
Squash, summer (including zucchini)	Q.I.: Firm, heavy, and crisp; tender skins, no blemishes. Prep.: Wash or scrub well. Trim ends.	90%
Squash, winter	Q.I.: Heavy and firm. Hard rind. No blemishes. Prep.: Wash. Cut in half. Scrape out seeds and fibers. Cut into portion sizes. For puréed or mashed squash, either steam or bake and then remove peel; or peel, dice, and then steam.	65–85%
Tomatoes	Q.I.: Firm but not hard, with little or no green core. Smooth, without bruises, blemishes, cracks, or discoloration. If underripe, let stand 2–3 days at room temperature. Prep.: For use with skin on: wash, remove core. To peel: plunge into boiling water for 10–20 seconds (riper tomatoes take less time). Cool immediately in ice water. Slip skins off and remove core. See Figure 16.8 for further techniques.	90% (peeled)
Turnips and rutabagas	Q.I.: Firm and heavy, with good color and no blemishes. White turnips over 2½ inches (6–7 cm) in diameter may be woody or spongy. Prep.: Peel heavily by hand or in machine to remove thick skin (see Figure 16.9). Rinse.	75–80%
Watercress	Q.I.: Bright green, crisp, unbruised leaves. Prep.: Wash well. Remove heavy stems and discolored leaves.	90%

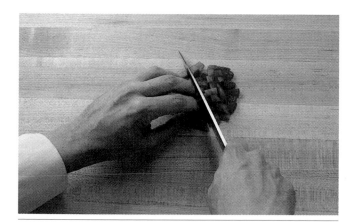

(b) Dice the seeded tomato or chop it coarsely.

FIGURE 16.9   **Peel rutabagas and turnips deeply enough to remove the full thickness of skin, as pointed out in this photograph.**

HANDLING PROCESSED VEGETABLES

It is generally agreed that the quality of frozen or canned vegetables can never equal that of the best quality fresh product, at its peak of maturity, prepared properly, and cooked while still fresh. However, because of the high perishability of fresh produce, because of seasonal variations in availability and price, and because of the amount of labor required to handle fresh produce in commercial kitchens, food service relies to a great extent on processed vegetables. Therefore, it is important to know how to handle processed foods properly. Your goal should be to make them as close as possible in quality to the best fresh produce.

The quality of processed vegetables varies greatly. For example, frozen cauliflower always lacks the slightly crunchy texture of properly cooked fresh cauliflower. In fact, most frozen vegetables are a bit mushier than fresh, because cell walls rupture during freezing. On the other hand, frozen peas are almost universally accepted, not just for their convenience, but for their dependably high quality, in comparison with the highly perishable fresh product.

In the section of Chapter 7 called "Handling Convenience Food," we learned that convenience foods are products that have been partially or completely prepared or processed by the manufacturer. This means that you should treat frozen and canned vegetables as though they are partially or fully cooked fresh vegetables, which deserve the same care in handling, heating, seasoning, and presentation.

Handling Frozen Vegetables

Checking Quality

Examine all frozen products when received to make sure there has been no loss of quality. Check in particular for the following:

1. **Temperature.**

    Check the temperature inside the case with a thermometer. Is it still 0°F (−18°C) or below, or has it begun to thaw during shipment?

2. **Large ice crystals.**

    A little frost is normal, but lots of ice means poor handling.

3. **Signs of leaking on the carton.**

    This is another obvious sign of thawing.

4. **Freezer burn.**

    Open a package and check the vegetables themselves. Is the color bright and natural, or is there any yellowing or drying on the surface?

Cooking

Frozen vegetables have been partially cooked, so final cooking time is shorter than for fresh products.

Cook from the frozen state. Most vegetables need no thawing, but can go directly into steamer pans or boiling salted water.

Exceptions: Corn on the cob and vegetables that freeze into a solid block, such as spinach and squash, should be thawed in the cooler first, for more even cooking.

Seasoning: Most frozen vegetables have been slightly salted during processing, so add less salt than you would for fresh products.

Handling Canned Vegetables

Checking Quality

1. **Reject damaged cans on receipt.**

    Puffed or swollen cans indicate spoilage. Small dents may be harmless, but large dents may mean that the can's protective lining has been damaged. Avoid rusted or leaking cans.

2. **Know the drained weight.**

    This varies with different grades of different vegetables and should be specified when ordering. Typical drained weights are 60 to 65 percent of total contents. You must know this drained weight in order to calculate the number of servings the can contains.

    Some canned products, such as tomato sauce or cream-style corn, have no drained weight, because the entire contents are served.

3. **Check the grade.**

    Grades are determined by the packers or by federal inspectors. They are based on factors like color, absence of defects, and sieve size (size of individual pieces). Check to make sure you receive the grade you ordered (and paid for).

    Federal grades are

    U.S. Grade A or Fancy.

    U.S. Grade B or Extra Standard (for vegetables) or Choice (for fruits).

    U.S. Grade C or Standard.

Cooking

1. Wipe the top of the can clean before opening. Use a clean can opener.

2. Drain the vegetable, and place half the liquid in cooking pot. Bring it to a boil. This shortens the heating time of the vegetable.

3. Add the vegetable and heat to serving temperature. *Do not boil for a long time.* Canned vegetables are fully cooked—in fact, usually overcooked. They need only to be reheated.

    (Note: Health officials recommend holding vegetables at 190°F (88°C) for 10 minutes or more—20 to 30 minutes for nonacid vegetables like beets, green beans, or spinach—to eliminate the danger of botulism. See Chapter 2.)

4. Heat as close to serving time as possible. Do not hold in steam table for long periods.

5. Season and flavor with imagination. Canned vegetables require more creativity in preparation than fresh, because they can be pretty dreary when just served plain.

6. Season the liquid while it is coming to a boil, before you add the vegetable. This will give the flavors of the herbs and spices time to blend.

7. Butter will enhance the flavor of most vegetables and it carries the flavors of other seasonings that you choose to add.

8. Dress up the vegetables with added flavors and garnishes, such as beets or sauerkraut with caraway, limas or green beans with crisp crumbled bacon, corn with sautéed minced onion and green or red pepper, carrots with butter and tarragon, or with orange juice and brown sugar.

    The combinations suggested in the table in Chapter 17 apply to canned vegetables as well as to fresh and frozen.

Handling Dried Vegetables

There are two basic kinds of dried vegetables:

1. ***Dried legumes.***

    Dried beans, peas, and lentils have been used for food for thousands of years. They are handled in these stages:

    a. Pick over to remove any foreign particles and rinse well.

    b. Soak overnight in three times their volume of water. (Split peas and some lentils do not require soaking. Check package directions.)

    c. Simmer, covered, until tender. Do not boil, or the vegetables may toughen. Some beans require up to 3 hours of simmering.

    d. If you forget to soak beans overnight, an alternative method can be used. Put the beans in a cooking pot with three times their volume of cold water. Bring to a boil. When water boils, cover tightly and remove from the heat. Let stand 1 hour. Then proceed with step *c* above.

2. ***Freeze-dried and other dehydrated vegetables.***

    Modern technology has made possible dried potatoes, onions, carrots, celery, beans, peppers, tomatoes, mushrooms, and many other products.

    Follow manufacturers' directions for reconstituting these products. Many need to be soaked in cold or warm water for specific lengths of time. They continue to absorb water as they are simmered.

    Instant dried products, especially potatoes, require only the addition of a boiling liquid and seasonings to be ready to serve. Again, manufacturers' directions vary with different brands.

PRODUCTION AND HOLDING PROBLEMS IN QUANTITY COOKING

We have emphasized throughout this chapter that vegetables should be cooked as close as possible to serving time. They lose quality rapidly when held in a steam table.

In quantity cooking, however, it is rarely possible to cook individual vegetable portions to order. After 20 to 30 minutes at steam table temperatures, even carefully prepared vegetables are usually overcooked.

Two systems have been devised to help solve this problem. *Batch cooking* is especially well suited to set-meal service, and the *blanch and chill* method is most helpful in extended meal service. Needs vary from institution to institution, and you will probably find both techniques useful in one kitchen.

Batch Cooking

Rather than cooking all your vegetables in one batch large enough for the entire meal service, this method (described in Chapter 7, p. 103) involves dividing the food into smaller batches and cooking them one at a time as needed.

Procedure

1. Steamers and small tilting trunnion kettles behind the service line are the most useful kinds of equipment for vegetable batch cooking.

2. Divide each vegetable into batches small enough to be served within 20 to 30 minutes. Arrange in steamer pans ready to be placed in steamers or in containers ready for pouring into the kettles.

3. Keep the prepped vegetables in the cooler until needed.

4. Cook batches as needed. In planning, allow time for loading and unloading the equipment, for cooking, for finishing the product with desired seasoning, sauce, or garnish, and for carrying to the serving line.

5. Undercook slightly if the vegetable must be held before serving.

6. Have all your seasonings, sauces, and garnishes ready for finishing the dish.

7. Do not mix batches. They will be cooked to different degrees, and colors and textures will usually not match.

Blanch and Chill Method

It is usually impractical to cook vegetables completely to order. Too much time is required. But if the vegetables have been partially cooked, the time needed to finish them to order is short.

Partially cooking, chilling, and finish-cooking is not as good, nutritionally, as cooking completely to order, but it is almost as good. It's certainly better than holding them for hours at serving temperature, and it gives the cook complete control over the degree of doneness when served.

Procedure

1. Steam or simmer the vegetable until partially cooked to desired degree. (In the case of french fries, blanch by deep-frying.)

   The amount of cooking required depends on the vegetable and on the method by which it will be reheated or finished. Frozen vegetables need less cooking than fresh. Often they need only be thawed.

2. Chill immediately in ice water. (Needless to say, french fries are an exception.)

3. Drain and keep chilled until needed.

4. Finish to order by desired cooking method.

   For example, one or more portions can be placed in a strainer and lowered briefly into a ready pot of boiling water.

   Sautéing in butter is a popular method for finishing such items as peas, green beans, and carrots.

   Potato croquettes are an example of a more complicated application of this same method. The potatoes are boiled or steamed, puréed, seasoned, formed, and breaded in advance. They are then deep-fried to order.

STORAGE

Fresh Vegetables

1. Potatoes, onions, and winter squash are stored at cool temperatures (50–65°F/10–18°C) in a dry, dark place.

2. Other vegetables must be refrigerated. To prevent drying, they should be kept covered or wrapped, or the humidity in the cooler must be high. Allow for some air circulation to help prevent mold.

3. Peeled and cut vegetables need extra protection from drying and oxidation. Cover or wrap, and use quickly to prevent spoilage. Potatoes, eggplant, and other vegetables that brown when cut should be treated with an acid or antioxidant. As an alternative, they can be blanched to destroy the enzymes that cause browning. Raw, cut potatoes are sometimes held in cold water for a short time.

4. Store all fresh vegetables for as short a time as possible. They lose quality rapidly. Peas and corn lose sweetness even after a few hours in storage.

5. Keep refrigerators and storage areas clean.

Frozen Vegetables

1. Store at 0°F (−18°C) or colder, in original containers, until ready for use.

2. Do not refreeze thawed vegetables. Quality will be greatly reduced.

Dried Vegetables

1. Store in a cool (less than 75°F/24°C), dry, well-ventilated place.

2. Keep well sealed and off the floor.

Canned Vegetables

1. Keep in a cool, dry place, away from sunlight and off the floor.

2. Discard cans that show signs of damage or spoilage (swollen, badly dented, or rusted cans). "When in doubt, throw it out."

Leftovers

1. The best way to store leftovers is not to create them in the first place. Careful planning and small batch cooking reduce leftovers.

2. Don't mix batches.

3. Store leftover creamed vegetables only 1 day. Then either use or discard. Before storing, cool rapidly by placing the container on ice.

TERMS FOR REVIEW

al dente	anthocyanins	trimming loss	sieve size
pigment	carotenoids	AP weight	batch cooking
plant acids	chlorophyll	EP weight	blanch and chill
flavones			

QUESTIONS FOR DISCUSSION

1. Give two reasons for not adding baking soda to the cooking water for green vegetables.

2. Besides appearance, why is proper, uniform cutting of vegetables important?

3. What are some advantages of steam cooking vegetables over boiling or simmering?

4. You are trying a recipe for blueberry muffins. When you break open a finished muffin, you see that the baked dough around each berry is green. What caused this? How can you correct it? (Hint: The batter is made with buttermilk and leavened with baking soda.)

5. Discuss the reasons for cooking green vegetables in a large quantity of water and in just enough water to cover.

6. You are to prepare buttered, steamed asparagus and must produce fifty 3-ounce portions. How much untrimmed fresh asparagus will you need?

CHAPTER 17

COOKING VEGETABLES

Now that you have studied the
whys and wherefores of vegetable cooking, you should be able to proceed to actual
preparation with a clear understanding of what you are doing.

This chapter outlines briefly the basic methods of
vegetable preparation. Successful performance of these methods relies on your
knowledge of the principles we have discussed.

The recipes given here reinforce your understanding
through actual practice. The emphasis is on the method, rather
than on the particular vegetable used, because each method applies to many
vegetables. For this reason, variations listed after basic recipes are used rather
than separate complete recipes. As in other chapters, recipes for sauces
served with vegetables are not repeated here from Chapter 8.

Most of the recipes are applicable to fresh, frozen,
or canned vegetables, even though variations are not listed for each. You
have learned how to handle these different products in order to make proper
substitutions. Review pages 398 to 399 if necessary.

Potatoes and other starchy foods, such as rice
and pasta, are covered in the next chapter. However, the basic cooking methods here
apply to potatoes as well as to other vegetables.

After reading this chapter, you should be able to

1. Cook vegetables by boiling and steaming.

2. Cook vegetables by sautéing and pan-frying.

3. Cook vegetables by braising.

4. Cook vegetables by baking.

5. Cook vegetables by broiling.

6. Cook vegetables by deep-frying.

BOILING AND STEAMING

Nearly all vegetables may be cooked by boiling or by steaming, and these are the two most frequently used methods, because they are easy, economical, and can be adapted to a great variety of preparations.

Boiling and steaming are basic cooking methods. In most cases, additional steps are required after the basic cooking is completed, in order to make the product ready for serving. These steps include adding butter, seasonings, flavorings, and sauces.

In other cases, the product is only partially cooked by boiling or steaming and finished by another cooking method, such as sautéing or baking. Recipes of this sort are usually included under the *final* cooking method.

"Boiling" is actually an inaccurate term. In most cases, vegetables should be simmered rather than boiled. The agitation and high temperatures of boiling break up delicate vegetables and destroy nutrients.

Steaming as a method for cooking vegetables is becoming more and more widely used, especially as more varieties of advanced equipment become available. It may be the ideal method for cooking certain vegetables, such as broccoli, that easily become broken or turn watery or mushy when simmered.

Procedure for Boiling Vegetables

1. Collect all equipment and food products.

2. Trim, peel, and cut vegetables as required. See Table 16.2 for preprep requirements.

3. Add required amount of water to pot (sauce pot, steam-jacketed kettle, tilting skillet, or whatever equipment you are using).

    Most vegetables are cooked in just enough water to cover. Many green vegetables and strong-flavored vegetables may be cooked in a large quantity of water (two or three times their volume). See pages 385–386 for discussion.

4. Add salt (approximately 1½ to 2 tablespoons per gallon of water, or 6 to 8 grams per liter) and bring to a boil.

5. Place the vegetables in the pot and return the water to a boil.

6. Reduce heat to a simmer and cook the vegetables, covered or uncovered as indicated, to required doneness.

    a. Green vegetables and strong-flavored vegetables are cooked uncovered.

    b. Other vegetables are cooked covered.

7. Drain the vegetable quickly to avoid overcooking.

8. If the vegetable is to be served at once, complete the recipe and serve.

9. If the vegetable is not to be served at once, cool the vegetable (except potatoes) in cold water, drain, and refrigerate until needed.

Variation

In some instances, the vegetable may be placed in a cooking utensil and boiling salted water added to it, as when broccoli is cooked in steam table pans (see recipe, p. 408). The advantage of this procedure is that you don't have to estimate how much water is needed to cover the vegetable, as in step 3. The disadvantages are that two pots are required instead of one, and that there is a safety factor in the possibility of spilling boiling water.

Procedure for Steaming Vegetables

This method is used both for pressurized and non-pressurized compartment steam cookers and for simple range-top steamers that consist of a perforated basket over a pot of boiling water.

1. Know your equipment. Read all operating instructions supplied with your equipment. Every model is a little different.

2. Collect all equipment and food products.

3. Trim and cut vegetables as required.

4. Preheat the steamer.

5. Arrange vegetables in pans or baskets for cooking. Make shallow, even layers for uniform cooking.

    Use perforated pans for best steam circulation.

    Use solid pans if cooking liquid must be retained.

6. Insert pans or baskets in steamer and close door or lid.

7. Steam for required time. Consult timing charts supplied with your model of steamer.

8. Remove vegetable from steamer. If it is a pressure steamer, *pressure must return to zero before door is opened.*

9. Finish vegetable according to recipe and serve at once, or cool quickly for later use.

Vegetables that form compact layers do not steam well. They do not allow the steam to circulate, so they cook unevenly. Examples: spinach and other greens, peas, whole-kernel corn, frozen puréed squash.

RECIPE 151   Buttered Peas and Carrots

Portions: 15   **Portion size:** 3 oz (100 g)

U.S.	Metric	Ingredients	Procedure
1 lb	500 g	Carrots	1. Peel carrots and cut into ¼-inch (½-cm) dice.
2 lb	1 kg	Peas, frozen	2. Bring salted water to a boil in a saucepan. Add carrots. Return to a boil, lower heat, and simmer until tender.
1 tbsp	15 mL	Sugar	
2 oz	60 g	Butter, melted	
		Salt	3. Bring a second pan of salted water to a boil. Add the frozen peas and the sugar. Return to a boil and simmer until tender. Frozen peas have already been blanched and need very little cooking.
		White pepper	
			4. Drain the two vegetables and combine them in a steam table pan.
			5. Ladle the butter over the vegetables and season to taste.

Note: Proportion of peas and carrots may be varied as desired.

Variations

151A. À la Carte Service: Drain cooked vegetables and cool immediately in cold water. Drain and refrigerate. Sauté portions to order in butter or, if appropriate for the vegetable, olive oil. Season to taste.

151B. Buttered Vegetables: The following vegetables may be cooked by simple boiling or steaming method and dressed with butter for service, as in basic recipe:

Asparagus	Cabbage	Parsnips
Beans, green or yellow	Carrots	Peas
Beans, lima	Cauliflower	Rutabagas
Beets	Celery	Spinach
Broccoli (see note)	Corn (on cob, or whole kernel)	Turnips
Brussels sprouts	Kohlrabi	

Note: Dress each portion of broccoli spears with butter just when served. Butter runs off them quickly. Do not sauté for à la carte service. Reheat in boiling water and then add butter. Other large vegetables, such as cauliflower, may also be prepared like broccoli.

151C. Herbed Vegetables: Season buttered vegetables with fresh chopped parsley or other appropriate fresh or dried herbs (see table on p. 426). Dried herbs should be heated a few minutes with the vegetable to release flavor.

151D. Amandine: Especially for green beans, broccoli, celery, cauliflower. For each 2 lb (900 g) EP of vegetable, sauté 2 oz (60 g) slivered or sliced almonds in 2–3 oz (60–90 g) butter until lightly browned. (Caution: Almonds darken quickly.) Combine with cooked vegetable.

(Continues)

RECIPE 151 **Buttered Peas and Carrots** *(Continued)*

151E. *Hollandaise:* Especially for broccoli, asparagus, cauliflower, brussels sprouts, leeks, and artichoke hearts or bottoms. At serving time, nap each portion of vegetable with 2 oz (60 mL) Hollandaise Sauce.

151F. *Polonaise:* Especially for cauliflower, broccoli, brussels sprouts, and sometimes asparagus and green beans. For each 5 lb EP (2.3 kg) of vegetable, sauté 1½ pt (750 mL) fresh bread crumbs in about 6 oz (175 g) butter until golden. Chop the whites and yolks of 2 to 4 hard-cooked eggs separately. Combine the crumbs, chopped egg, and 4 tbsp (60 mL) chopped parsley. Sprinkle this mixture over the cooked vegetable immediately before serving.

RECIPE 152 **Puréed Butternut Squash**

		Portions: 25		**Portion size:** 3 oz (90 g)

U.S.	Metric	Ingredients	Procedure
7½ lb	3.5 kg	Butternut squash	1. Peel the squash, cut in half, and scrape out seeds. Cut into large dice.
6 oz	175 g	Butter	
3 oz	90 g	Brown sugar	2. Place in perforated steamer pan. Steam until tender. (Alternative method: Place in heavy pot. Add 1 inch of water, cover, and cook slowly until tender. Drain well.)
2 tsp	10 mL	Salt	
		White pepper	
		Nutmeg or ginger	3. Purée the squash through a food mill. Add the butter, sugar, and seasonings. Whip until light, but do not overwhip or squash will become watery. Note: If squash is too wet, cook out some of the moisture in a shallow pan over medium heat.

Variations

Add 3–4 oz (90–125 mL) heavy cream, heated. Sugar may be reduced or omitted if the squash has a good flavor.

152A. *Mashed Rutabagas or Yellow Turnips:* Prepare as in basic recipe. If desired, a small amount of whipped potato may be added.

RECIPE 153   **Creamed Spinach**

		Portions: 25	**Portion size:** 3½ oz (100 g)

U.S.	Metric	Ingredients	Procedure
10 lb AP 3½ pt	4.5 kg 1.7 L	Spinach, fresh Cream Sauce, hot Nutmeg Salt White pepper	1. Trim spinach and wash carefully in several changes of water. Drain. 2. Place 2 inches (5 cm) of water in a heavy pot, cover, and bring to a boil. Add the spinach. Stir several times so that it cooks evenly. 3. As soon as the spinach is thoroughly wilted, drain in a colander, pressing with the back of a kitchen spoon to squeeze out excess liquid. 4. Chop the spinach coarsely. 5. Combine with the Cream Sauce in a hotel pan. Season to taste with nutmeg, salt, and pepper. (The spinach must not taste strongly of nutmeg.)

Note: For frozen chopped spinach, partially thaw 2½ packages (2½ lb / 1.1 kg each). Cover with boiling salted water and break spinach apart. Cook only until hot and drain. Squeeze out excess liquid and combine with Cream Sauce.

Variations

153A. Creamed Vegetables: The following vegetables, cut into small pieces if necessary, may be cooked by boiling or steaming and combined with Cream Sauce, as in basic recipe. For 25 portions, use 5–6 lb EP (about 2½ kg) vegetables and 2½–3½ pt (1.2–1.7 L) Cream Sauce.

Asparagus	Cauliflower
Beans, green or yellow	Celery
Beans, lima	Kohlrabi
Broccoli	Okra
Brussels sprouts	Onions, small white
Cabbage	Peas
Carrots	

RECIPE 154   **Broccoli Mornay**

| | | | **Portions:** 24 | **Portion size:** 3½ oz (100 g) broccoli 2 oz (60 mL) sauce |

U.S.	Metric	Ingredients	Procedure
7½ lb	3.4 kg	Broccoli	1. Trim and wash broccoli. Separate large pieces into smaller serving pieces. Split or peel stems for even cooking.
1½ qt	1½ L	Mornay Sauce, hot	
			2. Arrange broccoli in hotel pan with flowers to the outside, stems in center.
			3. Pour in boiling salted water to partially cover. Cover with clean, wet towels and set on range top.
			4. Simmer until blossom parts are nearly tender. Fold back towels from edges to uncover blossoms. This releases steam and helps avoid overcooking. Leave stems covered and continue to simmer until stems feel tender but *al dente* when pierced with a knife. Drain well.
			5. Nap each portion with 2 oz (60 mL) Mornay Sauce at service time. Ladle the sauce across the stems, without covering the blossoms.

Note: This method of cooking in a shallow pan is used to prevent damaging the blossom ends, which are easily broken. Other delicate vegetables, such as asparagus, are also sometimes cooked in shallow water in hotel pans or sauté pans.

Broccoli may be cooked in a steamer, following basic steaming method.

Variations

154A. Broccoli with Cheddar Cheese Sauce: Prepare as in basic recipe, but substitute Cheddar Cheese Sauce for the Mornay Sauce.

Other vegetables served with cheese sauce: cauliflower and brussels sprouts.

RECIPE 155   **Cauliflower au Gratin**

Portions: 25   **Portion size:** 3 oz (90 g) cauliflower
2 oz (60 g) sauce
and topping

U.S.	Metric	Ingredients	Procedure
5 lb EP	2.3 kg	Cauliflower	1. Separate the cauliflower into florets.
1 tbsp	15 mL	Lemon juice (see note)	2. Place the cauliflower and lemon juice into boiling, salted water. Return to boil, lower heat, and cover. Simmer until just tender. Do not overcook, as it will cook further in the sauce. Drain.
1½ qt	1.5 L	Béchamel or Mornay Sauce, hot	
1½ oz	45 g	Dry bread crumbs	3. Butter the bottom of a baking pan or hotel pan and place the cauliflower in it about 2 inches (5 cm) deep. (Individual oven-proof serving dishes may be used instead.)
1½ oz	45 g	Parmesan cheese, grated	
2½ oz	75 g	Butter, melted	4. Cover with the hot sauce.
			5. Mix together the bread crumbs and cheese and sprinkle evenly over the top. Drizzle melted butter over the top.
			6. Bake at 350°F (175°C) for about 20 minutes to heat through. Brown the top under the broiler or salamander.

Note: Adding lemon juice to cooking water helps to keep white vegetables white. It may be omitted if desired.

Variations

Substitute Cheddar Cheese Sauce for the Béchamel or Mornay, and use grated cheddar cheese instead of parmesan for topping.

155A. ***Other Vegetables Prepared au Gratin:*** Asparagus, Belgian endive, broccoli, brussels sprouts, celery, celery root, leeks, and turnips.

RECIPE 156 **Artichokes Clamart**

....

Portions: 10   **Portion size:** 1 artichoke heart
1 oz (30 g) peas

U.S.	Metric	Ingredients	Procedure
10 1	10 1	Artichokes, large Lemon, cut in half	1. Prepare artichoke bottoms by trimming as shown in Figure 16.1. Rub the cut surfaces with the lemon as you work, to keep them from darkening.
1 oz 3 pt 1½ oz 1 tbsp	30 g 1.5 L 50 mL 15 mL	Flour Cold water Lemon juice Salt	2. Mix the flour with a little water, then add it to the remaining water in a saucepan. Add the lemon juice and salt. Bring to a boil. This mixture is called a *blanc*. It helps keep the artichokes white as they cook. 3. Add the artichokes to the *blanc* and simmer until just tender, about 30 minutes. Drain.
10 oz 3 oz pinch	300 g 90 g pinch	Peas, frozen Butter Salt White pepper Basil	4. Place the peas in a saucepan with boiling salted water and simmer until just heated through. Drain. 5. Heat 1 oz (30 g) of the butter in a sauté pan and sauté the peas briefly. Season with salt, pepper, and basil, tossing over heat briefly so that the basil can release its flavor. 6. At the same time, heat remaining 2 oz (60 g) butter in another sauté pan. Place the cooked artichoke bottoms in the pan and sauté over medium heat until the artichokes are well coated with butter and are hot. Season with salt and pepper. 7. Arrange artichokes in a hotel pan and fill with the peas. (Do not do this in advance, because the lemon juice in the artichokes will discolor the peas.)

Variations

Artichoke bottoms can be filled with other vegetables, such as asparagus tips, tiny tournéed carrots, tournéed turnips, or mushrooms. They may also be used as containers for a sauce served with grilled meat items. Either way, they are used mostly as garnish for meats.

....

RECIPE 157   White Beans Bretonne Style

Yield: about 6 lb (3 kg)   **Portions:** 20   **Portion size:** 5 oz (150 g)

U.S.	Metric	Ingredients	Procedure
2 lb	1 kg	Dried white beans	1. Soak the beans overnight in cold water.
1	1	Carrot, small	
1 stem	1 stem	Celery	2. Drain the beans and place in a pot with enough water to cover by 1 inch. Add the carrot, celery, onion, and spice bag. Simmer until the beans are tender, but not soft or broken (1–3 hours, depending on the beans). Drain but save the liquid. Discard the vegetables and spice bag.
1	1	Onion, small, peeled	
		Spice bag (tied in cheesecloth):	
1	1	Bay leaf	
6–8	6–8	Parsley stems	
3–4	3–4	Peppercorns	
1	1	Clove	
pinch	pinch	Thyme	
4 oz	125 g	Butter	3. Heat the butter in a large sauce pot or brazier. Sauté the onion and garlic until soft. Add the tomatoes and cook a few minutes to reduce liquid.
8 oz	250 g	Onion, diced	
2	2	Garlic cloves, chopped	
1 lb	500 g	Canned tomatoes, with juice, coarsely chopped	4. Add the beans to this mixture and stir carefully. Simmer until heated through and flavors are blended. If too dry, add some of the bean cooking liquid. Add pan drippings, if you are using them. Season to taste.
		Pan juices from roast lamb (optional; see note)	
		Salt	
		Pepper	

Note: This preparation is often served with roast leg of lamb or other lamb roast. If so, the pan drippings may be used to flavor the beans.

RECIPE 158   Glazed Carrots I

                                 Portions: 25   **Portion size:** 3 oz (90 g)

U.S.	Metric	Ingredients	Procedure
6½ lb	3 kg	Carrots	1. Trim and peel the carrots. Cut them into uniform pieces. Tournéed carrots (see Figure 18.1 for technique) are often prepared by this method.
3 oz	90 g	Butter	
2 oz	60 g	Sugar	
		Salt	2. Place the carrots in a saucepan with boiling salted water to cover. Simmer until tender. Drain.
			3. Heat the butter in a sauté pan. Add the carrots and sprinkle with the sugar and salt to taste. Sauté until the carrots are well glazed.

Variation

158A. Glazed Vegetables: Turnips, rutabagas, parsnips, celery root, pearl onions, and chestnuts may be glazed by this method.

RECIPE 159   **Glazed Carrots II (Carrots Vichy)**

Portions: 25   **Portion size: 3 oz (90 g)**

U.S.	Metric	Ingredients	Procedure
6½ lb	3 kg	Carrots	1. Trim, peel, and slice the carrots.
		Water (see note)	2. Place them in a saucepan or straight-sided sauté pan. Add water to barely cover the carrots. Add the butter, sugar, and salt.
5 oz	150 g	Butter	
2 tbsp	30 g	Sugar	
2 tsp	10 mL	Salt	3. Bring to a boil. Lower heat and simmer until the carrots are tender and the water is nearly evaporated. If done properly, these should happen at the same time. Toss the carrots so that they are well coated with the glaze that is left in the pan.
		White pepper	
		Chopped parsley	
			4. Garnish with chopped parsley.

Note: Sometimes Vichy water or other bottled mineral water is used, but it is not necessary.

SAUTÉING AND PAN-FRYING

Remember that the main differences between sautéing and pan-frying are in the amount of fat used and in the cooking time. Sautéing means cooking quickly in a small amount of fat. The product is often tossed or flipped in the pan over high heat. Pan-frying means cooking in a larger amount of fat, usually for a longer time at lower heat, and the product is not tossed or flipped. In practice, the two methods are sometimes very similar, and the distinction between them is hard to draw.

Both methods may be used for finish-cooking precooked or blanched vegetables as well as for completely cooking vegetables from the raw state. Sautéing in butter is especially popular for finishing precooked and chilled vegetables for service.

Stir-frying is a quick-cooking technique used in Oriental cookery. In effect, it is similar to sautéing, except that the pan is left stationary and the items being cooked are stirred and flipped in hot fat with spatulas or other tools.

Procedure for Sautéing Vegetables

This method is used for precooked or blanched vegetables and for tender, small-cut vegetables that cook quickly.

1. Collect all equipment and food products.

2. Prepare vegetables as required.

3. Place sauté pan on high heat.

4. When the pan is hot, add a small amount of clarified butter, oil, or other fat, enough to coat the bottom of the pan. (Clarified butter is used because the milk solids in whole butter burn quickly at the high heat necessary for sautéing.)

5. As soon as the fat is hot, add the vegetable. DO NOT overload the pan, or the temperature will be lowered too much, and the vegetables will simmer instead of sauté.

6. After the heat has had time to recover, flip the pan a few times to turn and toss the vegetables (see Figure 17.1). Let the pan set again over the heat.

7. Continue to flip the vegetables as often as necessary for them to cook or heat evenly and become coated with the cooking fat. (Don't flip more than necessary, however. It may be fun

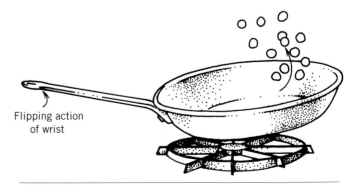

Flipping action of wrist

FIGURE 17.1   **To flip foods in a sauté pan, give the handle a sharp twist upward with the wrist. Be sure to move the pan back far enough to catch the foods as they come down.**

and a good way to show off, but it's a waste of time and accomplishes nothing except breaking fragile vegetables. Also, the heat must have time to recover between flips.)

8. As soon as the vegetables are cooked, or heated through if precooked, remove from the pan and serve. Browning may or may not be desirable, depending on the vegetable and the particular preparation.

Procedure for Pan-frying Vegetables

Note: A griddle is often used for this procedure if only a small amount of fat is required.

1. Collect all equipment and food products.

2. Prepare vegetables as required.

3. Place a sauté pan or cast iron skillet on moderately high heat. Add required amount of fat to the pan and let it heat up.

4. Place prepared vegetables in the pan. Adjust the heat so that the product cooks through with the desired amount of browning, but without burning the outside.

5. Turn vegetables with a spatula and continue to cook until done.

6. Remove from pan. If necessary, drain on absorbent paper to eliminate excess fat.

RECIPE 160   **Pan-fried Eggplant with Tomato Sauce**

Portions: 24		**Portion size:** 3½ oz (100 g) eggplant	
		2 oz (60 mL) sauce	

U.S.	Metric	Ingredients	Procedure
6½ lb	3 kg	Eggplant	1. Wash and trim eggplants. Pare if skins are tough. Cut crosswise into ¼-inch (½-cm) slices.
		Breading:	
6 oz	175 g	Flour	
1½ tsp	7 mL	Salt	2. Hold in strongly salted cold water up to 30 minutes. (This step may be omitted, but it helps prevent darkening and eliminates some bitter flavors.)
½ tsp	2 mL	White pepper	
1 pt	500 mL	Egg wash	
1¼ lb	600 g	Bread crumbs	
		Oil for frying	3. Set up breading station, seasoning the flour with the salt and pepper.
			4. Drain the eggplants and dry them well. Pass through Standard Breading Procedure (see p. 114).
			5. Heat ¼ inch (½ cm) of oil in a heavy iron skillet or sauté pan. Pan-fry the breaded eggplant on both sides until browned. Remove from pan with slotted spatula and drain on absorbent paper.
1½ qt	1.5 L	Tomato Sauce	6. Serve 2–3 slices per portion, depending on size. Nap each portion with 2 oz (60 mL) Tomato Sauce. Ladle the sauce in a band across the eggplant; do not cover completely.

Variations

Instead of Standard Breading Procedure, simply dredge slices in seasoned flour and pan-fry.

160A. *Pan-fried Eggplant Creole:* Use Creole Sauce instead of Tomato Sauce.

160B. *Eggplant Parmigiana:* Pan-fry as in basic recipe. Top each fried slice with a thin slice of mozzarella cheese. Arrange in layers in a baking pan, covering each layer with Tomato Sauce and sprinkling with parmesan cheese. Bake 30 minutes at 350°F (175°C).

RECIPE 161   **Sautéed Zucchini**

Portions: 25   **Portion size:** 3½ oz (100 g)

U.S.	Metric	Ingredients	Procedure
6 lb	2.7 kg	Zucchini	1. Wash and trim the zucchini. Cut crosswise into thin slices.
6 oz	175 g	Butter, clarified, or olive oil	
6 oz	175 g	Shallots or onions, minced	2. Heat the butter or oil in two or three sauté pans (or sauté in several batches—do not overload the pans). Add the shallot or onion and sauté until soft but not browned.
		Salt	
		White pepper	3. Add the zucchini and sauté until lightly browned but still somewhat crisp.
			4. Season to taste.

Variations

Cut zucchini into other shapes, but keep them small enough to cook quickly. Examples: batonnet, julienne, dice, and shredded on coarse grater.

161A. *Zucchini Sauté Provençale:* Sauté as in basic recipe, using olive oil for the fat and add 3–4 cloves chopped garlic with the onion. Garnish with chopped parsley.

161B. *Zucchini with Tomatoes:* Sauté as in basic recipe. When half cooked, add 2½ pt (1.2 L) drained, chopped, canned tomatoes or fresh tomatoes concassé (pp. 396–397), and finish cooking. Season with oregano or basil.

161C. *Zucchini with Cream:* Shred zucchini on grater. Salt lightly and let stand in a colander 30 minutes. Press out excess liquid. Sauté as in basic recipe, but without browning. Add 2½ cups (600 mL) heavy cream and simmer 2 minutes.

RECIPE 162   **Corn Sauté Mexicaine**

Portions: 25   **Portion size:** 3 oz (90g)

U.S.	Metric	Ingredients	Procedure
5 lb	2.2 kg	Corn, frozen whole kernel	1. Place corn in sauce pot with boiling salted water. Simmer until heated through. Drain well. Cool if to be held for later service.
4 oz	100 g	Butter	
8 oz	200 g	Green pepper, chopped fine	2. Heat butter in sauté pan and sauté green pepper about 1 minute.
4 oz	100 g	Pimiento (canned), chopped fine	3. Add corn and pimiento. Sauté until hot and well blended. Season to taste.
		Salt	
		White pepper	

Note: Canned corn may be used, but it does not need to be simmered first. Just drain well and add to sauté pan.

Variations

162A. *Corn O'Brien:* Prepare as in basic recipe, but sauté 6 oz (175 g) chopped onion with the green pepper. Cook 8 oz (250 g) diced bacon until crisp and add at service time. Bacon fat may be used instead of butter for sautéing, if desired.

162B. *Corn and Zucchini Sauté:* Prepare as in basic recipe, but replace green pepper with 2½ lb (1.1 kg) zucchini, cut in ¼-inch (½-cm) dice. Omit pimiento.

RECIPE 163   **Sautéed Mushrooms**

		Portions: 25		**Portion size:** 3½ oz (100 g)

U.S.	Metric	Ingredients	Procedure	
6½ lb 10 oz	3 kg 300 g	Mushrooms, fresh Clarified butter, or half oil, half butter Salt Pepper	1.	Rinse the mushrooms quickly and dry them with towels. Trim off the bottoms of the stems and slice the mushrooms.
			2.	Heat two or three sauté pans over high heat (or sauté in several batches—do not overload pans). Add the fat to the pans. Place the mushrooms in the pan and sauté over high heat until browned. Do not overcook, or the mushrooms will shrivel and lose a great deal of moisture.
			3.	Season with salt and pepper.

Note: If mushrooms must be kept light in color, add lemon juice to the pan when the mushrooms are added. Use about 1 oz (30 mL) lemon juice per pound of mushrooms.

Variations

Garnish with chopped parsley.

Instead of slicing, leave small mushroom caps whole, or cut in halves or quarters.

163A. Creamed Mushrooms: Prepare as in basic recipe, using lemon juice to keep light color. Combine with 2½ pt (1.2 L) hot Cream Sauce. Season with a little nutmeg.

163B. Duxelles: Chop mushrooms very fine. Squeeze out moisture in a towel. Sauté in butter with 3 oz (90 g) minced shallot or onion until dry. Season with salt, pepper, nutmeg. Used in vegetable and meat stuffings. May be moistened with heavy cream or stretched with bread crumbs.

BRAISING

Braising, as you know, is a slow, moist-heat cooking method using a small amount of liquid. When meats are braised, they are seared or browned in fat before any liquid is added. Braised vegetables are not always cooked in fat before liquid is added, although some kind of fat is used in the preparation.

Braised vegetable preparations tend to be more complex than boiled or steamed vegetables, and the cooking times are longer. Unfortunately, there are so many variations of braised vegetables that it is not possible to prescribe a single basic procedure. Instead, we will discuss the procedures in general terms and use the recipes to illustrate them.

Characteristics of Vegetable Braising Procedure

1. Fat is added to a braising or baking pan or a saucepan and heated. Finely diced mirepoix or other flavoring ingredients may be cooked briefly in the fat. The fat contributes to flavor and eating quality.

2. The vegetable (blanched or raw) is placed in the pan. It may or may not be cooked in the fat before the liquid is added, depending on the recipe.

3. Liquid is added—stock, water, wine, or a combination of liquids. The liquid generally covers the vegetable only part way.

4. The pot or saucepan is covered and the vegetable is cooked slowly in the oven or on the range top.

5. The flavorful cooking liquid is served with the vegetable. It is sometimes drained off and reduced over high heat before serving, in order to concentrate flavor.

RECIPE 164 **Braised Red Cabbage**

Portions: 25			**Portion size:** 5 oz (150 g)

U.S.	Metric	Ingredients	Procedure
6 lb AP	3 kg	Red cabbage	1. Remove outer leaves of cabbage and cut into quarters. Remove core and shred with a knife (Figure 16.4) or power shredder attachment. Do not chop; cabbage should be in long, fine shreds.
12 oz	375 g	Bacon, diced	
1 lb	500 g	Onions, sliced	
1 oz	30 g	Sugar	
1½ pt	750 mL	White stock (chicken, pork, veal) or water	2. Render the bacon in a large, heavy pot. Add the onions and sugar and cook until the onion is soft.
1 lb	500 g	Apples, cored, diced, peel left on	3. Add cabbage and stir over heat until the cabbage is coated with fat.
4	4	Cloves	4. Add the stock, apples, and the spices tied in a cheesecloth bag. Cover and simmer until cabbage is nearly tender, about 30 minutes.
6	6	Whole allspice	
1 piece	1 piece	Stick cinnamon	
4 oz or more	125 mL	Cider vinegar or red wine vinegar	5. Add the vinegar and red wine and simmer another 10 minutes. Remove spice bag.
1 cup	250 mL	Red wine (or more vinegar)	6. Taste and correct seasoning. If not tart enough or color is not red enough, add more vinegar.
		Salt	
		Pepper	

Variations

Substitute lard, salt pork, or chicken fat for the bacon. Vegetable oil may be used, but it does not contribute to flavor.

Eliminate cinnamon, cloves, and allspice. Add 1 tablespoon (15 mL) caraway seeds to onions when sautéing them.

164A. *Braised Green or White Cabbage:* Prepare as in the basic recipe, but season with 1 bay leaf, 6–8 parsley stems, 6 peppercorns, and a pinch of thyme, instead of the cinnamon, cloves, and allspice. *Omit* sugar, apples, wine, and vinegar. Butter may be used as cooking fat if desired.

RECIPE 165   **Sauerkraut**

| | | Portions: 25 | | Portion size: 4½ oz (125 g) |

U.S.	Metric	Ingredients	Procedure
1 No. 10 can		Sauerkraut	1. Rinse sauerkraut in cold water. Drain and press out water. Taste and rinse again if still too briny. (See Appendix 2, p. 794, for can sizes and substitutions.)
2 oz	60 g	Lard or bacon fat	
1 lb	500 g	Onions, sliced	
1 pint	500 mL	Dry white wine (optional)	
1½ qt (approx.)	1.5 L	Chicken stock	2. Heat lard in heavy pot and sauté onions until soft. Add sauerkraut, wine (if used) and enough stock so that the kraut is covered by about three-fourths. Tie the spices and garlic in cheesecloth and add to the pot.
5	5	Juniper berries	
2	2	Bay leaves	
2	2	Whole cloves	
1 tsp	5 mL	Caraway or cumin seed	3. Cover and simmer for 1½ hours on range top or in slow oven (300°F/150°C).
2	2	Garlic cloves	4. Remove spice bag. Taste kraut and adjust seasoning.
		Salt	

Variation

165A. ***Choucroute Garni:*** Double quantities per portion. Cook a variety of fresh and smoked pork products and sausages in the sauerkraut. Add each item at the proper time so that it is in the kraut for its correct cooking time. Suggestions: fresh or smoked pork chops, slab bacon, bratwurst, frankfurters, smoked pork shoulder. Serve as a main course. Accompany with boiled potatoes.

RECIPE 166   **Peas à la Francaise**

| | | Portions: 16 | | Portion size: 3 oz (90 g) |

U.S.	Metric	Ingredients	Procedure
3 oz	90 g	Butter	1. Heat the butter in a saucepan. Add the onions and sauté lightly.
2 oz	60 g	Chopped onion or whole tiny pearl onions, peeled	
2½ lb	1.1 kg	Peas, frozen	2. Add the peas, lettuce, parsley, salt, and sugar. Cook over moderate heat, stirring a few times, until the vegetables begin to steam.
8 oz	225 g	Lettuce, shredded	
2 tbsp	30 mL	Chopped parsley	
1 tsp	5 mL	Salt	3. Add the stock or water. Bring to a boil, cover, and simmer over low heat or in oven until peas are tender.
2 tsp	10 mL	Sugar	
4 oz	125 mL	Chicken stock or water, hot	4. Stir in a little beurre manié to thicken the cooking liquid and simmer another 2–3 minutes. Adjust seasoning. (For larger quantities, drain off liquid and thicken separately.)
1 tbsp	15 mL	Beurre manié	

RECIPE 167   Braised Celery

Portions: 25			**Portion size:** 3 oz (90 g)

U.S.	Metric	Ingredients	Procedure
6 lb AP	3 kg	Celery	1. Trim and wash celery. If very stringy, peel outside of ribs, or use the tender inner stems and save the outside ones for the mirepoix. Cut into 1½-inch (4-cm) lengths. Split broad pieces lengthwise so all pieces are about the same size.
4 oz	125 g	Butter	
3 pt	1.5 L	Brown stock or	
	approximately	chicken stock	
		Salt	
		Pepper	2. Heat the butter in a braising pot and add the celery. Cook over moderate heat until the celery is just beginning to soften.
			3. Add enough stock to cover the celery by about two-thirds. Cover and cook slowly in oven or on range top until tender, about 20–30 minutes.
		Optional: beurre manié (p. 133)	4. Drain celery and keep warm in a steam-table pan. Reduce the stock over high heat to about 2½ pt (1.25 L). If desired, thicken slightly with beurre manié. Adjust seasonings and pour over celery.

Variations

Bacon fat may be used instead of butter. For extra flavor, add finely diced mirepoix to the fat in the pan before adding celery.

167A. Braised Celery Hearts: Prepare as in basic recipe, but use celery hearts (the tender inner stalks, connected at the root), cut into wedges.

167B. Braised Celery with Brown Sauce: Add 2½ pt (1.25 L) Brown Sauce or Demiglace to the reduced cooking liquid and reduce again to reach desired consistency. Add to celery.

167C. Braised Celery Root: Prepare as in basic recipe, using sliced, blanched knob celery (celeriac).

167D. Braised Lettuce: Blanch romaine lettuce to wilt leaves. Fold leaves into neat, portion-size bundles. Arrange on finely cut, sautéed mirepoix and braise as in basic recipe, without sautéing the lettuce.

RECIPE 168   **Ratatouille**

The method for this preparation is unlike that for the other braised vegetables in this section, because no liquid is added. It is classified as a braised item because the vegetables are first sautéed in fat, then simmered in their own juices.

Portions: 20		**Portion size:** 4 oz (125 g)	

U.S.	Metric	Ingredients	Procedure
1 lb	500 g	Zucchini	1. Prepare the vegetables: Cut the zucchini into ½-inch (1-cm) slices. Peel the eggplant and cut into large dice. Slice the onions. Remove the cores and seeds of the peppers and cut into 1-inch (2½-cm) dice. Chop the garlic. Peel and seed the tomatoes and cut into large dice (leave canned tomatoes whole; they will break up during cooking).
1 lb	500 g	Eggplant	
1 lb	500 g	Onions	
4	4	Green peppers	
4 cloves	4 cloves	Garlic	
2 lb	1 kg	Tomatoes (canned may be used if necessary)	
6 oz or more as needed	200 mL	Olive oil	2. Sauté the zucchini in a little of the olive oil until it is about half cooked. Remove from pan.
½ cup	125 mL	Chopped parsley	3. Sauté the eggplant in olive oil until half cooked. Remove from pan.
1	1	Bay leaf	
¼ tsp	1 mL	Thyme	4. Sauté the onions and peppers until half cooked. Add the garlic and sauté another minute.
		Salt	
		Pepper	5. Combine all vegetables and seasonings in a brazier or heavy saucepan. Cover and cook in slow oven (325°F/160°C) about 30 minutes, until vegetables are tender and flavors are well blended. If the vegetables are too juicy, cook uncovered on range top for a few minutes to reduce. Be careful not to scorch the vegetables on the bottom.
			6. Adjust seasonings. Serve hot or cold.

BAKING

You could, if you wished, cook carrots by placing them in a pot of boiling water, placing the pot in a hot oven, and cooking until tender. This is not a different cooking technique, however. It's plain old simmering. You'd just be using the heat of the oven rather than the range top to simmer the water.

When we talk about baking vegetables, we usually mean one of two things:

1. Cooking starchy vegetables, such as potatoes, winter squash, and sweet potatoes, and other moist, densely textured vegetables such as tomatoes, beets, eggplant, onions, and turnips, from the raw to the finished state. Starch vegetables are baked because the dry heat produces a desirable texture. Baked potatoes, for example, do not have the same texture as boiled or steamed potatoes.

In some areas, it is fashionable to refer to such baked vegetables as "roasted."

In theory, any vegetable with enough moisture could be baked like potatoes, but the drying effects of the oven and the long cooking time make it undesirable for most small vegetables, such as peas and green beans.

2. Finishing certain vegetable combinations, sometimes known as casseroles. The vegetables in these items are usually parcooked by simmering or steaming before they are baked.

Vegetable casseroles are baked for either of two reasons:

a. The slow, all-around heat allows the product to cook undisturbed. The agitation and stirring of range-top cooking is not always desirable. Baked beans could be finished on top of the range, but they would be mushier and more broken up. Corn pudding would be pourable, not firmly set. And can you imagine boiling stuffed tomatoes?

b. The dry heat produces desirable effects, such as browning and caramelizing of sugars. For example, you could put a pan of candied potatoes in a steamer, but the moist heat would not allow a glaze to form.

Procedure for Baking Vegetables

1. Collect all equipment and food products.

2. Prepare vegetables as required.

3. Place in appropriate pan and set in preheated oven.

4. Bake to desired doneness.

RECIPE 169 **Baked Acorn Squash**

Portions: 24   **Portion size:** ½ squash

U.S.	Metric	Ingredients	Procedure
12	12	Acorn squash, small	1. Wash and cut squash in half lengthwise. Scrape out seeds. (If using large squash, cut into portion sizes.)
as needed		Butter, melted	
5 oz	150 g	Brown sugar	2. Brush cut surfaces and cavity with melted butter. Place close together cut side down on baking sheet. (This helps squash cook faster without drying by retaining steam.)
2½ tsp	12 mL	Salt	
2 oz	60 mL	Sherry (optional)	3. Bake at 350°F (175°C) until almost tender, about 30–40 minutes.
			4. Turn cut side up and brush again with butter. Sprinkle cavities with sugar and salt. Add a few drops of sherry to each if desired.
			5. Bake 10–15 minutes more, until surface is glazed.

Variations

Hubbard, buttercup, and other winter squash varieties may be cut into portion sizes and baked as in basic recipe.

169A. *Gingered Squash:* Mix 1½ tsp (7 mL) powdered ginger with the sugar in basic recipe.

169B. *Puréed Squash:* Bake cut Hubbard squash until tender. Remove from shell and purée in food mill. Add butter, salt, and pepper to taste.

RECIPE 170   Glazed Sweet Potatoes

| | | **Portions:** 25 | | **Portion size:** 5 oz (150 g) |

U.S.	Metric	Ingredients	Procedure
8 lb AP	3.6 kg	Sweet potatoes	1. Scrub the sweet potatoes and boil or steam until nearly tender. Do not overcook.
			2. Spread the potatoes on a sheet pan to cool.
			3. Peel when they are cool enough to handle. Remove dark spots. Cut into neat, uniform pieces for easy portioning. Arrange them in a buttered baking pan.
6 oz	175 mL	Water	4. Place the water, syrup, and sugar in a saucepan. Stir over heat until sugar is dissolved. Add the remaining ingredients and boil until the mixture is reduced to about 1½ pt (700–800 mL) and forms a heavy syrup.
1½ cups	350 mL	Light corn syrup or maple syrup	
6 oz	175 g	Brown sugar	
8 oz	250 mL	Orange juice	
2 oz	60 mL	Lemon juice	5. Pour the syrup over the potatoes.
2 oz	60 g	Butter	6. Bake at 350°F (175°C) until potatoes are thoroughly cooked and glazed, about 45–60 minutes. Baste with the syrup several times during baking.
1 tsp	5 mL	Cinnamon	
¼ tsp	1 mL	Ground cloves	
½ tsp	2 mL	Salt	

RECIPE 171   Corn Pudding

| | | **Portions:** 20 | | **Portion size:** 4 oz (125 g) |

U.S.	Metric	Ingredients	Procedure
2½ lb	1.25 kg	Frozen whole kernel corn	1. Thaw the corn or blanch it quickly in boiling water and drain.
1	1	Small onion, chopped fine	2. Sauté the onion in butter until translucent but not brown. Cool slightly.
2 oz	60 g	Butter	3. Combine the corn, onion, and butter with the remaining ingredients and pour into a buttered baking pan.
1 qt	1 L	Milk	
8	8	Eggs, beaten	
		Salt	
		White pepper	4. Bake in a hot-water bath (see note) at 325°F (160°C) until set, about 1 hour.

Note: The purpose of the water bath is to prevent the custard mixture (milk and eggs) from overcooking and curdling.

Variations

Fresh or dried bread crumbs may be added to make a drier, firmer product.

For a lighter product, beat the egg whites separately and fold into the corn/milk mixture.

RECIPE 172 **Baked Beans, New England Style**

....

Portions: 20			**Portion size: 4½ oz (125 g)**	

U.S.	Metric	Ingredients	Procedure	
2 lb	900 g	Dried beans, navy or great northern	1.	Soak the beans overnight in enough water to cover by 2 inches (5 cm).
		Bouquet garni:	2.	Place the beans and liquid in pot and add the bouquet garni. Bring to a boil and skim foam. Reduce heat to a simmer. Cover and simmer 45 minutes to 1 hour, or until beans are just tender but not soft. Add more water if necessary during cooking.
1	1	Bay leaf		
6–8	6–8	Parsley stems		
¼ tsp	1 mL	Thyme		
		A few celery tops		
			3.	Drain the beans, but save the cooking liquid. Discard the bouquet garni.
1 cup	250 mL	Molasses	4.	Mix together the molasses, brown sugar, dry mustard, salt, and 1 qt (1 L) of the bean cooking liquid. If there is not enough bean liquid, add water to make up the difference.
2 oz	60 g	Brown sugar		
1 tbsp	15 mL	Dry mustard		
1 tbsp	15 mL	Salt		
8 oz	225 g	Salt pork, medium dice	5.	Mix the beans, molasses mixture, and salt pork in a 4 qt (4 L) pot or deep baking pan.
			6.	Bake covered at 300°F (150°C) for 2–2½ hours. Add additional liquid if necessary during baking.

Variation

172A. *Michigan Baked Beans:* Reduce molasses to ¼ cup (60 mL) and add 2 cups (500 mL) tomato sauce or tomato purée.

....

BROILING AND GRILLING

Broiling is not widely used for cooking vegetables, because most vegetables would burn on the surface under a broiler's intense heat before cooking through. Only soft, quick-cooking items such as tomatoes are successfully broiled from the raw state.

Grilled quick-cooking vegetables such as peppers, zucchini, large mushroom caps, and eggplant are pleasant accompaniments to grilled and roasted meats and poultry. Cut the vegetables into broad slices, brush with oil, and grill until lightly cooked and lightly browned. Heavy browning may produce an unpleasant burned taste. Grilled vegetables are often dressed with vinaigrette.

Broiling is also used to finish cooked or partially cooked vegetables by browning or glazing them on top. Bread crumbs are sometimes used to give a pleasing brown color and to prevent drying. Casseroles or gratin dishes that do not brown sufficiently in the oven may be browned for a few seconds under the broiler or salamander.

RECIPE 173 **Broiled Tomato Slices**

Portions: 10		**Portion size:** about 2 slices	
		3–4 oz (100 g)	

U.S.	Metric	Ingredients	Procedure
2½ lb	1.1 kg	Tomatoes	1. Wash tomatoes, cut out core end, and slice crosswise into ½-inch (1-cm) slices.
2 oz	60 g	Butter, melted (or olive oil)	
		Salt	2. Place the slices in a single layer on an oiled baking sheet.
		White pepper	
			3. Drip melted butter or oil over the tomatoes and sprinkle with salt and pepper.
			4. Place in broiler, 4 inches from heat, and broil just until bubbling and hot but still firm enough to hold shape.
			5. Serve 2 slices per portion, depending on size.
		Optional topping:	
1 cup	100 g	Dry bread crumbs	Cook tomatoes halfway. Combine topping ingredients and sprinkle over tomatoes. Brown under broiler.
4 oz	100 g	Melted butter, or olive oil	
1 oz	30 g	Onion, minced very fine	

Variations

173A. Herbed Broiled Tomatoes: Top tomatoes with ¼ cup (60 mL) chopped parsley and ½ tsp (2 mL) basil or oregano before broiling, or mix herbs with crumb topping.

173B. Parmesan Broiled Tomatoes: Add ½ cup (125 mL) grated parmesan cheese to crumb topping.

DEEP-FRYING

The principles of deep-frying that you have already learned are applied to vegetables as well as to other foods.

- Review Deep-frying, Chapter 4, page 58.
- Review Breadings and Batters, Chapter 7, page 114.

Potatoes (covered in the next chapter) and onion rings are the most popular fried vegetables, but many others may be fried, too.

Deep-fried vegetables may be divided into five categories:

1. Vegetables dipped in batter and fried.

2. Vegetables breaded and fried.

3. Vegetables fried without a coating.

    Potatoes are the obvious example. Other starchy vegetables, such as sweet potatoes, may be fried without breading or batter if they are cut thin to reduce cooking time. The sugar in them burns easily if they are cooked too long.

4. Small vegetables or cuts mixed with a batter and dropped with a scoop into hot fat. The term "fritter" is used for this preparation, as well as for that in category 1.

5. Croquettes: thick vegetable purées or mixtures of small pieces of vegetable and a heavy béchamel or other binder, formed into shapes, breaded, and fried.

Procedure for Deep-frying Vegetables

1. Collect all equipment and food products.

2. Preheat fryer to proper temperature.
    Most vegetables are fried at from 325°F to 350°F (160°C to 175°C).

3. Prepare food items as required. Apply breading or batter if necessary.

4. Place proper amount of food in fryer—do not overload.

5. Fry to desired doneness.

6. Remove food from fryer and let fat drain from it.

7. Serve at once, or if necessary, hold uncovered in a warm place for shortest possible time.

Vegetables for Deep-frying

Most vegetables large enough to coat with breading or batter may be fried. Tender, quick-cooking vegetables can be fried raw. Others must be precooked by simmering or steaming briefly to reduce the cooking time they need in the frying fat.

Raw vegetables for frying in breading or batter:

Eggplant

Mushrooms

Onion rings

Peppers

Tomatoes

Zucchini

Blanched or precooked vegetables for frying in breading or batter:

Artichoke hearts

Asparagus

Beans, green and yellow

Broccoli

Brussels sprouts

Carrots

Cauliflower

Celery

Celery root

Cucumbers

Fennel

Okra

Parsnips

Turnips

RECIPE 174 **Onion Rings**

	Portions: 20		**Portion size:** 3 oz (90 g), 8–10 pieces

U.S.	Metric	Ingredients	Procedure
2	2	Eggs, beaten	1. Combine the eggs and milk in a bowl.
1 pint	500 mL	Milk	2. Mix the flour, baking powder, salt, and paprika together and add to the milk. Mix well. The batter should have the consistency of thin pancake batter.
10 oz	300 g	Cake flour	
2 tsp	10 mL	Baking powder	
½ tsp	2 mL	Salt	
½ tsp	2 mL	Paprika (optional: for color)	
3 lb AP	1.4 kg	Large onions Flour	3. Peel the onions and cut crosswise into ¼-inch (½-cm) slices. Separate into rings (save unusable pieces for another purpose).
			4. Place the onions in cold water if they are not used immediately, to maintain crispness.
			5. Drain and dry the onions thoroughly.
			6. Dredge with flour and shake off excess. (This step isn't always necessary, but it helps the batter adhere.)
			7. Dip a few pieces at a time in the batter and fry in deep fat (350°F/175°C) until golden brown.
			8. Drain and serve immediately.

Variations

174A. Beer Batter: Substitute light beer for the milk. Omit baking powder, because the carbonation of the beer will act as a leavener.

174B. Buttermilk Batter: Substitute buttermilk for the milk, and use 1 tsp (5 mL) baking soda instead of the 2 tsp baking powder.

174C. Other Fried Vegetables: Any of the vegetables on the list at the beginning of this section may be fried in these batters.

RECIPE 175   Vegetable Fritters

Portions: 20   **Portion size:** 3 oz (90 g)
                                                                 2 pieces

U.S.	Metric	Ingredients	Procedure
		Batter:	1. Combine eggs and milk.
6	6	Eggs, beaten	2. Mix flour, baking powder, salt, and sugar.
1 pt	500 mL	Milk	Add to milk and eggs and mix until smooth.
1 lb	500 g	Flour	
2 tbsp	30 mL	Baking powder	3. Let stand several hours in refrigerator.
1 tsp	5 mL	Salt	
1 oz	30 g	Sugar	
1½ lb EP	700 g	Vegetables: Choice of corn, cooked diced carrots, baby lima beans, diced asparagus, diced celery or celery root, turnip, egg-plant, cauliflower, zucchini, parsnips	4. Stir cold, cooked vegetables into batter.
			5. Drop with a No. 24 scoop into deep fat at 350°F (175°C). Hold the scoop just above the hot fat when dropping. Fry until golden brown.
			6. Drain well and serve.

Variations

For lighter fritters, beat egg whites separately and fold into batter.

175A. Fruit Fritters: Increase sugar to 2 oz (60 g). Use fresh, frozen, or canned fruits such as blueberries, diced pineapple, or apple. Fruit must be well drained. Dust each portion with powdered sugar at service time. (Batter may be seasoned with cinnamon, vanilla, brandy, or other appropriate flavoring.)

Some Suggested Vegetable Seasonings, Flavorings, and Combinations

Asparagus	Lemon juice, brown butter, mustard sauce, parmesan cheese; hard-cooked egg, peas, artichokes, mushrooms
Beans, green	Dill, basil, tarragon, oregano, garlic, brown butter, soy sauce; almonds, sesame seed, onion, tomato, celery, mushrooms, bacon
Beans, lima	Oregano, sage, thyme, sour cream, cheddar cheese; corn, peas, onions, mushrooms, pimiento, bacon
Beets	Lemon, allspice, caraway, cloves, dill, ginger, horseradish, bay leaf, orange, sour cream, onion
Broccoli	Lemon, mustard sauce, almonds, buttered toasted bread crumbs, hard-cooked egg
Brussels sprouts	Caraway, dill, parmesan cheese, cheddar cheese, chestnuts
Cabbage	Caraway, celery seed, dill, mustard, nutmeg, garlic; bacon, ham, carrots, onion
Carrots	Parsley, dill, fennel, tarragon, ginger, nutmeg, bay leaves, caraway, mint, orange; celery, peas, zucchini

Some Suggested Vegetable Seasonings, Flavorings, and Combinations *(Continued)*

Cauliflower	Dill, nutmeg, mustard, curry, cheese, tomato sauce; hard-cooked egg, peas, almonds
Celery	Parsley, tarragon, onion, green or red pepper, potatoes
Corn	Chili powder, mild cheddar or jack cheese, tomato, bacon, lima beans
Cucumber	Dill, garlic, mint, tarragon; peas
Eggplant	Garlic, marjoram, oregano, parsley, parmesan cheese; tomato, chopped walnuts
Mushrooms	Nutmeg, parsley, lemon, paprika, dill, sherry, parmesan cheese, cayenne, heavy cream; peas, spinach, artichokes, green beans
Okra	Garlic, coriander, sage; tomatoes, corn
Onions	Nutmeg, sage, thyme, cheese sauce, sour cream; peas
Peas	Mint, basil, dill, sage; mushrooms, pearl onions, turnips, potatoes, carrots, water chestnuts, Jerusalem artichokes
Spinach	Nutmeg, garlic, heavy cream; mushrooms, hard-cooked egg, cheese
Squash, summer (including zucchini)	Cumin, basil, oregano, mustard seed, rosemary, garlic, parmesan cheese, parsley; tomato, carrots (with zucchini), onion, almonds, walnuts
Squash, winter	Cinnamon, nutmeg, allspice, cloves, ginger; apples, bacon, pecans
Sweet potatoes	Allspice, cinnamon, cloves, nutmeg, ginger, brandy, orange; almonds, apples, bananas
Tomatoes	Basil, bay leaf, garlic, celery seed, oregano, thyme, rosemary, chili powder; peppers, black olives
Turnips	Parsley, chives, nutmeg; mushrooms, potatoes, peas

QUESTIONS FOR DISCUSSION

1. Which of the following vegetables would you simmer uncovered?

Asparagus	Cauliflower
Green beans	Peas
Beets	Sweet potatoes
Brussels sprouts	Rutabagas
Carrots	Turnips

2. Why are greens such as spinach not well suited to cooking in a compartment steamer?

3. In the recipe for Buttered Peas and Carrots, why could you not save a step and cook the two vegetables together in one pot?

4. Why is it important to drain vegetables well before combining with a cream sauce?

5. Which of the two recipes for glazed carrots might be more appropriate for à la carte service, or cooking to order? Why?

6. We have learned that green vegetables are supposed to be cooked in a neutral liquid, because acids destroy green pigments. But the recipe for artichokes says to cook them with lemon juice. What's going on here, anyway?

7. Describe briefly how you would make breaded, fried onion rings rather than onion rings with batter.

CHAPTER 18

POTATOES AND OTHER STARCHES

The eating habits of most nations place a great deal of importance on a category of foods we call starches. In the United States, the most important of these foods are potatoes, rice, pasta, and bread. It is true that we do not depend on these high-carbohydrate foods as much as many of the world's people who eat far less meat than we do. Nevertheless, starches appear at nearly all our meals.

Because we eat them often and have devised a great many ways of preparing them, starchy foods require some extra study beyond that which we have given to other vegetables. In this chapter we turn our attention primarily to the preparation of potatoes, rice, and pasta, and we also take a short detour to look at some other grains as well as a group of products called dumplings.

After reading this chapter, you should be able to

1. Distinguish the major types of potatoes and the best uses for each.

2. Select potatoes of high quality and store them properly.

3. Cook potatoes by boiling and steaming, and prepare potato purée.

4. Cook potatoes by baking, sautéing, pan-frying, and deep-frying.

5. Distinguish the major types of rice.

6. Prepare rice by boiling and steaming and by the pilaf and risotto methods.

7. Distinguish major kinds and shapes of commercial pasta, and determine their quality.

8. Prepare fresh and commercial pasta products.

POTATOES

*T*he potato is in the strange position of being one of the most popular American foods and at the same time one of the most neglected. The potato is one of the most important staple foods in American kitchens. And because it functions both as a vegetable and as a starch, it appears in all three meals more often than any other food.

Sadly, however, the potato is so often taken for granted that it is nothing more than the second half of the phrase "meat and potatoes," something everyone wants plenty of but no one pays much attention to. So instead of steaming, snowy-white baked potatoes and crispy, golden, flavorful hashed browns, we are often served heavy, soggy, gray baked potatoes and burned, greasy, tasteless hashed browns.

Because potatoes are so popular, the experienced cook knows how to gain the enthusiasm of customers with well-prepared potato items. Because they can be prepared in so many ways, they add variety to the menu. Offer your customers something in addition to the same old "baked, french fries, and mashed."

UNDERSTANDING POTATOES

Types

Potatoes are classified according to their starch content. The amount of starch determines the use for which they are most suitable.

1. **Waxy or new potatoes.**

   High moisture content, high sugar content, low starch content.

   Small, round in shape, with thin, smooth skin. May be red, white, or yellow.

   Hold shape well when cooked. Firm, moist texture.

   Use for boiling whole, for salads, soups, hashed browns, and any preparation where the potato must hold its shape.

   Do not use for deep-frying. High sugar content will cause dark streaks and poor texture.

2. **Mature or starchy potatoes.**

   High starch content, low moisture and sugar. Light, dry, and mealy when cooked.

   a. **Russets or Idahos.**

   Long, regularly shaped potatoes with slightly rough skin.

   Ideal for baking. Best potato for french fries, because the high starch content produces an even, golden color and good texture. Also, there is little trimming loss because of the regular shape.

   May be used for mashing, but generally too expensive.

   Sizes are indicated by count per 50-pound carton. For example, "100's" would average 8 oz each.

   b. **All-purpose** (sometimes called "chef potatoes").

   Not always as dry and starchy as russets.

   Irregularly shaped, less expensive than russets.

   Suitable for most purposes except baking (due to shape). Especially useful for puréeing or mashing, or any preparation in which the shape of the whole potato is not important.

   Note: Very knobby potatoes are wasteful when pared in a mechanical peeler.

Checking for Quality

Look for these signs of high-quality potatoes:

1. Firm and smooth, not soft or shriveled.

2. Dry skins.

3. Shallow eyes.

4. No sprouts. Sprouting potatoes are high in sugar.

5. No green color. Green areas develop on potatoes stored in light. These areas contain a substance called solanine, which has a bitter taste and is poisonous in very large quantities. All green parts should be cut off before cooking.

6. Absence of cracks, blemishes, and rotten spots.

Storing

Keep in a cool, dry, dark place, ideally at 55°F to 60°F (13°C to 16°C). If they will be used quickly, you may keep them at room temperature.

Do not refrigerate. Temperatures below 45°F (7°C) convert potato starch to sugar. Refrigerated potatoes must be stored at 50°F (10°C) for 2 weeks to change the sugar back to starch.

New potatoes do not keep very well. Purchase only a week's supply at a time.

Market Forms

The demands of time and labor have made processed potato products widely used, and many forms are available. Many of these products are very good, and there is no doubt that they save time. However, for best quality, there is no substitute for fresh potatoes, *if they are well prepared.*

1. *Fresh, unprocessed.*

2. *Peeled. Treated to prevent browning.*

   Keep refrigerated (below 40°F/4°C) for up to 5 to 7 days.

3. *Canned whole, cooked.*

4. *French fries. Blanched in deep fat and frozen.*

   Available in wide variety of sizes and cuts. Cook from the frozen state.

   Refrigerated french fries are also available.

5. *Other frozen, prepared products.*

   Available as hashed browns, puffs, stuffed baked, and croquettes; in casseroles with a variety of sauces.

6. *Dehydrated.*

   Granules or flakes for mashed potatoes to be reconstituted with hot water or milk, and butter or other desired flavorings.

Other products: many varieties and preparations. May need soaking in water before cooking.

COOKING POTATOES

Some potato recipes are very simple, but many are complex and use a combination of cooking methods. For example, to make potato croquettes, you must first boil to steam the potatoes, purée them and combine the purée with other ingredients, shape them, bread them, and finally deep-fry them.

Cooking methods are essentially the same as the methods for vegetables in the previous chapter. If necessary, review these methods before proceeding with the following recipes.

Boiling and Steaming Potatoes

These methods for cooking potatoes are given in the first recipe in this section. Boiled or steamed potatoes are served as is and are also the basis for many other preparations.

Two points should be noted:

1. Boiled potatoes are generally started in cold water rather than in hot water. This allows for more even cooking and heat penetration from outside to inside during the relatively long cooking time required.

2. Potatoes are never cooled in cold water, unlike most vegetables. This would make them soggy.

RECIPE 176 **Boiled Potatoes (Pommes Natures)**

· ·

Portions: 25   **Portion size:** 5 oz (150 g)

U.S.	Metric	Ingredients	Procedure
10 lb AP	4.5 kg	Potatoes	1. Peel and eye potatoes. Be sure that all traces of dark peel are removed.
			2. Cut potatoes into 25 uniform portions, 1 or 2 pieces per portion. Trim pieces to shape (see note). Save trimmings for other use.
			3. Place in pot and cover with salted water. Bring to boil, lower heat, and simmer until tender.
			4. Drain and let the potatoes steam dry in the colander for a minute.
			5. Serve immediately, or place in hotel pan, cover with a clean, damp towel, and hold for service.

Note: Potatoes may be cut, shaped, or trimmed as desired. They may be left in neat but irregular shapes, trimmed or tournéed into large, medium, or small sizes (see Figure 18.1), or cut with a ball scoop (see Figure 18.2) for parisienne boiled potatoes. Allow for greater trimming loss if preparing tournéed or parisienne potatoes.

Variations

176A. Steamed Potatoes (Pommes Vapeurs): Prepare as in basic recipe, but steam in perforated pan instead of boiling.

176B. Parsley Potatoes: Prepare as in basic recipe. Brush or pour 4 oz (125 mL) melted butter onto the potatoes and sprinkle with chopped parsley.

176C. New Potatoes: Prepare as in basic recipe, using small new potatoes. Scrub well but do not peel. Serve 1–3 per portion, depending on size. Optional: peel a narrow band around potato before cooking to prevent skin from splitting.

176D. Creamed Potatoes: Prepare new potatoes or all-purpose potatoes as in basic recipe. Cut or slice to desired size, or leave small new potatoes whole. Combine with 2 qt (2 L) hot Cream Sauce. Heat over low heat, but do not boil, and hold for service.

· ·

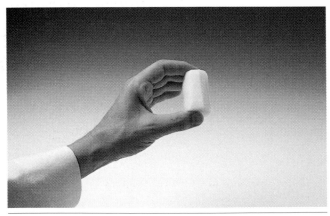

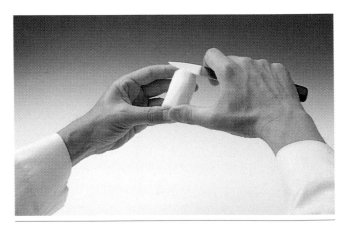

FIGURE 18.1 **Tournéing potatoes and other root vegetables.**
(a) Cut the potatoes roughly into pieces slightly larger than the final size desired. Cut off the top and bottom of each piece, so that they are flat and parallel.

(b) Hold the potato between the thumb and forefinger, and place the paring knife against the top edge as shown and the thumb of the cutting hand firmly against the potato. Your hand should be far enough up on the blade to maintain steady control.

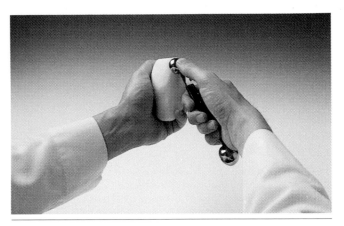

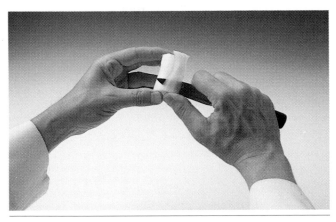

(c) Cut downward toward your thumb with a curving movement of the blade.

FIGURE 18.2   **Cutting parisienne potatoes.**
(a) Place the ball cutter against the potato as shown.

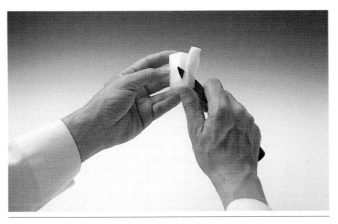

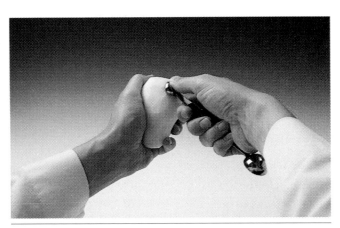

(d) Turn the potato slightly (one-seventh of a full turn, to be exact) and repeat the motion.

(b) With the thumb, press the cutter firmly into the potato as far as it will go.

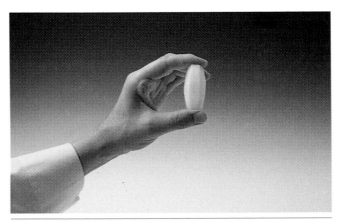

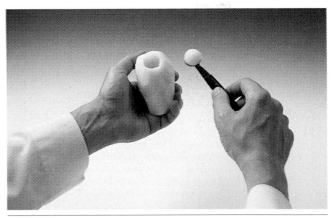

(e) The finished product. If perfectly done, it should have seven sides (but usually the customers won't count them).

(c) Lift the handle of the cutter outward, twist the cutter around, and remove the ball.

RECIPE 177 **Hungarian Potatoes**

Portions: 25   **Portion size:** 4 oz (125 g)

U.S.	Metric	Ingredients	Procedure
4 oz	125 g	Butter	1. Heat the butter in a large saucepan and add the onion and paprika. Cook until onion is soft.
8 oz	250 g	Onion, chopped	
2 tsp	10 mL	Paprika	
1 lb EP	500 g	Tomatoes, peeled, seeded, diced	2. Add the tomatoes and potatoes. Pour in enough stock just to cover the potatoes. Add a small amount of salt (about 2 tsp/10 mL) but undersalt, because liquid will reduce.
5 lb EP	2.5 kg	Potatoes, peeled and cut into thick slices	
1 qt approximately	1 L	Chicken or beef stock, hot	3. Simmer until potatoes are cooked and liquid is mostly evaporated or absorbed. Stir gently from time to time.
		Salt	
		Pepper	
½ cup	125 mL	Chopped parsley	4. Season to taste.
			5. Garnish with chopped parsley at service time.

Variation

177A. Bouillon Potatoes: Prepare as in basic recipe but omit paprika and tomatoes. Slice onion instead of chopping it, and sauté 6 oz (175 g) carrot, cut julienne, with the onion. Trim the potatoes into portion-size pieces instead of slicing them.

Potato Purée

Potato purée is an important product in most kitchens, even though it is not served as is. It is the basis of many popular preparations, including mashed or whipped potatoes, duchesse potatoes, and potato croquettes.

In order to prepare these products successfully, you must first understand the method for making a basic purée.

Procedure for Making Potato Purée

1. Select starchy potatoes rather than new or waxy potatoes.

2. Wash, peel, and eye carefully.

3. Cut into uniform sizes for even cooking.

4. Simmer or steam until tender. Potatoes for purée must be thoroughly cooked or the purée will be grainy. But they must not be overcooked or they will be watery.

5. Drain in a colander (if simmered). Set the colander on a sheet pan and place in an oven for several minutes to dry out the potatoes. If potatoes are too moist, they will be too loose or slack when additional liquid is added later.

6. Pass the potatoes through a food mill or ricer to purée. A mixer with the paddle attachment may be used to break up the potatoes for whipped potatoes, but there is no guarantee that it will remove all lumps.

Equipment used for puréeing should not be cold, or it will cool the potatoes too much. Heat equipment under hot water before use.

RECIPE 178   **Duchesse Potatoes**

			Portions: 25		Portion size: 4 oz (100 g)

U.S.	Metric	Ingredients	Procedure
7 lb EP	3 kg	Potatoes, peeled and quartered	1. Steam potatoes or simmer in salted water until tender. Drain in a colander and let dry in oven for several minutes.
4 oz	100 g	Butter, melted	2. Pass potatoes through a food mill or ricer.
		Salt	3. Add butter and mix to a smooth paste. Season to taste with salt, pepper, and just a little nutmeg (the potatoes should not taste strongly of nutmeg).
		White pepper	
		Nutmeg	
10	10	Egg yolks	
			4. If the potatoes are very moist, stir over a low flame to stiffen. *They must be much stiffer than mashed potatoes.*
			5. Add the egg yolks (off the fire) and beat until smooth.
			6. Put the mixture in a pastry bag with a star tube and bag out into desired shapes on sheet pans or as platter borders (see Figure 18.3). Cone-shaped spiral mounds are most popular for individual portion service.
		Egg wash, optional	7. If desired, brush lightly with egg wash for greater browning.
			8. At service time, place potatoes in hot oven (400–425°F/200–230°C) until lightly browned. Platter borders may be browned under the salamander.

Variations

Duchesse Potato mixture is also used as the base for Potato Croquettes (p. 450) and is considered one of the basic hot kitchen preparations.

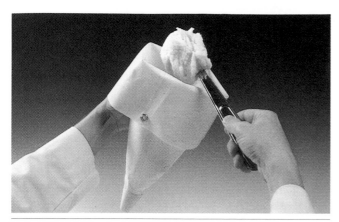

FIGURE 18.3 Using the pastry bag: Duchesse Potatoes. (a) Turn down the top of the pastry bag as shown. Slip your hand under this collar and hold the top open with your thumb and forefinger while you fill it with duchesse potato mixture.

(c) Duchesse Potatoes are often used to decorate platters, as in this illustration. This same technique is also used in decorating cakes and desserts with icing, whipped cream, or meringue.

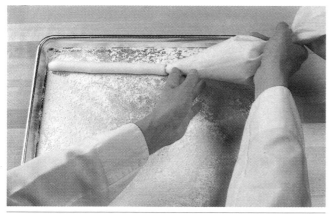

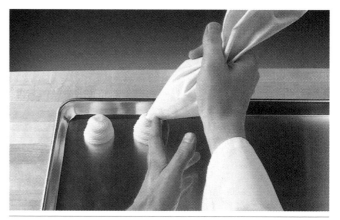

(b) Turn the top of the bag up again, and gather the loose top together again as shown. Hold the bag shut with your thumb and forefinger. To force out the potatoes, squeeze the top of the bag in the palm of your hand. The free hand is used to guide the tip or hold an item being filled or decorated. Potato Croquettes can be made quickly by forcing out the potato mixture in long strips, using a large plain tube. Cut the strips into 2-inch (5-cm) lengths with a knife.

(d) Single portions of Duchesse Potatoes are usually piped out into a tall spiral shape. They are then browned in the oven.

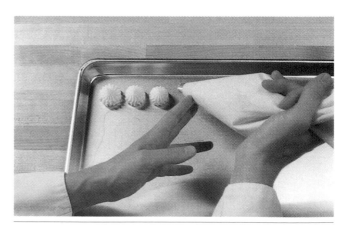

(e) Dauphine and Lorette Potatoes (see recipes p. 451) may be bagged out into many shapes, such as these small stars. Some cookies are also shaped this way.

RECIPE 179   **Whipped or Mashed Potatoes**

| | **Portions:** 25 | | **Portion size:** 5 oz (150 g) | |

U.S.	Metric	Ingredients	Procedure
9 lb AP	4 kg	Potatoes	1. Peel and eye potatoes and cut into uniform sizes. Simmer in salted water to cover until tender.
6 oz	175 g	Butter	
1 cup	250 mL	Light cream, hot	
	as needed	Milk, hot	2. Drain well and let potatoes steam dry for a few minutes.
		Salt	
		White pepper	3. Pass the potatoes through a food mill or ricer into the bowl of a mixer.

3. (cont.) Alternative method: Place potatoes in mixer with paddle attachment. Mix until well broken up. Replace paddle with whip and beat until well puréed. Do not overwhip, or potatoes will become pasty.

4. Beat in butter, then cream.

5. Add enough hot milk to bring potatoes to proper consistency. They should be soft and moist, but firm enough to hold their shape, not runny.

6. Add salt and white pepper to taste.

7. Whip *briefly* at high speed until potatoes are light and fluffy. Do not overwhip.

Baking

Preparing baked potatoes is a very simple procedure, which, for some reason, is widely misunderstood and needlessly complicated. Properly baked potatoes are white, fluffy, mealy, and steamy. Poorly baked potatoes, unfortunately very common, are grey and soggy.

Procedure for Baking Potatoes

1. Select russet potatoes or other regularly shaped *starchy* potatoes.

2. Scrub well and pierce the ends with a fork or skewer so steam can escape.

3. For crisp skins, rub lightly with oil. For more tender skins, leave dry.

4. Place on sheet pans or on sheet pan racks in preheated 400°F (200°C) oven and bake until done, about 1 hour. To test doneness, squeeze gently. Done potatoes will yield to gentle pressure.

   Note: Using sheet pan racks will eliminate the hard spot that forms where the potato is in contact with the sheet pan.

5. Remove from oven.

6. To hold for service, keep warm and uncovered, so potatoes will not be made soggy by trapped steam. Hold no more than an hour, if possible, though they will keep longer with some loss of quality.

   Note that nothing was said about wrapping potatoes in foil. Foil-wrapped potatoes do not bake but rather steam in their own moisture. The texture of a steamed potato is entirely different from that of a baked potato. Save yourself the trouble and expense of wrapping in foil and serve a better product.

RECIPE 180 **Baked Potatoes**

....

Portion size: 1 potato

U.S.	Metric	Ingredients	Procedure
as needed		Idaho or baking potatoes Vegetable oil, optional	1. Scrub potatoes well and pierce ends with skewer or fork to allow steam to escape. 2. Leave potatoes dry or oil lightly if a crisp skin is desired. 3. Place on sheet pan in 400°F (200°C) oven. Bake until done, about 1 hour. Test for doneness by squeezing potato gently.

....

RECIPE 181 **Stuffed Baked Potatoes**

....

Portions: 10   **Portion size:** 1 potato

U.S.	Metric	Ingredients	Procedure
10	10	Baking potatoes, about 7–8 oz (200–225 g) each	1. Bake potato according to basic method. 2. Remove from oven. Cut a slice off the top of each potato and scoop out the pulp, leaving a shell about ¼ inch (½ cm) thick.
2 oz	60 g	Butter, melted	
4 oz	100 mL	Light cream or milk, hot	3. Pass the pulp through a food mill or ricer. Beat in the butter and enough cream or milk to make a smooth purée. Season to taste. (Note that this preparation is basically the same as Whipped Potatoes.)
or as needed		Salt White pepper	4. Fill the potato shells with the purée, using a pastry bag or kitchen spoon. (A pastry bag is faster and neater.) Place on baking sheet.
3 tbsp	45 mL	Dry bread crumbs	5. Mix the bread crumbs and parmesan cheese and top the potatoes with this mixture. Sprinkle with melted butter.
3 tbsp	45 mL	Parmesan cheese, grated	
1 oz	30 g	Butter, melted	6. Place in hot oven (400°F/200°C) until potatoes are heated through and tops are browned, about 15 minutes.

Variations

For each variation listed, add the indicated ingredients to the potato purée mixture. Proportions are for about 2½ to 3 lb (1.1–1.4 kg) purée.

1. 2 oz (60 g) grated parmesan cheese
2. 8 oz (225 g) minced onion, sautéed in butter
3. 4 oz (100 g) cooked ham, small dice
   4 oz (100 g) mushrooms, chopped and sautéed in butter
4. 8 oz (225 g) bacon, diced and cooked crisp
   1 green pepper, chopped and sautéed in butter or bacon fat

....

RECIPE 182   **Oven Roast Potatoes**

	Portions: 25		Portion size: 4 oz (125 g)

U.S.	Metric	Ingredients	Procedure
10 lb AP	4.5 kg	Potatoes Vegetable oil Salt White pepper	1. Peel and eye potatoes. Cut into 25 uniform portions and trim pieces to shape. Save the trimmings for other use. 2. Dry potatoes well and rub with oil. Place in oiled baking pan and season with salt and pepper. 3. Place in 400°F (200°C) oven and bake until browned and cooked through, about 1 hour. Halfway through baking time, turn potatoes and brush with additional oil.

Baked "En Casserole"

A number of preparations call for potatoes baked in a baking pan or casserole, with or without liquid added. The most well known is scalloped potatoes. A characteristic of most of these preparations is that they are baked uncovered at least part of the time so that a brown crust forms on top.

RECIPE 183   **Dauphinoise Potatoes**

	Portions: 15		Portion size: 5 oz (150 g)

U.S.	Metric	Ingredients	Procedure
3 lb AP ½ lb	1.4 kg 225 g	Potatoes Salt White pepper Nutmeg Gruyère cheese, grated	1. Peel and eye potatoes. Cut into very thin slices. 2. Place some of the potatoes in a layer in a buttered baking pan. Season with salt, pepper, and a very small amount of nutmeg. Sprinkle with a little of the cheese. Repeat until all the potatoes and about three-fourths of the cheese are used up.
1½ cups 1 cup	375 mL 250 mL	Milk Heavy cream	3. Combine the milk and cream and heat to a simmer. 4. Pour the milk and cream over the potatoes. Top with remaining cheese. 5. Bake uncovered at 350°F (175°C) until done, about 45–60 minutes.

Variation

183A. Savoyarde Potatoes: Prepare as above, but use chicken stock instead of milk.

RECIPE 184 **Scalloped Potatoes**

....

Portions: 25			**Portion size:** 5 oz (150 g)

U.S.	Metric	Ingredients	Procedure
2½ qt 3 oz 3 oz 2 tsp	2.5 L 90 g 90 g 10 mL	Milk Butter Flour Salt White pepper	1. Make a thin white sauce (Béchamel) using the ingredients listed (see p. 138). Keep hot while preparing potatoes.
7½ lb AP	3.5 kg	Potatoes	2. Peel and eye the potatoes. Cut into ⅛-inch thick (3-mm) slices. 3. Place the potatoes in a buttered baking pan, making several layers. 4. Pour in the white sauce. Lift the potatoes slightly so that the sauce can run between the layers. 5. Cover with foil or greased paper and place in oven at 350°F (175°C) for 30 minutes. 6. Uncover and continue to bake until top is lightly browned and potatoes are tender.

Note: Unthickened milk may be used instead of a thin white sauce, but the milk is more likely to curdle. The roux helps prevent curdling.

Variations

184A. Scalloped Potatoes with Onions: Add 1¼ lb (600 g) sliced onions to baking pan with the potatoes.

184B. Scalloped Potatoes with Cheese: Add 1 lb (500 g) shredded cheddar cheese to baking pan with potatoes. Top with additional cheese before browning.

184C. Scalloped Potatoes with Ham: Add 2½ lb (1.4 kg) diced ham.

....

RECIPE 185 **Boulangère Potatoes**

Portions: 25			**Portion size:** 5 oz (150 g)

U.S.	Metric	Ingredients	Procedure
2½ lb AP	1.1 kg	Onions, sliced	1. Sauté onions in butter or fat until they are translucent and just beginning to brown.
5 oz	150 g	Butter or fat drippings from roast (see note)	2. Add the potatoes and toss until the potatoes are coated with fat.
7½ lb AP	3.5 kg	Potatoes, peeled and cut into thick slices	3. Place in baking pan or in roasting pan under partially cooked roast. Pour in hot stock. Season.
1 qt	1 L	Stock, chicken or lamb (if available), hot	4. Bake 1 to 1½ hours at 350°F (175°C) or at roasting temperature of lamb, until potatoes are done. Add additional stock during cooking if necessary to keep potatoes from drying out.
		Salt	
		Pepper	

Note: Boulangère potatoes may be cooked separately, but they are usually cooked with a roast, especially leg of lamb (see p. 225). If potatoes are cooked with a roast, they must be added to the pan at the right time so that the meat and potatoes will be done at the same time.

RECIPE 186 **Potatoes au Gratin**

Portions: 25			**Portion size:** 6 oz (175 g)

U.S.	Metric	Ingredients	Procedure
7½ lb AP	3.5 kg	Potatoes	1. Scrub potatoes and simmer or steam until tender but still firm.
2 qt	2 L	Cheese Sauce (p. 139), hot	2. Drain and spread on sheet pan to cool.
⅔ cup	150 mL	Dry bread crumbs	3. When cool enough to handle, peel and cut into uniform ⅜-inch (1-cm) dice.
2 tsp	10 mL	Paprika	4. Combine with hot cheese sauce in baking pan.
2 oz	60 g	Butter, melted (optional)	5. Mix bread crumbs and paprika and sprinkle over potatoes. Drip butter evenly over top.
			6. Bake at 350°F (175°C) about 30 minutes, until hot and browned.

Note: (1) Cream sauce may be used instead of cheese sauce. (2) Grated cheese (cheddar or parmesan) may be sprinkled over potatoes before topping with bread crumbs.

RECIPE 187 Anna Potatoes

Portions: 10   **Portion size:** 5 oz (150 g)

U.S.	Metric	Ingredients	Procedure
4 lb AP 12 oz	1.8 kg 350 g	Boiling potatoes Butter Salt White pepper	1. Select round, uniformly sized potatoes. The appearance of this dish is important, so slices should be neat and even. 2. Peel and eye the potatoes and cut into thin slices. Hold in cold water until ready to use. 3. Clarify the butter (see p. 147). 4. Heat about ¼ inch (½ cm) of butter in a heavy, 9-inch (23-cm) cast iron skillet. (The skillet must be well seasoned so that the potatoes will not stick.) Remove from heat. 5. Drain the potatoes and dry them well. Select the most uniform slices for the bottom layer. Arrange the slices in circles in the bottom of the pan. Shingle the slices and reverse the direction of each circle. See Figure 18.4 for illustration of technique. Season this layer with salt and pepper and ladle some clarified butter over it. 6. Continue making layers, seasoning and buttering each layer, until ingredients are used up. The potatoes will be mounded over the top of the pan, but they will compress as they cook. There will be a great deal of butter in the pan, but it will be drained after cooking and can be reused. 7. Place the pan over a moderate fire and heat until the pan is sizzling. Shake the pan lightly to make sure the potatoes are not sticking. 8. Cover with foil and bake in a hot oven (450°F/230°C) about 40 minutes, until potatoes are tender. Test for doneness by piercing center with paring knife. Remove the foil and bake 10 minutes more. 9. Drain off excess butter (remember that it's hot!) and carefully invert the potato cake onto a baking sheet. The potatoes should have stayed intact in a round cake, but if any slices have fallen off, put them back in place. Set the potatoes back in the oven if necessary for even browning. 10. Cut into wedges for service.

Note: Small molds may be used instead of the large pan for individual service.

Variation

187A. Voisin Potatoes: Prepare as in basic recipe, but sprinkle each layer of potatoes with grated Swiss cheese.

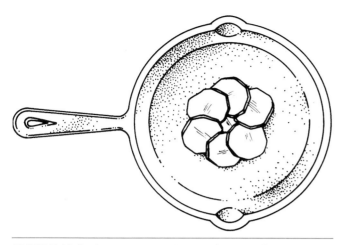

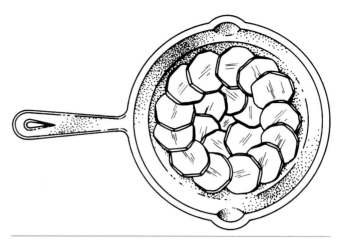

FIGURE 18.4   Anna potatoes (see recipe p. 442).
(a) Place one potato slice in the center of the prepared pan. Make a circle of overlapping slices around it.

(b) Make another circle of overlapping slices around this, but reverse the direction, as shown. Continue building up layers of potatoes, butter, and seasonings as directed in the recipe.

Sautéing and Pan-frying

The procedures for sautéing and pan-frying potatoes are basically the same as for other vegetables (p. 412).

There are many varieties of sautéed and pan-fried potato preparations. Some are made with raw potatoes, others with precooked or blanched potatoes. Many of these recipes are especially useful because they are excellent ways to utilize leftover boiled potatoes.

This group of recipes may be divided into two categories, based on production technique.

*1.   **Potatoes mixed or tossed while cooking.***

The procedure for sautéing vegetables, page 412, is used for these preparations. The potatoes are cut into pieces or into small shapes and cooked in a small amount of fat, turning or tossing them in the pan so that the pieces brown on all sides. This category includes rissolé, parisienne, noisette, chateau, and American fried or home fried potatoes.

*2.   **Potatoes cooked and served in compact cakes.***

The procedure for pan-frying vegetables, page 413, is the basic method used for these preparations. The potatoes are not mixed while cooking, but are made into cakes, which are browned on both sides. This category includes hashed browns and variations, as well as potato pancakes and macaire potatoes.

RECIPE 190 **Lyonnaise Potatoes**

Portions: 25		**Portion size:** 4½ oz (125 g)	

U.S.	Metric	Ingredients	Procedure
6½ lb EP	3 kg	Cooled, peeled, boiled potatoes	1. Cut the potatoes into slices about ¼ inch (½ cm) thick.
1½ lb	700 g	Onions	2. Peel the onions, cut in half lengthwise, and slice into julienne.
8 oz	225 g	Clarified butter, vegetable oil, or mixture of oil and butter	3. Heat half the fat in a sauté pan and sauté the onions until they are golden. Remove from the pan with a slotted spoon and set aside.
		Salt	4. Put the rest of the fat into the pan. Set the pan on high heat and add the potatoes.
		White pepper	5. Sauté the potatoes, tossing them in the pan until well browned on all sides.
			6. Add the onions and continue to sauté for another minute, until onions and potatoes are well mixed and the flavors are blended.
			7. Season to taste.

Note: This preparation may be made on a griddle instead of a sauté pan.

Variations

190A. *Home Fries or American Fries:* Prepare as in basic recipe, but omit onions.

190B. *Potatoes O'Brien:* Cook 10 oz (300 g) diced bacon until crisp. Remove bacon from pan. Sauté 10 oz onion (300 g), in fine dice, and 10 oz (300 g) green pepper, in fine dice, in bacon fat. Sauté 6½ lb (3 kg) diced potatoes as in basic recipe and add vegetables. Add the crisp bacon and 4 oz (125 g) diced pimiento to finish, and season to taste.

RECIPE 191   **Potato Pancakes**

		Portions: 20		**Portion size:** 2 pancakes, about 2 oz (60 g) each

U.S.	Metric	Ingredients	Procedure
6 lb AP	2.7 kg	Potatoes	1. Peel the potatoes and onions. Grate them together into a stainless steel bowl. Juice the lemons, add the juice to the potatoes to prevent discoloration, and toss to mix.
1 lb	450 g	Onions	
2	2	Lemons	
6	6	Eggs	
¼ cup	60 mL	Chopped parsley, optional	2. Place the potatoes in a china cap and squeeze out the excess liquid. Hold the liquid and let the starch settle out. Drain off the liquid from the starch.
2 tsp	10 mL	Salt	
½ tsp	2 mL	White pepper	
2 oz or more	60 g	Flour (see note)	3. Return the potatoes to a stainless steel bowl and add the potato starch.
		Oil for pan-frying	4. Beat in the eggs, parsley, salt and pepper.

5. Stir in enough flour to bind the potato mixture. (If batter is too thin, the pancakes will fall apart in the pan. Test-fry a little first, and add more flour if necessary.)

6. Pour about ¼ inch (½ cm) of oil into a heavy iron skillet. Heat the oil over moderately high heat. (Oil should reach about 325°F/160°C.)

7. Measuring portions with a solid kitchen spoon, place portions of the batter in the pan to make individual pancakes.

8. Pan-fry, turning once, until golden brown on both sides.

9. Remove from pan with slotted spoon or spatula and drain briefly on absorbent paper.

10. Alternative method: Lightly brown in oil and place in one layer on sheet pan. Finish in oven (375°F/190°C) until brown and crisp.

Note: Matzoh meal or dried potato starch may be used instead of flour for binding the batter.

RECIPE 192   Macaire Potatoes

			Portions: 25	Portion size: 4 oz (125 g)

U.S.	Metric	Ingredients	Procedure
10 lb	5 kg	Baking potatoes	1. Scrub potatoes and bake in 400°F (200°C) oven until done (see p. 437 for procedure for baking potatoes).
7 oz	200 g	Butter, soft	
		Salt	
		White pepper	2. Scoop out the pulp and mash it with a fork, or break it up in a mixer with the paddle attachment.
8 oz	250 g	Clarified butter or mixture of butter and oil	
			3. Add soft butter and mix in well. Season to taste.
			4. Heat a small sauté pan over high heat and ladle in a little of the clarified butter.
			5. Place one portion of the potatoes in the pan with a kitchen spoon and flatten it into a thick pancake.
			6. Cook until golden brown on the bottom and flip over or turn with an offset spatula. Brown other side.
			7. Repeat with remaining potatoes.
			8. These potatoes do not hold well and should be served very hot.

Variations

This procedure may be employed for utilizing leftover whipped potatoes. Egg yolks and/or grated cheese may be added for variations.

Deep-frying

All the rules of deep-frying that you learned in Chapter 4 apply to potatoes. Review page 58 if you need to refresh your memory.

There are two kinds of deep-fried potato preparations:

1. Potatoes fried raw.

These are potatoes that are simply cut into various shapes and deep-fried until golden and crisp. They include all the varieties of french fries, as well as potato chips.

Russet or Idaho potatoes are most suitable for frying because of their high starch content and their regular shape, which permits less trimming loss.

2. Preparations made from cooked, puréed potatoes.

Most of these products are made from Duchesse Potato mixture. They include potato croquette variations, Dauphine Potatoes, and Lorette Potatoes.

Starchy potatoes are used for these recipes, as they are for Duchesse Potatoes, because they make a good dry, mealy purée.

French Fries

Since french fries, or deep-fried potatoes, are one of the most popular items in American food service, you must know how to prepare them well. Most french fries served are made from blanched, frozen products, but it is also important to know how to make them from fresh potatoes.

The recipe on page 449 gives the complete procedure for preparing french fries. Note that they are fried in two stages. It is possible to cook them in one step, but this is impractical in a volume operation because of the long cooking time. The more common practice is to *blanch* them in frying fat. This is done at lower temperature so that they will cook through without becoming brown. They are then drained and refrigerated until service time. Portions can then be finished to order in a few minutes.

Frozen products have been prepared through step 5 in the recipe and then frozen. To use them, it is only necessary to begin with step 6.

RECIPE 193   **French Fries**

Portions: as needed [2¼ lb AP (1 kg) potatoes will yield about 1 lb (450 g) cooked potatoes]

U.S.	Metric	Ingredients	Procedure
		Potatoes, Idaho	1. Peel and eye potatoes.
			2. Cut into strips ⅜ inch (1 cm) square and about 3 inches (7½ cm) long. (See Figure 7.9 for cutting procedure.) Hold the cut potatoes in cold water until needed, to prevent discoloring.
			3. Line sheet pans with several layers of brown paper and have them ready by the deep fryer.
			4. Drain and dry the potatoes well. Deep-fry in fat heated to 325°F (160°C) until they are just beginning to turn a pale golden color. At this point they should be cooked through and soft.
			5. Remove them from the fryer and turn them out onto the sheet pans in a single layer to drain. Refrigerate until service time.
			6. At service time, fry in small quantities in fat heated to 350–375°F (175–190°C) until brown and crisp.
			7. Drain well. Salt them lightly *away from the fryer* or let customers salt their own. Serve immediately.

Variations

193A. Pont-Neuf Potatoes: Prepare as in basic recipe, but cut the potatoes in thicker strips, about ½ inch (1¼ cm) square or slightly larger. Blanching time will be slightly longer.

193B. Allumette Potatoes (Shoestring or Matchstick Potatoes): Cut the potatoes into thin strips, slightly less than ¼ inch thick (about ½ cm). Because they are so thin, they are usually fried in one step (without blanching) until very crisp.

193C. Straw Potatoes: Cut into very thin strips, about ⅛ inch (3 mm) thick. Fry in one step in hot fat (375°F/190°C).

193D. Steakhouse Fries: Scrub but do not peel Idaho potatoes. Cut in half lengthwise, then cut each half lengthwise into 4–6 wedges, depending on size. Prepare as in basic recipe.

193E. Potato Chips: Cut potatoes into very thin slices, less than ⅛ inch (3 mm) thick. Fry in one step in hot fat (375°F/190°C).

193F. Waffle or Gaufrette Potatoes: Set the fluted blade of a mandoline (a special slicer) so that it cuts very thin slices. Cut potatoes into round slices, turning the potato about 90° between slices so that you cut waffle shapes (see Figure 18.5). Fry like potato chips.

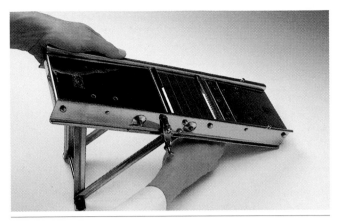

FIGURE 18.5 **Gaufrette Potatoes (see recipe p. 449).**
(a) Set the fluted blade of the mandoline so that it cuts very thin slices.

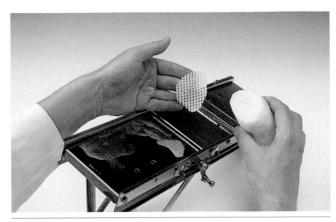

(c) You may need to adjust the thickness of the cut after the first slice or two. The slices should be thin enough so that there are holes in them.

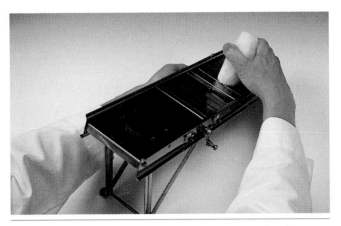

(b) Slice the potatoes, turning the potato about 90° between slices so that the ridges on the two sides of each slice cross each other.

RECIPE 194 Potato Croquettes

Note: These are made from Duchesse Potato mixture. The procedure for Duchesse Potatoes is repeated here for the sake of convenience.

		Portions: 20	**Portion size:** 3 pieces, 1½ oz (40 g) each
U.S.	Metric	Ingredients	Procedure
7 lb EP	3 kg	Potatoes, peeled and quartered	1. Steam potatoes or simmer in salted water until tender. (Steaming is preferable because it results in a drier product.) Drain in a colander (if simmered) and let dry in oven for a few minutes.
4 oz	100 g	Butter Salt White pepper Nutmeg	2. Pass potatoes through a food mill or ricer.
10	10	Egg yolks	3. Add butter and mix to a smooth paste. Season to taste with salt, pepper, and nutmeg.

RECIPE 194   **Potato Croquettes** *(Continued)*

U.S.	Metric	Ingredients	Procedure
			4. Set over moderate fire and stir the mixture to dry it out well. If it is not dry enough, the croquettes will not hold their shape. Alternative method: Add enough cornstarch or dry potato starch to absorb excess moisture and stiffen the mixture.
			5. Remove from the fire, add the egg yolks, and beat in thoroughly.
			6. To shape croquettes, two methods are available: (a) Spread the mixture out to cool in a pan, cover with plastic or buttered paper to keep a crust from forming, and refrigerate. Dust hands with flour and shape potatoes by hand into cylinders the shape of corks, about 2 inches (5 cm) long. They should be about 1½ oz (40 g) each. (b) Dust sheet pans with flour. Place the warm potato mixture in a pastry bag fitted with a large, plain tip. Bag out the potatoes into long strips on the pans (see Figure 18.3). With a knife, cut the strips into 2-inch (5-cm) lengths.
		Standard Breading Procedure: Flour Egg wash Bread crumbs	7. Set up the breading station and pass potatoes through Standard Breading Procedure (p. 114).
			8. At service time, fry croquettes in deep fat at 350°F (175°C) until golden brown. Drain well.
			9. Serve immediately, 3 pieces per portion.

Variations

Other shapes may be used, as desired.

Add 8 oz (225 g) of any one of the following to the potato mixture:

Grated cheese	Minced, sautéed onion	Chopped, sautéed mushrooms
Chopped ham	Finely chopped nuts	

*194A. **Berny Potatoes:*** Shape into small balls. Bread with finely slivered almonds instead of bread crumbs. (In classical cuisine, minced truffles are added to the potato mixture.)

*194B. **Dauphine Potatoes:*** For each pound of Duchesse or Croquette Potato mixture, add ⅓ lb Pâte à Choux or cream puff paste (p. 763) made without sugar and with half the amount of butter. To fry, bag out into desired shapes on greased brown paper. Slide into hot fat. Remove paper when potatoes float loose. Method 2: Hold pastry bag over deep fryer. Force out potato mixture and cut off short lengths with the back of a knife, letting them drop into the hot fat.

*194C. **Lorette Potatoes:*** Prepare like Dauphine Potatoes and add 1 oz of grated parmesan cheese per pound of mixture (60 g per kg). Shape as desired (the classic shape is a small crescent) and fry without breading.

RICE

UNDERSTANDING RICE

Types and Characteristics

Regular Milled White Rice

This rice has been milled to remove the outer bran coating. This process removes some vitamins and minerals, but it produces a white, lighter-textured product that most people prefer.

> *Enriched rice* has received a coating of vitamins to compensate for some of the nutrients lost in milling.
>
> *Short-grain* and *medium-grain* rice have small, round kernels that become sticky when cooked. They are used for such preparations as rice pudding and rice molds. In addition, the regular boiled rice used in Japanese cuisine for everyday eating and for making sushi is short-grain rice.
>
> *Long-grain* rice has long, slender grains that stay separate and fluffy when properly cooked. It is used for side dishes, entrées, casseroles, and so on.

Parboiled or Converted Rice

This is a specially processed long-grain rice. It has been partially cooked under steam pressure, redried, and then milled or polished. This process results in a higher vitamin and mineral content.

Parboiled rice is the most widely used in food service. The grains stay firm, separate, and light, and the product holds well in the steam table without becoming mushy or sticky. However, the flavor and texture are not like those of regular long-grain rice, so it is not always preferred by all customers.

Converted rice takes slightly more liquid and longer time to cook.

Instant Rice

This product has been precooked and dried so that it can be prepared quickly. It does not hold well after cooking and the grains quickly lose their shape and become mushy.

Brown Rice

This rice has had the bran layer left on, giving it a light brown color, slightly coarse crunchy texture, and nutty flavor. Brown rice is available as short, medium, or long grain.

Brown rice takes about twice as long to cook as white rice.

Specialty Rices

A number of different types of rice are used in various international cuisines. Perhaps the most important to us are the following three types.

> *Arborio rice* is one of several Italian varieties of a type of short-grain rice that is essential for making the highest-quality risotto (see p. 457). It is the variety most often found here and the variety specified in recipes.
>
> *Basmati rice* is an extra-long-grain rice widely used in India and surrounding countries. It has a unique nutty flavor.
>
> *Glutinous rice* is a sweet-tasting, short-grain rice that becomes quite sticky and chewy when cooked. It is used for a number of special dishes, including desserts, in Chinese and Japanese cuisines. Contrary to what you may read elsewhere, however, it is not the rice used for sushi, which is made with regular Japanese short-grain rice.

Handling and Storage

Washing

Regular milled rice should be rinsed in cold water before boiling or steaming. This removes excess starch that makes rice sticky.

The American rice industry recommends *not* washing rice, because it washes off some of the vitamin coating of enriched rice. But that's probably a small price to pay for a more attractive product. This is a decision you will have to make in your own operation.

Do not buy low-grade rice, which tends to be dirty, or rice that has been coated with talc.

Rice cooked by the pilaf method (p. 455) does not need to be washed (unless it is dirty), because the fat coating each kernel helps keep the grains separate and reduces stickiness.

Converted rice and instant rice do not need to be washed.

Storing

Keep raw rice at room temperature in a dry place and in a tightly sealed container to keep out moisture and insects. White rice will keep for many months. Brown rice is somewhat more perishable.

OTHER GRAINS COOKED LIKE RICE

Several other cereal products can be served as side dishes to add variety to your menu.

Wild Rice

Wild rice is not actually rice, but is harvested from a kind of grass native to northern United States and Canada. The grains are long, slender, hard, and dark brown or nearly black in color. Because of its unique nutty flavor, its scarcity, and its high price, it is considered a luxury food.

Wild rice should always be washed before cooking. It is simmered in 3 pints water per pint of grain, for 45 minutes. The grains burst open when cooked.

Wild rice may be mixed with long-grain white rice, *cooked separately*, to decrease the cost per serving.

Barley

Pearled barley has been milled to remove outer bran layers. It is commonly used in soups, but it can also be cooked by the pilaf method and served like rice, although it has a longer cooking time.

Cracked Wheat

Whole wheat grains that have been cut into smaller pieces are called *cracked wheat*. This product also can be cooked like pilaf.

Bulgur is a type of cracked wheat that has been partially cooked or parched. It is usually available in coarse, medium, and fine granulations. Its cooking time is shorter than regular cracked wheat, and in fact the fine granulations can be prepared simply by pouring boiling water over them and letting them stand for a half hour. This type of bulgur is often served cold, mixed with lemon juice, olive oil, chopped scallions, and fresh herbs.

Kasha

Kasha refers to whole buckwheat groats, which are especially popular in Eastern European and Jewish cooking. Kasha is also cooked like pilaf, requiring 2 pints liquid per pint of grain, and 15 minutes cooking time. Sometimes eggs are added (2 eggs per pint of grain) while the kasha is being sautéed in the fat.

COOKING RICE

There seems to be very little agreement among chefs regarding the best ways to cook rice. The methods outlined here have been shown to produce good results. Your instructor may have developed other methods or variations. In any case, consult your instructor if you have questions.

Boiling and Steaming Rice

Below are basic procedures for preparing plain boiled or steamed rice on top of the range, in the oven, or in a steamer.

Everyone agrees that the key to properly cooked rice is correct proportions of rice to water and correct cooking times. Unfortunately, no one agrees on what those proportions and times should be.

The proportions given here indicate slightly less liquid than has been used in the past. Even so, they produce a very moist product. Apparently American-grown rice is less dry than it used to be. *You may wish to reduce the quantity of liquid as much as 25 percent.*

The proportion of liquid needed depends on

1. Tightness or looseness of the cover (degree of moisture loss during cooking).

2. Desired moistness of the finished product.

3. Variety, age, and moisture content of the rice used.

RECIPE 195 Boiled and Steamed Rice

Yield: about 3 lb (1.4 kg)

	Portions:	Portion size:
	10	4½–5 oz (140 g)
	12	4 oz (115 g)
	16	3 oz (90 g)

Proportions	U.S.	Metric
Regular long-grain white rice		
Rice	1 lb	475 g
Water	1 qt	1 L
Salt	1 tsp	5 mL
Butter	1 oz	30 g
Parboiled long-grain rice		
Rice	1 lb	475 g
Water	4½ cups	1.1 L
Salt	1 tsp	5 mL
Butter	1 oz	30 g
Medium-grain white rice		
Rice	18 oz	525 g
Water	1 qt	1 L
Salt	1 tsp	5 mL
Butter	1 oz	30 g
Brown rice		
Rice	12 oz	350 g
Water	1 qt	1 L
Salt	1 tsp	5 mL
Butter	1 oz	30 g

Procedures

Range Top	Oven	Steamer
1. Wash rice in cold water until water is clear (optional step; see p. 452 for note on washing rice).	1. Wash rice in cold water until water is clear (optional step; see p. 452 for note on washing rice).	1. Wash rice in cold water until water is clear (optional step; see p. 452 for note on washing rice).
2. Combine all ingredients in a heavy pot. Bring to boil. Stir. Cover and cook over very low heat.	2. Bring salted water to boil. Combine all ingredients in a shallow steamer pan. Cover with foil or tight lid. Place in 375°F (175°C) oven.	2. Bring salted water to boil. Combine all ingredients in a shallow steamer pan. Place uncovered pan in steamer for cooking time recommended by equipment manufacturer.
Cooking times: Long- and medium-grain: 15–20 minutes Parboiled: 20–25 minutes Brown: 40–45 minutes	Cooking times: Long- and medium-grain: 25 minutes Parboiled: 30–40 minutes Brown: 1 hour	Cooking times: Depend on type of steamer.

RECIPE 195 **Boiled and Steamed Rice** *(Continued)*

....

Procedures

Range Top	*Oven*	*Steamer*
3. Test rice for doneness. Cook 2–4 minutes more if necessary.	3. Test rice for doneness. Bake 2–4 minutes more if necessary.	3. Test rice for doneness. Steam 2–4 minutes more if necessary.
4. Turn rice out into a hotel pan. Fluff with fork or slotted spoon to let steam escape.	4. Fluff rice with fork or slotted spoon to let steam escape.	4. Fluff rice with fork or slotted spoon to let steam escape.

The Pasta Method

Rice may also be cooked in a large quantity of boiling water like pasta (see p. 460). This method is very good for producing separate, unsticky grains. However, some nutrients are lost in the cooking water, so chefs disagree about the value of this method.

1. Drop rice into a large pot of boiling, salted water, 4 qt per pound of rice (4 liters per 500 grams).

2. When just tender, pour rice into a strainer and drain well.

3. Place in a hotel pan. Cover and steam dry in oven 5–10 minutes, or leave uncovered and place in a steamer to steam dry.

To Reheat Cooked Rice

Add 4 oz water per quart of cooked rice (125 mL per liter). Cover and heat slowly in oven or on range. Or reheat in a steamer, uncovered, without additional water.

To Store Cooked Rice

Cover tightly and refrigerate.

The Pilaf Method

This is equivalent to braising. The rice is first sautéed in fat, then cooked in liquid—preferably in the oven for uniform heating—until the liquid is absorbed. The fat helps keep the grains separate and adds flavor.

It is normal to measure the rice by volume when making pilaf, since the proportions are based on volume measure. One pint of raw rice weighs about 14 oz, or 1 lb measures about 2¼ cups. (Metric: 1 liter weighs about 875 grams, or 1 kilogram measures 1.15 liters.) Regarding exact measurements, see the note following the pilaf recipe.

RECIPE 196 **Rice Pilaf**

Yield: about 3 lb (1.4 kg)   **Portions:** 10   **Portion size:** 5 oz (150 g)
                                      12   4 oz (125 g)
                                      16   3 oz (90 g)

U.S.	Metric	Ingredients	Procedure
2 oz	60 g	Butter	1. Heat the butter in a heavy saucepan. Add the onion and sauté until it begins to soften. Do not brown.
3 oz	90 g	Onions, fine dice	
1 pt	500 mL	Long-grain rice	
	(see note)		2. Add the rice, without washing. Stir over heat until the rice is completely coated with butter.
1½–2 pt	750 mL–1 L	Chicken stock	
	(see note)	or water, boiling	3. Pour in the boiling liquid. Return the liquid to a boil with the rice. Taste and adjust seasonings, and cover tightly.
		Salt	
			4. Place in a 350°F (175°C) oven and bake for 18–20 minutes, until liquid is absorbed and rice is dry and fluffy. Taste the rice, and if it is not done, replace in oven 3–5 minutes.
			5. Turn out into a hotel pan and fluff the rice with a fork. This releases steam and prevents further cooking. Keep hot for service.
			6. If desired, additional raw butter may be stirred into finished rice.

Note: Rice for pilaf is measured by volume rather than by weight. Use 1½ to 2 times its volume in stock or water (1¾ times is the normal proportion for long-grain rice). Use 2 pints liquid per pint of rice if you desire a moister product or if you are using parboiled rice. Use 1½ pints liquid if you desire a drier product and if your cover is tight enough to retain most of the steam.

Variations

196A. Tomato Pilaf: Prepare as in basic recipe, using 12–16 oz (375–500 mL) chicken stock and 1½ lb (700 g) chopped canned tomatoes with juice.

196B. Spanish Rice: Prepare like Tomato Pilaf, but use bacon fat, and sauté 6 oz (175 g) diced green pepper, 1 crushed clove garlic, and 1 tbsp (15 mL) paprika with the onion.

196C. Turkish Pilaf: Sauté ¼ tsp (1 mL) turmeric with the rice. To finished rice, add 4 oz (125 g) tomato concassée or drained, chopped canned tomatoes, 4 oz (125 g) cooked peas, 4 oz (125 g) raisins (soaked and drained). Let stand 10–15 minutes before serving.

196D. Cracked Wheat Pilaf: Prepare as in basic recipe, using cracked wheat instead of rice.

196E. Orzo Pilaf: Prepare as in basic recipe, using orzo (rice-shaped) pasta instead of rice.

196F. Barley Pilaf: Prepare as in basic recipe, using pearled barley instead of rice. Use 2½ pints (1.25 L) of stock, and bake 45 minutes. Mushrooms are often added to barley pilaf.

Additions to rice pilaf:

Pimiento	Peas	Ham, diced or julienne
Chopped nuts	Green pepper, diced	Raisins or currants
Celery, diced	Spinach, chopped	Water chestnuts
Carrot, diced or grated	Mushrooms	Bacon
Scallions	Olives, chopped or sliced	

Risotto

Risotto is a classic Italian preparation made by a special procedure that is like neither the boiling method nor the pilaf method. After sautéing the rice, one adds a small amount of stock and stirs until the liquid is absorbed. This procedure is repeated until the rice is cooked but still firm. Risotto should be served quickly and does not hold well. The finished product has a creamy consistency, due to the starch that is cooked out of the rice. The grains are not fluffy and separate.

Because of the labor required, the risotto served in restaurants is not always cooked by the true risotto method. Instead, chefs often prepare a basic pilaf, using the special Italian Arborio rice, and then finish it with extra stock, butter, and cheese.

The restaurant method appears after the basic recipe below. The true risotto method is given here because, if you are going to make an imitation risotto, you first have to know what you are imitating. Otherwise, you won't know how good your imitation is. Anyway, risotto is a preparation you should be familiar with as a professional cook.

RECIPE 197   **Risotto alla Parmigiana**

Portions: 10   **Portion size:** 5 oz (150 g)

U.S.	Metric	Ingredients	Procedure
1 oz	30 g	Butter	1. Heat the butter and oil in a large, straight-sided sauté pan. Add the onion and sauté until soft. Do not brown.
1 oz	30 mL	Vegetable oil	
1 oz	30 g	Onion, chopped fine	
1 lb	450 g	Italian Arborio rice	2. Add the rice and sauté until well coated with the fat.
1½ qt approximately	1.4 L	Chicken stock, hot	3. Using a 6-oz (150-mL) ladle, add one ladle of stock to the rice. Stir the rice over medium heat until the stock is absorbed and the rice is almost dry.
			4. Add another ladle of stock and repeat procedure. Do not add more than one ladleful of stock at a time.
			5. Stop adding stock when the rice is tender but still firm. It should be very moist and creamy, but not runny. The cooking should take about 30 minutes.
1 oz	30 g	Butter	6. Remove from the heat and stir in the raw butter and parmesan cheese. Salt to taste.
3 oz	90 g	Parmesan cheese, grated	
		Salt	

Variations

197A. Restaurant Method: Prepare basic pilaf (p. 456) using 1 lb Italian Arborio rice to 1 qt chicken stock (500 g to 1 L stock). To finish for service, place desired number of portions in a sauté pan and moisten with additional stock. Simmer until slightly moist and creamy, as in basic recipe. Finish with raw butter and parmesan cheese.

197B. Risotto Milanese: Prepare as in basic recipe, but add ¼ to ½ tsp (1–2 mL) saffron, soaked in 1 cup (200 mL) of the stock. Add the saffron-flavored stock near the end of cooking.

197C. Risotto with Mushrooms: Add 4–8 oz (100–200 g) mushrooms, chopped and sautéed in butter, near the end of cooking time.

197D. Risi Bisi: Add 1 lb (450 g) cooked peas and ¼ cup (60 mL) chopped parsley to basic risotto. (This is not authentic Risi Bisi, which is considered a thick soup in Italy. However, it is similar.)

PASTA AND DUMPLINGS

UNDERSTANDING PASTA

Macaroni products, or pastas, are popular alternatives to other starch foods. The name "pasta" is the Italian word for "paste," so called because pasta is made from a mixture of wheat flour and water and sometimes eggs.

Not so many years ago, Americans knew only spaghetti with tomato sauce and elbow macaroni with cheese, among all pasta products. Today, thanks to the influence of Italian cooks, we have a choice of a great variety of pasta dishes.

Kinds, Characteristics, and Quality Factors

1. Commercial pasta is made from dough that has been shaped and dried.

Macaroni refers to pastas made from flour and water. These include spaghetti, lasagne, elbow macaroni, and many other shapes.

Egg pastas contain at least 5½% egg solids in addition to the flour and water. They are usually sold as flat noodles of various widths.

Checking quality. The best pastas are made from *semolina*, a high-protein flour from the inner part of durum wheat kernels. Lower-quality products are made from farina, a softer flour.

Look for a good yellow color, not grey-white. The product should be very hard, brittle, and springy, and it should snap with a clean, sharp-edged break. When cooked, it should be firm and hold its shape well. Poor-quality pastas are soft and pasty when cooked.

2. Fresh egg pasta is made from flour and eggs and sometimes a small quantity of water and/or oil. Soft egg noodle products are also available fresh and frozen from manufacturers. They take less time to cook than dried macaroni products.

Shapes and Their Uses

There are hundreds of shapes and sizes of pasta. Each shape is appropriate for different kinds of preparations, because of the way different kinds of sauce cling to them, or the way their textures complement the texture of the topping. Figure 18.6 shows some of the most popular kinds. Table 18.1 describes the most common shapes and gives suggestions for use.

TABLE 18.1 **Commercial Pasta Shapes and Uses**

Name	*Description*	*Suggested Uses*
Spaghetti	Long, round	With great variety of sauces, especially tomato sauces
Spaghettini	Thin, long, round	Like spaghetti, especially with olive-oil-and-seafood sauces
Vermicelli	Very thin	With light, delicate sauces and, broken, in soups
Linguine	Looks like slightly flattened spaghetti	Like spaghetti; popular with clam sauces
Fusilli	Long, shaped like a corkscrew	Thick, creamy sauces
Macaroni	Long, hollow, round tubes	Especially good with hearty meat sauces
Elbow macaroni	Short, bent macaroni	Cold, in salads; baked, in casseroles
Penne or mostaccioli	Hollow tubes, cut diagonally; may be smooth or ridged	Baked, with meat sauce or with tomato sauce and cheese; or freshly cooked, with tomato sauce
Ziti	Short, hollow tubes, cut straight	
Rigatoni	Larger tubes, with ridges	

(Continues)

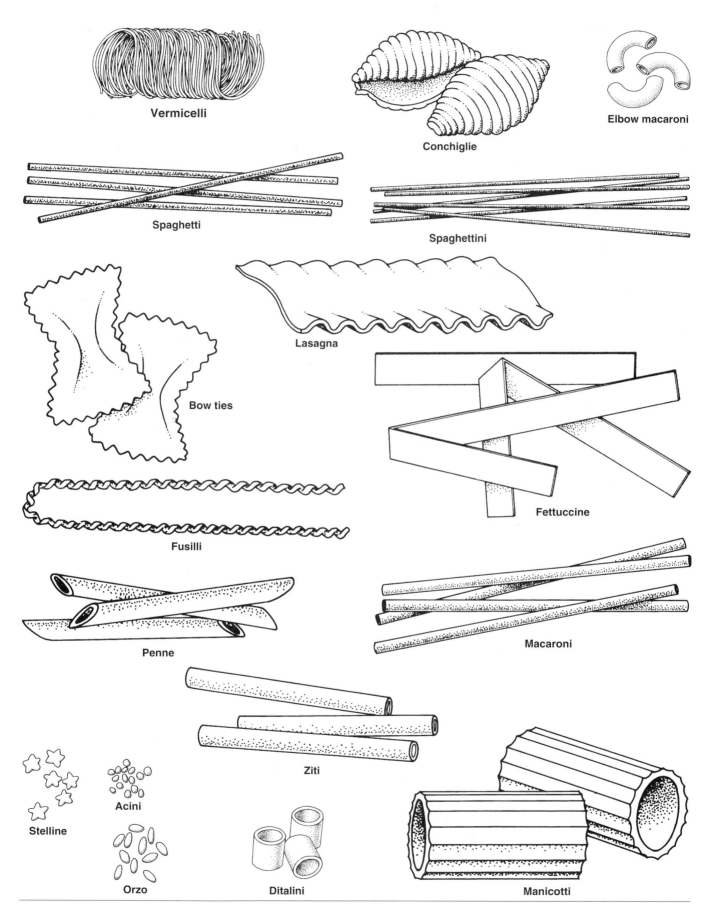

Vermicelli

Conchiglie

Elbow macaroni

Spaghetti

Spaghettini

Bow ties

Lasagna

Fettuccine

Fusilli

Penne

Macaroni

Ziti

Stelline

Acini

Orzo

Ditalini

Manicotti

FIGURE 18.6 **Some of the hundreds of pasta shapes available.**

TABLE 18.1   *(Continued)*

Name	Description	Suggested Uses
Manicotti	Large hollow tubes, sometimes with ridges (sometimes called cannelloni, which are actually rolled from fresh egg noodle dough)	Stuff with cheese or meat filling
Fettuccine	Flat egg noodles	Rich cream sauces or meat sauces
Lasagne	Broad, flat noodles, often with rippled edges	Bake with meat, cheese, or vegetable fillings
Conchiglie	Shell shaped	With seafood or meat sauces; small sizes can be used in salads
Bow ties		With sauces containing chunks of meat, sausage, or vegetables
Pastina (little pasta)		In soups; cold, in salads; buttered, as a side dish
Ditalini	Very short, hollow tubes	
Orzo	Rice shaped	
Stelline	Tiny stars	
Acini	"Peppercorns"	

COOKING PASTA

Doneness

Pasta should be cooked *al dente,* or "to the tooth." This means that cooking should be stopped when the pasta still feels firm to the bite, not soft and mushy. Much of the pleasure of eating pasta is its texture (that's why there are so many shapes), and this is lost if it is overcooked.

Testing Doneness

Many suggestions have been made for testing doneness, but none is more reliable than breaking off a very small piece and tasting it. As soon as the pasta is *al dente,* the cooking must be stopped at once. Half a minute extra is enough to overcook it.

Cooking times differ for every shape and size of pasta. Timing also depends on the kind of flour used and the moisture content. Times indicated on the package are often too long.

Fresh egg pasta, if it has not been allowed to dry, takes only a minute or minute and a half to cook after the water has returned to a boil.

Pasta is best if cooked and served immediately. Whenever possible, you should try to cook pasta to order. Fresh pasta, in particular, cooks so quickly that there is little reason to cook it in advance. In volume operations, however, commercial pasta may have to be cooked ahead of time. The following procedures are used for quantity cookery.

Procedure for Cooking Pasta

1. Use at least 4 qt boiling, salted water per pound of pasta (4 L per 500 g). Use about 1½ tbsp (25 g) salt per 4 qt (4 L) water.

2. Have the water boiling rapidly, and drop in the pasta. As it softens, stir gently to keep it from sticking together and to the bottom.

3. Continue to boil, stirring a few times.

4. As soon as it is *al dente,* drain immediately in a colander and rinse with cold, running water until the pasta is completely cooled. Otherwise, it would continue to cook and become too soft. (If you are cooking just a few portions to serve immediately, just drain well and do not cool. Sauce and serve without a moment delay.)

    If the pasta is to be used cold in a salad, it is ready to be incorporated into the recipe as soon as it has cooled.

5. If the pasta is to be held, toss gently with a small amount of oil to keep it from sticking.

6. Measure portions into mounds on trays. Cover with plastic film, and refrigerate until service time. (Do not store pasta in cold water. The pasta will absorb water and become soft, as though it had been overcooked.)

7. To serve, place desired number of portions in a china cap and immerse in simmering water to reheat. Drain, plate, and add sauce.

Alternative Method: Steam Table Service

Pasta gradually becomes soft and mushy when kept hot for service, but it will hold reasonably well for 30 minutes. It will not be as good as if freshly cooked, however.

1. Follow steps 1 to 3 above.

2. Drain while still slightly undercooked. Rinse briefly in cool water, enough to stop the cooking and rinse off starch, but not enough to cool the pasta. Pasta should still be quite warm.

3. Transfer to steam table pan and toss with oil to prevent sticking.

4. Hold up to 30 minutes.

Yields

One pound (450 g) uncooked dried pasta yields about 3 pounds (1.4 kg) cooked pasta. This is enough for 4 to 6 main-course portions, or 8 to 10 side-dish or first-course portions.

One pound (450 g) uncooked fresh pasta yields about 2 to 2½ pounds (900 to 1100 g) cooked pasta.

RECIPE 198   Tomato Sauce for Pasta

Yield: 3 qt (3 L)	Portions: 24		Portion size: 4 oz (125 g)

U.S.	Metric	Ingredients	Procedure
1 pt	500 mL	Olive oil	1. Heat the olive oil in a large sauce pot. Add the onions, carrots, and celery and sauté lightly for a few minutes. Do not let them brown.
½ lb	225 g	Onion, chopped fine	
½ lb	225 g	Carrot, chopped fine	
½ lb	225 g	Celery, chopped fine	
1 No. 10 can		Whole tomatoes	2. Add remaining ingredients. (See Appendix 2 for can sizes and substitutions.) Simmer uncovered about 45 minutes, until reduced and thickened.
2	2	Garlic cloves, minced	
1 oz	30 g	Salt	
1 tbsp	15 mL	Sugar	
			3. Pass through a food mill. Taste and adjust seasonings.

Variations

198A. Meat Sauce: Brown 2 lb (1 kg) ground beef, ground pork, or a mixture of beef and pork, in oil or rendered pork fat. Add 8 oz (250 mL) red wine, 2 qt (2 L) Tomato Sauce, 1 qt (1 L) beef or pork stock, and parsley, basil, and oregano to taste. Simmer 1 hour, uncovered.

198B. Tomato Cream Sauce: Use butter instead of olive oil in basic recipe. At service time, add 1 cup heavy cream per quart of tomato sauce (250 mL per liter). Bring to simmer and serve.

198C. Tomato Sauce with Sausage: Slice 3 lb (1.4 kg) fresh Italian sausage and brown in oil. Drain and add to basic tomato sauce. Simmer 20 minutes.

198D. Tomato Sauce with Sausage and Eggplant: Prepare like Tomato Sauce with Sausage, but use 1½ lb (700 g) each sausage and peeled, diced eggplant.

198E. Tomato Sauce with Ham and Rosemary: Cook 1 lb (450 g) ham, cut into fine dice, and 2 tbsp (30 mL) dried rosemary leaves in a little olive oil for a few minutes. Add to basic tomato sauce (after it has been passed through the food mill) and simmer 5 minutes.

Note: Except for meat sauce, most Italian sauces are cooked less than American-style tomato sauce and have fewer ingredients. As a result, they have a more pronounced fresh tomato taste.

RECIPE 199   **Fresh Egg Pasta**

Yield: 1½ lb (700 g)

U.S.	Metric	Ingredients	Procedure
1 lb	450 g	Bread flour	1. Put the flour in a mound on a work surface. Make a well in the center and add the eggs, oil, and salt.
5	5	Eggs	
½ oz	15 mL	Olive oil	2. Working from the center outward, gradually mix the flour into the eggs to make a dough.
pinch	pinch	Salt	
			3. When the dough is firm enough to knead, begin kneading the dough, incorporating more of flour. If the dough is still sticky when all the flour has been incorporated, add more flour a little at a time. Knead well for at least 15 minutes.
			4. Cover the dough and let it rest for at least 30 minutes.
			5. Cut the dough into 3 to 5 pieces. Set the rollers of a pasta machine at the widest opening. Pass the pieces of dough through the machine, folding them in thirds after each pass and dusting them lightly with flour to keep them from getting sticky. Continue passing each piece through the machine until it is smooth.
			6. Working with one piece of dough at a time, decrease the width between the rollers one notch and pass the dough through them again. After each pass, turn the rollers one notch narrower, dust the dough with flour, and pass it through again. Continue until the dough is as thin as desired. The pasta is now ready to cut into desired shapes and to cook. See variations below for cutting instructions.

Variations

*199A. **Cutting Instructions:***

Fettuccine or Tagliatelle: Roll dough thin and cut with wide cutting rollers.

Taglierini: Roll dough thin and cut with narrow cutting rollers.

Papardelle: Cut by hand, using a fluted cutting wheel, into long noodles about ¾-inch (18-mm) wide.

Tonnarelli: Roll dough to the same thickness as the width of the narrow cutting roller. Cut with the narrow cutting rollers. The result is like square spaghetti.

Bow ties: Cut into rectangles about 1½ × 3 inches (4 × 8 cm). Pinch in the middle to make a bow (see Figure 18.6).

Lasagne: Cut by hand into broad strips about 8 to 12 inches (20 to 30 cm) long.

*199B. **Spinach Pasta:*** Clean 1 lb (450 g) AP spinach, discarding stems. Simmer 5 minutes in salted water. Drain, rinse in cold water, and squeeze dry. Chop as fine as possible. Incorporate in basic pasta recipe, adding it to the flour at the same time as the eggs. Reduce the quantity of eggs to 4.

*199C. **Other Colored Pastas:*** Other colored vegetables, in small quantities, cooked until tender and puréed or chopped fine, can be substituted for spinach to color pasta. For example, try experimenting with beets, red bell peppers, and carrots.

RECIPE 200   **Fettuccine Alfredo**

			Portions: 10	Portion size: 6–7 oz (175–200 g)
U.S.	*Metric*	*Ingredients*	*Procedure*	
1 cup 2 oz	250 mL 60 g	Heavy cream Butter	1. Combine the cream and butter in a sauté pan. Bring to a simmer, reduce by one-fourth, and remove from heat.	
1½ lb	700 g	Fresh fettuccine	2. Drop the noodles into boiling salted water, return to a full boil, and drain. The noodles must be slightly undercooked because they will cook further in the cream.	
1 cup 6 oz	250 mL 175 g	Heavy cream Freshly grated parmesan cheese Salt Pepper	3. Put the drained noodles in the pan with the hot cream and butter. Over low heat, toss the noodles with two forks until they are well coated with the cream. 4. Add the remainder of the cream and the cheese and toss to mix well. (If the noodles seem dry at this point, add a little more cream.) 5. Add salt and pepper to taste. 6. Plate and serve immediately. Offer additional grated cheese at the table.	

Variations

*200A. **Fettuccine with Vegetables I (Fettuccine Primavera):*** Fresh, lightly cooked vegetables can be added to fettuccine to make a great variety of dishes. In the basic recipe, use about half the quantity of cream and one-third to one-half the quantity of cheese. Select 4 to 6 fresh vegetables, cook them until al dente, cut into appropriately small sizes and shapes, and add them to the pasta when it is being tossed in the cream. The following are examples of appropriate vegetables:

Mushrooms	Tiny green beans
Peas	Asparagus
Broccoli	Artichoke hearts
Red or green bell pepper	Zucchini

Small quantities of finely diced ham, prosciutto, or bacon can also be added as a flavor accent.

*200B. **Fettuccine with Vegetables II:*** Prepare like Fettuccine with Vegetables I, but omit all butter and cream. Instead, toss the freshly cooked fettuccine and cooked vegetables with olive oil. Add parmesan cheese as desired.

*200C. **Fettuccine with Seafood:*** Use half the quantity of cream and cheese in the basic recipe. Prepare like Fettuccine with Vegetables I, adding only 1 to 3 types of vegetables. At the same time, add desired quantity of cooked seafood, such as shrimp, scallops, crab, or lobster. For a fuller flavor, reduce a small amount of fish stock and white wine with the cream in the first step.

*200D. **Fettuccine with Gorgonzola:*** Prepare as in basic recipe, except use light cream instead of heavy cream in the first step. Omit the second quantity of heavy cream, and instead add 6 oz (175 g) gorgonzola cheese (Italian blue cheese). Reduce the quantity of parmesan cheese to 2 oz (60 g).

RECIPE 201 Pesto (Fresh Basil Sauce)

Yield: about 3 cups (750 mL) **Portions:** 12 **Portion size:** 2 oz (60 mL)

U.S.	Metric	Ingredients	Procedure
2 qt	2 L	Fresh basil leaves	1. Wash the basil leaves and drain well.
1½ cups	375 mL	Olive oil	2. Put the basil, oil, nuts, garlic, and salt in a blender or food processor. Blend to a paste, but not so long that it is smooth. It should have a slightly coarse texture.
2 oz	60 g	Walnuts or pine nuts (pignoli)	
6	6	Garlic cloves	
1½ tsp	7 mL	Salt	
5 oz	150 g	Freshly grated parmesan cheese	3. Transfer the mixture to a bowl and stir in the cheese.
1½ oz	50 g	Freshly grated romano cheese	4. To serve, cook pasta to order according to the basic procedure. Just before the pasta is done, stir a little of the hot cooking water into the pesto to thin it out, if desired. Toss the drained pasta with the pesto and serve immediately. Pass additional grated cheese.

RECIPE 202 Spaghettini Puttanesca

Portions: 10 **Portion size:** approximately 12 oz (350 g)

U.S.	Metric	Ingredients	Procedure
3½ lb	1.6 kg	Tomatoes, preferably fresh	1. Peel, seed, and dice the tomatoes, and let them stand in a colander. If using canned tomatoes, drain them and chop them coarsely.
2 oz	60 mL	Olive oil	2. Heat the olive oil in a sauté pan over moderate heat. Add the garlic and sauté for a minute.
5	5	Garlic cloves, chopped	
15	15	Anchovy fillets, chopped	3. Add the anchovy fillets and sauté for a few seconds.
3 tbsp	30 g	Capers, drained	4. Add the tomatoes, capers, and olives. Bring to a boil. Cook 2 to 3 minutes.
5 oz	150 g	Black olives, pitted and sliced	
½ tsp	2 mL	Oregano	5. Remove from heat. Add the oregano, the parsley, and the second quantity of olive oil. Season to taste with salt and pepper.
3 tbsp	45 mL	Chopped parsley	
1 oz	30 mL	Olive oil	
		Salt	
		Pepper	
2 lb	900 g	Spaghettini	6. Boil the spaghettini, drain, toss with the sauce, and serve immediately. Grated cheese is usually not served with this dish.

RECIPE 203 **Linguine with White Clam Sauce**

Portions: 10   **Portion size:** approximately 12 oz (350 g)

U.S.	Metric	Ingredients	Procedure
4 dozen	4 dozen	Cherrystone clams	1. Open the clams. Strain and reserve 1 pt (500 mL) of their juice. Chop the clams coarsely.
1 cup	250 mL	Olive oil	2. Heat the olive oil in a large sauté pan. Add the garlic and brown it very lightly. Do not let it get too brown, or it will be bitter.
4–6	4–6	Garlic cloves, sliced thin	
½ tsp	2 mL	Red pepper flakes	3. Add the red pepper, and then, very carefully, add the wine. (If the pan is very hot, you may want to cool it a little first, to prevent dangerous spattering when the liquid is added.) Reduce the wine by half.
½ cup	125 mL	Dry white wine (optional)	
2 tsp	10 mL	Oregano	4. Add the reserved clam juice and reduce by half.
			5. Add the oregano.
2 lb	900 g	Linguine	6. Drop the linguine into boiling, salted water and boil until al dente. Drain and plate.
4 tbsp	60 mL	Chopped parsley	
		Black pepper	7. While the linguine is boiling, add the chopped clams and the parsley to the olive oil mixture. Heat gently just until the clams are hot. Do not overcook them or they will be tough.
			8. Add pepper to taste. (Since clams are salty, the sauce will probably not need any salt, but taste to make sure.)
			9. Spoon the sauce over the hot linguine and serve at once.
			10. Many people prefer this dish without parmesan cheese, but provide it on the side to those who want it.

RECIPE 204   **Baked Lasagne**

			Portions: 24	**Portion size:** 8 oz (225 g)
U.S.	*Metric*	*Ingredients*	*Procedure*	
1½ lb 2 oz 2	700 g 60 g 2	Ricotta cheese Parmesan cheese Eggs Salt Pepper	1. Mix together the ricotta, parmesan, and eggs. Season to taste with salt and pepper.	
2 lb	900 g	Fresh pasta or 　spinach pasta	2. Cut the fresh pasta into lasagne noodles. Cook them in boiling salted water, drain, and rinse in cold water. Lay them out in a single layer on oiled sheet pans.	
3 qt 1½ lb 4 oz	3 L 700 g 125 g	Meat sauce (p. 461) Mozzarella cheese, 　shredded Parmesan cheese	3. Ladle a little meat sauce into a standard 12 × 20-inch (20 × 50 cm) hotel pan. Spread it across the bottom. 4. Arrange a layer of noodles in the pan. Then add a layer of the ricotta mixture, a layer of noodles, a layer of sauce, and a layer of mozzarella. 5. Continue making layers of noodles, ricotta, sauce, and mozzarella until all ingredients are used up. Top with parmesan cheese. 6. Bake at 375°F (190°C) for about 45 minutes. Cover lightly with foil at first to keep it from drying out, but remove the foil for the last 15 minutes of baking time.	

Variations

Other ingredients can be added to lasagne, such as sliced, cooked meatballs, sausages, zucchini, eggplant, and so forth. It is best to add only one or two ingredients, so that the lasagne doesn't seem like a catchall for leftovers.

If meat items are added to the lasagne, you may use plain tomato sauce instead of meat sauce. The ricotta mixture may also be omitted, especially if other protein items are added, or if the quantity of mozzarella is increased.

DUMP

Dumpling
doughs o

RECIPE 2

U.S.

2½ lb EP

12 oz
2 tsp
2

4 oz
4 oz

Variation

One or
(125 g)
fat.

RECIPE 205   **Ravioli with Cheese Filling**

Portions: 25   **Portion size:** 5 oz (150 g) uncooked
or approx.
7 oz (200 g) cooked

U.S.	Metric	Ingredients	Procedure
3 lb	1.4 kg	Ricotta cheese	1. Mix together the ricotta cheese, parmesan, egg yolks, parsley, and seasonings.
8 oz	250 g	Parmesan cheese	
5	5	Egg yolks	
¾ cup	50 g	Chopped parsley	
½ tsp	2 mL	Nutmeg	
		Salt	
		White pepper	
4½ lb	2 kg	Fresh pasta	2. Roll out the pasta into thin sheets.

3. Over half the pasta, make small mounds of the cheese filling about 1 tsp (5 mL) each, arranging them in a checkerboard pattern about 1½ to 2 inches (4 to 5 cm) apart.

4. Lay the remaining pasta over the top and press down between the mounds of cheese to seal well. While doing this, try to avoid sealing large air bubbles inside the ravioli. Note: If the pasta is fresh and moist, the layers will seal together if pressed firmly. If it is dry, moisten the bottom layer lightly between the mounds of cheese, using a brush dipped in water. Do not get the pasta too wet.

5. Cut the ravioli apart with a pastry wheel. Check each piece to be sure it is completely sealed.

6. The cheese filling does not keep well, so the ravioli should be cooked the same day they are made. They can be held briefly on sheet pans covered with dry, clean towels; turn them over from time to time so that they do not stick. Or cook them immediately, in boiling salted water, keeping them slightly underdone. Drain and rinse under cold water, drain, and toss with oil or melted butter. Spread in a single layer on a sheet pan and refrigerate. They can then be reheated to order by sautéing them briefly in butter or oil, or by dipping them in boiling water.

7. Serve with your choice of sauce, such as Tomato Sauce, Meat Sauce, Tomato Cream Sauce, or just melted butter and parmesan cheese.

PART FIVE

THE PANTRY AND OTHER SPECIAL SUBJECTS

From the pantry come salads, dressings, and other cold foods and breakfast items. An exploration of appealing food presentation and a collection of recipes from around the world complete the many subjects in this part.

Salads and Salad Dressings

Sandwiches and Hors d'Oeuvres

Breakfast Preparation, Dairy Products, and Coffee and Tea

Food Presentation and Garnish

Recipes from International Cuisines

SALADS

*B*ecause the number and variety of salad combinations is nearly endless, it is helpful to divide salads into categories in order to understand how they are produced. For the pantry chef, the most useful way to classify salads is by ingredients: green salads, vegetable salads, fruit salads, and so on. This is because production techniques are slightly different for each kind. We will use this kind of classification when we discuss specific recipes later in this chapter.

But before the pantry chef can produce the salads, first it has to be decided exactly what salads should be made. Therefore, you should know what kinds of salads are best for different purposes. For this reason, salads are also classified according to their function in the meal. Keep in mind that there are no exact dividing lines between the types of salads discussed below. For example, a salad that is suitable as the first course of a dinner may also be an excellent main course on a luncheon menu.

....

TYPES OF SALADS

Appetizer Salads

Many establishments serve salads as a first course, often as a substitute for a more elaborate first course. Not only does this ease the pressure on the kitchen during service, but it gives the customers a satisfying food to eat while their dinners are being prepared.

In addition, more elaborate composed salads are popular as appetizers (and also as main courses at lunch) in many elegant restaurants. These often consist of a poultry, meat, or fish item, plus a variety of other vegetables and garnishes, attractively arranged on a bed of greens.

1. Appetizer salads should stimulate the appetite. This means they must have fresh, crisp ingredients; a tangy, flavorful dressing; and an attractive, appetizing appearance.

2. Preportioned salads should not be so large as to be filling, but they should be substantial enough to serve as a complete course in themselves. (Self-service salad bars, of course, avoid this problem.) Tossed green salads are especially popular for this reason, because they are bulky without being filling.

3. The combination of ingredients should be interesting, not dull or trite. Flavorful foods like cheese, ham, salami, shrimp, and crabmeat, even in small quantities, add appeal. So do crisp raw or lightly cooked vegetables. A bowl of poorly drained iceberg lettuce with a bland dressing is hardly the most exciting way to start a meal.

4. Attractive arrangement and garnish are important, because visual appeal stimulates appetites. A satisfying, interesting starter puts the customer in a good frame of mind for the rest of the meal.

Accompaniment Salads

Salads can also be served with the main course. They serve the same function as other side dishes (vegetables and starches).

1. Accompaniment salads must balance and harmonize with the rest of the meal, like any other side dish. For example, don't serve potato salad at the same meal at which you are serving french fries or another starch. Sweet fruit salads are rarely appropriate as accompaniments, except with such items as ham or pork.

2. Side-dish salads should be light and flavorful, not too rich. Vegetable salads are often good choices. Heavier salads, such as macaroni or high-protein (meat, seafood, cheese, etc.) salads should not be served unless the main course is light. Combination salads with a variety of elements are appropriate accompaniments to sandwiches.

Main-course Salads

Cold salad plates have become very popular on luncheon menus, especially among nutrition- and diet-conscious diners. The appeal of these salads is in variety and freshness of ingredients.

1. Main-course salads should be large enough to serve as a full meal and should contain a substantial portion of protein. Meat, poultry, and seafood salads, as well as egg salad and cheese, are popular choices.

2. Main-course salads should offer enough variety on the plate to be a balanced meal, both nutritionally and in flavors and textures. In addition to the protein, a salad platter should offer a variety of vegetables, greens, and/or fruits. Examples are chef's salad (mixed greens, raw vegetables, and strips of meat and cheese), shrimp or crabmeat salad with tomato wedges and slices of avocado on a bed of greens, and cottage cheese with an assortment of fresh fruits.

3. The portion size and variety of ingredients give the chef an excellent opportunity to use imagination and creativity to produce attractive, appetizing salad plates. Attractive arrangements and good color balance are important.

Separate-course Salads

Many finer restaurants serve a refreshing, light salad after the main course. The purpose is to "cleanse the palate" after a rich dinner and to refresh the appetite and provide a pleasant break before dessert.

Salads served after the main course were the rule rather than the exception many years ago, and the practice deserves to be more widespread. A diner who may be satiated after a heavy meal is often refreshed and ready for dessert after a light, piquant salad.

Separate-course salads must be very light and in no way filling. Rich, heavy dressings, such as those made with sour cream and mayonnaise, should be avoided. Perhaps the ideal choice is a few delicate greens, such as Bibb lettuce or Belgian endive, lightly dressed with vinaigrette. Fruit salads are also popular choices.

Dessert Salads

Dessert salads are usually sweet and may contain items such as fruits, sweetened gelatin, nuts, and cream. They are often too sweet to be served as appetizers or accompaniments and are best served as dessert or as part of a buffet or party menu.

INGREDIENTS

Freshness and variety of ingredients are essential for quality salads. Lettuce, of course, is the first choice for most people, but there are many other foods that can make up a salad.

The following tables list, by category, most of the ingredients used in popular American salads. You will be able to think of others. Add them to the lists as they occur to you or as they are suggested to you by your instructors. The lists will be useful to you when you are creating your own salad ideas.

Following these lists are detailed descriptions of two groups of foods that have not been covered in previous chapters and belong especially in the pantry: salad greens and fresh fruits (Table 19.1).

Salad Greens

    Iceberg lettuce
    Romaine lettuce
    Boston lettuce
    Bibb or limestone lettuce
    Loose-leaf lettuce
    Escarole
    Chicory or curly endive
    Belgian endive
    Chinese cabbage or celery cabbage
    Spinach
    Dandelion greens
    Watercress
    Arugula
    Radicchio

Vegetables, Raw

    Bean sprouts
    Broccoli
    Cabbage, white, green, and red
    Carrots
    Cauliflower
    Celery
    Celeriac (celery root)
    Cucumbers
    Jerusalem artichokes
    Kohlrabi
    Mushrooms
    Onions and scallions
    Peppers, red, green, and yellow
    Radishes
    Tomatoes

Vegetables, Cooked, Pickled, and Canned

    Artichoke hearts
    Asparagus
    Beans (all kinds)
    Beets
    Carrots
    Cauliflower
    Corn
    Cucumber pickles (dill, sweet, etc.)
    Hearts of palm
    Leeks
    Olives
    Peas
    Peppers, roasted and pickled
    Pimientos
    Potatoes
    Water chestnuts

Starches

Dried beans (cooked or canned)

Potatoes

Macaroni products

Rice

Bread (croutons)

Fruits, Fresh, Cooked, Canned, or Frozen

Apples

Apricots

Avocados

Bananas

Berries

Cherries

Coconut

Dates

Figs

Grapefruit

Grapes

Kiwi fruit

Mandarin oranges and tangerines

Mangos

Melons

Oranges

Papayas

Peaches and nectarines

Pears

Persimmons

Pineapple

Plums

Prunes

Pomegranates

Raisins

Protein Foods

Meats (beef, ham)

Poultry (chicken, turkey)

Fish and shellfish (tuna, crab, shrimp, lobster, salmon, sardines, anchovies, herring, any fresh cooked fish)

Salami, luncheon meats, etc.

Bacon

Eggs, hard-cooked

Cheese, cottage

Cheese, aged or cured types

Miscellaneous

Gelatin (plain or flavored)

Nuts

Lettuce and Other Salad Greens
(see Figure 19.1)

Iceberg Lettuce (Figure 19.1a)

The most popular salad ingredient. Firm, compact head with crisp, mild-tasting pale green leaves. Valuable for its texture, because it stays crisp longer than other lettuces. Can be used alone, but best mixed with more flavorful greens such as romaine, because it lacks flavor itself. Keeps well.

Romaine or Cos Lettuce (Figure 19.1b)

Elongated, loosely packed head with dark green, coarse leaves. Crisp texture, with full, sweet flavor. Keeps well and is easy to handle. Essential for Caesar Salad. For elegant service, the center rib is often removed.

Boston Lettuce (Figure 19.1c)

Small, round heads with soft, fragile leaves. Deep green outside, shading to nearly white inside. The leaves have a rich, mild flavor and delicate, buttery texture. Bruises easily and does not keep well. Cup-shaped leaves excellent for salad bases.

Bibb or Limestone Lettuce (Figure 19.1d)

Similar to Boston lettuce but smaller and more delicate. A whole head may be only a few inches across. Color ranges from dark green outside to creamy yellow at the core. Its tenderness, delicate flavor, and high price make it a luxury in some markets. The small, whole leaves are often served by themselves, with a light vinaigrette dressing, as an after-dinner salad.

Loose-leaf Lettuce (Figure 19.1e)

Forms bunches rather than heads. Soft, fragile leaves with curly edges. May be all green or with shades of red. Wilts easily and does not keep well, but is inexpensive and gives flavor, variety, and interest to mixed green salads.

Escarole or Broad-leaf Endive (Figure 19.1f)

Broad, thick leaves in bunches rather than heads. Texture is coarse and slightly tough, and flavor is somewhat bitter. Mix with sweeter greens to vary flavor and texture, but do not use alone, because of bitterness. Escarole is frequently braised with olive oil and garlic and served as a vegetable in Italian cuisine.

FIGURE 19.1 **Salad greens.**
(a) Iceberg lettuce.

(d) Bibb or limestone lettuce.

(b) Romaine or cos lettuce.

(e) Loose-leaf lettuce.

(c) Boston lettuce.

(f) Escarole or broad-leaf endive.

(g) Chicory or curly endive.

(i) Chinese cabbage.

(h) Belgian endive or witloof chicory.

(j) Spinach.

Chicory or Curly Endive (Figure 19.1g)

Narrow, curly, twisted leaves with firm texture and bitter flavor. Outside leaves are dark green; core is yellow or white. Attractive when mixed with other greens or used as a base or garnish, but may be too bitter to be used alone.

Belgian Endive or Witloof Chicory (Figure 19.1h)

Narrow, lightly packed, pointed heads resembling spearheads, 4 to 6 inches (10 to 15 cm) long. Pale yellow-green to white in color. Leaves are crisp, with a waxy texture and pleasantly bitter flavor. Usually expensive. Often served alone, split in half or into wedges, or separated into leaves, accompanied by a mustard vinaigrette dressing.

Chinese Cabbage (Figure 19.1i)

Elongated, light green heads with broad, white center ribs. Available in two forms: narrow, elongated head, often called celery cabbage, and thicker, blunt head, called nappa cabbage. Tender but crisp, with a mild cabbage flavor. Adds excellent flavor to mixed green salads. Also used extensively in Chinese cooking.

Spinach (Figure 19.1j)

Small, tender spinach leaves are excellent salad greens, either alone or mixed with other greens. A popular salad is spinach leaves garnished with sliced, raw mushrooms and crisp, crumbled bacon. Spinach must be washed very thoroughly and the coarse stems must be removed.

Watercress (Figure 19.1k)

Most commonly used as a garnish, watercress is also excellent in salads. Small, dark green, oval leaves with a pungent, peppery flavor. Remove thick stems before adding to salads.

Arugula (Figure 19.1l)

Also known as Rugula or Rocket, these pungent, distinctively flavored greens are related to mustard and to watercress. They are tender and perishable, and they often are very sandy, so they must be washed carefully. Arugula was once found almost exclusively in Italian restaurants, but it has since become more widely available and is increasingly popular.

Radicchio (Figure 19.1m)

This red-leafed, Italian variety of chicory (whose name is pronounced ra-dik-ee-oh) has creamy white ribs or veins and generally comes in small, round heads. It has a crunchy texture and a slightly bitter flavor. Radicchio is expensive, but only a leaf or two are needed to add color and flavor to a salad.

Dandelion Greens

The familiar lawn ornament is also cultivated for use in the kitchen. Only young, tender leaves must be used. Older leaves are coarse and bitter, though cultivated varieties are milder than wild dandelion. Best in spring.

Precleaned, precut salad greens are sold in large, sealed plastic bags. They save labor costs in large operations, but they are more perishable than unprocessed greens. Keep refrigerated, and do not open until ready to use. Unopened bags will keep 2 or 3 days. Taste before serving to make sure the greens do not have too much antioxidant on them, making them bitter.

(k) Watercress.

(l) Arugula or rocket.

(m) Radicchio.

TABLE 19.1   **Fruit Pre-preparation**

Note: This chart is a continuation of Table 16.2: Vegetable Pre-preparation

Product	Quality Indicators and Pre-preparation	Percentage Yield
Apples	Quality Indicators (Q.I.): Mature apples have fruity aroma, brown seeds, and slightly softer texture than unripe fruit. Overripe or old apples are soft and sometimes shriveled. Avoid apples with bruises, blemishes, decay, or mealy texture. Summer varieties (sold until fall) do not keep well. Fall and winter varieties keep well and are available until summer.	75%
	Prep.: Wash. Pare (if desired), quarter and remove core, or leave whole and core with special coring tool. Use stainless steel knife for cutting. After paring, dip in solution of lemon juice (or other tart fruit juice) or ascorbic acid to prevent browning.	
Apricots	Q.I.: Accept only tree-ripened fruits, golden yellow, firm, and plump. Avoid fruit that is too soft or with blemishes, cracks, or decay.	94%
	Prep.: Wash, split in half, and remove pit. Does not need to be peeled.	
Avocados	Q.I.: Two main types: with rough green skin turning black when ripe; with smoother skin that stays green. Fresh appearance, heavy for size, turning soft when ripe. Avoid soft spots and bruises.	75%
	Prep.: Ripen at room temperature, 2 to 5 days. Cut in half lengthwise and remove pit. Peel (skin pulls away easily from ripe fruit). Dip or rub with lemon juice immediately to prevent browning.	
Bananas	Q.I.: Plump and smooth, without bruises or spoilage. Avoid overripe fruit.	70%
	Prep.: Ripen at room temperature for 3 to 5 days (full ripe fruit is all yellow with small brown flecks and no green). Do not refrigerate, or fruit will discolor. Peel and dip in fruit juice to prevent browning.	
Berries (blackberries, blueberries, cranberries, currants, raspberries, strawberries)	Q.I.: Full, plump and clean, with bright, fully ripe color. Watch for mold or spoiled fruits. Wet spots on carton indicate damaged fruit.	92–95%
	Prep.: Refrigerate in original container until ready to use. Except for cranberries, berries do not keep well. Sort out spoiled berries and foreign materials. Wash with gentle spray and drain well. Remove stems from strawberries. Handle carefully to avoid bruising.	
Cherries	Q.I.: Plump, firm, sweet, and juicy, with uniform dark red to almost black color (except Royal Anne variety, which is creamy white with red blush). No blemishes or bruises.	82% (pitted)
	Prep.: Refrigerate in original container until ready to use. Remove stems and damaged fruit. Rinse and drain well. Remove pits with special cherry pitting tool.	
Coconuts	Q.I.: Shake to hear liquid inside. Avoid cracked fruits and fruits with wet "eyes."	50%

TABLE 19.1   (Continued)

Product	Quality Indicators and Pre-preparation	Percentage Yield
	Prep.: Pierce eyes with ice pick or nail and drain liquid (which may be used in curries and similar dishes). Crack with a hammer and remove meat from shell (easier if placed in 350°F (175°C) oven for 10 to 15 minutes). Peel off brown skin with paring knife or vegetable peeler.	
Figs	Q.I.: Plump, soft fruits without spoilage or sour odor. Calimyrna figs are light green when ripe; Missions are nearly black. Rinse and drain (handle carefully). Remove stem ends. Very perishable. Store as short a time as possible.	95% (80–85% if peeled)
Grapefruit	Q.I.: Firm, smooth skins, heavy for size. Avoid puffy, soft fruits or those with pointed ends. Cut and taste for sweetness.	45–50% (flesh without membrane); 40–45% (juiced)
	Prep.: For grapefruit halves, cut in half crosswise and free flesh from membranes with grapefruit knife. For sections and slices, peel and section or slice as illustrated in Figure 7.11.	
Grapes	Q.I.: Firm, ripe, well-colored fruits in full bunches that should be firmly attached to stems, not fall off when shaken. Watch for shriveling or rotting at stem ends.	90%
	Refrigerate in original container. Wash and drain. Leave on bunches if desired for dining room presentation, or pull from stems. Cut in half and remove seeds (except for seed-less variety).	
Kiwi fruit	Q.I.: Firm but slightly soft to touch when ripe. No bruises or excessively soft spots.	80%
	Prep.: Pare thin outer skin with paring knife. Cut crosswise into slices.	
Lemons and limes	Q.I.: Firm, smooth skins. Color may vary: limes may be yellow, and lemons may have some green on skin.	40–45% (juiced)
	Prep.: Cut in wedges, slices, or other shapes for garnish, or cut in half crosswise for juicing.	
Mangoes	Q.I.: Plump and firm, with clear color and no blemishes. Avoid rock hard fruits, which may not ripen properly.	75%
	Prep.: Let ripen at room temperature until slightly soft. Peel and cut flesh away from center stone, or cut in half before peeling, working a thin bladed knife around both sides of the flat stone.	
Melons	Q.I.: Cantaloupes: Smooth scar on stem end, with no trace of stem (called "full slip," meaning melon was picked ripe). Yellow rind, with little or no green. Heavy, with good aroma. Honeydew: Good aroma, slightly soft, heavy, creamy white to yellowish rind, not green. Large sizes have best quality. Crenshaws, Casabas, Persians: Heavy, with rich aroma and slightly soft blossom end. Watermelon: Yellow underside, not white. Firm and symmetrical. Large sizes have best yield. Velvety surface, not too shiny. When cut, look for hard dark brown seeds and no "white heart" (hard white streak run-ning through center).	Watermelons: 45%; other: 50–55%

(Continues)

TABLE 19.1   **Fruit Pre-preparation** *(Continued)*

Product	Quality Indicators and Pre-preparation	Percentage Yield
	Prep.: Hollow types: Wash, cut in half, and remove seeds and fibers. Cut into portion-size wedges or cut balls with ball cutter. Watermelon: Wash. Cut into desired portions, or cut in half and cut balls with ball cutter.	
Nectarines	Same as for peaches, except do not need to be peeled.	86%
Oranges and mandarins (including tangerines)	Oranges: Same as for grapefruit. Mandarins: May feel puffy, but should be heavy for size. Peel by hand and separate sections. Discard fibers between sections.	60–65% (sections with no membranes); 50% (juiced)
Papayas	Q.I.: Firm and symmetrical, without bruises or rotten spots. Avoid dark green papayas, which may not ripen properly.	65%
	Prep.: Let ripen at room temperature, until slightly soft and nearly all yellow, with only a little green. Wash. Cut in half lengthwise and scrape out seeds. Peel if desired, or serve like cantaloupe.	
Peaches	Q.I.: Plump and firm, without bruises or blemishes. Avoid green fruits, which are immature and will not ripen well. Select Freestone varieties; Clingstone varieties require too much labor.	75%
	Prep.: Let ripen at room temperature, then refrigerate in original container. Blanch in boiling water about 10 to 20 seconds, until skins slip off easily, and cool in ice water. Peel, cut in half, remove pits, and drop into fruit juice, sugar syrup, or ascorbic acid solution to prevent darkening.	
Pears	Q.I.: Clean, firm, and bright; no blemishes or bruises.	75% (peeled and cored)
	Prep.: Wash. Peel, if desired, cut in half or quarters and remove core.	
Persimmons	Q.I.: Firm, plump, and smooth, with good red color and stem cap attached.	80%
	Prep.: Ripen at room temperature until very soft, then refrigerate (unripe fruits make your mouth feel as though hair is growing in it). Remove stem cap, cut as desired, and remove seeds, if any.	
Pineapple	Q.I.: Plump and fresh looking, orange-yellow color, abundant fragrance. Avoid soft spots, bruises, and dark, watery spots. Large sizes have best yield.	50%
	Prep.: Store at room temperature for a day or two to allow some tartness to disappear, then refrigerate. May be cut in many ways. For slices, chunks, and dice, cut off top and bottom and pare like a grapefruit (see Figure 7.11), using stainless steel knife. Remove all eyes. Cut into quarters lengthwise and cut out hard center core. Slice or cut as desired.	
Plums	Q.I.: Plump and firm but not hard, with good color and no bruises or blemishes.	95% (pitted only)
	Prep.: Wash, cut in half and remove pits, or serve whole.	
Rhubarb	Q.I.: Firm, crisp, tender, with thick stalks, not thin and shriveled. Rhubarb is not actually a fruit but a stem.	85–90% (no leaves)
	Prep.: Cut off all traces of leaf (which is poisonous). Trim root end if necessary. Cut into desired lengths.	

ARRANGEMENT AND PRESENTATION

The Structure of a Salad

There are four basic parts of a salad: base, body, garnish, and dressing. Salads may or may not have all four parts.

1.   *Base or underliner.*

Leafy greens usually form the base of a salad. They add greatly to the appearance of many salads, which would look naked on a bare plate.

Cup-shaped leaves of iceberg or Boston lettuce make attractive bases. They give height to salads and help to confine loose pieces of food.

A layer of loose, flat leaves (such as romaine, loose-leaf, or chicory) or of shredded lettuce may be used as a base. This kind of base involves less labor and food cost, since it is not necessary to separate whole cup-shaped leaves from a head.

Tossed green salads or salads served in a bowl rather than on a plate usually have no base or underliner.

2.   *Body.*

This is the main part of the salad and this part receives most of our attention in this chapter.

3.   *Garnish.*

The purpose of garnish is to give eye appeal to the salad, though it often adds to the flavor as well. It should not be elaborate or dominate the salad. Remember this basic rule of garnishing: keep it simple.

Garnish should harmonize with the rest of the salad ingredients and, of course, be edible. It may be mixed with the other salad ingredients (for example, shreds of red cabbage mixed into a tossed green salad), or it may be added at the end.

Often the main ingredients of a salad form an attractive pattern in themselves, and no garnish is necessary.

Nearly any of the vegetables, fruits, and protein foods listed on pages 477–478, cut into simple, appropriate shapes, may be used as garnish.

4.   *Dressing.*

Dressing is a seasoned liquid or semiliquid that is added to the body of the salad to give it added flavor, tartness, spiciness, and moistness.

The dressing should harmonize with the salad ingredient. In general, use tart dressings for green salads and vegetable salads, and use slightly sweetened dressings for fruit salads. Soft, delicate greens like Boston or Bibb lettuce require a light dressing. A thick, heavy one will turn them to mush.

Dressings may be added at service time (as for green salads), served separately for the customer to add, or mixed with the ingredients ahead of time (as in potato salad, tuna salad, egg salad, and so on). A salad mixed with a heavy dressing, like mayonnaise, to hold it together is called a *bound salad.*

Remember: Dressing is a *seasoning* for the main ingredients. It should accent their flavor, not overpower or drown them. Review the rules of seasoning in Chapter 4.

Arranging the Salad

Perhaps even more than with most other foods, the appearance and arrangement of a salad is essential to its quality. The colorful variety of salad ingredients gives the creative chef an opportunity to create miniature works of art on the salad plate.

Unfortunately, it is nearly as difficult to give rules for arranging salads as it is for painting pictures, because the principles of composition, balance, and symmetry are the same for both arts. It is something you have to develop an eye for, by experience and by studying good examples.

Guidelines for Arranging Salads

1.   *Keep the salad off the rim of the plate.*

Think of the rim as a picture frame, and arrange the salad within this frame. Select the right plate for the portion size, not too large or too small.

2.   *Strive for a good balance of colors.*

Plain iceberg lettuce looks pretty pale and sickly all by itself, but it can be livened up by mixing in some darker greens and perhaps a few shreds of carrot, red cabbage, or other colored vegetable. On the other hand, don't go overboard. Three colors are usually enough, and sometimes just a few different shades of green will create a beautiful effect. Too many colors may look messy.

3.   *Height helps make a salad attractive.*

Ingredients mounded on the plate are more interesting than if they are spread flat. Lettuce cups as bases add height. Often just a little height is enough. Arrange ingredients like fruit wedges or tomato slices so that they overlap or lean against each other rather than lay them flat on the plate.

4. **Cut ingredients neatly.**

Ragged or sloppy cutting makes the whole salad look sloppy and haphazard.

5. **Make every ingredient identifiable.**

Cut every ingredient into large enough pieces so that the customer can recognize them immediately. Don't pulverize everything in the buffalo chopper or VCM. Bite-size pieces are the general rule, unless the ingredient can be cut easily with a fork, such as tomato slices. Seasoning ingredients, like onion, may be chopped fine.

6. **Keep it simple.**

A simple, natural arrangement is pleasing. An elaborate design, a gimmicky or contrived ar-rangement, or a cluttered plate is not pleasing. Besides, elaborate designs take too long to make.

RECIPES AND TECHNIQUES

Thorough *pre-preparation* is extremely important in salad making. There is little cooking involved, but a great deal of time-consuming handwork. Salads can be made quickly and efficiently only if the station is set up properly.

Basic Procedures

Most salads are made in quantity, so an assembly-line production system is most efficient. Figure 19.2 illustrates this technique.

1. Prepare all ingredients. Wash and cut greens. Prepare cooked vegetables. Cut all fruits, vege-

FIGURE 19.2 Efficient production of salads in quantity. (a) Prepare all ingredients ahead. Arrange cold salad plates on trays for easy refrigeration.

(c) Place body of salad (in this case, potato salad) on all plates.

(b) Place lettuce bases on all plates.

(d) Garnish all salads. Refrigerate until service.

tables, and garnish. Mix bound and marinated salads (egg salad, potato salad, three bean salad, etc.). Have all ingredients chilled.

2. Arrange salad plates on work tables. Line them up on trays for easy transferring to refrigerator.

3. Place bases or underliners on all plates.

4. Arrange body of salad on all plates.

5. Garnish all salads.

6. Refrigerate until service. Do not hold more than a few hours or salads will wilt. Holding boxes should have high humidity.

7. Do not add dressing to green salads until service, or they will wilt.

Green Salads

Principles

Salad greens must be fresh, clean, crisp, cold, and well drained, or the salad will lack quality. Good greens depend on proper preparation.

Moisture and air are necessary to keep greens crisp:

1. Leaves wilt because they lose moisture. Crispness can be restored by washing and refrigerating. The moisture that clings to the leaves after thorough draining is usually enough. Too much water drowns them and dissolves out flavor and nutrients.

2. Air circulation is essential for the greens to "breathe." Do not seal washed greens too tightly or pack too firmly. Refrigerate in colanders covered with clean, damp towels, or in specially designed perforated plastic bins. These protect from drying while still allowing air circulation.

Browning or "rusting" occurs when cut greens are held too long. This can be partially avoided by rinsing them in a very mild antioxidant and by using stainless steel knives. Better yet, plan purchasing and production so that you don't need to hold them too long.

Basic Procedure for Green Salads

1. **Wash greens thoroughly.**

   Remove core from head lettuce by striking the core gently against the side of the sink and twisting it out. Do not smash it or you'll bruise the entire head. Cut through the core of other greens or separate the leaves so that all traces of grit can be removed. Wash in several changes of cold water, until completely clean. For iceberg lettuce, run cold water into the core end (after removing core) and then turn over to drain.

2. **Drain greens well.**

   Lift greens from the water and drain in a colander. Tools and machines are available that will quickly spin-dry greens. Poor draining results in a watered-down dressing and a soupy, soggy salad.

3. **Crisp the greens.**

   Refrigerate them in a colander covered with damp towels or in a perforated storage bin to allow air circulation and complete drainage.

4. **Cut or tear into bite-size pieces.**

   Many people insist on tearing leaves instead of cutting, but this is a very slow method if you have a large quantity to do. Also, you are more likely to crush or bruise the leaves.

   Use sharp stainless steel knives for cutting. Bite-size pieces are important as a convenience to the customer. It is difficult to eat or cut large leaves with a salad fork.

5. **Mix the greens.**

   Toss *gently* until uniformly mixed. Nonjuicy raw vegetable garnish such as green pepper strips or carrot shreds may be mixed in at this time. Just make sure the vegetables are not cut into compact little chunks that will all settle to the bottom of the bowl. Broad, thin slices or shreds stay better mixed.

6. **Plate the salads (including underliners, if used).**

   Cold plates, please. Don't use plates right out of the dishwasher.

   Avoid plating salads more than an hour or two before service, or they are likely to wilt or dry.

7. **Garnish.**

   Exceptions: (a) Garnish that is tossed with the greens in step 5. (b) Garnish that will not hold well (croutons will get soggy, avocado will discolor, etc.). Add these at service time.

8. **Refrigerate.**

9. **Add dressing immediately before service, or serve it on the side.**

   Dressed greens wilt rapidly.

RECIPE 209   **Mixed Green Salad**

Portions: 25		**Portion size: 2½–3 oz (70–90 g)**	

U.S.	Metric	Ingredients	Procedure
2 heads	2 heads	Iceberg lettuce	1. Review guidelines and method for preparing green salads (p. 487).
2 heads	2 heads	Romaine	
½ head	½ head	Curly endive (chicory)	2. Wash and drain greens thoroughly. Chill in refrigerator.
1 bunch	1 bunch	Watercress	3. Cut or tear the greens into bite-size pieces.
			4. Place in a large mixing bowl and toss gently until the greens are uniformly mixed.
			5. Plate the salads on cold salad plates or bowls.
			6. Refrigerate until service.
			7. Serve with any appropriate dressing. Serve the dressing in a separate container or add it just before service.

Variations

Any combination of salad greens may be used. The number of heads needed will vary, since the size of the heads is not always the same. Plan on 2½–3 oz (70–90 g) EP (edible portion) per serving. For 25 portions, you will need about 4½ lb (2 kg) trimmed greens.

Vegetable ingredients, if they are not juicy, may be tossed with the greens. See page 477 for a listing. Shredded carrot and red cabbage are useful because a small amount gives an attractive color accent.

Garnishes may be added after the salads are plated, such as
    Tomato wedges
    Cherry tomatoes
    Cucumber slices
    Radishes
    Pepper rings
    Croutons
    Hard-cooked egg wedges or slices

Service variation: Instead of plating and holding the salads, toss the greens with dressing immediately before service. For 25 portions, use about 1½ pt (700 mL) dressing. Use a vinaigrette variation or Emulsified French. Mayonnaise dressings are too thick for tossing. Plate and serve immediately.

RECIPE 210   **Spinach Salad**

Portions: 25			**Portion size:** 3 oz (90 g)

U.S.	Metric	Ingredients	Procedure
3 lb	1.4 kg	Spinach leaves, trimmed (no stems)	1. Wash the spinach in several changes of cold water until there is no trace of sand on them. Drain well. Chill in the refrigerator.
12 oz	350 g	Bacon	2. Cook the bacon on a griddle or in the oven on a sheet pan until crisp. Drain and let cool.
			3. Crumble the bacon.
1 lb	450 g	Fresh, white mushrooms	4. Wash the mushrooms and dry them well. Trim off the bottoms of the stems. Cut the mushrooms into thin slices.
6	6	Hard-cooked eggs	5. Chop the eggs coarsely.
			6. Place the spinach in a large bowl. Tear large leaves into smaller pieces. Smaller leaves may be left whole.
			7. Add the mushrooms. Toss to mix thoroughly.
			8. Portion the salad onto cold salad plates.
			9. Sprinkle the salads with the chopped eggs.
			10. Hold for service in refrigerator.
			11. At serving time, sprinkle with the crumbled bacon.
			12. Serve with a vinaigrette variation or with Emulsified French Dressing.

Note: Bacon may be added to salads when they are assembled (step 9). However, it will be less appetizing, because the fat congeals in the refrigerator. For best quality, cook the bacon as close to serving time as possible.

RECIPE 211 **Caesar Salad**

This famous salad is frequently prepared at the customer's table by the waiter, and most recipes are written for à la carte service. The recipe included here has been adapted for kitchen preparation, so that larger quantities can be prepared, if desired. The ingredients are traditional, even if the method is not.

Portions: 25 **Portion size:** 3 oz (90 g) lettuce, plus dressing

U.S.	Metric	Ingredients	Procedure
5 lb	2.3 kg	Romaine leaves	1. Wash and drain the greens thoroughly. Chill in refrigerator.
12 oz 2–4 oz	350 g 60–125 mL	White bread Olive oil	2. Trim the crusts from the bread. Cut the bread into small cubes, about ⅜ inch (1 cm). 3. Heat a thin layer of olive oil in a sauté pan over moderate high heat. Add the bread cubes and sauté in the oil until golden and crisp. Add more oil as needed. 4. Remove the croutons from the pan and hold for service. Do not refrigerate.
25 2 tsp (variable) 4 6 oz 2½ cups	25 10 mL 4 175 mL 600 mL	Dressing: Anchovy fillets (optional) Garlic, crushed Eggs, beaten (see note) Lemon juice Olive oil Salt	5. Mash the anchovies and garlic together to make a paste. 6. Beat in the eggs and lemon juice until smooth. 7. Beating constantly with a wire whip, slowly add the olive oil. 8. Season the dressing to taste.
2 oz	60 g	Parmesan cheese, grated	9. Cut or tear the romaine into bite-size pieces. Place in a large bowl. 10. Immediately before service, pour the dressing over the greens and sprinkle with the parmesan cheese. Toss until all the leaves are coated with the dressing. 11. Add the croutons and toss again. 12. Plate and serve immediately *Alternative method:* If speed of service is critical, plate the lettuce and hold for service in the refrigerator. At service time, ladle on the dressing and top with cheese and croutons.

Note: Coddled eggs are often used instead of raw eggs. To coddle eggs, simmer in water 1 minute and cool in cold water. Some chefs prefer to use yolks only.

RECIPE 211   **Caesar Salad** *(Continued)*

Variation

Tableside service: Using the same proportions of ingredients, use the following method:

1. Have the lettuce and croutons prepared ahead of time.
2. Ask the customers how much garlic they would like. Depending on their answer, either rub the salad bowl with a cut clove of garlic and remove it, or leave it in the bowl and crush it with the anchovies.
3. Mash the anchovies (and garlic, if used) to a paste.
4. Beat in about half of the olive oil.
5. Add the greens and toss to coat with the oil mixture.
6. Break the egg over the bowl and drop it in. Toss the lettuce well.
7. Add the lemon juice, the rest of the oil, the parmesan cheese, and a little salt. Toss again until well mixed.
8. Add the croutons and toss a final time.
9. Plate and serve.

RECIPE 212   **Garden Salad**

Portions: 25		**Portion size:** 3 oz (90 g)	
		plus garnish	

U.S.	Metric	Ingredients	Procedure
3½ lb	1.6 kg	Mixed salad greens	1. Include some firm-textured crisp lettuce in the mixed greens, such as romaine or iceberg.
8 oz	250 g	Cucumbers	2. Wash and drain greens thoroughly. Chill in refrigerator.
4 oz	125 g	Celery	
4 oz	125 g	Radishes	3. Score the cucumbers lengthwise with a fork (see p. 595). Peel them if they have been waxed. Cut into thin slices.
4 oz	125 g	Scallions	
4 oz	125 g	Carrots	
1½ lb	700 g	Tomatoes	4. Cut the celery into thin slices on the bias.

5. Trim the radishes and cut into thin slices.
6. Trim off the roots and wilted tops of the scallions. Cut in half crosswise. Then slice lengthwise into thin shreds.
7. Trim and peel the carrots. Shred on a medium grater.
8. Remove the core end of the tomatoes. Cut into wedges, 8–10 per tomato, depending on size.
9. Cut or tear the lettuce and other greens into bite-size pieces.
10. Place all ingredients except tomatoes in a large mixing bowl. Toss until evenly mixed.
11. Plate the salads on cold plates or bowls.
12. Garnish with tomato wedges.
13. Hold for service in refrigerator.
14. Serve with an appropriate dressing.

Vegetable Salads

Principles

Vegetable salads are salads whose main ingredients are vegetables other than lettuce or other leafy greens. Some vegetables are used raw, such as celery, cucumbers, radishes, tomatoes, and green peppers. Some are cooked and chilled before including in the salad, such as artichokes, green beans, beets, and asparagus. See pages 477–478 for lists of vegetables that can be used.

Sometimes cooked pasta or a protein item such as meat, poultry, fish, or cheese is added to a vegetable salad. If the proportion of these ingredients is high, the salad may be more like the cooked salads discussed in the next section. There is no exact dividing line between these types of salads. It helps to keep the guidelines for both types of salads in mind when you are preparing these recipes.

Guidelines for Making Vegetable Salads

1. Neat, accurate cutting of ingredients is important, because the shapes of the vegetables add to eye appeal. The design or arrangement of a vegetable salad is often based on different shapes, such as long, slender asparagus and green beans, wedges of tomato, slices of cucumber, strips or rings of green pepper, and radish flowers.

2. Cut vegetables as close as possible to serving time, or else they may dry or shrivel at the edges.

3. Cooked vegetables should have a firm, crisp texture and good color. Mushy, overcooked vegetables are unattractive in a salad. See Chapter 16 for vegetable cooking principles.

4. After cooking, vegetables must be thoroughly drained and well chilled before being included in the salad.

5. Vegetables are sometimes *marinated*, or soaked in a seasoned liquid, before being made into salads, as for three bean salad and for mushrooms à la Grecque. The marinade is usually some form of oil and vinegar dressing, and also serves as the dressing for the salad. Do not plate marinated salads too far ahead of time, or the lettuce base will wilt. Use crisp, sturdy greens (such as iceberg, romaine, or chicory) as bases, since they do not wilt as quickly.

RECIPE 213 Cucumber and Tomato Salad

Portions: 25   **Portion size:** about 3 oz (90 g)

U.S.	Metric	Ingredients	Procedure
10	10	Tomatoes, medium size	1. Wash the tomatoes and cut out the core at the stem end. Cut each tomato into 5 slices of uniform thickness.
3	3	Cucumbers	2. Wash the cucumbers. Score them lengthwise with a fork or flute them with a channel knife (see Figure 22.1). If the cucumbers have been waxed, peel them.
25	25	Lettuce leaves for underliners	
½ cup	125 mL	Chopped parsley	3. Cut the cucumbers on the bias into ⅛-inch (3-mm) thick slices.
			4. Arrange the washed, crisped lettuce leaves on cold salad plates.
			5. On top of the lettuce, overlap 2 slices of tomato alternating with 2 slices of cucumber. Make sure the most attractive side of each slice is facing up.
			6. Sprinkle the salads with chopped parsley.
			7. Hold for service in refrigerator.
1⅔ cups	400 mL	French Dressing	8. At service time, dress each salad with 1 tbsp (15 mL) dressing.

RECIPE 213   **Cucumber and Tomato Salad** (*Continued*)

Variations

213A. ***Tomato and Cucumber Salad with Capers:*** Omit chopped parsley, and sprinkle the salads with capers.

213B. ***Tomato Salad:*** Omit cucumbers. Use 15 tomatoes and serve 3 slices per portion, overlapping on the plate.

213C. ***Tomato and Spinach Salad:*** Prepare like Tomato Salad, but use spinach leaves instead of lettuce as the salad base.

213D. ***Tomato and Watercress Salad:*** Prepare like Tomato Salad, but use watercress instead of lettuce as the salad base.

213E. ***Tomato and Onion Salad:*** Substitute sweet Bermuda onion for the cucumber in the basic recipe. Alternate slices of tomato and onion on the plate.

213F. ***Tomato and Green Pepper Salad:*** Substitute green peppers for the cucumber in the basic recipe. Alternate slices of tomato and pepper (rings) on the plate.

213G. ***Tomato and Avocado Salad:*** Substitute avocado for the cucumber. Dip avocado slices in French Dressing or lemon juice to keep them from darkening. Alternate slices of tomato and avocado on the plate.

RECIPE 214   **Cucumbers and Onions in Sour Cream**

| **Portions:** 25 | | | **Portion size:** 3½ oz (100 g) |

U.S.	Metric	Ingredients	Procedure
1 pt	500 mL	Cider vinegar	1. Combine the vinegar, water, sugar, salt, and pepper in a stainless steel bowl. Stir to dissolve the sugar and salt.
1 cup	250 mL	Water	
1 oz	30 g	Sugar	
2 tsp	10 mL	Salt	2. Add the sliced cucumbers and onions. Mix.
½ tsp	2 mL	White pepper	3. Cover and marinate in refrigerator for at least 2 hours.
4 lb EP	1.8 kg EP	Cucumber, peeled and sliced thin	
1 lb EP	450 g EP	Onions, peeled and sliced thin	
1 pt	500 mL	Sour cream	4. Mix together the sour cream and mayonnaise until smooth.
1 cup	250 mL	Mayonnaise	
25	25	Lettuce leaves for underliners	5. Drain the cucumbers and onions and add them to the dressing. Mix together. Adjust the seasoning.
3 tbsp	45 mL	Cut chives	6. Arrange the lettuce on cold salad plates. Place a portion of the cucumbers on each plate. Garnish with a light sprinkling of chives.
			Alternative method: Instead of mixing cucumbers with sour cream dressing, just drain off the marinade and plate the salads. Top each with 1 oz (30 mL) of the sour cream mixture.

(Continues)

RECIPE 214   Cucumbers and Onions in Sour Cream (*Continued*)

Variations

Marinating step may be omitted. Just mix the sliced cucumbers and onions with the sour cream dressing and season to taste. (Flavor and texture will be different.)

214A.   Cucumber and Onion Salad (without sour cream): Omit sour cream dressing. Add 1 cup (250 mL) salad oil to the marinade. If desired, add 1 tbsp (15 mL) dried dill or 3 tbsp (45 mL) fresh chopped dill to the marinade.

RECIPE 215   Coleslaw

Portions: 25   **Portion size:** 3 oz (100 g)

U.S.	Metric	Ingredients	Procedure
1½ pt	750 mL	Mayonnaise	1. Combine the mayonnaise, vinegar, sugar, salt, and pepper in a stainless steel bowl. Mix until smooth.
2 oz	60 mL	Vinegar	
1 oz	30 g	Sugar (optional)	
2 tsp	10 mL	Salt	2. Add the cabbage and mix well.
½ tsp	2 mL	White pepper	3. Taste and, if necessary, add more salt and/or vinegar.
4 lb EP	2 kg EP	Cabbage, shredded	
25	25	Lettuce cups for underliners	4. Arrange the lettuce leaves on cold salad plates.
			5. Using a No. 12 scoop, place a mound of coleslaw in the center of each plate.
			6. Hold for service in refrigerator.

Variations

215A.   Dressing Variations:
1. Use Cooked Dressing (p. 523) instead of mayonnaise. Reduce or omit vinegar.
2. Substitute sour cream for *half* of the mayonnaise.
3. Substitute heavy cream for 1 cup (250 mL) of the mayonnaise.
4. Substitute lemon juice for the vinegar.
5. Use 1 pt (500 mL) Basic French Dressing and omit mayonnaise and vinegar. Flavor with 2 tsp (10 mL) celery seed and 1 tsp (5 mL) dry mustard.
6. Add 2 tsp (10 mL) celery seed to the basic mayonnaise dressing.

215B.   Mixed Cabbage Slaw: Use half red cabbage and half green cabbage.

215C.   Carrot Coleslaw: Add 1 lb (500 g) shredded carrots to the basic recipe. Reduce cabbage to 3½ lb (1.7 kg).

215D.   Garden Slaw: Add the following ingredients to the basic recipe: 8 oz (250 g) carrots, shredded; 4 oz (125 g) celery, chopped or julienne; 4 oz (125 g) green pepper, chopped or julienne; 2 oz (60 g) scallions, chopped. Reduce cabbage to 3½ lb (1.7 kg).

215E.   Coleslaw with Fruit: Add the following ingredients to the basic recipe: 4 oz (125 g) raisins, soaked in hot water and drained; 8 oz (250 g) unpeeled apple, cut in small dice; 8 oz (250 g) pineapple, in small dice. Use sour cream dressing (Dressing Variation 2 above), and use lemon juice instead of vinegar.

RECIPE 216 **Green Bean Salad**

. . . .

Portions: 25   **Portion size:** 3 oz (90 g)

U.S.	Metric	Ingredients	Procedure
5 lb	2.3 kg	Green beans (see note)	1. Trim off the ends of the green beans. Cut the beans into 2-inch (5-cm) lengths. 2. Cook them uncovered in boiling salted water until just tender. 3. Cool the beans thoroughly under cold running water or in ice water. Drain well.
1½ pt 4 tbsp ½ tsp	700 mL 60 mL 2 mL	Mustard vinaigrette (p. 518) or Italian Dressing Chives Garlic, chopped fine	4. Combine the beans, dressing, chives, and garlic. Mix well. 5. Refrigerate for 2–4 hours (see note).
6 oz 25	175 g 25	Red onions Lettuce leaves for underliners	6. Peel the onions and cut into very thin slices. Separate into rings. 7. Line salad plates with lettuce leaves. 8. Just before service, place a 3-oz (90-g) portion of marinated green beans on each lettuce underliner, using a solid spoon. 9. Garnish the tops of the salads with a few onion rings. 10. Keep chilled, but serve as soon as possible so that the lettuce doesn't wilt.

Note: Frozen or canned green beans may be used. Canned green beans need no further cooking. Just drain and mix with the dressing.

Green vegetables should be served the same day they are placed in the marinade. If held too long, they begin to turn brown.

Variations

Portion the beans with a slotted spoon. Place a tablespoon of mayonnaise on each salad.

Other cooked vegetables may be marinated in vinaigrette and served using the same procedure:
Artichoke hearts
Asparagus
Beets
Carrots
Cauliflower
Leeks
Dried beans: white beans, chick peas, etc., alone or in combination (see next variation).

216A. Three Bean Salad: Use only 1½ lb (700 kg) green beans. After beans are cooked, add 1½ lb (700 g) drained, canned kidney beans, 1½ lb (700 g) drained, canned chick peas, 4 oz (125 g) onion cut in small dice, 2 oz (60 g) green pepper cut in small dice, and 2 oz (60 g) drained chopped pimiento. Proceed to step 4 as in basic recipe.

RECIPE 217 **Mushrooms à la Grecque**

		Portions: 25	**Portion size:** 2½ oz (75 g)
U.S.	Metric	Ingredients	Procedure
4½ lb	2 kg	Small whole mushrooms	1. Wash and dry the mushrooms. Trim off the bottoms of the stems. Leave the mushrooms whole. (If only large ones are available, cut them into quarters.)
1 qt	1 L	Water	2. Place the water, olive oil, lemon juice, celery, and salt in a stainless steel saucepan. Tie the sachet ingredients in a piece of cheesecloth and add to the pan.
1 pt	500 mL	Olive oil	
6 oz	175 mL	Lemon juice	
1 rib	1 rib	Celery	
2 tsp	10 mL	Salt	3. Bring to a boil. Simmer 15 minutes to extract flavors from the spices.
		Sachet:	
2	2	Garlic cloves, crushed	4. Add the mushrooms. Simmer 5 minutes.
1½ tsp	7 mL	Peppercorns, lightly crushed	5. Remove the heat. Cool the mushrooms in the liquid.
2 tsp	10 mL	Coriander seeds	6. Remove the celery and sachet. Marinate the mushrooms overnight in the refrigerator. (The mushrooms will keep several days in the marinade.)
1	1	Bay leaf	
1 tsp	5 mL	Thyme	
25	25	Lettuce cups for underliners	7. Arrange the lettuce leaves on cold salad plates.
¼ cup	60 mL	Chopped parsley	8. Just before service, place a 2½-oz (75-g) portion of mushrooms in each lettuce cup, using a slotted spoon.
			9. Sprinkle with chopped parsley.

Variations

Other vegetables may be prepared à la Grecque, using this recipe. Increase cooking time as necessary, but keep the vegetables crisp.
   Artichoke hearts
   Carrots, sliced or diced
   Cauliflower, florets
   Leeks
   Pearl onions

RECIPE 218 **Carrot Salad**

		Portions: 25	**Portion size:** 3 oz (100 g)
U.S.	Metric	Ingredients	Procedure
5 lb	2.5 kg	Carrots	1. Peel the carrots. Shred them on a coarse grater.
1½ cup	375 mL	Mayonnaise	
1 cup	250 mL	Basic French Dressing	2. Combine the mayonnaise and French dressing. Mix until smooth.
		Salt	
25	25	Lettuce cups	3. Add the carrots and mix. Season to taste with salt.
13	13	Pitted black olives	

RECIPE 218 **Carrot Salad** *(Continued)*

Portions: 25   **Portion size:** 3 oz (100 g)

U.S.	Metric	Ingredients	Procedure
			4. Arrange the lettuce cups on cold salad plates.
			5. Using a No. 12 scoop, place a mound of carrot salad in each lettuce cup.
			6. Cut the olives in half lengthwise. Garnish the top of each salad with an olive half.

Variations

218A. Carrot Raisin Salad: Simmer 8 oz (250 g) raisins in water for 2 minutes. Cool and then drain. Mix raisins with the carrots.

218B. Carrot Pineapple Salad: Mix 12 oz (375 g) drained pineapple tidbits with the carrots.

218C. Carrot Celery Salad: Reduce the carrots to 3½ lb (1.7 kg). Mix 1½ lb (750 g) celery (cut julienne) or celery root (shredded) with the carrots.

218D. Celery Salad: Use celery or celery root instead of carrots in basic recipe. Cut stalk celery into thin slices instead of shredding it. Add 2 tbsp (30 mL) French or Dijon-type mustard to the dressing.

RECIPE 219 **Oriental Salad with Beef**

Portions: 25   **Portion size:** 5 oz (150 g)

U.S.	Metric	Ingredients	Procedure
2 lb	900 g	Bean sprouts	1. Mix together the bean sprouts, snow peas, carrots, water chestnuts, scallions, and almonds. Hold in refrigerator.
1 lb	450 g	Snow peas, trimmed and blanched	
8 oz	225 g	Carrots, julienne	
12 oz	350 g	Water chestnuts, sliced	
4 oz	125 g	Scallions, chopped	
4 oz	125 g	Slivered almonds, toasted	
1½ lb	700 g	Cold roast beef	2. Slice the beef about ¼ in. (6 mm) thick, then cut into thin strips.
1¾ pt	800 mL	Oriental Vinaigrette (p. 519)	3. About 2 hours before serving, marinate beef in the vinaigrette for 30 to 60 minutes.
			4. Add the mixed vegetables to the beef and vinaigrette mixture. Toss to mix well.
1½ lb	700 g	Chinese cabbage, shredded	5. Place a bed of shredded Chinese cabbage on salad plates.
50	50	Orange wedges	6. Portion the salad mixture onto the plates.
			7. Garnish each salad with two orange wedges.

Variations

Substitute chicken, turkey, ham, or duck meat for the beef.

RECIPE 220   Mixed Vegetable Salad with Pasta

Portions: 25   **Portion size:** 4 oz (125 g)

U.S.	Metric	Ingredients	Procedure
1½ lb	700 g	Cooked ditalini pasta, cold	1. Combine the pasta, beans, vegetables, and cheese in a large bowl. Toss to mix.
1 lb	450 g	Cooked chick peas or other dried beans, cold	2. No more than an hour or two before service, add the dressing and toss.
12 oz	350 g	Zucchini, medium dice, raw or blanched	
12 oz	350 g	Green beans, cooked and cut into ½-inch (1-cm) lengths	
8 oz	250 g	Red onions, diced	
6 oz	175 g	Small pitted black olives	
6 oz	175 g	Celery, diced	
4 oz	125 g	Diced green pepper	
4 oz	125 g	Diced red pepper	
¼ cup	60 mL	Capers, drained	
4 oz	125 g	Parmesan cheese	
1½ pt	700 mL	Italian dressing	
25	25	Lettuce leaves for underliners	3. Arrange the lettuce leaves on cold salad plates.
25	25	Tomato wedges or cherry tomatoes	4. Just before service, place a 4-oz (125-g) portion of the salad on each lettuce leaf.
			5. Garnish each salad with a tomato wedge.

Variations

Add 1 lb (450 g) diced or sliced salami, pepperoni, or mozzarella cheese to the salad mixture.

Cooked Salads

Principles

Cooked salads are those whose main ingredients are cooked foods, usually meat, poultry, fish, eggs, or starch products, and occasionally some vegetables. They are different from combination salads and from vegetable salads using cooked vegetables in that the cooked product is usually mixed with a thick dressing, generally mayonnaise, during preparation.

A salad that is mixed with a thick dressing to bind it together is also called a *bound salad*. Some bound salads, such as tuna, egg, or chicken salad, can also be used as sandwich fillings.

Popular choices for cooked salads are the following:

Chicken	Lobster
Turkey	Eggs
Ham	Potatoes
Tuna	Pastas
Salmon	Rice
Crab	Mixed vegetables
Shrimp	

Guidelines for Making Cooked Salads

1. Cooked ingredients must be thoroughly cooled before being mixed with mayonnaise, and the completed salad mixture must be kept chilled at all times. Mayonnaise-type salads are ideal breeding grounds for bacteria that cause food poisoning.

2. Cooked salads are good ways to use leftovers such as chicken, meat, or fish, but the ingredient must have been handled according to the rules of good sanitation and food handling. The product will not be cooked again to destroy any bacteria that might grow in the salad and cause illness.

3. Potatoes for salads should be cooked whole, then peeled and cut, in order to preserve nutrients.

4. Don't cut ingredients too small, or the final product will be like mush or paste, with no textural interest.

5. Crisp vegetables are usually added for texture. Celery is the most popular, but other choices might be green peppers, carrots, chopped pickles, onions, water chestnuts, or apples. Be sure that the flavors go together, however.

6. Bland main ingredients, such as potatoes or some seafoods, may be marinated in a seasoned liquid such as vinaigrette before being mixed with the mayonnaise and other ingredients. Any marinade not absorbed should be drained first to avoid thinning out the mayonnaise.

7. Fold in thick dressings gently to avoid crushing or breaking the main ingredients.

8. Bound salads are usually portioned with a scoop. This has two advantages: (a) It provides portion control. (b) It gives height and shape to the salad.

9. Choose attractive, colorful garnishes. A scoop of potato or chicken salad looks pretty pale and uninteresting without a garnish.

RECIPE 221 **Macedoine of Vegetables Mayonnaise**

Portions: 25		**Portion size:** 4 oz (125 g)	

U.S.	Metric	Ingredients	Procedure
2 lb	1 kg	Cooked carrots, ¼-inch (½-cm) dice	1. Chill all ingredients before combining.
2 lb	1 kg	Cooked white turnips, ¼-inch (½-cm) dice	2. Place all ingredients in a bowl and mix until evenly combined. Use only enough mayonnaise to bind. Season to taste with salt and white pepper.
1 lb	500 g	Cooked green beans, sliced in ¼-inch (½-cm) pieces	
1 lb	500 g	Cooked green peas	
1 pt or as needed	500 mL	Mayonnaise	
		Salt	
		White pepper	
25	25	Lettuce cups for underliners	3. Place lettuce bases on cold salad plates.
25	25	Tomato wedges	4. Using a No. 10 scoop, place a mound of salad on each plate. Garnish with tomato wedge.

RECIPE 222   Chicken or Turkey Salad

Portions: 25   **Portion size: 3½ oz (100 g)**

U.S.	Metric	Ingredients	Procedure
3 lb	1.4 kg	Cooked chicken or turkey, ½-inch (1-cm) dice	1. Combine all ingredients in a mixing bowl. Toss gently until thoroughly mixed.
1½ lb	700 g	Celery, ¼-inch (½-cm) dice	
1 pt	500 mL	Mayonnaise	
2 oz	60 mL	Lemon juice	
		Salt	
		White pepper	
25	25	Lettuce cups for underliners Parsley or watercress sprigs	2. Arrange lettuce on cold salad plates. 3. Using a No. 10 scoop, place a mound of chicken salad on each plate. Garnish with parsley or watercress. 4. Hold for service in refrigerator.

Variations

Additions to Chicken Salad: Add any of the following ingredients to the basic recipe:
1. 6 oz (175 g) broken walnuts or pecans
2. 6 hard-cooked eggs, chopped
3. 8 oz (225 g) seedless grapes, cut in half, and 3 oz (90 g) chopped or sliced almonds
4. 8 oz (225 g) drained, diced pineapple
5. 8 oz (225 g) diced avocado
6. 1 lb (450 g) peeled, seeded, diced cucumber, *substituted for* 1 lb of the celery
7. 8 oz (225 g) sliced water chestnuts

222A. *Egg Salad:* Substitute 28 diced, hard-cooked eggs for the chicken in the basic recipe.

222B. *Tuna or Salmon Salad:* Substitute 3 lb (1.4 kg) drained, flaked canned tuna or salmon for the chicken in the basic recipe. Add 2 oz (60 g) chopped onion. Optional ingredient: 4 oz (100 g) chopped pickles or drained capers.

RECIPE 223   **Potato Salad**

....

| | **Portions:** 25 | | **Portion size:** 4 oz (125 g) |

U.S.	Metric	Ingredients	Procedure
5 lb AP	2.5 kg AP	Potatoes, waxy type (see note)	1. Scrub the potatoes. Steam or boil until tender, but do not overcook. 2. Drain the potatoes and leave in colander or spread out on a sheet pan until cool enough to handle.
1½ cups 1½ tsp ¼ tsp	375 mL 7 mL 1 mL	Basic French Dressing (p. 518) Salt White pepper	3. Peel the warm potatoes. Cut into ½-inch (1-cm) dice. 4. Combine the dressing, salt, and pepper. Add the potatoes and mix carefully to avoid breaking or crushing them. 5. Marinate until cold. For the purpose of food safety, chill the potatoes in the refrigerator before proceeding with the next step.
12 oz 4 oz	375 g 125 g	Celery, small dice Onion, chopped fine (Optional ingredients—see variations below)	6. If any French Dressing has not been absorbed by the potatoes, drain it off. 7. Add the celery, onion, and, if desired, any of the optional ingredients listed below. Mix gently.
1 pt	500 mL	Mayonnaise	8. Add the mayonnaise. Mix carefully until evenly blended. 9. Keep refrigerated until ready to use.
25 50	25 50	Lettuce cups for underliners Pimiento strips	10. Arrange the lettuce on cold salad plates. 11. Using a No. 11 scoop, place a 4-oz (125-g) mound of potato salad on each plate. 12. Garnish each salad with 2 strips of pimiento placed crosswise on top. 13. Hold for service in refrigerator.

Note: See page 430 for explanation of potato types. Do not use starchy, mealy-type potatoes for salad, because they will not hold their shape.

Variations

Optional ingredients, to be added in step 7:
  4–6 hard-cooked eggs, diced
  2 oz (60 g) green peppers, small dice
  2 oz (60 g) pimientos, small dice
  4 oz (125 g) chopped pickles or capers or sliced olives
  ¼ cup (60 mL) chopped parsley

French Dressing marination (steps 4–5) may be omitted if necessary. In this case, chill the potatoes before mixing with the dressing. Add 2 oz (60 mL) vinegar to the mayonnaise and check carefully for seasonings. Refrigerate for 2 hours or more before serving.

Portions: 25   **Portion size:** 4 oz (125 g)

U.S.	Metric	Ingredients	Procedure
7 lb	3.5 kg	Potatoes, waxy type	1. Scrub the potatoes. Steam or boil until tender, but do not overcook.
			2. Drain the potatoes and leave in colander or spread out on a sheet pan until cool enough to handle.
8 oz	250 mL	Salad oil	3. Peel the potatoes while still hot. Cut into ¼-inch (½-cm) thick slices or into ½-inch (1-cm) dice.
6 oz	200 mL	Wine vinegar (white or red)	
4 oz	125 g	Onions or shallots, chopped fine	4. Mix potatoes with remaining ingredients. Allow to stand at least 15 minutes while the potatoes absorb the dressing.
¼ tsp	1 mL	Garlic, chopped fine	
¼ cup	60 mL	Chopped parsley	5. Serve warm or cold. This salad is a popular accompaniment to hot, cooked sausages.
1 tbsp	15 mL	Tarragon	
		Salt	
		Pepper	

Variation

224A. Hot German Potato Salad: Omit oil and tarragon from basic recipe. Cook 8 oz (250 g) diced bacon until crisp. Add the bacon, the bacon fat, and 1 cup (250 mL) hot chicken stock to the dressing ingredients. (More stock may be needed if the potatoes absorb a great deal.) Place the mixed salad in a hotel pan, cover, and heat in a 300°F (150°C) oven for about 30 minutes. Serve hot.

Portions: 25   **Portion size:** 3½ oz (100 g)

U.S.	Metric	Ingredients	Procedure
3 lb	1.4 kg	Cooked smoked ham, small dice	1. Combine all ingredients in a mixing bowl. Toss gently until evenly mixed. Adjust seasonings.
1 lb	450 g	Celery, small dice	
8 oz	225 g	Chopped pickles (sweet or dill) or drained pickle relish	2. Keep refrigerated until ready for use.
			3. Serve a 3½-oz (100-g) portion on a bed of lettuce. Garnish with tomato wedges, hard-cooked egg wedges, or pimiento.
2 oz	60 g	Onion, chopped fine	
1 pt	500 mL	Mayonnaise	
2 oz	60 mL	Vinegar	

Variations

225A. Ham Salad Spread: Grind the ham or chop very fine. Chop the celery very fine. Use for sandwiches.

225B. Deviled Ham: Grind the ham. Add 3 tbsp (45 mL) prepared mustard and 1 tsp (5 mL) hot red pepper sauce to the basic recipe. Increase the onion to 4 oz (125 g). Use as a canapé spread.

225C. Corned Beef Salad: Substitute corned beef for ham in the basic recipe.

225D. Beef Salad: Substitute cooked beef for ham in the basic recipe.

225E. Ham and Egg Salad: Reduce the ham to 2 lb (900 g) and add 10 diced hard-cooked eggs.

225F. Macaroni and Ham Salad: Reduce the ham to 12 oz (350 g) and add 3 lb (1.4 kg) cooked, drained, chilled elbow macaroni. Omit pickles and add 4 oz (125 g) diced green pepper and 2 oz (60 g) diced pimiento.

RECIPE 226   **Dilled Shrimp Salad**

Portions: 25   **Portion size:** 3½ oz (100 g)

U.S.	Metric	Ingredients	Procedure
3 lb	1.4 kg	Cooked, peeled, deveined shrimp	1. Cut the shrimp into ¼-inch (1-cm) pieces. (If the shrimp are very small, leave them whole.)
1½ lb	700 g	Celery, small dice	2. Combine the celery and shrimp in a bowl.
1 pt	500 mL	Mayonnaise	3. Mix together the mayonnaise, lemon juice, dill, and salt.
2 tbsp	30 mL	Lemon juice	
2 tsp	10 mL	Dried dillweed (or 2 tbsp/30 mL chopped fresh dill)	4. Add the dressing to the shrimp mixture. Mix in thoroughly.
½ tsp	2 mL	Salt	
25	25	Lettuce cups for underliners	5. Arrange the lettuce leaves on cold salad plates.
50	50	Tomato wedges	6. Using a No. 10 scoop, place a mound of shrimp salad on each plate.
			7. Garnish with tomato wedges, using 2 per salad.

Variations

226A. ***Crab or Lobster Salad:*** Prepare as in basic recipe, using crab or lobster meat instead of shrimp.

226B. ***Crab, Shrimp, or Lobster Louis:*** Use Louis Dressing (p. 521) instead of the mixture of mayonnaise, lemon juice, and dill. Serve on shredded lettuce. (If food cost permits, omit celery and increase shellfish to 4½ lb/2 kg.)

226C. ***Rice and Shrimp Salad:*** Reduce shrimp in basic recipe to 1 lb (450 g) and add 2 lb (900 g) cooked rice.

226D. ***Curried Rice Salad with Shrimp:*** Prepare Rice and Shrimp Salad but omit the dill. Instead, flavor the dressing with 1 tsp (5 mL) curry powder heated lightly in a teaspoon of oil and cooled. Optional: Substitute diced green pepper for half the celery.

Fruit Salads

Principles

As their name indicates, fruit salads have fruits as their main ingredients. They are popular as appetizer salads, as dessert salads, and as part of combination luncheon plates, often with a scoop of cottage cheese or other mild-tasting protein food.

Guidelines for Making Fruit Salads

1. Fruit salads are often arranged rather than mixed or tossed, because most fruits are delicate and easily broken. An exception is the Waldorf Salad, made of firm apples mixed with nuts, celery, and a mayonnaise-based dressing.

2. Broken or less attractive pieces of fruit should be placed on the bottom of the salad, with the more attractive pieces arranged on top.

3. Some fruits discolor when cut and should be dipped into an acid such as tart fruit juice. See page 482 for pre-preparation guidelines for individual fruits.

4. Fruits do not hold as well as vegetables after being cut. If you are preparing both vegetable and fruit salads for a particular meal service, the vegetable salads should usually be prepared first.

5. Drain canned fruits well before including them in the salad, or the salad will be watery and sloppy. The liquid from the canned fruit may be reserved for using in fruit salad dressing or other preparations.

6. Dressings for fruit salads are usually slightly sweet, but a little tartness is usually desirable as well. Fruit juices are often used in dressings for fruit salad.

RECIPE 227 **Waldorf Salad**

| | | | | | **Portions:** 25 | | **Portion size:** 3 oz (90 g) |

U.S.	Metric	Ingredients	Procedure
1½ cups	350 mL	Chantilly Dressing (p. 521)	1. Prepare the dressing. Place it in a large stainless steel bowl and have it ready in the refrigerator.
4 lb AP	1.8 kg AP	Crisp, red eating apples	2. Core and dice the apples (½-inch/1-cm dice) without peeling them.
1 lb	450 g	Celery, small dice	3. As soon as the apples are cut, add them to the dressing and mix in to prevent darkening.
4 oz	100 g	Walnuts, coarsely chopped	
25	25	Lettuce cups for lettuce	4. Add the celery and walnuts. Fold in until evenly mixed.
		Optional garnish:	5. Arrange the lettuce bases on cold salad plates.
2 oz	60 g	Chopped walnuts	6. Using a No. 12 scoop, place a mound of salad on each plate.
			7. If garnish is desired, sprinkle each salad with about 1 tsp (5 mL) chopped nuts.
			8. Hold for service in refrigerator.

Note: Plain mayonnaise may be used instead of Chantilly Dressing.

RECIPE 227   **Waldorf Salad** *(Continued)*

Variations

Any of the following ingredients may be added to the basic Waldorf mixture. If any of these changes are made, the item should no longer be called simply "Waldorf Salad." Change the menu name to indicate that the product contains other ingredients. For example: Pineapple Waldorf Salad or Apple Date Salad.

1. 8 oz (225 g) diced pineapple
2. 4 oz (100 g) chopped dates, *substituted for* the walnuts
3. 4 oz (100 g) raisins, plumped in hot water and drained
4. 1 lb (450 g) shredded cabbage or Chinese cabbage, *substituted for* the celery

RECIPE 228   **Orange and Grapefruit Salad**

		Portions: 25		**Portion size:** 3 oz (90 g)

U.S.	Metric	Ingredients	Procedure	
8	8	Oranges (see note)	1.	Peel and section the oranges and grapefruit as shown in Figure 7.11.
7	7	Grapefruit (see note)		
2 heads	2 heads	Leaf lettuce, trimmed, washed, and crisped	2.	Line cold salad plates with lettuce leaves.
			3.	Place 3 orange sections alternating with 3 grapefruit sections on each plate, arranging the fruits to resemble a pinwheel.
			4.	Hold for service in refrigerator.
25 oz	750 mL	Basic French Dressing made with lemon juice instead of vinegar *or* Honey Lemon Dressing	5.	At service time, ladle 1 oz (30 mL) dressing over each salad.

Note: The number of oranges and grapefruits needed will vary, depending on the size of the fruits.

Variations

228A. Orange, Grapefruit, and Avocado Salad: Alternate the orange and grapefruit sections with thin slices of avocado, which have been dipped in citrus juice to prevent discoloring.

228B. Grapefruit and Avocado Salad: Prepare like Orange, Grapefruit, and Avocado Salad, but use all grapefruit instead of the oranges.

RECIPE 229 Fresh Fruit Chantilly

....

| | | | **Portions:** 25 | | **Portion size:** 4 oz (125 g) |

U.S.	Metric	Ingredients	Procedure
1½ lb	750 g	Orange sections	1. Prepare orange and grapefruit sections as shown in Figure 7.11. Be sure to save the juice. Cut the grapefruit sections in half.
1¼ lb	625 g	Grapefruit sections	
1 lb	500 g	Diced apples	2. Drain the orange and grapefruit in a china cap or strainer and collect the juice in a stainless steel bowl.
1 lb	500 g	Sliced bananas	
12 oz	375 g	Grapes	3. Place the apples and bananas in the citrus juice as soon as they are cut to prevent darkening.
			4. Cut the grapes in half lengthwise. If they are not seedless, remove the seeds.
1 cup	250 mL	Heavy cream	5. Just before service, whip the cream until it forms soft peaks.
1 cup	250 mL	Mayonnaise	6. Stir about one-fourth of the cream into the mayonnaise to lighten it. Then fold in the rest of the cream.
			7. Drain the fruits well and fold into the dressing.
25	25	Lettuce leaves for underliners	8. Arrange the lettuce leaves on cold salad plates.
		Suggested garnish (one only):	9. Place a 4-oz (125-g) portion of fruit salad on each plate. Garnish as desired.
		Mint sprigs	10. Serve immediately, or hold in refrigerator up to 30 minutes.
		Strawberries	
		Red or Black grapes	
		Fresh cherries	

Note: Other fresh fruits in season may be used. The fruits here were chosen because they are available all year. Canned or frozen fruits may be used, but the word "fresh" must then be removed from the menu title.

....

RECIPE 230 Banana Pineapple Nut Salad

Portions: 25   **Portion size:** 3 oz (90 g)

U.S.	Metric	Ingredients	Procedure
4 lb AP	1.8 kg AP	Bananas	1. Peel the bananas and cut into ¼-inch (½-cm) thick slices.
1 cup	250 mL	Tart fruit juice, such as grapefruit, orange, lemon, or pineapple	2. Gently toss the banana slices with the fruit juice to prevent discoloring.
2 lb	900 g	Diced pineapple (drained if canned)	3. Drain the bananas and mix with the pineapple.
25	25	Lettuce leaves for underliners	4. Arrange the lettuce leaves on cold salad plates.
25 oz	750 mL	Sour Cream Fruit Salad Dressing (p. 522)	5. Place a 3-oz (90-g) portion of fruit on each plate.
8 oz	225 g	Chopped walnuts or pecans	6. Top each portion with 1 oz (30 mL) dressing, placed in the center of the salad.
			7. Sprinkle each portion with about 1 tbsp (15 mL) nuts.

Variations

230A. Banana Orange Nut Salad: Substitute fresh orange sections or drained canned mandarin orange sections for the pineapple.

230B. Mixed Fruit Salad: Decrease bananas to 2 lb (900 g). Add 2 or 3 of the following fresh or canned fruits, using a total of 2 lb (900 g): grapes, sliced peaches, sliced pears, diced apples, orange sections, grapefruit sections, cherries, strawberries, blueberries, sliced kiwi fruit.

Combination Salads

Principles

Combination salads get their name because they are combinations of different kinds of ingredients. They may even consist of two or more different salads in an attractive arrangement, for example, chicken salad and sliced cucumber and tomato salad arranged on a bed of greens. Probably the most popular combination salad is the chef's salad, mixed greens with strips of turkey, ham, and cheese, and usually several raw vegetables such as tomato and green pepper.

Because they are more elaborate and can usually be quite substantial in size, combination salads are often served as main courses. Because combination salads are often made up of other kinds of salads, there are really only two guidelines for their production:

1. Observe the guidelines for preparing the different components, such as greens, vegetables, cooked salads, and fruit salads.

2. Observe the guidelines for attractive salad arrangement.

RECIPE 231 **Chef's Salad**

Portions: 25

U.S.	Metric	Ingredients	Procedure
6 lb	3 kg	Mixed salad greens, washed, trimmed, and crisped	1. Place the greens in cold salad bowls, approximately 4 oz (125 g) per portion.
1½ lb	700 g	Turkey breast, cut into thin strips	2. Arrange the turkey, ham, and cheese strips neatly on top of the greens. Keep the items separate—do not mix them all together.
1½ lb	700 g	Pullman ham, cut into thin strips	3. Arrange the remaining items attractively on the salad.
1½ lb	700 g	Swiss cheese, cut into thin strips	4. Hold for service. If salads must be held for over 1 hour, they should be covered, so that the meats and cheese don't dry out.
50	50	Tomato wedges or cherry tomatoes	
50	50	Hard-cooked egg quarters	5. Serve with any appropriate salad dressing, served on the side in a separate container.
25	25	Radishes	
8 oz	225 g	Carrots, cut into sticks (batonnet)	
25	25	Green pepper rings	

Variations

Other vegetable garnish may be used in addition to or in place of the items in the basic recipe. See lists on pages 477–478.

RECIPE 232 **Stuffed Tomato Salad with Tuna**

Portions: 24   **Portion size:** 1 tomato

U.S.	Metric	Ingredients	Procedure
24	24	Tomatoes, small (about 4 oz/125 g each) Salt	1. Wash the tomatoes and remove the core at the stem end.
			2. Set the tomatoes on the cutting board, stem end down. Cut into eighths to within ½ inch (1 cm) of the bottom—that is, leave the sections attached at the bottoms.
			3. Carefully spread the sections apart slightly. Sprinkle the insides with salt and turn upside down on a sheet pan to drain for 15–20 minutes.
3 lb	1.5 kg	Tuna salad (p. 500)	4. Fill the tomatoes with tuna salad, using 2 oz (60 g) per portion.
24	24	Lettuce cups for underliners	
24	24	Small parsley sprigs	5. Arrange the lettuce on salad plates and place a filled tomato on each. Garnish the tops with parsley.
			6. Hold for service in the refrigerator.

RECIPE 232   **Stuffed Tomato Salad with Tuna** *(Continued)*

Variations

Tomatoes may be stuffed with any of the following:
 Chicken salad and variations (p. 500)
 Egg salad (p. 500)
 Shrimp salad and variations (p. 503)
 Ham salad (p. 502)
 Cottage cheese

Alternative Method: Tomatoes may be hollowed out for stuffing by cutting off the tops and scooping out the insides, being careful not to pierce the sides. Large tomatoes may be cut in half and hollowed out.

RECIPE 233   **Shrimp in Avocado**

			Portions: 24	**Portion size:** ½ avocado

U.S.	Metric	Ingredients	Procedure	
3 lb	1.4 kg	Cooked, peeled, deveined shrimp	1.	Cut the shrimp into ½-inch (1-cm) pieces or, if they are very small, leave them whole.
12 oz	350 g	Mayonnaise	2.	Combine the shrimp, mayonnaise, and lemon juice in a bowl. Mix until evenly combined. Add salt to taste.
2 oz	60 mL	Lemon juice		
		Salt	3.	Keep refrigerated until needed.
12	12	Avocados, ripe	4.	Wash the avocados. As close as possible to serving time, cut them in half lengthwise. Remove the pits. (Do not peel.)
4 oz	125 mL	Lemon juice		
or as needed			5.	Dip the cut sides of the avocados in lemon juice to prevent darkening.
2 heads	2 heads	Leaf lettuce, washed, trimmed, and crisped	6.	Line cold salad plates with lettuce leaves.
			7.	Place an avocado half on each plate. Top with a 2½-oz (75-g) portion of the shrimp mixture.
6	6	Tomatoes		
			8.	Cut each tomato into 8 wedges. Place 2 wedges on each plate. Serve.

Variations

Crab meat may be used instead of shrimp for avocado filling. Or use Shrimp Salad (p. 503) or any of its variations.

French Dressing (Vinaigrette) may be used instead of mayonnaise.

RECIPE 234   **Salad Niçoise**

Portions: 25

U.S.	Metric	Ingredients	Procedure
3 lb	1.4 kg	Potatoes, waxy type, scrubbed	1. Cook the potatoes in boiling salted water until just tender. Drain and let cool. Peel. Cut into thin slices. Hold in refrigerator, covered.
3 lb	1.4 kg	Green beans, washed and trimmed	
			2. Cook the beans in boiling salted water. Drain and cool under cold running water. Cut into 2-inch (5-cm) pieces. Hold in refrigerator.
3 heads	3 heads	Leaf lettuce or Boston lettuce, washed, trimmed, and crisped	3. Line the bottoms of cold salad bowls with the lettuce leaves (see note).
			4. Combine the potatoes and green beans. Divide the mixture among the salad bowls, about 3 oz (90 g) per portion.
1 60-oz can	1 1700-g can	Tuna, solid pack or chunk	
25	25	Anchovy fillets	5. Drain the tuna and break it into chunks. Place a 1½-oz (50-g) portion in the center of each salad.
50	50	Olives, black or green	
50	50	Hard-cooked egg quarters	6. Arrange the anchovy fillets, olives, egg quarters, and tomato wedges attractively on the salads.
100	100	Tomato wedges	
½ cup	60 mL	Chopped parsley	7. Sprinkle the salads with chopped parsley.
			8. Hold for service in refrigerator.
		French Dressing:	9. Combine the dressing ingredients and mix well. Just before service, mix again and dress each salad with 1½ oz (50 mL) of the dressing.
1 qt	1 L	Olive oil	
1 cup	250 mL	Wine vinegar	
1 tsp	5 mL	Garlic, chopped fine	
1 tbsp	15 mL	Salt	
½ tsp	2 mL	Pepper	

Note: Salade Niçoise (nee-swahz) may be plated on large platters or bowls to serve 2–6 portions each.

RECIPE 235   **Chicken Breast Salad with Walnuts and Blue Cheese**

Portions: 10

U.S.	Metric	Ingredients	Procedure
10	10	Boneless, skinless chicken breasts, about 4 oz (125 g) each Chicken stock	1. Poach the chicken breasts in a flavorful, seasoned chicken stock, using just enough to cover them. (See Chapter 13 for information on poaching chicken.) When they are just done but still juicy, remove from the heat and cool in the poaching liquid.
1 lb	450 g	Fresh, white mushrooms	2. Shortly before serving, slice the mushrooms. Toss them with about 4 oz (125 mL) of the vinaigrette and with the parsley so that they are lightly coated with the dressing.
1 pt	500 mL	Mustard Vinaigrette made with olive oil	
2 tbsp	30 mL	Chopped parsley	
1 lb 4 oz	575 g	Mixed salad greens (see note)	3. Arrange the greens on large salad plates or dinner plates.
2–3 heads	2–3 heads	Belgian endive	4. Cutting across the grain, slice each chicken breast on slant into slices about ¼ inch (6 mm) thick. On one side of each salad plate, arrange a sliced breast single-fashion, fanning out the slices.
3 oz	90 g	Walnuts, coarsely chopped	
3 oz	90 g	Blue cheese, crumbled	
			5. Separate the endive into leaves. Arrange some of the leaves on the other half of each plate.
			6. Place a small mound of the mushroom slices on top of the endive.
			7. Sprinkle the salads with the nuts and the blue cheese.
			8. Just before serving, spoon about 1 oz (30 mL) of the dressing over each salad.

Note: Use tender, dark green salad greens. Iceberg lettuce is not appropriate for this salad. If possible, include some red leaf lettuce or some radicchio to add color.

Variation

When plating the salads to order, toss the mixed salad greens with some of the salad dressing before plating.

Gelatin Salads

Principles

Gelatin salads have a distinguished history. Their ancestors are aspics, the highly ornamented appetizers and elaborate buffet pieces made with meat and fish stocks rich in natural gelatin extracted from bones and connective tissue. Aspics are part of the glory of classical cuisine and still an important part of modern buffet work.

It's no longer necessary to extract gelatin from bones in your kitchen, since purified, granular gelatin and gelatin sheets have long been available for use in the pantry. Many excellent gelatin-based salads can be made with little labor using these products. However, most gelatin products today are made with sweetened prepared mixes, whose high sugar content and heavy reliance on artificial color and flavor make their appropriateness as salads somewhat questionable. (Often in a cafeteria line you will see in the salad section little squares of gelatin with a lettuce leaf underneath and a dab of mayonnaise on top; and in the dessert section the identical product, without the lettuce leaf and with a dab of whipped cream in place of the mayo.)

Nevertheless, as professional cooks you need to know how to prepare these products, because your customers will expect them. You should also know how to prepare salads using unflavored gelatin, relying on fruit juices and other ingredients for flavor. Unflavored gelatin is especially valuable for preparing molded vegetable salads, because shredded cabbage and other vegetables make a poor combination with a highly sweetened dessert gelatin.

Guidelines for Making Gelatin Salads

1. It is important to use the right amount of gelatin for the volume of liquid in the recipe. Too much gelatin makes a stiff, rubbery product. Too little makes a soft product that will not hold its shape.

   Basic proportions for unflavored gelatin are 2½ oz dry gelatin per gallon of liquid (19 g per liter), BUT you will almost always need more than this because of acids and other ingredients in the recipe. Basic proportions for sweetened, flavored gelatin are 24 oz per gallon of liquid (180 g per liter).

   Acids, such as fruit juices and vinegar, weaken the gelatin set, so a higher proportion of gelatin to liquid is needed, sometimes as much as 4 oz or more per gallon (30 g per liter). The setting power is also weakened by whipping the product into a foam and by adding a large quantity of chopped foods. It is impossible to give a formula for how much gelatin to use, since it varies with each recipe. Test each recipe before using it.

2. Gelatin dissolves at about 100°F (38°C), but higher temperatures will dissolve it faster.

   To dissolve unflavored gelatin, stir it into cold liquid to avoid lumping, and let it stand for 5 minutes to absorb water. Then heat it until dissolved, or add hot liquid and stir until dissolved.

   To dissolve sweetened, flavored gelatin, stir it into boiling water. It will not lump, because the gelatin granules are held apart by sugar granules, much the way starch granules in flour are held separate by the fat in a roux.

3. To speed setting, dissolve the gelatin in up to half of the liquid and add the remainder cold to lower the temperature. For even faster setting, add crushed ice in place of an equal weight of cold water. Stir until the ice is melted.

4. Do not add raw pineapple or papaya to gelatin salads. They contain enzymes that dissolve the gelatin. If cooked or canned, however, these fruits may be added.

5. Add solid ingredients when the gelatin is partially set—very thick and syrupy. This will help keep them evenly mixed, rather than floating or settling.

6. Canned fruits or other juicy items must be well drained before being added or they will dilute the gelatin and weaken it.

7. For service, pour into pans and cut into equal portions when set, or pour into individual molds.

8. To unmold gelatin:

   a. Run a thin knife blade around the top edges of the mold to loosen.

   b. Dip the mold into hot water for one or two seconds.

   c. Quickly wipe the bottom of the mold and turn it over onto the salad plate (or invert the salad plate over the mold and flip the plate and mold over together). Do not hold in the hot water for more than a few seconds or the gelatin will begin to melt.

d. If it doesn't unmold after a gentle shake, repeat the procedure. You may also wrap a hot towel (dipped in hot water and wrung out) around the mold until it releases, but this is more time-consuming.

9. Refrigerate gelatin salads until service to keep them firm.

RECIPE 236 **Basic Flavored Gelatin with Fruit**

Portions: 25   **Portion size:** 4 oz (125 g)

U.S.	Metric	Ingredients	Procedure
12 oz	375 g	Flavored gelatin mix	1. Place the gelatin in a bowl.
1 qt	1 L	Boiling water	2. Pour in the boiling water. Stir until dissolved.
1 qt	1 L	Cold water or fruit juice	3. Stir in the cold water or juice.
			4. Chill until thick and syrupy but not set.
2 lb	1 kg	Fruit, well drained	5. Fold the fruit into the gelatin mixture.
			6. Pour into molds or into a half-size hotel pan.
			7. Chill until firm.
			8. Unmold. If using a hotel pan, cut 5 × 5 into portions.

Variations

The number of combinations of fruits and flavored gelatin is nearly limitless. The following suggestions are only a few possibilities. Note: When using canned fruits, use the syrup from the fruits as part of the liquid in step 3.

1. Lime-flavored gelatin; pear halves or slices.
2. Black cherry-flavored gelatin; bing cherries.
3. Raspberry-flavored gelatin; peach slices or halves.
4. Strawberry, raspberry, or cherry-flavored gelatin; canned fruit cocktail.
5. Orange-flavored gelatin; equal parts sliced peaches and pears.
6. Cherry-flavored gelatin; equal parts crushed pineapple and bing cherries.
7. Lime-flavored gelatin; grapefruit sections.

RECIPE 237 **Perfection Salad**

Portions: 25			**Portion size:** 4 oz (125 g)

U.S.	Metric	Ingredients	Procedure
2 oz	60 g	Unflavored gelatin	1. Stir the gelatin into the cold water. Let stand at least 5 minutes to soften.
1 cup	250 mL	Cold water	
3 pt	1.5 L	Boiling water	2. Add the boiling water, sugar, and salt. Stir until the gelatin and sugar are dissolved. Let cool.
12 oz	350 g	Sugar	
2 tsp	10 mL	Salt	
1 cup	250 mL	Cider vinegar	3. Stir in the vinegar and lemon juice.
2 oz	60 mL	Lemon juice	4. Chill the mixture until it is thick and syrupy, but not set.
1 lb	500 g	Shredded cabbage	5. Fold the vegetables into the gelatin mixture.
12 oz	375 g	Celery, chopped fine	6. Pour into individual ½-cup molds (see note). Chill until firm.
2 oz	60 g	Green pepper, chopped fine	
3 oz	90 g	Pimientos, drained and chopped	
25	25	Lettuce leaves for underliners	7. Line cold salad plates with lettuce leaves.
			8. Unmold the salads and place on the plates.
1⅔ cups	400 mL	Mayonnaise	9. Hold for service in refrigerator.
			10. At service time, top each salad with about 1 tbsp (15 mL) mayonnaise.

Note: Hotel pans may be used instead of individual molds. For 25 portions, use a half-size pan. When gelatin is firm, cut 5 × 5 into rectangles. For 24 portions, cut 6 × 4.

RECIPE 238 **Jellied Coleslaw**

Portions: 25			**Portion size:** 4 oz (125 g)

U.S.	Metric	Ingredients	Procedure
2 oz	60 g	Unflavored gelatin	1. Stir the gelatin into the cold water. Let stand for 5 minutes.
1 cup	250 mL	Cold water	
1 pt	500 mL	Boiling water	2. Add the boiling water, sugar, and salt. Stir until the gelatin and sugar are dissolved.
2 oz	60 g	Sugar	
1 tbsp	15 mL	Salt	3. Cool until syrupy but not set.
4 oz	125 mL	Vinegar	4. Add the vinegar, mayonnaise, and white pepper to the gelatin. Beat with a wire whip or in mixing machine until thoroughly mixed.
1 pt	500 mL	Mayonnaise	
½ tsp	2 mL	White pepper	
3½ lb	1.6 kg	Shredded cabbage	5. Fold in the scallions and cabbage.
2 oz	60 g	Chopped scallions	6. Pour the mixture into individual half-cup molds. Chill until set.
		Lettuce for lining plates	7. When firm, unmold and place on salad plates lined with lettuce. Garnish the tops with pimiento strips or small parsley sprigs.
		Pimiento strips or parsley garnish	

RECIPE 239   Jellied Fruit Salad

| | | **Portions:** 25 | | **Portion size:** 4 oz (125 g) |

U.S.	Metric	Ingredients		Procedure
1 No. 2 can		Pineapple cubes	1.	Drain the pineapple and reserve the juice. You should have about 12 oz (350 g) drained fruit.
8 oz	250 g	Grapefruit sections		
12 oz	375 g	Orange sections	2.	Cut grapefruit and orange sections into ½-inch (1-cm) dice. (See p. 111 for cutting citrus sections.)
8 oz	250 g	Grapes		
			3.	Cut the grapes in half. Remove seeds, if any.
			4.	Place the fruit in a colander or strainer over a bowl and hold in refrigerator.
2 oz	60 g	Unflavored gelatin	5.	Stir gelatin into the cold water and let stand at least 5 minutes.
1 cup	250 mL	Cold water		
	as needed	Fruit juice: grape-fruit, orange, or pineapple	6.	Add enough fruit juice (or part juice and part water) to the liquid from the pineapple to measure 3½ pt (1.75 L).
6 oz	175 g	Sugar	7.	Bring fruit juice to a boil in a stainless steel pan. Remove from heat.
¼ tsp	1 g	Salt		
3 oz	90 mL	Lemon juice	8.	Add the sugar, salt, and softened gelatin. Stir until gelatin and sugar are dissolved.
			9.	Cool the mixture. Add the lemon juice.
			10.	Chill until thick and syrupy but not set.
			11.	Fold the drained fruits into the gelatin mixture.
			12.	Pour into individual molds or into a half-size hotel pan. Chill until firm.
25	25	Lettuce leaves for underliners	13.	Line cold salad plates with lettuce leaves.
1⅔ cups	400 mL	Chantilly Dressing (p. 521)	14.	Unmold the salads or, if a hotel pan was used, cut 5 × 5 into rectangles.
			15.	Place a gelatin salad on each plate. Hold for service in refrigerator.
			16.	At service time, top each salad with a tablespoon (15 mL) of dressing.

Salad Bars and Buffet Service

Salad bars have become regular fixtures in American restaurants and are popular with both customer and restaurateur. The customer enjoys being able to custom make a salad with selections from a large bowl of greens, smaller containers of assorted condiments, and a variety of dressings. The restaurateur likes them because they take some of the pressure off the dining room staff during service. Many restaurants have designed unique salad bars that have become almost a trademark.

For successful salad bar service, it is important to keep several points in mind:

1. Keep it attractive and well stocked from the beginning until the end of service. Refill containers before they begin to look depleted, wipe the edges of dressing containers, and clean up debris that has been scattered by customers.

2. Keep it simple but attractive. Elaborately arranged salad bowls lose their effect as soon as two or three customers have dug into them.

3. Select a variety of condiments to appeal to a variety of tastes. Try both familiar and unusual items to make your salad bar something different. There is no reason to restrict yourself to the same old stuff everyone else is serving.

   There are two basic kinds of salad bar condiments:

   a. *Simple ingredients.* Nearly any item in the salad ingredient list on page 477 might be selected. Your choice will depend on balance of flavors and colors, customer preference, as well as cost.

   b. *Prepared salads.* Marinated vegetable salads, such as three bean salad, and cooked salads, like macaroni salad, are especially suitable. The choice is very large.

4. Arrange the salad bar in the following order (see Figure 19.3):

   a. Plates.
   b. Mixed greens.
   c. Condiments (put the expensive ones at the end).
   d. Dressings.
   e. Crackers, breads, etc., if desired.

5. Make sure your setup conforms to your state health department regulations.

6. Some portion control can be achieved by selecting the right size plates, condiment servers, and dressing ladles.

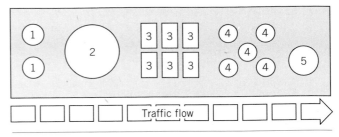

FIGURE 19.3 **Suggested arrangement of a salad bar. Key: (1) plates; (2) large bowl of salad greens; (3) condiments; (4) dressings; (5) crackers, breads, etc.**

SALAD DRESSINGS

Salad dressings are liquids or semiliquids used to flavor salads. They are sometimes considered cold sauces and they serve the same functions as sauces; that is, they flavor, moisten, and enrich.

Most of the basic salad dressings used today can be divided into three categories:

1. Oil and vinegar dressings (most unthickened dressings).

2. Mayonnaise-based dressings (most thickened dressings).

3. Cooked dressings (similar in appearance to mayonnaise dressings, but more tart, and with little or no oil content).

There are also a number of dressings whose main ingredients include such products as sour cream, yogurt, and fruit juices. Many of these are designed specifically for fruit salads or for low-calorie diets.

INGREDIENTS

Since the flavors of most salad dressings are not modified by cooking, their quality depends very directly on the quality of the ingredients.

Most salad dressings are made primarily of an oil and an acid, with other ingredients added to modify the flavor or texture.

Oils

Kinds

Corn oil is widely used in dressings. It has a light golden color and is nearly tasteless, except for a very mild cornmeal-type flavor.

Cottonseed oil, soybean oil, canola oil, and *safflower oil* are bland, nearly tasteless oils. *Vegetable oil* or *salad oil* is a blend of oils and is popular because of its neutral flavor and relatively low cost.

Peanut oil has a mild but distinctive flavor and may be used in appropriate dressings. It is somewhat more expensive.

Olive oil has a very distinctive, fruity flavor and aroma and a greenish color. The best olive oils are called *virgin* or *extravirgin,* which means they are made from the first pressing of the olives. Because of its flavor, olive oil is not an all-purpose oil but may be used in specialty salads such as Caesar Salad.

Walnut oil has a distinctive flavor and a high price. It is occasionally used in elegant restaurants featuring specialty salads. Other nut oils, such as hazelnut oil, are sometimes used.

Quality Factors

All-purpose oils for dressings should have a mild, sweet flavor. Strongly flavored oils can make excellent salad dressings but are not appropriate with every food.

Winterized oil should be used with dressings that are to be refrigerated. These are oils that have been treated so they will remain a clear liquid when chilled.

Rancidity is a serious problem with oils, because even a hint of a rancid flavor can ruin an entire batch of dressing. A thin film of oil, such as might be left on containers through careless washing, becomes rancid very quickly. Clean all dressing containers thoroughly, and never pour a fresh batch into a jar containing older dressing.

Vinegar

Kinds

Cider vinegar is made from apples. It is brown in color and has a slightly sweet, appley taste.

White or distilled vinegar is distilled and purified so that it has a neutral flavor.

Wine vinegar may be white or red, and it has, naturally, a winey flavor.

Flavored vinegars have had another product added to them, such as tarragon, garlic, or raspberries.

Sherry vinegar is made from sherry wine and, consequently, has the distinctive flavor of that wine.

Balsamic vinegar is a special wine vinegar that has been aged in wooden barrels. It is dark brown in color and has a noticeably sweet taste.

Other specialty vinegars include malt vinegar, rice vinegar, and vinegars flavored with fruits, such as raspberry.

Quality Factors

Vinegars should have a good, clean, sharp flavor for their type.

Strength of acidity determines the tartness of the vinegar—and of the dressing made from it. Most salad vinegars are about 5 percent acidity, but some range as high as 7 or 8 percent. Read the label for this information. Vinegar that is too strong should be diluted with a little water before it is measured for a recipe.

White vinegar is used when a completely neutral flavor is desired for a dressing. Other vinegars are used for their characteristic flavors. Wine vinegars are usually preferred for the best-quality oil-and-vinegar dressings.

Lemon Juice

Fresh lemon juice may be used in place of or in addition to vinegar in some preparations, when its flavor is desired.

Egg Yolk

Egg yolk is an essential ingredient in mayonnaise and other emulsified dressings. Only fresh eggs should be used, and the finished product should be refrigerated to guard against spoilage.

Seasonings and Flavorings

Nearly any herb or spice can be used in salad dressings. Remember that dried herbs and spices need extra time to release their flavors if they are not heated in the product. This is why most dressings are best made at least 2 or 3 hours before serving. Review Chapter 4 to refresh your memory on the use of herbs and spices.

Other ingredients added for flavoring include mustard, catsup, worcestershire sauce, and various kinds of cheeses.

A note on blue cheese and Roquefort cheese: Many restaurants sell what they call "Roquefort dressing," when it is actually blue cheese dressing. Roquefort is a brand name for a special kind of blue cheese made in Roquefort, France. It is made of sheep's milk, has a distinctive taste, and is expensive. Never use the term "Roquefort" for blue cheese dressings unless you are actually using this brand of cheese.

EMULSIONS IN SALAD DRESSINGS

As you know, oil and water do not normally stay mixed but separate into layers. Salad dressings, however, must be evenly mixed for proper service, even though they are made primarily of oil and vinegar. A uniform mixture of two unmixable liquids is called an *emulsion*. One liquid is said to be in *suspension* in the other.

Temporary Emulsions

A simple oil and vinegar dressing is called a temporary emulsion, because the two liquids always separate after being shaken up.

The harder the mixture is beaten or shaken, the longer it takes for it to separate. This is because the oil and water are broken into smaller droplets, so they take longer to separate. (When milk is homogenized, the milk fat or cream is broken into such tiny droplets that they stay in suspension.)

The disadvantage of oil and vinegar dressings is that they must be shaken or stirred before each use.

Permanent Emulsions

Mayonnaise is also a mixture of oil and vinegar, but the two liquids do not separate. This is because the formula also contains egg yolk, which acts as an emulsifier. This means that the egg yolk forms a layer around each of the tiny droplets and holds them in suspension.

The harder the mayonnaise is beaten to break up the droplets, the more stable the emulsion becomes. Also all emulsions, whether permanent or temporary, form more easily at room temperature, because a chilled oil is harder to break up into small droplets.

Other stabilizers besides egg yolks are used in some preparations. Cooked dressing uses starch in addition to eggs. Commercially made dressings may use such emulsifiers as gums, starches, and gelatin.

OIL AND VINEGAR DRESSINGS

Basic French Dressing, the first recipe in this section, is a simple mixture of oil, vinegar, and seasonings. It can be used as is, but it is usually the base for other dressings, such as the variations that follow.

Incidentally, the thickened, sweet, tomato-based dressing often served as "French Dressing" is unknown in France. This is not to say that the product cannot be a good one. But to avoid confusion and to help standardize food service terminology, it would be helpful if it were called by another name, such as "Tomato French" or "American French."

The ratio of oil to vinegar in Basic French Dressing is 3 parts oil to 1 part vinegar. This is not a divine law, however, and the proportions may be changed to taste. Some chefs prefer a 2-to-1 ratio, while others prefer a 4-to-1 or even 5-to-1 ratio. Less oil makes the dressing more tart, while more oil makes it taste milder and oilier.

A very strong vinegar, more than 5% acid, may have to be diluted with water before being measured and added to the recipe.

RECIPE 240 Basic French Dressing or Vinaigrette

Yield: 2 qt (2 L)

U.S.	Metric	Ingredients	Procedure
1 pt	500 mL	Wine vinegar	1. Combine all ingredients in a bowl and mix well.
2 tbsp	30 mL	Salt	
2 tsp	10 mL	White pepper	2. Mix or stir again before using.
3 pt	1.5 L	Salad oil	

Variations

Substitute olive oil for all or part of the salad oil.

240A. Mustard Vinaigrette: Add 2 to 4 oz (60 to 125 g) prepared mustard (French or Dijon type) to the basic recipe. Mix with vinegar before adding oil.

240B. Herbed Vinaigrette: Add to the basic recipe or to the Mustard French variation 1 cup (60 g) chopped parsley and 4 tsp (20 mL) of one of the following dried herbs: basil, thyme, marjoram, tarragon, chives.

RECIPE 240 **Basic French Dressing or Vinaigrette** *(Continued)*

240C. *Italian Dressing:* Use all or part olive oil. Add to the basic recipe 1 tbsp (15 mL) minced garlic, 2 tbsp (30 mL) oregano, ½ cup (125 mL) chopped parsley.

240D. *Piquante Dressing:* Add to the basic recipe 4 tsp (20 mL) dry mustard, ¼ cup (60 mL) finely chopped onion, 4 tsp (20 mL) paprika.

240E. *Chiffonade Dressing:* Add to the basic recipe the following ingredients, all chopped fine: 4 hard-cooked eggs, 8 oz (250 g) cooked or canned beets (drained), 4 tbsp (60 mL) parsley, 2 oz (60 g) onion or scallion.

240F. *Avocado Dressing:* Add 2 pt (1 kg) puréed avocado to basic recipe or to Herbed Vinaigrette. Beat until smooth. Increase salt to taste.

240G. *Blue Cheese or Roquefort Dressing:* Mix 8 oz (250 g) crumbled blue or Roquefort cheese and 8 oz (250 mL) heavy cream in a mixer with paddle attachment. Gradually beat in 3 pt (1.5 L) Basic French Dressing.

240H. *Low-fat Vinaigrette:* Prepare basic vinaigrette or any of the variations, substituting a *jus lié* (see p. 143) made with a white stock, vegetable stock, or vegetable juice for *two-thirds* of the oil.

RECIPE 241 **American French or Tomato French**

Yield: 2 qt (2 L)

U.S.	Metric	Ingredients	Procedure
4 oz	125 g	Onion	1. Grate onion on hand grater or grind in food chopper.
1 qt	1 L	Salad oil	
12 oz	375 mL	Vinegar, cider	2. Combine all ingredients in a stainless steel bowl.
2½ cups	625 mL	Catsup	
4 oz	125 g	Sugar	3. Mix with a wire whip until well combined and sugar is dissolved. Chill.
1 tsp	5 mL	Garlic, mashed	
1 tbsp	15 mL	Worcestershire sauce	4. Beat or stir again before serving.
1 tsp	5 mL	Paprika	
¼ tsp	1 mL	Hot pepper sauce (such as Tabasco)	
½ tsp	2 mL	White pepper	

RECIPE 242 **Oriental Vinaigrette**

Yield: 1½ pt (250 mL)

U.S.	Metric	Ingredients	Procedure
¾ cup	200 mL	Rice vinegar or white vinegar	1. Combine all ingredients except salt in a bowl and mix well.
¼ cup	60 mL	Soy sauce	
1¾ cup	425 mL	Salad oil	2. Taste the dressing and add salt if necessary (the soy sauce may contain enough salt).
¼ cup	60 mL	Oriental sesame oil	
1 tbsp	15 mL	Grated fresh ginger	3. Mix or stir again before using.
2 tsp	10 mL	Pepper	
¼ tsp	1 mL	Garlic, crushed	
½ tsp	2 mL	Hot pepper sauce	
		Salt, if needed	

EMULSIFIED DRESSINGS

Mayonnaise is the most important emulsified dressing. It is sometimes used by itself as a salad dressing but more often serves as the base for a wide variety of other dressings. Mayonnaise-based dressings are generally thick and creamy. In fact, many of them are made with the addition of sour cream.

Emulsified French Dressing is similar to Basic French Dressing, except that egg yolk has been added to keep the oil and vinegar from separating. Its preparation is similar to that of mayonnaise. Emulsified French Dressing is given a red-orange color and a subtle flavoring through the addition of Spanish paprika.

Preparation of Mayonnaise

Good-quality prepared mayonnaise is readily available on the market, and few establishments make their own. But it is such a basic preparation and, like the mother sauces you studied in Chapter 8, the foundation of many others. Therefore it is important to know how to make it.

Homemade mayonnaise is not as stable as the commercial product, which has been prepared with special equipment that creates a finer emulsion, and which may have added stabilizers to increase its shelf life. Also, the commercial product is usually less expensive. Nevertheless, making mayonnaise in your operation takes only minutes with a power mixer, and by carefully selecting your ingredients, you can make a superior-tasting product.

To make mayonnaise, you must observe several conditions in order to get an emulsion. Study these guidelines before proceeding with the recipe:

1. **Use fairly bland ingredients if the mayonnaise is to be used as a base for other dressings.**

   The mayonnaise will be more versatile as a base if it has no strong flavors. Olive oil and other ingredients with distinctive flavors may be used for special preparations.

2. **Use the freshest eggs possible for the best emulsification.**

3. **Have all ingredients at room temperature.**

   Cold oil is not easily broken into small droplets, so it is harder to make an emulsion.

4. **Beat the egg yolks well in a bowl.**

   Thorough beating of the yolks is important for a good emulsion.

5. **Beat in the seasonings.**

   It is helpful to add a little of the vinegar at this time, as well. The emulsion will be easier to form, because the acidity of the vinegar helps to prevent the curdling of the egg yolk proteins. Also, the vinegar helps to disperse the spices and dissolve the salt.

6. **Begin to add the oil very slowly, beating constantly.**

   It is critical to add the oil slowly at first, or the emulsion will break. When the emulsion has begun to form, the oil may be added more quickly. But never add more oil at once than the amount of mayonnaise that has already formed in the bowl, or the emulsion may break.

7. **Gradually beat in the remaining oil alternately with the vinegar.**

   The more oil you add, the thicker the mayonnaise gets. Vinegar thins it out. Add a little vinegar whenever the mayonnaise gets too thick to beat.

   Beating with a power mixer using the wire whip attachment makes a more stable emulsion than beating by hand.

8. **Add no more than 8 oz (240 mL) of oil per large egg yolk, or no more than 1 qt (950 mL) per 4 yolks.**

   The emulsion may break if more oil is added than the egg yolks can handle.

9. **Taste and correct the seasonings.**

   Finished mayonnaise should have a smooth, rich but neutral flavor, with a pleasant tartness. Its texture should be smooth and glossy, and the mayonnaise should be thick enough to hold its shape.

10. **If the mayonnaise breaks, it can be rescued.**

    Beat an egg yolk or two or some good prepared mayonnaise in a bowl, and very slowly begin to beat in the broken mayonnaise, as in step 6. Continue until all the mayonnaise has been added and reformed.

RECIPE 243   Mayonnaise

Yield: 2 qt (2 L)

U.S.	Metric	Ingredients	Procedure
8 2 tbsp 2 tsp 2 tsp pinch	8 30 mL 10 mL 10 mL pinch	Egg yolks Vinegar Salt Dry mustard Cayenne	1. Review guidelines for making mayonnaise, page 520. 2. Place the egg yolks in the bowl of a mixer and beat with the whip attachment until well beaten. 3. Add 2 tbsp (30 mL) vinegar and beat well. 4. Mix together the dry ingredients and add to the bowl. Beat until well mixed.
3½ pt 4 tbsp 3–4 tbsp	1.7 L 60 mL 50–60 mL	Salad oil Vinegar Lemon juice	5. Turn the mixer to high speed. *Very slowly*, almost drop by drop, begin adding the oil. When the emulsion forms, you can add the oil slightly faster. 6. When the mayonnaise becomes thick, thin out with a little of the vinegar. 7. Gradually beat in the remaining oil alternately with the vinegar. 8. Adjust the tartness and the consistency by beating in a little lemon juice.

Mayonnaise-based Dressings

For each of the following dressings, add the listed ingredients to *2 qt (2 L) Mayonnaise* as indicated.

243A. Thousand Island Dressing: 1 pt (500 mL) chili sauce, 2 oz (60 g) minced onion, 4 oz (125 g) finely chopped green pepper, 4 oz (125 g) chopped drained pimiento, and (optional ingredient) 3 chopped hard-cooked eggs.

243B. Louis Dressing: Prepare Thousand Island Dressing without the chopped eggs. Add 1 pt (500 mL) heavy cream.

243C. Russian Dressing: 1 pt (500 mL) chili sauce or catsup, ½ cup (125 mL) drained horseradish, 2 oz (60 g) minced onion, and (optional ingredient) 1 cup (500 mL) lumpfish or whitefish caviar.

243D. Chantilly Dressing: 1 pt (500 mL) heavy cream, whipped. (Fold the whipped cream into the mayonnaise carefully to retain volume. Do this as close as possible to service time.)

243E. Blue Cheese Dressing: ½ cup (125 mL) white vinegar, 2 tsp (10 mL) worcestershire sauce, a few drops of hot red pepper sauce, and 1 lb (500 g) crumbled blue cheese. Thin out to desired consistency with 1–2 cups (250–500 mL) heavy cream or half-and-half.
Variation: Substitute sour cream for up to half of the mayonnaise.

RECIPE 244 **Emulsified French Dressing**

Yield: 2 qt (2 L)

U.S.	Metric	Ingredients	Procedure
2	2	Eggs, whole	1. Place the eggs in the bowl of a mixer and beat with the whip attachment until well beaten.
1 tbsp	15 mL	Salt	
1 tbsp	15 mL	Paprika	2. Mix together the dry ingredients and add to the bowl. Beat until well mixed.
1 tbsp	15 mL	Dry mustard	
½ tsp	2 mL	White pepper	3. Turn the mixer to high speed. *Very slowly* begin adding the oil, as when making mayonnaise.
3 pt	1.4 L	Salad oil	
8 oz	250 mL	Cider vinegar	4. When the dressing becomes thick, thin out with a little of the vinegar.
4 oz	125 mL	Lemon juice	
			5. Gradually beat in the remaining oil alternatively with the vinegar.
			6. Beat in the lemon juice.
as needed		Vinegar, lemon juice, or water	7. The dressing should be pourable, not thick like mayonnaise. If it is too thick, *taste for seasonings first.* If it is not tart enough, thin out with a little vinegar or lemon juice. If it is tart enough, thin out with water.

OTHER DRESSINGS

Cooked salad dressing is similar in appearance to mayonnaise, but it has a more tart flavor, while mayonnaise is richer and milder. Cooked dressing is made with little or no oil and with a starch thickener. It may be made in the kitchen or purchased ready prepared. Formerly it was little used in commercial kitchens because of its stronger flavor and tartness, but now it is preferred to mayonnaise in some regions of the country.

You will find in many cookbooks a great variety of other dressings based on neither mayonnaise nor oil and vinegar. They include sour cream-based dressings, fruit juice- and yogurt-based dressings for fruit salads, and low-calorie dressings that appeal to the dieter. The important thing to remember is that these dressings should have well-balanced flavors with a pleasant tartness, and that they should harmonize with and complement the salad with which they are served.

RECIPE 245 **Sour Cream Fruit Salad Dressing**

Yield: About 2½ pt (1.25 L)

U.S.	Metric	Ingredients	Procedure
4 oz	125 g	Currant jelly	1. Place the jelly and lemon juice in a stainless steel bowl. Set over hot water or low heat and stir until melted.
4 oz	125 mL	Lemon juice	
2 pt	1 L	Sour cream	2. Remove from heat and beat in the sour cream a little at a time. Chill the dressing.

Variation
245A. ***Yogurt Fruit Salad Dressing:*** Prepare as in basic recipe, using 1 cup (250 mL) sour cream and 3 cups (750 mL) plain yogurt.

RECIPE 246   **Cooked Salad Dressing**

Yield: 2 qt (2 L)

U.S.	Metric	Ingredients	Procedure
4 oz	125 g	Sugar	1. Mix the sugar, flour, salt, mustard, and cayenne in a stainless steel bowl.
4 oz	125 g	Flour	
2 tbsp	30 mL	Salt	2. Add the eggs and yolks and beat until smooth.
2 tbsp	30 mL	Dry mustard	
¼ tsp	1 mL	Cayenne	3. Place the milk in a saucepan and bring to a simmer. (Be careful not to scorch it.)
4	4	Eggs, whole	
4	4	Egg yolks	4. Gradually beat about half the milk into the egg mixture. Then return the mixture to the saucepan.
3 pt	1.5 L	Milk	
			5. Cook over low heat, stirring constantly, until very thick and no raw flour taste remains.
4 oz	125 g	Butter	6. Remove from heat and stir in the butter.
12 oz	375 mL	Vinegar, cider	7. When the butter is melted and mixed in, stir in the vinegar.
			8. Immediately transfer the dressing to a stainless steel container. Cover and cool.

RECIPE 247   **Fruit Salad Dressing**

Yield: 1 qt (1 L)

U.S.	Metric	Ingredients	Procedure
6 oz	175 g	Sugar	1. Mix the sugar and cornstarch in a stainless steel bowl.
1 oz	30 g	Cornstarch	
4	4	Eggs	2. Add the eggs and beat until the mixture is smooth.
1 cup	250 mL	Pineapple juice	3. Heat the fruit juices in a saucepan and bring to a boil.
1 cup	250 mL	Orange juice	
½ cup	125 mL	Lemon juice	4. Gradually beat the hot juices into the egg mixture.
			5. Return the mixture to the saucepan and bring to a boil, stirring constantly.
			6. When the mixture has thickened, immediately pour it out into a stainless steel bowl or bain marie and chill.
1 cup	250 mL	Sour cream	7. Beat the sour cream into the chilled fruit mixture.

RECIPE 248   **Honey Lemon Dressing**

Yield: 1 pt (500 mL)

U.S.	Metric	Ingredients	Procedure
1 cup	250 mL	Honey	1. Mix honey and lemon juice together until thoroughly mixed.
1 cup	250 mL	Lemon juice	
			2. Serve with fruit salads.

Variations

248A. Honey Cream Dressing: Mix 1 cup (250 mL) heavy cream with the honey before adding the lemon juice.

248B. Honey Lime Dressing: Use lime juice instead of lemon juice.

TERMS FOR REVIEW

appetizer salad	full slip	cooked salad	winterized oil
accompaniment salad	four parts of a salad	fruit salad	vinegar strength
main-course salad	bound salad	combination salad	Roquefort
separate-course salad	green salad	gelatin salad	emulsion
dessert salad	vegetable salad	marinated	French dressing

QUESTIONS FOR DISCUSSION

1. List three or four salads that may be served as appetizers, as accompaniments, as main dishes, as separate-course salads, and as desserts. Give reasons for your choices.

2. What is the effect of salad dressings on the crispness of salad greens, and what are some ways to solve this problem?

3. You are asked to prepare 250 Waldorf salads for a banquet. Explain the procedure you will use for the preparation. List each step, from raw ingredients to plated salads. (You may refer to the recipe on p. 504.)

4. How can you ensure that salad greens will be crisp?

5. You are making mixed green salads and have the following ingredients to choose from. Which would you toss together and which would you add after plating or at service time? Why?

Iceberg lettuce   Chicory
Shredded red cabbage   Avocado slices
Carrot strips or shreds Tomato wedges
Watercress   Romaine lettuce
Sliced celery

6. You are preparing tossed green salads, potato salads, and avocado and grapefruit salads for luncheon service. How will you plan your preparation (what will you do first, second, and so on)?

7. You are trying a new recipe for a molded vegetable salad using unflavored gelatin. After evaluating the flavor, you decide it isn't tart enough and more vinegar should be added. Should you make any other adjustments?

8. When you are making mayonnaise, there are a number of precautions you should take to make sure a good emulsion is formed. Name as many as you can. If you forget one of these and your mayonnaise breaks, what can you do?

CHAPTER 20

SANDWICHES AND HORS D'OEUVRES

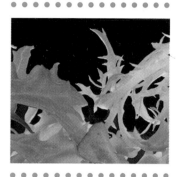

The sandwich is without a doubt America's favorite lunchtime food. It is quickly made and served, convenient, and adaptable to so many variations that it satisfies nearly every taste and nutrition requirement.

Sandwiches have long been the domain of the pantry department, along with salads and other cold preparations. However, when you consider that the most popular sandwich in America today is the hamburger, you realize that sandwich preparation is as much the responsibility of the short-order cook as it is of the pantry cook.

Preparing hot and cold sandwiches to order is one of the fundamental skills required in modern food service. In this chapter we start by looking at the fundamentals of sandwich making, the basic ingredients and basic sandwich types. We then look at the setup of the sandwich station and methods for efficient production.

The subject of sandwiches leads us to the study of another category of foods that are handled by the pantry department: hors d'oeuvres. One of the most important types of hors d'oeuvre is the canapé, which is actually a tiny, open-faced sandwich. In the last part of this chapter, we discuss not only canapés but also other basic kinds of hors d'oeuvres.

After reading this chapter, you should be able to

1. Select, store, and serve fresh, good-quality breads for sandwiches.

2. Use sandwich spreads correctly.

3. List most popular sandwich fillings.

4. Set up a sandwich station.

5. Prepare the major types of sandwiches to order.

6. Prepare sandwiches in quantity.

7. Prepare canapés and other popular hors d'oeuvres.

SANDWICHES

BREADS

One of the functions of the bread in a sandwich is to provide an edible casing for the food inside. Ideally, though, the bread should do more than this. Good-quality breads provide variety, texture, flavor, and eye appeal to sandwiches, as well as providing bulk and nutrients.

Types

1. Pullman or sandwich loaves of white bread are most frequently used. These are long, rectangular loaves that provide square slices of specified thickness, from ⅜ inch to ⅝ inch (10 mm to 16 mm) thick.

   Commercial sandwich bread should be of fine rather than coarse texture and firm enough to spread well. Supermarket white bread is unsuitable because it is too soft for spreading and for holding most fillings, and it becomes pasty in the mouth.

   Because of its neutral flavor, white bread is suitable for the largest variety of fillings.

2. Other kinds of breads add variety and interest, provided that they harmonize with the filling. The following are some possibilities:

   Rolls, including hard and soft rolls, hamburger and hot dog rolls, long rolls for submarine sandwiches

   French or Italian bread, split horizontally

   Whole wheat

   Cracked wheat

   Rye and pumpernickel

   Pita bread

   Raisin bread

   Cinnamon bread

   Fruit and nut breads

Storage

Fresh bread is essential for top-quality sandwiches. Stale or dry bread is undesirable. The following measures can be taken to ensure freshness.

1. Daily delivery, or as frequent as possible, depending on your location. Bread stales rapidly, and day-old bread has lost much of its freshness.

2. Keep bread tightly wrapped in moisture-proof wrapping until it is used. This prevents drying and also guards against absorption of odors.

3. French bread and other hard-crusted breads should not be wrapped, or the crusts will soften. These breads stale rapidly and should be used the day they are baked.

4. Store at room temperature, away from ovens or hot equipment. Do not refrigerate, because refrigerated bread becomes stale faster.

5. If bread must be kept more than a day, it may be frozen. Thaw frozen bread without unwrapping.

6. Day-old bread may be used for toasting, without loss of quality.

SPREADS

Purposes of Spreads

1. To protect the bread from soaking up moisture from the filling.

2. To add flavor.

3. To add moisture or "mouth feel."

Butter

Butter should be soft enough to spread easily without tearing the bread. It may be softened by whipping in a mixer or by simply letting it stand at room temperature for half an hour.

Whipping gives the butter greater volume and this cuts food cost. However, whipped butter does not keep as well because the incorporated air speeds the development of rancidity.

Some operators whip a small amount of water or milk into the butter. This not only increases spreadability but also increases volume. However, it adds nothing to the quality of the sandwich and increases the likelihood of soaking the bread.

Margarine is sometimes used instead of butter, if food costs require it or if customers request it.

Flavored butters, such as those listed on page 537, may be used with appropriate fillings.

Mayonnaise

Mayonnaise is often preferred to butter as a spread because it contributes more flavor. However, it does not protect the bread from moisture as well as butter does.

Because of the danger of food-borne disease, sandwiches made with mayonnaise should be served immediately or refrigerated at once and kept refrigerated until served.

FILLINGS

The filling is the heart of the sandwich. As we have already said, nearly any kind of food may be served between two slices of bread. The following are some possible fillings, which may be used separately or in combination.

Meats and Poultry

Most meats for sandwiches are precooked, though some are cooked to order. Sliced meats dry out and lose flavor, so avoid slicing farther ahead than necessary and keep sliced meats covered or wrapped.

Leftovers may be used, but only if they are of good quality and have been properly handled and stored to avoid contamination.

Thin slices are tenderer and the sandwich is easier to eat. Also, many thin slices make a thicker sandwich than one or two thick slices of the same total weight.

1. *Beef.*
    Sliced roast beef, hot or cold
    Hamburger patties
    Small steaks
    Corned beef
    Pastrami
    Tongue, fresh or smoked

2. *Pork products.*
    Roast pork
    Ham, all kinds
    Bacon
    Canadian bacon

3. *Poultry.*
    Turkey breast
    Chicken breast

4. *Sausage products.*
    Salami
    Frankfurters
    Bologna
    Liverwurst
    Luncheon meats

Cheese

Like meats, cheese dries out rapidly when unwrapped and sliced. When slicing is done ahead, the slices should remain covered until service time. See Chapter 21 for a summary of cheese varieties.

The most popular sandwich cheeses are

    Cheddar types
    Swiss types
    Provolone
    Cream cheese
    Process cheese
    Cheese spreads

Fish and Shellfish

Most seafood fillings for sandwiches are highly perishable and should be kept well chilled at all times.

Some popular seafood fillings are

    Tuna
    Sardines
    Smoked salmon and lox
    Shrimp
    Anchovies
    Fried fish portions

Mayonnaise-based Salads

Refer to page 498 for preparation of cooked salads. The most popular salads for sandwich fillings are tuna salad, egg salad, chicken or turkey salad, and ham salad.

Vegetable Items

Lettuce, tomato, and onion are indispensable in sandwich production. In addition, nearly any vegetables used in salads may also be included in sandwiches. See page 477 for a listing.

Miscellaneous

    Peanut butter
    Jelly
    Hard-cooked egg
    Fruits, fresh or dried
    Nuts (such as sliced almonds)

TYPES OF SANDWICHES

Hot Sandwiches

1. *Simple hot sandwiches* consist of hot fillings, usually meats, between two slices of bread or two halves of a roll. They may also contain items that are not hot, such as a slice of tomato or raw onion on a hamburger.

    Hamburgers and hot dogs and all their variations are the most popular hot sandwiches.

2. *Open-faced hot sandwiches* are made by placing buttered or unbuttered bread on a serving plate, covering with hot meat or other filling, and topping with a sauce, gravy, cheese, or other topping. Some versions are browned under the broiler before serving. This type of sandwich is eaten with a knife and fork.

3. *Grilled sandwiches*, also called toasted sandwiches, are simple sandwiches that are buttered on the outside and browned on the griddle or in a hot oven. Sandwiches containing cheese are popular for grilling.

4. *Deep-fried sandwiches* are made by dipping sandwiches in beaten egg and sometimes in bread crumbs and then deep-frying. This type of sandwich is often cooked on a griddle or in a hot oven instead, since deep-frying makes it greasy.

Cold Sandwiches

1. *Simple cold sandwiches* are those made with two slices of bread or two halves of a roll, a spread, and a filling. They are called "simple" because they are made with just two slices of bread, not because they are necessarily simple in construction. Simple cold sandwiches range from a single slice of cheese or meat between two slices of buttered bread to complex constructions like the submarine sandwich (also called a hero sandwich or grinder), a long Italian roll filled with salami, ham, capicolla, mortadella or bologna, provolone cheese, peppers, onions, olives, tomatoes, and more.

    Most popular sandwiches fall into this category.

2. *Multidecker sandwiches* are made with more than two slices of bread (or rolls split into more than two pieces) and with several ingredients in the filling.

    The *club sandwich* is a popular multidecker sandwich, made of three slices of toast and filled with sliced chicken or turkey breast, mayonnaise, lettuce, tomato, and bacon. It is cut into four triangles, as shown in Figure 20.1.

3. *Open-faced sandwiches* are made with a single slice of bread, like large canapés, which is what they are. Like canapés, the filling or topping should be attractively arranged and garnished. Canapé ingredients and method are discussed later in this chapter.

4. *Tea sandwiches* are small, fancy sandwiches generally made from light, delicate ingredients and bread that has been trimmed of crusts. They are often cut into fancy shapes. Fillings and spreads can be the same as those for canapés.

MAKING SANDWICHES

The preparation of sandwiches requires a great deal of handwork. Many individual motions may be required, especially if the sandwiches are multideckers or have several ingredients. Whether you are making sandwiches in quantity or to order, your goal must be to reduce your motions to make the production as efficient and quick as possible.

Setting Up the Station for Prepared-to-Order Sandwiches

A station setup depends on the menu and on the available equipment and space, so there is no single correct way to set up.

Any setup involves two elements: ingredients and equipment.

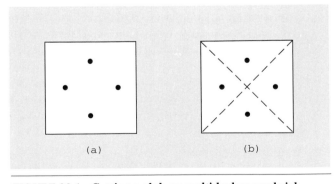

FIGURE 20.1 **Cutting a club or multidecker sandwich.**
(a) Place four picks in the sandwich in the location shown by the dots in the illustration.
(b) Cut the sandwiches into quarters from corner to corner. Plate the sandwich with the points up (see Figure 20.3).

Ingredients

This phase of the setup has two parts:

1. *Prepare ingredients.* Mix fillings, prepare spreads, slice meats and cheeses, separate lettuce leaves, slice tomatoes, prepare garnishes, and so on. In other words, have everything ready ahead of time, so there is nothing left to do but put the ingredients together.

2. *Arrange or store ingredients for maximum efficiency.* To reduce your movements to a minimum, the ideal setup has everything you need within easy reach of both hands. Depending on the kitchen layout, this may not be possible, especially if the sandwich menu is very large. But try to get as close to it as possible.

    Arrange ingredients so you can use both hands. For example, while the left hand reaches for the bread, the right hand reaches for the butter spreader. Then, while the right hand puts the spreader back, the left reaches for the sliced ham. The right hand, on its way back from the butter, picks up a slice of cheese and so on. On a busy sandwich station, every second counts.

Two other considerations are important while we're talking about ingredients:

1. *Sanitation.* Because cold sandwiches are subjected to a lot of handling and are not cooked, it is especially important that ingredients be properly refrigerated and protected at all times. A refrigerated table—sort of a cold version of a steam table—is usually used. Refrigerated drawers or under-the-counter reach-ins are used for less frequently needed items.

2. *Portion control.* Sliced items are portioned by the count and by weight. If portioning is by the count, you must take care, during pre-prep, to slice to the proper thickness. If done by weight, each portion can be placed on squares of waxed paper and stacked in a container.

Equipment

The equipment needed for a sandwich station depends, of course, on the menu and the size of the operation.

1. *Storage equipment* for ingredients includes refrigeration equipment for cold ingredients and a steam table for hot ingredients, such as roasted meats.

2. *Hand tools* are basic requirements for sandwich making and are often the only tools necessary.

These include spreaders, spatulas, and knives, including a serrated knife and a sharp chef's knife for cutting the finished sandwich. A cutting board, of course, is also required. A power slicer may be necessary for any slicing not done ahead.

3. *Portion control equipment* includes scoops for fillings and a portion scale for other ingredients.

4. *Cooking equipment* is necessary for most hot sandwiches. Griddles, grills, broilers, and deep fryers are all used for cooking sandwich ingredients to order. Microwave ovens are sometimes used to heat ingredients or finished sandwiches.

Setting Up and Preparing Sandwiches in Quantity

Once the ingredients are prepared and the hand tools assembled, all that's needed for a complete sandwich station is a large table.

Assembly line production is the most efficient method, because it simplifies movements. This is the same method applied to producing salads in quantity in Chapter 19.

Procedure for Making Simple Cold Sandwiches in Quantity

1. Prepare and assemble all ingredients.

2. Assemble necessary equipment, including wrapping materials.

3. Arrange bread slices in rows on the table top.

4. Spread each slice with butter or whatever spread is required.

5. Place fillings evenly and neatly on alternate slices, leaving the other slices plain. Fillings should not hang over the edges of the bread. If the filling is spreadable, spread it evenly to the edges. See Figure 20.2 for spreading technique.

6. Top the filled slices with the plain buttered slices.

7. Stack two or three sandwiches and cut with a *sharp* knife.

8. To hold, do one of the following:

    a. Wrap separately in plastic, waxed paper, or sandwich bags.

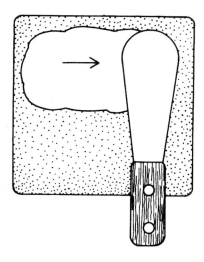

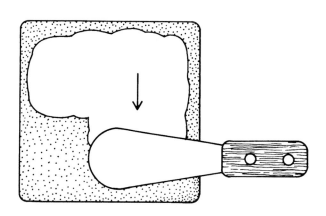

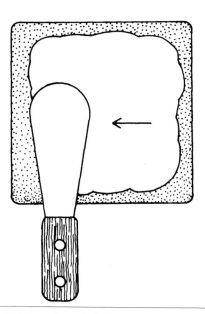

FIGURE 20.2 **Spread sandwiches efficiently with three quick strokes as shown.**

b. Place in storage pans, cover tightly with plastic wrap, and cover with clean, damp towels. The towels must not touch the sandwiches; their purpose is to provide a moisture barrier to help prevent drying.

9. Refrigerate immediately, and hold until served.

Service

With a few exceptions—such as hamburgers and hot dogs—sandwiches are cut before serving. Cutting serves two purposes:

1. It makes the sandwich easier to handle and eat.

2. It makes a more attractive presentation possible.

The first purpose is usually accomplished by simply cutting the sandwich in half, or if it is very large or thick, into thirds or quarters.

The second purpose can be served by displaying the cut edges to the outside rather than the crust edges. If the sandwich was neatly made, of good ingredients, and tastefully garnished (see Chapter 22), it will be appetizing and attractive. Little purpose is served by cutting and arranging the sandwich in complicated ways. That sort of presentation is seen more often in textbooks than in busy kitchens.

Hamburgers and other uncut sandwiches may be presented open faced to display the attractive ingredients. For example, a hamburger version often called a California Burger is presented with the meat on the bottom half of the bun and, along side, a lettuce leaf and a slice of tomato on the top half of the bun.

Figure 20.3 shows some examples of sandwich presentation.

Cold Sandwich Combinations

The following suggestions are only a few of the many sandwiches that can be made from the ingredients listed in the first part of this chapter.

1. Roast beef on rye bread spread with a mixture of softened cream cheese and horseradish.

2. Beef tongue, lettuce, tomato on onion roll with mayonnaise.

3. Bologna, provolone cheese, tomatoes, and chopped pimiento on hard roll; mayonnaise.

4. Liverwurst, onion slices, and sour pickles on pumpernickel; mayonnaise or butter.

5. Corned beef or ham, Swiss cheese, mustard, and dill pickle slices on rye; mayonnaise or butter.

FIGURE 20.3   Sandwich presentation need not be elaborate to be attractive.
(a) California Burger.

(c) Club Sandwich.

(b) Tuna Salad Sandwich with an assortment of fruits.

(d) Monte Cristo Sandwich with Tomato and Cucumber Salad.

6. Corned beef, cole slaw (well drained), and Swiss cheese on rye; mayonnaise or butter.

7. Ham, salami, tomato slice, Russian dressing, and lettuce on rye toast.

8. Chicken or turkey, ham, Swiss cheese, and lettuce on white or whole wheat toast; mayonnaise.

9. Chicken and cucumber slices on whole wheat; mayonnaise.

10. Turkey, bacon, Swiss cheese, and lettuce on white or whole wheat toast; mayonnaise.

11. Deviled ham, pineapple slice, and lettuce on white toast.

12. Tuna salad, lettuce, tomato, and shredded cheddar cheese on white toast.

13. Sardines and onion slices on dark rye spread with cream cheese; served open faced.

RECIPE 249 California Burger

Yield: 1 sandwich

U.S.	Metric	Ingredients	Procedure
1	1	Hamburger patty, 4 oz (125 g)	1. Cook the hamburger patty on a griddle or grill to desired doneness.
1	1	Hamburger roll	
as needed		Butter	2. While the meat is cooking, prepare the roll. Butter the bottom half very lightly. Spread the top half with mayonnaise.
2 tsp	10 mL	Mayonnaise	
1	1	Lettuce leaf	
1	1	Thin slice of onion (optional)	3. Place the two halves of the roll side by side on a serving plate.
1	1	Tomato slice	4. On the top half, place the lettuce leaf, the onion slice (if used), and the tomato slice.
			5. When the hamburger patty is cooked, place it on the bottom half of the roll. Serve immediately, open faced.

Variations

249A. California Cheeseburger: Prepare as in basic recipe, except place a slice of cheddar or American cheese on top of the hamburger patty 1 minute before it is done. Cook until the cheese melts.

249B. Cheeseburger (plain): Omit mayonnaise, lettuce, onion, and tomato, but add the slice of cheese as in California Cheeseburger.

249C. Cheeseburger with Bacon: Prepare like a Cheeseburger, but place two half strips of bacon on top of the cheese.

249D. California Cheeseburger Deluxe: Prepare like a California Cheeseburger, but place two half strips of bacon on top of the cheese.

RECIPE 250 Submarine Sandwich

Yield: 1 sandwich

U.S.	Metric	Ingredients	Procedure
1	1	Submarine roll	1. Split the roll horizontally, but leave it hinged on one side.
2 tbsp	30 mL	Mayonnaise	
1 oz	30 g	Salami, cut in thin slices	2. Spread the roll with mayonnaise.
1 oz	30 g	Ham, cut in thin slices	3. Arrange the meats and cheese in the sandwich in layers. If the slices of meat are too wide to fit, fold them in half.
1 oz	30 g	Bologna, cut in thin slices	
1 oz	30 g	Provolone cheese, cut in thin slices	4. Arrange the tomato, onion, and pepper slices on top of the meats and cheese.
2	2	Tomato slices	5. Close the sandwich. Leave it whole or cut it in half for service.
2	2	Onion slices, very thin	
3	3	Green pepper rings	6. Serve the sandwich with mustard and olives or pickles on the side.

RECIPE 251   **Club Sandwich**

Yield: 1 sandwich

U.S.	Metric	Ingredients	Procedure
3 slices	3 slices	White bread, toasted Mayonnaise	1. Place the 3 slices of toast on a clean work surface. Spread the tops with mayonnaise.
2 leaves	2 leaves	Lettuce	
2 slices	2 slices	Tomato, about ¼ inch (½ cm) thick	2. On the first slice, place 1 lettuce leaf, then 2 slices of tomato, then 3 strips of bacon.
3 strips	3 strips	Crisp cooked bacon	
2 oz	60 g	Sliced turkey or chicken breast	3. Place the second slice of toast on top, spread side down.
			4. Spread the top with mayonnaise.
			5. On top of this, place the turkey or chicken, then the other lettuce leaf.
			6. Top with the third slice of toast, spread side down.
			7. Place frilled picks on all 4 sides of the sandwich as shown in Figure 20.1.
			8. Cut the sandwich from corner to corner into 4 triangles. Each triangle will have a pick through the center to hold it together.
			9. Place on a plate with the points up. The center of the plate between the 4 pieces may be filled with potato chips, french fries, or other garnish or accompaniment.

Variation

251A. Bacon, Lettuce, and Tomato Sandwich (BLT): Using only 2 slices of toast, prepare basic recipe through step 3. Omit remaining ingredients. Cut the sandwich in half diagonally for service.

RECIPE 252 **Grilled Cheese Sandwich**

Yield: 1 sandwich

U.S.	Metric	Ingredients	Procedure
2 slices	2 slices	White bread	1. Place the slice of cheese between the 2 slices of bread.
1 oz	30 g	Cheddar or American cheese: 1 slice cut to the size of the bread	2. Butter the outsides of the sandwich and place on a griddle preheated to 350–375°F (175–190°C).
		Butter	3. Cook until golden brown on one side. Turn over and cook until the second side is golden brown and the cheese starts to melt.
			4. Remove from griddle. Cut in half diagonally and serve immediately.

Variations

252A. *Grilled Ham and Swiss Sandwich:* Make the sandwich with a ½-oz (15-g) slice of Swiss cheese and a 1-oz (30-g) slice of ham. Griddle as in basic recipe.

252B. *Grilled Cheese and Bacon Sandwich:* Make the sandwich with 1 oz (30 g) cheddar or American cheese and 2 strips of crisp cooked bacon. Griddle as in basic recipe.

RECIPE 253 **Reuben Sandwich**

Yield: 1 sandwich

U.S.	Metric	Ingredients	Procedure
2 slices	2 slices	Dark rye bread	1. Place the two slices of bread on a clean work surface.
4 tsp	20 mL	Russian or Thousand Island Dressing	2. Spread each slice with about 2 tsp (10 mL) dressing.
2 oz	60 g	Corned beef, sliced very thin	3. On one of the slices, place the corned beef, then the sauerkraut, then the cheese.
1 oz	30 g	Sauerkraut, well drained	4. Place the second slice of bread on top, spread side down.
1 oz	30 g	Swiss cheese (1 or 2 slices)	5. Butter the top of the sandwich and place buttered side down on a preheated griddle. Immediately butter the other side of the sandwich, which is now on top. (This method is less messy than buttering both sides before placing it on the griddle.)
		Butter	6. Griddle the sandwich, turning once, until browned on both sides and hot all through.
			7. Cut the sandwich into halves and serve immediately.

RECIPE 254   **Monte Cristo Sandwich**

Yield: 1 sandwich

U.S.	Metric	Ingredients	Procedure
2 slices	2 slices	White bread	1. Place the bread on a clean work surface. Spread the tops with butter.
1 oz	30 g	Sliced turkey or chicken breast	2. Place the turkey, ham, and cheese slices on one of the pieces of bread. Top with the remaining slice of bread, buttered side down.
1 oz	30 g	Sliced ham	
1 oz	30 g	Sliced Swiss cheese	3. Secure the sandwich with two picks placed in opposite corners.
1	1	Egg, beaten	4. Beat the egg and milk together.
2 tbsp	30 mL	Milk	5. Dip the sandwich in the batter until it is completely coated and the liquid has partially soaked into the bread.
			6. Fry the sandwich in deep fat at 375°F (190°C) until golden brown. *Alternative method:* Omit the picks and cook on a griddle until browned on both sides.
			7. Cut in half and serve immediately.

RECIPE 255   **Barbecued Pork or Beef Sandwich**

Portions: 25   **Portion size:** 1 sandwich with 3 oz (90 g) filling

U.S.	Metric	Ingredients	Procedure
3 lb	1.3 kg	Cooked pork or beef	1. Using a slicing machine or chef's knife, cut the meat into very thin slices.
2¼ pt	1 L	Barbecue Sauce (p. 155)	2. Combine the meat and sauce in a saucepan. Simmer uncovered over low heat for 10–15 minutes, until the meat has absorbed some of the flavor of the sauce and the liquid has reduced and thickened slightly.
25	25	Hamburger rolls Butter	
			3. Keep the meat hot for service.
			4. For each order, butter a hamburger roll. Place a 3-oz (90-g) portion of the meat mixture on the bottom half of the roll. Close the sandwich and serve immediately.

HORS D'OEUVRES

*I*n addition to salads and salad dressings, the pantry department is generally responsible for the small food items variously known as *appetizers* or *hors d'oeuvres*. The function of these foods is to enliven the appetite before dinner, often to the accompaniment of drinks, so they are generally small in size and spicy or piquant in flavor.

There is some confusion as to the distinction, if any, between the terms appetizer and hors d'oeuvre. Most books prescribe definitions of these words. The trouble is, everyone has different definitions for them, and they rarely correspond to the general way most people use the terms.

Rather than add to the confusion, let's just note that, in general, the first course of a multicourse meal is often called an *appetizer*, and the various kinds of finger foods served at receptions and with cocktails are called *hors d'oeuvres*. In some parts of the country, however, the terms are used interchangeably.

This section deals not with first courses but with special kinds of foods that are usually encountered away from the dinner table—foods that are the special domain of the pantry chef. They include "finger foods" such as canapés and relishes, indispensible accompaniments to receptions and parties.

The French expression *hors d'oeuvre* is literally translated "outside the work," meaning "apart from the main meal or main part of the meal." Incidentally, in French the term is not spelled or pronounced with an "s" at the end to make it plural, so you will often see the plural form spelled that way.

. . . .

CANAPÉS

Canapés may be defined as bite-size, open-faced sandwiches. The variety of combinations possible is nearly unlimited. Most canapés consist of three parts: base, spread, and garnish.

Base

Canapé bases may be made from several different items:

> Bread cutouts
>
> Toast cutouts
>
> Crackers
>
> Melba toasts

Tiny unsweetened pastry shells

Profiteroles (miniature unsweetened cream puff shells, p. 764)

Many of these items, such as crackers and melba toasts, can be purchased ready made, but bread and toast cutouts are the most widely used and offer the lowest food cost, though they require more labor.

Untoasted bread for canapés should be firm enough to allow the finished product to be handled easily. It may be cut thick and flattened slightly with a rolling pin to make it firmer. Toast is, of course, firmer, and it gives a pleasing texture and crispness to the canapés.

Procedure for Preparing Canapés from Toast

Method 1

1. You may use ready-sliced bread (after trimming the crusts), but it is usually most efficient to use long unsliced pullman loaves. Cut the crusts from all sides (save for bread crumbs). Slice the bread horizontally into ¼-inch-thick slices, as shown in Figure 20.4.

2. Toast the slices in the oven or in a large toaster.

3. Let the toasts cool.

4. Cover with a thin, even layer of the chosen spread and cut into desired shapes with a knife (see Figure 20.5). Make the cuts neat and uniform.

    Or cut the toasts into desired shapes with small cutters and reserve the trim for bread

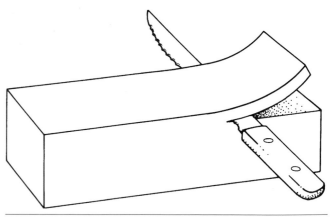

FIGURE 20.4 **For canapés, trim the crusts from a pullman loaf. With a serrated knife, cut horizontally into thin slices.**

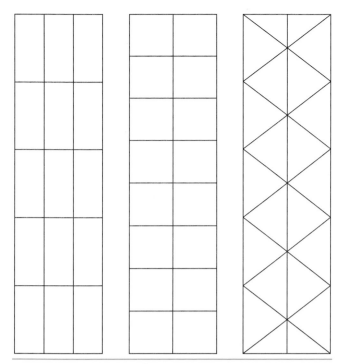

FIGURE 20.5   Bread slices for canapés can be cut into several basic shapes with no waste.

crumbs. Spread each cutout with desired topping. (This method is more time-consuming, but it may be used with round or odd-shaped cutters if you desire to save food cost by not losing spread on unused trimmings.)

5.   Garnish the cutouts as desired.

Method 2

1.   Cut bread slices as in step 1 above.

2.   Cut into desired shapes. Brush both sides of each cutout with melted butter and arrange on sheet pans. Place in a hot oven (450°F/230°C) until golden brown and very crisp, about 6 to 8 minutes.

3.   Let the bases cool.

4.   Assemble the canapés.

This method is more costly but gives a crisper base that holds up better with a moist spread.

Spread

Canapé spreads may be as simple as butter or softened cream cheese, but it is better to use a more highly flavored spread, because sharp or spicy flavors are better for stimulating the appetite.

The spread should be thick enough so that it clings well to the base and so that the garnish sticks to it without falling off.

Spreads may be divided into three basic categories, as follows:

Flavored Butters

Basic procedures for making flavored or compound butters are explained in Chapter 8 (see recipes on p. 148). Most types of flavored butters are made simply by blending the flavoring ingredients with the softened butter until completely mixed. Solid ingredients should be pureéd or chopped very fine, so that the butter can be spread smoothly.

Proportions of flavoring ingredients to butter can be varied widely, according to taste. For example, to make anchovy butter, you could double the quantity of anchovies indicated in the recipe on page 148 to get a stronger flavor, or you could decrease it to get a milder flavor. Because of this variability, and because the basic procedure is so simple, you should be able to make many kinds of flavored butters without needing individual recipes. Use the recipes in Chapter 8 and the following list as guides. Popular and versatile flavors for butter spreads include

> Lemon
>
> Parsley
>
> Tarragon
>
> Chive
>
> Anchovy
>
> Caviar
>
> Mustard
>
> Horseradish
>
> Pimiento
>
> Blue cheese
>
> Shrimp
>
> Olive
>
> Shallot or scallion
>
> Curry
>
> Caper

Flavored Cream Cheese

Flavored cream cheese spreads are made like flavored butters, except that you substitute cream cheese for the butter. Or you can use a mixture of cream cheese and butter, blended together well. Flavor variations are the same as those listed above for butter.

In addition, cream cheese is often blended with sharper, more flavorful cheeses that have been mashed or grated. Adding cream cheese to firmer cheese helps make them more spreadable. A liquid such as milk, cream, or port wine may be added to make the mixture softer. Such cheese spreads are often flavored with spices and herbs such as paprika, caraway seeds, dry mustard, parsley, or tarragon.

Meat or Fish Salad-type Spreads

You can use many cold meat or fish mixtures, such as cooked salads, to make canapé spreads. Popular examples include tuna salad, salmon salad, shrimp salad, chicken salad, deviled ham, and liver pâté.

To convert a salad recipe (see pp. 498–503) to a spread recipe, you may need to make one or more of the following modifications:

1. Chop the solid ingredients until very fine, or grind or purée them, so that the mixture is spreadable and not chunky.

2. Do not add the liquid ingredients and mayonnaise all at once. Add them a little at a time, just until the mixture reaches a thick, spreadable consistency.

3. Check the seasonings carefully. You may want to increase the seasonings to make the spread more stimulating to the appetite.

Garnish

The garnish of a canapé is any food item or combination of items placed on top of the spread. It may be a major part of the canapé, such as a slice of ham or cheese, or it may be a small tidbit that is selected for color, design, texture, or flavor accent, such as a pimiento cutout, a slice of radish, a caper, or a dab of caviar. Even the spread can be used as a garnish. For example, you may make a canapé with a mustard butter spread and a slice of ham, and then decorate the ham with a border or design of mustard butter piped on with a paper cone.

Here are some of the many food items that may be used alone or in combination to decorate canapés:

Vegetables, Pickles, and Relishes

Radish slices

Olives

Pickles

Capers

Pimiento

Pickled onions

Chutney

Asparagus tips

Cucumber slices

Cherry tomato slices or halves

Watercress leaves

Marinated mushrooms

Parsley

Fish

Smoked oysters and clams

Smoked salmon

Smoked trout

Herring

Shrimp

Rolled anchovy fillets

Caviar

Salmon or tuna flakes

Crabmeat

Lobster chunks or slices

Sardines

Meats

Ham

Salami

Chicken or turkey breast

Smoked tongue

Roast beef

Other

Cheese

Hard-cooked egg slices

Guidelines for Assembling Canapés

1. **Pre-preparation is essential.**

    Preparing thousands of canapés for large functions can be tedious work, so it is essential that all bases, spreads, and garnishes be prepared ahead of time in order that final assembly may go quickly and smoothly.

2. **Assemble as close as possible to serving time.**

    Bases quickly become soggy and spreads and garnish dry out easily. As trays are completed, they may be covered lightly with plastic and held for a short time under refrigeration. Be sure to observe all rules for safe food handling and storage, as you learned in Chapter 2.

3. ***Select harmonious flavor combinations in spreads and garnish.***

    For example, caviar and chutney or anchovy and ham are not appealing combinations, but these combinations are:

    Mustard butter and ham

    Lemon butter and caviar

    Pimiento cream cheese and sardine

    Horseradish butter and smoked salmon or smoked tongue

    Tuna salad and capers

    Anchovy butter, hard-cooked egg slice, and olive

4. ***Be sure that at least one of the ingredients is spicy or pronounced in flavor. A bland canapé has little value as an appetizer.***

5. ***Use quality ingredients.***

    Canapés can be a good way to utilize leftovers, but only if the leftovers have been carefully handled and stored to retain freshness.

6. ***Keep it simple.***

    Simple, neat arrangements are more attractive than elaborate, overworked designs. Besides, you don't have time to get too fancy. Also, be sure that the canapés hold together and do not fall apart in the customers' hands.

7. ***Arrange the canapés carefully and attractively on trays.***

    Much of the appeal of canapés is eye appeal, and the customer never sees just one at a time, but a whole trayful. Each tray should carry an assortment of various flavors and textures, so there is something for every taste.

    Figure 20.6 shows a tray of simple, attractive canapés.

COCKTAILS

The term *cocktail* is used not only for alcoholic beverages and vegetable and fruit juices, but also for a group of appetizers made of seafood or fruit, usually

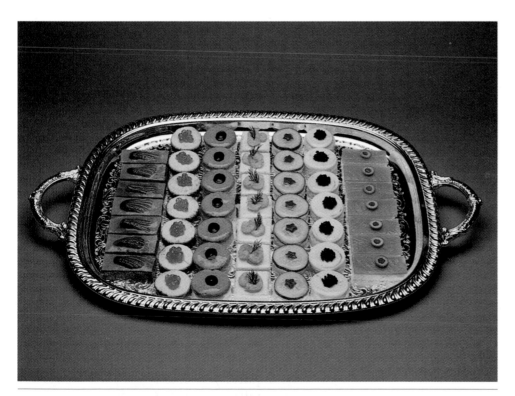

FIGURE 20.6   **Assorted canapés, from left: Row 1: mustard butter, ham, sour pickle. Row 2: lemon butter, salmon caviar. Row 3: chive butter, liver pâté, black olive. Row 4: lemon butter, shrimp, fresh dill. Row 5: curry butter, cucumber, pimiento. Row 6: shallot butter, hard-cooked egg slice, caviar. Row 7: chive cream cheese, smoked salmon, stuffed olive slice.**

with a tart or tangy sauce. Such cocktails are always served well chilled, often on a bed of crushed ice.

Oysters and clams on the half-shell are popular seafood cocktails, as are shrimp, crabmeat, lobster, and firm, flaked white fish with an appropriate sauce. Recipes for a standard tomato-based cocktail sauce and for a lighter sauce called Mignonette are included in Chapter 8.

Fresh oysters and clams on the half-shell should be opened just before they are served (see pp. 336–338) and arranged on flat plates, preferably on a bed of ice. Provide cocktail sauce in a small cup in the center or at the side of the plate. Lemon wedges should also be provided.

Cocktails of shrimp and other cooked seafood are generally served in a stemmed glass or in a small, cup-shaped bowl, which may be nestled in a bed of ice. The cocktail sauce may be put in the glass first and the seafood then arranged on top, partially immersed. Or the cocktail sauce may be added to the seafood as a topping. A third alternative is to serve the sauce separately in a small cup, as for raw oysters. Garnish the dish attractively with lettuce or other salad greens and with lemon wedges.

Fruit cups served as cocktails should be pleasantly tart and not too sweet. Many fruit salads (see Chapter 19) may be served as cocktails. Adding fresh lemon or lime juice to fruit mixtures or serving with a garnish of lemon or lime wedges will provide the necessary tartness. A simple wedge of melon with lime is a refreshing cocktail.

A few drops of a flavored liqueur can also be used to perk up the flavor of a fruit cocktail.

RELISHES

The term *relish* covers two categories of foods, raw vegetables, and pickled items.

Raw Vegetables

These are also known as *crudités* (croo-dee-tays; "cru" in French means "raw").

Any vegetable that can be eaten raw may be cut into sticks or other attractive, bite-size shapes and served as relishes. Most popular are celery, carrots, and radishes. Other good choices are green and red peppers, zucchini, cucumber, scallions, cauliflower and broccoli florets, peeled broccoli stems, peeled kohlrabi, cherry tomatoes, and Belgian endive leaves. Crudités are often served with an appropriate dip (see the next section).

Raw vegetables must be served crisp and well chilled, just as in salads. Use the freshest, most attractive vegetables possible. If they are a little wilted, they can be recrisped by holding them for a short time in ice water. Serving vegetables embedded in crushed ice will maintain their crispness.

An imaginative pantry chef can make an attractive, colorful bouquet of raw vegetables.

Pickled Items

A wide variety of items such as dilled cucumber pickles, gherkins, olives, watermelon pickles, pickled peppers, spiced beets, and other preserved vegetables and fruits are served as relishes. These items are rarely made in-house but are purchased already prepared. Like raw vegetables, they should be served chilled.

DIPS

Savory dips are popular accompaniments to potato chips, crackers, and raw vegetables.

Proper consistency is important for any dip you prepare. It must not be so thick that it cannot be scooped up without breaking the chip or cracker, but it must be thick enough to stick to the items used as dippers. Proper consistency means thickness at *serving temperature*. Most dips become thicker when held in the refrigerator.

Many mixtures used as spreads (see Canapés) can also be used as dips. Thin or soften them by adding a little mayonnaise, cream, or other appropriate liquid.

The recipes here are examples of typical dips. Salsa Cruda (p. 627) is also popular as a dip.

RECIPE 256   **Blue Cheese Dip**

Yield: 1 qt (1 L)

U.S.	Metric	Ingredients	Procedure
12 oz	375 g	Cream cheese	1. In a mixer with the paddle attachment, beat the cream cheese at low speed until soft and smooth.
5 oz	150 mL	Milk	
6 oz	175 g	Mayonnaise	
1 oz	30 mL	Lemon juice	2. With the machine running, slowly beat in the milk.
1 oz	30 g	Onion, minced	
½ tsp	2 mL	Hot red pepper sauce	3. Add the rest of the ingredients and blend in well.
½ tsp	2 mL	Worcestershire sauce	4. Taste and adjust seasonings. Chill.
10 oz	300 g	Blue cheese, crumbled	

Variations

256A. *Cheddar Cheese Dip:* Substitute grated sharp cheddar cheese for the blue cheese. If desired, add chopped chives.

256B. *Garlic Cheese Dip:* Add mashed garlic to taste to Cheddar Cheese Dip.

256C. *Bacon Cheese Dip:* Add crumbled crisp bacon to Cheddar Cheese Dip.

256D. *Cheese and Chili Dip:* Flavor Cheddar Cheese Dip with canned green chilies, chopped.

RECIPE 257   **Hummus (Chickpea Dip)**

Yield: 1 qt (1 L)

U.S.	Metric	Ingredients	Procedure
1 lb	500 g	Cooked or canned chickpeas, drained	1. Purée the chickpeas with the tahini, garlic, lemon juice, and olive oil.
8 oz	250 g	Tahini (sesame paste)	2. If necessary, thin out the purée with a little water or with additional lemon juice, depending on the taste.
¼ oz	8 g	Garlic, crushed	
4 oz	125 mL	Lemon juice	
1 oz	30 mL	Olive oil	3. Season with salt to taste and with cayenne.
		Salt	4. Chill for at least an hour to allow the flavors time to blend.
pinch	pinch	Cayenne	
1–2 oz	30–50 mL	Olive oil	5. Spoon the hummus into serving bowls. Drizzle additional olive oil over each bowl before serving.

Variation

257A. *Babaganouj:* Substitute eggplant purée for the chickpeas. Make the eggplant purée as follows. Toast whole eggplants under a broiler, over a gas burner, or directly on a flattop range until the skin is charred and the eggplant is soft. Peel off the charred skin under running water and cut off the tops. Remove large clumps of seeds if desired. Let stand in a china cap or sieve to let excess moisture drain, then purée the pulp. Reduce the lemon juice to 2–3 oz (60–90 mL) and the tahini to 4 oz (125 g). Double the olive oil.

RECIPE 258   **Spiced Clam Dip**

Yield: 1 qt (1 L)

U.S.	Metric	Ingredients	Procedure
1 lb 4 oz	625 g	Cream cheese	1. Using a mixer with a paddle attachment, soften the cream cheese at low speed.
3 oz	100 mL	Milk or clam juice	
2 oz	60 g	Dijon-style mustard	2. Slowly blend in the milk or clam juice and the mustard.
1 oz	30 mL	Worcestershire sauce	
1 tsp	5 mL	Horseradish	3. Add the Worcestershire sauce, horseradish, onion, and hot pepper sauce. Mix in well.
1½ oz	45 g	Grated onion	
½ tsp	2 mL	Hot pepper sauce	4. Mix in the clams.
12 oz	375 g	Canned, minced clams, drained	5. Season to taste with salt and white pepper.
		Salt	6. Chill until serving time.
		White pepper	

Variations

258A. *Shrimp Dip:* Use chopped, cooked shrimp instead of clams. Omit the milk or clam juice, mustard, and Worcestershire sauce. Use chili sauce to thin the mixture, or use part chili sauce and part mayonnaise or sour cream.

258B. *Tuna Dip:* Use canned tuna instead of clams. Omit the milk or clam juice, and use only half the mustard and Worcestershire sauce. Use mayonnaise or sour cream to thin out the mixture.

RECIPE 259   **Guacamole**

Yield: approx. 1 qt (1 L)

U.S.	Metric	Ingredients	Procedure
4	4	Medium-sized ripe avocados	1. Pit and peel the avocados. Mash the pulp coarsely. It should not be a smooth purée but should be slightly lumpy.
2 oz	60 g	Onion, grated	
1	1	Small, hot, green chili, such as jalapeño, minced	2. Mix in the onion, minced chili, lime or lemon juice, olive oil, and salt to taste.
1 oz	30 mL	Lime or lemon juice	3. If desired, peel, seed and dice the tomato and mix it into the avocado.
1 oz	30 mL	Olive oil	
		Salt	4. Cover tightly with plastic wrap placed on the surface of the guacamole. This is to protect it from air, which will darken it. For the same reason, guacamole should not be made too long before serving time. Chill the guacamole until ready to serve.
12 oz	375 g	Fresh tomato (optional)	

Note: If fresh chilies are not available, used canned chilies or a few dashes of hot red pepper sauce.

Variation

259A. *Sour Cream Avocado Dip:* Use 1 oz (30 g) onion. Omit the olive oil and tomato. Mash the avocado to a smooth purée. Add ½–¾ pt (250–375 mL) sour cream.

MISCELLANEOUS HORS D'OEUVRES

A great variety of other foods, both hot and cold, can be served as hors d'oeuvres. If they are to be served away from the dinner table, it is best if one is able to eat them with the fingers or to spear them with a pick. At a cocktail reception at which many hors d'oeuvres are served, it is all right if a few of them must be eaten with forks from small plates, but finger food is much easier for the guests, who are likely to be standing and holding a wine glass or cocktail glass while eating.

Of course, there are many thousands of hors d'oeuvre recipes, including many that have been adapted from the cuisines of other lands. Those included here are a sampling of some popular types.

Many of the recipes given elsewhere in this book can be adapted as hors d'oeuvre recipes. In most cases, unit size or portion size should be decreased. For example, meatballs should be made small enough to be eaten in one or two bites. Among the items most readily adapted are the following (check the Index or Recipe Table of Contents for page numbers):

Barbecued Spareribs

Shish Kebab

Deep-Fried Chicken (using wing sections)

Baked Clams Oreganata

Broiled Shrimp, Scampi Style

Broiled Scallops

Fried Breaded Scallops, Shrimp, Oysters, or Clams

Steamed Mussels (served on the half-shell, with a sauce)

Cod Cakes or other fish cakes

Vegetable Fritters

Many salads

Quiche

Cheese Wafers and Straws

Italian cuisine is particularly rich in hors d'oeuvres, or *antipasti*, as they are called (singular form: *antipasto*). Many books give a recipe for a mixed salad called antipasto. This is misleading, however, because the Italian term does not refer to a specific recipe but to any typically Italian hors d'oeuvre, hot or cold.

Many menus of Italian-style restaurants in America offer a cold antipasto plate or platter, comprising an assortment of flavorful tidbits. Typical components include the following:

Cured meats, such as salami, prosciutto, bologna, or boiled ham.

Seafood items, especially canned or preserved items such as sardines, anchovies, and tuna.

Cheese such as provolone and mozzarella.

Hard-cooked eggs and stuffed eggs.

Relishes such as raw carrots, celery, fennel, radishes, cauliflower, and tomatoes, and cooked or pickled items such as olives, artichoke hearts, small hot peppers, and onions.

Mushrooms and other vegetables prepared à la grecque. (p. 496)

Cooked dried beans and other firm vegetables in a piquant vinaigrette.

RECIPE 260   **Cheese Nachos**

Yield: 100 pieces

U.S.	Metric	Ingredients	Procedure
6 oz	175 g	Canned green chili peppers, drained	1. Chop the chilies.
1 lb 4 oz	600 g	Monterey jack or cheddar cheese	2. Grate the cheese.
100	100	Tortilla chips	3. Arrange the chips on sheet pans. Sprinkle with the cheese and the chilies.
			4. Broil until the cheese is melted. Serve warm.

RECIPE 261   **Spinach Boreks**

Yield: 50 pieces

U.S.	Metric	Ingredients	Procedure
2 lb	900 g	Spinach	1. Trim, wash, and steam or boil the spinach just until it is thoroughly wilted.
			2. Drain, cool under cold running water, and squeeze dry. Chop fine.
4 oz	100 g	Butter	3. Heat the butter in a sauté pan. Sauté the onions and scallions over low heat until soft.
4 oz	100 g	Onion, chopped fine	
1 oz	30 g	Scallions, chopped fine	4. Remove from the heat and add the spinach and dill. Mix to coat the spinach lightly with butter.
1 oz	30 g	Fresh dill, chopped	5. Mix in the cheese.
1 lb	450 g	Feta cheese, crumbled	6. Season to taste with salt and pepper.
		Salt	
		Pepper	
25 sheets	25 sheets	Phyllo dough (about 1 lb or 450 g)	7. Thaw the phyllo if it is frozen. Unwrap and unfold the stack of sheets and cut them in half lengthwise. Keep them covered to prevent drying.
approx. 8 oz	approx. 225 g	Melted butter	8. Taking one sheet at a time, brush it lightly with melted butter. Fold it in half lengthwise and butter it again.
			9. Put a small mound (about ½–⅔ oz or 15–20 g) of the spinach mixture toward the bottom of the strip and a little to one side, as shown in Figure 20.7.
			10. Fold up into triangular packets as indicated in the illustration.
			11. Arrange the triangles on baking sheets with the loose ends of the phyllo on the bottom. Brush the tops with melted butter.
			12. Bake at 375°F (190°C) until golden brown and crisp, about 20–25 minutes.
			13. Serve warm.

Variations

Many other fillings can be baked wrapped in phyllo, as long as they are not too juicy. The following are some suggestions:

Diced ham, cheddar cheese, and prepared mustard.

Gruyère cheese, blue cheese, walnuts.

Feta and cream cheese (2 parts feta to 1 part cream cheese) mixed together, plus 1 egg yolk per 12 oz (350 g) cheese.

Sautéed mushrooms and onions, crumbled bacon, parsley, parmesan cheese.

Diced cooked chicken, mozzarella cheese, sun-dried tomatoes, basil.

Crabmeat, sautéed shellfish, cream cheese, hot pepper sauce.

Ratatouille (p. 419).

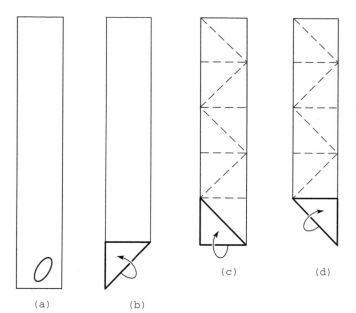

FIGURE 20.7 **Folding phyllo dough triangles.**
(a) Place the filling at the bottom of the strip of buttered phyllo dough and a little to one side.
(b) Fold the bottom corner over at a 45-degree angle to form a triangle.
(c–d) Continue folding the triangle as shown in the diagram.

RECIPE 262 **Rumaki**

Yield: 60 pieces

U.S.	Metric	Ingredients	Procedure
15	15	Chicken livers	1. Trim the chicken livers and cut them into quarters.
8 oz	250 mL	Soy sauce	
1	1	Garlic clove, cut in half	2. Marinate them overnight with the soy sauce, garlic, and ginger.
3 slices	3 slices	Fresh ginger root (optional)	
15 (approx.)	15 (approx.)	Water chestnuts	3. Cut each water chestnut into 3–5 pieces, so that you have the same number as liver pieces.
30 strips	30 strips	Bacon	4. Cut each slice of bacon in half.
			5. Wrap each liver piece together with a water chestnut piece in a piece of bacon and secure with a pick.
			6. Bake at 400°F (200°C) until the bacon is cooked, about 15 minutes. Brush with the marinade 2 or 3 times during baking.

RECIPE 263 **Deviled Eggs**

Yield: 50 pieces

U.S.	Metric	Ingredients	Procedure
25	25	Hard-cooked eggs	1. Halve the eggs lengthwise and remove the yolks.
½ pt	250 mL	Mayonnaise	
1 oz	30 mL	Lemon juice or vinegar	2. Mash the yolks or force them through a sieve.
1 tsp	5 mL	Dry mustard	3. Add the remaining ingredients (except the garnish) and mix to a smooth paste.
1 tsp	5 mL	Worcestershire sauce	
		Salt	
		White pepper	4. Using a pastry bag with a star tip, fill the egg white halves.
		Cayenne	
		Assorted garnish, such as:	5. Using a variety of garnishes, decorate the top of each egg.
		chopped parsley	
		tiny dill sprigs	
		capers	
		diced pimiento	
		sliced stuffed olives	
		paprika	
		red or black caviar	

Variations

Vary the flavor of stuffed eggs by adding any of the following ingredients to the egg yolk mixture in the basic recipe.

Anchovy: 2–3 oz (60–90 g) anchovy paste.

Curried: 2 tbsp (30 mL) curry powder, heated very gently with a little oil and cooled.

Blue cheese: 6 oz (175 g) mashed blue cheese.

Parmesan: 3 oz (90 g) grated parmesan cheese.

Tarragon: use tarragon vinegar in the filling and add 2 tsp (10 mL) tarragon.

Tuna: 6 oz (175 g) well-mashed, drained tuna.

RECIPE 264 **Sausage Puffs**

Yield: as desired

U.S.	Metric	Ingredients	Procedure
as needed	as needed	Pepperoni or other spicy sausage	1. Slice the sausage about ⅛ inch (3 mm) thick. Depending on the size of the sausage, cut the slices into quarters or squares, no more than ½–¾ inch (12–15 mm) across.
as needed	as needed	Puff paste (p. 757)	
as needed	as needed	Egg wash	
			2. Roll out puff paste into two sheets, each about ⅛ inch (3 mm) thick.
			3. Arrange rows of sausage checkerboard-fashion on one of the sheets, using two slices in each stack. Leave about 1 inch (2.5 cm) between rows.
			4. Lightly brush between rows with egg wash or water to moisten the dough slightly.
			5. Place the second sheet of puff paste on top and carefully press down between the rows of sausage to seal the two sheets of dough together.
			6. Brush the top with egg wash.
			7. With a wheel knife, cut the sausage-filled pieces apart between the rows. Prick the tops lightly so that steam can escape.
			8. Chill for at least one hour.
			9. Bake at 400°F (200°C) until puffed and brown.
			10. Serve warm. The puffs can be reheated by placing them in a moderate oven, uncovered.

Variations

Other hors d'oeuvres can be made with puff paste, either by substituting other fillings for the sausage, or by using other methods such as the following:

Cut small circles from a sheet of puff paste about ¼ inch (½ cm) thick. Egg wash the tops and bake. Split horizontally and fill with desired spread or filling.

Cheese allumettes: Cut a sheet of puff paste into strips about 3 inches (7 cm) long and ½ inch (1 cm) wide. Egg wash and sprinkle generously with grated parmesan cheese. Bake.

Anchovy allumettes: These are filled puffs made by the same general method as used for the sausage puffs, except that anchovy paste is used as the filling. It is piped onto the bottom sheet in thin stripes, and the filled paste is cut into strips like cheese allumettes.

RECIPE 265   **Miniature Gougère Puffs**

Yield: about 160 pieces

U.S.	Metric	Ingredients	Procedure
2½ lb	1.1 kg	Eclair paste (p. 763)	1. Mix together the eclair paste and the cheese.
8 oz	225 g	Gruyère cheese, grated	2. Using a pastry bag with a small, plain tip, pipe small mounds of about a tablespoon each onto sheet pans lined with parchment. See page 763 for guidelines on making tiny cream puff shells or profiteroles, which is essentially what these are.
		Egg wash	
			3. Bake at 400°F (200°C) until puffed and brown, about 20–30 minutes.
			4. Make a little slit in side of each to allow steam to escape. Put the puffs in a warm oven until they are dry.
			5. Serve warm or at room temperature.

RECIPE 266   **Chicken Liver Pâté**

Yield: 2½ lb (1.2 kg)

U.S.	Metric	Ingredients	Procedure
2 lb	1 kg	Chicken livers	1. Trim fat and sinews from the livers.
		Salt	2. Sprinkle them lightly with salt. Add milk to cover and let stand overnight, refrigerated. This step is optional, but it results in a slightly milder flavor and lighter color.
		Milk	
4 oz	125 g	Onion, chopped	3. Sauté the onion lightly in the butter until tender but not brown.
3 oz	90 g	Butter	
½ tsp	2 mL	Oregano	4. Add the livers (drained and rinsed), herbs, and spices. Brown the livers lightly and cook them until they are still slightly pink in the center. Remove from the heat and cool.
¼ tsp	1 mL	White pepper	
pinch	pinch	Nutmeg	
pinch	pinch	Ginger	
pinch	pinch	Ground cloves	
1 tsp	5 mL	Salt	
12 oz	375 g	Cream cheese	5. Grind the livers and onions in a grinder or buffalo chopper.
1–2 oz	30–60 mL	Brandy, madeira, or port (optional)	6. Add cream cheese and continue to process to obtain a uniformly mixed paste.
		Salt	7. Add brandy or wine to taste. Add additional salt if necessary.
			8. Pack the mixture into containers and chill overnight.

RECIPE 267   **Prosciutto and Melon Balls**

Yield: as desired

U.S.	Metric	Ingredients	Procedure
		Melon (canteloupe, honeydew, crenshaw, etc.) Lime juice Prosciutto ham	1. Using a ball cutter, cut melon into small balls. 2. Sprinkle the melon balls with lime juice and let stand 10 minutes. 3. Using a slicing machine, cut ham into paper-thin slices. Cut large slices in half crosswise. 4. Shortly before serving, wrap each melon ball in a slice of ham and fasten with a pick.

Variations

Other fruits may be substituted for the melon, such as pineapple sticks or chunks, fresh figs (whole, halves, or quartered), fresh pear or peach slices. Pears and peaches must be coated with lime or lemon juice to prevent darkening.

RECIPE 268   **Mushrooms Stuffed with Tapenade**

Yield: 50 pieces

U.S.	Metric	Ingredients	Procedure
8 oz	250 g	Pitted Mediterranean or Greek black olives	1. In a blender or food processor, purée the olives, capers, anchovies, tuna, mustard, oil, lemon juice, and herbs.
1 oz	30 g	Capers, drained	2. Chill the mixture several hours to let the flavors blend.
1 oz	30 g	Anchovies, drained	
1 oz	30 g	Tuna, drained	
1 tsp	5 mL	Dijon-style mustard	
2½ oz	75 mL	Olive oil	
1 tsp	5 mL	Lemon juice	
2 tbsp	30 mL	Chopped parsley	
pinch	pinch	Thyme	
		Salt	
		Pepper	
50	50	Small to medium fresh white mushrooms Pimiento	3. Remove the stems from the mushrooms and clean the caps. 4. Fill each cap with a small spoonful of the tapenade. 5. Garnish the top of each with a dot of pimiento.

RECIPE 269 **Spiced Shrimp**

Yield: 3–3½ lb (1.4–1.6 kg)

U.S.	Metric	Ingredients	Procedure
5 lb	2.3 kg	Peeled, deveined shrimp, any size	1. Combine all ingredients in a stainless steel saucepan. Add just enough water to barely cover the shrimp.
8 oz	250 mL	Lemon juice or white wine vinegar	
2 oz	60 mL	Olive oil	2. Bring to a boil, then reduce heat to a slow simmer. Cook shrimp slowly, about 1 to 2 minutes, until just barely cooked. Cooking time depends on the size of the shrimp. They will cook further in the hot liquid as they cool.
1 tbsp	15 mL	Peppercorns, crushed	
2–4 cloves	2–4 cloves	Garlic, crushed	
4 oz	125 g	Onion, sliced	
3	3	Bay leaves	
1½ tsp	7 mL	Cayenne	3. Let shrimp cool in the liquid.
2 oz	60 g	Salt	
		Water	
3 pt	1.5 L	Italian Dressing or Piquante Dressing (see p. 519)	4. Drain well and add the dressing. Marinate overnight.
			5. Drain well just before serving. These can be served as is or with an appropriate dip, such as herbed mayonnaise, cocktail sauce, or guacamole.

TERMS FOR REVIEW

pullman loaf	open-faced sandwich	tea sandwich	cocktail
simple sandwich	(hot or cold)	hors d'oeuvre	crudité
(hot or cold)	club sandwich	canapé	dip
			antipasto

QUESTIONS FOR DISCUSSION

1. If you cannot get daily bread delivery, what are some other measures you can take to ensure that the bread in the sandwiches you serve is always fresh?

2. What precautions must you take when using mayonnaise as a sandwich spread?

3. Briefly describe the setup of a short-order sandwich station.

4. How does a setup for preparing sandwiches in quantity differ from a short-order sandwich setup?

5. Why are most sandwiches cut before serving?

6. How can you avoid soggy canapé bases?

7. In order to use a ham salad recipe to make a ham spread, you may need to change the recipe slightly. What are three modifications that you may need to make?

8. What is the difference between a fruit salad and a fruit cocktail?

9. What is the proper consistency or thickness for a dip?

CHAPTER 21

BREAKFAST PREPARATION, DAIRY PRODUCTS, AND COFFEE AND TEA

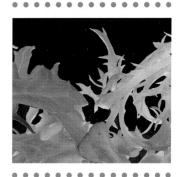

When we speak of breakfast cookery, we are not just talking about a particular meal. We are referring to a particular small group of foods that appears on perhaps every breakfast menu in America. These items not only appear on breakfast menus, but are popular for brunches, snacks, and late suppers. Many establishments offer a breakfast menu all day long.

Eggs, of course, are the most popular breakfast food and are the primary subject of this chapter. In addition, this chapter examines the preparation of other breakfast staples: pancakes, waffles, French toast, and breakfast meats. We then turn our attention to dairy products in general, specifically milk, cream, butter, and cheese. Finally, we study the preparation of two items essential not only at breakfast but at every meal: coffee and tea.

After reading this chapter, you should be able to

1. Describe the composition of eggs and the major differences among grades.

2. Store eggs properly.

3. Prepare the following egg items: hard-, medium-, and soft-cooked eggs; poached eggs; fried eggs; shirred eggs; scrambled eggs; omelets; entrée soufflés; and savory custards.

4. Prepare pancakes, waffles, and French toast.

5. Prepare cooked breakfast cereals.

6. Prepare breakfast meats.

7. Describe the major milk, cream, and butter products.

8. Heat and cook with milk without curdling or scorching.

9. Whip cream.

10. Describe the most important kinds of cheese used in American kitchens.

11. Store and serve cheese properly.

12. Cook with cheese.

13. Prepare coffee and tea.

EGGS

Contrary to popular opinion, there is no law that says one must have eggs or cereal or pancakes or pastries for breakfast and *must* not have shrimp curry or chili or spaghetti and meatballs. Although most Americans would think these last suggestions rather strange for the morning meal, there is probably no food that someone, somewhere, does not enjoy for breakfast. No doubt many Japanese, who have soy bean soup and sour pickles for their first meal of the day, think our breakfast habits are strange.

However, the egg remains America's favorite breakfast food, even as we become more adventurous and explore ethnic cuisines. For such apparently simple items, eggs are used in many ways in the kitchen and require special study. We will examine not only the usual breakfast preparation, but other egg items as well, such as soufflés and custards.

. . . .

UNDERSTANDING EGGS

Composition

A whole egg consists primarily of yolk, a white, and a shell. In addition, it contains a membrane that lines the shell and forms an air cell at the large end, and two white strands called chalazae that hold the yolk centered. Figure 21.1 is a cross-sectional diagram that shows the location of these features.

1. The yolk is high in both fat and protein, and it contains iron and several vitamins.

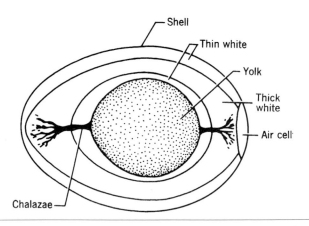

FIGURE 21.1 **The parts of an egg. The diagram shows, in simplified form, the location of the parts of an unbroken egg, as described in the text.**

Its color ranges from light to dark yellow, depending on the diet of the chicken.

2. The white is primarily albumin protein, which is clear and soluble when raw, but white and firm when coagulated. The white also contains sulfur.

    There are two parts to the white: a thick white that surrounds the yolk, and a thinner, more liquid part on the outside of this.

3. The egg shell is not the perfect package, in spite of what you may have heard. Not only is it fragile, but it is very porous, allowing odors and flavors to be absorbed by the egg, and allowing the egg to lose moisture even if unbroken.

Grades and Quality

1. *Grades.*

    Eggs are graded for quality by the U.S. Department of Agriculture. There are three grades: AA, A, and B.

    The best grade has a firm yolk and white that stand up high when broken onto a flat surface and do not spread over a large area. In the shell, the yolk is well centered, and the air sac is small.

    As eggs age, they lose density. The thin part of the white becomes larger, and the egg spreads over a larger area when broken. Also, the air sac becomes larger as the egg loses moisture through the shell. Figure 21.2 shows the difference among grades AA, A, and B.

2. *Maintaining quality.*

    Proper storage is essential for maintaining quality. Eggs keep for weeks if held at 36°F (2°C) but lose quality quickly if held at room temperature. In fact, they can lose a full grade in one day at warm kitchen temperatures. There's no point in paying for Grade AA eggs if they are Grade B by the time you use them.

    Store eggs away from other foods that might pass on undesirable flavors or odors.

3. *Grades and use.*

    One glance at Figure 21.2 will show you why Grade AA is the best to use for fried or poached eggs. Lower grades spread out too much to produce a quality product.

    For hard-cooked eggs, use either Grade A eggs or Grade AA that have been held a few days in the refrigerator. Very fresh eggs are difficult to peel when cooked in the shell.

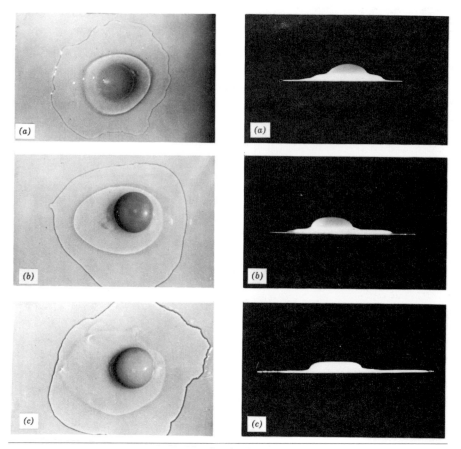

FIGURE 21.2   **(a) Grade AA, (b) Grade A, and (c) Grade B eggs, as seen from the top and side. Note how the white and yolk lose thickness and spread out more in the lower grades.**

Grade B eggs are suitable for use in baking. If you are certain they have developed no strong flavors, they may be used for scrambled eggs, where the firmness of the whole egg is less important.

Size

Eggs are also graded by size. Table 21.1 gives the minimum weight per dozen (including shell), according to size category. Note that each size differs from the next by 3 ounces.

Most food service operations use large eggs, and recipes are based on this size.

Market Forms

1. *Fresh eggs or shell eggs.*

   These are most often used for breakfast cookery and are the main subject of this section.

2. *Frozen eggs.*
   a. Whole egg
   b. Whites
   c. Yolks
   d. Whole eggs with extra yolks

TABLE 21.1   **Egg Size Classifications**

	Minimum Weight per Dozen	
Size	*U.S.*	*Metric*
Jumbo	30 oz	850 g
Extra large	27 oz	765 g
Large	24 oz	680 g
Medium	21 oz	595 g
Small	18 oz	510 g
Peewee	15 oz	425 g

Frozen eggs are usually made from high-quality fresh eggs and are excellent for use in scrambled eggs, omelets, French toast, and in baking. They are pasteurized and are usually purchased in 30-lb cans. These take at least 2 days to thaw at refrigerator temperatures.

3. **Dried eggs.**

   a. Whole
   b. Yolks
   c. Whites

Dried eggs are used primarily for baking. They are not suggested for use in breakfast cookery.

Unlike most dehydrated products, dried eggs are not shelf stable and must be kept refrigerated or frozen, tightly sealed.

General Cooking Principles

The most important rule of egg cookery is a very simple one: *avoid high temperatures and long cooking times.* In other words, do not overcook. This should be a familiar rule by now.

Overcooking produces tough eggs, causes discoloration, and affects flavor.

Coagulation

Eggs are largely protein, so the principle of coagulation (p. 52) is important to consider.

Eggs coagulate at the following temperatures:

Whole eggs, beaten	about 156°F/69°C
White	140 to 149°F/60 to 65°C
Yolks	144 to 158°F/62 to 70°C
Custard (whole eggs plus liquid)	175 to 185°F/79 to 85°C

Note that whites coagulate or cook before yolks do. This is why it is possible to cook eggs with firm whites but soft yolks.

Note also that when eggs are mixed with a liquid, they become firm at a higher temperature. However, 185°F is still much lower than the temperature of a sauté pan or skillet over high heat. As the temperature of coagulation is reached, the eggs change from semiliquid to solid, and they become opaque. If their temperature continues to rise, they become even firmer. *An overcooked egg is tough and rubbery.* Low temperatures produce the best-cooked eggs.

If egg–liquid mixtures such as custards and scrambled eggs are overcooked, the egg solids separate from the liquids, or *curdle.* This is often seen in tough, watery scrambled eggs.

Sulfur

The familiar green ring that you have often seen in hard-cooked eggs is caused by cooking at high temperatures or cooking too long.

The same green color appears in scrambled eggs that are overcooked or held too long in the steam table.

This is caused when the sulfur in the egg whites reacts with the iron in the yolk to form iron sulfide, a compound that has a green color and a strong odor and flavor.

The best way to avoid green eggs is to use *low temperatures and short cooking and holding times.*

Foams

Beaten egg whites are used to give lightness and rising power to soufflés, puffy omelets, cakes, some pancakes and waffles, and a number of other products. The following guidelines will help you handle beaten egg whites properly.

1. **Fat inhibits foaming.**

   When separating eggs, be careful not to get any yolk in the whites. Yolks contain fats. Use very clean equipment when beating whites.

2. **Mild acids help foaming.**

   A small amount of lemon juice or cream of tartar gives more volume and stability to beaten egg whites. Use about 2 tsp cream of tartar per pound of egg whites (20 mL per kg).

3. **Egg whites foam better at room temperature.**

   Remove them from the cooler an hour before beating.

4. **Do not overbeat.**

   Beaten egg whites should look moist and shiny. Overbeaten eggs look dry and curdled, and have lost much of their ability to raise soufflés and cakes.

5. **Sugar makes foams more stable.**

   When making sweet puffed omelets and dessert soufflés, add some of the sugar to the partially beaten whites and continue to beat to proper stiffness. (This will take longer than when no sugar is added.) The soufflé will be more stable before and after baking.

COOKING EGGS

Simmering in the Shell

The term "hard-boiled egg" is not a good one to use, since eggs should be simmered instead of boiled.

Eggs may be simmered to the soft-, medium-, or hard-cooked stage by simmering in water, according to the following methods.

Procedures for Simmering Eggs in the Shell

Method 1

1. Collect equipment and food items.

2. Bring eggs to room temperature by (a) removing them from cooler 1 hour before cooking, or (b) placing them in warm water for 5 minutes and draining. Cold eggs are more likely to crack when placed in boiling water.

3. Place eggs in boiling water and return the water to a simmer.

4. Simmer, do not boil, for required time:

Soft cooked	3 to 4 minutes
Medium cooked	5 to 7 minutes
Hard cooked	12 to 15 minutes

   Exact cooking time depends on temperature of eggs, size of eggs, and amount of water used.

5. Drain immediately and cool under cold running water to stop the cooking. Cool just a few seconds if eggs are to be served hot. Cool further if they are to be held for later use.

6. To peel, crack shell and pull away shell, starting at large end (where air sac is located). For easier peeling, peel while still warm, and hold under running water to help loosen shell. Very fresh eggs are hard to peel. Eggs for cooking in shell should be several days old.

Method 2

1. Collect equipment and food items.

2. Place eggs in saucepan and cover with cold water.

3. Bring water to a boil.

4. Reduce heat and simmer for required time:

Soft cooked	1 minute
Medium cooked	3 to 5 minutes
Hard cooked	10 minutes

Method 3, for Hard-cooked Eggs Only

Proceed as in Method 2, but remove pan from heat and cover as soon as it comes to a boil. Let stand off heat for 20 minutes.

Standards of Quality for Hard-cooked Eggs

1. Evenly coagulated whites and yolks.

2. Whites glossy and firm but tender, not tough or rubbery.

3. No dark color on outside of yolk.

4. Pleasing flavor.

Poaching

The principles of cooking eggs in the shell are applicable to poached eggs. The only difference between the two items is the shell.

This difference, of course, adds some complications to the cooking process, as emphasized in the following procedure. The object is to keep the eggs egg-shaped, in a round, compact mass rather than spread out all over the pan.

Procedure for Poaching Eggs

1. Collect equipment and food items.

2. Use the freshest Grade AA eggs, whenever possible, for best results. These maintain their shape best because yolks and whites are firm.

3. If eggs are not very fresh, add 1 tsp salt and 2 tsp distilled vinegar per quart of water (5 mL salt, 10 mL vinegar per liter).

   The vinegar helps coagulate the egg white faster, so that it will keep a better shape.

   Vinegar is not necessary if very fresh eggs are used. Omit in this case, because whites will be tougher and not as shiny if cooked with vinegar.

4. Bring water to a simmer.

   If water is boiling, eggs will toughen and may be broken up by the agitation.

   If water is not hot enough, eggs will not cook quickly enough and will spread.

5. Break eggs one at a time into a dish or a small plate and slide into the simmering water. Eggs will hold shape better if they slide in against the edge of the pan.

6. Simmer 3 to 5 minutes, until whites are coagulated and yolks are still soft.

7. Remove eggs from pan with slotted spoon or skimmer.

8. To serve immediately, drain very well. For better appearance, trim off ragged edges.

9. To hold for later service, plunge immediately into cold water to stop the cooking. At service time, reheat briefly in hot water.

Standards of Quality for Poached Eggs

1. Bright, shiny appearance.

2. Compact, round shape, not spread or flattened.

3. Firm but tender whites; warm, liquid yolks.

RECIPE 270 Eggs Benedict

Yield: 1 portion (see note)

U.S.	Metric	Ingredients	Procedure
½	½	English muffin Butter	1. Toast the muffin half. Spread it with butter and place on a serving plate.
1	1	Egg, fresh Grade AA	2. Poach the egg according to the basic procedure given in this section.
1 slice	1 slice	Canadian bacon or ham, cooked (about 2 oz/60 g)	3. While the egg is poaching, heat the Canadian bacon or ham for a minute on a hot griddle or in a sauté pan. Place the meat on top of the toasted muffin.
1½ oz	50 mL	Hollandaise Sauce	4. Drain the poached egg well and place it on top of the Canadian bacon.
			5. Ladle Hollandaise Sauce over the top. Serve immediately.

Note: To prepare Eggs Benedict in quantity, the eggs may be poached ahead of time, cooled in cold water, and refrigerated. At service time, reheat the eggs in simmering water for 30 to 60 seconds. Drain, plate, and serve.

Variations

270A. Eggs Florentine: Instead of the muffin and bacon, place the egg on a bed of hot, buttered, cooked spinach (about 2 oz/60 g). Cover with Mornay Sauce instead of Hollandaise. Optional: Sprinkle with parmesan cheese and brown under the salamander or broiler.

270B. Eggs Bombay: Instead of the muffin and bacon, place the egg on a bed of hot rice pilaf (about 2 oz/60 g). Cover with Curry Sauce instead of Hollandaise.

Frying

Fried eggs are the most popular breakfast preparation in this country. They should always be cooked to order and served immediately. For best quality, observe each step in the following procedure.

Choice of cooking fat is a matter of taste and budget. Butter has the best flavor, but margarine or oil may be used. Use bacon fat only if that flavor is desired by customer.

Procedure for Frying Eggs to Order

1. Collect all equipment and food items.

   Eggs may be fried in small, individual sauté pans (omelet pans) or on the griddle. Griddled eggs are not as attractive, since they tend to spread more. See page 559 for procedure for conditioning sauté pans to avoid sticking.

2. Select very fresh Grade AA eggs for best results.

3. Add about ⅛ inch of fat to the sauté pan and set it over moderate heat or preheat griddle to 325°F (165°C) and ladle on a small quantity of fat. Too much fat will make the eggs greasy. Not enough will cause them to stick, unless a pan with a no-stick coating is used.

4. Break the eggs into a dish. This lessens the chance of breaking the yolks.

5. When the fat is hot enough so that a drop of water sizzles when dropped into it, slide the eggs into the pan (or onto the griddle).

   If the fat is not hot enough, the eggs will spread too much and may stick. If it is too hot, the eggs will become tough or even crisp.

6. Reduce heat to low (if using sauté pan) and cook the eggs to order as indicated below. See Figures 21.3 and 21.4 for flipping and turning techniques.

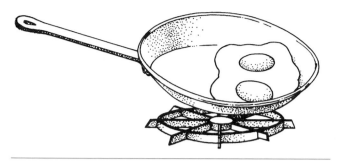

FIGURE 21.3   **Flipping eggs in a pan.**
(a) Lift the handle of the pan, and slide the eggs to the far edge with a quick jerk.

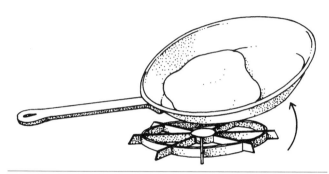

(b) With a quick flip of the wrist as shown by the arrow, turn the egg over. Do not flip the egg too hard, or the yolk may break when it lands.

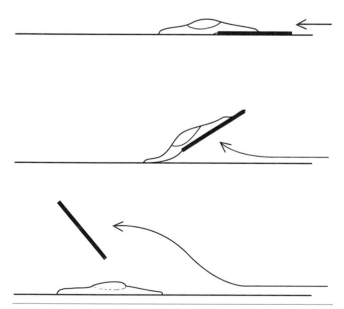

FIGURE 21.4   **When frying the eggs on a griddle, turn them with one smooth motion of the spatula, as shown. The left corner of the egg never actually leaves the surface of the griddle.**

Sunny side up.   Cook slowly without flipping until white is completely set and yolk is still soft and yellow. Heat must be low or bottom will toughen or burn before top is completely set.

Basted.   Do not flip. Add a few drops of water to pan and cover so steam cooks the top. Yolk will have a thin film of coagulated white covering it. Yolk should remain liquid. Note: This preparation is sometimes called *country style*. The term "basted" is used because the same effect may be achieved by spooning hot fat over the egg as it fries. This method may make the eggs excessively greasy, however.

Over easy.   Fry and flip over. Cook just until white is just set and yolk is still liquid.

Over medium.   Fry and flip over. Cook until yolk is partially set.

Over hard.   Fry and flip over. Cook until yolk is completely set.

Standards of Quality for Fried Eggs

1.   White should be shiny, uniformly set, and tender, not browned, blistered, or crisp at edges.

2.   Yolk should be set properly according to desired doneness. Sunny side up yolks should be yellow and well rounded. In other styles, yolk is covered with thin layer of coagulated white.

3.   Relatively compact, standing high. Not spread out and thin.

Shirred Eggs

Shirred eggs resemble fried eggs, except that they are baked in individual serving dishes rather than fried.

They may also be baked with or garnished with a variety of meats and sauces, as indicated in the variations that follow.

Procedure for Making Shirred Eggs

1.   Collect equipment and food items.

2.   Butter individual portion casseroles or baking dishes.

3.   Break eggs into dish.

4.   Set over moderate heat until the eggs begin to coagulate on the bottom.

5.   Place in oven at 350°F (175°C) and cook to desired doneness.

6.   Serve in the same dish or casserole.

Shirred Egg Variations

Any of the following may be placed in the buttered shirred egg dish *before* adding the egg:

> Ham or Canadian bacon, thin slice, lightly browned on griddle or in sauté pan
>
> Bacon, cooked crisp, 3 or 4 half strips
>
> Corned beef hash, beef hash, or ham hash
>
> Cheese, such as cheddar, Swiss, or Gruyère, grated
>
> Diced chicken in cream sauce
>
> Tomato concassée, sautéed in butter

Any of the following may be added to shirred eggs *after baking*. Place solid garnish off to one side. Spoon sauces around the outside. Do not cover the yolk:

> Heavy cream, hot
>
> Brown sauces such as Bordelaise, Madeira, or Demiglaze
>
> Tomato sauce
>
> Soubise sauce
>
> Sauted chicken livers and brown sauce
>
> Small grilled sausages
>
> Mushrooms sautéed in butter or in cream sauce
>
> Asparagus tips

Scrambled Eggs

Like other egg preparations, scrambled eggs are best if cooked to order. However, they may be made in larger quantities. They should be undercooked if they are to be held for volume service, as they will cook more in the steam table.

If scrambled eggs must be held over 30 minutes, they will be more stable if the eggs are mixed with a medium white sauce before cooking. Use about 8 oz sauce per quart of eggs (250 mL per liter).

Do not overcook scrambled eggs or hold them too long. Overcooked eggs are tough and watery, and they eventually turn green in the steam table.

Scrambled eggs should be soft and moist, unless the customer requests "scrambled hard."

Procedure for Scrambling Eggs

1. Collect equipment and food items.

2. Break eggs into a stainless steel bowl and beat until well blended. Season with salt and white pepper.

Do not use aluminum, which may discolor the eggs.

3. If desired, add a small amount of milk or cream, about 1 to 1½ tbsp (15 to 20 mL) for 2 eggs, or 8 to 12 oz per quart of eggs (250 to 375 mL per liter).

   Too much liquid may make cooked eggs watery and dilutes the flavor. Heavy cream adds richness but also adds cost.

4. Heat butter in a small sauté pan (for cooking to order) or in a large skillet, as for fried eggs.

   Note: Steam kettles or tilting skillets may be used for scrambling large quantities of eggs.

5. When fat is just hot enough to make a drop of water sizzle, pour in eggs.

6. Cook over low heat, stirring gently from time to time as the eggs coagulate. Lift portions of coagulated egg so that uncooked egg can run underneath.

   Too much stirring breaks up eggs into very small particles.

   Do not let the eggs brown. Keep heat low.

7. When eggs are set but still soft and moist, remove from heat. Turn out onto plate or into steam table pan.

Additions to Scrambled Eggs

Flavor variations may be created by adding any of the following ingredients to scrambled eggs before serving:

> Chopped parsley and/or other herbs
>
> Grated cheese (cheddar, Swiss, parmesan)
>
> Diced ham
>
> Crumbled bacon
>
> Sautéed diced onion and green pepper
>
> Diced smoked salmon
>
> Sliced cooked breakfast sausage

Omelets

Making omelets is like riding a bicycle. When you are learning, it seems very difficult, and you can't imagine how anyone can do it. But once you have mastered the technique, it seems very easy, and you don't understand how anyone could have any trouble doing it.

We are talking about the plain or French omelet. There are several kinds, as described below, but the French omelet remains the most popular. It is a technique worth mastering.

French Omelet

Omelets may be described as sophisticated scrambled eggs. The first part of the technique is similar to that for making scrambled eggs. But the similarities end there, and the omelet emerges from the pan not as a shapeless pile of curds but an attractive oval with a light, delicate texture.

Two elements are necessary for making omelets:

1. High heat. This seems like a contradiction to our basic principle of low temperature egg cookery. But the omelet cooks so fast that its internal temperature never has time to get too high.

2. A conditioned omelet pan. First, the pan must have sloping sides and be the right size, so that the omelet can be shaped properly. Second, it must be well seasoned or conditioned to avoid sticking.

Procedure for Conditioning an Omelet Pan

The following method is only one of many. Your instructor may show you another. The object is to seal the surface of the metal with a layer of baked-on oil.

1. Rub the clean pan with a thin film of vegetable oil.

2. Set the pan over moderately high heat until it is very hot.

3. Remove from heat and let cool.

4. Do not scour the pan or wash with a detergent after use. Rub with salt, which will scour the pan without harming the primed surface. Rinse only after pan has cooled, or wipe with a clean towel.

5. Reseason as often as necessary, or after each day's use.

Procedure for Making a French Omelet

(See Figure 21.5 for illustration of technique.)

1. Collect all equipment and ingredients.

2. Beat 2 or 3 eggs in a small bowl just until well mixed. Do not whip until frothy. Season with salt and pepper.

   If desired, 1 tbsp (15 mL) of water may be added to make the omelet lighter.

For extended service, a large quantity of eggs may be beaten. Each portion is then measured out with a ladle.

3. Place an omelet pan over high heat.

4. When the pan is hot, add about 1 tbsp (15 mL) clarified butter and swirl it around to coat the inside of the pan. Give it a second to get hot.

   Raw butter may be used, but great care is necessary to keep it from burning.

5. Add the eggs to the pan. They should begin to coagulate around the edges and on the bottom in a few seconds.

6. With one hand (the left, if you are right handed), vigorously shake the pan back and forth. At the same time, stir the eggs with a circular motion with the bottom side of a fork, but do not let the fork scrape the pan.

   This is the difficult part. The most common errors are not shaking and stirring vigorously enough and using too low heat. The purpose of this action is to keep the eggs in motion so that they coagulate uniformly.

7. Stop shaking and stirring when the eggs are almost set but still very moist. If you continue stirring, you will have scrambled eggs instead of an omelet.

8. Tilt the handle up and shake the pan so that the omelet slides to the opposite side of the pan and begins to climb up the opposite slope.

9. For a filled omelet, spoon the filling across the center of the egg, at right angles to the handle.

10. With the fork fold the sides of the omelet over the center. The omelet should now be resting in the corner of the pan and have an approximately oval shape.

11. Grasp the handle of the pan with your palm underneath and tilt the omelet out onto a plate, so that it inverts and keeps an oval shape.

The whole procedure should take less than a minute.

The finished omelet should be moist on the inside, tender on the outside, and yellow or only slightly browned.

Suggested Omelet Fillings

Cheese

Sautéed or creamed mushrooms

Creamed or curried chicken

Creamed or buttered spinach

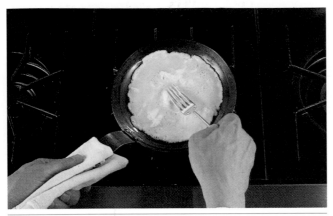

FIGURE 21.5 Making a French omelet. Read the accompanying text for a full description of the steps shown here. (a) As soon as the eggs are added to the hot pan, shake the pan back and forth with one hand, and stir the eggs in a circular motion with a fork.

(d) Fold over the side of the omelet to make an oval shape.

(b) When the eggs are almost set, tilt the pan and shake the eggs down to the opposite side of the pan. Rapping the handle sharply helps move the eggs.

(e) Grasp the handle of the pan with your palm underneath, and tilt the omelet onto a plate.

(c) Spoon the filling, if used, across the center.

(f) The finished omelet should have a neat, oval shape. Some chefs prefer omelets that are lightly browned. Others feel that they should not be browned at all.

Sautéed onions with or without bacon

Sautéed onions and diced potatoes

Seafood newburg or in a cream sauce

Red caviar

Thick Spanish sauce (p. 146)

Ratatouille (p. 419)

American-Style Omelet

This style of omelet is usually called a French omelet, but it is not a French omelet. It was probably devised by cooks who hesitated to tackle the French method.

It is made somewhat like a French omelet, except that low heat is used, and the eggs are not stirred or agitated. Instead, the edges of the cooked portion are lifted with a fork or spatula allowing the uncooked portion to flow underneath. The finished omelet may be folded in half or like a French omelet.

The advantage of this method is that it is easier to learn.

The disadvantages are that the omelet is not as light or delicate in texture, and that the method is much slower—a serious disadvantage in a busy kitchen.

Fluffy Omelet or Soufflé Omelet

These are made by beating the egg whites separately and folding them into the beaten yolks, which may have some milk added. The mixture is poured into a hot, buttered omelet pan and the omelet is finished in the oven. It is folded in half for service.

Fluffy omelets are not often made in food service because of the time they take to make.

Frittatas and Other Flat Omelets

A frittata is a flat omelet that originated in Italy. The same basic techniques are used for many popular American preparations. Flat omelets are made by mixing beaten eggs with a variety of ingredients, such as vegetables, meats, or cheese, and cooking the mixture over low heat without stirring. To finish, it is either flipped over or run under the broiler until the top is set.

A popular American frittata (actually derived from the Chinese egg foo yung) is the Western omelet, containing diced sautéed onion, green pepper, and ham.

Soufflés

Soufflés are not normally featured on breakfast menus. However, they are important basic egg preparations with which you should be familiar.

Soufflés are often considered by amateur cooks to be difficult to make. Actually, they are relatively easy preparations. Many restaurants have no difficulty turning out large numbers of soufflés to order. The only hard part is making sure the waiter picks up the order when it is ready.

A standard entrée soufflé consists of three elements:

Base—usually a heavy Béchamel Sauce.

Flavor ingredient—cheese, vegetables, seafood, etc.

Egg whites, beaten.

General Procedure for Preparing Entrée Soufflés

1. Prepare a heavy Béchamel Sauce.

2. Combine with egg yolks.

3. Prepare flavor ingredient: grate cheese, cook and chop vegetables, and so on.

4. Combine base and flavor ingredient.

5. Beat egg whites and fold in.

6. Bake in soufflé dish, which has been buttered and dusted with parmesan cheese.

7. Serve immediately.

À la Carte Service

Prepare through step 4 and hold in refrigerator.

Or, if several flavors are offered, prepare single large batch of base and keep flavor ingredients separate.

For each order, beat egg whites and combine with measured amount of base.

RECIPE 271 Cheese Soufflé

	Portions: 12		Portion size: 4 oz (125 g)

U.S.	Metric	Ingredients		Procedure
		Butter		1. Select three 1½-qt (1½-L) soufflé dishes (4 portions each) or two 2-qt (2-L) dishes (6 portions each). Butter the insides of the dishes well. Sprinkle with cheese or crumbs so that the bottom and sides are completely coated.
		Parmesan cheese or dry bread crumbs		
		Roux:		2. Make a white roux with the butter and flour. Cook the roux a few minutes.
2½ oz	75 g		Butter	
2½ oz	75 g		Flour	3. Beat in the hot milk. Bring to a boil, while stirring. Cool and stir until very thick and smooth.
1½ pt	750 mL	Milk, hot		
1½ tsp	7 mL	Salt		
1 tsp	5 mL	White pepper		4. Remove from the heat. Stir in the salt, pepper, cayenne, and nutmeg.
pinch	pinch	Cayenne		
pinch	pinch	Nutmeg		
12	12	Egg yolks		5. Add the egg yolks to the hot sauce and quickly mix in with a wire whip.
10 oz	300 g	Gruyère cheese, coarsely grated (see note)		6. Stir in the cheese.
12–15	12–15	Egg whites		7. Beat the egg whites with the salt until they form stiff peaks. (The larger number of egg whites will make a lighter soufflé.)
¼ tsp	1 mL	Salt		
				8. Fold the egg whites into the cheese mixture.
				9. Pour the mixture into the prepared soufflé dishes.
				10. Place the dishes in a preheated 375°F (190°C) oven. Bake for 40 minutes without opening the oven door. After this time, check for doneness by *very gently* shaking the dishes. If the centers are firm and do not jiggle, the soufflés are done. If necessary, bake another 5–10 minutes.
				11. Remove from oven and serve *immediately*.

RECIPE 271   **Cheese Soufflé** *(Continued)*

Note: Other cheeses may be used: sharp cheddar, Swiss, a mixture of Swiss and Gruyère, or a mixture of Swiss or Gruyère and Parmesan.

Variations

271A. À la Carte Service: Prepare the basic recipe through step 6. Chill the mixture quickly and hold in refrigerator. For each order, scale off 3½ oz (100 g) of the mixture. Beat 1 egg white and fold in. Bake in an individual soufflé dish about 20 to 30 minutes.

271B. Spinach Soufflé: Reduce cheese to 5 oz (150 g). Add 5 oz (150 g) well-drained, chopped, cooked spinach.

271C. Spinach and Ham Soufflé: Add 2 oz (60 g) ground or finely chopped ham to Spinach Soufflé.

271D. Mushroom Soufflé: Reduce cheese to 5 oz (150 g). Add 4 oz (125 g) cooked, chopped mushrooms.

271E. Other Vegetable Soufflés: Follow the procedure for Spinach Soufflé, using chopped cooked vegetables such as broccoli, asparagus, or carrots.

271F. Salmon Soufflé: Make the sauce base with milk, plus liquid from canned salmon. Add 1½ oz (45 g) tomato paste to the base. Reduce cheese to 4 oz (125 g) and add 8 oz (250 g) flaked canned salmon.

Custards

A *custard* is a liquid that is thickened or set by the coagulation of egg protein.

There are two basic kinds of custards:

1. *Stirred custard,* which is stirred as it cooks and remains pourable when cooked.

2. *Baked custard,* which is not stirred, and which sets firm.

One basic rule governs the preparation of both custards: *Do not heat custards higher than an internal temperature of 185°F (85°C).*

This temperature, as you know, is the point at which egg–liquid mixtures coagulate. If they are heated more than this, they tend to curdle. An overbaked custard will become watery, because the moisture separates from the toughened protein.

Most custards are sweet. These preparations are covered in the baking and dessert section of this book. You may have already encountered a savory custard in the recipe for Corn Pudding (p. 421).

The *quiche* (keesh), which is a custard baked in a pastry shell, is probably the most popular form of a savory custard. The following recipe illustrates the technique for preparing savory custards.

RECIPE 272   Quiche au Fromage (Cheese Tart)

Yield: four 8-inch tarts   **Portion:** 24   **Portion size:** ¼ of tart
                                              16   ⅙ of tart

U.S.	Metric	Ingredients	Procedure
2 lb	900 g	Mealy Pie Dough (p. 745)	1. Scale the dough into four 8-oz (225-g) pieces. 2. Roll the dough out into 4 circles ⅛ inch (3 mm) thick. 3. Fit the dough into four 8-inch (20-cm) pie pans or tart pans. 4. Hold the pie shells in the refrigerator until needed (see note).
1 lb	450 g	Swiss or Gruyère cheese, grated	5. Sprinkle 4 oz (110 g) cheese into the bottom of each tart shell.
12	12	Eggs, beaten	6. Beat together the eggs, cream, milk, and seasonings. Pour into the tart shells.
1 pt	500 mL	Heavy cream	
2 pt	950 mL	Milk	7. Place the tarts in a 375°F (190°C) oven on the bottom shelf or, if using a deck oven, directly on the deck.
2 tsp	10 mL	Salt	
¼ tsp	1 mL	White pepper	8. Bake until the filling is set, about 20–30 minutes.
⅛ tsp	0.5 mL	Nutmeg	
			9. Serve hot or cold. Cut into wedges of desired size.

Note: Pastry shells may be partially baked before filling, if uncooked bottoms tend to be a problem. This is sometimes the case if you are using shiny aluminum pie pans or if the bottom heat of the oven isn't strong enough. See page 748 for procedure.

Variations

272A. *Quiche Lorraine:* Dice 1 lb (450 g) bacon strips and cook until crisp. Drain and add to pie shell in step 5. Omit cheese or leave it in, as desired. (Quiche Lorraine was originally made without cheese.)

272B. *Onion Quiche:* Sauté 2 lb (900 g) sliced onions very slowly in 2 oz (60 g) butter until golden and tender. Cool and add to empty pie shells. Reduce cheese to 8 oz (225 g).

272C. *Spinach Quiche:* Sauté 3 oz (90 g) chopped onion in 3 oz (90 g) butter until soft. Add 1½ lb (700 g) cooked, drained, chopped spinach. Sauté until most of the liquid has evaporated. Cool and add to empty pie shell. Omit cheese.

272D. *Mushroom Quiche:* Sauté 2 lb (900 g) sliced mushrooms and 3 oz (90 g) chopped onion in 3 oz (90 g) butter. Add 1 tbsp (15 mL) lemon juice to keep the mushrooms white. Cook until juices have evaporated. Cool and add to the empty pie shell. Omit cheese.

272E. *Seafood Quiche:* Substitute 8 oz (225 g) cooked diced shrimp and 8 oz (225 g) cooked, diced crabmeat for the cheese. Add 3 oz (90 mL) sherry and 2 oz (60 g) tomato paste to the egg mixture.

BREAKFAST BREADS, CEREALS, AND MEATS

*B*read items probably play a more important role than even eggs. Hardly an order of eggs is sold without an order of toast on the side. And for the diner who prefers a continental breakfast, coffee and a bread item such as a roll or pastry constitute the entire breakfast.

Except for toast, very few breakfast breads are prepared to order. Most operations purchase such items ready made. These products include muffins, doughnuts, Danish pastries, sweet rolls, and regional favorites such as bagels and cornbread.

In this section we consider three items that are made to order: pancakes, waffles, and French toast. You may not think of pancakes and waffles as breads, but they actually are a form of quick bread, a category of foods that we consider in more detail in the baking section of this book.

. . . .

PANCAKES AND WAFFLES

Waffles and pancakes, also called griddle cakes and hot cakes, are made from pourable batters. Pancakes are made on a griddle, while waffles are made on a special tool called a waffle iron.

Both items should be cooked to order and served hot. Waffles lose their crispness very quickly, and pancakes toughen as they are held. However, batters may be prepared ahead and are often mixed the night before.

Serve with butter and with maple syrup or syrup blends (pure maple syrup is very expensive). Other condiments that may accompany these items are fruit syrups, jams and preserves, applesauce, and fruits such as strawberries or blueberries.

Ingredients and Procedures

Instead of presenting these items in usual recipe format, we will list the ingredients and methods in parallel columns, so you can see the similarities and differences at a glance.

Note how much alike the batters are, with some important exceptions:

1.   Waffle batter contains more fat.

2.   Waffle batter contains less liquid, so it is slightly thicker.

3.   Waffles are given extra lightness by beating the egg whites separately and folding into the batter. (Some recipes omit this step.)

A standard-size pancake requires ¼ cup batter. The amount of batter needed for waffles depends on the size of the waffle iron.

Pre-preparation for Volume Service

Pancake and waffle batters leavened by *baking powder only* may be mixed the night before and stored in the cooler. Some rising power may be lost, so baking powder may have to be increased.

Batters leavened by *baking soda* should not be made too far ahead, because the soda will lose its power. Mix dry ingredients and liquid ingredients ahead and combine just before service.

Batters using beaten egg whites and baking powder may be partially made ahead, but *incorporate the egg whites just before service.*

RECIPE 273   **Pancakes and Waffles**

Ingredients for 3½ pt (1.75 L) batter

	Pancakes		Waffles	
	U.S.	Metric	U.S.	Metric
Dry ingredients				
Flour	1 lb 4 oz	625 g	1 lb 4 oz	570 g
Sugar	2 oz	60 g	—	—
Salt	1 tsp	5 mL	1 tsp	5 mL
Baking powder	2 tbsp	30 mL	2 tbsp	30 mL
Liquid ingredients				
Eggs, beaten	4	4	—	—
Egg yolks, beaten	—	—	6	6
Milk	1 qt	1 L	1½ pt	750 mL
Melted butter or oil	4 oz	125 g	8 oz	250 g
Egg whites	—	—	6	6
Sugar	—	—	2 oz	60 g

Buttermilk pancakes and waffles: Use buttermilk instead of milk. Reduce baking powder to 1 tbsp (15 mL) and add 2 tsp (10 mL) baking soda. Buttermilk makes a thick batter. You may need to thin the batter out with a little plain milk.

Procedures

Pancakes	*Waffles*
1. Sift together dry ingredients.	1. Sift together dry ingredients.
2. Combine liquid ingredients.	2. Combine liquid ingredients.
3. Add liquid ingredients to dry ingredients. Mix just until dry ingredients are thoroughly moistened. Do not overmix. Overmixing causes toughness by developing the gluten in the flour (see p. 658).	3. Add liquid ingredients to dry ingredients. Mix just until dry ingredients are thoroughly moistened. Do not overmix. Overmixing causes toughness by developing the gluten in the flour (see p. 658).
	4. Beat the egg whites until they form soft peaks. Add sugar and beat until stiff peaks form. Fold the egg white foam into the batter.
4. Using a 2-oz ladle or No. 16 scoop, measure ¼-cup (60-mL) portions onto a greased, preheated griddle (375°F/ 190°C), allowing space for spreading.	5. Pour enough batter onto a lightly greased, preheated waffle iron to almost cover the surface with a thin layer. Close the iron.
5. Griddle the pancakes until the tops are full of bubbles and begin to look dry, and the bottoms are golden brown. Turn and brown other side.	6. Cook waffles until signal light indicates they are done, or until steam is no longer emitted.
6. Remove from griddle and serve.	7. Remove from iron and serve.

FRENCH TOAST

Different versions of French toast are popular in many regions of the country, and they have the added advantage of being an excellent way to utilize day-old bread.

Basic French toast consists of slices of bread dipped in a batter of eggs, milk, a little sugar, and flavorings. French toast is cooked on a griddle like pancakes.

Variations may be created by changing the basic ingredients:

Bread. White pullman bread is standard. Specialty versions can be made with French bread, rich egg bread, or whole-grain breads.

Batter. Milk is the usual liquid, mixed with egg in various proportions. Deluxe versions may include cream or sour cream.

Flavorings. Vanilla, cinnamon, or nutmeg are popular choices. Other possibilities are grated lemon or orange rind, ground anise, or rum or brandy.

The most common fault in making French toast is not soaking the bread long enough to allow the batter to penetrate. If the bread is just dipped in the batter, the final product is just dry bread with a little egg on the outside.

French toast is dusted with powdered sugar and served, like pancakes, with accompanying butter, syrups, preserves, or fruits.

CEREALS

Hot, Cooked Cereals

Cooked cereals are of two types:

1. Whole, cracked, or flaked cereals, such as oatmeal (rolled oats), Scotch oatmeal (cracked oats), and cracked wheat. The particles are large and can be added to boiling water without lumping.

2. Granular cereals, such as farina and cornmeal. The particles are small and tend to lump when added to boiling water.

Procedure for Cooking Whole, Cracked, or Flaked Cereals

1. Collect equipment and ingredients.

2. Measure correct amount of water and salt into pot and bring to a boil. Read package directions for quantities.

   Using milk or part milk makes a richer cereal, but a more expensive one. Be careful not to scorch the milk if you use it.

3. Measure correct amount of cereal.

4. Add cereal slowly, stirring constantly.

5. Stir until some thickening takes place, then stop stirring. Too much stirring makes cereal gummy.

6. Reduce heat to a slow simmer, cover, and cook until desired doneness and consistency are reached. Cooking times vary greatly.

7. Keep covered until served, to prevent drying.

Procedure for Cooking Granular Cereals

Procedure is the same as above, except that the cereal is mixed with a little cold water before adding to boiling water. This separates the grains and prevents lumping. The cold water must be calculated as part of the total amount of liquid.

Cold Cereals

Cold, dry cereals are purchased ready prepared and need no preparation by the kitchen. Like hot cereals, they are served with accompanying milk or cream, sugar, and sometimes fruit such as berries or sliced bananas.

BREAKFAST MEATS

Meats and meat cooking methods are covered in previous chapters, but we mention them again because three meats in particular—bacon, sausage, and ham—appear on most breakfast menus.

Bacon

Bacon is a cured, smoked pork product. It is available in whole slabs, but is almost always purchased presliced. Thickness of slices is specified by number of slices per pound, usually 18 to 22 (40 to 48 per kilogram).

Low-temperature cooking applies to bacon as well as to other meats. Bacon is about 70 percent fat and shrinks a great deal. However, cooking at low temperatures minimizes shrinkage. The oven is most often used for cooking bacon in quantity, though a griddle or sauté pan may also be used.

To cook in the oven, lay out the bacon strips on sheet pans in a single layer, or even better, on racks over sheet pans. (Bacon may be purchased already laid out on parchment.) Bake at 300°F to 350°F (150°C to 175°C) until about three-fourths done. Remove from oven, being very careful not to spill the hot fat. Finish individual portions to order on the griddle or in the oven, cooking them until crisp.

Ham

Ham for breakfast service is almost always precooked. Slices in 3- to 4-oz portions need only be heated and browned slightly on a griddle or under the broiler.

Canadian bacon is boneless pork loin that is cured and smoked like ham. It is handled like ham in the kitchen.

Sausage

Breakfast sausage is simply fresh pork that has been ground and seasoned. It is available in three forms: patties, links, and bulk.

Because it is fresh pork, sausage must be cooked well done. This does not mean, however, that it should be cooked until it is just hard, dry, shrunken little nuggets, as it often is.

Most kitchens cook sausages by the same methods as bacon. For volume service, it is partially cooked in the oven and then finished to order. Link sausages hold better than patties, because the links are protected from drying by their casings.

DAIRY

MILK AND CREAM

Categories and Definitions

1. *Fresh milk.*

   Whole milk is fresh milk as it comes from the cow, with nothing removed and nothing (except vitamin D) added. It contains 3½ percent fat (known as milk fat or butterfat), 8½ percent nonfat milk solids, and 88 percent water.

   Fresh milk is available in several forms:

   Pasteurized milk has been heated to kill disease-producing bacteria and then cooled. Most milk and cream products on the market have been pasteurized.

   Raw milk is milk that has not been pasteurized. It is not often used and in fact is generally not legal.

   Certified milk is produced by disease-free herds under very strict sanitary conditions. It may be raw or pasteurized.

   Homogenized milk has been processed so that the cream doesn't separate out. This is done by forcing the milk through very tiny holes, which break up the fat into particles so small that they stay distributed in the milk.

   The above terms apply not just to whole milk but to most of the following forms:

   Skim or nonfat milk has had most or all of the fat removed. Its fat content is 0.5 percent or less.

   Low-fat milk has a fat content of 0.5 to 3 percent. Its fat content is usually indicated.

   Fortified nonfat or low-fat milk has had substances added to increase its nutritional value, usually vitamins A and D and extra nonfat milk solids.

   Flavored milks, such as *chocolate milk,* have had flavoring ingredients added. A label such as *chocolate milk drink* or *chocolate-flavored drink* indicates that the product does not meet the standards for regular milk. Read ingredient labels.

2. *Cream.*

   Whipping cream has a fat content of 30 to 40 percent. Within this category, you may find *light whipping cream* (30 to 35 percent) and *heavy whipping cream* (36 to 40 percent). Whipping cream labeled *ultrapasteurized* will keep longer than regular pasteurized cream. Pure ultrapasteurized cream does not whip as well as regular pasteurized cream, so it may contain additives such as vegetable gums to make it more whippable.

   Light cream, also called *table cream* or *coffee cream,* contains 16 to 22 percent fat, usually about 18 percent.

   Half-and-half has a fat content of 10 to 12 percent, too low for it to be called cream.

3. *Fermented milk products.*

   Sour cream has been cultured or fermented by added lactic acid bacteria, which make it thick and slightly tangy in flavor. It has about 18 percent fat.

Buttermilk is fresh, liquid milk, usually skim milk, which has been cultured or soured by bacteria. It is usually called *cultured buttermilk* to distinguish it from the original buttermilk, which was the liquid left after buttermaking. Buttermilk is used in recipes calling for *sour milk*.

Yogurt is milk (whole or low-fat) cultured by special bacteria. It has a custardlike consistency. Most yogurt has additional milk solids added, and some of it is flavored and sweetened.

4. **Milk products with water removed.**

Evaporated milk is milk, either whole or skim, with about 60 percent of the water removed. It is then sterilized and canned. Evaporated milk has a somewhat "cooked" flavor.

Condensed milk is whole milk that has had about 60 percent of the water removed and is heavily sweetened with sugar. It is available canned and in bulk.

Dried whole milk is whole milk that has been dried to a powder. *Nonfat dry milk* is skim milk that has been dried in the same way. They are available in regular form and in *instant* form, which dissolves in water more easily.

Artificial Dairy Products

A wide variety of imitation cream and dessert topping products are available. They are made from various fats and chemicals, which are listed on the label. They are used in some institutions because they keep longer and are generally less expensive than dairy products. Some people feel they are acceptable, but many find their flavors objectionable.

Problems in Cooking Milk and Cream Products

Curdling

Curdling is a process by which milk proteins solidify and separate from the whey. Curdling is usually caused by acids, tannins, salt, and heat. The mild acids in many vegetables and the tannins in potatoes are often enough to curdle milk.

Starches partially stabilize milk and cream. This is why it is possible to make soups and sauces with both milk or cream and acid ingredients. Avoid combining milk or cream with strong acids unless a starch is present.

Reducing temperatures and cooking times also helps. Curdling is more likely at high heat or with prolonged cooking.

Salt lightly, unless the milk has been stabilized by starch.

When adding milk or cream to a hot liquid, heat it first in a separate pot, or temper it by stirring a little of the hot liquid into it first.

Reconstituted dry milk is more likely to curdle than fresh milk.

Scorching

Scorching occurs when milk that is being heated coagulates on the bottom of the pan due to the high heat. This deposit is likely to burn if cooking continues.

To avoid scorching, heat milk in a double boiler, steamer, or steam-jacketed kettle rather than over direct heat.

Skin formation

Formation of scum or skin on top of heated milk or milk sauces is caused by coagulation of proteins in contact with air. Prevent by covering the utensil or by coating the surface with a layer of melted fat.

Whipping Cream

Cream with a fat content of 30 percent or more can be whipped into a foam. One quart or liter of cream will produce up to 2 quarts or liters of whipped cream.

For best results, observe the following guidelines:

1. Have cream and all equipment well chilled.

2. Do not sweeten until the cream is whipped. Sugar decreases stability and makes the cream harder to whip. Use powdered sugar instead of granulated sugar for best stability.

3. Do not overwhip. Stop beating when the cream forms stiff peaks. If it is whipped longer, it first becomes granular and then turns into butter and whey.

4. Cream to be folded into other ingredients should be underbeaten, since the action of folding it in whips it more and may overwhip it.

BUTTER

Butter Characteristics and Grades

Fresh butter consists of about 80 percent milk fat. The remainder is milk solids and water.

Butter is graded according to USDA standards for flavor, body, color, and salt content, although grading is not mandatory. Grades are AA, A, B, and C. Most operations use grades AA and A, because the lower grades may have off flavors.

Most butter on the market is lightly *salted*. *Sweet*, or *unsalted*, butter is more perishable but has a fresher, sweeter taste.

Because of its flavor, butter is the preferred cooking fat for most purposes. It has no equal in sauce making, and is used as a sauce itself, as is discussed in Chapter 8.

Clarified butter (see p. 147 for production procedure) is used as a cooking fat more often than whole butter, because the milk solids in whole butter burn easily.

The smoke point of butter fat is only 260°F to 265°F (127°C to 130°C), so another product such as vegetable oil should be used when high cooking temperatures are required.

Storing

Have you ever been served butter that tasted like onions? Butter absorbs odors and flavors easily, so it should be kept well wrapped and away from other foods that might transfer odors to it in the refrigerator.

Best storage temperature is 35°F (2°C).

Margarine

Margarine is a manufactured product that is intended to resemble butter in taste, texture, and appearance. It is made from various vegetable and animal fats, plus flavoring ingredients, emulsifiers, coloring agents, preservatives, and added vitamins. Like butter, it is about 80 percent fat.

Flavors of different brands should be evaluated carefully, because they vary considerably. Margarine should have a reasonably clean, fresh flavor, although you should not expect even the best to taste like high-grade butter.

Margarines that include an emulsifier called lecithin will foam and brown like butter when heated. Those without lecithin will not. In all other respects, margarine is handled and stored like butter.

CHEESE

Composition

Cheese is a food produced by separating milk solids from whey by curdling or coagulation. This curdling is brought about by introducing selected bacteria or an enzyme called *rennet* into the milk. The resulting curds are drained, processed, and cured or aged in a variety of ways.

There are so many variations in processing techniques that from a single basic ingredient (milk from cows, sheep, or goats) it is possible to produce hundreds of kinds of cheese, from cottage cheese to parmesan, from cheddar to Swiss, from blue to Limburger. These variations include the type of milk used, the method of curdling and the temperatures during curdling, the method of cutting and draining the curd, the way the curds are heated, pressed, or handled, and all the conditions of ripening or curing.

Ripening is the process that converts freshly made curds into distinctive, flavorful cheeses. This ripening is brought about by certain bacteria or molds that are introduced during manufacture. Much of a cheese's final character is determined by the kind of ripening agent and the way it acts on the cheese.

Cheeses can be classified by the kind of ripening agent and whether it ripens from the inside or the outside.

Bacteria ripened, from inside: Cheddar, Swiss, Gouda, Parmesan.

Bacteria ripened, from outside: Limburger, Liederkranz.

Mold ripened, from inside: Blue cheeses, including Roquefort and Stilton.

Mold ripened, from outside: Brie, Camembert, St. André.

Unripened: Cottage, cream, baker's cheese.

The three major components of cheese are water, fat, and protein. The water content of cheese ranges from about 80 percent for a fresh, soft cheese like cottage cheese, to about 30 percent for a very hard, aged cheese like Parmesan.

The fat content of cheese, when it is listed on a label, generally refers to the percentage of solids. In other words, if a cheddar cheese has a 50 percent fat content, this means that the cheese would be 50 percent fat if all the moisture were removed. In fact, the cheese may have a moisture content of about 40 percent, and its actual fat content may be about 30 percent of the total.

Double-crème (at least 60 percent fat) and triple-crème (at least 75 percent fat, dry weight) are very rich cheeses. Most of these originated in France, but they have become very popular and are now made in many countries. Most of them fall into the unripened, soft-ripened, or blue-veined categories, discussed below.

Varieties

Only a few of the many hundreds of the world's cheeses find their way into American commercial kitchens. The following are the most frequently used (see Figure 21.6).

1. **Unripened cheeses.**

   These are soft, white, freshly made cheeses.

   Cottage cheese is a moist, loose-curd cheese that may or may not have cream added. *Baker's cheese* or *pot cheese* is similar but drier. It is used in cheesecakes and pastry.

   Ricotta cheese is sometimes called Italian cottage cheese, but it is smoother, moister, and has a sweeter flavor.

   Cream cheese is a smooth, mild cheese with a high fat content. It is extensively used in making sandwiches, canapés, and hors d'oeuvres and in baking.

   Neufchâtel is similar but has less fat. An Italian cream cheese called *Mascarpone* is very soft and rich, and it looks almost like whipped cream. It has a slightly tangy taste that goes with fruits as a dessert.

   Mozzarella is a soft, mild cheese made from whole milk or part skim milk. It has a stringy texture that comes from being pulled and stretched during production. It is widely used in pizzas and Italian-style dishes. The freshly made mozzarella one finds in Italian neighborhoods is moister and tenderer than the packaged varieties.

   Mozzarella di Bufala, made from the milk of water buffaloes, is imported from Italy and is available in some areas at a somewhat high price. It is much softer and more delicate in texture than regular mozzarella, and it has a slightly acidic flavor that is refreshing.

   Feta is a crumbly, curdy cheese from Greece and other Balkan countries. Instead of being aged or cured, it is pickled in brine. This, plus the fact that it is generally made from goat's or sheep's milk, gives it a unique, salty flavor.

2. **Semisoft cheeses.**

   Bel Paese and *Fontina* from Italy, *Port Salut* from France, and American *munster* and *brick* cheeses are the best known of a larger group of cheeses that range from bland and buttery when young to more earthy and full flavored when somewhat older. They are often used as dessert cheeses and as hors d'oeuvres.

   France produces many soft cheeses, often with orange rinds and with flavors that range from mild to pungent. Among the better known

FIGURE 21.6   **An assortment of cheeses. Back row, left to right: Port Salut, Danish Blue, Jarlsberg, New York Cheddar, Edam. Center: large Brie. Front, left to right: Limburger, slightly aged domestic Chèvre, fresh Chèvre coated with dill, Crottin de Chavignol, Camembert, Explorateur, Chaource, Saga Blue.**

ones are *Pont L'Evêque* and *Livarot* from Normandy and *Muenster* from Alsace. (These cheeses might also be categorized as soft ripened cheeses, below.)

3. Soft ripened cheeses.

These cheeses ripen from the outside toward the center. When very young, they are firm and cakey and have little flavor. As they mature they gradually become softer and when fully ripe may be actually runny.

Brie and *Camembert* from France are ripened by mold. They are made in flat, round shapes and are covered with a crust that varies from white to straw colored. When ripe, they are creamy and flavorful, but they develop a sharp odor of ammonia when overripe.

Liederkranz, made in the United States, and its Belgian cousin *Limburger* are ripened by bacteria rather than mold, but they also become softer as they age. They are widely misunderstood because of their aroma. Actually, when not over-ripe, these cheeses are not nearly as strong as most people expect, and they have a pleasant, smooth texture. Liederkranz and Limburger are served as dessert cheeses, like *Brie* and *Camembert.*

Many rich double- and triple-crème cheeses fall in this category, including *Explorateur, Brillat-Savarin, St. André, Boursault,* and *Boursin* (which may be flavored with pepper or with garlic and herbs). *Chaource* is similar in texture and appearance to a double-crème cheese but is actually closer in composition to Brie, having a fat content of 45 to 50 percent.

4. Hard ripened cheeses.

These are cured cheeses with a firm texture and varying degrees of mildness or sharpness, depending on their age.

Cheddar is an English invention, but American versions of it are so popular that it is often thought of as a distinctly American cheese. It ranges in flavor from mild to sharp, and in color from light yellow to orange. Cheddar is eaten as is and is also widely used in cooking. *Colby* and *Monterey jack* are similar to very mild cheddars. Monterey jack is usually sold when quite young. In this case it is more like American munster and belongs in the semisoft category.

Swiss-type cheeses are also very popular in the United States. *Domestic Swiss* is the largest seller, but the original Swiss cheese from Switzerland, *Emmenthaler,* is more flavorful. These are very firm, slightly rubbery cheeses with a nutty taste. Their large holes are caused by gases formed during ripening. *Gruyère* is another Swiss-type cheese, from either Switzerland or France. It has smaller holes and a sharper, earthier flavor, Gruyère is very important in cooking and it, plus Emmenthaler, are widely used for sauces, soufflés, fondue, and gratinéed items. Other cheeses related to Swiss are *Comté* from France, *Appenzeller* and *Raclette* from Switzerland, and *Jarlsberg* from Norway.

Edam and *Gouda* are the familiar round Dutch cheeses with the yellow and red wax rinds. Hard in texture, with a mellow, nutlike flavor, they are often seen on buffet platters and among dessert cheeses.

Provolone is an Italian cheese that resembles mozzarella when very young, but becomes sharper as it ages. It is also available smoked.

5. Blue-veined cheeses.

These cheeses owe their flavor and appearance to the blue or green mold that mottles their interiors. The most famous of the blue cheeses is *Roquefort,* made in France from sheep's milk and cured in limestone caves near the town of Roquefort. *Stilton,* from England, is a mellower, firmer blue cheese that the English call "Roquefort with a college education." Italy's *Gorgonzola* is a soft, creamy cheese with an unmistakable pungency. Less expensive than these three, and thus more widely used here, are a number of blue cheeses made in the United States and in Denmark.

Less widely known but worth seeking out are a number of special blues, including *Bleu de Bresse, Fourme d'Ambert,* and *Pipo Crem'* from France, *Saga Bleu* from Denmark, and *Bavarian Blue* and *Blue Castello* from Germany. The last four of these are double- or triple-crèmes.

6. Goat cheeses.

Cheeses made from goat's milk are made in dozens of varieties in France, where this type of cheese, called *chèvre,* is very popular. It has also become well known in the United States, and now there are several American producers. With a few exceptions, most goat cheeses are small, ranging in size from tiny buttons to logs, cakes, cones, and pyramids weighing up to 5 or 6 ounces.

Fresh, unaged chèvres are the most popular and the mildest in flavor. Their paste is very white, with a soft but interestingly dry texture. They have a distinctive peppery, slightly acidic taste. The most widely available fresh French chèvre is probably the cylindrical *Montrachet*, either plain or with a coating of ash. Other fresh goat cheeses, both domestic and imported, may be available in different localities, and many may have no name other than Chèvre.

As goat cheese ages, it becomes firmer, and the peppery, acidic flavor becomes stronger. Cheeses two or three months old can be quite powerful, while the youngest might taste almost like the unaged ones. Some names of chèvres are *Boucheron, Banon* (wrapped in chestnut leaves), *Pyramide, Crottin de Chavignol, Chabis, Rocamadour,* and *Saint-Marcellin* (part cow's milk).

7. *Hard grating cheeses.*

The hard grating cheeses, typified by Italian *Parmesan*, are called *grana* cheeses, referring to their grainy textures. The very best of all granas is called *Parmigiano Reggiano.* It is the true Parmesan, aged at least 2 years, and is very expensive. It is imitated widely around the world, and the imitations vary from bad to very good. Another Italian grana is *Romano.* Italian Romanos are made with sheep's milk, but American versions are usually made with cow's milk. Romano is stronger and saltier than Parmesan.

These cheeses are very often sold already grated. This is a convenience for commercial kitchens, of course, but unfortunately, pregrated cheese has much less flavor than freshly grated cheese. A merchant was once arrested for selling what he claimed was grated Parmesan cheese but was actually grated umbrella handles. A large share of pregrated cheese sold today resembles grated umbrella handles in flavor.

8. *Process cheeses.*

Up to now we have been talking about so-called natural cheeses, made by curdling milk and ripening the curds. *Process cheese,* by contrast, is manufactured by grinding one or more natural cheeses, heating and blending them with emulsifiers and other ingredients, and pouring the mixture into molds to solidify. Process cheese is a uniform product that does not age or ripen like natural cheese. Thus, it keeps very well. It is usually very mild in flavor and has a gummy texture.

Because of its melting quality and low price, it is often used in cooking. However, it is not as good a value as its price implies. Because it is relatively flavorless, you have to use much more of it to get the same flavor as from a smaller quantity of sharp cheddar.

In addition to its price and keeping qualities, its chief advantages are that it melts easily and its blandness appeals to many people who don't like a more flavorful cheese.

The term *American cheese* usually refers to process cheese, although some people use this name for cheddar. In this country, most process cheeses are made from cheddar, while European process cheeses more often contain Swiss-type cheeses. Among them is a process cheese called *Gruyère,* which bears little resemblance to true *Gruyère.*

Process cheese food and *process cheese spread* contain a lower percentage of cheese and more moisture than a product labeled simply *process cheese. Cold pack* or *club cheese,* on the other hand, is not heated and pasteurized like process cheese, but is simply ground and mixed with flavorings and seasonings, to a spreadable consistency. Some brands are fairly flavorful.

Storage and Service

1. *Storing.*

Keeping qualities of cheese vary considerably. In general, *the firmer and more aged the cheese, the longer it will keep.* Cottage cheese must be used within a week, while a whole, uncut Parmesan may keep a year or more.

Soft ripened cheeses like Brie, Camembert, and Liederkranz deteriorate rapidly once they have reached maturity. They are difficult cheeses to purchase, because in their whole life span there may be only 1 week when they are neither underripe nor overripe.

Other ripened cheeses are not so fussy, as long as you store them under refrigeration and well wrapped to prevent drying. Cut cheeses dry especially quickly, so they must be wrapped in plastic at all times.

2. *Serving.*

Serve cheese at room temperature. This is the single most important rule of cheese service. Only at room temperature will the full flavors develop. (This does not apply to unripened cheese like cottage cheese.)

Cut cheese just before service, to prevent drying. Better yet, set out whole cheese and large pieces when possible, so that portions can be cut to order by the customer or the service personnel.

Cooking with Cheese

1. Three varieties account for the majority of cheese used in cooking.

   Cheddar is the most frequently used in American dishes, especially in sauces, as casserole ingredients, and as a melted or gratinéed topping.

   Swiss-type cheeses are used more often in European-style dishes. Emmenthal and Gruyère are essential ingredients for fondue, Mornay Sauce, gratinéed dishes, soufflés, and quiches.

   Parmesan-type cheeses are used in grated form for toppings and for seasoning and flavoring purposes.

Many other varieties are called for in specialized recipes, such as mozzarella and ricotta in Italian-style dishes.

2. The following guidelines should be kept in mind when cooking with cheese.

   Use low temperatures. Cheese contains a high proportion of protein, which toughens and becomes stringy when heated too much. Sauces containing cheese should not be boiled.

   Use short cooking times, for the same reasons. Cheese should be added to a sauce at the end of cooking. Stirring it into the hot sauce *off the heat* is usually enough to melt it.

   Grate cheese for faster and more uniform melting.

   Aged cheeses melt and blend into foods more easily than young cheeses.

   Aged cheese adds more flavor to foods than young, mild cheeses, so you need less of it.

RECIPE 274 **Welsh Rabbit**

Portions: 25   **Portion size:** 4 oz (125 g)

U.S.	Metric	Ingredients	Procedure
3 tbsp	45 mL	Worcestershire sauce	1. Mix the Worcestershire sauce and spices in a heavy saucepan.
2 tsp	10 mL	Dry mustard	
pinch	pinch	Cayenne	2. Add the beer or ale. Heat almost to a simmer.
2½ cups	625 mL	Beer or ale	
5 lb	2.5 kg	Sharp cheddar cheese, grated	3. Set the pan over very low heat. Add the grated cheese, a little at a time. Stir constantly. Continue to stir over low heat until the mixture is smooth and thick.
			4. Remove from heat. The mixture may be kept warm in a steam table or bain marie, but it is better if served immediately.
25 slices	25 slices	White bread	5. Toast the bread.
			6. For each portion, place a slice of hot toast on a plate. Ladle 4 oz (125 mL) cheese mixture over the toast. Serve.

Note: This dish is sometimes called "Welsh Rarebit," although "Rabbit" is the correct name.

RECIPE 275   **Swiss Fondue**

....

| | **Portions:** 4 | | **Portion size:** 8 oz (250 g) |

U.S.	Metric	Ingredients	Procedure
1 clove	1 clove	Garlic	1. Cut the garlic clove in half. Rub the inside of a 1½-qt (1½-L) fondue pot or casserole with the garlic.
1 pt	500 mL	Dry white wine	
1 lb	500 g	Grated Swiss Emmenthaler cheese, or half Emmenthaler and half Gruyère	2. Add the wine to the pot and set over moderate heat. Heat the wine until it is hot but not simmering. Do not boil.
1 tsp	5 mL	Cornstarch	3. Add the cheese to the wine, about one-fourth at a time. Stir well between each addition.
3 tbsp	45 mL	Kirsch (see note)	
		Salt	4. Dissolve the cornstarch in the kirsch. Stir into the cheese mixture. Stir over very low heat until smooth and slightly thickened.
		White pepper	
		Nutmeg	
			5. Season to taste with salt, white pepper, and just a trace of nutmeg.
2	2	Small loaves French bread, cut into bite-size pieces	6. Set the casserole over a chafing-dish-type heating element for service. Serve the bread cubes in baskets. To eat fondue, the diner spears a cube of bread on a special fondue fork and swirls it in the cheese mixture, which is kept hot over the heating element.

Note: Kirsch is a white (that is, clear) alcoholic beverage distilled from cherries. While it is traditional in Swiss fondue, it may be omitted if unavailable. In this case, dissolve the cornstarch in cold water or mix it with the grated cheese.

....

RECIPE 276 Cheese Wafers

Yield: about 150 wafers

U.S.	Metric	Ingredients	Procedure
1 lb	500 g	Sharp cheddar cheese, grated	1. Combine all ingredients in the bowl of a mixer. Mix at low speed with the paddle attachment until the mixture forms a dough.
8 oz	250 g	Butter, softened	
12 oz	375 g	Bread flour	2. Remove from the mixer and knead lightly on a floured board until the dough holds together well.
½ tsp	2 mL	Salt	
¼ tsp	1 mL	White pepper	
			3. Divide the dough into 4 or 5 pieces. Roll each piece into a cylinder 1 inch (2½ cm) in diameter. Wrap in waxed paper or plastic film and chill.
			4. Slice the dough into thin rounds a little less than ¼ inch (½ cm) thick. Place on greased baking sheets.
			5. Bake at 450°F (230°C) about 10 minutes, until crisp and lightly browned.
			6. Serve hot or cold as an hors d'oeuvre or as a soup accompaniment.

Variation

276A. *Cheese Straws:* Roll the dough out like pie dough, slightly less than ¼ inch (½ cm) thick. Cut into ¼ × 3-inch (½ × 7½-cm) strips. Bake as in basic recipe.

RECIPE 277 Sirniki (Russian Fried Cheese Cakes)

	Portions: 25		**Portion size:** 3½ oz (100 g)

U.S.	Metric	Ingredients	Procedure
5 lb	2.3 kg	Pot cheese	1. Place the pot cheese in a strainer lined with cheesecloth. Fold the overhanging cloth over the top of the cheese so that it is covered. Set the strainer over a bowl and refrigerate for 24 hours to drain the cheese.
6 oz	175 g	Bread flour	2. Force the cheese through a sieve or food mill into the bowl of a mixer.
8	8	Egg yolks	
½ tsp	2 mL	Salt	3. Add the flour, egg yolks, salt, and sugar.
2 oz	60 g	Sugar	4. With the paddle attachment, mix until smooth.
		Butter, for frying	
			5. Divide the dough into 3 parts. Roll each part into a cylinder about 3 inches (7½ cm) thick. Wrap in plastic film. Refrigerate 2 hours or more.
			6. At service time, cut the cheese rolls into cakes about ¾ inch (2 cm) thick.

RECIPE 277   **Sirniki (Russian Fried Cheese Cakes)** *(Continued)*

U.S.	Metric	Ingredients	Procedure
			7. Heat about ⅛ inch (3 mm) butter in a heavy sauté pan. Pan-fry the cakes over low heat until golden brown on both sides. Turn very carefully with a spatula.
2½ pt	1.2 L	Confectioners' sugar Sour cream	8. Plate the cakes and sprinkle lightly with confectioners' sugar. Place about 1½ tbsp (20 mL) sour cream on the plate next to the cake. Serve immediately.

Note: This dish is often served as the main course for brunch or lunch. In this case, portion sizes may be increased. Sirniki may also be served with strawberry or other preserves.

COFFEE AND TEA

COFFEE

Many people judge a restaurant by its coffee. Regardless of the quality of the food, one of the things they are most likely to remember about an establishment is whether the coffee is good or bad.

Whether or not that seems fair to you, it is at least a clear signal that you ought to learn to make coffee properly. Coffee making is basically a very simple procedure. All you do is pass hot water through ground coffee. The care with which you perform this operation, with attention to all the details, makes the difference between a rich, aromatic, satisfying beverage and a bitter, unpleasant liquid.

Varieties, Roasts, and Blends

Coffee beans are the berries of a tropical shrub. Coffee is grown in many tropical countries around the world, and each producing area is known for certain quality and flavor characteristics. Many connoisseurs feel that the finest coffee comes from Colombia. Excellent coffees are grown in Brazil, Venezuela, Mexico, and nations in Africa, the Middle East, and Indonesia.

Most ground coffees are blends of different varieties. Blending enables the processor to combine desirable quantities from a number of beans to produce a well-balanced beverage.

Coffee beans are roasted to develop their flavor. The degree of roasting—light, medium, dark—affects the flavor. Americans generally prefer medium roast, while dark roast coffees are popular in Europe and are often served as after-dinner beverages in French and Italian restaurants.

The most important fact about coffee varieties for you to know as a professional cook is that many blends at different prices and quality levels are available. You do have a choice—all coffee is not alike. Your selection will be based on your own taste evaluation, the needs of your establishment, the preferences of your customers, and your cost constraints.

In addition to the standard American blends, the following coffee varieties are sometimes served.

1. **Instant coffee** is a powdered, soluble extract from coffee beans. To simplify somewhat, instant coffee is made by brewing regular coffee and drying it. In the process, the coffee loses a portion of its flavor and aroma. Most coffee lovers agree that it does not taste as good as freshly brewed coffee. Instant coffee is rarely used in food service, with the major exception of decaffeinated coffee.

2. **Decaffeinated coffee.**   Caffeine is a chemical stimulant that occurs naturally in coffee, tea, and chocolate. Decaffeinated coffee is coffee from which the caffeine has been removed by solvents. It is often specially requested by some customers. In the past, most restaurants offered decaffeinated coffee only in the instant form. Recently, however, due to increased demand, more and more restaurants are serving freshly brewed decaffeinated coffee.

3. **Espresso** or **expresso** is a strong, dark coffee made from beans roasted until they are almost black

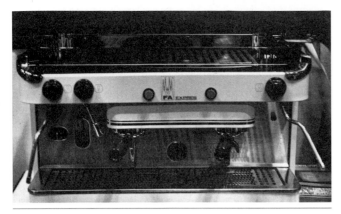

FIGURE 21.7 **An espresso maker.**

and ground to a powder. It is brewed in special machines (Figure 21.7) that force water through the ground coffee under steam pressure. Espresso is served in small cups as an after-dinner beverage.

4. *Demitasse* means "half cup." It refers to strong, black coffee served in small cups after dinner.

5. *Cappuccino* is a combination of equal parts espresso and frothy, steamed milk. It is served in tall cups, often topped with whipped cream and cinnamon.

6. *Iced coffee* is made double strength to compensate for dilution by melting ice.

Basic Principles of Coffee Making

Coffee is made by extracting flavors from ground coffee by dissolving them in hot water. The essence of making good coffee is to extract enough of these solids to make a flavorful beverage, but not to brew so long as to extract those solids that make the coffee bitter.

With this principle in mind, study the following guidelines for making good coffee. The list is long, and every item is important.

1. *Use fresh coffee.*

   Once it is ground, coffee loses flavor and aroma rapidly. To maintain freshness, store coffee tightly sealed in a cool, dry place. Even with the best storage, however, you should not use coffee more than a week old. Vacuum-packed coffee keeps longer, but it too deteriorates as soon as it is opened. If you can't grind your own coffee daily (some restaurants do), at least you can arrange for frequent delivery.

2. *Use the right grind and the right brewing time.*

   A coarse grind requires more time for extraction than a fine grind. You must use the grind that is suited to your equipment.

Grind	Extraction Time
Fine or vacuum	2 to 4 minutes
Drip or urn	4 to 6 minutes
Regular (percolator)	6 to 8 minutes

3. *Use the right proportions.*

   Always measure. Recommended proportions are 1 pound of coffee and 1¾ to 2½ gallons of water, or 500 grams of coffee and 7.5 to 10.5 liters of water, depending on the strength desired.

   To make weaker coffee, add more hot water after removing the used grounds. Using more water while actually making the coffee extends the brewing time, resulting in overextraction and bitterness. In fact, many experts feel that passing no more than 2 gallons of water through a pound of ground coffee (8 liters to 500 grams) and then diluting to taste is the surest way to avoid bitterness.

   Coffee strength is a matter of customer preference and varies from region to region. For example, people in New York generally prefer stronger coffee than people in Chicago. In some areas, the preferred ratio is 1 lb (500 g) coffee to 3 gallons (12 liters) of water.

4. *Use fresh water.*

   Fresh, cold water brought to a boil contains some dissolved air. Water that has been kept hot for a long time does not, so it tastes flat, and it makes flat-tasting coffee.

   Tap water is usually best to use. Special filtration systems are available for tap water that has off flavors or is heavily chlorinated. Do not use chemically softened water.

5. *Use water at the right brewing temperature: 195°F to 200°F (90°C to 93°C).*

   Water that is too hot will extract bitter solids. Water that is too cold will not extract enough flavor, and the coffee will be too cool for serving.

6. *Use a good brewing procedure.*

   Most operations use either urns, for large volume, or automatic drip makers, which make one pot at a time (see Figure 21.8). These machines can make excellent coffee because water passes through the grounds only once.

FIGURE 21.8   Coffee-brewing equipment.
(a) Twin urn.

(b) Decanter-type automatic drip coffee maker.

Percolator-type coffee makers should not be used. They boil the coffee as it is being brewed and pass it through the grounds repeatedly.

7. *Use clean equipment.*

Urns and coffee makers must be cleaned every day. Coffee leaves oily deposits that quickly turn rancid or bitter and that can ruin the next batch of coffee.

8. *Use good filters.*

Good filters are the only way to ensure sparkling, clear coffee. Most operations use paper filters, which are discarded after use. If cloth filters are used, they must be perfectly clean and free from odors.

9. *Use proper holding procedures.*

Proper holding temperature is 185°F to 190°F (85°C to 88°C). Higher temperatures decompose the coffee quickly. Lower temperatures mean that the customer gets cold coffee.

Do not hold coffee more than 1 hour. After an hour, loss of flavor is considerable. Loss of customers might also be considerable. Plan production so that coffee is always fresh. Discard old coffee.

Procedure for Making Coffee in an Urn

1. Be familiar with your equipment. Models differ in details.

2. Check to make sure the urn holds sufficient fresh water at the proper temperatures for brewing.

3. Fit the filter securely in place.

4. Spread a measured amount of coffee evenly in the filter. An even bed is necessary for uniform extraction.

5. Pass the correct amount of water through the ground coffee. If the urn is manual, pour the water slowly in a circular motion. If it is automatic, all you need to do is make sure the nozzle is in place.

6. Keep the top covered during brewing to retain heat.

7. Remove the filter with the used grounds as soon as brewing has been completed. Leaving the grounds in the urn will result in overextraction and bitterness.

8. Mix the coffee. Because the coffee at the bottom is stronger, you must draw out some of it—about a gallon (4 liters) per pound (500 grams) of coffee—and pour it back into the top of the urn.

9. Hold at 185°F to 190°F (85°C to 88°C) for up to 1 hour.

10. Clean urn thoroughly after use.

Using special urn brushes, clean inside of urn as well as inside spigots and glass gauges. Rinse and fill with several gallons of fresh water if urn is to stand for a time. Empty and rinse with hot water before next use.

Twice a week, clean thoroughly with urn cleaning compound, following manufacturer's instructions.

TEA

The United States is the second largest importer of tea in the world. This may come as a surprise to a coffee-drinking nation like ours. Actually, tea is a much more popular beverage in the home than in the restaurant. Part of the difference may be due to mishandling in the restaurant and indifference on the part of restaurateurs.

Food service professionals would do well to pay more attention to tea. First of all, it is much less expensive to serve. A pound (500 grams) of tea yields 200 servings, as compared with 40 from a pound of coffee. Moreover, tea is one of the simplest of beverages to serve and does not require the equipment or the labor of coffee service.

Varieties

All the world's varieties of tea are produced from one species of evergreen shrub. Most of the differences in varieties are the results of growing conditions and modifications in processing techniques.

As in the case of coffee, different regions produce teas of different quality and flavor characteristics. Most of the tea consumed in the United States is imported from India and Sri Lanka (Ceylon).

Variations in processing produce three categories of tea.

Black tea is fermented by allowing the freshly harvested leaves to oxidize in a damp place.

Green tea is dried without fermenting.

Oolong tea is partially fermented to a greenish-brown color.

Specialty teas and flavored teas are also available.

Black teas are graded by leaf size, according to a rather complicated system. This is important to remember, because most people think of Orange Pekoe as a variety of tea, whereas it is actually a specific leaf size of any black variety.

After grading, the teas are blended to ensure consistency and uniformity. A blend may contain as many as 30 individual teas.

Many excellent blends are available from many purveyors. A smart food service operator would do well to shop around, rather than serve the same mediocre blend that the competition serves.

Packaging and Market Forms

Tea is packaged in bulk as loose tea and in tea bags of various sizes. Standard cup-size bags are packaged 200 to the pound, while the pot-sized bag (that is, individual service pot) is packaged at 150 to 175 per pound. This is important for you to know if you are purchasing tea, because the larger bags would not be as economical if the service in your establishment is by the cup.

Larger tea bags are available, containing 1 or 2 oz (30 to 60 g) of tea for brewing larger quantities, especially for iced tea.

Instant tea is a soluble extraction made by brewing a very strong tea, using lesser grades, and drying the liquid to obtain a powder. This product is used primarily for iced tea, because the processing results in the loss of much of the flavor and aroma essential to a good hot tea.

Preparing Tea

In most restaurants, it seems, when one orders tea, one receives a cold cup, a tea bag in a little package, and a pot of warm water that has been standing in an urn for hours. This is absolutely the worst possible way to serve tea, with the possible exception of brewing a large quantity and keeping it warm all day. No wonder most people don't order tea.

Here is the right way:

Procedure for Making Hot Tea

1. Use proper proportions of tea and water. One teaspoon of loose tea or one single service tea bag makes a 6-oz (175-mL) cup.

2. Rinse the teapot with hot water to warm it. Use china, glass, or stainless steel. Other metals may give an off flavor.

3. Bring fresh, cold water to a boil. Water that has been kept warm for a time makes flat-tasting tea.

4. Place the loose tea or tea bag in the pot and pour the water directly over it.

5. Let the tea steep 3 to 5 minutes. Then remove the tea bag or strain off the tea from the loose leaves.

     Establishments specializing in tea service present the customer with the pot of tea and a pot of hot water so that they can dilute the tea to taste.

6. Serve immediately. Tea does not hold well.

Procedure for Making Iced Tea

The following method makes 1 gallon or 4 liters. The tea is brewed stronger to allow for melting ice.

1. Place 2 oz or 60 g of tea in a pot.

2. Bring 1 qt (1 L) of water to a boil and pour over the tea.

3. Steep 5 minutes. Remove tea bags, or strain out loose leaves.

4. Add 3 qt (3 L) cold tap water.

5. Hold at room temperature up to 4 hours. Refrigerating may make the tea cloudy.

6. Serve over ice.

TERMS FOR REVIEW

sunny side up	breakfast sausage	sour cream	double-crème cheese
over easy	pasteurized	buttermilk	triple-crème cheese
shirred egg	homogenized	yogurt	chèvre
conditioned pan	skim milk	evaporated milk	process cheese
frittata	whipping cream	condensed milk	instant coffee
soufflé	light cream	nonfat dry milk	espresso
custard	half-and-half	ripened cheese	demitasse
quiche			

QUESTIONS FOR DISCUSSION

1. Which grade of eggs would you choose to prepare poached eggs? Hard-cooked eggs? Fried eggs? Scrambled eggs? Why?

2. Is it possible to prepare hard-cooked eggs in a pressure steamer? Give reasons for your answer.

3. When separating eggs, many chefs advise breaking them one by one over a small bowl, and then transferring each white to the larger bowl as it is separated. Can you give a reason for this advice?

4. Give two reasons for being careful not to add too much vinegar to egg poaching water.

5. In the recipe for waffles, what is the purpose of beating the sugar into the egg whites rather than combining it with the other dry ingredients?

6. What special precautions might you take if you were making French toast from thick slices of French bread?

7. What is curdling, and how can you prevent it when cooking with milk?

8. Why does cheese combine more smoothly with a sauce at low heat than at high heat?

9. Why is using the proper grind important in making coffee?

10. Describe the proper method for making tea.

CHAPTER 22

FOOD PRESENTATION
AND GARNISH

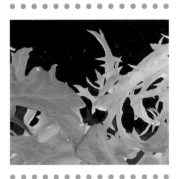

The setting is a dining room in
an elegant restaurant or hotel. The tables are set with the finest crystal,
china, and linen. On cue the waiters appear with gleaming, ornate silver platters
bearing, perhaps, a roast saddle of lamb or a loin of veal, juicy, brown, and aromatic,
surrounded by a colorful array of vegetables, carefully cut and arranged.
After an opening like that, the food could taste like nearly
anything and everyone would still be happy.

That's an exaggeration, of course. We still want
food that tastes good. But the example emphasizes the importance of
the appearance of food. Throughout this book we have stressed making food look
good as well as taste good. We have talked about accurate, neat cutting of vegetables
and fruits, about proper trimming of meats, poultry, and fish, about
grill-marking steaks, about maintaining color in cooked
vegetables, and about attractive plating of salads.

In this chapter we continue the discussion of making food
attractive. With your instructor's guidance, you will learn effective ways to present
food beyond simply adding that same old sprig of parsley.

After reading this chapter, you should be able to

1. Explain the importance of attractive food presentation.

2. Serve food that is attractively arranged on the plate or platter, with proper balance of color, shape, and texture.

3. Identify common terms from classical garniture that are still in general use today.

4. Garnish a banquet platter with attractive and appropriate vegetable accompaniments.

5. Produce and use correctly a wide variety of simple garnishes.

6. Plan and arrange attractive food platters for buffets.

HOT FOOD PRESENTATION

THE IMPORTANCE OF APPEARANCE

We eat for enjoyment as well as for nutrition and sustenance. Cooking is not just a trade but an art that appeals to our sense of taste, smell, and sight.

"The eye eats first" is a well-known maxim. Our first impressions of a plate of food set our expectations. The sight of food stimulates our appetites, starts our digestive juices flowing, and makes us eager to "dig in." Our meal becomes exciting and stimulating.

On the other hand, if the food looks carelessly served, tossed onto the plate in a sloppy manner, we assume it was cooked with the same lack of care. If the colors are pale and washed out, with no color accent, we expect the flavors to be bland and monotonous. If the size of the plate makes the steak *look* small (even if it's not), we go away unsatisfied.

Your job as cooks and chefs then is to get your customers interested in your food or, better yet, excited about it. You can't afford to turn them off before they even taste it. Your success depends on making your customers happy.

Making food look good requires first of all that you use proper cooking techniques. If a fish is overcooked and dry or a green vegetable is drab and mushy, it won't look good no matter what you do with it

Second, serving attractive food is largely a matter of being neat and careful and using common sense. This is an aspect of the professionalism we discussed in Chapter 1. Professionals take pride in their work and in the food they serve. They don't put up a plate with sauce dribbled all over the rim and maybe a thumbprint or two for extra effect—not because their supervisors told them not to or because a rule in a textbook says "don't dribble sauce all over the rim of the plate," but because it's not professional.

Third, beyond just being neat, effective food presentation depends on developing an understanding of techniques involving balance, arrangement, and garniture. These are the subjects of our next sections.

FUNDAMENTALS OF PLATING

We've said before that a plate of food is like a picture, and the rim of the plate is the frame. This does not mean that you have to spend as much time arranging the plate as Rembrandt did painting a portrait, but it does mean that you think a little like an artist and strive for a pleasing arrangement.

One caution: Don't get carried away. A plate that's too elaborate can be as bad as one that's too careless. Besides, you want that hot dinner to be still hot when it reaches the customer, and you don't have time to get too fancy.

Balance

Balance is a term we used when talking about menu planning in Chapter 6. The rules of good menu balance also apply to plating. Select foods and garnishes that offer variety and contrast, while at the same time avoiding combinations that are awkward or jarring.

1. *Colors.*

   Two or three colors on a plate are usually more interesting than just one. Visualize this combination: poached chicken breast with suprême sauce, mashed potatoes, and steamed cauliflower. Appetizing? Or how about fried chicken, french fries, and corn? Not quite so bad, but still a little monotonous.

   Many hot foods, especially meats, poultry, and fish, have little color other than shades of brown, gold, or white. It helps to select vegetables or accompaniments that add color interest—one reason why green vegetables are so popular.

   Garnish is often unnecessary, especially if the accompaniments have color, but it is very important in some cases. The classic American combination of broiled steak (brown) and baked potato (brown and white) looks a little livelier with even the simple addition of a healthy sprig of watercress or parsley.

2. *Shapes.*

   Plan for variety of shapes and forms as well as of colors. For example, you probably do not want to serve brussels sprouts with meatballs and new potatoes. Your customers might get up a game of marbles. Green beans and whipped potatoes might be better choices for accompaniment.

   Cutting vegetables into different shapes gives you great flexibility. Carrots, for example, which can be cut into dice, rounds, or sticks (batonnet, julienne, etc.), can be adapted to nearly any plate.

3. **Textures.**

   Textures are not strictly visual considerations, but they are important in plating as in menu planning (Chapter 6).

   Good balance requires a variety of textures on the plate. Perhaps the most common error is serving too many soft or puréed foods, such as baked salmon loaf with whipped potatoes and puréed squash.

4. **Flavors.**

   You can't see flavors, either, but this is one more factor you must consider when balancing colors, shapes, and textures on the plate. Consult the menu planning guidelines in Chapter 6.

Portion Size

Portion sizes are important for presentation as well as for costing.

1. ***Match portion sizes and plates.***

   Too small a plate makes an overcrowded, jumbled, messy appearance. Too large a plate may make the portions look skimpy.

2. ***Balance the portion sizes of the various items on the plate.***

   One item, generally a meat, poultry, or fish preparation, is usually considered the main item on the plate. It is the center of attention and is larger than the accompaniments. Don't let the main item get lost amid excessive garnish and huge portions of vegetable and starch items.

   Where there is no main item, as in some vegetable plates, strive for a logical balance of portions.

Arrangement on the Plate

Until recent years, plated main courses followed a standard pattern: meat or fish item at the front of the plate (closest to the diner), vegetable and starch items at the rear.

This arrangement is still the most commonly used, because it is one of the simplest and most convenient. Nevertheless, many creative chefs are eager to display their creativity with imaginative plating presentations.

The following patterns are examples of today's plating styles. Figure 22.1 illustrates some of these styles, using recipes from this book.

- The classic arrangement: main item in front, vegetables, starch items, and garnish at the rear.

- The main item alone in the center of the plate, sometimes with a sauce or simple garnish.

- The main item in the center, with vegetables distributed randomly around it, sometimes with a sauce underneath.

- The main item in the center, with neat piles of vegetables carefully arranged around it in a pattern.

- A starch or vegetable item heaped in the center; the main item sliced and leaning up against it; additional vegetables, garnish, and/or sauce on the plate around the center items.

- Vegetable in center of plate, sometimes with sauce; main item (in slices, medallions, small pieces, etc.) arranged around it toward the outside of the plate.

- Slices of the main item arranged shingle-fashion on a bed of vegetables or a purée of vegetables or starch. Perhaps additional garnish to one side or around.

- Various asymmetrical or random-looking arrangements that don't seem to follow any pattern. These often create the impression that the food was rushed to the dining room the instant it was cooked, without thought to the design. Of course, to be effective these arrangements are carefully thought out in advance.

The following guidelines will help you plate attractive, appealing food, no matter what plating style you are using.

1. ***Keep food off the rim of the plate.***

2. ***Arrange the items for the convenience of the customer.***

   Put the best side of the meat forward. The customer should not have to turn the item around to start on it. The bony or fatty edge of the steak, the back side of the half duckling, the boniest parts of the chicken pieces, and so on, should face *away* from the customer.

3. ***Keep space between items.***

   Don't pile everything together in a jumbled heap. Each item should have its own identity.

FIGURE 22.1 **Examples of traditional and modern plating styles and patterns.**
(a) **Tournedos Rossini; berny potatoes, braised lettuce.**

(b) **Veal cutlet Viennese style.**

(c) Sautéed veal chop; zucchini with tomatoes.

(d) Sautéed chicken breast, ivory sauce; broccoli, parisienne potatoes.

(e) **Roast rack of lamb; white beans bretonne, steamed brussels sprout leaves.**

(f) **Paupiettes of sole Dugléré; buttered spinach, steamed potatoes.**

(g) Spicy shrimp sauté; steamed rice, sautéed grated zucchini.

(h) Roast duckling, Bohemian style; braised red cabbage, potato dumplings; green beans.

This is of course related also to selecting the right plate size.

4. *Maintain unity.*

Basically, there is unity when the plate looks like *one* meal that happens to be made up of several items, rather than like several unrelated items that just happen to be on the same plate.

Create a center of attention and relate everything to it. The meat is generally the center of attention and is often placed front and center. Other items are placed around and behind it so as to balance it and keep your eyes centered rather than pulled off the edge of the plate.

5. *Make the garnish count.*

Garnishes are added not just for color. Sometimes they are needed to balance out a plate by providing an additional element. Two items on a plate often look unbalanced, but adding a garnish completes the picture.

On the other hand, don't add unnecessary garnishes. In many or even most cases, the food is attractive and colorful without garnish, and adding it clutters the plate and increases your food cost as well.

6. *Don't drown every plate in sauce or gravy.*

Sometimes ladling sauce all over an item hides colors and shapes. If the item is attractive by itself, let the customer see it. Ladle the sauce around or under it, or possibly covering only part of it, as with a band of sauce across the center.

7. *Keep it simple.*

As you have heard before, simplicity is more attractive than overworked, contrived arrangements or complicated designs. Unusual patterns are occasionally very effective, but avoid making the food look too cute or too elaborate.

One of the simplest plating styles can also be one of the most attractive if it is carefully done—that is, placing only the meat or fish item and its sauce, if any, in the center of the plate. Vegetable accompaniments are then served in separate dishes. This method is widely used in restaurants to simplify service in the kitchen. However, it is usually best to use this method for only some of the menu items, in order to avoid monotony.

Temperature

Serve hot foods hot, on hot plates.

Serve cold foods cold, on cold plates.

Your arrangement of beautiful food will not make much of a final impression if you forget this rule.

GARNISH

What Is Garnish?

The word "garnish" is derived from a French word meaning "to adorn or to furnish." In English, we use the word to mean to decorate or embellish a food item by the addition of other items. The word also is used for these decorative items.

This definition at first seems too vague, because it could include just about anything. But, in fact, the term has been used for a great variety of preparations and techniques in the history of classical and modern cuisines. Let's look at some of these styles of garnish and what they mean to today's cooks and chefs.

First, however, we'll briefly define some similar words that are often confused.

Garnish refers to decorative edible items used to ornament or to enhance the eye appeal of another food item.

To garnish means to add such a decorative item to food.

Garniture is the French word for garnish and means the same thing. Garniture also means "the act or process of garnishing."

Garni means "garnished." It does not refer to the decorative item but describes the main food item by stating that it has had garnish added to it. In other words, you say "steak garni" (garnished steak), not "steak with garni."

Classical Garnish

In classical French cooking, the terms garnish and garniture have been used the way we use the term *accompaniments.* In other words, garnishes are any items placed on the platter or plate or in the soup bowl in addition to the main item. It happens that these accompaniments also make the food look more attractive, but that is not the emphasis.

The classical French chef had a tremendous repertory of simple and elaborate garnishes, and they all had specific names. A trained chef, or a well-informed diner for that matter, knew that the word Rachel on the menu meant that the dish was served with artichoke bottoms filled with poached marrow and that Portugaise meant a garnish of stuffed tomatoes.

There were so many of these names, however, that no one could remember them all. So they were catalogued in handbooks for the use of chefs. *Le Répertoire de la Cuisine,* one of these handbooks, has 209 listings in the garnish section alone, not to mention nearly 7,000 other preparations, all with their own names. The garnishes may be as simple as the one called Concorde or as complex as the one called Tortue, quoted here to give you an idea of the complexity and elaborateness of classical garnish.

> *Concorde (for large joints)*—Peas, glazed carrots, mashed potatoes.

> *Tortue (for Entrées)*—Quenelles, mushroom heads, gherkins, garlic, collops of tongue and calves' brains, small fried eggs, heart-shaped croutons, crayfish, slices of truffles. Tortue sauce.

Classical Terms in the Modern Kitchen

Many of the classical names for garnishes are still used in American kitchens, although they have lost the precise meanings they once had. You will encounter these terms frequently, so it is worthwhile learning them.

Remember that the following definitions are not the classical ones, but simply the garnish or accompaniment generally indicated by the terms in today's kitchens.

Bouquetière: "bouquet" of vegetables.

Jardinière: "garden" vegetables.

Printanière: spring vegetables.

Primeurs: first spring vegetables.

These four terms refer to assortments of fresh vegetables, including carrots, turnips, peas, pearl onions, green beans, cauliflower, sometimes asparagus, artichokes.

Clamart: peas.

Crécy: carrots.

Doria: cucumbers (cooked in butter).

Dubarry: cauliflower.

Fermière: carrots, turnips, onions, and celery, cut into uniform slices.

Florentine: spinach.

Forestière: mushrooms.

Judic: braised lettuce.

Lyonnaise: onions.

Niçoise: tomatoes concassée cooked with garlic.

Parmentier: potatoes.

Princesse: asparagus.

Provençale: tomatoes with garlic, parsley, and sometimes mushrooms and/or olives.

Vichy: carrots (especially Vichy carrots, p. 412).

Modern Hot Platter Garnish

In classical cuisine, food was nearly always brought to the dining room on large platters and then served, rather than being plated in the kitchen as is most often done today.

This practice is still widely used for banquets, and nothing stimulates appetites as much as a succulent roast on a silver platter, sumptuously adorned with a colorful variety of vegetable garnishes.

The classical garnitures most often adapted to modern platter presentation are those called Bouquetière, Jardinière, and Printanière. At one time these were very specific vegetable assortments cut in prescribed ways. But today they are taken in a more general way, meaning colorful assortments of various fresh vegetables.

Platter garnish need not be elaborate or difficult to prepare. A simple assortment of colorful vegetables, carefully cut and properly cooked to retain color and texture, is appropriate to the most elegant presentation. Stuffed vegetables, such as tomato halves filled with peas, are a little fancier, but still easy to prepare. Borders of duchesse potatoes are also popular (see p. 435).

Many of the rules of proper plating apply to platter arrangement as well, for example, those that call for neatness, balance of color and shape, unity, and preserving the individuality of the items. Following are a few other guidelines that apply to hot platter presentation and garnish. Examples of hot platters are included with the color plates.

1. ***Vegetables should be in easily served units.***

    In other words, don't heap green peas or mashed potatoes on one corner of the platter. More suitable are vegetables such as cauliflower, broccoli, boiled tomatoes, asparagus spears, whole green beans, mushroom caps, or anything that comes in large or easy-to-handle pieces. Small vegetables such as peas can be easily served if they are used to fill artichoke bottoms, tomato halves, or tartlet shells.

2. *Have the correct number of portions of each item.*

Vegetables like brussels sprouts and tournéed carrots are easily portioned in the dining room if they are arranged in little portion-size piles.

3. *Arrange the garnishes around the platter to get the best effect from the different colors and shapes.*

The meat, poultry, or fish is usually placed in the center of the platter, or in a row or rows, and the garnishes are arranged around it.

4. *Avoid being too elaborate.*

While it is sometimes desirable to make very ornate platters, simplicity is usually preferable to an overworked appearance. Let the attractiveness of the food speak for itself. The garnish should never dominate or hide the meat, which is the center of attention.

5. *Serve extra sauce or gravy in a sauceboat.*

If it is appropriate, dress or nap the meat or fish items with some of the sauce, but don't drown the entire platter with it.

6. *Serve hot foods hot, on a hot platter.*

Don't spend so much time arranging the food that it's cold by the time it reaches the dining room.

Simple Plate Garnish

To many people, the word "garnish" means a sprig of parsley. What this implies is that garnish is often nothing more than an afterthought, a meaningless scrap of something routinely planted on the plate without regard to its function or appropriateness.

Just as bad is the practice in some restaurants of adopting a single garnish, such as a cinnamon apple ring on a leaf of lettuce, and using it routinely on every plate, from prime rib to batter-fried shrimp. No one garnish is appropriate for every plate, and in the case of the apple ring, it is appropriate for very few.

The only solution to this problem is to learn a wide variety of garnishes and to give more thought and imagination to garniture.

Let's consider two approaches to plating, from the point of view of garnish.

1. *No garnish.*

Many or even most plates need no added garnish. If the accompanying vegetables and starches provide an attractive balance and color combination, the garnish may just clutter it up. Leave it off.

Actually, this is much the same as classical garniture, as we discussed above. The accompaniments become the garnish because they do the job of balancing out the plate for an attractive presentation.

2. *Simple garnish.*

Sometimes it is necessary to serve the accompanying vegetables in side dishes. Sometimes the accompaniments do not add much contrast to the plate, such as a baked potato served with a steak or french fries served with fried chicken or fish. A simple garnish may then be helpful to provide a color accent or balance to the plate.

A simple garnish should be

- Edible.
- Appropriate to the food.
- Planned into the plate layout, not just stuck on haphazardly.

Although modern plating styles have made simple garnishes less frequently used than in years past, they sometimes play a useful role. Table 22.1 lists some popular simple garnishes and appropriate foods. Techniques for producing specific garnishes follow the table, with illustrations. These are, with a few exceptions, uncooked or ready prepared (for example, pickled) garnishes. Most cooked garnishes are more on the order of accompaniments or side dishes. Salad and soup garnishes are discussed in their respective chapters.

Note: Appropriate foods indicated on the chart are *for general guidelines only.* There will be many exceptions among individual recipes.

TABLE 22.1 **Simple Garnishes**

	Beef	Veal	Lamb	Pork, Ham, Duck, Goose	Chicken, Turkey	Eggs	Fish	Vegetables	Other
Herbs and leafy garnish									

Parsley
  Sprigs
  Chopped
  Fried (technique 1)
	x	x	x	x	x	x	x	x	

Watercress, sprigs	x	x	x	x	x		x		
Chives, cut						x	x	x	Cheese dishes
Mint, sprigs			x						Entreés with fruit-based sauces or accompaniments
Dill, sprigs						x	x	x	Cold meat plates
Chicory, leaves	x	x	x	x	x				
Vegetables									

Tomato
  Wedge
  Slice, raw or broiled
  Half, raw or broiled
  Cherry tomato
	x	x	x	x	x	x	x		

Cucumber
  (technique 2)
  Slice, plain or fluted
  Twist
  Cup
						x			Cold meat plates

Mushrooms
  (technique 3)
  Slices
  Caps, plain or fluted
	x	x	x	x	x	x	x	x	

Radishes (technique 4)
  Slices
  Roses
  Fans
	x	x	x	x	x	x	x		

Green pepper
  Rings
  Dice
						x	x	x	Cold meat plates

Onions
  Rings, raw or deep-fried
  Scallions
  (technique 5)
	x	x	x	x	x		x	x	

Duchesse potatoes
  Borders, rosettes, etc.
  (see Figure 18.3)
	x	x	x	x	x	x	x	x	

Horseradish, grated	x			x					Smoked fish, seafood cocktails

(Continues)

TABLE 22.1 **Simple Garnishes** *(Continued)*

	Beef	Veal	Lamb	Pork, Ham, Duck, Goose	Chicken, Turkey	Eggs	Fish	Vegetables	Other
Vegetables (Continued)									
Olives, green, black, stuffed—whole or sliced	x	x	x	x	x	x	x	x	

Pickles
  Slices
  Spears
  Fans (technique 6)
	x	x		x					Pâté, sausages

Pimiento
  Strips
  Cutouts
	x	x			x	x	x	x	

Artichokes Bottoms filled with appropriate sauce (see p.410)	x	x	x	x	x	x	x	x	
Fruits									

Lemon (technique 7)
  Slices
  Wedges
  Halves
		x		x	x	x	x	x	

Orange Cut like lemon				x	x	x	x	x	
Lime Cut like lemon				x	x	x	x	x	
Apple Spiced rings and crabapples, with leafy underliner	x	x	x	x					
Grapes (technique 8) Frosted or plain				x	x	x			

Pineapple
  Rings
  Sticks
				x	x				

Peaches
  Halves
  Slices
				x	x				

Cranberries
  Relish
  Sauce
  Jelly
				x	x				

Kumquats
  Fresh
  Preserved
				x	x				

TABLE 22.1   **Simple Garnishes** *(Continued)*

	Beef	Veal	Lamb	Pork, Ham, Duck, Goose	Chicken, Turkey	Eggs	Fish	Vegetables	Other
Miscellaneous									

Hard-cooked eggs
    Slices
    Halves
    Wedges
    Chopped white
    Chopped yolk
					x	x		x	Cold meat plates

Anchovy
    Flat or rolled fillets,
    often combined with
    sliced lemon or egg
	x	x				x	x		

Almonds
    Whole, toasted
    Sliced
					x	x	x	x	

Toast points (technique 9)					x	x	x	x	Creamed dishes
Paprika, Spanish		x		x	x	x	x	x	

Technique 1.   Fried Parsley

1. Separate sprigs and remove coarse stems.

2. Wash. Dry *thoroughly*.

3. Deep-fry for just a few seconds, until crisp but still green.

4. Drain on absorbent paper. Serve immediately.

Technique 2.   Cucumbers (see Figure 22.2)

1. For decorative slices, score unpeeled cucumber with a fork or flute with a channel knife before slicing.

2. For twists, cut slices three-fourths of the way across, twist open, and stand on plate.

3. For cups, cut fluted cucumber in one-inch sections, hollow out slightly with a melon ball cutter or spoon, and fill with an appropriate condiment or sauce.

FIGURE 22.2   Cucumber garnishes can be made more decorative by scoring the cucumber.
(a) With a fork.

(b) With a channel knife before slicing or cutting. See Technique 2.

Technique 3. Mushroom Caps

1. Fluting mushrooms is a technique that takes a great deal of practice to get the knack of. Follow the steps in Figure 22.3, or watch your instructor demonstrate. Then, whenever you have to slice mushrooms, practice fluting a few. Eventually you'll get it.

2. To keep mushrooms white, simmer 2 to 3 minutes in salted water with a little butter and lemon juice.

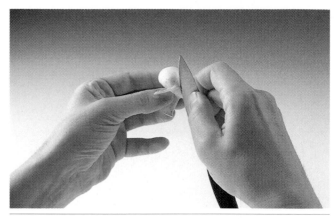

(c) The first cut is completed.

FIGURE 22.3 **There are two basic methods for fluting mushrooms (Technique 3).**
(a) Grasping the blade of a paring knife as shown, hold the edge of the blade against the center of the mushroom cap at a sharp angle as shown.

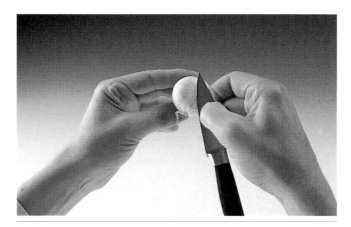

(d) Rotate the mushroom a few degrees and cut a second groove next to the first.

(b) Begin to rotate the blade toward the edge of the cap so that the blade cuts a shallow groove in the mushroom.

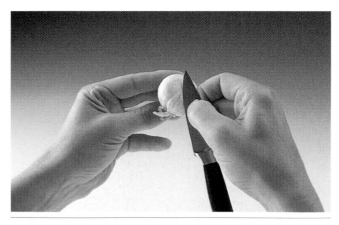

(e) Continue making cuts all around the mushroom.

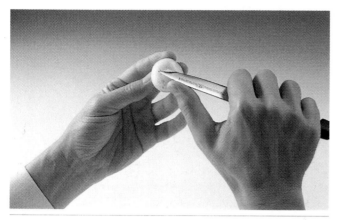

(f) The second method is similar, except that the edge of the blade is away from you. The thumb of your knife hand rests on the mushroom and braces the back of the blade. Rotate the knife, using your thumb as the pivot point.

(i) The fluted mushroom cap.

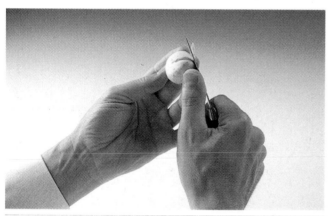

(g) Turn the knife until the groove extends to the edge of the mushroom cap.

(j) To decorate the center of the cap, you can press the point of the knife into the mushroom to form a star.

(h) Continue cutting grooves as in the first method.

Technique 4. Radishes

1. Radishes can be cut in many ways to make decorative garnishes, as illustrated in Figure 22.4.

2. After cutting, soak the radishes in ice water until they open up.

Technique 5. Scallion Brushes

1. Cut off the root ends of the scallions, including the little hard core. Cut the white part into 2-inch sections.

2. With a thin-bladed knife, split both ends of the scallion pieces with cuts ½ inch (15 mm) deep. Make enough cuts to separate the ends into fine shreds, as shown in Figure 22.5.

3. Soak in cold water until the ends curl up.

FIGURE 22.4 **Radishes can be cut into many decorative forms, including those shown here (Technique 4).**

FIGURE 22.5 **Scallions for garnish can be cut as described in Technique 5.**

Technique 6. Pickle Fans

1. With the stem end of the pickle away from you, make a series of thin vertical slices the length of the pickle, but do not cut through the stem end (Figure 22.6).

2. Spread the pickle into a fan shape as shown.

Technique 7. Lemons

1. Fluted lemon slices and twisted slices are cut the same way as for cucumbers (technique 2). Slices placed directly on fish or meat are cut from *peeled* lemons.

2. Dip half the slice in paprika or finely chopped parsley for a colorful effect, as shown in Figure 22.7a. For just a line of paprika down the center, bend the slice between the fingers, as shown in the illustration, and dip lightly in paprika.

3. Wedges are often more attractive if the ends of the lemons are cut off first (Figure 22.7a). For added color, dip the edge of the wedge in paprika as shown.

4. For lemon halves, first cut a thin slice from each end of the lemon so the halves will stand straight. Cut a long strip from the outer edge of the lemon half as shown in Figure 22.7b, but do not detach it. Tie a knot in the strip, being careful not to break it. Or you may cut two strips, one from either side, and make two knots. Decorate with parsley.

5. For a sawtooth edge, cut the pattern as shown in Figure 22.7c, piercing all the way to the center of the lemon with the knife. Separate the two halves. Decorate with parsley, or dip the points of the teeth in paprika.

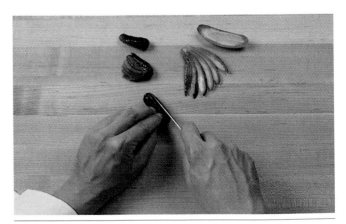

FIGURE 22.6 **Pickle fans (Technique 6) may be cut from tiny gherkins or from slices of larger dill pickles.**

FIGURE 22.7   **Lemon garnishes (Technique 7).**
(a) Lemon slices and wedges may be decorated with paprika or chopped parsley. Peeled lemon slices may also be used.

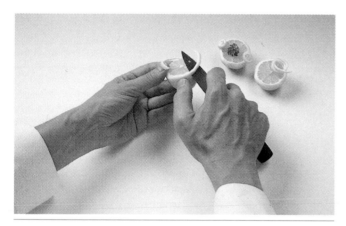

(b) Simple lemon halves are made more decorative by cutting as shown.

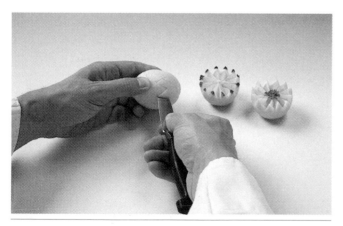

(c) This illustration shows another way of presenting lemon halves as garnish. After cutting, the halves may be decorated with paprika or parsley.

Technique 8.   Frosted Grapes

1.   Separate the grapes into small bunches. Brush with lightly beaten egg white and sprinkle with granulated sugar.

2.   Let dry before serving.

Technique 9.   Toast Points

1.   Cut slices of pullman bread in half diagonally. Trim the crusts off and cut each piece into a heart shape as shown (Figure 22.8). Save the trimmings for bread crumbs.

2.   Sauté the pieces in butter and oil until golden on both sides.

3.   Dip the tips into the sauce that is being served with the dish the toast points are to garnish, and then into chopped parsley.

FIGURE 22.8   **To prepare toast points, cut bread slices into triangles or heart shapes as shown. Fry the bread shapes in butter and dip the tips in sauce and then in parsley.**

COLD FOOD PRESENTATION AND BUFFET SERVICE

*T*he buffet is a popular and profitable form of food presentation in nearly every kind of food service operation across the country. There are at least three reasons for this popularity:

1. *Visual appeal.* An attractive presentation of foods has the effect of lavishness and ample quantity, and careful arrangement and garnish suggest quality as well.

2. *Efficiency.* The buffet allows the restaurant to serve a large number of people in a short time with relatively few service personnel.

3. *Adaptability.* Buffet service is adaptable to nearly every kind of food (except items that must be cooked to order, like broiled or deep-fried foods), and to all price ranges, occasions, restaurant styles, and local food customs.

· · · · · · · · ·

BUFFET ARRANGEMENT AND APPEARANCE

The buffet's visual appeal is perhaps its greatest attraction for the customer. Eye appeal of food is always important, but perhaps nowhere more important than on a buffet, because it is the appearance that sells the food. A buffet is not just food service, it is food display.

Lavishness and Abundance

Above all else, a buffet should look lavish and plentiful. The appearance of an abundance of food beautifully laid out is exciting and stimulating to the appetite. There are many ways to create this look.

1. *Color.* A variety of colors is vital on a buffet as it is on a single plate. Plan menus and garnish so that you have enough color on the table.

2. *Height.* Flat foods on flat trays on flat tables are uninteresting to the eye.

 A centerpiece is an important feature, giving height and focus to the buffet. Ice carvings, tallow sculptures, and floral or fruit displays are some possibilities. They should be on a separate table behind the food table.

Centerpieces on individual platters also add height. Large food items such as large cheeses and whole roasts being carved at the table are also effective. Multilevel tables, when available, are used to good effect.

3. *Full platters and bowls.* Replenish items as they become depleted. A nearly empty bowl isn't as appetizing as a full one.

 Arrange platters so that they still have interest even when portions have been removed (more on this later).

4. *Proper spacing.* While you shouldn't crowd the items, don't spread them so far apart that the table looks half empty.

Simplicity

This sounds like a contradiction to "lavishness," but it's not. You need to strike a good balance between the two. Lavishness is not the same as clutter.

1. Overdesigned, overdecorated food scares people from eating it. How many times have you heard someone say, "Oh, it's so pretty I don't want to touch it"? Even if they don't say it, they'll think it.

 Too much design detracts from the food. Sometimes the food is so overdecorated that it no longer looks like food. This is completely defeating the purpose. The customer should at least be able to identify it.

2. Excessive garnish is quickly destroyed as customers take portions.

Orderliness

A buffet should look like it was planned, not like it just happened. Customers prefer food presentations that look carefully done, not just thrown together.

1. Simple arrangements are much easier to keep neat and orderly than complicated designs.

2. Colors and shapes should look lively and varied, but make sure they go together and do not clash.

3. Keep the style consistent. If it's formal, then everything should be formal. If it's casual or rustic, then every part of the presentation should be casual or rustic. If it's a Mexican fiesta, don't include German sauerbraten just because your specialty happens to be sauerbraten.

 This is true not only of the food but of the dishes and serving pieces, too. Don't use ornate silver serving pieces for a country theme, for example.

Menu and Serving Sequence

Practical reasons as well as visual appeal determine the order in which foods are arranged on the buffet. As far as possible, it is good to have items in the proper menu order (for example, appetizers first, main course afterward, desserts last) if only to avoid confusing the customers, who might otherwise wonder what the food is and how much they should take. But there are many reasons for changing the order. The following should be taken into account when arranging a buffet.

1. Hot foods are best served last. Otherwise they would cool off while the guests make other selections from the cold foods. Also, it is more effective, visually, to place the decorative cold platters first and the less attractive chafing dishes last.

2. The more expensive foods are usually placed after the less expensive items. This gives you some control of food cost, since the guests' plates will be nearly full of other attractive foods by the time they get to the costly items.

3. Sauces and dressings should be placed next to the items with which they are to be served. Otherwise the customer might not match them with the right foods.

4. A separate dessert table is often a good idea. It allows guests to make a separate trip for their desserts without interfering with the main serving line. It is also possible, if the menu is large, to have a separate appetizer table.

5. Plates, of course, must be the first items on the table. Silverware, napkins, and other items not needed until the guest sits down to eat should be at the end of the buffet table or set in place on the dining tables.

The Cocktail Buffet—an Exception

One kind of buffet doesn't conform to this menu-order pattern. The cocktail buffet displays appetizers intended to accompany drinks and other refreshments at receptions, cocktail parties, and cocktail hours preceding banquets and dinners. There is no serving line—or looking at it a different way, there is a separate line for each item.

1. Only appetizer-type foods are served: tasty, well-seasoned foods in small portions.

2. Stacks of small plates are placed beside each item, rather than at the beginning of the table.

3. The table or tables must be easy to get to from all parts of the room and must not block traffic. Do not place them next to the entry, because guests gather around them, blocking movement into and out of the room.

COLD PLATTER PRESENTATION

The cold platter is the mainstay of the buffet and offers the most opportunity for visual artistry. It also can be one of the most demanding forms of food presentation, particularly show platters, which require great precision, patience, and a good artistic sense.

Cold platters can range from a simple tray of cold cuts to elaborate constructions of patés, meats, poultry, or fish decorated with aspic, truffles, and vegetable flowers. In this chapter we have space only for a discussion of general guidelines that you can apply both to formal buffet platters and to simple cold food arrangements. To learn more detailed, complex techniques, you will have to depend on your instructors, on more advanced courses, and on on-the-job experience. But this section should help you take the foods available in whatever kitchen you find yourself working and produce an attractive, appetizing buffet.

Basic Principles of Platter Presentation

1. The three elements of a buffet platter:

   a. Centerpiece or *grosse pièce* (gross pyess). This may be an uncut portion of the main food item, such as a pâté or a cold roast, decorated and displayed whole. It may be a separate but related item, such as a molded salmon mousse on a platter of poached slices of salmon in aspic. It may be something as simple as a bowl or *ravier* (an oval relish dish—pronounced rahv-yay) of sauce or condiment. Or it may be strictly for decoration, such as a butter sculpture or a squash vase filled with vegetable flowers. Whether or not the grosse pièce is intended to be eaten, it should be made of edible materials.

   b. The slices or serving portions of the main food item, arranged artistically.

   c. The garnish, arranged artistically, in proportion to the cut slices.

2. The food should be easy to handle and serve, so that one portion can be removed without ruining the arrangement.

3. A simple design is best. Simple arrangements are easier to serve, are more appetizing than

overworked food, and are more likely to be still attractive when they are half demolished by the guests.

Simple arrangements may be the hardest to produce. Everything has to be perfect because there is less decoration to divide the attention.

4. Attractive platter presentations may be made on silver or other metals, on mirrors, china, plastic, wood, or on many other materials, as long as they are presentable and suitable for use with food. Metal platters that might cause discoloration or metallic flavors are often covered with a thin layer of aspic before the food is placed on them.

5. Once a piece of food has touched the tray, do not remove it. Shiny silver or mirror trays are easily smudged, and you'll have to wash the tray and start over again. This shows the importance of good preplanning.

Following this rule also helps eliminate over-handling of food, which is a bad sanitary practice.

6. Think of the platter as part of the whole buffet. It must look attractive and appropriate not only by itself but among the other presentations on the table. The arrangement should always be planned from the same angle from which it will be seen on the buffet.

Designing the Platter

1. *Plan ahead.*

Making a sketch is a good idea. Otherwise you might have half the food on the platter and suddenly realize you have to start over because everything doesn't fit the way you had hoped. The result is wasted time and excessive handling of food.

One way to start a sketch is to divide the platter into six or eight equal parts, as in Figure 22.9. This helps you avoid lopsided or crooked arrangements by giving you equally spaced markers to guide you. It is relatively easy, then, to sketch in a balanced, symmetrical layout, as the examples show.

2. *Get movement into your design.*

This doesn't mean that you should mount the food on little wheels. It means that a good design makes your eyes move across the platter following the lines you have set up.

Most food for platters consists of single small portions arranged in rows or lines. The trick is

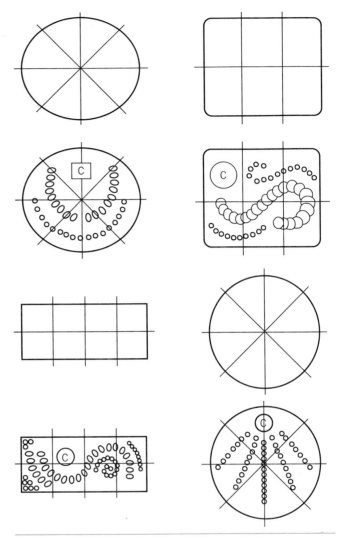

FIGURE 22.9 Begin your planning sketch of a buffet platter by dividing the tray into six or eight sections. This helps you lay out a balanced, symmetrical design. The examples shown here indicate the placement of the main items (usually slices of foods), the centerpiece (labeled "c"), and the garnish (shown as tiny circles).

to put movement into those lines by curving or angling them, as shown in Figure 22.10. In general, curves and angles are said to have movement. Square corners do not.

3. *Give the design a focal point.*

This is the function of the centerpiece, which emphasizes and strengthens the design by giving it direction and height. This may be done very directly, by having the lines point directly to it, or more subtly by having them angle toward it or sweep around it in graceful curves. Again, see Figures 22.9 and 22.10.

FIGURE 22.10 **Arranging rows of foods in curves or in angled lines gives movement to the design.**

Note that the centerpiece isn't always in the center, in spite of its name. Because of its height, it should be at the back or toward the side, so it doesn't hide the food. Remember, you are designing the platter from the customer's point of view.

It's not necessary for every platter on the buffet to have a centerpiece. Some of them should, however, or the buffet will lack height and be less interesting to the eye.

4. *Keep items in proportion.*

The main items on the platter—the slices of meat, pâté, or whatever—should *look* like the main items. The centerpiece should not be so large or so tall that it totally dominates the platter. The garnish should enhance, not overwhelm, the main item in size, height, or quantity. The number of portions of garnish should be in proportion to the amount of the main item.

The size of the platter should be in proportion to the amount of food. Don't select one that is so small as to become crowded or so large as to look almost empty even before the first guest has arrived.

Keep enough space between items or between rows so that the platter doesn't look jumbled or confused.

Figure 22.9 indicates placement of garnish as well as of the main item. Note how the arrangement of garnish reflects or accents the pattern established by the sliced foods.

5. *Let the guest see the best side of everything.*

Angle overlapping slices and wedge-shaped pieces toward the customer. And make sure that the best side of each slice is face up.

Cheese Platters

Cheese trays are popular on both luncheon buffets as a main course item and on dinner buffets as a dessert item. Cheeses are presented much differently from the other cold buffet foods we have been talking about.

First, whole cheeses or cheeses in large pieces are generally more attractive than an arrangement of slices. This also helps the guest identify the varieties. Be sure to supply several knives, so guests can cut their own portions.

Second, an assortment of fresh fruit is often included on a cheese tray. It adds a great deal to the appearance of a cheese presentation, and its flavors go well with cheese. Figure 22.11 shows an example of a cheese and fruit presentation.

A Note on Sanitation

Cold food for buffets presents a special sanitation problem. This is because the food spends a great deal of time out of refrigeration while it is being assembled and decorated and again while it sits on the buffet. For this reason it is particularly important to follow all the rules of safe food handling. Keep foods refrigerated whenever they are not being worked on. Also, keep them chilled until the last minute before they are to be brought out for service.

For a buffet service that lasts a long time, it is a good idea to make each course or item on a number of small platters rather than on one big one. The replacements can then be kept refrigerated until needed.

FIGURE 22.11   **One type of cheese and fruit presentation for buffet service.**

HOT FOODS FOR BUFFETS

Everything we have learned about the preparation and holding of hot foods in quantity applies to hot foods for buffets. Hot items are nearly always served from chafing dishes, which may be ornate silver affairs or simple steam table pans kept warm over hot water. These foods cannot be elaborately decorated and garnished the way cold foods can. On the other hand, the bright, fresh, juicy appearance and good aroma of properly cooked hot food is generally sufficient to arouse appetites.

Hot foods for chafing dishes should be easily portioned (such as vegetables served with a kitchen spoon) or already portioned in the pan (braised pork chops, sliced baked ham, and poached fish fillets, for example). Items less suitable for buffets are those that must be cooked to order and served immediately, such as most broiled or deep-fried foods.

Whole roasts are popular items at buffets, carved to order by a member of the kitchen staff. Especially attractive are large roasts such as hams, turkeys, and large cuts of beef such as steamship round.

As we have said, hot foods are best placed at the end of the buffet, so that they will not cool off on the guests' plates before they are seated, and so that the decorated cold foods can steal the show.

TERMS FOR REVIEW

unity of arrangement	Bouquetière	Dubarry	Lyonnaise
garnish	Jardinière	Fermière	Parmentier
garniture	Printanière	Florentine	grosse pièce
garni	Clamart	Forestière	ravier
classical garnish			

QUESTIONS FOR DISCUSSION

1. Discuss the idea of professionalism and how it applies to the presentation of food.

2. Following are several popular food combinations. Describe what plating problems they present, if any, and how you might efficiently and economically solve them.

Fish and chips (deep-fried fillets and french fries).

Prime rib of beef and baked potato.

Meat loaf, mashed potatoes, and gravy.

Open-faced hot turkey sandwich.

Beef stroganoff and egg noodles.

Chicken à la king in a patty shell.

3. What is meant by plating food for the convenience of the customer, and how does this affect other rules of plating?

4. When is it a good idea *not* to add a garnish to a plate?

5. What is the difference between a cocktail buffet and a luncheon or dinner buffet?

6. Customers like to see a lot of food on a buffet. Is it correct to say, then, that the best way to please customers is to put out as much food as possible? Explain your answer.

7. When you are preparing a cold buffet platter, why is it a good idea to plan ahead by making a sketch? What would you include in the sketch? What do the terms movement and focal point mean in platter design?

CHAPTER 23

RECIPES FROM INTERNATIONAL CUISINES

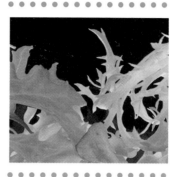

The popularity of ethnic and
international cuisines is booming. While there is a surge of interest in American
cuisine, at the same time there are more ethnic restaurants than ever before. Japanese,
Chinese, and Mexican restaurants, among others, are springing up not just in
big cities but in suburbs and small towns as well.

Many of our most creative chefs have been inspired by these
cuisines and have borrowed some of their techniques. For example, many
American and French chefs, looking for ways to make their own cooking lighter and
more elegant, have found ideas in the cuisine of Japan. And in the American
Southwest, a number of chefs have transformed Mexican influences
into an elegant and original cooking style of their own.

Foreign influences are not new, of course. Classical cuisine is full
of terms that reveal foreign inspiration, like *Espangnole, Hongroise,* and
Japonaise. It is important to remember, however, that a dish inspired by a foreign
cuisine may not be the same as an authentic dish from that cuisine. For example, we fill
a French omelet with a type of tomato sauce and call it Spanish. But in Spain,
the classic omelet is a thick, flat mixture of eggs, potatoes, and onions.

This chapter can present only a small selection of typical recipes
from some of the cuisines that have been influential here. After having had experience
with this small sampling, students are encouraged to continue their own research. The
bibliography at the end of the book lists some titles that can help.

At the end of the chapter is a short glossary of foreign
words and phrases used in this chapter instead of the usual Terms for Review.

*After reading this chapter, you should be able to prepare some typical recipes
from Japan, China, Mexico, and from Italy and other European countries.*

JAPANESE

Many people are surprised when they first taste typical Japanese dishes. Expecting something like Chinese food, they discover that it is very different. For example, stir-frying is perhaps the most characteristic cooking technique in Chinese cooking, while simmering, steaming, and grilling may be more typical of Japanese. While many Chinese dishes are highly seasoned, most Japanese foods are very delicately seasoned.

The appearance of the food in Japan is very important. In most cases each dish is presented carefully and attractively in a separate bowl or dish. Portions are generally small, and a formal dinner consists of a sequence of many small dishes.

Fish dominates the cuisine of this island country. Dishes like sashimi (sliced raw fish), sushi (vinegared rice, usually served with raw fish), and simple grilled fish are frequently encountered. The basic stock, called *dashi*, is made from dried, shaved bonito (a type of fish) and a kind of seaweed. It is used in soups, simmered dishes, and sauces.

RECIPE 278 **Dashi**

Yield: 2 qt (2 L)

U.S.	Metric	Ingredients	Procedure
4½ pt	2.25 L	Cold water	1. Put the water in a pot and add the kombu. Bring to a boil over moderately high heat.
2 oz	60 g	Kombu (giant kelp for stock)	
1½ oz	50 g	Katsuobushi (dried bonito flakes)	2. Just as the water comes to a boil, remove the kombu.
			3. Remove from the heat and immediately add the bonito flakes. Let the flakes settle to the bottom. This will take a minute or two.
			4. Strain through a china cap lined with cheesecloth. Use the dashi within a day.

Variations

Instant dashi is also available. Its quality is good enough for simmered dishes and miso soup, but not for good clear soup. Follow label instructions.

278A. Vegetarian Dashi: Omit the bonito flakes and use only the kombu.

RECIPE 279 **Clear Soup with Shrimp**

	Portions: 10		**Portion size:** 6 oz (200 mL)

U.S.	Metric	Ingredients	Procedure
2 qt	2 L	Dashi Salt	1. Bring the dashi to a simmer. Carefully add salt to taste.
1 tbsp	15 mL	Japanese soy sauce	2. Add soy sauce. (The soup should be crystal clear.)
		Garnish:	3. Cut lemon zest into very fine julienne.
1–2 strips	1–2 strips	Lemon zest, yellow part only	4. Trim and wash the snow peas. Cut them crosswise at an angle, making diamond shapes. Blanch them 1 minute in boiling water. Drain and cool.
15	15	Snow peas	
10	10	Medium shrimp	
			5. Peel and devein the shrimp. Blanch them in boiling water just until cooked, no more than a minute. Drain.
			6. Rinse soup cups or bowls in hot water to warm them. In each bowl put one shrimp, a few pieces of snow peas, and a few threads of lemon zest.
			7. Make sure that the soup is very hot—almost at the boiling point—and ladle 6 oz (200 mL) into each bowl. Serve at once.

Variations

Garnish: Clear soup garnish can be varied considerably. Always use just a few carefully chosen items. Don't clutter the bowl. The effect should be like an elegant little still-life painting seen through the perfectly clear soup. All cutting should be done carefully and neatly. Some items for garnish include the following:

Tofu, cut in small cubes.

Cooked pork loin or chicken breast, in small dice, batonnet, or julienne.

Lobster tail, in thin slices.

Cooked fish, separated into flakes (use a type that separates into large, firm flakes, such as snapper or cod).

Small clams, steamed and removed from shell (the broth can be clarified, diluted, and used for soup base instead of dashi).

Carrots, julienne.

Fresh white mushrooms, in thin slices.

Dried shiitake mushrooms, soaked, simmered, and cut into julienne.

Wakame (a type of seaweed); soak it until soft, cut it into small pieces and discard the hard ribs, and simmer it in the soup 2 minutes.

Chinese cabbage, shredded.

Watercress leaves.

Fresh ginger, cut into fine shreds (use only a few shreds per serving).

Bamboo shoots, in thin slices.

White radish, in thin slices or shreds.

(Continues)

RECIPE 279 Clear Soup with Shrimp (*Continued*)

279A. *Miso Soup:* Miso soup is made simply by dissolving some *miso* (fermented paste made of soybeans, barley, and/or rice) in dashi. The two main categories of miso are *white miso*, which is actually light yellowish in color and has a sweet, mild taste, and *red* or *dark* miso, which comes in varying shades of reddish brown and is stronger and saltier in taste. General proportions for soup are 4 tbsp (60 mL) red miso or 6 tbsp (90 mL) white miso per quart (or liter) of dashi. Put the miso in a small bowl and carefully stir in a ladleful of hot dashi. Stir until completely lump-free. Add enough dashi so that the miso is thin and pourable. (Do not add miso directly to soup or it will not mix in properly.) Carefully stir the dissolved miso into the remaining hot dashi. Season to taste and, if desired, add a teaspoon or two of soy sauce. Add desired garnish as for clear soup, except that the garnish can be added directly to the soup kettle. Because this is a heartier soup, it is more often garnished with tofu and vegetables rather than more delicate seafood. Stir before serving, because the miso settles out.

RECIPE 280 Sushi Rice

Yield: about 2½ lb (1.1 kg)

U.S.	Metric	Ingredients	Procedure
3 cups	750 mL	Japanese short-grain rice (see note)	1. Wash the rice in several changes of cold water. Drain well.
3½ cups	900 mL	Cold water	2. Put the drained rice in a heavy saucepan and add the measured water. Cover tightly and let stand at least 30 minutes.
			3. With the cover in place, set the pan over high heat and bring to a boil. When boiling, reduce the heat to medium and let cook until all the water is absorbed. Do not remove the cover to check, but listen to the sounds: the bubbling will stop, and there will be a faint hissing sound.
			4. Reduce the heat to very low and cook another 5 minutes. Then remove from heat and let stand at least 15 minutes before removing the cover. You now have the basic white rice that is eaten with Japanese meals.
3–4 oz	100–125 mL	Sushi vinegar (see note)	5. In Japan, mixing in the vinegar is done in a special wooden tub that is used only for this purpose (to avoid off flavors). The advantage of wood is that it absorbs excess moisture. If you use a nonabsorbent mixing bowl, transfer the rice to a clean bowl whenever the mixing bowl becomes coated with moisture. Using a wooden paddle or plastic spatula, break up the hot rice to get rid of all lumps. At the same time fan the rice to cool it down.

U.S.	Metric	Ingredients	Procedure
			6. When the rice is slightly warm to the touch, begin adding the sushi vinegar. Add a little at a time, while mixing gently. The rice is ready when it has a glossy appearance and a very mild taste of the vinegar. The vinegared rice is best if used within 2 or 3 hours, and it must not be refrigerated.

Note: Do not confuse Japanese short-grain rice with glutinous rice, which is an entirely different product. Sushi vinegar is commercially available, but it can also be made in the kitchen. Combine 1 pint (500 mL) Japanese rice vinegar, 8 oz (250 g) sugar, and 4 oz (125 g) salt. Heat and stir until the sugar and salt are dissolved, then cool.

Variations

280A. Nigirizushi (Finger Sushi):

1. Prepare *wasabi* (green horseradish) by mixing wasabi powder with a little water to form a thick paste. Let stand, covered, a few minutes to allow flavor to develop.
2. Prepare sushi toppings by cutting very fresh fish fillets (use saltwater fish; smoked salmon can also be used) into slices about 1½ by 2½ inches (4 by 6 cm). Tuna, the most popular fish for sushi, is tender and is usually cut about ¼ inch (6 mm) thick. Other fish are cut thinner.
3. Wet your hands with cold water to keep the rice from sticking to them, then pick up about 2 tbsp (30 mL) sushi rice. Shape it into firm oval about 1½ inches (4 cm) long (see Figure 23.1). Pick up a slice of fish in one hand. Dip a finger of the other hand in the wasabi and spread a very small amount on the underside of the fish slice. Drape the fish over the oval of rice, with the wasabi underneath next to the rice, and press it gently but firmly in place. Serve with soy sauce for dipping.

280B. Kappa-maki (Cucumber Roll):
To make rolled sushi, you will need a special bamboo mat called a *sudare* (see Figure 23.1). You could also use a sheet of parchment, but the roll will be harder to make.

1. Peel a cucumber. Cut it in half and scrape out the seeds. Cut lengthwise into julienne.
2. Cut a sheet of *nori* (a type of seaweed for rolled sushi) in half crosswise. Toast it by holding it passing it briefly above a burner flame, being careful not to burn it.
3. Put the bamboo mat on the table in front of you with the bamboo strips horizontally. Put the half sheet of nori on the mat smooth side down.
4. Cover the two-thirds of the nori closest to you with a layer of sushi rice about ¼ inch (6 mm) thick.
5. Spread a light streak of wasabi from right to left across the middle of the rice.
6. Lay strips of cucumber evenly on top of the strip of wasabi.
7. Lift the edge of the mat closest to you and roll up firmly. This is best done by lifting the mat with the thumbs while holding the cucumber in place with the fingers. Press the roll in the mat gently but firmly to make it tight.
8. Wipe the blade of a very sharp knife, then cut the roll in half crosswise. Do not saw the roll but cut it cleanly with a single stroke. Wiping the blade on a damp cloth after every cut, cut each half roll into four pieces.

280C. Tekka-maki (Tuna Roll):
Make *kappa-maki*, but instead of cucumber, use raw tuna cut into batonnet strips.

280D. Chirashizushi (Scatter Sushi):
Fill a serving bowl half full of sushi rice. Carefully and attractively arrange an assortment of raw fish, cooked shrimp, crab meat, and neatly cut vegetables such as snow peas, cucumber, carrots, mushrooms, and pickled ginger on top of the rice.

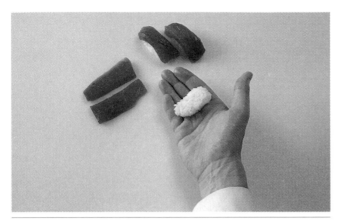

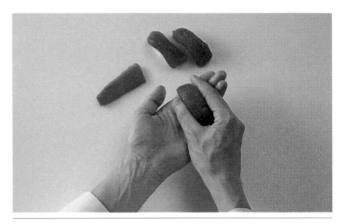

FIGURE 23.1 Making sushi.

(a) For nigirizushi, wet your hands with cold water to keep the rice from sticking to them. Form a bit of rice into a small oval in one hand.

(d) Turn it over and press the same way. Then press the sides with the thumb and forefinger to finish shaping it.

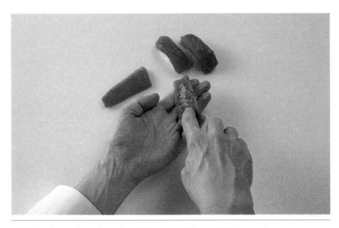

(b) In the other hand, pick up a slice of fish and smear a dab of wasabi on the bottom of it.

(e) For rolled sushi, put a half piece of nori on the sudare (bamboo mat). Wetting your hands with cold water to keep the rice from sticking to them, spread a layer of sushi rice over the bottom two-thirds of the nori.

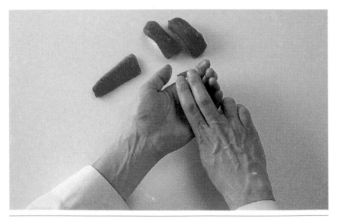

(c) Top the rice with the fish, wasabi side against the rice, and press in place in the palm of one hand with two fingers of the other.

(f) Lay strips of the filling across the middle of the rice.

(g) Holding the filling in place with the fingers, lift the corner of the mat with the thumbs and roll up.

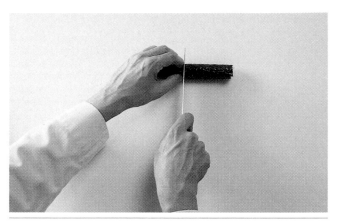

(i) Cut the roll in half with a single forward stroke, using a dampened knife.

(h) Press the mat firmly and evenly to make a tight roll.

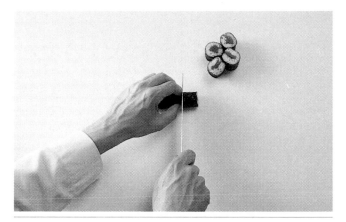

(j) Wipe the blade between cuts, and cut each half roll into three or four pieces.

RECIPE 281   **Shrimp and Vegetable Tempura**

Portions: 16   **Portion size:** 3 shrimp,
                                                     plus vegetables

U.S	Metric	Ingredients	Procedure
48	48	Large shrimp	1. Peel the shrimp, leaving the tails attached. Devein and butterfly them.
4	4	Green peppers	
1 lb 4 oz	600 g	Sweet potatoes	2. Core and seed the peppers. Cut each one lengthwise into 8 wedges or strips.
32	32	Small mushrooms (or halves or quarters of large mushrooms)	3. Peel the sweet potatoes. Cut into slices about ⅙ inch (4 mm) thick.
			4. Clean the mushrooms and trim the bottoms of the stems.
1½ lb	750 g	Cake flour or other low-gluten flour	5. Sift the flour into a mixing bowl.
			6. Mix together the water and egg yolks.
1½ pt	750 mL	Water, ice cold	7. Mix the liquid into the flour until they are just combined. Do not worry about a few lumps. The batter should be somewhat thinner than pancake batter.
6	6	Egg yolks	
1½ pt	750 mL	Dashi	8. Make a dipping sauce by combining the dashi, soy sauce, and mirin.
5 oz	150 mL	Soy sauce	
3 oz	100 mL	Mirin (sweet rice wine)	
		Flour for dredging	9. Divide the shrimp and vegetables equally among the 16 portions. Fry the vegetables first, then the shrimp, by dredging with flour, shaking off the excess, then dipping in the batter and dropping into clean frying fat at 350°F (175°C). Fry just until lightly golden.
8 oz	250 g	Grated daikon (large white Japanese radish)	
3 tbsp	45 mL	Grated fresh ginger	10. Drain and serve at once. Tempura is traditionally served on a bamboo tray covered with a clean piece of absorbent paper. Accompany with about 2 oz (60 mL) dipping sauce in a shallow bowl. Put a small mound each of grated daikon and grated ginger on each serving tray. The diner mixes these to taste into the dipping sauce.

RECIPE 282 Oyako Donburi

	Portions: 16		**Portion size:** see procedure

U.S.	Metric	Ingredients	Procedure
2 qt	2 L	Dashi	1. Combine the dashi, soy sauce, sugar, and saké in a saucepan. Bring to a simmer to dissolve the sugar. Remove from heat and reserve.
5 oz	150 mL	Soy sauce	
5 oz	150 g	Sugar	
2 oz	60 mL	Saké (optional)	
3 qt	3 L	Raw Japanese short-grain rice	2. Cook the rice by following steps 1–4 in the recipe for sushi rice, page 610. Keep it hot.
1½ lb	725 g	Boneless, skinless chicken meat	3. Cut the chicken into inch-wide (2½-cm) strips, then slice diagonally ¼ inch (6 mm) thick.
16	16	Scallions	
16	16	Eggs	4. Trim off the roots and the coarser greens from the scallions, leaving tender green parts intact. Cut diagonally into ½-inch (1-cm) pieces.
			5. For each portion, put 1½ oz (45 g) chicken, 1 sliced scallion, and 4½ oz (125 mL) dashi mixture in a small sauté pan. Simmer until the chicken is nearly done.
			6. Break an egg into a bowl. Mix lightly but do not beat.
			7. Pour the egg in a stream around the chicken in the skillet. Continue to simmer until the egg is half-set.
			8. Put 1½ cups (375 mL) hot rice in a large, deep soup bowl.
			9. When the egg is nearly set, give the egg and chicken mixture a light stir and pour the contents of the skillet over the rice.

Note: The name of this dish, "oyako," means "parent and child," referring to the chicken and egg. A *donburi* is a type of serving bowl, and the word also refers to foods served in this type of bowl, generally rice with toppings and sauce.

Variation

282A. Tendon: Omit the chicken, scallions, and egg in the recipe above. Reduce the dashi to 1 qt (1 L), and double the amount of saké. Top each bowl of rice with one piece of shrimp tempura and two pieces of vegetable tempura. Pour about 2½ oz (75 mL) hot dashi mixture over the rice and serve. (The name of this dish comes from the first syllables of "tempura" and "donburi.")

RECIPE 283   **Chicken Teriyaki**

| | | | **Portions:** 16 | **Portion size:** 1 chicken breast or thigh |

U.S.	Metric	Ingredients	Procedure
		Teriyaki sauce:	1. Combine the saké, soy sauce, mirin, and sugar. Heat to a simmer to dissolve the sugar. Cool.
3 oz	75 mL	Saké	
7 oz	175 mL	Soy sauce	
6 oz	150 mL	Mirin (sweet rice wine)	
2 tbsp	25 mL	Sugar	
16	16	Boneless chicken breasts or thighs, skin on or off as desired Vegetable oil	2. Heat a thin film of oil in a skillet. Put in the chicken pieces skin side down. Cook until browned and half-done. Turn and cook the other side.
			3. Remove the chicken and degrease the pan.
			4. Deglaze the pan with the teriyaki sauce, and bring the sauce to a boil.
			5. Return the chicken to the pan, and turn it in the pan until it is lightly glazed.
			6. Remove the chicken from the pan and reserve the sauce. Cut each piece of chicken crosswise, on the diagonal, into half-inch-wide (1-cm) strips.
			7. Plate the chicken, keeping each piece assembled in its original form. Spoon a little of the sauce on top.

Variations

Other items, such as small beefsteaks, fish fillets, and scallops can be cooked this way. In the case of fish fillets, keep the skin on if possible, and use the skin side as the presentation side.

RECIPE 284   **Chawan Mushi**

| | | | **Portions:** 16 | **Portion size:** 7 oz (200 g) |

U.S.	Metric	Ingredients	Procedure
12 oz	375 g	Boneless, skinless chicken breast meat	1. Cut the chicken breast into ½-inch (1-cm) dice. Mix with the soy sauce and *saké* and marinate for 15 minutes. Drain.
1 tbsp	15 mL	Soy sauce	2. Divide the chicken, shrimp, scallions, and water chestnuts equally among 16 custard cups or other 8-oz (250-mL) heatproof cups.
1 tbsp	15 mL	*Saké* (optional)	
16	16	Small shrimp, peeled and deveined	
6	6	Scallions, sliced thin	
4 oz	125 g	Water chestnuts, sliced	

RECIPE 284   **Chawan Mushi** *(Continued)*

U.S.	Metric	Ingredients	Procedure
12	12	Large eggs	3. Beat the eggs lightly in a bowl.
2 qt	2 L	Dashi or chicken stock	4. Mix in the dashi or stock, soy sauce, and mirin. Season to taste with a little salt.
1 tbsp	15 mL	Soy sauce	5. Carefully remove any foam from the egg mixture and ladle the egg mixture into the cups (about 5½ oz or 160 mL in each). There should be no bubbles or foam on the surface.
2 tbsp	30 mL	Mirin (sweet rice wine)	
		Salt	6. Cover each cup tightly with foil and place in a steamer. Steam for about 15 minutes, or until the custard is set.
			7. Serve hot or cold. This savory custard is eaten with a spoon and with chopsticks for the solid pieces.

RECIPE 285   **Green Beans with Sesame Dressing**

	Portions: 16		**Portion size:** 2 oz (60 g)

U.S.	Metric	Ingredients	Procedure
1 cup	250 mL	White sesame seeds	1. Toast the sesame seeds in a dry skillet, stirring and tossing regularly, until light golden.
1½ oz	50 mL	Soy sauce	
2 tbsp	30 g	Sugar	
2 oz	60 mL	Dashi or water	2. Using a spice grinder or mortar and pestle, grind the sesame seeds to a paste.
			3. Mix in the soy sauce and sugar. Thin out with dashi or water. Set aside.
2 lb	1 kg	Green beans	4. Wash the green beans and trim off the ends. Cut into 1-inch (2½-cm) lengths.
			5. Cook the beans in boiling, salted water until crisp-tender, drain, cool under cold, running water, and drain again.
			6. Mix the beans with the dressing.

Variations

Other mild, green vegetables, such as spinach and asparagus, can be served the same way.

285A. Sesame Miso Dressing: Reduce the sesame seeds to ½ cup (125 mL). Omit the soy sauce and sugar, and add 4 oz (125 g) white or red miso. Use mirin (sweet rice wine) instead of dashi or water to thin out the dressing. Use as a dressing for vegetables, in the same manner as sesame dressing.

CHINESE

China is a vast country, and the climate and food resources vary greatly from region to region. Consequently, there is no single Chinese cooking style, but an array of regional styles. The styles of Peking in the north, Canton in the southeast, and Sichuan in the western interior, to name three of the most famous, are perhaps as different as the styles of Germany, France, and Italy.

Nevertheless, we can make some generalizations about Chinese cooking that may help clarify it. In the first place, meat does not play such a central role as it does in American and European cooking. Vegetables and grains are more important and supply the bulk of the diet. Rice is the most important grain, while noodles and other wheat products are also eaten frequently, especially in the north.

A typical meal has no main dish. Rather, cooked dishes are generally considered to be accompaniments for rice, which is the most important item in the meal. Portions of these "side dishes" are usually small, and a meal may consist of a large assortment of such dishes. Serving dishes are placed in the center of the table, and each diner takes a small quantity of each, as desired, to eat between bites of rice.

Although there are some foods that are stewed or simmered for a long time, in most cases cooking times are short, while preparation times are long. A great deal of trimming, cutting, and slicing is required, but once this is done, many dishes are cooked and sent to the table in a matter of minutes.

Many of the cooking techniques we are familiar with, including deep-frying, steaming, and simmering, have a place in Chinese cooking. From our point of view, perhaps the most important and typically Chinese cooking technique is stir-frying. The basic procedure is explained on page 619, and recipes are included that use this technique.

RECIPE 286 Egg Rolls or Spring Rolls

Yield: 16 pieces

U.S.	Metric	Ingredients	Procedure
1 oz	30 mL	Oil	1. Heat the oil in a wok or sauté pan. Stir-fry the meat, cabbage, scallions, bean sprouts, black mushrooms, bamboo shoots, and shrimp.
6 oz	175 g	Cooked meat or poultry, cut into fine julienne	
6 oz	175 g	Chinese cabbage, shredded	2. Add the soy sauce, sherry, and stock. Continue to stir and cook for another minute or two.
3	3	Scallions, shredded	
6 oz	175 g	Bean sprouts	3. Mix the cornstarch with the cold water. Stir into the vegetable mixture and cook until reduced and thickened.
5	5	Dried black mushrooms (stems discarded), soaked in boiling water, cut julienne	
2 oz	60 g	Bamboo shoots, julienne	4. Remove from the heat and adjust the seasonings. Cool thoroughly.
1½ oz	45 g	Raw shrimp, chopped	
2 tsp	10 mL	Soy sauce	
1 tsp	5 mL	Sherry or shaoxing wine	
3 oz	100 mL	Chicken stock	
1½ tsp	7 mL	Cornstarch	
1 tbsp	15 mL	Cold water	

RECICE 286   **Egg Rolls or Spring Rolls** *(Continued)*

U.S.	Metric	Ingredients	Procedure
16	16	Egg roll skins or spring roll skins	5. Lay an egg roll skin on the worktable, with one of the corners toward you. Spoon about 1½ oz (45 g) of the filling onto the lower half of the skin in a sort of sausage shape. (See Figure 23.2.)
	as needed	Egg, beaten	6. Fold the lower corner of the skin (the corner pointing at you) over the filling so that it is covered. Then start to roll it up like a cylinder, giving it just a half turn.
			7. Brush the left and right corners with a little beaten egg. Fold one corner over the filling, then the other, pressing down to seal. At this point it should look like an open envelope.
			8. Brush the top corner with beaten egg. Roll up into a firm, compact cylinder. Seal the top corner well.
			9. Repeat with the remaining skins and filling.
			10. Deep fry the egg rolls until the skins are crisp and brown. (Note: Egg roll skins are heavier than spring roll skins; they must be thoroughly fried or they will be doughy.) Drain and serve at once, with a little hot mustard or bottled duck sauce for dipping.

Basic Procedure for Stir-Frying

1. Heat a wok or sauté pan over high heat until very hot.

2. Add a small quantity of oil, and let it heat.

3. Add seasonings for flavoring the oil, one or more of the following: salt, garlic, ginger root, scallions.

4. If meat, poultry, or seafood items are part of the dish, add them now. As when sautéing, do not overload the pan. Leave it untouched for a few moments, so that it begins to brown properly. Then stir and toss it with a spatula so that it sears and cooks evenly.

5. If any liquid seasonings for the meat are used, such as soy sauce, add it now, but only in small quantities, so that the meat continues to fry and does not start to simmer or stew.

6. Remove the meat from the pan or leave it in, depending on the recipe. If a small quantity of quick-cooking vegetables is used, the meat can sometimes be left in the pan and the vegetables cooked with it. Otherwise, remove the meat when it is almost done and keep it on the side while cooking the vegetables.

7. Repeat steps 2 and 3 if necessary.

8. Add the vegetables to the pan and stir-fry. If more than one vegetable is used, add the longest-cooking one first, and the quick-cooking ones last.

9. Some dishes are dry-fried, meaning prepared without liquid or sauce. In this case, simply return the meat item, if any, to the pan to reheat with the vegetables, and serve. Otherwise, proceed to the next step.

10. Add liquid ingredients, such as stock or water, and continue to cook and stir until the vegetables are almost cooked.

11. Add the meat item, which was removed in step 6, to the pan so that it will reheat.

12. Optional but widely used step: Add a mixture of cornstarch and water to the pan and cook until lightly thickened.

13. Serve at once.

FIGURE 23.2 **Rolling egg rolls.**
(a) Lay an egg roll skin on the bench with one corner toward you. Place the filling as shown.

(d) Fold them over the filling, so that the skin resembles an open envelope.

(b) Fold the lower corner of the skin over the filling and roll it up about one-third of the way.

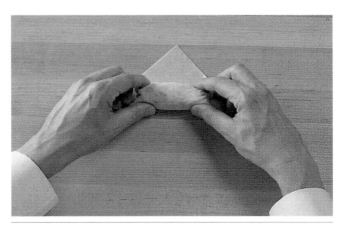

(e) Brush the top edge with egg and roll up tightly.

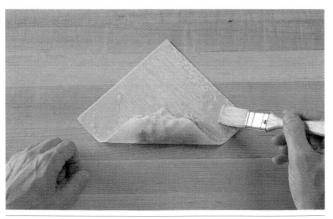

(c) Brush the left and right corners of the skin with beaten egg.

(f) When completely rolled, egg rolls are ready to be cooked.

RECIPE 287 Stir-Fried Beef with Green Peppers

....

Portions: 16			Portion size: 4 oz (125 g)

U.S.	Metric	Ingredients	Procedure
2½ lb 4 oz 1 oz 5 tsp	1.2 kg 125 mL 30 mL 25 mL	Flank steak Soy sauce Sherry or shaoxing wine Cornstarch	1. Cut the flank steak lengthwise (with the grain) into strips 2 inches (5 cm) wide. Then cut the strips crosswise into very thin slices. (This is easier if the meat is partially frozen.) 2. Toss the meat with the soy sauce, sherry, and cornstarch. Let marinate 30 minutes or longer.
6 4 slices 1–2 2 oz	6 4 slices 1–2 60 g	Green peppers Ginger root Garlic cloves, sliced Scallions, sliced	3. Core and seed the peppers. Cut them into large dice. 4. Have the ginger, garlic, and scallions ready in separate containers.
3–4 oz ½ tsp 2 oz	90–125 mL 2 mL 60 mL	Oil Salt Chicken stock	5. Stir-fry the beef in 3 or more batches, depending on the size of the pan or wok. Use a little of the oil for each batch, as needed. 6. As each batch of the beef is cooked, remove it from the pan and set it aside. 7. Heat additional oil in the pan and add the salt, ginger, garlic, and scallions. Stir-fry for a few seconds to develop flavor. 8. Add the peppers and stir-fry until lightly cooked but still crisp. 9. Add the broth and toss the vegetables a few times. 10. Return the meat to the pan. Toss the meat with the vegetables until it is hot and evenly combined with the peppers. Serve at once.

Variations

Other vegetables may be used instead of the peppers, such as celery, broccoli, snow peas, green beans, asparagus, mushrooms, and bok choy. Or use two or three fresh vegetables, plus water chestnuts and/or bamboo shoots.

Chicken or pork may be used instead of beef. If chicken is used, cut it into medium dice or batonnet. Also, reduce the quantity of soy sauce to avoid discoloring the light meat of the chicken.

....

RECIPE 288   Stir-Fried Mixed Vegetables

| | **Portions:** 16 | | **Portion size:** 4 oz (125 g) |

U.S.	Metric	Ingredients	Procedure
1½ lb	750 g	Chinese cabbage	1. Cut off the root end of one cabbage and separate the leaves. Cut out the thick center ribs, then cut them crosswise into 2-inch (5-cm) chunks. Cut the thin, leafy parts into shreds.
16	16	Dried black mushrooms	
6 oz	175 g	Bamboo shoots, drained	2. Soak the mushrooms in boiling water to cover. When soft, drain and squeeze dry, reserving the liquid. Discard the stems and cut the caps into julienne.
4 oz	125 g	Celery	
4 oz	125 g	Carrots	3. Cut the bamboo shoots into thin slices.
15-oz can	425-g can	Baby corn	4. Cut the celery on the diagonal into thin slices.
4	4	Scallions	5. Cut the carrot into julienne.
			6. Drain the baby corn.
			7. Slice the scallions at a sharp angle into shreds.
2–3 oz	60–90 mL	Oil	8. Heat the oil in a wok or large sauté pan.
1 clove	1 clove	Garlic, crushed (optional)	9. Add the garlic and cook about 15 seconds to flavor the oil, then remove and discard the garlic.
5 slices	5 slices	Ginger root	
1 tsp	5 mL	Salt	10. Add the ginger root and salt and let cook about 15 seconds.
12 oz	350 mL	Water or chicken stock	
1 oz	30 mL	Soy sauce (optional)	11. Add the cabbage ribs and stir-fry for 1–2 minutes.
¼ cup	25 g (60 mL)	Cornstarch	12. Add the remaining vegetables, except for the shredded cabbage leaves. Continue to stir-fry for another minute or two. Then add the shredded cabbage.
3 oz	100 mL	Cold water	
1 tsp	5 mL	Sesame oil (optional)	13. Add the stock and soy sauce and continue to stir and cook until the vegetables are cooked but still crisp.
			14. Mix the cornstarch with the cold water, then stir it, a little at a time, into the vegetables to thicken the sauce. Do not add it all at once, because you may not need it all. The sauce should not be too thick, about the consistency of a light velouté sauce.
			15. Stir in the sesame oil and serve at once.

Variations

This is a basic procedure for stir-fried vegetables. One or two vegetables, or any harmonious assortment, can be cooked using the same recipe, merely substituting different vegetable ingredients.

RECIPE 289   **Basic Fried Rice**

. . . .

Portions: 16   Portion size: 6 oz (175 g)

U.S.	Metric	Ingredients	Procedure
4 lb	1.8 kg	Cold cooked rice	1. Break up the rice to remove all lumps.
4–6 oz	125–175 mL	Oil	2. Cook the fried rice in several batches, depending on the size of the pan or wok. Do no more than 1–2 lb (½–1 kg) rice at once.
1 lb	450 g	Cooked meat (cut into shreds) or seafood (flaked or sliced)	
3 oz	90 g	Scallions, sliced thin	3. Heat a small amount of oil in the wok. Add the meat and stir-fry for a minute or two.
1 lb	450 g	Vegetables (see variations), shredded or small dice	
4–6 oz	125–175 mL	Soy sauce (optional) Salt, to taste	4. Add the scallions and stir-fry for a minute.
4–8	4–8	Eggs, beaten	5. Add any raw vegetables and stir-fry until almost done.
			6. Add the rice and stir-fry until it is hot and lightly coated with oil.
			7. Add any cooked vegetables and mix in.
			8. Add soy sauce, if used, and salt.
			9. Add beaten egg and mix in. Stir-fry lightly to cook the egg, then serve.

Variations

The quantities given in the basic recipe are only guidelines, but the rice should be the predominant ingredient. You can omit the meat or fish items. For plain rice, you can omit the vegetables too.

Eggs can be omitted, or they can be added to fried rice in several other ways:

1. Remove the meat and raw vegetables from the pan when they are cooked. Add the egg to the pan and scramble. Add the rice, return the meat and vegetables to the pan, and continue with the recipe.
2. In step 9, push the rice to the sides of the pan. Add the egg to the well in the middle. When it starts to set, gradually mix in the rice.
3. Scramble the eggs separately and add to the rice at the end.
4. Mix the raw beaten egg with the cold cooked rice before cooking.

Suggested Ingredients:

Meats: cooked pork, beef, chicken, duck, ham, bacon, Chinese sausage.

Seafoods: shrimp (diced or whole), crab, lobster.

Vegetables: bamboo shoots, bean sprouts, celery, peas, mushrooms, onions, peppers, water chestnuts.

RECIPE 290 **Pearl Balls**

....

Yield: about 40 pieces

U.S.	Metric	Ingredients	Procedure
2 cups	500 mL	Glutinous rice	1. Wash the rice in several changes of cold water. Drain. Add enough fresh water to cover by 1 inch (2½ cm). Let soak for at least 30 minutes.
3 tbsp	45 mL	Cornstarch	2. Mix together the cornstarch and water.
1 oz	30 mL	Cold water	3. Combine all ingredients except the glutinous rice and mix together.
2 lb	900 g	Ground pork	
4	4	Scallions, minced	4. Form the meat mixture into small meatballs about 1 oz (30 g) each.
8	8	Water chestnuts, minced	
2 tsp	10 mL	Fresh ginger, minced	5. Drain the rice. Roll the balls in the rice so that they are well coated.
2	2	Eggs, beaten	
1 oz	30 mL	Soy sauce	6. Line a rack or perforated steamer pan with cheesecloth. Arrange the meatballs in the pan, allowing about ½ inch (1–2 cm) between them.
1 oz	30 mL	Sherry or shaoxing wine	
2 tsp	10 mL	Sugar	
1½ tsp	7 mL	Salt	7. Steam for 30–45 minutes, until the rice is translucent and the pork is done.

Variations

290A. Fried Pork Balls: Omit the rice coating, and cook the meatballs by deep-frying them.

290B. Wontons: The pork mixture can be used for wonton filling. Put a small spoonful of meat in the center of a wonton skin. Moisten the edges with beaten egg, then fold the skin in half to make a triangle (or, if you are using round wonton skins, a semicircle) enclosing the filling. Moisten one of the two corners (on the folded edge) with egg, then twist the wonton to bring the two corners together. Press the corners together to seal. Makes 60 or more wontons, depending on size.

Wontons can be cooked by simmering, steaming, or deep-frying. They are often served in chicken broth as wonton soup.

....

RECIPE 291 **Eggplant Sichuan Style**

....

| | **Portions:** 16 | | **Portion size:** 2–2½ oz (60–75 g) |

U.S.	Metric	Ingredients	Procedure
2 oz	60 mL	Chili paste with garlic (sichuan paste)	1. Mix together the chili paste, soy sauce, wine, vinegar, sugar, and stock or water.
1 oz	30 mL	Soy sauce	
2 oz	60 mL	Sherry or shaoxing wine	
1 oz	30 mL	Red wine vinegar	
1 tsp	5 mL	Sugar	
2 oz	60 mL	Chicken stock or water	

RECIPE 291 **Eggplant Sichuan Style** (*Continued*)

U.S.	Metric	Ingredients	Procedure
2½ lb	1.1 kg	Eggplant	2. Peel the eggplant if the skin is tough. Otherwise leave it on. Cut the eggplant into 1-inch (2½-cm) dice.
4	4	Garlic cloves	
1 tsp	5 mL	Ginger root	3. Mince the garlic, ginger, and scallions.
6	6	Scallions	
2–3 oz	60–90 mL	Oil	4. Heat the oil in a sauté pan and sauté the eggplant until lightly browned.
1 tbsp	15 mL	Sesame oil	5. Add the garlic, ginger, and scallions and sauté another minute.
			6. Add the chili paste mixture and stir in. Cover and cook over low heat until the eggplant is tender, about 15–20 minutes.
			7. Uncover. The sauce should be quite thick, so if necessary, cook uncovered for a few minutes to reduce the liquid.
			8. Add the sesame oil and serve.

RECIPE 292 **Red-Cooked Chicken**

Portions: 16   **Portion size:** ⅛ chicken

U.S.	Metric	Ingredients	Procedure
2	2	Chickens, about 4 lb (1.8 kg) each	1. Cut each chicken into eighths.
2 cloves	2 cloves	Star anise	2. Tie the star anise, ginger root, and sichuan peppercorns in a cheesecloth bag.
3 slices	3 slices	Ginger root	
1 tbsp	15 mL	Sichuan peppercorns	3. Combine the soy sauce and water or stock in a pot and add the spice bag, sugar, scallions, and sherry. Bring to a boil.
½ pt	250 mL	Soy sauce	
2 pt	1 L	Water or chicken stock	
1 oz	30 g	Sugar	
2	2	Scallions	4. Add the chicken. Simmer until tender.
2 oz	60 mL	Sherry or shaoxing wine	5. Serve the chicken hot or cold. If it is to be served cold, cool it down and store it in the cooking liquid. The liquid may be reused for another batch.

Variations

The star anise and sichuan peppercorns may be omitted for a simpler version of this dish.

Other meats (using cuts appropriate for simmering) may be cooked this way, including pork, beef, tripe, and duck.

RECIPE 293 **Tea-Smoked Duck**

Yield: 1 duck

U.S.	Metric	Ingredients	Procedure
3 tbsp 1 tbsp	45 mL 15 mL	Coarse salt Sichuan peppercorns	1. Toast the salt and sichuan peppercorns in a dry skillet over moderate heat, until the peppercorns are fragrant. 2. Cool the mixture, then crush with a rolling pin.
1	1	Duck, about 5 lb (2.3 kg)	3. Clean the duck well, removing excess fat. Flatten the duck slightly by pressing down on the breastbone to break it. 4. Rub the duck inside and out with the salt and peppercorn mixture. 5. Put the duck in a hotel pan, weight it down, and refrigerate it for 1–2 days.
6 4 slices	6 4 slices	Scallions, trimmed Ginger root	6. Rinse the duck. 7. Put the scallions and ginger slices in the cavity. 8. Steam the duck for 1 to 1½ hours, until tender.
3 oz ½ cup 2 oz	90 g 125 mL 60 g	Raw rice Brown or black tea leaves Sugar	9. Line a large wok or other heavy pan with aluminum foil. 10. Mix together the rice, tea leaves, and sugar. Put the mixture in the bottom of the wok. 11. Put the duck on a rack over the tea mixture and cover the pan tightly. 12. Set the pan over high heat for 5 minutes, then over moderate heat for 20 minutes. Turn the heat off and let stand another 20 minutes without uncovering. 13. Cool the duck. Chop it into 1- or 2-inch (3- to 5-cm) pieces, bones and all. Or bone it out and cut the meat into inch-wide strips. This dish is normally served at room temperature.

Variations

For spicier duck, add 1 tsp (5 mL) five-spice powder to the dry marinade after toasting.

293A. Crispy Duck: This variation may be made with smoked duck or with steamed but unsmoked duck (step 8). When the duck is cool, cut it into quarters. You may bone it if desired, but try to keep it in its original shape. Deep-fry until the skin is crisp. Drain, cut up, and serve at once. (Optional step: Rub some cornstarch into the skin before deep-frying.)

MEXICAN

Much of what we think of as Mexican cuisine does not really represent the great range of dishes in that country. The land and climate vary so much within Mexico's large area that the cooking of Sonora and Chihuahua in the north have little in common with the cooking of Oaxaca and Yucatan in the south. The style of the dishes familiar to us—the well-known tacos and enchiladas, for example—is based primarily on northern Mexican influences. These influences combine with the culinary traditions of the southwestern United States to form a cuisine sometimes called Tex-Mex, as well as related styles in New Mexico and other regions of the southwestern United States.

The recipes in this section go beyond the usual Tex-Mex dishes, but in such a short space it is impossible even to begin to give an idea of the richness of Mexican cooking. This chapter restricts itself to a sampling of some of the more well-known dishes. (In addition, another Mexican classic, guacamole, is found in Chapter 20.)

One of the most familiar dishes, the *enchilada*, can be defined as a tortilla moistened with a sauce made with chiles and filled with meat or cheese. Because enchiladas can be made in hundreds of different varieties, they can perhaps be better explained by means of a procedure rather than a recipe.

The recipes for Ancho Sauce, Salsa Verde Cocida, Salsa Roja, Carnitas, and Picadillo can be used for enchilada ingredients. Unless Mexican cheeses are available, the most appropriate American cheeses to use in Mexican cooking are Monterey jack, American munster, and mild cheddar or colby.

General Procedures for Making Enchiladas

Method 1

1. Fry tortillas quickly to soften them (do not fry until crisp). Keep them warm and moist between towels.

2. Dip the tortillas in sauce.

3. Fill with desired meat or cheese filling and roll up. Arrange in baking dish.

4. Ladle a little sauce over the enchiladas.

5. Top with grated cheese.

6. Bake at 350°F (175°C) until hot, about 15–20 minutes.

Method 2

1. Dip tortillas in sauce to coat lightly.

2. Fry quickly in shallow oil.

3. Fill and roll up.

4. Serve immediately. (Or bake with a sauce and topping as in method 1.)

RECIPE 294   **Salsa Cruda**

Yield: 1 qt (1 L)

U.S.	Metric	Ingredients	Procedure
1 lb 4 oz	600 g	Fresh tomatoes	1. Chop the tomatoes fine. (You may peel them, but it is not necessary.)
6 oz	175 g	Fresh green chiles such as jalapeño or serrano	2. Remove the stem end of the chiles. Chop the chiles fine.
6 oz	175 g	Onion	3. Mince the onion.
½–1 oz	15–30 g	Fresh coriander leaves, chopped	4. Mix together the tomato, chiles, onion, coriander, and lime juice or vinegar. Dilute with water or tomato juice to make thick, chunky sauce.
1 tbsp	15 mL	Lime juice or vinegar	
2–4 oz	60–125 mL	Cold water or tomato juice	
1½ tsp	7 mL	Salt	5. Add salt to taste.
			6. This sauce is used as a table condiment with many dishes, including eggs, broiled meats, tacos, tortillas, and beans. It is best if used within a few hours.

RECIPE 295   Salsa Verde Cocida

Yield: 1 qt (1 L)

U.S.	Metric	Ingredients	Procedure
4	4	13-oz (368-g) cans whole tomatillos (Mexican green tomatoes)	1. Drain the tomatillos.
2 oz	60 g	Onion, chopped	2. Combine the tomatillos, onion, garlic, chiles, and coriander in a blender. Blend to a smooth purée.
4 cloves	4 cloves	Garlic, chopped	
2–4	60–125 g	Green chiles, such as jalapeno or serrano, canned or fresh	
1 oz	30 g	Fresh coriander leaves (optional)	
1 oz	30 mL	Oil Salt	3. Heat the oil in a large saucepan. Add the purée and cook 4–5 minutes, until slightly thickened. 4. Season to taste with salt.

Variations

295A. Salsa Roja: Substitute 2 lb (1 kg) red, ripe tomatoes, peeled, or canned red tomatoes for the tomatillos. The onion may be included or omitted to create slightly different flavors.

295B. Tomato Broth for Chiles Rellenos: Prepare as for Salsa Roja, using the onion but omitting the chiles and coriander. After step 3, add 3 pt (1.5 L) pork stock (including the cooking liquid from making picadillo for the filling for the chiles) and/or chicken stock. Also, add a sachet containing 6 whole cloves, 10 peppercorns, 2 bay leaves, and 1 small cinnamon stick. Simmer until slightly thickened with the consistency of a thick broth or thin sauce.

RECIPE 296   Ancho Sauce

Yield: about 1½ pt (750 mL)

U.S.	Metric	Ingredients	Procedure
8	8	Dried ancho chiles	1. Toast the chiles lightly in a dry skillet, until softened. Split them open. Remove and discard the seeds and core. 2. Soak the chiles for about 30 minutes in enough hot water to cover. Drain.
2 oz	60 oz	Onion, chopped	3. Combine the chiles, onion, garlic, and water or stock in a blender. Blend to a smooth purée.
3 cloves	3 cloves	Garlic, chopped	
1 pt	500 mL	Water or chicken stock	
1 oz	30 mL	Oil Salt	4. Heat the oil in a saucepan and add the chile purée. Simmer 2–3 minutes. 5. Season to taste with salt.

Variation

Blend 8 oz (250 g) chopped tomato with the chiles in step 3.

RECIPE 297   **Shredded Pork (Carnitas)**

Yield: about 3½ lb (1.6 kg)

U.S.	Metric	Ingredients	Procedure
6 lb	2.8 kg	Pork butt or shoulder, boned	1. Remove most of the large chunks of fat from the pork, leaving a little of it on. Cut the meat into 1-inch by 2-inch (2.5 × 5 cm) strips.
1	1	Medium onion, cut in half	2. Put the pork in a large pot with the rest of the ingredients. Add water to barely cover the meat.
1 clove	1 clove	Garlic, chopped	
1 tbsp	15 mL	Salt	3. Bring to a boil, reduce heat, and simmer slowly, uncovered, until all the liquid has evaporated. By this time, the meat should be tender. If it is not, add more water and continue to cook until it is.
¼ tsp	1 mL	Pepper	
1 tsp	5 mL	Oregano	
1 tsp	5 mL	Cumin seeds	
			4. Remove the onion, and discard it.
			5. Lower the heat, and let the meat cook in the rendered fat, stirring from time to time, until the meat is browned and very tender. Shred the meat slightly.
			6. Serve as a snack or appetizer, or as a filling for tortillas either as it is or moistened with any of the sauces in this section or with guacamole.

Variation

297A. *Picadillo:* Add a little extra water to the basic recipe so that there will be some liquid left when the meat is tender. Drain and degrease the liquid and use it to make Tomato Broth for Chiles Rellenos (p. 631). Heat 3 oz (90 g) oil or lard and sauté 6 oz (175 g) onion, medium dice, and 4 cloves garlic, chopped. Add the meat, plus a sachet containing 10 peppercorns, a small cinnamon stick, and 6 cloves, and brown slowly. Add 4 oz (125 g) raisins, 4 oz (125 g) slivered almonds, and 2 lb (900 g) peeled, seeded, chopped tomatoes. Cook slowly until almost dry. Serve as is or as a stuffing for Chiles Rellenos (p. 631).

297B. *Short Cut Picadillo:* Instead of preparing Shredded Pork, use 5 lb (2.3 kg) raw ground pork. Sauté it with the onion and garlic in the Picadillo recipe, then proceed as directed with the rest of the recipe.

RECIPE 298   Mole Poblano de Pollo *or* de Guajolote

....

Portions: 16   **Portion size:** 3 oz (90 mL) sauce

chicken or turkey

quantity variable

U.S.	Metric	Ingredients	Procedure
15	15	Mulato chiles (see note)	1. Remove and discard the seeds and stem ends from the chiles. Grind the chiles to a powder.
1½ oz	45 g	Sesame seeds	
4 oz	125 g	Almonds	2. Grind the sesame seeds in a spice grinder or with a mortar and pestle. Set them aside and grind the almonds in the same way.
3	3	Tortillas	
6 oz	175 g	Lard, or rendered chicken fat, turkey fat, or pork fat	3. Fry the tortillas in the fat for about 30 seconds. Drain and reserve the fat for step 6. Break the tortillas into pieces.
¼ tsp	1 mL	Cloves, ground	
½ tsp	2 mL	Cinnamon	4. Put the ground sesame, ground almonds, tortillas, cloves, cinnamon, pepper, and coriander into the container of a blender.
½ tsp	2 mL	Black pepper	
¼ tsp	1 mL	Coriander, ground	
8 oz	225 g	Tomatoes, canned or fresh	5. Peel the tomatoes if they are fresh. Add the tomatoes and the garlic to the blender. Blend to a smooth purèe. If the mixture is too thick to blend, add a little chicken or turkey broth or water.
4 cloves	4 cloves	Garlic, chopped	
1 oz	30 g	Bitter (unsweetened) chocolate, grated or broken into pieces	
			6. Heat the reserved fat from step 3 in a sauce pot over moderate heat. Add the powdered chiles and cook for about 30 seconds. Be careful not to let it burn.
			7. Add the purée from the blender. Cook 5 minutes, stirring constantly. The mixture will be very thick.
			8. Add the chocolate. Stir constantly until the chocolate is completely blended in. *The sauce may be prepared to this point a day or two ahead of time and held in the refrigerator.*
10–14 lb	4.5–6.5 kg	Chicken (pollo) or turkey (guajolote), disjointed	9. Put the poultry, onion, carrot, garlic, peppercorns, and salt in a large pot. Add enough water to cover.
6 oz	175 g	Onion, chopped	10. Simmer until the poultry is tender.
2 oz	60 g	Carrot, chopped	11. Remove the poultry from the broth and set aside to keep warm.
1 clove	1 clove	Garlic	
8	8	Peppercorns	
4 tsp	20 mL	Salt	12. Strain the broth. Measure 3 pt (1.5 L) of the broth and stir it into the chile sauce base. Simmer slowly 30–45 minutes, until the flavors have blended and the mixture has the consistency of a light sauce. (Reserve remaining broth for another use.)
		Water	

RECIPE 298   **Mole Poblano de Pollo** *or* de Guajolote *(Continued)*

U.S.	Metric	Ingredients	Procedure
		Lard Salt	13. Heat the lard in a sauté pan and brown the cooked poultry pieces lightly. (This step is optional.) 14. Add the poultry to the sauce and simmer a few minutes until quite hot. 15. Adjust the seasoning with salt, if necessary, and serve.

Note: Instead of mulato chile peppers, you may use ancho or pasilla chiles or a mixture of different kinds. If none of these is available, you may substitute about 1 cup (125 g) chile powder.

RECIPE 299   **Chiles Rellenos**

Portions: 16		**Portion size:** 1 pepper	

U.S.	Metric	Ingredients	Procedure
16 3 lb (approx.)	16 1.4 kg (approx.)	Chiles Poblanos (see note) Picadillo (see note)	1. Char the chiles over a gas flame until the skin is blackened. Rub off the blackened skin under running water. 2. Slit one side of each pepper and remove the seeds, but be careful to keep the peppers intact. 3. Stuff the peppers with picadillo.
12 1 oz 1 oz ½ tsp 12	12 30 mL 30 g 2 mL 12	Egg yolks Water Flour, sifted Salt Egg whites Flour for dredging	4. Beat the egg yolks and water slightly, then mix in the flour and salt. 5. Whip the whites until they form soft peaks. Fold them into the yolk mixture. 6. Carefully dust the filled peppers with flour, then dip in the egg batter. Deep-fry at 350°F (175°C) until lightly browned. (Hint: Carefully lower each pepper into the fat with the slit side up. If the slit tends to open up, spoon a little of the batter over the slit. This helps keep opening sealed and the filling in the pepper.)
3–4 pt	1.5–2 L	Tomato Broth for Chiles Rellenos (p. 628)	7. For each portion, ladle 3–4 oz (90–125 mL) broth into a broad serving bowl or soup plate. Place one chile in the center of the bowl and serve at once.

Note: Anaheim peppers or frying peppers may be used if poblanos are not available, but the results will not be as flavorful. Exact amount of filling needed depends on the size of the peppers.

Variations

For cheese-filled chiles, use chunks of American munster or Monterey jack cheese instead of the picadillo.

For baked Chiles Rellenos, omit the egg batter and simply bake the stuffed chiles in a casserole until they are heated through. Serve with the tomato broth as in the basic recipe.

Portions: 16–20   **Portion size:** 4 oz (125 g)

U.S.	Metric	Ingredients	Procedure
1½ lb	750 g	Pinto beans or pink beans	1. Combine the beans, water, onion, garlic, and chile in a pot. Bring to a boil, reduce heat, and simmer, covered, for 1½ hours. Check the pot from time to time and add more water, if needed, to keep the beans covered.
3 qt	3 L	Cold water (see note)	
6 oz	175 g	Onion, sliced thin	
1–2 cloves	1–2 cloves	Garlic, chopped	
1	1	Jalapeño or other green chile, chopped (optional)	2. Add the lard and salt. Continue to simmer until the beans are tender. Do not let the beans go dry. There should always be some broth. Add hot water if necessary.
2 oz	60 g	Lard or rendered pork fat	3. The beans will hold refrigerated for several days.
2 tsp	10 mL	Salt	

Note: The beans may be soaked overnight, if desired (although many Mexican cooking authorities feel that the results are not as good). If they are soaked, reduce the water for cooking to 1½ pt (750 mL).

Variation

300A. *Frijoles Refritos:* For the quantity of beans in the basic recipe, make in at least three batches. Mash the beans coarsely. Heat 2 oz (60 g) lard in a large sauté pan. Add 2 oz (60 g) chopped onion and fry until soft, but do not brown. Add one-third of the cooked, mashed beans (about 1½ lb or 750 g, including broth) to the pan. Stir and mash the beans over heat until the beans start to dry out and pull away from the sides of the pan. Roll the mass out of the pan like an omelet. Sprinkle with grated cheese (mild cheddar or Monterey jack) and serve with tortilla chips.

Portions: 16   **Portion size:** 3½ oz (100 g)

U.S.	Metric	Ingredients	Procedure
6	6	Anaheim chiles (see note)	1. Char the chiles over an open flame or under a broiler until the skin is black. Rub off the blackened skin under running water.
4 oz	125 g	Onion	
2 oz	60 g	Butter	2. Remove and discard the seeds and stem ends from the chiles. Cut the chiles into medium dice.
2½ lb	1.2 kg	Whole kernel corn (frozen or fresh)	
		Salt	3. Cut the onion into small dice. Cook it slowly in the butter until it is soft. Do not brown.
10 oz	300 g	Mild cheddar cheese, grated	
			4. Add the diced chile and cook 5 minutes.
			5. Add the corn and cook over moderate heat until the corn is thawed (if using frozen corn) or no longer raw (if using fresh corn).
			6. Add salt to taste.
			7. Put the corn in a shallow baking pan, or in individual gratin dishes, and bake at 350°F (175°C), covered, for 10 minutes.

RECIPE 301   **Elote con Queso** *(Continued)*

U.S.	Metric	Ingredients	Procedure
			8. Uncover and top with the grated cheese. Bake until very hot and the cheese is melted and bubbling.

Note: Canned, diced chiles (10–12 oz/300–350 g, drained) may be used in place of the fresh Anaheims. Omit steps 1 and 2 in the procedure.

Variations

If you wish, this may be cooked entirely on top of the range. Simply mix in the grated cheese before serving.

Fresh zucchini, cut into small dice, may be substituted for one-third to one-half of the corn. Add it to the onion at the same time as the chiles.

RECIPE 302   **Arroz Mexicana**

Portions: 16   **Portion size:** 4½ oz (125 g)

U.S.	Metric	Ingredients	Procedure
1½ lb	700 g	Long-grain rice	1. Rinse the rice well to remove excess starch. Soak in cold water for at least 30 minutes. Drain well.
3 oz	90 mL	Oil	
12 oz	350 g	Tomato purée	
3 oz	90 g	Onion, chopped fine	2. Heat the oil in a pot and add the rice. Stir over moderate heat until it begins to brown lightly.
2 cloves	2 cloves	Garlic, mashed to a paste	
3½ pt	1.75 L	Chicken stock	3. Add the tomato purée, onion, and garlic. Cook until the mixture is dry. Be careful not to let it burn.
1 tbsp	15 mL	Salt	

4. Add the chicken stock and stir. Simmer uncovered over medium heat until most of the liquid has been absorbed.

5. Cover, turn the heat to very low, and cook for 5–10 minutes, until the rice is tender.

6. Remove from the heat and let it stand, without removing the cover, for 15–30 minutes before serving.

Variation

302A. Arroz Verde: Omit the tomato purée. Purée in a blender the onion and garlic along with the following: 6 oz (175 mL) water, 3 tbsp (45 mL) chopped fresh coriander leaves, ¾ cup (45 g or 200 mL) chopped parsley, and 3 oz (90 g) green chiles (or part green chiles and part green bell peppers). Use this purée in place of the tomato purée. Reduce the quantity of stock to 3 pt (1.5 mL) (you may use water instead of stock).

ITALIAN

Italian foods have long enjoyed great popularity in this country. The style of cooking we know the best was developed in the kitchens of Italian immigrants, most of whom came from the southern part of Italy. Many of these Italian-American dishes are excellent in their own right, but they are not really typical of Italian cooking as a whole.

It is nearly impossible to generalize about Italian cooking, because it varies so much from region to region. It is often said that the cooking of southern Italy is based on olive oil and tomatoes, while that of the north is based on butter and cream, but that is too simplistic to be completely accurate.

We can make a few generalizations about Italian cooking, but keep in mind that there are many exceptions. In the first place, it is true that tomatoes are important in Italian cooking, but most Italian dishes are made without tomato sauce. There are even many pasta dishes made without tomatoes.

Second, sauces and other dishes simmered for hours, or heavy casseroles loaded with sauce and cheese, are not wholly typical of Italian cooking. They do exist, of course, but there are just as many, if not more, simple grilled, boiled, and fried dishes, quickly prepared and enhanced with just a few seasonings to highlight the natural flavor of the basic ingredients.

The recipes in this section are selected to give you a little idea of the range of Italian dishes. Most of them, by the way, are made without tomato sauce. In addition, there are a number of Italian dishes elsewhere in this book. Look especially for the pasta and risotto recipes in Chapter 18.

RECIPE 303   Zuppa di Ceci e Riso

Portions: 16   **Portion size:** 6 oz (175 mL)

U.S.	Metric	Ingredients	Procedure
3 oz	90 mL	Olive oil	1. Heat the oil over moderate heat. Add the garlic and rosemary. Cook for a few seconds.
1 clove	1 clove	Garlic, chopped	
1½ tsp	7 mL	Rosemary, chopped fine	2. Add the tomatoes. Bring to a boil, then simmer until most of the juice has evaporated.
1 lb	450 g	Canned Italian-style plum tomatoes, crushed or chopped	3. Add the stock and the rice. Simmer for 15 minutes.
5 pt	2.5 L	White stock (chicken, veal, or pork)	4. Add the chick peas and continue to simmer until the rice is tender and the flavors are well blended.
6 oz	175 g	Rice (raw)	5. Season to taste with salt and pepper.
1½ lb	700 g	Cooked chick peas, drained	6. Sprinkle each portion with a little chopped parsley.
		Salt	
		Pepper	
3 tbsp	45 mL	Chopped parsley	

RECIPE 304 Polenta

Yield: about 5 lb (2.5 kg)

U.S.	Metric	Ingredients	Procedure
5 pt	2.5 L	Water	1. Bring the water and salt to a boil in a sauce pot.
1 tbsp	15 mL	Salt	
1 lb	500 g	Polenta (Italian coarse-grained yellow cornmeal)	2. Very slowly sprinkle the cornmeal into the boiling water, while stirring constantly. This must be done slowly and carefully to avoid lumps.
			3. Cook over low heat, stirring almost constantly. The polenta will become thicker as it cooks and will eventually start to pull away from the sides of the pot. This will take about 20–30 minutes.
			4. Lightly moisten a large flat surface, such as a wooden board or a platter.
			5. Pour out the polenta onto this board or platter. Serve immediately, hot, or let cool and use in any of a number of ways, including some of the variations below.

Variations

Freshly made hot polenta is good with many kinds of stews and other braised dishes that provide plenty of flavorful juices for the polenta to soak up. It is also served with grilled dishes.

304A. Polenta con Sugo di Pomodoro: Serve hot polenta with Tomato Sauce or with Meat Sauce (p. 461).

304B. Polenta con Salsicce: Serve hot polenta with pork sausages cooked with tomatoes or tomato sauce.

304C. Polento al Burro e Formaggio: Stir 6 oz (175 g) fresh butter and 2–3 oz (60–90 g) grated parmesan cheese into hot polenta as soon as it is cooked.

304D. Polenta Fritta or Grigliata: Let polenta cool and cut it into slices ½ inch (1 cm) thick. Pan-fry in oil until a thin crust forms. Or heat slices on a grill or broiler until hot and lightly grill-marked.

304E. Polenta Grassa: This can be prepared in two ways. (1) Pour a layer of hot polenta into a buttered baking dish. Cover with sliced fontina cheese and dot with butter. Cover with another layer of polenta, then another layer of cheese and butter. Bake until very hot. (2) Prepare as in the first method, but instead of the hot, freshly made polenta, use cold polenta cut into thin slices.

304F. Polenta Pasticciata: Prepare Meat Sauce (p. 461) using some pork sausage in addition to the beef. Also, add some sautéed sliced mushrooms to the sauce. Cut cold polenta into thin slices. Fill a baking pan with alternating layers of polenta slices, Meat Sauce, and parmesan cheese. Bake until hot.

RECIPE 305 **Pesce con Salsa Verde**

		Portions: 16	**Portion size:** one piece of fish, plus 1½ oz (45 mL) sauce

U.S.	Metric	Ingredients	Procedure
		Court bouillon:	1. Combine the court bouillon ingredients in a pot. Simmer for 15 minutes.
4 oz	125 g	Onion, sliced	
1 oz	30 g	Celery, chopped	
6–8	6–8	Parsley stems	
1	1	Bay leaf	
¼ tsp	1 mL	Fennel seeds	
1½ tsp	7 mL	Salt	
1 pt	500 mL	White wine	
3 qt	3 L	Water	
		Salsa verde:	2. Soak the bread in the vinegar for 15 minutes, then squeeze it out.
3 slices	3 slices	White bread, crusts removed	3. Combine the parsley, garlic, capers, and anchovies on a cutting board, and chop them very well.
4 oz	125 mL	Wine vinegar	
1½ oz	50 g	Parsley, leaves only	
1 clove	1 clove	Garlic	4. Mash the egg yolks and the bread pulp together in a bowl, then add the chopped parsley mixture and mix together until well combined.
3 tbsp	45 mL	Capers, drained	
4	4	Anchovy fillets	
3	3	Hard-cooked egg yolks	
1 pt	500 mL	Olive oil	5. Very slowly beat in the olive oil as though you were making mayonnaise. When all the oil has been added, the sauce should have a creamy texture, not as thick as mayonnaise.
		Salt	
		Pepper	
			6. Season to taste with salt and pepper.
16	16	Fish steaks, fillets, or small whole fish	7. Poach the fish in the court bouillon.
			8. Drain well. Top each portion with 1½ oz (45 mL) sauce, and serve immediately.

Note: Some of the fish that can be used for this recipe are halibut, sea bass, striped bass, red snapper, bluefish, and porgy.

RECIPE 306 Mozzarella in Carozza

		Portions: 16	

U.S.	Metric	Ingredients	Procedure
1 lb	450 g	Mozzarella cheese (see note)	1. Cut the mozzarella into slices. Make 16 sandwiches with the bread.
32 slices	32 slices	White bread	2. Beat the eggs with a large pinch of salt.
8–10	8–10	Eggs	3. Dip the sandwiches in the eggs to coat both sides.
		Salt	
		Oil for pan-frying	4. Pan-fry (or deep-fry) until both sides are golden brown and the cheese is melted. Serve at once.

Note: If possible, use freshly made mozzarella cheese or mozzarella di bufala (p. 571). Commercial low-moisture mozzarella, formulated for pizzas, does not have the same fresh milk flavor.

Variations

This appetizer is sometimes served with a sauce made by heating butter and a little olive oil with mashed anchovies. Because this sauce is almost all fat, however, it is not really appropriate to a fried dish. This sauce is more appropriate to the following:

306A. *Spiedini alla Romana:* Cut fresh mozzarella, preferably mozzarella di bufala, into half-inch-thick (1-cm) slices. Also, cut a loaf of thin Italian bread into 1½-inch-thick (4-cm) slices. Alternate four slices of bread with three slices of mozzarella on skewers, beginning and ending with bread. Heat very carefully in a broiler or on a grill to toast the bread and lightly heat the cheese. Serve with the anchovy sauce described above.

RECIPE 307 **Zuppa di Vongole**

Portions: 16

U.S.	Metric	Ingredients	Procedure
15 lb	7 kg	Small clams, such as littlenecks	1. Scrub the clams under cold water to remove sand and grit from the shells.
1 pt	500 mL	Water	2. Put the clams and water in a heavy, covered pot, and heat gently just until the clams open. Set the clams aside. Strain and reserve the liquid.
			3. Depending on how you wish to serve them, you can leave the clams in the shell, or you can shell all but 4–6 of them per portion to use as garnish.
6 oz	175 mL	Olive oil	4. Heat the olive oil in a large pot. Sauté the onion until soft but not brown.
5 oz	150 g	Onion, small dice	
3–5 cloves	3–5 cloves	Garlic, chopped	5. Add the garlic and cook another minute.
6 tbsp	90 mL	Chopped parsley	6. Add the parsley and the wine, and boil for a minute.
12 oz	350 mL	White wine	
1½ lb	700 g	Canned plum tomatoes, with juice, coarsely chopped	7. Add the tomatoes and the reserved clam juice. Simmer 5 minutes.
			8. Taste for seasonings and adjust if necessary.
			9. Add the clams and reheat them gently. Do not overcook, or the clams will be tough.
			10. Serve with plenty of crusty bread for dipping in the broth.

Variations

307A. *Zuppa di Cozze:* Substitute mussels for the clams.

307B. *Zuppa di Frutti di Mare:* Use a mixture of clams, mussels, squid (cut up), and shrimp (shelled). Keep all the items separate. Cook the clams and mussels as in the basic recipe. Add the squid at the same time as the tomatoes and broth, and simmer slowly, covered, until tender. Add the shrimp and cook just a minute before adding the clams and mussels.

307C. *Zuppa di Pesce:* Use a mixture of shellfish and fin fish, as desired. Add each type of fish just long enough before the end of cooking so that it cooks through without overcooking.

RECIPE 308 Costolette di Vitello Ripiene alla Valdostana

Portions: 16			**Portion size:** 1 chop

U.S.	Metric	Ingredients	Procedure
16	16	Veal rib chops	1. Remove the chine and featherbones so that only the rib bone is attached to each chop.
			2. Cut a pocket in each as shown in Figure 11.4.
			3. Flatten the chops lightly with a cutlet pounder to increase the diameter of the eye. Be careful not to tear a hole in the meat.
12 oz	350 g	Fontina cheese Salt White pepper	4. Cut the cheese into thin slices.
as needed	as needed	Standard Breading Procedure: Flour Egg wash Bread crumbs	5. Stuff the chop with the cheese, making sure all of the cheese is inside the pockets, with none hanging out. Press the edges of the pocket together and pound lightly to seal. If this is done carefully, you don't need to skewer them shut.
1½ tsp	7 mL	Rosemary Butter	6. Season the chops with salt and pepper.
			7. Set up a breading station. Crumble the rosemary, and mix it with the bread crumbs.
			8. Bread the chops.
			9. Sauté the chops in butter and serve immediately.

Variation

308A. Costolette alla Milanese: Omit the cheese stuffing and the rosemary. Do not cut pockets in the meat. Flatten the chops with a cutlet pounder until they are half their original thickness. Bread and sauté them as in the basic recipe.

RECIPE 309 Saltimbocca alla Romana

Portions: 16			**Portion size:** 2 pieces

U.S.	Metric	Ingredients	Procedure
32	32	Veal scaloppine, about 1½–2 oz (45–60 g) each Salt White pepper	1. Pound the scaloppine with a cutlet pounder. Season with salt and white pepper. Put a slice of prosciutto and a sage leaf on top of each and fasten with a toothpick.
32	32	Thin slices of prosciutto, about the same diameter as the scaloppine	2. Sauté briefly in butter on both sides.
32	32	Sage leaves	3. Add the wine and continue to cook until the meat is done and the wine is partly reduced, no more than 5 minutes.
4 oz	125 g	Butter	
12 oz	350 mL	White wine	4. Remove the meat from the pan and serve, ham side up, with a spoonful of the pan juices over each.

RECIPE 310   **Lombatine di Maiale alla Napoletana**

	Portions: 16		**Portion size:** 1 chop, 3–4 oz (90–125 g) vegetables

U.S.	Metric	Ingredients	Procedure
6	6	Italian peppers or bell peppers; red or green	1. Char the peppers over a gas flame until the skin is black. Rub off the blackened skin under cold, running water. Remove and discard the seeds and core and cut the peppers into batonnet. (See note.)
1 lb 8 oz	700 g	Mushrooms	
3 lb	1.4 kg	Tomatoes	
			2. Slice the mushrooms.
			3. Peel, seed, and chop the tomatoes.
6 oz	175 mL	Olive oil	4. Heat the olive oil in a large sauté pan or brazier. Add the garlic cloves. Sauté them until they are light brown. Then remove and discard them.
2	2	Garlic cloves, crushed	
16	16	Pork loin chops	
		Salt	5. Season the chops with salt and pepper. Brown them in the olive oil. When they are well browned, remove and set them aside.
		Pepper	
			6. Add the pepper and mushrooms and sauté briefly, until wilted.
			7. Add the tomatoes and return the chops to the pan. Cover and cook on the range or in a low oven until the pork is done. The vegetables should give off enough moisture to braise the chops, but check the pan from time to time to make sure it is not dry.
			8. When the chops are done, remove them from the pan and keep them hot. If there is a lot of liquid in the pan, reduce it over high heat until there is just enough to form a little sauce for the vegetables.
			9. Adjust the seasoning. Serve the chops topped with the vegetables.

Note: Charring and peeling the peppers is optional, but it improves the flavor, and it removes the peel, which would otherwise come off during cooking and make the vegetable mixture less attractive.

Variations

310A. ***Pollo con Peperoni all'Abruzzese:*** Double the quantities of peppers. Increase the tomatoes to 4½ lb (2 kg). Omit the mushrooms and garlic. Add 1 lb (450 g) sliced onions, and sauté them with the peppers. Instead of pork, use 8–10 lb (3.6–4.5 kg) chicken parts. Season with a little basil.

If desired, reduce the quantity of chicken in the above recipe and add some Italian pork sausages.

RECIPE 311   Spinaci alla Romana

Portions: 16   **Portion size:** 3 oz (90 g)

U.S.	Metric	Ingredients	Procedure
6 lb	2.7 kg	Spinach	1. Trim and wash the spinach. Cook in a small quantity of boiling water until wilted. Drain, cool under running water, and drain again. Press excess water out of the spinach, but do not squeeze too dry.
1½ oz	45 mL	Olive oil	
1½ oz	45 g	Fat from prosciutto or pork, small dice	
1½ oz	45 g	Pine nuts	
1½ oz	45 g	Raisins	
		Salt	2. Heat the oil in a pan. Add the fat and render it. Remove and discard the cracklings (solid pieces remaining from the fat).
		Pepper	
			3. Add the spinach, pine nuts, raisins. Sauté until hot.
			4. Season with salt and pepper.

Variations

Chopped garlic may be added (sautéed in the fat before the spinach is added).

Lean prosciutto, sliced thin, then diced, may be added.

311A. Spinaci alla Piemontese: Omit the oil, fat, nuts, and raisins. Heat chopped anchovy fillets and 2 chopped garlic cloves in 4 oz (125 g) butter, then add the boiled, drained spinach and sauté.

RECIPE 312   Cipolline in Agrodolce

Portions: 16   **Portion size:** 3½ oz (100 g)

U.S.	Metric	Ingredients	Procedure
4½ lb	2 kg	Pearl onions	1. Blanch the onions for a minute. Drain and peel.
1 pt	500 mL	Water	
2 oz	60 g	Butter	2. Put the onions in a sauté pan in a single layer. Add the water and cook slowly, uncovered, for about 20 minutes, until fairly tender. Add a little water if necessary during cooking so that the pan does not become dry. Stir gently from time to time.
3 oz	90 mL	Wine vinegar	3. Add the vinegar, sugar, and salt. Cover lightly. Cook over low heat until very tender and the liquid is syrupy, about 30 minutes. If necessary, remove the cover toward the end of the cooking time to let the liquid reduce. The onions should be lightly browned by the time they are done.
1½ oz	45 g	Sugar	
1½ tsp	7 mL	Salt	

EUROPEAN CLASSICS

This last section is a collection of recipes from many parts of Europe. Its main purpose is simply to give you additional experience with a variety of international dishes.

Sometimes it is impossible to draw the line between international and American recipes. As a nation with a widely diverse cultural heritage, we have inherited our culinary traditions largely from Europe. Many of our familiar, everyday dishes originated in Europe, but we have adopted them and made them our own. Even names from other languages, like "pizza" for example, have become so familiar that we no longer think of them as foreign.

Throughout this book you can find recipes from many European countries, such as Borscht and Sirniki, from Russia; Scotch Broth and Welsh Rabbit, from the British Isles; Coq au Vin, Ratatouille, and Choucroute Garni, from different regions of France; Sauerbraten, from Germany; Avgolemono, from Greece; and Swedish Meatballs (called Köttbullar in Swedish) from Scandinavia. The recipes that follow are an addition to that list.

RECIPE 313   Brandade de Morue (France)

Yield: about 2½ lb (1.25 kg)

U.S.	Metric	Ingredients	Procedure
2 lb	1 kg	Salt cod	1. Soak the salt cod in cold water for 24 hours, changing the water several times.
			2. Put the cod in a pot with enough water to cover. Bring to a boil, reduce heat, and simmer 5–10 minutes, just until the cod is cooked and flakes. Do not overcook or it will not absorb liquids well in the next steps. Remove the fish from the water, flake it, and remove the skin and bones.
1–2 cloves	1–2 cloves	Garlic, crushed to a paste	3. Work the fish, while it is still hot, into a smooth, lump-free paste. This can be done by hand with a bowl and wooden spoon or with a mixer with the paddle attachment. (A food processor may also be used, but be careful not to process the fish until it is totally puréed.)
8 oz	250 mL	Olive oil	
8 oz	250 mL	Milk, cream, or half-and-half	
		White pepper	4. Warm the oil and milk or cream in separate pans.
		Salt	5. Gradually beat in the oil alternately with the milk, adding just a little at a time, until the mixture is the consistency of mashed potatoes.
		Toast points fried in olive oil (see p. 599)	
			6. Add white pepper to taste. Salt may not be necessary, because the dried cod is very salty.
			7. Serve warm as a dip, with toast points for dipping.

Variations

Brandade can be reheated if it is done slowly over low heat, stirring frequently.

Brandade can be mixed with mashed potatoes in varying proportions.

If you add too much oil or cream in step 5, or if you add it too quickly, the brandade can break or curdle. It can usually be rescued by beating it vigorously. If this doesn't work, add a little mashed potatoes.

RECIPE 314 **Rohkostsalatteller (Germany)**

Portions: 16   **Portion size:** see procedure

U.S.	Metric	Ingredients	Procedure
6 oz	175 mL	White wine vinegar	1. Make a dressing by mixing together the vinegar, sour cream, salt, sugar, and chives. Set aside.
1 pt	500 mL	Sour cream	
2 tsp	10 mL	Salt	
½ tsp	2 mL	Sugar	
2 tbsp	30 mL	Chopped chives	
1 lb	450 g	Carrots	2. Peel the carrots. Shred them on a coarse grater.
2 tbsp	30 mL	Horseradish, drained well	3. Mix the carrots with the horseradish, then with 6 oz (175 mL) of the sour cream dressing, or just enough to bind. Season to taste with salt.
		Salt	
1 lb 6 oz	625 g	Cucumbers	4. Peel the cucumbers. Cut them into thin slices. Toss with the coarse salt and let stand for 1–2 hours.
1 tbsp	15 mL	Coarse salt	
2 oz	60 mL	White wine vinegar	5. Press the juices out of the cucumbers. Rinse off excess salt and drain.
3 oz	90 mL	Water	
1 tbsp	15 mL	Sugar	6. Mix together the vinegar, water, sugar, dill, and white pepper.
2 tsp	10 mL	Fresh dill, chopped	
pinch	pinch	White pepper	7. Mix this dressing with the cucumbers. If necessary, add salt to taste.
1 lb 4 oz	575 g	Celery root	8. Peel the celery root. Grate it on a coarse grater. Immediately mix with the lemon juice.
1½ oz	50 mL	Lemon juice	
5 oz	150 mL	Heavy cream	
		Salt	9. Mix in the cream. Season with salt and white pepper.
		White pepper	
2 lb	900 g	Bibb or Boston lettuce greens	10. If necessary, thin out the remaining sour cream dressing with a little water, until it is the consistency of heavy cream.
16	16	Tomato wedges	11. Toss the greens with dressing. Plate in the center of large salad plates.
			12. Around the outside edge of each plate, arrange one tomato wedge and about 1 oz (30 g) each of the carrot, cucumber, and celery salads.

RECIPE 315   **Caldo Verde (Portugal)**

Portions: 16   **Portion size:** 10 oz (300 mL)

U.S.	Metric	Ingredients	Procedure
2 oz	60 mL	Olive oil	1. Heat the oil in a soup pot. Add the onion and garlic. Cook slowly until soft, but do not brown.
12 oz	350 g	Onion, chopped fine	
1 clove	1 clove	Garlic, chopped fine	
4 lb	1.8 kg	Potatoes, peeled and sliced	2. Add the potatoes and water. Simmer until the potatoes are very tender.
4 qt	4 L	Water	3. Purée the soup, or for a coarser texture, simply mash it in the pot.
1 lb	450 g	Hard, spicy garlic sausage (see note)	4. Cut the sausage into thin slices. Heat slowly in a sauté pan to cook off some of the fat. Drain.
		Salt	
		Pepper	5. Add the sausage to the soup. Simmer 5 minutes. Season to taste.
2 lb	900 g	Kale	6. Remove the hard center ribs from the kale. Shred as fine as possible, about as thin as threads.
			7. Add to the soup. Simmer 5 minutes. Check the seasoning.
			8. This soup should be accompanied by chunks of coarse peasant bread.

Note: Because authentic Portuguese *chouriço* sausage is not widely available, you may substitute Spanish *chorizo* or Italian pepperoni.

RECIPE 316   Carbonnade à la Flammande (Belgium)

....

	Portions: 16		**Portion size:** 6–7 oz (175–200 g)

U.S.	Metric	Ingredients	Procedure
3 lb	1.4 kg	Onions Beef fat or vegetable oil	1. Peel the onions. Cut them into small dice. 2. Cook over moderate heat in a little fat until golden. Remove from the heat and set aside.
6 oz 2 tsp 1 tsp 5 lb	175 g 10 mL 5 mL 2.3 kg	Flour Salt Pepper Beef chuck, cut into 1-inch (2.5-cm) dice	3. Season the flour with salt and pepper. Dredge the meat in the flour. Shake off the excess flour. 4. Brown the meat well in a sauté pan. Do a little at a time to avoid overcrowding the pan. As each batch is browned, add it to the pot with the onions.

2½ pt
2½ pt
 	
2
1 tsp
8
8
1 tbsp
	1.25 L
	1.25 L
	
	2
	5 mL
	8
	8
	15 mL
		Dark beer
		Brown stock
		Sachet:
		   Bay leaves
		   Thyme
		   Parsley stems
		   Peppercorns
		Sugar
			5. Deglaze the sauté pan with the beer and add it to the pot. Add the stock, sachet, and sugar.
			
			6. Bring to a boil, cover, and transfer to the oven. Cook at 325°F (160°C) until very tender, about 2–3 hours.
			
			7. Degrease. Adjust the consistency of the sauce: if it is too thin, reduce over moderately high heat. If it is too thick, dilute with brown stock.
			
			8. Taste and adjust the seasonings. Serve with plain boiled potatoes.

....

RECIPE 317   **Dillkött (Sweden)**

Portions: 16			**Portion size:** 6 oz (175 g)

U.S.	Metric	Ingredients	Procedure
7 lb	3.2 kg	Boneless, trimmed veal shoulder, breast, or shank	1. Cut the veal into 1-inch (2.5-cm) dice.
1	1	Medium onion stuck with 2 cloves	2. Put the meat in a pot with the onion, sachet, water, and salt. Bring to a boil and skim well.
		Sachet:	3. Reduce the heat and add the dill. Simmer slowly until the meat is very tender, about 1½–2 hours.
1	1	Bay leaf	
5–6	5–6	Parsley stems	
6	6	Peppercorns	4. Strain off the broth into another pan. Discard the onion and the sachet.
2 qt	2 L	Water	
1 tbsp	15 mL	Salt	
2 tbsp	30 mL	Fresh dill, chopped (see note)	
		Roux:	5. Reduce the broth over high heat to 1 qt (1 L).
2 oz	60 g	Butter	
2 oz	60 g	Flour	6. Make a blond roux with the flour and butter. Thicken the broth with it.
1 oz	30 mL	Lemon juice or wine vinegar	
1½ tsp	7 mL	Brown sugar	7. Add the lemon juice, brown sugar, dill, and capers. Adjust the seasonings.
2 tbsp	30 mL	Fresh dill, chopped	
2 tbsp	30 mL	Capers, drained	

Note: If fresh dill is not available, substitute one-third its quantity of dried dill.

Variation

317A. **Dillkött på Lamm:** Substitute lamb shoulder or shank for the veal.

RECIPE 318   Paella (Spain)

....

Portions: 16			**Portion size: see procedure**

U.S.	Metric	Ingredients	Procedure
2	2	Chickens, 2½–3 lb (1.1–1.4 kg) each	1. Cut each chicken into 8 pieces.
as needed	as needed	Olive oil	2. In a large sauté pan, brown the chicken in olive oil. Remove and set aside.
8 oz	225 g	Chorizo sausage (see note)	3. Using additional oil as needed, briefly sauté the sausage, pork, shrimp, squid, and peppers. Do each ingredient separately, then remove to separate containers.
2 lb	900 g	Lean pork, cut into large dice	
16	16	Large shrimp, peeled and deveined	
2 lb	900 g	Squid, cleaned (p. 346), cut into rings	
2	2	Red bell peppers, large dice	
2	2	Green bell peppers, large dice	
16	16	Small clams	4. Combine the clams and mussels with the water in a covered pot. Steam them just until they open.
16	16	Mussels	
8 oz	250 mL	Water	
as needed	as needed	Chicken stock	5. Remove the shellfish and set them aside. Strain the liquid, then add enough chicken stock to measure 2 qt (2 L).
1 tsp	5 mL	Saffron	6. Add the saffron to the stock mixture.
12 oz	350 g	Onion, small dice	7. In the skillet used for browning the meats, sauté the onion and garlic until soft. Use additional olive oil if necessary.
6 cloves	6 cloves	Garlic, minced	
2 lb	900 g	Tomatoes, chopped	8. Add the tomatoes and rosemary. Cook until most of the liquid has evaporated and the tomatoes form a rather dry paste.
2 tsp	10 mL	Rosemary	
2 lb	900 g	Short-grain rice, such as Italian arborio	9. Add the rice and stir. Add the chicken, sausage, pork, squid, and peppers.
2 tsp	10 mL	Salt	10. Bring the stock mixture to a boil in a separate pot, then add to the rice and stir. Add salt and pepper to taste.
		Pepper	11. Bring to a simmer, cover, and put in an oven heated to 350°F (175°C) for 20 minutes. (This dish is traditionally made uncovered on top of the stove, but making it in the oven is more practical for restaurants, because it requires less attention.)

RECIPE 318 **Paella** *(Continued)*

U.S.	Metric	Ingredients	Procedure
4 oz	125 g	Cooked green peas	12. Remove the pan from the oven. Check the moisture level and add more stock if necessary. It should be quite moist but not soupy.
16	16	Lemon wedges	
			13. Sprinkle the peas over the top of the rice. Then arrange the shrimp, clams, and mussels on top. Cover loosely and let stand 10 minutes to heat the shellfish.
			14. For each portion, allow 8 oz (225 g) rice and vegetables, one shrimp, one clam, one mussel, one piece of chicken, and at least one piece each of pork, sausage, and squid. Garnish each portion with a lemon wedge.

Note: If chorizos are not available, use pepperoni sausage or other hard, spicy sausage. You may cut the sausage into half-ounce (15-g) chunks before sautéing or cut them up just before serving.

RECIPE 319 **Lecsó (Hungary)**

| | | **Portions: 16** | **Portion size: 4 oz (125 g)** |

U.S.	Metric	Ingredients	Procedure
1 lb 8 oz	750 g	Onions	1. Peel the onion and cut into fine dice.
3 lb	1.5 kg	Green peppers, or Hungarian or Italian frying peppers	2. Core and seed the peppers. Cut into thin slices.
			3. Peel, seed, and chop the tomatoes.
3 lb	1.5 kg	Tomatoes, as ripe as possible	4. Heat the lard over low heat. Add the onion and cook slowly for 5–10 minutes, until it is quite soft.
3 oz	100 g	Lard	
3 tbsp	20 g	Hungarian paprika	5. Add the peppers and cook for another 5–10 minutes.
		Salt	6. Add the tomatoes and paprika. Cover and simmer for 15–20 minutes, until vegetables are tender.
		Sugar	
			7. Season to taste with salt. Add a pinch or two of sugar if desired.

Variations

This dish may be used as a vegetable or appetizer or served with rice or boiled noodles. Smoked sausages are often added to it as a luncheon dish, or it may be served with eggs prepared in a variety of ways. The portion size indicated is rather large, because this dish is often served as part of a main course. For a side dish portion, you may want to reduce the portion size to 2½–3 oz (75–100 g).

RECIPE 320 **Moussaka (Greece)**

Portions: 16		**Portion size: 9 oz (250 g)**	

U.S.	Metric	Ingredients	Procedure
1 lb	450 g	Onion, small dice	1. Sauté the onion and garlic in the olive oil until soft. Remove with a slotted spoon.
3 cloves	3 cloves	Garlic, chopped	
2 oz	60 mL	Olive oil	2. Add the meat to the pan and brown lightly.
3½ lb	1.6 kg	Ground lamb or beef	3. Return the onion and garlic to the pot and add the tomato, wine, parsley, oregano, and cinnamon. Simmer, uncovered until the liquid has reduced and the mixture is thick.
2 lb 4 oz	1 kg	Tomato, canned or fresh, peeled and chopped, with juice	
4 oz	100 mL	Red wine	4. Season to taste with salt and pepper.
2 tbsp	30 mL	Chopped parsley	
1½ tsp	7 mL	Oregano	
¼ tsp	1 mL	Cinnamon	
		Salt	
		Pepper	
4 lb	1.8 kg	Eggplant	5. Peel the eggplant if the skin is tough. Cut into half-inch (1-cm) slices.
		Olive oil	
		Salt	6. Fry the eggplant slices in olive oil until tender. Set aside and season with salt.
1 qt	1 L	Bechamel, cold	7. Season the bechamel (which should be quite thick when cold) with a little salt, white pepper, and nutmeg.
		Salt	
		White pepper	
		Nutmeg	8. Beat the eggs and mix into the bechamel.
4	4	Eggs	
		Olive oil	9. Oil the bottom of a hotel pan or other 12 × 20-inch (30 × 50-cm) pan with olive oil. Sprinkle lightly with bread crumbs.
		Bread crumbs	
2 oz	60 g	Romano or parmesan cheese, grated	10. Arrange the eggplant slices in the pan so that they completely cover the bottom. Push them together as necessary.
			11. Put the meat mixture on top of the eggplant in a smooth layer.
			12. Pour the bechamel over the top and sprinkle with the grated cheese.
			13. Bake at 350°F (175°C) until hot and the top is golden, about 45–60 minutes.
			14. Cut into squares to serve.

RECIPE 321 **Colcannon (Ireland)**

	Portions: 16		**Portion size:** 5 oz (150 g)	

U.S.	Metric	Ingredients	Procedure
4 lb	1.8 kg	Potatoes	1. Peel and eye the potatoes. Cut them into uniform sizes. Simmer in salted water until tender.
2 lb	900 g	Cabbage	
6 oz	175 g	Leeks or scallions	
4 oz	125 g	Butter	2. While the potatoes are cooking, trim the cabbage and cut into wedges. Steam until tender.
6 oz	175 mL	Milk or cream, hot	
2 tbsp	30 mL	Chopped parsley (optional)	3. Cook the leeks or scallions very slowly in a little of the butter until tender.
		Salt	4. Mash the potatoes and add the leeks or scallions and the rest of the butter. Mix in the milk or cream and the parsley.
		White pepper	
		Additional hot milk or cream as needed	5. Chop the cabbage fine and stir it into the potatoes until well mixed. Season with salt and white pepper.
			6. If the mixture seems dry, mix in additional milk or cream to bring to a smooth, moist consistency.

FOREIGN TERMS USED IN THIS CHAPTER

Following are brief explanations of the foreign-language terms for food items and cooked dishes in this chapter. The language that the term comes from is indicated in parentheses. Please note that this may not correspond to the country that the food comes from. For example, many of the foods whose names are in Spanish are not from Spain but from Mexico.

The following abbreviations are used: J. = Japanese; Ch. = Chinese; Sp. = Spanish; It. = Italian; Fr. = French. The first six entries, by the way, all refer to place names in Italy.

all'Abruzzese (It.): in the style of Abruzzo.

alla Milanese (It.): in the style of Milan.

alla Napoletana (It.): in the style of Naples.

alla Piemontese (It.): in the style of Piedmont.

alla Romana (It.): in the style of Rome.

alla Valdostana (It.): in the style of the Val d'Aosta.

ancho chile (Sp.): see chile.

arroz (Sp.): rice.

arroz verde (Sp.): green rice; rice cooked with herbs.

brandade de morue (Fr.): purée of salt cod.

burro (It.): butter.

caldo verde (Portuguese): a Portuguese soup made with potatoes, kale, and sausages.

carbonnade à la Flammande (Fr.): Flemish-style beef braised in beer.

carnitas (Sp.): "little meats"; browned pieces of pork.

ceci (It.): chickpeas.

chawan mushi (J.): savory steamed custard.

chile (Sp.): any of a variety of hot capsicum peppers, which may be fresh and green (such as poblano, jalapeño, and serrano) or red-ripe and dried (such as ancho, pasilla, and mulato).

chiles rellenos (Sp.): stuffed chiles.

chirashizushi (J.): scatter sushi, various fish and other garnish arranged on a bed of sushi rice.

cipolline in agrodolce (It.): sweet-and-sour pearl onions.

colcannon (Irish/English): a mixture of mashed potatoes and cabbage.

costellete di vitello ripiene (It.): stuffed veal chop.

cozze (It.): mussels.

daikon (J.): giant white radish.

dashi (J.): Japanese soup stock.

dillkött (Swedish): meat stew flavored with dill.

elote con queso (Sp.): corn with cheese.

enchilada (Sp.): a tortilla moistened with a sauce made with chiles and filled with meat or cheese.

formaggio (It.): cheese.

frijoles (Sp.): beans.

frijoles refritos (Sp.): "well-fried beans"; often called "refried beans."

fritta (It.): fried.

frutti di mare (It.): "fruits of the sea"; shellfish.

grassa (It.): fat.

grigliata (It.): grilled.

guajolote (Sp.): turkey.

kappa-maki (J.): rolled sushi filled with cucumber.

lecsó (Hungarian): cooked mixture of peppers, tomatoes, and onions.

lombatine di maiale (It.): pork loin chop.

mirin (J.): sweet rice wine.

miso (J.): a fermented paste made of soybeans, barley, or rice.

mole poblano (Sp.): a spicy chile sauce generally seasoned with bitter chocolate, or a dish (most often turkey or chicken) made with this sauce.

moussaka (Greek): a layered casserole made with eggplant and spicy ground lamb or other meat.

mozzarella in carrozza (It.): "mozzarella in a carriage"; a fried mozzarella sandwich.

mulato chile (Sp.): see chile.

nigirizushi (J.): finger sushi, or small ovals of sushi rice with topping.

nori (J.): a type of seaweed made into thin sheets, often used for sushi.

oyako donburi (J.): "parent-and-child bowl"; rice topped with chicken and egg in a thin sauce or broth.

paella (Sp.): an elaborate rice casserole containing a variety of meats, seafood, and vegetables.

pasilla chile (Sp.): see chile.

pasticciata (It.): made like a pie or pastry.

pesce (It.): fish.

picadillo (Sp.): a spiced ground or shredded meat, often used as a stuffing or filling.

poblano chile (Sp.): see chile.

polenta (It.): Italian cornmeal.

pollo (It., Sp.): chicken.

pollo con peperoni (It.): chicken with peppers.

riso (It.): rice.

rohkostsalatteller (German): raw vegetable salad plate.

saké (J.): rice wine.

salsa cruda (Sp.): uncooked sauce.

salsa roja (Sp.): red sauce.

salsa verde (Sp., It.): green sauce.

salsa verde cocida (Sp.): cooked green sauce.

salsicce (It.): sausages.

saltimbocca (It.): "jump in the mouth"; a dish of veal cutlets with ham and sage.

sashimi (J.): sliced raw fish.

serrano chile (Sp.): see chile.

shaoxing (Ch.): a Chinese wine similar to sherry.

sichuan (Ch.) peppercorns: a dried bud used as a spice.

spiedini (It.): skewers.

spinaci (It.): spinach.

sudare (J.): a bamboo mat used for rolling sushi.

sugo di pomodoro (It.): tomato sauce.

sushi (J.): vinegared rice, garnished with raw fish or other foods.

tekka-maki (J.): rolled sushi filled with raw tuna.

tempura (J.): Japanese-style batter-fried foods.

tendon (J.): rice topped with tempura and a seasoned broth.

teriyaki (J.): broiled, grilled, or griddled foods with a soy sauce glaze.

tomatillo (Sp.): a Mexican vegetable resembling a small, green tomato.

vongole (It.): clams.

wakame (J.): a type of seaweed.

wasabi (J.): Japanese green horseradish.

wonton (Ch.): meat-filled dumpling.

zuppa (It.): soup.

QUESTIONS FOR DISCUSSION

1. Explain the basic procedure for making dashi.

2. Explain how to make miso soup.

3. Describe the composition of sushi rice.

4. Describe a basic procedure for stir-frying.

5. Give one basic procedure for assembling an enchilada.

6. True or false: Most Italian dishes are served with tomato sauce. Discuss.

Fruit torte, page 709

PART SIX

THE BAKESHOP

· ·

· · · · · · · · · · · · · · · · · · · *To many people, a meal is not complete without bread or dessert. These chapters introduce the student to the baker's demanding art.*

■

Bakeshop Production: Basic Principles and Ingredients

Yeast Products

Quick Breads

Cakes and Icings

Cookies

Pies and Pastries

Creams, Custards, Puddings, Frozen Desserts, and Sauces

CHAPTER 24

BAKESHOP PRODUCTION: BASIC PRINCIPLES AND INGREDIENTS

At one time it was common for food service establishments to produce all their own breads, desserts, and other baked goods. Today, most operations find it more economical to buy these products from commercial bakeries. However, many owners and chefs have discovered that offering fresh, "home-baked" breads, cakes, and pastries attracts customers and increases profits. With little more than an oven and a mixer, many cooks turn out attractive baked items that set their operations apart from competitors.

For this reason, it is important for you to learn the fundamentals of baking, even if you intend to become a cook rather than a baker. These chapters will not make a professional baker out of you. A baker requires far more technical and specialized information than can be presented in this short space. But you will learn the basic methods that will enable you to produce a wide variety of breads, desserts, and pastries, with only the simplest of resources.

In this chapter you will be introduced to bakeshop production with a discussion of the basic processes and ingredients common to nearly all baked goods. This will give you the understanding necessary to proceed to actual production in the succeeding chapters.

After reading this chapter, you should be able to

1. Explain the importance of weighing baking ingredients.

2. Use a baker's balance scale.

3. Use formulas based on baker's percentages.

4. Explain the factors that control the development of gluten in baked products.

5. Explain the changes that take place in a dough or batter as it bakes.

6. Prevent or retard the staling of baked items.

7. Discuss the major ingredients of baked goods and their functions and characteristics.

BASIC PRINCIPLES OF BAKING

*W*hen you consider that most bakery products are made of the same few ingredients—flour, shortening, sugar, eggs, water or milk, and leavenings—then you should have no difficulty understanding the importance of accuracy in the bakeshop, because slight differences in proportions or procedures can mean great differences in the final product.

If you have begun your food service studies in a kitchen production laboratory, you have surely been told many times of the importance of measurement, not only for portion control and cost control but also for consistency in the quality of the final product. However, you have no doubt also learned that there is a great deal of margin for error, that it is possible (if not desirable) to cook many foods without measuring anything. Coming into the bakeshop, where measurement is absolutely essential, may be a bit of a shock to you after your kitchen experiences, but it should reinforce the habits of accuracy that you may have let slip.

If, on the other hand, you are beginning your practical studies in the bakeshop, then you will do well to pay particular attention to the principles of measurement you will learn here. They will be valuable to you throughout your career.

· · · · · · · · · · · · · ·

FORMULAS AND MEASUREMENT

Bakers generally talk about "formulas" rather than "recipes." If this sounds more to you like the chemistry lab than the kitchen, it is with good reason. The bakeshop is very much like a chemistry laboratory both in the scientific accuracy of all the procedures and in the complex reactions that take place during mixing and baking.

Measurement

All ingredients must be weighed. Accuracy of measurement, as we have already said many times, is critical in the bakeshop. Measurement is by weight rather than by volume measure, because weighing is much more accurate. Unlike in homemakers' recipes, you will not see a professional baker's formula calling for 6 cups of flour.

To demonstrate to yourself the importance of weighing rather than measuring by volume, measure a cup of flour in two ways. (1) Sift some flour and lightly spoon it into a dry measure. Level the top and

weigh the flour. (2) Scoop up some unsifted flour into the same measure and pack it lightly. Level the top and weigh the flour. Note the difference. No wonder home recipes can be so inconsistent!

The baker's term for weighing out ingredients is *scaling*.

The following ingredients may be measured by *volume*, because they weigh *one pound per pint*:

Water   Milk   Eggs

Thus, if a formula calls for 2 lb of eggs, you may measure 2 pt (1 qt). (Liquid flavoring ingredients, such as vanilla extract, normally measured in very small quantities, may also be measured by volume; 1 tablespoon equals one-half ounce.) In the metric system, one milliliter of water weighs one gram; one liter weighs one kilogram. All other liquid ingredients (such as corn syrup or molasses) and all dry ingredients are normally weighed.

Procedure for Using a Baker's Balance Scale

The principle of using a baker's scale (Figure 24.1) is very simple: The scale must balance before setting the weights, and it must balance again after scaling.

1. Set the scale scoop or other container on the *left* side of the scale.

2. Balance the scale by placing counterweights on the *right* side and/or adjusting the ounce weight on the horizontal bar.

3. Set the scale for the desired weight by placing weights on the *right* side and/or by moving the ounce weight. For example, to set the scale for 1 lb 8 oz, place a 1-lb weight on the *right* side, and move the ounce weight to the *right* 8 oz. If

FIGURE 24.1   **A baker's balance scale.**

the ounce weight is already over 8 oz, so that you cannot move it another 8, add 2 lb to the right side of the scale, and subtract 8 oz by moving the ounce weight 8 places to the *left*. The result is still 1 lb 8 oz.

4. Add the ingredient being scaled to the left side until the scale balances.

Baker's Percentages

Bakers use a simple but versatile system of percentages for expressing their formulas. Baker's percentages express the amount of each ingredient used as a percentage of the amount of flour used.

To put it differently, the percentage of each ingredient is its total weight divided by the weight of the flour, multiplied by 100%, or

$$\frac{\text{weight of ingredient}}{\text{weight of flour}} \times 100\% = \% \text{ of ingredient}$$

Thus, flour is always 100%. (If two kinds of flour are used, their total is 100%.) Any ingredient that weighs the same as the flour is also given as 100%. The following ingredients from a cake formula illustrate how these percentages are used. Both U.S. and metric examples are given. (Note that numbers may be rounded off for practical measuring.) Check the figures with the above equation to make sure you understand them.

Ingredient	Weight	Percentage
Cake flour	5 lb	100%
Sugar	5 lb	100%
Baking powder	4 oz	5%
Salt	2 oz	2.5%
Emulsified shortening	2 lb 8 oz	50%
Skim milk	3 lb	60%
Egg whites	3 lb	60%
	18 lb 14 oz	377.5%

Ingredient	Weight	Percentage
Cake flour	2500 g	100%
Sugar	2500 g	100%
Baking powder	125 g	5%
Salt	60 g	2.5%
Emulsified shortening	1250 g	50%
Skim milk	1500 g	60%
Egg whites	1500 g	60%
	9435 g	377.5%

The advantage of using *baker's percentages* is that the formula is easily adapted for any yield, and single ingredients may be varied without changing the whole formulation.

Procedure for Calculating the Weight of an Ingredient if the Weight of Flour Is Known

1. Change the ingredient percentage to decimal form by moving the decimal point two places to the left.

2. Multiply the weight of the flour by this decimal to get the weight of the ingredient.

    Example: A formula calls for 20% sugar and you are using 10 pounds of flour. How much sugar do you need?

    20% = 0.20
    10 lb × 0.20 = 2 lb sugar

    Note: In the U.S. system, weights must normally be expressed all in one unit, either ounces or pounds, in order for the calculation to work, as explained in Chapter 5.

    Example (Metric):   A formula calls for 20% sugar and you are using 5000 grams (5 kg) of flour. How much sugar do you need?

    20% = 0.20
    5000 g × 0.20 = 1000 g sugar

Procedure for Converting a Formula to a New Yield

1. Change the total percentage to decimal form by moving the decimal point two places to the left.

2. Divide the desired yield by this decimal figure to get the weight of flour.

3. If necessary, round off this number to the next highest figure. This will allow for losses in mixing, makeup, and panning, and it will make calculations easier.

4. Use the weight of flour and remaining ingredient percentages to calculate the weights of the other ingredients, as in the previous procedure.

    Example: In the sample cake formula above, how much flour is needed if you require 6 pounds (or 3,000 grams) of cake batter?

6 lb = 96 oz
377.5% = 3.775
96 oz ÷ 3.775 = 25.43 oz
    or, rounded off, 26 oz (1 lb 10 oz)

3000 g ÷ 3.775 = 794.7 g
    or, rounded off, 800 g

Clearly, the percentage system we have been discussing is used only when flour is a major ingredient, such as in breads, cakes, and cookies. For these formulas, we use a written format different from our regular recipe format in this book.

In these formulas, the indicated yield is the total weight of the ingredients. This figure indicates the weight of the batter or dough. It is the figure that we need to know for the purpose of scaling the dough or batter into loaves or pans. The finished weight of the baked goods will be less, because moisture is lost during baking.

Also, please note that all yields, including percentage totals, are rounded off to the next lower whole number. This eliminates unimportant fractions and makes reading and calculating easier.

Selection of Ingredients

In addition to measuring, there is another basic rule of accuracy in the bakeshop: *Use the exact ingredients specified.*

As you will learn in this chapter, different flours, shortenings, and other ingredients do not function alike. Baker's formulas are balanced for specific ingredients. Do not substitute bread flour for pastry flour or regular shortening for emulsified shortening, for example. They won't work the same way.

Occasionally a substitution may be made, such as active dry yeast for compressed yeast (see p. 664), but not without adjusting the quantities or rebalancing the formula.

MIXING AND GLUTEN DEVELOPMENT

What Is Gluten?

Gluten is a substance made up of proteins present in wheat flour; it gives structure and strength to baked goods.

In order for gluten to be developed, the proteins must first absorb water. Then, as the dough or batter is mixed or kneaded, the gluten forms long, elastic strands. As the dough or batter is leavened, these strands capture the gases in tiny pockets or cells, and we say the product "rises." When the product is baked, the gluten, like all proteins (see p. 52), coagulates or solidifies and gives structure to the product.

How Does the Baker Control Gluten?

Flour is mostly starch, but it is the protein or gluten content, not the starch, that concerns the baker most. Without gluten proteins to give structure, baked goods would not hold together.

The baker must be able to control the gluten, however. For example, we want French bread to be firm and chewy, which requires much gluten. On the other hand, we want cakes to be tender, which means we want very little gluten development.

Ingredient proportions and mixing methods are determined in part by how they affect the development of gluten. The baker has several methods for adjusting gluten development:

1. *Selection of flours.*

   Wheat flours are classified as *strong* or *weak,* depending on their protein content.

   Strong flours come from *hard wheat* and have a high protein content.

   Weak flours come from *soft wheat* and have a low protein content.

   Thus, we use strong flours for breads and weak flours for cakes.

   Only wheat flour will develop gluten. To make bread from rye and other grains, the formula must be balanced with some high-gluten flour, or the bread will be heavy.

2. *Shortening.*

   Any fat used in baking is called a shortening because it shortens gluten strands. It does this by surrounding the particles and lubricating them so they do not stick together. Thus, *fats are tenderizers.* A cookie or pastry that is very crumbly, due to high fat content, is said to be "short."

   You can see why French bread has little or no fat, while cakes contain a great deal.

3. *Liquid.*

   Because gluten proteins must absorb water before they can be developed, the amount of water in a formula can affect toughness or tenderness. Pie crusts and crisp cookies are made with very little liquid, to keep them tender.

4. *Mixing methods.*

In general, the more a dough or batter is mixed, the more the gluten develops. Thus, bread doughs are mixed or kneaded for a long time to develop the gluten. Cakes, pie crusts, muffins, and other products that must be tender are mixed for a short time.

It is possible to overmix bread dough, however. Gluten strands will stretch only so far. They will break if the dough is overmixed.

THE BAKING PROCESS

The changes undergone by a dough or batter as it bakes are basically the same for all baked products, from breads to cookies and cakes. You should know what these changes are so you can learn how to control them.

The stages in the baking process take place as follows:

1. *Formation and expansion of gases.*

Some gases are already present in the dough, as in proofed bread dough and in sponge cake batters. As they are heated, the gases expand and leaven the product.

Some gases are not formed until heat is applied. Yeast and baking powder form gases rapidly when first placed in the oven. Steam is also formed as the moisture of the dough is heated.

Leavening and leavening agents are discussed in more detail beginning on page 664.

2. *Trapping of the gases in air cells.*

As the gases are formed and expand, they are trapped in a stretchable network formed by the proteins in the dough. These proteins are primarily gluten and sometimes egg protein.

Without gluten or egg protein, the gases would escape, and the product would not be leavened. Breads without enough gluten are heavy.

3. *Coagulation of proteins.*

Like all proteins, gluten and egg proteins coagulate or solidify when they reach high enough temperatures. It is this process that gives structure to baked goods.

Correct baking *temperature* is very important. If it is too high, coagulation will start too soon, before the expansion of gases has reached its peak. The product will have poor volume or a split crust. If the temperature is too low, the proteins will not coagulate soon enough, and the product may collapse.

4. *Gelatinization of starches.*

The starches absorb moisture, expand, and become firmer.

5. *Evaporation of some of the water.*

This takes place throughout the baking process.

6. *Melting of shortenings.*

Different shortenings melt—and release trapped gases—at different temperatures, so the proper shortening should be selected for each product.

As the fats melt, they surround the air cells and make the product tenderer.

7. *Browning of the surface and crust formation.*

Browning occurs when sugars caramelize and starches and proteins undergo certain changes. This contributes to flavor. Milk, sugar, and egg increase browning.

A crust is formed as water evaporates from the surface and leaves it dry.

STALING

Staling is the change in texture and aroma of baked goods due to the change in structure and the loss of moisture by the starch granules. Stale baked goods have lost their "fresh baked" aroma and are firmer, drier, and more crumbly than fresh products.

Prevention of staling is a major concern of the baker, because most baked goods lose quality rapidly.

Staling can be slowed by these techniques:

1. *Protecting the product from air.*

Wrapping bread in plastic and covering cakes with icing are two examples.

Unfortunately, hard-crusted breads, which stale very rapidly, should not be wrapped, or the crusts will become soft. These bread products should always be served fresh.

2. *Adding moisture retainers to the formula.*

Fats and sugars are good moisture retainers, and products high in these ingredients keep best.

Some of the best French bread has no fat at all, and it must be served within hours of baking or it will begin to stale. For longer keeping, bakers often add a very small amount of fat and/or sugar to the formula.

3. *Freezing.*

Baked goods frozen *before* they become stale maintain quality for longer periods. They should be served very quickly after thawing. Frozen breads may be reheated with excellent results if they are to be served immediately.

Refrigerating actually seems to speed staling rather than slowing it. Only baked goods that could develop health hazards, such as those with cream fillings, are refrigerated.

Loss of crispness is caused by absorption of moisture, so it is in a sense the opposite of staling. This is a problem with low-moisture products such as cookies and pie crusts. The problem is usually solved by proper storage in airtight wraps or containers to protect the products from moisture in the air. Prebaked pie shells should be filled as close to service time as possible.

INGREDIENTS

*T*he following introduction to baking ingredients is necessarily simplified. If you decide to pursue a career as a baker, you will need to learn a great deal of technical information. However, the basic information is here, enough to enable you to produce a full range of baked items in a small bakeshop or restaurant kitchen.

. . . .

FLOURS, MEALS, AND STARCHES

White Wheat Flour

White wheat flour is milled from wheat kernels after the outer covering, called bran, and the germ have been removed. Wheat flour contains about 63 to 73 percent starch and 7 to 15 percent protein. The rest is moisture, fat, sugar, and minerals.

Wheat flour is the source of the protein called *gluten,* which you remember is one of the most essential elements in baking. Bakers select flour on the basis of its gluten content. Flours high in protein are called "strong," those low in protein are called "weak."

For our purposes in the small bakeshop, we need to know about three kinds of wheat flour:

1. *Bread flour* is a strong flour that is used for making breads, hard rolls, and any product that requires high gluten. The best bread flours are called *patents. Straight* flours are also strong flours.

2. *Cake flour* is a weak or low-gluten flour made from soft wheat. It has a very soft, smooth texture and a pure white color. Cake flour is used for cakes and other delicate baked goods that require low gluten content.

3. *Pastry flour* is lower in gluten than bread flour but higher than cake flour. It has the same creamy white color as bread flour, not the pure white of cake flour. Pastry flour is used for cookies, pie pastry and some sweet yeast doughs, and for biscuits and muffins.

Being able to identify these three flours by sight and touch is an important skill, because sooner or later, someone dumps a bag of flour into the wrong bin, and you will want to be able to recognize the problem.

Bread flour feels slightly coarse when rubbed between the fingers. If squeezed into a lump, it falls apart as soon as the hand is opened. Its color is creamy white.

Cake flour feels very smooth and fine. It stays in a lump when squeezed in the palm of the hand. Its color is pure white.

Pastry flour feels more like cake flour but has the creamy color of bread flour.

All-purpose flour, seen in retail markets, is not often found in bakeshops. This flour is formulated to be slightly weaker than bread flour so that it can be used for pastries as well. A professional baker, however, prefers to use flours that are formulated for specific purposes, because these give the best results.

Whole Wheat Flour

Whole wheat flour is made by grinding the entire wheat kernel, including the bran and germ. The germ, which is the embryo of a new wheat plant, is high in fat, which can become rancid. So whole wheat flour does not keep as well as white flour.

Because it is made from wheat, whole wheat flour contains gluten, so it can be used alone in bread making. However, a bread made with 100 percent whole wheat will be heavy, because the gluten strands are cut by the sharp edges of the bran flakes. Also, the fat from the wheat germ contributes slightly to the shortening action. This is why most whole wheat breads are strengthened with white bread flour.

Bran flour is flour to which bran flakes have been added. The bran may be coarse or fine, depending on specifications.

Rye Flour

Next to white and whole wheat, rye is the most popular flour in bread making. Since rye flour does not develop gluten, breads made with it will be heavy unless some hard wheat flour is added.

Rye flour is available in three shades, *light, medium,* and *dark. Rye meal* or *pumpernickel* is a coarse meal made from the whole rye grain. It looks something like oatmeal.

Rye blend is a mixture of rye flour and hard wheat flour.

Other Flours

Products milled from other grains are occasionally used to add variety to baked goods. These include corn meal, buckwheat flour, soy flour, potato flour, oat flour, and barley flour. The term "meal" is used for products that are not as finely ground as flour.

All these products must normally be used in combination with wheat flour, because they do not form gluten.

Starches

In addition to flours, some other starch products are also used in the bakeshop. Unlike flour, they are used primarily to thicken puddings, pie fillings, and similar products. The principles of thickening with starches are covered in Chapter 8.

The most important starches in dessert production are as follows:

1. *Cornstarch* has a special property that makes it valuable for certain purposes. Products thickened with cornstarch set up almost like gelatin when cooled. For this reason, it is used to thicken cream pies and other products that must hold their shape.

2. *Waxy maize* and other *modified starches* also have valuable properties. They do not break down when frozen, so are used for products that are to be frozen. Also, they are very clear when cooked, and give a brilliant, clear appearance to fruit pie fillings.

   Waxy maize does not set up firm like cornstarch but makes a soft paste, which has the same consistency hot and cold. Thus, it is not suitable for cream pie fillings.

3. *Instant starches* have been precooked or pregelatinized, so they will thicken cold liquids without further cooking. They are useful when heat will damage the flavor of the product, as in fresh fruit glazes (such as strawberry).

FATS

We have said that one of the main functions of fats in baking is to shorten gluten strands and tenderize the product. We can summarize the reasons for using fats in baked items as follows:

- To tenderize the product and soften the texture.
- To add moistness and richness.
- To increase keeping quality.
- To add flavor.
- To assist in leavening, when used as creaming agents or when used to give flakiness to puff pastry, pie dough, and similar products.

Shortenings

Any fat acts as a shortening in baking, because it shortens gluten strands and tenderizes the product. However, we usually use the word shortening to mean any of a group of solid fats, usually white and tasteless, that have been especially formulated for baking.

Because shortenings are used for many purposes, manufacturers have formulated different kinds of fats with different properties. There are three main types:

1. *Regular shortenings.*

   These are called "plastic" shortenings because they have a tough, waxy texture, and small particles of the fat tend to hold their shape in a dough or batter; also this type of shortening does not melt until a high temperature has been reached.

   Regular shortening has a good creaming ability. This means that a large quantity of air can be mixed into it to give a batter lightness and leavening power. Therefore, it is used in products mixed by the creaming method, such as certain cookies.

   Because of its texture, this type of shortening is used for flaky products such as pie crusts and biscuits. It is also used in breads and in many other pastries. Unless another shortening is specified, regular shortening is generally used.

2. *Emulsified shortenings.*

These are soft shortenings that spread easily throughout a batter and quickly coat the particles of sugar and flour. Because of their easy spreading, they give a smoother and finer texture to cakes and make them moister.

Emulsified shortening is often used whenever the weight of sugar in a cake batter is greater than the weight of flour. Because this shortening spreads so well, a simpler mixing method can be used, as explained in Chapter 27. Such cakes are referred to as *high-ratio cakes,* so emulsified shortening is sometimes called high-ratio shortening.

In addition, emulsified shortening is used in icings, because it can hold more sugar and liquid without curdling.

3. *Puff pastry shortenings.*

These are firm and plastic like regular shortening. They are especially formulated for puff pastry and other doughs that form layers, such as Danish pastry. Like margarine, but unlike shortening, these fats have a significant water content, which helps give leavening power to the dough when it forms steam.

Butter and Margarine

Shortenings are manufactured to have certain textures and hardness. Butter, on the other hand, is a natural product that doesn't have these advantages. It is hard and brittle when cold, and very soft at room temperature, and it melts easily. Consequently, doughs made with butter are much harder to handle. Margarine is a little easier to handle, but it has many of the same disadvantages.

On the other hand, butter and margarine have two major advantages:

1. *Flavor.* Shortenings are intentionally flavorless, but butter has a highly desirable flavor.

2. *Melting qualities.* Butter melts in the mouth. Shortenings do not. After eating pastries or icings made with shortening, one can be left with an unpleasant film of shortening coating the mouth.

For these reasons, many bakers and pastry chefs feel that the advantages of butter outweigh its disadvantages for some purposes.

Oils

Oils are liquid fats. They are not often used as shortenings in baking, because they spread through a batter or dough too thoroughly and shorten too much. Their usefulness in the bakeshop is limited primarily to greasing pans and proofing bowls, to deep-frying doughnuts, and to serving as a wash for some kinds of rolls. A few quick breads and cakes use oil as a shortening.

Lard

Lard is the rendered fat of hogs. Because of its plastic quality, it was once highly valued for making flaky pie crusts. Since the development of modern shortenings, it is not often used in the bakeshop.

SUGARS

Sugars or sweetening agents are used for the following purposes in baking:

- To add sweetness and flavor.
- To create tenderness and fineness of texture by weakening the gluten structure.
- To give crust color.
- To increase keeping qualities by retaining moisture.
- To act as creaming agents with fats.

We customarily use the term "sugar" for regular refined sugars derived from sugar cane or beets. The chemical name for these sugars is sucrose. However, other sugars of different chemical structure are also used in the bakeshop. The following are the more important sugars:

Regular Refined Sugars, or Sucrose

Refined sugars are classified by the size of grains.

1. *Granulated sugar.*

Regular granulated, also called *fine granulated* or *table sugar,* is the most familiar and the most commonly used.

Very fine and *ultrafine* are finer than regular granulated. They are prized for making cakes and cookies, because they make a more uniform batter and can support higher quantities of fat.

Sanding sugars are coarser and are used for coating doughnuts, cakes, and other products.

2. *Confectioners' or powdered sugars.*

These sugars are ground to a fine powder and mixed with a small amount of starch to prevent caking. They are classified by coarseness or fineness.

10X is the finest sugar. It gives the smoothest textures in icings.

6X is the standard confectioners' sugar. It is used in icings, toppings, and cream fillings.

Coarser types (*4X* and *XX*) are used for dusting or for any purposes for which 6X and 10X are too fine.

Molasses and Brown Sugar

Molasses is concentrated sugar cane juice. *Sulfured molasses* is a by-product of sugar refining. It is the product that remains after most of the sugar has been extracted from cane juice. *Unsulfured molasses* is not a by-product but is a specially manufactured sugar product. It has a less bitter taste.

Molasses contains large amounts of sucrose, plus other sugars, acids, and impurities.

Brown sugar is mostly sucrose, but it also contains varying amounts of molasses and other impurities. The darker grades contain more molasses.

Because molasses and brown sugar contain *acids,* they can be used with baking soda to provide leavening (see p. 665).

Molasses retains moisture in baked goods and so prolongs freshness. However, crisp cookies made with molasses become soft very quickly, for the same reason.

Corn Syrup

Corn syrup is a liquid sweetener consisting mainly of a sugar called glucose or dextrose. It is made by converting cornstarch into simpler sugar compounds by the use of enzymes.

Corn syrup aids in retaining moisture and is used in some icings and in candy making.

Honey

Honey is a natural sugar syrup consisting largely of glucose and fructose, in addition to other compounds that give it its flavor. Honeys vary considerably in flavor and color, depending on their source. Flavor is the major reason for using honey, especially because it can be expensive.

Honey contains *invert sugar,* which means that it stays smooth and resists crystallizing. Like molasses, it contains *acid,* which enables it to be used with baking soda as a leavening.

Malt Syrup

Malt syrup is used primarily in yeast breads. It serves as food for the yeast and adds flavor and crust color to the breads.

LIQUIDS

Gluten cannot be developed without moisture, so liquids are essential to the baking process.

Pie crusts provide a good illustration of how liquids function in baking. If too much water is incorporated in a pie dough, a lot of gluten will be developed and the crust will be tough. If no water at all is used, no gluten will develop and the crust will not hold together.

Some of the moisture in doughs and batters changes to steam during baking. This contributes to leavening.

Water

Water is the basic liquid in baking, especially in breads.

Tap water is normally suitable for most baking purposes. However, in some localities, the water may be very *hard,* meaning that it contains many dissolved minerals. These minerals interfere with proper gluten development. In these areas the water may have to be treated for use in baking.

Milk and Cream

Milk products, as described in Chapter 21, are important in baking. These products include liquid whole and skim milk, buttermilk, and dry milk solids.

Milk contributes to the texture, flavor, nutritional value, keeping quality, and crust color of baked goods.

1. Whole milk contains fat, which must be calculated as part of the shortening in a dough. For this reason, whole and skim milk are not interchangeable in a formula, unless adjustments are made for the fat.

2. Buttermilk, which is slightly acid, is often used for quick breads, in conjunction with baking soda as a leavening agent.

3. Cream is not often used as a liquid in doughs and batters, except in a few specialty products. In these instances, it is used as a shortening as well as a liquid, because of its fat content.

Cream is more important in the production of fillings and toppings.

4. Dry milk is often used because of its convenience and low cost. In some formulas, it is not necessary to reconstitute it. The milk powder is included with the dry ingredients, and water is used as the liquid.

Other Sources of Liquids

Eggs, honey, molasses, and even butter (about 15% water) contribute moisture to a dough or batter. In many cookies, for example, eggs are the only liquid in the formula.

EGGS

Forms

As we discussed in Chapter 21, eggs are purchased in the following forms:

1. Whole shell eggs.

2. Frozen: whites, yolks, whole, and whole with extra yolks.

3. Dried: whole, whites, yolks.

Functions

Eggs perform the following functions in baking:

1. *Structure.*

    Like gluten protein, the egg protein coagulates to give structure to baked products. This is especially important in high-ratio cakes, where the high sugar and fat content weakens the gluten.

    If used in large quantities, eggs give toughness or chewiness to baked products, unless balanced by high fat and sugar, which are tenderizers.

2. *Emulsifying of fats.*

    Egg yolks contain natural emulsifiers, which help produce smooth batters. This contributes to volume and to texture.

3. *Leavening.*

    Beaten eggs incorporate air in tiny cells or bubbles. In a batter, this trapped air expands when heated and aids in leavening.

4. *Shortening action.*

    The fat in egg yolks acts as a shortening. This is an important function in products that are low in other fats.

5. *Moisture.*

    Whole eggs are about 70 percent water, egg whites about 86 percent water, and egg yolks about 49 percent water. This moisture must be calculated as part of the total liquid in a formula.

6. *Flavor.*

7. *Nutritional value.*

8. *Color.*

    Yolks impart a yellow color to doughs and batters. Also, eggs brown easily and contribute to crust color.

LEAVENING AGENTS

Leavening is the production or incorporation of gases in a baked product to increase volume and to produce shape and texture. These gases must be retained in the product until the structure is set enough (by the coagulation of gluten and egg protein) to hold its shape.

Exact measurement of leavening agents is important, because small changes can produce major defects in baked products.

Yeast

Fermentation is the process by which yeast acts on carbohydrates and changes them into carbon dioxide gas and alcohol. This release of gas produces the leavening action in yeast products. The alcohol evaporates completely during and immediately after baking.

Yeast is a microscopic plant. As a living organism, it is sensitive to temperatures.

45°F (7°C)	Inactive; storage temperature
60° to 70°F (15° to 20°C)	Slow action
70° to 90°F (20° to 32°C)	Best growth; proofing temperature for bread doughs
Above 100°F (38°C)	Reaction slows
140°F (60°C)	Yeast is killed

Yeast is available in two forms: compressed and active dry. Most bread formulas call for compressed yeast. *To convert to active dry yeast, use only 40 percent of the weight of compressed yeast specified.* In other words, in place of 1 lb of compressed, use 6.5 oz dry yeast (0.40 × 16 oz). Dry yeast must be dissolved in four times its weight of warm water (about 110°F/43°C) before use.

Yeast also contributes flavor, in addition to leavening action.

Chemical Leaveners

Chemical leaveners are those that release gases produced by chemical reactions.

1. **Baking soda.**

    Baking soda is the chemical sodium bicarbonate. If *moisture* and an *acid* are present, soda releases carbon dioxide gas, which leavens the product.

    Heat is not necessary for the reaction (although the gas will be released faster at higher temperatures). For this reason, products leavened with soda must be baked at once or gases will escape and leavening power will be lost.

    Acids that react with soda in a batter include honey, molasses, buttermilk, fruits, cocoa, and chocolate. Sometimes cream of tartar is used for the acid. The amount of soda used in a formula is generally the amount needed to balance the acid. If more leavening power is needed, baking powder, not more soda, is used.

2. **Baking powder.**

    Baking powders are mixtures of baking soda plus an acid to react with it.

    Because baking powders do not depend for their leavening power on acid ingredients in a formula, they are more versatile.

    Single-acting baking powders require only moisture to be able to release gas. Like baking soda, they can be used only if the product is to be baked immediately after mixing.

    Double-acting baking powders release some gas when cold, but they require heat for complete reaction. Thus, cake batters made with these can incorporate the leavening agent early in the mixing period and can stand for some time before being baked.

    Do not include more baking powder than necessary in a formula, because undesirable flavors may be created.

3. **Baking ammonia.**

    Baking ammonia is the chemical ammonium carbonate. It decomposes during baking to form carbon dioxide gas and ammonia gas. Only heat and moisture are necessary for it to work. No acids are needed.

    Because it decomposes completely, it leaves no residue that could affect flavor. However, it can be used only in small products like cookies, which allow the ammonia gas to be completely driven off.

    Baking ammonia releases gases very quickly, so it is sometimes used in products like cream puffs, where rapid leavening is desired.

Air

Air is incorporated into a batter primarily by two methods, creaming and foaming. This air expands during baking and leavens the product.

1. *Creaming* is the process of beating fat and sugar together to incorporate air. It is an important technique in cake and cookie making. Some pound cakes and cookies are leavened almost entirely by this method.

2. *Foaming* is the process of beating eggs, with or without sugar, to incorporate air. Foams made with whole eggs are used to leaven sponge cakes, while angel food cakes, meringues, and soufflés are leavened with egg white foams.

Steam

When water turns to steam, it expands to 1,600 times its original volume. Because all baked products contain some moisture, steam is an important leavening agent.

Puff pastry, cream puffs, popovers, and pie crusts use steam as their major or only leavening agent.

If the starting baking temperature for these products is high, steam will be produced rapidly and leavening will be greatest.

SALT, FLAVORINGS, AND SPICES

Salt

Salt plays a very important role in baking. It is more than just a seasoning or flavor enhancer. It also has these functions:

1. Salt strengthens gluten structure and makes it more stretchable. Thus, it improves the texture of breads.

2. Salt inhibits yeast growth. It is therefore important for controlling fermentation in bread doughs and in preventing the growth of undesirable wild yeasts.

For these reasons, the quantity of salt in a formula must be carefully controlled.

Chocolate and Cocoa

Chocolate and cocoa are derived from cocoa or cacao beans. When the beans are roasted and ground, the resulting product is called *chocolate liquor,* which contains a white or yellowish fat called *cocoa butter.*

Cocoa is the dry powder that remains after part of the cocoa butter is removed from chocolate liquor.

Dutch process cocoa is processed with an alkali. It is slightly darker, smoother in flavor, and more easily dissolved in liquids.

Bitter or *unsweetened chocolate* is straight chocolate liquor. In some less expensive brands, some of the cocoa butter may be replaced by another fat.

Sweet chocolate is bitter chocolate with the addition of sugar in varying amounts. If the percentage of sugar is low, it is sometimes called *semisweet* or *bittersweet.*

Milk chocolate is sweet chocolate with the addition of milk solids. It is used primarily in candy making. (None of the recipes in this book call for milk chocolate.)

Cocoa and chocolate are high in starch. When cocoa is added to a cake formula, it is sometimes considered part of the flour proportion for this reason.

Spices

Spices are discussed in detail in Chapter 4. The most important spices in the bakeshop are cinnamon, nutmeg, mace, cloves, ginger, caraway, cardamom, allspice, anise, and poppy seed.

Because spices are used in small quantities, it is not much more expensive to use the best quality, and the results will be superior.

Spices should be measured by weight, unless the quantity is so small that measuring spoons are necessary.

Extracts and Emulsions

Extracts are flavorful oils and other substances dissolved in alcohol. These include vanilla, lemon, and bitter almond.

Emulsions are flavorful oils mixed with water with the aid of emulsifiers such as vegetable gums. Lemon and orange are the most frequently used emulsions.

The flavorings of extracts and emulsions may be natural or artificial. Natural flavorings give the best results, but are often expensive. Artificial flavorings must be used in moderation, to avoid creating strong or undesirable flavors in baked items.

TERMS FOR REVIEW

gluten	cake flour	emulsified shortening	single- and double-
strong flour	pastry flour	sucrose	acting baking powders
weak flour	whole wheat flour	confectioners' sugar	creaming
shortening	rye blend	leavening	foaming
staling	pumpernickel	fermentation	extract
bread flour	regular shortening	chemical leavener	emulsion

QUESTIONS FOR DISCUSSION

1. Below are ingredients for a white cake. The weight of the flour is given, and the proportions of other ingredients are indicated by percentages. Calculate the weights required for each.

Cake flour	3 lb or 1500 g (100%)
Baking powder	4%
Shortening	50%
Sugar	100%
Salt	1%
Milk	75%
Egg whites	33%
Vanilla	2%

2. Discuss four factors that affect the development of gluten in doughs and batters.

3. Why do some cakes fall if they are removed from the oven too soon?

4. Which kind of cake would you expect to have better keeping qualities, a sponge cake, which is low in fat, or a high-ratio cake?

5. Why is white wheat flour used in rye breads? In whole wheat breads? Some bakeries in Europe produce a kind of pumpernickel bread with 100 percent rye flour. What would you expect its texture to be like?

6. Describe how to distinguish among bread, pastry, and cake flours by touch and sight.

7. What is the difference between regular and emulsified shortenings?

8. Shortbread is a type of cookie made with flour, butter, and sugar, but no liquid. What would you expect its texture to be like? Why?

YEAST PRODUCTS

In its simplest form, bread is
nothing more than a baked dough of flour and water, leavened by yeast. In
fact, some hard-crusted French breads contain only these ingredients, plus salt. Other
kinds of bread contain additional ingredients, including sugar, shortening, milk,
eggs, and flavorings. But flour, water, and yeast are still the basic
building blocks of all breads.

Yet for something that seems so simple, bread can
be one of the most exacting and complex products to make. Success
in bread making depends largely on your understanding two basic principles:
gluten development, which we discussed in the previous chapter,
and yeast fermentation, which we have touched on and
which we will study in greater detail here.

This chapter focuses on the production of many
kinds of yeast products, including breads, dinner rolls, sweet rolls, Danish
pastry, and croissants.

After reading this chapter, you should be able to

1. Produce breads and dinner rolls.

2. Produce sweet dough products.

3. Produce Danish pastry and croissants.

UNDERSTANDING YEAST PRODUCTS

YEAST PRODUCT TYPES

Although all yeast doughs are made according to essentially the same basic principles, it is useful to divide yeast products into categories such as the following.

Regular Yeast Dough Products

1. *Lean dough products.*

    A lean dough is one that is low in fat and sugar.

    a. Hard-crusted breads and rolls, including French and Italian breads, kaiser rolls and other hard rolls, and pizza. These are the leanest of all bread products.
    b. Other white breads and dinner rolls. These have a higher fat and sugar content and sometimes also contain eggs and milk solids. Because they are slightly richer, they generally have soft crusts.
    c. Whole grain breads. Whole wheat and rye breads are the most common. Many varieties of rye breads are produced with light or dark flours or with pumpernickel flour and with various flavorings, especially molasses and caraway seeds.

2. *Rich dough products.*

    There is no exact dividing line between rich and lean doughs, but in general, rich doughs are those that contain higher proportions of fat, sugar, and sometimes eggs.

    a. Nonsweet breads and rolls, including rich dinner rolls and brioche. These have a high fat content but low enough sugar so that they can be served as dinner breads. Brioche dough is especially rich, made with a high proportion of butter and eggs.
    b. Sweet rolls, including coffee cakes and many breakfast and tea rolls. These have high fat and sugar and usually eggs. They are usually made with a sweet filling or topping.

Rolled-in Yeast Dough Products

Rolled-in doughs are those in which a fat is incorporated into the dough in many layers, by using a rolling and folding procedure. The alternating layers of fat and dough give the baked product a flaky texture.

1. Nonsweet rolled-in doughs: croissants.
2. Sweet rolled-in doughs: Danish pastry.

MIXING METHODS

Mixing yeast doughs has three main purposes:

1. To combine all ingredients into a uniform, smooth dough.
2. To distribute the yeast evenly throughout the dough.
3. To develop gluten.

Two principal mixing methods are used for yeast doughs: the straight dough method and the sponge method.

Straight Dough Method

There is only one step in this method, as practiced by many bakers:

Procedure

Combine all ingredients in the mixing bowl and mix.

Some bakers dissolve the compressed yeast in some of the water before adding the remaining ingredients. Others omit this step. Active dry yeast, on the other hand, must be rehydrated before mixing.

The advantage of softening the yeast in some of the water is that it helps to ensure that the yeast is evenly distributed in the dough.

Modified Straight Dough Method for Rich Doughs

For rich sweet doughs, the method is modified to ensure even distribution of the fat and sugar.

Procedure

1. Soften the yeast in part of the water.
2. Combine the fat, sugar, salt, milk solids, and flavorings and mix until well combined, but do not whip until light.

3. Add the eggs gradually, as fast as they are absorbed.

4. Add the liquid and mix briefly.

5. Add the flour and yeast. Mix into a smooth dough.

Sponge Method

Sponge doughs are prepared in two stages.

Procedure

1. Combine the liquid (or part of the liquid), the yeast, and part of the flour (and sometimes part of the sugar), and mix into a thick batter or soft dough. Let ferment until double in bulk.

2. Punch down and add the rest of the flour and remaining ingredients. Mix to a uniform, smooth dough.

STEPS IN YEAST DOUGH PRODUCTION

There are 12 basic steps in the production of yeast breads. These steps are applied to yeast products in general, with some variations depending on the particular product.

1. Scaling ingredients.

2. Mixing.

3. Fermentation.

4. Punching.

5. Scaling.

6. Rounding.

7. Benching.

8. Makeup and panning.

9. Proofing.

10. Baking.

11. Cooling.

12. Storing.

As you can see, mixing of ingredients into a dough is only one part of a complex procedure.

Scaling Ingredients

All ingredients must be weighed accurately. The only items that may be measured by volume are water, milk, and eggs, which may be scaled at 1 pint per pound (or 1 liter per kilogram).

Mixing

Use the *dough arm* attachment when using a vertical mixer. Mix for the specified time.

The first two purposes of mixing—combining the ingredients into a dough and distributing the yeast—are accomplished during the first part of mixing. The remaining time is necessary to develop the gluten. Overmixed and undermixed doughs have poor volume and texture. (Review "Gluten Development," p. 658.)

It is necessary for you to learn to tell by sight and feel when a dough is thoroughly mixed. This can be done only through experience and through the guidance of your instructor. A properly developed dough should feel smooth and elastic. A lean dough should not be sticky.

Sometimes it is necessary to add a little more flour if the dough hasn't lost its stickiness after most of the mixing time has passed.

Rich doughs are generally undermixed slightly, because a greater tenderness is desired for these products.

Note: Mixing times given in bread formulas in this book are only guidelines. Small mixers might be damaged if they are run at too high a speed with a stiff dough. In such cases, use a lower speed and extend the mixing time as necessary. Depending on the mixer, developing a dough at first or slow speed requires about twice as much mixing time as at second speed. Follow the manufacturer's recommendations.

Fermentation

Fermentation is the process by which yeast acts on the sugars and starches in the dough to produce carbon dioxide gas and alcohol.

Procedure

1. Place the dough in a lightly oiled container and oil the surface to prevent a crust from forming. (This may not be necessary if humidity is high—about 75%.)

2. Cover the container lightly and let the dough rise at a temperature of about 80°F (27°C).

3. Fermentation is complete when dough has doubled in volume. If fermentation is complete, a dent will remain after the hand is pressed into the top of the dough.

Gluten becomes smoother and more elastic during fermentation. An underfermented dough will not develop proper volume, and the texture will be coarse. A dough that ferments too long or at too high a temperature will become sticky, hard to work, and slightly sour.

An underfermented dough is called a *young dough.* An overfermented dough is called an *old dough.*

Doughs with weak gluten, such as rye doughs and rich doughs, are usually underfermented or "taken to the bench young."

Punching

Punching is *not* hitting the dough with your fist. It is a method of deflating the dough that *expels carbon dioxide, redistributes the yeast* for further growth, *relaxes the gluten,* and *equalizes the temperature* throughout the dough.

Procedure

Pull up the dough on all sides, fold over the center, and press down. Then turn the dough upside down in the bowl.

A second fermentation and punching may or may not take place, depending on the product.

Scaling

Using a baker's scale, divide the dough into pieces of uniform weight, according to the product being made.

During scaling, allowance is made for weight loss due to evaporation of moisture in the oven. This weight loss is approximately 10 to 13 percent of the weight of the dough. Allow an extra 1½ to 2 ounces of dough for each 1 pound of baked bread or 50 to 65 grams per 500 grams.

Rounding

After scaling, the pieces of dough are shaped into smooth, round balls. This procedure forms a kind of skin by stretching the gluten on the outside of the dough into a smooth layer. Rounding simplifies later shaping of the dough and also helps retain gases produced by the yeast.

Your instructor will demonstrate rounding techniques. Machines are also available which divide and round portions of dough automatically. Figure 25.1 illustrates a piece of dough being rounded by hand.

Benching

Rounded portions of dough are allowed to rest on the bench for 10 to 15 minutes. This relaxes the gluten to make shaping the dough easier. Also, *fermentation* continues during this time.

Makeup and Panning

The dough is shaped into loaves or rolls and placed in pans or on baking sheets. For all loaves and rolls, the seam must be centered on the bottom to avoid splitting during baking.

Breads and rolls take a great many forms. A variety of shapes and techniques are presented in the next section.

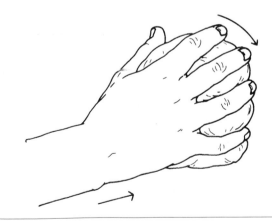

FIGURE 25.1 **To round a piece of dough, roll the dough on the bench with the palm of your hand. As you rotate the dough, the edge of your hand should pinch the dough against the bench. This movement stretches the surface of the dough so that it is completely smooth except for a seam at the bottom where it was pinched together.**

Proofing

Proofing is a continuation of the process of yeast *fermentation,* which increases the volume of the shaped dough. Bakers use two different terms so they can distinguish between fermentation of the mixed dough and proofing of the made-up product before baking. Proofing temperatures are generally higher than fermentation temperatures.

Procedure

Place the panned products in a proof box at 80° to 95°F (27° to 35°C) and about 85 percent humidity. Proof until double in bulk.

If a proof box is not available, come as close to these conditions as you can by covering the products to retain moisture and setting them in a warm place.

Underproofing results in poor volume and dense texture. Overproofing results in coarse texture and some loss of flavor.

Rich doughs are slightly underproofed, because their weaker gluten structure will not withstand too much stretching.

Baking

As you recall from the previous chapter, many changes take place in the dough during baking. The most important changes are these:

1. *Oven spring,* which is the rapid rising in the oven due to production and expansion of trapped gases as a result of the oven heat. The yeast is very active at first but is killed when the temperature inside the dough reaches 140°F (60°C).

2. Coagulation of proteins and gelatinization of starches. In other words, the product becomes firm and holds its shape.

3. Formation and browning of the crust.

Load the ovens carefully, because proofed doughs are fragile until they become set by baking.

Oven temperatures must be adjusted for the product being baked. Rolls spaced apart are baked at a higher temperature than large loaves, so that they become browned in the short time it takes to bake them. In general, popular American lean breads are baked at 400°F to 425°F (200°C to 220°C), while some French breads and rolls are baked at 425° to 475°F (220° to 245°C). Rich doughs and sweet doughs are baked at a lower temperature, 350° to 400°F (175° to 200°C), because their fat, sugar, and milk content makes the crust brown faster.

Hard-crusted breads are baked with steam injected into the oven during the first part of the baking period. This aids the formation of a thin, crisp crust.

Rye breads also benefit from baking with steam for the first 10 minutes.

A break on the side of the loaf is caused by continued rising after the crust is formed. To allow for this final expansion, hard-crusted breads are cut or *scored* before baking by making shallow slashes on the top of the loaf with a sharp knife or razor.

Small rolls bake completely without a break, so they are usually not scored.

Baking times vary considerably, depending on the product. A golden brown crust color is the normal indication of doneness. Loaves should sound hollow when thumped, if they are done.

Cooling

After baking, bread must be removed from pans and cooled rapidly on racks to allow the escape of excess moisture and alcohol created during fermentation.

Rolls baked apart from each other on sheets may be left on them, because they will get adequate air circulation.

If soft crusts are desired, breads may be brushed with melted shortening before cooling.

Do not cool in a draft, or crusts may crack.

Storing

Breads to be served within 8 hours may be left on racks. For longer storage, wrap cooled breads in moisture-proof bags to retard staling. Bread must be thoroughly cool before wrapping, or moisture will collect inside the bags.

Wrapping and freezing maintains quality for longer periods. Refrigeration, on the other hand, increases staling.

Hard-crusted breads should not be wrapped (unless frozen), or the crusts will soften.

Because of the complexity of bread production, many things can go wrong. To remedy common bread faults, check Table 25.1 for possible causes and correct your procedures.

TABLE 25.1 **Bread Faults and Their Causes**

Fault	*Causes*
Shape	
Poor volume	Too much salt
	Too little yeast
	Weak flour
	Under- or overmixing
	Improper fermentation or proofing
	Oven too hot
Too much volume	Too little salt
	Too much yeast
	Too much dough scaled
	Overproofed
Poor shape	Too much liquid
	Improper molding or makeup
	Improper proofing
	Too much steam in oven
Split or burst crust	Overmixing
	Underfermented
	Improper molding—seam not on bottom
	Oven too hot
	Not enough steam in oven
Texture and crumb	
Too dense or close grained	Too little yeast
	Underproofed
	Too much salt
	Too little liquid
Too coarse or open	Too much yeast
	Too much liquid
	Incorrect mixing time
	Improper fermentation
	Overproofed
	Pan too large
Streaked crumb	Improper mixing procedure
	Poor molding or makeup techniques
	Too much flour used for dusting
Poor texture or crumbly	Fermentation time too long or too short
	Overproofed
	Baking temperature too low
	Flour too weak
	Too little salt
Grey crumb	Fermentation time or temperature too high
Crust	
Too dark	Too much sugar or milk
	Underfermented ("young dough")
	Oven temperature too high
	Baking time too long
	Insufficient steam at beginning of baking
Too pale	Too little sugar or milk
	Overfermented ("old dough")
	Overproofed
	Oven temperature too low
	Baking time too short
	Too much steam in oven

TABLE 25.1   *(Continued)*

Fault	Causes
Too thick	Too little sugar or fat Overfermented ("old dough") Baked too long and/or at too low a temperature Too little steam
Blisters on crust	Too much liquid Improper fermentation Improper shaping of loaves
Flavor	
Flat taste	Too little salt
Poor flavor	Inferior, spoiled, or rancid ingredients Poor bakeshop sanitation Under- or overfermented

DOUGH FORMULAS AND TECHNIQUES

BREAD AND ROLL FORMULAS

The basic yeast dough mixing and baking methods discussed earlier in this chapter apply to the following formulas. Therefore, the methods are not repeated in detail for each formula. The basic procedures are indicated, and you should refer to the first part of this chapter if you need to refresh your memory for details.

Makeup techniques for loaves, rolls, and other items are described and illustrated after this recipe section.

RECIPE 322   **Hard Rolls**

Ingredients	U.S.	Metric	Percentage
Water	1 lb 8 oz	700 g	55%
Yeast	1½ oz	45 g	3.5%
Bread flour	2 lb 12 oz	1250 g	100%
Salt	1 oz	30 g	2.25%
Sugar	1 oz	30 g	2.25%
Shortening	1 oz	30 g	2.25%
Egg whites	1 oz	30 g	2.25%
Yield:	4 lb 9 oz	2115 g	167%

Mixing: Straight dough method.
        10 minutes, 2nd speed (see note, p. 671).

Fermentation: About 1 hour at 80°F (27°C).

Scaling and makeup: Rolls—1 lb (500 g) per dozen. French-type loaf—18 oz (550 g) per loaf.
                See makeup techniques after recipe section.
                Dock after proofing. Brush with water.

Baking: 425°F (220°C). Steam for first 10 minutes.

RECIPE 323   **Soft Rolls**

Ingredients	U.S.		Metric	Percentage
Water	1 lb	4 oz	600 g	45%
Yeast		2 oz	60 g	4.5%
Bread flour	2 lb	12 oz	1300 g	100%
Salt		1 oz	30 g	2.25%
Sugar		4 oz	125 g	9%
Nonfat milk powder		2 oz	60 g	4.5%
Shortening		2 oz	60 g	4.5%
Butter or margarine		2 oz	60 g	4.5%
Eggs		4 oz	125 g	9%
Yield:	5 lb	1 oz	2420 g	183%

Mixing: Straight dough method.
          10–12 minutes at 2nd speed (see note, p. 671).

Fermentation: 1½ hours at 80°F (27°C).

Scaling and makeup: 16–20 oz (450–600 g) per dozen rolls.
          See makeup techniques after recipe section.

Baking: 400°F (200°C).

RECIPE 324   **French Bread**

Ingredients	U.S.		Metric	Percentage
Water	1 lb	12 oz	875 g	58%
Yeast		1½ oz	45 g	3%
Bread flour	3 lb		1500 g	100%
Salt		1 oz	30 g	2%
Yield:	4 lb	14 oz	2450 g	163%

Mixing: Straight dough method. Dissolve yeast in water before adding flour and salt.
          3 minutes at 2nd speed; rest 2 minutes; 3 minutes more at 2nd speed (see note, p. 671).

Fermentation: 1½ hours at 80°F (27°C).
          Punch down.
          1 hour at 80°F (27°C).

Scaling and makeup: French loaves—12 oz (350 g).
          Round loaves—18 oz (550 g).
          Rolls—16–20 oz (450–600 g) per dozen.
          See makeup techniques after recipe section.

Baking: 400°F (200°C). Steam for first 10 minutes.

RECIPE 325   **White Pan Bread**

Ingredients	U.S.	Metric	Percentage
Water	1 lb 8 oz	750 g	60%
Yeast	1½ oz	45 g	3.75%
Bread flour	2 lb 8 oz	1250 g	100%
Salt	1 oz	30 g	2.5%
Sugar	1½ oz	45 g	3.75%
Nonfat milk powder	2 oz	60 g	5%
Shortening	1½ oz	45 g	3.75%
Yield:	4 lb 7 oz	2225 g	178%

Mixing: Straight dough method.
   10 minutes at 2nd speed (see note, p. 671).

Fermentation: 1 hour at 80°F (27°C).

Makeup: Pan loaves. See makeup techniques after recipe section.

Baking: 400°F (200°C).

Variation

325A. Whole Wheat Bread: Prepare basic White Pan Bread, using

Bread flour	1 lb	500 g	40%
Whole wheat flour	1 lb 8 oz	750 g	60%

RECIPE 326   **Rye Bread and Rolls**

Ingredients	U.S.	Metric	Percentage
Water	1 lb 8 oz	750 g	60%
Yeast	2 oz	60 g	5%
Rye flour	1 lb	500 g	40%
Bread flour	1 lb 8 oz	750 g	60%
Salt	1 oz	30 g	2.5%
Shortening	1 oz	30 g	2.5%
Molasses	1 oz	30 g	2.5%
Caraway seeds	½ oz	15 g	1.25%
Yield:	4 lb 5 oz	2165 g	173%

Mixing: Straight dough method.
   5–6 minutes at 2nd speed (see note, p. 671).

Fermentation: 1 hour at 80°F (27°C).

Scaling and makeup: 1 lb (500 g) per pan loaf.
   1 lb (500 g) per dozen rolls.
   See makeup techniques after recipe section.

Baking: 400°F (200°C). Steam for first 10 minutes.

RECIPE 327 **Brioche**

Ingredients	U.S.	Metric	Percentage
Milk	8 oz	250 g	20%
Yeast	2 oz	60 g	5%
Bread flour	8 oz	250 g	20%
Eggs	1 lb 4 oz	625 g	50%
Bread flour	2 lb	1000 g	80%
Sugar	2 oz	60 g	5%
Salt	½ oz	15 g	1.25%
Butter, softened	1 lb 8 oz	750 g	60%
Yield:	6 lb	3010 g	241%

Mixing: Sponge method:

1. Scald milk and cool to lukewarm. Dissolve yeast. Add flour and mix to make a sponge. Let rise until double.
2. Gradually mix in eggs and then dry ingredients (using the paddle attachment) to make a soft dough.
3. Beat in butter a little at a time until completely absorbed and dough is smooth. Dough will be very soft and sticky.

Fermentation: Cover with plastic film and place in retarder overnight.

Makeup: 1½ oz (50 g) per roll. See makeup techniques after recipe section. Dough is very soft and is easiest to make up when chilled.
Egg wash after proofing.

Baking: 400°F (200°C).

Variation

To make the dough less sticky and less difficult to handle, reduce the butter to 35–50% (14 to 20 oz/450 to 625 g). This adjustment also reduces cost. However, the brioche will not be as rich and delicate.

RECIPE 328   **Sweet Roll Dough**

Ingredients	U.S.	Metric	Percentage
Milk	1 lb	500 g	40%
Yeast	3 oz	100 g	7.5%
Butter/margarine/shortening (see note)	8 oz	250 g	20%
Sugar	8 oz	250 g	20%
Salt	½ oz	15 g	1.25%
Eggs	6 oz	175 g	15%
Bread flour	1 lb 12 oz	875 g	70%
Pastry flour	12 oz	375 g	30%
Yield:	5 lb 1 oz	2540 g	203%

Note: Any of the fats listed may be used either alone or in combination.

Mixing: Modified straight dough method:
1.   Scald milk. Cool to lukewarm. Dissolve yeast in milk.
2.   Mix fat, sugar, and salt until smooth, using paddle. Beat in eggs.
3.   Add liquid and flour. With dough arm, mix 4 minutes at 2nd speed.

Fermentation: 1½ hours at 80°F (27°C).

Makeup: See makeup techniques after recipe section.

Baking: 375°F (190°C).

Variation

328A. Raised Doughnuts: Prepare basic sweet roll dough but reduce the fat and sugar by half. Mace, nutmeg, or other spices may be added.

Scaling: 1½ oz (50 g) each.
　　　Give full proof.

Frying: 360°F (182°C).
　　　Drain. Roll in cinnamon sugar or 6X sugar when cool.

ROLLED-IN DOUGHS: DANISH PASTRY AND CROISSANTS

Rolled-in doughs contain many layers of fat sandwiched in between layers of dough. These layers create the flakiness that you are familiar with in Danish pastry.

Two basic kinds of rolled-in yeast doughs are made in the bakeshop:

Sweet: Danish pastry

Nonsweet: Croissants

Rolled-in doughs are mixed only slightly, because the rolling-in procedure continues to develop the gluten.

The preferred fat for flavor and melt-in-the-mouth qualities in rolled-in doughs is butter. Specially formulated shortenings are available when lower cost and greater ease of handling become more important considerations.

RECIPE 329   Danish Pastry

Ingredients	U.S.	Metric	Percentage
Milk	1 lb	400 g	40%
Yeast	3 oz	75 g	7.5%
Butter	5 oz	125 g	12.5%
Sugar	6 oz	150 g	15%
Salt	½ oz	12 g	1.25%
Cardamom	1 tsp	2 g (5 mL)	0.2%
Eggs	8 oz	200 g	20%
Bread flour	2 lb 4 oz	900 g	90%
Cake flour	4 oz	100 g	10%
Butter	1 lb 4 oz	500 g	50%
Yield:	6 lb 2 oz	2464 g	246%

Mixing: Modified straight dough method:
1. Scald milk. Cool to lukewarm. Dissolve yeast in milk.
2. Mix butter, sugar, salt, and spice until smooth, using paddle. Beat in eggs.
3. Add liquid (from step 1) and flour. With dough arm, mix 3–4 minutes on 2nd speed.
4. Rest in retarder 20–30 minutes.
5. Roll in remaining butter and give three 3-folds, as shown in Figure 25.2.

Makeup: See makeup techniques after recipe section.

Proofing: 90°F (32°C) with little steam. Egg wash after proofing.

Baking: 375°F (190°C).

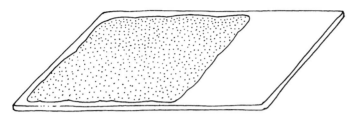

FIGURE 25.2   Rolling-in procedure for Danish and croissant dough.

(a) Roll out the dough ½ to ¾ inch (1 to 2 cm) thick into a rectangle about three times as long as it is wide.

(b) Spot the butter over two-thirds of the length of the dough as shown, leaving a 1-inch (2½-cm) margin at the edges.

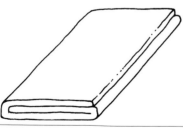

(c) Fold the third without fat over the center third.

(d) Fold the remaining third on top. Rest the dough in the retarder (under refrigeration) 20 to 30 minutes to allow the gluten to relax.

(e) Place the dough on the bench at right angles to its position in step *d*. This step must be taken before each rolling-out of the dough, so that the gluten is stretched in all directions, not just lengthwise.

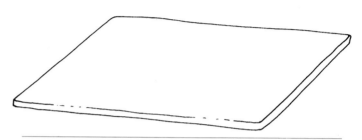

(f) Roll out the dough into a rectangle.

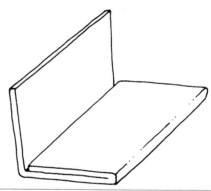

(g) Fold again into thirds. Be sure to brush off excess dusting flour from between the folds. You have now completed the first turn or fold; incorporating the butter doesn't count as a turn. Press one finger in the dough near the end to make one indention. This indicates "1 turn" to anyone who may have to take up where you left off, or to you if you have several batches going. Refrigerate the dough 20 to 30 minutes to relax the gluten. Repeat the above rolling and folding procedures for a second and third turn, resting the dough between turns. Mark the number of turns in the dough with two or three fingers. After the third turn, rest the dough in the retarder for several hours or overnight. Cover it with plastic film to prevent crusting. The dough is then ready for makeup.

RECIPE 335   **Almond Filling**

Yield: 3 lb (1500 g)

U.S.	Metric	Ingredients	Procedure
1 lb	500 g	Almond paste	1. With paddle attachment, mix almond paste and sugar at low speed until evenly mixed.
1 lb	500 g	Sugar	
8 oz	250 g	Butter and/or shortening	2. Mix in fat and flour until smooth.
4 oz	125 g	Pastry or cake flour	3. Beat in eggs, a little at a time, until smooth.
4 oz	125 g	Eggs	

RECIPE 336   **Cheese Filling**

Yield: 4½ lb (2250 g)

U.S.	Metric	Ingredients	Procedure
2 lb	1 kg	Baker's cheese	1. Using the paddle attachment, cream the cheese, sugar, and salt until smooth.
10 oz	300 g	Sugar	
¼ oz	7 g	Salt	
6 oz	200 g	Eggs	2. Add the eggs, butter, vanilla. Blend in.
6 oz	200 g	Butter and/or shortening, soft	
1 tbsp	15 mL	Vanilla	
3 oz	100 g	Cake flour	3. Add the cake flour. Blend until just absorbed.
6 oz or more	200 g or more	Milk	4. Add the milk a little at a time, adding just enough to bring the mixture to a smooth, spreadable consistency.
8 oz	250 g	Raisins (optional)	5. Stir in the raisins, if desired.

MAKEUP TECHNIQUES

The object of yeast dough makeup techniques is to shape the dough into rolls or loaves that bake properly and have an attractive appearance. When you shape a roll or loaf correctly, you are stretching the gluten strands on the surface into a kind of smooth skin. This tight gluten surface holds the item in shape. This is especially important for loaves and rolls that are baked freestanding, not in pans.

Units that are not made up correctly will develop irregular shapes and splits and may flatten out on the pan.

Following are a few of the many different makeup techniques for yeast doughs.

Hard Rolls and Breads

Round Rolls

1. Scale the dough as indicated in the recipes, usually 1 lb (450 g) per dozen.

2. Round each unit as shown in Figure 25.3.

3. Place rolls 2 inches (5 cm) apart on sheet pans sprinkled with cornmeal.

Round Loaves

1. Flatten the rounded, benched dough into a circle. Fold the four sides over the center, then round again.

2. Place on sheet pans sprinkled with cornmeal.

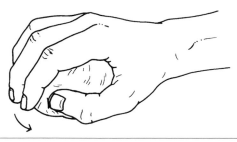

FIGURE 25.3   **Rounding small rolls is nearly the same as rounding large loaves, except that the whole ball fits under the hand. Roll the piece of dough vigorously in a tight circle on the bench, using the edge of the thumb and little finger to stretch the dough across the top of the roll into a seam on the bottom—the same way you use the edge of your hand in Figure 25.1.**

Club Rolls

1. Make up as shown in Figure 25.4.

2. Place 2 inches (5 cm) apart on sheet pans sprinkled with cornmeal.

Crescent Rolls

1. Scale dough into 20-oz (600-g) units.

2. After rounding and benching, flatten dough and roll out into a circle 12 inches (30 cm) across.

3. With a pastry wheel, cut the dough circle into 12 equal wedges or triangles. (Alternative method: For large quantities of dough, roll out into a rectangle and cut like croissant dough, Figure 25.18.)

4. Roll the triangles into crescents using the same technique as for croissants (Figure 25.18).
    Note: If using soft roll dough, brush the dough with butter before cutting into triangles. Do not use any fat with hard roll doughs.

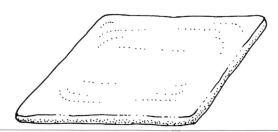

FIGURE 25.4   **Making club rolls.**
(a) Flatten the piece of dough roughly into a rectangle.

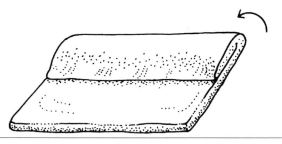

(b) Begin to roll up the dough by folding over the back edge of the rectangle. Press the seam firmly with the fingertips.

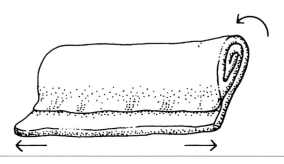

(c) Continue to roll the dough, always pressing the seam firmly after each turn. As you roll up the dough, the front edge will appear to shrink. Stretch the front corners as shown by the arrows to keep the width uniform.

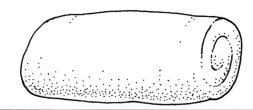

(d) When the roll is finished, seal the seam well so that you have a tight roll.

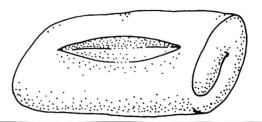

(e) Docking the proofed roll with a single slash gives the baked roll this appearance.

French-type Loaves

1. Scale the dough into 12 to 18 oz (350 to 500 g) units.

2. Form into long, thin loaves following the general procedure used for club rolls, except that the ends should be tapered. Roll the loaf on the bench under the palms of the hands to even out the shape. This will produce an elongated, oval-shaped loaf. The ends should be tapered and rounded, not pointed.

3. If a longer, thinner loaf is desired, relax these units again for a few minutes. Flatten them with the palms of the hands and stretch the dough lightly to increase its length. Once again, roll up tightly and seal the seam well. Roll on the bench under the palms of the hands to even it out and to stretch it to the desired shape and length.

4. Place well apart, seam side down, on sheet pans sprinkled with cornmeal.

Soft Roll Doughs

Tied or Knotted Rolls

1. Scale dough 16 to 20 oz (450 to 600 g) per dozen.

2. With the palm of the hand, roll each unit on the workbench into a strip or rope of dough.

3. Tie rolls as shown:

   Single-knot rolls: Figure 25.5.
   Double-knot rolls: Figure 25.6.
   Braided rolls: Figure 25.7.
   Figure eight rolls: Figure 25.8.

4. Place 2 inches (5 cm) apart on greased baking sheets.

5. Egg wash after proofing.

Pan Rolls

1. Scale dough 16 to 20 oz (450 to 600 g) per dozen.

2. Make up as for round hard rolls.

3. Place on greased pans ½ inch (1 cm) apart.

Parker House Rolls

1. Scale dough 16 to 20 oz (450 to 600 g) per dozen.

2. Make up as shown in Figure 25.9.

3. Place on greased baking sheet ½ inch (1 cm) apart.

Cloverleaf Rolls

1. Scale dough 16 to 20 oz (450 to 600 g) per dozen.

2. Make up and pan as shown in Figure 25.10.

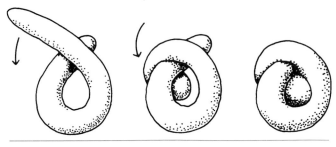

FIGURE 25.5 **Tying a single-knot roll.**

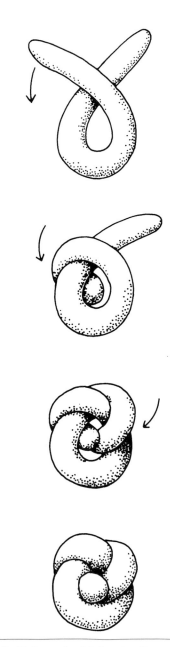

FIGURE 25.6 **Tying a double-knot roll.**

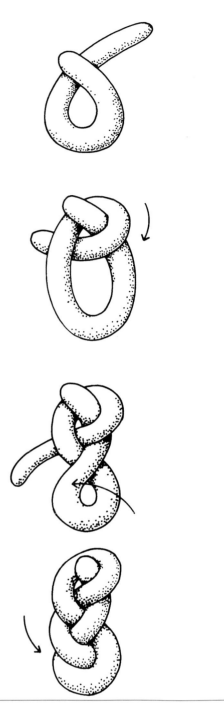

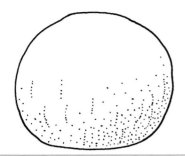

FIGURE 25.9 Parker House rolls.
(a) Round the scaled piece of dough.

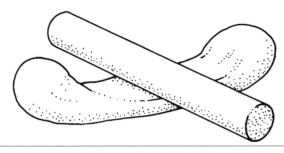

(b) Flatten the *center* of the dough with a thin rolling pin as shown.

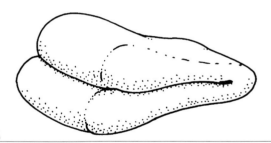

(c) Fold the dough over and press down on the folded edge to make a crease.

FIGURE 25.7 Tying a braided roll.

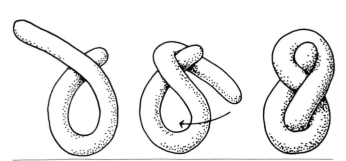

FIGURE 25.8 Tying a figure eight roll.

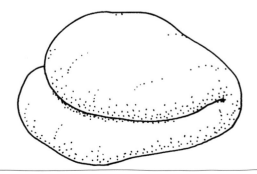

(d) The baked roll has this shape.

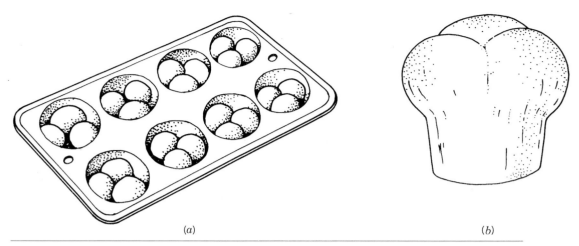

(a)   (b)

FIGURE 25.10   **Cloverleaf rolls. (a) Divide each piece of dough into three equal parts, and shape into balls. Place three balls in the bottom of each greased muffin tin. (b) The baked roll has this appearance.**

Butterflake Rolls

Make up as shown in Figure 25.11.

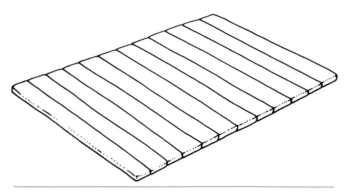

FIGURE 25.11   **Butterflake rolls.**

(a) Roll the dough out very thin into a rectangular shape. Brush with melted butter. Cut into strips 1 inch (2½ cm) wide.

(c) Place the pieces on end in greased muffin tins. Proof.

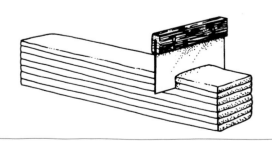

(b) Stack up six strips. Cut into 1½-inch (3½-cm) pieces.

(d) The baked rolls have this appearance.

Pan Loaves

Shaping dough into loaves to be baked in loaf pans is illustrated in Figure 25.12.

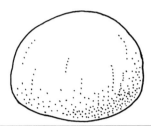

FIGURE 25.12   **Pan loaves.**
(a) Start with the rounded, benched dough. Flatten it with the palms of the hands.

(b) Stretch it out into a long rectangle.

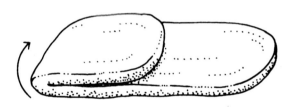

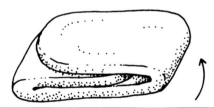

(c, d) Fold into thirds.

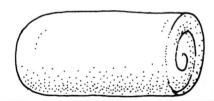

(e) Roll the dough into a tight roll that has the same length as the pan it is to be baked in. Seal the seam very well and place the dough seam side down in the greased pan.

Brioche

Brioche dough may be made into many shapes, but the traditional shape is shown in Figure 25.13.

FIGURE 25.13   **Making brioches.**
(a) For a small brioche, roll the dough into a round piece.

(b) Using the edge of the hand, pinch off about one-fourth of the dough without detaching it. Roll the dough on the bench so that both parts are round.

(c) Place the dough in the tin large end first. With the fingertips, press the small ball into the larger one as shown.

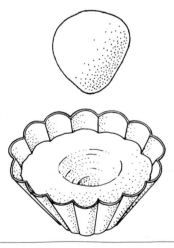

(d) For large brioche, separate the two parts of the dough. Place the large ball in the tin and make a hole in the center. Form the smaller ball into a pear shape and fit it into the hole.

(e) A baked large brioche.

Sweet Dough Products

Note: Many sweet dough products may be glazed with clear glaze (p. 683) and/or iced with flat icing (p. 721) after baking. Flat icing is drizzled over the cooled products, so that it doesn't cover them completely.

Cinnamon Rolls (see Figure 25.14)

1. Scale dough into 20-oz (600-g) units. On a floured board, roll each piece of dough into a rectangle 9 × 12 inches and about ¼ inch thick (23 × 30 × ½ cm).

2. Brush with butter and sprinkle with 2 oz (60 g) cinnamon sugar.

3. Roll up like a jelly roll 12 inches (30 cm) long, as shown in the illustration.

4. Cut into 1-inch (2½-cm) rolls

5. Place cut side down in greased muffin tins or on greased sheet pans. One full-size 18 × 26-inch (46 × 66-cm) pan holds 48 rolls placed 6 by 8.

For variations on the basic cinnamon roll shape, see Figure 25.14.

Cinnamon Raisin Rolls

Prepare like cinnamon rolls, but add 2 oz (60 g) raisins to the filling.

Caramel Rolls

1. Prepare like cinnamon rolls.

2. Before panning, spread the bottoms of the pans or muffin tins with the following mixture. Use about 1 oz (30 g) of the mixture per roll.

    2 lb (1 kg) brown sugar

    8 oz (250 g) corn syrup

    10 oz (300 g) butter

    4 oz (125 mL) water

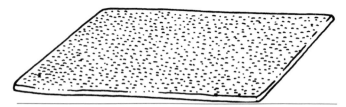

FIGURE 25.14   **The filled dough roll is the starting point for a variety of sweet dough and Danish products.**
(a) Roll the dough out into a rectangle. Brush with butter and sprinkle with cinnamon sugar, or spread with desired filling.

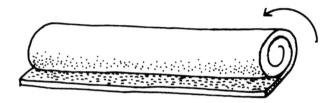

(b) Roll up like a jelly roll.

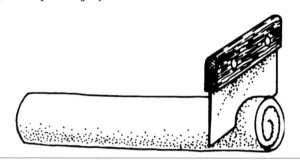

(c) For cinnamon rolls and similar products, cut off 1-inch (2½-cm) pieces.

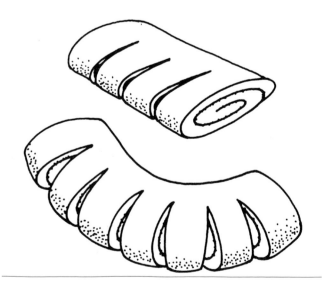

(d) For combs or bear claws, make the roll thinner and cut into longer pieces. Flatten slightly and cut part way through each piece in three to five places as shown. Leave straight, or bend into a curve to open up the cuts.

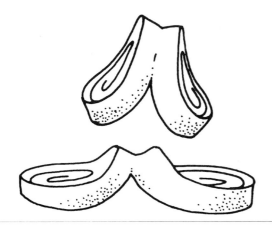

(e) For figure eight cinnamon rolls, cut the rolls almost through as shown. Open them up, and lay them flat on the baking sheet.

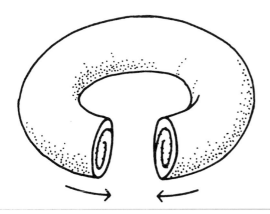

(f) To make a wreath-shaped coffee cake, join the ends of the dough roll to make a circle.

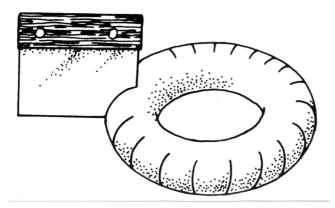

(g) Cut part way though the dough at 1-inch (2½-cm) intervals as shown.

(h) Twist each segment outward to open the cuts.

Cream the sugar, corn syrup, and butter. Beat in the water.

Quantities given are enough for 1 sheet pan of 48 rolls.

Caramel Nut Rolls or Pecan Rolls

Prepare like caramel rolls, but sprinkle the sugar–butter mixture in the pans with chopped nuts or pecan halves before placing the rolls in the pans.

Wreath Coffee Cake

1. Make a filled dough roll as for cinnamon rolls, but do not cut into separate pieces. Other fillings, such as prune or date, may be used instead of butter and cinnamon sugar.

2. Shape the roll into a circle as shown in Figure 25.14*f–h*. Place on a greased baking sheet. Cut and shape as shown in the illustration.

3. Egg wash after proofing.

Filled Coffee Cake

1. Scale dough into 12-oz (350-g) units.

2. Roll each unit into a rectangle 9 × 18 inches (23 × 46 cm).

3. Spread half of each rectangle with desired filling, using about 6 oz (175 g) filling.

4. Fold the unspread half over the spread half to make a 9-inch (23-cm) square.

5. Place in greased 9-inch (23-cm) square pan.

6. Sprinkle with Streusel Topping, about 4 oz (125 g) per pan.

7. Proof and bake.

Braided Coffee Cake

Make up as shown in Figure 25.15. Egg wash after proofing.

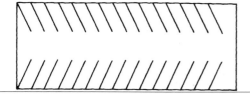

FIGURE 25.15   **Braided coffee cake.**

(a) Roll out the dough into a rectangle 8 inches (20 cm) wide, 12 to 18 inches (30 to 46 cm) long, and less than ¼ inch (½ cm) thick. Make diagonal cuts from the outer edges 1 inch (2½ cm) apart and 3 inches (7½ cm) long, as shown.

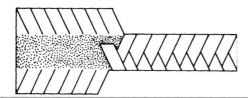

(b) Spread the filling down the center and fold alternate strips of dough over the filling.

Rolled-in Dough Products

Danish Rolls and Coffee Cakes

Most of the techniques given in the previous section for sweet dough products may be used for Danish pastry.

In addition, two other methods are illustrated in Figures 25.16 and 25.17.

Baked Danish dough products are frequently glazed with clear glaze (p. 683) and/or iced with flat icing (p. 721).

Croissants

The method for making up croissants is illustrated in Figure 25.18.

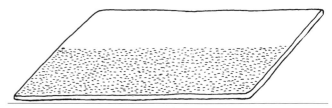

FIGURE 25.16   **Spiral Danish rolls.**

(a) Roll out the dough into a rectangle 16 inches (40 cm) wide and less than ¼ inch (½ cm) thick. (The length of the rectangle depends on the quantity of dough.) Brush the dough with melted butter. Sprinkle half of it with cinnamon sugar as shown.

(b) Fold the unsugared half over the sugared half. You now have a rectangle 8 inches (20 cm) wide. Roll the dough very gently with a rolling pin to press the layers together.

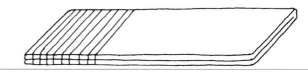

(c) Cut the dough into strips ½ inch (1 cm) wide.

(d) Place one strip crosswise in front of you on the bench.

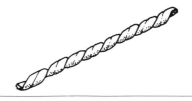

(e) With the palms of your hands on the ends of the strip, roll one end toward you and the other away from you, so that the strip twists. Stretch the strip slightly as you twist it.

(f) Curl the strip into a spiral shape on the baking sheet. Tuck the end underneath and pinch it against the roll to seal it in place. If desired, press a hollow in the center of the roll and place a spoonful of filling (such as a fruit filling) in the center.

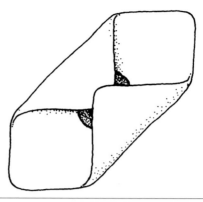

(b) Fold two opposite corners over the center. Press down firmly to seal them together. (If desired, rolls may be left in this shape.)

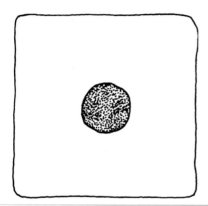

FIGURE 25.17   **Danish pockets.**
(a) Roll out the dough less than ¼ inch (½ cm) thick and cut into 5-inch (13-cm) squares. Place desired filling on the center of each square. Brush the four corners lightly with water—this helps them seal when pressed together.

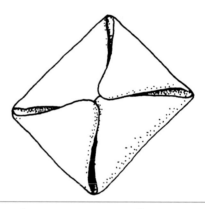

(c) Fold the other two corners over the center, and again press them firmly together.

FIGURE 25.18 **Making croissants.**
(a) Roll the dough out into a rectangle 10 inches (26 cm) wide and about ⅛ inch (3 mm) thick. (The length depends on the amount of dough used.)

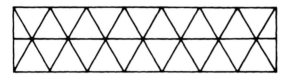

(b) Cut into triangles as shown. Special roller cutters are available that do this very quickly.

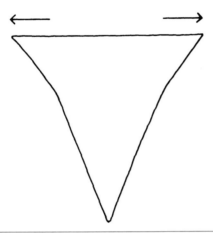

(c) Place one of the triangles on the bench in front of you. Stretch the back corners outward slightly, as shown by the arrows.

(d) Begin to roll up the dough toward the point.

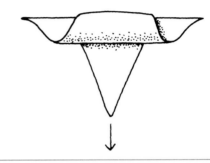

(e) Stretch out the point of the triangle slightly as you roll it up.

(f) Finish rolling up the dough.

(g) Bend the roll into a crescent shape. The point of the triangle must be toward the inside of the crescent and tucked under the roll so that it won't pop up during baking.

TERMS FOR REVIEW

lean dough	sponge method	young and old doughs	proofing
rolled-in dough	fermentation	punching	oven spring
straight dough method			

QUESTIONS FOR DISCUSSION

1.   What are the three major purposes of mixing yeast doughs?

2.   Explain the difference in procedure between the straight dough method and the sponge method. How is the straight dough method sometimes modified for sweet doughs, and why is this necessary?

3.   What are the 12 steps in the production of yeast products? Explain each briefly.

4.   Judging from what you know about fermentation of doughs, do you think it might be necessary for bakers to modify procedures from winter to summer? How?

5.   As you know, butter is very hard when cold and melts easily at warm temperatures. What precautions do you think are necessary when using butter as the rolling-in fat for Danish pastry?

CHAPTER 26

QUICK BREADS

Quick breads are the perfect
solution for those operations that want to offer their patrons fresh,
homemade bread products but can't justify the labor cost of making yeast
breads. Also, quick breads have the advantage of being easily made in almost
unlimited varieties, using such ingredients as whole wheat flour, rye flour,
cornmeal, bran, oatmeal, and many kinds of fruits, nuts, and spices.

As their name implies, quick breads are quick to make.
Because they are leavened by chemical leaveners and steam, not by yeast,
no fermentation time is necessary. And because they are usually tender products
with little gluten development, mixing them takes just a few minutes.

Although prepared biscuit and muffin mixes
are available, the only extra work that making these products
"from scratch" requires is the time to scale a few extra ingredients. With a careful
and imaginative selection of ingredients and an understanding of basic
mixing methods, you can create superior products.

You may already have studied two kinds of quick breads in
the breakfast chapter: pancakes and waffles. In this chapter you will
study two basic mixing methods and apply them to biscuits, muffins, quick loaf
breads and coffee cakes, and corn breads. In addition, you will also
learn to prepare popovers, which are leavened only by steam.

After reading this chapter, you should be able to

1. Prepare baking powder biscuits and variations.
2. Prepare muffins, loaf breads, coffee cakes, and corn breads.
3. Prepare popovers.

MIXING AND PRODUCTION METHODS

Types of Doughs

Dough mixtures for quick breads are generally of two types:

1. *Soft doughs* are used for biscuits. These products are rolled out and cut into desired shapes. They are mixed by the biscuit method.

2. *Batters* may be either *pour batters,* which are liquid enough to pour, or *drop batters,* which are thicker and will drop from a spoon in lumps.

Most quick-bread batters are mixed by the muffin method, except for drop biscuits, which are mixed by the biscuit method, and some rich cakelike muffins and coffee cakes, which are mixed by a cake-mixing method called the creaming method. The biscuit and muffin methods are presented in this chapter. The creaming method is presented in Chapter 27, along with other cake methods.

The muffins and loaf breads in this chapter should be thought of as breads rather than as tea cakes. They are lower in fat and sugar than some of the rich, cakelike muffins sometimes seen.

Gluten Development in Quick Breads

Only slight gluten development is desired in most quick breads. Tenderness is a desirable quality, unlike the chewy quality of yeast breads.

In addition, chemical leavening agents do not create the same kind of textures that yeast does and are not strong enough to create a light, tender product if the gluten is too strong.

1. Muffin, loaf bread, and pancake batters are mixed as little as possible, only until the dry ingredients are moistened. This, plus the presence of fat and sugar, keeps gluten development low.

   Overmixing muffins produces not only toughness, but also irregular shapes and large, elongated holes inside the product. This latter condition is called *tunneling.*

2. Biscuit dough is often lightly kneaded, enough to develop some flakiness but not enough to toughen the product.

3. Popovers are the exception among quick breads. They are made with a thin batter and leavened only by steam. Very large holes develop inside the product during baking, and the structure must be strong enough to hold without collapsing. Thus, bread flour is used, and the batter is mixed well to develop the gluten. The high percentage of egg in popovers also helps build structure.

The Biscuit Method

Procedure

1. Scale all ingredients accurately.

2. Sift the dry ingredients together into a mixing bowl.

3. Cut in the shortening using the paddle attachment or the pastry knife attachment. Or, if preferred, you may also cut in the fat by hand, using a pastry blender or your fingers. Continue until the mixture resembles a coarse cornmeal.

4. Combine the liquid ingredients. Biscuits may be prepared in advance up to this point. Portions of each mixture may then be scaled and combined just before baking.

5. Combine the liquid ingredients.

6. Add the liquid to the dry ingredients. Mix just until the ingredients are combined and a soft dough is formed. Do not overmix.

7. Bring the dough to the bench and knead it lightly by pressing it out and folding it in half. Rotate the dough 90° after each fold.

8. Repeat this procedure about 10 to 20 times, or about 30 seconds. The dough should be soft and slightly elastic, but not sticky. Overkneading toughens the biscuits. The dough is now ready for makeup.

Variations on the basic procedure produce different characteristics in the finished product:

1. Using slightly more shortening and cutting it in less—until the pieces are the size of peas—produces a flakier biscuit.

2. Omitting the kneading step produces a very tender, crustier biscuit, but with less volume.

Makeup of Biscuits

1. Roll the biscuit dough out into a sheet about ½ inch (1 cm) thick, being careful to roll it evenly and to a uniform thickness.

   Biscuits will approximately double in height during baking.

2. Cut into desired shapes.

    When using round hand cutters, cutting straight down produces the best shape after baking. Do not twist the cutter. Space the cuts closely to minimize scraps.

    Cutting into squares or triangles with a pastry cutter or knife eliminates scraps that would have to be rerolled. Roller cutters also eliminate or reduce scraps. Reworked scraps will be tougher.

3. Place the biscuits ½ inch (1 cm) apart on baking sheet for crisp-crusted biscuits, or touching each other, for softer biscuits. Bake as soon as possible.

    If desired, the tops may be brushed with egg wash or milk before baking to aid browning.

The Muffin Method

This mixing method is used not only for muffins but also for pancakes, waffles, quick loaf breads, and coffee cakes. Loaf breads and coffee cakes are sometimes higher in fat and sugar than muffins, so they can withstand more mixing without toughening.

Procedure

1. Thoroughly combine the dry ingredients. Sifting them together is best but is not necessary if mixing is thorough.

2. Combine all liquid ingredients, including melted fat or oil.

3. Add the liquids to the dry ingredients and mix just until all the flour is moistened. The batter will look lumpy. Do not overmix.

4. Pan and bake immediately. The dry and liquid mixtures may be prepared in advance. But once they are combined, the batter should be baked without delay, or loss of volume may result. When portioning batter into muffin tins, be careful not to stir the mix and toughen it. Scoop the batter from the outside edge for best results.

Summary: Biscuit and Muffin Methods

Biscuit Method	*Muffin Method*
1. Combine dry ingredients and cut in fat.	1. Combine dry ingredients.
2. Combine liquid ingredients.	2. Combine liquid ingredients, including melted fat.
3. Add liquid and dry ingredients and mix just until combined.	3. Add liquid to dry ingredients and mix just until combined.
4. If required, knead very lightly.	

FORMULAS

RECIPE 337   Biscuits

Ingredients	U.S.	Metric	Percentage
Bread flour	1 lb 4 oz	600 g	50%
Pastry flour	1 lb 4 oz	600 g	50%
Salt	¾ oz	25 g	2%
Sugar	2 oz	60 g	5%
Baking powder	2½ oz	75 g	6%
Shortening (regular) and/or butter	14 oz	425 g	35%
Milk	1 lb 10 oz	775 g	65%
Yield:	5 lb 5 oz	2560 g	213%

Mixing and makeup: Biscuit method.

Scaling: Approximately 1 lb (500 g) per dozen 2-inch (5 cm) biscuits.

Baking: 425°F (220°C), about 15 minutes.

Variations

337A. Buttermilk Biscuits: Use buttermilk instead of regular milk.

337B. Cheese Biscuits: Add 30% (12 oz/350 g) grated cheddar cheese to dry ingredients.

337C. Currant Biscuits: Add 15% (6 oz/175 g) dried currants to dry ingredients. Increase sugar to 10% (4 oz/125 g). Sprinkle tops with cinnamon sugar before baking.

337D. Herb Biscuits: Add 5% (2 oz/60 g) fresh chopped parsley to the dry ingredients.

RECIPE 338   Plain Muffins

Ingredients	U.S.	Metric	Percentage
Pastry flour	2 lb 8 oz	1250 g	100%
Sugar	12 oz	375 g	30%
Baking powder	2½ oz	75 g	6%
Salt	½ oz	15 g	1.25%
Eggs, beaten	8 oz	250 g	20%
Milk	2 lb	1000 g	80%
Melted butter or shortening	12 oz	375 g	30%
Yield:	6 lb 11 oz	3340 g	267%

Mixing: Muffin method.

Scaling and panning: Grease and flour muffin tins, or use paper liners. Scale batter with No. 16 scoop, 2 oz (60 g) per unit.

Baking: 400°F (200°C), about 20 minutes.

RECIPE 338   **Plain Muffins** *(Continued)*

Variations

338A.   Raisin Spice Muffins: Add 20% raisins (8 oz/250 g), 2 tsp (10 mL) cinnamon, and ½ tsp (2 mL) nutmeg to the dry ingredients.

338B.   Date Nut Muffins: Add 15% (6 oz/175 g) *each* chopped dates and chopped walnuts to the dry ingredients.

338C.   Blueberry Muffins: Gently fold 40% (1 lb/500 g) well-drained blueberries into the finished batter.

338D.   Whole Wheat Muffins: Use 70% (1 lb 12 oz/875 g) pastry flour and 30% (12 oz/375 g) whole wheat flour. Reduce baking powder to 4% (1½ oz/50 g) and add ¾% (2 tsp/10 mL) baking soda. Add 10% (4 oz/125 g) molasses to the liquid ingredients.

338E.   Corn Muffins: Use 75% (1 lb 14 oz/950 g) pastry flour and 25% (10 oz/300 g) yellow corn-meal. (See also following Corn Bread formula.)

338F.   Bran Muffins: Use 30% (12 oz/375 g) bran, 40% (1 lb/500 g) bread flour, and 30% (12 oz/375 g) pastry flour. Add 15% (6 oz/175 g) raisins to the dry ingredients. Add 15% (6 oz/175 g) molasses to the liquid ingredients. Increase eggs to 30% (12 oz/375 g).

338G.   Crumb Coffee Cake: Increase sugar and fat to 50% (1 lb 4 oz/625 g) *each*. Pour into greased, paper-lined sheet pan and spread smooth. Top with 80% (2 lb/1 kg) Streusel Topping (p. 683). Bake at 360°F (180°C), about 30 minutes.

RECIPE 339   **Banana Bread**

Ingredients	U.S.		Metric	Percentage
Pastry flour	1 lb	8 oz	700 g	100%
Sugar		10 oz	275 g	40%
Baking powder		1¼ oz	35 g	5%
Baking soda		1 tsp	3.5 g (5 mL)	0.5%
Salt		2 tsp	9 g (10 mL)	1.25%
Chopped walnuts		6 oz	175 g	25%
Eggs		10 oz	275 g	40%
Ripe banana pulp, puréed	1 lb	8 oz	700 g	100%
Oil or melted shortening or butter		8 oz	225 g	33%
Yield:	5 lb	4 oz	2397 g	344%

Mixing: Muffin method.

Scaling: 1 lb 10 oz (750 g) per 8½ × 4½ inch (22 × 11 cm) loaf pan.

Baking: 375°F (190°C), about 50 minutes.

RECIPE 340 **Corn Bread, Muffins, or Sticks**

Ingredients	U.S.		Metric	Percentage
Pastry flour	1 lb	4 oz	600 g	50%
Cornmeal	1 lb	4 oz	600 g	50%
Sugar		6 oz	175 g	15%
Baking powder		2½ oz	75 g	6%
Salt		¾ oz	25 g	2%
Eggs, beaten		8 oz	250 g	20%
Milk	2 lb	2 oz	1000 g (1 L)	85%
Melted butter or shortening		12 oz	350 g	30%
Yield:	6 lb	7 oz	3075 g	258%

Mixing: Muffin method.

Scaling: 60 oz (1700 g) per half-size sheet pan (13 × 18 inches/33 × 46 cm).
24 oz (725 g) per 9-inch (23 cm) square pan or per dozen muffins.
10 oz (300 g) per dozen corn sticks.
Grease and flour pans well.

Baking: 400°F (200°C) for corn bread, 25–30 minutes.
425°F (220°C) for muffins or sticks, 15–20 minutes.

RECIPE 341 **Orange Nut Bread**

Ingredients	U.S.		Metric	Percentage
Sugar		12 oz	350 g	50%
Grated orange zest		1 oz	30 g	4%
Pastry flour	1 lb	8 oz	700 g	100%
Nonfat dry milk		2 oz	60 g	8%
Baking powder		1 oz	30 g	4%
Baking soda		2 tsp	10 g	1.4%
Salt		2 tsp	10 g	1.4%
Chopped walnuts		12 oz	350 g	50%
Eggs		5 oz	150 g	20%
Orange juice		6 oz	175 g	25%
Water	1 lb		450 g	65%
Oil or melted butter or shortening		2½ oz	75 g	10%
Yield:	5 lb	2 oz	2390 g	329%

Mixing: Muffin method. Blend the sugar and orange zest thoroughly before adding remaining dry ingredients, to ensure even distribution.

Scaling: 1 lb 10 oz (750 g) per 8½ × 4½-inch (22 × 11 cm) loaf pan.

Baking: 375°F (190°C), about 50 minutes.

RECIPE 342   **Popovers**

Ingredients	U.S.		Metric	Percentage
Eggs	1 lb	4 oz	625 g	125%
Milk	2 lb		1000 g (1 L)	200%
Salt		¼ oz	8 g	1.5%
Melted butter or shortening		2 oz	60 g	12.5%
Bread flour	1 lb		500 g	100%
Yield:	4 lb	6 oz	2193 g	439%

Mixing: 1. Beat eggs, milk, and salt together with whip attachment, until well blended.
2. Replace whip with paddle. Mix in flour until completely smooth.

Scaling and panning: Grease every other cup of muffin pans—popovers need room for expansion. Fill cups about ⅔ full, about 1½ oz (50 g) batter per unit.

Baking: 450°F (230°C) for 10 minutes. Reduce heat to 375°F (190°C) for 20–30 minutes. Before removing them from oven, be sure popovers are dry and firm enough to avoid collapsing. Remove from pans immediately.

TERMS FOR REVIEW

pour batter   tunneling   biscuit method   muffin method
drop batter

QUESTIONS FOR DISCUSSION

1.   If you made a batch of muffins that came out of the oven with strange, knobby shapes, what would you expect was the reason?

2.   What is the most important difference between the biscuit method and the muffin method?

3.   Why do popovers require more mixing than other quick breads?

CAKES AND ICINGS

Cakes are the richest and
sweetest of all the baked products we have studied so far. From the
baker's point of view, producing cakes requires as much precision as producing
breads, but for completely opposite reasons. Breads are lean products that
require strong gluten development and careful control of yeast action
during the long fermentation and proofing periods.

Cakes, on the other hand, are high in both fat and sugar.
The baker's job is to create a structure that will support these ingredients
and yet keep it as light and delicate as possible. Fortunately, producing cakes in
quantity is relatively easy if the baker has good, well-balanced formulas, scales
ingredients accurately, and understands basic mixing methods well.

Cakes owe their popularity to their richness and
sweetness, but also to their versatility. Cakes can be presented in
many forms, from simple sheet cakes in cafeterias to elaborately decorated works
of art for weddings and other important occasions. With only a few basic
formulas and a variety of icings, the chef or baker can construct
the perfect dessert for any occasion or purpose.

After reading this chapter, you should be able to

1. Perform basic cake mixing methods.

2. Understand the characteristics of basic cake types.

3. Produce both high-fat or shortened cakes and low-fat or foam-type cakes.

4. Prepare basic icings.

5. Assemble and ice cakes.

UNDERSTANDING CAKE MAKING

BASIC MIXING METHODS

The mixing methods presented in this chapter are the basic ones for most types of cakes prepared in the modern bakeshop. Each of these methods is used for particular types of formulas.

High-fat or shortened cakes.

Creaming method.

Two-stage or blending method.

Low-fat or foam-type cakes.

Foaming or sponge method.

Angel food method.

Chiffon method.

We will discuss these cake types in detail after you have had a chance to study the actual procedures.

Creaming Method

This method, also called the *conventional method,* was for a long time the standard method for mixing butter cakes. Recently, the development of emulsified or high-ratio shortenings has led to the development of simpler mixing methods for shortened cakes. But the creaming method is still used for many types of butter cakes.

Procedure

1. Scale ingredients accurately. Have all ingredients at room temperature.

2. Place the butter or shortening in the mixing bowl. With the paddle attachment, beat slowly until the fat is smooth and creamy.

3. Add the sugar and cream the mixture at moderate speed until the mixture is light and fluffy.
    Some bakers prefer to add the salt and flavorings with the sugar to ensure uniform distribution.
    If melted chocolate is used, it is added during creaming.

4. Add the eggs a little at a time. After each addition, beat until the eggs are absorbed before adding more. The mixture should be light and fluffy after the eggs are beaten in.

5. Scrape down the sides of the bowl to ensure even mixing.

6. Add the sifted dry ingredients (including the spices if they were not added in step 3) alternating with the liquids. This is done as follows:

    a. Add one-fourth of the dry ingredients. Mix just until blended in.
    b. Add one-third of the liquid. Mix just until blended in.
    c. Repeat until all ingredients are used. Scrape down the sides of the bowl occasionally for even mixing.

    The reason for adding dry and liquids alternately is that the batter may not absorb all the liquid unless some of the flour is present to aid in absorption.

    Cocoa, if used, is included with the flour.

Two-Stage Method

This method, also called the *blending method,* was developed for use with modern high-ratio shortenings (see Chapter 24). It is simpler than the creaming method, but produces a very smooth batter that bakes up into a fine-grained, moist cake. It is called two-stage because the liquids are added in two stages.

Procedure

1. Scale ingredients accurately. Have all ingredients at room temperature.

2. Sift the flour, baking powder, soda, and salt into the mixing bowl and add the shortening. With the paddle attachment, mix at low speed for 2 minutes. Stop the machine, scrape down the bowl and beater, and mix again for 2 minutes.
    If melted chocolate is used, blend it in during this step.
    If cocoa is used, sift it with the flour in this step or with the sugar in step 3.

3. Sift the remaining dry ingredients into the bowl and add part of the water or milk. Blend at low speed for 3 to 5 minutes. Scrape down the sides of the bowl and the beater several times to ensure even mixing.

4. Combine the remaining liquids and lightly beaten eggs. With the mixer running, add this mixture to the batter in three parts. After each part, turn off the machine and scrape down the bowl.

Continue mixing for a total of 5 minutes in this stage.

The finished batter will normally be quite liquid.

Variation

This variation combines steps 2 and 3 above into one step.

1. Scale ingredients as in basic method.

2. Sift all dry ingredients into the mixing bowl. Add the shortening and part of the liquid. Mix on low speed for 7 to 8 minutes. Scrape down the sides of the bowl and the beater several times.

3. Continue with step 4 in the basic procedure.

Foaming or Sponge Method

All egg-foam cakes are similar in that they contain little or no shortening and depend for most or all of their leavening on the air trapped in beaten eggs.

One mixing method is usually presented as the basic method for all foam cakes. However, since whole-egg foams and egg-yolk foams are handled differently from egg-white foams, we will discuss two separate, although similar, methods. A third method, for chiffon cakes, is somewhat unusual. It combines an egg-white foam with a high-fat batter made with oil.

First, the method for sponge cakes:

Procedure

1. Scale ingredients accurately. Have all ingredients at room temperature.

    If butter is included, it must be melted.

    If liquid and butter are included, heat them together, just until the butter is melted.

2. Combine the eggs and sugar and warm to about 110°F (43°C). This may be done in one of two ways.

    a. Stir the egg–sugar mixture over a hot-water bath.

    b. Warm the sugar on a sheet pan in the oven (do not get it too hot) and gradually beat it into the eggs.

    The reason for this step is that the foam will attain greater volume if warm.

3. With the whip attachment, beat the eggs at high speed until very light and thick. This may take 10 to 15 minutes.

This step is very important. One of the most frequent causes of failure in the sponge method is not whipping the eggs and sugar enough. The foam must be very thick. When the beater is lifted from the bowl, the foam falls slowly from it and makes a ribbon that slowly sinks into the batter in the bowl.

4. Fold in the sifted flour, being careful not to deflate the foam. Many bakers do this by hand.

    If other dry ingredients are used, such as cornstarch or baking powder, they are first sifted with the flour.

5. If melted butter or a butter–liquid mixture is being used, fold in at this point. Be careful not to overmix, or the cake will be tough (because of developed gluten).

6. Immediately pan and bake the batter. Delays will cause loss of volume.

Variations

Some formulas contain water or some other liquid, but no butter (so you cannot heat the liquid and butter together, as in the basic procedure). In this case, the liquid is usually added after step 3 and before folding in the flour. Either whip it in in a steady stream or stir it in, as indicated in the recipe.

In some formulas the egg yolks and whites are separated. Use the yolks and part of the sugar to make the foam in steps 2 and 3. Use the remaining sugar to whip with the whites. Fold the egg-white foam into the batter after step 5.

Angel Food Method

Angel food cakes are based on egg-white foams and contain no fat. For success in beating egg whites, review the principles of egg foams in Chapter 21.

Procedure

1. Scale ingredients accurately. Have all ingredients at room temperature. The egg whites may be slightly warmed for achieving better volume.

2. Sift the flour with half the sugar. This step helps the flour mix more evenly with the foam.

3. Beat the egg whites, using the whip attachment, until they form soft peaks.

    Salt and cream of tartar are added near the beginning of the beating process.

4. Gradually beat in the sugar that was not mixed with the flour. Continue to beat until the egg whites form soft, glossy peaks. Do not overbeat.

5. Fold in the flour–sugar mixture just until it is thoroughly absorbed, but no longer.

6. Pan and bake immediately.

Chiffon Method

Chiffon cakes and angel food cakes are both based on egg-white foams. But here the similarities in the mixing methods end. In angel food cakes, a dry flour–sugar mixture is folded into the egg whites. But in chiffon cakes, a batter containing flour, egg yolks, vegetable oil, and water is folded into the whites.

Egg whites for chiffon cakes should be whipped until they are a little firmer than those for angel food cakes, but do not overwhip them until they are dry. Chiffon cakes contain baking powder, so they do not depend on the egg foam for all their leavening.

Procedure

1. Scale all ingredients accurately. Have all ingredients at room temperature. Use a good-quality, flavorless vegetable oil.

2. Sift the dry ingredients, including part of the sugar, into the mixing bowl.

3. Mixing with the paddle attachment at second speed, gradually add the oil, then the egg yolks, water, and liquid flavorings, all in a slow, steady stream. While adding the liquids, stop the machine several times and scrape down the bowl and the beater. Mix until smooth, but do not overmix.

4. Whip the egg whites until they form soft peaks. Add the cream of tartar and sugar in a stream and whip to firm, moist peaks.

5. Fold the whipped egg whites into the flour–liquid mixture.

6. Immediately deposit batter in ungreased center-tube pans (like angel food cakes) or in layer pans that have had the bottoms greased and dusted, but not the sides (like sponge layers).

Prepared Mixes

Many mixes are available that contain all ingredients except water and sometimes egg. These products also contain added emulsifiers to ensure even blending of ingredients. To use them, follow the package instructions exactly.

Most mixes produce cakes with excellent volume, texture, and tenderness. Whether or not they also taste good is a matter of opinion. On the other hand, cakes made "from scratch" are not necessarily better. They will be better only if they are carefully mixed and baked, and prepared from good, tested formulas, using quality ingredients.

CAKE FORMULA TYPES

The proper mixing method for a particular formula depends on the balance of ingredients. A baker can look at the ingredients in a formula and know immediately which mixing method to use.

If *fat is high,* use creaming method or two-stage method.

Two-stage method may be used if the percentage of sugar is over 100 percent, and if the fat is emulsified shortening.

In other cases, the creaming method is used.

If *fat is low* and *eggs and sugar are high,* use an egg-foam method.

High-Fat Cakes

The creaming method's major disadvantage is the labor it requires. The two-stage method is quicker, but because the flour is mixed for a long time, two conditions are necessary to prevent the gluten from developing toughness:

1. Increased percentage of sugar (sugar is a tenderizer).

2. Emulsified shortening, which will blend very thoroughly to prevent toughness.

Cakes made by the two-stage method have good volume and lightness, fine velvety texture, and great tenderness. Butter cakes made by the creaming method are usually graded lower because the texture is coarser and the tenderness is generally somewhat less.

One factor seems to be neglected when cakes are rated, however—flavor. Shortening contributes no flavor to cakes, only texture. Butter, on the other hand, is highly prized for its flavor. It also influences texture, because it melts in the mouth, while shortening does not. Thus, butter cakes are and always will be in demand. As long as they are, the creaming method will be important for you to know.

Low-Fat Cakes

High-fat cakes depend on air incorporated by the creaming action of the fat and sugar for some of their leavening and much of their texture. Low-fat or no-fat cakes obviously cannot. They must depend on the foaming action of eggs.

Sponge cakes have a springy texture and are tougher than shortened cakes. This makes them valuable for many kinds of desserts that require much handling to assemble. For example, many European-style cakes or tortes are made by cutting sponge cake layers horizontally into thinner layers and stacking them up with a variety of rich fillings, creams, icings, and fruits.

Even if a high-ratio cake survived all this without breaking into crumbs, it would probably disintegrate when it absorbed moisture from the fillings. In addition, sponge layers in this kind of cake are usually moistened with a flavored sugar syrup to compensate for their lack of moisture.

The *fruit torte* (illustrated on p. 652) is an example of this type of cake. Genoise layers are split, moistened with dessert syrup (p. 772), layered and iced with whipped cream, and topped with attractively arranged fruit pieces. The fruit is then coated with glaze (p. 724) to protect it and enhance its appearance.

Sponge sheets for jelly rolls and other rolled cakes are made without any shortening, so that they do not crack when rolled.

Flour for sponge cakes must be very weak to avoid making the cake tough. Cornstarch is often added to cake flour for sponge cakes to weaken the flour further.

SCALING AND PANNING

Pan Preparation

Prepare pans before mixing cake batters, so that cakes can be baked without delay as soon as they are mixed.

1. For high-fat cakes the bottoms of layer pans must be greased, preferably with a commercial pan greasing preparation. If this is not available, dust the greased pan with flour and tap out the excess.

2. For sheet cakes, line the pan with greased parchment.

3. For angel food cakes, do not grease the pan. The batter must be able to cling to the sides in order to rise.

4. For sponge cake layers with a small percentage of fat, grease the bottoms but not the sides.

Procedure for Scaling Creaming Method Batters

These batters are thick and do not pour easily. Scale cakes as follows:

1. Place prepared cake pan on left side of balance scale. Balance the scale out by placing another pan on right side.

2. Set scale for desired weight.

3. Add batter to left pan until scale balances.

4. Remove pan from scale and spread batter smooth with spatula.

5. Repeat with remaining pans.

6. Give the pans several sharp raps on the bench to free large trapped air bubbles. Bake immediately.

Procedure for Scaling Two-Stage Batters

These batters are more liquid than creamed batters. They may be scaled like creamed batters, or for greater speed, they may be scaled as follows:

1. Place empty volume measure on left side of balance scale. Balance the scale out to zero.

2. Set scale for desired weight.

3. Pour batter into measure until scale balances.

4. Note the volume of batter in the measure.

5. Pour batter into prepared pan, quickly scraping out the measure to get all the batter.

6. Scale remaining cakes with the volume measure, using the volume noted in step 4.

7. Give the pans several sharp raps on the bench to free large trapped air bubbles. Bake immediately.

Procedure for Scaling Foam Cakes

Foam cake batters should be handled as little as possible and baked immediately in order to avoid deflating the beaten eggs. Although they may be scaled like creamed batters, many bakers prefer to "eyeball" them in order to minimize handling.

1. Have all prepared pans lined up on the bench.

2. Scale first pan as for creamed batters.

3. Quickly fill remaining pans to the same level as the first pan, judging the level by eye.

4. Spread the batter smooth and bake immediately.

See Table 27.1 for average scaling weights, as well as baking temperatures and times.

TABLE 27.1 **Average Cake Scaling Weights, Baking Temperatures, and Times**

Pan Type and Size	Scaling Weight[a]		Baking Temperature		Approximate Baking Time in Minutes
	U.S.	Metric	U.S.	Metric	
High-fat cakes					
Round layers					
6 in. (15 cm)	8–10 oz	230–285 g	375°F	190°C	18
8 in. (20 cm)	14–18 oz	400–510 g	375°F	190°C	25
10 in. (25 cm)	24–28 oz	680–800 g	360°F	180°C	35
12 in. (30 cm)	32–40 oz	900–1100 g	360°F	180°C	35
Sheets and square pans					
18 × 26 in. (46 × 66 cm)	7–8 lb	3.2–3.6 kg	360°F	180°C	35
18 × 13 in. (46 × 33 cm)	3½–4 lb	1.6–1.8 kg	360°F	180°C	35
9 × 9 in. (23 × 23 cm)	24 oz	680 g	360°F	180°C	30–35
Loaf (pound cake)					
2¼ × 3½ × 8 in. (6 × 9 × 20 cm)	16–18 oz	450–500 g	350°F	175°C	50–60
2¾ × 4½ × 8½ in. (7 × 11 × 22 cm)	24–27 oz	680–765 g	350°F	175°C	55–65
Cupcakes per dozen	18 oz	510 g	385°F	195°C	18–20
Foam-type cakes					
Round layers					
6 in. (15 cm)	5–6 oz	140–170 g	375°F	190°C	20
8 in. (20 cm)	10 oz	280 g	375°F	190°C	20
10 in. (25 cm)	16 oz	450 g	360°F	180°C	25–30
12 in. (30 cm)	24 oz	700 g	360°F	180°C	25–30
Sheets (for jelly roll or sponge roll)					
18 × 26 in., ½ in. thick (46 × 66 cm, 12 mm thick)	2½ lb	1.2 kg	375°F	190°C	15–20
18 × 26 in., ¼ in. thick (46 × 66 cm, 6 cm thick)	28 oz	800 g	400°F	200°C	7–10
Tube (angel food and chiffon)					
8 in. (20 cm)	12–14 oz	340–400 g	360°F	180°C	30
10 in. (25 cm)	24–32 oz	700–900 g	350°F	175°C	50
Cupcakes per dozen	10 oz	280 g	375°F	190°C	18–20

[a] The weights given are averages. Weights may be increased by 25% if thicker layers are desired. Baking times may then need to be increased slightly.

BAKING AND COOLING

Baking

Cake structure is very fragile, so proper baking conditions are essential for quality products. The following guidelines will help you avoid cake failures:

1. Preheat the ovens. (But to conserve expensive energy, don't preheat longer than necessary.)

2. Make sure ovens and shelves are level.

3. Do not let pans touch each other in oven. If pans touch, air circulation is inhibited and the cakes rise unevenly.

4. Bake at correct temperature. Too hot an oven causes the cake to set unevenly or to set before it has fully risen. Crusts will be too dark.

   Too slow an oven causes poor volume and texture because the cake doesn't set fast enough and may fall.

5. Do not open ovens or disturb cakes until they have finished rising and are partially browned. Disturbing the cakes before they are set may cause them to fall.

6. If steam in the oven is available, use it for creamed and two-stage batters. These cakes bake with a flatter top if baked with steam because the steam delays the formation of the top crust.

7. Tests for doneness:

   a. Shortened cakes will shrink away from sides of pan slightly.
   b. Cake will be springy. Center of top of cake will spring back when pressed slightly.
   c. A cake tester or pick inserted in center of cake will come out clean.

Cooling and Removing from Pans

1. Cool layer cakes and sheet cakes 15 minutes in pans and turn out while slightly warm. They are too fragile to turn out when hot, and they may break.

2. Turn out layer cakes onto racks to finish cooling.

3. To turn out sheet cakes:

   a. Sprinkle top lightly with granulated sugar.
   b. Set an empty sheet pan on top, bottom side down.
   c. Invert both pans.
   d. Remove top pan.
   e. Peel parchment off cake.

4. Cool angel food cakes upside down in pans. Support the edges of the pan so that the top of the cake is off the bench. When cool, loosen cake from sides of pan with knife or spatula, and pull out carefully.

Common Cake Faults and Their Causes

Errors in mixing, scaling, baking, and cooling cakes cause many kinds of defects and failures. For easy reference, these various defects and their possible causes are summarized in the trouble-shooting guide in Table 27.2.

TABLE 27.2 **Common Cake Faults and Their Causes**

Fault	Causes
Volume and shape	
Poor volume	Too little flour
	Too much liquid
	Too little leavening
	Oven too hot
Uneven shape	Improper mixing
	Batter spread unevenly
	Uneven oven heat
	Oven racks not level
	Cake pans warped
Crust	
Too dark	Too much sugar
	Oven too hot
Too light	Too little sugar
	Oven not hot enough
Burst or cracked	Too much flour or flour too strong
	Too little liquid
	Improper mixing
	Oven too hot
Soggy	Underbaked
	Cooling in pans or with not enough ventilation
	Wrapping before cool
Texture	
Dense or heavy	Too little leavening
	Too much liquid
	Too much sugar
	Too much shortening
	Oven not hot enough
Coarse or irregular	Too much leavening
	Too little egg
	Improper mixing

(Continues)

TABLE 27.2 **Common Cake Faults** *(Continued)*

Fault	Causes
Texture	
Crumbly	Too much leavening
	Too much shortening
	Too much sugar
	Wrong kind of flour
	Improper mixing
Tough	Flour too strong
	Too much flour
	Too little sugar or shortening
	Overmixing
Poor flavor	Poor-quality ingredients
	Poor storage or sanitation
	Unbalanced formula

ALTITUDE ADJUSTMENTS

At high altitudes, atmospheric pressure is much less than at sea level. This factor must be taken into account in cake baking. Formulas must be adjusted to suit different baking conditions above 2,000 or 3,000 feet above sea level.

Although general guidelines can be given, the exact adjustments required will vary for different kinds of cakes. Many manufacturers of flour, shortening, and other bakery ingredients will supply detailed information and adjusted formulas for any given locality.

In general, the following adjustments must be made above 2,000 or 3,000 feet elevation. See Table 27.3 for more specific adjustments.

Leavening

Leavening gases expand more when air pressure is lower, so baking powder and baking soda must be *decreased*.

Creaming and foaming procedures should also be reduced so that less air is incorporated.

Tougheners: Flour and Eggs

Cakes require firmer structure at high altitudes. Both eggs and flour must be increased to supply proteins for structure.

Tenderizers: Shortening and Sugar

For the same reasons, shortening and sugar must be decreased so that the structure will be firmer.

Liquids

At high altitudes, water boils at a lower temperature and evaporates more easily. Liquids must be *increased* to prevent excess drying both during and after baking. This also helps compensate for the decrease in moisturizers (sugar and fat) and the increase in flour, which absorbs moisture.

Baking Temperatures

Increase baking temperatures about 25°F (14°C) above 3,500 feet.

Pan Greasing

High-fat cakes tend to stick at high altitudes. Grease pans more heavily. Remove baked cakes from pans as soon as possible.

Storing

Wrap or ice cakes as soon as they are cool to prevent drying.

TABLE 27.3 **Approximate Formula Adjustment in Shortened Cakes at High Altitudes**

Ingredient	Increase or Decrease	Percentage Adjustment		
		2,500 Feet	5,000 Feet	7,500 Feet
Baking powder	Decrease	20%	40%	60%
Flour	Increase	—	4%	9%
Eggs	Increase	2½%	9%	15%
Sugar	Decrease	3%	6%	9%
Fat	Decrease	—	—	9%
Liquid	Increase	9%	15%	22%

To make adjustments, multiply the percentage indicated by the amount of ingredient and add or subtract as indicated.

Example: To adjust 1 lb (16 oz) eggs for 7,500 feet:
   0.15 × 16 oz = 2.4 oz
   16 oz + 2.4 oz = 18.4 oz

CAKE FORMULAS

CREAMING METHOD

RECIPE 343   **Yellow Butter Cake**

Ingredients	U.S.	Metric	Percentage
Butter	1 lb 2 oz	550 g	60%
Sugar	2 lb 8 oz	725 g	80%
Salt	¼ oz (1½ tsp)	9 g (8 mL)	1%
Eggs	14 oz	400 g	45%
Cake flour	1 lb 14 oz	900 g	100%
Baking powder	1½ oz	45 g	5%
Milk	1 lb 4 oz	600 g	67%
Vanilla	½ oz	15 g	1.5%
Yield:	6 lb 12 oz	3244 g	359%

Mixing: Creaming method.

Scaling and Baking: See Table 27.1.

RECIPE 344   **Brown Sugar Spice Cake**

Ingredients	U.S.	Metric	Percentage
Butter and/or shortening	1 lb 2 oz	600 g	60%
Brown sugar	1 lb 14 oz	1100 g	100%
Salt	½ oz	15 mL	1.5%
Eggs	1 lb 2 oz	600 g	60%
Cake flour	1 lb 14 oz	1000 g	100%
Baking powder	1½ oz	30 g	3%
Baking soda	¾ tsp	3 g (3 mL)	
Cinnamon	1 tbsp	5 g (15 mL)	
Cloves, ground	1½ tsp	3 g (7 mL)	
Nutmeg	¾ tsp	2 g (3 mL)	
Milk	1 lb 8 oz	800 g	80%
Yield:	7 lb 9 oz	4058 g	404%

Mixing: Creaming method.

Scaling and baking: See Table 27.1.

Variation

344A. Carrot Nut Cake: Reduce the milk to 70% (1 lb 5 oz/700 g). Add 40% (12 oz/400 g) grated fresh carrots, 20% (6 oz/200 g) finely chopped walnuts, and 2 tsp (6 g or 10 mL) grated orange zest after eggs are beaten in. Omit cloves.

RECIPE 345 Chocolate Butter Cake

Ingredients	U.S.	Metric	Percentage
Butter, or part butter and part shortening	1 lb	500 g	67%
Sugar	1 lb 12 oz	875 g	116%
Salt	⅓ oz (2 tsp)	10 g (2 tsp)	1.5%
Unsweetened chocolate, melted	8 oz	250 g	33%
Eggs	12 oz	375 g	50%
Cake flour	1 lb 8 oz	750 g	100%
Baking powder	1 oz	30 g	4%
Milk	12 oz	375 g	50%
Vanilla	2 tsp	10 mL	1.5%
Yield:	6 lb 5 oz	3175 g	423%

Mixing: Creaming method. Blend in the melted chocolate after the fat and sugar are well creamed.

Scaling and baking: See Table 27.1.

RECIPE 346 Old-Fashioned Pound Cake

Ingredients	U.S.	Metric	Percentage
Butter, or butter and shortening combined	1 lb	500 g	100%
Sugar	1 lb	500 g	100%
Vanilla	2 tsp	10 mL	2%
Eggs	1 lb	500 g	100%
Cake flour	1 lb	500 g	100%
Yield:	4 lb	2000 g	402%

Mixing: Creaming method. Add the eggs and the cake flour alternately to avoid curdling the mixture.

Scaling and baking: See Table 27.1.

Variations

Mace or grated lemon or orange zest may also be used to flavor pound cake.

346A. Raisin Pound Cake: Add 25% (4 oz/125 g) raisins or dried currants, which have been soaked in the boiling water and drained well.

346B. Chocolate Pound Cake: Add 25% (4 oz/125 g) unsweetened chocolate to the butter and sugar after the creaming stage.

346C. Marble Pound Cake: Fill pans one-third full of the basic yellow batter. Add a layer of Chocolate Pound Cake batter, and then finish with the yellow batter. Run a spatula blade through the mixture to marble the mixture.

TWO-STAGE METHOD

RECIPE 347   **White Cake**

Ingredients	U.S.	Metric	Percentage
Cake flour	1 lb 8 oz	700 g	100%
Baking powder	1½ oz	45 g	6.25%
Salt	½ oz	15 g	2%
Emulsified shortening	12 oz	350 g	50%
Sugar	1 lb 14 oz	875 g	125%
Skim milk	12 oz	350 g	50%
Vanilla	2 tsp	10 mL	1.5%
Almond extract	1 tsp	5 mL	0.75%
Skim milk	12 oz	350 g	50%
Egg whites	1 lb	475 g	67%
Yield:	6 lb 12 oz	3175 g	452%

Mixing: Two-stage method.
Scaling and baking: See Table 27.1.

Variations

Use water instead of milk, and add 10% (2½ oz/70 g) nonfat dry milk powder to the dry ingredients.

Flavor with lemon extract or emulsion instead of vanilla and almond.

347A. Yellow Cake: Reduce shortening to 45% (11 oz/325 g). Substitute whole eggs for egg whites, using the same total weight (67%). Use 2% vanilla (½ oz/15 g), and omit almond extract.

RECIPE 348   **Devil's Food Cake**

Ingredients	U.S.	Metric	Percentage
Cake flour	1 lb 8 oz	700 g	100%
Cocoa	4 oz	125 g	17%
Salt	½ oz	15 g	2%
Baking powder	¾ oz	20 g	3%
Baking soda	½ oz	15 g	2%
Emulsified shortening	14 oz	400 g	58%
Sugar	2 lb	925 g	133%
Skim milk	1 lb	475 g	67%
Vanilla	2 tsp	10 mL	1.5%
Skim milk	12 oz	350 g	50%
Eggs	1 lb	475 g	67%
Yield:	7 lb 8 oz	3500 g	500%

Mixing: Two-stage method.
Scaling and baking: See Table 27.1.

FOAMING METHODS

RECIPE 349   Sponge Cake (Genoise)

Ingredients	U.S.	Metric	Percentage
Eggs	2 lb 4 oz	1050 g	150%
Sugar	1 lb 8 oz	700 g	100%
Cake flour	1 lb 8 oz	700 g	100%
Butter, melted	8 oz	225 g	33%
Vanilla (or lemon flavor)	½ oz	15 g	2%
Yield:	5 lb 12 oz	2690 g	385%

Mixing: Sponge method.

Scaling and baking: See Table 27.1.

Variations

349A. Chocolate Genoise: Substitute 4 oz (125 g) of cocoa powder for 4 oz (125 g) of the flour.

349B. Sponge Roll or ***Jelly Roll:*** Prepare basic formula, but omit butter. Add the vanilla to the beaten eggs just before folding in the flour. Spread *evenly* in parchment-lined pans. When baked and cooled, trim off the edges. Cut in half or into quarters. Spread each rectangle with desired filling (jelly, buttercream, etc.) and roll up so that the long side of the rectangle becomes the length of the roll. Ice or sprinkle with 6X sugar.

RECIPE 350   Milk and Butter Sponge

Ingredients	U.S.	Metric	Percentage
Sugar	1 lb 4 oz	625 g	125%
Eggs, whole	12 oz	375 g	75%
Egg yolks	4 oz	125 g	25%
Salt	¼ oz	7 g	1.5%
Cake flour	1 lb	500 g	100%
Baking powder	½ oz	15 g	3%
Skim milk	8 oz	250 g	50%
Butter	4 oz	125 g	25%
Vanilla	1 tbsp	15 mL	3%
Yield:	4 lb	2037 g	407%

Mixing: Sponge method. Heat the milk and butter until the butter is melted; fold into batter
(step 5 in basic procedure).

Scaling and baking: Cake layers; see Table 27.1.

RECIPE 351   **Jelly Roll Sponge**

Ingredients	U.S.	Metric	Percentage
Sugar	11 oz	325 g	100%
Eggs, whole	10 oz	300 g	90%
Egg yolks	2 oz	65 g	20%
Salt	¼ oz	7 g (7 mL)	2%
Corn syrup	1½ oz	45 g	14%
Water	1 oz	30 g	10%
Vanilla	1 tsp	5 mL	1.5%
Hot water	4 oz	125 g	36%
Cake flour	11 oz	325 g	100%
Baking powder	1 tsp	5 g (5 mL)	1.5%
Yield:	2 lb 8 oz	1232 g	375%

Mixing: Sponge method. Add the syrup, the first quantity of water, and the vanilla to the sugar and eggs in the first mixing stage. When the foam is completely whipped, stir in the second quantity of water.

Scaling and baking: See Table 27.1. One recipe makes one sheet pan. Line the pans with greased paper. Immediately after baking, turn out of pan onto a sheet of parchment and remove the paper from the bottom of the cake. Spread with jelly and roll up tightly. When cool, dust with confectioners' sugar.

RECIPE 352   **Yellow Chiffon Cake**

Ingredients	U.S.	Metric	Percentage
Cake flour	1 lb 4 oz	500 g	100%
Sugar	1 lb	400 g	80%
Salt	½ oz	12 g (12 mL)	2.5%
Baking powder	1 oz	25 g	5%
Vegetable oil	10 oz	250 g	50%
Egg yolks	10 oz	250 g	50%
Water	15 oz	375 g	75%
Vanilla	½ oz	12 g (12 mL)	2.5%
Egg whites	1 lb 4 oz	500 g	100%
Sugar	10 oz	250 g	50%
Cream of tartar	1¼ tsp	2.5 g (5 mL)	0.5%
Yield:	6 lb 7 oz	2576 g	515%

Mixing: Chiffon method.

Scaling and baking: See Table 27.1.

Variation

352A. *Chocolate Chiffon Cake:* Add 20% cocoa (4 oz/100 g); sift it with the flour. Increase the egg yolks to 60% (12 oz/300 g). Increase the water to 90% (1 lb 2 oz/450 g).

RECIPE 353 Angel Food Cake

Ingredients	U.S.	Metric	Percentage
Egg whites	2 lb	1000 g	267%
Cream of tartar	¼ oz (1 tbsp)	8 g (15 mL)	2%
Salt	1 tsp	5 g	1.5%
Sugar	1 lb	500 g	133%
Vanilla	2 tsp	10 mL	2.5%
Almond extract	1 tsp	5 mL	1.25%
Sugar	1 lb	500 g	133%
Cake flour	12 oz	375 g	100%
Yield:	4 lb 12 oz	2403 g	640%

Mixing: Angel food method.

Scaling and baking: See Table 27.1.

Variation

353A. Chocolate Angel Food Cake: Substitute 3 oz (90 g) cocoa for 3 oz (90 g) of the flour.

ICINGS: PRODUCTION AND APPLICATION

PRODUCING AND HANDLING BASIC TYPES

Icings or frostings (the two terms mean the same thing) are sweet coatings for cakes and other baked goods. Icings have three main functions:

1. They improve the keeping qualities of the cake by forming a protective coating around it.

2. They contribute flavor and richness.

3. They improve appearance.

There are six basic kinds of icings:

Fondant.
Buttercreams.
Foam-type icings.
Fudge-type icings.
Flat-type icings.
Royal or decorator's icing.

In addition, we will consider two other preparations for cakes:

Glazes.
Fillings.

Use top-quality flavorings for icings, so that they will enhance the cake rather than detract from it. Use moderation when adding flavorings and colors. Flavors should be light and delicate. Colors should be delicate, pastel shades—except chocolate, of course.

Fondant

Fondant is a sugar syrup that is crystallized to a smooth, creamy white mass. It is familiar as the icing for napoleons, eclairs, petits fours, and some cakes. When applied, it sets up into a shiny, nonsticky coating.

Because it is difficult to make in the bakeshop, fondant is almost always purchased already prepared, either in the ready-to-use moist form or in the dry form, which requires only the addition of water.

Guidelines for Using Fondant

1. Heat fondant over a warm-water bath, stirring constantly, to thin out the icing and make it pourable. *Do not heat over 100°F (38°C)*, or it will lose its shine.

2. If still too thick, thin out with a little simple sugar syrup or water (simple syrup blends in more easily).

3. Flavorings and colorings may be added as desired.

4. To make *chocolate fondant,* stir melted bitter chocolate into warm fondant until desired color and flavor are reached. Chocolate will thicken the fondant, so the icing may require more thinning with sugar syrup.

5. Apply fondant by pouring over the item or by dipping items into it.

Buttercreams

Buttercream icings are light, smooth mixtures of fat and confectioners' sugar. They may also contain eggs to increase their smoothness or lightness.

These are popular icings used for many kinds of cakes. They are easily flavored and colored to suit a variety of purposes.

There are three basic kinds of buttercreams:

1. *Simple buttercreams* are made by creaming together fat and sugar to the desired consistency and lightness. A small quantity of egg whites may be whipped in.

Decorator's buttercream is a simple buttercream used for making flowers and other cake decorations. It is creamed only a little, because too much air beaten into it would make it unable to hold delicate shapes.

2. *Meringue-type buttercreams* are prepared by first beating egg whites and adding a boiling syrup or just sugar. Soft butter is then mixed into the meringue. This is a very light, smooth icing.

3. *French buttercreams* are similar to the meringue type, but the foam is made with egg yolks (and sometimes whole eggs) and boiling syrup. This is a very rich, light icing.

Butter, especially sweet, unsalted butter, is the preferred fat for buttercreams because of its flavor and melt-in-the-mouth quality. Icings made with only shortening can be unpleasant because the fat congeals and coats the inside of the mouth and does not melt. However, butter makes a less stable icing because it melts so easily. There are two ways around this problem:

1. Use buttercreams only in cool weather.

2. Blend a small quantity of emulsified shortening with the butter to stabilize it.

RECIPE 354 **Simple Buttercream**

Yield: 6 lb 6 oz (3175 g)

U.S.	Metric	Ingredients	Procedure
1½ lb	750 g	Butter	1. Cream together the butter, shortening, and sugar until well blended, using the paddle attachment.
8 oz	250 g	Emulsified shortening	
4 lb	2 kg	Confectioners' sugar (10X)	2. Add the egg whites, lemon juice, and vanilla. Blend in at medium speed. Then mix at high speed until light and fluffy.
5 oz	150 g	Egg whites	
2 tsp	10 mL	Lemon juice	
1 tbsp	15 mL	Vanilla	

Variations

354A. Decorator's Buttercream: Use 2 lb (1 kg) regular shortening, no butter. Omit lemon juice and vanilla. Reduce egg whites to 2 oz (60 g). Blend at low speed until smooth; do not whip.

354B. Cream Cheese Icing: Substitute cream cheese for the butter and shortening. Omit egg whites. If necessary, thin the icing with cream or milk. If desired, flavor with grated lemon or orange zest instead of vanilla.

RECIPE 355 French Buttercream

Yield: 5 lb 8 oz (2750 g)

U.S.	Metric	Ingredients	Procedure
2 lb 8 oz	1 kg 250 mL	Sugar Water	1. Combine the sugar and water in a saucepan. Bring to a boil, while stirring to dissolve the sugar. 2. Continue to boil until the syrup reaches a temperature of 240°F (115°C).
12 oz	375 g	Egg yolks	3. While the syrup is boiling, beat the yolks with the whip attachment until they are thick and light. 4. As soon as the syrup reaches 240°F, pour it *very slowly* into the beaten yolks, while the mixer is running at second speed. 5. Continue to beat until the mixture is *cool* and the yolks are very light and thick.
2 lb 8 oz 1 tbsp	1.25 kg 15 mL	Butter, soft Vanilla	6. With the mixer still running, add the butter a little at a time. Add it just as fast as it can be absorbed by the mixture. 7. Beat in the vanilla. If the icing is too soft, refrigerate until it is firm enough to spread.

Variations

Flavored buttercreams are made by adding the desired flavoring to any of the three basic buttercream recipes. In addition to the two variations given below, extracts and emulsions such as lemon, orange, and almond may be used.

355A. Chocolate Buttercream: Add 4–5 oz (125–150 g) sweet chocolate, melted and cooled, to each pound (500 g) of buttercream.

355B. Coffee Buttercream: For each pound (500 g) of buttercream, add 1½ tbsp (22 mL) instant coffee dissolved in 2 tsp (10 mL) hot water.

RECIPE 356 Meringue-Type Buttercream

Yield: 5 lb 12 oz (2900 g)

U.S.	Metric	Ingredients	Procedure
2 lb 8 oz	1 kg 250 mL	Sugar Water	1. Combine the sugar and water in a saucepan. Bring to a boil, while stirring to dissolve the sugar. 2. Continue to boil until the syrup reaches a temperature of 240°F (115°C).

RECIPE 356 **Meringue-Type Buttercream** *(Continued)*

U.S.	Metric	Ingredients	Procedure
1 lb	500 g	Egg whites	3. While the syrup is boiling, beat the egg whites in a clean, grease-free bowl, using the whip attachment, until they form firm, moist peaks. Do not overbeat.
			4. As soon as the syrup reaches 240°F, pour it *very slowly* into the egg whites, while the mixer is running at second speed.
			5. Continue to beat until the meringue is *cool* and forms stiff peaks. (You have now made an Italian Meringue. For more information, see Chapter 29.)
2 lb	1 kg	Butter, soft	6. With the mixer still running at medium speed, begin adding the butter a little at a time. Add it just as fast as it can be absorbed by the meringue.
8 oz	250 g	Emulsified shortening	
2 tsp	10 mL	Lemon juice	7. When all the butter is beaten in, add the shortening in the same way.
1 tbsp	15 mL	Vanilla	8. Beat in the lemon juice and vanilla.

Foam-type Icings

Foam icings, sometimes called boiled icings, are simply meringues made with a boiling syrup. Some also contain stabilizing ingredients like gelatin.

Foam-type icings should be applied thickly to cakes and left in peaks and swirls.

These icings are not stable. They should be used the day they are prepared. *Italian Meringue,* discussed in Chapter 29, is the simplest foam-type icing. Follow the recipe on page 765, but add 8 oz (250 g) corn syrup to the sugar and water for the boiled syrup. It is usually flavored with vanilla.

Flat Icings

Flat icings, also called water icings, are simply mixtures of 10X sugar and water, and sometimes corn syrup and flavoring. They are used mostly for coffee cakes, Danish pastry, and sweet rolls. Flat icings are warmed to 100°F (38°C) for application and are handled like fondant.

Fudge-type Icings

Fudge-type icings are rich, cooked icings. Many of them are made somewhat like candy. Fudge icings are

RECIPE 357 **Flat Icing**

Yield: 5 lb (2.5 kg)

U.S.	Metric	Ingredients	Procedure
4 lb	2 kg	Confectioners' sugar (10X or 6X)	1. Mix all ingredients together until smooth.
12 oz	375 g	Water, hot	2. To use, place desired amount in a double boiler. Warm to 100°F (38°C) and apply to the product to be iced.
4 oz	125 g	Corn syrup	
1 tbsp	15 mL	Vanilla	

heavy and thick, and they may be flavored with a variety of ingredients. They are used on cupcakes, layer cakes, loaf cakes, and sheet cakes.

Fudge icings are stable and hold up well on cakes and in storage. Stored icings must be covered tightly to prevent drying and crusting.

To use stored fudge icing, warm in a double boiler until it is soft enough to spread.

Fudge-type icings do not necessarily contain chocolate. Plain white fudge icings may be flavored with vanilla, almond, maple, coffee, or other desired flavoring.

RECIPE 358 Caramel Fudge Icing

Yield: 4 lb (2 kg)

U.S.	Metric	Ingredients	Procedure
3 lb	1500 g	Brown sugar	1. Combine the sugar and milk in a saucepan. Bring to a boil, stirring to dissolve the sugar. Using a brush dipped in water, wash down the sides of the saucepan to prevent sugar crystals from forming. (See sugar cooking, Chapter 30.)
1½ pt	750 mL	Milk	
12 oz	375 g	Butter or shortening	
¼ tsp	1 mL	Salt	
1 tbsp	15 mL	Vanilla	
			2. Boil the mixture slowly, without stirring, until it reaches 240°F (115°C).
			3. Pour the mixture into the bowl of a mixer. Add the butter and salt. Mix in with the paddle attachment.
			4. Turn off the machine, and let the mixture cool to 110°F (43°C).
			5. Add the vanilla and turn the machine on low speed. Beat the icing until it is smooth and creamy in texture. If it is too thick, thin it with a little cream or milk.
			6. Spread on cooled cake while the icing is warm, or rewarm it in a double boiler.

RECIPE 359 Quick White Fudge Icing

Yield: 5 lb 3 oz (2600 g)

U.S.	Metric	Ingredients	Procedure
8 oz	250 mL	Water	1. Place the water, butter, shortening, syrup, and salt in a saucepan. Bring to a boil.
4 oz	125 g	Butter	
4 oz	125 g	Emulsified shortening	
3 oz	90 g	Corn syrup	
½ tsp	2 mL	Salt	

RECIPE 359   **Quick White Fudge Icing** *(Continued)*

U.S.	Metric	Ingredients	Procedure
4 lb	2 kg	Confectioners' sugar (10X or 6X)	2. Sift the sugar into the bowl of a mixer.
1 tbsp	15 mL	Vanilla	3. Using the paddle attachment and with the machine running on low speed, add the boiling water mixture. Blend until smooth. Icing will become lighter the more it is mixed.
			4. Blend in the vanilla.
			5. Use while still warm, or rewarm in a double boiler. If necessary, thin out with hot water.

Variation

359A. ***Quick Chocolate Fudge Icing:*** Omit the butter in the basic recipe. Beat in 12 oz (375 g) melted unsweetened chocolate after the boiling water has been added. Thin out with more hot water as needed.

RECIPE 360   **Cocoa Fudge Icing**

Yield: 4 lb 12 oz (2375 g)

U.S.	Metric	Ingredients	Procedure
2 lb	1 kg	Granulated sugar	1. Combine the sugar, syrup, water, and salt in a saucepan. Bring to a boil, stirring to dissolve the sugar. Boil the mixture until it reaches 240°F (115°C). (See sugar cooking, Chapter 30.)
10 oz	300 g	Corn syrup	
8 oz	250 mL	Water	
1 tsp	5 mL	Salt	
8 oz	250 g	Butter, or part butter and part emulsified shortening	2. While the sugar is cooking, mix the fat, sugar, and cocoa until evenly combined, using the paddle attachment of the mixer.
1 lb	500 g	Confectioners' sugar (10X or 6X)	3. With the machine running at low speed, very slowly pour in the hot syrup.
6 oz	175 g	Cocoa	4. Mix in the vanilla. Continue to beat until the icing is smooth, creamy, and spreadable. If necessary, thin out with a little hot water.
	to taste	Vanilla	
	as needed	Hot water	5. Use while still warm, or rewarm in a double boiler.

Variation

360A. ***Vanilla Fudge Icing:*** Use evaporated milk or light cream instead of water for the syrup. Omit cocoa. Adjust consistency with additional confectioners' sugar (to thicken) or water (to thin out). Other flavorings may be used in place of vanilla, such as almond, maple, peppermint, or coffee.

Royal Icing

This icing, also called decorating or decorator's icing, is similar to flat icings except that it is much thicker and is made with egg whites, which make it hard and brittle when dry. It is used almost exclusively for decorative work.

To prepare royal icing:

1. Place desired amount of 10X sugar in a mixing bowl. Add a small quantity of cream of tartar (for whiteness)—about ⅛ tsp per pound of sugar (1 g per kilogram).

2. Beat in egg white a little at a time, until the sugar forms a smooth paste. You will need 2 to 3 oz of egg whites per pound of sugar (125 g per kilogram).

3. Keep unused icing covered with a damp cloth at all times to prevent hardening.

Glazes

Glazes are thin, glossy, transparent coatings that give shine to baked products and also help prevent drying.

The simplest glaze is a sugar syrup or diluted corn syrup brushed onto coffee cakes or Danish while it is hot. See Chapter 25 for recipe. Syrup glazes may contain gelatin or waxy maize starch. Fruit glazes, the most popular being apricot, are available commercially prepared. They are melted, thinned out with a little water, and brushed on while hot.

Fruit glazes may also be made by melting apricot or other preserves and forcing them through a strainer.

One of the most common uses of glazes in cakemaking is to coat the fruit arranged on the top of fruit tortes (see p. 709).

Fillings

Fillings are sometimes used instead of icings between cake layers. They are also used in such products as jelly rolls, Danish, and other pastries.

1. *Fruit fillings.*

Fruit fillings may be cooked or uncooked.

Cooked fruit fillings are chopped or puréed fruits or fruit juices thickened with starch or eggs. They are prepared somewhat like pie fillings (see Chapter 29).

Uncooked fruit fillings include jellies and preserves and dried fruits that have been ground and flavored (see recipes in Chapter 25). Fresh fruits, such as the strawberries in strawberry shortcake, are also used.

Many ready-to-use fruit fillings are on the market.

2. *Cream fillings.*

Cream fillings include pastry cream (recipes in Chapter 30) and various pudding-type preparations.

Desserts with cream fillings should be assembled as close to service time as possible and kept refrigerated to avoid health hazards.

3. *Whipped cream.*

Whipped cream is used as a dessert topping, filling, and frosting. See page 569 for instructions on whipping and handling heavy cream.

Artificial whipped toppings resemble whipped cream in appearance. They should be used only if your customers actually like them.

ASSEMBLING AND ICING CAKES

Selection of Icing

The flavor, texture, and color of the icing must be compatible with the cake.

1. **In general, use heavy frostings with heavy cakes and light frostings with light cakes.**

   For example, ice angel food cakes with a simple flat icing, fondant, or a light fluffy, boiled icing.

   High-ratio cakes go well with buttercreams and fudge-type icings.

   Shortened sponge layer cakes (genoise) are often combined with fruits or fruit fillings, light French or meringue-type buttercream, whipped cream, or flavored fondants.

2. **Use the best-quality flavorings, and use them sparingly. The flavor of the frosting should not be stronger than the cake.**

   Fudge-type icings may be flavored more strongly, as long as the flavor is of good quality.

3. **Use coloring sparingly. Light, pastel shades are more appetizing than loud colors.**

   Paste colors give best results. Mix a little color with a small portion of the icing, then use this icing to color the rest.

Procedure for Assembling Layer Cakes

1. Cook cake layers completely before assembling and icing.

2. Trim layers, if necessary.

a. Remove any ragged edges.

b. Slightly rounded tops are easily covered by icing, but excessively large bumps may have to be cut off.

c. If desired, layers may be split in half horizontally. This makes the cake higher and increases the proportion of filling to cake. See Figure 27.1.

3. Brush all crumbs from cakes. Loose crumbs make icing difficult.

4. Place the bottom layer *upside down* (to give a flat surface for the filling) on a cardboard cake circle of the same diameter. Place the cake in the center of a cake turntable.

   If a cake circle or turntable is not available, place the cake on a serving plate and slip sheets of waxed paper or parchment under the edges of the cake to keep the plate clean.

5. Spread filling on bottom layer out to the edges. If the filling is different from the frosting for the outside of the cake, be careful not to spread the filling over the edges.

   Use proper amount of filling. If applied too heavily, it will ooze out when top layer is placed on.

6. Place top layer on bottom layer, right side up.

7. Ice the cake:

   a. If a thin or light icing is used, pour or spread the icing onto the center of the cake. Then spread it to the edges and down the sides with a spatula.

   b. If a heavy icing is used, it may be necessary to spread the sides first, then place a good quantity of icing in the center of the top and *push* it to the edges with the spatula.

      Pushing the icing rather than pulling or dragging it with the spatula prevents pulling up crumbs and getting them mixed with the icing.

      Use enough icing to cover the entire cake generously, but not excessively, with an even layer.

      Smooth the icing with the spatula, or leave it textured or swirled, as desired.

      The finished, iced cake should have a perfectly level top and perfectly straight, even sides.

Small Cakes

1. Cupcakes are iced by dipping the tops in a soft icing. Twist the cakes slightly and pull them out quickly in one smooth motion.

   Cupcakes may also be iced by spreading icing on with a spatula. Practice is necessary to develop speed and efficiency.

2. Petits fours are tiny cakes cut from sheet cakes. Select a cake that doesn't crumble easily, and carefully cut it into desired shapes. Remove all crumbs and place the cakes on a rack over a sheet pan. Ice them by pouring fondant or flat icing over them to cover completely.

Sheet Cakes

Sheet cakes are ideal for volume service because they require little labor to bake, ice, or decorate, and they keep well as long as they are uncut.

For special occasions, sheet cakes are sometimes decorated as a single unit with a design or picture in colored icing, a "Happy Special Occasion" message, and so on. It is more common, however, to ice them for individual service as in the following procedure.

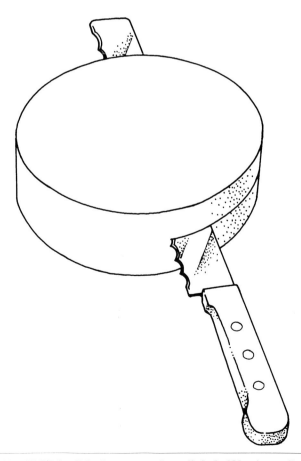

FIGURE 27.1 **Cake layers may be split in half horizontally, using a long-bladed, serrated knife.**

Procedure for Icing Sheet Cakes

1. Turn out the cake onto the bottom of another sheet pan or tray, as described on page 711. Cool the cake thoroughly.

2. Trim the edges evenly with a serrated knife.

3. Brush all crumbs from the cake.

4. Place a quantity of icing in the center of the cake, and, with a spatula, push the icing to the edges. Smooth the top with the spatula, giving the entire cake an even layer of icing.

5. With a long knife or spatula, mark the entire cake off into portions, as in Figure 27.2, by press-

18 X 26 inch sheets

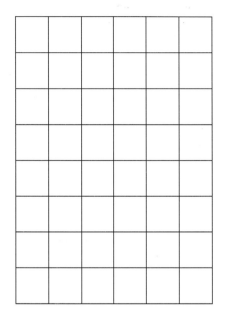

6 X 8 = 48 portions

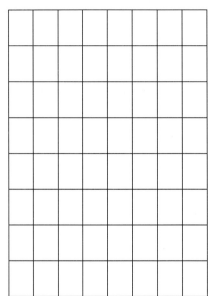

8 X 8 = 64 portions

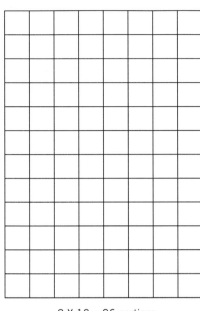

8 X 12 = 96 portions

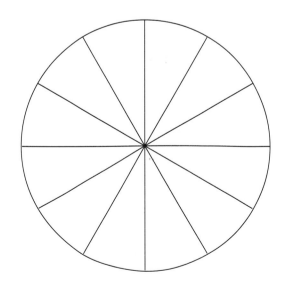

8-10 inch layers
12 portions

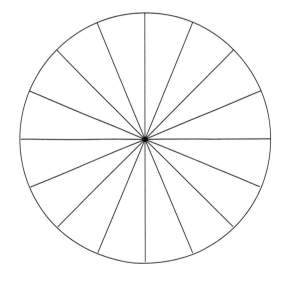

10-12 inch layers
16 portions

FIGURE 27.2   Cake-cutting guides for sheet cakes and round layer cakes. For 13 × 18-inch (33 × 46-cm) sheets, simply divide the above diagrams for full-sized sheet cakes in half.

ing the back of the knife lightly into the icing. Do not cut the cake.

6. Using a paper cone or pastry bag fitted with a star tube, pipe a rosette or swirl of icing onto the center of each marked-off portion. Or select another decoration, as desired. Whatever decorations you use, keep them simple, and make them the same for every portion. The finished sheet cake will resemble that in Figure 27.3.

7. Hold for service. Cut as close as possible to service time to keep the cake from drying.

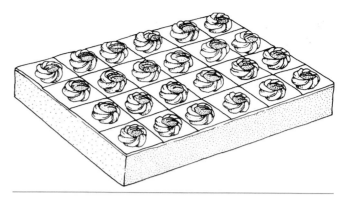

FIGURE 27.3   **A finished sheet cake marked off into portions and decorated so that each portion is identical.**

TERMS FOR REVIEW

creaming method	angel food method	fondant	fudge icing
two-stage method	chiffon method	buttercream	royal icing
blending method	high-fat cakes	foam icing	glaze
foaming method	low-fat cakes	flat icing	

QUESTIONS FOR DISCUSSION

1. Briefly list the steps in each of the four basic cake mixing methods that are presented in this chapter.

2. What are the reasons, in the creaming method, for creaming the butter and sugar until the mixture is light and fluffy?

3. In both the creaming method and the two-stage method, there is a lot of emphasis on scraping down the sides of the bowl. Why is this necessary?

4. What might the finished product be like if you tried to mix a low-fat cake by the two-stage method? Explain.

5. Examine the following cake formulas and indicate which mixing method you would use for each.

Cake 1

2 lb	Cake flour	1 kg
1 lb 2 oz	Emulsified shortening	525 g
1 oz	Salt	30 g
1½ oz	Baking powder	45 g
2 lb 8 oz	Fine granulated sugar	1250 g
1 lb	Skim milk	500 g
1 lb 5 oz	Whole eggs	650 g
10 oz	Skim milk	300 g

Cake 2

3 lb	Whole eggs	1.5 kg
1 lb	Egg yolks	500 g
2 lb 4 oz	Sugar	1125 g
2 lb	Cake flour	1 kg
6 oz	Cornstarch	175 g
6 oz	Melted butter	175 g

Cake 3

1 lb	Butter	500 g
8 oz	Shortening	250 g
4 lb	Sugar	2 kg
1 oz	Vanilla	30 g
1 lb 4 oz	Whole eggs	625 g
3 lb 8 oz	Cake flour	1750 g
10 oz	Cocoa powder	300 g
1½ oz	Baking soda	45 g
3 lb	Buttermilk	1.5 kg
1 lb 8 oz	Water	750 g

6. What is the most important rule to consider when using fondant?

7. Compare the keeping qualities of simple buttercreams and meringue-type buttercreams.

8. List the steps in assembling and icing a three-layer cake.

CHAPTER 28

COOKIES

The word "cookie" means "small cake," and that's exactly what a cookie is. In fact, some cookies are made from cake batter. For some products, such as certain kinds of brownies, it's difficult to know whether to classify them as cakes or cookies.

Most cookie formulas, however, call for less liquid than cake formulas do. Cookie doughs range from soft to very stiff, unlike the thinner batters for cakes. This difference in moisture content means some differences in mixing methods, although the basic procedures are much like those for cakes.

The most apparent differences between cakes and cookies are in the makeup. Because most cookies are individually formed or shaped, there is a great deal of hand labor involved. Learning correct methods and then practicing diligently are essential for efficiency.

After reading this chapter, you should be able to

1. Understand the causes of crispness, softness, chewiness, and spread in cookies.

2. Prepare cookie doughs by the three basic mixing methods.

3. Prepare seven basic types of cookies: dropped, bagged, rolled, molded, icebox, bar, and sheet.

4. Bake and cool cookies properly.

COOKIE CHARACTERISTICS AND THEIR CAUSES

Cookies come in an infinite variety of shapes, sizes, flavors, and textures. Characteristics that are desirable in some are not desirable in others. For example, we want some cookies to be crisp and others to be soft. We want some to hold their shape and others to spread during baking. In order to produce the characteristics we want and to correct faults, it is useful to know what causes these characteristics.

Crispness

Cookies are crisp if they are very low in moisture. The following factors contribute to crispness:

1. Low proportion of liquid in the mix. Most crisp cookies are made from a stiff dough.

2. High sugar and fat content.

3. Evaporation of moisture during baking due to high temperatures and/or long baking.

4. Small size or thin shape, so the cookie dries faster during baking.

5. Proper storage. Crisp cookies can become soft if they absorb moisture.

Softness

Softness is the opposite of crispness, so it has the opposite causes, as follows:

1. High proportion of liquid in mix.

2. Low sugar and fat.

3. Honey, molasses, or corn syrup included in formulas. These sugars are *hygroscopic*, which means they readily absorb moisture from the air or from their surroundings.

4. Underbaking.

5. Large size or thick shape, therefore retaining more moisture.

6. Proper storage. Soft cookies can become stale and dry if not tightly covered or wrapped.

Chewiness

Moisture is necessary for chewiness, but other factors are also required. In other words, all chewy cookies are soft, but not all soft cookies are chewy.

1. High sugar and liquid content, but low fat content.

2. High proportion of eggs.

3. Strong flour, or gluten developed during mixing.

Spread

Spread is desirable in some cookies, while others must hold their shape. Several factors contribute to spread or lack of spread.

1. *Sugar.*

   High sugar content increases spread. Coarse granulated sugar increases spread, whereas fine sugar or confectioners' sugar reduces spread.

2. *Leavening.*

   High baking soda or baking ammonia content encourages spread. So does long creaming, which incorporates air.

3. *Temperature.*

   Low oven temperature increases spread. High temperature decreases spread because the cookie sets up before it has a chance to spread too much.

4. *Liquid.*

   A slack batter—that is, one with a high liquid content—spreads more than a stiff dough.

5. *Flour.*

   Strong flour or activation of gluten decreases spread.

6. *Pan grease.*

   Cookies spread more if baked on a heavily greased pan.

MIXING METHODS

Cookie mixing methods are very much like cake mixing methods. The major difference is that less liquid is usually incorporated, so that mixing is somewhat easier.

Less liquid means that gluten will become less developed by the mixing. Also, it is a little easier to get a smooth, uniform mix.

There are three basic cookie mixing methods:

One stage

Creaming

Sponge

These methods are subject to many variations, due to differences in formulas. The general procedures are as follows, but always be sure to follow the exact instructions when a formula indicates a variation in the procedure.

One-stage Method

This method is the counterpart of the blending or two-stage cake mixing method, which was discussed in the previous chapter. Cake batters have more liquid, so it must be added in two or more stages in order to blend uniformly. Low-moisture cookies, on the other hand, can be mixed all in one stage.

Procedure

1. Scale ingredients accurately. Have all ingredients at room temperature.

2. Place all ingredients in mixer. With the paddle attachment, mix at low speed until uniformly blended. Scrape down the sides of the bowl as necessary.

Creaming Method

This is nearly identical to the creaming method for cakes. Since cookies require less liquid, it is not necessary to add the liquid alternately with the flour. It can be added all at once.

Procedure

1. Scale ingredients accurately. Have all ingredients at room temperature.

2. Place the fat, sugar, salt, and spices in the mixing bowl. With the paddle attachment, cream these ingredients at low speed.

   For light cookies, cream until the mix is light and fluffy, to incorporate more air for leavening.

   For a dense, chewier cookie, cream only slightly.

3. Add the eggs and liquid if any and blend in at low speed.

4. Sift in the flour and leavening. Mix until just combined.

Sponge Method

This method is essentially the same as the egg-foam methods for cakes. The procedure varies considerably, depending on the ingredients. Batches should be kept small because the batter is delicate.

Procedure

1. Scale all ingredients accurately. Have all ingredients at room temperature, or warm the eggs slightly for greater volume, as for sponge cakes.

2. Following the procedure given in the formula used, whip the eggs (whole, yolks, or whites) and the sugar to the proper stage: soft peaks for whites, thick and light for whole eggs or yolks.

3. Fold in remaining ingredients as specified in the recipe. Be careful not to overmix or to deflate the eggs.

TYPES AND MAKEUP METHODS

We can classify cookie types by makeup methods as well as by mixing methods. Grouping by the makeup method is perhaps more useful from the point of view of production, because mixing methods are relatively simple, whereas makeup procedures vary considerably.

In this section, you will learn basic procedures for producing seven cookie types:

    Dropped
    Bagged
    Rolled
    Molded
    Icebox
    Bar
    Sheet

No matter what makeup method you use, follow one important rule: *Make all cookies of uniform size and thickness.* This is essential for even baking. Since baking times are so short, small cookies may be burnt before large ones are done.

Dropped Cookies

Dropped cookies are made from a soft dough or batter. They are fast and easy to make up.

Many sponge or foam-type batters are made up as dropped cookies.

1. Select the proper size scoop for accurate portioning.

   A No. 30 scoop makes a large cookie, about 1 oz (30 g).

   A No. 40 scoop makes a medium cookie.

   Nos. 50, 60, or small scoops make small cookies.

2. Drop the cookies onto the prepared baking sheets. Allow enough space between cookies for spreading.

3. Rich cookies will spread by themselves. But if the formula requires it, flatten the mounds of batter slightly with a weight dipped in sugar.

Bagged Cookies

Bagged or pressed cookies are also made from soft doughs. The dough must be soft enough to be forced through a pastry bag, but stiff enough to hold its shape.

1. Fit a pastry bag with a tip of desired size and shape. Fill the bag with the cookie dough. Review Figure 18.3 for tips on use of the pastry bag.

2. Press out cookies of desired shape and size directly onto prepared cookie sheets.

Rolled Cookies

Cookies rolled and cut from a stiff dough are not often made in commercial food service, because they require excessive labor. Also, there are always scraps left over after cutting. When rerolled, these scraps make inferior, tough cookies.

1. Chill dough thoroughly.

2. Roll dough out ⅛ inch (3 mm) thick on a floured canvas or floured work bench. Use as little flour as possible for dusting, because this flour can toughen the cookies.

3. Cut out cookies with cookie cutters and place on prepared baking sheets. Cut as close together as possible to reduce the quantity of scraps.

Molded Cookies

The first part of this procedure (steps 1 and 2) is simply a fast and fairly accurate way of dividing the dough into equal portions. Each piece is then molded into the desired shape. This usually consists of simply flattening the pieces out with a weight. For some traditional cookies, special molds are used to flatten the dough and at the same time stamp a design onto the cookie.

The pieces may also be shaped by hand into crescents, fingers, or other shapes.

1. Roll the dough out into long cylinders about 1 inch (2½ cm) thick, or whatever size is required. (Refrigerate the dough if it is too soft to handle.)

2. With a knife or bench scraper, cut the roll into 1-oz (30-g) pieces, or whatever size is required.

3. Place the pieces on prepared baking sheets, leaving 2 inches (5 cm) of space between each.

4. Flatten cookies with a weight (such as a can) dipped in granulated sugar after pressing each cookie.

   A fork is sometimes used for flattening the dough, as for peanut butter cookies.

5. Alternative method: After step 2, shape the dough by hand into desired shapes.

Icebox Cookies

The icebox or refrigerator method is ideal for operations that wish to have freshly baked cookies on hand at all times. The rolls of dough may be made up in advance and stored. Cookies can easily be cut and baked as needed.

1. Scale dough into pieces of uniform size, from 1½ lb (700 g) if you are making small cookies, to 3 lb (1400 g) for large cookies.

2. Form the dough into cylinders from 1 to 2 inches (2½ to 5 cm) in diameter, depending on the size cookie desired.

   For accurate portioning, it is important to make all the cylinders of dough the same thickness and length.

3. Wrap the cylinders in parchment or waxed paper, place them on sheet pans, and refrigerate overnight.

4. Unwrap the dough and cut into slices of *uniform thickness*. The exact thickness required depends on the size of the cookie and how much the dough spreads during baking. The usual range is from ⅛ to ½ inch (3 to 12 mm).

A slicing machine is recommended for ensuring even thickness. Doughs containing nuts or fruits should be sliced by hand with a knife.

5. Place the slices on prepared baking sheets, allowing 2 inches (5 cm) of space between cookies.

Bar Cookies

1. Scale the dough into 1¾-lb (800-g) units (1-lb units, or 500-g units, may be used for smaller cookies).

2. Shape the pieces of dough into cylinders the length of the sheet pans. Place three strips on each greased pan, spacing them well apart.

3. Flatten the dough with the fingers into strips about 3 to 4 inches wide and about ¼ inch thick (8 to 10 cm wide, 6 mm thick).

4. If required, brush with egg wash.

5. Bake as directed in the formula.

6. After baking, while cookies are still warm, cut each strip into bars about 1¾ inches (4½ cm) wide.

Sheet Cookies

Sheet cookies vary so much that it is nearly impossible to give a single procedure for all of them. Some of them are almost like sheet cakes, only denser and richer. They may even be iced like sheet cakes. Others consist of two or three layers added and baked in separate stages. The following procedure is only a general guideline.

1. Spread cookie mixture into prepared sheet pans. Make sure the thickness is even.

2. If required, add topping or brush with an egg wash.

3. Bake as directed. Cool.

4. Apply icing or topping, if any.

5. Cut into individual squares or rectangles.

PANNING, BAKING, AND COOLING

Preparing the Pans

1. Use clean, unwarped pans.

2. Lining the sheets with parchment or silicone paper is fast, and it eliminates the necessity of greasing the pans.

3. A heavily greased pan increases the spread of the cookie. A greased and floured pan decreases spread.

4. Some high-fat cookies can be baked on ungreased pans.

Baking

1. Most cookies are baked at a relatively high temperature for a short time.

2. Too low a temperature increases spreading and may produce hard, dry, pale cookies.

3. Too high a temperature decreases spreading and may burn the edges or bottoms.

4. Even a minute of overbaking can burn cookies, so watch them closely. Also, the heat of the pan continues to bake the cookies even after they are removed from the oven.

5. Doneness is indicated by color. The edges and bottoms should just be turning a light golden color.

6. With some rich doughs, burnt bottoms may be a problem. In this case, *double-pan* the cookies by placing the sheet pan on a second pan of the same size.

Cooling

1. Remove cookies from pans while they are still warm, or they may stick.

2. If cookies are very soft, do not remove from pans until they are cool enough and firm enough to handle. Cookies may be soft when hot but become crisp when cool.

3. Do not cool too rapidly or in cold drafts, or cookies may crack.

4. Cool completely before storing.

RECIPE 361   Chocolate Chip Cookies

Ingredients	U.S.	Metric	Percentage
Butter and/or shortening	12 oz	350 g	60%
Granulated sugar	10 oz	300 g	50%
Brown sugar	10 oz	300 g	50%
Salt	¼ oz (1½ tsp)	8 g (7 mL)	1.25%
Eggs	6 oz	175 g	30%
Vanilla	2 tsp	10 mL	1.5%
Water	2 oz	60 g	10%
Pastry flour	1 lb 4 oz	600 g	100%
Baking soda	¼ oz (1½ tsp)	8 g (7 mL)	1.25%
Chocolate chips	1 lb 4 oz	600 g	100%
Chopped walnuts or pecans	8 oz	250 g	40%
Yield:	5 lb 8 oz	2661 g	444%

Mixing: Creaming method. Blend in chocolate chips and nuts last.

Makeup: Drop method. Use greased or parchment-lined baking sheets.

Baking: 375°F (190°C), 8–12 minutes, depending on size.

Variation

361A. Brown Sugar Nut Cookies: Omit granulated sugar and use 100% (1 lb 4 oz/600 g) brown sugar. Omit chocolate chips, and increase nuts to 100% (1 lb 4 oz/600 g).

RECIPE 362   Oatmeal Raisin Cookies

Ingredients	U.S.		Metric	Percentage
Butter and/or shortening		8 oz	250 g	67%
Brown sugar	1 lb		500 g	133%
Salt		1 tsp	5 g	1.5%
Eggs		4 oz	125 g	33%
Vanilla		2 tsp	10 mL	3%
Milk		1 oz	30 g	8%
Pastry flour		12 oz	375 g	100%
Baking powder		½ oz (1 tbsp)	15 g	4%
Baking soda		¼ oz (1½ tsp)	8 g	2%
Rolled oats (quick cooking)		10 oz	300 g	83%
Raisins (see note)		8 oz	250 g	67%
Yield:	3 lb 11 oz		1858 g	500%

RECIPE 362   **Oatmeal Raisin Cookies** *(Continued)*

Note: If raisins are hard and dry, soak them in hot water 30 minutes, drain, and dry well before adding to cookie dough.

Mixing: Creaming method. Combine oats with other dry ingredients after they are sifted. Mix raisins into dough last.

Makeup: Drop method. Use greased or parchment-lined baking sheets.

Baking: 375°F (190°C), 10–12 minutes, depending on size.

RECIPE 363   **Tea Cookies**

Ingredients	U.S.		Metric	Percentage
Butter, or half butter and half shortening	1 lb		500 g	67%
Granulated sugar		8 oz	250 g	33%
Confectioners' sugar		4 oz	125 g	17%
Eggs		6 oz	175 g	25%
Vanilla (or almond extract)		1½ tsp	8 mL	1%
Cake flour	1 lb	8 oz	750 g	100%
Yield:	3 lb	10 oz	1823 g	243%

Mixing: Creaming method.

Makeup: Bagged method. Make small cookies about the size of a quarter, using a star tube or plain tube. Bag out onto ungreased or parchment-lined baking sheets.

Baking: 375°F (190°C), about 10 minutes.

Variations

363A. Almond Tea Cookies: Add 17% (4 oz/125 g) almond paste. Blend it thoroughly with the sugar before adding the butter.

363B. Sandwich-Type Cookies: Select cookies with the same size and shape. Turn half of them over and dot the centers of the flat sides with a small amount of jam or fudge icing. Sandwich with the remaining cookies.

363C. Chocolate Tea Cookies: Substitute 6 oz (175 g) cocoa for 6 oz (175 g) of the flour.

RECIPE 364   **Ladyfingers**

Ingredients	U.S.	Metric	Percentage
Egg yolks	8 oz	250 g	80%
Sugar	5 oz	150 g	50%
Pastry flour	10 oz	300 g	100%
Vanilla (optional)	1½ tsp	8 g	2.5%
Egg whites	12 oz	350 g	120%
Sugar	5 oz	150 g	50%
Yield:	2 lb 8 oz	1208 g	402%

(enough for about 8 dozen ladyfingers)

Mixing: Sponge method

1. Beat egg yolks 1 minute at medium speed, using whip attachment. With machine running, gradually add the first amount of sugar. Continue to whip until thick and light.
2. Sift the flour and fold into the yolks. If desired, add the vanilla.
3. Whip the egg whites until they form soft peaks. Add the sugar and beat until stiff but still moist.
4. Fold the whites into the batter.

Makeup: Bagged method. Use plain tube. Bag out 3-inch-long strips × ¾ inch wide (7½ × 2 cm) onto pans that have been lined with parchment or greased and floured.

Baking: 375°F (190°C), about 10 minutes.

RECIPE 365   **Coconut Macaroons (Meringue Type)**

Ingredients	U.S.	Metric
Egg whites	8 oz	250 g
Cream of tartar	1 tsp	2 g (5 mL)
Sugar	1 lb 4 oz	625 g
Vanilla (or rum flavor)	½ oz	15 g
Macaroon coconut	1 lb	500 g
Yield:	2 lb 12 oz	1392 g

Mixing: Sponge method

1. Beat the egg whites and cream of tartar until they form soft peaks. Gradually beat in the sugar. Continue to beat until stiff and glossy.
2. Fold in the coconut.

Makeup: Bagged method. Bag out with a star tube onto parchment-lined baking sheets.

Baking: 300°F (150°C), about 30 minutes.

RECIPE 366   **Sugar Cookies**

Ingredients	U.S.	Metric	Percentage
Butter and/or shortening	1 lb	500 g	40%
Sugar	1 lb 4 oz	625 g	50%
Salt	2 tsp	10 g	0.9%
Eggs	4 oz	125 g	10%
Milk	2 tsp	125 g	10%
Vanilla	½ oz	15 g	1.25%
Cake flour	2 lb 8 oz	1250 g	100%
Baking powder	1¼ oz	35 g	3%
Yield:	5 lb 5 oz	2685 g	215%

Mixing: Creaming method.

Makeup: Rolled method. Before cutting the rolled-out dough, wash with milk and sprinkle with granulated sugar. Use greased or parchment-lined baking sheets.

Baking: 375°F (190°C), 8–10 minutes.

Variations

Lemon rind, extract, or emulsion may be used in place of vanilla.

366A. Rolled Brown Sugar Cookies: Increase butter to 50% (1 lb 4 oz/625 g). Omit granulated sugar, and use 60% (1 lb 8 oz/750 g) brown sugar.

366B. Rolled Chocolate Cookies: Substitute 4 oz (125 g) cocoa for 4 oz (125 g) of the flour.

RECIPE 367   **Shortbread Cookies**

Ingredients	U.S.	Metric	Percentage
Butter	1 lb 8 oz	750 g	75%
Sugar	1 lb	500 g	50%
Salt	¼ oz (1½ tsp)	8 g	0.75%
Egg yolks (see note)	8 oz	250 g	25%
Optional flavoring (see note)			
Pastry flour	2 lb	1000 g	100%
Yield:	5 lb	2508 g	250%

Note: Traditional Scottish shortbread is made with butter, flour, and sugar, no eggs, flavoring, or liquid. Because the dough is very crumbly, it is not rolled out but is pressed into pans or molds and baked. For the recipe given here, you may make the cookies without added flavoring or flavor to taste with vanilla, almond, or lemon.

Mixing: Creaming method.

Makeup: Rolled method. Roll dough ¼ inch (½ cm) thick (this is thicker than most rolled cookies). Use greased or parchment-lined baking sheets.

Baking: 350°F (175°C), about 15 minutes.

RECIPE 368   **Cinnamon Cookies**

Ingredients	U.S.		Metric	Percentage
Butter and/or shortening	1 lb		500 g	80%
Granulated sugar		8 oz	250 g	40%
Brown sugar		8 oz	250 g	40%
Salt		1 tsp	5 g	0.9%
Cinnamon		⅓ oz (1½ tbsp)	10 g	1.7%
Eggs		3 oz	90 g	15%
Milk		1 oz	30 g	5%
Pastry flour	1 lb	4 oz	625 g	100%
Yield:	3 lb	8 oz	1760 g	282%

Mixing: Creaming method.

Makeup: Molded method. Roll cut pieces in cinnamon sugar before placing on greased baking
sheets and pressing flat.

Baking: 375°F (190°C), about 10 minutes.

Variation

368A. Chocolate Cinnamon Cookies: Substitute 4 oz (125 g) cocoa for 4 oz (125 g) of the flour.

RECIPE 369   **Raisin Spice Bars**

Ingredients	U.S.		Metric	Percentage
Sugar	1 lb 8 oz		700 g	100%
Butter and/or shortening	8 oz		225 g	33%
Eggs	8 oz		225 g	33%
Molasses	4 oz		125 g	17%
Pastry flour	1 lb 8 oz		700 g	100%
Cinnamon	2 tsp		4 g (10 mL)	0.6%
Cloves, ground	½ tsp		1 g (2 mL)	0.16%
Ginger	1 tsp		2 g (5 mL)	0.3%
Baking soda	¾ tsp		3 g (3 mL)	0.5%
Salt	1 tsp		5 g (5 mL)	0.75%
Raisins (see note)	1 lb		475 g	67%
Yield:	5 lb 4 oz		2465 g	350%

Note: If raisins are hard and dry, soak them in hot water 30 minutes, drain, and dry well before
adding to the mix.

Mixing: One-stage method.

Makeup: Bar method. Egg wash with whole eggs or egg whites.

Baking: 350°F (175°C), about 15 minutes.

RECIPE 370   **Peanut Butter Cookies**

Ingredients	U.S.	Metric	Percentage
Butter and/or shortening	12 oz	375 g	75%
Brown sugar	8 oz	250 g	50%
Granulated sugar	8 oz	250 g	50%
Salt	1 tsp	5 g (5 mL)	1%
Peanut butter	12 oz	375 g	75%
Eggs	4 oz	125 g	25%
Pastry flour	1 lb	500 g	100%
Baking soda	1 tsp	5 g (5 mL)	1%
Yield:	3 lb 12 oz	1885 g	377%

Mixing: Creaming method. Cream peanut butter with the fat and sugar.

Makeup: Molded method. Use a fork instead of a weight to flatten the cookies. Use greased or parchment-lined baking sheets.

Baking: 375°F (190°C), 8–12 minutes, depending on size.

RECIPE 371   **Icebox Cookies**

Ingredients	U.S.	Metric	Percentage
Butter and/or shortening	2 lb	1000 g	67%
Granulated sugar	1 lb	500 g	33%
Confectioners' sugar	1 lb	500 g	33%
Salt	½ oz	15 g	1%
Eggs	8 oz	250 g	17%
Vanilla	½ oz	15 g	1%
Pastry flour	3 lb	1500 g	100%
Yield:	7 lb 9 oz	3780 g	252%

Mixing: Creaming method.

Makeup: Icebox method. Scale dough strips 1½ lb (750 g) each. Slice cookies ¼ inch (½ cm) thick. Bake on ungreased pans.

Baking: 375°F (190°C), about 12 minutes.

Variations

To reduce spread, use all confectioners' sugar.

371A. Butterscotch Icebox Cookies: In place of sugars in basic recipe, use 67% (2 lb/1 kg) brown sugar, and use only butter. Increase eggs to 25% (12 oz/375 g). Add 1 tsp (5 g or 5 mL) baking soda to the flour.

371B. Chocolate Icebox Cookies: Add 17% (8 oz/250 g) melted unsweetened chocolate to the creamed butter and sugar.

371C. Nut Icebox Cookies: Add 25% (12 oz/375 g) finely chopped nuts to the sifted flour in the basic recipe or the Butterscotch or Chocolate Cookie recipes.

RECIPE 372 **Brownies**

Ingredients	U.S.	Metric	Percentage
Unsweetened chocolate	1 lb	450 g	100%
Butter	1 lb 8 oz	675 g	150%
Eggs	1 lb 8 oz	675 g	150%
Sugar	3 lb	1350 g	300%
Salt	¼ oz (1½ tsp)	7 g (7 mL)	1.5%
Vanilla	1 oz	30 g	6%
Cake flour	1 lb	450 g	100%
Chopped walnuts or pecans	1 lb	450 g	100%
Yield:	9 lb 1 oz	4087 g	907%

Mixing: Foaming method`
   1. Melt chocolate and butter together in a double boiler. Stir so that the mixture is smooth. Let it cool to room temperature.
   2. Blend the eggs, sugar, and salt until well mixed, but do not whip. Add the vanilla.
   3. Blend in the chocolate mixture.
   4. Sift the flour and fold it in.
   5. Fold in the nuts.

Makeup: Sheet method. Grease and flour the pans or line them with parchment. Quantity of basic recipe is enough for one full 18 × 26 inch (46 × 66 cm) sheet pan, or two half-size sheet pans, or four 9 × 13 inch (23 × 33 cm) pans or six 9-inch (23 cm) square pans.

If desired, batter may be sprinkled with additional 50% (8 oz/225 g) chopped nuts after panning.

Baking: 325°F (165°C), about 60 minutes. For 2-inch (5 cm) square brownies, cut sheet pan 8 × 12, to yield 96 pieces.

Variation

372A. Butterscotch Brownies or **Blondies:** Omit chocolate. Use brown sugar instead of white granulated sugar. Increase flour to 1 lb 6 oz (600 g).

TERMS FOR REVIEW

spread	sponge method	rolled cookies	bar cookies
one-stage method	dropped cookies	molded cookies	sheet cookies
creaming method	bagged cookies	icebox cookies	

QUESTIONS FOR DISCUSSION

1. What makes cookies crisp, and how can you keep them crisp after they are baked?

2. If you baked some cookies that were unintentionally chewy, how would you correct them in the next batch?

3. Describe briefly the difference between the creaming method and the one-stage method.

4. Besides cost control, why is accurate scaling and uniform sizing important when making up cookies?

CHAPTER 29

PIES AND PASTRIES

On the American frontier it was
not uncommon for the pioneer housewife to bake 21 pies a week—one for
every meal. Pies were so important to the settlers that in winter, when fruits were
unavailable, cooks would bake pies for dessert out of whatever materials
were available, such as potatoes, vinegar, and soda crackers.

Few of us today eat pie at every meal. Nevertheless,
pies are still the favorite American dessert. Most customers will order
and pay a higher price for a piece of chocolate cream pie than for chocolate
pudding, even if the pie filling is the same as the pudding, and
even if they leave the crust uneaten.

In this chapter you will study the preparation
of pie crusts and fillings. In addition, you will also learn to make puff pastry,
eclair paste, meringues, and fruit desserts.

After reading this chapter, you should be able to

1. Prepare flaky and mealy pie doughs.

2. Prepare crumb crusts and short or cookie crusts.

3. Assemble and bake pies.

4. Prepare pie fillings.

5. Prepare puff pastry dough and puff dough products.

6. Prepare eclair paste and eclair paste products.

7. Prepare standard meringues and meringue desserts.

8. Prepare fruit desserts.

PIES

PIE DOUGHS

Before you begin studying this section, it would be a good idea for you to review the section on gluten development in Chapter 24. Pie pastry is a very simple product in terms of its ingredients: flour, shortening, water, and salt. Yet success or failure depends on how the shortening and flour are mixed and how the gluten is developed. The key to making pie dough is proper technique, and you will remember the techniques better if you understand why they work.

Ingredients

1. *Flour.*

   Pastry flour is the best choice for pie doughs. It has enough gluten to produce the desired structure and flakiness, yet is low enough in gluten to yield a tender product, if handled properly.

   If stronger flours are used, the percentage of shortening should be increased to provide more tenderness.

2. *Fat.*

   Regular hydrogenated shortening is the most popular fat for pie crusts because it has the right plastic consistency to produce a flaky crust. It is firm and moldable enough to make an easily workable dough. Emulsified shortening should not be used because it blends too quickly with the flour, making a flaky pastry difficult to achieve.

   Butter contributes excellent flavor to pie pastry, but it is not frequently used in volume production for two reasons: it is expensive, and it melts very easily, making the dough difficult to work.

   It is desirable, if costs permit, to blend a quantity of butter into the shortening used for pie crusts, to improve flavor. The quantity of pie crust that is dumped in the garbage after customers have eaten out the filling is evidence that many people are not satisfied with the taste of pie crusts made with shortening.

   If all butter is used in place of shortening, the percentage of fat in the formula should be increased by about one-fourth. (If 1 lb shortening is called for, use 1 lb 4 oz butter.) The liquid should be reduced slightly, since butter contains moisture.

   Lard is an excellent shortening for pies because it is firm and plastic. Some people dislike its flavor, however, so it is not widely used in food service.

3. *Liquid.*

   Water is necessary to develop some gluten in the flour and give structure and flakiness to the dough. If too much water is used, the crust will become tough because of too much gluten development. If not enough water is used, the crust will fall apart.

   Milk makes a richer dough that browns more quickly. However, the crust is less crisp and the production cost is higher.

   Whether water or milk is used, it must be added cold (40°F/4°C or colder) to maintain proper dough temperature.

4. *Salt.*

   Salt has some tenderizing and conditioning effect on the gluten. However, its main contribution is to flavor.

   Salt must be dissolved in the liquid before adding to the mix, in order to ensure even distribution.

Temperature

Pie dough should be kept cool, about 60°F (15°C), during mixing and makeup, for two reasons.

1. Shortening has the best consistency when cool. If it is warm, it blends too quickly with the flour. If it is very cold, it is too firm to be easily workable.

2. Gluten develops more slowly at cool temperatures than at warm temperatures.

Pie Dough Types

There are two basic types of pie dough:

> Flaky pie dough
>
> Mealy pie dough

The difference between the two doughs is how the fat is blended with the flour. Complete mixing procedures are given later. First, it is important to understand the basic distinction between the two types.

Flaky Pie Dough

For flaky dough, the fat is cut or rubbed into the flour until the particles of shortening are about the size of peas or hazelnuts. That is, the flour is not completely blended with the fat, and the fat is left in pieces. (Many bakers distinguish between this crust, which they call *short-flake*, and *long-flake* crusts in which the fat is left in pieces the size of walnuts, and the flour is even less coated with shortening.)

When water is added, the flour absorbs water and develops some gluten. When the dough is rolled out, the lumps of fat and moistened flour are flattened and become flakes of dough separated by layers of fat.

Mealy Pie Dough

For mealy dough, the fat is blended into the flour more thoroughly, until the mixture looks like coarse cornmeal.

Because the flour is more completely coated with fat:

- The crust is very "short" and tender, because less gluten can develop.

- Less water is needed in the mix, because the flour won't absorb as much as in flaky dough.

- The baked dough is less likely to absorb moisture from the filling and become soggy.

Mealy dough is used for bottom crusts in baked fruit pies and soft or custard-type pies, because it resists sogginess. Flaky doughs are used for top crusts and for prebaked pie shells.

Trimmings

Reworked scraps or trimmings will be tougher than freshly made dough. They may be combined with mealy dough and used for bottom crusts only.

Mixing Pie Doughs

Hand mixing is best for small quantities of dough, especially flaky dough, because you have more control over the mixing. Quantities up to 10 pounds (or 5 kilograms) can be mixed almost as quickly by hand as by machine.

For machine mixing, use a pastry knife or paddle attachment, and blend at low speed.

Procedures for rolling out pie doughs and lining pie pans are discussed in the next section, "Assembly and Baking."

RECIPE 373   Flaky Pie Dough
RECIPE 374   Mealy Pie Dough

Ingredients	Flaky			Mealy		
	U.S.	Metric	Percentage	U.S.	Metric	Percentage
Pastry flour	5 lb	2300 g	100%	5 lb	2300 g	100%
Shortening	3 lb 8 oz	1600 g	70%	3 lb 4 oz	1500 g	65%
Salt	1½ oz	45 g	2%	1½ oz	45 g	2%
Water	1 lb 8 oz	700 g	30%	1 lb 4 oz	575 g	25%
Yield:	10 lb 1 oz	4645 g	202%	9 lb 9 oz	4420 g	191%

Mixing:
1. Collect all equipment.
2. Collect and scale ingredients.
3. Dissolve salt in water. Set aside.
4. Place flour and shortening in mixing bowl.
5. Rub or cut shortening into flour to the proper degree:
    For mealy dough—until it resembles coarse cornmeal.
    For flaky dough—until fat particles are the size of peas or hazelnuts.
6. Add salt and water. Mix very gently, just until water is absorbed. Do not overwork the dough.
7. Place the dough in pans, cover with plastic film, and place in refrigerator or retarder for several hours.

Other Pie Crusts

Crumb Crusts

Graham cracker crusts are popular because they have an appealing flavor and are much easier to make than pastry crusts. For variations, vanilla or chocolate wafer crumbs or gingersnap crumbs may be used instead of graham cracker crumbs. Ground nuts may be added for special desserts.

Crumb crusts are used only for unbaked pies, such as cream pies and chiffon pies. Be sure that the flavor of the crust is compatible with the filling. A lime chiffon pie with a chocolate crumb crust is not an appealing combination. Some cream fillings are so delicate that they would be overwhelmed by a crust that is too flavorful.

Baking the crust makes a firmer, less crumbly crust and increases flavor.

Short-Dough Crusts

Short pastry is actually a kind of cookie dough. It is richer than regular pie pastry and contains butter, sugar, and eggs. Because it is difficult to handle, it is used primarily for small fruit tarts.

RECIPE 375   **Graham Cracker Crust**

Yield: 2 lb (900 g)

Crusts for: four 9-inch pies
five 8-inch pies

U.S.	Metric	Ingredients	Procedure
1 lb	450 g	Graham cracker crumbs	1. Mix crumbs and sugar in mixing bowl.
8 oz	225 g	Granulated sugar	2. Add butter and mix until evenly blended and crumbs are all moistened by the melted butter.
8 oz	225 g	Butter, melted	
			3. Scale the mixture into pie pans: 8 oz (225 g) for 9-inch pans 6 oz (175 g) for 8-inch pans
			4. Spread mixture evenly on bottom and sides of pan. Press another pan on top to pack crumbs evenly.
			5. Bake at 350°F (175°C) for 10 minutes.
			6. Cool thoroughly before filling.

Variations

Substitute chocolate or vanilla wafer crumbs or gingersnap crumbs for the cracker crumbs.

RECIPE 376   **Short Dough**

Yield: 6 lb 5 oz (3.1 kg)

U.S.	Metric	Ingredients	Procedure
2 lb	1 kg	Butter, or part butter and part shortening	1. Using the paddle attachment, mix the butter, sugar, and salt at low speed until smooth and evenly blended.
12 oz	375 g	Sugar	
1 tsp	5 g	Salt	
9 oz	275 g	Eggs	2. Add the eggs and mix until just absorbed.
3 lb	1.5 kg	Pastry flour, sifted	3. Add the flour. Mix just until evenly blended.
			4. Chill several hours before using.

Procedure for Making Small Fruit Tarts

1. Roll out chilled short dough on a floured surface until it is slightly less than ¼ inch (5 mm) thick.

2. With a round cutter about ½ inch (1 cm) larger than the top diameter of your individual tart shells, cut the dough into circles.

3. For each shell, fit a circle of dough into a tin and press it well against the bottom and sides. If you are using fluted tins, make sure the dough is thick enough on the sides so that it won't break apart at the ridges.

4. Fit paper liners inside the shells and fill with dried beans to keep the dough from blistering or puffing while baking.

5. Bake at 400°F (200°C) about 15 minutes until the shells are fully baked. Remove the paper liners and the beans.

6. Cool the shells completely and remove from the tins.

7. Fill the shells half full of vanilla pastry cream (see Chapter 30).

8. Arrange well-drained fresh, cooked, or canned fruits over the pastry cream.

9. Brush the top with apricot glaze, melted currant jelly, or other desired glaze (see Chapter 27).

10. Keep refrigerated until service.

ASSEMBLY AND BAKING

Types of Pies

Pies may be classified into two groups, based on method of assembling and baking.

1. **Baked pies.**

    Raw pie shells are filled and then baked. *Fruit pies* contain fruit fillings and usually have a top crust.

    Soft pies are those with custard-type fillings or, in other words, liquid fillings that become firm when their egg content coagulates. They are usually baked as single-crust pies.

2. **Unbaked pies.**

    Baked pie shells are filled with a prepared filling, chilled, and served when the filling is firm enough to slice.

Cream pies are made with pudding or boiled custard-type fillings.

Chiffon pies are made with fillings that are lightened by the addition of beaten egg whites and sometimes whipped cream. Gelatin or starch gives them their firm consistency.

Procedure for Rolling Pie Dough and Lining Pans

1. **Scale the dough.**

    8 oz (225 g) for 9-inch (23-cm) bottom crusts.
    6 oz (175 g) for 9-inch (23-cm) top crusts.
    6 oz (175 g) for 8-inch (20-cm) bottom crusts.
    5 oz (150 g) for 8-inch (20-cm) top crusts.

    Experienced bakers are able to roll out crusts using less dough, because less needs to be trimmed when dough is rolled to a perfect circle of the exact size needed.

2. **Dust the bench and rolling pin lightly with flour.**

    Too much dusting flour toughens the dough. Use no more than needed to prevent sticking.

3. **Roll out dough.**

    Flatten the dough lightly and roll it out to a uniform ⅛-inch (3-mm) thickness. Use even strokes and roll from the center outward in all directions. Lift dough frequently to make sure it is not sticking. Finished dough should be a perfect circle.

4. **Place dough in pan.**

    To lift dough without breaking, roll it lightly around the rolling pin. Allow the dough to drop into the pans and press it into the corners without stretching the dough. Stretched dough will shrink during baking. There should be no air bubbles between the dough and the pan.

5. **For single-crust pies, flute edges if desired and trim off excess dough.**

    Some bakers feel that fluted edges add to the appearance of the product. Others feel that fluting takes too much time and only produces a rim of heavy dough that customers leave on their plates.

6. **For two-crust pies:**

    Fill with cold filling, place second crust on top, and seal top and bottom crusts together at edges. Flute if desired and trim excess dough. Apply desired wash or glaze to top.

7. **Bake as directed in recipe.**

TABLE 29.1 **Scaling Instructions for Baked Pies**

Pie Size		Weight of Filling	
U.S.	Metric	U.S.	Metric
8 inch	20 cm	26–30 oz	750–850 g
9 inch	23 cm	32–40 oz	900–1150 g
10 inch	25 cm	40–50 oz	1150–1400 g

Note: Weights are guidelines only. Exact weights may vary, depending on the filling and the depth of the pans.

Procedure for Preparing Baked Pies

Note: For pies without a top crust, omit steps 3 through 7.

1. Line pie pans with pie dough as in basic procedure.

2. Fill with *cooled* fillings. See Table 29.1 for scaling instructions.

3. Roll out dough for top crust.

4. Cut perforations in top crust to allow steam to escape during baking.

5. Moisten the rim of the bottom crust to help seal it to the top crust.

6. Fit the top crust in place. Trim excess dough and seal edges together firmly. Rim may be fluted if desired.

7. Brush tops with desired wash: milk, cream, eggs and milk, or water. Sprinkle with granulated sugar if desired.

8. Bake at 425°F to 450°F (220°C to 230°C) for first 10 minutes. The high initial heat helps set the bottom crust to avoid soaking. Fruit pies are usually baked at this high heat until done. For custard pies, reduce heat to 325°F to 350°F (165°C to 175°C) to avoid overcooking and curdling custard. Custard pies include all those containing large quantities of egg, such as pumpkin pie and pecan pie.

The Soggy Bottom

Common pie faults are underbaked bottom crusts or crusts that have soaked up moisture from the filling.

Soggy bottoms can be avoided in several ways.

1. Use mealy dough for bottom crusts. Mealy dough absorbs less liquid than flaky dough.

2. Use high bottom heat, at least at the beginning of baking, to set the crust quickly. Bake the pies at the bottom of the oven.

3. Do not add hot fillings to unbaked crusts.

4. Use dark metal pie tins, which absorb heat. (If you use disposable aluminum pans, choose pans with the bottoms colored black.)

Procedure for Preparing Unbaked Pies

1. Line pie pans with pie dough as in basic procedure.

2. Dock the crust well with a fork to prevent blistering of the crust.

3. Place another pan inside the first one, so that the dough is between two pans. This is called *double-panning*.

4. Place the pans upside down in preheated oven at 450°F (230°C). Baking upside down helps keep the dough from shrinking down into the pan.

    Some bakers like to chill the crusts before baking to relax the gluten and help reduce shrinkage.

5. Bake at 450°F (230°C) for 10 to 15 minutes. The top pan may be removed during the last part of baking so that the crust can brown.

6. Cool the baked crust completely.

7. Fill with cream or chiffon filling. Fill as close as possible to service time to prevent soaking the crust.

8. Chill the pie until it is set enough to slice.

FILLINGS

Starches for Fillings

Many kinds of pie fillings, especially fruit fillings and cream fillings, depend on starch for their thickness.

Types

Cornstarch is used for cream pies because it sets up into a firm gel that holds its shape when sliced. Cornstarch may also be used for fruit pies.

Waxy maize and other *modified starches* are best for fruit pies because they are very clear when set and make a soft paste rather than a firm gel. Waxy maize should be used for pies that are to be frozen, because this starch is not broken down by freezing.

Flour, tapioca, and other starches are used less frequently. Flour has less thickening power than other starches and makes the product cloudy.

Instant or pregelatinized starch needs no cooking because it has already been cooked. When used with certain fruit fillings, it eliminates the need to cook the filling before making up the pie. It has no advantage, however, if the filling must be cooked anyway, in order to cook such ingredients as raw fruit or eggs.

Starches differ in thickening power, so follow the formulas exactly.

Cooking Starches

To avoid lumping, starches must be mixed with a cold liquid or with sugar before being added to a hot liquid.

Sugar and *strong acids* reduce the thickening power of starch. When possible, all or part of the sugar and strong acids like lemon juice should be added *after the starch has thickened.*

Fruit Fillings

Fruit pie fillings consist of fruits and fruit juices, sugar, spices, and a starch thickener.

Fruits for Pie Fillings

Fresh fruits make excellent pies if they are at their seasonal peak. Fresh apples are used extensively for high-quality pies. But the quality of fresh fruits can vary considerably, and they require a lot of labor.

Frozen fruits are widely used for pies because they are consistent in quality and readily available.

Canned fruits can also be of high quality. Solid pack (with little juice) gives a higher yield of fruit per can than syrup or water pack.

Dried fruits must be rehydrated by soaking and usually simmering before they are made into pie fillings.

Fruits must have sufficient acid (tartness) to make flavorful fillings. If they lack natural acid, you may need to add some lemon, orange, or pineapple juice to supply the acid.

Cooked Juice Method

The advantage of this method is that only the juice is cooked. The fruit retains better shape and flavor because it is subjected to less heat and handling. This method is used when the fruit requires little or no cooking before filling the pie. Examples: cherry, blueberry and other berries, peach, most frozen or canned fruits.

Procedure

1. Drain juice from fruit.

2. Measure juice and, if necessary, add water or other fruit juice to bring to desired volume.

3. Bring the juice to a boil.

4. Dissolve starch in cold water, and stir into boiling juice. Return to boil and cook until clear and thickened.

5. Add sugar, salt, and flavorings and stir until dissolved.

6. Pour thickened juice over drained fruit and mix gently. Be careful not to break or mash the fruit.

7. Cool.

Cooked Fruit Method

This method is used when the fruit requires cooking or there is not enough liquid for the cooked juice method. Examples: fresh apple, raisin, rhubarb.

Procedure

1. Bring fruit and juice or water to a boil. Some sugar may be added to the fruit to draw out juices.

2. Dissolve starch in cold water and stir into the fruit. Return to a boil and cook until clear and thickened. Stir while cooking.

3. Add sugar, salt, flavorings, and other ingredients, and stir until dissolved.

4. Cool as quickly as possible.

Old-Fashioned Method

This method is best suited for pies made with fresh apples or peaches. It is not as widely used in food service as the other methods because it is more difficult to control the thickening of the juices.

Procedure

1. Mix the starch and spices with the sugar until uniformly blended.

2. Mix the fruit with the sugar mixture.

3. Fill unbaked pie shells with the fruit.

4. Place lumps of butter on top of the filling.

5. Cover with top crust or with streusel (p. 683) and bake.

Cooked Juice Method

RECIPE 377 Apple Pie Filling (Canned Fruit)

Yield: about 9½ lb (4.5 kg)
five 8-inch (20-cm) pies
four 9-inch (23-cm) pies
three 10-inch (25-cm) pies

U.S.	Metric	Ingredients	Procedure
6 lb 8 oz	3 kg	Canned apples (one No. 10 can)	1. Drain the apples and save the juice.
as needed	as needed	Water	2. Add enough water to the juice to measure 1½ pt (750 mL).
8 oz	250 mL	Cold water	3. Mix the cold water and starch.
3 oz	90 g	Cornstarch or modified starch	4. Bring the juice mixture to a boil.
			5. Stir in the starch mixture and return to a boil.
1 lb 4 oz	575 g	Sugar	6. Add the remaining ingredients (except the drained apples). Simmer until the sugar is dissolved.
¼ oz (1¼ tsp)	7 g (6 mL)	Salt	
¼ oz (4¼ tsp)	7 g (21 mL)	Cinnamon	7. Pour the syrup over the apples and mix gently. Cool completely.
1 tsp	2 g (5 mL)	Nutmeg	
3 oz	90 g	Butter	8. Fill pie shells. Bake at 425°F (220°C) about 30–40 minutes.

Variations

377A. Dutch Apple Pie Filling: Simmer 8 oz (250 g) raisins in water. Drain and add to Apple Pie Filling.

377B. Cherry Pie Filling: Use one No. 10 can sour cherries instead of apples. Increase starch to 4 oz (125 g). Add 1½ oz (45 mL) lemon juice in step 6. Increase the sugar to 1 lb 12 oz (800 g). Omit cinnamon and nutmeg. Add almond extract to taste (optional). If desired, color with 2 to 3 drops red coloring.

377C. Peach Pie Filling: Use one No. 10 can sliced peaches, preferably solid or heavy pack, instead of apples. Omit cinnamon and nutmeg.

377D. Pineapple Pie Filling: Use one No. 10 can crushed pineapple instead of apples. Increase liquid in step 1 to 1 qt (1 L). Increase starch to 4 oz (125 g). Use 1 lb 8 oz (700 g) sugar and 8 oz (250 g) corn syrup. Omit cinnamon and nutmeg.

RECIPE 378   Blueberry Pie Filling (Frozen Fruit)

Yield: about 10 lb (4.3 kg)
    five 8-inch (20-cm) pies
    four 9-inch (23-cm) pies
    three 10-inch (25-cm) pies

U.S.	Metric	Ingredients	Procedure
7 lb	3.2 kg	Frozen unsweetened blueberries	1. Thaw blueberries in original container without opening.
as needed	as needed	Water	2. Drain the berries. Add enough water to the juice to measure 1 pt (500 mL). Stir in the sugar.
8 oz	250 g	Sugar	
8 oz	250 mL	Cold water	3. Mix the cornstarch and cold water.
4 oz	125 g	Cornstarch or modified starch	4. Bring the juice mixture to a boil. Stir in the starch. Return to a boil to thicken.
1 lb 2 oz	500 g	Sugar	5. Stir in the sugar, salt, cinnamon, and lemon juice. Stir over heat until the sugar is dissolved.
¼ oz (1¼ tsp)	7 g (6 mL)	Salt	
¼ oz (4¼ tsp)	7 g (21 mL)	Cinnamon	6. Pour the syrup over the drained blueberries. Mix gently. Cool completely.
2 oz	60 mL	Lemon juice	
			7. Fill pie shells. Bake at 425°F (220°C), about 30 minutes.

Variations

378A. Apple Pie Filling: Use 7 lb (3.2 kg) frozen apples instead of blueberries. Reduce second quantity of sugar to 12 oz (350 g). Reduce starch to 3 oz (90 g). Add 1 tsp (5 mL) nutmeg and 4 oz (125 g) butter in step 5.

378B. Cherry Pie Filling: Use 7 lb (3.2 kg) frozen cherries instead of blueberries. Increase liquid in step 2 to 1½ pt (750 mL). Decrease starch to 3½ oz (100 g). Reduce second quantity of sugar to 14 oz (400 g). Omit cinnamon and reduce lemon juice to 1 oz (30 mL).

RECIPE 379   Fresh Strawberry Pie Filling

Yield: about 12 lb (5.5 kg)
     six 8-inch (20-cm) pies
     five 9-inch (23-cm) pies
     four 10-inch (25-cm) pies

U.S.	Metric	Ingredients	Procedure
9 lb	4.1 kg	Fresh whole straw-berries	1. Hull, wash, and drain the berries. Set aside 7 lb (3.2 kg) of the berries. These may be left whole if small, or cut in halves or quarters if large.
1 pt	500 mL	Cold water	
			2. Mash or purée the remaining 2 lb (900 g) of the berries. Mix with the water. (If a clear filling is desired, this mixture may be strained.)
1 lb 12 oz	800 g	Sugar	3. Mix together the sugar, starch, and salt. Stir into the cold juice and water mixture until no lumps remain.
4 oz	125 g	Cornstarch or modi-fied starch	
1 tsp	5 mL	Salt	4. Bring to a boil, stirring constantly. Cook until thickened.
2 oz	60 mL	Lemon juice	
			5. Remove from heat and stir in the lemon juice.
			6. Cool to room temperature but do not chill.
			7. Stir to eliminate lumps. Fold in the reserved berries.
			8. Fill baked pie shells and chill (do not bake).

Cooked Fruit Method

RECIPE 380   Rhubarb Pie Filling

Yield: about 11 lb (5 kg)
six 8-inch (20-cm) pies
five 9-inch (23-cm) pies
four 10-inch (25-cm) pies

U.S.	Metric	Ingredients	Procedure
7 lb	3.2 kg	Fresh rhubarb	1. Cut the rhubarb into 1-inch (2½-cm) pieces.
1 pt	500 mL	Water	
1 lb	450 g	Sugar	2. Combine the rhubarb, water, and sugar in a saucepan. Bring to a boil and simmer 2 minutes.
8 oz	250 mL	Water	3. Mix the water and starch. Stir into the rhubarb and boil until thick and clear.
5 oz	150 g	Cornstarch	
1 lb	450 g	Sugar	4. Add the remaining ingredients. Stir gently until the sugar is dissolved and the butter is melted.
2 tsp	10 mL	Salt	
2 oz	60 g	Butter	
			5. Cool completely.
			6. Fill pie shells. Bake at 425°F (220°C), about 30–40 minutes.

Variations

380A. Fresh Apple Pie Filling: Use 10 lb (4.5 kg) fresh peeled and sliced apples instead of rhubarb. Omit orange zest and instead flavor with 1 tbsp (15 mL) cinnamon, 1 tsp (5 mL) nutmeg, and 1–2 oz (30–60 mL) lemon juice.

RECIPE 381   Raisin Pie Filling

Yield: about 10½ lb (4.8 kg)
six 8-inch (20-cm) pies
five 9-inch (23-cm) pies
four 10-inch (25-cm) pies

U.S.	Metric	Ingredients	Procedure
4 lb	1.8 kg	Raisins	1. Combine the raisins and water in a saucepan. Simmer 5 minutes.
2 qt	2 L	Water	
8 oz	250 mL	Cold water	2. Mix the water and starch. Stir into the raisins and simmer until thickened.
2½ oz	75 g	Cornstarch or modi- fied starch	
1 lb 4 oz	575 g	Sugar	3. Add the remaining ingredients. Stir until sugar is dissolved and mixture is uniform.
2 tsp	10 mL	Salt	
3 oz	90 mL	Lemon juice	4. Cool thoroughly.
1 tbsp	15 mL	Grated lemon zest	
1 tsp	5 mL	Cinnamon	5. Fill pie shells. Bake at 425°F (220°C), about 30–40 minutes.
3 oz	90 g	Butter	

Old-Fashioned Method

RECIPE 382 **Old-Fashioned Apple Pie Filling**

Yield: about 11 lb (5 kg)
      six 8-inch (20-cm) pies
      five 9-inch (23-cm) pies
      four 10-inch (25-cm) pies

U.S.	Metric	Ingredients	Procedure
9 lb EP	4.1 kg EP	Fresh peeled, sliced apples	1. Select firm, tart apples.
2 oz	60 mL	Lemon juice	2. Combine apple slices and lemon juice in a large mixing bowl and toss to coat apples with the juice.
2 lb	900 g	Sugar	3. Mix together the sugar, starch, salt, and spices.
3 oz	90 g	Cornstarch	
¼ oz (1¼ tsp)	7 g (6 mL)	Salt	4. Add to the apples and toss gently until well mixed.
¼ oz (4¼ tsp)	7 g (21 mL)	Cinnamon	
1 tsp	5 mL	Nutmeg	
3 oz	90 g	Butter	5. Fill pie shells. Dot the tops with butter before placing on top crusts. Bake at 400°F (200°C), about 45 minutes.

Custard or Soft Fillings

Custard, pumpkin, pecan, and similar pies are made with an uncooked liquid filling containing eggs. The eggs coagulate when the pie is baked, setting the filling.

The greatest difficulty in cooking soft pies is cooking the crust completely yet not overcooking the filling. Start the pie at the bottom of a hot oven (425°F to 450°F/220°C to 230°C) for first 10 minutes to set the crust. Then reduce heat to 325°F to 350°F (165°C to 175°C) to cook the filling slowly.

To test for doneness:

1. Shake the pie very gently. If it is no longer liquid, it is done. The center will still be slightly soft but will continue cooking in its own heat after it is removed from oven.

2. Insert a thin knife 1 inch from the center. It will come out clean if the pie is done.

RECIPE 383 **Custard Pie Filling**

Yield: 8 lb (3.6 kg)
      five 8-inch (20-cm) pies
      four 9-inch (23-cm) pies
      three 10-inch (25-cm) pies

U.S.	Metric	Ingredients	Procedure
2 lb	900 kg	Eggs	1. Beat the eggs lightly. Add sugar, salt, and vanilla. Blend until smooth. Do not whip air into the mixture.
1 lb	450 g	Sugar	
1 tsp	5 mL	Salt	
1 oz	30 mL	Vanilla	

U.S.	Metric	Ingredients	Procedure
2½ qt	2.5 L	Milk (see note)	2. Stir in the milk. Skim off any foam.
1–1½ tsp	5–7 mL	Nutmeg	3. Pour into the unbaked pie shells.
			4. Sprinkle tops with nutmeg.
			5. Bake at 450°F (230°C) 15 minutes. Reduce heat to 325°F (165°C) and bake until set, about 20–30 minutes more.

Note: For a richer custard, use part milk and part cream.

Variation

*383A. **Coconut Custard Pie Filling:*** Use 10 oz (275 g) unsweetened, flaked coconut. Sprinkle coconut into pie shells before adding custard mixture. Coconut may be toasted lightly in oven before adding to pies, if desired. Omit nutmeg.

RECIPE 384   **Pumpkin Pie Filling**

Yield: about 8½ lb (4 kg)
five 8-inch (20-cm) pies
four 9-inch (23-cm) pies
three 10-inch (25-cm) pies

U.S.	Metric	Ingredients	Procedure
3 lb 6 oz	1.5 kg	Pumpkin purée, 2 No. 2½ cans or ½ No. 10 can	1. Place pumpkin in a bowl of a mixer fitted with whip attachment.
2 oz	60 g	Pastry flour	2. Sift together the flour, spices, and salt.
4 tsp	20 mL	Cinnamon	3. Add the flour mixture and sugar to the pumpkin. Mix at 2nd speed until smooth and well blended.
½ tsp	2 mL	Nutmeg	
½ tsp	2 mL	Ginger	
¼ tsp	1 mL	Cloves	
2 tsp	10 mL	Salt	
1 lb 4 oz	575 g	Brown sugar	
12 oz	350 g	Eggs	4. Add eggs and mix in. Scrape down the sides of the bowl.
4 oz	125 g	Corn syrup, or half corn syrup and half molasses	5. Turn machine to low speed. Gradually pour in the syrup/molasses mixture, then the milk. Mix until evenly blended.
1½ qt	1.5 L	Milk	6. Fill pie shells. Bake at 450°F (230°C) for first 15 minutes. Lower heat to 350°F (175°C) and bake until set, about 30–40 minutes more.

Variations

*384A. **Sweet Potato Pie Filling:*** Substitute canned sweet potatoes, drained and puréed, for the pumpkin.

*384B. **Squash Pie Filling:*** Substitute puréed squash for the pumpkin.

RECIPE 385 **Pecan Pie Filling**

Yield: 8 lb (3.6 kg) filling plus 1 lb 4 oz (575 g) pecans
  five 8-inch (20-cm) pies
  four 9-inch (23-cm) pies
  three 10-inch (25-cm) pies

U.S.	Metric	Ingredients	Procedure
2 lb	900 g	Granulated sugar (see note)	1. Using the paddle attachment at low speed, blend the sugar, butter, and salt until evenly blended.
8 oz	225 g	Butter	
1½ tsp	7 mL	Salt	
2 lb	900 g	Eggs	2. With the machine running, add the eggs a little at a time, until they are all absorbed.
3 lb 8 oz (about 2½ pt)	1.6 kg	Dark corn syrup	3. Add the syrup and vanilla. Mix until well blended.
1 oz	30 mL	Vanilla	
1 lb 4 oz	575 g	Pecans	4. To assemble pies, distribute pecans evenly in pie shells. Fill with syrup mixture.
			5. Bake at 450°F (230°C) for 10 minutes. Reduce heat to 325°F (165°C). Bake about 40 minutes more, until set.

Note: Brown sugar may be used if darker color and stronger flavor are desired.

Cream Pie Fillings

Cream pie fillings are the same as puddings, which in turn are the same as a basic pastry cream with added flavorings, such as vanilla, chocolate, coconut. Lemon filling is made by the same method, using water and lemon juice instead of milk.

The one difference between puddings and pie fillings that you should note is that *cream pie fillings are made with cornstarch,* so that slices will hold their shape when cut. Puddings may be made with flour, cornstarch, or other starches.

Techniques and recipes for these fillings are included in Chapter 30, along with other basic creams and puddings.

Chiffon Pies

Chiffon fillings are made by adding gelatin to a cream filling or to a thickened fruit and juice mixture; egg whites and/or whipped cream are then folded into the mixture. It is then poured into baked pie shells and allowed to set.

These preparations are the same as chiffon desserts, bavarians, and some mousses and cold soufflés.

To avoid unnecessary repetition, techniques and recipes for these products are included in Chapter 30, with other puddings and creams.

PASTRIES, MERINGUES, AND FRUIT DESSERTS

Although pie dough is the most frequently produced pastry in American bakeshops and kitchens, two other pastries also have great importance: *puff pastry,* used for such products as napoleons and turnovers, and *eclair* or *choux paste,* used for eclairs and cream puffs. In addition, both these products are used in the hot food kitchen and the pantry, in the preparation of a number of hors d'oeuvres, entrées, and side dishes.

Meringues and fruit desserts are also covered in this section. Meringues are not only important as pie toppings, but they can also be formed, baked until crisp, and then used in many of the same ways as pastry shells for desserts.

PUFF PASTRY

Puff pastry is one of the most remarkable products of the bakeshop. Although it includes no added leavening agent, it can rise to eight times its original thickness when baked.

Puff pastry is a rolled-in dough, like Danish and croissant dough. This means that it is made up of many layers of fat sandwiched in between layers of dough. Unlike Danish dough, however, puff pastry contains no yeast. Steam, created when the moisture in the dough layers is heated, is responsible for the spectacular rising power of puff pastry.

Puff pastry or puff dough is one of the most difficult of all bakery products to prepare. Because it consists of over 1,000 layers, many more than in Danish dough, the rolling-in procedure requires a great deal of time and care.

Like so many other products, there are nearly as many versions of puff pastry as there are bakers. Both formulas and rolling-in techniques vary. The formula provided here contains no eggs, for example, although some bakers add them.

The folding-in technique used here differs somewhat from that used by European pastry chefs, although it is widely used by American bakers.

Butter is the preferred fat for rolling in, because of its flavor and melt-in-the-mouth quality. Special puff pastry shortening is also available. This shortening is much easier to work with than butter because it is not as hard when refrigerated and it doesn't soften and melt as easily as butter at warm temperatures. It is also less expensive than butter. However, puff pastry shortening can be unpleasant to eat because it tends to congeal and coat the inside of the mouth.

Skill at producing puff pastry requires careful attention to your instructor and diligent practice. Take special note of any alternative methods your instructor may present.

RECIPE 386   **Puff Pastry**

Ingredients	U.S.		Metric	Percentage
Bread flour	3 lb		1500 g	75%
Cake flour	1 lb		500 g	25%
Butter, soft		8 oz	250 g	12.5%
Salt		1 oz	30 g	1.5%
Cold water	2 lb	4 oz	1125 g	56%
Butter	4 lb		2000 g	100%
Bread flour (see note)		8 oz	250 g	12.5%
Yield:	11 lb	5 oz	5655 g	282%

Note: The purpose of the 8 oz (250 g) of bread flour is to absorb some of the moisture of the butter. Omit if puff paste shortening is used instead of butter.

Mixing:

1. Place the first quantities of flour and butter in a mixing bowl. With a paddle attachment, mix at low speed until well blended.
2. Dissolve the salt in the cold water.
3. Add the salted water to the flour and mix at low speed until a soft dough is formed. Do not overmix.
4. Remove the dough from the mixer and let rest in refrigerator for 20 minutes.
5. Cream the last quantities of butter and flour at low speed in the mixer until it is about the same consistency as the dough, neither too hard nor too soft.
6. Roll the butter into the dough following the procedure shown in Figure 29.1. Give the dough *four 4-folds* or *six 3-folds.*

FIGURE 29.1 Rolling-in procedure for puff pastry.
(a) Dust the bench lightly with flour. Roll out the dough about ½ inch (1–1½ cm) thick into a rectangle about three times as long as it is wide. Make the corners as square as possible.

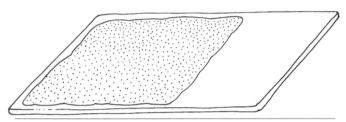

(b) Spot the butter *evenly* over two-thirds of the length of the dough as shown, leaving a 1-inch (2½-cm) margin at the edges. The butter should be about the same consistency as the dough. If it is too hard, it will puncture the dough and not spread evenly. If it is too soft, it will ooze out when rolled.

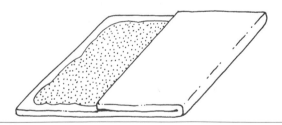

(c) Fold the third without fat over the center third.

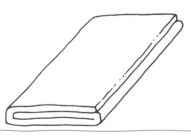

(d) Fold the remaining third on top. All ends and corners should be folded evenly and squarely. This procedure, enclosing the butter in the dough, does not count as one of the folds. The folding procedure starts with the next step.

(e) Turn dough 90 degrees on bench, so that the length becomes the width. This step must be taken before each rolling out so that the gluten is stretched in all directions, not just lengthwise. Failure to do this will result in products that deform or shrink unevenly when they bake.

(f) Roll dough out into a rectangle. Make sure the corners are square. Roll smoothly and evenly. Do not press down when rolling, or layers may stick together and the product will not rise properly.

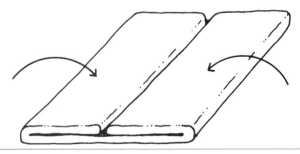

(g) Brush excess flour from top of dough. Fold the two ends to the center. Make sure corners are square and even. Again brush off excess flour.

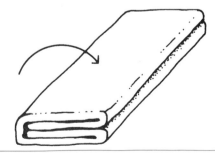

(h) Fold the dough in half like closing a book. You have now given the dough *one 4-fold*. Refrigerate the dough for 15 to 20 minutes to relax the gluten. Do not refrigerate it too long or the butter will become too hard. (If it does, let soften a few minutes at room temperature before proceeding.) Give the dough another *three 4-folds*, as in steps *f* to *h* . After another rest, the dough is ready to be rolled out and made up into the desired products. (Alternative method: Instead of giving the dough *four 4-folds*, you may give it *six 3-folds*.) See Figure 25.2 for the 3-fold method.

Blitz Puff Pastry

This product is much easier and quicker to make than classic puff dough. ("Blitz" is the German word for "lightning.") It does not rise nearly as high as true puff pastry, so it is not suitable for patty shells and other products where a high, light pastry is desirable. However, it bakes up very crisp and flaky and is perfectly suitable for napoleons and similar desserts that are layered with cream fillings.

Blitz puff paste, as you will see, is actually a very flaky pie dough that is rolled and folded like regular puff dough.

General Guidelines for Makeup of Puff Dough Products

1. Dough should be cool and firm when it is rolled and cut. If it is too soft, layers may stick together at the cuts, preventing proper rising.

2. Cut with straight, firm, even cuts.

3. Avoid touching the cut edges with the fingers, or layers may stick together.

4. For the same reason, avoid letting egg wash run down the edges.

5. Rest madeup products for 30 minutes in a cool place or in the refrigerator before baking. This relaxes the gluten and reduces shrinkage.

6. Trimmings may be pressed together, keeping the layers in the same direction. After being rolled out and given another 3-fold, they may be used again, although they will not rise as high.

Procedure for Making Turnovers (see Figure 29.2)

1. Roll out puff pastry dough ⅛ inch (3 mm) thick.

2. Cut into 4-inch (10-cm) squares. Wash the edges of each with water.

3. Portion desired filling into center of each square.

4. Fold diagonally and press edges together.

5. Puncture tops with a knife in two or three places to allow steam to escape. Rest 30 minutes.

6. Brush tops with egg wash, if desired, or brush with milk or water and sprinkle with sugar.

7. Bake at 400°F (200°C) until crisp and brown.

RECIPE 387 **Blitz Puff Pastry**

Ingredients	U.S.	Metric	Percentage
Bread flour	1 lb	500 g	50%
Pastry flour	1 lb	500 g	50%
Butter, slightly softened	2 lb	1000 g	100%
Salt	½ oz	15 g	
Cold water	1 lb	500 g	50%
Yield:	5 lb	2515 g	250%

Mixing:
1. Sift the two flours together into a mixing bowl.
2. Cut the butter into the flour as for pie dough, but leave the fat in very large lumps, 1 inch (2½ cm) across.
3. Dissolve the salt in the water.
4. Add the water to the flour/butter mixture. Mix until the water is absorbed.
5. Let the dough rest 15 minutes. Refrigerate if the bakeshop is warm.
6. Dust the bench with flour and roll out the dough into a rectangle. Give the dough *three 4-folds.*

Variation

Reduce the butter to 75% (1 lb 8 oz/750 g).

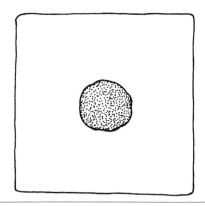

FIGURE 29.2 **Makeup of turnovers.**
(a) Cut the dough into 4-inch (10-cm) squares. Wash the edges with water and place filling in center of each square.

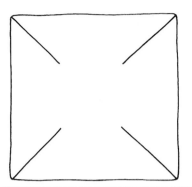

FIGURE 29.3 **Makeup of pinwheels.**
(a) Cut the dough into 5-inch (12-cm) squares. Wash centers with water. Cut diagonally from corners to 1 inch (2½ cm) from center.

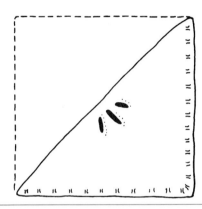

(b) Fold over diagonally and press the edges together. Puncture two or three steam holes in top.

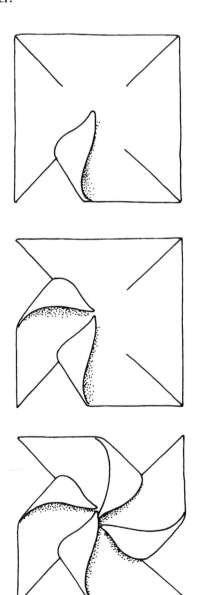

(b–d) Fold every other corner to center and press down. Fill center with fruit filling before or after baking.

Procedure for Making Pinwheels (see Figure 29.3)

1. Roll out puff dough ⅛ inch (3 mm) thick.

2. Cut into 5-inch (12-cm) squares.

3. Wash centers with water.

4. Cut diagonally from the corners to about 1 inch (2½ cm) from center.

5. Fold every other corner into the center and press in place.

6. Bake at 400°F (200°C).

7. Let cool. Spoon desired fruit filling into centers. Dust lightly with confectioners' sugar. (Pinwheels may also be filled before baking if the filling is thick and not likely to burn.)

Procedure for Making Patty Shells (see Figure 29.4)

1. Roll out puff dough ⅛ inch (3 mm) thick.

2. Roll out a second piece of dough ¼ inch (6 mm) thick.

3. Cut out the same number of circles from each piece of dough with a round 3-inch (7½-cm) cutter.

4. With a 2-inch (5-cm) cutter, cut out the centers of the *thick* circles.

5. Wash the thin circles with water or egg wash and place one of the rings on top of each. Wash the top carefully with egg wash (do not drip wash down the edges). Rest 30 minutes.

6. Place a sheet of greased parchment over the tops of the shells to prevent their toppling over while baking.

7. Bake at 400°F (200°C) until brown and crisp.

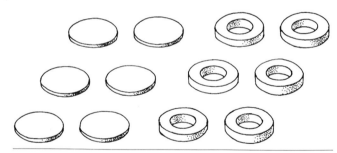

FIGURE 29.4 **Makeup of patty shells.**
(a) Roll out one sheet of puff dough ½ inch (3 mm) thick and another sheet ¼ inch (6 mm) thick. Cut out an equal number of 3-inch (7½-cm) circles from each. Cut out the centers of the thick circles with a 2-inch (5-cm) cutter.

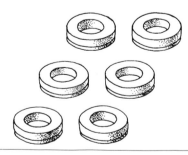

(b) Wash the thin circles with water or egg wash and place the thick circles on top.

Procedure for Making Cream Horns (see Figure 29.5)

1. Roll out puff dough into a sheet ⅛ inch (3 mm) thick and about 15 inches (38 cm) wide.

2. Cut out strips 1¼ inches (3 cm) wide by 15 inches (38 cm) long.

3. Wash the strips with water.

4. With the washed side out, roll the strips diagonally onto cream horn tubes, making a spiral. Overlap the edges by about ⅜ inch (1 cm). If you are using conical tubes, start at the small end.

5. Roll in granulated sugar and lay on baking sheets. The end of the dough strip should be on the bottom so that it will not pop up during baking. Rest 30 minutes.

6. Bake at 400°F (200°C) until brown and crisp.

7. Slip out tubes while still warm.

8. Just before service, fill the horns from both ends with whipped cream or pastry cream, using a pastry bag with a star tip. Dust with confectioners' sugar.

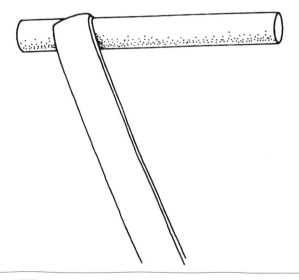

FIGURE 29.5 **Makeup of cream horns.**
(a) Roll out puff dough ⅛ inch (3 mm) thick, and cut into strips 1¼ inch (3 cm) wide and 15 inches (38 cm) long. Wash the strips with water, and press one end (washed side out) onto one end of cream horn tube as shown. *(Continues)*

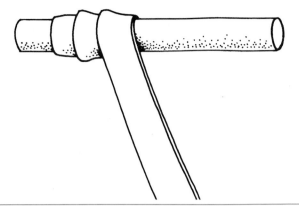

(b) Roll up the dough strip in a spiral by turning the tube. Overlap the edges by about ⅜ inch (1 cm). Do not stretch the dough.

(c) Roll up completely and press the end in place to seal.

Procedure for Making Napoleons

1. Roll puff dough into a very thin sheet about the size of a sheet pan. Blitz puff paste or rerolled trimmings may be used.

2. Place on sheet pan and let rest 30 minutes.

3. Dock with a fork to prevent blistering.

4. Bake at 400°F (200°C) until brown and crisp.

5. Trim the edges of the pastry sheet and cut with a serrated knife into equal strips 4 inches (10 cm) wide. Set the best one aside for the top layer. (If one of the strips breaks, don't be upset. It can be used as the middle layer.)

6. Spread one rectangle with pastry cream (p. 774) or with a mixture of pastry cream and whipped cream.

7. Top with second sheet of pastry.

8. Spread with another layer of pastry cream.

9. Place third pastry rectangle on top, flattest side up.

10. Ice top with fondant (p. 718).

11. To decorate, pipe four strips of chocolate fondant lengthwise on the white fondant. Draw a spatula or the back of a knife across the top in opposite directions, 1 inch apart, as shown in Figure 29.6.

12. Cut into strips 2 inches (5 cm) wide.

FIGURE 29.6 **Decorating napoleons.**
(a) Spread the top of the assembled napoleon with white fondant. With a paper cone, pipe on four strips of chocolate fondant.

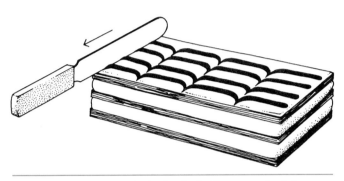

(b) Draw a spatula or the back of a knife across the icing at 2-inch (5-cm) intervals.

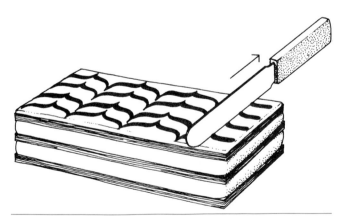

(c) Draw the spatula in the opposite direction in the center of these 2-inch intervals as shown.

(d) Cut the napoleon into strips 2 inches (5 cm) wide.

ECLAIR PASTE

Eclairs and cream puffs are made from a dough called eclair paste or choux paste. The French name *pâte à choux* (pot a shoo) means "cabbage paste," referring to the fact that cream puffs look like little cabbages.

Unlike puff pastry, eclair paste is extremely easy to make. The dough itself can be prepared in just a few minutes. This is fortunate, because for best baking results the dough should not be prepared ahead of time.

In principle, eclair paste is similar to popover batter, even though one is a thick dough and the other a thin batter. Both products are leavened by steam, which expands the product rapidly and forms large holes in the center of the item. The heat of the oven then coagulates the gluten and egg proteins to set the structure and make a firm product. A strong flour is necessary for sufficient structure.

Eclair paste must be firm enough to hold its shape when piped from a pastry bag. Occasionally you may find a formula that produces too slack a dough. Correct such a formula by reducing the water or milk slightly.

Proper baking temperatures are important. Start at a high temperature (425°F to 475°F/215°C to 245°C) for the first 10 minutes to develop steam. Then reduce the heat to 375°F to 425°F (190°C to 215°C) to finish baking and set the structure. The products must be firm and dry before being removed from the oven. If they are removed too soon or cooled too quickly, they may collapse. Some bakers like to leave them in a turned off oven with the door ajar. However, if the oven must be heated again for other products, this may not be the best idea, especially in these times of high energy costs. It may be better to bake the products thoroughly, remove them carefully from the oven, and let them cool slowly in a warm place.

RECIPE 388   **Eclair Paste**

Ingredients	U.S.	Metric	Percentage
Water *or* milk *or* half water and half milk	1 lb	500 g	133%
Butter or regular shortening	8 oz	250 g	67%
Salt	1 tsp	5 mL	1.5%
Bread flour	12 oz	375 g	100%
Eggs	1 lb 4 oz	625 g	167%
Yield:	3 lb 8 oz	1755 g	468%

Note: If a sweeter product is desired, add ½ oz (15 g) sugar to the liquid, fat, and salt.

Mixing:
1. Combine liquid, butter, and salt in a heavy saucepan and bring to a boil.
2. Remove pan from heat and add the flour all at once. Stir quickly.
3. Return the pan to moderate heat and stir vigorously until the dough forms a ball and pulls away from the sides of the pan.
4. Transfer the dough to the bowl of a mixer. Or if you wish to mix by hand, leave it in the saucepan.
5. With the paddle attachment, mix at low speed until the dough has cooled slightly. It should be about 140°F (60°C), still very warm, but not too hot to touch.
6. At medium speed, beat in the eggs a little at a time. Add no more than a fourth of the eggs at once, and wait until they are completely absorbed before adding the remainder. When all the eggs are absorbed, the paste is ready to use.

Procedure for Making Cream Puffs

1. Line sheet pans with silicone paper.

2. Fit a large pastry bag with a plain tube. Fill the bag with the choux paste.

3. Pipe out round mounds of dough about 1½ inches (4 cm) in diameter onto the lined baking sheets. Or, if preferred, dough may be dropped from a spoon.

4. Bake at 425°F (215°C) for 10 minutes. Lower heat to 375°F (190°C) until well browned and very crisp.

5. Remove from oven and cool slowly in a warm place.

6. When cool, cut a slice from the top of each puff. Fill with whipped cream, pastry cream (p. 774), or desired filling, using a pastry bag with a star tube.

7. Replace the tops and dust with confectioners' sugar.

8. Fill the puffs as close to service as possible. If cream-filled puffs must be held, keep refrigerated.

9. Unfilled and uncut puffs, if they are thoroughly dry, may be held in plastic bags in the refrigerator for a week. Recrisp in oven for a few minutes before use.

Procedure for Making Eclairs

1. Proceed as for cream puffs, except pipe the dough out into strips about ¾ inch (2 cm) wide and 3 to 4 inches (8 to 10 cm) long. Bake as for cream puffs.

2. Fill baked, cooled eclair shells with pastry cream. Two methods may be used:

   a. Make a small hole in one end of the shell and fill with a pastry bag or a doughnut filling pump.

   b. Cut a slice lengthwise from the top and fill with a pastry bag.

3. Dip the tops of the eclairs in chocolate fondant (p. 719).

4. For service and holding, see cream puffs.

Variation: Frozen Eclairs or Profiteroles

1. Fill eclairs or small cream puffs (profiteroles) with ice cream. Keep frozen until service.

2. At service time, top with chocolate syrup.

Procedure for Making French Crullers or French Doughnuts

1. Cut sheets of parchment paper to the same width as your deep fryer.

2. Using a pastry bag with a star tube, pipe choux paste onto the parchment into circles (doughnut shapes) about 2 inches (5 cm) across.

3. Slide the paper with the paste into deep fryer heated to 375°F (190°C). Remove the paper as the doughnuts release and float free.

4. Fry the doughnuts on both sides until golden brown. French doughnuts must be completely fried or they may collapse when cooling. Remove and drain on absorbent paper.

5. When cooled, drizzle fondant icing over the tops.

MERINGUES

Meringues are beaten egg whites sweetened with sugar. Their most frequent use in this country is for pie toppings and cake icings (known as boiled icing). They are also used to give volume and lightness to buttercream icings and to such preparations as dessert soufflés.

Another excellent use for meringues is to bake them in a slow oven until crisp. In this form, they can be used in place of cake layers or pastry shells to make very light, elegant desserts. Chopped nuts may be folded into meringue before forming and baking, to make these desserts more flavorful.

Basic rules for beating egg whites are discussed in Chapter 21, page 554. Please review this section before attempting to make any of the following preparations. We repeat one rule here because it is so important:

Make sure that all equipment is free of any trace of fat or grease, and that the egg whites have no trace of yolk in them. Even a small trace of fat will prevent the whites from foaming properly.

Soft meringues, those used for pie toppings, may be made with as little as 1 pound of sugar per pound of egg whites. *Hard meringues,* those which are baked until crisp, are made with up to twice as much sugar as egg whites.

Basic Meringues

The stiffness to which meringues are beaten may vary, as long as they are not overbeaten until they are too stiff and dry. For most purposes, they are beaten until they form stiff or nearly stiff, moist peaks.

1. *Common meringue* is made from egg whites at room temperature, beaten with sugar. It is the easiest to make, and it is reasonably stable due to the high percentage of sugar.

2. *Swiss meringue* is made from egg whites and sugar that are warmed over a double boiler while beat-

ing. This warming gives the meringue better volume and stability.

3. *Italian meringue* is made by beating a hot sugar syrup into the egg whites. This meringue is the most stable of the three because the egg whites are actually cooked by the heat of the syrup. When flavored with vanilla, this meringue is also known as boiled icing. It is also used in meringue-type buttercream icings.

RECIPE 389   **Meringue**

	Common Meringue	*Swiss Meringue*	*Italian Meringue*
Egg whites	1 lb/500 g	1 lb/500 g	1 lb/500 g
Sugar	2 lb/1 kg	2 lb/1 kg	2 lb/1 kg
Water	—	—	8 oz/250 mL

Note: For soft meringues to top pies, use half the amount of sugar.

Procedure for Making Common Meringue

1. With the whip attachment, beat the egg whites at high speed until they form soft peaks.

2. Gradually add the sugar with the machine running.

3. Continue to beat until the meringue forms stiff but moist peaks.

Procedure for Making Swiss Meringue

1. Place the egg whites and sugar in a stainless steel bowl or the top of a double boiler. Beat with a wire whip over hot water until the mixture is warm (about 120°F/50°C).

2. Transfer the mixture to the bowl of a mixing machine and whip at high speed until stiff peaks form.

Procedure for Making Italian Meringue

1. Heat the sugar and water in a saucepan until the sugar dissolves and the mixture boils. Boil until a candy thermometer placed in the mixture registers 240°F (115°C).

2. While the syrup is cooking, beat the egg whites in a mixing machine until they form soft peaks.

3. With the machine running, very slowly beat in the hot syrup.

4. Continue beating until the meringue forms firm peaks.

Meringue Desserts

Procedure for Making Pie Topping

1. Make Common Meringue or Swiss Meringue using equal parts sugar and egg whites. Beat until just stiff.

2. Spread a generous amount (2 to 3 cups/500 to 700 mL) of meringue on still-warm pies. Mound it slightly and be sure to attach it to the edge of the crust all around. If this is not done, the meringue may slide around on the finished pie. Leave the meringue in ripples or peaks.

3. Bake at 400°F (200°C) until the surface is attractively browned.

4. Remove from oven and cool.

Procedure for Making Baked Meringue Shells

1. Beat Common or Swiss Meringue until stiff.

2. Using a pastry bag or a spoon, form the meringue into small nest shapes on a parchment-lined baking sheet.

3. Bake at 200°F to 225°F (about 100°C) until crisp but not browned. This will take 1 to 3 hours.

4. Cool the shells and remove from the parchment. Be careful, because they may be very fragile.

5. Use in place of pastry shells for fruit tarts, fill with whipped cream and fresh strawberries or raspberries, or place a scoop of ice cream in shell and garnish with chocolate or raspberry sauce. Crisp meringues with ice cream make a dessert called *meringue glacée* (glah say).

Procedure for Making Japonaise Meringues

These flavorful meringue layers (pronounced zhah-po-nez) are used like cake layers. They may be filled and iced with light buttercreams, chocolate mousse, whipped cream, or similar light icings and creams.

1. Prepare 1 recipe (1 lb egg whites plus 2 lb sugar) Swiss Meringue.

2. Quickly but carefully, fold in 1 lb (500 g) finely chopped hazelnuts.

3. With a pastry bag or spatula, form circles of desired size, and about ½ inch (1½ cm) thick, on parchment-lined sheet pans.

4. Bake as for meringue shells.

Procedure for Making Baked Alaska

1. Pack softened ice cream into a dome-shaped mold of desired size. Freeze solid.

2. Prepare a layer of sponge cake the same size as the flat side of the mold and about ½ inch (1½ cm) thick.

3. Unmold the frozen ice cream onto the cake layer, so that the cake forms a base for the ice cream.

4. With a spatula, cover the entire dessert with a thick layer of meringue. If desired, decorate with more meringue forced from a pastry bag.

5. Bake at 450°F (230°C) until meringue is golden brown.

6. Serve immediately.

FRUIT DESSERTS

Fruit desserts are included here because many of them are very similar to pies or pie fillings. Special American favorites include cobblers, which are very much like fruit pies made in large baking pans, without bottom crusts; crisps, which are like cobblers, but with brown-sugar streusel topping instead of a pastry crust; and bettys, which have alternate layers of rich cake crumbs and fruit.

Also, don't overlook fresh fruits for dessert, served plain, lightly sweetened, or with cream.

RECIPE 390   Fruit Cobbler

Yield: 1 pan 12 × 20 inches (30 × 50 cm)   **Portions:** 48   **Portion size:** about 5 oz (150 g)

U.S.	Metric	Ingredients	Procedure
12–15 lb	5.5–7 kg	Fruit pie filling (apple, cherry, blueberry, peach, etc.)	1. Place fruit filling in a 12 × 20-inch (30 × 50-cm) bake pan (see note).
2 lb	1 kg	Flaky pie pastry	2. Roll out the pastry in a rectangle to fit the top of the bake pan. Place on top of filling and seal edges to side of pan. Pierce small holes in the pastry to allow steam to escape.
			3. Bake at 425°F (220°C) about 30 minutes, until top is browned.
			4. Cut the dessert 6 × 8 to make 48 portions. Serve warm or cold.

Note: If possible, use stainless steel instead of aluminum pans. The acid of the fruit will react with aluminum and create an undesirable flavor.

RECIPE 391   Apple Betty

Yield: 1 pan 12 × 20 inches (30 × 50 cm)   **Portions:** 48   **Portion size:** 4 oz (125 g)

U.S.	Metric	Ingredients	Procedure
8 lb EP	4 kg EP	Apples, peeled and sliced	1. Combine the apples, sugar, salt, nutmeg, lemon zest, and lemon juice in a bowl. Toss gently until well mixed.
1 lb 8 oz	750 g	Sugar	
1½ tsp	7 mL	Salt	
1 tsp	5 mL	Nutmeg	
1 tbsp	15 mL	Grated lemon zest	
2 oz	60 mL	Lemon juice	
2 lb	1 kg	Yellow or white cake crumbs	2. Place one-third of the apple mixture in an even layer in a well-buttered 12 × 20-inch (30 × 50-cm) bake pan.
8 oz	250 g	Melted butter	3. Top with one-third of the cake crumbs.
			4. Continue until all the apples and crumbs have been used. You will have 3 layers of fruit and 3 layers of crumbs.
			5. Pour the melted butter evenly over the top.
			6. Bake at 350°F (175°C) about 1 hour, until fruit is tender.

RECIPE 392   Apple Crisp

Yield: 1 pan 12 × 20 inches (30 × 50 cm)   **Portions:** 48   **Portion size:** 4 oz (125 g)

U.S.	Metric	Ingredients	Procedure
8 lb EP	4 kg EP	Apples, peeled and sliced	1. Toss the sliced apples gently with the sugar and lemon juice.
4 oz	125 g	Sugar	2. Spread the apples evenly in a 12 × 20-inch (30 × 50-cm) bake pan (see note).
2 oz	60 mL	Lemon juice	
1 lb	500 g	Butter	3. Rub the butter, sugar, cinnamon, and flour together until well blended and crumbly.
1 lb 8 oz	750 g	Brown sugar	
2 tsp	10 mL	Cinnamon	4. Sprinkle evenly over the apples.
1 lb 8 oz	750 g	Pastry flour	5. Bake at 350°F (175°C) about 45 minutes, until top is browned and apples are tender.

Note: If possible, use stainless steel instead of aluminum pans. The acid of the fruit will react with aluminum and create an undesirable flavor.

Variations

392A. Peach, Cherry, or Rhubarb Crisp: Substitute the indicated fruit for the apples. If rhubarb is used, increase the sugar in step 1 to 12 oz (350 g).

RECIPE 393   Poached Pears

Portions: 24   **Portion size:** 2 pear halves

U.S.	Metric	Ingredients	Procedure
2 qt 3 lb 4 tsp	2 L 1.5 kg 20 mL	Water Sugar Vanilla	1. Combine the water and sugar in a trunnion kettle or large sauce pot. Bring to a boil, stirring until the sugar is dissolved. 2. Remove from heat and add the vanilla.
24	24	Pears	3. Peel the pears. Cut them in half and remove the cores with a melon ball cutter. 4. Add the pears to the syrup and simmer very slowly until just tender. 5. Let the pears cool in the syrup. When cool, refrigerate in the syrup until needed for service.

Variations

393A. Pears in Wine: Substitute red or white table wine for the water. Omit vanilla. Add one sliced lemon to the syrup. Peel the pears but leave them whole.

393B. Poached Peaches: Substitute peaches for pears in basic recipe.

393C. Peaches in Wine: Substitute peaches for pears in recipe for Pears in Wine.

RECIPE 394   Raspberry or Cherry Gratin

Portions: 1

U.S.	Metric	Ingredients	Procedure
1 3 oz	1 90 g	Genoise layer (see step 2) Raspberries or sweet, pitted cherries	1. Select a shallow gratin dish or other heat-proof dish large enough to hold the fruit in a shallow layer. 2. Cut a thin slice of genoise (about ⅜ inch or 1 cm thick) to cover the bottom of the dish. 3. Arrange the fruit on top of the genoise.
2 oz 1 oz to taste	60 g 30 g to taste	Pastry cream Whipped cream Optional flavoring: kirsch, orange liqueur, or raspberry or cherry brandy	4. Combine the pastry cream, whipped cream, and flavoring. Spread the mixture over the fruit to cover completely.
¼ oz ¼ oz	7 g 7 g	Sliced almonds Melted butter Confectioners' sugar	5. Mix the almonds and butter and sprinkle over the pastry cream. Dredge the top heavily with confectioners' sugar. 6. Place under a broiler or in the top of a hot oven for a few minutes to brown the top. Serve hot.

TERMS FOR REVIEW

flaky pie dough	chiffon pie	blitz puff pastry	hard meringue
mealy pie dough	instant starch	napoleon	common meringue
crumb crust	cooked juice method	eclair paste	Swiss meringue
short dough	cooked fruit method	pâte à choux	Italian meringue
fruit pie	puff pastry	profiteroles	meringue glacée
soft pie	4-fold	soft meringue	Baked Alaska
cream pie			

QUESTIONS FOR DISCUSSION

1. Discuss the various factors that affect tenderness, toughness, and flakiness in pie dough. Why should emulsified shortening not be used for pie dough?

2. What kind of crust or crusts would you use for a pumpkin pie? An apple pie? A banana cream pie?

3. What would happen to a flaky pie dough if you mixed it too long before adding the water? After adding the water?

4. How can you prevent shrinkage when baking pie shells?

5. What are the remedies for soggy or undercooked bottom pie crusts?

6. What starch would you use to thicken apple pie filling? Chocolate pie filling? Lemon pie filling? Peach pie filling?

7. Why is lemon juice added to lemon pie filling after the starch has thickened the water? Wouldn't this thin out the filling?

8. Why is it important to bake cream puffs and eclairs thoroughly and to cool them slowly?

9. Briefly describe the difference between common, Swiss, and Italian meringues.

CHAPTER 30

CREAMS, CUSTARDS, PUDDINGS, FROZEN DESSERTS, AND SAUCES

A quick glance at this last chapter may give you the impression that you will be overwhelmed with a great many recipes and techniques within a few pages. Among the subjects covered are custard sauces, pastry cream, puddings, custards, mousses, bavarians, soufflés, ice cream, and dessert sauces.

It's all much simpler than it seems. Once you have learned three basic preparations—vanilla custard sauce, pastry cream, and baked custard—you will have learned most of the rest. Vanilla custard sauce, also called crème anglaise (krem awng-glezz) or English cream, is the basis for bavarians, ice cream, and some dessert sauces. Pastry cream, with a variety of flavorings, is also used for pie fillings and puddings and is the basis for some soufflés. Many baked puddings are baked custard with added starch or fruit ingredients.

There seems little point in giving you recipes for cream pie fillings in the pie section, a recipe for pastry cream filling for napoleons in the puff pastry section, and recipes for boiled puddings in the pudding section, and never tell you that they are all basically the same preparation. You are not just learning a collection of unrelated recipes; you are learning to cook and to understand what you are cooking.

After reading this chapter, you should be able to

1. Cook sugar syrups to various stages of hardness.
2. Prepare vanilla custard sauce, pastry cream, and baked custard.
3. Prepare starch-thickened puddings and baked puddings.
4. Prepare bavarians, chiffons, mousses, and dessert soufflés.
5. Assemble frozen desserts.
6. Prepare dessert sauces.

SUGAR COOKING

Understanding sugar cooking is important in the preparation of desserts and confections because sugar syrups of various strengths are often required (see, for example, Italian Meringue, p. 765).

Basic Principles

The principle of sugar cooking is fairly simple: a solution of syrup of sugar and water is boiled to evaporate part of the water. As the water is boiled off, the temperature of the syrup gradually rises. When all the water has evaporated, what you have left is melted sugar. The sugar will then begin to *caramelize* or turn brown and change flavor. If heating continues, the sugar will continue to darken and then burn.

A syrup cooked to a high temperature will be harder when it is cooled than will a syrup cooked to a lower temperature. For example, a syrup cooked to 240°F (115°C) will form a soft ball when cooled. A syrup cooked to 300°F (150°C) will be hard and brittle when cooled.

One pint (one pound) of water is enough to dissolve and cook 3 to 4 lb of sugar. There is no point in adding more water than is necessary, because you just have to boil it off again.

Simple Syrup

Simple syrup is a solution of equal weights of sugar and water. For example, combine 1 pt of water and 1 lb of granulated sugar in a saucepan, stir, and bring to a boil to dissolve the sugar. Cool the syrup.

Dessert syrup is a flavored simple syrup used to moisten and flavor some cakes (see p. 709). (Many chefs use 2 or 3 parts water to 1 part sugar for a less sweet syrup.) Flavorings may be extracts, such as vanilla, or liquors, such as rum or kirsch. Add flavorings after the syrup has cooled, because flavor may be lost if they are added to hot syrup. Syrups may also be flavored by boiling them with lemon or orange rind.

Crystallization

Graininess is a common fault in many candies and desserts. Graininess results when cooked sugar crystallizes or turns to tiny sugar crystals rather than staying dissolved in the syrup. If even one sugar crystal comes in contact with a cooked syrup, it can start a chain reaction that turns the whole thing into a mass of sugar crystals.

To avoid crystallization during the first stages of boiling, use one of the following techniques.

TABLE 30.1 Stages of Doneness in Sugar Cooking

Stage	Temperature °F	Temperature °C
Thread	230	110
Soft ball	240	115
Firm ball	245	118
Hard ball	250–260	122–127
Small crack	265–270	130–132
Crack	275–280	135–138
Hard crack	290–310	143–155
Caramel	320–340	160–170

1. Wash down the sides of the saucepan with a brush dipped in water. This will remove crystals that may "seed" the whole batch.

2. When first bringing the syrup to a boil, cover the pan and boil for several minutes. Condensed steam will wash down the sides of the pan. Uncover and finish cooking without stirring.

Sometimes an acid such as cream of tartar is added to a syrup before cooking. Acids change some of the sugar to *invert sugar*, which resists crystallizing. Corn syrup is sometimes added for the same reason.

Stages of Sugar Cooking

Testing the temperature with a candy thermometer is the most accurate way to determine the desired doneness of a syrup.

In the old days, syrups were tested by dropping a little syrup into a bowl of cold water and checking the hardness of the cooled sugar. The stages of doneness were given names that described their hardness.

Table 30.1 lists these stages of sugar cooking.

BASIC CUSTARDS AND CREAMS

The three preparations presented in this section are some of the most basic and useful preparations in the bakeshop. All three can be classified as custards, because they consist of a liquid thickened by coagulation of eggs.

Vanilla custard sauce, also known as crème anglaise, is a stirred custard. It consists of milk, sugar, and egg yolks stirred over very low heat until lightly thickened, and flavored with vanilla.

Pastry cream contains starch thickeners as well as eggs, resulting in a much thicker and more stable product. It is used as a cake and pastry filling, as a filling for cream pies, and as a pudding. With more liquid added, it is used as a custard sauce.

Baked custard, like vanilla custard sauce, also consists of milk, sugar, eggs, and flavoring (usually whole eggs are used for greater thickening power). But unlike the sauce, it is baked rather than stirred over heat, so that it sets and becomes firm. Baked custard is used as a pie filling, as a dessert by itself, and as a basis for many baked puddings.

All of these preparations are subject to a wide range of variations. Because all of these recipes are based on eggs, it would be helpful for you to review the basic egg cooking principles discussed in Chapter 21.

Vanilla Custard Sauce

The following recipe gives the method for preparing custard sauce or crème anglaise. Special care is necessary in preparing this sauce, because the eggs can curdle very easily if overcooked. The following guidelines will help you be successful.

1. Use clean, sanitized equipment, and follow strict sanitation procedures. Egg mixtures can easily be contaminated by bacteria that cause food poisoning.

2. Heat the milk to scalding (just below simmering) in a double boiler before combining with the egg yolks. This makes the final cooking much shorter.

3. *Slowly* beat the hot milk into the beaten eggs and sugar. This raises the temperature of the eggs gradually and helps prevent curdling. (The same principle is used in tempering a cream/egg yolk liaison in sauce making.)

4. Heat the mixture slowly in a double boiler, stirring constantly, in order to prevent curdling.

RECIPE 395 **Vanilla Custard Sauce (Crème Anglaise)**

Yield: about 2½ pt (1¼ L)

U.S.	Metric	Ingredients	Procedure
12 8 oz	12 250 g	Egg yolks Sugar	1. Review the guidelines for preparing vanilla custard sauce preceding this recipe. 2. Combine the egg yolks and sugar in the bowl of a mixer. Beat with the whip attachment until thick and light.
1 qt	1 L	Milk	3. Scald the milk in a double boiler. 4. With the mixer running at low speed, very gradually pour the scalded milk into the egg yolk mixture. 5. Pour the mixture back into the double boiler. Heat it slowly, stirring constantly, until it thickens enough to coat the back of a spoon (or until it reaches 185°F/85°C).
1 tbsp	15 mL	Vanilla	6. Immediately remove the top part of the double boiler from the heat and set it in a pan of cool water. Stir in the vanilla. Stir the sauce occasionally as it cools.

Variation

395A. Chocolate Custard Sauce: Melt 6 oz (175 g) sweetened chocolate. Stir into the Custard Sauce while it is still warm (not hot).

5. To test for doneness, two methods are available. Keep in mind that this is a very light sauce, so you can't expect a lot of thickening.

   a. Check the temperature with a thermometer. When it reaches 185°F (85°C), the sauce is cooked. Never let the temperature go above 190°F (87°C).

   b. When the mixture lightly coats the back of a spoon instead of running off like milk, the sauce is cooked.

6. *Immediately* cool the sauce by setting the pan or bowl in ice water. Stir occasionally to cool it evenly.

7. If the sauce accidentally curdles, it is sometimes possible to save it. Immediately stir in an ounce or two of cold milk, transfer the sauce to a blender, and blend at high speed.

Pastry Cream

Although it requires more ingredients and steps, pastry cream is easier to make than custard because it is less likely to curdle. Pastry cream contains a starch thickening agent that stabilizes the eggs. It can actually be boiled without curdling. In fact, it must be brought to a boil, or the starch will not cook completely and the cream will have a raw, starchy taste.

Strict observance of all sanitation rules is essential when preparing pastry cream, because of the danger of bacterial contamination. Use clean, sanitized equipment. Do not put your fingers in the cream, and do not taste except with a clean spoon. Chill the finished cream rapidly in shallow pans. Keep the cream and all cream-filled products refrigerated at all times.

The procedure for preparing pastry cream is given in the following recipe. Note that the basic steps are similar to those for custard sauce. In this case, however, a starch is mixed with the eggs and half the sugar to make a smooth paste. (In some recipes with lower egg content, it is necessary to add a little cold milk to provide enough liquid to make a paste.) Meanwhile, the milk is scalded with the other half of the sugar (the sugar helps protect the milk from scorching on the bottom of the pan).

The egg mixture is then tempered with some of the hot milk and then returned to the kettle and brought to a boil. Some chefs prefer to add the cold paste gradually to the hot milk, but the tempering procedure given here seems to give better protection against lumping and curdling.

Pastry Cream Variations

Cream pie fillings and puddings are actually pastry cream, flavored with various ingredients.

Cornstarch should be used as the thickening agent when the cream is to be used as a pie filling, so

---

RECIPE 396 Vanilla Pastry Cream

Yield: about 2¼ qt (2¼ L)

U.S.	Metric	Ingredients	Procedure
2 qt 8 oz	2 L 250 g	Milk Sugar	1. In a heavy saucepan or trunnion kettle, dissolve the sugar in the milk and bring just to a boil.
8 4 5 oz 8 oz	8 4 150 g 250 g	Egg yolks Whole eggs Cornstarch Sugar	2. With a whip, beat the egg yolks and whole eggs in a stainless steel bowl. 3. Sift the starch and sugar into the egg. Beat with the whip until perfectly smooth. 4. Temper the egg mixture by slowly beating in the hot milk in a thin stream. 5. Return the mixture to the heat and bring to a boil, stirring constantly.
4 oz 1 oz	125 g 30 g	Butter Vanilla	6. When the mixture comes to a boil and thickens, remove from the heat. 7. Stir in the butter and vanilla. Mix until the butter is melted and completely blended in.

RECIPE 396   **Vanilla Pastry Cream**   *(Continued)*

U.S.	Metric	Ingredients	Procedure
			8. Pour out into a clean, sanitized hotel pan or other shallow pan. Dust lightly with sugar and cover with waxed paper to keep a crust from forming. Cool and chill as quickly as possible.
			9. For filling pastries such as eclairs and napoleons, whip the chilled pastry cream until smooth before using.

Variations

For a lighter pastry cream filling, fold whipped heavy cream into the chilled pastry cream. Quantities may be varied to taste. For every 2 qt (2 L) pastry cream, whip 1–2 cups (250–500 mL) heavy cream.

396A. Chocolate Pastry Cream: Melt together 4 oz (125 g) sweetened chocolate and 4 oz (125 g) unsweetened chocolate. Stir into the hot pastry cream.

396B. Coffee Pastry Cream: Add 4 tbsp (60 mL) instant coffee powder to the milk in step 1.

Cream Pie Fillings [quantities for four 8-inch (20-cm) pies]

396C. Vanilla Cream Pie Filling: This is the same as Vanilla Pastry Cream. Fill prebaked pie shells with cooled but not chilled filling.

396D. Coconut Cream Pie Filling: Add 8 oz (250 g) toasted unsweetened coconut to Vanilla Pastry Cream.

396E. Banana Cream Pie Filling: Using vanilla cream filling, pour half the filling into the pie shells, cover with sliced bananas, and fill with remaining filling. (Bananas may be dipped in lemon juice to help prevent browning.)

396F. Chocolate Cream Pie Filling I: This is the same as Chocolate Pastry Cream, above.

396G. Chocolate Cream Pie Filling II: In step 1, use only 3½ pt (1.75 L) milk. Add 3 oz (90 g) cocoa to dry ingredients (sugar and cornstarch) in basic Vanilla Pastry Cream recipe. Add 8 oz (250 mL) cold milk to the eggs.

396H. Butterscotch Cream Pie Filling: Combine 2 lb (900 g) brown sugar and 10 oz (300 g) butter in a saucepan over low heat. Heat and stir until butter is melted and ingredients are blended. Omit all the sugar from the basic Pastry Cream recipe (steps 1 and 3). Increase the starch to 6 oz (175 g). As the mixture is nearing a boil in step 5, gradually stir in the brown sugar mixture. Finish as in basic recipe.

396I. Lemon Pie Filling: Follow the procedure for Vanilla Pastry Cream, but make the following ingredient adjustments:

1. Use water instead of milk.
2. Increase sugar in step 1 to 1 lb (450 g).
3. Increase the cornstarch to 6 oz (175 g).
4. Add the grated zest of 2 lemons to the egg mixture.
5. Add 8 oz (250 mL) lemon juice to the finished, hot cream *instead of* the vanilla.

Cream Puddings

396J. Vanilla Pudding
396K. Coconut Pudding
396L. Banana Cream Pudding
396M. Chocolate Pudding I and II
396N. Butterscotch Pudding

For each of these puddings, prepare the corresponding pie filling but use only *half* the cornstarch.

that the cut slices will hold their shape. For other uses either cornstarch or flour may be used. Remember that twice as much flour as cornstarch is required for the same thickening power. Other variations are possible, as you will see in the recipes. Sometimes whipped cream is folded into cold pastry cream to lighten it and make it creamier.

Lemon pie filling is also a variation of pastry cream. It is made with water instead of milk, and it is flavored with lemon juice and grated lemon rind.

Baked Custard

Baked custard is a mixture of eggs, milk, sugar, and flavorings, which is baked until the eggs coagulate and the custard is set. A good custard holds a clean, sharp edge when cut.

The following recipe gives the procedure for making baked custard. Note these points in particular:

1. Scald the milk before beating it slowly into the eggs. This reduces cooking time and helps the product cook more evenly.

2. Remove any foam that would mar the appearance of the finished product.

3. Bake at 325°F (165°C). High temperatures increase the risk of overcooking and curdling.

4. Bake in a water bath, so that the outside edges are not overcooked before the inside is set.

5. To test for doneness, insert a thin-bladed knife about an inch or two from the center. If it comes out clean, the custard is done. The center may not be completely set, but it will continue to cook in its own heat after removal from the oven.

RECIPE 397 **Baked Custard**

Portions: 24　　　　　　　　　　　　　　　　　　　**Portion size:** 5 oz (150 g)

U.S.	Metric	Ingredients	Procedure
2 lb	1 kg	Eggs	1. Combine the eggs, sugar, salt, and vanilla in a mixing bowl. Mix until thoroughly blended, but do not whip.
1 lb	500 g	Sugar	
1 tsp	5 mL	Salt	
1 oz	30 mL	Vanilla	
2½ qt	2.5 L	Milk	2. Scald the milk in a double boiler or in a saucepan over low heat.
			3. Gradually pour the milk into the egg mixture, while stirring constantly.
			4. Skim off all foam from the surface of the liquid.
			5. Arrange custard cups in a shallow bake pan. (Butter the insides of the cups if the custards are to be unmolded.)
			6. Carefully pour the custard mixture into the cups. If any more bubbles form during this step, skim them off.
			7. Set the bake pan on the oven shelf. Pour enough hot water into the pan around the cups so that the level of the water is about as high as the level of the custard mixture.
			8. Bake at 325°F (165°C) until set, about 45 minutes.
			9. Carefully remove from the oven and cool. Store covered in refrigerator.

Variation

397A. *Crème Caramel:* Cook 1½ lb (750 g) sugar and 4 oz (125 g) water until it caramelizes (see the section on sugar cooking at the beginning of this chapter). Line the bottoms of the custard cups with this hot caramel. (Be sure the cups are clean and dry.) Fill with custard and bake as in basic recipe.

PUDDINGS

It is difficult to give a definition of pudding that includes everything by that name. The term is used for such different dishes as chocolate pudding, blood sausages (blood puddings), and steak-and-kidney pudding. In this chapter, however, we are considering only popular American dessert puddings.

Two kinds of puddings, starch thickened and baked, are the most frequently prepared in food service kitchens. These are the types we will discuss here. A third type, steamed pudding, is less often served, and then mainly in cold weather, because steamed puddings are usually rather heavy and filling.

Starch-thickened Puddings

These are also called boiled puddings, because they are boiled in order to cook the starch that thickens them.

1.   *Cornstarch pudding or blanc mange.*

Cornstarch pudding consists of milk, sugar, and flavorings, thickened with cornstarch (or sometimes another starch). If enough cornstarch is used, the hot mixture may be poured into molds, chilled, and unmolded for service.

2.   *Cream puddings.*

Cream puddings, as you learned in the previous section, are the same as pastry cream. Puddings are usually made with less starch, however, and may contain any of several flavoring ingredients, such as coconut or chocolate. Butterscotch pudding is given its flavor by using brown sugar instead of white sugar.

If you will look again at the recipe for pastry cream, you will see that the only difference between cornstarch puddings and cream puddings is that the latter contain eggs. In fact, cream puddings may be made by stirring hot cornstarch pudding into beaten eggs and then heating the entire mixture to just below the simmer. Care must be taken to avoid curdling the eggs if this method is used.

A basic recipe for cornstarch pudding follows. Recipes for cream puddings are included among the variations following the recipe for Vanilla Pastry Cream, page 775.

RECIPE 398   **Blanc Mange English Style**

Portions: 24   **Portion size:** 4 oz (125 g)

U.S.	Metric	Ingredients	Procedure
2 qt 12 oz ½ tsp	2 L 375 g 2 mL	Milk Sugar Salt	1. Combine the milk, sugar, and salt in a heavy saucepan and bring to a simmer.
8 oz 1 pt	250 g 500 mL	Cornstarch Milk, cold	2. Mix the cornstarch and cold milk until perfectly smooth. 3. Pouring in a thin stream, add about 1 cup (250 mL) of the hot milk to the cornstarch mixture. 4. Stir this mixture back into the hot milk. 5. Stir over low heat until the mixture thickens and comes to a boil.
1 tbsp	15 mL	Almond or vanilla extract	6. Remove from heat and add desired flavoring. 7. Pour into half-cup molds. Cool and then chill. Unmold for service.

Note: French blanc mange is very different from the English style. The French style is made with almond milk and gelatin.

Variations

Blanc mange or cornstarch pudding may be flavored in any way that cream puddings are. See the variations following the Vanilla Pastry Cream Recipe.

Baked Puddings

Baked puddings are custards that contain additional ingredients, usually in large quantities. Bread pudding, for example, is made by pouring a custard mixture over pieces of bread in a pan and baking it in the oven. Rice pudding is another popular item, made of cooked rice and custard.

The procedure for making baked puddings is the same as for making baked custard. A water bath may not be necessary if the starch content of the pudding is high.

Soft pie fillings, such as pumpkin, could also be considered as baked puddings.

RECIPE 399 **Rice Pudding**

| | | | Portions: 25 | Portion size: 5 oz (150 g) |

U.S.	Metric	Ingredients	Procedure
1 lb	450 g	Rice (medium or long grain)	1. Wash the rice well. Drain.
3 qt	3 L	Milk	2. Combine the rice, milk, vanilla, and salt in a heavy saucepan. Cover and simmer over very low heat until the rice is tender, about 30 minutes. Stir occasionally to be sure the mixture doesn't scorch on the bottom. Remove from heat when cooked.
2 tsp	20 mL	Vanilla	
½ tsp	2 mL	Salt	
2	2	Whole eggs	3. Combine the eggs, yolks, sugar, and cream in a mixing bowl. Mix until evenly combined.
4	4	Egg yolks	
1 lb	450 g	Sugar	4. Ladle some of the hot milk from the cooked rice into this mixture and mix well. Then very slowly stir the egg mixture back into the hot rice.
1 pt	500 mL	Light cream	
		Cinnamon	5. Pour into a buttered 12 × 20-inch (30 × 50-cm) bake pan. Sprinkle the top with cinnamon.
			6. Bake in a water bath at 350°F (175°C) for 30–40 minutes, until set. Serve warm or chilled.

Variation

399A. **Raisin Rice Pudding:** Add 8 oz (250 g) raisins to the cooked rice and milk mixture.

RECIPE 400 **Bread and Butter Pudding**

| | | | Portions: 25 | Portion size: 6½ oz (200 g) |

U.S.	Metric	Ingredients	Procedure
2 lb	1 kg	White bread, in thin slices	1. Cut each slice of bread in half. Brush both sides of each piece with melted butter.
8 oz	250 g	Melted butter	2. Arrange the bread overlapping in a buttered 12 × 20-inch (30 × 50-cm) bake pan.

RECIPE 400   **Bread and Butter Pudding** *(Continued)*

U.S.	Metric	Ingredients	Procedure
2 lb	1 kg	Eggs	3. Mix together the eggs, sugar, salt, and vanilla until thoroughly combined.
1 lb	500 g	Sugar	
1 tsp	5 mL	Salt	4. Gradually stir in the milk.
1 oz	30 mL	Vanilla	
2½ qt	2.5 L	Milk	
		Cinnamon	5. Pour the custard mixture over the bread slices in the pan. Let stand, refrigerated, for an hour or longer, so that the bread absorbs the custard mixture.
		Nutmeg	
			6. Sprinkle the top lightly with cinnamon and nutmeg.
			7. Set the pan in a larger pan containing about an inch of hot water.
			8. Place in the oven preheated to 350°F (175°C). Bake about 1 hour, until set.
			9. Serve warm or cold with whipped cream, light custard sauce, or dusted with confectioners' sugar.

Variation

400A. Cabinet Pudding: Prepare in individual custard cups instead of a bake pan. Substitute diced sponge cake for the bread and omit the melted butter. Add about 1 tbsp (15 mL) raisins to each cup before pouring in the custard mix.

BAVARIANS, CHIFFONS, MOUSSES, AND SOUFFLÉS

All the preparations in this section have one thing in common: they all have a light, fluffy or puffed texture, which is created by the addition of whipped cream, beaten egg whites, or both.

Although these particular products may be new to you, you should have little trouble learning to prepare them if you have already studied the previous chapter and the first part of this chapter. Once you have learned how to prepare custard sauce, pastry cream, starch-thickened fruit fillings, meringues, and whipped cream, and have learned how to work with gelatin (please read p. 512 if you have not yet studied gelatin), all you have to do is combine these products in different ways to make bavarians, chiffons, mousses, and soufflés.

Let's look at these four items separately to see what they are made of. Afterward, we will examine the procedures for assembling them.

Bavarians

A bavarian, also known as bavarian cream or bavaroise, is made of three basic elements: custard sauce (flavored as desired), gelatin, and whipped cream.

That's all there is to it. Gelatin is softened in cold liquid, stirred into the hot custard sauce until dissolved, and chilled until almost set. Whipped cream is then folded in, and the mixture is poured into a mold until set. It is unmolded for service.

Accurate measuring of the gelatin is important. If not enough gelatin is used, the dessert will be too soft to hold its shape. If too much is used, it will be too firm and rubbery.

Chiffons

Chiffons are most popular as fillings for chiffon pies, but they may also be served more simply as puddings and chilled desserts.

The major difference between chiffons and bavarians is the use of beaten egg whites in place of or in addition to whipped cream. In other words, chiffons are made of a base plus gelatin plus beaten egg whites. (Some chiffons also contain whipped cream in addition to the egg whites.)

Bases for chiffons include the following three main types:

1. ***Thickened with starch.*** The procedure is the same as for fruit pie fillings made by the cooked juice or cooked fruit method, except that the fruit is finely chopped or puréed. Most fruit chiffons are made this way.

2. ***Thickened with egg.*** The procedure is the same as for custard sauce or crème anglaise. Many chocolate chiffons are made this way, as is pumpkin chiffon.

3. ***Thickened with egg and starch.*** The procedure is the same as for pastry cream. Lemon chiffon is usually made this way.

Mousses

There are so many varieties of mousses that it is impossible to give a rule for all of them. In general, we could define a mousse as any soft or creamy dessert that is made light and fluffy by the addition of whipped cream or beaten egg whites or both. Note that bavarians and chiffons fit this description. In fact, they are often served as mousses but with the gelatin reduced or left out so that the mousse is softer.

There are many kinds of bases for mousses. They may be nothing more than melted chocolate or puréed fresh fruit, or they may be more complex, like the bases for chiffons.

Some mousses contain both beaten egg whites and whipped cream. When this is the case, most chefs prefer to fold in the egg whites first, even though they may lose some volume. The reason is that if the cream is added first, there is more danger that it will be overbeaten and turn to butter during the folding and mixing procedure.

If egg whites are folded in a *hot* base, they will be cooked or coagulated, and the mousse will be firmer and more stable. Whipped cream should never be folded into hot mixtures, or it will melt and deflate.

Dessert Soufflés

Soufflés are lightened with beaten egg whites and then baked. Baking causes the soufflé to rise like a cake, because the air in the egg foam expands when heated.

To understand their structure, we can divide the preparation of dessert soufflés into four stages:

1. ***Base.*** There are many kinds used for dessert soufflés, but most of them are heavy, starch-thickened preparations, such as pastry creams or sweetened white sauces.

2. ***Egg yolks.*** When used, these are added to the base.

3. ***Egg whites.*** Whenever possible, egg whites should be whipped with some of the sugar. This makes dessert soufflés more stable than entrée soufflés.

4. ***Baking.*** Please review the section on entrée soufflés (p. 561), so that you understand the general principles of baking soufflés.

Summary and Comparison

1. ***Bavarian.***

   Base: custard sauce.

   Gelatin.

   Whipped cream.

2. ***Chiffon.***

   Base: a. Starch thickened (fruit filling type).

   　　　 b. Egg thickened (custard type).

   　　　 c. Egg and starch thickened (pastry cream type).

   Gelatin.

   Egg whites.

   (Optional whipped cream).

3. ***Mousse.***

   Base: many varieties.

   Little or no gelatin.

   Egg whites and/or whipped cream.

4. ***Soufflé***

   Base: many varieties, but generally contain egg yolk.

   Egg whites.

   Baked.

General Procedure

The following procedure is only a general one. It is not a detailed method for one specific dessert but will give you a basic understanding that will help you tackle many different recipes. These basic steps apply to most bavarians, chiffons, mousses, and soufflés.

1. Prepare base.

2. If gelatin is used, soften it in cold liquid and stir it into the hot base until dissolved. Chill until almost set.

3. Fold in beaten egg whites and/or whipped cream.

4. Chill (for bavarians, chiffons, and mousses) or bake (for soufflés).

RECIPE 401 Bavarian Cream

Portions: 24   **Portion size:** 3 oz (90 g)

U.S.	Metric	Ingredients	Procedure
1½ oz	45 g	Gelatin (unflavored)	1. Soak the gelatin in cold water.
10 oz	300 mL	Cold water	
		Vanilla custard sauce:	2. Prepare the custard sauce: Whip the egg yolks and sugar until thick and light. Scald the milk and slowly stir it into the egg yolk mixture, beating constantly. Cook over a hot water bath, stirring constantly, until it just thickens slightly. (Review p. 773 for details on making custard sauce.)
12	12	Egg yolks	
8 oz	250 g	Sugar	
1 qt	1 L	Milk	
1 tbsp	15 mL	Vanilla	
			3. When the sauce is still hot, add the softened gelatin. Stir until the gelatin is dissolved.
			4. Cool in the refrigerator or over crushed ice, stirring occasionally to keep the mixture smooth.
1 qt	1 L	Heavy cream	5. While the custard sauce is cooling, whip the cream until it forms *soft*, not stiff, peaks. Do not overwhip.
			6. When the custard sauce is very thick but not yet set, fold in the whipped cream.
			7. Pour into molds or into serving dishes.
			8. Chill until completely set. If prepared in molds, unmold for service.

Variations

401A. Chocolate Bavarian Cream: Add 12 oz (350 g) sweetened chocolate, chopped or grated, to the hot custard sauce. Stir until completely melted and blended in.

401B. Coffee Bavarian Cream: Add 3 tbsp (45 mL) instant coffee powder to the hot custard sauce.

401C. Strawberry Bavarian Cream: Reduce the milk to 1 pt (500 mL) and the sugar to 6 oz (175 g) when making the custard sauce. Mash 1 lb (500 g) strawberries with 6 oz (175 g) sugar, or use 1½ lb (700 g) frozen, sweetened strawberries. Stir this purée into the custard sauce before adding the whipped cream.

401D. Raspberry Bavarian Cream: Prepare like Strawberry Bavarian Cream, using raspberries.

RECIPE 402 Strawberry Chiffon Dessert or Pie Filling

Yield: 6 lb 8 oz (3 kg)
six 8-inch (20-cm) pies
five 9-inch (23-cm) pies
four 10-inch (25-cm) pies

U.S.	Metric	Ingredients	Procedure
4 lb	1800 g	Frozen sweetened strawberries (see note)	1. Thaw and drain strawberries. Chop the strawberries coarsely.
1 tsp	5 g	Salt	2. Place the drained juice and salt in a saucepan. Bring to a boil.
1 oz	30 g	Cornstarch	
4 oz	125 mL	Water	3. Dissolve the cornstarch in the water and stir into the juice. Cook until thick. Remove from heat.
1 oz	30 g	Gelatin	4. Soften the gelatin in the water. Add to the hot, thickened fruit juice, and stir until completely dissolved.
8 oz	250 mL	Water, cold	
1 oz	30 mL	Lemon juice	5. Stir in the lemon juice and the drained strawberries.
			6. Chill the mixture until thickened but not set.
1 lb	450 g	Egg whites	7. Beat the egg whites until they form soft peaks.
12 oz	350 g	Sugar	8. Gradually add the sugar, and continue to beat until a thick, glossy meringue is formed.
			9. Fold the meringue into the fruit mixture.
			10. Portion into individual serving dishes or fill baked pie shells.
			11. Chill until set.

Note: To use fresh strawberries, slice or dice 3 lb (1.4 kg) fresh, hulled strawberries, and mix with 1 lb (450 g) sugar. Let stand 2 hours in refrigerator. Drain and reserve juice, and proceed as in basic recipe.

Variations

For a creamier chiffon, reduce egg whites to 12 oz (350 g). Whip 1 pt (500 mL) heavy cream, and fold in after the meringue.

402A. Raspberry Chiffon Dessert or Pie Filling: Substitute raspberries for strawberries in basic recipe.

402B. Pineapple Chiffon Dessert or Pie Filling: Use 3 lb (1.4 kg) crushed pineapple. Mix the drained juice with an additional 1 pt (500 mL) pineapple juice and add 8 oz (250 g) sugar.

402C. Frozen Strawberry or Raspberry Mousse: Omit gelatin and second quantity of water from basic recipe or from raspberry variation. Reduce egg whites to 8 oz (225 g). Whip 1½ pt (750 mL) heavy cream, and fold in after the meringue. Pour into molds or other containers and freeze.

RECIPE 403   **Chocolate Chiffon Dessert or Pie Filling**

Yield: 7 lb (3.2 kg)
    six 8-inch (20-cm) pies
    five 9-inch (23-cm) pies
    four 10-inch (25-cm) pies

U.S.	Metric	Ingredients	Procedure
10 oz	300 g	Unsweetened chocolate	1. Combine the chocolate and water in a heavy saucepan. Bring to a simmer, stirring constantly until smooth.
1½ pt	750 mL	Water	
1 lb	450 g	Egg yolks	2. Beat the egg yolks and sugar together with the whip attachment until thick and light.
1 lb	450 g	Sugar	
			3. With the mixer running, gradually pour in the chocolate mixture.
			4. Return the mixture to the saucepan and stir over very low heat until thickened. Remove from heat.
1 oz	30 g	Gelatin	5. Soften the gelatin in the water. Add to the hot chocolate mixture and stir until the gelatin is completely dissolved.
8 oz	250 mL	Water, cold	
			6. Chill until thick but not set.
1 lb 4 oz	575 g	Egg whites	7. Beat the egg whites until they form soft peaks.
1 lb 8 oz	700 g	Sugar	
			8. Gradually beat in the sugar. Continue beating until a firm, glossy meringue is formed.
			9. Fold into the chocolate mixture.
			10. Pour into serving dishes or into baked pie shells. Chill until set.

Variation

403A. Chocolate Cream Chiffon Pie Filling: For a creamier chiffon, reduce the egg whites to 1 lb (450 g). Whip 1 pt (500 mL) heavy cream and fold it in after the meringue.

RECIPE 404   Lemon Chiffon Dessert or Pie Filling

Yield: 7 lb (3.2 kg)
      six 8-inch (20-cm) pies
      five 9-inch (23-cm) pies
      four 10-inch (25-cm) pies

U.S.	Metric	Ingredients	Procedure
1½ pt	750 mL	Water	1. Dissolve the sugar in the water and bring to a boil.
8 oz	250 g	Sugar	
12 oz	375 g	Egg yolks	2. Beat together the egg yolks, water, cornstarch, sugar, and lemon zest until smooth.
4 oz	125 mL	Water, cold	
3 oz	90 g	Cornstarch	3. Gradually beat in the boiling water in a thin stream.
8 oz	250 g	Sugar	
		Grated zest of 4 lemons	4. Return the mixture to the heat and bring to a boil, beating constantly with a whip.
			5. As soon as the mixture thickens and boils, remove from the heat.
1 oz	30 g	Gelatin	6. Soften the gelatin in the cold water.
8 oz	250 mL	Water, cold	7. Add the gelatin to the hot lemon mixture. Stir until it is dissolved.
12 oz	350 mL	Lemon juice	8. Stir in the lemon juice.
			9. Chill until thick but not set.
1 lb	450 g	Egg whites	10. Beat the egg whites until they form soft peaks.
1 lb	450 g	Sugar	11. Gradually add the sugar and continue to beat until a thick, glossy meringue is formed.
			12. Fold the meringue into the lemon mixture.
			13. Pour into individual serving dishes or fill baked pie shells.
			14. Chill until set.

Variations

404A. Lime Chiffon Dessert or Pie Filling: Substitute lime juice and zest for the lemon.

404B. Orange Chiffon Dessert or Pie Filling: Use orange juice instead of water in step 1 and omit the first 8 oz (250 g) of sugar. Substitute orange zest for the lemon zest. Reduce the lemon juice to 4 oz (125 mL).

404C. Frozen Lemon Mousse: Omit the gelatin and the water used to dissolve it. Decrease egg whites to 12 oz (350 g). Whip 1 qt (1 L) heavy cream and fold in after meringue. Pour into molds or other containers and freeze.

RECIPE 405   **Pumpkin Chiffon Dessert or Pie Filling**

Yield: 7 lb 12 oz (3.4 kg)
    six 8-inch (20-cm) pies
    five 9-inch (23-cm) pies
    four 10-inch (25-cm) pies

U.S.	Metric	Ingredients	Procedure
2½ lb	1.2 kg	Pumpkin purée	1. Combine the pumpkin, sugar, milk, egg yolks, salt, and spices. Mix until smooth and uniform.
1 lb 4 oz	600 g	Brown sugar	
12 oz	350 g	Milk	
12 oz	350 g	Egg yolks, beaten	2. Place in a double boiler. Cook, stirring frequently, until thickened or until the temperature of the mix reads 185°F (85°C). Remove from heat.
1 tsp	5 mL	Salt	
4 tsp	20 mL	Cinnamon	
2 tsp	10 mL	Nutmeg	
1 tsp	5 mL	Ginger	
1 oz	30 g	Gelatin	3. Soften the gelatin in the water.
8 oz	250 mL	Water, cold	4. Add it to the hot pumpkin mixture and stir until dissolved.
			5. Chill until very thick but not set.
1 lb	450 g	Egg whites	6. Beat egg whites until they form soft peaks.
1 lb	450 g	Sugar	7. Gradually add the sugar, and continue to beat until a thick meringue is formed.
			8. Fold the meringue into the pumpkin mixture.
			9. Portion into individual serving dishes or fill baked pie shells. Chill until set.

Variation

405A. Pumpkin Cream Chiffon: Reduce the egg whites to 12 oz (350 g). Whip 1 pt (500 mL) heavy cream and fold in after the meringue.

RECIPE 406   Vanilla Soufflé

Portions: 10		**Portion size: 4½ oz (125 g)**	

U.S.	Metric	Ingredients	Procedure
3 oz 3 oz	90 g 90 g	Flour Butter	1. Work the flour and butter together to form a smooth paste.
1 pt 4 oz	500 mL 125 g	Milk Sugar	2. Dissolve the sugar in the milk and bring to a boil. Remove from the heat. 3. With a wire whip, beat in the flour paste. Beat vigorously to make sure there are no lumps. 4. Return the mixture to the heat and bring to a boil, beating constantly. Simmer for several minutes, until the mixture is very thick and no starchy taste remains. 5. Transfer the mixture to a mixing bowl. Cover and let cool for 5 to 10 minutes.
		Butter Sugar	6. While the mixture is cooling, butter the soufflé dishes well and coat with granulated sugar. For 1 recipe, use one 10-inch (25-cm) dish, two 7-inch (18-cm) dishes, or 10 single-portion dishes.
8 2 tsp	8 10 mL	Egg yolks Vanilla	7. Quickly beat the egg yolks and vanilla into the milk mixture.
8–10 2 oz	8–10 60 g	Egg whites Sugar	8. Beat the egg whites until they form soft peaks. Add the sugar and beat until the mixture forms firm, moist peaks. 9. Fold the egg whites into the soufflé base. 10. Pour the mixture into the prepared baking dishes and smooth the tops. 11. Bake at 375°F (190°C). Approximate baking times are 45 to 50 minutes for a 10-inch (25-cm) dish, 30 to 40 minutes for a 7-inch (18-cm) dish, and 15 minutes for single-portion dishes.

Variations

406A. Chocolate Soufflé: Add 3 oz (90 g) melted unsweetened chocolate and 1 oz (30 g) melted sweet chocolate to the base after step 5.

406B. Lemon Soufflé: Instead of vanilla, use the grated zest of 2 lemons for flavoring.

406C. Liqueur Soufflé: Flavor with 2–3 oz (60–90 mL) of desired liqueur such as kirsch or Grand Marnier, added after step 5.

406D. Coffee Soufflé: Flavor with 2 tbsp (30 mL) instant coffee powder, added to the milk in step 2.

RECIPE 407   **Chocolate Mousse**

Yield: about 5½ lb (2.5 kg)   **Portions:** 25   **Portion size:** 5 fl oz (150 mL)
        or 4 qt (4 L)

U.S.	Metric	Ingredients	Procedure
2 lb 8 oz 12 oz	900 g 225 g 350 g	Semisweet chocolate Butter Egg yolks	1. Melt the chocolate over hot water. 2. Remove from the heat and add the butter. Stir until the butter is melted and completely mixed in. 3. Add the egg yolks one at a time. Mix in each yolk completely before adding the next.
1 lb 5 oz	450 g 150 g	Egg whites Sugar	4. Beat the egg whites until they form soft peaks. Add the sugar and beat until the egg whites form stiff but moist peaks. Do not overbeat. 5. Fold the egg whites into the chocolate.
1 pt	500 mL	Heavy cream	6. Whip the heavy cream until it forms soft peaks. Fold it into the chocolate mixture. 7. Spoon the mousse into serving dishes or use a pastry bag fitted with a star tube. 8. Chill the mousse well before serving.

Note: This mixture may also be used as a filling for cakes, pastries, and baked meringues. For another, very different chocolate mousse recipe, see the variation following the recipe for Chocolate Chiffon earlier in this chapter.

FROZEN DESSERTS

The popularity of ice cream needs no explanation. Whether served as a plain scoop of vanilla ice cream in a dish or as an elaborate assemblage of fruits, syrups, toppings, and numerous flavors of ice cream and sherbet, frozen desserts appeal to everyone.

Classification

1. **Ice creams.**

   Ice cream is a smooth, frozen mixture of milk, cream, sugar, flavorings, and sometimes eggs. *Philadelphia-style* ice cream contains no eggs, while *French-style* ice cream contains egg yolks. The eggs add richness and help make a smoother product because of the emulsifying properties of the yolks.

   Ice milk is like ice cream, but with a lower butterfat content.

   Frozen yogurt contains yogurt in addition to the normal ingredients for ice cream or ice milk.

2. **Sherbets.**

   Sherbets and *ices* are made from fruit juices, water, and sugar. American sherbets usually contain milk or cream and sometimes egg whites. The egg whites increase smoothness and volume. Ices, also called *water ices*, contain only fruit juice, water, sugar, and sometimes egg whites. They do not contain milk products. The French word *sorbet* (sor-bay) is sometimes used for these products. *Granité* (grah-nee-tay) is coarse, crystalline ice, made without egg white.

3. **Still-frozen desserts.**

   Ice cream and sherbet are churn-frozen, meaning that they are mixed constantly while being frozen. If they were not churned, they would freeze into solid blocks of ice. The churning keeps the ice crystals small and incorporates air into the ice cream.

   Frozen soufflés and *frozen mousses* are made like chilled mousses and bavarians. That is, they have whipped cream or beaten egg whites or both folded into them to give them lightness. This allows them to be still-frozen in an ordinary freezer.

Production and Quality

Few establishments make their own ice cream, because of the labor involved, the equipment required, and the convenience of commercially made products. Also, strict health codes in many states make it difficult for all but large producers to make ice cream.

If you have access to an ice cream freezer, you will be happy to know that you probably already know how to make basic ice cream mix. Simply make a custard sauce or crème anglaise, using 12 oz sugar for every quart of milk (375 g per liter). Add 1 part heavy cream for every 2 parts of milk used in the sauce, and flavor as desired, with vanilla, melted chocolate, instant coffee, crushed strawberries, and so on. Chill thoroughly, then freeze according to the instructions for your particular equipment.

When the mix has frozen, it is transferred to containers and placed in a deep-freeze at below 0°F (–18°C) to harden. (Soft-frozen or soft-serve ice creams are served directly as they come from the churn freezer, without being hardened.)

Whether you make ice cream or buy it, you should be aware of the following quality factors.

1. *Smoothness* is related to the size of the ice crystals in the product. Ice cream should be frozen rapidly and churned well during freezing so that large crystals don't have a chance to form.

    Rapid hardening helps keep crystals small. So do eggs and emulsifiers or stabilizers added to the mix.

    Large crystals may form if ice cream is not stored at a low enough temperature (below 0°F/ –18°C).

2. *Overrun* is the increase in volume due to incorporation of air when freezing ice cream. It is expressed as a percentage of the original volume of the mix. (For example, if the ice cream doubles in volume, then the amount of increase is equal to the original volume, and the overrun is 100%.)

    Some overrun is necessary to give a smooth, light texture. If ice cream has too much overrun, it will be airy and foamy and will lack flavor. It was once thought that ice cream should have from 80 to 100 percent overrun and that less would make it heavy and pasty. This may be true for ice creams containing gums and other stabi-

lizers. However, some quality manufacturers are producing rich (and expensive) ice cream with as little as 20 percent overrun.

3. *Mouth feel* or body depends in part on smoothness and overrun, as well as on other qualities. Good ice cream will melt in the mouth to a smooth, not too heavy liquid. Some ice creams have so many stabilizers that they never do melt to a liquid. Unfortunately, many people have become so accustomed to these products that an ice cream that actually does melt strikes them as "not rich enough."

Storage and Service

1. Store ice creams and sherbets at 0°F (–18°C) or lower. This low temperature helps prevent the formation of large ice crystals.

2. For service, temper frozen desserts at 8°F to 15°F (–13°C to –9°C) for 24 hours, so that they will be soft enough to serve.

3. When serving, avoid packing the ice cream. The best method is to draw the scoop across the surface of the product, so that the product rolls into a ball in the scoop.

4. Use standard scoops for portioning ice cream. Normal portions for popular desserts are as follows:

Parfait	3 No. 30 scoops
Banana split	3 No. 30 scoops
"A la mode" topping for pie or cake	1 No. 20 scoop
Sundae	2 No. 20 scoops
Plain dish of ice cream	1 No. 10, 12, or 16 scoop

5. Measure syrups, toppings, and garnishes for portion control. For syrups, use pumps that dispense measured quantities, or use standard ladles.

Popular Ice Cream Desserts

1. *Parfaits* are made by alternating layers of ice cream and fruit or syrup in a tall, narrow glass. They are usually named after the syrup or topping. For example: *chocolate parfait*—three scoops of vanilla or chocolate ice cream, alternating with layers of chocolate syrup, topped with whipped cream and shaved chocolate.

2. *Sundaes* or *coupes* consist of one or two scoops of ice cream or sherbet in a dish or glass, topped

with any of a number of syrups, fruits, toppings, and garnishes. They are quick to prepare, unlimited in variety, and as simple or as elegant as you could wish—served in an ordinary soda fountain glass or in a silver cup or crystal champagne glass.

Two sundaes have become classics:

Peach Melba. Vanilla ice cream, topped with fresh, poached, or canned peach half, napped with sweetened raspberry purée (Melba sauce), garnished with slivered almonds.

Pear Belle Hélène. Vanilla ice cream, topped with poached or canned pear half, napped with chocolate sauce, garnished with toasted sliced almonds.

3. *Bombes* are ice cream molds made by lining a chilled mold with softened ice cream, freezing it hard, then filling the center with another flavor of ice cream or sherbet and freezing it again. (More than two flavors may be used.) The dessert is unmolded onto a cold platter for service and decorated as desired with whipped cream, fruits, and/or confections.

4. *Meringue glacée.* See meringues, pages 766.

5. *Baked Alaska.* See meringues, page 766.

6. *Frozen eclairs* and *profiteroles.* See eclair pastries, page 764.

DESSERT SAUCES

Most dessert sauces fall into three categories.

1. **Custard sauces.**

   Vanilla custard sauce or crème anglaise is presented early in this chapter. It is one of the most basic preparations in dessert cookery. Chocolate or other flavors may be added to create other varieties. See recipe on page 773.

2. **Fruit purées.**

   These are simply purées of fresh or cooked fruits, sweetened with sugar. Other flavorings and spices are sometimes added. Some fruit sauces are thickened with cornstarch or other starch.

   Raspberry sauce and *strawberry sauce,* two popular items, can be made by simply puréeing frozen sweetened berries or by puréeing fresh berries and adding sugar to taste. See also the recipe for Applesauce, page 154.

3. **Syrups.**

   This is a broad category that includes such products as chocolate sauce and caramel sauce. An understanding of sugar cooking is necessary to produce many of these sauces.

   The following recipes are popular examples of this category of sauce.

RECIPE 408   **Chocolate Sauce**

Yield: 2 qt (2 L)

U.S.	Metric	Ingredients	Procedure
1 qt	1 L	Water	1. Combine the water, sugar, and syrup and bring to a boil, stirring to dissolve the sugar.
4 lb	2 kg	Sugar	
12 oz	750 g	Corn syrup	2. Boil 1 minute and remove from heat. Let cool 1–2 minutes.
1 lb	500 g	Unsweetened chocolate, melted	3. Melt the chocolate and butter together over low heat. Stir until smooth.
4 oz	125 g	Butter	4. Very slowly stir the hot syrup into the chocolate.
			5. Place over moderate heat and bring to a boil. Boil for 4 minutes.
			6. Remove from heat and cool.

RECIPE 409   Caramel Sauce

Yield: 1½ qt (1½ L)

U.S.	Metric	Ingredients	Procedure
2 lb 8 oz 1 tbsp	1 kg 250 g 30 mL	Sugar Water Lemon juice	1. Combine the sugar, water, and lemon juice in a heavy saucepan. Bring to a boil, stirring to dissolve the sugar. 2. When the sugar is dissolved, cover the pan and boil for 2 minutes. 3. Uncover and cook to the caramel stage (see p. 772). Toward the end of the cooking time, turn the heat to very low to avoid burning the sugar or getting it too dark. It should be a golden color. 4. Remove from heat and cool 5 minutes.
3 cups	750 mL	Heavy cream	5. Bring the heavy cream to a boil. Add a few ounces of it to the caramel. 6. Stir and continue to add the cream slowly. 7. Return to the heat and stir until all the caramel is dissolved. 8. Let cool completely.
1 pt	500 mL	Milk	9. Stir the milk into the cooled caramel to thin it out.

Variations

409A. Hot Caramel Sauce: Prepare as directed through step 7. Omit the milk.

409B. Clear Caramel Sauce: Substitute 10–12 oz (300–350 mL) water for the heavy cream and omit the milk. If the sauce is too thick when cool, add more water.

TERMS FOR REVIEW

....

simple syrup	cream pudding	Philadelphia-style ice cream	still-frozen
dessert syrup	baked pudding	French-style ice cream	overrun
crystallize	bavarian	ice milk	parfait
crème anglaise	chiffon	sherbet	coupe
pastry cream	mousse	ice	Peach Melba
blanc mange	ice cream	granité	bombe

QUESTIONS FOR DISCUSSION

....

1. How can you avoid unwanted crystallization when cooking sugar syrups?

2. Light custard sauce and pastry cream both contain eggs. Why is it possible to boil pastry cream but not custard sauce?

3. Explain the importance of sanitation in the production of pastry cream. What specific steps should you take to ensure a safe product?

4. Light custard sauce, pastry cream, and baked custard are made with basic techniques that are also used for the following preparations. Identify which of the three techniques is used for each.

Coconut cream pie	French vanilla ice cream
Baked rice pudding	Pumpkin pie
Butterscotch pudding	Custard pie
Chocolate bavarian	Lemon meringue pie

5. Briefly describe the differences among bavarians, chiffons, mousses, and soufflés.

6. When making dessert soufflés, what is the advantage of beating the egg whites with part of the sugar?

7. What difficulty would you encounter, when making a bavarian or chiffon, if you chilled the gelatin mixture too long before folding in the whipped cream or egg whites?

APPENDIX 1

METRIC CONVERSION FACTORS

Weight

    1 ounce equals 28.35 grams

    1 gram equals 0.035 ounce

    1 pound equals 454 grams

    1 kilogram equals 2.2 pounds

Volume

    1 fluid ounce equals 29.57 milliliters

    1 milliliter equals 0.034 ounce

    1 cup equals 237 milliliters

    1 quart equals 946 milliliters

    1 liter equals 33.8 fluid ounces

Length

    1 inch equals 25.4 millimeters

    1 centimeter equals 0.39 inch

    1 meter equals 39.4 inches

Temperature

To convert Fahrenheit to Celsius:

    Subtract 32. Then multiply by $\frac{5}{9}$.

    Example: Convert 140°F to Celsius.
                   $140 - 32 = 108$
                   $108 \times \frac{5}{9} = 60°C$

To convert Celsius to Fahrenheit:

    Multiply by $\frac{9}{5}$. Then add 32.

    Example: Convert 150°C to Fahrenheit.
                   $150 \times \frac{9}{5} = 270$
                   $270 + 32 = 302°F$

Note: The metric equivalents in the recipes in this book are rounded off. See page 75 for complete explanation.

APPENDIX 2

STANDARD CAN SIZES

	Volume		Approximate Weight [a]	
Can Name	U.S.	Metric	U.S.	Metric
6 oz	5.75 fl. oz	170 mL	6 oz	170 g
8 oz	8.3 fl. oz	245 mL	8 oz	227 g
No. 1 picnic	10.5 fl. oz	311 mL	10½ oz	298 g
No. 211 cylinder	12 fl. oz	355 mL	12 oz	340 g
No. 300	13.5 fl. oz	399 mL	14 oz	397 g
No. 303	15.6 fl. oz	461 mL	16–17 oz	454–482 g
No. 2	20 fl. oz	591 mL	1 lb 4 oz	567 g
No. 2½	28.5 fl. oz	843 mL	1 lb 13 oz	822 g
No. 3 cylinder	46 fl. oz	1360 mL	3 lb	1360 g
No. 5	56 fl. oz	1656 mL	3 lb 8 oz	1588 g
No. 10	103.7 fl. oz	3067 mL	6½–7 lb	2722–2948 g

[a] Because the density of foods varies, net weights for any given size can will vary.

APPENDIX 3

APPROXIMATE WEIGHT-VOLUME EQUIVALENTS OF DRY FOODS

The following equivalents are rough averages only. Actual weight per volume varies considerably. For accurate measurement, all ingredients should be weighed.

Bread flour, sifted
- 1 lb = 4 cups
- 1 cup = 4 oz

Bread flour, unsifted
- 1 lb = 3⅓ cups
- 1 cup = 4.75 oz

Cake flour, sifted
- 1 lb = 4¼ cups
- 1 cup = 3.75 oz

Cake flour, unsifted
- 1 lb = 3½ cups
- 1 cup = 4.5 oz

Granulated sugar
- 1 lb = 2¼ cups
- 1 cup = 7 oz

Confectioners' sugar, sifted
- 1 lb = 4 cups
- 1 cup = 4 oz

Confectioners' sugar, unsifted
- 1 lb = 3½ cups
- 1 cup = 4.5 oz

Cornstarch, sifted
- 1 lb = 4 cups
- 1 cup = 4 oz
- 1 oz = 4 tbsp = ¼ cup
- 1 tbsp = 0.25 oz

Cornstarch, unsifted
- 1 lb = 3½ cups
- 1 cup = 4.5 oz
- 1 oz = 3½ tbsp
- 1 tbsp = 0.29 oz

Cocoa, unsifted
- 1 lb = 5 cups
- 1 cup = 3.2 oz
- 1 oz = 5 tbsp
- 1 tbsp = 0.2 oz

Gelatin, unflavored
- 1 oz = 3 tbsp
- ¼ oz = 2¼ tsp
- 1 tbsp = 0.33 oz
- 1 tsp = 0.11 oz

Baking soda
Baking powder (phosphate type and sodium aluminum sulfate type)
- 1 oz = 2 tbsp
- ¼ oz = 1½ tsp
- 1 tbsp = 0.5 oz
- 1 tsp = 0.17 oz

Cream of tartar
- 1 oz = 4 tbsp
- ¼ oz = 1 tbsp
- 1 tsp = 0.08 oz

Salt

    1 oz = 5 tsp

    ¼ oz = 1¼ tsp

    1 tsp = 0.2 oz

Cinnamon

    1 oz = 17 tsp

    ¼ oz = 4¼ tsp

    1 tsp = 0.06 oz

Ground spices (except cinnamon)

    1 oz = 14 tsp

    ¼ oz = 3½ tsp

    1 tsp = 0.07 oz

Grated lemon zest

    1 oz = 4 tbsp

    1 tsp = 0.08 oz

Dried beans

    1 cup = 6.5 oz

    1 lb = 2½ cups (yields 6 cups cooked)

Rice, long grain

    1 cup = 7 oz

    1 lb = 2¼ cups (yields 8 cups cooked)

APPENDIX 4

KITCHEN MATH EXERCISES— METRIC VERSIONS

This appendix includes metric sample calculations corresponding to the calculations in the text that use U.S. measures. Refer to the appropriate pages in the text for explanations.

Recipe Conversion, pages 75–77

Beef tenderloin tips and mushrooms à la crème
Portions: 8
Portion size: 250 g

Butter	60 g
Onions	125 g
Flour	15 mL
Mushrooms	250
Beef tenderloin	1250 g
White wine	125 mL
Prepared mustard	10 mL
Brown sauce	750 mL
Heavy cream	250 mL
Salt	to taste
Pepper	to taste

To determine quantities for 18 portions, divide new yield by old yield to find conversion factor:

$$\frac{\text{new yield}}{\text{old yield}} = \frac{18}{8} = 2.25$$

EXAMPLE 1

Ingredient	Quantity	Times	Conversion Factor	Equals	New Quantity (rounded off)
Butter	60 g	×	2.25	=	135 g
Onions	125 g	×	2.25	=	275 g
Flour	15 mL	×	2.25	=	35 mL
Mushrooms	250 g	×	2.25	=	575 g
Beef tenderloin	1250 g	×	2.25	=	2800 g
White wine	125 mL	×	2.25	=	275 mL
Prepared mustard	10 mL	×	2.25	=	23 mL
Brown sauce	750 mL	×	2.25	=	1700 mL
Heavy cream	250 mL	×	2.25	=	575 mL

To determine quantities for 40 portions at 175 grams each, first find the total yield of the old recipe. Multiply the portions by the portion size:

8 (portions) times 250 g equals 2000 g

Do the same calculation for the desired yield:

40 (portions) times 175 g equals 7000 g

Divide the desired yield by the old yield to find the conversion factor:

7000 ÷ 2000 = 3.5

EXAMPLE 2

Ingredient	Quantity	Times	Conversion Factor	Equals	New Quantity (rounded off)
Butter	60 g	×	3.5	=	200 g
Onions	125 g	×	3.5	=	450 g
Flour	15 mL	×	3.5	=	50 mL
Mushrooms	250 g	×	3.5	=	875 g
Beef tenderloin	1250 g	×	3.5	=	4375 g
White wine	125 mL	×	3.5	=	450 mL
Prepared mustard	10 mL	×	3.5	=	35 mL
Brown sauce	750 mL	×	3.5	=	2625 mL
Heavy cream	250 mL	×	3.5	=	875 mL

Completed Raw Yield Test Form (Metric)—p. 82

Item ....veal leg to scalop....   Test Number ....3........   Date ....3/16/94........

Purveyor ....ABC Meats....   Price per kg ....$11.00........   Total cost ....$148.50....

AP Weight (1) ..13.5 kg....   kg price (2) ....$11.00....   Total cost (3) ....$148.50....

Trim, salvage, and waste:

	Item	Weight	Value/kg	Total Value (kg × value)
(4)	fat	1.14 kg	$ .25	$ .29
(5)	bone	1.5 kg	$ .88	$1.32
(6)	ground veal	0.95 kg	$9.75	$9.26
(7)	stew meat	1.4 kg	$10.95	$15.33
(8)	unusable trim	0.4 kg	0	0
(9)	cutting loss	0.09 kg	0	0
(10)				

Total weight (4 thru 10) (11) ____5.48 kg____   Total value (4 thru 10) (12) ____$26.20____

Total yield of item (13) ....8.02 kg................

Net cost (3 minus 12) (14) _____$122.30_____

Cost per kg (14 divided by 13) (15) _____$15.25_____

Percentage of increase (15 divided by 2) (16) _____1.39 (139%)_____

Completed Cooked Yield Test Form (Metric)—p. 83

Item .... roast fresh ham ....   Test number ...... 2 ......   Date .... 9/4/94 ....

AP price per kg .... $7.75 ....

Cooking temperature ..... 325 ....

Net raw weight   (1) .... 5.5 kg ......   Net cost per kg   (2) .... $8.73 ....

    Total net cost   (3) .... $48.02 ....

Weight as served   (4) .... 3.75 kg ....

Cooked cost per kg (3 divided by 4)   (5) $12.81

Shrinkage (1 minus 4)   (6)   1.75 kg

Percentage of shrinkage (6 divided by 1)   (7)   32%

Total percentage of cost increase   (5 divided by AP price per kg)   (8)   165%

Metric Example: Costing a Recipe (p. 84)
Item: Baked Rice

Ingredient	Recipe Quantity	AP Quantity	Price	Total Amount
Rice, long grain	2 kg	2 kg	$1.59/kg	$3.18
Butter	375 g	0.375 kg	4.25/kg	1.59
Onions	500 g	0.5 kg	0.79/kg	0.40
Chicken stock	4 L	4 L	0.30/L	1.20
Salt	30 g	0.03 kg	0.35/kg	0.01
			Total cost	$6.38
			Number of portions	50
			Cost per portion	$0.13

BIBLIOGRAPHY

A

Amendola, Joseph. *The Bakers' Manual for Quantity Baking and Pastry Making*, 3rd ed. Rochelle Park, N.J.: Hayden, 1972.

Anderson, Jean. *The Food of Portugal*. New York: Morrow, 1986.

Anderson, Jean, and Hedy Wurz. *The New German Cookbook*. New York: Harper Collins, 1993.

Andoh, Elizabeth. *At Home with Japanese Cooking*. New York: Knopf, 1980.

B

Bayless, Rick. *Authentic Mexican*. New York: Morrow, 1987.

Bertolli, Paul, and Alice Waters, *Chez Panisse Cooking*. New York: Random House, 1988.

Bickel, Walter, ed. *Hering's Dictionary of Classical and Modern Cookery*. London: Virtue, 1987.

Bocuse, Paul. *Paul Bocuse's French Cooking*. New York: Pantheon, 1977.

Boni, Ada. *Italian Regional Cooking*. New York: Bonanza, 1969.

Bugialli, Giuliano. *The Fine Art of Italian Cooking*. New York: Times Books, 1977.

Bugialli, Giuliano. *Classic Techniques of Italian Cooking*. New York: Simon & Schuster, 1982.

C

Casas, Penelope. *The Foods and Wines of Spain*. New York: Knopf, 1987.

Claiborne, Craig, and Virginia Lee. *The Chinese Cookbook*. Philadelphia: Lippincott, 1972.

Cox, Beverly. *Cooking Techniques*. Boston: Little, Brown, 1981.

Culinary Institute of America. *The New Professional Chef*, 5th ed. New York: Van Nostrand Reinhold, 1991.

Culinary Institute of America. *The Professional Chef's Knife*. New York: CBI, 1978.

D

David, Elizabeth. *French Provincial Cooking*. Harmondsworth, England: Penguin, 1960.

David, Elizabeth. *Italian Food*. Harmondsworth, England: Penguin, 1954.

D'Ermo, Dominique. *The Modern Pastry Chef's Guide to Professional Baking*. New York: Harper & Row, 1962.

E

Educational Foundation of the National Restaurant Association. *Applied Foodservice Sanitation*, 4th ed. New York: Wiley, 1992.

Escoffier, A. *The Escoffier Cook Book*. New York: Crown, 1969.

G

Gisslen, Wayne. *Advanced Professional Cooking*. New York: Wiley, 1992.

Gisslen, Wayne. *Professional Baking*, 2nd ed. New York: Wiley, 1994.

Grausman, Richard. *At Home with the French Classics*. New York: Workman, 1988.

H

Haines, Robert G. *Food Preparation*. Homewood, Ill.: American Technical Publishers, 1988.

Hazan, Marcella. *The Classic Italian Cookbook*. New York: Knopf, 1976.

Hazan, Marcella. *More Classic Italian Cooking*. New York: Knopf, 1978.

Holden, Chet. *Cooking for Fifty*. New York: Wiley, 1993.

Hom, Ken. *Chinese Technique*. New York: Simon & Schuster, 1981.

K

Kennedy, Diana. *The Cuisines of Mexico*, 2nd ed. New York: Harper & Row, 1986.

Kennedy, Diana. *Mexican Regional Cooking*. New York: Harper & Row, 1978.

Knight, John B., and Lendel H. Kotschevar. *Quantity Food Production, Planning and Management.* New York: CBI, 1979.

Kotschevar, Lendal H. *Standards, Principles, and Techniques in Quantity Food Production,* 3rd ed. New York: CBI, 1974.

L

Lang, George. *The Cuisine of Hungary.* New York: Bonanza, 1971.

M

McClane, A. J. *The Encyclopedia of Fish.* New York: Holt, Rinehart & Winston, 1977.

McGee, Harold. *The Curious Cook.* San Francisco: North Point Press, 1990.

McGee, Harold. *On Food and Cooking.* New York: Scribners, 1984.

Miller, Gloria Bley. *The Thousand Recipe Chinese Cookbook.* New York: Grosset & Dunlap, 1970.

Mizer, David A., Mary Porter, and Beth Sonnier. *Food Preparation for the Professional,* 2nd ed. New York: Wiley, 1987.

Montagné, Prosper. *Larousse Gastronomique,* New American Edition. New York: Crown, 1988.

N

National Association of Meat Purveyors. *Meat Buyers Guide.* Reston, Virginia, 1992.

P

Pauli, Eugen. *Classical Cooking the Modern Way,* 2nd ed. New York: Van Nostrand Reinhold, 1989.

Pepin, Jacques. *The Art of Cooking.* New York: Knopf, 1987.

Pepin, Jacques. *La Technique: The Fundamental Techniques of Cooking: An Illustrated Guide.* New York: Quadrangle/Times Books, 1976.

Powers, Jo Marie. *Basics of Quantity Food Production.* New York: Wiley, 1979.

S

Saulnier, L. *La Répertoire de la Cuisine.* Woodbury, N.Y.: Barron's, 1976.

Schneider, Elizabeth. *Uncommon Fruits and Vegetables: A Commonsense Guide.* New York: Harper & Row, 1986.

Sheraton, Mimi. *The German Cookbook.* New York: Random House, 1965.

Shugart, Grace, and Mary K. Molt. *Food for Fifty,* 9th ed. New York: Macmillan, 1992.

Sonnenschmidt, Frederic H., and Jean F. Nicolas. *The Professional Chef's Art of Garde Manger,* 5th ed. New York: Van Nostrand Reinhold, 1993.

Stefanelli, John M. *Purchasing: Selection and Procurement for the Hospitality Industry,* 3rd ed. New York: Wiley, 1992.

Sultan, William J. *Practical Baking,* 4th ed. Westport, Conn.: AVI, 1986.

T

Torres, Marimar. *The Spanish Table.* Garden City, N.Y.: Doubleday, 1986.

Tsuji, Shizuo. *Japanese Cooking: A Simple Art.* Tokyo: Kodansha, 1980.

W

Waldner, George K., and Klaus Mitterhauser. *The Professional Chef's Book of Buffets.* New York: Van Nostrand Reinhold, 1971.

Willan, Anne. *La Varenne Pratique.* New York: Crown, 1989.

GLOSSARY

(*Note:* Phonetic guides are included for difficult French words, giving the approximate pronunciation using English sounds. Exact rendering is impossible in many cases, because French has a number of sounds that don't exist in English. For foreign terms used in Chapter 23, see glossary at the end of that chapter, page 650.)

A

Adductor Muscle The muscle with which a mollusk closes its shell. In the case of American scallops, this is usually the only part that is eaten.

Aging Holding meats in coolers under controlled conditions to allow natural tenderizing to take place.

À la Carte (1) Referring to a menu on which each individual item is listed with a separate price. (2) Referring to cooking to order, as opposed to cooking ahead in large batches.

Al Dente Firm, not soft or mushy, to the bite. Said of vegetables or pasta.

Allemande (1) German style. (2) A sauce made of Velouté (usually veal), a liaison, and lemon juice.

Allumette Cut into matchstick shapes; usually refers to potatoes.

Anthocyanins Red or purple pigments in vegetables and fruits.

Antipasto Italian hors d'oeuvre.

AP Weight As purchased; the weight of an item before trimming.

Arborio Rice A variety of short-grain rice from Italy.

Argenteuil (ar zhawn toy) Garnished with asparagus.

AS Weight As served; the weight of an item as sold or served, after processing and/or cooking.

Au Gratin (oh gra tan) Having a browned or crusted top, often made by topping with bread crumbs, cheese, and/or a rich sauce and passing under the broiler or salamander.

Au Jus (oh zhoo) Served with its natural juices. Usually unthickened pan drippings.

Au Sec (oh seck) Until dry.

Avgolemono Greek soup made of chicken stock, egg, and lemon juice.

B

Bacteria Microscopic organisms, some of which can cause disease, including food-borne disease.

Bain Marie A container of hot water used for keeping foods hot.

Bake To cook foods by surrounding them with hot, dry air. Similar to roast, but the term baking usually applies to breads, pastries, vegetables, and fish.

Baked Alaska A dessert consisting of ice cream on a sponge-cake base, covered with meringue and browned in the oven.

Barbecue To cook with dry heat created by the burning of hardwood or by the hot coals of this wood.

Bard To tie thin slices of fat, such as pork fatback, over meats with no natural fat cover to protect them while roasting.

Basmati Rice A variety of long-grain rice from India.

Batonnet Cut into sticks, about $\frac{1}{4} \times \frac{1}{4} \times 2\frac{1}{2}$–3 inches (6 mm $\times$ 6 mm $\times$ 6–7.5 cm).

Batter Semiliquid mixture containing flour or other starch used for the production of such products as cakes and breads and for coating products to be deep-fried.

Bavarian Cream A dessert made of custard sauce, gelatin, and whipped cream.

Béarnaise (bare nez) A sauce made of butter and egg yolks and flavored with a reduction of vinegar, shallots, tarragon, and peppercorns.

Béchamel A sauce made by thickening milk with a roux.

Beurre Manié (burr mahnyay) A mixture of equal parts raw butter and flour mixed together into a smooth paste.

Beurre Noir (burr nwahr) Butter heated until it is dark brown and flavored with vinegar.

Beurre Noisette (burr nwah zett) Whole butter heated until it is light brown.

Bisque A cream soup made from shellfish.

Blanch To cook an item partially and very briefly in boiling water or in hot fat. Usually a pre-preparation technique, as to loosen peels from vegetables, fruits, and nuts, to partially cook french fries or other foods before service, to prepare for freezing, or to remove undesirable flavors.

Blanc Mange (1) An English pudding thickened with cornstarch. (2) A French almond-flavored pudding containing gelatin and milk.

Blanquette A white stew made of white meat or poultry simmered without preliminary browning and served with a white sauce.

Boil To cook in water or other liquid that is bubbling rapidly, about 212°F (100°C) at sea level and at normal pressure.

Bombe A molded ice cream or sherbet dessert.

Bordelaise A brown sauce flavored with a reduction of red wine, shallots, pepper, and herbs and garnished with marrow.

Botulism A deadly food-borne intoxication usually associated with improperly canned foods.

Bouquet Garni A combination of fresh herbs tied together, used for flavoring.

Bouquetière (book tyair) Garnished with an assortment or "bouquet" of fresh vegetables, such as artichokes, carrots, turnips, green beans, peas, cauliflower, and potatoes.

Braise (1) To cook covered in a small amount of liquid, usually after preliminary browning. (2) To cook (certain vegetables) slowly in a small amount of liquid without preliminary browning.

Brioche Rich yeast dough containing large amounts of eggs and butter, or the products made from this dough.

Broil To cook with radiant heat from above.

Broth A flavorful liquid obtained from the simmering of meats and/or vegetables.

Brunoise (broo-nwahz) (1) Cut into very small (1/8 inch/3 mm) dice. (2) Garnished with vegetables cut in this manner.

Bulgur A type of cracked wheat that has been partially cooked.

Buttercream An icing made of butter and/or shortening blended with confectioners' sugar or sugar syrup and sometimes other ingredients.

Butterflied Cut partially through and spread open to increase the surface area.

C

Calorie The amount of heat needed to raise the temperature of 1 kg water by 1°C. Used as a measure of food energy.

Canapé (can ah pay) Tiny open-faced sandwiches, served as an hors d'oeuvre.

Capon A castrated male chicken.

Cappuccino Mixture of equal parts espresso and frothy, steamed milk.

Caramelization The browning of sugars caused by heat.

Carbohydrates Any of a group of compounds, including starches and sugars, which supply energy to the body.

Carême, Marie-Antoine Famous nineteenth-century French chef, often considered the founder of classical cuisine.

Carotenoids Yellow or orange pigments in vegetables and fruits.

Carry-over Cooking The rise in temperature in the inside of roast meat after it is removed from the oven.

Celsius Scale The metric system of temperature measurement, with 0°C set at the freezing point of water and 100°C set at the boiling point of water.

Centi- Prefix in the metric system meaning "one-hundredth."

Chasseur (sha sur) "Hunter style," usually referring to items served with a brown sauce containing mushrooms, tomato, and white wine.

Chef The person in charge of a kitchen or of a department of a kitchen.

Chèvre A cheese made from goat's milk.

Chiffon (1) A light, fluffy dessert or pie filling containing gelatin and beaten egg whites. (2) A type of cake made with an egg-white foam and with oil as a shortening.

China Cap A cone-shaped strainer.

Chlorophyll Green pigment in vegetables and fruits.

Cholesterol A fatty substance found in foods derived from animal products and in the human body; it has been linked to heart disease.

Chop To cut into irregularly shaped pieces.

Choucroute (shoo kroot) Sauerkraut.

Choucroute Garni Sauerkraut cooked with a variety of sausage, pork, and sometimes poultry products. A specialty of Alsace, France.

Chowder A hearty American soup made from fish, shellfish, and/or vegetables, usually containing milk and potatoes.

Clamart Garnished with or containing peas.

Clarified Butter Purified butterfat, with water and milk solids removed.

Clearmeat A mixture of ground meat, egg whites, and flavoring ingredients used to clarify consommés.

Club Sandwich A sandwich consisting of three slices of toast and filled with such ingredients as sliced chicken or turkey, lettuce, tomato, and bacon.

Coagulation The process by which proteins become firm, usually when heated.

Cocktail A type of appetizer generally made of seafood or fruit and often served with a tart or tangy sauce.

Collagen A type of connective tissue in meats that dissolves when cooked with moisture.

Complementary Proteins Protein supplied by foods that, if eaten together, supply all the amino acids necessary in the human diet.

Complete Protein A protein that supplies all the amino acids necessary in the human diet.

Compound Butter A mixture of raw butter and various flavoring ingredients.

Concasser To chop coarsely.

Conduction The transfer of heat from one item to something touching it or a cooler part of the first item.

Consommé A rich, flavorful, seasoned stock or broth that has been clarified to make it perfectly clear and transparent.

Convection The transfer of heat by the movement of a liquid or gas.

Convection Oven An oven in which hot air is circulated by a fan.

Convenience Food Any food product that has been partially or completely prepared or processed by the manufacturer.

Coq au Vin (coke oh van) A French dish of chicken braised in wine.

Coral The roe or eggs of certain shellfish.

Coupe A dessert consisting of one or two scoops of ice cream or sherbet in a dish or glass, topped with any of a number of syrups, fruits, toppings, and garnishes; sundae.

Course A food or group of foods served at one time or intended to be eaten at the same time.

Court Bouillon (koor bwee yohn) Water containing seasonings, herbs, and usually an acid; used for cooking fish.

Cream Soup A soup that is thickened with roux or other thickening agent and contains milk and/or cream.

Crecy (kray see) Garnished with or containing carrots.

Crème Anglaise (krem awng glezz) A light vanilla-flavored custard sauce made of milk, sugar, and egg yolks.

Critical Control Point An action that can be taken that will eliminate or minimize a food safety hazard.

Croissant A crescent-shaped roll made from a rich, rolled-in yeast dough.

Croquette (crow kett) Food that has been puréed or bound with a thick sauce, made into small shapes, breaded, and fried.

Cross-contamination The transfer of bacteria to food from another food or from equipment or work surfaces.

Crudité (croo dee tay) French term for raw vegetables served as a relish.

Crustaceans Sea animals with segmented shells and jointed legs, such as lobsters and shrimp.

Custard A liquid that is thickened or set firm by the coagulation of egg protein.

Cycle Menu A menu that changes every day for a certain period and then repeats the same daily items in the same order.

D

Danish A rich, sweet, flaky yeast dough containing layers of rolled-in fat.

Deci- Prefix in the metric system meaning "one-tenth."

Deep-fry To cook submerged in hot fat.

Deglaze To swirl a liquid in a sauté pan or other pan to dissolve cooked particles or food remaining on bottom.

Demiglaze A rich brown sauce that has been reduced by half.

Demitasse Literally, "half cup." Strong, black coffee served in small cups after dinner.

Doria Garnished with cucumbers cooked in butter.

Drawn With entrails removed.

Dressed (1) Poultry market form: killed, bled, and plucked. (2) Fish market form: viscera, scales, head, tail, and fins removed.

Drop Batter A batter that is too thick to pour but that will drop from a spoon in lumps.

Dry-heat Cooking Methods Methods in which heat is conducted to foods without the use of moisture.

Dubarry Garnished with or containing cauliflower.

Duchesse Potatoes (doo shess) Potato purée mixed with butter and egg yolks.

Dumpling Any of a variety of small starch products made from soft doughs or batter and cooked by simmering or steaming.

Duxelle A coarse paste or hash made of finely chopped mushrooms sautéed with shallots.

E

Elastin A type of connective tissue in meats that does not dissolve when cooked.

Emincer (em man say) To cut into very thin slices.

Emulsion A uniform mixture of two unmixable liquids.

Entremetier (awn truh met yay) The cook who prepares vegetables, starches, soups, and eggs.

EP Weight Edible portion: The weight of an item after all trimming and preparation is done.

Escoffier, Georges Auguste Great chef of the early twentieth century and the father of modern cookery.

Espagnole A sauce made of brown stock and flavoring ingredients and thickened with a brown roux.

Espresso, Expresso Strong dark coffee made from beans roasted until almost black, ground very fine, and brewed under steam pressure.

Étuver (ay too vay) To cook or steam an item in its own juices; to sweat.

Executive Chef The manager of a large kitchen or food production department.

Extended Meal Service Service of a meal at which customers eat at different times.

F

Fermentation The process by which yeast acts on carbohydrates to change them into carbon dioxide gas and alcohol.

Fermière (fair myair) Garnished with carrots, turnips, onions, and celery cut into uniform slices.

Fettuccine Flat egg noodles.

Fiber A group of indigestible carbohydrates in grains, fruits, and vegetables.

Fillet, Filet (1) Meat: Boneless tenderloin. (2) Fish: Boneless side of fish.

Flavones White pigments in vegetables and fruits.

Florentine Garnished with or containing spinach.

Flow of Food The path that food travels in a food service operation, from receiving to serving.

Foie Gras (fwah grah) Liver of specially fattened geese and ducks.

Fondant A smooth, creamy, white icing or candy consisting of very finely crystallized sugar syrup.

Fond Lié A sauce made by thickening brown stock with cornstarch or similar starch.

Fondue, Swiss A dish consisting of melted Gruyère and Emmenthaler cheeses and white wine into which cubes of bread are dipped and eaten. From the French word meaning "melted."

Food Danger Zone The temperature range of 45°F to 140°F (7°C to 60°C), in which bacteria grow rapidly.

Forestière Garnished with mushrooms.

French Dressing Salad dressing made of oil, vinegar, and seasonings.

French-Style Ice Cream Ice cream containing egg yolks.

Fricassée A white stew in which the meat is cooked in fat without browning before liquid is added.

Frittata A flat, unfolded omelet.

Fry To cook in hot fat.

Fumet A flavorful stock, usually fish stock.

G

Garde Manger (gard mawn zhay) (1) The cook in charge of cold food production, including salads and buffet items. (2) The department of a kitchen in which these foods are prepared.

Garni Garnished. Having had garnish added to it.

Garnish (1) Decorative edible items used to ornament or enhance the eye appeal of another food item. (2) To add such a decorative item to food.

Garniture (1) Garnish. (2) The act or process of garnishing.

Gazpacho A cold Spanish soup made of puréed raw vegetables.

Gelatinization The process by which starch granules absorb water and swell in size.

Genoise (zhen wahz) A French sponge cake.

Glace de Viande (glahss duh vee awnd) Meat glaze; a reduction of brown stock.

Glaze (1) A stock that is reduced until it coats the back of a spoon. (2) A shiny coating, such as a syrup, applied to a food. (3) To make a food shiny or glossy by coating it with a glaze or by browning under a broiler or in a hot oven.

Gluten A substance made up of proteins present in wheat flour that gives structure and strength to baked goods.

Glutinous Rice A type of short-grain rice that becomes sticky and chewy when cooked.

Goulash A Hungarian stew flavored with paprika.

Gram The basic unit of weight in the metric system; equal to about one-thirtieth of an ounce.

Granité (grah nee tay) Coarse, crystalline frozen dessert made of water, sugar, and fruit juice or other flavoring.

Green Meat Meat that has not had enough time after slaughter to develop tenderness and flavor.

Griddle To cook on a flat, solid cooking surface called a griddle.

Grill To cook on an open grid over a heat source.

Grillardin (gree ar dan) Broiler cook.

Gross Pièce (gross pyess) Centerpiece of a buffet platter.

H

HACCP A food safety system of self-inspection, designed to highlight hazardous foods and to control food handling to avoid hazards.

Hash (1) To chop. (2) A dish made of chopped foods.

Hazard A potentially dangerous food condition due to contamination, growth of pathogens, survival of pathogens, or the presence of toxins.

Herbs The leaves of certain plants, used in flavoring.

Hollandaise A sauce made of butter, egg yolks, and flavorings (especially lemon juice).

Homogenized Milk Milk that has been processed so that the cream doesn't separate out.

Hongroise (ong grwahz) Hungarian style.

Hygroscopic Readily absorbing moisture.

I

Infection Disease, including much food-borne disease, caused by bacteria in the body.

Intoxication Disease caused by poisons that bacteria produce while they are growing in food.

J

Jardinière (zhar din yair) Garnished with fresh "garden" vegetables, such as carrots, turnips, green beans, peas, cauliflower.

Judic Garnished with braised lettuce.

Julienne (1) Cut into small, thin strips, about 1/8 × 1/8 × 2½ inches (3 mm × 3 mm × 6½ cm). (2) Garnished with foods cut in this manner.

Jus (zhoo) Unthickened juices from a roast.

Jus Lié Thickened juices from a roast.

K

Kasha Whole buckwheat groats.

Kilo- Prefix in the metric system meaning "one thousand."

L

Lard (1) The rendered fat of hogs. (2) To insert strips of fat into meats low in marbling.

Lasagne Broad, flat egg noodles, or a baked, layered casserole made with these noodles.

Leading Sauce A basic sauce used in the production of other sauces. The five leading hot sauces are Béchamel, Velouté, Espagnole, Tomato, and Hollandaise. Mayonnaise and Vinaigrette are often considered leading cold sauces.

Leavening The production or incorporation of gases in a baked product to increase volume and to produce shape and texture.

Liaison A binding agent, usually made of cream and egg yolks, used to thicken sauces and soups.

Liter The basic unit of volume in the metric system; equal to slightly more than a quart.

London Broil Flank steak or other cut of beef broiled rare and cut in thin slices.

Lyonnaise (lee oh nez) Containing or garnished with onions.

M

Macaroni Noodle products made of flour and water and dried.

Maitre d'Hotel Butter (may truh doh tell) Compound butter containing parsley and lemon juice.

Marbling The fat that is deposited within muscle tissue.

Marinate To soak a food in a seasoned liquid.

Marsala A flavorful sweet to semidry wine from Sicily.

Mayonnaise A semisolid cold sauce or dressing consisting of oil and vinegar emulsified with egg yolks.

Meringue A foam made of beaten egg whites and sugar.

Meringue Glacée Baked meringue shells served with ice cream.

Meter The basic unit of length in the metric system: slightly longer than 1 yard.

(À la) Meunière Fish prepared by dredging in flour and sautéing, served with brown butter, lemon juice, and parsley.

Microwave Radiation generated in special ovens and used to cook or heat foods.

Milli- Prefix in the metric system meaning "one-thousandth."

Mince To chop into very fine pieces.

Minestrone Italian vegetable soup.

Mirepoix (meer pwah) A mixture of rough-cut or diced vegetables, herbs, and spices used for flavoring.

Mise en Place (meez on plahss) French term meaning "everything in place." The setup for production. All the preparations and organization that must be made before actual production can begin.

Moist-Heat Cooking Methods Methods in which heat is conducted to foods by water or other liquid or by steam.

Mollusk A soft-bodied sea animal, usually inside a pair of hinged shells, such as clams or oysters.

Monter au Beurre (mohn tay oh burr) To finish a sauce or soup by swirling in raw butter until it is melted.

Mornay A sauce made of Béchamel and Gruyère cheese.

Mousse A soft, creamy food, either sweet or savory, that is made light by the addition of whipped cream or beaten egg whites or both.

Mozzarella A mild, unripened cheese used in pizzas and many other Italian-style dishes.

N

Navarin A brown lamb stew.

New England Boiled Dinner A dish consisting of simmered corned beef and simmered vegetables, served together.

Niçoise (nee swahz) (1) Prepared in the style of Nice, France. (2) Garnished with or containing tomato concassée cooked with garlic.

Nouvelle Cuisine A modern style of cooking that emphasizes lightness of sauces and seasonings, shortened cooking times, and new and sometimes startling combinations of foods.

O

Offal Another name for variety meats.

Oolong A greenish-brown, partially fermented tea.

Oven Spring The rapid rise of yeast goods in the oven due to production and expansion of trapped gases as a result of the oven heat.

Overrun The increase in volume of ice cream or frozen dessert due to incorporation of air while freezing.

P

Pan Gravy A type of sauce made with the pan drippings of the meat or poultry it is served with.

Pan-broil To cook uncovered in a sauté pan or skillet without fat.

Pan-fry To cook in a moderate amount of fat in an uncovered pan.

(en) Papillote (on poppy yote) Wrapped in paper or foil for cooking so that the food is steamed in its own moisture.

Parboil To cook partially in a boiling or simmering liquid.

Parcook To partially cook by any method.

Parfait A dessert consisting of alternating layers of ice cream and fruit or syrup in a tall, narrow glass.

Parmentier (par mawn tyay) Garnished with or containing potatoes.

Pasta General term for any shape of macaroni product or egg noodles.

Pasteurized Heat-treated to kill bacteria that might cause disease or spoilage.

Pastry Cream A thick custard sauce containing eggs and starch.

Pâte à Choux (pot a shoo) A soft dough used for making eclairs and cream puffs. Also called eclair paste.

Pathogen A bacteria that causes disease.

Patissier (pa tees syay) Pastry cook.

Peach Melba A sundae consisting of vanilla ice cream, peach half, and Melba (raspberry) sauce.

Persillade (pear see yahd) A mixture of bread crumbs, parsley, and garlic, used to coat roast meat items, usually lamb.

Philadelphia-Style Ice Cream Ice cream containing no eggs.

Pigment Any substance that gives color to an item.

Pilaf Rice or other grain product that has been first cooked in fat and then simmered in a stock or other liquid, usually with onions, seasonings, or other ingredients.

Poach To cook very gently in water or other liquid that is hot but not actually bubbling, about 160°F to 180°F (71°C to 82°C).

Poissonier (pwah so nyay) Fish cook.

Portion Control The measurement of portions to ensure that the correct amount of an item is served.

Pot Roast A large cut of meat cooked by braising.

Poulette Allemande Sauce flavored with mushrooms, parsley, and lemon juice.

Pour Batter A batter that is liquid enough to pour.

Primal Cut One of the primary divisions of meat quarters, foresaddles, hindsaddles, and carcasses as they are broken down into smaller cuts.

Primeur (pree mur) Garnished with fresh spring vegetables such as carrots, turnips, green beans, peas, cauliflower, and small potatoes.

Princesse Garnished with asparagus.

Printaniere (pran tawn yair) Garnished with fresh spring vegetables, such as carrots, turnips, pearl onions, peas, green beans, asparagus.

Prix Fixe (pree fix) French term meaning "fixed price"; referring to a menu offering a complete meal, with a choice of courses, for one given price.

Process Cheese A product made by grinding and melting one or more cheeses, blending them with other ingredients, and pouring into molds to solidify.

Profiterole Tiny round pastry made from eclair paste; filled with savory fillings and served as an hors d'oeuvre, or filled with ice cream and served as a dessert.

Provençale (pro vawn sal) Garnished with or containing tomatoes, garlic, parsley, and sometimes mushrooms and olives.

Puff Pastry A very light, flaky pastry made from a rolled-in dough and leavened by steam.

Pullman Loaf Long, rectangular loaf of bread.

Pumpernickel (1) Coarsely ground rye flour. (2) Bread made with this flour.

Purée (1) A food product that has been mashed or strained to a smooth pulp. (2) To make such a pulp by mashing or straining a food.

Q

Quiche A savory tart or pie consisting of a custard baked in a pastry shell.

Quick Bread A bread leavened by chemical leaveners or steam rather than yeast.

R

Radiation The transfer of energy by waves, such as infrared or light waves.

Raft The coagulated clearmeat that forms when stock is clarified.

Ratatouille (ra ta tweey) A Southern French vegetable stew of onions, tomatoes, zucchini, eggplant, and green peppers.

Ravier (rahv yay) Oval relish dish.

Ravioli Dumplings consisting of egg noodles filled with any of a variety of fillings.

Recipe A set of instructions for producing a certain dish.

Reduce To cook by simmering or boiling until quantity is decreased; often done to concentrate flavors.

Reduction (1) A liquid that has been concentrated by cooking it to evaporate part of the water. (2) The process of making such a liquid.

Relish A type of appetizer consisting of raw or pickled vegetables.

Ricotta An Italian-style cheese similar to cottage cheese but smoother, moister, and sweeter in flavor.

Risotto A moist Italian dish of rice cooked in butter and stock.

Rissolé (riss oh lay) Browned. Often referring to potatoes cut in small shapes, parboiled, and browned in hot fat.

Roast To cook foods by surrounding them with hot, dry air, in an oven or on a spit over an open fire.

Roe Fish eggs.

Roesti Potatoes Boiled potatoes that have been grated, formed into small cakes, and pan-fried until crisp.

Rolled-in Dough Dough in which a fat is incorporated into the dough in many layers by using a rolling and folding procedure.

Roquefort A blue-veined cheese made in Roquefort, France, from sheeps' milk.

Rotisserie An item of cooking equipment that slowly rotates meat or other foods in front of a heating element.

Rotisseur (ro tee sur) Cook who prepares roasted, braised, and broiled meats.

Rough Prep The preliminary processing of ingredients to the point at which they can be used in cooking.

Roux A cooked mixture of equal parts flour and fat.

Royal Icing An icing made of confectioners' sugar and egg whites, used for decorating.

Russet Starchy potato often used for baking and deep-frying.

Rye Blend A mixture of rye flour and hard wheat flour.

S

Sachet (sa shay) A mixture of herbs and spices tied in a cheesecloth bag.

Salamander Small broiler used primarily for browning or glazing the tops of certain items.

Salmonella A widespread food-borne disease, spread by improper food handling and inadequate sanitation.

Sanitize To kill disease-causing bacteria, usually by heat or by chemical disinfectants.

Saturated Fat A fat that is normally solid at room temperature.

Sauce A flavorful liquid, usually thickened, that is used to season, flavor, and enhance other foods.

Saucier (so see ay) The sauce cook; prepares sauces and stews and sautés foods to order.

Sauerbraten A German dish consisting of beef marinated and then cooked with vinegar and other ingredients.

Sauté To cook quickly in a small amount of fat.

Scampi A kind of shellfish similar to large shrimp. In this country, the term is often used for large shrimp, especially if broiled with garlic butter.

Sear To brown the surface of a food quickly at high temperatures.

Semolina A hard, high-protein flour often used for the best-quality macaroni products.

Set Meal Service Service of a meal at which all the customers eat at one time.

Shirred Egg Egg baked in a shallow, buttered dish.

Short Having a high fat content, which makes the product (such as a cookie or pastry) very crumbly and tender.

Shortening (1) Any fat used in baking to tenderize the product by shortening gluten strands. (2) A white, tasteless, solid fat that has been formulated for baking or deep-frying.

Shred To cut into thin but irregular strips, either with the coarse blade of a grater or with a knife.

Sieve Size Size of individual pieces, usually of canned vegetables.

Simmer To cook in water or other liquid that is bubbling gently, about 185°F to 200°F (85°C to 93°C).

Sirniki Russian pan-fried cheesecakes.

Slurry A mixture of raw starch and cold liquid, used for thickening.

Small Sauce A sauce made by adding one or more ingredients to a leading sauce.

Solanine A poisonous substance found in potatoes that have turned green.

Sorbet (sor bay) Sherbet, usually made without milk products.

Soufflé A light, fluffy baked egg dish consisting of a base (such as a heavy white sauce) mixed with egg yolks and flavoring ingredients into which beaten egg whites are folded just before baking. May be sweet or savory.

Sous Chef (soo shef)   A cook who supervises food production and who reports to the executive chef.

Spaetzle   Small dumplings or noodles made from a thin egg and flour batter.

Spice   Any part of a plant, other than the leaves, used in flavoring foods.

Staling   The change in texture and aroma of baked goods due to the loss of moisture by the starch granules.

Standard Breading Procedure   The procedure for coating a food product with bread crumbs (or other crumbs or meal) by passing it through flour, then egg wash, then crumbs.

Standardized Recipe   A set of instructions describing the way a particular establishment prepares a particular dish.

Staphylococcus or "Staph"   A bacterium that causes food-borne disease by producing a toxin or poison in improperly stored foods.

Static Menu   A menu that offers the same dishes every day.

Station Chef   A cook in charge of a particular department in a kitchen or food production facility.

Steam   To cook by direct contact with steam.

Stew   (1) To simmer a food or foods in a small amount of liquid that is usually served with the food as a sauce. (2) A dish cooked by stewing, usually one in which the main ingredients are cut in small pieces.

Stock   A clear, thin (that is, unthickened) liquid flavored by soluble substances extracted from meat, poultry, and fish, and their bones, and from vegetables and seasonings.

Streusel (stroy zel)   A crumbly topping for baked goods, consisting of fat, sugar, and flour rubbed together.

Strong Flour   Flour with a high protein or gluten content.

Suprême Sauce   A sauce made of chicken velouté and heavy cream.

Sweat   To cook in a small amount of fat over low heat, sometimes covered.

Sweetbreads   The thymus glands of calves and young animals, used as food.

Swiss Steak   Beef round steaks braised in brown sauce.

T

Table d'Hote (tobble dote)   (1) Referring to a fixed-price menu with no choices. (2) Referring to a menu on which prices are listed for complete meals rather than for each separate item.

Tang   The portion of a metal knife blade that is inside the handle.

Temper   To raise the temperature of a cold liquid gradually by slowly stirring in a hot liquid.

Tomalley   The liver of lobsters and some other shellfish.

Tournant (toor nawn)   A cook who replaces other station cooks; relief cook or swing cook.

Tournedos (toor nuh doe)   A small beef steak cut from the tenderloin.

Trichinosis   A food-borne disease caused by a parasite sometimes found in undercooked pork.

Tripe   The muscular stomach lining of beef or other meat animals.

Truit au Bleu   Poached trout that was alive until cooking time and that turns blue when cooked in the court bouillon.

Trunnion Kettle   A steam-jacketed kettle that can be tilted for emptying.

Truss   To tie poultry into a compact shape for cooking.

Tunneling   A condition of muffin products characterized by large, elongated holes; caused by overmixing.

U

Unsaturated Fat   A fat that is normally liquid at room temperature.

V

Variety Meats   Various organs, glands, and other meats that don't form a part of the dressed carcass.

Velouté   A sauce made by thickening white stock with a roux.

Vent   To allow circulation or escape of a liquid or gas, such as by setting a pot of hot stock on blocks in a cold-water bath so that the cold water can circulate all around the pot.

Viande (vee awnd)   French word for meat.

Vichyssoise (vee she swahz)   Cold purée of leek and potato soup with cream.

Vin   Wine.

Vin Blanc   White wine.

Vin Rouge   Red wine.

Vinaigrette   Dressing or sauce made of oil, vinegar, and flavoring ingredients.

Vitamin   Any of a group of compounds that are present in foods in very small quantities and that are necessary for regulating body functions.

Volatile   Evaporating quickly when heated.

W

Wash   (1) To brush or coat a food item with a liquid such as egg wash or milk. (2) The liquid used in this procedure.

Waxy Potato A young potato high in sugar and low in starch.

Weak Flour Flour with a low protein or gluten content.

Welsh Rabbit A dish made of melted cheddar cheese and, usually, ale or beer. Sometimes called Welsh Rarebit.

Whitewash A thin mixture or slurry of flour and cold water.

Winterized Oil Vegetable oil that stays clear and liquid when refrigerated.

Z

Zest The colored part of the peel of citrus fruits.

INDEX